D0991285

THE AMERICAN NEGRO

HIS HISTORY AND LITERATURE

PROCEEDINGS

OF THE

CONSTITUTIONAL CONVENTION

OF

SOUTH CAROLINA

Volume I

ARNO PRESS and THE NEW YORK TIMES

NEW YORK 1968

General Editor
WILLIAM LOREN KATZ

IN JANUARY 1868, AFTER AN ELECTION WHICH HAD BEEN SUPER-
vised by Federal troops, delegates (a majority of whom were black)
arrived in Charleston, South Carolina and began to write a new
constitution for their state. For fifty-three days a strange mixture of
ex-slaves and their former masters, educated and illiterate men, rich
and poor, argued and debated as they wrote the state's first democratic constitution. The document that emerged from their deliberations infuriated those who believed that black skin was proof of
inferior mentality. The convention and the Negro-white governments
which followed it were denounced at the time by one newspaper as
"the maddest, most unscrupulous and infamous revolution in history." Another paper fulminated at white ruination beneath the
"unholy hoofs of African savages" and "gibbering, louse-eaten,
devil-worshipping barbarians, from the jungles of Dahomey, and
peripatetic buccaneers from Cape Cod. . . . Hell, and Boston."

Many historians have echoed this approach without its more
hysterical crudities. In so doing they have fashioned another great
southern myth to accompany and amplify that of "the contented
slave." But both the contributions of the Negro delegates and the
document they produced stand in sharp contrast to the vulgar
mouthings of their detractors.

This volume tells us what the delegates said and did during the
days of deliberation in that winter of 1868. Essentially they brought
the reforms of the Jacksonian era to a state that had been retarded
by slavery: the first public school system for all children, increased

women's rights, the state's first divorce law, the extension of voting rights to those who were black, and those who did not own property, power to elect state officials, up to and including the Governor. However, no "special" provisions were made for the state's black majority. "Mark you, we did not discriminate, although we had a majority," Joseph H. Rainey reminded his fellow congressmen years later.

Perhaps the highest compliment was paid this constitution by its greatest enemies, the white supremacists. When, in 1895 they convened to change it, they struck out not the document's many reforms, but rather denied its benefits to the state's black population. But a black delegate to the 1895 convention, Thomas E. Miller, made his fellow delegates take cognizance of the great truths of South Carolina's era of black power:

> We were eight years in power. We had built schoolhouses, established charitable institutions, built and mantained the penitentiary system, provided for the education of the deaf and dumb, rebuilt the jails and courthouses, rebuilt the bridges and reestablished the ferries. In short, we had reconstructed the state and placed it upon the road to prosperity. . . .

Sara Jackson
NATIONAL ARCHIVES

PROCEEDINGS

OF THE

CONSTITUTIONAL CONVENTION

OF

SOUTH CAROLINA,

Held at Charleston, S. C., beginning January 14th and ending March 17th, 1868.

———o———

INCLUDING THE

DEBATES AND PROCEEDINGS.

———o———

REPORTED BY J. WOODRUFF, PHONOGRAPHIC REPORTER.

VOL. I.

PUBLISHED BY ORDER OF THE CONVENTION.

CHARLESTON, S. C.
PRINTED BY DENNY & PERRY.
163 Meeting Street.
1868.

WHEREAS, it is important to the interests of the State, and necessary in a historical point of view, that the proceedings of this, the first Convention in the new era of South Carolina, should be permanently preserved; be it

Resolved, That a Committee of three be appointed to make such arrangements with one or more short hand reporters as will secure a faithful record of the proceedings and debates of this body, the compensation for the same to be not more than the sum paid to official reporters in Congress, and to be paid by the Treasurer of the State, on the presentation to the President of the Convention of the proceedings in manuscript, ready for the printer, in the bills receivable of this Commonwealth, at their market value, that amount to be paid by the Treasurer of the State, on the order of the President of the Convention.

B. F. WHITTEMORE, ⎫
NILES G. PARKER, ⎬ Committee.
S. LEE. ⎭

PREFACE.

SINCE the rupture of our colonial dependence on the mother country, seven Conventions have been held in South Carolina. The first of these, if that can be called a Convention, which was simply a self-constituted organization of the Colonial Congress into a General Assembly, without any special reference to the voice of the people, was held in March, 1776, and it then framed a temporary Constitution, which was tacitly accepted as the original law of the colony, until a reconciliation should be effected between Britain and its revolted provinces, a consummation, at that time, both wished and expected by many. This Constitution remained in force for two years only. In 1778, the Legislature of the State, assuming, by its own will, the province of a Convention, adopted a new Constitution, which, however irregularly formed, seems, evidently, to have been an improvement on the preceding instrument, since it diminished the prerogatives of the ruling powers, and extended the privileges of the people. Yet, neither of these Constitutions was framed in that regular and legitimate mode which would give to it the character and the value of a fundamental law; indeed, the Supreme Court of the State subsequently affirmed, with great distinctness, that the Constitutions of both 1776 and 1778, were merely ordinary statutes, repealable by the General Assembly.

Passing over the Convention of 1787, which was called only to ratify the Federal Constitution, we come to the fourth Convention of the State, which was convened in 1790, by the Legislature, under its ordinary legislative power. The Constitution framed by this Convention continued, with a few amendments enacted in 1808, and in 1816, to be the organic law of the State for seventy years.

In 1860, the General Assembly summoned a Convention for the express purpose of enacting an Ordinance of Secession, and attempted to withdraw the State from its connection with the National Government—an attempt whose signal failure is on the record of history. This Convention did not frame a new Constitution, but made those modifications in the old one which were rendered necessary by the supposed changed relations of the State to the Union. Of the illegality of this Convention, and of all the proceedings under it, it is unnecessary to make an argument.

The civil war having terminated by the defeat of the rebellious forces, the overthrow of the so-called Confederacy, and the restoration of the State to its primary and paramount allegiance to the General Government, the entire change in the internal organization of the State, consequent on the abolition of slavery, and the assumption by one-half of its population of the status of freemen and citizens, rendered the old Constitution of 1790 no longer applicable to the changed condition of things.

Accordingly, in 1865, the President of the United States, having appointed a Provisional Governor, directed the calling of a Convention, which assembled in September, 1865, and framed a new Constitution for the government of the people. This Constitution, although in some respects an improvement on that of 1790, was not such an instrument as the progressive spirit of the age demanded. Slavery, it is true, was abolished, although the abolition was ungracefully accorded to the demands of superior power; but the framers of the organic law had not yet learned the lessons of the war, and were too little imbued with the expansive spirit of the age to recognize the just and equal rights of all in the eye of the law.

We need not enter into the argument, whether the Convention of 1865 was legally called, or whether its acts could be of any binding force. That question has been definitively settled by the law-making power of the nation. Congress has decided that it was no part of the prerogative of the Executive to call Conventions, or to direct the adoption of Constitutions. That power it has reserved to itself, and, accordingly, under the Reconstruction Acts of Congress, a Convention of the State assembled in January, 1868, the result of whose labors has been accepted by those whom the Constitution is to govern, as the organic law of the land.

Of the legality of this Convention, there can be no doubt. The question whether a Convention should be called, was regularly submitted to the people, who, by a large majority of votes declared it to be their will that such a body should be convened, for the avowed purpose of presenting to it a proposition for a change of the organic law. At the same time delegates were elected by the people to represent them in that Convention. Under the express declaration of the people, their representatives assembled and framed a Constitution. This Constitution was, subsequently, submitted to the people for their rejection or their adoption. The people, in the exercise of their sovereign will, have chosen to adopt and ratify this Constitution as the form of civil polity under which they desire to live, and have expressed that desire by an overwhelming majority of votes, and no power but that of the people, in like manner, expressing a contrary will, can subvert that law.

Some very silly, and some very fanatical persons, have pretended to sneer at the constitutionality of the Convention of 1868. The sneers of the fool and the vituperations of the partisan are equally unworthy and incapable of being met by honest argument. If argument were available, on their own theory they could be convinced of error.

The enemies of congressional reconstruction, who alone have been the denouncers of the legality of the Convention of 1868, have never denied the constitutionality and legitimacy of that of 1865. But a comparison of the two will easily show how much the former surpasses the latter in all the elements of legality and constitutionality.

The preliminary steps towards the reconstruction of 1865, were inaugurated by the Executive in the exercise of what at best can only be deemed a doubtful prerogative. Those which led to the reconstruction of 1868 were authorized by Congress, the law-making power of the nation, and its prerogative to act in this matter has been denied by no one, although many have chosen to express discontent with the mode and manner of its exercise. The Convention of 1865 was called by a direct order of the President, and without any application to the people for their sanction and approval of the measure. That of 1868, although recommended by Congress, was not called until the people had, at the polls, by a large majority of votes, expressed their will that the Convention should assemble. The delegates to the Convention of 1865 were elected by only a part of the people, the great loyal element of the country being almost wholly ignored. Those of 1868 were chosen by all the people, save those who had been justly disqualified by their participation, directly or indirectly, in the crime of treason. The Constitution of 1865, when adopted by the Convention, was adopted as a finality, and the people were neither asked their consent to its provisions, nor permitted, if it were not popular, to reject it. They were called upon only to hear and obey. The Constitution of 1868, after it had been framed by the representatives of the people, was submitted to them for their approval. Its provisions were subjected to examination, and the question being propounded at the ballot box, the people, by a vote whose majority was more than forty thousand, declared that it was their will that the Constitution of 1868 should be the fundamental law under which they were to live, until in their wisdom they should, at some future time, choose to change it. If the Convention and the Constitution of 1865 were legal, then, *a fortiori*, the Convention and the Constitution of 1868 must have been equally so.

But to those who believe in the justice and the expediency of the system of construction adopted by Congress, and men of that opinion comprise much the larger portion of the people of the State, no such argument is necessary. Denying the legality of the Convention of 1865, they recognize that of 1868 as the only legitimate Convention that has assembled in the State of South Carolina since the year 1790. Of such a body, the proceedings cannot but be highly interesting, and, accordingly, before its adjournment, it took the necessary steps for publishing the record of its proceedings. These were carefully and accurately kept by Mr. Josephus Woodruff, a professional stenographer, who was officially employed by the Convention. The work has been faithfully performed, and is, under the authority of the Convention, submitted to the people of the State as an interesting record of a part of the history of the times.

ALBERT G. MACKEY,
President of the South Carolina Convention.

PROCEEDINGS

OF THE

Constitutional Convention

OF

SOUTH CAROLINA.

FIRST DAY.

Tuesday, January 14, 1868.

Pursuant to an Act of Congress of the United States, entitled an Act supplementary to an Act entitled "An Act to provide for the more efficient government of the rebel States," passed on the second day of March, eighteen hundred and sixty-seven, and the Act supplementary thereto, passed on the twenty-third day of March, eighteen hundred and sixty-seven, the Delegates from the several Election Districts of this State assembled in the Club House, in the city of Charleston, on this day, at 12 o'clock, M.

The Convention was called to order by Mr. TIMOTHY HURLEY, of Berkley District.

On motion of Mr. JAMES M. RUTLAND, of Fairfield, Mr. T. J. ROBERTSON, of Richland, was called to the Chair.

Mr. ROBERTSON on taking the Chair addressed the Convention as follows :

Gentlemen of the Convention :—We, the delegates of the loyal people of South Carolina, are assembled here for the purpose of restoring our State to her proper relations in the Federal Union.

It becomes us to frame a just an 1 liberal Constitution, that will guarantee equal rights to all, regardless of race, color or previous condition—a Constitution which will comply with the Reconstruction Acts of Congress, thereby insuring our speedy admission into the Union.

I trust there will be no class legislation here. I hope we will act harmoniously, promptly, judiciously and in such a manner as will reflect credit on ourselves, and secure the confidence of the people of the State, whom we represent. By your kind assistance I hope to speedily organize this Convention.

Mr. WM. J. McKINLAY, of Orangeburg, was chosen temporary Secretary.

By direction of the Chair, the Secretary read the following order convening the body :

HEADQUARTERS SECOND MILITARY DISTRICT,

CHARLESTON, S. C., December 28, 1867.

GENERAL ORDERS, }
   No. 160. }

At the election held in the State of South Carolina, on the 19th and 20th days of November, 1867, pursuant to General Orders No. 99, from these Headquarters, dated October 16, 1867, a majority of the registered voters of the said State having voted on the question of holding a Convention, and a majority of the votes cast being in favor of holding such Convention, the delegates elected thereto, and hereinafter named, are hereby notified, in conformity with the provisions of the fourth section of the Act of Congress of March 23, 1867, to assemble in convention in the city of Charleston, South Carolina, at noon, on Tuesday, the 14th day of January, 1868, for the purpose of framing a constitution and civil government according to the provisions of the aforesaid Act of the 23d day of March, 1867, and of the Act of the 2d day of March, 1867, to which it is supplementary.

A copy of this order will be furnished to each of the persons hereinafter named, and shall be the evidence of his having been elected as a delegate to the aforesaid Convention.

DELEGATES.

District of Abbeville—Hutson J. Lomax, Nelson Joiner, Jno. A. Hunter, Bailey Milford, Thomas Williamson.

District of Anderson.—William Perry, Dr. N. J. Newell, Samuel Johnson.

District of Barnwell.—Charles P. Leslie, Niles G. Parker, James N. Hayne, Julius Mayer, Charles D. Hayne, Abram Middleton.

District of Berkley.—Joseph H. Jenks, W. H. W. Gray, George Lee, A. C. Richmond, D. H. Chamberlain, Wm. Jervey, Timothy Hurley, M. F. Becker, Benjamin Byas.

District of Beaufort.—Francis E. Wilder. James D. Bell, Robert Smalls, J. J. Wright, R. G. Holmes, W. J. Whipper, L. S. Langley.

District of Charleston.—A. G. Mackey, F. A. Sawyer, A. J. Ransier, William McKinlay, Robt. C. DeLarge, Francis L. Cardozo, Gilbert Pillsbury, C. C. Bowen, Richard H. Cain.

District of Chester.—S. Sanders, P. Alexander, B. Burton.

District of Clarendon—Elias Dickson, William Nelson.

District of Colleton.—William M. Thomas, John K. Terry, William Driffle, William M. Viney, Jesse S. Craig.

District of Chesterfield.—R. J. Donaldson, H. L. Shrewsbury.

District of Darlington.—Jordan Lang B. F. Whittemore, Isaac Brockenton, Richard Humbird

District of Edgefield.—R. B. Elliott, George DeMeddis, John Wooley, Prince R. Rivers, John Bonum, David Harris, Frank-Arnim.

District of Fairfield.—Henry Jacobs, James M. Rutland, H. D. Edwards.

District of Georgetown.—Franklin F. Miller, Henry W. Webb, Joseph H. Rainey.

District of Greenville.—William B. Johnson, James M. Allen, James M. Runion, Wilson Cooke.

District of Horry.—Augustus R. Thompson, Henry Jones.

District of Kershaw.—J. K. Jillson, S. G. W. Dill, John A. Chestnut.

District of Lexington.—Lemuel Boozer, Simeon Corley.

District of Lancaster.—Albert Clinton, Charles Jones.

District of Laurens.—Nelson Davis, Joseph Crews, Harry McDaniels, Y. J. P. Owens.

District of Marlboro'.—Calvin Stubbs, George Jackson

District of Marion.—William S. Collins, H. E. Hayne, Benjamin A. Thompson, J. W. Johnson.

District of Newberry.—Lee Nance, B. Odell Duncan, James Henderson.

District of Orangeburg.—E. J. Cain, E. W. M. Mackey, Benjamin F. Randolph, T. L. Sasportas, W. J. McKinlay.

District of Pickens.—Alexander Boyce, M. Mauldin, Dr. L. B. Johnson.

District of Richland.—William B. Nash, Charles M. Wilder, Samuel B. Thompson, Thomas J. Robertson.

District of Spartanburg.—John S. Gentry, J. P. F. Camp, Rice Foster, Coy Wingo.

District of Sumter.—T. J. Coghlan, W. E. Johnston, Samuel Lee, F. J. Moses, Jr.

District of Union.—Abram Dogan, Samuel Nuckles, James H. Goss.

District of Williamsburg.—C. M. Olsen, S. A. Swails, William Darrington.

District of York—W. E. Rose, Dr. J. C. Neagle, J. H. White, John W. Mead.

By command of Brevet Major-General Ed. R. S. Canby :

LOUIS V. CAZIARC,

Aide-de-Camp, Actg. Asst. Adgjt. Genl.

Official :

LOUIS V. CAZIARC,

Aide-de-Camp, Actg. Asst. Adjt. Genl.

The roll of delegates being called by Districts, the following answered to their names :

Abbeville.—Hutson J. Lomax, Nelson Joiner, John A. Hunter, Thomas Williamson.

Anderson.—William Perry, Dr. N. J. Newell, Samuel Johnson.

Barnwell.—Charles P. Leslie, Niles G. Parker, James N. Hayne, Abraham Middleton.

Berkley.—Joseph H. Jenks, W. H. W. Gray, George Lee, A. C. Richmond, D. H. Chamberlain, Timothy Hurley, M. F. Becker, Benjamin Byas.

Beaufort —F. E. Wilder, James D. Bell, Robert Smalls, J. J. Wright. R. G. Holmes, W. J. Whipper, L. S. Langley.

Charleston.—A. G. Mackey, A. J. Ransier, William McKinlay, Robert C. DeLarge, Francis L. Cardozo, Gilbert Pillsbury, C. C. Bowen, Richard H. Cain.

Chester.—Sancho Sanders, B. Burton.

Clarendon.—Elias Dickson, William Nelson.

Colleton.—Wm. M. Thomas, Wm. Driffle, Wm. M. Viney, Jesse S. Craig.

Chesterfield.—H. L. Shrewsbury.

Darlington.—Jordan Lang, B. F. Whittemore, Isaac Brockenton, Richard Humbird.

Edgefield.—R. B. Elliott, Prince R. Rivers, John Bonum, David Harris, Frank Arnim.

Fairfield.—Henry Jacobs, James M. Rutland, H. D. Edwards.

Georgetown.—Franklin F. Miller, Henry W. Webb, Joseph H. Rainey.

Greenville.— William B. Johnson, James M. Allen, John M. Runion, Wilson Cooke.

Horry.—Henry Jones.

Kershaw.—J. K. Jillson, S. G. W. Dill, John A. Chestnut.

Lexington.—Simeon Corley.

Lancaster —Albert Clinton, Charles Jones.

Laurens.—Joseph Crews.

Marlboro'.—Calvin Stubbs, George Jackson.

Marion.—Wm. S. Collins, H. E. Hayne, Benj. A. Thompson, J. W. Johnson.

Newberry.—Lee Nance, B. Odell Duncan, James Henderson.

Orangeburg.—E. J. Cain, E. W. M. Mackey, Benjamin F. Randolph, T. K. Sasportas, W. J. McKinlay.

•Pickens.—Dr. L. B. Johnson.

Richland.—Wm. B. Nash, Charles M. Wilder, Samuel B. Thompson, Thomas J. Robertson.

Spartanburg.—John P. F. Camp, Rice Foster, Coy Wingo.

Sumter.—T. J. Coghlan, W. E. Johnston, Samuel Lee.

Union.—James H. Goss.

Williamsburg.—C. M. Olsen, S. A. Swails, William Darrington.

York.—W. E. Rose, J. H. White, John W. Mead.

Ninety-two delegates having answered, the President announced a quorum present, and the Convention ready for business.

Mr. B. F. WHITTEMORE moved that they proceed to a permanent organization, and that a Committee of seven be appointed by the Chair, to retire and report to the Conventien the names of candidates for permanent officers.

R. C., DeLARGE rose to a point of order, and asked how they were to know whether those answering to names when called were the men elected and entitled to their seats, and whether the officers elected by them would be entitled to· act as the legal officers of the Convention. He thought the first thing in order was the appointment of a Committee on Credentials, to examine and report.

The President decided that the possession of the military order was the best evidence of membership, and that ninety two members having responded, it was not necessary to go into any further investigation.

Mr. B. ODELL DUNCAN said he did not think the members of the Convention were prepared to go into an election for permanent officers. They had met for the first time together, did not know each other, and were acting in ignorance as to who were members of the Convention. A few caucuses would make them better acquainted, and better able to decide on the person best fitted for the position of President. He thought it better, therefore, to postpone the permanent organization for two or three days until they had some better knowledge of the members of the Convention. Much of the success of their work, he thought, would depend on the person selected for their permanent President. If they made a failure in this respect all their business might go wrong. The permanent President would have to appoint the committees, and upon them would depend, in a great measure, the success or failure of the Convention. He hoped, therefore, they would not go into the matter blindly. A majority of the members were not prepared to vote intelligently on the question, and he moved, as an amendment, that the permanent organization be postponed until 12 o'clock Thursday.

Mr. L. S. LANGLEY thought some further action necessary with reference to the identity of the persons who answered to names. Any one there might answer to a name and the Convention would not know whether the answer came from the person elected or from another. He was opposed, therefore, to going into a permanent organization until this question could be determined. He was in favor of the appointment of a Committee on Credentials.

Mr. DUNCAN mentioned that, in the Georgia Convention, a man attended and answered several days to the name of an absent delegate before he was discovered.

The question recurring on the amendment of Mr. DUNCAN to postpone,

Mr. N. G. PARKER moved to amend by substituting to-morrow at 12 M., instead of Thursday, which was accepted by the mover.

Mr. J. S. CRAIG said he had come to Charleston with limited means and did not wish to stay any longer than he could help. He was very anxious to effect organization as soon as possible, and to proceed with all possible haste to frame a new Constitution, or to make such changes in the old one as were necessary to secure a Republican form of Government.

Mr. C. C. BOWEN did not think the Convention sufficiently organized to go into an election for permanent officers. It might be presumed that every gentleman there was provided with the necessary order or credentials, but did the Chair know whether many of these orders might not have been transferred from one person to another. He would state that an individual was sitting here to-day with the certificate of another individual in his possession, so that it was absolutely necessary that they should determine whether all these persons were properly there or not. To this end, he moved that the question concerning the permanent organization be laid upon the table until the credentials of delegates could be examined.

The motion was agreed to.

Mr. DUNCAN moved that a Committee on Credentials be appointed by the Chair to consist of five. He regarded the possession of the order of General Canby (No. 160), as proper credentials, but thought that every man should show evidence that he is the member elected from the district he claimed to represent.

Mr. T. HURLEY moved to amend by adding that the Committee report forthwith.

Mr. T. K. SASPORTAS moved to amend by making the Committee to consist of one member from each District, such member to be chosen by each District delegation.

Mr. W. J. WHIPPER thought a Committee of five amply sufficient.

Mr. B. F. WHITTEMORE said there should certainly be one delegate from each District. He wished to know how a Committee of five of the members could be sure of either the person who presented a certificate or General Canby's order. These orders have been distributed all over the country ; any one might have an order, and some come in who had no right there. He was not afraid that such a Committee would be too cumbersome. He wanted to go to work properly, whatever time it required.

All he desired was simply the identification of the respective delegates by those who knew them; and in those cases where the certificates of General Canby have been lost or are wanting, they could be easily supplied from Headquarters. He was aware that there were some delegates present who held certificates from the Commissioner in Equity, and he knew of no higher authority than such an endorsement of a delegate by a proper official in the District which he represents. There certainly was no reason to be afraid of each other, and therefore he was disposed to settle this matter in the speediest way.

Mr. C. C. BOWEN said he was opposed to large Committees. A Committee of five is ample enough. If there was doubt concerning a delegate, he could easily be sent for and examined as to his identity. So far as regards the credentials, he contended that no certificate from a judge, or a clerk of any Court, or a Commissioner in Equity, was proper evidence here. Only the certified order of General Canby could be received as credentials, and those who were not supplied, must obtain a copy from the proper authority.

Mr. R. C. DeLARGE said that any difficulty of identity might be avoided by any gentleman sending for a member with whom he is acquainted, and who can vouch for him before the Committee.

Mr. B. F. RANDOLPH thought a Committee of one delegate from each District would facilitate business, as each delegate on the Committee could at once report on the credentials of the other members of his delegation, whereas five only would require time to make investigations.

Mr. N. J. NEWELL stated that none of the up-country delegations had been furnished officially with credentials.

The PRESIDENT said the gentlemen named in General Canby's official orders were regarded as members of the Convention.

The question being on agreeing to the motion to appoint a Committee of five, it was decided in the negative.

Mr. DUNCAN then moved that a Committee on Credentials, consisting of one from each District, be appointed by the Chair.

The motion was agreed to.

The PRESIDENT appointed the following:

Abbeville, John A. Hunter; Anderson, Dr. N. J. Newell; Barnwell, James N. Hayne; Berkley, Joseph H. Jenks; Beaufort, W. J. Whipper; Charleston, F. L. Cardozo; Chester, B. Burton; Clarendon, Elias Dickson; Chesterfield, H. C. Shrewsbury; Darlington, B. F. Whittemore; Edgefield, Frank Arnim; Fairfield, James M. Rutland; Georgetown, Joseph H. Rainey; Greenville, James M. Allen; Horry, Henry Jones; Kershaw, J. K. Jillson; Lexington, S. Corley; Lancaster, Chas. Jones; Laurens, Joseph Crews; Marlboro', Calvin Stubbs; Marion, H. E. Hayne; Newberry, B. Odell Duncan; Orangeburg, T. K. Sasportas;

Pickens, Dr. L. B. Johnson ; Richland, Chas. M. Wilder ; Spartanburg, J. P. F. Camp ; Sumter, T. J. Coghlan ; Union, James H. Goss ; Williams - burg, S. A. Swails ; York, John W. Mead.

The Committee then retired.

Mr. BOWEN moved that the Convention appoint John R. Pinckney and Peter Miller, temporary Sergeants-at-Arms.

Objection being made to the transaction of business during the ab- sence of the Committee, the motion was withdrawn.

On motion of Mr. WILLIAM J. McKINLAY, Secretary, the Convention took a recess for three quarters of an hour.

On re-assembling, M. DUNCAN, Chairman, made a verbal report of the Committee on Credentials, stating that the Committee examined first the credentials of each of its own members, and appointed a Chairman and Secretary. Finding their credentials correct, they then called in the delegates from other districts, and examined their credentials, which, on being proved, were signed by the Chairman and Secretary underneath the official signature of General Canby. This signature, on being shown to the doorkeeper, is to be taken as evidence that the bearer is a mem- ber, and entitled to admission in the Convention. Any member arriving afterwards, must be identified by the Chairman and Secretary of the Committee, which propose to continue its organization until all the mem- ber had arrived, or there was no further necessity for their services.

On motion of Mr. B. BYAS, the report of the Committee was adopted.

Mr. F. L. CARDOZO moved that a Committee of one from each Dis- trict be elected by the members of each respective District delegation to constitute a Committee to nominate suitable officers for the permanent organization of the Convention. He thought it essential to success that there should be a thorough and complete canvass for officers to fill those important positions. Upon the permanent President would depend much of the dignity and success of their legislation. He hoped there would be no smaller number appointed, as it would in that case be very apt to form a clique. One from each delegation, he felt sure, must give more satisfaction and be attended with better results.

Mr. HURLEY moved that the Convention proceed to a nomination at large.

The motion was not agreed to.

On motion of Dr. NEWELL, the Convention adjourned to meet to- morrow at 12 o'clock.

SECOND DAY.

Wednesday, January 15, 1868.

The Convention assembled at 12 M., and was called to order by the Chairman, Mr. T. J. ROBERTSON.

The proceedings were opened with prayer by the Rev. B. F. RANDOLPH as follows:

Almighty God, Creator and Ruler of the Universe, we praise and adore Thee for Thy goodness. which Thou hast manifested to us, Thy undeserving creatures. Thou seest the purposes for which we have assembled. We pray that we may be guided by Thy spirit and wisdom. Thou knowest the grave responsibilities resting upon us. Thou knowest we have assembled for the purpose of framing the Constitution for the legislative guidance of this State. We pray that Thou will fill our hearts with love for the general welfare of the citizens of the State, and that in all things Thy wisdom may guide us, and all our actions redound to Thy honor and glory. We pray that we may remember our accountability to Thee and the people of South Carolina. Help us, oh Lord, in these our great responsibilities. Help us in our work here, and when we finish our earthly course, receive us into that welcome abode in heaven; and all we ask is in the name of God our Father and Jesus our dear Redeemer. Amen.

The CHAIRMAN requested Mr. H. E. HAYNE, Delegate from Marion District, to act as temporary Assistant Secretary.

On the call of the roll, one hundred and nine Delegates answering to their names, the CHAIRMAN announced a quorum present.

The minutes of yesterday were read by the Secretary.

Mr. F. L. CARDOZO asked a correction of the minutes by inserting the motion offered by him previous to adjournment yesterday. He also thought that motion should be taken up as unfinished business.

Mr. T. HURLEY said he supposed his motion to proceed to a nomination at large was the last business of yesterday.

Mr. N. G. PARKER said the motion of the gentleman from Charleston, Mr. F. L. CARDOZO, was pending yesterday when the motion of the gentleman from Berkley, Mr. HURLEY, was offered, as a new motion, not as an amendment, and he thought, therefore, the first motion took precedence in the order of unfinished business.

Mr. B. O. DUNCAN moved that the Convention now proceed to ballot for a permanent President, the Convention voting by Districts, and that two tellers be appointed to count the votes.

3

Mr. B. F. RANDOLPH thought they should act first on the pending motion of yesterday, to appoint a Committee on permanent organization

Mr. RICHMOND called attention to the fact that a number of members had arrived since yesterday, whose credentials had not been examined.

The CHAIRMAN said that would be the duty of the Committee on Credentials.

Mr. DUNCAN said he had signed a number of credentials this morning, and the doorkeeper had been instructed not to admit any one whose credentials were not signed. He was informed, however, that no doorkeeper had been appointed, and moved that a temporary doorkeeper be appointed until a permanent organization was effected.

On motion of Mr. R. C. DeLARGE, the Janitor of the building was appointed temporary doorkeeper.

Mr. DUNCAN renewed his motion to proceed to a permanent organization.

Mr. F. L. CARDOZO called for the unfinished business of yesterday.

The CHAIRMAN decided that there was no unfinished business pending.

Mr. B. F. RANDOLPH said there was a motion pending at the hour of adjournment, and it ought to be disposed of.

Mr. DUNCAN moved that the unfinished business be laid upon the table, and the motion was agreed to.

Mr. DUNCAN again renewed his motion to proceed to balloting, amending it so that each delegate, when the Districts were called, should come up and vote.

Mr. R. C. DeLARGE moved to go into an informal ballot for President, with the view of obtaining the sense of the House. The motion was agreed to.

Mr. J. M. ALLEN moved that the two persons receiving the highes number of votes on the informal ballot should be considered candidates. The motion was agreed to.

Messrs. B. O. DUNCAN and T. K. SASPORTAS were appointed tellers.

On motion of Mr. ALLEN, the Convention took a recess of fifteen minutes.

On reassembling, the Secretary proceeded to call the roll of the delegates by Districts, and each delegate came forward to the President's desk and deposited his vote.

Mr. DUNCAN reported the result of the informal ballot as follows :

Dr. A. G. MACKEY 74, B. F. WHITTEMORE 37, T. J. ROBERT-SON 1, and J. M. RUTLAND 1. Total 113.

Mr. G. PILLSBURY moved that Dr. A. G. MACKEY be unanimously declared the President of the Convention.

Mr. WHITTEMORE begged the gentleman to withdraw the motion temporarily.

Mr. PILLSBURY assented.

Mr. WHITTEMORE then addressed the Convention as follows:

Mr. President: I understand that the election we have gone into thus far has simply been an informal election, and that the expression of the Convention thus far has been declared, as far as the two higher candidates are concerned, as favorably disposed towards Mr. Mackey and myself.

I arise to express my thankfulness to the gentlemen upon this floor for the kindness they have shown in their expression of a preference for and the presentation of my name in connection with the Chairmanship of this Convention. I assure them of my appreciation of the compliment and trust that I have truly merited its bestowment; but, in justice to myself, and that the most earnest wish of my heart may be gratified, I deem it proper to say, that I have not been, nor am I at the present an aspirant for any other position than that to which I have been, by my constituency. elected, namely, an humble delegate, with the freedom and privilege to labor on the floor or in the committee room. My earnest desire is that harmony may prevail in all the deliberations of this body—that the work for which we have been sent may be immediately prosecuted, and that success may attend our every honest effort. That, therefore, a permanent organization may be at once effected, I do respectfully withdraw my name from the canvass, and move that Hon. **A. G. Mackey** be unanimously declared as the choice of this Convention for President.

The motion was agreed to amid applause, and the CHAIRMAN announced that Dr. **A. G. MACKEY** was unanimously elected permanent President of the Convention.

Mr. A. J. RANSIER moved that a Committee of three be appointed to apprise Dr. MACKEY of his election, and conduct him to the Chair.

Mr. F. J. MOSES, Jr., moved as an amendment that a Committee of two, to consist of Messrs. B. F. WHITTEMORE and R. C. DeLARGE be appointed for the purpose.

The amendment was not adopted.

The motion of Mr. RANSIER was then agreed to, and the PRESIDENT appointed Messrs. A. J. RANSIER, B. F. WHITTEMORE and R. C. DeLARGE.

On motion of Mr. PARKER, the Convention took a recess for fifteen minutes.

After recess, Mr. WHITTEMORE, Chairman of the Committee appointed to wait upon the President elect, reported that they had discharged that duty, and now begged leave to state that they had the honor of introducing the President elect.

Dr. MACKEY was then conducted to the chair, and formally presented to the Convention by Mr. T. J. ROBERTSON, the Chairman.

In entering upon the duties of his office the PRESIDENT addressed the body as follows:

Gentlemen of this Convention :—While I return you my thanks for the honor that you have conferred on me, in selecting me to preside over your deliberations, I confess that I assume the Chair with great diffidence as to my capability to discharge its duties. I can, however, safely promise a determination to perform the important task with the strictest impartiality, and with all the judgment in my power.

The position in which your kindness has placed me, will necessarily preclude me from a general participation in the debates of the house, and will condemn me to silence on many questions, on which, if I were on the floor, I would wish to be heard. You will perhaps, therefore, pardon me, if I take the present occasion, once for all, to define my position and to express my sentiments on some of the great topics, which are now agitating our country.

The Convention in which we are now sitting is marked by two peculiarities, which has distinguished no other Convention that has preceded it in South Carolina—peculiarities which demand for it the commendation of every lover of liberty and respecter of human rights.

Convened, as I contend it has been—for else, I had not been here—by competent legal authority, it is the first Constitutional Convention in this State, in the selection of whose members, the ballot box, the true palladium of rational liberty, has been made accessible to every man who was not disqualified by legal or political crime. In the call for the five South Carolina Conventions which have preceded it, and which were held in 1776, in 1777, in 1790, in 1860, and in 1865, but a portion of the people were permitted to exercise the elective franchise, because slavery, that vile relic of barbarism, had thrown its blighting influence upon the minds of the people, and for the noble doctrine that governments were constituted for the good of the whole, was substituted that anti-republican one, that they were intended only for the benefit of one class at the expense of another. But in the call for this body, every true man who could labor for the support or fight for the defence of the commonwealth has been invited to a representation. Manhood suffrage has for the first time been invoked to convene a body which is to make the fundamental law for all. This is, then, truly and emphatically a people's Convention —a Convention by the representatives of all who have minds to think— and to think for themselves, or muscle to work—and to work for themselves.

Again. In the five Constitutional Conventions held in this State, to which I have already alluded, the fundamental law therein framed was made a finality. The people were ignored as a part of the body politic by the Convention, which declared itself possessed of despotic and **irrespon-sible authority** : and, in every instance, refused to submit its **proceedings,** and the Constitution which it had framed, to the people for their ratification. This was but a natural and necessary result of the influences of the political sentiment that then prevailed. It was but consistent that those who deemed one-half of their fellow-citizens to be chattels, should forget, or overlook the political rights of the other half.

But we, who in these days, when the rising beams of political truth, promise, after so much storm, a brighter sky for the republic ; we who are emerging from that cloud of false opinion, into the full sunshine of that truth, know and claim ourselves to be only the representatives of the people. We arrogantly assume no final action, no irresponsible power, but recognize the rights of all men, of all races, the poor as well as the rich, the ignorant as well as the wise—of all men who make the State their home and identify themselves with its interests. We dare not present to them an organic law for their government, as something with which they have nothing to do but to hear it and obey. Our work here is not to be considered as completed until the people shall have reviewed it and ratified it. Not we, ourselves, but they who sent us here, are to say whether we deserve the reward of a " well done, good and faithful servants." For the first time in the history of South Carolina, will the people be recognized as the true framers of their own organic law. Of such a Convention, organized on the great acknowledged principles of Democratic Republicanism, I am proud to be a member ; far more proud to sit here beneath the folds of that beloved flag which is this day floating from our roof, than I should have been to have been in that other body which met in this city in 1860, with no such loyal symbol to protect it, but which rather sought to tear its stripes to tatters and to dash its stars to the earth.

Yielding to none in sentiments of devotion for that flag of my fathers, and in abhorrence of every sentiment of disloyalty and treason to that Government, to which I owe a paramount allegiance, I yet have no vindictive feelings towards those of my fellow-citizens who were led by the abstractions of their political leaders, to entertain different and opposing sentiments—sentiments which I deemed errors, but which they believed to be truths. I grant to them that liberty of thought which I demand for myself. Hence, I profess myself to be a moderate man. I am opposed to all confiscations of property, because the confiscation of all the lands of rebel owners in the State can have no effect in promoting the welfare of that State in elevating its political condition or advancing its commercial and agricultural prosperity. I am opposed to any general disfranchisement of the masses of the people. It is too late now to disfranchise as a punishment for treason. Punishment should be inflicted for the sake of reform. To inflict it now would be only to gratify revenge. I want no more disfranchisement either as to number of persons or as to duration of time, than is absolutely necessary to secure the safety of the nation, and if that can be secured by none at all, then would I favor a general amnesty.

I call God to witness, that in taking my seat in this august body, I do so only because I desire to contribute what little abilities or influence I may have to the restoration of peace and harmony, and for the establishment of such a Constitution or form of government for my native State as will secure to every man in the commonwealth an equal share of political rights, will protect us in the future from the errors which have led to our present unhappy condition, and will speedily rehabilitate the State as a constituent part of the great national confederation.

With this expression of my sentiments, which will not, however, control me in the impartial administration of the duties of the office to which you have assigned me, I am now prepared to take my place as your presiding officer, at the same time invoking your indulgence for any unintentional errors that I may commit, and your earnest co-operation in preserving the dignity and decorum of the body.

Mr. W. J. WHIPPER, of Beaufort, offered the following resolution, which was agreed to:

Resolved, That pending the appointment and report of the Committee on Rules, the Convention adopt and be guided by the rules of the House of Representatives of the United States for its government.

Mr. R. C. DeLARGE moved that the thanks of the Convention be returned to Mr. T. J. ROBERTSON, of Columbia, temporary Chairman, for the dignity and impartiality with which he had presided over their deliberations.

The motion was unanimously agreed to.

Mr. R. G. HOLMES, of Beaufort, moved that the Convention proceed to the election of a Secretary by ballot.

Mr. A. J. RANSIER, of Charleston, moved that a Committee of one from each District be appointed to complete the permanent organization of the Convention, and that the Committee report on Thursday at twelve o'clock meridian.

Mr. W. J. WHIPPER, of Beaufort, opposed the motion, and said they were ready to go on and complete the organization without an adjournment. He thought the appointment of a Committee upon which the Convention was to wait for a report, not only foolish, but unjust. He wanted to go on with their work as rapidly as possible.

Mr. D. H. CHAMBERLAIN, of Berkley, also opposed the resolution and thought the elections could be better settled in open Convention. It would take less time than an unwieldy Committee, and give more general satisfaction. He hoped to get to work and accomplish what they had to do as early as possible.

Mr. R. G. HOLMES, of Beaufort, moved that the resolution be laid upon the table, which was carried.

Mr. HOLMES moved to proceed to the election of a Secretary by ballot.

The PRESIDENT decided the motion out of order, the Convention having adopted the rules of the House of Representatives, which require all elections to be *viva voce*. The rules, however, might be suspended for the time, by the unanimous consent of the Convention.

On motion, the Convention proceeded to the election of a Secretary, *viva voce.*

Mr. WHITTEMORE nominated Mr. Carlos J. Stolbrand, and moved that the calling of the roll be suspended, which was adopted.

On motion of Mr. WHITTEMORE, Mr. C. J. Stolbrand was declared elected permanent Secretary of the Convention by acclamation.

Mr. PARKER moved that they proceed at once to the election of an Assistant Secretary, an Engrossing Clerk, a Sergeant-at-Arms, an Assistant Sergeant-at-Arms, a Doorkeeper, an Assistant Doorkeeper, and a Chaplain.

Mr. F. J. MOSES, Jr., of Sumter. I would like to ask the mover of the resolution before the House, something in relation to its meaning. I would ask if he means that some person not a member of the Convention shall be elected chaplain ? I, for one, am opposed *in toto* to that part of the gentleman's resolution which refers to the election of a regular chaplain for this body. As far as I am individually concerned, I am utterly opposed to the services of any chaplain in this body. I am opposed to having our proceedings opened with prayer, for that practice so sacred in the past, has been so prostituted lately in all legislative bodies that it is to be feared it will be prostituted here, and instead of prayers we shall have political protestations. But it is not on that ground alone I object. I ask, gentlemen, whether it would not be best for us as members of the Convention, as responsible persons, sent to perform the work before us, as responsible to all the citizens of the State, is it not incumbent upon us to have as much respect for the Treasury of the State as possible, and to get along as cheaply as possible.

I disclaim, in what I have said, having reference to any one. It is simply my individual opinion in reference to the practice of opening our proceedings with prayer. I ask what necessity is there to put our hands into the Treasury of the State and pull out more money than necessary, when we have gentlemen here who no doubt are willing to give their services free of charge.

Mr. B. F. RANDOLPH, of Orangeburg. I am in favor of the election of a chaplain. My first reason is that it is a custom of all such legislative bodies to have a chaplain. The Congress of the United States has a chaplain. Our legislatures have chaplains, and so far as I have noticed the reports of all the conventions which have assembled under the reconstruction acts, they all elected chaplains. It would, therefore, be passing strange for South Carolina to assemble in Convention and not elect a chaplain.

The gentleman thinks we should respect the Treasury of the State. No one upon this floor is more than I am, disposed to respect that Treasury. But I am not disposed to ignore religion, forget God, and leave one of the most important offices, as I consider it, unnoticed by the Convention. I think, therefore, it is wise to have a chaplain. The quota of officers will not be complete unless we do. There will be a lack, a vacancy. I hope that out of the respect the Convention has for God, or if there is any respect at all in our religion, unless it is all a farce, we shall have a chaplain. If it is a farce let us have no prayers, let us say the Bible is a lie, and that God never hears prayer. Let us ignore the doctrine which says Jesus died to save all men. I believe that religion is a reality, and I hope we may regard it as such. If the Bible is truth, it is to become established throughout all the earth, and it should be respected, not only by such bodies as this, but by all men. It says every knee shall bow to Jesus, and every heart respect him. That day, in my humble opinion, is coming, and I hope, if it has been the general rule, we will have a chaplain, and do as other Conventions have done, elect one.

Mr. MOSES, Jr. I do not propose to answer the gentleman I do not think a single argument he has made was applicable. The closing part of his speech should convince every one that the view I took was right and proper, that we ought not to take so much money out of the Treasury. We have had a capital prayer since the argument was started.

Mr. L. S. LANGLEY, of Beaufort I agree in part with the views of the delegate from Sumter. I believe this Convention should not by the election or appointment of a chaplain, sacrifice or waste money belonging to the State. We have gentlemen here, honorable members of this body, who are perfectly competent to act as chaplain, and in the impoverished condition of the State Treasury, I think it would be better that the Chair should appoint some gentleman, or request some member in the body, to officiate as chaplain.

Mr. J. J. WRIGHT, of Beaufort, rose to a point of order. The resolution did not require that the chaplain should be paid, and the gentleman seemed to be discussing the question whether they should or should not pay a chaplain. The resolution simply called for the election of a chaplain.

The PRESIDENT decided the point of order was not well taken, the previous speaker having used his argument in stating his positions.

Mr. L. S. LANGLEY said, with regard to the remark of the gentleman from Sumter, as to the propriety of opening their proceedings with prayer, he was decidedly in favor of first invoking the divine blessing before commencing their deliberations. He certainly hoped that it could never be said that they, in the noon of the 19th century, refused to open their sessions with prayer. He believed this to be the sense of this body, which had assembled for the purpose of taking the proud Commonwealth of South Carolina back into the Union from which she was torn in 1860 He was in favor of the appointment of a chaplain, but not in favor of paying him eight dollars per day out of the State Treasury. There were able gentlemen in the body, whom he believed had sufficient patriotism, and were ready and willing to officiate without pay.

Mr. R. C DeLARGE called for the previous question, which was not sustained.

Mr. J. J. WRIGHT, of Beaufort, said he was in favor of the election of a chaplain to the body. The resolution did not require he should be elected outside of the body. The gentleman from Beaufort, and the gentleman from Sumter, perhaps, had the same reasons for taking the positions they had, that it was not necessary to have a chaplain. One of the gentlemen, and he did not know but the other, had only followed the examples set for him to respect money more than God.

Mr. T. HURLEY, of Berkley, moved to amend the resolution so as to read that "the Chaplain shall be appointed by the Chair."

Mr. N. G. PARKER accepted the amendment.

Mr. A. J. RANSIER, of Charleston, moved to amend so as to leave it to the Chair to appoint from among the Convention those willing to perform extra labor of Chaplain.

Mr. A. C. RICHMOND hoped it would be left open so that visiting clergymen could be invited to be present and open the proceedings with prayer. He hoped the proceedings would be opened with prayer because it was customary. He was of opinion though that the invocation of the divine blessing in the South Carolina Convention of 1860 was not of any great service to the cause for which it was invoked, nor was it in the Convention of 1865. But he did not wish to abolish it because the custom had been abused on other occasions. It was possible they might prove more serviceable.

Mr. PARKER said that he did not suppose, in offering the resolution, it would be debated. He did not think there was any gentleman in the House who wished to make a speech upon the question, and was surprised at the remarks made. He hoped the debate would stop and the question be at once disposed of.

4

The question then being taken the resolution was adopted.

The PRESIDENT read the following communication from Mr. F. A. Sawyer, a delegate from Charleston, resigning his position:

CHARLESTON, January 15, 1868.

To the President of the Convention of South Carolina:

SIR:—I regret the necessity which compels me to announce to you my inability to assume the duties of a member of the Constitutional Convention.

While I am grateful for the confidence of my fellow-citizens, manifested in my election, it is due to them to say that I should not have consented to become a candidate had I foreseen, or thought I had a reason to foresee, the pressure of official duties under which I *now* find myself, and which is greater than at any time in the last two years.

If I become a member of the Convention I must elect one or two alternatives, neither of which I am willing to accept; on the one hand, a neglect, to an unjustifiable extent, of my duties as an officer of the United States Government—duties, the due performance of which I am every way bound to provide for; or, on the other, an unsatisfactory and partial discharge of the obligations which would be imposed upon me as a member of the Convention. The duties of my office at this season are such that a large part of them can be devolved upon no other person, and must be personally performed in the hours appropriated to the sessions of the Convention.

The labors I might perform as a member of that body would be only auxiliary to those of other equally or more competent men.

With the hope that the action of the body over which you preside will be such as to merit the approval of good men everywhere, and receive the endorsement of all right-thinking men in our State,

I am, sir, very respectfully, your obedient servant,

FREDERICK A. SAWYER.

On motion of Mr. HURLEY, the resignation was accepted.

The PRESIDENT called the attention of the Convention to the fact that a vacancy was made in the Charleston delegation by the resignation of Mr. Sawyer, which would require to be filled by the action of the House.

Mr. PARKER moved to add, in the resolution just adopted, a Reading Clerk, an Engrossing Clerk, three Messengers, and an additional Doorkeeper.

Mr. HURLEY moved that the Messengers be appointed by the Chair.

The PRESIDENT said he preferred that the voice of the Convention should be heard in the selections of all its officers

Mr. R. C. DeLARGE was opposed to having so many hangers on and digging unnecessarily into the State Treasury. If they kept on they would soon have as many officers as delegates.

Mr. J. J. WRIGHT agreed with Mr. DeLARGE. Most of us, he

said, have been used to waiting on ourselves, and I think we can do it yet.

Mr. R. C. DeLARGE moved that the number "three" be substituted by "two."

The amendment was adopted, and the motion then agreed to.

On motion of Mr. WHITTEMORE the rules were suspended, and Mr. Paul M. Poinsett declared elected Assistant Secretary by acclamation.

Mr. Wm. R. Mitchell, on motion of Mr. H. E. HAYNE, was declared elected, by acclamation, Engrossing Clerk.

On motion of Mr. C. P. LESLIE, Mr. Hannifin, appointed Janitor of the building by General Canby, was elected Hall Keeper by acclamation.

On motion the Convention adjourned to 8 o'clock this evening.

EVENING SESSION.

The Convention assembled at 8 P. M., and the roll being called, one hundred and ten delegates responded to their names.

The Chair announced that the first business in order was the election of a Sergeant-at-Arms.

On motion of Mr. T. K. SASPORTAS, the rules of the house requiring a *viva voce* vote to elect were suspended, and the Convention proceeded to the election of a Sergeant-at-Arms by ballot.

At the request of a member, the President defined the duties of a Sergeant-at-Arms. He said these duties are very important. He is, under the President, the executive and financial officer of the Convention. It is his duty to carry into effect all orders in relation to keeping order, and to enforce all rules, regulations and order of the house. He is also the cashier of the house. It is his duty to take charge of all funds. He pays the members whatever is due them, keeps an account of the same, and is accountable for the proper disposition of the funds.

Mr. PARKER nominated Mr. T. W. Johnson.

Mr. R. C. DeLARGE moved that T. W. Johnson be elected by acclamation.

Mr. W. J. WHIPPER hoped the motion would not prevail, but that the vote would be by ballot, and that other candidates before the Convention would have the same fair chance to be voted for.

Mr. E. W. M. MACKEY moved that they proceed to an election by ballot, which was carried.

On the ballot being taken, the result was announced as follows :
T. W. Johnson, 53 ; Edward Conway, 46 ; Scattering 13.

The PRESIDENT announced that 57 being necessary to a choice, there was no election.

Dr. N. J. NEWELL moved that Mr. T. W. Johnson be declared unanimously elected by acclamation. Lost.

Mr. L. S. LANGLEY said he was given to understand that Mr. Johnson is not a Republican. If that was the case, he wanted to know it. He alluded to the report in order to give the gentleman an opportunity to clear himself. It came to him from pretty good authority.

Mr. WHITTEMORE moved that the Convention proceed to a second ballot for Sergeant-at-Arms, which was carried.

On counting the votes, the result was announced as follows :

Edward Conway, 67 ; T. W. Johnson, 45 ; Scattering 2.

The PRESIDENT announced that Edward Conway having received a majority of all the votes cast, was duly elected Sergeant-at-Arms.

A motion was made to suspend the rules and proceed by ballot, to the election of an Assistant Sergeant-at-Arms.

Mr. B. BYAS nominated Peter Miller.

Mr. DUNCAN nominated Mr. T. W. Johnson, and took occasion to say that the charge made against Mr. Johnson, was unjust. He also advocated taking the vote *viva voce*, as required by the rules adopted by the House.

Mr. CHAMBERLAIN favored the vote *viva voce*, as required by the rules under which they were working. He thought it would save time and labor.

Mr. E. W. M. MACKEY did not think the point well taken. He thought the vote by ballot much shorter, as whole delegations could come forward and deposit their votes at once ; whereas, by the *viva voce* plan, each member present was called upon to answer.

Mr. DUNCAN did not see why they should adopt the rules of the House of Representatives, and then in every instance depart from them.

On motion of Mr. H. E. HAYNE, the motion to suspend the rules, and proceed to vote by ballot, was laid on the table.

Mr. W. J. WHIPPER moved that when this house adjourn, it adjourn to meet to-morrow morning at ten o'clock. The motion was agreed to.

Mr. R. C. DeLARGE notified the Convention that he would, to-morrow, move for a reconsideration of the vote by which Mr. Conway was elected Sergeant-at-Arms, it having been proclaimed that the person aforesaid was incompetent to discharge the duties of the office.

Mr. F. J. MOSES, Jr., moved that the Convention do not adjourn until a permanent organization had been effected. This was opposed by Mr. LANGLEY, who said he had no notion of staying here. His contract with his constituents did not require it, and he wanted to go home in reasonable time.

The question being put, the motion was not agreed to.

The Convention proceeded to vote *viva voce* for Assistant Sergeant-at-Arms, which resulted in the election of Mr. Peter L. Miller.

In the same manner, after two ballots, Mr. Samuel Dickinson, of Charleston, was elected Doorkeeper, and Mr. John Fitzsimmons, of Columbia, Assistant Doorkeeper.

Mr. E. W. M. MACKEY moved to go into an election for two Messengers, but before taking the question, the Convention adjourned to meet at ten o'clock to-morrow morning.

THIRD DAY.

Thursday, January 16, 1868.

The Convention was assembled at 10 A. M., and was called to order by the President, A. G. MACKEY.

Prayer was offered by Rev. B. F. WHITTEMORE.

The roll was called, and seventy-nine members answering to their names, the PRESIDENT announced a quorum present, and the Convention ready to proceed to business.

The minutes of yesterday were read and approved.

Mr. B. O. DUNCAN moved a reconsideration of the resolution passed yesterday regarding the election of officers, so as to amend by leaving it to the President to invite any clergyman present to open the Convention with prayer.

Rev. B. F. RANDOLPH opposed the adoption of the amendment on the ground that they would, perhaps, frequently be without a clergyman in attendance, and also, that it was against the practice of Congress and other legislative assemblies to select one of their own members for opening the proceedings with prayer. From the fact, also, that clergymen in the Convention might conscientiously differ, and each see fit to advocate their peculiar views, he hoped the members would see the propriety of electing a Chaplain outside of the body.

The question being taken on the motion of Mr. DUNCAN, it was adopted.

Mr. B. O. DUNCAN then offered the following resolution, which was adopted:

Resolved, That the Doorkeeper be instructed to admit no one to this floor who has not his credentials properly signed, or has not been admitted to the floor as an officer, reporter of the press, or an officially invited guest.

The PRESIDENT read an official communication from Headquarters, amending a certificate of election to a delegate from Horry, by inserting the name of Augustus Reaves Thompson in place of Stephen H. Thompson, which was received as information.

Mr. R. C. DeLARGE moved that the Convention take up the unfinished business, and proceed to the election of a Messenger. He nominated Mr. Oliver Williams, of Charleston.

The PRESIDENT, in reply to a delegate, stated that no member could address the Convention upon any subject not actually before it, should any other member object.

Mr. DUNCAN asked whether they were not allowed to inquire into the fitness of candidates for office.

The PRESIDENT said the information upon which delegates in the Convention are expected to base their votes should be obtained outside of the Convention, and among the friends of the candidates.

Mr. WHITTEMORE stated that some fifteen votes had been lost last night by members mistaking the name of the boy fitting for College and a candidate for Messenger. He wished to inform them that his name was Peter Phillips. He also moved to suspend the calling of the roll.

Mr. BOWEN opposed the election of Peter Phillips as Messenger on the ground that he was a minor, and therefore ineligible. He understood this to be in the nature of a State office, to which no one under twenty-one years of age could be elected. He would have no objection to have him appointed, but was opposed to his election.

Mr. B. F. RANDOLPH suggested that he might be appointed as one of the pages of the Convention. They would need two or three pages, and he was in favor of electing three.

Mr. PARKER moved that they proceed at once to the election of a Messenger.

Mr. CRAIG asked whether it had been decided that the boy Phillips was ineligible to office.

The PRESIDENT stated that, by the rules of the House of Representatives. which had been adopted as rules of government for this body, no person under age was eligible to office.

Mr. T. HURLEY withdrew the name of Peter Phillips, and substituted that of William Elliott.

The Convention then entered into an election for a Messenger, which resulted as follows : William Elliott, 65 ; J. D. Price, 11 ; William Miller, 10 ; Scattering, 8. Total 94.

The PRESIDENT announced that William Elliott having received a majority of the votes cast, was duly elected Messenger of the Convention.

Mr. B. F. WHITTEMORE took the Chair, and the Convention entered into an election for an Assistant Messenger. On counting the votes the result was announced as follows : Whole number cast 95—J. D. Price received 56 ; Alexander Bryce, Jr., 23 ; William Miller, 6 ; Scattering 10.

Mr. J. D. PRICE was declared to be the duly elected Assistant Messenger.

Mr. J. K. JILLSON moved that the Convention proceed to the election of three Pages.

Mr. F. L. CARDOZO opposed the appointment of Pages. The Convention did not need them, and it was desirable to avoid all unnecessary expense, especially in the present empty condition of the State Treasury.

Mr. T. K. SASPORTAS moved to strike out the word three and substitute one.

Mr. DUNCAN said he agreed with the gentleman from Charleston, Mr. CARDOZO, and was opposed to the election of any more officers.

Mr. J. J. WRIGHT thought the elections might stop with the choice of one Page.

On motion of Mr. H. E. HAYNE, the motion and amendment were laid on the table.

Mr. J. J. WRIGHT—I wish to offer as a motion, that this Convention do all it can to sustain the Charleston Daily News and Charleston Courier for the correctness and impartiality with which they have thus far reported the proceedings of this Convention, and that we go as far as becomes gentlemen to cause the Mercury to "evaporate."

Cries all over the hall, " I'll second that motion."

Mr. C. P. LESLIE—Will the delegate from Beaufort reduce his motion to writing ?

Mr. L. S. LANGLEY—Does not this motion require more than one second ; for I want the pleasure of seconding it myself ?

Mr. N. G. PARKER—I move that the motion be laid upon the table. The motion was not agreed to.

Mr. W. J. WHIPPER—I trust, Mr. President, that the question raised will not be sustained. For one I desire to have no bickering with newspapers or newspaper dealers. It is true that some papers have reported us fairly, and that others, from pecuniary consideration, have indulged in burlesque; but we are here for some other purpose than to censure newspapers, and it will be time enough when our deliberations have ended to take action it the matter proposed. I care nothing whether the editor of the Mercury, or his representative, comes here to burlesque the proceedings of the Convention or the persons of its members. He does so for the purpose of making money, and I hope the Convention will not so far depart from its dignity as to interfere with him in this design. We have higher aims before us than to seek to control the columns of a journal which at best can do us no harm.

Mr. B. F. RANDOLPH. It seems to me that to support this resolution will be to endorse the sentiments of these two papers, the News and and Courier, and I do not understand that either of them has ever supported the Republican party, or does so at the present time. I am, of course, pleased to see that both of them exhibit a spirit of fairness, and manifest respect for the Convention, in making their reports of these proceedings; but I cannot recognize the necessity of endorsing them to the extent named in this resolution on that account alone.

Mr. J. J. WRIGHT. In offering my resolution, it was not with a view to endorse the political course of either of the papers named, but simply to commend them to the Convention for the fairness and correctness of their reports; and for the purpose of stopping further discussion, I now withdraw my motion.

Mr. B. F. RANDOLPH. I now move, Mr. President, that the reporters of the press be invited within the bar of this Convention.

Mr. L. S. LANGLEY. I move as an amendment, that the reporter of the Mercury be excluded. I do not propose to allow or extend facilities to the editor of the Mercury to burlesque this Convention. The manner in which we should sustain our dignity is to treat those who do not come here as gentlemen, as they really are. Now, ever since the Convention has been in session, the Mercury has burlesqued its members. I don't care any thing about burlesque myself, but I do believe that paper to be utterly incapable of a respectable or gentlemanly course, and I am not willing for that rebel sheet to burlesque this body. I want it to be excluded. I am willing to admit all who act like gentlemen, but all who are not gentlemen, but come here in the garb of gentlemen, I want to see go out.

Mr. F. J. MOSES, Jr. I hope that this question, having been opened, will be discussed fully, and until every delegate on the floor, who wishes to do so, shall have spoken upon it. I myself regard the motion as one of the most dangerous that could be introduced into this body. What has this Convention to do with the political course of a newspaper? When the resolution was offered by the gentleman from Beaufort, I was in favor of amending it to the effect that the reporters of the press were entitled thus far to the thanks of the Convention for the correct manner in which they had reported our proceedings ; but what can we gain by putting a seal of condemnation upon the Charleston Mercury ? We have nothing to do with the political opinions of any journal, and whether it represents us fairly or unfairly, is a matter which belongs to its own management. I go further ; I say that I do not agree with that dogma which has been set up here that no person in the State can be a gentleman, simply because he happens to differ with those upon this floor in political opinion. Great God, Mr. President, shall we abuse a newspaper on account of its mere opposition or burlesque of our course ? I do not stand here to vindicate the Mercury. It is no friend of mine. I have been abused by it since the Convention assembled more than any other man on the floor, and yet I hope this resolution will be voted down with the most emphatic censure, because I do not believe the influence of this Convention should be employed to deprive any paper in South Carolina of its patronage.

Mr. F. L. CARDOZO. I am not in favor of endorsing either of the newspapers named. Fair as the reports of the News and Courier may have been, they are not understood to be in favor of the constitutionality or legality of this Convention. As to the Mercury, it has burlesqued us, but to attempt to exclude its reporter from the bar of the Convention on that account, would be only to exhibit a smallness, a pettiness of spite, unworthy of our character. Let it come and pursue what course it may please; let us pursue our straightforward course, and the world will judge between us.

Mr. A. J. RANSIER. While I do not approve the course of either of the papers that have been mentioned, I agree with the gentleman from Sumter, that it is dangerous to discard or turn away any reporter on account of his political opinions or those of his paper. It is a stab at the liberty of the press; and I am surprised that so much attention has been given to the subject. I desire that all the journals shall be welcomed to the Convention. As to the Mercury, I think that it has contributed more to republican liberty than any other paper in the country. It has shown up the sentiments of those opposed to republican principles, and thereby benefitted the party. I therefore propose to let it go on, to give it my

5

hearty thanks for the service it has done, and continue to extend to its reporter a welcome to this Convention.

Mr. N. G. PARKER. In the present state of public opinion in South Carolina, I think that an attempt to exclude the Mercury or its reporter from the Convention, would do that paper more good than harm, and the Convention more harm than good. While I am opposed to the Mercury's manner of carricaturing this body as the "Ring-Streaked and Striped Negro Convention," I would give them all the latitude they asked. If we attempt to exclude the Mercury they will make money out of it, but give them rope enough and they will hang themselves.

Dr. N. J. NEWELL. I move that the Mercury be left to the temperature of the atmosphere.

Mr. J. H. JENKS. Mr. President, I cannot see the point of that joke; but, nevertheless, call for the previous question.

The call for the previous question was not sustained.

Mr. W. J. WHIPPER. I am glad that the motion for the previous question has not been sustained. While I exceedingly regret that any newspaper has chosen to burlesque the proceedings of the Convention, it is proper to say, that any newspaper is entitled to the exercise of the privilege, so that it does not garble the speech or defame the character of an individual, in which case, he certainly would have redress. Until that is done, we detract from the dignity of our proceedings by paying any attention to the matter. It is due to the Mercury to say that it has not violated its privileges as a public journal. Its editors have a right to burlesque if they choose to use it; but when they place an individual in a false position, he has clearly the right to demand correction. Until then, it is frivolous to notice it.

We have come here for a great purpose, and we should not be swerved from it by newspapers, whose chief purpose, while we the representatives of the people are here to make the laws of the Commonwealth, is simply to make five cent pieces.

Mr. J. S. CRAIG. I regret that this subject has been brought before the Convention. for I think the body should treat the Mercury with the silent contempt it deserves. No doubt the other papers are as much opposed to our action as that journal, yet they have taken a high-toned and gentlemanly stand in the treatment both of the Convention and its cause; and I am willing to give them credit for it. But as for the Mercury, I think it would have been far more becoming to it, not to have stooped to a low and degrading position. For myself I have no regard save for those who have proved themselves to be true Union men.

Mr. W. E. JOHNSTON. I am glad that this question is up, for I have had the honor of being raised higher by the Mercury than any man in the Convention. On Tuesday morning, the Mercury said "the Rev. Mr. Johnston, in his speeches will cry aloud and spare not." Now I hope the editor will be spared, and that the Convention will spare him until he hears Johnston line out, "not a foot of land do I possess,"— spare him long enough to see the end of this meeting, and that he will be converted before he leaves.

On motion of Mr. T. K. SASPORTAS, the whole matter was laid on the table.

On motion of Mr. W. J. McKINLAY, the reporters of the press were invited to seats within the bar.

Mr. J. J. WRIGHT offered the following resolution :

Resolved, That a Committee of three be appointed by the President, for the purpose of waiting on Major-General Canby, Brevet Brigadier-General R. K. Scott, and Governor James L. Orr, and inviting these gentlemen to seats in the Convention.

Dr. N. J. NEWELL said that he would state, in reference to Governor Orr, that he had advocated reconstruction since last July.

A VOICE—Not a very long time, that.

Dr. NEWELL. Ever since last Spring then, and although he may not have actually supported the Republican party, he has never thrown any obstacle in its way, and on all occasions has favored the call for the Convention. It has been customary, in all Conventions in South Carolina, to invite the distinguished officers of the State to a seat on its floor, and I hope no exception will be made in the case of Governor Orr.

Mr. N. G. PARKER moved that the name of General Clitz be inserted in the resolution.

The mover accepted the amendment.

Mr. S. A. SWAILS moved that the word "provisional" be inserted before the word Governor.

Mr. J. J. WRIGHT said he would accept the amendment to avoid discussion.

Mr. L. S. LANGLEY favored the original resolution, and desired to incorporate the name of the Mayor of the City, P. C. Gaillard, Esq.

Mr. WRIGHT accepted the amendment.

Mr. J. M. RUTLAND said he hoped the proposition to insert the words "provisional governor" would not be adopted, since it would look like half an insult, when it was intended to be a courtesy.

Mr. A. C. RICHMOND opposed the amendment inviting Mayor Gaillard, on the ground that he was known not to be a sympathiser with the purposes of the Convention. He would say nothing disrespectful of a brave man, who certainly had a right to entertain what political opinions he saw fit, but, nevertheless, could see no good reason for showing him the same respect that was shown to General Canby or Governor Orr.

Mr. R. C. DeLARGE said he was astonished to see a member of the Convention object to extending the common courtesy of the Convention to the civil magistrate of Charleston, simply on the ground of party politics. If they made that a basis for extending courtesies, there were others named in the resolution whose politics and his own did not agree. He trusted that Mayor Gaillard would not be invited simply as Mayor Gaillard, but as the representative of the entire people in his official capacity. He is the temporary executive officer of the city. This was the Constitutional Convention of the State, called by the Reconstruction Acts of Congress. They did not know Mayor Gaillard as a partisan, but only knew him in his official capacity. He hoped the amendment would prevail.

Mr. A. C. RICHMOND said he did not regard the Mayor of Charleston as a very distinguished character, and saw no reason why the same respect should be shown to him as to the Union Generals named. With reference to the Governor of the State, there was no reasonable ground for refusing to extend to him a common courtesy. He had the reputation of being a fair and moderate man, and his official capacity as the civil head of the Government entitled him to the same consideration that was bestowed on those who represented the military authority.

Mr. N. G. PARKER said it had not occurred to him to embrace the name of the Mayor in the invitation contemplated; but after hearing the reasons so ably set forth by the delegate from Charleston, Mr. R. C. DeLARGE, he should certainly vote for the amendment.

Mr. R. B. ELLIOTT, moved that the "Board of Aldermen and Common Council" be included in the invitation.

The motion was not agreed to.

Mr. E. W. M. MACKEY moved, as an additional amendment, that the chief of police be also invited.

The motion was laid upon the table.

The PRESIDENT read the amended resolution as follows:

Resolved, That a Committee of three be appointed by the President to wait upon Brevet Major-General E. R. S. Canby, Major-General R. K. Scott, Brevet Brigadier-General H. B. Clitz, and Provisional Governor James L. Orr, and his Honor Mayor Gaillard, of the city of Charleston, and invite these distinguished gentlemen to seats within the bar of this Convention.

The question was then taken on the adoption of the resolution, and it was decided in the affirmative.

Mr. F. J. MOSES, Jr., of Sumter, introduced the following resolution:

Resolved, That a Committee of three be appointed to wait upon his Excellency Governor James L. Orr, and request him to address this Convention, and that said Committee report to-morrow.

Mr. L. S. LANGLEY moved that the word "provisional" be inserted before the word "Governor."

Mr. MOSES accepted the amendment.

Mr. J. J. WRIGHT moved to lay the resolution upon the table.

The motion was not agreed to.

Mr. BEVERLY NASH. I want to say, Mr. President, that I am opposed to the resolution inviting Governor Orr to address this Convention. I am unwilling to concede the right to him which he has denied to me— the right of free speech. I hold in my hand now an order from General Canby, by which on Tuesday last I was called upon to stand before a military commission and give an account of a speech which I delivered in Fairfield District, in behalf of the Republican party, at which Governor Orr and his friends took umbrage. I am proud to say that the military board decided I had a right to say what I did on that occasion. The Constitution of this country guarantees free speech, and as Governor Orr has opposed it outside of this hall, I am opposed to men of the stripe of Governor Orr exercising the privilege of free speech inside of the hall. I am willing to concede the right of free speech under all circumstances, but am not one of those men who bow down and lick the boot of Governor Orr, because he happens to occupy the position of Provisional Governor of South Carolina. I do not believe his sentiments are those of a majority of the people of the State, or that, representing, as he does, a minority, we shall honor the people by inviting him to address this Convention.

A gentleman has said that Governor Orr has endorsed reconstruction since last July. So he has, as he understands it; but his understanding is not that of this Convention. His desire is not to come into this Convention, but to draw this Convention over to him, so that I do not think anything he would say could enlighten us the least bit, and if Governor Orr he invited to address this Convention, it should be from the steps outside.

We are here to provide a Constitution for South Carolina, not for the purpose of making converts. We didn't come here to see Governor Orr make a flight like a squirrel from one tree to another. I remember he said to me last spring, "better wait and find out whether this is going to be a failure or not; don't jine the Republican party yet;

don't jine the Democratic party." He wanted me to sit on the fence with him, and when he got ready to make one of his flights, I suppose he wanted me to follow him. No, gentlemen, I don't propose that Governor Orr shall come here to teach us ground and lofty tumbling. We don't want to tumble, and if he comes here, he will come to let us see one of the loftiest tumbles which he has ever made yet.

I come from a part of the country where the people are Republican; from a District where they would rather hear Governor Perry any time, because we know he is going to cuss us and abuse us every way he can; but Governor Orr! why, he tumbles so fast that it makes a man's head "dizzle" to look at him. I heard a man say, on the way down here, that the Governor told a delegate that he was very much in favor of the homestead law, and he was going to press the Convention to make some provision for the people in this respect, and he did'nt care whether they called him a nigger or anything else.

Now, Governor Orr is in a position which reminds me of what an old woman once told me about John Tyler. He's hanging upside down between two parties. The Conservatives are trying to kick him off; the Republicans don't want him, and I reckon he'll hang there until the blood runs down into his brains, and then we shall get rid of his body.

W. J. WHIPPER, of Beaufort. I cannot agree with the gentleman from Richland that we shall reap any disadvantage from the presence or speech of Governor Orr. Certainly I am not afraid of his eloquence; and although it has been said that his effort is to draw parties over to him, I take it that this Convention is composed of firmer material than will yield to a single effort, at any rate. For the protection of the gentleman from Richland, however, who appears to have reason to fear the Governor's power, I presume that the Convention will excuse him from attendance. I, however, desire to hear the Governor, and if it be true that he will make a grand and lofty tumble, for God's sake let him do it, provided he tumbles in the right direction. I think the gentleman from Richland must have been an imitator of these gymnastics, for if I remember rightly he has done some extraordinary lofty tumbling himself.

It is due to the Governor that he should be invited to address the Convention. It is a body which has assembled to frame a Constitution and civil government, and we must bring to our assistance everything in sympathy with us. If Governor Orr proposes thus to afford the aid of his counsel and experience, by all means let him be welcome. We have got to use the Provisional Governor of the State to carry out the the reconstruction policy, and if he is in sympathy with us, let us know it. If he is not in sympathy with us, let us know it also. We are not familiar with the condition of the State. We can learn it only from the heads of departments; and shall we at the outset ignore the very chief of its civil government? He has not been removed; he holds his office by the same authority which permits this Convention to sit here; and until he is removed there should be perfect unanimity of action between the Governor and representatives of the people.

The effort made to raise a laugh over the past career of Governor Orr meets with no sympathy from me. It is nothing to me what he has done. He is not worse than some of the delegates on this floor, and perhaps a great deal more sincere. I am willing that he shall defend himself, both as a man and an executive officer of the State. There are many men who were not in favor of reconstruction until it became a fixed fact; not in favor of equal suffrage until compelled to yield to the irresistible logic of events. I am willing to admit all such, even if they make the grand and lofty tumble of the gentleman from Richland. We can increase our numbers only by accession from other ranks, and we should be anxious and zealous to do so, and to ignore all petty prejudices and passions as unbecoming men who occupy our now responsible position.

Mr. G. PILLSBURY opposed the resolution on the ground that it would entail additional and unnecessary expense. The cost of the Convention to the State, he said, was about a thousand dollars a day, and between the discussion and the speech it would consume a considerable sum of money. He was, nevertheless, anxious to hear the Governor, with whom as yet, he had never been brought in contact, although he had been told that he was corporally large enough for any man to see, and suggested that he be invited to address a public meeting in some hall where the Convention could be provided with front seats.

Mr. E. W. M. MACKEY said he agreed with the remarks of the member from Charleston. He would be happy to hear from the distinguished gentleman, but desired, on the score of economy and not to consume the time of the Convention, that some other place than the hall be procured for the purpose.

Mr. F. J. MOSES, Jr., modified his resolution so as to appoint the hour for the Governor's address to-morrow (Friday) evening. He stated, also, that he had introduced it only as an evidence of respect that should be entertained by the Convention for the Chief Executive. He did not speak for him, and indeed knew nothing of his present political sentiments.

Mr. R. C. DeLARGE strongly favored the resolution, and thought that if it should cost ten thousand dollars to establish proper accord between the Governor and the Convention, it would be money well spent. Through his official position, he is better acquainted with the wants of the people of the various Districts than any other man now in the State, and even though he might disagree with the Convention in some of its political actions, the speaker believed that his counsel and experience would prove valuable in the determination of many matters of importance which were to come before the body.

Mr. DeLARGE concluded by moving the previous question.

The previous question was ordered, and the main question being put, the resolution as amended was unanimously agreed to.

The PRESIDENT appointed the following delegates as a Committee to wait upon Generals Canby, Scott and Clitz: Messrs. B. F. Whittemore, B. Odell Duncan and F. L. Cardozo ; as a Committee to wait on Governor Orr: Messrs. F. J. Moses, Jr., J. M. Rutland, and W. G. Whipper.

Mr. J. K. JILLSON presented the resignation of Mr. Edward J. Conway, the Sergeant-at-Arms elected last evening, which, on motion of Mr. WHITTEMORE, was accepted.

On motion of Mr. H. E. HAYNE, the PRESIDENT appointed a Committee, consisting of Messrs. F. J. Moses, Jr., S. A. Swails, H. E. Hayne, F. L. Cardozo, R. G. Holmes, W. M. Viney, E. W. M. Mackey, B. O. Duncan, J. M. Rutland, J. M. Allen, S. Johnson and J. A. Crews, to nominate a suitable person for the position.

Mr. N. G. PARKER offered a resolution appointing a Committee of three to make changes on the floor for the better accommodation of delegates, to provide desks and stationery, and secure the hall, for which, as he announced, two hundred and fifty dollars a week, or one thousand dollars for the session, was charged by Mr. J. P. M. Epping, the proprietor.

The resolution was adopted, and the PRESIDENT appointed Messrs. Parker, C. C. Bowen and B. O. Duncan as a Committee on the hall.

Mr. E. W. M. MACKEY moved that a Committee of nine be appointed by the Chair, to report what Standing Committees are necessary to conduct the business of the Convention.

The motion was agreed to, and the PRESIDENT appointed the following delegates : Messrs. B. F. Whittemore, F. L. Cardozo, F. J. Moses, Jr., J. J. Wright, J. M. Rutland, R. B. Elliott, B. O. Duncan, N. G. Parker and C. M. Wilder.

Dr. N. J. NEWELL, moved that when the Convention adjourn, it be to meet at 8 o'clock, P. M.

Mr. H. E. HAYNE moved to insert " ten o'clock, A. M., to-morrow," which was agreed to, and

On motion of Mr. C. M. WILDER, the Convention adjourned.

FOURTH DAY

Friday, January 17, 1868.

The Convention assembled at 10 A. M., and was called to order by the PRESIDENT.

Prayer was offered by Rev. F. L. CARDOZO.

The roll was called, and ninety members answering to their names, the President announced a quorum present, and the Convention ready to proceed to business.

The Journal of yesterday was read and approved.

Mr. F. J. MOSES, Jr., Chairman of the Committee appointed to recommend the name of a suitable person to fill the position of Sergeant-at-Arms, reported that they had not been able to perform satisfactorily the important duty assigned them, and requested that further time be granted.

The report was adopted and the request granted.

Mr. F. J. MOSES, Jr., from the Committee to wait upon his Excellency Governor James L. Orr, and to request that he would address the Convention, reported that they had performed that duty, and that his Excellency had accepted the invitation. The Committee recommend that when this Convention adjourns, it adjourn to meet this evening at half past seven o'clock, and that the Governor be introduced to the Convention at eight o'clock.

The report was adopted.

Mr. N. G. PARKER, from the Committee appointed to make alterations for the better accommodation of delegates, and to provide stationery and desks, reported that they had discharged the duty, furnished stationery and provided desks.

The report was adopted.

Mr. PARKER moved that the Convention proceed to an election for a printer.

Mr. DUNCAN hoped the employment or nomination of a printer to the Convention, would be left to one of the Standing Committees, whose business it might be to attend to that duty.

6

Mr. J. J. WRIGHT said as there were several candidates for printer, he thought the matter should be left to the decision of the Convention.

Mr. DUNCAN said the action of the Committee was not binding on the House but they could make the best terms and then submit the propositions to the House.

The motion to elect a printer was agreed to.

Mr. E. W. M. MACKEY nominated H. Judge Moore, publisher of the Charleston Advocate.

A delegate stated that Mr. Moore's facilities for doing the work were ample, and, moreover, that he had intimated his purpose, if given the printing of the Convention, to commence the publication of a daily Republican paper.

Dr. N. J. NEWELL moved to lay the subject on the table.

The motion was not agreed to.

Mr. DUNCAN moved that a Committee of three be appointed to communicate with the several printing establishments in the city, and ascertain the best terms and arrangements for the work that can be effected, and to report at the next session of the House.

The PRESIDENT stated as the motion to elect was adopted, no other motion could be entertained except a subsidiary motion.

Mr. R. C. DeLARGE moved to strike out all after the word "resolved," and insert "that a Committee of three be appointed by the House to receive bids for the printing of the Convention, the names of the respective parties and their proposals to be reported to-morrow morning "

The substitute was adopted.

Mr. DeLARGE moved a reconsideration of the motion just adopted, and that the motion for reconsideration be laid upon the table.

The PRESIDENT announced the following Committee on Printing : Messrs. R. C. DeLarge, Dr. J. C. Neagle, S. Corley, A. C. Richmond, B. F. Randolph, J. M. Runion, L. S. Langley.

Mr. J. M. RUTLAND offered the following :

Resolved, That it be referred to a Special Committee of five, to enquire as to the propriety of calling to the aid of this Convention one or more of the Solicitors of the State, for the purpose of preparing, in proper legal form, the Ordinances and other measures of this Convention, and that the said Committee report by resolution or otherwise.

Mr. E. W. M. MACKEY moved that the resolution be laid on the table, which was agreed to.

Dr. N. J. NEWELL called the attention of the President to the fact that a number of gentlemen had been appointed upon three out of five Committees yesterday, and some of them made Chairman of two. Other members, representing larger and more wealthy constituencies, had been ignored in these appointments. He believed this had occurred through inadvertence or in the hurry of business, and not from any partiality on the part of the President. To prevent its recurrence, however, he submitted the following resolution:

Resolved, That no delegation be allowed to serve upon more than one Standing Committee at a time, and that should it create inconvenience to the several Committees, the Convention shall so arrange its deliberations as to give them ample time to prepare business.

The PRESIDENT stated that one gentleman was appointed on three Committees, and, to his surprise, another had been made Chairman of two. This arose from his unavoidable temporary absence during the session of yesterday, and the occupancy of the Chair by another presiding officer, (Mr. WHITTEMORE.) Several gentlemen had been appointed by both officers to different Committees, and hence the labors of these gentlemen were much increased, to the regret of the President, who desired that the labors of the Convention in Committee work should be equally divided among the members. It was not the intention of the Chair to make appointments other than in the most impartial manner, or to make any gentleman work more than he should.

Dr. NEWELL begged leave, after these explanations, to withdraw his resolution.

Mr. B. BYASS offered a resolution that the Sergeant-at-Arms be required to reserve seats for the use of lady spectators.

Mr. L. S. LANGLEY moved to amend by striking out the words, "lady spectators," and insert ladies, which was agreed to.

The resolution as amended was adopted.

Mr. S. A. SWAILS offered a resolution for the appointment of a Committee of three to wait upon the Hon. George S. Bryan, United States District Judge, and Major D. T. Corbin, United States District Attorney, and invite them to a seat on the floor of the Convention.

Mr. R. C. DeLARGE moved to amend by inserting, "and all other Judges from Courts of Record in the city."

Mr. J. J. WRIGHT objected, as he might be placed upon that Committee, and he should dislike the responsibility of going round to invite all the Judges of the Courts of Record.

The amendment was not agreed to. The original resolution was then adopted.

On motion of Mr. E. W. M. MACKEY, a Committee of three was appointed to define the duties of the subordinate officers of the Convention.

The PRESIDENT announced the following Committee : E. W. M. Mackey, D. H. Chamberlain, and W. E. Rose.

Mr. L. S. LANGLEY offered the following :

Resolved, That, in the opinion of this Convention, the weal of the Republic and of the Commonwealth of South Carolina requires that the further confiscation of lands and disfranchisement for political offences should be forever abandoned.

On motion, the resolution was laid upon the table for the present.

Mr. WHITTEMORE, Chairman of the Committee to report what Standing Committees were necessary for the Convention, reported the following : Committee on Bill of Rights, Legislative Committee, Executive Committee, Committee on the Judiciary, Committee on Franchise and Elections, Committee on Education, Committee on Finance, Committee on Rules and Regulations, Committee on Petitions, Committee on Miscellaneous Matter, Committee on Review and Consolidation.

The Report was adopted and the Committee discharged.

Mr. WHITTEMORE, from the Committee appointed to wait upon Generals Canby Scott, Clitz, His Excellency Governor Orr, and the Mayor of the City, reported that having waited upon those gentlemen, they all expressed their thanks for the compliment, and requested the Committee to assure the Convention that they would take the earliest opportunity to visit the body.

The report was adopted, and on motion of Mr. R. C. DeLARGE, the Committee was discharged.

Mr. DUNCAN offered the following resolution which was adopted :

Resolved, That a Committee of five be appointed to consider what measures are necessary for the relief of the people of the State, and to report as early as possible.

On motion of Mr. R. C. DeLARGE it was

Resolved, That all resolutions and motions, save those of temporary character, be referred to the appropriate Standing Committees.

Mr. J. M. RUNION offered the following :

1. *Resolved,* That whatever differences of opinion may exist as to the late plan of reconstruction enacted by the Congress of the United States, however ultra men in the South or in the North may oppose or denounce them, there is but one course of action for the true patriots to pursue, and that is unhesitatingly and in good faith to carry out their enactments.

2. *Resolved,* That the reconstruction measures, as passed by Congress, should be recognized as being the supreme laws of the land, passed by

the constitutional authority of the United States, and are therefore entitled to the unhesitating support of every citizen of this great Republic.

3. *Resolved*, That those measures combined form a harmonious whole and constitute the chart by which twelve millions of people are to be guided into the haven of perpetual union on the basis of equal justice, without regard to race or color.

On motion of Mr. R. C. DeLARGE, the resolutions were referred to the Committee on Bill of Rights.

The PRESIDENT announced Messrs. NEWELL, JILLSON and KERSHAW as the Committee to wait upon Judge Bryan and District Attorney Corbin, and invite them to seats in the Convention.

Mr. B. F. RANDOLPH moved that a Committee on Militia, a Committee on Charitable Institutions, and a Committee on Incorporations be added to those named by the Committee on Standing Committees. Referred to the Committee on Miscellaneous Matters.

Mr. N. G. PARKER offered the following, which was referred to the Committee on the Legislative part of the Constitution :

Whereas, in every State of the United States, and in every unreconstructed State under the Government of the United States, the several divisions of the same are denominated counties, except the State of South Carolina and Louisiana ; therefore

Resolved, That the several Districts of this State shall hereafter be known and denominated Counties.

Mr. B. O. DUNCAN offered the following :

Resolved, That Major-General Ed. R. S. Canby be requested to suspend all executions of judgments or other forcible collections of debts contracted prior to the 30th June 1865, for the space of three months, or until further measures of relief can be matured by this Convention.

Mr. F. J. MOSES, Jr., said the resolution was entirely superfluous, as General Canby had already issued such an order.

Mr. WHITTEMORE asked if this resolution was designed for the protection of any of the gentlemen of the Convention.

Mr. DUNCAN said he was not aware that such was the case. It was not the case of the mover at any rate.

Mr. J. J. WRIGHT said he was utterly opposed to the proposition. General Canby had already issued an order securing to every person a home, which was evidently all the resolution aimed to accomplish ; but whether he had done so or not, it would be well for the Convention to pause before dictating measures which could not be carried out when enacted. It might be necessary to pass some laws of a legislative character, but it remained to be seen when or how they were to be enforced.

For one he preferred to see the Convention engaged in its legitimate work—namely, that of framing the Constitution and establishing the supreme law of the State. He hoped, therefore, the resolution would be voted down.

Mr. DUNCAN said he did not presume to dictate to General Canby. This is a simple request, and a Convention of the people of South Carolina had a right to make that request. General Canby's order does not include debts contracted prior to the secession of the State, but only those between the 19th of December, 1860 and the 30th of June, 1865. The debts now oppressing the people of the State are those contracted prior to the war. During the war, debts could be paid, but there was a regulation of the finances of the rebel Government which prevented the possibility of paying old debts. On that account the present order of General Canby does not cover the troubles of the country. These troubles are not known generally. Hundreds of farmers are burdened with debts contracted when property was in an entirely different condition and lands were more valuable. Now the sale of these lands will not pay the debts when sold, as they are at great sacrifice. The creditor is not paid, and the debtor is thrown out of house and home. The only class benefitted are the men who speculated during the war, and the lawyers who collect the debts. Nor are the freedmen benefitted, for they are deprived of employment by the breaking up of their old homes and employers. Pass such an order as this, however, and the farmers and planters will be enabled to procure farming implements and provisions.

Mr. J. H. RAINEY advocated the passage of the resolution. He believed it to be of vital importance; many debts had been contracted, for which bonds were given; for instance, debts due for the purchase of slaves. These bonds had matured, and the debtor being unable to meet his obligations, his lands were seized and property taken by the officers of the law. He thought the Convention should take measures to ameliorate the condition of the people at this time. If they had been able to accumulate any money during the past year, they should be allowed to keep it to purchase farming utensils and provisions to meet their necessities. If we allow them to be taken hold of by the law, our State will be more impoverished and no good will be gained. He had no doubt the gentleman from Beaufort, (Mr. J. J. WRIGHT,) was in favor of enforcing the law, as he is a lawyer and gets his bread by its enforcement. They, the representatives, were not lawyers, and they should be desirous of doing everything to ameliorate their condition.

Mr. F. L. CARDOZO. I am opposed to the passage of this resolution. The Convention should be certain that their acts are not of doubtful constitutionality. The laws of the United States do not allow a State to pass a law impairing the obligations of contracts. This, I think, is therefore a proper subject for the Judiciary. I am heartily in favor of relief, but I wish the Convention to have nothing to do with that matter.

The resolution was laid on the table.

Mr. R. C. DeLARGE moved that the resolution offered by Mr. L. S. LANGLEY, relative to non-confiscation and non-disfranchisement, which had been laid upon the table, be taken up.

Mr. DeLARGE called for the yeas and nays.

Mr. WM McKINLAY, of Charleston, rose to explain his vote, saying that he unhesitatingly made the declaration that he was in favor of the principle embraced in the resolution, but would vote against taking it up, because he thought the discussion of the question premature.

The yeas and nays being called, resulted as follows:

YEAS—Messrs. Leslie, Parker, Chamberlain, Hurley, Wilder of Beaufort, Bell, Whipper, Langley, Mackey of Charleston, DeLarge, Bowen, Dickson, Driffle, Elliott, Wooley, Rutland, Edwards, Webb, Rainey, Allen, Runion, Cooke, Hayne of Marion, Johnson of Marion, Thompson of Marion, Duncan, Mackey of Orangeburg, Randolph, Bryce, Johnson of Pickens, Nash, Wilder of Richland. Thompson of Richland, Coghlan, Lee, Moses, Johnson of Sumter, Goss, Olson, Darrington, Rose, Corley, C. D. Hayne, Camp, Wingo and Gentry—46.

NAYS—Lomax, Hunter, Perry, J. N. Hayne, Mayer, Middleton, Gray, Lee, Richmond, Jervey, Becker, Byas, Smalls, Wright, Holmes, Ransier, McKinlay of Charleston, Cardozo, Cain of Charleston, Sanders, Burton, Thomas, Viney, Craig, Shrewsbury, Lang, Whittemore, Brockington, Humbird, Rivers, Harris. Arnim, Jacobs, Miller, Johnson of Greenville, Thompson of Horry, Jones of Horry, Jillson, Dill, Chestnut, Clinton, Jones of Lancaster, Davis, McDaniels, Owens, Stubbs, Jackson, Collins, Nance, Henderson, Sasportas, McKinlay of Orangeburg, Maulden, Dogan, Nuckles, Swails, Neagle, White, Mead, Milford and Foster—61.

ABSENT—Williamson, Newell, Johnson of Anderson, Jenks, Pillsbury, Alexander, Nelson, Perry, Donaldson, DeMeddis, Bonum, Boozer, Crews, Cain of Orangeburg, and Robertson—16.

So the motion to take the resolution from the table was not agreed to.

The PRESIDENT announced Messrs. E. W. M. Mackey, D. H. Chamberlain and W. E. Rose, Committee to instruct the subordinate officers as to their various duties.

Mr. C. P. LESLIE offered the following resolution, which was referred to the Committee on the Legislative part of the Constitution.

WHEREAS, the financial condition of this State, considered in connection with the future prosperity of the people, requires the earnest attention of this body,

Resolved, That a fit and proper provision for homesteads be incorporated in the Constitution of this State.

On motion of Mr. R. C. DeLARGE, all the Judges of the State Courts now in the city, were invited to seats upon the floor of the Convention.

Mr. N. G. PARKER offered the following Ordinance, which was referred to the Committee on the Constitution :

AN ORDINANCE

TO ALLOW EACH HEAD OF A FAMILY IN SOUTH CAROLINA A HOMESTEAD, AND TO PREVENT THE LEVY AND SALE OF THE SAME UNDER ANY CIRCUMSTANCES.

Be it ordained, That hereafter each head of a family in this State shall be allowed to own a homestead, which shall consist of one hundred acres of land, with a dwelling house and other improvements thereon, if not exceeding the value of two thousand dollars ; *Provided,* That none of the above lands be within the limits of a city or incorporated town, or in lieu of the above land, real estate in a city or town not exceeding two thousand five hundred dollars. The above named homestead shall be exempt from levy and sale by virtue of any process whatever under the law of the State.

Mr. B. BYAS offered the following, which was referred to the Legislative Committee :

Resolved, That a Special Committee be appointed to take into consideration the political division of the State.

Mr. F. J. MOSES, Jr., gave notice that on to-morrow he would introduce the following :

Resolved, That it be referred to a Special Committee of ten to ascertain whether or not there exists any authority in this Convention to legislate beyond and independent of the Reconstruction Acts of the United States Congress.

Mr. T. HURLEY introduced the following Ordinance, which was referred to the Judiciary Committee :

AN ORDINANCE

TO ANNUL ALL CONTRACTS AND LIABILITIES FOR THE PURCHASE OF SLAVES WHERE THE MONEY HAS NOT YET BEEN PAID.

Be it ordained by the people of South Carolina, in regular Convention assembled, That all contracts and liabilities made for the purchase of slaves, whether by parole or under seal, where the money has not been paid, shall be null and void, and all Clerks of Courts of Common Pleas and Masters in Equity, be required on proper affidavits to annul the same.

On motion the Convention adjourned.

EVENING SESSION.

The Convention re-assembled and was called to order at half-past seven o'clock.

On motion of Mr. F. J. MOSES, Jr., it was ordered that when this Convention adjourns, it adjourn to meet at 12 M., Monday.

Mr. B. F. RANDOLPH gave notice that he would, on Monday, introduce a petition to the Congress of the United States, praying for the continuance of the Bureau of Freedmen, Refugees and Abandoned Lands, until the restoration of the civil government, and that then a Bureau of Education be established by the General Government.

On motion of Mr. R. C. DeLARGE, the floor of the Convention was thrown open to visitors for the evening.

General Canby and Staff here entered the hall, and was greeted with great enthusiasm, which was gracefully acknowledged by the General.

The PRESIDENT, after introducing the General to the Convention, said that the latter requested him to say that he was unable at present to make a speech, but hoped they would take the will for the deed and receive his kindest thanks.

His Excellency Governor Orr, arrived shortly after, and was escorted into the hall by the Committee.

On the stage were the President of the Convention and Generals Canby and Scott. The Governor on ascending the stage, was received by the PRESIDENT, who said:

Governor Orr : I am gratified that it becomes my duty as the organ of the Constitutional Convention of South Carolina, to welcome you to the floor of the house. The members of this Convention desire only to act for the good of the Commonwealth, whose people they represent. While they feel the most profound respect for the exalted official position which you occupy as the Chief Magistrate of the State, they are well aware that that position gives you an ample opportunity of becoming peculiarly cognizant of the condition and wants of their constituents. They, therefore, desire to hear your voice on those subjects, and profit by your knowledge and experience. I promise you in their behalf, a patient and attentive hearing, and a careful consideration of the topics you may present.

Gentlemen of the South Carolina Constitutional Convention, I have the honor to introduce to you His Excellency James L. Orr, Governor of the State.

Mr. President and Gentlemen of the Convention : I esteem the invitation which you have extended to me to address this Convention, as a compliment paid to the existing Executive authority of the State, more than to the individual who represents that authority ; therefore, in behalf of the State for your kind consideration I tender you my thanks.

7

You are here in Convention to frame a Constitution for the people of South Carolina, and have been elected in conformity to the laws of the United States.

Unfortunately, in my judgment, for the best interests of the people of the late Confederate States, serious differences have arisen between the President of the United States and the Congress. In 1865, immediately after the surrender of General Johnston, the President appointed Provisional Governors, and provided for the calling of Conventions in all of the Southern States. The programme which he adopted was not in unison with the views of Congress, and, after very considerable delay, the Reconstruction Acts of March were passed. The Congress claimed that the power to reconstruct the Southern States which were in rebellion against the authority of the United States, belonged to them and not to the President. Hence, they ignored his action. It is due to frankness that I should say that, in my judgment, the plan projected by the President, and which has been carried into execution in all its details, except as to the representatives in Congress, was not only liberal but wise. With reference to the latter point, however, Congress having taken a different view of the subject, determined that the Southern States shall not be admitted to representation and to equal privileges in the Union upon any other basis than that which has been prescribed. The Acts passed go even further. They assume that the South, in relation to the government stands in the position of conquered provinces, and that as a conqueror, it has a right to prescribe the terms and conditions upon which the South is to be admitted into the Union.

It is unnecessary, on the present occasion, that I should discuss the constitutionality or wisdom of the Acts of Congress. Let it suffice for me to say that they have become the law of the land. They are laws which have been adopted in strict accordance with all the forms prescribed by the Constitution of the United States, and as a law-abiding citizen, not only now, but from the time of the passage of these Acts in March last, I am one of those who believed that it was not only the duty, but the interest of the people of the Southern States to go to work in earnest and carry them into operation.

Hence, immediately after the passage of the bill in March last, I publicly advised the people of the State, of all complexions, who were entitled to register to do so, and then go to the ballot-box and vote for the very best men possible to frame a Constitution in conformity with the provisions of the Acts of Congress.

My advice upon the subject ought, I think, to have been received as disinterested, since the execution of these laws excluded me from all the privileges of a citizen, because I belonged to the disfranchised class.

At the extra session in July the Legislature made the restrictions even more stringent than they were before, and this harshness on the part of Congress has had much to do with the action of the white people of South Carolina, in refusing to go to the polls and participate in any respect whatever in the election of delegates to the Convention. In this, I think, a great mistake has been committed by the great majority of whites of South Carolina. My judgment was, and is, that every white man who registered should have gone to the polls and voted. I even go further. I think that the whites, who have the intelligence to a very large extent, should, in Convention or otherwise, have submitted to the colored people of the State propositions as to the privileges and franchises which they are entirely willing to extend to them, now that the whole of the race have been declared free, not only by the constitutional amendment, but by the action of the Convention of the State.

The fact cannot be disguised, however, that the white population has almost unanimously abstained from exercising the privilege, and your Convention is, therefore, strictly speaking, the representative only of the colored·population of South Carolina. This being the case, it cannot be denied that the intelligence, refinement and wealth of the State is not represented by your body. Hence, the very high duty is devolved upon you of discharging the important trusts confided to your care in such a manner as to commend your action to the confidence and support, not only of those by whom you were elected, but of those who refused to go to the polls and vote in the election.

I say to you, very frankly, that I regard this body as invested with the sovereign power of the State, and that the Constitution which you may adopt for the people of South Carolina is one which will not only be ratified and accepted by Congress, but one under which all classes in South Carolina will live for years to come.

The party which has passed the reconstruction laws has undisputed control of the Government in both houses of Congress, and will retain it until the 4th of March, 1869. Prior to that time a Presidential election will occur. The probability is that an individual representing the Conservative and Democratic element in the North and West will be elected President. It may be that a Conservative element will largely preponderate in the next election for members of the House of Representatives on the 4th day of March, 1869, who are Conservative or Democratic, and opposed to the legislation that may have been adopted, it will be impossible to effect a repeal of these acts, obnoxious as they are to the new party, prior to the 4th of March, 1871. Confirmed as I am, therefore, in the opinion that the legislation of the present and preceding Congress will remain in force until the 4th of March, '71, and that any Constitution adopted by this Convention will continue to be of force until that time at least, I have felt it to be my duty as the Executive of the State, and as an individual, to be present in Charleston during the sessions of your Convention, in the hope that through official, if not personal, influence, I may accomplish something in securing from the Convention a liberal, just, and wise Constitution.

If such a Constitution is adopted, harmony, good feeling and prosperity will prevail. If, however, extreme views and measures are engrafted upon that instrument, it will increase the interest which now exists between the two races, and force the whites of the State, who have the means to do so, to leave its borders and seek homes in other communities. It will produce discontent and disquiet everywhere, and confidence, trade and enterprise will all be paralyzed. As responsible duties are, therefore, devolved upon you as were ever devolved upon a similar body of men in any State, the interest and prosperity of South Carolina depend not only upon law and a good Constitution, but upon the kind relations which are to be established between the two races.

It is idle to disguise the fact that the white and colored races, where they have been thrown together, with equal privileges, have rarely, if ever, been able to harmonize.

The experiment of giving to the colored people of the South all of the privileges of the franchise of citizens is a novel one, and time only can determine whether it is to be a success or a failure. On the one hand it is said that the negro is utterly incapable of exercising the rights and privileges of a citizen. On the other hand it is said that the "rebel"— the man who participated in the war—should not be allowed to participate in the Government. Those of you who are to the manor born know the fact that very few white men in South Carolina abstained from some participation in the late war. You know further that the intelligence, wealth and virtue of South Carolina entered eagerly into that war, and that when it is attempted to disfranchise or denounce these persons as unworthy of public trust, it is to exclude the real intelligence and experience of the State from her councils. This is one of the reasons why so little experience is to be found in your body.

To supply this deficiency it is the duty of the Convention to give to every question that may be submitted the gravest and most potent consideration. When you appreciate the fact that the intelligence of the white population is antagonized to you; that all of your acts will be looked upon with distrust; when you remember that whatever you do will be subjected to the severest scrutiny at home and abroad; when you know that whatever errors are committed here will be reviewed by no friendly eye, the duty is doubly incumbent upon you of framing a Constitution which will challenge the criticism and condemnation of the most intelligent portion of the State.

Believing, as I have said to you, that you have assembled here with proper motives; that the Constitution framed by you will be the law under which the people of South Carolina will live for years to come, and, occupying the position of Chief Executive of the State, I am here to give to members of your body the benefit of whatever suggestions may occur to my mind, provided I can do so without seeming to intrude. My earnest desire is that this Convention shall adopt a Constitution which will meet with the cordial support and approval of the white as well as the black race. If it be just, wise and liberal, when the question comes up on its adoption, I shall certainly recommend my friends to vote for it. If unwise or unjust, I shall be equally free to urge its rejection.

It is proper to say here that in my judgment it was unfortunate that the election of delegates to this Convention should have been influenced by the politics of the day. Members should have been chosen without reference to their opinions upon national politics. It was immaterial whether they were Conservatives, Radicals or Democrats. The best men of each District, without reference to antecedents or to present political opinions, ought to have been selected for the great purpose of framing a Constitution. This was my advice to the people of the State months ago. It was a matter of little consequence who was elected as representatives of the State in the Senate or House of Representatives of the United States, whether Radical, moderate Republican or Democrat, as compared with the important duty of framing a Constitution for a people which was to last for years. The whites in the State have abstained from going to the polls, and the blacks mainly have been controlled by the Radical party. Although thus elected, let the members of the Convention remember that the Constitution which they adopt for the people of South Carolina may, in all probability, be the Constitution of the State for the next twenty years—when Radical, Republican and Democratic parties may have passed away and others have taken their place. Anything, therefore, which savors of a partisan purpose, incorporated in the Constitution may, in a very few years, find that it has outlived its purpose, its supporters, and its *proteges.*

In framing a Constitution, many improvements may be made upon the existing laws of the land. I beg very briefly to call your attention to some of them. If they are adopted, in my judgment, when the question is presented to the people of the State to ratify or reject the Constitution, you will be able to command in its favor a much larger vote than was polled in the election of delegates to the Convention.

First. Upon the question of the elective franchise, I desire most earnestly to recommend that you incorporate no disability whatever in it; that you allow every man in the State, even those who have been disfranchised under the Constitutional amendment to exercise the right of suffrage, and of holding office, with the restrictions that no one shall exercise that franchise unless he may be able to read and write, or has a property qualification such as you may determine.

In voting upon the ratification of the Constitution you may adopt, all registered voters will of course be included, which will of course secure its adoption. With the view of carrying out fully the views of the Convention, the first Legislature to be elected under the Constitution may be elected by all male voters over twenty-one years of age, but after that time, if not before, I urgently recommend that qualified suffrage extending to all classes and races be provided for in the Constitution. A man who goes to the polls after January 1, 1870, whether he be white or black, who is not able to read or write, should be excluded from the privileges of a voter.

Representing as you do, almost exclusively the colored element of South Carolina, you are not invisible to the fact, and to its legitimate results, that very many of the voters who have sent you here have not that intelligence with reference to men and measures which should entitle them to cast a vote. You know that thousands of them are utterly incompetent to exercise this high prerogative.

You may think that to perpetuate your power, and to preserve your organization, it is necessary to continue the franchise to this class of persons, but eventually you will find that you have been sadly mistaken. Many of the colored men of the State have an intelligence which entitles them, in their new relations, to the privileges of citizens; but very many are incompetent to exercise them with discretion or judgment. These will become the prey of evil, vicious and indisposed men. When an election is to occur with such voters, the bad will get their votes, and not the good.

In view of the fact that the colored population have a large majority in this State, and that the bulk of them are to be controlled by these evil influences, what kind of judges, legislators, and executive officers, can you hope for? Is vice and ignorance to elect your judges? Are the representatives of vice and ignorance to elect your legislators? If so, what security have you for the rights of life, liberty and property? I, therefore, in view of the responsibility before us, and in all probability in antagonism to the sentiments of a very large majority of this body, recommend earnestly that in framing that feature of the Constitution conferring the elective franchise, you establish an educational qualification for the voter, but—not being able to read or write—that you establish a property qualification.

Second. If you desire that this Convention should commend itself to the favorable consideration of the people of the State, white and colored, I recommend that you adopt in the Constitution a provision for a liberal homestead law—that you make it applicable to all those who now own a homestead and protect them against antecedent debts. The disasters resulting from the war, the abolition of slavery, and, thereby, the wiping out of the fortunes of very many of those who were wealthy prior to the war, as a matter of humanity demands that you should protect them as to the past by a liberal homestead law, and securing that home to its owner in the future. The homestead law which guarantees to a family fifty dollars or one hundred acres in the country, and a town lot or house in the city, is not only humane but patriotic. In the country, where the head of a family knows that his homestead is protected, he goes to work to beautify and adorn the same. He plants his orchard and his vineyard. He erects his buildings, decorates his dwelling, and makes all of his surroundings comfortable, and invites happiness and content to his hearth.

Perhaps one of the greatest troubles in American legislation has been in not protecting the homestead. It has made the American people almost as great wanderers as the Arabs. When a farmer planted an orchard or a vineyard, he had no assurance that five years thereafter the result of his care and labor would not pass into the hands of strangers. Grant, therefore, a liberal homestead law, providing against past and future debts so that the white man who has his home now, and the black man who may secure a home by industry and economy hereafter, can feel that it is secured to him, and you will find not only an increase in the prosperity and happiness of the State, but you will stimulate a patriotism which has not heretofore existed. Wherever you identify a man and his household with the soil upon which he lives you make that man, if from no higher considerations of love of country, a defender of the country when 'tis assailed, because the assault is upon his individual household.

Third. I urge you to provide for the abolishment of imprisonment for debt. I have always considered the incarceration of a human being for debt as senseless and cruel, except in cases of positive fraud. It is advocated that imprisonment for debt is right, for the purpose of assuring creditors in their demands, and that it curtails the capacity of an individual to secure credit, where this right is denied. In these views I do not concur. To be perfectly frank with you, I think that the universal credit extended to or claimed by a community is a great misfortune to that community, and if the homestead and exemption law, and the abolition of imprisonment for debt, will reduce the temptation to men to ask credit, and curtail the disposition of those who hold funds or goods to extend credit, it will be a blessing to our people. To the farming interest especially, the credit system is a curse, and the sooner that and all other interests, except perhaps the mercantile interest, dispense with it the better will it be for the general prosperity of the State.

Fourth. It is very important that this body should adopt some ordinance to provide relief to debtors prior to the war. The temporary orders of the military Commandant extend to debts contracted during the war. All debts now existing, where the consideration is for the purchase of slaves, should be absolutely wiped out by the Convention. If these debts are recognized, it is a recognition of that institution, of its propriety, its justice and morality. Most of the debts contracted prior to the war, were upon the faith and possession of property in slaves. That property has been destroyed, and a liberal provision should be made by this body with reference to debtors—the amount and time when they may make payment of the same. Do this, and you will commend your Constitution under the most favorable auspices to the consideration of that class in South Carolina who have not participated in the election of delegates to this Convention.

Fifth. Education is now the great desideratum of all the colored people of South Carolina. For obvious reasons it was the policy of the State, previous to emancipation, to exclude the slave population from the benefits and advantages of education. I will not discuss these reasons. But the relations of that population to the State are now materially changed. Hence it is of the utmost importance that the largest intelligence possible shall be communicated to that class. Men of intelligence have many more opportunities, through their reading and observation, of learning and appreciating the moral law and its requirements. Profound ignorance, almost universally couples with it crime and vice. Hence, the education of the black population—and, I am sorry to say, of many of the white population of the State—should command the earnest attention of this body.

In providing for it, I beg to guard you against attempting to levy taxes exclusively upon property. There is no taxation which is so universal, just and equitable as that upon the person or poll, for educational purposes, since all are interested in having an intelligent and virtuous population.

Sixth. With reference to the condition of the State, I have only to say to you that the Treasury is empty. The tax bill adopted by the last Legislature has failed, by three hundred thousand dollars, to produce the amount of taxes contemplated. We have, therefore, been compelled to rely upon bills what are known as the "bills receivable," issued by authority of the Legislature, to pay all officers and claims against the State. The great depreciation of property, and the general impoverishment of the State, has reduced the amount of taxes anticipated by the Legislature very materially, and consequently the financial condition of the State is greatly embarrassed. But it is very important that you should, in your deliberations, by ordinance or otherwise, declare—and nothing can more commend your body to the confidence of the people of the State, who represented its wealth—that all of the obligations of the State, all the bonds of the State created prior to the war, and all the obligations of the State since the war, shall be fully and faithfully redeemed. An ordinance announcing the validity of the obligations of the State, passed by you, will at once rapidly and largely appreciate the value of the bonds, now held at such low figures. The great discount upon the State bonds in the markets, here and elsewhere, grows out of a want of confidence in the will and determination of the new government to redeem them. This you should set at rest. And while you may, with propriety, repudiate all obligations contracted by the State for war purposes, the credit of the State for other obligations should not be tarnished either by repudiation or a semblance of repudiation.

In framing your Constitution, I cannot too earnestly commend to your favorable consideration the importance of removing the disability from all the white population of this State. When you look to the judiciary, I am very sure you can have no reasonable ground of complaint against their fairness or impartiality. Under the Constitutional amendment, most or nearly all are excluded from continuing in their position. Have you in the State members of the bar who are competent to discharge these high and important trusts with the ability or even the satisfaction to yourselves of those who would be required to retire from the public service, unless you make a modification retaining them in their present position? Is there any reasonable ground of complaint against your Appeal Court, the Judges of your Criminal Court or your Chancellors? While, under the Constitution, you may vacate these offices and subject all of the parties to the ordeal of an election before the Legislature, will it not be eminently wise and prudent for you to place the judiciary in a position where, if the Legislature elected under your Constitution think it expedient; they may re-elect such of the Judges and Chancellors as in their judgment are worthy to be continued in these positions.

This brings me to say that in South Carolina, at least, there is no reason why any man, white or colored, should be excluded from the privilege of voting or holding office. You are aware that the disfranchisement in the Reconstruction Acts of Congress excludes the intelligence and wealth of the State. In one of the Districts of the State, I know that the colored people waited upon certain gentlemen and requested them to become candidates for the Convention, but they were constrained to decline because they were disfranchised. This is an illustration of the condition of affairs which exists in all the Districts of South Carolina—the most intelligent men being excluded. In starting a new government all of this intelligence and experience should not be ignored. The State cannot afford to give it up. She is entitled to the counsel of such men and to their services.

The doctrine of State rights, as taught in South Carolina, has been exploded by the war. The allegiance of the citizen, according to the results of that controversy, is due to the Government of the United States, and not to the State. I recognize this doctrine to the fullest extent, and in my inaugural message as Governor of the State, I announced my judgment that hereafter the supremacy of the United States Government over the State was undisputed and indisputable. I am aware that many of my contemporaries deny the proposition, but I can properly comprehend the legitimate sequences of war, no other result presents itself to my mind.

Gentlemen of the Convention, I have merely outlined some of the subjects which in my judgment should command your earnest attention. As I have indicated, your body is here, not the representatives of the intelligence of the State. Your action, therefore, must be your passport to public favor, and while the great majority of the white population have failed to cast their votes in electing delegates, it will be your duty to adopt such a Constitution as will commend itself not only to the black, but to the white people of South Carolina.

As the Executive of the State during the trying times through which we have passed, I have earnestly endeavored to do equal and exact justice to all of our citizens. In the performance of my duties, I have known no distinction between race or color. When I have been called upon to exercise the high prerogative of Executive clemency in favor of those who have violated the laws, the records of my office will show that I have made reasonable allowance for the frailty and ignorance of the colored population, and that the commutations and pardons extended to them exceed those extended to the white race, whose opportunities for obtaining intelligence did not commend them with the same force to my judgment and sympathies.

As a citizen of South Carolina, born and raised on her soil, and desiring to lay my bones in this home of my fathers, I do not wish to see a Constitution adopted obnoxious to our people. If the instrument which you may frame be just and wise, as I trust it will be, I shall feel it to be a duty to recommend the adoption to my people. But if, on the other hand, it bears upon its face evidences of hostility to the true interests of the State, it will be calculated to create antagonisms, the results of which will be most deplorable, and I for one will pull up my stakes, and with my household remove to some other section of the country.

I am one of those who believe, as I have already said, that the Constitution you are to frame is the Constitution which the people of South Carolina are to live under for years to come, certainly for three, perhaps for twenty years. If I can talk to this Convention, or any member of the Convention, with the view of securing moderation, conservatism, or liberality in the framing of that Constitution, I feel as a citizen of South Carolina that it is my duty to come here and give you that counsel.

Born and raised as I have been in South Carolina, I desire that my bones shall repose in her soil. But if your Convention shall adopt a Constitution so obnoxious and unjust that, in my opinion, my wife and children cannot live under it, I shall pull up my stakes, remove my household and go to some other quarter. I do not desire such an alternative. I desire that this Convention should do what has not been done in Georgia, Alabama or elsewhere. In South Carolina the black population preponderates one hundred and twenty thousand over the white. It would, therefore, be not only generous but magnanimous of the black delegates who represent their constituency to tender to the people of

8

South Carolina such a Constitution as any just, fair and honorable man can accept.

As I have already stated to you, gentlemen, I do not choose to discuss before you the constitutionality of the reconstruction acts of Congress. Those laws, whether constitutional or not, have been adopted by Congress. Immediately upon their adoption I recommended the people of South Carolina, to go to work diligently and earnestly to carry them into effect. I have given the same advice to promiscuous gatherings in Charleston, Anderson, Columbia and elsewhere. Whatever may be my opinion of the reconstruction course of President Johnson, which I think liberal and just, the laws we are now acting under are the laws of Congress passed not by a majority simply, but by a two-thirds vote in both Houses of Congress. I am therefore disposed, disfranchised as I may be under these laws, to carry them into operation. Therefore when I see this Convention, with the black rather than the white element preponderating, with more colored delegates than whites occupying seats in the Convention, I feel it to be my duty to impress upon the Convention the propriety, yea the necessity, of framing a liberal Constitution. To the colored man there can be no reasonable objection to it. You have in the State, when you go to the ballot box, fifteen or twenty thousand votes over the whites, and if you act wisely and frame a Constitution which will commend itself to the white people of the State, then you will have accomplished a great result.

I say to you in all frankness, if you frame a just, wise and liberal Constitution, I for one will advocate its adoption before all the white as well as black people of South Carolina.

I presume that opposition will be made to those who favor this Convention. There will be opposition to you and opposition to me, but I have been too long in political life to be afraid of the small thunder which may be directed against me by newspapers. I have reached a period of indifference upon that question. If I know my own conscience, and if what I say is not true, I trust that that overruling Providence which guides and controls us will smite me for the falsehood—I have this day no other or higher motive, I care not whether it be public or private, no other political aspiration than to promote the interests of the people of South Corolina. I believe I said so some of my colored friends some months ago that I was tired of politics and desired to embark in some business that would enable me to support those who are dependent on me. I now go further and say to you I am disgusted with politics. I know of no position, State or Federal, that I would seek if it cost me the passage of a single step. Let me tell you that a man who embarks in political life, if he is honest, will be poor as long as he remains in it, and the sooner he gets out of it the better it will be for his wife, children and self. I intend to do it. I wish to go into retirement, and there is no office that your recommendation or votes could confer upon me that I would accept. I ask you, then, to have confidence in the statements that I have made.

I care not how much odium will attach to me, I care not what opposition may develope itself, what denunciation may be pronounced either from the press or from the public, if you make a Constitution liberal, fair and just, I pledge you my word I will advocate publicly its ratification by the people of South Carolina. But if you are proscriptive and unjust, I shall raise my voice against its adoption. I don't know that it will prevail—perhaps not. I have reached that point in my political life which will enable me to say yea or nay without any regard to whether it pleases or displeases the populace.

Gentlemen, I thank you for the attention which you have extended me this evening I am here, as I have stated, to make suggestions, to give information, and I will be pleased to give any information upon any subject connected with the Executive department of the Government which they may call for. If I can contribute anything whatever to your deliberations I will do so with the extremest pleasure.

I am not one of those that sneer at this Convention. I think its deliberations are of importance to the people of the State. I think it is of as much importance to my race as to the black race. In its deliberations, therefore, I hope you will exhibit wisdom and good sense in framing a Constitution, under which we can live in peace and quiet. If you attempt proscription and injustice, there will be a continual warring between the white and black races, which will result in the shedding of blood. God forbid that such shall be the case. As far as I have been able to see and confer with the members of this body, I believe their temper and disposition is to frame such a Constitution as that the white and black race can live in quiet and content.

In conclusion, I desire you to adopt a liberal and wise Constitution, under which the white and the black man can live together ; a Constitution which will protect the great interests of the State, and restore to it a degree of prosperity not heretofore enjoyed ; a Constitution that will dispel that distrust which unfortunately now prevails. You have a great problem to solve, such an one as has rarely been given to man ; you are to undertake an experiment which has not thus far in the experience of mankind been successful. That experience shows that, when placed upon terms of equality, the races have not harmonized. It is for you to demonstrate to the contrary.

Being hopeful myself, I believe that, with proper discretion and wisdom, you may form such a Constitution as will promote harmony, peace, and good will, and enlarge the prosperity of our State. And in the utmost sincerity, gentlemen of the Convention, I invoke the blessings of Heaven upon your deliberations, and trust that an overruling Providence may give you such wisdom as will secure peace and concord to this people.

FIFTH DAY.

Saturday, January 20, 1868.

The Convention assembled at 12 M., and was called to order by the PRESIDENT.

Prayer was offered by Rev. JAMES M. RUNION.

The roll was called, and one hundred and one members answering to their names, the PRESIDENT announced a quorum present, and the Convention ready to proceed to business.

The minutes of Friday were read and approved.

The PRESIDENT announced the following Standing Committees :

1. *Committee on a Bill of Rights*—B. F. Whittemore, Darlington ; A. J. Ransier, Charleston ; Dr. L. B. Johnson, Pickens ; R. B. Elliott, Edgefield ; W. J. McKinlay Orangeburg ; R. J. Donaldson, Chesterfield ; W. B. Nash, Richland ; T. J. Coghlan, Sumter ; James Henderson, Newberry.

2. *Committee on the Legislative part of the Constitution*—J. M. Rutland, Fairfield ; B. O. Duncan, Newberry ; W. J. Whipper, Beaufort ; E. W. M. Mackey, Orangeburg ; William McKinlay, Charleston ; James H. Goss. Union ; Samuel Johnson, Anderson ; Jesse S. Craig, Colleton ; Wilson Cook, Greenville.

3. *Committee on the Executive part of the Constitution*—F. J. Moses, Jr., Sumter ; J. H. Rainey, Georgetown ; R. G. Holmes, Beaufort ; C. M. Wilder, Richland ; S. Corley, Lexington ; A. Clinton, Lancaster ; J. M. Runion, Greenville ; W. H. W. Gray, Berkley ; M. Mauldin, Pickens.

4. *Committee on the Judiciary*—C. C. Bowen, Charleston ; J. J. Wright, Beaufort ; D. H. Chamberlain, Berkley ; A. Middleton, Barnwell ; Dr N. J. Newell, Anderson ; William E. Johnston, Sumter ; J. P. F. Camps, Spartanburg ; P. R. Rivers, Edgefield ; John A. Hunter, Abbeville.

5. *Committee on Franchise and Elections*—R. C. DeLarge, Charleston ; James D. Bell, Beaufort ; C. P. Leslie, Barnwell ; Isaac Brockenton, Darlington ; Elias Dixon, Clarendon ; John A. Chestnut, Kershaw ; H. W. Webb, Georgetown ; M. F. Becker, Berkley ; John S. Gentry, Spartanburg.

6. *Committee on Finance*—N. G. Parker, Barnwell ; T. J. Robertson, Richland ; Robert Smalls, Beaufort ; C. M. Olsen. Williamsburg ; John Bonum, Edgefield ; William Perry, Anderson ; P. Alexander, Chester ; George Jackson, Marlboro' ; J. H. White, York.

7. *Committee on Education*—F. L. Cardozo, Charleston ; J. K. Jillson, Kershaw ; L. S. Langley, Beaufort ; Dr. J. C. Neagle, York ; H. E. Hayne, Marion ; F. F. Miller, Georgetown ; H. L. Shrewsbury, Chesterfield ; Alexander Bryce, Pickens ; David Harris, Edgefield.

8. *Committee on Petitions*—William E. Rose York ; T. K. Sasportas, Orangeburg ; Frank Arnim, Edgefield ; S. B. Thompson, Richland ; Y. J. P. Owen, Laurens ; Lee Nance, Newberry ; J. H. Jenks, Berkley ; William M. Thompson, Colleton ; H. D. Edwards, Fairfield.

9. *Committee on Rules and Regulations*—S. A. Swails, Williamsburg ; S. G. W. Dill, Kershaw ; G. Pillsbury, Charleston ; George Lee, Berkley ; Henry Jones, Horry ; John Wooley, Edgefield ; William S. Collins, Marion ; J. K. Terry, Colleton ; H. J. Lomax, Abbeville.

10. *Committee on the Miscellaneous-Provisions of the Constitution*— L. Boozer, Lexington ; B. F. Randolph, Orangeburg ; Joseph Crews, Laurens ; R. H. Cain, Charleston ; F. E. Wilder, Beaufort ; J. A. Hayne,

Barnwell ; Bailey Milford, Abbeville ; J. M. Allen, Greenville ; Benjamin Byas, Berkley.

11. *Committee on the Review and Consolidation of the Constitution as a Whole*—L. Boozer, Lexington ; B. F. Whittemore Darlington ; F. L. Cardozo, Charleston ; F. J. Moses, Jr., Sumter ; R. C. DeLarge, Charleston ; William E. Rose, York ; J. M. Rutland, Fairfield ; C. C. Bowen, Charleston ; S. A. Swails, Williamsburg ; N. G. Parker, Barnwell.

The PRESIDENT stated that the last Committee under the suggestions of the Committee to whom was referred the subject of the appointment of Standing Committees, consists of the Chairman of the respective Committees, the object being, after the other Committees have prepared their matter, it may be consolidated into one whole, so as to be presented in a proper shape.

Mr. LEMUEL BOOZER, of Lexington, arose and said he understood from the announcement of the Committees, that he had been appointed upon one or more as chairman. I appreciate very highly, he said, the distinction conferred by the Chair in appointing me a Chairman of one of the Committees of this Convention. I am here to contribute my humble services to the business of the Convention, and am willing to add, in any way, so far as I am able. But under the peculiar circumstances, I do not believe that I can effectually discharge all the duties of Chairman of a Committee, more especially one of so much importance as that to which I have been assigned. The District Court of Lexington District must be held early in February. There is much business to be done, and many prisoners are in jail for trial. My duty imperatively demands that I shall attend that Court as District Judge, and it is altogether probable that the term may last two weeks. That will be the busy time when the most important business of this Convention will be progressing to maturity, and when the Chairman of each Committee should be at his place. This will be out of my power. The Convention will therefore readily perceive the reasonableness of the request, which I now make, to be excused from serving as Chairman of the Committees. I am willing to work in any other capacity, but I earnestly believe the business of the Convention will be facilitated and the interest of the State promoted by granting my request. I hope I may, therefore, be excused for the reason assigned, from serving on these Committees.

Mr. C. C. BOWEN moved that the excuse of the delegate from Lexington be made the special order for twelve M., to-morrow, which was agreed to.

Mr. F. J. MOSES, Jr., offered the following, which was adopted :

Resolved, That until the Committee on Review and Consolidation report a form of Constitution, this House will meet daily at twelve M., and adjourn at three P. M., so as to give the Committees ample time for the investigation of the subjects referred to them.

Mr. B. F. RANDOLPH asked leave to be excused from serving on the Committee on Miscellaneous Matters. Made the special order for twelve M., to-morrow, (Tuesday.)

Mr. S. A. SWAILS, of the Committee who were appointed to invite Judge Bryan and Major D. T. Corbin to seats on the floor of the House, reported that they had discharged that duty. The gentlemen named returned their sincere thanks for the honor, and desired the Committee to state that they would avail themselves of the earliest opportunity to visit the Convention.

The report was adopted and the Committee discharged.

Mr. R. C. DeLARGE, of the Committee on Printing, made a verbal report, and asked for further time, which was granted.

Mr. E. W. M. MACKEY, of the Committee to define the duties of subordinate officers, made a report, which recommended that the rules of the House of Representatives of the United States for the government of the subordinate officers, so far as they apply to this body, be adopted, and that the Committee be empowered to call before them the subordinate officers of the Convention, and instruct them with regard to their various duties.

The report was adopted.

Mr. F. J. MOSES, Jr., made a report of the Committee appointed to recommend the name of a suitable person to be elected Sergeant-at-Arms, and proposed Mr. Miles M. Johnson, of York District.

A motion was made that the report be adopted.

The question being put on the adoption of the report, Mr. BOOZER said it was usual, in legislative bodies of this character, for reports to stand over one day. The members of the Convention might desire a little time before going into an election. I have no choice, but merely rise to bring the matter to the notice of the Chair.

The Chair said, under the rules, the report would lie over one day unless taken up by unanimous consent.

Mr. WHITTEMORE moved that the rules be suspended for the purpose of taking up the report, which was agreed to.

The PRESIDENT read the report, and informed the Convention that if adopted, Mr. M. M. Johnson would be elected Sergeant-at-Arms.

Mr. B. O. DUNCAN moved its adoption.

Mr. WHITTEMORE said, I am perfectly well aware that it is necessary for us to go into an election for Sergeant-at-Arms. I am also well aware that we have been told by the highest functionary of the State that the treasury of the State is impoverished, and am cognizant of the fact that it is the desire of members of the Convention to impose as small a debt as possible on the State Treasury. In the matter of the election of a Chaplain to open the sessions, economy was brought forward as the principal reason why members on the floor should be called upon to perform the functions of Chaplain. Inasmuch as economy seems to pervade the minds of most members, I hope that those who are not clergymen may be considered as eligible to perform the duties of Sergeant-at-Arms, and that the balance of the Convention act as bondsmen for the members, as they are severally called upon, thereby saving to the State a very large expenditure.

Mr. F. J. MOSES, Jr., said, we are not debating whether we shall or not elect a Sergeant-at-Arms. The question before the House is whether the report shall be adopted, and Mr. Miles M. Johnson elected Sergeant-at-Arms.

Mr. W. J. WHIPPER asked whether the adoption of the report would be acting under the rules of the House of Representatives, which require elections to be *viva voce.* It seemed to him they would elect by acclamation, if they adopted the report.

Mr. CRAIG asked whether the Committee were instructed to report the name of one or more candidates.

Mr. MOSES said the mover of the resolution had informed him distinctly, it said candidate.

Mr. B. F. RANDOLPH agreed with the member from Darlington, (Mr. WHITTEMORE,) that they should curtail the expenses of the Convention, and was willing to dispense with the Sergeant-at-Arms.

Mr. WHITTEMORE moved that the report be recommitted to the Committee, with instructions to report two or more candidates.

Dr. NEAGLE asked whether that had precedence of the motion to adopt.

The PRESIDENT decided in the affirmative.

Mr. C. C. BOWEN said he noticed a disposition among members to retain the floor after being called to order, and moved that the rule in relation to that subject be read for the information of the House, which was agreed to, and the rule read.

Mr. DUNCAN opposed recommitment, and said the Committee having carefully examined the various candidates, found only one that possessed the necessary qualifications.

Mr. B. F. RANDOLPH moved a reconsideration of the resolution to appoint a Sergeant-at-Arms. He did it on the ground that they could dispense with a Sergeant-at-Arms as well as a Chaplain.

Mr. PARKER said no member could perform the duties of a Sergeant-at-Arms.

Dr. J. C. NEAGLE asked whether that duty could be imposed upon any member without his consent.

The PRESIDENT replied it could not.

Dr. NEAGLE moved to indefinitely postpone the subject.

The PRESIDENT said the question was on recommitment.

On the question being put it was lost.

Mr. W. J. WHIPPER asked whether the motion to suspend the rules of the Convention, simply as to laying over a matter for one day, also affects the election. He was told the consideration of the report was suspended as well as the election.

The PRESIDENT stated that the opinion of the Chair could be overruled by the House. The report recommends Mr. M. M. Johnson as a suitable person for Sergeant-at-Arms. The resolution is embodied in the report, which, under the rules, is laid over, but the rules having been suspended for the purpose of taking up the report, it was before the House for immediate action. If the House refuse to adopt the report, it goes to the wall; but if adopted, then the House elects Mr. Miles M. Johnson Sergeant-at-Arms.

Mr. L. S. LANGLEY. I have always been in the habit, before voting for a candidate, of knowing something of his antecedents. I know nothing of the gentleman proposed in the report, and hope I shall be enlightened by those who do know him.

Mr. R C. DeLARGE moved that the report be received and the House proceed to an election.

Mr. E. W. M. MACKEY said a motion had already been made to adopt the report.

Mr. L. S. LANGLEY. As none of the friends of Mr. Johnson think proper to respond to the invitation made by myself, I move that the report of the Committee be laid upon the table.

Mr. LANGLEY, at the request of Mr. NEAGLE, withdrew his motion.

Mr. NEAGLE. I had hoped that the report of the Committee would be altogether satisfactory. The Chairman of the Committee had stated that Mr. Johnson was the only candidate found suitable for the position, and supposed when the Committee was appointed they would examine into both the antecedents and qualifications of candidates, and that their recommendation would be sufficient. Mr. Johnson is from my district (York). All the members of our delegation. as well as others, have recommended him for the position. I had thought every member on the floor was fully satisfied as to the character, antecedents and status of Mr. Johnson. I would say they are altogether satisfactory to me as a Union Republican and also that he is the best man as far as capacity is concerned.

Mr. C. M. WILDER. I object to the election of one candidate without opposition I believe there is more than one man in South Carolina capable of filling the position. When I made the motion that a Committee be appointed to select, I was satisfied I said suitable persons.

Mr. H. E. HAYNE. I beg leave to correct the gentleman. I introduced the resolution, and that read that the Committee be instructed to nominate a suitable person for Sergeant-at-Arms.

Mr. WILDER. I offered an amendment, which was agreed to by the House. I move that the report of the Committee be laid on the table.

Mr N. G. PARKER. I hope the Convention will take up and adopt the report. We need a Sergeant-at-Arms. I have some experience of such a necessity since acting as Chairman of the Committee to provide suitable accommodation for the members. I have been appealed to by doorkeepers, messengers, members and others, to attend to their several wants. They want wood, coal, water and other things, all of which have to be provided by the Sergeant-at-Arms.

Mr. F J. MOSES, Jr. I consider it an extraordinary movement that the member who introduced the resolution to appoint the Committee should move to lay the report on the table. It is the first time I have ever heard of it. I believe the Committee performed their duty as well as it could possibly be performed. The Committee met. The first time they met, out of several canditates presented they nominated Mr. T. W. Johnson. After that gentleman had been made acquainted with the fact of his nomination, circumstances occurred which placed the Committee in an embarrassing position. They asked for further time, which was granted. A second time they met and had several candidates. They were very anxious to present a proper person and examined the candidates, propounding to them questions in regard to their reading and writing qualifications and mathematical knowledge. Those who know the candidate selected vouch for his capability to perform the duties of the office. If the report is to be recommitted I hope that the member from Darlington, or some other of the anxious gentlemen will be allowed to put up candidates.

Mr. PILLSBURY. I hope this matter will be brought speedily to a

9

close. We do not know to what dangers we are subjecting ourselves. A proposition has been offered to make the clergymen of the body responsible, and for all I know another proposition may be offered to make ex-agents of the Bureau responsible. If there are gentlemen in this Convention willing to respond for Mr. Miles M. Johnson, although a stranger to me, for the sake of facilitating business I am willing to try him, and if he proves incapable we can remove him. A question may occur as to whether the man of our choice is scrupulously honest, but that may not be important, as we have been given to understand there are no funds in the State Treasury. As the body is still unorganized, I do hope we will proceed to elect the candidate nominated by the Committee.

The question recurring on the adoption of the report, it was carried, and the PRESIDENT announced Mr. Miles M. Johnson elected Sergeant-at Arms.

On motion of Mr. L. S. LANGLEY, the Committee appointed to nominate a candidate for Sergeant at-Arms was discharged.

Mr. B. F. RANDOLPH offered the following resolution, which was referred to the Committee on Franchise and Elections:

Resolved, That in the opinion of this Convention the question of the confiscation of property and the disfranchisement of citizens for disloyalty should be left to the Federal Government.

Mr. J. M. RUTLAND offered the following, which was adopted:

Resolved, That it be referred to the Committee on Finance, to inquire into the condition of the State Treasury, and that they report to this Convention at the earliest practicable period.

Mr. F. J. MOSES, Jr., offered the following, which was referred to the Committee on Legislation:

WHEREAS, forced sales of property under legal processes, at the present unpropitious period, when cotton is so much depreciated in value, the daily necessaries of life so high, and the whole country in such an unsettled condition, that the entire planting interest is endangered, as well as almost every other solid interest in the State, depriving the planters of the power to continue preparations for their crops, and nearly all the laborers in the country of their homes, and the means of obtaining provisions for their daily subsistence; and, whereas, the general destitution that must inevitably ensue can result in benefit only to a small class of persons who live by speculating on the ruin of others; therefore, be it

Resolved, That we, the representatives of the people of South Carolina, in Constitutional Convention assembled, do hereby respectfully, but earnestly, petition Brevet Major General Ed. R. S. Canby, commanding

Second Military District, in order to afford this Convention the necessary time in which to mature proper measures of relief for the people of the State, to suspend for three months any execution or other legal processes under any judgment or decree rendered by the Courts of this State, for a debt or debts contracted prior to the 30th June, 1865.

Resolved, That the President of the Convention be requested to forward at the earliest practicable moment a certified copy of this preamble and resolution to Brevet Major General E. R. S. Canby.

Mr. J. C. NEAGLE moved that the rules be suspended, and that the preamble and resolution be adopted.

Mr. BOOZER. I object to the suspension of the rules. It is one of the gravest and most important questions to be presented to the Convention. A gentleman introduces a resolution to suspend the collection of debts, or rather to petition the military authorities to suspend the collection of debts for three months, and it is urged to press it before the Convention at once. I desire such a question to take the regular course, not being prepared to discuss its merits. The Convention should not proceed hastily in a matter of such grave importance. It was sprung upon them and he hoped the rules would not be suspended.

Mr. F. J. MOSES, Jr. I a glad to hear the gentleman acknowledge the question a grave one. If the member from Lexington had been in his seat last Friday, he would have known that a resolution covering the same ground was introduced and laid on the table. Three days had elapsed, and it really did seem that members had full time to make up their minds. It was a very common rule, when gentlemen wished to kill a resolution, to refer it to one of the Standing Committees. I am opposed to referring. It was important that such a resolution should be passed, and passed to-day. The first Monday of next month will be sales day, when a vast amount of property will be sacrificed under the hammer of the Sheriff if not checked in time. It is, therefore, time that the question should be considered, and without reference to some Committee of which the gentleman himself might be Chairman, to be there retained until too late to effect the beneficent object in view. If necessary, let us "rush" the measure through the Convention, and show to the people of the State that we are willing to rush anything through which is demanded for their good and welfare.

Mr. C. C. BOWEN. I oppose the suspension of the rules and the resolution as it stands. I understand there is to be some effort made to afford relief, which will be concurred in by a large majority of the members. But I wish to state that I am opposed to anything like class legislation, and this is strictly of that kind. It proposes to enumerate what class of people have a claim to protection from this body. I see no reason why this should not go to its appropriate Committee.

Mr. CRAIG said if the matter was referred to a Committee, it would delay it, and perhaps come up again too late to prevent sales of property by the Sheriff in February. It was important something should be done to prevent the immense sacrifice of property throughout the State. It is a mere request to General Canby to stop proceedings until we can do something to grant permanent relief. I hope the rules will be suspended.

On the question being taken, the Convention refused to suspend the rules, and, on motion of Mr. DUNCAN, it was referred to the Executive Committee, with instructions to report to-morrow.

Mr. DUNCAN moved that it be left to the discretion of the Chair to admit such visitors to the Convention as he might deem proper, which was agreed to.

Mr. J. M. ALLEN offered the following, which was referred to the Legislative Committee :

1. *Resolved*, That the personal property of every resident of this State, to consist of such property only as shall be designated by law, shall be exempted to an amount of not less than $1,000 from sale on execution or other final processes or court issued for the collection of any debt.

2. *Resolved*, That every homestead not exceeding one hundred and sixty acres of land and the dwelling house thereon, with the appurtenances to be selected by the owner, owned and occupied by any resident of this State and not exceeding in value $2,500, shall be exempt from forced sale for the collection of any debt or execution of other final process of any Court. Such exemption shall not extend to any mortgage thereon lawfully obtained, and such mortgage or other conveyance of such land by the owner thereof, if a married man, shall not be valid without the signature of the wife of the same.

3. *Resolved*, That no resident of this State owning and occupying a house on land not his own, and claiming the same as a homestead, shall be entitled to such house, to the benefits provided in this Article to the same extent as if he were the owner of such land, and such exemption shall not in any way impair the right of the owner to the said land.

4. *Resolved*, If the owner of a homestead dies or deserts his family, leaving a widow, or wife or children, such homestead shall be exempt from the payment of debts so long as the widow shall be without other homestead of her own, or while the deserted wife shall occupy such homestead.

5. *Resolved*, The real and personal estate of every woman acquired before marriage, and the property which she may afterwards become entitled by gift, grant or inheritance, or devised, shall be and remain the estate and property of such woman, and shall not be liable for the debts,

obligation or engagements of her husband, and may be devised, bequeathed and alienated by her as if she were unmarried.

Mr. ALLEN also offered the following :

Resolved, That the Judiciary Committee be instructed to inquire into the legality of extending the benefits of the homestead law to all exemptions of debts contracted prior to the passage of those Acts, and that they be empowered to call to their aid the best legal talent of this State, if by them considered necessary.

Mr. ALLEN. I have been informed by members of this body, whom I consider competent judges, that such a law would be unconstitutional. The Governor of the State, however. whom I also consider competent legal authority, has advised the passage of such an act. I merely introduce the resolution for the purpose of inquiring into the expediency or legality of the measure. It is intended for many of the most prominent men of this country, who, unless afforded relief, will be thrown as outcasts upon the land. The question being put upon its adoption, it was disagreed to.

Mr. L. S. LANGLEY, of Beaufort, submitted an ordinance to change the name of the election Districts of South Carolina into Counties, and to divide such Counties into Townships; said Townships to be not less than five miles, nor more than ten miles, which was referred to the Committee on Legislation.

Dr. J. C. NEAGLE offered the following :

Be it ordained, &c., That the President of this Convention do place his signature and official title, dated at Charleston, January 20, 1868, across the face of two hundred thousand dollars of the bills of this State, authorized by Act of the Legislature of this State, passed on the 21st of December, 1865, and known as "Bills Receivable." And that all such bills bearing said signature shall be "legal tender" for all debts, public or private, within the jurisdiction of this State, except in cases where the Government of the United States is a party.

Second. *Be it ordained, &c.,* That the public Treasurer of this State in Charleston is hereby authorized to sell, under the direction and control of His Excellency James L. Orr, Provisional Governor of the State, a sufficient amount of the aforesaid bills to raise ten thousand dollars in United States currency per week, or so much as may be necessary to pay the delegates of this Convention.

Third. *Be it ordained, &c.,* That the balance of the aforesaid bills remain in the Public Treasury of the State, to be expended in defraying the contingent expenses of the State under the appropriations authorized by General Orders, No. —, from the Headquarters, Second Military District, and under the control of His Excellency James L. Orr, Provisional Governor, or his successor in office.

Fourth. *Be it ordained, &c.,* That the Finance Committee are hereby directed to prepare and report at an early day an ordinance for the levy and collection of taxes in accordance with the Reconstruction Acts of Congress, under which this Convention is convened, that will amount to two hundred thousand dollars, to be collected between the first day of September and first day of December, 1871, which money shall be appropriated to the redemption of the aforesaid bills on and after the first of January, 1872, in such manner as this Convention may direct.

Dr. NEAGLE moved to refer the ordinance to the Committee on Finance, with instructions to report to morrow.

Mr. N. G. PARKER, Chairman of the Finance Committee, asked an extension of the time fixed in the proposed ordinance.

Mr. J. L. NEAGLE. Many of the delegates are in want of money to meet their expenses here, and it is very important we should provide for them at once. We desire to know where the money is to come from.

On motion, the ordinance was referred to the Finance Committee, to report at 12 o'clock M., Wednesday.

Mr. N. G. PARKER offered the following, which was considered immediately and adopted :

Resolved, That the Committee on Rules and Regulations be requested to report rules and regulations for the government of this body, and that one hundred and fifty copies be printed and laid upon the desks of the members at the earliest practicable moment ; also, that the names of the members be alphabetically arranged and published with those rules.

Mr. B. BYAS offered the following, which was referred to the Committee on Rules and Regulations :

Whereas, The exercise of wisdom and discretion is necessary in the action of this body ; therefore be it

Resolved, That no article, section, paragraph or clause, calculated to be embodied in the Constitution, shall receive its final adoption until the same shall receive at least two readings, and the lapse of twenty-four hours between each reading, and all ordinances be subjected to the same stipulations.

Mr. B. O. DUNCAN offered the following, which was referred to the Committee on the Judiciary :

Whereas, the institution of slavery has been abolished by the Government of the United States, and this action has been ratified by the State of South Carolina ; and

Whereas, still to recognize indebtedness or obligations for slaves, is still to recognize rights in slavery ; therefore be it

Resolved, That all debts or obligations of any kind for slaves, are herewith declared to be null and void, and shall forever after be so considered. Be it further

Resolved, That hereafter no State Court or State official shall entertain any suit, or recognize any claim on indebtedness or obligations contracted for slave property.

Mr. B. O. DUNCAN also offered the following, which was referred to the Committee :

WHEREAS, a long continued and bloody war has left our State in a most deplorable condition of poverty and demoralization ; and,

Whereas, property of all kind has depreciated to much less than half its former value, thus changing entirely the basis on which the debts were contracted ; and,

Whereas, a most vicious management of the rebel finances have left nearly all our people loaded down with old debts contracted prior to the war ; therefore be it

Resolved, That all debts contracted prior to the 30th of June, 1865, shall be reduced one-half; provided, however, that nothing in this ordinance shall be so construed as to interfere with any debt owed outside the State prior to the date above mentioned, and that it shall not relieve the State of any of its obligations except those contracted in aid of the rebellion, nor shall it relieve any individual, company or corporation of any obligations to the State.

Mr. J. N. HAYNE, of Barnwell, moved that the Clerk of the House furnish each member of the Convention with a copy of the daily papers of this city.

Mr PILLSBURY moved to amend by making it one copy of any daily paper a member may select.

Mr. A. J. RANSIER suggested that the Courier be selected. Another delegate said he preferred the Mercury.

Mr. B. F. WHITTEMORE moved to amend by adding that one weekly paper be furnished to the members.

Mr. CRAIG asked for information who was going to pay for the papers ; whether they proposed the members to pay for them themselves or to take the money out of the State Treasury.

The PRESIDENT stated all orders for money would have to be settled out of the State Treasury.

Mr. R. C. DELARGE moved to lay the resolution on the table, which was agreed to.

Mr. F. J. MOSES, Jr., offered the following, which was referred to the Committee on the Executive :

Whereas, by all Conventions in South Carolina heretofore, it has been a wise and salutary custom to have the assistance and aid of the State Solicitors in the legal preparation of ordinances and other papers ; and

Whereas, it is the earnest desire of this Constitutional Convention to perform the important duties entrusted to it in such a manner as will commend itself to the praise and approval of all law-abiding citizens; be it

Resolved, That the necessary steps be taken by the Convention to secure the legal services of Major D. C. Melton of York District, and that should he be willing to lend his aid in the hastening forward of the work of reconstruction, a room in this building shall be assigned to his use, and the per diem and mileage of delegates be allowed him.

Mr. BOWEN objected to the resolution.

Mr. CRAIG objected to the reference, and wished to act upon the resolution at once. Something of the kind, he said, was absolutely necessary to facilitate business.

Mr. DUNCAN moved that the Executive Committee be instructed to report to-morrow, which was agreed to.

Mr. B. F. RANDOLPH presented the following petition, which was referred to the Committee on Miscellaneous Provisions of the Constitution:

We, the undersigned people of South Carolina, in Convention assembled, do hereby recommend that the Bureau of Refugees, Freedmen and Abandoned Lands be continued until the restoration of civil authority; that then a Bureau of Education be established, in order that an efficient system of schools be established. Your humble servants and petitioners would respectfully represent that the reasons for making this recommendation are:

1. The necessity which first governed the existence of a Bureau remains the same, and demands its continuance until the restoration of civil government.

2. The want of an efficient system of public schools for the education of thousands who have been deprived of such school privileges.

3. The greatly impoverished condition of the State, and the financial difficulties of the people, render the establishment by the State government of such a system of public schools impossible for several years.

Mr. J. M. ALLEN offered the following, which was referred to the Committee on Legislation:

Be it ordained, &c., That the legislature shall, as soon as possible after the first assembling thereof, under the authority of this Convention, enact such laws as shall secure from levy and sale on any judgment or any final process of any court of this State, all the real or personal property of any debtor, contracted prior to the year 1865, and until such action shall have been taken by the Legislature, the levy on and sale of such property is suspended: *Provided*, it shall not extend beyond the year 1873, and any stay law passed by the Legislature shall not extend beyond the same time.

Mr. N. G. PARKER offered the following, which was referred to the Executive Committee :

Whereas, Governments are instituted to protect and insure the people in the enjoyment of their inalienable rights, "such as life and liberty, and the pursuit of happiness ;"

Whereas, happiness depends in a great measure upon the possession and security of property, to secure and protect which a revenue must be raised, and to the end that it shall be justly and equitably raised from all the property and people of the State, therefore

Resolved, That all taxes on property in this State, shall be assessed in exact proportion to the value of such property, both real and personal, and that the General Assembly may levy a poll tax, not to exceed $1 on each poll, which shall be applied exclusively in aid of the public school fund, and that no other tax shall be imposed upon the people of this State.

Dr. NEAGLE introduced the following :

Be it ordained, &c., That every delegate of this Convention shall receive as compensation for his services during his attendance on, and going to and from this Convention, eight dollars *per diem*, and twenty-five cents per mile by the most direct route from his home to the city of Charleston, each way; *Provided*, that any delegate, living in this city, and representing other districts, shall not receive mileage, only as the delegates of this city.

Referred to the Committee on Finance.

Dr. L. B. JOHNSON presented and read a petition praying the division of Pickens District into two parts, which was referred to a Special Committee of five, consisting of Messrs. L. B. Johnson, of Pickens ; J. M. Allen, of Greenville ; Dr. N. J. Newell, of Anderson ; C. M. Wilder, of Richland ; Jos. H. Rainey, of Georgetown.

Mr. H. D. EDWARDS offered the following :

WHEREAS, Ministers of the Gospel should, by their profession, dedicate their services to God and the care of souls, and ought not to be deterred from their great object; be it

Resolved, That no Minister of the Gospel, or public preacher of any persuasion whatever, whilst he continues in the exercise of his functions, shall be eligible to the office of Governor, Lieutenant-Governor, or a seat in the Senate or House of Representatives, or work upon any public road or streets, or do patrol duty.

Referred to the Legislative Committee.

Mr. T. HURLEY, of Berkley, introduced the following, which was referred to the Committee on the Judiciary :

Resolved, That there shall be incorporated in the Constitution of the State the following sections, to wit :

10

1. No person shall be elected or appointed to any office in this State unless he possesses the qualifications of an elector.

2. No person who shall hereafter fight a duel, assist in the same as a second, accept, or knowingly carry a challenge therefor, shall hold any office in this State.

3. Lotteries, and the sale of any lottery tickets, for any purpose whatsoever, shall be forever prohibited in this State.

4. There shall be no imprisonment for debt, except in case of fraud or absconding debtors.

Mr. S. B. THOMPSON, of Richland, introduced the following:

WHEREAS, it is currently reported and believed that the inmates in the State Penitentiary are maltreated, in direct violation of the rules of said institution, and that many are incarcerated within said walls that should be now at large; be it

Resolved, That a Committee, consisting of five members, be appointed to proceed to Columbia, with power to send for persons and papers to facilitate a thorough investigation of the above report, and lay the facts before this body.

Mr. B. O. DUNCAN, of Newberry, said he thought this was a question too important to be passed over hastily. It should be remembered that there is not a case in that Penitentiary which has not passed under the eye of the military probably as well as civil authorities; and it is to be presumed that the convicts there incarcerated, being found guilty by a jury of their countrymen, have been properly sentenced.

Mr. J. M. ALLEN. I know there are several men in the Penitentiary who would not be there but for the passions and prejudices of our opponents, and the enemies of this Convention—men who are the advocates of Ariel, have advocated the incarceration of some of these prisoners; and I call on this Convention to have the matter investigated. I care not whether their cases were examined by the military or executive department. I hope their cases will be inquired into by the Convention. They have been put there by men who would crush the poor men of this State. There are men there accused of murder, and all other heinous crimes, of which they are perfectly innocent, and have documents upon documents to prove it, but which will not be examined by those opposed to them. I second the motion for the appointment of a Committee of five.

Mr. B. BYAS moved that the resolution be referred to the Committee on Miscellaneous Provisions of the Constitution, to report to-morrow, which was agreed to.

Mr. W. B. NASH offered the following, which was referred to the Committee on Education:

Resolved, That all schools, academies, colleges and universities in this State, which are or may be endowed or supported in part or in whole from the revenue arising from taxes or donations to the State, cities or towns, shall be open for the reception of scholars, students and teachers of every grade, without any distinction or preference whatever, to all citizens of the State; also, it shall be the duty of the Legislature, at its first session, to divide the State into school districts, and establish free schools in every District, to be open to all citizens of the State.

Mr. F. J. MOSES, Jr., offered the following:

Resolved, That it be referred to the Judiciary Committee to inquire and report as to whether or not the reconstruction acts of the United States Congress confer upon this Convention authority to legislate on matters not involved in the formation of a State Constitution.

Mr. S. CORLEY offered the following, which was referred to the Committee on Miscellaneous Matters:

WHEREAS, a large majority of the people heretofore constituting the Government of the State of South Carolina have, by unjustifiable rebellion, forfeited their political rights as citizens of the State and of the United States, and are still hostile to every act of Congress for the restoration of the State to the Union—claiming, as they do, every political right they formerly enjoyed as citizens under the Constitution, which properly defines their late acts as treason, and authorized even the penalty of death for crimes thus committed, instead of equal rights with those who love the Government which they so madly attempted to destroy; and,

Whereas, the officers of the present Provisional Government of the State, from the highest to the lowest have generally exercised their influence, and used the emoluments of their various offices in a manner highly prejudicial to the claims of loyal citizens, and in opposition to the laws of Congress looking to a speedy restoration—the only competent authority that we recognize—and are now marshaling their forces to defeat any Constitution, however faultless it may be, that this Convention may frame as the fundamental law of the State; therefore, be it

Resolved, That we, the representatives of the loyal people of South Carolina, having accepted in good faith the terms offered by Congress for the restoration of the State to her proper relations in the Union, demand for ourselves and our constituents under the law and its Constitution, present and prospective, *every right* which these embittered and incorrigible enemies to the Government claim as exclusively their own.

Resolved, That the continued efforts of the present disloyal officers of the Provisional Government of the State to continue themselves in power as such, while looking to a speedy reinstatement to place in the Federal position, so lately and contemptuously deserted by many of them, and their systematic efforts to escape the just penalty of violated faith, while their active hostility to the essential principles of Republicanism remain, is substantial and positive proof that the safety of the Government and the welfare of the people demand their speedy removal.

Mr. GEORGE LEE, of Berkley, offered the following, which was referred to the Legislative Committee:

Resolved, That all persons shall enjoy equal rights and privileges while traveling in this State, and all places of amusement, entertainment, refreshment, or of any public nature whatever, shall be open to all persons alike.

Resolved, That no Company, Municipality, Parish or Corporation, shall make any rules or regulations creating any distinction between persons on account of race, color, or previous condition.

Mr. T. HURLEY offered the following, which was referred to the Committee on Franchise and Elections:

Resolved, That in all elections to be made by the people, or of any part thereof, for civil or political officers, every person shall be entitled to vote who has the following qualifications, to wit: Every person who has attained the age of twenty one years, and is not a pauper, nor a non-commissioned officer or private soldier of the army, nor a seaman or marine of the United States navy, provided he shall, for a period of one year next preceding the day of election, have been a citizen of this State, or for the same period an emigrant from Europe. who has declared his intentions to become a citizen of the United States according to the Constitution and laws of the United States.

Mr. N. G. PARKER offered the following, which was referred to the Committee on Franchise and Elections:

Resolved, That this Convention recommend to all persons in South Carolina, who are at present disqualified from registration under the Acts of Congress, who are willing to swear allegiance to the Constitution of the United States, and to the Constitution which this Convention shall adopt, to forward their names to this Convention, with recommendations from the Governor of the State, the Commanding officers of the several Military Districts, the United States Judges, Internal Revenue Collectors, District Attorney, or other United States officers, or Union men of note throughout the State, and this Convention will petition the Congress of the United States to remove their disablties.

On motion, the Convention adjourned.

SIXTH DAY.

Tuesday, January 21, 1868.

The Convention assembled at 12 M., and was called to order by the PRESIDENT.

Prayer was offered by Rev. A. WEBSTER.

The roll was called, and a quorum answering to their names, the PRESIDENT announced the Convention ready to proceed to business.

The Journal of Monday was read and approved.

The PRESIDENT called for reports of Standing Committees.

Mr. F. J. MOSES, Jr., from the Committee on the Executive part of the Constitution, to whom was referred a preamble and resolutions con-cerning a petition to General Canby, to suspend for three months all sales of property under execution for debts contracted prior to the 30th of June, 1865, reported that they had considered the same, and unani-mously recommend that they do pass.

Mr. B. O. DUNCAN moved the adoption of the report.

Mr. J. M. RUTLAND moved that the report be made the Special Order for one o'clock to-morrow, which was agreed to.

Mr. F. J. MOSES, Jr., from the same Committee, to whom was re-ferred the preamble and resolutions in relation to the employment by the Convention of the legal services of Major C. D. Melton, State Solicitor, in the preparation of Ordinances and other papers, reported that they had the same under consideration and unanimously recommend that it do pass; they also recommend that Major D. T. Corbin, United States District Attorney, be included in the resolution, and that he be requested to act as a Solicitor for this body, and that he be allowed the pay and mileage contemplated by the resolutions.

Mr. J. J. WRIGHT. I would like to ask whether the first gentle-man mentioned in the resolution is not disfranchised ?

Mr. MOSES. I will answer the question in the affirmative, together with the information that I introduced the resolution. The resolution° called for the employment of Major Melton's services as State Solicitor, an officer of the State government. His disfranchisement therefore would have nothing to do with it.

Mr. WRIGHT. That does not answer my question, which is, whether the gentleman is disfranchised under the constitutional amendment. I am informed that he is. If so, I am opposed to asking him to do this work for us. But I am not opposed to having a Solicitor If we elect the gentleman proposed, we elect one that cannot, as the law stands now, or as we regard it, be elected to any office in this State. Under that law no person can be elected to any office unless they are enfranchised, and provisions are made for enfranchisement. I presume there is no one in this Convention but what is willing from his heart to recommend the enfranchisement of any person desiring it.

Mr. J. M. RUTLAND. I think the gentleman from Beaufort has entirely misapprehended the question. It is not whether a State officer shall be elected to fill the position named, but whether he shall be called --be commanded as a State officer already, to aid in the performance of certain duties. Major Melton is not a candidate for any office in the gift of the Convention. He is already a Solicitor, and if this invitation be extended to him, I may say, from my personal acquaintance, there is no man in South Carolina of a higher order of talent, or more competent to aid in preparing business in proper shape for the consideration of the Convention.

The question being taken on the adoption of the report, it was decided in the affirmative.

The resolution is as follows :

WHEREAS, in all Conventions in South Carolina heretofore held, it has been a wise and salutary custom to have the assistance and aid of the State Solicitors in the legal preparation of ordinances and other papers ; and whereas, it is the earnest desire of this Constitutional Convention to perform the important duties entrusted to it in such a manner as will commend it to the praise and approval of all law-abiding citizens ; therefore be it

Resolved, That the necessary steps shall be taken by this Convention to secure the legal services of Major C. D. Melton, of York District, and Major D. T. Corbin, United States District Attorney, of Charleston, should they be willing to lend us their aid in hastening forward the work of reconstruction, a room in this building be assigned to their use, and the *per diem* and mileage of delegates be allowed to each of them.

Mr. LEMUEL BOOZER, of Lexington, from the Committee on the Miscellaneous Provisions of the Constitution, to whom was referred a resolution that a Committee of five shall be appointed to proceed to Columbia and investigate certain reports concerning the penitentiary, reported that they had considered the same, and that, in the opinion of the Committee, its subject matter was one which belonged exclusively to the Committee on the Judiciary, since the resolution was a proposition to appoint a commission to review the action of the Judiciary of the State.

Mr. C. C. BOWEN. The house having thought proper to refer those documents to that Committee, I do not think the Committee can come back and say to the house it is not a proper subject for their Committee.

It might at least have been discussed. I therefore move that the report be recommitted to the same Committee.

Mr. BOOZER. Nothing is more common, as every gentleman at all acquainted with legislative proceedings knows, than for Committees to be discharged from the consideration of subjects referred to them, when the subject properly belongs to some other Committee. The matter was not brought to the attention of the Convention yesterday when it was referred, but the Committee, on undertaking to investigate it, found that it did not properly belong to them, and they unanimously directed me to make the report presented to the house. The subject matter of the resolution is entirely of a judicial character, and has nothing to do with Miscellaneous Provisions of the Constitution.

Mr. R. H. CAIN moved that it be referred to the Judiciary Committee, which was agreed to.

Mr. R. C. DeLARGE made a verbal report of the Committee on Printing, and asked for further time, which was granted.

The PRESIDENT announced that the hour had arrived for the consideration of the Special Order, which was the excuses tendered by the delegates from Lexington and Orangeburg.

On motion of Mr. R. C. DeLARGE, the Special Order was discharged.

Mr. BOOZER asked how this action affected the applications to be excused from serving on Committees.

The PRESIDENT said the gentlemen would not be excused from serving.

Mr. B. F. RANDOLPH moved a reconsideration.

Mr. R. C. DeLARGE. The gentleman cannot move a reconsideration as he did not vote in the affirmative. I move a reconsideration.

The question was put, and the house refused to reconsider.

Mr. W. E. ROSE, offered the following, which was agreed to :

Resolved, That the President be authorized to appoint a Reading Clerk for this Convention.

Mr. R. C. DeLARGE moved a reconsideration, and that the motion to reconsider be laid on the table, which was agreed to.

Mr. T. HURLEY offered the following, which was referred to the Committee on Franchise and Elections :

Resolved, That all elections hereafter held in this State shall be free and voluntary ; that any elector allowing himself to be bribed or corrupted by meat, drink, money or otherwise, shall be punished therefor ; and if any person who shall directly or indirectly give promise of, or bestow any such rewards be elected, he shall thereby be rendered incapable to hold any office of trust for a period of ten years, and be punished by fine and imprisonment, as the law shall hereafter direct.

Mr. H. E. HAYNE moved to lay the resolution on the table, which was not agreed to.

Mr T. HURLEY also offered the following which was referred to the Committee on Miscellaneous Matters :

Resolved, That all able-bodied male citizens in the State between eighteen and forty-five years of age, except such persons as are exempt by law, shall be enrolled, armed, equipped and trained as the Legislature may provide. All officers shall be commissioned by the Governor, and hold their commissions during good behaviour. The Legislature shall organize the divisions in brigades and regiments. The Governor shall appoint all officers above the rank of major, and majors and other subordinate officers shall be elected by the several commands.

Mr. S. A. SWAILS offered the following :

Resolved, That the President be empowered to appoint a janitor for this building, and that the said janitor be authorized to appoint an assistant.

Mr. R. C. DeLARGE. I trust the motion will be voted down. We have enough persons serving the Convention in various capacities who can take care of the books and papers. The owner of the building has already taken the precaution to place the building in charge of a keeper who lives on the premises. I hope we will consider the condition of the State Treasury.

The resolution was not agreed to.

Mr. J. M. RUNION offered the following :

We the people of the State of South Carolina, by our delegates in Convention assembled, to ordain, That the inferior Courts of each District, known as District Courts, be, and the same are hereby, abolished, and all judgments and decrees of such Courts rendered after the passage of this Ordinance shall be null and void.

Mr. J. C. NEAGLE, of York, moved that the Convention go into Committee of the Whole on this subject.

The PRESIDENT explained that all resolutions whose object is of a permanent character are required by rule to be referred to a Committee before they can be considered, unless the Convention suspend the rules for the purpose of immediate consideration.

Mr. B. F. WHITTEMORE, of Darlington, moved to suspend the rules.

The motion was agreed to.

Mr. R. C. DeLARGE called for the ayes and noes.

Mr. L. S. LANGLEY desired to know if a member had a right to call the ayes and noes after a vote is announced.

The PRESIDENT. If the matter has not been recorded previous to the call for the ayes and noes, the call is in order.

The question being on resolving the Convention into Committee of the Whole was then taken, and likewise decided in the affirmative.

Mr. J. M. RUTLAND took the Chair.

Mr. R. C. DeLARGE. I desire to say but a few words on this subject. I trust the Ordinance as presented will not be adopted. I feel, and I suppose every gentleman on the floor feels, that it is one of the most important measures this Convention could enact. We propose to strike out one of the higher branches of the government of this State, the Judiciary. I hope that delegates who regard the State District Courts as superfluous will yet give the subject that grave consideration which its importance demands. I agree with the spirit of the ordinance. I believe these Courts unnecessary for the administration of justice. From their action I have always felt that many of them trifled with the rights and liberties of the parties brought up for trial. But opposed as I am to them, I am still more strongly opposed to hurrying through a matter of such grave importance. As I understand the resolution, it is to do away immediately with these Courts. I would like to know whether in abolishing these Courts now, we would not in some way retard justice. I hope it will be referred to the appropriate Committee, who can give the subject a careful consideration, and members, when it comes up again, may vote understandingly. I trust we will not allow our personal feelings to cause us to rush through this grave matter, requiring the utmost deliberation.

Mr. L. S. LANGLEY. I am opposed to the resolution, not only because I believe the Convention has no power to legislate, but because a resolution has already been introduced and referred to the Judiciary Committee, inquiring as to what power of legislation the Convention possesses. I am also opposed to pushing such important matters through hastily, and opposed to any legislation not necessary to the formation of a Constitution by this Convention. I hope it will be voted down. I do not believe the Convention has any right to legislate on any matter outside of the Constitution.

Mr. JOS. H. RAINEY. I cannot for one moment see how the abrogation of the District Courts will meet the aim intended by the mover. So long as the present code of laws of the State exist, there can be no remedy in that direction. It matters not in what Courts the different

11

cases will be tried, there will be a certain amount of injustice meted out, but which should not be. I am therefore opposed to the resolution and hope it will not pass.

Mr. T. HURLEY. I desire to have read for the information of the Convention the reconstruction acts of Congress. We will then know how far to go. [Mr. HURLEY here read the General Order of General Canby, convening the body.] I do not believe we have the power or authority to abolish any branch of the civil government of the State. We are simply here to frame a Constitution, which is to be submitted to the people for their acceptance or rejection. As regards the District Courts, they are perhaps as good as any other Courts in the State, but we should not abrogate them until we are prepared to substitute something better in their place. I therefore move that this subject be indefinitely postponed.

Mr. J. M. RUNION. I will state for the information of the Convention, that I supposed we had just as much right to abolish these Courts as the Convention of 1865 had the right to pass them. Furthermore, I have consulted the constituents of my District, white and colored, and they are almost unanimous in favor of the resolution. They complain that much injustice has been practiced in those Courts.

Mr. F. L. CARDOZO. I will state for the information of the Convention, that when the Committee called upon Governor Orr to invite him to a seat here, the Governor referred to this subject, and said that the Convention of 1865, which met to frame a Constitution, in his opinion, transgressed its limits in regard to the Judiciary, when they said the Legislature should establish such Superior and Inferior Courts as they in their judgment should determine, and also these District Courts. The Governor thought it would have been much better if the Convention had only said such superior and inferior Courts as the Legislature might determine. I think if that Convention had ordered the establishment of any Courts, surely this Convention has just as much right to abolish. In conversation with the Governor, the latter said he thought the District Courts highly inappropriate, and altogether objectionable; that they did not accomplish their purpose. At the same time, in abolishing the District Court, that did not perhaps reach the trouble. It is not the form of the Court, but rather the spirit of the Judges. If these are disposed to do injustice, the form of the Court will not prevent them from doing so.

Mr. WM. J. McKINLAY. I doubt whether we have authority to act in this matter, we are here for a specific purpose, the framing of a Constitution and form of civil Government, and until the Constitution is ratified by the people and accepted, no ordinance can be passed that will have any effect. That is the view I take of the subject, and for the life of me I cannot see what the abolishment of the District Courts, whether they were to be condemned or approved, has to do with this clear line of duty. No ordinance the Convention can adopt will have any effect until the Constitution is ratified by the people, and, therefore, this resolution can be of no possible use. The subject belongs exclusively to the Legislature.

Mr. B. F. RANDOLPH. I concur with the gentleman who last addressed the Convention, in the opinion that we are here for a specific purpose, but we are also at the same time to do all in our power to relieve the State of any financial embarrassment which may seem fit. The District Courts are a great expense to the State and needless for the ends of justice. I am in favor of the resolution, but the question is whether we have a right to pass this ordinance. If it was so deter_ mined, I would suggest the propriety of asking General Canby to issue an order abolishing these Courts. As to whether the people of the State have obtained justice through these Courts, I would leave that to be determined by others better acquainted with their government.

Mr. NEAGLE. It is urged against this measure that we are working hastily, but that I look upon as no argument. I am of the opinion that the delegates to the Convention came here with their minds made up on that question. We have been considering the matter of District Courts ever since the Act was passed for the establishment of those Courts, and I believe our constituents have almost universally condemned them. I am credibly informed that they cost the State not less than $50,000, and some estimate it at over $80,000 or $100,000. We are oppressed by heavy taxation, and I am in favor of relieving the State Treasury as soon as possible of these useless Courts. We have been told that this Convention has no right to legislate ; I want to know what is meant by the formation of a civil government of the State. We are here for a specific purpose, that is by others is urged to be the simple forming of a Constitution; my understanding is that we are here for a specific purpose, and that is to form a Constitution for the State of South Carolina, which shall be its organic law, and then to form a civil government also for the State of South Carolina. What good is there to form a Constitution and laws, and have no officers or government to carry those laws into execution ? I take it for granted that the government of a State means its organic laws, its Constitution, its laws throughout for the regulation of the State and the citizens therein. We must have officers to execute those laws, and I consider we have a perfect right, a perfect jurisdiction over every official position in this State. We cannot place any other construction upon the Reconstruction Acts of Congress. One gentleman on my right urges that no act passed by the Convention can have any effect until it is ratified by the people. I am prepared to admit that. I do not consider any act of this Convention can be enforced by the authority of the State until the Constitution is ratified by the people If that is ratified, then our laws are to be enforced. Who is to enforce those laws unless we have officers favorable to them? We are here to frame a Constitution, to establish a government, and unless we can make the machinery to put it in operation, we may as well go home. We must have the men and the machinery. I think we have a perfect jurisdiction over every Court, and every officer in the State.

Mr. A. G. MACKEY. I did not intend to obtrude on this Convention, but this is an occasion when I esteem it my duty to speak. I think this one of the most important actions that can come before the Convention, not so much in relation to the principle involved in the ordinance itself, which is simply the abolition of a court, of whose character and whose utility a very large number of people of all shades of political character are agreed, but because I think I see in this Convention a desire, in the introduction of an ordinance like that, not only to legislate upon matters not within its province, but also to hurry that legislation through in unseemly haste. In relation to the character of the District Courts, of the necessity of the abolition of those bodies, of their good or ill effects, I need not say anything. This, in my opinion, is neither the time nor the place to discuss these principles. The question is, what right has the Convention to pass any such ordinance? Is this Convention possessed of legislative powers outside of the specific purposes for which it was called together? That is the great question we have first to enquire into. Then, should we agree that we have such power, in the next place, is it the best way to exercise that power by thrusting through at once, without due consideration, one of the most important measures which can be submitted for its consideration and demand its action?

I contend that the Constitutional Convention of South Carolina was called under the Reconstruction Acts of Congress, and the order of the General Commanding convening this body for one specific purpose and no other. When called for a specific purpose, it is illegal and wrong to go beyond that purpose, or to enter into any other, which we are not authorized to review and consider.

I know if I were to say that a Constitutional Convention is possessed of legislative powers I should be, for the first time, in accord with what I believe to be the heretical side of the State. I know it has been generally held that Conventions of the people were sovereign and unlimited in their power, so much so that it was not deemed necessary to refer their actions to the people for ratification, because it was said they were the people themselves. That is a doctrine I have not held, and a doctrine not sanctioned by any jurist of reputation in this country. It is generally conceded that Constitutional Conventions are called to make Constitutions, not laws. This in my opinion is the intention of this body. It is a Convention to make a Constitution. We have not even the power of declaring what shall be the Constitution of South Carolina. Our powers are limited here as they ought to be in every other State, namely, to the simple proposition of what we believe would be a proper form of Constitution; and until the people shall ratify our action, it will be of no effect whatever. But even if we had the power of legislation we should not undertake to rush an ordinance through without the usual parliamentary form of a first, second and third reading, and giving to the body ample time to deliberate and form a correct judgment. Can we undertake to adopt an ordinance abolishing Courts which have been for two years in existence and in which the rights and property of citizens are in litigation? Have we a right, without referring our action to the people, to declare these Courts abolished, and in the language of the ordinance "that all processes and decrees, after the date of this ordinance, shall be null and void?" Called simply to frame a Constitution for the acceptance or non-acceptance of the people, have we the right to begin by declaring that we will change the whole Judiciary or to set it aside?

The gentleman who preceded me said he knew the ordinance could have no effect until submitted to and ratified by the people. With such a view of the case, it is wholly unnecessary for us to pass any such ordinance. We have appointed a Committee on the Judiciary, to whom is to be submitted all these questions for examination and discussion. That Committee, after laboriously and faithfully investigating all the points, with all the lights and assistance of such legal counsel as they may call to their aid in making up their judgment, are to determine as to what Courts are necessary. Did we appoint a Committee on the Judiciary that it might be a mere shadow without the substance; that after having appointed this Committee over that part of the Constitution which relates to the Courts, we are to take away its work, commence ourselves as a Committee on the Judiciary, and without examination, without consideration, without legal advice or counsel pass an ordinance which we all admit is a mere *brutum fulmen*—a harmless thunderbolt— which can have no effect until acted upon by the people? How much more rational, more prudent, more like a deliberative assembly, to say we will touch none of these things. Let us confine ourselves wholly and solely to the framing of a Constitution to be presented to the people for their acceptance or rejection. Heaven knows that task is sacred enough to engage any set of men. We will give to each portion of the Constitution that due deliberation to which it is entitled. We will divide the questions which arise among the appropriate Committees, and let these at their leisure uninfluenced by eloquence, or other considerations which might control them upon this floor, determine what is right or wrong, and present it here! Then, not now, will be time enough for us to talk about abolishing District or any other Courts. Then if we are to submit this act to the people let us submit it not in the form of an ordinance, but as a part of the Constitution which has been referred to and will be reported upon by the Judiciary Committee, who will recommend whether or not District Courts, after the adoption of this Constitution, shall be abolished. That would be the proper course for the Constitutional Convention to take. But if we commence by passing ordinances now, we know not where we shall stop.

From all the information I have been able to obtain upon the subject of preceding Constitutional Conventions, and from a study of the ablest jurists upon the subject, I believe that a Constitutional Convention has no right to pass any other ordinance than such as has been committed to it by the people. In this case there is but one ordinance that this Convention can pass, and that is to levy and collect a tax to pay its own expenses. Its next and only other business is to frame a Constitution.

In conclusion, I move that this resolution be referred to the Committee on the Judiciary, and that the Committee on the Whole do now rise and report to the house that they have considered the subject, and recommend that it be referred to the Judiciary Committee.

The motion was agreed to, and the Committee rose. Dr. MACKEY resumed the Chair.

Mr. RUTLAND made the report of the Committee of the Whole, which was adopted.

Mr. C. C. BOWEN introduced the following Bill of Rights, which was referred to the Committee on Bill of Rights :

WHEREAS, the people of the State of South Carolina, by their delegates in Convention assembled, on the twentieth day of December, in the year of our Lord one thousand eight hundred and sixty, did, by an ordinance commonly called the Act of Secession, lay violent hands upon the Government and rudely severed the ties which bound the said State, in common with other States, in a Union, by a social compact known as the "Articles of Confederation and Perpetual Union," of the United States of America, whereby the State was rendered a Territory, and deprived of her rights, privileges and immunities then guaranteed by the "Constitution of the United States ;"

And whereas, by the said "Act of Secession, no legal State Government has since existed, we, therefore, the representatives of the people, inhabiting the Territory formerly known as the State of South Carolina, assembled in Convention, at the city of Charleston, on the fourteenth day of January, in the year of our Lord one thousand eight hundred and sixty-eight, in pursuance of an Act of Congress entitled an 'Act to provide for the more efficient government of the rebel States," passed March second, eighteen hundred and sixty-seven, and the Acts supplementary thereto, thereby enabling the people of the said Territory to form a Constitution and State Government for the re-admission of such State back into the Union on an equal footing with the original States.

We, therefore, in order to establish justice, ensure tranquility, provide for our mutual defence, promote our common welfare, and to secure to ourselves and our posterity the blessings of liberty, acknowledging, with grateful hearts, the goodness of the Supreme Ruler of the Universe in affording us an opportunity so favorable to the design, and imploring his aid and direction in its accomplishment, do agree to form ourselves into a free and independent State, to be known as the State of South Carolina, for which we do ordain and establish the following declaration of rights and form of government as the Constitution thereof :

ARTICLE I.

DECLARATION OF RIGHTS.

That the general, great and essential principles of liberty and free Government may be recognized and established, we declare,

1st. That all men are born equally free and independent, and have certain natural, inherent and inalienable rights, among which are those of enjoying life and defending liberty, acquiring, possessing and protecting property, and of pursuing and obtaining safety and happiness.

2d. That neither slavery nor involuntary servitude shall exist in this State, except as a punishment for crime, whereof the party shall have been duly convicted ; nor shall any male person, who has arrived at the age of twenty-one years, nor female person, who has arrived at the age of eighteen years, be held to serve any person as a servant, under pretense of indenture or otherwise, unless such person shall enter into such indenture while in a state of perfect freedom, and on condition of a *bona fide* consideration, received or to be received for their service.

3d. That all power is inherent in the people, and all free governments are founded upon the authority of, and established for the peace, safety and happiness of the whole people. Therefore, no attempt shall ever be made to abridge or destroy the right of suffrage which is now enjoyed by any person or persons in this State, except as provided for in this Constitution.

4th. That all men have a natural and indefeasible right to worship Almighty God according to the dictates of their own conscience ; that no man shall be compelled to attend, erect or support any place of worship, or maintain any ministry against his consent; that no human authority ought in any case whatever, to control or interfere with the rights of conscience, therefore, the exercise and enjoyment of religious profession and worship without distinction, shall be forever free to all persons in this State : *Provided*, the right hereby declared and established shall not be so construed as to excuse acts of licentiousness or justify practices inconsistent with the peace and safety of the State.

5th. No preference shall ever be given by law to any religious sect or mode of worship.

6th. That no person shall be molested for his opinions on any subject whatever, nor suffer any civil or political incapacity, or acquire any civil or political advantage, in consequence of such opinions, except in cases provided for in this Constitution.

7th. Every citizen may freely speak, write and publish his sentiments, on all subjects, being responsible for the abuse of that liberty.

8th. No law shall ever be passed to curtail or restrain the liberty of speech or the press.

9th. In all prosecutions for the publication of papers investigating the official conduct of officers or men in a public capacity, where the matter published is proper for the public information, the truth thereof may be given in evidence ; and, in all indictments for libels the jury shall have a right to determine the law and the facts, under the direction of the Court as in other cases.

10th. The rights of the people to be secure in their persons, houses, papers and effects, against unreasonable searches and seizures, shall not be violated ; and no warrant shall issue but upon probable cause, supported by oath or affirmation, and particularly describing the place to be searched, and the person or things to be seized.

11th. That in all criminal prosecutions the accused hath a right to be heard by himself and counsel ; to demand the nature and cause of the accusation ; to be confronted by the witnesses against him ; to have compulsory process for obtaining witnesses in his favor ; and, in all prosecutions by indictment or information, a speedy public trial, by an impartial jury of the District; that he cannot be compelled to give evidence against himself, nor can he be deprived of his life, liberty, or property, but by due course of law.

12th. No person shall be accused, arrested or detained, except in cases ascertained by law, and according to the forms which the same has prescribed ; and no person shall be punished but in virtue of a law established and promulgated prior to the offence, and legally applied.

13th. That no person shall, for any indictable offence be proceeded against criminally by information, except in cases arising in the land or naval forces, or the militia, when in actual service, or by leave of the Court, for misdemeanor in office.

14th. No person shall, for the same offence, be twice put in jeopardy of life or limb, nor shall any person's property be taken or applied to public use without the consent of his representatives, and without just compensation being made therefor.

15th. That all Courts shall be open, and every person, for an injury done him in his lands, goods, person or reputation, shall have remedy by due course of law, and right and justice administered without denial or delay.

16th. That no person arrested or confined in jail shall be treated with unnecessary rigor, or be put to answer any criminal charge but by presentment, indictment or impeachment; and that no law shall ever be passed in this State, inflicting corporal punishment upon any person whatever.

17th. The right of trial by jury shall remain inviolate, and no person shall be convicted of any crime but by the unanimous verdict of the same.

18th. That no power of suspending the operation of the laws shall be exercised, except by the General Assembly or its authority.

19th. That excessive bail shall not be required, nor excessive fines imposed, nor cruel or unusual punishment inflicted.

20th. All penalties shall be proportioned to the nature of the offence, the true designs of all punishments being to reform, not to exterminate mankind.

21st. That all prisoners shall, before conviction, be bailable by sufficient securities, except for capital offences, when the proof is evident, or the presumption great; and the privilege of the writ of *habeas corpus* shall not be suspended, unless when in case of rebellion or invasion the public safety may require it.

22d. No person shall be imprisoned for debt in any civil action, or mesne or final process, unless upon refusal to deliver up his estate for the benefit of his creditors, in such manner as shall be prescribed by law, or in cases where there is strong presumption of fraud.

23d. That no *ex post facto* law, nor law impairing the obligation of a contract, shall be made, except such contracts as may have been made between the nineteenth day of December, eighteen hundred and sixty, and the fifteenth day of May, eighteen hundred and sixty-five, or contracts for the purchase of slaves.

24th. That no person shall be attainted of treason or felony by the Legislature, and no attainder shall work corruption of blood or forfeiture of estate.

25th. That treason against this State shall consist only in levying war against it, adhering to its enemies, giving them aid and comfort. No person shall be convicted of treason unless on the testimony of two witnesses to the same overt act, or confession in open Court.

26th. That the estates of suicides shall descend or vest as in cases of natural death, and if any person shall be killed by casualty, there shall be no forfeiture by reason thereof.

27th. That the citizens have a right, in a peaceable manner, to assemble together for their common good, to instruct their representatives, and to apply to those invested with the powers of government for redress of grievances or other proper purposes, by petition, address or remonstrance.

28th. Every citizen has a right to keep and bear arms in defence of himself and the State, and this right shall never be questioned.

29th. No standing army shall be kept up without the consent of the

12

General Assembly, and the military shall, in all cases and at all times, be in strict subordination to the civil power

30th. That no soldier shall, in time of peace, be quartered in any house without the consent of the owner, nor in time of war, but in a manner to be prescribed by law.

31st. That no hereditary emoluments, privileges or honors, shall ever be granted or conferred in this State.

32d. No citizen of this State shall be exiled or prevented from emigrating on any pretence whatever.

33d. No person shall be debarred from prosecuting or defending any civil cause for or against him or herself before any tribunal in this State, by him or herself, or counsel, or both.

34th. That every association of persons when regularly formed within this State, and having given themselves a name, may, on application to the General Assembly, be entitled to receive letters of incorporation to enable them to hold estates, real and personal.

35th. A frequent recurrence to the fundamental principles of the Constitution and a constant adherence to those of justice, moderation, temperance, industry and frugality, are absolutely necessary to preserve the advantages of liberty, and to maintain a free government. The people ought, therefore, to pay particular attention to all those principles, in the choice of their officers and representatives, and they have a right to require of their law-givers and magistrates an exact and constant observance of them in the formation and execution of all laws necessary for the good administration of the State.

36th. That as religion, morality and knowledge, being essentially necessary to the good government and the happiness of mankind, schools and the means of instructions shall forever be encouraged by legislative provision.

37th. That no laws shall ever be passed to prevent the poor in the several Districts within this State, from an equal participation in the Schools, Academies, Colleges and Universities within the State, which are endowed, in whole or in part, from the revenue arising from the donations made by the United States, or otherwise, for the support of Schools and Colleges, and the doors of said Schools, Academies and Universities shall be open for the reception of scholars, students and teachers, of every grade, without any distinction or preference whatever.

38th. This enumeration of certain rights shall not be construed to deny or disparage others retained by the people, and to guard against any encroachments on the rights herein retained, or any transgression of any of the high powers herein delegated, we declare that every thing in this article is excepted out of the general powers of Government, and shall forever remain inviolate, and that all laws contrary thereto, or to the following provisions, shall be void.

Mr. T. K. SASPORTAS offered the following, which was referred to the Committee on the Judiciary.

WHEREAS, the bulwark of life and liberty depends upon the intelligence of those who sit in judgment on their fellow men, be it

Resolved, That all persons may sit on juries without regard to race, color, or previous condition, provided they are registered voters, and are able to read and write legibly.

Mr. B. O. DUNCAN presented and read a petition to Congress praying for a repeal of the cotton tax, so as to cover the crop of 1867, and setting forth the reasons therefor.

Referred to the Committee on Petitions.

Mr. J. M. RUNION offered a resolution, providing for the election of Justices of the Peace and Constables in each District; also, a resolution prescribing that the General Assembly shall, from time to time, regulate and define the duties of said officers, and providing that Justices of the Peace shall not have jurisdiction over sums not exceeding $100.

Referred to the Committee on Franchise and Elections.

Mr. RUTLAND moved that the Secretary be requested to inform Messrs. Melton and Corbin of their election, and request their attendance at as early a day as practicable, which was agreed to.

Mr. B. F. WHITTEMORE offered the following, which was referred to the Committee on Franchise and Elections :

Resolved, That every male citizen of the United States, and every male person of foreign birth who may have declared his intention to become a citizen of the United States according to law, not less than one year, nor more than five years before he offers a vote, who is over the age of twenty-one years, who is not disqualified under ths provisions of the Constitution of this State, and who shall have complied with its requirements, and have resided in this State one year next preceding any election, or next preceding his registration as a voter, and during the last six months of that period shall have resided in the county, city or town where he offers to vote, or seeks registration as a voter, shall be entitled to vote at such election. No person shall vote elsewhere than in the election precincts of which he is at the time a resident.

Mr. JAMES N. HAYNE submitted an Ordinance providing for the formation of a new Judicial District, to be called " Sumner," out of contiguous portions of Edgefield, Barnwell, Lexington, and Orangeburg Districts, which was referred to the Committee on the legislative part of the Constitution.

Mr. L. S. LANGLEY offered the following, which was referred to the Committee on Bill of Rights :

WHEREAS, the pernicious doctrine of States Rights, as believed in and taught by a mistaken son of South Carolina, Hon. John C. Calhoun, has cost our beloved country many thousand valuable lives and many millions of treasure ; and, whereas, it is highly necessary that the new Constitution which this Convention is about to frame should not be silent on the subject, therefore be it

Resolved, That the allegiance of the citizens of this date is due to the Federal Government and to South Carolina, only so long as she continues a component part of the American Union.

Mr. J. H. RAINEY offered the following, which was referred to the Committee on the Judiciary :

Resolved, That it is the sense and wish of this Convention that the next Legislature take measures for a revision of the code of State laws as speedily as possible after its assembling.

Mr. W. E. JOHNSTON offered the following, which was referred to the Committee on Franchise and Elections :

WHEREAS, it has been proposed to this Convention that all ministers shall be debarred from participating in all political affairs, be it
Resolved, That all men, whether ministers or otherwise, shall be liable to any position in the government that the people in their judgment may honor them with, providing that said minister or man be qualified to fill the offices they may be called to serve in.

Mr. A. J. RANSIER offered the following, which was referred to the Committee on Education :

Resolved, That the Committee on Education inquire into the expediency of establishing a Board of Education, consisting of three from each Congressional District.   Such Board shall have power to divide the State into school districts, and provide for a thorough system of common schools, elect a Superintendent from among their number, and make all needful regulations for the education of youth, no discrimination to be made in favor of any class of persons.

On motion of R. C. DeLARGE, the Convention adjourned to meet at 12 M. to-morrow.

SEVENTH DAY.
Wednesday, January 22, 1868.

The Convention assembled at 12 M., and was called to order by the PRESIDENT.

Prayer was offered by the Rev. F. L. CARDOZO.

The roll was called, and a quorum answering to their names, the PRESIDENT announced the Convention ready to proceed to business.

On motion of Mr. N. G. PARKER, the reading of the Minutes was dispensed with.

The PRESIDENT announced the first business in order to be the reports of Special Committees.

Mr. C. C. BOWEN made a report of the Committee on the Judiciary on a resolution in relation to contracts, where the consideration was for the purchase of slaves, stating that they had considered the same, and recommend for adoption the following Ordinance.

We, the People of the State of South Carolina, by our Delegates in Convention, do hereby ordain and declare, That all contracts, whether under seal or not, the consideration of which were for the sale of slaves, are null and void and of non-effect.

2. No suit, either at law or equity, shall be commenced or prosecuted on such contracts and proceedings for the satisfaction and payment of judgments and decrees which at any time heretofore have been recorded, rendered, enrolled, or entered upon such contracts, are hereby forever prohibited.

3. All orders relative to such contracts which may at any time heretofore have been made in any Court of this State, either of law or equity, whereby any property, real or personal, is held subject to decision as to the validity of such contracts, are also declared null and void, and of non-effect.

The PRESIDENT stated that the Convention having at an early session of the body adopted the rules of the House of Representatives, and regarding the term ordinance in the Convention as synonymous with bill in the Legislative Assembly, the Chair was compelled to decide that no ordinance can pass the Convention until it has received three readings. The Chair decided therefore that this ordinance had received its first reading.

Mr. WM. McKINLAY. It is my opinion that all matters coming from Committees in the shape of ordinances or resolutions should be printed for the use of the members, so that they may have as much light as is possible to be thrown upon the subject. I therefore move that all ordinances and reports coming from Committees, intended to be passed into permanent laws by this Convention, be printed, and copies laid upon the table of the members.

Mr. R. J. DONALDSON. I think that course will entail a great deal of unnecessary expenses, and delay the business of the Convention. I move as an amendment, that ordinances and resolutions shall only be printed after the second reading. A great many resolutions may be introduced here, which if printed simply when offered, may get no further than the hands of the printer, and would, therefore, be a useless expense; but if they pass after a second reading, then they should be printed.

Mr. L. BOOZER. After a second reading a measure is considered as passed. It is true the Convention still has the subject under its control, and may reject at the third reading, or may depart from the usual course, and consider the subject at the third reading. What I mean to say is that the discussion on all subjects generally take place at the second reading; that is the usual course of all legislative bodies, and to print all reports of Committees. The members will then be able to understand better, with copies before them, and as there was no necessity for hurrying through our proceedings, we can deliberate more carefully and cautiously. I hope everything will be printed as it comes from the Committee.

Mr. WHITTEMORE moved, as an amendment to the original motion, that all ordinances and reports be printed after the first reading.

Mr. WM. McKINLAY. I merely desire to state that I am not at all convinced, from what has been said, that the printing of the resolutions and ordinances after the second reading will entail less expense upon the Convention than what it will at first. If only a certain number be printed, it will not cost more to print at first than afterwards.

Mr. R. J. DONALDSON said his motion was to postpone until after the second reading.

The question was then taken on the original motion, and decided in the affirmative.

Mr. C. C. BOWEN made a report of the Committee on the Judiciary, on a resolution appointing a Committee of five to investigate affairs in the Penitentiary, and report relative to the treatment of prisoners in the State Penitentiary, stating that the subject matter is beyond the jurisdiction of the Convention, the Penitentiary being under the control of the Provisional Government of this State, and subject to the military authorities of the United States. The Committee recommend that the matter be referred to General Canby, with a request that an investigation be made of the charges contained in the resolution. Adopted.

Mr. C. C. BOWEN, from the same Committee, to whom had been referred a resolution relating to jurors, reported it back, with the recommendation that it be referred to the Committee on Legislative Provisions of the Constitution.

The report was not adopted.

Mr. N. G. PARKER made the following report, which was adopted:

The Committee on Finance, to whom was referred an ordinance relative to the validation of a portion of the bills receivable of the State, and the sale thereof, and the manner of levying and collecting the tax authorized by Act of Congress, to defray the expenses of the Convention, with instructions to report thereon this morning, beg leave respectfully to report, that they are in correspondence with Major-General E. R. S. Canby, the Governor of the State, and other State officials, from whom information is asked, and that it was impossible to arrive at any conclusion at so early a day, and respectfully ask further time, with the assurance that an early report may be expected.

Mr. S. A. SWAILS, from the Committee on Rules and Regulations, made the followig report, which was read, and, on motion of Mr. PARKER, one hundred and fifty copies were ordered to be printed:

SOUTH CAROLINA CONSTITUTIONAL CONVENTION, ⎱
CHARLESTON. S. C., January 22, 1868. ⎰

The Committee appointed for the purpose of drafting Rules and Regulations for the Government of this Convention, beg leave to report through their Chairman, that they have had the matter under consideration, and respectfully submit the following:

I. ORDER OF BUSINESS OF THE DAY.

1st. This Convention shall meet at twelve o'clock, M., and continue in session until three o'clock. P. M., each day, unless otherwise ordered.

2d. Prayer by the Chaplain.

3d. Calling the Roll of Delegates, a majority of whom being present shall constitute a quorum for the transaction of business.

4th. Reading and disposing of the journal of the preceding session.

5th. Report of Standing Committees.

6th. Report of Special Committees.

7th. Receiving Petitions and Resolutions.

8th. Unfinished Business.

II. No member shall absent himself from the service of this Convention without the consent of the Convention, under penalty of losing the pay for the day absent, unless he shall give a reasonable excuse.

III. No member shall be allowed to speak more than twice on the same question, nor for more than fifteen minutes each time, unless by the consent of the Convention, and for the purpose of explaining some point in question.

IV. No Article, Section, Paragraph or Clause, intended to be embodied in the Constitution, or a Petition to or from the Convention, shall receive its final adoption, until it has received at least two readings: *Provided*, That twenty-four hours shall elapse after the first reading And all amendments thereto shall be subject to the said stipulation.

V. It shall be the duty of the subordinate officers of this Convention to attend the meetings of all Committees held in this building.

VI. So much of the Rules of the House of Representatives as do not conflict with the foregoing Rules are hereby adopted for the government of this body.

Respectfully submitted,

S. A. SWAILS, Chairman.

Mr. L. B. JOHNSON made a report of the Special Committee, to whom was referred a petition for the division of Pickens into two Districts, one to be known by its original name Pickens, the other to be called Oconee. The Committee report an Ordinance, and recommend its adoption or reference to the Judiciary Committee, with instructions to incorporate such portions in the Constitution as may be necessary to carry out the object of the ordinance.

The ordinance appoints commissioners to select proper sites, lay out a new town for a Court House and jail, sell property. apply proceeds, and make titles to purchasers of lots in the name of the State.

Mr. J. J. WRIGHT moved that the report be retained by the PRESIDENT until the Legislature has assembled, and that it then be referred to them.

Mr. JOHNSON hoped the Convention would take some more direct action. This division of Pickens District was earnestly desired by all classes and parties in that section of country. A very strong petition had been sent here, signed by all the officers of the Court residing at Pickens Court House, including the Clerk of the Court, Sheriff, Commissioner in Equity, Judge, the United States and State Tax Collectors, all the lawyers, and other prominent citizens. There are only thirteen families residing in Pickens Court House, most of them officers of the District. They are all willing to sacrifice their property to get another Court House. The present Court House is located in a very poor section of country. Oconee District, when the division takes place, will contain one thousand four hundred and six square miles. Pickens District will contain one thousand two hundred and twenty-five square miles.

Mr. N. G. PARKER said he sympathised with the gentleman from Pickens in his desire to to have the District divided. He knew something of that District, but to facilitate business he would lay on the table the motion to refer it to the next Legislature of the State, in order to have it referred to its appropriate Committee. He deemed it, however, a fit subject for the Legislature and not of this Convention.

Mr. R. C. DeLARGE moved that it be made the Special Order for to-morrow (Wednesday) at one o'clock, which was agreed to.

Mr. B. F. WHITTEMORE offered the following, which was referred to the Committee on Legislation:

Resolved, That it shall be the duty of the General Assembly, as soon as circumstances will permit, to form a penal code, founded on the principles of reformation and not of vindictive justice, and also to provide one or more farms to be an asylum for those persons, who, by reason of age, infirmity, or other misfortunes, may have a claim upon the aid of the benevolence of society, that such persons may therein find employment and every reasonable comfort, and lose by their usefulness the degrading sense of dependence.

Mr. J. K. JILLSON offered the following which was referred to the Committee on the Judiciary:

The Judicial power of this State shall be vested in one Supreme Court, and in such inferior Courts as the Legislature may from time to time ordain and establish.

The several Courts shall have such jurisdiction as may from time to time be prescribed by law. Chancery powers may be conferred on the Supreme Court, or on any other Court, to no greater extent than may be hereafter provided by law.

The Judges of the Supreme Court shall, in all trials, instruct the jury in the law. They shall also give their written opinion upon any question of law, whenever requested by the Governor or by either House of the Legislature

The Judges of the Supreme Court shall be elected by the two Houses in Grand Committee. Each Judge shall hold his office until his place be declared vacant by a resolution of the Legislature to that effect, which resolution shall be voted by a majority of all the members elected to the House in which it may originate. and be concurred in by the same majority of the other House. Such resolution shall not be entertained at any other than an annual session for the election of public officers, and in default of the passage thereof at said session, the Judge shall hold his place as herein provided. But a Judge of any Court shall be removed from office if, upon impeachment, he shall be found guilty of any official misdemeanor.

In case of vacancy by death, resignation or removal from the State, or from office, refusal or inability to serve, of any Judge of the Supreme Court, the office may be filled by the Grand Committee until the next annual election, and the Judge then elected shall hold his office as before provided.

In cases of impeachment or temporary absence or inability, the Governor may appoint a person to discharge the duties of the office during the vacancy caused thereby.

The Judges of the Supreme Court shall receive a compensation for their services, which shall not be diminished during their continuance in office.

Mr. R. J. DONALDSON objected to the introduction of such resolutions, as wasting the time of the Convention on subjects properly belonging to the Standing Committees. He considered it a piece of impertinence, entrenching upon the business of the Committees which had been appointed to prepare such amendments to the Constitution as might be deemed necessary, and he thought it was not flattering to the good sense of the members to be continually offering suggestions to those Committees. He hoped the Convention would discountenance them.

13

Mr. J. J. WRIGHT. As one of the members of the Committee on the Judiciary I certainly would be pleased to receive any suggestions or resolutions in that Committee the Convention might deem fit to send it.

Mr. L. S. LANGLEY called for the Special Order, which was the report of the Committee recommending a petition to General Canby to suspend, for three months, the collection of all debts contracted prior to the 30th of June, 1865.

Mr. T. J. ROBERTSON said he understood under the rules this should lay over until the third reading.

The CHAIR said under the rules it would have to lay over until a third reading.

Mr. B. F. WHITTEMORE moved a suspension of the rules, the order discharged, and the resolution printed for consideration to-morrow (Wednesday.)

Mr. F. J. MOSES, Jr. I hope the motion will not prevail. The object of the motion is very plainly to be seen, and that is to kill the resolution or the purposes of the resolution. As I announced the other day, the object of that resolution was to request General Canby in time for him to issue an order before the first Monday in February, which is sales day. I know the fact that there is an organized opposition to it, and this is the first move they have made. I hope gentlemen who oppose this measure will come up and face the question like men. The Chair had said that this was no new matter, and consequently, having been made the order of the day, it came up for discussion now. I hope the matter will be disposed of at once. There is really no necessity to post-pone, unless it is to advance the wishes of those who desire to kill this question of relief. The question has been before the House several days, allowing ample time for every member to obtain the fullest infor-mation on the subject.

Mr. R. C. DeLARGE. I concur with the member from Sumter. This question has been before the House in two or three different forms, and I hope will be acted upon. Some relief to the people of the State is necessary, and even if this measure be not adopted the question will con-tinue to come up, and, like Banquo's ghost, "will not down at our bidding."

Mr. N. J. NEWELL. I desire to state, for the information of the Convention, that I received this morning a letter from a distinguished lawyer of the State, who says there are over twenty thousand decrees obtained up to this time which will be put in execution in February. These decrees involve property to an amount of over two hundred thousand dollars. I hope the Convention will give the subject its earliest consideration.

Mr. B. F. WHITTEMORE. My object in calling for the printing of this resolution is that members may have an opportunity of duly considering the question. I have no desire to ask that this measure shall be killed, and when any gentleman supposes I rise for the purpose of murdering a resolution, and declares in the presence of the Convention that that is my object, he is doing more than he has any authority for doing. I consider this matter of too grave an import to be acted upon hastily. When we are touching upon matters of debts and individual liabilities it becomes us to consider well how far we can go before committing ourselves upon the question. I believe as an individual member I have a right, whenever it seems good in my mind, to present any resolution, and I do not impugn the motives of any member in the presentation of a resolution. I simply ask that the Convention may duly and properly consider this matter, in order that, whenever passed upon, their action will be justified, at least, by a fair and impartial discussion of the question. I hope the resolution will prevail. I hope that no spirit of animosity will prevail here that will prevent others from the introduction of such other measures as they desire to offer. I do not know whether this proposition may be the best that can be offered. I am perfectly willing to consider it, and if convinced that it is the best, I will give it my hearty support, and if not the best, my hearty objection.

Mr. W. J. WHIPPER. I hope the motion to postpone will not prevail. I hope the house will take up the resolution and consider it. This matter has already been before the house for four or five days. It came up yesterday and was made the Special Order for this day at one o'clock, that they might have time to consider or discuss the matter. I do not propose to say what course we should take, but I do think if there is any necessity of bringing it up at all, it should be considered immediately. As I have said, it has been before us four or five days, and it is now asked to be put off. Another continuance on probably more frivolous grounds, may be asked, until it gets so near the day on which these sales are to be held, that it will be impossible for the Commanding General to prevent the executions, even if disposed to do so. I feel that we have a right to ask that the subject be taken up and considered. I do not see the necessity of waiting until to-morrow, simply to have it printed. The facts will be elicited in discussion, and the mere fact of printing will add but little information to the question one way or the other. There are, perhaps, gentlemen here who have long speeches already prepared and I am willing to hear them now, that the facts may all be brought out, and if we decide in favor of the resolution, asking the General Commanding to issue his order of relief, I hope it will be done at once, more especially as one gentleman has told us over two hundred thousand dollars worth of real estate in the interior is so shortly to be levied upon or sold under execution by the sheriff. I trust we will not put off this question for any frivolous reasons.

Mr. L. S. LANGLEY. I hope the resolution of the gentleman from Darlington will prevail. Two or three days ago a resolution was referred to the Judiciary Committee to inquire as to whether this Convention had legislative powers or not. I am informed by the Chairman of the Committee that that resolution has not been handed to him. If we should vote to lay the motion of the gentleman from Darlington on the table, or if we consider the subject to-day, I hope we will hear first from the Judiciary Committee as to what are the legislative powers of this Convention.

Mr. B. BYAS moved that the whole matter be discharged.

Mr. B. F. WHITTEMORE. I move that the Special Order be postponed until two o'clock to-morrow.

Mr. F. J. MOSES, Jr., called for the yeas and nays.

The yeas and nays were ordered, and being taken, resulted yeas 46, nays 68.

Mr. S. G. W. DILL. I move to lay the whole matter upon the table. The yeas and nays were again taken, and resulted yeas 28, nays 82.

Mr. T. J. ROBERTSON moved that the whole matter be indefinitely postponed.

The yeas and nays were again called for.

Mr. R. J. DONALDSON. I protest against this waste of time. I appeal to the good sense of the house. It is a matter of no importance. The whole resolution is no more than so much waste paper.

The yeas and nays being ordered, were taken, and resulted yeas 24, nays 86.

Mr. J. M. RUTLAND. I move that it be recommitted to the same Committee, with instructions to its Chairman, to give his reasons more at length, and especially on the legal points involved in the matter.

Mr. R. C. DeLARGE. I move that the Committee report within ten minutes.

Mr. F. J. MOSES, Jr. I think what I said in reference to an organized opposition to defeat this measure of relief, has been plainly proved by the action of that opposition on this question of postponement. I see in this motion to recommit nothing but another stride towards the wish for a defeat of this important measure. The Committee to whom that resolution was referred, did not deem it proper to embody with the report an argument in favor of its adoption by this house. That may have suited the opposition. But it was the object of the Committee to bring it back as soon as possible, knowing that every eye in the State is turned to the Convention to see what we will do for them. We are not looking to the interests of any particular class of citizens. There is not a man but what demands relief. Now, for the mere purpose of killing the resolution and defeating its object, it is proposed by the opposition to send it back to the Committee for the purpose of getting the legal argument and reasons of the Chairman. So far as my individual opinion is concerned, I think such a motion is unprecedented, and could only arise in the brain of any man who is compelled to some dernier resort to accomplish his end in defeating a measure.

This question should be discussed on the floor of the house, where gentlemen can meet each other, and not in the Committee room. I therefore trust this motion to recommit will be voted down. It is true, as far as a vote on the subject is concerned, I think the Convention has shown itself in favor of the measure. At the same time the organized opposition is so perfect, and they have so many members ready to jump up at the proper time to make motions, and they are so admirably drilled on this particular subject, that they have staved it off until it is close upon three o'clock, the hour of adjournment. We shall therefore be compelled to postpone further consideration, but we shall beat them to-morrow.

Mr. B. F. WHITTEMORE. I will go as far as any one else in the support of measures for the relief of the people of the State. The gentleman from Sumter, is, apparently, quite sure that he will be able to carry through his proposition to-morrow, and I am not convinced that he may not then persuade me over to his side of the question. The subject of relief has often been brought to my mind since I have been a resident of South Carolina, and it is no new question with which I have to deal. In order therefore that the gentleman may have an opportunity of adding as many friends to his measure as possible, I move as an amendment, that the further consideration of the subject be postponed until half-past one o'clock to-morrow.

The question being taken, it was decided in the affirmative, and on motion of Mr. R. C. DeLARGE, the Convention adjourned.

EIGHTH DAY.

Thursday, January 23, 1868.

The Convention assembled at 12 M., and was called to order by the PRESIDENT.

Prayer was offered by the Rev. R. H. CAIN.

The roll was called, and a quorum answering to their names, the President announced the Convention ready to proceed to business.

The Journal was read and approved.

Mr. J. J. WRIGHT, from the Committee on the Judiciary, to whom was referred a resolution of inquiry as to the legislative powers of the Convention, reported that the Committee are of the opinion that the Convention has the power to legislate as far as they may consider it for the good of the people.

On motion of Mr. F. J. MOSES, Jr., the report was made the Special Order for one o'clock to-morrow.

From the same Committee, Mr. J. J. WRIGHT reported that the Ordinance providing for the abolition of the District Courts, which had been referred to them for consideration, was, in their opinion unnecessary, since the subject would be embodied in the report of the Committee with reference to the Judiciary of the State.

The report was adopted.

Mr. C. M. OLSEN offered the following resolution, which was referred to the Committee on Finance :

Resolved, That all Banks and Savings Institutions in this State, which suspended payment during the rebellion, shall immediately after the ratification of the State Constitution go into liquidation.

Mr. N. G. PARKER called for the report of the Committee on Printing. He stated that the work of the Convention was delayed from the want of a Printer. Orders had been issued for the printing of documents which ought then to be upon the tables of members.

Mr. R. C. DeLARGE replied that these documents were already in the possession of the gentleman who had been elected as printer—Mr. H. Judge Moore. He promised to have them here at eleven o'clock, but had failed to do so.

Mr. DeLARGE then stated that the Committee on Printing received two bids for the work ; one from H. Judge Moore, publisher of the

Charleston Advocate, and the other from Messrs. McMillan & Jowitt, Job Printers. The bid of H. J. Moore was $1.25 per thousand "ems" for 200 copies of the Journals and Resolutions not in pamphlet form, or $2.25 per page in pamphlet form. The bid of Messrs. McMillan & Jowitt was the same. Both were submitted for the consideration of the Convention.

Mr. LEMUEL BOOZER said that as he presumed the Convention did not understand the terms of the report, he would move to lay the matter on the table until further information could be received.

The motion was not agreed to.

Dr. J. C. NEAGLE moved that the Convention proceed to the election of printer at once.

The motion was not agreed to.

Mr. C. C. BOWEN desired to know the size of the page, quality of paper and manner in which the work was to be executed, and as this information was not in possession of the Committee, he thought it prudent to recommit the report to the Committee.

On motion of Mr. H. E. HAYNE, the report was then recommitted with instructions to report at one o'clock to-morrow.

Mr. B. F. RANDOLPH offered the following resolution, which was referred to the Committee on Franchise and Elections:

WHEREAS, incentives are necessary to a more speedy attainment of learning and intelligence, which are the sure guards of Republican liberty; therefore be it

Resolved, That the forthcoming Constitution of the State shall provide that all persons coming of age after the first of January, 1875, shall possess the qualifications of reading and writing intelligently in order to be able to vote.

Referred to the Committee on Franchise and Elections.

Mr. S. A. SWAILS offered the following, which was referred to the Committee on Petitions:

WHEREAS, certain citizens of the State of South Carolina were appointed as Assistant Assessors of Internal Revenue for the year 1866, and served in that capacity until April, 1867, without compensation, by reason of not being able to subscribe to the oath prescribed by the Act of July, 1862, and

Whereas, they did discharge those duties with fidelity to the Government, therefore be it

Resolved, That this body do earnestly recommend to the Congress of the United States the extreme necessity of adopting some measure for the relief of those persons.

Mr. B. F. WHITTEMORE offered the following, which was referred to the Committee on Education :

No township or school district shall receive any portion of the public school fund, unless a free school shall have been kept therein for not less than three months during the year, for which the distribution therein shall have been made. The Legislature shall have the power to require by law, that every child of sufficient mental and physical ability shall attend the public schools, during the period between the ages of five and eighteen years, for a term equivalent to sixteen months, unless educated by other means.

Mr. R. G. HOLMES offered the following, which was referred to the Committee on the Legislative part of the Constitution :

Resolved, That no debt contracted by the State of South Carolina while in rebellion against the United, shall be legalized or paid by any Act of any Legislature of this State.

Mr. ROBERT SMALLS offered the following, which was referred to the Committee on Education :

Whereas, the maintenance of an intelligent government, faithful to the interests and liberties of the people, must in a great measure depend upon the intelligence of the people themselves; and,

Whereas, the experience of those States which have opened to the poor and rich alike the opportunities of instruction has demonstrated the utility of common schools in elevating the intellectual character of their population; therefore,

Resolved, That the Committee on the Constitution be directed to report an article providing for a system of common schools, of different grades, to be open without charge to all classes of persons.

Resolved, That for the purpose of making effective the common school system, it be required that all parents and guardians send their children between the ages of seven and fourteen to some school, at least six months for each year, under penalties for non-compliance, to be fixed by law, unless from sufficient cause any may be excused in writing by some proper legal authority, appointed to direct or superintend the public schools.

Mr. B. F. RANDOLPH introduced the following, which, on motion of Mr. J. J. WRIGHT, was indefinitely postponed :

Whereas. distinction and inequality in law would be destructive to peace and harmony, and would be a source of general dissatisfaction, as well as make a large majority of citizens of the State discontented by social conflict among citizens, be it

Resolved, That the forthcoming Constitution shall not itself make any distinction on account of color, and shall provide that no distinction whatever on account of color in any law, legislative or municipal, shall be made in this State.

Resolved, That there shall be no distinction on account of color in any institution which depends on the public for its support.

Mr. J. M. RUNION offered the following:

Resolved, That Sheriffs, Coroners, Clerks of the Court of Common Pleas, Commissioners in Equity, Justices of the Peace and Constables, shall be elected by the people of their respective districts or beats for the term of four years, and that for four years thereafter they shall be ineligible to office.

The PRESIDENT announced that the hour had arrived for the consideration of the Special Order, namely, an Ordinance for the division of Pickens District.

Mr. W. J. WHIPPER moved that the Special Order be discharged.

Mr. L. B. JOHNSON, of Pickens. I earnestly hope the Convention will not postpone this matter. The petition has been signed by citizens all over the District. There is not a corner, not a beat, not a settlement in that District the citizens of which have not signed the petition. Another petition to the same effect has been received by me from Walhalla. If gentlemen knew the extent of Territory of that District, and the pressing need for another Court House, I am confident that they would withdraw their opposition. In consequence of the present poverty of Pickens Court House, there are no accommodations for citizens, from a great distance, who are obliged to attend Court, and it is often impossible to get a meal of victuals. I hope, therefore, so important a matter may not be hastily disposed of without a full consideration of the merit of the application, and its bearing upon the welfare of the people.

Mr. N. G. PARKER, of Barnwell. I certainly can see no harm likely to result from the adoption of this Ordinance, although my opinion is that is a subject that belongs more properly to the Legislature.

Mr. B. O. DUNCAN. I think there is no disposition among the members of this Convention to oppose the division of Pickens District; but there are various applications of the kind before the body, and if we begin, where shall we end? Divide one, and it will be claimed we should divide other Districts. As the Legislature will sit in a few weeks, I trust the matter will be postponed until that time.

Mr. R. C. DeLARGE. I believe it is the intention of the Convention to give to all petitions sent here a respectful consideration. At the same time, one of the Committees has already before it a proposition to re-arrange the State into counties and towns, and it was at least advisable to wait until the report of that Committee had been made.

14

Mr. R. J. DONALDSON. I trust that the gentlemen who oppose this petition will give us some more substantial reasons for so doing than I have heard on this floor. The people of Pickens are surely more familiar with the wants of that locality than we can possibly be, and hence their prayer deserves of our hands that consideration and action which the importance of the subject demands.

Mr. C. C. BOWEN. I am opposed to the division of Pickens District, on the general principle that if you can grant the division of one District every other District and county town may send their applications here and ask the Convention to do likewise with regard to it; in fact, I doubt whether they will be able to raise money enough to erect the necessary buildings.

Mr. J. M. ALLEN, of Greenville. The citizens of Pickens propose to erect the Court House by taxing themselves. I agree with the delegate from Pickens (Mr. JOHNSON,) as to the poverty and want of accommodations at Pickens Court House, travellers having frequently to take their provisions and whiskey with them, but the eastern side of that District is a fertile country, capable of supporting large and flourishing towns, which we propose to form into the District of Oconee, and if the people want to erect another Court House themselves, I can not see why the Convention should object to it.

Mr. W. J. WHIPPER, of Beaufort. In making the motion to discharge the Special Order, it was not with the view of defeating the object of this petition. I appreciate the necessities of that people; but my own District, which contains a larger number of inhabitants than Pickens, has equal claims upon the consideration of this Convention, and, therefore, as a matter of expediency, I deem it best that the whole subject shall be referred to the Legislature. I cannot recognize the consistency of gentlemen who question the legislative power of this body and still insist on a division, which of necessity is an act of legislation. If we once commence the work of legislation, no one can tell where it will end, and we may be kept here a month longer than is absolutely necessary. I therefore hope the Special Order may be discharged.

Mr. C. P. LESLIE, of Barnwell. This matter ought to have been disposed of without debate. Other districts will now come up for division. It is not usual to insert in the Constitution of a State the changing of a name or the division of a county. The gentleman from Edgefield (Mr. ELLIOTT,) for instance, refuses to divide Barnwell District, because he is unwilling to locate the Court House at Blackville. He is not willing to make the change from Barnwell Court House. It could not possibly be done by any rational means. He intimates I have been log-rolling, but I appeal only to the good sense of the house. Prior to the war and since, the white people of Barnwell District did not think fit to divide that District, and they certainly knew as much then as they know now of their wants. Their status has not actually changed. To bring these questions before the Convention and ask it to hurry them through does seem to smack somewhat of the ridiculous. Some have said the people will pay the expenses of erecting the Court Houses in the new districts. I believe they will at last come back on the State.

Mr. F. J. MOSES, Jr. With the consent of the mover of the resolution, I move to discharge the Special Order to-day, and to make it the Special Order for Tuesday next at one o'clock.

Mr. J. J. WRIGHT. While I am as deeply interested in the question of the division of Pickens District as any other man in the house, I am opposed to any legislation in this body, except such as is required by the exigencies of the time. We have been sent here for a specific purpose, namely, to form a Constitution for South Carolina, and we should leave to the Legislature the settlement of all questions as that which is pending at this moment. I, therefore, hope the resolution will be voted down at once.

The question being taken on the postponement of the Special Order, it was not agreed to.

Mr. WILLIAM J. McKINLAY. If we are here to legislate at all, I think the majority should be consulted. We do not know whether the majority favor the division of Pickens District. All that we know is, that certain persons are appointed Special Commissioners to select a proper site.

Mr. J. M. ALLEN. We have a petition signed by nearly all the prominent citizens of Pickens District.

Mr. F. L. CARDOZO. I desire to direct the attention of the Convention to one view of this subject not advanced by any gentleman I have heard. It is this : a number of gentlemen have questioned the legality of this Convention to enter into any such matters at all. I regard the Legislature as the only proper body to consider these questions. If we divide Pickens, we shall be inundated with petitions from a dozen or more Districts. Our Constitution may be defeated solely on that ground. Let us keep free from all doubtful questions, the Constitution we frame, so as to make it as unobjectionable as possible. Let us do nothing to incur the opposition or displeasure of any person of this State.

Mr. W. J. WHIPPER. I again move that the Special Order be discharged.

Mr. F. J. MOSES, Jr. I move to amend by discharging the Special

Order and making it the Special Order for Monday next at one o'clock, which was agreed to.

The next Special Order of the day was the petition to General Canby for the stay of all executions on debts contracted prior to the 30th of June, 1865.

Mr. N. G. PARKER moved to amend the resolution by inserting after the words "30th June, 1865," the words, "except wages of laborers or liens on the crops to secure advances made by factors or others."

Mr. PARKER said:

Mr. President: Before the vote is taken upon this resolution, I desire to define my position upon it. I desire to accomplish all that it is possible for this Convention to do, to relieve the people of South Carolina from the terrible distress which they are now suffering, and the danger that threatens them. My sympathies lead me to wish that we, as a Convention, had more power and authority to relieve them than are delegated to us. Resolutions providing various measures of relief have been presented to this Convention, and referred to appropriate Committees. They have not yet been discussed. In due time they will be re-reported back to this body, and will be discussed, and, in all probability, some of them, or part of them, will be adopted as a portion of the Constitution of this State.

While, sir, a resolution declaring null and void all contracts where slaves were the consideration, yet remains to be disposed of, shall we refuse to ask General Canby to suspend the collection of debts for a period of three months, and thus set quietly by and see the processes of collection go on daily, when slaves were the consideration?

If, sir, we contemplate the adoption of the Ordinance just alluded to, and adopt it as a portion of the Constitution of South Carolina, are we willing to let this matter rest until we shall have done so? It seems to me, sir, that we should be acting like school boys to do so. Perhaps, sir, we shall not adopt any measure whatever of relief, what then? The collections will only have been suspended for three months, provided General Canby complys with our request. It is a short time; no great harm can be done by this act.

But, sir, the desire to defeat the resolution does not seem to stop here. We have a right to presume, sir, that those who oppose this resolution, oppose any measure of relief to the State. If this is the fact, it might as well be fought out now as at any other subsequent time, and if this resolution is lost, give up the attempt to pass any whatever. Contracts for slaves, war debts, homesteads, and all.

In advocating this measure, I am aware that I may be charged by some with possessing more sympathy than judgment; but, sir, I would rather be subjected to that charge than to be accused of a lack of human sympathy. I thank God that the milk of human kindness forms a large part of the material of which I am composed, and my life long devotion to the interests of the down-trodden and oppressed, cannot be questioned. I desire the prosperity of this State, the whole State, not a part of it;

the people of this State, the whole people, not a portion of them, and I undertake to say that no portion of them can prosper at the expense of any other portion.

To relieve the present suffering debtor, in my opinion, is to relieve those also who do not owe debts or own property, but who are dependent upon those persons who do own property, for the employment which enables them to earn their bread.

I sincerely hope this measure will pass.

Mr. C. C. BOWEN moved to amend the resolution by substituting " all debts contracted previous to 1st of January, 1868, for " 30th June, 1865."

Mr. R. B. ELLIOTT moved to amend by inserting " prior to the passage of this Ordinance."

Mr. B. F. WHITTEMORE moved to lay the amendment on the table.

The PRESIDENT stated that laying the amendment on the table carried with it the whole subject matter.

Mr. B. F. WHITTEMORE moved to strike out the time and insert " up to the reception of this petition by General Canby."

Mr. B. O. DUNCAN. The *animus* of these amendments are clearly to be seen. It is an attempt of the party that were fillibustering yesterday to kill a measure absolutely essential to the welfare of the people of the State and the success of the party. The basis upon which that resolution was made, was the changed relations since the close of the war, and the changed relations on which funds were based. If we include all debts contracted since the close of the war, we ignore the intent and meaning of the resolution. I am opposed to any amendments upon this question.

Mr. R. C. DeLARGE called for the previous question, which was agreed to.

A number of delegates rose to ask for information and the reading of the Ordinance, when Mr. WHITTEMORE moved a reconsideration, which was agreed to.

Mr. T. J. ROBERTSON. Mr. President, the gentlemen who have spoken on this subject have frequently alluded to the impoverished condition of the country; I wish to ask them who brought it about : it was certainly not the poor man, or the loyal man; it was those who claim to have all the wisdom, intelligence and wealth of the country. These are now the very men clamoring for stay laws and homesteads. I venture the assertion right here, and do not believe it can be successfully contradicted, that any man who only pays his debts at the end of the law, was ever known to pay them when he could evade them by taking shelter under the protection of a stay law. I have seen and known the most ruinous consequences follow the passage of the stay law of 1861. Parties I know who were deeply in debt at that time, who never did pay or tried to pay, but who were pressed for payment, were suddenly relieved by the passage of that law, and have never since, to my knowledge, paid any of their just obligations, and these very parties, who are now in possession of large tracts of land, are the strongest advocates of stay laws; yet these same parties cry out that they cannot live in this country with colored men, and proclaim a war of races inevitable. The principal and largest debtors in this State are those who staked their all on secession. Many of them could have discharged their obligations during the war, or at its close, from the proceeds of cotton in their possession at that time, and for which they realized between forty and fifty cents per pound, but they do not want to pay, and intend never to do so as long as they have unconstitutional laws under which they may claim protection. The first stay law was passed on the 21st of December, 1861—this was continued in force until the end of the war. By an Act of the General Assembly, passed December 21st, 1865, the stay law was again continued in force for one year longer. This was followed by the celebrated stay law of General Sickles, known as Order No. 10, which expires on the 11th of April, 1868, as yet nearly three months off. The United States Government not having passed any stay law, a creditor in this State can sell and transfer his claims to a citizen of another State, and this latter party can immediately institute an action in the United States Court against the debtor.

This creates a distinction between the citizens of the several States, constituting this great and glorious republic. The stay law, too, is in direct violation of the Constitution of the United States, which says, "no State shall pass any law impairing the obligation of contract." A stay law, therefore, is not only unconstitutional, but in my opinion, calculated to unsettle business, and keep our people in a constant state of confusion and turmoil. I for one am willing to see the property of the country, if necessary, change hands, and if lands are sold cheap, so much the better for working men. It will enable poor men to provide themselves with a home, and identify each one more closely with the soil. I am in favor of a liberal homestead law which can injure no one. If, for instance, a man owns one hundred acres of land, I would exempt forty acres for a homestead. He then has sixty upon which he may obtain credit, or so to speak, he may bunk upon it. Forty acres I consider sufficient to support a family, however large it may be. But would it be right and proper for this Convention, or a future Legislature, to exempt from levy and sale the balance of the one hundred acres on which a person may have obtained credit, and thus destroy the right of the creditor, besides impairing the obligations of contracts. The Court of Errors, the highest judicial tribunal in this State, wherein was assembled the intelligence, wisdom and learning of the whole bench, decided with but one dissenting voice, that stay laws are unconstitutional and in direct conflict with the Constitution of the State and the Constitution of the United States. Under the reconstruction laws of Congress, passed March 2d, 1867, I contend we have no right to pass any law or resolution of the character proposed. The men asking relief, with but few exceptions, are those who do not recognize the validity of the Reconstruction Acts of Congress, and who refused to vote at the election for delegates to this Convention. Some of them call this Convention a menagerie, a collection of wild animals. Is this menagerie to protect their property at the expense of the loyal citizens, and the working men of the country, or are we to obey the laws which recognize no such measures? The resolution before us only asks a stay of three months, and what does that mean? They will then bring it up before the Legislature and ask for it to be extended until fall, to allow the crop to be made and gathered, and then the price of cotton not being high enough to suit their views, they will clamor for its continuance, and there will be no end to it. A stay law has been in operation for more than six years, and gentlemen ask for more time. I see no disposition on the part of the creditors of this State to oppress the debtors, where they are making the least effort to discharge their obligations. Stay laws are the legitimate offspring of secession and rebellion, and are we, who claim to be loyal, to continue to foster and cherish that offspring? Let them take the fate of their alma mater. In what I have said, there may have been some expressions which would appear harsh to some of my unreconstructed friends, but I can truly say I entertain no unkind feelings to any opponent for his political opinions.

Mr. R. H. CAIN. This question is one that certainly affects the poor man as well as the rich. I did not intend to obtrude my thoughts upon the Convention were it not I believe that at this stage of our proceedings, when bills or propositions fraught with so much interest to the country and the State are brought up, there should be a frank expression of the views of the members. I am in favor of relief, but I wish to review the *modus operandi*, in which it is to be given. The rich man has suffered greatly in the breaking up of all the relations that have heretofore existed, but I think the poor man has suffered a great deal more. I have several reasons which I propose to give, to show why I am opposed to the passage of the resolution introduced by the member from Sumter, (Mr. F. J. MOSES, Jr.) My first reason for opposing the passage of this resolution is, that the Convention has been called for the purpose of framing a Constitution for the future government of the State, and to that business I think we are legitimately committed, and ought to confine our operations. Second. Whatever Acts, Ordinances or Resolutions it may pass are inoperative, so far as their bearings are concerned, on the immediate execution of existing laws, and, therefore, we should be careful, as well as reasonable, in the presentation of these resolutions. I believe no act, so far as it relates to the immediate relief of creditors and debtors, can affect the State so as to profit either. Another reason I would give is, that to suspend executions now pending, will be an act of injustice which ought not to be perpetrated, because these actions are brought by co-equal citizens, who are demanding their claims under the laws of the State, which laws apply to all such citizens who are parties to these suits and actions. If, therefore, we pass acts and make distinctions between citizens, what good can they affect. The right of one citizen in the State is as sacred as the other. The right of the poor man is equally as sacred to the Convention or to the Commanding General as the right of the rich man. The large landholders have been for years the recipients of all the benefits from these lands. They entered heart and soul into all acts of rebellion. They have made their money ; they have amplified their domains by virtue of speculations in lands. They are that very class of men who have been standing out against the government, against the Constitution. Men who have endeavored to thwart the existence of this Convention, who have been laying schemes ever since the first Reconstruction Act of Congress passed for the ostensible purpose of defeating these Acts of Congress. These men have sacrified money and time to defeat the assembling of this Convention. Ought they not, therefore, be compelled to pay their honest debts. Their contracts were legitimate when made, and made with their mutual consent in good faith. That seems to me to be a very pertinent question. They should be kept and executed according to law. They made the contracts themselves. This Convention did not make them, neither did the members of the Convention help to make them. They run out into the great sea of speculation, they run the hazard of the die, and should take the consequences. We have been informed by one gentleman, that over two hundred thousand dollars worth of property is now involved, and we are informed by the gentleman from Sumter, that if no relief is given by the Convention, the hammer of the Sheriff will take away, in February, all the possessions of a large class of the people of the State. In answer to that, I refer to the order of the Commanding General of the Department, who has made ample provisions to meet all contingencies.

(Mr. CAIN here read General Canby's Order.) The Commanding General has certainly secured the poor man upon the plantation, and in consideration of that fact, I think it unnecessary for this Convention to make any further application to him. He has been adequate to the task, and seems to have grasped hold of this great question with consummate statesmanship. I am prepared to trust him still. The men who desire this relief were foreshadowed on the stage where a certain party came to make their lofty tumbling, and would have made that lofty flight if it could have been made with safety. The same party came with the professed cry of homesteads for the poor man, but just behind the veil is the charmer asking all the law and all the rights for the rich man. The gentleman who addressed the Convention a few nights ago took the ground that something must be done. I wish to show the consistency of this class of men. There is a class of men who denominate this Convention the "ring-streaked and speckled," like Jacob's cattle. That class, including some of the great minds of the State, have been opposed to the assembling of this Convention, and opposed to every man here. Some thinking it rather possible it might succeed, have run the hazzard of the die, have thought it best to get into the boat, and try to paddle it on their side. Are the men who opposed the General Government in its efforts to restore these States to the Union on the basis of Republican liberty, who have opposed all measures passed by Congress, have refused to vote when they could vote, who counsel "masterly inactivity" to their followers—are these men to be clothed with all the powers necessary to save their property from the law? They did not, nor do they now, recognize the validity of this body. Shall we, therefore, in the capacity of a Convention, however hybrid it may be, act the part of hybrids and fee and endow men, who do not recognize us at all, with the means of saving their property. Far be it from me to do aught that would impair the well being of every class of citizens. I am for the well being of the State, but I do not believe that in the passage of such an act the poor man will be benefitted. I believe it will result only to the benefit of those who have their large broad acres, the rich and the luxurious, who once rode in their carriages, who made the war which has brought them to destruction. I do not believe these men care about the interest of the Convention only so far as their own interests are concerned. The President had said in his opening address that for the first time in the history of the State, a Convention of the people was assembled. This being a Convention of the people, it is not a Convention for the benefit exclusively of that class of men who do not recognize the people. We should do justice to all the people. If a man owes a debt, let him pay it, and

15

the poor man cannot be the worse off. It is possible that about twenty thousand in this State might be benefitted by the passage of the resolution, but there were perhaps six or seven hundred thousand whose homes, by the order of the Commanding General, are just as secure without it. The orders of the Commanding General, he believed, would be sufficient until reconstruction is completed by this Convention. Until reconstruction is completed, the Commanding General is supreme in this State ; until the machinery of civil government is in operation, until the State has voted upon the Constitution, until Congress has passed upon that Constitution, the General Commanding is "monarch of all he surveys." With all due respect for the efforts of my friend from Sumter, and with all due respect for the best interests of the State, I believe the good of the people demands not the passing of this seeming stay law, because then we shall open the door to emigration. If we pass this resolution, the large landholders will keep the lands in their hands. If they are obliged to sell their lands, the poor man will have a chance to buy. If we want to see this State blossom like the garden of Eden, if we want to see prosperity at once spring up in our land, if we want to see commerce flourish, if we want to see emigration from the East, West, North and South, let us make this State the garden State. If we want to made this State a power, if we want to make it great, grand and glorious, let us begin by doing equal and exact justice to all men.

On motion, the Convention then adjourned.

NINTH DAY.

Friday, January 24, 1868.

The Convention assembled at 12 M., and was called to order by the PRESIDENT.

Prayer was offered by Rev. W. C. SMITH.

The roll was called, and a quorum answering to their names, the PRESIDENT announced the Convention ready to proceed to business.

The Journal was read and approved.

The PRESIDENT announced that he had appointed Mr. J. Hume Simons Reading Clerk.

The PRESIDENT read the following communication from General Scott :

HEADQUARTERS ASSISTANT COMMISSIONER
BUREAU R. F. AND A. L.,
CHARLESTON, S. C., DISTRICT SOUTH CAROLINA,
January 23, 1868.

Hon. A. G. Mackey, President South Carolina Constitutional Convention, Charleston, S. C :

SIR:—I have the honor to transmit for your consideration, and for the action of the Convention over which you have the honor to preside, (if in your judgment it may seem best to lay the matter before it,) the enclosed letter.

It is one of many complaints which I have received during the past few weeks, and as the condition of affairs described therein arises from what appears to be a gradually growing sentiment on the part of the freed people throughout the State, I think an expression of some kind from the Convention, in the form of a resolution, announcing the sense of the Convention on the subject, would be productive of most beneficial results.

The sooner that such ideas as those held by the freed people upon the plantation of Mr. Irving are eradicated, the better it will be for both planter and laborer.

I would also respectfully suggest that such an expression as I have alluded to, on the part of the Convention, would do more than any act of the military authorities, or myself, to disabuse the minds of the people of the idea that the Convention has lands at its disposal for distribution.

I have the honor to be, very respectfully, your obedient servant,
(Signed)   R. K. SCOTT,
Brevet Major-General, Assistant Commissioner.

KENSINGTON, EASTERN BRANCH OF COOPER RIVER,
January 14, 1868.

Captain F. W. Leidtke :

DEAR SIR :—A condition of things has arisen on this plantation among the freedmen which it is necessary to inform you of at once, and to request that you will communicate with me at once upon the subject I have offered General Scott's contract to the people on the plantation for their acceptance, but was answered with a flat refusal to make any contract at all.   They went on to say that they would work the lands, but until something was decided in their favor by the sitting of the Convention, they would not sign any agreement or make any terms with me whatsoever. Now this is like taking possession of my lands out and out, and I am not disposed to submit without every effort to establish my authority over what I consider my own property.

I am not disposed to be harsh in my measures, believing as I do that all this is the result of false teaching, but simply wish that you would advise me as the proper method to pursue, either compel them to sign this contract of General Scott's, or to quit my premises at once, so that I may have a chance of procuring other labor before it is too late.   I have given these people full warning that if they insist upon working my lands without a contract, they do it at their own risk, and I am not bound now to contract with any of them against my will or recognize their work in any way. If my plantation affairs are to await the deliberations of the Convention, you will readily perceive the necessity of immediate action in order to disabuse their minds of the prevailing idea that something is to be done for their especial benefit by the Convention.

You will oblige me by sending a reply to this at once through Oakley Postoffice, Northeastern Rail Road.

Respectfully yours,
S. EMELIUS IRVING.

The communication was laid upon the table until the disposal of the unfinished business.

Mr. R. C. DeLARGE moved that the Convention go into Committee of the Whole, which was agreed to.

Mr. LEMUEL BOOZER, of Lexington, took the Chair.

The consideration of the resolution to request General Canby to suspend all debts contracted prior to the 30th June, 1865, was resumed.

Mr. L. S. LANGLEY moved to add after the words "excepting wages for laborers" the words "and mechanics."

Mr. F. J. MOSES, Jr. accepted the amendment.

Mr. R. C. DeLARGE obtained the floor. I had not intended to speak, Mr. President, upon this subject, but finding those who, acting from purely personal motives, are interested in the defeat of the measure from no higher object than that of filling their own coffers, who get up and raise objections to such a measure in face of the impoverished condition of the people of the State standing in need of relief. I feel that duty to myself and my constituents require I should not remain silent. If they had been content to go no further than in Convention, I might have been induced to keep quiet. But when members go outside the Convention, and use threats to intimidate others, I for one will let them and their satellites see that there is one member who will not be intimidated by their threats.

Mr. T. J. ROBERTSON rose, and said if the gentleman had any reference to him he would pronounce the charge false.

Mr. DeLARGE disclaimed any reference to the honorable gentleman. It has been said in opposition to this measure that the proposed legislation was for a certain class. If I did not feel that some of the gentlemen have allowed their zeal to get beyond their judgment, I would be tempted to believe they did not know of what they were speaking. That the resolution as first presented to the Convention had the appearance of a class measure I will not attempt to deny, but after the adoption and incorporation of the amendment offered by the member from Darlington,

(Mr. WHITTEMORE,) with the original resolution, no gentleman can conscientiously rise and argue that the proposed measure is for the benefit of any specific class. I hold in my hand letters from almost every section of the State, addressed to members of the Convention crying out for relief. These letters depict, in strong language, the impoverished condition of the people, and demand that something shall be done to relieve them in their present condition. I deny in toto that this is a piece of class legislation, and I believe nothing but the zeal of the members who spoke yesterday induced them to speak of it as such. It is simply a request to General Canby to relieve the necessities of a large part of the people of the State. Some members had gone further, and attempted to prove it was a scheme to keep the freedmen from becoming purchasers and owners of land. I claim to be as much interested in the welfare of my race as any member upon the floor, and I think my claim will be substantiated by that race much more than the claims of gentlemen having thousands of dollars upon the issue, and who desire to defeat the measure for the benefit of their private coffers.

Mr. R. J. DONALDSON called the gentleman to order for introducing personalities into the debate.

The CHAIR decided the point of order not well taken.

Mr. DeLARGE continued: It has been argued that the execution of the laws compelling the sale of the lands will benefit the poor man by affording him an opportunity to get possession of the lands. That argument I am confident cannot be sustained. If they are sold, they will be sold at public sales, and sold in immense tracts, just as they are at present. They will pass into the hands of the merciless speculator, who will never allow a poor man to get an inch unless he can draw his life blood from him in return. The poor freedmen are the poorest of the poor, and unprepared to purchase lands. The poor whites are not in a condition to purchase land. The facts are, the poor class are clamoring, and their voices have been raised far beyond the limits of South Carolina, away to the seat of government, appealing for assistance and relief from actual starvation. If this measure was intended for only one class of men, I would be the first to raise my voice against it. I know I am on the unpopular side of the question, but I am willing, and hope others are, to sacrifice any mere personal popularity, personal friends, or even the friendship of relatives, for the welfare of the whole people of South Carolina. I trust you will by no action of yours allow the voice of the impoverished people of the State asking relief to pass by unheeded. I have been astonished to witness the unchristian feeling exhibited during the discussion. Even admitting, for the sake of argument, that the passage of this resolution is to benefit only those who have been in arms against the Government, who have done everything to oppress my race; admitting this measure to benefit them only, a position which I deny, still the Word of God extends far beyond the littleness of man and says, "Do unto others as ye would that men should do unto you." I propose to do it. Other gentlemen, with perhaps more claim to Christianity than I have, and who would be expected to bring forward these doctrines of Almighty God, have thought fit to differ. I would like to ask if there is a member so dull to the commonest ideas of finance, so devoid of reason, as to believe that any further impoverishment of the rebel classes will result in any good to any set of people. I believe there are none. Fortunately for mankind the various grades of society and various classes are dependent upon each other. I deny that the class of people who warred against the Government are the only ones to be benefitted. It is well known that the planters in the low country have much larger tracts of land than those in the up country. In the up country the land is more generally divided into small farms, ranging from one hundred to three hundred acres, and if it was not already known, it should be known, that the class of men, both white and black, in those upper districts possessing small farms, are most loyal to the Government. Some were forced into the Confederate army, and many driven into the mountains and swamps of the State for protection, and while these men, who were conscripted, persecuted or driven from their homes, were away, their families were compelled to get provisions to sustain life from the very class of men who are now trying to enforce these executions. I do not believe there is a member upon the floor who would give his verdict in favor of punishing this class simply because he might fail of an opportunity to punish some who deserve it. It has also been said that while there is a large class of debtors, there was an equal number of creditors. No business man would attempt to make such an assertion. Again, it was said it is unconstitutional for this Convention to legislate; but this is not legislation. It is simply a request to the party that has the power to suspend the enforcement of these executions. It is not intended to repudiate debts or to defraud creditors. To show how property has been sacrificed under the Sheriff's hammer, permit me to relate an instance of very recent occurrence. One of the Secretaries of this Convention owned a three story brick house, which was sold under a forced execution. In ordinary times it would have brought at least $4,000. It was sold by the Sheriff for the paltry sum of $750 He felt that it was incumbent upon them to do all they cou'd to relieve the sufferings of their fellow-men. I know members have attempted to persuade others that if they voted in favor of this resolution for staying executions for debts for three months, they give the debtor an opportunity of defrauding his creditor. There were none, however, so ignorant as to believe that the staying of the collection of a debt prevents the creditor from going before the court, obtaining a judgment or decree and placing it in the hands of an officer of the law. Then if the debtor attempts any fraud, the creditor may have the execution enforced, and I feel confident that those interested will take good care to see they are not defrauded.

But what is our duty? Is there a man upon this floor who does not feel it encumbent upon him to do every thing possible to relieve the sufferings of his fellow men. Coming, as the members do, from every portion of the State, they should be cognizant of the condition of their people. I am myself aware of the unfortunate condition of the people in the various upper and middle Districts of the State, and I say, without fear of contradiction, that the men to be relieved by this proposed measure are more loyal than most of their creditors. While I doubt the constitutionality of the stay law, I believe the voice of the Convention will be heard by the Commanding General, and acted upon. Already there are scattered throughout this State a heartless class of speculators, with no interest in the State but that of purchasing these lands at an enormous sacrifice. They do not propose to invest capital in their cultivation, but to keep them until they can demand an exorbitant price. If a wise scheme of taxation is adopted hereafter, none of the present owners will find it profitable to keep any more than he can well cultivate, and the result will be, the poor whites and the poor freedmen will, after they have succeeded in raising a crop, be able to buy these lands as they are thrown into the markets. I am here in defence of no class of men. I love my country, love my native State, love the entire people of my native State; love my race, and the adoption of this measure I feel, will redound to the interest of my race. The defeat of this measure may lead to the defeat of the ratification of the Constitution framed by this Convention. I feel that the defeat of this measure will be the defeat of the people with whom I am allied and identified.

Mr. F. L. CARDOZO said. In discussing this measure, I would say to the gentleman who preceded me, and those who will follow, that they will accomplish their object much sooner and with much more satisfaction by not impugning the motives of those with whom they differ. The gentleman who spoke last, made gratuitous assumptions and ascribed mercenary motives, that were it not for personal friendship, might be retorted upon him with perhaps worse effect than he made them. He asserted that the gentlemen who opposed him, opposed his race. I intend to show that his race is not at all connected with the matter. In giving my view of the measure, I shall not resort to mere declamations or appeals to passion or prejudice. In the first place, I doubt its legality. It is true, it is said the Convention does not propose to legislate, but I contend that a request from this body carries a certain moral influence. It shows what it would do if it had the power. It is virtually legislation. I regard any stay law as unjust and unconstitutional. It is unjust to the creditors. Let every man who contracts a debt, pay it. If he is an honest man he will pay his debts at any sacrifice. In our country it is unfortunate, as Americans, that we have a character by no means enviable as repudiators. Look at the attempt to repudiate the national debt. As an American, I protest against any further repudiation whatever, either in the form of a stay law or illegal legislation. I deem it inappropriate for us to touch the matter at all. We are sent here to form a Constitution. To travel outside of our proper province, will probably be to incur odium, displeasure and dissatisfaction. I wish to confine the action of this Convention to its proper sphere. The first question that arises is, what claim have these debtors on our sympathies more than creditors? Are the debtors greater in number than creditors? If we legislate in favor of any, will it be doing the greatest good to the greatest number? I maintain it will not. It is a class measure. This will be but the beginning. We will be burdened with applications, and the burden will be upon those who introduced this measure, not upon those who refused to legislate for other special favorite classes. I ask not only what are the claims of the debtors, but also what are the nature of these sales? Was it the transfer of real estate? I think every one here will say no. Nine-tenths of the debts were contracted for the sale of slaves. I do not wish we should go one inch out of the way to legislate either for the buyer or seller. They dealt in that kind of property, they knew its precarious tenure, and, therefore, let them suffer. When the war commenced every rebel sold their property to give money to "a common cause. And their slaves were sold for the same object, to maintain a war waged for the purpose of perpetually enslaving a people. That was the object. The ladies of the South stripped themselves of their jewels, and the men sold their lands and their slaves for that object. Now, let them suffer for it. As the gentleman from Charleston very ably said, "they have cast the die, let them take the chances."

There is also another reason, and one of the strongest, why the Convention should not take any action on the subject, but postpone it indefinitely. One of the greatest bulwarks of slavery was the infernal plantation system, one man owning his thousand, another his twenty, and another fifty thousand acres of land. This is the only way by which we will break up that system, and I maintain that our freedom will be of no effect if we allow it to continue. What is the main cause of the prosperity of the North. It is because every man has his own farm and is free and independent. Let the lands of the South be similarly divided. I would not say for one moment they should be confiscated, but if sold to maintain the war, now that slavery is destroyed, let the plantation system go with it. We will never have true freedom until we abolish the system of agriculture which existed in the Southern States. It is useless to have any schools while we maintain this stronghold of slavery as the agricultural system of the country. The gentleman has said that if these plantations were sold now, they would pass into the hands of a few mercenary speculators. I deny it, and challenge a single proof to sustain the assertion. On the contrary I challenge proof to show that if the plantations are not sold, the old plantation masters will part with them. If they are sold, though a few mercenary speculators may purchase some, the chances are that the colored man and the poor man would be the purchasers. I will prove this, not by mere assertion, but by facts. About one hundred poor colored men of Charleston met together and formed themselves into a Charleston Land Company. They subscribed for a number of shares at $10 per share, one dollar payable monthly. They have been meeting for a year. Yesterday they purchased 600 acres of land for $6,600 that would have sold for $25,000 or $50,000 in better times. They would not have been able to buy it had not the owner through necessity been compelled to sell. This is only one instance of thousands of others that have occurred in this city and State. I look upon it, therefore, as the natural result of the war that this system of large plantations, of no service to the owner or anybody else, should be abolished.

I think Providence has not only smiled upon every effort for abolishing this hideous form of slavery, but that since the war it has given unmistakeable signs of disapprobation wherever continued, by blasting the cotton crops in that part of the country. Men are now beginning not to plant cotton but grain for food, and in doing so they are establishing a system of small farms, by which not only my race, but the poor whites and ninety-nine hundredths of the other thousands will be benefitted. The real benefit from this legislation would inure to not more than thirty thousand landholders against the seven hundred thousand poor people of the State. If we are to legislate in favor of a class at

16

all, any honest man, any man who has the interest of the people at heart will legislate in favor of the greater number. In speaking against the landholders. and in taking this position I do not cherish one feeling of enmity against them as a class or individuals. But this question takes a larger range, and is one in which the whole country is involved. I can never sacrifice the interests of nine or ten millions to the interests of three hundred thousand, more especially when the three hundred thousand initiated the war and were the very ones who established an infernal negro code, and want to keep their lands until better times. They do not want that a nigger or a Yankee shall ever own a foot of their land. Now is the time to take the advantage. Give them an opportunity, breathing time, and they will reorganize the same old system they had before the war. I say, then, just as General Grant said when he had Lee hemmed in around Petersburg, now is the time to strike, and in doing so we will strike for our people and posterity, and the truest interest of our country.

Mr. B. O. DUNCAN, of Newberry, said:

Mr. President: I undertake to defend this measure of relief—not in the form in which it now stands, but as it was originally introduced—as one pre-eminently wise, just and humane. I shall make no appeals to passions or prejudice. I shall make no attempt to veil the truth. But I shall endeavor to bring it to light where it has been obscured by others. I shall endeavor to prove by argument that the position we have taken is right, and I wish my arguments to be judged only in the light of reason. Hoping for the attention of the Convention, and for calm deliberation before decision, I will proceed at once to the question before us.

The propriety of the petition to General Canby instead of an ordinance I regard as undoubted. There is no doubt of his authority in the case; and by the petition we recognize that authority more fully than if we were to pass an ordinance that we could not enforce without the assistance of the military authorities. We cannot, of course, know whether General Canby will accede to our request or not. But we know that General Meade has put in force the relief measures enacted by the Conventions of Georgia and Alabama. We know that General Hancock has denied the Convention of Louisiana jurisdiction in the case. If we judge General Canby by comparison with Generals Meade and Hancock, we may reasonably suppose that he will readily comply with a petition from this Convention. for relief to the people of the State.

The legality in the case was first settled by General Sickles in his famous order No. 10, and on the 31st of December last by General Canby, in his order modifying order No. 10 of Sickles. And here let me say in reply to the gentleman from Columbia, who stated that the order of General Sickles would not expire for nearly three months, that, so far as relates to the stay of executions, it has been out since the 31st of December, when General Canby's order took its place. I know not if this was ignorance of the gentleman, or if it was an attempt to veil the truth. So much, Mr. President, on the propriety of asking General Canby to give us temporary relief.

And now, sir, I will proceed in the attempt to show that measures of relief are required by justice. Were the terms *justice* and *law* synony-mous, as in some countries I might mention, where they are very much nearer it in fact than in our own. the point of law upon which the gen-tleman dwelt so long and persistently would be much stronger than it is. But here, unfortunately, we have had laws in all times past which ignored justice, and were made only for a class; laws before which the poor man and the slave had no chance to obtain justice; laws that have ever furnished a cloak for the most glaring and monstrous acts of injus-tice. And yet these are the laws that are now appealed to by the gen-tleman in the name of justice.

Let us test the justice of measures of relief by a few examples. Sup-pose I sold my neighbor in 1859 or '60, 500 acres of land at $20 per acre. This was a very ordinary price at that time. The debt was $10,000. The war come on and the rebel government took from the people the power to pay this debt with rebel money. Now the debt would amount to $16,000 or $17,000, and the land would probably bring from $250–500. This pitiful sum would scarcely pay the bills of the lawyers and Sheriffs. The creditor is no better off and the debtor is ruined. Again, the case of a town lot with dwelling worth $5,000. The owner owes probably a few store accounts, in all say $7–800. The war breaks out and the debts have to stand over. Now his house and lot under the Sheriff's hammer would bring probably $3–400. Who is the gainer? Not the creditor who gets scarcely anything. Not the debtor who is ruined. But only the lawyer, the Sheriff and the speculator. No wonder that these classes are clamoring against relief, and urging the necessity of obeying these unjust laws. Now how stands it with the banker compared with the owners of real estate? A bank pays 5, 10, 15 or 20 cents on the dollar as may be regarded the value of his paper. Why this discrimination in favor of banks? Why may not the owner of real estate have the same advantage from the change of circumstances? Gentlemen, I tell you it is the principle of Shilock to attempt to make the debtor pay up in full the demands against him during and prior to the war. The Jew had the right by *contract* to demand the pound of flesh from nearest Antonio's heart. But was it just for him to demand it ? As entirely just as it now is to ruin thousands of families for old debts contracted on an entirely different basis.

Justice demands relief for all classes of the people. But especially for the poor, both white and colored. I would like to hear any one show by argument—not by appeals to passion—how the poor man, either white or colored is to be benefitted by the ruin of the present real estate owners in South Carolina. Is there any one in this Convention so ignorant of the condition of the freedmen and poor whites in the country as to imagine that one in a hundred would be able to buy land even if it were all to be sold? Or if they had the lands given them, where would they find the means to cultivate them ?

Let us now consider for a moment what class of men would be benefitted by the ruin that is threatening the country. First are the lawyers. These were our former politicians. These are responsible for the unjust laws we have always had. These are responsible more than any other one class for secession and the ruin which has attended it. These are the men who now cry out loudest against the legality of any measure of relief. These are the men who are looking for the lions' share in the general ruin, and they do not wish to see it escape them. There are a few honorable exceptions, and these, of course, are not included. Next come the Sheriffs, those executioners in times like the present of the public welfare. Then come the speculators. These are the men who in various ways have managed to save money in these hard times. Some bought cotton during the war with rebel money and have since sold it at a high price for gold. Some bought bonds and obligations of various kinds for almost nothing, and now demand payment in full. But the most numerous class in the country are such as have worked the freedmen since the war, and have in various ways defrauded them of their wages. Some have sold them provisions at such exorbitant prices as to consume their hire. Others have kept a few articles of merchandize, and sold out to the poor deluded freedmen at one, two, and three hundred per cent. These are the men who now have the means to buy in the lands sacrificed under the Sheriff's hammer ; and to these the freedmen will have to look in the future for homes and a subsistence.

Without relief, the best class of men in the country will be ruined, and the lands and wealth of the country go into much more dangerous hands. The dishonest man you will leave untouched, for he will have conveyed away his titles, or have his business so smuggled up that the law cannot reach him. Only the man who is too honest to resort to such means will be reached and ruined.

At the same time, the best class of freedmen who choose to live with honest men, who will deal fairly with them, will be temporarily, at least, thrown out of house and home, and the means of subsistence for their families. This Convention may do much for the poor and ignorant of the country. Let our Committee on Education be careful to introduce such a public school system as will enable the largest number possible to enjoy the benefits of at least a primary education. In this direction, none will go farther than I. Let our Committee on the Judiciary frame such a measure as will secure to the laborer quick and cheap justice. Here, too, none will go farther than I. Let every means be taken by us as a body and individually to urge the necessity of habits of industry and economy. In this way we may do the laboring classes a great and permanent good. But never by teaching them that their interests demand the ruin of honest and intelligent white men. Those who teach such doctrines, directly or indirectly, are the worst enemies of the colored race and of humanity. It would be easy to prove by reference to the history of other countries that wherever there has been antagonism between peasantry and nobility, or between laborers and capitalists, there has been no prosperity for either. But where the relations are friendly between these two classes, and just and wise laws secure impartial justice to all, there we find all prosperous and happy. Our duty is then clear. We are, for weal or for woe, the citizens of one common country. By promoting the prosperity of all, we promote our own. By ruining others, we ruin ourselves. We are all Carolinians. Let it be our aim to do whatever will best promote the interest of Carolina. I heard a distinguished gentleman of the opposition say a few days ago he was ashamed of being a South Carolinian. Gentlemen, I cannot call these the words of a patriot. Whatever may have been her faults, she is still our country ; and instead of being ashamed of her, we should use every effort to raise her to a position of which any of her sons may be proud. I heard the same gentleman say he had rather see reconstruction defeated, than that this Convention should pass any measures of relief. I regret exceedingly that the gentleman has so much personal interest in this matter, as to make him prefer the defeat of the Republican party in this State, rather than that the people of the State should be afforded any relief. The gentleman could not have well considered what would be the consequences of the defeat of our party before reconstruction is *au fait accompli*. The colored race would assuredly be deprived of all political rights for an indefinite period, and the few whites, who have entered the party, would have to leave the country, or fall a prey to a set of outlaws called *bushwhackers*.

It seems to me that we now have the very best opportunity afforded us of forming a party regardless of race or color. Let us adopt some wise but moderate measures of relief, and thousands of fair minded honest men would join us, who have hitherto stood aloof from want of confidence. Then we could henceforth control the State, in spite of all efforts of disloyal men, aided and abetted by the Democratic party. But if we fail to do any thing for the relief of the people, I believe it will be exceedingly doubtful if we can carry any Constitution we may adopt. A sufficient number to defeat the work of this body of the best freedmen in the country will fail to see that the ruin of their employer is of any benefit to them. But let us do what justice, good policy and humanity alike demand, and we secure our position beyond the reach of danger.

A word on the subject of the legality of legislative measures on our part, and I have done. Neither the words of the reconstruction acts, nor the universal usage of Conventions, leaves any doubt in my mind on this subject. The reconstruction act gives us the power to '· frame a Constitution and civil government." Now, who ever heard of civil government being framed without legislation? But the gentleman from Richland, from some very strange cause, could only learn that we had power to " frame a Constitution." It is, I believe, the universal usage of Conventions to insert a clause continuing in force all existing law s that do not come in conflict with the work done by the Convention. This is, so to speak, re-enacting the entire previous legislation. And yet, gentlemen pretend to doubt our power to legislate. Mr. President, I am sure no one is more impressed than I am with the necessity of confining ourselves to the main work before us—that of framing a Constitution. But where the public welfare demands an act of legislation, I do not for a moment doubt our power to perform it.

Mr. W. J. WHIPPER said: Mr. President, since this matter has come up for discussion, I hope it will result in the adoption of the resolution. In the discussion of this subject, I was sorry that there should be anything like crimination or recrimination. I feel we can afford to discuss it frankly and fairly, for it is in discussions like these, where eye meets eye and face meets face, that the evidence can be produced, and the facts elicited which will enable us to judge of the matter under consideration. To appeal to the prejudice of this body may answer the purposes of an attempt to defeat or carry temporarily the object, but such appeals have no permanent effect; and a people deceived, when they find they have been deceived, only think the less of the party that deceives them. Hence, the only object we have in view, is to establish, by argument, that which is for the general good. I for one have no other object, no other purpose. With regard to the resolution upon which there has been so much said, it simply asks that the Commanding General suspend, for a given time, certain executions that are to take effect on the 4th of next month. It has been stamped very ingeniously with the brand of a stay law—a law to which much odium in this country very naturally attaches. I shall not enter into a discussion of the constitutionality or unconstitutionality of a stay law, but I have simply to say this is not a stay law, it is a resolution by this body simply asking the Commanding General to stay certain executions now likely to be enforced at a given time. This is all to which the body would commit itself. Why is it asked? It is asked simply so as to give to this Convention, or the body it may create, time to adopt a general measure of relief, and to afford immediate relief to certain parties that must necessarily be distressed by the threatened executions in February. Right here I wish to reply to the gentleman from Charleston, (Rev. F. L. CARDOZO.) He remarks that nine-tenths of the debts were contracted for slaves, and that the parties having purchased that kind of property, knowing its precarious tenure, ought to suffer. This sentiment was concurred in by the gentleman who spoke yesterday, (Rev. R. H. CAIN.) I do not know but that this may be the true Christian feeling. It, however, does not comport with my idea of Christianity, although I have not the honor of having put on the professional garb of the clerical gentleman.

Rev. R. H. CAIN. I rise to a point of order; I wish to know whether or not we have Christianity under discussion.

Mr. W. J. WHIPPER. If the gentleman pays attention he will, probably, very soon discover what is under discussion without any assistance from the Chair. What I say is that the idea to which I have alluded has been concurred in by both the clerical gentlemen from Charleston.

Rev. F. L. CARDOZO. As one of the gentlemen from Charleston who wear the clerical garb, I would like to ask the member speaking if he thinks it comports with the dignity of that garb to regard the seller of human flesh, or forgive the man that sells it?

Mr. W. J. WHIPPER. The gentleman wishes to know if it would comport with the dignity of the clerical garb to forgive the seller of human flesh. I am not prepared to say, just how much dignity attaches to the clerical garb; but I am prepared to say that it does comport with my idea of Christianity to forgive a man whenever I believe he is repentant.

Mr. L. S. LANGLEY. I wish to know whether the gentleman has thrown away all his skepticisms.

Mr. W. J. WHIPPER. That question is below the dignity of a member of this body, and I will not deign to notice it. With regard to these debts being for slave property, that is one of the strongest reasons why we should suspend, at least for the present, these executions, or why they should be suspended altogether. If certain parties who dealt in human flesh, men who brought slaves to this country, or men whose province it was to sell slaves to the man who cultivated the land, who made their living and their fortunes from selling human flesh, have not succeeded in obtaining their money, I am not one desirous or willing to assist them in obtaining it. But on the other hand, I am anxious they who held them should be relieved, for the fact is, the thing for which the debt was contracted, has been relieved, and there was no property given in consideration of those debts. I am anxious that the innocent should not suffer. It would only distress, in great part, the young or helpless women and children who had no control or hand in this business, who had nothing left but their homes, and who, if these executions are enforced, will be thrown out of doors upon the cold charities of the world. Taking the ground, then, that nine-tenths of these debts are for what was termed slave property, that of itself should induce us to ask that the sales be suspended. The Convention has already before it an Ordinance setting aside all debts where the consideration was for slaves, and when that measure comes up, we will be prepared to say whether it shall pass ; but until that question is decided, we may surely ask that judgments for slave property should be suspended. If an Ordinance of that kind is passed, why allow these creditors for slaves to go on selling and enforcing the executions before the 4th of February ? Why not let them all wait until they knew just exactly what position the Convention will take with regard to that class of debts ? Why allow hundreds of people to be thrown out of doors who had no more to do with the buying and selling for which the debts were incurred, than the gentlemen from Charleston ? Many wives, daughters, and some who have been brought into existence since, have to suffer alike with the men who purchased slaves years ago. Does this idea of distressing innocent children, born since the debt was created, of distressing women and the young, who had nothing to do with the matter of compelling them to pay these debts, comport with the gentleman's idea of clerical dignity ? Who is it to be paid to ? It is to be paid to the men who traded all his life in slave property, who made their money by it, and who secured the passage of that odious fugitive slave law which enabled them to go North, hunt down freemen and bring them to South Carolina and sell them ; and if they have not been paid, the two gentlemen from Charleston wants to make these innocent people pay the debts thus created.

Rev. F. L. CARDOZO. I said it did not comport with the clerical dignity to regard the seller of human flesh, but whenever any person repents, it does comport with the clerical dignity to forgive. But I do not believe they have repented.

Mr. W. J. WHIPPER. The gentleman says he does not believe they have repented. I have not been able to ascertain what has been their action in this particular. I question very much whether he has ever seen or knows a single man amongst those to be sold out at these executions. As I have stated already, I am not ready to assist any of those men who gathered up and sold the slaves throughout the Southern States, and those are the men to be benefitted by the recovery of those debts where the consideration was slave property. It might in some instances, too, have been the case where this identical property was stolen under the infamous law to which I have just alluded, and under that opinion, operations on the Southern mind, those parties got rid of their slaves. Now, after years have passed, to assist that class in recovering their property, certainly does not comport with my idea of Christianity.

The opponents of the resolution have also labored hard and zealously by an appeal to the passions of the poor man, to show that this measure was against his interest, and that if adopted it would be against him. And this is one of the hobbies by which they propose to defeat this measure. I cannot see how or in what way the poor of South Carolina, white or black, were to be benefitted by the sale of large landed estates at this time, at a time when, perhaps, there is not one man out of ten, who has the means of living comfortably, or able to raise a crop, while there are hundreds and thousands living only by aid obtained from charitable institutions and the assistance of the Government. This is the condition of affairs. It would be perfect folly to entertain the opinion that in the present miserable destitution of the South the poor people will become the owners of the vast tracts of land if thrown into the market. This land will become the property of Northern capitalists, many of them non-residents, speculators, who will be large land monopolists. Should this course be adopted the total ruin of the State will be accomplished.

Mr. L. S. LANGLEY. I would like to know whether the large land speculators have not always been willing to sell their lands at reasonable prices.

Mr. WHIPPER. With regard to the land monopolist of the West,
17

I can answer from ten years experience that they have done more to retard the progress of the country than any other people. They go in whenever a site for a county town was prescribed, purchased all the land around, necessarily compelling the emigrant to buy from them; and when the land rises in value, by the labor of the emigrant, they sell at enormous prices. Their object is to buy all the land around, where they suppose the land will rise in value by the labor of others. If that is the class of men wanted here as better calculated to develope the resources of the country, then they had better defeat the resolution, and invite them to these shores.

Mr. L. S. LANGLEY. Do you consider twelve dollars per acre, for such land as is sold by these capitalists, an exorbitant price?

Mr. WHIPPER. Land in Illinois, in the new portion of that country, is sold by the Government at $1.25 per acre. If a land speculator purchases it for $1.00, the emigrant who settles there, raises the value of the land by his labor, and is compelled to pay $12.00 per acre.

That is just what they propose to do here. While using their influence to have this Convention defeat that resolution, they hope, on the 4th day of February next, to purchase those acres of land, that must pass under the hammer of the auctioneer; and knowing the labor is already here, that the people must cultivate the lands, and rent them for the purpose of obtaining the necessities of life, knowing that the land will in a very short time raise in value, and they will then be able to sell, they are zealous to see this measure opposed, and we should be equally zealous in our efforts to defeat them.

Whenever non-residents of the State purchase large tracts of land, it is against the best interests of the State; whenever owned by capitalists in New York, Boston or elsewhere; whenever that state of things exist then are the prospects of the State blasted. The men who hold the land are wedded to it by all that endears a man to any portion of country. It is their home, the land of their birth, and all their dearest associations are here. Their weal depends upon the prosperity of the State, and over them to-day hangs executions for debts, many perhaps just, and should be paid. But it is not my desire, nor the desire of the large majority who have argued upon the same side of the question, for any person to be sold out under the hammer of the auctioneer, at a time, too, when the whole proceeds will hardly pay the expenses of sale. All we ask is that the Commanding General stay these executions until such measures of relief can be adopted as will enable these lands to be sold at a reasonable value, and by that time parties living in the State may be able to purchase. The present owners, from inevitable necessity, will be compelled, ere long, to sell portions of their lands, and sell them to freedmen, or whoever can pay for them. But if sold now, they will be sold in large bodies, or large tracts, so that nobody but capitalists will be able to buy.

The harangue made yesterday, that it was for the interest of the poor man to defeat this measure, and would give him an opportunity to buy land, was simply for effect. It may defeat the purpose of the resolution, but every man who is deceived by getting land, will realize that he has been made a puppet merely for a purpose. It will recoil on those who defeated the resolution. There has already been too much holding out this idea whereby a poor man shall be a land owner without any help of his own. We know that the large majority of them, at present, are not able to buy food much less land. The resolution does not injure the poor man. It does not prevent him from collecting debts honestly owing him. The resolution, as amended, allows the execution to go into effect where the consideration is for labor, or for advances made in obtaining the crop.

The argument of the constitutionality or unconstitutionality of the measure is simply balderdash. It is only a request that the order be issued by the military authority to afford relief.

The gentleman from Charleston said yesterday that anything this Convention does will not have any effect until the Constitution is ratified. I will say here that an ordinance passed by this Convention is of force from the date of its passage, and is not to be submitted to the people. The Constitution is to be submitted to the people, but the ordinances are not to be tied to that Constitution, either for the purpose of carrying it through or for the purpose of defeating it. The ordinances are entirely separate, and are only a part of the civil government that this body feels is necessary for the protection and relief of the people.

But the great object of this Convention is to frame a Constitution and civil government which will tend to the prosperity of all the people of the State, black or white. For God's sake let us inquire whether the passage of the resolution is for the best interests of the State. There is nothing in it that looks like class legislation. It would be a lamentable state of affairs, indeed, indicative of a miserable feeling on the part of the Convention, if anybody could say that unless a colored man, a man steeped in Radicalism, or a red headed man, be relieved, we will withhold the arm of protection. Then we would indeed fall far short of our mission.

I hope that all of us will feel that petty prejudices against the people we represent are to be quashed as far as legislation is concerned. I will admit frankly that I entertain perhaps as much prejudice as any other man. I have spent two years of the morning of my life in the war carried on for the purpose of crushing the rebellion of this people. All these things should be forgotten now. We are not here to incorporate these prejudices and hatreds into the Constitution and ordinances that we adopt. We are not to pass laws to represent vengeance that we may individually entertain against anybody. Nor are we to withhold relief from any class of persons because they happen to be in a position heretofore of open hostility to us. Nor are we to withhold relief because they choose to defame us in our present capacity. Indeed, it would be giving them the power, the cue with which to whip us hereafter. Assembled as we are now, representing the people of South Carolina, our sole object should be to pass laws that will benefit the whole people of South Carolina. And if we see any class of people suffering here, it is our duty, our privilege, to relieve them. I care not where they belong, what they have been heretofore, what they may be hereafter; I care not what they may be belching forth to the community, whether they are people crying "ring-streaked-and-striped" or not, these things should have nothing to do with the action of any man that has been elevated to the dignity of a member of this body. Here we should forget all preju_dices, and not be swerved from our purposes for anything so far below the dignity of the body to which we belong. We should now, if we never have before, examine critically, as representatives, the position of the people. Every man here should feel that he is the representative of the people of South Carolina. No matter what may be the opinions of others; no matter what the Governor may have said with regard to the representative portion of the people; no matter what may be the opinions of the journals of this city, I say every member of this body who does not feel that he is the representative of the entire people is unworthy of the position he occupies. And if you are the representatives of the people of South Carolina, you know the needs, wants and necessities of that people, and should do that which is best calculated for their good.

Now I come to the question. Is this measure one of the best calculated for the good of the people of South Carolina. I say unhesitatingly that there may be some circumstances in which the poor man of South Carolina would be benefitted by these sales, but in a great number of instances, from the very nature of things, and from all the circumstances existing, the property thus sold must pass into the hands of the land sharks, and you have declared in your platform that large land monopolies are ruinous to the best interests of the State. That is the platform upon which every member of this body was elected. Yet we are to set here in dumb silence whilst, under the auctioneer's hammer, a very large portion of the lands of the people of the State passes from the people, passes from those whose object is to cultivate, into that of a merciless set of legalized robbers. I ask you, gentlemen, are you ready and willing to suffer this act of injustice to take place, or by the passage of that resolution stay the hand of angry justice.

These are matters that must come home to you. Will you suffer this land to pass, as it necessarily will, into the hands of land monopolists? Will you allow it without an attempt on your part to stay their hands? Will you allow these lands to be sold, and see whole families thrown upon the cold charities of the world? Remember the many, too, that are to be made the victims of these sales, are perfectly innocent of the crimes which brought desolation to their homes; many of them have been ushered into existence since the war was settled; many were in a position that rendered them innocent. In many instances these executions are upon the estates of those who were forced into the war by a power they could not resist, and by the fate of war have been carried down to an untimely grave. Is the auctioneer's hammer to carry into the hands of these land monopolists these estates, when we, the representatives of the people, are assembled in a body, and can extend a helping hand, if that is the first thing to be done? What will then be the amount left to the creditor? In nine cases out of ten the creditor will get nothing, and the debtor will be thrown out of doors, and the land passed into the hands of the land monopolist. Another mistaken idea is, that the men who are going to buy the land will be of that class who will sell it out for the benefit of the people. They are not coming here for the special interest of the poor man; they seek only their own interest. When once they gobble up the lands, they will sell only at their own fixed price, and they will wait until the land rises in value before they sell.

The land monopolist can sit securely in New York, Ohio, Massachusetts, and wait the rise in value of these lands, while we, the representatives of the people, will then too late regret our mistake.

I hope there is not a man in this body, whatever may be his course, will suffer himself to be swayed by passion or prejudice. I hope whatever you do here, you will do it, at least, feeling that it is for the good and for the best interests of the people you represent. I hope it will not be done in the feeling manifested by the gentlemen from Charleston who addressed you yesterday. I hope it will not be done as a measure of punishment to a people already punished too severely. Whatever you do, above all I hope it will not be done for the purpose of revenge. The time was when I, as much perhaps as any man, was anxious to see some of these men hung. When General Lee surrendered, I would have hung every leader of the rebellion. I would have given them a short, shrift, and a speedy death ; but that time is past.

When I left the army at the close of the war, I was zealous to see the leaders of the rebellion hung, and every man engaged in it disfranchised and their lands confiscated. The government of the country has thought proper to pursue a different course. I think for us to act now and suffer anything to be done that savors of anything like vengeance is wrong, cruel, and unjust. If we are truly the representatives of the people, we will suffer nothing of the kind. I shrink from no responsibility, but I will oppose anything that savors of vengeance. These executions. as I have said, must of necessity punish a very large number that were not at all engaged in the rebellion, or in any way responsible for it.

This measure is far short of what we should have done, and what I would have it do. I believe we have a right to pass an Ordinance for the relief of the people. We should have passed an Ordinance suspending these debts for any time necessary, and asked the military to enforce it. This is the course we should have pursued, what, in my opinion, we should have done, and what we had a right to do. But knowing the existing feelings, I consented to the present measure. I am willing to attribute to the opposition, honesty in their position. I am not disposed to argue against it. I think them mistaken with regard to the benefit the poor people of the South are to reap from the sale of these lands, for the very people to be sold out are as poor as it is possible for them to be, saving entire bankruptcy. And I say more than that. The creditor is not to be benefitted by the measure, or at least, not in extent to the waste of property that must necessarily follow. If you sell the lands, what is the result ? The lawyer is to be paid, the Sheriff is to be paid, and all the whole string of officers who had a hand in getting up these executions.

Again, it has been shown that the very men to be benefitted, are the lawyers, men who have been leaders, who hatched up treason and brought on the war. They are responsible for it. Who was it carried this State out of the Union ? Was it the poor honest farmer, who lived far away in the country, coming, perhaps, once or twice a year to town, or was it the men who will reap the benefit of these executions, the lawyers ? How many leading men were there in South Carolina before the war ? They may be counted, perhaps, only by the dozen. But those they have wronged, those they have deceived, may be counted by hundreds, yea, by thousands. The Government having magnanimously declined to punish the men who led the State into ruin, I ask that we should save the men who were forced into rebellion by those leaders. I ask it as a matter of justice. As the supreme power of the State of South Carolina, we should interpose our arm for the protection of suffering humanity. This is my earnest desire, prompted only by the feelings of a warm heart toward every citizen of our State.

Mr. F J. MOSES, Jr. I move that the Committee do now rise and report that we have had the subject committed to us under consideration, and have come to no conclusion. I desire to state that I make this motion not with any view to stop discussion, but that the Convention may adjourn at the time fixed by rules of the house.

Mr. R. J. DONALDSON. I move as an amendment, that we rise and report progress.

Mr. L. S. LANGLEY. I am decidedly opposed, after the opposition have fired off their big gun, and suppose they have now sufficient influence to carry their measure through, to adjourn without a reply. If we do this, the previous question may be sprung upon us.

Mr. R. J. DONALDSON. The motion of the gentleman from Sumter, was not seconded in parliamentary form. No member can second a motion without rising and addressing the Chair.

Mr. R. C. DeLARGE. I rose and seconded the motion.

The Chair decided the motion of the gentleman from Sumter, to be before the house.

Mr. R. B. ELLIOTT. I rise simply to make a correction. The gentleman from Sumter offered as an excuse for this motion, that the rules by which we are governed, would compel us to adjourn at 3 o'clock.

Mr. B. F. WHITTEMORE asked if the Committee of the Whole were governed by the rules of the house.

Mr. J. J. WRIGHT. I am in favor of the Committee rising and submitting the question to the house and decided there.

Mr. F. J. MOSES, Jr. My motion was strictly parliamentary and in order.

Mr. B. F. WHITTEMORE. I move that when this Committee does rise, it shall rise at three o'clock.

Mr. T. HURLEY. I move as an amendment, that the Committee rise five minutes before three o'clock.

The amendment was agreed to, the Committee rose and reported progress, and the Convention then adjourned.

TENTH DAY.

Saturday, January 25, 1868.

The Convention assembled at 12 M., and was called to order by the PRESIDENT.

Prayer was offered by the Rev. T. W. LEWIS.

The roll was called, and a quorum answering to their names, the PRESIDENT announced the Convention ready to proceed to business.

The journal of the preceding session was read and approved.

The PRESIDENT read the following communication, which was received as information :

OFFICE OF THE DISTRICT ATTORNEY UNITED STATES,
DISTRICT OF SOUTH CAROLINA.

CHARLESTON, S. C., January 23, 1868.

Hon. C. J. STOLBRAND,

Secretary of Constitutional Convention, Charleston, S. C.:

SIR : I have the honor to acknowledge the receipt of yours of the 21st, informing me that by a resolution of the Convention I have been elected one of the Solicitors of your honorable body, and entitled to such per diem and mileage as are accorded to delegates.

I beg leave to thank the Convention for this high honor so unexpectedly conferred upon me, and though greatly distrusting my ability to assist, will accept the position and do all in my power to aid in the great work which the Convention has in hand.

I am, very respectfully,
Your obedient servant,

D. T. CORBIN.

The PRESIDENT. I deeply regret that in consequence of a monition from the United States District Court, it will be necessary for me to be present at that Court on Monday. I may not be present at the opening of the Convention, and if I hear of no objection, I will appoint Mr. LEMUEL BOOZER President during my temporary absence.

Mr. L. S. LANGLEY. I object to an appointment by the President, I think the Convention should appoint its own Chairman.

The PRESIDENT. The objection is well taken, I hope the Convention will elect a member to preside during my absence.

Mr. R. C. DeLARGE. I move that Mr. LEMUEL BOOZER, delegate from Lexington, be chosen temporary Chairman during the PRESIDENT'S absence.

Mr. L. S. LANGLEY. I nominate Mr. F. L CARDOZO.

Mr. F. L. CARDOZO. I decline the honor in favor of my friend, Mr. W. J. WHIPPER, of Beaufort.

Mr. W. J. WHIPPER, declined the honor.

Dr. J. L. NEAGLE nominated Mr. L S. LANGLEY, of Beaufort.

Mr. L. S. LANGLEY declined.

Mr. R. C. DeLARGE. I call for the previous question.

The call for the previous question was sustained, and on being put, Mr. LEMUEL BOOZER was chosen temporary President.

Reports of Standing Committees were called for.

Mr. N. G. PARKER, of the Committee on Finance, reported that on Monday they would present for the consideration of the Convention, an ordinance regulating and ordaining the pay and mileage of members, the manner of levying and collection of taxes, and an ordinance in relation to bills receivable of the State.

Mr. R. C. DeLARGE, from the Special Committee on Printing, reported the following bids, which he submitted for the consideration of the Convention :

CHARLESTON, S. C., January 20, 1868.

To the Committee on Printing,
  South Carolina Constitutional Convention :

GENTLEMEN : We beg leave to hand you an estimate for printing for your Convention. We will print not exceeding two hundred copies of any resolutions, proceedings, ordinances. etc., when in pamphlet form, at the rate of $2.25 per page, (pamphlet pages to be five and a half by nine inches,) and for matter not in pamphlet form, at the rate of $1.23 per one thousand ems.

The above includes cost of paper, press work, binding, etc., but for tabular or figure work, double the above price. When the work is ordered on extra fine or heavy paper, an addition will be made to the above prices, the only difference being in the cost of the paper. Hoping for a favorable consideration on our estimate,

I am your obedient servant,

H. JUDGE MOORE.

N. B.—I propose to use long primer type.

CHARLESTON, S. C., January 21st, 1868.

To the Committee on Printing Constitutional Convention :

Two hundred copies pamphlet form $2 25 per page ; two hundred copies of Bills, Ordinances, Resolutions, &c., $1 25 per 1000 ems. This estimate includes press work, paper, &c. Where cap paper is used, an additional charge will be made to cover actual cost of paper. Tabular

18

work double price. One thousand copies of proceedings, paper included, $3 50 per page. Every additional five hundred copies, $1 per page.

Very respectfully,

McMILLAN & JOWITT.

Mr. S. CORLEY. I move that H. Judge Moore be elected printer for this Convention.

Mr. A. J. RANSIER. Before that motion is put, I trust the Chairman of the Committee on Printing, will enlighten the Convention as to which of the two bids presented is the lowest.

Mr. R. C. DeLARGE. They are almost identically the same. The bid of H. Judge Moore is about two cents lower.

Mr. T. HURLEY. I object to the acceptance of the report. The bids do not specify whether the printed matter will be made solid or leaded. Any practical printer, or any one that knows any thing about printing, knows that the difference between brevier and long primer, is from fifty to seventy-five per cent. in favor of the latter or solid matter. Mr. Moore's bid might be two or three cents lower, and still the estimate of the other parties be about fifteen or twenty cents cheaper. The difference is made up in the amount of matter furnished. I move, as an amendment to the motion of the delegate from Lexington, (Mr. CORLEY) that the report be recommitted, with instructions to the Committee to obtain further information from the bidders, as to whether the work will be solid or leaded, and also to specify the size of the pages.

Mr. B. F. RANDOLPH. I hope the motion will not be seconded, and that the Convention will elect Mr. H. Judge Moore printer. The subject has been before the house several times, and we have been a whole week without a printer. It is enough to know that Mr. Moore can do the printing, and we know he is in sympathy with the Convention. I hope the matter will not be postponed.

Mr. C. C. BOWEN. I am opposed to giving the printing to H. Judge Moore. I understand, and am prepared to prove the assertion, that Mr. Moore has entered into a combination with other printers, whereby other bids were kept out. It is one of the rules laid down, that where a party enters into a combination with another, he is not to be a contractor under any consideration whatever. I move, therefore, that the printing be given to Messrs. McMillan & Jowitt. It is not altogether decorous for the delegate from Orangeburg (Mr. RANDOLPH) to urge the election of H. Judge Moore. The delegate is connected with the press, which expects to reap the benefit of this printing. I am opposed to the contrac being given to Mr. Moore on that ground also.

Mr. B. F. RANDOLPH. I am connected with the paper published

by Mr. H. Judge Moore, but not with the job printing department. I favor Mr. Moore because I know him to be in sympathy with the party. It may be that Mr. Moore has entered into a combination with other printers to assist him. What I object to is to give the printing to the other parties who are not in sympathy with our party.

Mr. J. M. ALLEN. I think it is time we entered into an election. The question seems to be how to save two hundred dollars to the State, and we have already lost about three hundred by this discussion.

Mr. R. C. DeLARGE. I would ask the house to receive the report as information, and then appoint a Special Committee to investigate the subject.

Mr. J. J. WRIGHT called for the previous question, which was sustained.

Mr. R. C. DeLARGE, Chairman of the Committee on Printing, said: I hope the vote in relation to this matter will not be taken to-day. I am opposed to taking a dollar out of the State Treasury that can by any possibility be allowed to remain. Both bids appear to leave a large margin for speculation. I do not know the facilities of Mr. H. Judge Moore for doing the work, but I do know that all the printing thus far has been executed by him. Neither can I state whether Messrs. McMillan & Jowitt can execute the work more satisfactorily. Both parties are anxious for the work. Messrs. McMillan & Jowitt stated to me they would do it five per cent. lower than any other establishment in the city. But as both bids allow the widest range for speculation, it may be in the making up of their charges by the parties. The Convention will have to pay more than has ever heretofore been paid for similar work. I feel confident if the Convention will postpone until Monday, and appoint another Committee, they will be able to obtain better and more definite offers for the work. As a matter of principle, I would be disposed to give it to the person allied with the party, but it is stated that the party directly interested with Mr. Moore, has no more sympathy with us than Messrs. McMillan & Jowitt.

The main question being on the motion to elect H. Judge Moore Printer, it was decided in the affirmative, and Mr. Moore declared Printer to the Convention.

Mr. J. J. WRIGHT, of Beaufort, offered the following resolution :

Resolved, That this Convention respectfully request that Major-General Ed. R. S. Canby, commanding the Second Military District, immediately issue an order exempting from levy or sale, for a period of four months, one hundred acres of land which now, or which may, prior to the expiration of the four months, be under execution.

Mr. WRIGHT said: I offer this resolution in hopes of it adoption. It is the desire of the Convention to secure the homestead, and I believe it their intention to pass a Homestead Act. The object of the resolution is to save out of all lands now liable to execution and in process of being carried into effect, one hundred acres, or so much as will secure the homestead.

Mr. A. J. RANSIER. I move that the resolution be referred to the Committee on the Legislative part of the Constitution.

Mr. E. W. M. MACKEY. I move to amend by inserting, "and that they be required to report Monday morning next."

Mr. L. S. LANGLEY. We have had before us for several days, a question bearing some analogy to the one involved in the resolution. I believe we are willing to exempt from levy and sale, a homestead to each landholder in this State, and as there is a necessity for speedy relief, I would propose that the resolution be considered at once. I am anxious that every man who owns land in this State, should be secured in his homestead. And as we have been told there is danger of some families being turned out of doors, I move we proceed to take up the matter, and hope the resolution will be adopted.

Mr. R. H. CAIN. Last Thursday I rose in my place as an humble delegate to this Convention, to express my views on a question then pending, and similar to the one now before the Convention. At that time I expressed a wish and desire that every possible relief to the poor and suffering in this State might be afforded. I regret exceedingly that gentlemen on the other side have felt called upon to misstate and misrepresent my views. No man will go further than myself to afford all possible relief to the citizens of this State, through and by the law. But I am decidedly opposed to all violations or abrogations of law to suit any class of men. I claim to be a law abiding man, and until the law is abrogated by recognized authority, I am in favor of its enforcement. With this view, I opposed the resolution then pending before the Convention. But I am in favor of exempting every man's property and giving a homestead which can be saved from any execution for debt. Gentlemen have misrepresented my views and made it appear that I am opposed to a certain class in the State. I deny it. No man has gone farther to bring about peace and harmony. I claim to be a citizen of the State, have made large purchases of lands and am involved to a very large extent. If the stay law does not pass, I myself will probably be a loser to the amount of six or seven thousand dollars. But the reason why I am opposed to the resolution under discussion on Thursday is, as I showed, that the Commanding General had made ample provision for the execution of the law, and at the same time extended protection to every man's household.

As I have said, no one will go farther than I myself, to secure a homestead, for I believe the future prosperity of the country, the hope and future well-being of the State, depends upon a homestead law, securing to every man, white or black, rebel or union, the right to maintain himself and family from executions of law. I go further than the gentleman from Beaufort, Mr. WHIPPER. He said he came into the State habited in the garb of a soldier, determined, if possible, to hang the leaders of the rebellion as high as Haman, but he was now willing to extend the olive branch of peace. I came simply as a messenger of peace, and it has been my province and desire ever since I have been in the State, to counsel moderation, patience and obedience to law, in all departments whatever. I am in favor of doing right and giving equal justice to all mankind. I would ask no man with regard to the past. I recognize the fact that we are assembled in Covention. It is our duty to state our views, and should not be called into question as to motives because we do not think as other gentlemen. I believe the question of homesteads will enter into the deliberations of the Convention ; and that it is in our power to lay the foundation of a homestead law, to allow of its formation, and then within the province of the legislative department to so arrange the details as to do justice to all men. I am in favor of securing to every man a homestead against all or any execution whatsoever. I contend, however, that we are asking General Canby to do what he has already done. I believe, as I said last Thursday, he has ample powers, and will do everything that is right to protect the interest and safety of all the people of this Commonwealth. I feel we may repose implicit confidence in him, and for that reason, I was opposed to the introduction of resolutions, like the one offered Thursday, into this Convention. I think we have a certain line of duty marked out, and having fulfilled that, to adjourn, and present to the people for ratification such a Constitution as can be adopted by every right minded man, so that we may have our representatives knocking at the door of Congress at the proper time.

The expenses of the Convention are going on, and we have been informed by the Governor of the State that there is no money in the State Treasury. We will have to resort to taxation to meet the expenses of the Convention. I am opposed, therefore, to any measure being discussed by the Convention which properly can be left to the Legislature. The Commanding General, in my view, has done enough, and it will come within the province of the Legislature to make good whatever is necessary, or has been left undone by the General Commanding.

These are my views on this question. I regret I have been misrepresented. It has been stated that I came here for the purpose of seeking revenge, and that it did not comport with the dignity and position which I assume as a clergyman. In all my remarks last Thursday I made no allusion nor indicated any desire of vindictiveness to any class in the State of South Carolina. I simply confined myself to arguments to show the reason why the motion then pending should not prevail. I have several reasons I might introduce here, but will not detain the Convention.

I want a Constitution that shall do justice to all men. I have no prejudices, and feel above making any distinctions as much as my friend of the *News*, who proposed "Daddy Cain" should do certain things. I agree with the sentiment that every class of men should reap the benefits of this Convention. Far be it from me to put down one man simply because he rebelled, or raise another simply because he was a Union man. I hope we will take hold high upon the highway of human progress, lay the foundation broad and deep, and rear a superstructure whose grand proportions shall give shelter and justice to the rich man as well as the poor. I want to see this State take its place in the Congress of the United States. I want to see internal improvements, the railroads rebuilt, and, in fact, the whole internal resources of the State so developed that she shall be brought back more happy and prosperous than she ever was. I believe, under the ægis of freedom and liberty, she will take such a bound forward as has never before been witnessed in this country. It had been said that it was dangerous to introduce Northern men here. I regret that this should come from one who, if his logic was good, ought to be back in Michigan to-day. The introduction of Northern men will be a sure means of redeeming the State. I am in favor of bringing in men of every class. Already societies had been organized by the prudent, thrifty and far-seeing Germans for the purpose of bringing emigrants into the State. I am for giving to each and all, native and adopted, a homestead. But while I am in favor of securing a homestead, I am not willing to give license to rascality. I am in favor of giving relief to the merchant, the mechanic, the farmer, the machinist, the laboring man. I am in favor of giving relief to all classes of the State, and not confining our action to one particular class. I desire to do whatever will contribute to the well being of the State.

Mr. F. J. MOSES, Jr. I call for the previous question.

The call was sustained, and the PRESIDENT decided that the question before the house was on the adoption of the resolution offered by the delegate from Beaufort (Mr. J. J. WRIGHT.)

Mr. B. F. RANDOLPH. Does not that lie over for one day, or under the rules is it not required to be referred to a Committee?

The PRESIDENT decided that as the resolution was not of a permanent character it did not come under the rule adopted by the house in regard to matters affecting the Constitution.

Mr. J. J. WRIGHT. We have been for several days past considering the question of relief to the people of South Carolina. I have not been able to see how the proposed measure of the delegate from Sumter (Mr. MOSES) is to grant relief. I therefore submitted the resolution offered this morning. It differs entirely from the first resolution offered, because that was simply a request to General Canby to stay for three months the debts and the executions now pending in the courts, so that certain person's lands might not be sold. It was to stay it for three months for what? Was it a measure of relief to the people? To what people? It would grant relief to the people in debt, because it simply stays executions for three months. During that period they could get all their property out of their hands. It would be relief to but few. They could cause poor people to contract with them; they could cheat them out of their wages or their labor, and perhaps get money enough to pay the debt. It is granting no measure of relief. It is simply allowing a transfer, from one party to another, property sufficient to cover the debt.

Mr. W. J. WHIPPER. I would ask the member as a lawyer, how a man would dispose of his property after judgment has been rendered, and the execution on that judgment merely suspended?

Mr. J. J. WRIGHT. If I had a farm or plantation on which there was a judgment, I could put all my property out of my hands that that judgment does not cover.

Mr. W. J. WHIPPER. Suppose the judgment covered all the property.

Mr. J. J. WRIGHT. I might, during the stay of that judgment, get money enough by cheating the people to relieve me of that judgment. The resolution I offer, embodies a practicable measure of relief, and I hope it will be adopted without reference to a Committee. We can then ask General Canby to exempt from levy or sale on execution one hundred acres of land. We propose to incorporate into the Constitution a homestead law that shall give to every person in the State of South Carolina who now owns a fee simple, forever of one hundred acres. If the Courts allow these executions to take place, many families will be sold out of house and home.

Mr. F. L. CARDOZO. General Canby has already exempted from executions property to the amount of two thousand dollars.

Mr. J. J. WRIGHT. That is true, but General Canby's order does not say land. It seems simply to apply to personal property.

Mr. F. L. CARDOZO. General Canby's order exempts twenty acres of land.

Mr. J. J. WRIGHT. But that is not what we propose to do. We propose to exempt one hundred acres. Land is so poor along the sea coast that it takes from three to four acres to make as much as could be raised on one acre of good soil. We believe a man may live as he ought to live on one hundred acres of land, and we desire General Canby to exempt that much until we get the State restored to the Union.

The question being put on referring the resolution to the Judiciary Committee, to report Monday morning, it was not agreed to.

The main question was then put, on the adoption of the resolution, and it was agreed to.

Mr. F. J. MOSES, Jr. I now call up the resolution reported back by the Committee, and on that, call for the previous question.

The call for the previous question was sustained.

Mr. F. J. MOSES, Jr. In the commencement of my remarks, on this important subject, I desire to state, for the information and comfort, perhaps, of all the gentlemen in the opposition, that I know and understand exactly what rights I had in debate, according to parliamentary usages, and these I intend to maintain. I rise in a spirit of all kindness towards every delegate on this floor. Although the discussion of this question, so far, has been characterized with a bitterness which I hardly expected to see in so grave a body as this; although rage, and spite, and venom, have been the distinguishing features of some of the speeches made on the subject, I desire to say, if those shafts were sent towards the members who agree with me on this subject, they have fallen harmless at our feet, and I rise, as their representative, in the best of humor with every body on the floor. I know, according to parliamentary usage, I have the right to keep this Convention listening to me for the space of one hour. I desire to say, however, I do not intend to make a speech. I desire simply to have a plain, quiet, confidential conversation with all the members of this Convention. The subject does not admit of elaborate argument. I do not believe the majority of us have been impressed with the force of a single remark, for I cannot dignify the speeches made with the name of argument that has fallen from the lips of the opposition. Further, it would be unkind, unjust, and regardless of the feelings of the members of the Convention, after having been kept three days listening to speeches on this dry subject, to bring forth now an elaborate argument in reference to this question. It is, perhaps, astonishing that those to whom we should have looked for examples of charity, forbearance, kindness and brotherly love, were the first to throw down the gauntlet of defiance from one race to another, and attempt to set up a spirit of antagonism between the two classes of this country, which, I venture to say, does not exist, nor can any of the efforts of those gentlemen bring into existence. We have been regaled this morning with an argument by the gentleman from Charleston, who spoke last Thursday, after the gentleman from Richland, Mr. R. H. CAIN, and I am delighted to see that he has changed his standpoint entirely, and with all the candor for which he is remarkable, confesses that from the beginning he has never seen how any good or evil result could flow to any class from the passage of this resolution.

Mr. R. H. CAIN. I entertain the same opinions I did on Thursday last. I do not concur in the original resolution, but am in favor of the one adopted this morning.

Mr. F. L. CARDOZO said he did not object to the exemption of one hundred acres of land from execution of debt, as embraced in the resolution just adopted, but to the fifty or eighty thousand covered by the resolution offered by the speaker.

Mr. MOSES continued. The gentleman did vote in favor of the resolution of the gentleman from Beaufort (Mr. WRIGHT.) I now repeat that the gentleman from Charleston have changed ground most completely, in reference to the question under discussion. The gentleman who spoke this morning, said he preferred the resolution of the gentleman from Beaufort, to the one introduced by myself, because he thought that measure will help a great many persons, and the resolution proposed the other day did neither. Why then does he stand forth and oppose with so much bitterness and venom, a resolution which he says can endanger no one. And I was delighted to see that it was the sense of the house to adopt that resolution, because I believe that vote evidence of a determination to sustain the resolution which I have the honor to represent. I believed when I came to this Convention as a delegate, I came a representative of the State of South Carolina. I came to labor for the interest of every man in the State, and not in the interest of any particular class or set of men whatever. I do not know one white man in this State who voted for me as a member of this Convention. But though they did not vote for me, they are my constituents, and I would be recreant to every sentiment of honor, recreant to every prompting of duty were I to forget their interest simply because they did not vote to send me.

I believed it was coming to a Convention of the people of the State,

19

and not to an inquisition or star chamber. If the feelings exhibited here are the true ones, if a spirit of enmity exists to the persons embraced in that resolution, if it is the desire to take from men every thing they own in this world, then let those who desire it come up and do it openly and manfully, and if necessary put the hatchet at once to the hearts and brains of their victims. But come not in the guise of friends, in the guise of representatives of the people, and make the deepest stab that could possibly be made. I ask you, for God's sake, do not do this. Abstain from all prompting of enmity. If these executions under sales are allowed to go on, the State of South Carolina will be in the most distressing position in which any commonwealth has ever been placed?

It seems to me that this is too late an hour for gentlemen to call for information. It seems to me that the representatives from the upper part of this State know the destitution and desolation that prevails, and need not be reminded of it by one in whose District there is not so much destitution as in any other. We can, however, look around us and see the desolation. We know we are at the end of a terrible war ; that we have just emerged from a conflict which devastated the whole Southern land and drenched it in blood. Almost every landmark of prosperity has been swept away. Nothing but ruins mark the spot where temples used to stand. The people everywhere call for relief. They ask it of their representatives, of every man upon this floor. They come in their bitterness of heart and anguish, and say you alone are able to give us this relief. Will you put your feet on our necks now that we are crushed to earth, or will you, like brothers, as you should be, extend a helping hand and lift us up on the platform you occupy yourselves. Which is it to be ? What message shall we send forth from the Convention ? Shall we send forth an edict declaring that these men deserve punishment when the Government has refused to punish ? Shall we be deaf to the call for mercy ? I do not believe that will be the edict. I believe when the resolution is voted upon, the voice of happiness and cheering will greet the heart of every family in the State, and bring forth tears of joy and happiness at the action of this Convention. If otherwise, if the sales under the Sheriff's hammer go on ; if nothing is left to the poor shivering mother and children ; if nothing is left to clothe their scantily clothed limbs, who shall be responsible for it ? Gentlemen who have brought up this bitterness from the depths where it had been forgotten in the midst of the desolation, may hear the cry coming forth directed to some of them, saying : ." Cain, Cain, why slewest thou thy brother ?"

I was never more surprised than when I introduced this resolution, and asked that it should be passed, to find delegates with white skins denouncing me as bringing it in favor of class legislation for the colored citizens of this State. I believed it would do more good to the laboring class of the State of South Carolina than it could possibly do to any other class. Hence my astonishment at being denounced as a man, in the words of the clerical gentleman from Charleston, guilty of legislating for a class of men opposed to the objects of this Convention. That was the idea, and it was carried out with a degree of intensity, warmth, enthusiasm and excitement which I, for one, was not prepared to meet.

[Mr. F. J. MOSES, Jr., here read the resolution.]

The only reason why I had not inserted the words after added, viz : "except for wages, liens on crops, etc.," was because I thought those already amply protected by the order of General Canby, who with that sense of justice, which has characterized him ever since he has commanded this Military District, has up to this time secured to laborers and mechanics the wages due them.

The resolution, as it stands, is a simple request to General Canby. We are the representatives of the people of South Carolina. We come from every District in this State. We are either prepared to know the wants and necessities of every District, or we have not prepared ourselves for the performance of our duties. I believe I know the wants and necessities of Sumter District, and I am responsible for the statement, that not one of the citizens, in the length and breadth of Sumter District, white or colored, but desires that this relief should be extended. I am happy to say in my District there is no consideration of class. As far as equity and justice are concerned, they are all on one broad platform. They all live in friendship and amity with one another. If the condition is different from this in any other District, I should be grieved to hear it. If the gentlemen from Charleston do not know the wants of their District, then I undertake to say they have not performed their duty as well as I have mine.

The argument about the constitutionality or unconstitutionality of this measure, and about its being legislation, is simply stuff and nonsense. I am surprised that any member should be able to keep a smooth countenance when they hear a protest that it is unconstitutional. I desire to ask the question, if a certain individual, say a citizen of Sumter District, were to go to General Canby and make a request, that in order to meet the necessities of the District, he would issue such and such an order, would the gentleman from Charleston say it was unconstitutional ? I see the members smiling now who have been trying this argument on the Convention. This is simply an effort to induce General Canby to stop sales under executions, in order to afford the Convention time to mature proper measures of relief for the people of the State. I suppose this Convention will not adjourn without adopting some permanent measure of relief.

This resolution commits no one. It is simply an expression on the part of the Convention that it would be good for the people of South Carolina that the sales of property under executions should be stopped for three months. Why? In order to afford the Convention the necessary time in which to mature proper measures of relief for the people of the State. I suppose this Convention is determined to grant some measure of relief, and I think I have a right to say so, because I believe there is but one gentleman who is in opposition, all the rest have shown or expressed an intense desire to give at least a homestead. How long will it be before we can afford relief. No member expects to be here longer than three weeks, and I earnestly hope we will not be kept longer than two. But it may happen that Congress may pass a new Bill, and send it to us to carry out its provisions. We might, in that event, be kept here for three months. This is the explanation in reference to the duration of time mentioned in the resolution. To rid the mind of the gentleman from Richland (Mr. T. J. ROBERTSON) of a ghastly nightmare, giving rise to visions of repudiation, of greenbacks flying from him, of eluding his grasp, I would say to him, as the mover of the resolution, that it does not look to repudiation, does not stoop to repudiation, and that is not the intention of the resolution. This was only another word hunted up to frighten us off.

Mr. ROBERTSON asked if six years was not time enough for paying debts; if not, how much longer time was necessary?

Mr. MOSES. I do not believe the people of South Carolina do not desire to pay their debts. It is the first time I have heard this charged against them. I know the people of South Carolina. I know there exists not in this broad land a more honorable people in reference to the performance of their contracts. I know most of them have promptly paid their debts whenever due. It lies not in the mouth of a South Carolinian to brand them with an unwillingness to pay their debts. The people of South Carolina simply now ask to be allowed to discharge their debts in a manner which will save them something and their creditors something. They desire relief now as much in behalf of the men they owe money as in their own behalf. What is the consequence of pressing men at the present time? I have seen it at my own Court House. I have seen the finest land in Sumter District sacrificed under the Sheriff's hammer. I have seen the owner standing by and heard the bid at which everything was swept from him. Everything was taken away from the

poor debtor. Yet South Carolinians have been branded with the dis-
honor of not being willing to pay their debts. In the name of South
Carolinians I protest against the charge.

Mr. ROBERTSON. Does the gentleman claim to be more identified
with the interests of South Carolina than I do or other gentlemen here
to the manor born?

Mr. MOSES. I do not claim to represent South Carolina more than
any other South Carolinians on this floor. The only difference that
exists between myself and the gentleman is, that while we agree on the
question as to the political mistakes, which South Carolinians have made,
we do not agree in reference to the estimation of the character of South
Carolinians. I think they have always paid their debts whenever they
were able. He has a great many debts coming to him, and he ought to
know whether they pay their debts.

Mr. ROBERTSON. They do not come.

Mr. MOSES. I hope the gentleman will not succeed in making them
come for three months yet.

We sit here as representatives of every District in the State, and are
presumed by General Canby to know the wants and necessities of our
people, and the passing of the resolution is an expression of the sense of
the Convention that the people of South Carolina desire relief. They
have not asked it of this Convention. I for one have not heard of any
such request. As far as I am individually concerned, I can say in all
sincerity I have not been approached by a South Carolinian in reference
to the granting by this Convention of measures of relief. On the contrary, South Carolinians have expressed the hope that this Convention
will give them no relief, that the Convention will shut out entirely the
old class of South Carolinians and legislate entirely and solely for the
newly enfranchised citizens. That is what I complain of. The opponents of the measure are playing into the hands of their enemies. They
are playing into the hands of those who desire to defeat reconstruction,
who desire nothing more than that this Convention should adopt a Constitution and pass every measure solely in the interest of the newly
enfranchised citizens.

I appeal to the colored delegates, those who are supposed to have at
heart the interests of their people, to listen not to the voice of these
charmers, who seek to destroy you. Listen not to those men who tell
you it will benefit you to vote down this resolution. If you do, rest
assured that vote will result in the defeat of our Constitution. Then,
when that time comes, go to the men who have betrayed you on this
measure, come not to me, for "thou canst not say I did it." Be not

swerved from your duty to yourselves and the country by the appeals made to passion and prejudice.

I am no prophet, nor the son of a prophet, but I will stake my reputation as a prophet against the clerical gentlemen from Charleston, and I prophesy if this measure of relief is refused to the people of the State, and if that is done because of the convenience of a certain delegate's interests, our Constitution will be defeated, and he will be held responsible, and will reap the fruits of everything with which he has been instrumental in forcing upon them. I have not been able to see any argument on the other side. I have seen passion appealed to; an attempt made to raise prejudice, but I cannot for one moment imagine that those gentlemen with whom I have set in Convention for the last week or ten days, will allow their minds to be so wrought upon by prejudice as to yield to speeches that have not the slightest force or reason.

In answer to the gentleman from Richland (Mr. ROBERTSON), I would say it is not the rich men of the country that are asking relief. It is the poor man. It is the rich men who desire to sell out the poor men and take from their families every thing they possess.

Mr. ROBERTSON. I have refused to sell out poor men.

Mr. MOSES. I deny emphatically that the men who staked all on secession are the debtors who seek relief. The largest number, I believe, were not secessionists. I know there are a great many men on this floor who know the fact as well as I do, that many of the men now deeply in debt, were Union men, and many became more largely involved because they were more oppressed. They were oppressed more than those who staked their all on secession. But even if it were true that it is the secessionists who are asking for relief, what is that but an appeal to passion and prejudice?

The gentleman from Richland says he is in favor of homes for the laboring man. I am glad that just there we can shake hands. This resolution intends to secure a home for the poor man. That was one reason why it was introduced. I contend that if these laws or executions are carried out, the poor man will not be able to get a home.

The gentleman from Beaufort (Mr. WHIPPER) was attacked for his views on emigration. That gentleman did not object to thrifty, industrious, active men coming to buy the land. He was opposed to the land monopolists; those Northern men who come here to seek investments. Some of these men are already in the city of Charleston prepared to buy up every foot of land sold at auction in February. The poor man will get none of that land. It will be sold in large tracts.

In conversation with a distinguished gentleman,. familiar with the present condition of the State, he stated that at present not a laboring man can purchase land, even if sold in small tracts, for they have no money. Last year the laborers failed to make scarcely any thing, and at the end of the year, received little or nothing. It may be, some laboring men in Charleston have saved a little money. But in my District, and other Districts of the country, I venture to say not one in two thousand laboring men can buy an acre of land. I say they have not the money. I come to this Convention desiring relief for the entire people of the State. I desire relief for the newly enfranchised. I thank God I have come here to do all in my power to give them relief. Suspend these sales for three months. Probably as the Legislature may interfere and put off the sales still longer, at the end of the year the laboring men may be able to buy the lands. One of the delegates had said one hundred and twenty thousand homes could be procured for the laboring class at two dollars per acre. The people of South Carolina are desirous to have the laboring class around them. I grant, at the close of the war, there was a spirit against them, but that spirit has been eradicated. Some go so far as to prefer the colored to any other kind of men to whom they will offer their lands for sale. And these men will sell the lands to be paid for by the freedmen in their labor. Yet we are met with the bold assertion that the poor colored men cannot get lands because the rich men or large landholders are not willing to sell to them. I wish to see this measure adopted, for it will materially aid in the ratification of our Constitution. It will wrest from nearly every man in this State his approval, no matter how much he may be opposed to us. One of the delegates from a large and flourishing District, told me that the majority of citizens promised if we passed a measure of relief, they would vote for our Constitution.

Mr. T. J. ROBERTSON. I would like to know from the gentleman if the large number of his constituents voted for him as a member of this body.

Mr. F. J. MOSES, Jr. I have already said that not one that I know of voted for me; but I think it my duty, nevertheless, to attend to their interest when it does not conflict with the other class. I ask you to recollect what I have said; I believe this a highly important matter to the well being of reconstruction. There is not a man in the length and breadth of Sumter District who did not desire the people should have relief. All those men who did vote for me, gave it as their instruction that the people of South Carolina should have relief. I ask now if it is not the sentiment of every heart on this floor, because I do not believe the delegates here would wish to represent Districts where one race was at enmity against us. They will live in peace and security, and the newly enfranchised class ask me to give relief to even those who opposed the calling of the Convention. I ask you to forget all the past, to go nobly, manfully, bravely forward in the path that will lead to glory, looking only to the true interest of all the people, without distinction of race or color.

The hour having expired, the question was taken by ayes and nays on the adoption of the resolution, and the vote stands as follows :

YEAS—The President. and Messrs. Allen, Alexander, Bowen, Bryce, Camp, Coghlan, Cooke, Collins, Corley, Craig, Crews, Davis, LeLarge, Dickson, Duncan, Elliott, Gentry, Goss, Gray, Harris, Charles D. Hayne, Holmes Hunter, Hurley, Samuel Johnson, Wm. B. Johnson, J. W. Johnson Dr. L. B. Johnson, W. E. Johnson, Joiner, Lang, Samuel Lee, Leslie, Mackey, Mayer, Mauldin, Milford, Moses, Neagle, Nuckles, Olsen, Parker, Perry, Pillsbury, Rainey, Richmond, Rivers, Rose, Runion, Sanders, Smalls. Swails. Whipper, White, C. M. Wilder, and Wooley.

NAYS—Messrs. Bell, Bonum, Brockenton, Byas, Richard H. Cain, F. J. Cain, Cardozo, Chamberlain, Chestnut, Clinton, Darrington, Dill, Dogan, Driffle, Edwards, Foster, H. E. Hayne, Henderson, Humbird, Jackson, Jacobs, Jervey, Jillson, Henry Jones, Charles Jones, Langley, George Lee, W. J. McKinlay, Wm. McKinlay, McDaniels, Mead, Miller, Nance, Nash, Nelson, Owens, Randolph, Ransier, Robertson, Rutland, Sasportas, Shrewsbury, Stubbs, Thomas, Augustus Thompson, Benj. A. Thompson, Samuel B. Thompson, Viney, Whittemore, Williamson, Wingo, and Wright.

Total ayes 57 ; nays 52.

Mr. R. C. DELARGE made a motion that the question be reconsidered, and that the motion to reconsider be laid upon the table.

The PRESIDENT explained that the effect of this motion would be to put the question forever beyond the further consideration of the Convention.

It was decided in the affirmative.

Mr. B. F. WHITTEMORE, of Darlington, offered the following resolution, which was agreed to :

Resolved, While the members of this Convention will not favor any scheme for the repudiation of debts, the violation of the obligation of contracts, or the taking of lands from the hands of the lawful owners of the same, without reasonable compensation, yet we are willing to further any measure of relief consistent with the powers delegated to us by the Reconstruction Acts of Congress.

The Convention then adjourned.

ELEVENTH DAY.

Monday, January 27, 1868.

The Convention assembled at 12 M., and was called to order by Mr. LEMUEL BOOZER, temporary Chairman.

Prayer was offered by Rev. B. F. JACKSON.

The roll was called, and a quorum answering to their names, the Convention proceeded to business.

The Journal was read and approved.

The PRESIDENT, Mr. A. G. MACKEY, here appeared and took his seat.

Major D. T. Corbin, United States District Attorney, appeared in Convention, and was introduced by the PRESIDENT.

Reports of Standing Committees were called up.

Mr. F. J. MOSES, Jr., made a report of the Executive Committee, to whom was referred the preamble and resolutions, declaring that the safety of the Government and the welfare of the State, demand the speedy removal of the officers of the State Provisional Government. The Committee say they have considered the same, and believing that the removal of the present State officers would be highly prejudicial to South Carolina, recommend that the preamble and resolutions be laid upon the table, and that the whole question of removing State officers and electing others in their stead be left to the people of the State, unless otherwise ordered by the United States Congress.

Mr. B. F. WHITTEMORE moved the adoption of the report, which was carried.

Mr. N. G. PARKER, Chairman of the Committee on Finance, made the following report:

The Committee on Finance, to whom was referred the Ordinance in reference to pay and mileage of members, also the Ordinances authorizing this Convention to pledge the faith and credit of the State for the redemption of "$200,000 of the bills receivable by the State," and the "sale of a portion of them to defray the expenses of this Convention," and an Ordinance "directing this Committee to report at an early day some plan for the levy and collection of a tax on the property of this State, authorized by Congress, to meet the expenses of this Convention," beg leave to submit the following report:

That, in view of the pressing necessities of members of this Convention, your Committee have prepared the measures herein set forth at a much earlier day than they otherwise should, and at considerable risk of being charged with a slight consideration of a very important matter.

20

Your Committee has reported a section in the Ordinance pledging the faith and credit of the State for the redemption of the $500,000 of bills receivable, authorized by the Act of Assembly of South Carolina of December, 1865, and a Supplemental Act in September, 1866.

This is indispensable, not only to secure to members of the Convention compensation and immediate relief, but also a fund by which the Legislature, when it assembles, under our new Government, may be paid its per diem and mileage.

The pledge herein given will, in the opinion of your Committee, secure confidence in this currency, which is now at a discount, causing it to appreciate in value, and the failure to make this pledge will cause a loss to the State, a loss to the members of the Convention, and when the Legislature assembles there will be no fund whatever from which its expenses can be paid.

The small amount of those bills, now outstanding, $99,919, in view of the fact that one-half of the taxes ordered to be collected, under General Order No. 139, are to be paid during the month of March, and which will, it is estimated, yield to the Treasury $175,000 by the middle of April, will leave not a dollar of the bills in circulation, (provided prompt payment is made,) even including the $75,000 necessary to defray the expenses of this Convention, and the disbursement of $80,000 more, which it is estimated it will take to meet the wants of the present Provisional Government during this period, in payment of quarterly salaries, &c. ; but there would be a balance of $50,000 in greenbacks in the Treasury. But we can safely leave that off as no such prompt payment will be made.

The endorsement will relieve the new Legislature from embarrassment, and that body can proceed with its work in framing such legislation as may be necessary to carry out the provisions of the new Constitution. The several operations of the Government must also be carried on—the Lunatic Asylum, Penitentiary, Prisons and Courts, must all be sustained, so that society shall be protected, and the life, liberty and property of the citizen be secured.

In any view which the Convention may take of the matter, whether additional Acts of Reconstruction may be passed, whether the present Provisional Government may be continued until the new Constitution has been ratified by the people, accepted by Congress, and the new Government placed in operation, these expenses must be met ; and inasmuch as these bills receivable are the only currency which can be relied upon, it behooves every citizen of the State to give them the largest value. In doing so, an unqualified pledge for their redemption, according to the terms of the Act authorizing this issue, ought to be made.

The Treasurer of the State is a bonded officer, and there is no reason to distrust his fidelity. No portion of these bills receivable can be paid from the Treasury, except in conformity to the appropriations of the order of General Canby and the existing law.

There is, therefore, no danger of the fund being squandered inasmuch as it is regulated by law, and its custodian, the Treasurer, is under bonds of $100,000, with abundant securities.

Your Committee also think it important that this Convention should give a solemn pledge that all the obligations of the State should be liquidated and paid at the earliest practical day, and with the least inconvenience to the people. The same reasons may be urged in behalf of this proposition that have been mentioned in connection with the bills receivable, since the enforcement of these obligations by this Convention would tend to restore the bonds by which they are represented to their former value, and to secure the confidence of capitalists at home and abroad in the same.

Your Committee, therefore, have reported a section making such an endorsement, taking care, however, to declare null and void all obligations entered into by the State, either to aid the State of South Carolina or the so-called Confederate States in the rebellion against the Government and authority of the United States. An unequivocal declaration that this class of claims against the State shall never be paid, should, we think, be made by this body, and thus put at rest all apprehension that at any future time any citizen of South Carolina shall be taxed one cent to pay a debt to destroy the Union. Your Committee, after full consideration and consultation with the Commanding General, are of the opinion that the taxes levied may be most conveniently collected by the means suggested by General Canby in his General Order No. 139, and he has promised his hearty co-operation in that work. They, therefore, recommend that the same persons shall collect the taxes. they being officers duly appointed by law and under heavy bonds, and to transfer the same to the Treasury of the State for the immediate pay of the mileage and per diem of the members of this body, together with its necessary expenses. When the public observes that while the Convention places $75,000 of these bills in circulation in addition to those already out, a tax is levied to be collected, half in March and the other in July, to reimburse the Treasury for the outlay which it will make to this Convention, it will, in the judgment of your Committee, prevent the depreciation of these bills, and, with the pledges given, we see no reason why they should not, at an early day, appreciate very nearly to their full value.

In considering this report, the Committee hope that the Convention will keep constantly in view the important fact that our State finances are one of the important matters, not only of this Convention, but of the people of the State—the whole people, not only now, but in the future. We are not legislating or framing a Constitution for to-day, but for the future.

It must be borne in mind that if a Constitution is adopted by this Convention and accepted by the people, it is almost absolutely certain that it will be by Congress. That such will be the result, this Committee have no shadow of doubt; hence a Legislature will, within a short time, assemble, when large additional expenses for the State will be incurred. Was this the last expense that the new government which is about to be organized could inflict upon the State, and our interest as citizens of the State should cease here, a very different plan than the one proposed might be recommended; but with the firm conviction that this is only the beginning, and with a conscientious desire to discharge our duties to the State with fidelity—with a desire to increase the confidence of all the people of the State and elsewhere—place the credit of the State upon a firm basis, and in the belief that the adoption of the course herein recommended will accomplish much to bring about such a result, your Committee have unhesitatingly made the recommendations herein contained. This body is in want of money now. The Congress of the United States gives us power to levy and collect a tax. Under that authority it is already in the province of this body to authorize the levy and the collection within five days; but it would be impossible to execute such an order. We might order it in ten, fifteen or thirty days, but it could not be collected within that period. A reasonable time would be asked and given. The dictates of humanity would demand it, if there were not other weighty reasons for it.

It certainly would not be wise for this body to offend every citizen of the State in the very first act, by levying a tax to meet the expenses of this Convention, and forcing the collection of it in the shortest possible time. And though the most arbitrary measures be resorted to to collect a tax if imposed, it is not sure that it would all be paid, and within a reasonable time. There is a stringent law for the collection of taxes now, there always has been, and yet there are, delinquents; there always will be. In view of the facts set forth, and in view of another fact, viz: that there is no money now in the State Treasury, that is, no State currency, and that if there was, there is no absolute certainty that we could at once get possession of it, inasmuch as we have no authority to appropriate such money, but only power to levy a tax and collect it. Although your Committee have not been met by such objections, and have no reason to expect any, yet in view of the facts just mentioned, and all the circumstances enumerated, together with other considerations of importance, they have deemed it best, in order to insure :—

1st. The most speedy payment of a portion due the members and officers of the Convention.

2d. To protect the credit of the State, and to restore confidence and increase prosperity.

3d. Levy a tax upon the property of the State according to law, and give the most liberal time for the payment thereof, and not distress the people, who are already overburdened and oppressed.

4th. With the view of acting in harmony with the power whose authority we must obtain before we can take any money from the State Treasury (the Major General commanding the Military District), your Committee respectfully recommend that a tax shall be levied, collected and paid in the manner and form herein annexed :

AN ORDINANCE

To levy a Special Tax to defray the Expenses of this Convention and preserve the Credit of the State.

We, the people of the State of South Carolina, by our Delegates in Convention met, do ordain, That there shall be assessed and collected by the Tax Collectors of the several districts and parishes in this State, in addition to the tax already levied, under General Orders No. 139, issued from headquarters Second Military District, by Brevet Major General E.

R. S. Canby, dated Charleston, S. C , December 3, 1867, commanding said District, the following taxes, which shall be collected by the persons and at the times, and in the manner prescribed by the said General Orders.

On all real estate 75 cents on every $100, excepting such lands as are exempted in article 1st, of said General Order.

On all articles manufactured for sale, barter or exchange, between the first day of January, 1868, and the first day of January, 1869, ten cents on every $100, to be paid by the manufacturers.

On buggies, carriages, gold and silver plate, watches, jewelry and pianos on hand or to first day of January, 1868, except when held by dealers for purposes of sale, twenty-five cents on every $100.

From the sale of goods, wares and merchandize, embracing all the articles of trade, sale, barter or exchange, (the cotton tax of the United States excepted.) which any person shall make between the first day of January, 1868, and the 31st day of December, 1869, ten cents on every one hundred dollars.

Upon each hack, stage coach, buggy, wagon and omnibus drawn by two or more horses, there shall be paid a tax of $5 ; and on each dray, cart, buggy and express wagon drawn by one horse, a tax of $2 50 ; and upon each and every person keeping a dog or dogs, shall pay a tax of 50 cents.

And the Tax Collectors, Sheriffs, or any other person whose duty it may be to collect, or the Treasurer of the State, whose duty it is to receive, shall be liable upon their respective official bonds for neglecting or refusing to collect, safely keep, pay over and disburse the same in conformity to the order of the Convention.

SEC. 2. *Be it further ordained*, That a sufficient amount of the same thus realized, is hereby appropriated to refund to the Treasurer of the State of South Carolina any sum or sums which may be advanced by the order of Brevet Major General E. R. S. Canby, or otherwise, for the payment of the per diem, mileage, or other expenses of this Convention.

SEC. 3. *Be it further ordained*, That the funds on the credit of the State, are hereby pledged for the redemption of bills receivable of the State of South Carolina, issued in conformity to an Act of the General Assembly of the said State, of December, 1865, and subsequently the Act of September, 1866, and also for the payment of the bonds and other obligations of the State ; provided, that all obligations created for the purpose of aiding the rebellion, and maintaining a hostile government to the laws and authorities of the United States are hereby declared to be null and void, and shall never be paid by any tax to be imposed upon the people of South Carolina.

SEC. 4. That for the purpose of defraying the current expenses of this Convention, the payment of its officers, members and contingent accounts, Brevet Major General E. R. S. Canby, Commanding Second Military District, be requested to issue from time to time, as may be necessary, such orders upon the Treasury of the State of South Carolina, for the payment of such sums as may be authorized by this Convention, in such amounts as may be agreed upon between the President of this Convention and the General Commanding, to the officers and members of this body for their per diem and mileage, and for the current expenses of the same, and that the amount of the tax herein authorized to be levied, shall be placed in the Treasury of the State, to reimburse said advances.

SEC. 5. *Be it further ordained,* That if the taxes levied and assessed under this Ordinance should be in excess of the whole expenses of the Convention, it shall be retained in the Treasury, subject to the future order and in conformity to the provisions of the Constitution to be adopted by this Convention. Should there be any deficiency in the sum required to be raised by taxation under this Ordinance, to reimburse the Treasury for its ontlay, the first Legislature which assembles hereafter shall make such further provisions as may be necessary to raise funds for this purpose.

SEC. 6. *Be it further ordained,* That the per diem of the President and members of this Convention shall be—President, $12 ; Members, $9 ; Sergeant-at-Arms $9 ; Secretary, $9 ; Doorkeeper, $6 ; two Messengers, each, $4 ; Assistant Sergeant-at-Arms. $7 ; Assistant Secretary, $7 ; Engrossing Clerk, $7 ; Reading Clerk, $6 ; Assistant Doorkeeper $5.

SEC. 7. *Be it further ordained,* That the mileage of members and officers of this Convention shall be twenty (20) cents per mile to and from the Convention, by the usual mail routes.

SEC. 8. *Be it further ordained,* That all payments made, in conformity to the several provisions of this Ordinance, shall be upon the authority of the President of this Convention, upon the recommendation of the Finance Committee.

Your Committee would furthermore state that the pay recommended per diem might have been less, if there has been no doubt whatever about the value of the bills receivable, which is the only money available to meet the present demand ; but your Committee confidently believe that if the recommendation of this Convention to guarantee the entire amount of the bills receivable is adopted, that the value of such bills will be so increased that they will go up from 80 or 85 to 90 or 95 cents, or even more, as the time draws near, when a considerable portion of the tax levied becomes due, and while a discount is allowed for prompt payment. [See Sec. 12, General Order No. 139, from which the tax recommended to be levied in this report is a portion.]

It is believed to be a peculiarly favorable time to put into circulation a considerable amount of these bills receivable, inasmuch as one-half of the taxes levied by General Order No. 139, referred to, is due on or before the 31st day of March next, and the balance on or before the 30th day of June next.

Your Committee could not recommend that a portion only of these bills should be secured ; it would, in their opinion, have rendered the balance almost worthless. It would, in their opinion, have destroyed confidence, weakened credit, and been both unjust and unwise. They have, therefore, recommended the guarantee of all the bills receivable of the State, issued by the Provisional Government of this State, trusting to meet, not only the exigencies of to-day, but the no distant future, by bringing these bills into general use, and holding them to their full value.

Your Committee could not recommend the sale of them, or any portion of them, at public auction. To pursue such a course, would, in the opinion of the Committee, be very unwise. They would be bought up solely by speculators at a reduced price, the State would suffer, and we should be mainly responsible for it.

We should show that we are willing to take the bills ourselves of the State that we make. We may be compelled to sacrifice a small amount upon a portion of it for immediate use, but the great bulk of it can be carried to your homes, and not a dollar will be sacrificed. It may be urged that the Convention should not touch these bills receivable, and that they should issue bonds to the amount of $200,000, place them upon the market, convert them into greenbacks, and pay the expenses of this Convention.

There are grave objections to that course, besides this objection, that to pursue such a course would not, in all probability, realize any money for at least thirty days, and in all human probability within sixty or ninety at least, without a far greater discount than this Convention would be willing to inflict upon the value of such bonds, and the consequent injury it would inflict upon the State of South Carolina.

It may be urged that the bonds could not be issued and competent business men be entrusted to take them North—say to Boston or New York, and negotiate them at the best rate for greenbacks, and that our friends—those who are in sympathy with the present plan of reconstruction—would loan us the money at 6 or 7 per cent. But your Committee believe it is not yet time to take such a step. Northern capital has not yet commenced floating Southward for investment. Another year of experiment has yet to be tried before there is any reasonable hope that it will.

Such a plan would be unwise and impracticable at the present juncture of affairs.

And the Committee are, furthermore, of the opinion that such bonds would not sell at all in this market, and grave doubts are entertained about their selling in any market.

In addition to this report, your Committee would state that they have a communication from Headquarters, Second Military District, containing the views of the Major-General Commanding, and for the information of this body will read that portion which expresses opinion:

[From Headquarters, Second Military District—21.]

The law of the United States, of March 23, 1867, limits the Convention in providing for the payment of its expenses to "the levy and collection of such taxes upon the property of such States as may be necessary."

If the rules established by the tax laws of the State should be followed, and for convenience and economy in making the levy and collection, this course is recommended, the subjects of taxation will be as follows:

1. Real Estate valued at _____$70,507,075
2. Personal Property (articles of luxury)_____2,052,985

$72,560,060

A tax of one-half on the 1st item will yield_____$35,253 53
And of two and a half will on the same_____5,132 44

    Total_____$40,385.97

Taxes upon manufactures and upon sales, although as assessed as income taxes, are, in reality, taxes upon property, and may properly be included in the levy which the Convention is authorized to make.

Articles manufactured in 1868, at the estimated value_____$1,164,314
Sales of goods, wares, etc., in 1868, at the estimated value___14,582,602

    Making a total of_____$15,744,916
    Will yield with a tax of 1 mill_____15,746,91

In addition to the foregoing, there are articles of personal property subject to specific taxes under existing laws, which are estimated to yield at the rates established by these laws as follows :

5. Dogs _____ $20,000
6. Omnibuses, etc., drawn by two or more horses_____1,000
8. Carts _____3,000

    Total ____   ____   _____$24,000

An additional tax of 50 per cent. upon the first item will
    yield _____$10,000
Upon the 2d_____250
Upon the 3d_____750

    Total _____$11,000

RECAPITULATION.

1. Tax on Real Estate _____$35,253 53
2. Luxuries _____5,132 56
3. Manufactures _____15,741 96
4. Dogs, etc., Omnibuses, Drays, etc_____11,000 00

    Total _____$67,128 05

Discount for commissions, taxes, etc., 12 per cent_____$8,055 36

    Leaving for net revenue_____$59,072 69

There is, of course, other property subject so taxation under the law of March 23, 1867 ; but as the imposition of a tax upon such property would involve the introduction of new subjects of taxation, with which the people are not familiar, and the necessity of making at great cost new assessments, it is not considered expedient to adopt that course. If the plan above suggested be adopted, the assessors will only have to add the new levy to the assets already made, or about to be made, and the collection will come with the collections of the regular taxes.

The amount of " bills receivable" now outstanding is $99,919. It is virtually essential to the credit of the State that this amount should not be increased if it be possible to avoid it, and that the issue should be absorbed as speedily as possible. Any action of the Convention looking towards a repudiation of these bills, or any other of the legitimate debts of the State, or any increase in the amount now authorized, or any discrimination in their application, would have an unfortunate effect upon financial credit of the State, and be reflected disastrously upon all its people. I cannot see any reason for apprehending, that with an economical administration, the expenses of the State for the current year, and of the Convention, may not be met without resorting to any further increase, or to any other mode of raising supplies, and I think that as soon as these questions have been definitely acted upon by the Convention, market value of the " bills receivable" will be enhanced.

Your Committee have, also, a letter from His Excellency the Governor of the State, written in reply to a request for information, which they will read :

CHARLESTON, S. C., January 25, 1868.

N. G. PARKER, Esq.,

Chairman Committee on Finance, etc., Charleston, S. C.:

SIR : On the receipt of your communication of the 21st, I addressed a letter to Wm. Hood, Esq., Treasurer of the State, requesting him to furnish the information which you seek, with reference to the financial condition of the State.

From his reply you will observe that a very small amount of national currency is in the Treasury. You will also note that of the $500,000 of bills receivable authorized to be issued by the Act of Assembly of December, 1865, there has been printed only $390,000. Of this amount but $222,000 has been "signed, registered and carried to cash for circulation," and there is now in the vault of the Treasury in these bills receivable $122,081, which leaves the outstanding circulation $99,919.

The unpaid taxes of the State, whereon executions are now in the hands of various Sheriffs, will reach about $130,000. What amount of these executions can be made available, I am not prepared to say.

If the Convention should consider it expedient to make any pledges for the redemption of these bills receivable, in connection with the debt of the State existing before the war, it would, in my judgment, materially appreciate their value, and bring them nearly up to par. The tax order issued by Gen. Canby will, if faithfully executed by the different officers in the State, yield about $330,000. If these taxes are collected, all of the bills which every month may be required to be issued to carry on the civil government of the State, will be absorbed by these taxes and returned to the Treasurer.

There is no good reason why these bills receivable are now at so great a discount.

I have the honor to be.

Your obedient servant,

JAMES L. ORR,

Governor of South Carolina.

21

The Ordinance was read by its title, and on motion of Mr. E. W. M. MACKEY, was ordered to be printed, and made the special order for one o'clock Tuesday.

The PRESIDENT. I beg leave to make a personal explanation, with a view of preventing debate on this subject hereafter, in reference to the pay of the President, referred to in the above Ordinance. When first nominated by my constituents of Charleston as a delegate to this Convention, I made a determination from which I have not seen any cause to deviate. As an officer of the Government of the United States, I receive compensation for my services. I do not think it right and proper, therefore, to receive any compensation for services while acting President of the Convention.

I beg leave therefore, to state that it is my fixed and unalterable determination to receive no compensation from the Convention for my services, either as President or delegate.

Dr. L. B. JOHNSON called for the Special Order, namely : "An Ordinance to divide Pickens District."

Mr. J. J. WRIGHT moved that the Special Order be indefinitely postponed.

Dr. L. B. JOHNSON called for the ayes and nays, which was sustained.

The PRESIDENT stated the question to be on the indefinite postponement of the consideration of the bill which would have come up for its second reading.

The Secretary called the roll, which resulted : ayes 38 ; nays 79.

Mr. E. W. M. MACKEY. I desire to offer the following substitute :

AN ORDINANCE

To divide Pickens into two Election and Judicial Districts, or Counties, as the case may be.

We, the people of South Carolina, in Convention assembled, do declare and ordain, and it is hereby declared and ordained, That it shall be the duty of the Legislature, at its first session, held in pursuance of the new Constitution, to enact the necessary laws for submitting the question of division of Pickens District to the people of said District. And in case the question is decided in favor of a division, the Legislature shall then enact the necessary laws for the division of Pickens District : *Provided,* that the people of said District are willing to bear the expense of the division.

Mr. T. J. ROBERTSON. I move to amend by striking out of the original Ordinance all of sections 2d, 3d, 4th, and a part of section 5th. so that the 5th section may become the 2d, and read, "That it shall be the duty of the Legislature that shall assemble by authority of the Constitution adopted by this Convention, at its first session, to perfect the division and complete the organization of the said Districts of Pickens and Oconee, as well as the other Judicial and Election Districts of the State."

Mr. ROBERTSON. This amendment simply gives the power to the Legislature to divide the Districts whenever the inhabitants of a District consent.

Mr. J. M. RUTLAND. I would state for the information of the Convention that the Committee on the Legislative part of the Constitution have had under consideration a section in relation to this matter, not for Pickens alone, but for the whole State of South Carolina. The proposed section will enable the Legislature to make a new division in any District wherever necessary, limiting each District to a certain number of square miles. It seems to me these motions to divide single Districts consume the time of the Convention unnecessarily, when a single section of the bill from the Committee on the Legislative Department may embrace the whole State. I suggest to the gentleman who introduced the Ordinance to withdraw the matter, and let it come up when the question of re-districting the State is discussed.

Mr. E. W. M. MACKEY. The substitute introduced by myself is intended as a compromise, making it the duty of the Legislature to divide certain Districts. It will make it incumbent upon the Legislature to divide Pickens District.

Mr. J. J. WRIGHT. Is it intended to incorporate this Ordinance into the Constitution? I merely ask for information, as I have never seen a Constitution composed of Ordinances.

Mr. E. W. M. MACKEY. It is intended whenever the Constitution is submitted, to submit the Ordinances attached to it.

Mr. J. M. RUTLAND. I am not opposed to the division of Pickens District, but as I believe we can dispose of the matter with so much more ease when it comes up to be voted on by sections in the Constitution, I move that the whole matter be laid on the table.

The PRESIDENT. The question will be upon passing the Ordinance to a third reading. If the Convention objects, and votes against passing it to a third reading, the Ordinance goes to the wall.

Mr. T. J. ROBERTSON. If a majority of the people of Pickens District agree to this division, and are willing to pay the expenses of erecting a new Court House in the new District, I think we should act upon it at once.

Mr. A. C. RICHMOND. I have taken some pains to look over the map, and certainly sympathise with the people of that District, as they are compelled to walk up one side of the mountain to get to Court, and down the other side to get home. The District is large enough to be divided, and I see no reason why it should not be done, and the act go immediately into operation.

Mr. B. F. RANDOLPH. We are sent for a specific purpose, but there are other duties which come properly within our legislative powers, and which I hope we shall perform. The people of the State are undoubtedly looking to us to do whatever is legitimate for us to do to help them. The delegates from Pickens District, tell us that the people of that District implore the Convention to divide it for their welfare. If we can do it legitimately, I see no other reason why we should not act now upon the matter, and not postpone it. I do not wish this power of dividing Districts taken out of the hands of the Legislature. On the contrary, I hope it will be invested with it. But the Convention can also listen to a petition of citizens, and if they desire to divide their District, we should not turn a deaf ear to them. I shall vote for the division. It is a matter really of internal improvements, and I am in favor of doing all in our power to advance internal improvements in any part of the State.

Mr. T. J. ROBERTSON called for the previous question, which was sustained.

The question being put on the amendments and substitute offered, they were not agreed to.

The PRESIDENT then put the main question, " Shall this Ordinance be engrossed for a third reading."

Dr. L. B. JOHNSON. I call for the yeas and nays on that question.

The call was sustained, and on the call of the roll, resulted yeas 65, nays 49.

On motion of Mr. E. W. M. MACKEY, the third reading of the Ordinance was made the Special Order for Wednesday at one o'clock.

Mr. E. W. M. MACKEY offered the following resolution :

Resolved, That a clause be incorporated in the Constitution providing that hereafter in the sales of all lands, either for taxes or under executions, or other final process, of any Court issued for the collection of debt, the lands shall be sold in tracts not exceeding one hundred and sixty acres, so that the opportunity of purchase may be extended to all classes of the community whose industry and frugality will enable them to obtain a home.

Mr. R. C. DeLARGE called the previous question, which was not sustained.

Mr. T. J. ROBERTSON. I must express my surprise at the course adopted by some members of this house. They seem disposed to spring important measures upon the house for action, and rush them through by calls for the previous question, without giving the Convention an opportunity scarcely to know what is being voted upon. Such a resolution as that should be referred to the appropriate Committee. It involves the interests of thousands of people of the State, and to attempt to pass it through without argument or reflection is a matter of not only surprise, but amazement.

Mr. R. C. DeLARGE. I am more than surprised to find a gentleman upon this floor entertaining such a trifling opinion of the intelligence of the members of this body as to suppose for one moment that they could not understand a simple resolution like the one just offered. I am the more surprised at the objection coming from the quarter it does. The resolution simply proposes that in all sales of lands to be made hereafter under execution for taxes, those lands be divided into small tracts to enable poor, frugal, industrious men to purchase homes. I did not think a single member of the Convention could object to such a proposition.

Mr. T. J. ROBERTSON. The member, from his remarks, appears to think I am opposed to the measure. That is not my objection. My objection is to the hasty manner in which it was attempted to be rushed through the Convention without due consideration.

Mr. R. C. DeLARGE. I had supposed that every member had made up his mind on this matter, and was ready to vote upon it. I do not see, therefore, what is to be gained by argument. The resolution does not propose to take away the rights of any man. We all know that tracts of land sold in small divisions will be more speedily bought up and realize better prices than when sold by thousands of acres. This is a measure to benefit poor men, and benefit future generations. I believe the member himself is in favor of such a proposition, for he has frequently expressed a desire to alleviate the condition of the poor, honest people of the State. I trust the resolution will pass.

Mr. F. J. MOSES, Jr. As far as I am individually concerned, I am not opposed to the resolution. But I do think it would be dangerous to rush through such a matter which has been sprung upon the house without a reference to some proper Committee.

Mr. F. L. CARDOZO. I concur with the view of the member from Richland (Mr. ROBERTSON.) It would seem as if a few here desire to assume all the powers of the government of this body. One offers a resolution and the other jumps up and moves the previous question. Such extraordinary action ought to be discountenanced by the house. Let us have at least twenty-four hours to think on matters brought before the Convention. I am in favor of a homestead law, such as that proposed by the gentleman from Beaufort (Mr. WRIGHT) exempting one hundred acres, but not in favor of the other measure passed here Saturday, by which a landholder can save eighty thousand acres.

The PRESIDENT. I have the pleasure of introducing to the house Major D. T. Corbin, District Attorney of the United States, who comes as your invited guest.

Major Corbin on being introduced, said :

Gentleman of the Convention : I come here as a casual visitor and not to make any lengthy remarks, but simply to thank you for the honor you have conferred upon me in electing me one of your Solicitors. Hoping that you may frame a Constitution that will meet the approval of your State and country, and be successful in restoring the State to the Union, I wish you God speed.

The debate on the question before the house was resumed.

Mr. T. J. ROBERTSON. The member from Charleston has misunderstood my position. I will go further than the mover of the resolution now before the house. I propose, at the proper time, to offer a substitute and divide all saleable lands into eighty acres instead of one hundred and sixty. thus affording a still better opportunity to the poor man to purchase a homestead. But I am opposed to all hasty legislation.

Mr. A. J. RANSIER. I may agree, after sufficient time to consider it, to favor the resolution now under discussion. I appreciate the distressed situation of the people of this State, and yield to none in the desire to relieve them by any legitimate action we may take. But I must protest against any member introducing such important matters, and before this body has had time to consider it, move the previous question. Like many others who voted in the negative last Saturday, I have been put in a false position. I would have favored the measure that passed Saturday, could I have seen in it a measure that really would benefit the people of the State. But I believed at the outset, it was wrong in principle and practice. I would have favored it could I have believed that it would benefit the people of South Carolina as a whole or a respectable majority. I believed it wrong in principle, as having a tendency to impair the obligations of contracts. I also believed the Commanding General had done what was necessary and proper, and we were, therefore, wasting the time of the Convention in useless discussion. I protest, however, against the application of the gag law, which has been attempted in this body. I trust every member who desires to define his position, or speak upon any measure before the house, will be allowed the opportunity to do so, and no further attempts made to quash legitimate debate by the use or misuse of the gag law. I hope the resolution will be referred to a Special Committee to report to this house.

Mr. W. B. NASH. I hope the resolution will pass, and allow the gentlemen who have repented of the sin they committed last Saturday, to at least give poor people a chance to divide lands what they then, by their votes provided, shall not be sold. I think it would be in such good taste for them to sustain this measure. I am in favor of the amendment making it eighty acres as a matter of policy, and to oblige the gentleman who offered the resolution, I will vote for it, and hope the vote will be taken at once, as it is a matter of great importance to some of the members that it should be done. I believe every member of the Convention perfectly appreciates the position of those repentant gentlemen. Perhaps it would have been better for the mover if he had provided that one hundred and sixty acres should be sold as soon as possible. The Convention on Saturday passed a resolution requesting General Canby to prohibit the sale of lands under execution for debts, for three months, yet we find the friends of that measure introducing a resolution to-day, to sell the same land in small lots of one hundred and sixty acres.

Mr. R. C. DeLARGE. Will the gentleman from Richland allow me the floor for a few words.

Mr. NASH. No, sir, I cannot. I think the gentleman from Charleston occupies the floor too much altogether. I want to see the land sold in small parcels. If sold now, they would be sold in immense tracts. If we pass the resolution, making it obligatory upon the Legislature to provide in the Constitution that these tracts shall not be sold in lots of more than one hundred and sixty acres, I do not think the freedman or the poor man, when they are sold, will get any opportunity to purchase; and the capitalists or land monopolists cannot, of course, buy but one hundred and sixty acres in a lot, but may take as many lots as he desires. I do not see the necessity of referring this resolution to any special or regular Committee, and believe the majority are ready to adopt it immediately.

Mr. D. H. CHAMBERLAIN moved to amend by adding, "And that General Canby be earnestly requested to enforce the foregoing provision in all forced sales prior to the adoption of the new Constitution."

Mr. C. P. LESLIE. I always like to keep perfectly good natured. The delegate from Charleston (Mr. DeLARGE) on several occasions, has deemed it proper to move the previous question, and I do not know why any of the old fogies in the Convention should object. There is something so peculiarly graceful about his manner and the style in which he urges it. Besides, everybody knows that he understands parliamentary tactics better than any one else on the floor, and consequently more capa-- ble of pressing his points. After all, the man that has the money will get the land. It has always been so, and always will be so. There are some men who want to incorporate into the Constitution, a provision fixing the prices of labor. The demand for labor will always govern its price, and it is exactly so with regard to the sale and purchase of lands.

All these propositions appear simply to gain some *eclat* with poor people. I unfortunately run a plantation once in my own District (Barnwell), did it as well as I could, and ought to know something about the subject. I carried it on as extensively as any one in my District Poor land seldom produced more than six bushels to the acre, and unless this land was fenced, it was not worth much. I do not think one hundred and sixty acres are enough for a poor man. It is all gammon for the gentleman to talk about the poor, for it does not amount to one cent. I move that the resolution be referred to the appropriate Committee.

Mr. W. J. WHIPPER. I certainly am not prepared to vote upon this matter, and hope it will be referred to the appropriate Committee. One gentleman has said they should vote on this resolution immediately, because it was necessary for those who supported the resolution Saturday to do something for the poor man. I feel bound to say that in voting on that resolution, the expression on either side was simply a matter of opinion ; but I feel confident that we did more for the poor man in that expression of opinion than was intended in the other measure, which was then also adopted. But I desire to see this resolution referred, so that the Committee can deliberate upon it, ascertain how it would effect the Constitution of the United States, and make their report. The Convention would then consider it, and, with all the light before them, vote intelligently. But to spring matters of this kind on the Convention, and effect a decision by a snap vote, is certainly unusual, and is adopting a course that may make us do many things of which we will be ashamed hereafter.

Mr. J. J. WRIGHT. I concur with the gentleman who has just taken his seat, and hope the resolution will be referred. The call for the previous question, and the effort made to rush this matter through, was as much a source of surprise to me as to any other member in the house. It is a question of some importance, and requires due consideration. I do not desire to refer to the action of Saturday, but I do wish to say that we do contemplate incorporating into the Constitution a homestead provision, and it is, therefore, all the more necessary that all resolutions of this character should go to a Committee to consider and recommend what action should be taken by the House.

Mr. F. L. CARDOZO. I move to amend the resolution by striking out "one hundred and sixty," and inserting "fifty."

The amendment was not agreed to.

Mr. E. W. M. MACKEY moved that the resolution be referred to a Special Committee of five, to report on Thursday morning.

The motion was not agreed to, and the PRESIDENT decided that the resolution be referred to the Committee on Miscellaneous Provisions of the Constitution.

Mr. B. F. WHITTEMORE offered the following, which was referred to the Committee on Petitions:

WHEREAS, the general distress of the people of this State demands the sympathy and consideration of this Convention, which can in no wise be expected to enter into a measure of relief for a class; and,

Whereas, thousands of laborers of this commonwealth are suffering for the actual necessaries of life, and have been compelled on account of the claims which their employers held against them, to turn over the entire proceeds of their toil for the year 1867; and,

Whereas, many have not been paid their honest dues, which the contracts they entered into defined since the close of the war; and,

Whereas, a certain resolution has been passed by this body calling for a suspension of the collection of certain debts that only benefits the property holders of the State, therefore

Resolved, That this Convention most respectfully requests Brevet Major-General Edw. R. S. Canby, Commanding General of the Second Military District, to stay the further withholding of such portions of the crops as the laborers are entitled to by the terms of their agreements; also, that all notes or obligations given for labor shall be settled at once; also, that no debts shall be collected from the laborers which they may owe their employers, or others, for four months from the date of the ratification of the Constitution which this Convention may adopt.

Mr. R. B. ELLIOTT offered the following:

Resolved, That the Legislative Committee, to whom was referred a resolution for the formation of a new Judicial District, out of the contiguous portions of Barnwell, Edgefield, Lexington, and Orangeburg Districts, be instructed to report thereon on Wednesday next.

Before taking the question, the hour of three having arrived, the Convention adjourned.

TWELFTH DAY.

Tuesday, January 28, 1868.

The Convention assembled at 12 M., and was called to order by the PRESIDENT.

Prayer was offered by Rev. ISAAC BROCKENTON.

The roll was called, and a quorum answering to their names, the PRESIDENT announced the Convention ready to proceed to business.

The journal of the preceding day was read and approved.

Mr. E. W. M. MACKEY rose to make a personal explanation. I desire to express to the Convention my regret that on yesterday I so far forgot myself as to make an assault upon a certain individual after the adjournment, within the bar of the House. I have to offer as my excuse the excitement under which I labored after reading a series of base falsehoods uttered against my father, and contained in the columns of a dirty, scurrilous and infamous journal of this city. But while apologizing to the House for this infringement of its privileges, I have no regrets to offer to the low individual whom I justly chastised.

On motion of Mr. L. S. LANGLEY, the apology of the delegate from Orangeburg was received.

Mr. J. M. RUTLAND, of the Legislative Committee, made a report recommending that the resolution in reference to the qualifications of voters, and referred to that Committee, be referred to the Committee on Franchise and Elections, and asking that the Legislative Committee be discharged from its further consideration.

The report was adopted.

Mr. B. F. RANDOLPH made a majority report of the Committee on Miscellaneous Matters, in reference to the petition to Congress for the continuance of the Freedmen's Bureau. The Committee recommend that the Convention petition Congress to continue the Bureau until the restoration of the Civil Government; also that a Bureau of Education be established as soon as practicable.

Mr. L. BOOZER made a minority report of those members of the Committee dissenting from the above, for the reason that they are unable to perceive the propriety of the proposed application, as before the time for the propose discontinuance of the Bureau by Act of Congress, namely, 16th of July, 1868, in all probability the Constitution and Civil Government will be adopted and established in this State; and it seems to be admitted by all that after that has been effected, this Bureau will be unnecessary. Such is understood, also, to be the opinion of General R. K. Scott, Assistant Commissioner. If the effort now being made to frame a Constitution and Civil Government shall fail, Congress will provide for the emergency.

The minority of the Committee, however, concurred with the majority to recommend the establishment of a Bureau of Education.

On motion of Mr. J. J. WRIGHT, the reports were made the Special Order for one o'clock Wednesday.

The PRESIDENT read a letter of resignation from Mr. JOHN K. PERRY, a delegate elect from Colleton, stating that unforseen circumstances compelled him to resign, and that it would have afforded him great pleasure to have assisted in framing a Constitution for the State of South Carolina. He hoped the Convention would not, one moment, think he was not with them in spirit, and felt confident that the good material of which the Convention was composed would do credit to themselves, and frame a Constitution they should all be proud of.

The letter was received as information, and the resignation accepted.

The PRESIDENT also read a telegraphic dispatch from Mr. M. M. JOHNSON, Sergeant-at-Arms elect, returning his grateful thanks for the honor conferred upon him, but stating that, owing to sickness in his family, he would not be able to serve.

Mr. Y. J. P. OWENS moved that the President be authorized to appoint a Sergeant-at-Arms.

Mr. F. L. CARDOZO moved to amend by authorizing the Finance Committee to take charge of all financial affairs of the Convention, including the pay of members &c.

Mr. N. G. PARKER said as they had got along very well thus far without a Segeant-at-Arms, and as they had an Assistant Sergeant-at-Arms, he seconded the amendment that the finances of the Convention be left to the Finance Committee.

The amendment was adopted.

Mr. D. H. CHAMBERLAIN offered the following:

Resolved, That the Secretary of the Convention be, and is hereby directed, to cause to be printed and distributed upon the tables of the members of the Convention, each morning, one hundred and fifty copies of the Journal of the Convention for the preceding day's session.

Mr. C. P. LESLIE. I regret that I am compelled to say a word upon this resolution. I do not rise for the purpose of saying anything funny or ridiculous, but I am not aware that any such resolution was ever entertained by a body that was of a legislative character. I have heard so much, both inside and outside of this hall, in regard to the contract by the printer, that, though personally friendly to the gentleman who has the contract, I cannot go out of the usual routine adopted by legislative bodies for the purpose of adding to the expenses of the people of the State.

Mr. E. W. M. MACKEY. I desire to correct the statement made by the gentleman from Barnwell, that it is out of the usual routine for legislative bodies to have the journals of their proceedings printed. I think the gentleman is entirely mistaken. It is always customary for legislative bodies to have their daily journal of proceedings printed, and if it is not done by this Convention, it will be an exception.

Mr. J. J. WRIGHT. I agree with the gentleman from Barnwell, that it is wholly unnecessary, and I was going to say, supremely ridiculous. The expenses of this Convention will be a heavy drain upon the pockets of the people of the State, and I hope we shall act both wisely and judiciously. I would favor the printing of the journal did I not consider it totally unnecessary. There are not ten members, perhaps, who would read the journals if printed. We have a reading clerk and a Secretary who reads the journals. Every delegate, therefore, who wishes to know his standing on any question, can have the journal read.

Mr. N. G. PARKER. I differ with the gentleman entirely. I think it is necessary to have the journals printed. I hope we shall have not only the journals regularly printed, but also the proceedings of each day we have already been in session. We have just dispensed with the services of a Sergeant-at-Arms, and this expense of printing will be comparatively light.

The question being taken on the original motion to print one hundred and fifty copies, it was adopted.

The Special Order, "An Ordinance to levy a special tax to defray the expenses of this Convention, and preserve the credit of the State," was taken up.

Mr. PARKER, Chairman of the Committee on Finance, begged leave to make some corrections in the printed Ordinance. Instead of seventy-five cents on every hundred dollars of real estate, it should have been seven and a half cents on every hundred and one-fifth per cent. on every hundred dollars of manufactured articles. He also proposed to exempt from this tax all hacks and other vehicles, these being already overtaxed in the city.

Mr. J. M. RUNION moved to strike out the tax on dogs.

Mr. N. G. PARKER. I move to amend as follows: "That each and every person that keeps a dog or dogs shall pay a tax upon every dog or dogs in excess of one for each family."

Mr. W. J. WHIPPER. I move that the Ordinance, with the amendments, be recommitted to the Committee, to report in half an hour.

Mr. WM. McKINLAY. I move to amend by requiring the Committee to report at 12 o'clock to-morrow. When the Ordinance was first read I was under the impression that the taxes assessed was a per centage upon the tax assessed by General Canby. But upon reading the paper, I found that seventy-five cents upon every one hundred's worth of real estate is to be collected. This I consider excessive and disproportionate to the tax upon other property. I think the Ordinance had better be recommitted. The Committee may find other taxes levied in unequal proportions.

The question being on the motion to recommit, it was not agreed to.

The next question was on the motion of the delegate from Greenville (Mr. J. M. RUNION) to strike out the provision for a tax upon dogs.

Mr. N. G. PARKER. If we strike out the tax on dogs we reduce the amount proposed to be raised by the Ordinance ten thousand dollars.

Mr. J. K. JILLSON moved to strike out "fifty" and insert "one dollar."

Mr. J. M. RUTLAND. This tax is to be levied upon property. I submit that dogs, in a general sense, are not property.

Mr. B. O. DUNCAN. I think a dog quite as much property as a cow, horse, or any other property. There is no tax more proper than a dog tax. In the country we have too many dogs, and levying a high tax may rid us of some very worthless animals.

Mr. A. BRYCE. Will my friend take the dogs for the taxes?

Mr. NEAGLE moved to lay all the amendments on the table, with the exception of the amendment offered by the delegate from Barnwell (Mr. PARKER), to tax all dogs in excess of one.

The question was taken on the motion of the delegate from Greenville (Mr. RUNION) to strike out the tax on dogs, which was agreed to.

Mr. E. W. M. MACKEY moved to amend by striking out "two and a half" and inserting "ten" cents in the eleventh line of the Ordinance, so as to make a tax of ten cents on every hundred dollars' value of watches, jewelry and pianos. This increase would make up for the loss of the tax which had been calculated to be raised on dogs.

Mr. N. G. PARKER. I desire to know how much money that would raise. It is a matter of considerable importance to the Committee to know in what manner they are to raise the $75,000 called for by the Ordinance. Their earnest desire is to raise it in the most equitable manner possible. The dog tax just stricken out was suggested by General Canby, and was estimated to raise $10,000. The rate of taxation imposed on personal property will give $5,132; making it five cents additional on every hundred dollars will make it $10,000, and cover the deficiency from the dog tax.

Mr. B. F. WHITTEMORE moved to reconsider the vote on striking out the dog tax, and to insert that each and every person keeping a dog in excess of one shall pay a tax of fifty cents. It was evident that the Committee had given this ordinance a great deal of attention, and if they attempted to mutilate it they would certainly have to recommit it to the Committee.

The motion to reconsider was agreed to.

Mr. H. E. HAYNE moved to amend by inserting one dollar as the tax on dogs instead of fifty cents.

Mr. W. E. JOHNSON moved to lay the amendment on the table, which was agreed to.

The amendment proposed by Mr. E. W. M. MACKEY, in the 11th line, relative to the tax on gold watches, jewelry, etc., was laid on the table.

Mr. J. J. WRIGHT. If we make a tax of fifty cents on every person keeping a dog, the tax will not be collected, because the people will kill their dogs. I believe 25 cents amply sufficient.

Mr. J. M. RUTLAND. I would like to ask the Chairman of the Committee on Finance, whether the tax proposed is two and a half per cent., or two and a half cents on every hundred dollars worth of property. Some gentlemen read one way and some the other. It makes a very wide difference.

The PRESIDENT. As the bill stands before the Chair, it reads two and a half cents.

Mr. N. G. PARKER. It should be two and a half per cent.

Mr. B. F. WHITTEMORE. I hope the clause taxing dogs will be retained. I do not propose to put a tax upon the guardian of a house, but upon all unnecessary dogs.

The motion to retain was agreed to.

Mr. C. P. LESLIE asked the Chairman of the Committee on Finance the estimated value of real estate to be levied upon in the State, and how much they expected to realize from the tax.

Mr. N. G. PARKER said it was intended to raise $52,505.29.

Mr. L. S. LANGLEY moved that the report be recommitted to the Committee.

Mr. R. C. DeLARGE moved that it be made the Special Order for half-past one o'clock Wednesday.

Mr. A. J. RANSIER moved that the Committee report the amount expected to be raised upon each species of property.

Mr. N. G. PARKER. This has already been given in the full report, which has appeared in the newspapers.

Mr. C. P. LESLIE. I move that the subject be made the Special Order for one o'clock to-morrow.

The motion was agreed to.

The Ordinance defining the pay and mileage of members and officers of the Convention was next taken up.

Mr. J. S. CRAIG. I suggest the propriety of postponing action on this Ordinance until we can ascertain what kind of money we are to receive. If we are to be paid in a depreciated currency, we ought to have a very liberal per cent. I move, therefore, that the subject be postponed until after the Ordinance providing the means of raising funds for the Convention be acted upon.

Mr. T. J. ROBERTSON. I hope that motion will not prevail. The Finance Committee have looked over the whole ground, and could find no other means of raising money to pay the expenses of the Convention, but by endorsing the bills receivable of the State. Some of the members report that they are now much distressed, and in need of money. That being the case, the quicker they acted upon this Ordinance the better for these members. This Ordinance could be acted upon separately. According to the Ordinance, the members were to be paid nine dollars per day. The present discount on the bills receivable of the State is about 20 per cent., making the real value of the per diem of the members seven dollars and twenty cents in greenbacks. Very few members spend daily more than one-third of that amount The balance, by carrying it home and circulating it through the country, would furnish a medium for paying taxes, which would increase their value perhaps fifteen per cent., leaving only a discount of five per cent. to the members. There was now $99,000 outstanding bills receivable. $390,000 have been stricken off to this date, of which $222,000 only have been signed and carried to cash account. The amount on hand is reported to be $122,000 The amount of unpaid taxes in the hands of the Sheriffs for collection is $130,000. General Canby's order requires the raising of $330,000, and the sum to be raised by the Convention is estimated at $70,000, making a total amount of $530,000 to be raised by taxation. Should all the taxes be paid, they will not only absorb all the bills receivable authorized by the Act of the Legislature in 1865, but in addition $30,000 in United States currency or greenbacks.

It has been proposed to issue bonds to the amount of $200,000 and sell them. I have consulted with some of the best financiers of the State and city, and, in their judgment, these bonds would not sell at any price. They would not bring five cents on the dollar.

Mr. G. PILLSBURY. I conceive a very great propriety in the suggestion made by the gentleman from Colleton. I think I may safely pledge that most of the members of this Convention will be perfectly satisfied, if his Excellency Gov. Orr, in connection with the Commanding General, guarantees us $5 a day in greenbacks.

Mr. T. J. ROBERTSON. I will advance the gentleman $5 a day in greenbacks for his $9 per diem in bills receivable.

Mr. G. PILLSBURY. The difficulty with me is, what effect the action of this Convention in relation to the bills receivable of the State, will have upon the community or upon the inhabitants of the State. From what little experience I have had, I know they are unfavorably regarded. Occasionally through mistake, I have received State bills, and I have carried them in my pocket until nearly worn out. I have presented them to various merchants upon the streets, and they have invariably refused them. If I had faith in the predictions of the gentleman from Richland (T. J. ROBERTSON), I should favor the amount *per diem* as it is fixed, running the risk of the per centage.. But it is my candid opinion that any action of this Convention, endorsing those bills by fixing their per diem and mileage in bills receivable, will have a tendency to still further depreciate that currency. Let us wait until we can ascertain what these bills will bring in the market, and then we can establish a just per diem.

Mr. T. J. ROBERTSON. It is impossible for these bills to go as low as the gentleman thinks, for the Provisional Government under which we are living have legalized these bills; the Governor and General Canby recognizes them, and the Convention by its action will strengthen these bills. We provide for twenty per cent. discount in our estimates.

Mr. N. G. PARKER. I desire to state in behalf of myself and the Committee of which I am Chairman, that no motives of self-consideration governed them in the conclusions to which they came. Personal considerations alone would have led them to different conclusions. Nor does your Committee make any pretensions to a higher regard for the welfare of the State, than other members of this body. They do, however, regard the credit of the State of paramount importance, and believe that this Convention should do whatever they can to improve and maintain it. We cannot afford to let it suffer. The Constitution that we shall adopt will become the organic law of the State.' The expenses of the State Government, it is fair to presume, will be greatly increased. The cause of education alone will add greatly to it. We who make the Constitution are deeply interested in advancing this cause, for upon this rests our hope of perpetuating the Government we ordain. To realize the greatest practical benefit from the new Government we create, we must adopt such measures as will sustain such Government. I trust every member of this body realizes this important fact. We are not legislating for to day. If we were, and had no higher object in view than to complete the work before us, and to get as large a sum as possible for it, we might pursue a very different course. But no plan has yet suggested itself to us, nor has any plan been recommended to us, whereby a sum sufficient to meet the requirements of this Convention could be realized in greenbacks in such time as your wants demand. Were it a question of time and money merely, and the course might be pursued, a tax might be imposed and collected in greenbacks, but while you are waiting for it, you might suffer worse than you possibly can by the mode we recommend. No tax could be assessed and collected at once. It is true, we have the power to levy and collect, but it takes time. It would be most unwise and injudicious it seems to me, to assess a tax of $75,000 upon the property of the State and attempt to force the collection of it in an unreasonable short period. Four months would be a short period. We cannot afford to use harsh measures, even to collect a tax, in the peculiar condition of our unfortunate people. Supposing we should not pass this measure, pledging the faith of the State for the payment of her debts, and guaranteeing the bills receivable, and adopt the latter course of levying and collecting a tax in greenbacks, how then should we stand in the future? Where would the money come from and how to meet the expenses of the Legislature?

This is a question which concern us. We should prepare for it, unless we do, they will be in precisely the same condition as we are now. Only they will want a far greater sum, for no one will doubt for a moment but that they will want, to meet their expenses, nearly double as much as this Convention. Some people ask why not issue bonds and borrow the money? I answer this cannot be done by the authority we have. When we are a Legislature, we shall have the authority. Then we can make the attempt. Let us first do what we can to establish the credit of the State. The very first Legislature that we have may be compelled to do it. To do so, or to attempt it now, would be a failure. I do not believe that we could get ten cents on a dollar for any bond that we could make now, nor until after the Legislature should legalize an act. Where is the authority of the Convention to issue bonds and to dispose of them

23

for greenbacks? Is it in the Acts of Congress? Certainly not. Where is the men, or where is the set of men who would take the responsibility to do this? When it is hardly probable, or even possible, that if such bonds were issued, that they would bring ten cents on the dollar, who would want to sanction an act authorizing the issue of $700,000 of bonds to raise the sum of $70,000? Such an act would forever damn this Convention, and all that they might do. I do not believe that we could sell them at any price. I would not like to bear the odium that would attach to such a measure. We might give each member a certificate of indebtedness, or a promise to pay on demand, the amount of his pay and mileage, and if they are willing to take this and hold it until they can get greenbacks for it, the matter might be settled at once, but how would it be settled? It would be settled until the greenbacks could be raised. This might be sometime between this and June next. Can the members wait for this? I have been asked why not sell these bills at auction and get greenbacks for them? I will answer that I do not think it expedient to do so. It is very probable that if they were sold in that manner, that the speculators would purchase them, and at a much lower price than they are worth. There is another reason. You must bear in mind that we cannot get these bills except by permission of Gen. Canby. He sees objections to selling them.

In view of the probability of the entire transfer of this State government into the hands of this new power, and that within a brief period, can we afford to do this, you will perceive that the course recommended by your Committee, has the sanction of one whom we cannot accuse of any selfish ends, and of one whom we must at present, at least, look to aid us, without whose sanction we cannot touch a dollar of these bills, and that is the Major General Commanding this District. This act is one of self-protection. It has the sanction of the best business men in the State. The member from Richland, one of your Committee, himself a good judge of financial matters, can vouch for this. There is no other way under the sun whereby we can secure immediate funds to meet the payment of the expenses of this Convention. We want ready means; we have got it; only pledge the faith of the State for its redemption. Sir, we must legalize the acts of the General Assembly which created these bills. Let us sanction them; let us add our approval of them. Then with bills guaranteed by the Provisional Government, and further guaranteed by the government we create, under the sanction of the Congress of the United States, we can move onward to the accomplishment of the great ends in view, viz: the establishment and perpetuation of freedom, justice, civilization, education and the prosperity of the entire State.

Mr. C. C. BOWEN. There seems to be a great anxiety by some parties to dodge this question of the tendency of bills receivable to depreciate in value. I do not propose to enter on the record that we are receiving nine dollars a day, when it would be perhaps not more than two dollars and fifty cents. It is proposed to put $50,000 of bills receivable in the hands of one hundred and twenty delegates. Let these bills receivable be distributed or let them go out to-morrow, and before 10 o'clock they will not be worth twenty-five cents on the dollar. There is a large amount of this money already out in the hands of brokers and others. I think I see in this move a disposition to launch out another large amount of this money for the simple purpose of letting those people get hold of it at a still lower figure. When the delegates get paid they are obliged to spend their money immediately, and those sharpers know it. I am, therefore, in favor of placing on the record only what we get in greenbacks or their equivalent.

Mr. CRAIG. There is another very important reason why bills receivable should depreciate in value and are not in reality worth anything to-day. Article 10 of the Constitution of the United States says, "No State shall coin money or emit bills of credit," &c. Now I cannot see where is the difference between bills of credit and the bills receivable of the State. I think, therefore, the bills receivable proposed to be issued are unconstitutional, and if you levy a tax of that kind the people will protest against it, and they will have the law on their side of the question. I am willing to take five dollars if the Convention says so; but if you put me on the record as receiving nine dollars I want nine dollars. If I am put on as receiving five dollars I want but five, and I am satisfied; I did not come here to make a fortune. I do not regard the pay. I would not have been slandered as I have been since I came to this Convention by the *Mercury* for five hundred dollars per day. I came to do the business of the Convention, to do it as cheap as I could, and go back to the people, and advocate the adoption and ratification of the new Constitution. But I did not come to violate the Constitution of the United States, and I wish to enter my protest against this measure, which I regard as unconstitutional.

Mr. B. F. RANDOLPH. We have an excellent Committee on Finance, and I understand that that Committee have made all the necessary investigations in regard to these bills. They have reported these bills receivable as worth eighty cents on the dollar. It strikes me we could fix on pay in these bills at their market value in greenbacks.

Mr. B. F. WHITTEMORE. In order to allay the fears existing upon the minds of members in regard to what they may or may not have, I move that the pay per diem of the members shall be equivalent in greenbacks to what is in the Ordinance defined the pay and mileage of the officers and members of this Convention, and so recorded on the journal.

Mr. PARKER moved to strike out "nine dollars" and insert "ten dollars" wherever nine occurred.

Mr. CRAIG moved to amend by saying "seven dollars or its equivalent in greenbacks.

On motion, the amendment was laid on the table.

Mr. L. S. LANGLEY moved that the pay per diem be twelve dollars in bills receivable.

On motion of Mr. C. M. WILDER, the motion to insert twelve dollars was laid on the table.

Mr. J. J. WRIGHT moved that ten dollars be inserted.

The PRESIDENT stated that that had already been put and laid on the table.

Mr. N. G. PARKER moved to fix the pay at eleven dollars per day.

Mr. C. P. LESLIE. I desire to say a word before that resolution is passed, and be put right on the record. I am perfectly willing to receive three dollars per day in greenbacks for my services here. I think that sum all they are worth ; and, further, if I got any more, it would be so much more than I have been in the habit of receiving, I might possibly go on a spree and lose the whole of it. I know this is a delicate subject to speak upon, but there is a great deal of farce, too, about this business of money matters. I am here to do what is right and just. Now I ask any of the delegates in this body if they were called upon to pay a similar body of men out of their own pockets, how much they would be willing to pay each member. I will stake my existence on it they would not pay more than one dollar and a half per day to each member. I want to be recorded as always opposed to a high tariff, but not against any reasonable compensation. But this eight or nine dollars per day, when we consider all the surroundings and condition of the people, looks too much like a fraud.

Mr. W. J. WHIPPER. I shall certainly not object to the gentleman from Barnwell taking but a dollar and a half per day for his services if he wishes, but I shall certainly not rate my own at that price. I hope the matter will be speedily settled. We have been two days engaged on subjects that if I was asked what we had been doing, I should be embarrassed for an answer. It appears to me if we take bills receivable at 20 per cent. discount, with the probability of a further decrease in value, by the large amount likely to be thrown upon the market, eleven dollars a day in bills receivable will be small enough. The fact that those gentlemen who are able to carry them will realize their value, is no argument for those who will be compelled to sell them for debts already incurred.

Mr. B. F. WHITTEMORE. I desire to renew my motion that the pay per diem shall be equivalent in greenbacks to the amount mentioned in the Ordinance defining the pay and mileage of officers and members of this Convention, and that an amount of bills receivable, sufficient to cover the same, shall be drawn by the Committee on Finance, who shall be authorized to negotiate said bills receivable.

The question was taken on the motion to strike out $9 and insert $11, and was decided affirmatively.

Mr. B. F. WHITTEMORE. As the Ordinance reads now, the members are to receive $11 per day. It will be flashed all over the wires before night that the members of the South Carolina Constitutional Convention have voted themselves $11 per day. It will be the understanding throughout the country that we are absolutely receiving that sum, whereas we are taking it in bills receivable on $11, or which we might not probably realize $8 per day. I propose to add the words after $11 per day, "which is equivalent to about $8 in United States currency."

Mr. J. H. CRAIG. I agree with the gentleman. I am decidedly opposed to an appearance of voting myself $11 per day, when in fact I do not receive half that amount.

Mr. F. J. MOSES, Jr. We can meet the difficulty by inserting after the word "each" on the last line, the words, "and that the sums mentioned shall be paid to said members and officers in bills receivable of the State of South Carolina."

The question was then taken on this amendment, which was agreed to, and the Ordinance passed to its third reading, as follows : The pay of members, $11 per day ; Secretary, $11 per day ; Assistant Sergeant-at-Arms, $8 ; Assistant Secretary, $8; Engrossing Clerk, $8 ; Reading Clerk, $7 ; Doorkeeper, $7 ; Assistant Doorkeeper, $6 ; two Messengers, $5 per day, each. And the sums mentioned aforesaid shall be paid to the members and officers in bills receivable of the State of South Carolina. The mileage of members and officers of the Convention, shall be twenty cents per mile to and from the Convention by the usual mail routes.

All payment made in conformity to the several provisions of this Ordinance or Ordinances, shall be upon the recommendation of the Finance Committee and upon the authority of the President of the Convention.

On motion, the Convention adjourned.

THIRTEENTH DAY.

Wednesday, January 29, 1868.

The Convention assembled at 12 M., and was called to order by the PRESIDENT.

Prayer was offered by the Rev. J. M. RUNION.

The roll was called, and a quorum answering to their names, the PRESIDENT announced the Convention ready to proceed to business.

The Journal of the preceding day was read and approved.

The PRESIDENT explained to the Convention that in consequence of a misapprehension in relation to the passage of the resolution requiring the printing of the Journal, it was omitted. The error would be corrected, and the Journal of yesterday, and of all subsequent sessions, would be regularly published.

Mr. T. J. COGHLAN, of Sumter, offered the following resolution :

Resolved, That the reporter of the Mercury be excluded from the floor and the privileges of the House.

The motion was agreed to, and Mr. R. T. Logan, reporter of the Mercury, retired.

The PRESIDENT ordered the Sergeant-at-Arms to exclude the reporter of the Mercury from the floor of the House.

Mr. F. J. MOSES, Jr., rose and requested that several members who desired, and did vote against the resolution, might be allowed to enter their names on the record as so voting. The following members then rose and announced their names as voting against the resolution : F. J. Moses, Jr., Dr. L. B. Johnson, L. Boozer, C. M. Olsen, S. A. Swails, W. J. Whipper, Bailey Milford, T. Hurley, John A. Hunter, Dr. N. J. Newell, Wm. Perry, C. P. Leslie, Dr. J. L. Neagle, Rev. J. M. Runion.

The PRESIDENT asked the privilege of recording his vote against the resolution, as no reason had been assigned for the exclusion of the reporter ; he, therefore, voted no.

Mr. R. C. EELARGE voted no, because he thought the members ought to be able to protect themselves, and not seek it of the Convention.

Mr. J. J. WRIGHT moved a reconsideration.

Mr. L. S. LANGLEY moved to lay the motion to reconsider on the table, which was agreed to.

Mr. J. K. JILLSON moved that the rules and regulations as reported by the Chairman of the Committee on the subject, be amended in the fourth section, so as to require all articles, sections, etc., of the new Constitution to be read three times, instead of two, before final adoption, and the report was adopted.

Mr. B. F. RANDOLPH moved an amendment, so as to change the hours of meeting from 12 M. to 10 A. M., and to make the hour of adjournment 1 P. M. instead of 3 P. M. Laid on the table.

The question was then taken on the motion of Mr. JILLSON, and the report of the Committee, as amended, adopted.

Mr. R. B. ELLIOTT, of Edgefield, read the petition of W. J. Mixon, setting forth the following facts: That for many years before the war, he held a magisterial position, was opposed to the action of the State, and refused to vote for delegates to the secession Convention of 1860; but believing his first allegiance was due to the State, he volunteered as a soldier in her defence, and fought her battles with all his zeal; that after the war, he took the oath of allegiance from Capt. N. G. PARKER, then in command of colored troops in Barnwell, renewed his allegiance, and adopted the principles of the Republican party; that in consequence of having held magisterial office, he has been deprived of the elective franchise, and the petitioner, therefore, prays that his case may be presented to the Congress of the United States, with the prayer that his disability be removed. Referred to the Committee on Petitions.

The PRESIDENT also referred to that Committee a letter on the same subject, from the individual named.

Mr. S. A. SWAILS, of Williamsburg, presented petitions of Elizabeth Gordon and H. T. Cooper, citizens of said District, praying for a divorce.

Referred to the Committee on Petitions.

Mr. C. P. LESLIE said he would like to know what color they were.

Mr. SWAILS. "Both white."

Mr. S. CORLEY offered the following, which was referred to the Legislative Committee:

WHEREAS, bankruptcy and financial ruin, the inevitable results of a bloody and protracted civil war, stare us in the face at every turn; and, whereas, the ordinary resources of the State are swept away, and the people are clamoring for relief; therefore be it

Resolved, That the State shall be authorized to issue bonds to the amount of —— millions, the same to be paid in twenty years, and, if possible, secure thereon the endorsement of Congress, in order to make them available, and shall also pledge for the redemption of said bonds all the lands which a loan based upon these bonds will purchase, at the lowest cash price when forced into the market. That a Commissioner or Commissioners be elected for each County or District, whose duty it shall be to purchase, on the application of the owner—who shall show that he is loyal to the Constitution which this Convention shall adopt, by a sworn allegiance thereto—each and every tract of land forced into the market by execution or other legal process, when sold at a rate equal to or below the value of the same prior to the 20th of December, 1860. Of the said tracts, each, the said Commissioners shall cause to be surveyed one hundred acres, the same to be reserved to the late owner as a homestead, at the price paid per acre for the whole tract, adding thereto the incidental expenses of the transfer, and the value of the improvements thereon. If there be a disagreement as to the value thereof, each may choose his man and the two a third, to whom it shall be submitted, and their decision shall be final. A title shall be given by the State, and the said homestead shall be exempt from levy and sale forever, except to the State for the purchase money. The said homstead shall be paid for by annual, graduated instalments, during a period of twenty years, with interest at seven per cent., payable annually—the same homestead to be pledged, by mortgage or otherwise, to the State, for the stipulated payments. The remaining tracts of land, in each case, shall be held for sale to any citizen, like qualified, not in the possession of lands ; will obligate himself to settle on and improve the same, and, who will enter into a like contract, at like rates, and under similar liabilities, not over one hundred acres being sold to each individual, and the said homestead to be guaranteed forever against all debts and all executions whatsoever ; be it further

Resolved, That any person, like qualified, indebted beyond the supposed value of his property, either as principal or surety, against whom any suit to the value of five dollars has been entered, may make application to the said Commissioner or Commissioners, for the sale of his effects at public auction, for the benefit of his creditors ; and the said Commissioner or Commissioners, being hereby empowered to effect such sale or sales, shall, to that end, receive a schedule of all the papers and property of said debtor, not legally exempted from levy and sale, and the said schedule being sworn to and duly advertised for the space of one month, for the inspection of his creditors, who shall be allowed to disapprove the correctness of the same, which proof shall invalidate the claims of the debtor so offending, and if not disproved, said debtor shall be entitled to all the privileges of this Ordinance, and his creditors shall accept the proceeds of any and every sale so affected as final in the liquidation of all such debts, no creditor to receive more than his equal per centage, without preference or partiality, through any attempted forced sales for his own benefit, to the detriment of more lenient creditors.

Resolved, That this plan of relief and for securing homesteads to the people be referred to the Legislative Committee with instructions to report thereon in one week, with such alterations and amendments as they deem proper.

Mr. F. ARNIM submitted the following, which was referred to the Committee on Petitions :

We, the people of the State of South Carolina, by our delegates in Convention assembled, in consideration of the general destitution existing throughout the State, and the great lack of capital to develope the natural resources of the State, to give employment to the poor and destitute, and to enable them to secure a homestead,

Resolved, That the Congress of the United States be requested to appropriate three millions of dollars, the net amount collected from the cotton tax in this State, and that the same be loaned to the State, to be repaid in five equal instalments in 20, 25, 30, 35 and 40 years, to be used and secured as follows:

First. The State of South Carolina shall be responsible for the amount received from the United States.

Second. There shall be appointed a Comptroller, General Receiver, and a Receiver for each Collection District.

The duty of the Comptroller will be to ascertain the correctness of the title of the land purchased or sold, and all transactions must be approved by him.

The General Receiver shall, upon application, and with the approval of the Comptroller, purchase or sell land in behalf of the State.

The Receiver of each Collection District shall be the proper person to whom all applications to sell or buy land must be made.

The head of a family, whether male or female, at the age of twenty-one years or over, without distinction of color, but loyal to the government of the State and United States, shall, upon application, be entitled to purchase not over one hundred and sixty acres of land.

The security of money obligations of the parties concerned, the duties of the officers and salary shall be regulated by legislation.

Mr. D. H. CHAMBERLAIN rose and said he desired to offer the following resolution, as an explanation of the action of the Convention at the present session, and moved its adoption:

WHEREAS, R. B. Rhett & Brother, Editors, and R. M. Fuller and Roswell T. Logan, Assistant Editors of the Charleston *Mercury*, a scurrilous and libellous paper published in this city, have published false reports of this body, and through blackguardism of its members proved themselves to be wholly unworthy of the privileges of this floor, which should only be extended to gentlemanly conductors of the press; therefore,

Resolved, That the said R. B. Rhett & Brother, R. M. Fuller and Roswell T. Logan are hereby expelled and excluded from the floor of this Convention.

Resolved, That the President be requested to see this order of the house enforced.

The PRESIDENT decided the motion of the member offering the resolution to be a question of privilege, and could therefore be entertained·

Mr. J. J. WRIGHT. I am glad this resolution has been offered. The first resolution offered excluding the reporter of the *Mercury* from this floor was rushed through with such rapidity that no time was given

24

for an expression of opinion. I am opposed, totally opposed to excluding any person from the floor of the House. I did not vote either way, nor ask that my vote might be recorded. But if I had voted and asked that my vote might be recorded it would have been in the affirmative, notwithstanding my opposition to the exclusion of any reporter or editor. From what I have seen and heard, I think it requisite that the reporter of the *Mercury* should be excluded. A day or two ago they had a fight, the first I have ever witnessed, and I learned there were others upon the floor who would not take the slander of the reporter of the *Mercury*. As they had to choose between two evils I would take the least, and exclude the reporter, though I am opposed to any such course. If the reporter had remained, and the *Mercury* had continued as in the past, there are persons here who would, no doubt, have attacked him, blood would have been spilled, and perhaps persons in the house perfectly innocent have suffered. I am, therefore, perfectly willing the reporter should be excluded. But I wanted an opportunity to express myself and show the people that I am opposed to such a course. This was simply setting up an old standard, which, for many years, had been regarded as the standard of a people who had stooped below the dignity of men. When men resort to strong arms they lower their dignity. If there are persons in the Convention who will stoop so low, as to notice a little mean sheet, making its living by meanness, it would be coming down very far beneath the dignity of gentlemen. I am in favor of free speech and a free press. An editor is perfectly responsible for anything he does, and the law is open to all persons irrespective of color. But I am in favor of expulsion to avoid a greater evil.

A call was made for the previous question, which was sustained.

Mr. D. H. CHAMBERLAIN. The privilege of a seat upon the floor of this house by any member of the press is simply obtained by the consent of the body. It is a courtesy which is ordinarily and almost universally extended to members and representatives of the press by all similar bodies. But it is not a right which any man can claim. It is not a right which any member of the press can claim, and when the body which extends that courtesy feels that that courtesy has been abused; when the representatives of the press, instead of confining themselves to their legitimate business, descend to libels and scurrilous sketches of individual members, it becomes the right, if not the duty, of the body to withdraw the courtesy and privileges extended. The members of the Convention feel that the course pursued by the representative of the *Mercury* tends to a breach of its peace, and it is upon that ground mainly that this resolution has been offered, and will be supported by the members of the Convention. It is upon the same ground that libellous articles may be punished by law, and tend hence to a breach of the peace. The members do not want the excitement and disgrace of personal encounters within the walls of the house or anywhere else, in consequence of articles published in the papers of the city. Upon the ground, then, that they had a right to do it, and that it is necessary to prevent a possible breach of the peace between the man who descends to this business and the man who feels himself aggrieved, this resolution is offered.

The question being taken on its passage, the resolution was adopted.

Mr. F. J. MOSES, Jr., rose and desired to have his vote recorded in in the negative.

Mr. L. BOOZER also desired to have his vote recorded in the negative.

Mr. R. C. DeLARGE asked to be allowed to change his vote on the first resolution, which was made in the negative, in consequence of the rapidity with which it was rushed through. He now desired to be recorded as voting yea, which was granted.

Mr. N. G. PARKER moved for a reconsideration of the motion of Tuesday, dispensing with the election of a Sergeant-at-Arms. The Assistant Sergeant-at-Arms could not well perform the duty, and the Chairman of the Committee on Finance could not. As it was proposed to make the PRESIDENT responsible for all the amounts disbursed, the PRESIDENT desires a Sergeant-at-Arms who can perform the duties of Clerk.

The motion to reconsider was adopted.

Mr. N. G. PARKER moved that the PRESIDENT be authorized to appoint a Sergeant-at-Arms.

The PRESIDENT stated that in conversation with the Chairman of the Finance Committee, he found that by the arrangement proposed, the amount of money necessary for liquidating the expenses of the Convention would be placed in the PRESIDENT'S hands. For his own safety, as well as for the convenience of the members, it was proper they should have an officer to countersign checks, and keep the accounts and vouchers of the body.

The resolution was adopted.

Mr. B. BYAS offered the following:

Resolved, That the rules and regulations prepared by the Committee on Rules and Regulations be applied to the Convention when resolved in a Committee of the Whole, when they are applicable.

Resolved, That the Sergeant-at-Arms be required to place a clock over the PRESIDENT'S Chair, that speakers can time themselves in accordance with the rules of the house.

On motion of Mr. L. BOOZER, the first resolution was referred to the Committee on Rules and Regulations; and, on motion of Mr. J. S. CRAIG, the second was laid on the table.

Mr. B. F. WHITTEMORE offered the following resolution, which was referred to the Legislative Committee :

Resolved, That all persons shall be eligible to take or retain a seat in the House of Representatives who shall have attained the age of twenty-one years, and have been citizens and residents of this State one year next preceding the day of election, and for the last six months of time, and shall continue to be residents of the District which they are to represent.

Mr. R. B. ELLIOTT offered a resolution, instructing the Legislative Committee to report on Thursday upon the resolution referred to them, for the formation of a new Judicial District out of contiguous portions of Barnwell, Lexington, Edgefield, and Orangeburg Districts.

Laid on the table.

Mr. D. H. CHAMBERLAIN moved to take up an Ordinance reported by the Judiciary Committee, invalidating contracts for the purchase and sale of slaves, and that the same be passed to its second reading.

The motion was agreed to, and the Ordinance taken up and passed to its second reading.

Mr. DUNCAN moved that the Ordinance be engrossed, and made the Special Order for 1 o'clock to-morrow, (Thursday.)

Mr. S. A. SWAILS moved to amend by inserting half-past 1 o'clock, which was agreed to.

The hour having arrived for taking up the Tax Ordinance, which had been made a Special Order,

Mr. N. G. PARKER, Chairman of the Finance Committee, reported an amendment The amount proposed to be raised is $75,592.76, to raise which it is proposed to impose a tax of seven and a half cents on every hundred dollars of real estate ; fifteen cents on every hundred dollars of articles manufactured for sale, barter and exchange, etc., and fifty cents on every hundred dollars invested in buggies, carriages, gold and silver plate, etc., and fifteen cents on the sale of every hundred dollars of goods, wares, or merchandize, etc.

The various amendments proposed by the Committee since last before the House were read, when Mr. N. G. PARKER moved the adoption of the Ordinance.

Mr. B. O. DUNCAN made a motion to recommit, which was lost.

Mr. WM. McKINLAY moved that its further consideration be postponed, and it be made the Special Order for Thursday at one o'clock.

Laid on the table.

The Ordinance then passed to its second reading, and the several sections successively adopted.

Dr. J. L. NEAGLE moved the adoption of the Ordinance.

The PRESIDENT stated that the question would be, shall the Ordinance be engrossed and go a third reading, which was agreed to.

Mr. B. O. DUNCAN offered the following resolution, which was referred to the Committee on Petitions :

Resolved That a Committee, consisting of one from each District, be appointed by the Chair to report to this Convention, the name of such persons as, in their opinion, this Convention shall petition to Congress to remove all disqualifications from on account of past political offences.

Mr. B. F. WHITTEMORE offered the following, which was referred to the Legislative Committee :

Resolved, That all persons shall be eligible to take or retain a seat in the Senate of the State who have attained the age of thirty years, have been citizens and residents of the State two years next preceding the day of election, and have been six months a resident of the District they are to represent.

Mr. Y. J. P. OWENS offered the following:

Whereas, the officers of the present Provisional Government of the State of South Carolina are exercising their influence prejudicial to the claims of loyal citizens, rendering it difficult for persons of known loyalty to give an official bond,

Be it ordained by this Convention assembled, That hereafter no official bond shall be required from persons elected or appointed to office in the State of South Carolina, but providing a fine and imprisonment, and perpetual disfranchisement for malfeasance in office.

Mr. F. J. MOSES, Jr., moved to lay the resolution on the table, which was agreed to.

Mr. W. B. NASH offered the following resolution, which, on motion, was referred to the Committee on Finance :

Resolved, That all taxation shall be equal and uniform throughout the State, and all property shall be taxed in proportion to its value, which shall be ascertained in such manner as may be prescribed by law : *Provided*, That all clear lands not cultivated shall be taxed one per cent. more than cultivated lands, which tax shall be for the benefit of free schools.

On motion of Mr. PARKER, the rules of the House were suspended, in order to take up the Tax Ordinance, and pass it to its third reading.

The Ordinance was taken up, read a third time, adopted, and on motion of Dr. NEAGLE, ordered to be engrossed, as follows :

AN ORDINANCE

To levy a Special Tax to defray the Expenses of this Convention and preserve the Credit of the State.

We, the people of the State of South Carolina, by our Delegates in Convention met, do ordain, That there shall be assessed and collected by the Tax Collectors of the several districts and parishes in this State, in addition to the tax already levied, under General Orders No. 139, issued from headquarters Second Military District, by Brevet Major General E. R. S. Canby, Commanding said District, dated Charleston, December 3, 1867, the following taxes, which shall be collected by the persons and at the times and in the manner prescribed by the said General Orders : On all real estate seven and a half cents on every hundred dollars, excepting such lands as are exempted in Article I, of said General Order. On articles manufactured for sale, barter or exchange, between the first day of January, 1868, and the first day of January, 1869, fifteen cents on every hundred dollars, to be paid by the manufacturer. On buggies, carriages, gold and silver plate, watches, jewelry and pianos, on hand on the 1st day of January, 1868, except when held by dealers for purposes of sale, fifty cents on every hundred dollars. From the sale of goods, wares or merchandize, embracing all the articles of trade, sale, barter, or exchange, (the cotton tax by the United States excepted,) which any person shall make between the first day of January, 1868, and the thirty-first day of December, 1868, fifteen cents on every one hundred dollars. And the Tax Collectors, Sheriffs, or any other persons whose duty it may be to collect, or the Treasurer of the State, whose duty it is to receive, shall be liable upon their respective official bonds for neglecting or refusing to collect, safely keep, pay over, and disburse the same in conformity to the orders of this Convention.

SEC. 2. *Be it further ordained,* That a sufficient amount of the sum thus realized is hereby appropriated to refund to the Treasurer of the State of South Carolina any sum or sums which may be advanced by the order of General Canby, or otherwise, for the payment of the per diem, mileage, or other expenses of this Convention, in bills receivable of the State.

SEC. 3. *Be it further ordained,* That the faith and credit of the State are hereby pledged for the redemption of bills receivable of the State of South Carolina, issued in conformity to an Act of the General Assembly of the said State in December, 1865, and subsequently the Act of September, 1866 ; and also for the payment of the bonds and other obligations of the State ; *Provided,* That all obligations created for the purpose of aiding the rebellion, and for maintaining a hostile Government to the laws and authorities of the United States, are hereby declared to be null and void, and shall never be paid by any tax to be imposed upon the people of South Carolina.

[Mr. J. M. ALLEN, of Greenville, moved to strike out of Section 3, the endorsement of the "bonds and other obligations of the State," which was not agreed to.]

SEC. 4. *Be it further ordained,* That for the purpose of defraying the current expenses of this Convention—the payment of its officers, members and contingent accounts—Brevet Major General E. R. S. Canby, Commanding the Second Military District, be requested to issue from time to time, as may be necessary, such orders upon the Treasury of the State of South Carolina, for the payment of such sums as may be authorized by this Convention, in such amounts as may be agreed upon between the President of the Convention and the General Commanding, to the officers and members of this body, for their per diem and mileage, and for the current expenses of the same ; and that the amount of tax herein authorized to be levied, shall be placed in the Treasury of the State to reimburse said advances.

SEC. 5. *Be it further ordained,* That if the taxes levied and assessed under this Ordinance, should be in excess of the whole expenses of this Convention, it shall be retained in the Treasury subject to the future order of the Convention, or of the General Assembly, which may meet in conformity to the provisions of the Constitution to be adopted by this Convention. Should there be any deficiency in the sum required to be raised by taxation under this Ordinance, to reimburse the Treasury for its outlay, the first General Assembly which shall assemble hereafter shall make such further provision as may be necessary to raise funds for the purpose.

Mr. HURLEY moved a reconsideration of the vote on the passing of the Ordinance, and that the motion of reconsideration be laid upon the table.

Mr. PARKER moved that the President be instructed to request Gen. Canby to provide for the Convention at once $12,000 in bills receivable of the State.

Dr. NEAGLE moved to amend by making it $20,000.

Mr. L. S. LANGLEY moved $25,000.

Mr. C. M. WILDER moved to make it $37,500.

The amendments were lost, and the original motion agreed to.

The Special Order for the hour, being an Ordinance for the divison of Pickens District, was taken up.

Mr. C. P. LESLIE. I desire to withdraw my objections against the passage of this Ordinance. I have examined the subject fully, and am satisfied that the people, white and colored, of the District are united in the desire to have the District divided. Having conversed with many of the most substantial men of the District, who all concur as to the exigencies of the case, I am willing to waive all objection, take up this matter out of the ordinary course of business, and give the measure my earnest vote.

Mr. B. BYAS moved that the matter be indefinitely postponed, which was not agreed to.

The question being taken on the passage of the Ordinance, the yeas and nays were ordered, and resulted, yeas 86, nays 25.

On motion, the Ordinance was ordered to be engrossed, the title to remain "An Ordinance for the division of Pickens District."

Mr. B. F. RANDOLPH moved that the motion whereby the Ordinance was passed be reconsidered, and that the motion to reconsider be laid on the table. The motion was agreed to.

Mr. L. B. JOHNSON offered the following, which was agreed to.

Resolved, That the Ordinance for the division of Pickens District, be reported to the appropriate Committee, with instructions to incorporate the name of Oconee District in the Constitution with the name of the other Districts.

Mr. L. S. LANGLEY offered the following:

WHEREAS, many members of this Convention have been absent without leave, and whereas it is the opinion of this body that no member should be paid his per diem during said absence, therefore

Resolved, That no member of this Convention shall receive any pay for the day or days during which he has been absent, unless said member has been sick, or received leave of absence from this body.

Resolved, That each member be, and is, hereby required to state on oath to the Sergeant-at-Arms the number of days he has attended the sessions of the Convention.

Mr. RUTLAND. That looks like an *ex post facto* affair. Such a motion in higher bodies is unconstitutional. If it had been agreed to at the commencement of the Convention it might have been of some service. I think it should be amended so as to embrace only future absentees.

Mr. DUNCAN moved that the word "affirmation" be substituted for that of "oath," which was agreed to.

Mr. W. J. WHIPPER. I certainly hope that resolution will pass. There are very good reasons why it should have a retroactive effect. The gentleman himself, I think, has been away several days. I hope every one will be required to swear how many days he has been in attendance, and, unless he has been sick or can give a sufficient excuse, will receive no pay. It is very convenient for gentlemen who plant rice on Goose Creek to receive pay here while attending to their crops.

Mr. L. S. LANGLEY. If there is any member here who did not know that he was elected to serve his constituents, and paid for his time and services in the Convention, I am willing to excuse him. But I am not willing that those knowing the fact and neglecting their duty should receive compensation.

On motion of Mr. W. J. WHIPPER, the resolution was referred to the Committee on Rules and Regulations, to report at 1 o'clock to-morrow.

Mr. N. G. PARKER called up the Ordinance providing for the pay of members.

Mr. B. F. WHITTEMORE introduced the following as a substitute:

AN ORDINANCE

Defining the Pay and Mileage of Members and Officers of this Convention.

SECTION 1. *And be it ordained,* That the pay per diem of the President shall be $12; members, $8; Sergeant-at-Arms, $8; Secretary, $8; Assistant Sergeant-at-Arms, $6; Assistant Secretary, $6; Engrossing Clerk, $6; Reading Clerk, $5; Doorkeeper, $5; Assistant Doorkeeper, $4; two Messengers, $4 each.

SEC. 2. *And be it further ordained,* That the mileage of members and officers of the Convention shall be (20) twenty cents per mile to and from the Convention, by the usual mail routes.

SEC. 3. *And be it further ordained,* That all payments made in conformity to the same shall be made in the bills receivable of the State of South Carolina at their market value, so that the amount of per diem and milage shall be the same as if paid in greenbacks or United States legal tender notes; all such payments shall be made upon the recommendation of the Finance Committee and authority of the President of the Convention.

Mr. B. F. WHITTEMORE. I desire to impress upon the minds of members present that it has already gone abroad and received as a fact that we are receiving $11 per pay for our services in this Convention. I desire to show to the world what we really are receiving. If it be $8 in United States currency let us say so, but not enter upon the journals $11 as the amount, when in fact we may not be receiving more than $5 per day. I am unwilling such a statement should go to the people of this Commonwealth and future generations that would lead them to believe we received $3 more per day than the members of any other Convention voted themselves. It should be distinctly understood that the bills receivable of the State are depreciated in value. Let us fix the pay at $8 in greenbacks, and receive its equivalent in bills receivable.

25

Mr. N. G. PARKER: I sympathize with everything the gentleman has said, but we cannot at this time take the risk of adopting that amendment. We are between two fires. The Commanding General may interpose if we fix our pay at a stated amount in one currency, and propose to make up that amount by receiving its equivalent in another. We might possibly negotiate these State bills without putting them up at auction. If there was any way by which we could let the world know we are not receiving $11 a day in United States currency, but in State bills at a depreciated value, I should be happy to have it done. It is already stated that we receive $11 in State bills, and it may be that outsiders will endeavor to give the impression that we are receiving that amount in United States currency, but that is one of the accidents we cannot avoid.

Mr. W. J. WHIPPER. I hope some stated sum, whether in greenbacks or bills receivable, will be fixed upon. Hardly two men in the Convention, perhaps, would agree as to the market value of the bills receivable, and there might be a continual difficulty between the Finance Committee and the members when about to be paid off. If we want $8 in greenbacks, let us say so and make it definite.

Mr. C. C. BOWEN. I have only one question to ask. Suppose the market value of bills receivable to day is eighty cents, when there are so few on the market, and we put $12,000 more out now, can any man say what will be the result? I doubt whether you could pay your fare on any railroad with it, or make any purchase in a store without submitting to an enormous discount. I shall, speaking for myself, be satisfied with whatever action the Convention may deem it proper to take. I was in favor of fixing the pay at $8 in United States currency, but have been informed that arrangements cannot be made for the payment of the members in that currency. If so, we will have to take the bills receivable for what they are worth.

Mr. B. O. DUNCAN. I think we should have no hesitation in voting $11 per day in bills receivable. They are now selling at 80 and 90 cents on the dollar, and we have been told by a gentleman in a position to know, that there will be no further depreciation, but that the bills receivable are likely to rise in value to 90 or 96 cents by our guaranteeing the bills.

Dr. J. L. NEAGLE. The gentleman's amendment conflicts with the Ordinance passed this morning. Section 4 provides that the per diem and mileage of the members and other expenses of the Convention shall be paid in bills receivable of the State.

Mr. H. E. HAYNE. I will state for the information of the Convention, that the bills receivable have depreciated five cents since yesterday.

Mr. B. F. WHITTEMORE. I do not see how it is possible for the amendment to come in conflict with the second section of the Ordinance referred to. We can appropriate a certain sum of bills receivable as will amount, when sold in the market, to what we declare shall be our per diem.

The hour of three having arrived, the Convention adjourned.

FOURTEENTH DAY,

Thursday, January 30, 1868.

The Convention assembled at 12 M, and was called to order by the PRESIDENT.

Prayer was offered by the Rev. B. F. WHITTEMORE.

The roll was called, and a quorum answering to their names, the PRESIDENT announced the Convention ready to proceed to business.

The journal of the preceding day was read, corrections made, and on motion of Mr. B. F. WHITTEMORE, was ordered to be reprinted.

The PRESIDENT stated that before entering on the regular business, he had a question of privilege to lay before the Convention. Upon coming to the Convention this morning he was met by a Sergeant of the City Police, who handed him a document which would be read by the Reading Clerk.

A communication from General Clitz to Mayor Gaillard was then read by the Clerk, requesting of the Mayor that a Sergeant and five Policemen should be sent to the Convention to be in attendance at the Club House during the hours of the session of the Convention, with instructions to maintain the peace.

The PRESIDENT said the matter was entirely unknown to him. He had not been consulted on the subject by General Clitz or any other officer, and the request to the Mayor had been made without his knowledge. As the presiding officer, he deemed it his duty to lay before the Convention what appeared to affect their privileges. He did not know the object of it. He did not feel authorized to act himself, and had therefore directed the doorkeeper to permit no policemen to come upon the floor of the Convention until the pleasure of the body on the subject had been known. He submitted the whole subject to the Convention to take such action as it might deem advisable.

Mr. B. F. WHITTEMORE moved that a Committee of three be appointed to wait upon General Clitz, Commandant of the Post of Charleston, and inquire of him why he has considered it necessary to send the protection mentioned in his communication to the Convention, which was agreed to.

The PRESIDENT named as the Committee to wait upon General Clitz, Messrs. B. F. Whittemore, A. J. Ransier and W. E. Rose.

Mr. W. J. WHIPPER moved that, pending the report of that Committee, no policeman be allowed on the floor of the Convention.

The PRESIDENT announced the motion unanimously agreed to.

Mr. S. A. SWAILS made a report of the Committee on Rules and Regulations, on a resolution in reference to the pay of absent members. The Committee say, inasmuch as the rules of the house already contain a clause on the subject, they recommend that the resolution be laid on the table. Report adopted.

Mr. S. A. SWAILS also made a report of the same Committee, amending the resolution referred to them, requiring members to " state, on oath or affirmation, the number of days they have been in attendance," by striking out the latter, and inserting " to certify on his word of honor." Adopted.

The PRESIDENT presented a communication from J. P. M. Epping, United States Marshal, which, on motion of Mr. C. C. BOWEN, was read by the Reading Clerk and referred to the Committee on Petitions.

The following is the communication :

To the President and Members of the
Constitutional Convention of South Carolina:

GENTLEMEN : The undersigned respectfully submits the following plan for the settlement of the land and labor question to the Convention, with the suggestion that Congress be memorialized by a resolution of the Convention, to grant the boon herein prayed for, and it is thought that the same will be readily and promptly granted, in view of providing homes for the freedmen throughout the South, and of relieving the prevalent general distress for want of a sufficient circulation of ready capital.

Particularly would the now dominant great Republican party, it is thought, gladly avail itself of the opportunity of showing its kindness and interest, in the welfare of the Southern States, and thereby secure the everlasting gratitude and good will of all races and color alike.

It is a well known fact in political economy, that for a State or community to flourish, three elements are requisite. First is land ; second, labor ; third, capital or money. Throughout the Southern States lands are plenty, labor is abundant, *but the capital is wanting.*

A disorganization of society, and an utter absence of remunerative industry is, consequently, everywhere felt.

Congress having abolished slavery, owes it to itself and the country to take proper care of their wards—the freedmen who have been turned loose upon the world. It owes it not only to itself and the freedmen, but to the entire Union, to set in motion the now obstructed wheels of commerce, agriculture and manufactures throughout the South.

Two of the elements named already exist here; the third only is wanting, and yet can easily be supplied.

The freedmen are, in a manner, like children turned out of doors by their parents. They have been wilfully kept in ignorance while in the state of slavery, and, consequently, have neither the knowledge, ability, nor means, to establish themselves independently of their former masters and owners, while the latter are themselves in a situation equally embarrassing, because with all their landed possessions, they have not the funds necessary for the payment of remunerative wages to the laborer, and thus develop the capacities and resources of these possessions, and there is not capital sufficient in all these Southern States to buy the lands, and to put them into successful cultivation by means of hired free labor.

It is, therefore, for the General Government to step in, and, besides affording its protection to the one class, lend its material aid to the other, in order that existing difficulties may be overcome.

Hence, the proposition is now made, that Congress, in the amplitude of its power, furnish a limited amount of capital, not to individuals, but to the States, in the shape of a loan, for the benefit of the two classes referred to.

A sum equal to the amount collected from the agricultural products of the former slaveholding States, in one year, in the way of taxes on cotton, would, it is believed, be sufficient for this purpose.

There are, for instance, in the State of South Carolina between twenty and thirty thousand persons, who own plantations of five hundred acres and upwards, and who could spare very readily from one-fourth to one-third of the same.

With such a fund as has been described put in the hands of the Governor of the State, and managed by a Board possessing supervisory powers, consisting of the Governor, chief agent of the Freedman's Bureau, and one or two other authorized Commissioners, these surplus lands may be purchased at a very moderate rate, and sold and transferred to such freedmen on credit as formerly belonged to the respective plantations, or any others upon which they desire to locate, and the State give to the purchaser a cheap and perfect title, which is very seldom and even difficult to obtain now in this State, where lands are purchased from individuals.

Enough land would thus come into the possession of the freedmen to give each a homestead at a moderate price, while the planter making such a disposition would receive money enough to pay cash wages to his employees, and carry forward his yearly labor to the satisfaction of all.

The present pernicious system of working by contract for a share of the crop, has been a cause of great confusion and distress since the cessation of hostilities, and ought, for the welfare of the community, to be avoided in future ; but the plan now proposed, it is thought, will supply the capital necessary for the payment of cash wages, and likewise secure permanent homes for the freedmen.

Respectfully submitted,

J. P. M. EPPING.

Charleston, S. C., January 28, 1868.

Mr. N. G. PARKER offered the following, which was agreed to:

Resolved, That the PRESIDENT of the Convention cause to be forwarded to the Major-General commanding this Military District, a certified copy of the Ordinance, entitled "An Ordinance to Levy a Special Tax to defray the expenses of the Convention, and to preserve the credit of the State."

Mr. N. G. PARKER also offered a resolution that all Ordinances adopted by the Convention shall be engrossed and ratified, on being signed by the President and Secretary, which was agreed to.

Mr. B. F. WHITTEMORE offered the following, which was agreed to:

WHEREAS, it is important to the interests of the State, and necessary in a historical point of view, that the proceedings of this, the first Convention in the new era of South Carolina, should be permanently preserved; be it

Resolved, That a Committee of three be appointed to make such arrangements with one or more short hand reporters as will secure a faithful record of the proceedings and debates of this body, the compensation for the same to be not more than the sum paid to official reporters in Congress, and to be paid by the Treasurer of the State, on the presentation to the President of the Convention of the proceedings in manuscript, ready for the printer, in the bills receivable of this Commonwealth, at their market value, that amount to be paid by the Treasurer of the State, on the order of the President of the Convention.

The PRESIDENT named as the Committee, B. F. WHITTEMORE, of Darlington; N. G. PARKER, of Barnwell, and S. LEE, of Sumter.

Mr. J. M ALLEN, on behalf of John S. Gentry, of Spartanburg submitted the following:

AN ORDINANCE TO ESTABLISH RENTS.

Resolved, That the landlords shall receive as rents one-third of all grain crops and one-fourth of the cotton and tobacco crops raised on their lands by the lessees, where the lessor furnishes all the labor and capital.

Resolved, That landlords furnishing the stock and feed for stock shall receive one-half the productions of his lands of any crop whatever.

Resolved, That any one receiving from tenants more crop from the productions of his lands than herein is provided, shall be deemed guilty of a misdemeanor, which shall be punished with fine and imprisonment

Laid on the table.

Mr. J. M. RUNION offered the following:

Resolved, That it is essential to the preservation of the rights of every individual, his life, liberty, property and character that there shall be an impartial interpretation and just administration of the laws, and that every citizen should be tried by free, independent and impartial judges.

Resolved, That it is not only the best policy for the country at large, but for the better security of its rights and of the rights of citizens of this great Republic, that all officers of State, from the highest to the lowest, shall be elected by the people, and that said officers have reasonable and honorable salaries, to be established by law; *Provided,* That the judges of the Supreme Judicial Court and United States Senators may be elected by the General Assembly.

Laid on the table.

Mr. J. M. ALLEN presented the petitions of sundry citizens of Pickens District, praying the enactment of some measure of relief to parties who had sold their property during the war, and had been brought to a condition of squalid poverty by receiving therefor worthless money in notes and bonds of the Confederate States. The petitioners pray for a measure that will afford relief and effect a fair and equitable settlement between the seller and purchaser.

Mr. W. J. WHIPPER moved that the petitions be laid upon the table.

The motion was lost and the documents referred to the Committee on Petitions.

Mr. F. J. MOSES, Jr., moved the following, which was referred to the Committee on the Judiciary:

WHEREAS, the present system of pleadings, by which the administration of justice is regulated in the courts of law in this State, is very expensive and tends to much delay, be it

Resolved, That the Committee on the Judiciary be instructed to inquire into, and report upon, the propriety and expediency of inserting in the State Constitution a clause to the following effect:

"The Legislature, at its first session after the adoption of this Constitution, shall, by Act, abolish the present system of pleadings in the courts of law in this State, and provide in lieu thereof, that all actions in the courts of law shall be by petition, and the Legislature shall at the same time prescribe rules and regulations for the conduct of such processes."

Mr. A. J. RANSIER offered the following, which was referred to the Committee on the Judiciary:

Resolved, That the proper and legitimate work of this Convention is that of framing "a Constitution and Civil Government" for this State, (South Carolina,) and of providing for the pay of members and other expenses that may be necessarily incurred; that whilst some scheme ought to be adopted by which the planters and others in straightened circumstances may be relieved, and whilst petitions from any quarter ought to be treated with the utmost respect, this Convention will not undertake to act upon any subject that properly belongs to the Legislature, when convened under the Constitution which we shall frame.

Mr. R. H. CAIN offered the following, which was referred to the Committee on Petitions:

WHEREAS, the condition of the freedmen of this State is most deplorable. in consequence of the failure of the crops, in some respects, and by the non-payment by the employers of the laborers for their services the last year, leaving them in a worse condition pecuniarily than two years ago; and whereas, it is of vital importance that all classes of a community should be placed in a condition of self sustanance by their labor and production, which adds to the material prosperity of the State or country in which they live, giving strength and stability to the Government, and augmenting the value of the lands, and adding to the revenue;

And whereas, these people have been freed by the operations of the war, and left penniless by slavery, with no means at their command to purchase lands with, and have become the wards of the National Government of the United States, whose duty it is to protect them and afford them every opportunity of supporting themselves;

And whereas, the lands in the State of South Carolina belong to the citizens of the State who are willing to sell the same at reasonable prices to the freedmen or the agents of the Government, (not being able by reason of their present embarrassments to pay for labor to till the soil); and whereas, the prosperity of this State imperatively demands capital to meet the wants of the inhabitants, and believing that the Government is willing to afford every means of immediate relief to all the citizens of this Commonwealth, as well as to encourage the freedmen in their efforts to procure homes and become industrious producers, as well as consumers; therefore,

Resolved, That this Convention do petition, and they do hereby petition the Fortieth Congress of the United States to make an appropriation of one million dollars of the funds in the possession of the Bureau of Refugees, Freedmen and Abandoned Lands, for the purpose of purchasing lands in this State, now offered for sale in this State or to be offered, for the freedmen, and such other persons who may come within its jurisdiction, or may apply for aid through said Bureau; and that said lands when so purchased shall be sold to the freedmen as homes, in parcels of 10, 20, 40, 50, 60, 80 and 100 acres, to suit the purchasers; and the purchases of said lands shall be made under the supervision of Major General O. O. Howard, Commissioner of the Freedman's Bureau; and that when said lands are so purchased and sold, the purchaser thereof shall enter into an obligation to the Government to pay the amount of the value of said land purchased by him, her, or them, from the Government, and the Government shall hold claim to said lands by bonds, &c., as in all other cases of land conveyances by law, and at the expiration of five years the person so purchasing shall make full payment to the Commissioner or Commissioners of the Freedman's Bureau, or such persons as shall be authorized to receive the same, the full amount of the purchase money paid by the Government for the lands which he purchased from the same.

Resolved, That this measure should be passed and made effective as soon as possible, as a measure of speedy and immediate relief to the suffering thousands of both races in this State, thereby saving thousands of dollars to the Government, which will necessarily be expended to save the people from starvation in the interior of this State.

Resolved, That we do earnestly pray the Congress to take immediate action that relief may be afforded the hundreds of thousands of homeless and penniless sufferers in this State, and that in these appropriations provisions be made to supply the wants of agricultural implements and seeds for the farms—the war having destroyed all the means available to these people.

Resolved, That the President of this Convention be requested to transmit a copy of this preamble and resolutions to the Congress of the United States at as early a day as practicable.

The PRESIDENT announced that in obedience to the order of the house he had appointed Mr. JOHN P. HUGHES, Sergeant-at-Arms for the Convention.

The Special Order for one o'clock, viz. : the report of the Committee on Miscellaneous Matters, on a petition to Congress for the continuance of the Freedman's Bureau, was taken up.

Mr. B. F. RANDOLPH moved that the majority report, recommending that the Convention petition Congress for the continuance of the Bureau, be adopted.

Mr. B. BYAS. As one of the minority of the Committee, I wish to say a word and give my reasons for dissenting from the majority. While I admit the necessity for the continuance of the Freedman's Bureau, I deem the petition the Congress unnecessary. Congress has already continued the Bureau from time to time, and it was natural to suppose would have the magnanimity to again prolong its existence if civil government was not restored before the 16th of July, the time fixed for its expiration. I am in favor, however, of a petition to Congress for the establishment of a Bureau of Education.

Mr. B. F. RANDOLPH. The petition can do no harm, and Congress had asked to be informed by petition or otherwise, from the people of the Southern States, whether the continuance of the Bureau was necessary. In reference to the opinion of General Scott, the latter had stated that if civil government was not restored by the 16th of July, the Bureau would have to be continued. With reference to a Bureau of Education, they all knew the necessity for that, and the Federal Government

26

was able to give the South from its great revenue, a few millions for the education of the children of its impoverished people.

The question being taken on the adoption of the majority report, it was agreed to.

The next Special Order, a report of the Committee on the Judiciary, on a resolution of inquiry as to the legislative powers of the Convention, on motion of Mr. E. W. M. MACKEY, was laid on the table.

Mr. J. M. RUTLAND. I am not prepared to make a speech on this question, but it does occur to me that this is not a proper subject for the consideration of the Convention. All matters of this kind should be left to the Courts to determine, whether they are valid or not. In my opinion, it smacks somewhat of the spirit of revenge, upon a class of people who have been identified with the institutions of the past. I do not stand here to advocate the moral right of slavery; I never did believe it right for one man to hold another in bondage, and call him property. But such was the law of the land. Slaves were property; were bought and sold, and the country was bound to recognize them as property as long as the institution existed. If this Ordinance was intended to punish all those who dealt in slaves, it did not effect its object at all. If these contracts were to be declared null and void, the result would be simply to punish one party—he who sold the slaves, and to pay a premium to the man who bought; and both were morally guilty. Aside from this fact, however, the Convention is assembled to frame a Constitution, and not to decide questions, the decision of which clearly belongs to the Courts of law.

Mr. S. CORLEY. Mr. President: The Ordinance invalidating all contracts, the consideration of which was the purchase or sale of slaves, is of doubtful utility, and highly dangerous as a precedent, for the guidance of future legislation. The Constitution of the United States denies the right of any State to pass an *ex post facto* law, or any law impairing the obligation of contracts. It is proposed, in the adoption of this resolution, to violate this plain principle of the Constitution, thus clearly expressed. We are framing a Constitution for the purpose of reconstructing this State, that she may take once more the proud position of an equal in the great sisterhood of States composing the "Great Republic." And is it possible that any one here expects her to be admitted the sooner to so noble and honorable a position by endorsing, contrary to the letter of the Constitution, the repudiation of any debts or contracts whatever? Certainly we cannot be so completely deluded! The idea that because a man cannot be rightfully held as property, there is not, and cannot be, any legal right to his services as such, is fallacious in the

premises, and, therefore, entirely false in the conclusion, and utterly un-
tenable in fact and every day practice. Perhaps more than half the
members of this Convention can testify that they were once held as slaves,
bought and sold as property, and legally held as such, under the lash of
the task-master—against the injustice of which there was no appeal,
either in State or Federal Courts. This being admitted, what reason can
be urged for setting aside any such contracts ? Is there any difference
between the seller and buyer in a moral sense ? If the act of the speculator in the bones and muscles of man was criminal, that of the purchaser
was equally, and even more so. The slave trader made no pretensions
to piety, as he tore the child from the mother's arms to be sold as a
brute, and separated from her forever under the sanction of the pious
priest, who denounced the act. and yet purchased the child. I can see
no good reason for denying the seller's right to collect the purchase
money from him, whose pious clamor now denounces the contract as an
outrage upon justice and right. If the pious purchaser were not an
idiot, incapable of entering into a contract—if he got, in his own estimation, at that time, value received for his obligation to pay, it is not the
right nor the legitimate business of this Convention to decide whether or
not he was a fool in accepting as property that which, I trust, we all hold
could not be rightfully claimed as such. It does not alter the case to
argue that this species of property was held by force, and the pressure
being removed by violence—by relentless, cruel, bloody war—therefore,
the obligation is impaired. He who sells a horse for cash or on credit,
does not thereby obligate himself to secure to the purchaser the services
of that animal during his natural life. The owner may so use him as to
forfeit his right and title in him, and if he does forfeit that right by violation of law, then there remains no right with him to deny the payment
of the consideration. The slaveholders of the South concocted the rebellion for the express purpose of perpetuating slavery. They madly raised
their hands against the best government on earth simply to keep themselves in office, and rivet more firmly the chains of the unfortunate slave.
By that rash act, and by using the services of the slave to sustain it,
they forfeited all rights of property in the same, under the Constitution,
which defines treason and authorizes its punishment. The legal right
of the master being forfeited, and the United States Government denying
the moral right to hold such property, the legal right again reverted to the
original owner, which is the slave himself. It does not matter whether
he or his former master has the bill of sale, the fact is patent, and the
gladdened freedman feels that he is his own master and has the right to
exercise his own body and mind in the pursuit of happiness.

But if we admit the validity of such contracts, will that admission in any way subject the United States to a liquidation of the claims of loyal masters, whose property was wrenched from their hands by the war? Certainly not. By permitting themselves, and the said property, to be used in the interest of the rebellion, they forfeited every such right, by simply remaining in bad company. Lot saved himself by leaving Sodom, but if he had remained all his righteousness would have been inadequate. The innocent must suffer with the guilty, because they acted with them. The man who was loyal, and was forced in the rebel army, though he loved the Government and was shot as a rebel, was thus compelled to accept the situation in the sacrifice of life to rebel perverseness; and, certainly, those who could not, or did not prevent their property from being used by the rebellion for its success, cannot expect to be paid by the Government for its loss, particularly when, as a military necessity, its destruction, as property, was essential to save the life of the nation. The poor man lost his life and these slave drivers-only their property; and I think the latter have greatly the advantage, and may thank God that they have still their heads on. As the Government cannot replace the heads of loyal men, I know it never will the property of those who have lost less than life. I am willing to go as far as any one, by inserting the strongest clauses in our Constitution that can be written, to perpetuate freedom and equal rights to all, but I am not willing to relieve one class of our citizens from their obligations at the expense of another, simply because they have lost their property by an illegal process, to right themselves by wronging others. We have already pledged this same Convention against repudiation, and the United States Courts in this State have decided in favor of these contracts, and it is certainly too late to defy the law, reason and common sense. I can not consent to relieve this class of creditors; while my poorer neighbors, whose debts for property, more wisely and judiciously contracted, are, at least, as jusly entitled to relief by repudiation as any of those quondom slaveholders. There is no justice in the demand, and the precedent itself will be fatal to our success.

When I remember that those who are indebted for slaves were stronger props in the rebellion than those who felt slavery insecure, and sold out—and that they exempted themselves from the perils of the battle-field to watch over and protect their slaves, while I, with thousands of my poor countrymen, were forced to face the leaden hail of the Union army, simply to keep them in power as our masters and as yours (alluding to the colored members), I cannot respect myself longer by relieving them of their foolish obligations, while I bind myself and you to ours. Let me say for once and for all, that personally, I have no interest in the matter. I have no axe to grind. I have never sold or bought a slave. I have had the means to have done so, but while yet a boy I vowed eternal hostility to slavery, and determined never to claim for myself any right which I denied to others. For the last twenty-five years I have been persecuted and spit upon, because of my devotion to the Union and to freedom. I have been hunted down like a wild beast, threated with death, and subjected to attempted expatriation, simply because of my public avowal of belief in the great principles of the Declaration of American Independence. Thank God, the spell has been broken at last, and the blow which struck the shackles from the hands of the slave has also made me free. I thank God that I have at last the opportunity, as the representative of the free people of my native District, to vindicate my right to free speech upon the floor of this Convention ; and, still claiming for myself no right which I deny to others, I demand that while I and my non-slaveholding friends are required to pay our debts, that every quondam slaveholder shall pay his, or show some better reason for his delinquencies than any vote of mine shall afford, in the settlement of this question on the floor of this house.

On motion of Mr. B. F. WHITTEMORE, the further consideration of the subject was postponed until one o'clock on Monday.

The Special Order being the unfinished business of yesterday, the Ordinance providing for the pay of members was taken up.

Mr. F. L. CARDOZO moved to amend by substituting ten cents for twenty cents to pay the mileage of members, which was not agreed to.

Mr. C. C. BOWEN moved to amend the third section by striking out after the words "be it ordained," and inserting the following: "In addition to the above, the actual expenses in traveling to the Convention by the ordinary route of travel, and returning therefrom once during the session, and no more, shall be paid upon the draft of the PRESIDENT to every member who has seasonably attended in the judgment of the Convention, and has not departed without leave." Laid on the table.

Mr. E. W. M. MACKEY moved to insert in the sixth line, "and the Janitor $4 a day."

Mr. B. F. WHITTEMORE moved to amend the amendment by inserting "$5 a day."

Mr. ALLEN moved to lay that amendment on the table, which wat agreed to.

Mr. B. F. WHITTEMORE then accepted the first amendment offered by the gentleman from Orangeburg (Mr. E. W. M. MACKEY.)

The question was next taken on the following amendment to the first section offered by Mr. B. F. WHITTEMORE: "That the members and officers of this Convention be paid in the 'Bills Receivable' of this State, which are not on a par with United States currency."

Mr. B. F. WHITTEMORE. It was understood yesterday that payment of the members is to be made in an amount of Bills Receivable of the State, equivalent to $8 in greenbacks or legal tender.

Mr. F. J. MOSES, Jr. Suppose the members are paid off this afternoon, and they are given a certain amount of State money to make up $8 in greenbacks, and to-morrow morning there is a change. If I purchase gold with the State money how is the difference to be arranged?

Mr. B. F. WHITTEMORE. If I purchase gold to day, and pay one dollar and a half for it, and it goes down to-morrow to one dollar and twenty five cents, I will be compelled to sell it at that rate, if I wish to make an exchange.

Mr. R. J. DONALDSON. I understood the gentleman from Darlington (Mr. B. F. WHITTEMORE), proposed that each member should have the privilege of receiving pay in greenbacks or bills receivable.

Mr. B. F. WHITTEMORE. My desire is that the Journal should show what we are actually receiving. In the present shape of the Ordinance, we are made to appear as if we are receiving eleven dollars per day, whereas we are not receiving that amount in legal tender. We are receiving eleven dollars in bills receivable of the State, subject to all the fluctuations of the market. Now if we are to receive eight dollars in United States currency, let us announce that distinctly. If the Convention fixes upon five dollars, let it be five dollars in United States currency. If we are to receive our pay in bills receivable at eighty cents on the dollar, I desire that a sufficient amount of those bills should be sold to make up the pay agreed upon in United States currency.

Mr. C. C. BOWEN. I have the same objection to the amendment that I made yesterday. I stated then I was willing to take whatever the majority of the Convention thought fit. If we cannot be paid in United States currency, we are compelled to take whatever we can get. The proposition to pay a fixed sum in United States currency, has not and cannot be made. I am, therefore, opposed to any amendment. The proposition is to take this money at its market value, which to-day is eighty cents on the dollar. We get an amount to-day at that rate sufficient to make up eight dollars in greenbacks. Our names go on the record as receiving that much, and to-morrow before we have an opportunisy of disposing of the bills receivable they may go down to twenty-five cents on the dollar. If we have to take these bills receivable, and take the chances of a depreciation, I am willing to let the Ordinance stand as it is.

Mr. B. F. RANDOLPH. I am in favor of the Ordinance as it stands, so that we can be paid off, even if the bills go down to twenty-five cents on the dollar.

Mr. DUNCAN. I think the fears of the gentleman from Charleston are altogether groundless. It must be remembered that this money is receivable for all State taxes, which will be about $350,000. I have already heard of persons writing from the country offering ninety cents on the dollar, for the purpose of paying their taxes. I do not think we need have any apprehension of these bills falling so low.

Mr. A. J. RANSIER. I really think nothing is better calculated to depreciate this currency than the arguments made on the floor of the Convention. They would almost lead to the impression that these bills are worth nothing. I understand from dealers they are now worth about eighty-five cents on the dollar, and as the faith of the State is pledged for their redemption, I cannot see even if $75,000 be thrown upon the market why they should depreciate more than thirty per cent. at the farthest. Being in favor of fixing the per diem at not more than $6, or $7 at the utmost, I will vote for the original Ordinance as reported by the Committee. Even if the bills depreciate fifteen per cent. more, the pay under the Ordinance would amount to $7.25 per day, and that ought to satisfy every reasonable man.

Mr. N. G. PARKER. As Chairman of the Finance Committee, I wish to say that while I sympathise with the views of the gentleman from Darlington (Mr. WHITTEMORE), I do not advocate his amend. ment. I do not see any other way for the prompt payment of the members than the one proposed. There is due now $50,000 in taxes, which must be paid on or before the 31st of March. When I visited the Tax Collector to-day to pay my taxes, he informed me that the money is coming in rapidly. That shows that those who wish to pay their taxes are now seeking bills receivable, for fear they will rise in value. I think there is no doubt this money will appreciate continually from now to the 31st of March.

Mr. W. J. WHIPPER. I hope the amendment of the gentleman from Darlington will be lost. I am willing to take whatever a majority of the house decides upon. The Finance Committee have informed us that it will be impossible to pay off in greenbacks. I am willing, therefore, to let the amount of our pay be fixed in bills receivable, and take the chances of a rise or fall. One thing is certain, the taxes can be paid in these bills, and I feel assured the members will have an interest in keeping up the value of these bills, and will not rush the money unnecessarily upon the market; that they will sell them only as they are compelled to supply their immediate wants. I move that the amendment be laid upon the table.

The question was taken on the motion to lay the amendment on the table, and was agreed to.

The question was then taken on the passage of the Ordinance to a third reading, which was decided in the affirmative and the Ordinance ordered to be engrossed, as follows:

AN ORDINANCE

Defining the Pay and Mileage of Members and Officers of this Convention.

SECTION 1. *And be it ordained,* That the pay per diem of the President shall be $00; members, $11; Sergeant-at-Arms, $11; Secretary, $11; Assistant Sergeant-at-Arms, $8; Assistant Secretary, $8; Engrossing Clerk, $7; Reading Clerk, $7; Doorkeeper, $8; Assistant Doorkeeper, $6; two Messengers, $5 each; Janitor, $4; in bills receivable of the State, which have not the par value of United States currency.

SEC. 2. *And be it further ordained,* That the mileage of members and officers of the Convention shall be (20) twenty cents per mile to and from the Convention, by the usual mail routes.

SEC. 3. *And be it further ordained,* That all payments made in conformity to the several provisions of this Ordinance, or Ordinances, shall be upon the recommendation of the Finance Committee and upon the authority of the President of the Convention.

The Convention adjourned.

FIFTEENTH DAY.

Friday, January 31, 1868.

The Convention assembled at 12 M., and was called to order by the PRESIDENT.

Prayer was offered by the Rev. W. E. JOHNSTON.

The roll was called, and a quorum answering to their names, the PRESIDENT announced the Convention ready to proceed to business.

The journal of the preceding day was read and approved.

Mr. J. M. RUTLAND, from the Committee on the Legislative part of the Constitution, made the following report, which was adopted:

The Committee, to whom was referred the resolutions requesting the organization of a new judicial district out of contiguous portions of Barnwell, Edgefield, Lexington, and Orangeburg, beg leave respectfully to report that they have had the same under consideration, and recommend that the subject be left to the future action of the Legislature, the Committee having incorporated in the Legislative part of the Constitution a section providing for all such cases.

Respectfully submitted,

J. M. RUTLAND, Chairman.

The PRESIDENT stated to the Convention that he had a personal conference with General Canby last evening, and was satisfied from the statement received from the General Commanding, that the object of sending the police force was to protect the Convention rather than to take any supervision of the body. It was ordered for the purpose of protecting the Convention from what, according to outside rumors, brought to his notice, he thought might occur. The PRESIDENT said he had not seen or had any conference with General Clitz. On his arrival here this morning, a Sergeant of Police with a squad of men were outside. The Sergeant informed him that he was ordered by the Mayor to report to the PRESIDENT of the Convention for orders. As the matter was in the hands of the body, and a resolution adopted to have no policemen on the floor until the Committee appointed on the subject was heard from, he had directed them to remain outside until the pleasure of the Convention was known.

Mr. T. J. COGHLAN offered the following, which was referred to the Committee on Miscellaneous Matters :

WHEREAS, the prosperity of the State, like that of families, depends on the harmony existing among its members, and the precepts of true religion teaches us to do unto others as we would they should do unto us ; and

Whereas, our newly enfranchised citizens have displayed their good sense and strong love of country by a cordial and unassuming co-operation with the rest of their fellow citizens, in promoting the true interests of our beloved State and glorious Republic ; be it

Resolved, That this Convention take such action as it may in its wisdom deem compatible with its powers, and conducive to the public weal, to expunge forever from the vocabulary of South Carolina, the epithets " negro," " nigger," and " Yankee," as used in an opprobious sense.

Resolved, That the exigencies and approved civilization of the times demand that this Convention, or the legislative body created by it, enact such laws as will make it a penal offence to use the above epithets in the manner described against an American citizen of this State, and to punish the insult by fine or imprisonment.

27

Mr. B. F. RANDOLPH said : As a member of the Committee on Miscellaneous Matters, he hoped the gentleman who introduced the above resolutions would also give the Committee some instructions upon them.

Mr. B. F. RANDOLPH offered the following, which was referred to the Committee on Miscellaneous Matters :

Resolved, That institutions for the benefit of the insane, blind, deaf and dumb, and the poor, shall always be fostered and supported by this State, and shall be subject to such regulations as the General Assembly may direct.

Resolved, That the Directors of the Penitentiary shall be elected or appointed as the General Assembly may direct.

Resolved, That the Trustees of benevolent and other State institutions as may be hereafter created, shall be appointed by the Governor, by and with the consent of the Senate ; and upon all nominations made by the Governor, the questions shall be taken by yeas and nays, and entered upon the Journals.

Resolved, That the Governor shall have power to fill all vacancies that may occur in the offices aforesaid, and said appointees shall hold over to the next meeting of the General Assembly, and until a successor is qualified and confirmed by the Senate.

Mr. S. CORLEY offered the following, which was referred to the Committee on the Judiciary :

WHEREAS, the rebel Legislature of South Carolina did authorize guardians to invest the funds of their several wards in Confederate bonds ; and

Whereas, the present Provisional Government fully endorses the said Act, by the operation of which many innocent and helpless orphans have lost their entire estates, and the said bonds are now being tendered by guardians in lieu of United States currency toward a final settlement of all such claims ; therefore,

Resolved, That in the opinion of this Convention the legislation authorizing a tender of Confederate bonds by guardians in settling the claims of their wards is a monstrous wrong, contrary to the Constitution and laws of the United States, and therefore null and void ; and that all the parties concerned are now in the same legal relation as though no such legislation had ever been enacted.

Resolved, That the Committee on the Judiciary be directed to prepare an Ordinance, which will reach all classes of this complicated swindle ; and determine whether or not guardians who sold property, or invested the proceeds, during the rebellion, are entitled to any exception or favor on that particular ground.

Mr. J. J. WRIGHT moved to lay the above resolutions on the table, which was not agreed to.

Mr. CORLEY also offered the following, which was referred to the Committee on the Judiciary :

WHEREAS, the people of South Carolina have now the advantage of a penitentiary system for the punishment of criminals; and

Whereas, the State is now in a condition to protect the lives, property and best interests of every class of its population, without resort to extreme modes of punishment; and

Whereas, there is no imperative demand for capital punishment when society can otherwise protect itself against the depravity and violence of the lawless; therefore

Resolved, That it be referred to the Legislative Committee to determine whether or not the following, or a similar clause, shall be incorporated in the Constitution of the State, to wit:

"That no violation of the laws of this State shall be deemed a capital offence; that imprisonment for life shall be substituted for the death penalty; and for a less offence than murder, the period of incarceration shall be graduated to accord with the moral progress of the criminal, in conformity to the provisions of a wholesome prison discipline."

Mr. CORLEY offered the following, which was referred to the Finance Committee:

WHEREAS, the several Banks of the State have, by the suspension of specie payments during the war and since, forfeited their charters; and, whereas, by their complicity in the Confederate swindle, they have forfeited the respect and confidence of the people of this commonwealth, therefore

Resolved, That the Committee be requested to report some action designed to secure the people, in the future, against such a system of legalized swindling, by requiring that hereafter no such corporations shall be allowed to conduct any banking operations whatever, otherwise than upon the real amount of capital employed, and that the members of all such corporations shall be held amenable to the common law enacted for the government of all other citizens of the State.

Resolved, That whether or not the issues of the Bank of the State, prior to the war, are pledges by the people to the people of this commonwealth, and if they are, having pledged this Convention against the repudiation of every form, it remains for us to distinguish between repudiation in a collective and in an individual capacity, and, failing to do so, that some plan to redeem their pledges be reported.

Mr. B. O. DUNCAN, in view of the statement of the President regarding the police force, moved that the action of the house yesterday on the subject be reconsidered, and that the matter be left with the President to give instructions to the police hereafter.

Mr. B. BYAS moved to lay the motion on the table, which was not agreed to.

Mr. R. J. DONALDSON asked that the original motion be withdrawn until the Committee to wait on General Clitz could be heard from.

Mr. B. O. DUNCAN thought the report of the President sufficient.

Mr. W. J. WHIPPER hoped the motion would be voted down, as the Committee were then out, and, on their arrival, it would be time enough to act. The report of the Committee might throw some light on the subject requiring different action.

The question was taken, and the Convention refused to reconsider its action of the previous day.

Mr. J. M. RUTLAND moved that when the Convention adjourn, it stand adjourned until 12 o'clock Monday. Mr. RUTLAND stated that his object in offering the resolution was to give time to the Committee to have a conference in reference to the Constitution, in order to shape it for presentation to the Convention Monday.

The motion was agreed to.

Mr. S. A. SWAILS presented the petion of sundry citizens of Williamsburg District, which was referred to the Committee on Petitions.

Mr. N. G. PARKER offered the following, which was referred to the Committee on Miscellaneous Matters :

Resolved, That it shall be the duty of the General Assembly to provide for the organization of cities and incorporation of towns, and to restrict their powers of assessment and taxation.

Mr. A. C. RICHMOND offered the following:

WHEREAS, considering that several members of this body deem it desirable to offer numerous and divers resolutions, apprehending possibly that the voice of the people may be heard asking why all the delegates do not offer resolutions for the good of this people, that the homeless shall have homes, the houseless houses, the landless lands, the moneyless money, and that debtors shall be debtors no more, Confederate scrip no scrip, that all shall sin no more ; therefore be it

Resolved, That of one blood were made all the nations of the earth, that the poor shall always be with us, that the hungry will always need food, the naked clothing, the landless land, the homeless homes, and the moneyless money ; in fine that all future legislation should be in the interests of humanity, of justice and protection to the poor, and justice and security to the rich.

Mr. T. HURLEY moved that the above be referred to a Committee on Spiritualism.

The resolution and motion not being seconded, were not received, and no question taken on their adoption.

The Ordinance defining the pay of members was taken up, read a third time, and adopted as follows :

AN ORDINANCE

Defining the Pay and Mileage of Members and Officers of the Convention.

Sec. 1. *And be it ordained,* That the pay per diem of the Members shall be (eleven dollars) $11; Sergeant-at-Arms (eleven dollars) $11; Secretary (eleven dollars) $11; Assistant Sergeant-at-Arms (eight dollars) $8; Assistant Secretary (eight dollars) $8; Engrossing Clerk (eight dollars) $8; Reading Clerk (seven dollars) $7; Doorkeeper (eight dollars) $8; Assistant Doorkeeper (six dollars) $6; Two Messengers (five dollars) $5 each; and Janitor (four dollars) $4, in bills receivable of the State, which have not the par value of United States currency.

Sec. 2. *And be it further ordained,* That the mileage of members and officers of the Convention, shall be (20) twenty cents per mile to and from the Convention by the usual mail routes.

Sec. 3. *And be it further ordained,* That all payments made in conformity to the several provisions of this Ordinance or Ordinances, shall be upon the recommendation of the Finance Committee, and upon the authority of the PRESIDENT of the Convention.

Messrs. B. O. DUNCAN, Dr. N. J. NEWELL, and WM. B. JOHNSTON, asked leave to record their votes in the negative.

Mr. L. S. LANGLEY moved that the vote by which the above Ordinance was passed be reconsidered, and that the motion to reconsider be laid upon the table. Carried.

Mr. N. G. PARKER moved that the printer be paid weekly.

Mr. C. P. LESLIE moved to amend, by adding the words "after this week." If this was not done, the printer would want the whole $12,000 received from Columbia.

The amendment was adopted.

Mr. J. K. JILLSON called for the report of the Committee appointed to wait upon General Clitz.

Mr. B. F. WHITTEMORE, Chairman of the Special Committee appointed to wait upon General Clitz, reported that they had seen that gentleman, and he had stated that by order of General Canby, he requested the Mayor of the city to furnish, yesterday, a Sergeant and five policemen, to be in attendance at the Hall of the Convention, and to be ready for any order they may receive from the PRESIDENT. General Clitz said the police were sent to prevent occurrences similar to that which occurred on the floor of the Convention the other day between a member of the body and a representative of the press of the city.

General Clitz also remarked that the Sergeant had no instructions to come upon the floor of the house, but to remain outside, ready for any call made by the PRESIDENT, and that he transcended his orders in coming inside the Convention.

Mr. F. J. MOSES, Jr., offered the following:

Resolved, That the house receive the explanation tendered to the Committee by General Clitz, of the motives which led him in ordering the Mayor to send a body of policemen to the Convention as satisfactory, and that the Committee be discharged. Carried.

The PRESIDENT stated that the resolution adopted by the Convention yesterday that no policeman be admitted to the floor until the report of the Committee, expired by its own limitation. It was now proper for the Convention to take such action as they might think proper with reference to the policemen sent to this body.

Mr. B. F. WHITTEMORE moved that the policemen remain outside of the door of the Convention, subject to the order of the PRESIDENT, which was agreed to.

Mr. T. HURLEY moved to reconsider the vote whereby the Ordinance annulling all contracts for slaves, was made the Special Order for one o'clock Monday, which was not agreed to.

Mr. B. BYAS moved to take up from the table a resolution offered by him to have a clock placed ever the PRESIDENT'S chair, which was not agreed to.

On motion of Mr. N. G. PARKER, the Convention adjourned.

SIXTEENTH DAY.

Monday, February 3, 1868.

The Convention assembled at 12 M., and was called to order by the PRESIDENT.

Prayer was offered by the Rev. H. D. EDWARDS.

The roll was called, and a quorum answering to their names, the PRESIDENT announced the Convention ready to proceed to business.

The Journal of Friday's proceedings were read and approved.

The PRESIDENT stated that he had been informed since his arrival that several of the Standing Committees on the Constitution were ready to report. It would be proper, if the Convention so desired it, to have the reports printed, and made the order of some day, giving time to the printer to have them ready to lay upon the tables of the members. If the reports were read, the hour for the Special Order would intervene, and the reports would have to be suspended.

Mr. B. O. DUNCAN moved that the reports be read by their title, and printed, which was agreed to.

Mr. F. L. CARDOZO moved to suspend the Special Order, which was not agreed to.

Mr. R. B. ELLIOTT moved to amend by making the reports the Special Order for one o'clock Wednesday, which was agreed to.

Mr. B. F. WHITTEMORE, Chairman, presented the Bill of Rights.

Mr. J. M. RUTLAND presented the report of the Committee on the Legislative part of the Constitution.

Mr. C. C. BOWEN presented the report of the Committee on the Judiciary.

Mr. F. L. CARDOZO presented the report of the Committee on Education.

Mr. B. F. RANDOLPH rose to say that the press of the country was doing them injustice, as they were everywhere reported as receiving $11 per day. He therefore offered the following :

Resolved, That the Present of the Convention be requested to inform the Associated Press at the North that the actual pay of the delegates of this body is only about seven dollars and a half per day in United States currency.

Mr. W. J. WHIPPER moved that the gentleman be requested to forward the information himself.

On motion of Mr. F. J. MOSES, Jr., the resolution was laid on the table.

Mr. B. F. RANDOLPH offered the following, which was referred to the Committee on the Miscellaneous Provisions of the Constitution :

Resolved 1st. The General Assembly shall provide for the organization and equipment of an efficient militia, which the Governor shall have power to call forth to execute the laws, suppress insurrection and repel invasion.

2d. All male citizens, residents of this State, being eighteen years of age, and under forty-five years of age, shall be enrolled in the militia, except those persons exempted by the laws of the United States.

3d. Persons whose religious tenets, or conscientious scruples, forbid them to bear arms, shall not be compelled to do so, but shall pay an equivalent for personal service.

4th. The Adjutant-General and Quartermaster-General shall be appointed by the Governor, but all other officers shall be appointed, elected, and serve as the General Assembly may direct.

Mr. B. O. DUNCAN offered the following resolution, which was agreed to :

Resolved, That a Committee, consisting of two from each Congressional District of the State, as they existed in 1860, prior to the act of secession of the 19th December, 1860, be appointed by the President, to inquire and report to this Convention, what number of representatives it will be proper, according to the present law of the United States, that this State shall elect to the Congress of the United States ; and that the Committee shall also report on a suitable construction of the Congressional Districts, according to representatives allowed us.

Mr. DUNCAN also offered the following, which was referred to the Committee on the Judiciary :

WHEREAE, a large proportion of the executors, administrators, guardians, and other fiduciary agents, appointed in this State prior to and during the late rebellion, either actually did or fraudulently pretended to have invested the funds and estates of their *cestui que trusts* in the securities of the rebel States, created for the purpose of carrying on war against the United States;

And whereas, investments made in such securities in aid of the said rebellion, was not only treason against the United States, but when made by trustees and other fiduciary agents, a fraud upon the rights of the persons whom they were appointed to represent, and who were legally incompetent to protect their own interests ; be it therefore

Resolved, That all investments of the funds and estates of infants, married women, idiots, lunatics, and other *cestui que trusts*, in the securities of the late rebel government, or in the securities of any one of the rebel States, created for the purpose of carrying on war against the United States, by executors, administrators, guardians, masters and commissioners in equity, trustees, and other judiciary agents, are, and shall forever hereafter, be held to be absolutely null and void, and no plea or pretence of any such investments shall avail in any court of law or equity in this State to bar or hinder any *cestui que trust* from recovering his, her or their estate in lawful money of the United States of America.

Resolved, That it be referred to the Committee on the Judiciary, to draft a provision to this effect, to be inserted in the Constitution to be framed by this Convention.

Mr. R. G. HOLMES presented the petition of sundry citizens of Beaufort, praying for the change of the location of the Court House of that District to that town. Referred to the Committee on Petitions.

Mr. J. K. JILLSON offered the following, which was referred to the Committee on Franchise and Elections :

Resolved, That every male person of the age of twenty-one years, or upwards, belonging to either of the following classes, who shall have resided in the State for one year next preceding any election, shall be deemed a qualified voter at the time of each election :

1st. Citizens of the United States.

2d. Persons of foreign birth who shall have declared their intention become citizens, conformably to the laws of the United States on the subject of naturalization, and the provisions of the Constitution of the United States.

3d. No person under guardianship, *non compos mentis*, or insane, shall be qualified to vote at any elections; nor shall any person convicted of treason or rebellion against this State, or the United States, or of felony, be qualified to vote at any election, unless restored to civil rights.

All votes shall be given by ballot except for such township officers as may, by law, be directed by the Legislature to be otherwise chosen.

No person shall be deemed to have lost his residence in this State by reason of absence on business of the United States or of this State.

Laws may be passed excluding from the right of suffrage all persons who have been or may be convicted of bribery or of larceny, or of any infamous crime, and depriving every person who shall make or become directly or indirectly interested in any bet or wager depending upon the result of any election, from the right to vote at such election.

No soldier, seaman, or marine, in the army or navy of the United States, shall be deemed a resident of this State in consequence of being stationed within the same.

Mr. C. P. LESLIE, as a member of the Committee on Franchise and Elections, said the Committee would be ready to report at an early day, and returned his thanks to the gentleman offering the above resolutions for the magnanimity and generosity they displayed.

Mr. J. H. RAINEY offered the following, which was agreed to:

Resolved, That this Convention do hereby declare to the people of South Carolina, and to the world, that they have no land or lands at their disposal, and in order to disabuse the minds of all persons whatever throughout the State who may be expecting a distribution of land by the Government of the United States through the Bureau of Refugees, Freedmen and Abandoned Lands, or in any other manner, that no act of confiscation has been passed by the Congress of the United States, and it is the belief of this Convention that there never will be, and that the only manner by which any land can be obtained by the landless will be to purchase it.

Mr. J. H. RAINEY also offered the following resolution, which was referred to the Committee on Legislation:

WHEREAS, the general good, which it is the theory and policy of the law to promote, has been heretofore prejudiced by the mal-practice of conducting in Charleston proceedings for and effecting, by Charleston officers, sales of property located in the country Districts; and, whereas, this objectionable practice is at once violative of the aforesaid theory and policy, and destructive to a certain extent of the interest of whole communities; therefore be it

Resolved, That it be referred to the Committee on Legislation to inquire into and report to this Convention upon the expediency of provid-

28

ing by Ordinance that all public sales of property hereafter made in this State, shall take place in the several Districts in which the property sold is situated, and that all titles, warrants and other papers, in reference to said sales, shall be only recorded or deposited in the proper public offices of such District

The hour for the consideration of the Special Order having arrived, "An Ordinance to annul all contracts and liabilities for the purchase of slaves, where the money has not been paid," Mr. C. C. BOWEN stated that the Judiciary Committee had reported an Ordinance, which was read.

Mr. B. O. DUNCAN. The question before us to day, is one of relief in a different form from the one we had up last week. As that measure was stamped by its opponents as a *stay-law*, for the sake of killing it, and as it has become fashionable for every one to set himself right on the question of relief, it may be allowable for me to state here more clearly what was my understanding of the petition to General Canby, and my idea of relief. I wish it definitely understood, once for all, that I am no repudiationist, and no advocate for stay-laws. I am opposed to both in principle, and on constitutional grounds. I thought at first, and still think, that, as a matter of abstract justice, old debts should be scaled, somewhat to accord with the present value of property, or that the property itself should be returned as pay. That, however, I do not regard as at all like repudiation. But even that idea I have now given up, and will be satisfied if we succeed in the measure now before us, and in establishing a liberal homestead law, to be retrospective. I believe we can establish both, so they will stand the test of the courts : and, as to the absolute necessity of affording all the relief possible to the country, I am confident no intelligent man in this Convention for one moment doubts. Indeed, there is scarcely a prominent member in the Convention, who has not spoken out freely in favor of relief. It is so manifest that the future welfare of the country demands relief for all classes alike, that no one is willing to have his name recorded as opposed to it.

Now, as I understood the petition to General Canby, it was only to gain time to mature other measures of relief—not to repudiate, or to enact a stay-law of longer duration.

One of the measures proposed, we have before us now ; the other, we will have before us in the discussion of the homestead law in the Constitution.

We will now enter upon the examination of the question before us, and hope to establish clearly, that we have the power to annul all debts or obligations of any kind for slaves, and that justice and the future welfare of the country demand that we should do so. I am well aware that the most troublesome point in the way is the right of contract. But is not the very essence of every contract, value for value ? If I sell a piece of property, and it is afterwards found that the property is not sound, or that the titles to it are not good, I am not entitled to pay for it, because there has not been value for value. It makes no difference whatever, as to whether or not I knew the property was not sound, or the titles not safe. Is not this exactly the case with contracts for slaves ? The very essence of all contracts—value for value— has been violated in all contracts for slaves during the last ten or twenty years. The titles to slave property have been found entirely unsound, and are consequently in the eyes of the law null and void. So that in either view of the case, as to the validity of the titles, or as to the sacredness of contracts, we are entitled to set aside all these contracts, as in the eyes of the law, absolutely illegal, null and void.

Again, all of us in this Convention admit that slavery was a great moral and political evil—a crime against civilization and Christianity. In the light of justice and of true Christianity, it never would have legally existed. The institution was a relic of barbarism, inherited from our fathers, and from the very scum of all lawless desperadoes, the African slave traders. Shall we now, after having succeeded in getting free from this terrible curse, still continue to recognize its legality in any shape or form ? Was it not bad enough to be forced to recognize it while it existed, without continuing to do so since it has ceased to exist ? Then, we had a most potent reason for recognizing it ; we could not help it. But now it depends entirely upon ourselves. I am convinced, that properly considered, leaving out prejudice and personal interest, no one in this Convention would think of opposing this measure, which proposes to annul forever all rights growing out of slavery. But here, we are not left to our own resources. These contracts have been set aside in various places. If I am not mistaken, the United States District Court of Louisiana has decided against their validity. General Sickles, who is an able lawyer as well as a true Republican General, set aside all debts for the purchase of slaves. See his order No. 10. This he did in his capacity of military commander. But is it not clear, that he would not have done so, had he considered them valid like other debts ? Again, the Congress of the United States, on the 18th of March, 1867, passed a bill annulling a previous contract to pay for all slaves drafted into the United States army. All of the Republicans and some of the Democrats voted in favor of this, thus clearly showing that they regarded all contracts for slaves as null and void. In view of all these facts, should we, as a Convention, hesitate to do what every principle of justice so clearly demands?

Again, I contend that still to recognize debts or obligations of any kind for slaves, is still to recognize rights in slavery. Are we, the representatives of a party opposed to every principle of slavery, willing that it shall be said of us that we recognize any right growing out of slavery? I believe not. I believe it would little correspond with the professed principles of any white member of this body to do so. Nor do I believe it would comport with the dignity and sense of justice of any colored man to recognize that rights for slaves do now, or ever did legally exist. While I cannot agree with my very enlightened and accomplished friend from Charleston, who says he can never forgive one who has bought or sold a slave, I do most heartily agree with him as to the great wrong of slavery; and I trust that he will agree with me as to the necessity of destroying now and forever, every vestige of slavery, and every semblance of a recognition of rights or obligations of slavery in whatever kind. The opportunity is now afforded us to set aside such claims forever. It is said by some. let the Courts decide this. But I would reply that the Courts must decide according to law, and let us make a law by which they may decide. We are the representatives, direct from the people, with the power to make a Constitution and laws for the people, and Courts to be governed by; even more, to make the Courts themselves. The Courts are our creatures, and without our action they would have no existence.

If we make a Constitution and laws which will be accepted by the people, I believe no State Court will venture to set it aside. Nor do I believe the day is far distant, when the Supreme Court of the United States will cease to recognize any obligations based on slavery. It is the great fundamental principle of our party, that slavery and every thing connected with it, or growing out of it, shall cease to exist. I have all confidence that a principle so just and so noble will overcome all obstacles. Let us, as the representatives of such principles in South Carolina, not fail at the very threshhold to do our duty.

A few words in reply to the gentleman from Fairfield, who opposed this measure last week. I can imagine two reasons why he, as a lawyer, should oppose this proposition. The one—his great desire that there should not be even a semblance of violation of law. But if he will go back of the law, to what should be the foundation of all law, to the principles of justice, his objection on this point must fall to the ground. The other reason is one common to all lawyers, and which may account in some measure for nearly every lawyer opposing any measure of relief, the desire to have as many law suits as possible, and as many people ruined, so they can secure the loaves and fishes. I have too much confidence in my friend from Winnsboro', to think that this latter motive has any influence with him. But I cannot, for the life of me, find any reason why he, as an individual desirous of the prosperity and welfare of the whole people, should oppose a measure, so wise and just, and calculated to afford so much relief.

Mr. J. J. WRIGHT. Mr. President and gentlemen of the Convention : I hope gentlemen who are on the other side of this question, who have been piling up so much for several days past, will not be afraid to discharge it. I presume the gentleman who spoke last, believed that all the members of the legal profession in this Convention were opposed to this Ordinance

Mr. B. O. DUNCAN. I do not think so.

Mr. J. J. WRIGHT. I am decidedly in favor of the measure. I came entertaining no malice, hatred or prejudice, against any person or persons that ever held slaves. I contend that the institution of American slavery never was a legal institution, that it never was so by any Act or law. It was simply regulated by law, and as necessary to regulate it by law as other processes entered into and carried on by men. It was necessary to make very stringent laws in order to protect those who held persons in bondage, because they held in bondage men endowed with all the powers of intellect, capable of being trained and developed. When the intellect of these men were drawn out and developed, then it was that the men who held them began to tremble for their lives, because they were in danger of having their throats cut, or something of the kind. This very fact is sufficient to show that those persons they held were men in every sense of the definition of man. We have, therefore, in order to show the justice of this measure, shown that there can be no property in man. To do this, we only refer to the decisions given by the highest courts in the old world, and those rendered in our own courts, to prove conclusively, that there never has been, nor never could be, property in man. Therefore I lay down this proposition, that whenever a debt was contracted, the proposed consideration of which was a slave, there was no consideration received, and where there was no consideration the debt was null and void. In thus repudiating these debts we do no more than follow the example set us in history, and the example of our own government, which has given us the power to assemble in Convention.

I know it is said by our opponents that we are an unlawful assembly, that we are an unconstitutional body. I do not propose to discuss whether we are or are not, an unlawful or unconstitutional body. I know we are here under the laws of the Congress of the United States, lawfully called together for the discharge of certain duties, and the repudiation of debts contracted for slaves. We are not here to establish any new precedents. I need only refer you to the fourth section of the Constitutional Amendment, which reads as follows: "Any obligation incurred in aid of the rebellion, or any claim for the loss or emancipation of any slave, shall be illegal and void." That is a provision of the Constitutional Amendment which all the Legislatures of the South refused to accept. Under the Reconstruction Act we must adopt this amendment before our State can be restored to the Union. This amendment repudiates all claims for slaves, and would it be wise for us to refuse to carry out the laws under which we are acting? There is another reason why we should repudiate these debts. We are here to lay the foundation for a new government. We are here, I trust, as I have already said, with hatred and malice towards no man who has held a slave. I trust we are here to extend the right hand of fellowship to all, and that our hearts will be filled with the milk of human kindness towards all. But we should repudiate these debts, from the very fact that we are here to lay the foundation for a new government, and in the laying the foundation of a new government it becomes our duty to have no litigation going on in our Courts where the consideration is for slaves.

It is the duty of the Convention to do what? It is our duty to destroy all the elements of the institution of slavery. If we do not, we recognize the right of property in man. We are not to recognize the right of our Courts to go on contending and fighting over these matters. We should not allow them to proceed bringing in their witnesses on each side, and continuing the cases perhaps for half a century, contending over slavery, and discussing whether one man had the right of property in another man.

It is not necessary for us to turn back or appeal to the moral code. It is not necessary for us to look up the decisions of the Courts. It is enough to know that we are men; that the object of the Convention is to give every man an equal chance before the law, and then if he does not show himself a man, then the fault is his and cannot be charged to the Convention. Therefore, let every one of us give our voices and votes in favor of repudiating these debts, and show to the people of South Carolina and to the world that we advocate the broad principles of humanity. I deny that this is a class measure. I believe this measure to be one of the best we can give the people of South Carolina. It is not generally the purchaser who will be the loser, but the seller. Many of these men to whom these debts are due, are those who trafficked in slaves and came from all parts of the United States. They came from the Northeast and the West. They came with vessels bringing a cargo of slaves, sold them to the people of the South, put what money they could in their pockets, and went back where they belonged. Many of them are now around with their bonds expecting to get their money, and they ought to suffer. I believe the repudiation of these debts will save many a widow and orphan from starvation, and perhaps from death. I hope we will show to the people of South Carolina, and to the world, that we are not afraid to do our duty, so that those who shall come hereafter cannot rise up and say when this Convention had the privilege of proclaiming that man was a man anywhere and everywhere, at all times, they refused to do it. God forbid that any man in the Convention should vote against the repudiation of these bonds.

Mr. R. C. DeLARGE. I did not think any extended argument in favor of the repudiation of these bonds necessary. I believe every member upon the floor, with one or two exceptions, have already decided that these debts shall and must be repudiated. I simply rise, as no one on my side of the house has attempted to reply to the delegate from Newberry. The opposition have failed to respond, but have worked hard and have been vigilant amongst the members before the meeting of the Convention. I desire to correct a misapprehension made upon the minds of members by the remarks of the delegate from Lexington last week. In his speech he argued that in the repudiation of these bonds only one class of landholders would suffer, and the other class go free. The only way to make both classes, seller and purchaser, suffer, is to repudiate these bonds. A simple incident would illustrate this. At the sale of a certain estate in the city, a slave broker purchased three families, took them to New Orleans, and from thence to Montgomery, Alabama, but failed to realize the profits anticipated. The brother of the deceased. whose estate was sold, wrote to the broker, and purchased twenty-two of the slaves, agreeing to pay $22,000. Of this amount he paid $11,000 in cash, giving a bond for the other half. The slave broker became insolvent, and the estate never realized anything from the sale of the slaves, but the broker since then has realized his interest on the $11,000 due up to the 1st of January, 1863. The interest accruing since that time would amount to three or four thousand dollars. If, therefore. they fail to repudiate these bonds, they protected one class of slaveholders against another. Again, the State Convention of 1865 abolished slavery, and it would be unjust to require a purchaser to pay for so-called property, taken from him by the Act of the State without any compensation. If they failed now to repudiate these debts, the day might come when the once holders of slaves will clamor for compensation. I hope no member allied to my race will say to the world that he is less than man, or that he acknowledged that he is a fit subject to become property.

Mr. J. M. RUTLAND. I had not intended to speak upon the subject, in consequence of being somewhat indisposed, but I am surprised to hear the gentleman from Newberry set out with a very remarkable assertion that he is no repudiationist, no stay law man, and then repudiate in the very next breath.

In order to get at this question at all, in order to have an opportunity for argument, they had, in the first place, to set aside the Constitution and laws of the United States, and the Constitution and laws of South Carolina, as they have heretofore existed ; and the opposite side had commenced by tirades and appeals upon a question which is peculiarly a legal one and peculiarly within the province of the Courts for their decision, and not for this Convention to waste its time upon. They speak of getting rid of legislation, as one argument in favor of the passage of this Ordinance. I would like to know of the party favoring repudiation, how they are to do justice and carry out their doctrines to do justice, without more legislation than was ever heard of in this country. I would like to know if the man who purchased a slave and paid cash for him was not entitled then to bring action to recover what he had paid, as well as the man whose debt and note for $1,000 or more, were declared null and void. If the slave was not property, the man who paid has a right to recover his thousand dollars.

Mr. J. J. WRIGHT. Is it your desire that the Constitutional Amendment should be adopted when the Legislature assembles ?

Mr. RUTLAND. I am in favor of the Reconstruction laws of Congress, and if the Government of the United States undertake to repudiate these debts, I would say nothing against it, for they have the power. But I contend that this Convention has not the power to repudiate these debts, and the same litigation in reference to them would be carried on in the Courts as if the Ordinance was not passed. They would declare it an unconstitutional Ordinance, which, according to the old laws of the United States, and the laws of South Carolina, it undoubtedly is. I never did believe one man had the right to make property of another. But they were bound to respect the laws as they existed, and he wished to let the Courts decide whether a warrant or title to property to make it binding, should ensure against revolutions, earthquakes, and every thing else. Conversing with a gentleman on the subject, I put two or three questions to him. I asked where the cash was paid for a slave, what would he do in a case like that? He replied he would make the seller pay the money. I then asked what course he would take where the man had used slaves twelve or sixteen years, without payment of either principal or interest? He replied he would demand payment for the time they were used.

The result of the action of the Convention in repudiating these debts would be to saddle the country with a litigation which would have no end. It would run back as far as slavery itself. There would be no such thing as a statute of limitations, and the litigation would devour the country and ruin it. General Sickles' celebrated order No. 10 has been quoted as sustaining the position of those on the other side. I think, however, we should not quote the orders of a military chieftain who has despotic power, and can pass any order he pleases. General Sickles had a right to pass any order and enforce it by the bayonet, and General Canby has the same power. But they certainly cannot be viewed as legal authority on the great questions involved here. If this measure succeeds, I look upon it as another entering wedge to a general repudiation of all indebtedness. The next step will be a repudiation of some other debts. It will go forth to the world that this Convention is a body of repudiationists. I contend it is a class measure. It is repudiating a debt in favor of one party, rewarding the man who purchased the slave and has not paid for him, and punishing the seller to extent of the value of the purchase. A great appeal is made in behalf of widows and orphans. I think the appeal would come more properly from my side. Many of the estates of widows and orphans consists entirely of notes of this character. Their estates were sold and the money given in notes and bonds. If this Ordinance passes, more widows and orphans will suffer from it than from any other measure we could pass. When the head of a family dies, it has been the custom of this country, in almost all instances to sell the property and convert it into bonds. These bonds are now in existence belonging to widows and orphans.

I say we have no right to consider the consequences of any measure we pass. Our duty is to do justice, and let the consequences take care of themselves. I will illustrate my opinion upon this subject by a homely comparison. Two strange dogs have commenced fighting over a bone, and they are fighting for that bone. This Convention has nothing to do with the fight, and I say let them fight it out in the proper place, and which ever wins the bone let him have it. We have nothing to do with it, and I hope we will not. If we get the country involved in this

29

quarrel, we will increase litigation to an extent of which no man can conceive.

Mr. B. F. WHITTEMORE. I had hoped this subject would have been referred to a period so distant that the Convention would not be called upon to consider it. The Convention had declared it would not enter into any scheme of repudiation. It was the fear that some question of repudiation might spring up that compelled me to vote against the resolution requesting relief of General Canby in the collection of debts. I wish to know if the Convention, called for the specific purpose of framing a Constitution, is really willing to lend all their efforts in the repudiation of debts and the impairing of the obligations of the people, and willing to acknowledge that fact not only to the State, but to the whole country. One gentleman had said that value for value is the foundation of all contracts, and that no value has been received when the bill payable has been given for a human body. I ask are we not compelled to acknowledge with shame, and a blush on our faces, that the United States has protected the right of property in man.

A man who purchased a slave, giving his note payable at a certain date, received what was acknowledged in South Carolina, and throughout the entire South, by the Constitution of this State and the Constitution of the country, a fair consideration.

The people of this portion of the country have said to the world that they went into the war with their property, their lives, and all that they possessed, even their sacred honor, and they claim, even as they came up from the field of carnage, that they had lost everything but their honor; and now, gentlemen, would sully that honor by endeavoring to wipe out their responsibilities and impair their obligations. God knows there is no desire on my part to do aught that would acknowledge the right of property in man I would go as far as any gentleman on this floor in denying any such right, but we are compelled to acknowledge that our country has acknowledged the right of property in man. It is no new virtue in me that I entertain anti-slavery principles, having been educated where every institution and everything I looked upon was free. It is no new virtue in me that I believed the right of property in man, as acknowledged by my country, was one of the most abominable creations that ever entered into the heart or mind of man ; but I am compelled to acknowledge that my government has acknowledged that right. I am compelled to believe with my legal friend, that we have no right to pass this Ordinance ; that in doing it we are passing an *ex post facto* law, by saying that one gentleman shall not pay the debts he owes to another. If the debtor and creditor both desire it, let them come before the Convention and express their desire. I would leave this matter in the hands of the Courts, to where it properly belongs.

Although I do not pretend to be a man of legal attainments, I may say I place a different construction on that part of the fourth section of the Constitutional Amendment which has been quoted by my friend from Beaufort (Mr. J. J. WRIGHT) It reads, " neither the United States, or any State, shall assume or pay any obligation or any claim, or loss created by the war or by emancipation." By this clause, as I conceive it, the United States Government intends to convey the idea that neither South Carolina, Georgia, or any other Southern State that entered into insurrection, can have claims against the United States Government, or claim any indemnity for the loss of any slaves. Much has been said with regard to admitting the right of property in man, by compelling the purchaser of a slave to pay his obligations. I contend we have nothing to do with that question—that question is already settled.

Mr. J. J. WRIGHT. Do you intend to give your influence and vote in favor of the Constitutional Amendment to be adopted by the Legislature ?

Mr. B. F. WHITTEMORE. I spent a good part of last year in bringing about this Convention, and I intend still further to work and uphold all bills which Congress may enact. But I say the question of the right of property in man has already been settled by the effect and results of the war, and these obligations are now existing. I believe if the voice of the people of this commonwealth, if their hearts and minds could be reached, it would show that they have no desire that this Convention shall pass upon their contracts or obligations. It has been my fortune, not only to have conversations with gentlemen of standing, but I have received letters upon this subject, and in no instance, save one, has there been any desire expressed by any one to have such an Ordinance passed as would nullify their debts contracted for the purchase of of slaves. They claim to be gentlemen of honor, and whatsoever may be the action of the State with regard to their obligations and contracts, they intend to keep them inviolate. To ask them to do otherwise would be the occasion of a call upon Citadel Green, or somewhere else, to settle a little affair of honor, such as has been the custom in the past. When the enemy of the United States entered into a joint compact to overthrow the power of the United States, as I have said, they entered into it with their property and their lives. They made use of their slaves against the United States, and they were declared contraband of war. But that had nothing to do with existing contracts.

The gentleman from Beaufort says he wants to repudiate these debts because the traffickers came from the North, East and West. I care not from what part they come; if they bought and sold slaves, when they entered their obligations they knew what they were about and took their chances We have no right to stand between the debtor and the creditor, or sit in judgment upon an obligation made between two individuals, and say to one he shall not pay, or to the other he shall not receive what is due him. It appears to me our duty is to proceed at once upon the work of framing a Constitution, and not to dig up the past or trouble ourselves about those who have become involved into such difficulties as debts on account of the rebellion against the Government. Let them pay the penalty of their rebellion. I trust all these matters will be referred to the Legislature and Courts to decide.

Mr. L. S. LANGLEY. I have been both interested and astonished by the argument advanced by the gentleman who has just resumed his seat. I am still more astonished when I reflect that the Executive of this State, with all his conservative views, has expressed an opinion entirely contrary to that of the gentleman who has last spoken. We find in the history that the slave trade has been declared by christendom for many years as piracy. That principle was based upon the declaration that there could be no property in man. And I would ask the gentleman what is the difference between the slave trade on the high seas and the slave trade that existed in South Carolina. The same principle that rendered null and void property in man on the high seas, as acknowledged by christendom, is the same that should render null and void in South Carolina property in man.

I do not concur in the views of my colleague (Mr. WRIGHT), that the fourth section of the Constitutional Amendment has any reference to these points. It prohibits the United States, and the States respectively, from assuming debts incurred by selling slaves, but it is not applicable to individuals. I hold all law founded in justice, and if it is right for individuals to pay for slaves, it is right for the Government to pay for them. To be consistent, therefore, if I were to give my vote in this body against the Ordinance we are considering, I would also raise my voice in favor of the Government of the United States paying for every slave emancipated by virtue of the laws of the United States. I would not charge the opposition with the intentoin of advancing their cause, and as a preliminary, asking the General Government to pay for slaves emancipated by the proclamation of Abraham Lincoln. I will not be so illiberal, but I do believe that if we allow these claims to be collected against the citizens of the State, although I must confess, both seller and purchaser are equally guilty, we contradict ourselves and the principles we have heretofore advocated.

I hope the Ordinance will be adopted, and that it will go forth to the State, and to the world, as the opinion of this body, as the opinion of the radical republican party of South Carolina, that there is not, nor cannot be, any right of property in man. I believe that party to be founded on the immutable principles of right and justice. If we at this time are to assume the responsibility of allowing these bonds to be paid, we may as well tear down the flag that to-day floats so proudly over us, and declare to the representatives of the "lost cause" that we have been for the last six years occupying a false position, that we have found ourselves mistaken, that we humbly beg their pardon, and also beg that the former state of things may be restored.

I make no appeal in behalf of orphans or widows, as has been made here to-day. I regret the unfortunate position in which they are placed, if made to suffer by the adoption of this Ordinance. But, if I know myself, I can say in all truth, in all sincerity, my desire is to let principle live forever and always be triumphant, and I therefore cannot, for the sake of a few widows and orphans, take into consideration their sufferings on account of the repudiation of these bonds. We cannot afford to sacrifice principle on their account. If we did, we would acknowledge by our action that the doctrine that existed in South Carolina that slavery was a Divine institution was correct, and that many of the members of this body should return to their former position.

Mr. B. F. RANDOLPH. I have made no attempt heretofore to detain this Convention with a lengthy speech. My health has forbidden it. Neither do I propose to-day to do anything more than to raise my voice in favor of the repudiation of these debts. Two of the gentlemen who have spoken, one from Fairfield and the other from Darlington, have made two propositions. The gentleman from Fairfield, Mr. RUTLAND, has said if two dogs were fighting for a bone he would let them continue to fight. I am not disposed to accuse the gentleman with a lack of generosity, but it seems to me that charity would induce the gentleman to interfere and prevent the poor creatures from injuring each other. If the people of South Carolina propose to fight for a bone, I think this Convention should interfere and not let them tear or destroy themselves.

The gentleman from Darlington (Mr. WHITTEMORE), dwells upon any act of repudiation as wrong. I differ with him. Repudiation is a policy which has been practiced by other nations before us. England has practiced it, and she is regarded as one of the wisest nations in the world ; one whose government has been a model heretofore, and her example followed by other nations. This government has practiced repudiation, and we come here to day to propose that slave debts shall be repudiated. Why ? For no other reason in the world but that we propose to disallow the principle of the right of property in human flesh. If we vote down this Ordinance, we will declare it as our opinion that to hold human flesh as property was right. It well becomes this body to declare that no such ever did, or ever can exist, and if we vote to repudiate these debts, we will, in my opinion, do something which will result to the general welfare of the people of the South. I am here for one to cater to no prejudices whatever. I am aware that in South Carolina there is a class of men who fought for the perpetuation of slavery ; that there is a class who staked their lives, their fortunes, their all in the attempt to perpetuate slavery, and I know that some of the same class of men did all in their power to defeat the assembling of this Convention. These men I know are the enemies of republicanism ; but while I know that to be the fact, I shall not give my voice or vote to a measure which results in the injury of that or any other class of men. We are to act in the interest of the whole people of South Carolina, and I hope we will show that we have acted not in behalf of any particular class, but in the interests of the whole people of the State. I hope we will be above all personal feelings and prejudices, and look only to the general welfare. I think if these debts are repudiated, it will be a wholesale beneficial measure.

As one gentleman who has preceded me (Mr. J. J. WRIGHT) has said, we are here to lay the foundation of a new government for South Carolina. It becomes us to lay it in justice, in righteousness, to show to the world that we know no class or race of men by color or condition. I will give my vote for the repudiation of these slave debts.

Mr. R. B. ELLIOTT. The importance of this subject overcomes my reluctance to obtrude my feeble opinion. I preferred that the matter should have been left to the judicial tribunals of the land ; but it has been presented here, and I deem it the duty of every gentleman in the Convention to express himself candidly, and vote according to his honest convictions. That a system of slave dealing in this State did exist is a fact that cannot be denied. I am aware that it is urged that contracts made in the traffic of slaves were *bona fide* contracts, and have been legalized by the laws of the State. That may also be true. It is urged that Congress by legislation had sanctioned such laws in the State, and such slave dealing by individuals therein. That is also true. But if Congress did sanction it, it does so no longer. If under the laws of the State these slave contracts were *bona fide* contracts, they are so no longer. Congress has declared that no legal government exists in this State. Gentlemen say by passing this Ordinance we will repudiate the obligation of contracts. I contend there never was, nor never can be, any claim to property in man. I regard the seller of the slave as the principal, and the buyer as the accessory. A few years ago the popular verdict of this country was passed upon the slave seller and the slave buyer, and both were found guilty of the enormous crime of slavery. The buyer of the slave received his sentence, which was the loss of the slave, and we are now to pass sentence upon the seller. We propose that he shall be punished by the loss of his money.

I do not intend to discuss this matter at length, but simply desire to express my conviction that it is no more than right to pass this Ordinance, and that it will benefit the people of this State. I hope we will vote unanimously upon this Ordinance, and put our stamp of condemnation upon this remnant of an abominable institution, which was such a stigma upon the justice of this country. I hope we will do away with everything connected with this bastard of iniquity. I feel assured if we pass this Ordinance we will get rid of a question that is calculated, if not stopped, to bring about more trouble and misery than was ever brought upon the country before.

Mr. F. L. CARDOZO. This question is somewhat different from that upon which we voted a fortnight ago. The question then before us was a stay law, a measure of relief for the people by preventing the execution or sale of landed property under the hammer of the Sheriff. This question is in relation to the payment of debts for the purchase of slaves. As I said before, I do not care in the least either about the buyer or seller of a slave. I think them both equally guilty, and should be both equally punished. But in discussing this subject some reflections have been brought in, which are entirely irrelevant. While I admit the force of the arguments used, I cannot regard them as conclusive.

In the first place, the gentleman from Newberry said, that the very essence of all contracts, which was value received, did not exist in this case. I would reply to that by saying that the contractors thought so, and therefore they did exist in their estimation. So it is in all contracts, all sales. If I and another man choose to regard the transfer of a piece of property, we are the parties, we are satisfied, and should in honor abide by our contract. I contend that the buyer did receive the value of his money, and buying a slave, under all the circumstances, he ought to be made to stand by his contract. There is more than that. The buyer not only received the value of his money, but he bought that slave in the midst of a war waged for the abolition of slavery, the corner stone of the war. Every person of ordinary intelligence knew that the existence of slavery was involved in that contest, and yet, in the face of all these circumstances, the buyer of men goes forward and says I will receive your slaves; I will pledge myself to pay five or ten thousand dollars for them. Notwithstanding all the risks I run, I will take them. If then, in spite of all these circumstances, which he knew perfectly well, he took the responsibility, let him, like a man of honor, stand to his contract. I hope, therefore, that point is disposed of. I say that the buyer received the value for his slave and that makes it a legitimate contract, and makes it obligatory upon him to pay for the slave.

Again, a number of gentlemen on the other side said if we make these buyers pay for their slaves, we acknowledge the right of property in man. I cannot see the force of that inference at all. I think it is entirely illogical and untrue, both in fact inference. Here are two men who believe in it; they choose to deal in it; I do not desire to go forward to relieve them of the consequences. They both traded in slaves and suffered the natural result of their risks.

With regard to the effect on the slaveholder, that ought not and can not be legitimately brought into the question at all. I think the gentleman who spoke last gave the true key to the motives which instigated a number of the opposition. He said that the buyer of the slave suffered in the loss of his slave, that the Government had inflicted that loss upon him, and now he is anxious to make the seller suffer also. That is the true character of the Ordinance. We are trying to make the seller suffer also. The true result of the passing of that Ordinance will be to punish the seller. Yet many gentlemen who advocated this measure, have imputed uncharitable motives to those who are willing to let the law take its course. Who, I ask, are the most uncharitable, the men who are desirous to punish the seller, or those willing to leave it entirely to the law? But there is more involved in this question than any gentleman on the opposite side has referred to. These are the last dying throes of the slaveholder. It is the result of a system based upon wrong, and I think we should not go one foot out of our way to help them. Let all those who trafficked in slavery suffer the consequences of their action, and by so doing we stamp indellibly the wrongfulness of the institution. A number of gentlemen have said it is our duty to legislate for the relief of these sufferers. I maintain it is not our duty. We have come here to frame a Constitution, and we should begin our action entirely anew, and not refer to any other existing condition of things whatever.

Again, I am satisfied this measure is a piece of class legislation. It is simply to punish the seller of slaves. Why should we go out of our way to punish anybody? Why should we regard them in any light whatever? It has been argued that we should be free from all class legislation. So we should, and, therefore, for that reason, we should not touch this matter which would only benefit a minority of the people. The very argument brought forward is sufficient to condemn it. We all know that half legislation is class legislation. This kind of legislation has heretofore been the curse of South Carolina and all the slave States.

I shall not condescend to imitate the action of a number of gentlemen who have spoken by imputing motives to their adversaries. It has been done freely by the opposition. I will only say that I hope my tongue may cleave to the roof of my mouth, my right hand be paralized before I urge the oppression of any. I shall always count it a pride to defend the weak and the down-trodden. But I hope we shall have no class legislation. Let us go on and frame our Constitution, looking only to the future, and taking the past as a warning, that will enable us to avoid all actions which have been the cause of so much misery and trouble.

A cunning appeal has been made to the prejudices of the colored people and gentlemen; especially the colored gentlemen on the other side of the question have thought it right and proper to refer to the feelings of the colored man. They said they hoped no colored man would vote against the measure. I, for one, shall vote against it, and I hope many of my colored friends will have the wisdom to do it, notwithstanding the unfounded and inflammatory appeals made by the opposition. It is only to benefit a class, the buyers, and punish the sellers of slaves. I hope we will postpone the subject indefinitely.

Mr. W. J. WHIPPER. I certainly agree as to the importance of this Ordinance as much so as any one here, but should have remained silent had not one main point been overlooked by the parties engaged in the discussion.

It has been said by those of the opposite side that we did not have the power to legislate in this matter. I differ with the gentleman in this respect. We have already acted in our legislative capacity, as has been the case in every Convention. It was the case with Conventions held heretofore in this State, and has been the case with all Conventions of which we have any history, even going as far back as the Conventional Parliament which met before King Charles the Second. It was called an entirely irregular body, but it did legislate, did restore the King, and passed laws and Ordinances, many of which are in force to this day.

Mr. J. M. RUTLAND. I do not contend that this Convention, as a Convention, has no right to legislate on any other matter. I did contend that it had no right to legislate on this particular matter, because I

30

consider it in contravention of the Constitution of the United States to do so.

Mr. W. J. WHIPPER. It has been asserted by several of the members of this body that we obtain our power from the Congress of the United States. I beg leave to differ. While this body was summoned by the Congress of the United States, we derive our power from the people we represent, and being a representative body, a Convention of the people, we have the power to do all that is necessary to relieve or benefit the people we represent. We are not a legislative body whose powers are delegated to us, or limited by any Constitution. It is a Convention of the people, possessed of supreme, absolute powers to do what-ever may be necessary for the relief of the people, just as did the Convention which met after the revolution of 1688, after the throne was abdicated, which not only restored the King, but passed laws yet in force.

But I pass from this question and ask, is there a necessity for the Ordinance we propose to pass? It is an Ordinance intended to do away with a large amount of obligations—obligations that arose in transactions that pertained and belonged to a system that has gone down beneath the wrath of God, giving place to a brighter civilization.

The question now is, shall we wipe out these obligations? I am zealous to see this Ordinance passed, to see the last vestige of that hated institution burried so deep in the sea of oblivion that no resurrection air shall ever reach it in its loathsome walls.

Members speak loud about the obligation of a contract. There was no obligation to the contract. There was no consideration, and therefore no contract. The facts are simply these: men in this portion of the country, for a long period of time, had been conniving at wholesale robbery—robbing, stealing and selling human plunder. Such has been the decision of the Courts of law, such the decision of the immutable laws of God from time immemorial. And whilst men had so far departed from the true principle, government has allowed this system to go on, and men agreed to pay these obligations. If there was a band of horse-thieves in this country, buying and selling horses, and parties buy, knowing they are stolen, other parties sell when stolen, and another man is arrested and brought to justice, is there a Court anywhere that would enforce obligations payable to robbers, legalized though they might be for the time being. If there is anything in this case at all, it is that there was such a law at that time. But admitting there was a law, there is a rule to be applied where wrong or inconvenience is likely to result that local law shall not prevail. Nobody will question but what this was strictly a local law, one that has outraged humanity everywhere, one that has blighted the fair prospects of the fairest portion of our country, destroyed its commerce and desolated its fields. This was tolerated by local law, and local law shall not prevail where great inconvenience and harm is to result from it.

One gentleman says we do not say there is property in man in the enforcement of these debts. If there was the obligation of a contract, there was property in the thing sold. If there was no property in the thing sold there was no obligation, and I hold that men cannot be the subject of property by whatever law you may claim. Just so long then as man is not property now, he never was, and hence there never was an obligation. Again it is said to be be an *ex post facto* law. It is as far from an *ex post facto* law as it is possible for a man to conceive. We are told, also, that this is a quarrel between two gentlemen, and it is proposed to let them fight it out. I am willing they shall, and that the buyer and seller shall settle upon whatever terms they choose, but I am not willing that the machinery of our Courts should be used for the purpose of wringing the bone from the two dogs. I ask, then, that we wipe out this thing forever. We are told to leave it to the Courts. This will only open up avenues for continued agitation.

Mr. F. L. CARDOZO. On what principle do you decide which dog is the meanest?

Mr. WHIPPER. The dog that went and stole the bone first in Africa or elsewhere, is the meanest, and that is the dog the gentleman proposes to pay. Be it said to the eternal honor of South Carolina, she opposed the institution, and it was not until a renegade dog forced the bone upon her, and made it into dollars and cents, that she consented to it.

Again, the man who sold the property, the dog who brought the bone, the seller says upon paper, and makes it as solemn as possible, I will warrant and defend this property. He, at least, is no longer able to warrant and defend. The country that once tolerated the injustice has said it was a crime to hold persons as property. They have said they will attach fine and imprisonment to it, and now, will we say different, and enforce the payment of these so-called obligations?

Whatever course other men may take, I, for my part, will vote for the Ordinance; I feel assured that a large majority will vote for it, not as a matter of expediency, but as a matter of right and as a matter of justice between the parties themselves. I hope we may establish a system of laws that will stand the favorable criticism of a holier and brighter civilization even than our own. For it is to be remembered that we are now doing what is to go down to future generations, to be criticised by ages that will judge us from the past. Let us see here that we, as far as possible, act so as to meet a favorable judgment from posterity.

I contend that we have to wipe out of existence that class of debts which belong to that evil institution tolerated here for so many years.

Mr. President, I have done ; and have only to say, in conclusion, that I hope the vote will not simply be a majority. I trust we will show that it will not be a mere majority, but that we give such an overwhelming majority as to show to the world that we recognize the word of light and of truth.

The hour of three having arrived, the Convention adjourned.

SEVENTEENTH DAY,

Tuesday, February 4, 1868.

The Convention assembled at 12 M., and was called to order by the PRESIDENT.

Prayer was offered by the Rev. F. L. CARDOZO.

The roll was called, and a quorum answering to their names, the PRESIDENT announced the Convention ready to proceed to business.

The Journal of the preceding day was read and approved.

The PRESIDENT informed the Convention that the Ordinance levying a tax to pay the expenses of the Convention, and the Ordinance defining the pay and mileage of members had been duly engrossed, and signed by the President and Secretary of the Convention.

The PRESIDENT called for the reports of Standing Committees.

Mr. WM. E. ROSE, from the Committee on Petitions, submitted the following, which was, on motion, adopted :

The Committee on Petitions, to whom was referred the resolution relative to the collection of wages and debts of laborers, ask leave respectfully to report that they have considered the same, and recommend that the said resolution be laid on the table.

Mr. WM. E. ROSE also made the following report :

The Committee on Petitions, to whom was referred the resolution in regard to the pay of assistant assessors of internal revenue who could not take the official oath required by the Act of July 2, 1862, ask leave respectfully to report, that it is inexpedient for this Convention to take any action on the subject, and they recommend that it be laid on the table.

Mr. J. J. WRIGHT. I really hope that report will not be adopted. I object to that matter being rushed through without due consideration it would be a bad precedent for the Convention to set. We cannot, of course, undertake to compensate those who could not take the oath required by law, but it is a matter for Congress to consider.

Mr. N. G. PARKER. I am glad the gentleman from Beaufort has taken the view he has of this case. If in order, I move that the report be recommitted to the Committee, with instructions to report that we do petition Congress in behalf of these petitioners. I happen to know some of the parties who have applied to this Convention for aid. The Assistant Assessor, from Kingstree, has given me a full history of his case. [Mr. C. P. LESLIE. Give me his name, Mr. PARKER.] His name is S. W. Maurice. He discharged the duties of Assistant Assessor with great ability and fidelity but received no pay. A Northern man who served since that time has been receiving pay, and I think it hard that an officer who did discharge the duty faithfully for some time should not be paid. A petition to Congress by this Convention, in behalf of such an officer, might do some good.

Mr. C. P. LESLIE. Having been unfortunately an officer of the Internal Revenue department, I know something about the doings and transactions of the officers of that department. I know there are a great many reasons, secret reasons, why certain officers are not paid. The Government does not think fit to divulge these reasons. I do not think the country or this Convention understands the reasons of the Government, but it is sufficient for us to know, that when these officers present their claims they are not paid. One reason has been given, and that is that they were not legal officers. What the other reasons are, we do not know. It is within the power of the Assistant Assessors, or Deputy Collectors to urge the Government to pay them, and ask Congress to pay them. We all know that when any honest, fair, legitimate claim has been rendered by any person, or set of persons, against the Government, Congress has never kept the claimants out of their money. I say, therefore, there are reasons why Congress does not propose to pay these claims; yet when these men find themselves baffled by Congress, they ingeniously slip round to this body because they think we have influence with that body. Such a foolish, nonsensical proposition was never entertained anywhere, except by the men cunning enough to present it. The Chairman of the Committee, in my judgment, in the recommendation to lay the matter on the table, has made a sensible report, and I hope it will be adopted.

Mr. B. F. WHITTEMORE. I believe in giving exact justice to all men. These gentlemen for whom this petition was asked, were entitled not only to their sympathy, but to their influence with Congress. They had served the Government, and never received one dollar's compensation for their services. This Convention had committed itself to measures of relief; and I am in favor, if it is extended in one particular, of extending it in all particulars.

Mr. S. A. SWAILS read a letter from C. W. Dudley, Esq., to S. W. Maurice, Esq., one of the gentlemen who had served as Assistant Assessor, testifying to his fidelity and ability, as deserving the compensation attached to the office.

On motion of Mr. E. W. M. MACKEY, the report was laid on the table.

Mr. WM. E. ROSE, Chairman of the Committee on Petitions, submitted the following report, which, on motion of Mr. A. J. RANSIER, was adopted:

The Committee on Petitions, to whom was referred the petition of W. J. Mixson, praying that this Convention recommend to Congress that his political disabilities be removed and he be restored to the elective franchise, have considered the same, and respectfully report that your Committee are satisfied of the loyalty of the petitioner, and recommend that the prayer of his petition be granted.

Mr. B. O. DUNCAN moved a reconsideration of the following resolution, which was adopted yesterday

Resolved, That a Committee consisting of two from each Congressional District of the State as they existed in 1860, prior to the act of secession of the 19th December, 1860, be appointed by the President, to inquire and report to this Convention what number of representatives it will be proper according to the present law of the United States, that this State shall elect to the Congress of the United States; and that the Committee shall also report on a suitable construction of the Congressional Districts, according to the number of Representatives allowed us.

The motion to reconsider was adopted, whereupon Mr. B. O. DUNCAN offered the following resolution, which was adopted:

Resolved, That a Committee consisting of eight be appointed by the President to inquire and report to this Convention what number of representatives it will be proper, according to the present law of the United States, that this State shall elect to the Congress of the United States, and that the Committee shall also report a suitable construction of the Congressional Districts, according to representatives allowed us.

The PRESIDENT presented the following communication from the Commanding General, which was read to the Convention :

HEADQUARTERS SECOND MILITARY DISTRICT. ⎱
CHARLESTON, S. C., January 31, 1868. ⎰

President of the Constitutional Convention, Charleston, S. C. :

SIR :—I have the honor to acknowledge the receipt from you of the preamble and resolutions adopted by the Convention on the 25th instant, requesting me " to suspend for three months all sales of property under execution or other legal process, under any judgment or decree rendered by Courts of this State for a debt or debts contracted, up to the acceptance by General Canby of this resolution, except for laborers and mechanics, and liens upon crops to secure advances made by factors and other persons."

The subject of this resolution has been one of serious consideration from the moment I entered upon this command, and to aid me in that consideration, I have endeavored to gather from the sources of information, within my reach, all the facts that bore directly or indirectly upon a question so important and so delicate. It is not proper that I should enter into any discussion of the principles involved in the solution of the financial questions suggested by the resolution.

These come properly under the consideration of your body, or of the Legislature, by which it will be followed. My own action on the immediate question must be determined, in a measure, by other considerations.

The resolutions, although general in terms, is divided by the effect of the action heretofore taken upon the subject. The first decision, embracing debts contracted prior to the 19th of December, 1860, and the second, those contracted subsequent to the 15th of May, 1865, the intermediate period being covered by the stay provided for in General Orders No. 10, of April 11, 1867. The debts embraced in the first decision were also stayed by the same order, but proceedings for their recovery was revived by the modifications made by General Orders No. 164, so far as they were covered by judgments rendered prior to the 19th of December, 1860, or subsequent to the organization of the Provisional Government and the re-establishment of the United States Courts under the President's proclamation of June 30, 1865.

The object of the modification of General Orders No. 10 by General Orders No. 164, was to bring the class of cases affected by the former order within the limits established by the decisions of the Supreme Court of the United States, and arrest, as far as possible, a flood of litigation that would be fruitful only in imposing additional burdens.

The experience of the last thirty days has demonstrated the fact that there are still many cases of this class, in which either the contract itself, or the consideration of the contract, or the proceeding by which it is sought to be enforced, may be questioned hereafter as unlawful, or as against public policy.

The apprehension that the proceedings in these cases are not final, together with the depressed financial condition of the State, has produced a state of affairs that is ruinous to the interest of both creditor and debtor. I have endeavored to meet the wishes of the Convention by the enclosed General Orders, which will operate as a stay in all cases where the property would be sacrificed by the immediate sale under execution.

In the case of debts contracted subsequent to the 29th of April, 1865, the action heretofore taken, both by civil and by the military authorities, has been such that an application of the resolution to these debts would not only be beyond the limit of any proper exercise of the military authority, but be productive of far greater ultimate evil than of immediate good, and reflect disastriously upon every interest and upon almost every individual in the community.

I have also the honor to acknowledge the receipt of the resolution requesting an extension of the homestead exemption to one hundred acres of land. Before acting upon this I think it proper to invite attention to the unequal operation of the resolution, and the serious difficulties in applying it, unless there be some pecuniary limit dependent upon the value of the land exempted.

It was the constant occurrence of the difficulties of this kind that led to the modification of Paragraph VII. of General Orders No. 10, and it would be unwise to renew them, even for a short period.

Very respectfully. your obedient servant,
(Signed)   ED. R. S CANBY,
                                    Brevet Major General Commanding.

Mr. A. J. RANSIER moved to take up the unfinished business of yesterday, namely, the Ordinance in reference to making null and void debts for slaves, which was agreed to.

Mr. A. J. RANSIER. I had wished that we were all of one mind on this important question. This, it seems, is not the case. I agree with my learned friend from Beaufort, who spoke yesterday on this qu estion, that we should pass this measure, and that too by a handsome vote. But I understood him to claim for this Convention supreme power to legislate for the people of this State, and on that point I beg to differ with him. I deny that we have the power to legislate at all.

We are here, sir, in pursuance of an Act of Congress and the Acts supplementary thereto, to frame a Constitution and civil government for this State. The civil government which we shall put into operation is that for which we are to provide in the Constitution we are here to frame

These Acts declare that no legal State governments exists in the States of Virginia, North Carolina, South Carolina, &c., &c.; that the said States shall be divided into Military Districts and made subject to the military authority of the United States; that it shall be the duty of each officer assigned to these Districts to protect all persons in their rights, &c., suppress disorders, punish or cause to be punished all offenders, &c., &c.; that all interference under color of State authority with their authority under these Acts shall be null and void; that when the people of any of said States shall have formed a Constitution and government in conformity with the Constitution of the United States; and when such Constitution shall be ratified by the people and approved by Congress, and when your Legislature, elected under said Constitution, shall do a certain thing, and when your Senators and Representatives are admitted into Congress, then these Acts will cease.

Now, sir, I contend that until we shall have done all of these things, and are restored to our normal relations in the Union, we have no power in or out of this Convention to make or enforce any law whatever, save by permission. We may enact measures here, but unless they are approved and sanctioned by General Canby, they will not have the force of law. No, sir, the supreme law making power of this State, or that which amounts to the same thing, now resides not with the people, nor yet in this Convention, but with the military commander, under the Acts of Congress, which invests him with paramount authority.

I question, therefore, whether we pass this measure it will have the force of law. Still, it is brought here, and I am in favor of an expression going forth to the world, that we deny, most solemnly and emphatically, that there ever was, or ever can be, property in man. I voted against the recommendation of a stay law the other day, and I did so on principle. I think stay laws are wrong in principle, and injurious in their effects, however necessary they may seem to be in certain contingencies. They can only be defended on the dangerous principle that the end justify the means.

The gentleman from Lexington says that this measure impairs the obligation of contracts; for this, and other reasons, he objects to it. In my humble judgment it does no such thing, for the simple reason that any contract, the proposed consideration of which was based on man as property, never did have, never can have, any binding force. It was void of itself; void from the very nature of the case; void because it was and is violative of the fundamental principle of the moral law; a principle recognized by the founders of this Government, and expressed in unmistakeable language in our declaration of independence; void because it is violative of the natural and inalienable right of man to liberty and the pursuit of happiness. Believing that God wills the happiness of all mankind, and that human slavery was, and is, destructive of this great end, therefore these parties, who have banded themselves together as buyers and sellers of human beings, thus contributing to defeat the purposes of the Almighty himself in the moral government of the world, must be judged by this standard. They have been judged, and the just judgment of the civilized world have pronounced them guilty. How can you impair obligations, then, when there was none? The pre-existing obligation upon each of these parties, and upon all of us, is, and upon this we are told in the inspired word, rests all the laws, "do unto others as you would that they should do unto you."

The gentleman says that slavery was wrong, and says that *both* parties to such a contract are morally guilty. My learned friend from Charleston District (Mr. CARDOZO) also regards both as morally guilty; therefore he thinks both should be punished. Leave them alone; let them fight over the bone, says the gentleman from Fairfield (Mr. RUTLAND). That both are morally guilty none will deny, but how will both be punished by leaving them alone? If the purchaser who has lost "property" is made to pay for it, which you propose to compel him to do, *he, only,* will be the loser, and, though both are morally guilty, you propose to reward one by compelling the purchaser to pay, thus regarding the contract as valid; thus conceding and establishing the sellers right to treat his fellows as chattels.

The gentleman from Fairfield also stated that were this measure to be adopted, it would lead to interminable litigations or law suits. It strikes me, then, that if I were a lawyer, this would be an additional incentive to support the measure.

It is not as a punishment for the crime of slaveholding that I advocate this measure. As far as it is safe and practicable, I propose, so far as I am concerned, to let the dead bury its dead. I think the sooner the wounds made by the late terrible fratracidal war are healed the better for all parties. I am willing to forget past injuries. I would be untrue to myself and faithless to my obligations as a man and a Christian, looking at this measure as I do, and most certainly every man has a right to his own opinions, were I to vote against this measure. Somebody would be the losers; but am I, and those who, like me, sustains this bill, responsible. No, sir. If I said these debts should be paid, I recognize the binding force of a contract that I regard as having no binding force, and concede that there is such a thing as property in man, which cannot be.

Mr. C. C. BOWEN. I may say that I have been both amused and surprised at the course this question has taken. Questions have been lugged in here that have had nothing to do with the issue. I am particularly surprised at the course of some of the legal gentlemen who have spoken. If they were to go to the Supreme Court of the United States, they would have to go on a better ground than any I have yet heard set forth. It has been said that when men were captured in the city of Boston who were fugitive slaves, they were returned under the law of the land. Such may have been the fact, such may have been the law then, but such is not the law now. Whether it was right then, is a question which was then and still is undecided. One party passed the law, another repealed it. It has been said that property in man was recognized by the laws of the country. They have gone further, and say that it has been recognized by the Constitution of the United States, which proposition I deny. Strange that gentlemen should come in here and make propositions in regard to the law without reference to the book in which it is contained. But taking for granted that such are the facts, admitting, for the sake of argument, that property in man was recognized by the Constitution of the United States, high as the Constitution is, I would appeal to an authority still higher—I mean the patent held by man directly from his God, by which his liberty and the right to its enjoyment was guaranteed. It existed before Constitutions or even societies themselves. The image stamped upon him at his birth was the sign of the covenant, and should have forever been a shield against its violations. I see no necessity of appealing to a higher law ; the question to be considered in this matter is the validity of a bond, the consideration of which was the purchase of slaves.

How were these slaves conveyed ? Usually by a bill of sale from the obligee to the obligor, which bill of sale always contained a covenant to forever *warrant and defend the premises to the obligor*, his heirs and assigns forever.

What next followed. In ninety-nine cases out of every hundred, the slaves were cotemporaneously re-conveyed by an instrument called a mortgage from the obligor to the obligee, as a security for or in payment of the bond. The slaves in·question were emancipated by the Proclamation of President Lincoln, which Proclamation was afterwards ratified by the Convention of South Carolina ; still gentlemen come in and set up that Article in the Constitution of the United States which speaks about no State impairing the obligation of a contract. I would say, in reply to that, the party who holds the bill of sale, the man who gave the bond, has just as much right to demand security of the party who holds the bond, and who has warranted to defend the person sold unto the heirs and assigns of the purchaser forever.

The bill of sale, bond and mortgage, constitute but one transaction. It is purely a question in law, over which the Court of Equity has no jurisdiction.

The only question then is, what is the condition of a mortgage at common law ? It is a conditional sale of property. The condition is, if I fail to pay the money the property is yours (the sellers.) Suppose you had given a bond and mortgage for a slave purchased in 1858, and the condition of that bond is broken, the remedy would be for the seller to take his property wherever he could find it. The title was never vested in the purchaser. It has always been ruled in South Carolina that the failure of consideration either partially or totally, was a good ground to set aside a contract. The decisions of the Supreme Court of South Carolina contain many such cases.

In the Convention of 1865, every man, woman and child in the State was supposed to be represented. The Convention admitted slaves were free, and by a voluntary act passed an Ordinance of emancipation. Both the man who held the bond, and the man who held the bill of sale, was represented in that Convention. It was agreed there that slavery should be abolished, and by that act all contracts for the purchase of slaves were rescinded.

I have not the slightest doubt but that if a case of this kind goes up to the Supreme Court of the United States, it will be so decided.

The gentleman from Fairfield (Mr. RUTLAND) argued that this measure would open the door to endless litigation. I do not see it in that light. The mere fact of the Convention passing this Ordinance has nothing to do with its constitutionality. The man who sold a slave in 1858, sues on his bond. I plead the Ordinance of this Convention, and the holder of the bond sets sets up the plea that the Ordinance is unconstitutional. The Convention has only to cast the onus upon the holder of the bond to show by a competent tribunal that the Ordinance is unconstitutional, and he can get his money.

There is no necessity of appealing to the passions or prejudices of the members of the Convention, as this is purely a question of law. A somewhat different version to any that I have ever heard before, was yesterday given by the gentleman to that portion of the Constitution of the United States which refers to an *ex post facto* law, and though it has been largely quoted, it can never have any thing to do with this question. If an action is ever brought in any of these cases, it must be a civil one, while an *ex post facto* law relates only to criminal matters, and therefore has nothing to do with this question. The Supreme Court of Louisiana decided last summer that all contracts entered into for the purchase of slaves were null, void and of no effect, upon the ground that the emancipation proclamation of President Lincoln destroyed the property, and that the party holding the bill of sale had just as much right to go into Court and ask the party to make good his warranty as the other party had to ask for the payment of the bond. The onus always has been, and always will be, upon the party holding the bond. In my opinion, when this case is decided, several questions will be presented, and all slaves sold since the 1st day of January, 1863, no matter what was the consideration, the Courts will decide to be no contracts at all. But to bring suit for the services of a slave purchased previous to that time would present an entirely different case. There are many other cases or views of the subject that might demand special action, but it was thought proper by the Committee to report an Ordinance that would cover all cases in regard to slaves from beginning to end.

With regard to the assertion that the Constitution of the United States recognized the right of property in man, I have not been able yet to find any such recognition. I do recollect the decision of the Supreme Court of the United States, known as the Dred Scott decision. That, however, was upon citizenship and nothing else. Now that the fight against an institution of which not only the people of the United States, but the whole world, was tired, and freedom established, we certainly cannot be asked to record our vote on that side, which would cause us to acknowledge that the struggle which passed over this land was a great humbug.

Mr. D. H. CHAMBERLAIN. Mr. President, I am extremely anxious that the measure which we are now considering, should receive the approval of a very large majority of the Convention, and it is with the hope that I may say something to add to that majority, that I take the time of the Convention. Let me say at the outset that I am not a repudiationist, that I am as far as any man here, as far even, to say, as far as my friend from Fairfield, from having any sympathy with any measure that looks either in principle or in fact towards repudiation; and when my friend from Fairfield yesterday took occasion to call us who favor the present measure repudiationists, and charged that this was but the initial step, the entering wedge of repudiation, he made a statement which every friend of this Ordinance denies, and which neither the gentleman from Fairfield, nor any other gentleman has proved. I am neither in favor of repudiating nor scaling, nor staying by so much as one hour, any honest and just debt. I do not believe that this community, nor any community can ever reach sound and substantial financial prosperity until it abandons, utterly and finally, all attempts to obstruct, delay, or forbid the speedy collection by due process of law, of any and all just legal claims of one citizen upon another. It was upon this principle and in this spirit that I recorded my vote against the stay measure which passed this body a week ago, and it is with this principle in view and in this spirit, that I now approach this question. If I thought that the existing claims for slaves fell within the category of just, legal debts. I know that I have no prejudice against the system out of which they sprang so strong, as to lead me to favor any measure which would impair their validity or delay their collection; and it is only because I am persuaded that the nature of the debts, and the circumstances in which they now stand, are such as to take them out of the catalogue and companionship of just, legal claims; upon high considerations I say of justice and of law, not at all from feeling or prejudice, that I favor the present measure which forever extinguishes and bars such claims. My friend from Fairfield told us yesterday that this measure grows out of our prejudice against slavery, which led us to forget and overlook the legal merits of the case. I desire for one to say to my friend that it is precisely upon the legal aspects of these claims, that I favor the Ordinance before us.

Mr. President, the existing claims for slaves, of which there are thousands in this community, grew out of the peculiar institution of slavery. By special legislation, by positive municipal law, human beings were considered property in this State. They were not property naturally and without law—God and nature, the common, unwritten laws of human society, made them men. It was solely by the force of positive enactments against natural justice and the law of nature, by virtue only of a positive, artificial code that they became property; wherever such a code did not exist, men were not property; or wherever having once existed, it ceased to exist, men ceased to be property and assumed their natural condition. The nature and tenure of slave property, was consequently at all times and under all circumstances peculiar and precarious. It rested not like other property upon nature and the original constitution of human society; but unlike any other property, in rested solely and exclusively on written, positive, special, municipal regulations. Such was the case in the slaveholding States of the Union; and while I do not deny or seek to evade the fact that slaves were by the statues of South Carolina property, and that this property was tolerated and even recognized by the General Government, yet I do claim that from its very nature, property in human beings was of a peculiar, limited, uncertain nature, liable to dangers to which no other property was exposed and held, by whomsover it was held, at a peculiar risk, and by a tenure liable to be broken by the same process by which it was created.

This, therefore, is my first observation; that at all times, even in its palmy days, when the mountain of slavery stood strong, when the dogmas of Calhoun and Hammond passed unchallenged, and South Carolina in the insolent frenzy of her madness was ready to throw down the gauntlet to the world, even then human beings were only a limited, peculiar *de facto* property, held by a peculiar tenure and at peculiar risks. It results, then, from this position that such property, property in human beings, could never claim the same sanctity, the same inviolability, the same legal consideration at our hands which we universally accord to other property.

But, Mr. President, a controversy arose touching this same property; one section of the Union sought its universal recognition; the other sought at first only its restriction, but at last its destruction. The controversy was not a sudden one. It did not burst, with sudden surprise, upon those who had invested in that property. The storm, the crisis, were foreseen by the blindest. It was to every man's vision a struggle which should settle this precise question, "shall human beings continue to be property?"

Both parties recognized and admitted the issue. Like a great suit at law the pleadings on either side had at last narrowed the entire controversy to this single and vital issue, *"shall human beings be property?"* That issue was joined. Every man knew that he held his slave property subject to the decision of that issue. Every man had due notice that any investment he might make or had made in any claim he might acquire to property of that sort, was subject to that decision; that is, was good or bad, valid or invalid, according as victory should rest on the banners of Lee and Johnson, or of Grant and Sherman; according as the hateful symbol of a slave-holding confederacy, or the glorious banner of a free Republic, should finally float from the battlements in yonder harbor. That was the whole question. It was taken out of the courts. It was referred to the dread arbitrament of war.

Do I need to appeal to native South Carolinians around me to attest the fact which I state, that every man felt and knew that his slaves were property, that his slave bonds and slave securities were good or bad, according as the confederacy stood or fell; who imagined that if the fortunes of war went against South Carolina it would ever be so much as a question anywhere whether any claim based on slave property would be valid?

No, Mr. President, the whole controversy, the whole issue, was then and there decided. A tribunal, from which there is no appeal, then and there recorded its decision that human beings were not property in South Carolina; and in whatever condition slave property stood, then and there, I contend, it must forever stand. The confederacy fell, and with it fell slavery; with it fell property in man; with it fell every claim and every obligation which rested on the basis of slavery. I say, then, that the strictly legal effect of the success of the arms of the Union under the President's proclamation, was to finally extinguish slavery and to invalidate all titles and claims based on slave property.

These, then, Mr. President, are my two positions: 1st. That property in human beings was originally a peculiar, *de facto* property, entitled to no consideration outside of the force of the positive, municipal laws which created and upheld it. 2nd. That the precise question of its validity, after long argument and all due notice, was submitted to decision in the struggle of South Carolina against the Union; that when South Corolina yielded to the arms of the republic, slavery, as a legal consequence, with all its incidents, all its obligations, all its concomitants, became finally extinct. We are not, therefore, Mr. President, repudiating any debt. The war settled the debt. We are not staying any debt. The war *satisfied* the debt. The rude hand of revolution swept the docket, stayed from every action, quashed forever every proceeding, and forever arrested every judgment. And I state it here to-day, as a legal proposition, fully capable of defence, that this Ordinance is no more than a mere declaration and announcement of the strictly legal consequences of the failure of South Carolina to maintain the issue which was submitted to the tribunal of war.

Now, Mr. President, if these principles are correct, I do not need to meet any special objection to this Ordinance. If this Ordinance rests on good and sufficient legal grounds, the incidental hardships it may work to individuals cannot change our action. But I maintain that no hardship will arise from the Ordinance which was not the necessary result of emancipation. It is true that slave bonds are worthless, and so are the slaves. Suppose the widows and orphans whose slaves were sold for bonds, had kept them until the close of the war, would they not have lost them? It is said that many widows and orphans and minors are to be ruined by the invalidation of these bonds. Are there not many, I ask, of the same classes who were ruined by the setting free of their slaves? But do we propose to remunerate them for slaves set free? No; Mr. President, when slavery went down, everything based on slavery, deriving its force and obligation from slavery, went down with it, as a legal, inevitable consequence; and that in future no doubt may rest on this question, no further litigation may be wasted upon this issue, we declare and ordain by this Ordinance that all such controversies shall cease, that the doors of our Courts shall not be open to contest claims which a war of four years has proved, in the face of the world, to be invalid.

For myself, sir, I do rejoice, I confess, that my moral abhorrence of that institution in which these claims originated, is also expressed in the Ordinance before us; that while the Ordinance rests on safe, sufficient legal grounds, it also enables us to fasten the stigma of our moral reprobation upon human slavery.

The day has at last come when law and morality join in saying with Lord Brougham, that it is a wild and guilty fantasy that man can hold property in man.

I remember, sir, with my friend from Darlington, when the slave hunter bore away his property from the streets of Boston. which we had fondly called free; but there were even those that day who swore by the living God that they would leave no stone unturned till Anthony Burns could walk the streets of Boston with his name on his forehead, and defy the Carolinas to come and take him. That day has come. That institution, by force of which alone Anthony Burns was property, staked its existence, its validity, its life on the issue of the struggle which began seven years ago in this very city. The decision was made against South Carolinians, and now, Mr. President, I do desire that through the mouth of the first legal assembly of South Carolina since that act of December, 1860, it shall be announced to the world that in that great suit, slavery was defeated, and, as a legal consequence, everything which rested for its force and validity upon slavery, fell with it; and that henceforth, no issue arising out of slavery shall be joined in our Courts, and no judgment for claims based upon property in human beings shall be enforced by authority.

Mr. G. PILLSBURY. The subject before this Convention last week, concerning the staying for three months of certain executions, and to which I gave my support, thereby causing the censure of some of my friends, is very similar to the question before us to-day, with the exception, as perhaps Erin would say, of an astonishing difference. They are both questions of relief from certain obligations, and this constitutes their similarity. The "astonishing difference" consists in this: that while the former proposition contemplates (for the purpose of preventing a summary and ruinous stagnation in the business interests of the State,) temporary suspension of collecting debts contracted for horses, cattle, lands and provisions, commodities which the whole civilized world recognize as legitimate for the purposes of trade, the latter debars payment forever of debts contracted where the asserted "value received" was human beings, whom no divine law does, and no human law can constitute as property. In a charitable point of view both propositions struck me favorably, for relief is a word which ever falls pleasantly upon my ear. The creditor usually possesses every advantage over the debtor.

32

They, together, occupy positions somewhat similar to those of the lion and the lamb. It is not usually the lion that petitions for mercy. There may be, occasionally, an exceptional lion, a sick lion, a very sick lion, that might consent to have his pains assuaged by the ministrations of the lamb; but it is usually the lamb, as he feels the huge talons of his powerful rival lacerating his flesh, that raises his dejected, imploring eyes for mercy. But I base my action upon the question now before us upon grounds higher than that of relief. I base it upon a principle that man is man, and not an article of merchandise, and that any contract made between two men where the body and soul of a third man is the consideration bandied between them, "as value received," is null and void.

Much has been said upon the other side about the inviolability of a contract. Indeed, the whole argument there against the proposition before us has been based upon the single idea, that every man is sacredly bound to perform whatever he has covenanted to do. Perhaps it may be a source of congratulation to those who take this ground, that Judas did not set us an example as a repudiator; but that after covenanting for the thirty pieces of silver, he walked straight up to the *scratch* like a man, and performed the betrayal. But it was his last contract, because you will recollect that the "price of blood" gave even to him slight uneasiness, which he quieted with the halter.

To show the fallacy of this single argument, and to demonstrate that the validity of a contract, and the obligation for its fulfilment, depend much upon the character and condition of the commodity entering into it, allow me to institute a comparison; no, not a comparison, for "comparisons are sometimes odious," as was the case yesterday. where the gentleman from Darlington compared a *man* to another man's *coat ;* but I will institute a contrast between my watch in my pocket and a man. Take first the watch, sometime since it was missing, and only recently I discovered it in the pocket of the gentleman from Charleston. Although I believe him to be both honest and honorable, I still demand of him my property. He replies: "The watch is mine, I purchased it from the gentleman from Fairfield. What have you to do with any contract I have made with another party? But not viewing the question in precisely the same light with him, I take my watch, and he at once repairs to the gentleman from Fairfield for redress. This kind party informs him that he obtained the watch by fair and honest purchase from the gentleman from Darlington, paying him the ready money, which certainly should make the covenant sacred to all interests and purposes. After being compelled to refund, he resorts for satisfaction to the gentleman from Darlington, who informs him that he came honestly by the watch, but that there can be no doubt it was stolen property. Therefore we all *club* together, trace out the original thief, and punish him with fine and imprisonment. Now, therefore, my watch, a little lump of inanimate matter, has been able, through me its representative, to vindicate its right to my pocket, thereby nullifying, at least, three different contracts, and causing condign punishment to be visited upon one thief.

Consider now the other side of the contest. A man! an immortal being, for aught I know, a jewel flashed from the diadem of the Almighty; and what can he not do? What contracts can he not annul? Take the last slave that was sold; trace him back through all the bargains and contracts which have been made for his head, and you will certainly find the original thief and robber. Now the contracts of the three honorable gentlemen mentioned, for the watch, were null and void, from the fact, that they bargained for what never properly belonged to either of them, but was the property of another. How much more would this be the case, where a *man*, and not a *watch*, was at issue!

But we are reminded that the passage of this Ordinance might not prove a Constitutional act. However that may be, if this Convention, standing upon the battlements of the Constitution, and peering outward to witness the fantastic pranks which are being played outside, should seem to incline too much outward, and be in danger of losing its equilibrium, and plunging headlong, the warning would come in bad taste from Southern men, who have done nothing for fifty years but fiddle and dance around the Constitution; and who for the last six or eight years have held perfect carnival outside, in every direction. But the able constitutional arguments by the two legal gentlemen who preceded me, upon the question at issue, have cleared up the doubts which weighed upon my mind; and I am satisfied we can stand firm and erect upon the ramparts, with no fear of tumbling outward amidst the ruins that have been caused around us.

It was stated in the debate upon this question yesterday, that recreant Yankees had come down from the North, and trafficked largely in slaves, and that they hold large numbers of the notes and bonds which the Ordinance under discussion proposes to repudiate. If any renegade son of my native State, Massachusetts, so far forgot his puritanical training, and outraged the moral and Christian sentiment of that people, as to come down here and prostitute himself to the base purpose of dealing in human blood, and bones, and brains, if his notes and bonds lie piled up as high as the spire of St. Michael's, I would repudiate every dollar of them;

and I would do it with the greater zest, *because* he is a renegade son of Massachusetts.

I was not instrumental in bringing this question before this Convention Perhaps if it had depended upon me, it would not have been done. But now that it is here, and we are summoned to act upon it, I connot by my vote, give the lie to my life-long belief. I have never supposed that one man could either morally or legally own another man, as property; and when called upon to pronounce against the validity of notes and bonds arising from such illegal, inhuman traffic, I shall give an unqualified yea.

The question recurring on the adoption of the Ordinance, Mr. F. J. MOSES, Jr., called for the yeas and nays, which was sustained.

Mr. B. F. WHITTEMORE asked to be allowed to explain the reasons of his vote, which was granted.

Mr. WHITTEMORE said the manner in which this question had been debated, would evidently put any gentleman who might vote against the passage of the Ordinance, in the position of one who acknowledged the right of property in man. There was no person upon the floor who had a longer record against the denial of the right of property in man than himself. He did not, therefore, vote in the negative because of any recognized right of property in man or any moral right, but because he believed in the enforcement of legally acknowledged contracts mutually formed of whatever nature they may be.

Mr. F. L. CARDOZO also desired to state that he would vote against the Ordinance on the same ground as his friend from Darlington. He did not think the right of property at all involved in the question.

The yeas and nays on the passage of the Ordinance was then taken, and resulted as follows:

YEAS—The President, Messrs. Allen, Arnim, Becker, Bell, Bowen, Bonum, Burton, Brockenton, Bryce, Byas, Cain, R. H., Cain, F. J., Camp, Coghlan, Chamberlain, Cooke, Crews, Darrington, Davis, De-Large, Dickson, Dogan, Donaldson, Driffle, Duncan, Edwards, Foster, Gentry, Goss, Gray, Harris, Haynes, James N., Hayne H. E., Henderson, Holmes, Humbird, Hunter, Hurley, Jackson, Jacobs, Jervey, Johnson, Samuel, Johnson, W. B., Johnson, J. W., Johnston, W. E., Joiner, Jones, Henry, Jones, Chas., Lang, Langley, Lee, Geo., Lee, Sam'l., Lomax, Leslie, Mackey, E. W. M., Mayer, Middleton, Milford, Moses, F. J. Jr., Nance, Nash, Neagle, Newell, Nuckles, Parker, Pillsbury, Randolph, Rainey, Ransier, Richmond, Rivers, Rose, Runion, Sanders, Sasportas, Shrewsbury, Smalls, Stubbs, Swails, Thomas, Thompson, Augustus, Thompson, B. A., Viney, Webb, Whipper, White, Wilder, Chas. M., Wingo and Wright.

NAYS—Alexander, Cardozo, Chestnut, Corley, Dill, Jenks, Jillson,

Mauldin, McKinlay, W. J., McKinlay, Wm., McDaniels, Mead, Miller, Owens, Rutland, Whittemore, Williamson, Wilder, and Francis, E.

The Ordinance having passed its second, was ordered to be engrossed for a third reading.

Mr. W. J. WHIPPER moved that the rules be suspended for the purpose of passing the Ordinance to its third reading, which was agreed to.

The Ordinance was then read a third time, passed, and ordered to be engrossed with its present title

Mr. W. J. WHIPPER moved to reconsider the motion by which the Ordinance was passed, and to lay the motion to reconsider on the table, which was agreed to.

The following is the Ordinance as passed :

AN ORDINANCE

Declaring null and void all Contracts and Judgments and Decrees heretofore made or entered up, where the consideration was for the purchase of Slaves.

We, the people of South Carolina, by our delegates in Convention assembled, do hereby declare and ordain, 1st. That all contracts, whether under seal or not, the considerations of which were the purchase of slaves, are hereby declared null, void, and of no effect ; and no suit, either at law or in equity, shall be commenced or prosecuted for the enforcement of such contracts.

2d. That all proceedings to enforce satisfaction or payment of judgment or decrees rendered, recorded, enrolled or entered upon such contracts in any Court of this State, are hereby prohibited.

3d. That all orders heretofore made in any Court in this State in relation to such contracts, whereby property is held subject to decision, as to the validity of such contracts, are also hereby declared null, void, and of no effect

Mr. B. BYAS offered a series of resolutions for the compensation of persons retained in service without pay after the passage of the proclamation of emancipation of the 1st January, 1863. The resolutions proposed to pay ten dollars per month to those of age prior to that time, and eight dollars per month to minors.

On motion, the resolutions were laid on the table.

Mr. W. J. WHIPPER offered the following, which was referred to the Committee on Miscellaneous Matters :

Resolved, That it shall be binding and obligatory upon the Legislature of this State to grant charters for any proposed railroad, when the said charters shall be applied for by any twelve respectable citizens of the

State ; *Provided*, that the route of such road, or proposed road, shall not run within ten miles on a parallel line with any road then in existence within the State.

Mr. W. J. WHIPPER also introduced the following :

AN ORDINANCE

Declaring null and void all Ferry Charters, Grants and Exclusive Privileges whatever.

Be it ordained by the people of South Carolina, in Constitutional Convention assembled, and by the authority of the same, That all ferry charters, grants and exclusive privileges whatsoever, that may have been heretofore granted by legislation, are hereby declared null and void and of no effect after the assembling of the first Legislature under the Constitution of 1868.

Referred to the Committee on Miscellaneous Matters.

Mr. B. F. WHITTEMORE offered the following, which was referred to the Committee on Miscellaneous Matters :

The Legislature shall pass no Special Act conferring corporate powers Corporations may be formed under general laws, but all such laws may from time to time be altered or repealed.

The property of corporations now existing, or hereafter to be created, shall forever be subject to taxation.

No right of way shall be appropriated to the use of any corporation until full compensation therefor shall be first made in money, or first secured by a deposit of money to the owner, irrespective of any benefit from any improvement proposed by such corporations, which compensation shall be ascertained by a jury of twelve men in a Court of Record, as shall be prescribed by law.

Dues from Corporations shall be secured by such individual liability to the stockholders and other means as may be prescribed by law.

Mr. W. J. McKINLAY offered the following, which was referred to the Committee on Miscellaneous Matters :

WHEREAS, it is incumbent upon the people of any commonwealth to do all in their power to develop the wealth and resources of their State, and that all legislation should have a tendency to encourage rather than impede such developments ; be it therefore

Resolved, That the authorities of no township, corporation or municipality shall be allowed to enact any law, or laws, whereby the owner of a lot, or lots, may be deprived of the right to clear said lot with a view to improve the same, provided said lot, or lots, be enclosed.

Mr. J. J. WRIGHT offered the following resolution, which was, on motion of Mr. B. BYAS, laid on the table :

Resolved, That no member of this Convention be permitted to absent himself from the floor, to remain for the space of thirty minutes, without the consent of the Chair, under the penalty of losing one day's pay.

Mr. J. M. ALLEN submitted the following resolution:

Resolved, That the President be requested to draw from the Treasury of this State thirty thousand dollars ($30,000) in bills receivable for the purpose of paying the per diem and mileage of the members of this Convention, and that the same be paid on Saturday, the 8th of February, 1868, at 3 o'clock, P. M.

Pending the resolution of Mr. ALLEN, the Convention adjourned.

EIGHTEENTH DAY,

Wednesday, February 5, 1868.

The Convention assembled at 12 M., and was called to order by the PRESIDENT.

Prayer was offered by the Rev. WM. M. THOMAS.

The roll was called, and a quorum answering to their names, the PRESIDENT announced the Convention ready to proceed to business.

The Journal of the previous day's proceedings was read and approved.

Mr. LEMUEL BOOZER. I observe in the Journal of yesterday a resolution introduced in regard to absentees. I suppose it has reference more particularly to those not present when the vote was taken upon the Ordinance passed in regard to annulling contracts and liabilities for the purchase of slaves. Unfortunately I was absent, and I desire to explain that it was not for the purpose of dodging the question, but owing to the fact of indisposition. which prevented me from remaining in the house during the entire sitting. If I had been present I would have voted "no," and I desire to have my name so recorded.

On motion of Mr. C. C. BOWEN, the gentleman was allowed to record his vote as desired.

The PRESIDENT stated that the various reports of the Committees already read by their title had been printed and laid upon his table.

Mr. C. P. LESLIE offered the following resolution, which was adopted:

Resolved, That the President of this Convention be requested to appoint a Special Committee, to consist of three members of this body, to be designated a Committee of Audit of Contingent Expenses, whose duty it shall be to investigate and enquire into, as to the correctness of all bills of all contingent expenses which have been, or may be hereafter incurred, during the sitting of the Convention ; and that no money be paid, in settlement or on account of such alleged indebtedness, until such Committee shall have examined and investigated the same, and reported the facts to this house, together with their recommendation thereon.

Mr. N. G. PARKER seconded the motion.

Mr. S. G. W. DILL moved to lay the resolution on the table. Lost.

Mr. W. J. WHIPPER moved that the resolution be adopted, which was agreed to.

Mr. L. S. LANGLEY moved to take up the unfinished business of yesterday, a resolution offered by Mr. J. M. ALLEN in reference to changing the hours of the sittings of the Convention.

The PRESIDENT stated that the unfinished business was the resolution offered by Mr. J. M. ALLEN in reference to a draft of $30,000 upon the State Treasury for the purpose of paying next Saturday the per diem of the members.

Mr. N. G. PARKER moved to amend by adding "for the purpose of paying the per diem of the members and officers of this Convention and such other expenses."

Mr. C. P. LESLIE moved to amend as follows : "Provided that no contingent expenses shall be paid until the same shall have been acted on by the Committee of Audit and approved by the House."

Mr. R. H. CAIN. I hope the amendment will not pass. The Finance Committee has charge of these matters, and it seemed to be calling in question their management to appoint a Committee to audit the accounts.

Mr. W. J. WHIPPER hoped, as a matter of relief to the Finance Committee, the amendment would be adopted.

Mr. N. G. PARKER. As Chairman of the Committee on Finance, when the motion was made to draw the money, I only desired to bring it to the consideration of the house that the money should be drawn. In order to be paid they might make any arrangements they deemed proper. Anything would be satisfactory to the Chairman or other members of the Committee on Finance. I do, however, want to pay the printer as soon as possible.

Mr. B. F. RANDOLPH. I am in favor of the first amendment, which requires that the officers and all other expenses be paid. If we receive our pay as delegates, and leave all incidental expenses unpaid, it will look as if we were disposed to feather our own pockets and let everybody else go. I hope the amendment will be adopted, and that the printer will be paid as well as all other expenses.

Mr. C. P. LESLIE. I offered my amendment simply to carry out the object intended by the appointment of an Auditing Committee, as called for in the resolution just before adopted. Unless the expenses were regularly audited, they might wake up some bright morning and find all the $75 000, which it was estimated would pay all the expenses of the Convention, had disappeared and left them still in session, with no money·

I want what the Auditing Committee has to do to be explicitly defined and certain. It has been intimated here that the business of the Finance Committee, among other things, is to pay these bills and to audit them. That is incorrect. It is the business of the Finance Committee to provide the ways and means, and to raise money, but not to disburse it· Now, yesterday on the floor of this house I did say, and to-day I have said, and I expect to say it as long as I have my reason and good sense, that I never will vote to pay one dollar of the contingent expenses of this Convention until I see that it is just and fair. I had the honor to sit on the Finance Committee at the time the estimate of $75,000 to pay the expenses of the Convention was made. It was supposed to be amply sufficient to pay the per diem and mileage of members of the house and the contingent expenses. This amendment in no way affects the pay or mileage of members. But I propose that no bills outside that be paid until regularly audited and passed upon by the house. If a printer's bill is twice as much as it ought to be, if the bill for coal is ten tons and we have only had five tons, and the Auditing Committee report these facts to the house, then the members can vote intelligently with regard to every bill that comes before them. The Finance Committee have no such authority, and every step they have taken in that direction has been an encroachment on the rights of the members of this body. I do not mean to imply or impute any personal misconduct on the part of the Chairman of the Finance Committee. But I deny that it is the duty or province of the Chairman of the Finance Committee, or any member of it, to say to the house such contingent expenses are paid. I will never consent to the payment of one dollar of money until a proper Committee be appointed, whose duty it shall be to report upon the correctness of the bills presented, and we can vote intelligently upon them. As the case now stands, I doubt whether $75,000 will be sufficient. That estimate was made on the basis of $9 per day to each member, and it was thought the amount of $75,000 would pay the per diem, mileage and all other expenses.

33

Mr. N. G. PARKER It was estimated that $65,000 would pay all expenses, including mileage, per diem, &c., and we thought $75,000 would leave a margin.

Mr. LESLIE. It is that little margin I desire to protect, and hope the house will take means to protect it. I say, after all the facts with regard to any bill are properly investigated and reported to the house, then the Convention can judge of the propriety of ordering it paid. I know not whether the printing, as contracted for, is just or not. I know not whether any member of this house has any interest, either di_rectly or indirectly, in that printing. I know not whether the charges that have been made on this floor, that certain persons had altogether too much interest in the printing contract, is true or not. One thing I do know; every time a contingent expense bill comes before the house they are in a great hurry to rush it through on a snap vote. We find them in season and out of season, in place and out of place, insisting that the printer's bill, before all others, ought to be paid. And they tell you that any report of their having an interest in the printing is abso-lutely false.

The object of the resolution to appoint an auditing Committee, and to have all bills examined by them and reported to the house, is to see that they are correct. I presume the house sees the necessity for its passage. I want to know, and the house wants to know, what the bill is for the rotten yellow paper we find on our table; paper that no man on the face of the earth of ordinary intelligence would have brought in this body. I hope the amendment will pass.

The question was then taken on the resolution as amended, and it was agreed to.

Mr. B. F. RANDOLPH offered the following, and moved that it be referred to the Committee on Franchise and Elections:

Resolved, That a Committee of five be appointed to confer with Major-General E. R. S. Canby in regard to a plan of voting upon the ratifica-tion of the forthcoming Constitution, said Committee to report said plan to this Convention.

Mr. C. P. LESLIE moved to lay the resolution on the table.

Mr. B. F. RANDOLPH. I hope the resolution will go to the Com-mittee proposed. If they see fit to report favorably, the house can then take further action; if not, that will be the end of it.

Mr. C. P. LESLIE. If you refer it to the Committee on Franchise and Elections, that will be the last of it. I do not think that body can be got together if Gabriel should blow his trumpet.

Mr. R. C. DeLARGE. As Chairman of that Committee, I desire to state that if the balance of the Committee are as tardy in getting together as the honorable gentleman from Barnwell is in putting in an appearance, the Convention never will get a report. The report of that Committee is completed, and the gentleman from Barnwell came in this morning and went out without knowing what was done.

Before the vote on the motion was taken, the PRESIDENT announced the hour for the consideration of the Special Order had arrived.

The following reports of Committees were then read for a first time, and, on motion of Mr. F. J. MOSES, Jr., made the Special Order for half-past twelve o'clock, Thursday:

We, the People of the State of South Carolina, in Convention assembled, Grateful to Almighty God for this opportunity, deliberately and peaceably of entering into an explicit and solemn compact with each other, and forming a new Constitution of civil government for ourselves and posterity, recognizing the necessity of the protection of the body politic in all that pertains to their freedom, safety and tranquility, and imploring the direction of the Great Legislator of the Universe, do agree upon, ordain and establish the following

Declaration of Rights and Form of Government as the Constitution of the Commonwealth of South Carolina.

ARTICLE I.

DECLARATION OF RIGHTS.

SECTION 1. All men are born free and equal—endowed by their Creator with certain inalienable rights, among which may be reckoned the right of enjoying and defending their lives and liberties, acquiring, possessing and protecting property, and seeking and obtaining their safety and happiness.

SEC. 2. Slavery shall not exist in this State, nor involuntary servitude, otherwise than for the punishment of crime, whereof the party shall have been duly convicted.

SEC. 3. All political power is vested in and derived from the people only; therefore they have the right, at all times, to modify their form of government in such manner as they may deem expedient, when the public good demands.

SEC. 4. Every citizen of this State owes paramount allegiance to the Constitution and Government of the United States, and no law or Ordinance of this State in contravention or subversion thereof can have any binding force.

SEC. 5. This State shall ever remain a member of the American Union, and all attempts, from whatever source, or upon whatever pretext, to dissolve said Union, ought to be resisted with the whole power of the State.

Sec. 6. The right of the people, peaceably to assemble to consult for the common good, and to petition the Government, or any department thereof, shall never be abridged.

Sec. 7. All persons resident in this State, born in the United States, or who have been naturalized, and shall have legally become citizens of the United States, are hereby declared citizens of South Carolina, possessing equal, civil and political rights and public privileges as hereinafter declared by this Constitution.

Sec. 8. All persons may freely speak, write and publish their sentiments on any subject, being responsible for the abuse of that right; and no laws shall be enacted to restrain or abridge the liberty of speech or of the press.

Sec. 9. In prosecutions for the publication of papers investigating the official conduct of officers or men in public capacity, or when the matter published is proper for public information, the truth thereof may be given in evidence; and that in all indictments for libel, the jury shall have the right to determine the law, and the facts under the direction of the Court.

Sec. 10. No person shall be deprived of the right to worship God according to the dictates of his own conscience; *Provided*, That the liberty of conscience hereby declared shall not justify practices inconsistent with the peace and moral safety of society.

Sec. 11. No form of religion shall be established by law; but it shall be the duty of the Legislature to pass suitable laws to protect every religious denomination in the peaceable enjoyment of its own mode of worship.

Sec. 12. The right of trial by jury shall remain inviolate.

Sec. 13. No person shall be disqualified as a witness, or be prevented from acquiring, holding and transmitting property, or be liable to any other punishment for any offence, or be hindered in acquiring education, or be subjected in law to any other restraints or disqualifications in regard to any personal rights than such as are laid upon others under like circumstances.

Sec. 14. No person shall be held to answer for any crime or offence until the same is fully, fairly, plainly, substantially and formally described to him; or be compelled to accuse or furnish evidence against himself; and every person shall have a right to produce all proofs that may be favorable to him, to meet the witnesses against him face to face, to have a speedy and public trial by an impartial jury, and to be fully heard in his defence of himself or by his counsel, as he may elect.

Sec. 15. No person shall be arrested, imprisoned, despoiled or dispossessed of his property, immunities or privileges, put out of the protection of the law, exiled or deprived of his life, liberty, or estate, but by the judgment of his peers or the law of the land. And the Legislature shall not enact any law that shall subject any person to punishment without trial by jury; nor shall he be punished but by virtue of a law already established, or promulgated prior to the offence, and legally applied.

Sec. 16. All Courts shall be open, and every person, for any injury that he may receive in his lands, goods, person or reputation, shall have remedy by due course of law and justice administered without unnecessary delay.

SEC. 17. All persons shall, before conviction, be bailable by sufficient sureties, except for capital offences, when the proof is evident or the presumption great; and excessive bail shall not, in any case, be required, nor corporal punishment inflicted.

SEC. 18. The privilege of the writ of *habeas corpus* shall not be suspended, except in case of insurrection, rebellion or invasion, as the public safety may require it.

SEC. 19. No person, after having been once acquitted by a jury, can again, for the same offence, be put in jeopardy of his life or liberty.

SEC. 20. No person shall be proceeded against, criminally, by information, for any indictable offence except in cases arising in the land or naval service, or in the militia when in actual service in the time of war or public danger, or by leave of the Court, for oppression or misdemeanor in office.

SEC. 21. No person shall be imprisoned for debt except in cases of fraud; and a reasonable amount of property, as a homestead, shall be exempted from seizure or sale for the payment of any debts or liabilities, except for taxes, that may be contracted after the adoption of this Constitution.

SEC. 22. No bill of attainder, *ex post facto* law, nor any law impairing the obligation of contracts, shall ever be enacted; and no conviction shall work corruption of blood or forfeiture of estate.

SEC. 23. Treason against the State shall consist in levying war against the same, or in adhering to its enemies, giving them aid and comfort. No person shall be convicted of treason unless on the testimony of two witnesses to the same overt act or on confession in open Court.

SEC. 24. All persons have a right to be secure from unreasonable searches or seizure of their persons, houses, papers or possessions. All warrants, therefore, are contrary to this right, if the cause or foundation of them be not previously supported by affirmation or oath, and if the order in the warrant to a civil officer to make search in suspected places, or to arrest one or more suspected persons, or to seize their property, be not accompanied with a special designation of the persons or objects of search, arrest or seizure; and no warrant shall be issued but in cases and with the formalities prescribed by the laws.

SEC. 25. Private property shall not be taken or applied for public use, or for the use of corporations, other than municipal or for private use, without the consent of the owner and a just compensation being made therefor; *Provided, however,* That laws may be made securing to persons or corporations the right of way over the lands of either persons or corporations, and for works of internal improvement, the right to establish depots, stations, turnouts, etc., but a just compensation, in all cases, shall be first made to the owner.

SEC. 26. The power of suspending the laws, or the execution of the laws, ought never to be exercised but by the Legislature, or by authority derived from it; to be exercised in such particular cases only as the Legislature may expressly provide for.

SEC. 27. No person shall, in any case, be subject to law martial, or to any pains or penalties by virtue of that law, except those employed in the army or navy, and except the militia in actual service, but by authority of the Legislature.

SEC. 28. In the government of this Commonwealth, the Legislative Department shall never exercise the executive and judicial powers, or either of them; the executive shall never exercise the legislative and judicial powers, or either of them; the judicial shall never exercise the legislative and executive powers, or either of them, to the end it may be a government of laws and not of men.

SEC. 29. The Legislature ought frequently to assemble for the redress of grievances—for correcting, strengthening and confirming the laws, and for making new laws as the common good may require.

SEC. 30. The people have a right to keep and bear arms for the common defence. As in times of peace, armies are dangerous to liberty, they ought not to be maintained without the consent of the Legislature. The military power shall always be held in an exact subordination to the civil authority and be governed by it.

SEC. 31. In time of peace no soldier ought to be quartered in any house without the consent of the owner; and, in time of war, such quarters ought not to be made but in a manner prescribed by law.

SEC. 32. No person who conscientiously scruples to bear arms shall be compelled to do so, but he may pay an equivalent for personal service.

SEC. 33. All elections shall be free and open, and every inhabitant of this Commonwealth possessing the qualifications provided for in this Constitution, shall have an equal right to elect officers and be elected for public employments.

SEC. 34. No property qualification shall be necessary for an election to or the holding of any office, and no office shall be created the appointment to which shall be for a longer time than good behavior. After the adoption of this Constitution, any person who shall fight a duel, or send or accept a challenge for that purpose, or be an aider or abetter in fighting a duel, shall be deprived of holding any office of honor or trust in this State, and shall be otherwise punished as the law shall prescribe.

SEC. 35. The right of suffrage shall be protected by laws regulating elections, and prohibiting, under adequate penalties, all undue influences from power, bribery, tumult or improper conduct.

SEC. 36. Representation shall be apportioned according to population, and no person in this State shall be disfranchised or deprived of any of the rights or privileges now enjoyed except by the law of the land or the judgment of his peers.

SEC. 37. Temporary absence from the State shall not forfeit a residence once obtained.

SEC. 38. All property subject to taxation ought to be taxed in proportion to its value. Each individual of society has a right to be protected in the enjoyment of life, property and liberty according to standing laws. He should, therefore, contribute his share to the expense of his protection and give his personal service when necessary.

SEC. 39. No subsidy, charge, impost tax or duties ought to be established, fixed, laid or levied, under any pretext whatsoever, without the consent of the people or their representatives lawfully assembled.

Sec. 40. Excessive fines shall not be imposed nor cruel and unusual punishment inflicted, nor shall witnesses be unreasonably detained.

Sec. 41. No title of nobility or distinction, or hereditary emolument shall ever be granted in this State.

Sec. 42. All navigable waters shall remain forever public highways, free to the citizens of the State and the United States, without tax, impost or toll imposed; and, no tax, toll or impost or wharfage shall be imposed, demanded or received from the owner of any merchandise or commodity, for the use of the shores or any wharf erected on the shores, or on or over the waters of any navigable stream, unless the same be expressly authorized by the Legislature.

Sec. 43. The enumeration of rights in this Constitution shall not be construed to impair or deny others retained by the people, and all powers not herein delegated remain with the people.

ARTICLE —.

JUDICIAL DEPARTMENT.

Sec. 1. The judicial power of this State shall be vested in a Supreme Court, in two Circuit Courts, to wit: A Court of Common Pleas, having civil jurisdiction and a Court of General Sessions, with criminal jurisdiction only, in District and Probate Courts, and in Justices of the Peace. The General Assembly may also establish such municipal and other inferior Courts as may be deemed necessary.

Sec. 2. The Supreme Court shall consist of three Judges, two of whom shall constitute a quorum. They shall be elected by a joint vote of the General Assembly for the term of six years, and shall continue in office until their successors shall be elected and qualified.

Sec. 3. They shall be so classified that one of the Judges shall go out of office every two years; and the Judge holding the shortest classification shall be Chief Justice of the Court during his term of office, and so on in rotation.

Sec. 4. The General Assembly, immediately after said election, shall determine by lot which of the three Judges elect shall serve for the term of two years, which for the term of four years, and which for the term of six years; and having so determined the same, it shall be the duty of the Governor to commission them accordingly.

Sec. 5. The Supreme Court shall have appellate jurisdiction only in cases of Chancery, and shall constitute a Court for the correction of errors at law, under such regulations as the General Assembly may by law prescribe: *Provided*, The said Court shall always have power to issue writs of injunction, *mandamus, quo warranto, habeas corpus,* and such other original and remedial writs as may be necessary to give it a general supervisory control over all other Courts in the State.

Sec. 6. The Supreme Court shall be held at least once in each year, at the seat of Government, and at such other place or places in the State as the General Assembly may direct.

Sec. 7. No judge shall preside on the trial of any cause in the event of which he may be interested, or where either of the parties shall be connected with him by affinity or consanguinity, within such degrees as may be prescribed by law, or in which he may have been counsel, or have presided in any inferior Court, except by consent of all the parties. In case all or any of the Judges of the Supreme Court shall be thus disqualified from presiding on any cause or causes, the Court or the Judges thereof shall certify the same to the Governor of the State and he shall immediately commission, specially, the requisite number of men of law knowledge for the trial and determination thereof. The same course shall be pursued in the circuit and inferior Courts as prescribed in this section for cases of the Supreme Court.

SEC. 8. There shall be appointed by the Judges of the Supreme Court a reporter and clerk of said Court, who shall hold their offices two years, and whose duties and compensation shall be prescribed by law.

SEC. 9. The Judges of the Supreme Court shall give their opinion upon important questions of constitutional law, and upon solemn occasions when required by the Governor, the Senate, or the House of Representatives; and all such opinions shall be published in connection with the reported decisions of said Court.

SEC. 10. When a judgment or decree is reversed or affirmed by the Supreme Court, every point made and distinctly stated in writing in the cause, and fairly arising upon the record of the case, shall be considered and decided; and the reasons therefor shall be concisely and briefly stated in writing, and preserved with the records of the case.

SEC. 11. The Judges of the Supreme Court and Circuit Courts shall, at stated times, receive a compensation for their services, to be fixed by law, which shall not be diminished during their continuance in office. They shall not be allowed any fees or perquisites of office, nor hold any other office of trust or profit under this State, the United States, or any other power.

SEC. 12. No person shall be eligible to the office of Judge of the Supreme Court or Circuit Courts who is not at the time of his election a citizen of the United States, and has not attained the age of thirty years, and been a resident of this State for five years next preceding his election, or from the adoption of this Constitution.

SEC. 13. All vacancies in the Supreme Court or other inferior tribunals shall be filled by election; *Provided*, That if the unexpired term does not exceed one year, such vacancy may be filled by Executive appointment. All judges, by virtue of their office, shall be conservators of the peace throughout the State.

SEC. 14. In all cases decided by the Supreme Court, a concurrence of two of the judges shall be necessary to a decision.

SEC. 15. The State shall be divided into convenient circuits, and for each circuit a judge shall be elected by the qualified electors thereof, who shall hold his office for a term of four years, and during his continuance in office he shall reside in the circuit of which he is judge.

SEC. 16. Judges of the Circuit Court shall interchange circuits with each other in such manner as may be determined by law.

SEC. 17. The Courts of Common Pleas shall have exclusive jurisdiction in all cases of divorce, and exclusive original jurisdiction in all civil cases and actions *ex delicto*, which shall not be cognizable before justices of the peace, and appellate jurisdiction in all such cases as may be provided by law. They shall have power to issue writs of *mandamus*, prohibition, *scire facias*, and all other writs which may be necessary for carrying their power fully into effect.

SEC. 18. The Court of Common Pleas shall sit in each Judicial District in this State at least twice in every year, at such stated times and places as may be appointed by law. It shall have full jurisdiction in all matters of equity, but the Courts heretofore established for that purpose shall continue as now organized until the first day of January, one thousand eight hundred and sixty-nine, for the disposition of causes now pending therein.

SEC. 19. The General Assembly shall provide by law for the preservation of the records of the Courts of Equity, and also for the transfer to the Court of Common Pleas and Probate Courts for final decision of all causes that may remain undetermined.

SEC. 20. The Court of General Sessions shall have exclusive jurisdiction over all criminal cases which shall not be otherwise provided for by law. It shall sit in each Judicial District in the State at least three times in each year, at such stated times and places as the General Assembly may direct.

SEC. 21. The qualified electors of each Judicial District shall elect three persons for the term of two years, who shall constitute a District Court which shall have full jurisdiction over roads, highways, ferries, bridges, and in all matters relating to taxes, disbursement of money for District purposes, and in every other case that may be necessary to the internal improvement and local concerns of the respective Districts.

SEC. 22. A Court of Probate shall be established in each Judicial District, with jurisdiction in all matters testamentary and of administration, in business appertaining to minors and the allotment of dower in cases of idiocy and lunacy, and persons *non compotes mentis*. The judge of said Court shall be elected by the qualified electors of the respective Districts for the term of two years.

SEC. 23. A competent number of the Justices of the Peace and Constables shall be chosen in each District by the qualified electors thereof, in such manner as the General Assembly may direct; they shall hold their offices for a term of two years, and until their successors are elected and qualified. They shall reside in the District, city or beat for which they are elected, and the Justices of the Peace shall be commissioned by the Governor.

SEC. 24. Justices of the Peace, individually, or two or more of them jointly, as the General Assembly may direct, shall have original jurisdiction in cases of bastardy, and in all matters of contract, and actions for the recovery of fines and forfeitures where the amount claimed does not exceed one hundred dollars, and such jurisdiction as may be provided by law in actions *ex delicto*, where the damages claimed does not exceed one hundred dollars; and prosecution for assault and battery and other penal offences less than felony punisable by fines only.

SEC. 25. They may also sit as examining Courts and commit, discharge or recognize persons charged with offences not capital, subject to such regulations as the General Assembly may provide; they shall also have

34

power to bind over to keep the peace, or for good behavior. For the foregoing purposes they shall have power to issue all necessary process.

Sec. 26. Every action cognizable before Justices of the Peace instituted by summons or warrant, shall be brought before some Justice of the Peace in the District or city where the defendant resides, and in all such causes tried by them, the right of appeal shall be secured under such rules and regulations as may be provided by law.

Sec. 27. The Judges of Probate, District Court Judges, Justices of the Peace, and Constables, shall receive for their services such compensation and fees as the General Assembly may from time to time by law direct.

Sec. 28. No person who has arrived at the age of seventy years, shall be appointed or elected to, or shall continue in the office of Judge in this State.

Sec. 29. Judges shall not charge juries in respect to matters of fact, but may state the testimony and declare the law.

Sec. 30. There shall be elected in each judicial District, by the electors thereof, one clerk for the Court of Common Pleas, who shall hold his office for the term of three years, and until his successor shall be elected and qualified. He shall, by virtue of his office, be clerk of all other Courts of record held therein; but the General Assembly may provide by law for the election of a clerk, with a like term of office, for each or any other of the Courts of record, and may authorize the Judge of the Probate Court to perform the duties of clerk for his Court, under such regulations as the General Assembly may direct. Clerks of Courts shall be removeable for such cause, and in such manner as shall be prescribed by law.

Sec. 31. There shall be an Attorney-General for the State, who shall reside at the seat of Government, and shall perform such duties as may be prescribed by law. He shall be elected by a joint vote of both branches of the General Assembly for the term of two years, and shall receive for his services a compensation to be fixed by law.

Sec. 32. There shall be one Solicitor for each circuit, who shall reside therein, to be elected by the qualified electors of the circuit, who shall hold his office for the term of four years, and shall receive for his services a compensation to be fixed by law. In all cases where an Attorney for the State, of any circuit, fails to attend and prosecute, according to law, the Court shall have power to appoint an Attorney *pro tempore*.

Sec. 33. The qualified electors of each District shall elect a Sheriff, a Coroner, and a District Surveyor, for the term of two years, and until their successors are elected and qualified; they shall be commissioned by the Governor, reside in their respective Districts during their continuance in office, and be disqualified for the office a second time, if it should appear that they or either of them are in default for moneys collected by virtue of their respective offices.

Sec. 34. All writs and process shall run, and all prosecutions shall be conducted in the name of the State of South Carolina; all writs shall be attested by the clerk of the court from which they shall be issued; and all indictments shall conclude against the peace and dignity of the State.

Sec. 35. The General Assembly shall provide by law for the speedy publication of the decisions of the Supreme Court made under this Constitution.

ARTICLE —.

JURISPRUDENCE.

SECTION 1. The General Assembly shall pass such laws as may be necessary and proper to decide differences by arbitrators, to be appointed by the parties who may choose that summary mode of adjustment.

SEC. 2. It shall be the duty of the General Assembly to pass the necessary laws for the change of venue in all cases, civil and criminal, over which the Circuit Courts have original jurisdiction, upon a proper showing, supported by affidavit, that a fair and impartial trial cannot be had in the District where such trial or prosecution was commenced.

SEC. 3. The General Assembly, at its first session after the adoption of this Constitution, shall make provision to revise, digest and arrange, under proper heads, the body of our laws, civil and criminal, and form a penal code, founded upon principles of reformation, and have the same promulgated in such manner as they may direct; and a like revision, digest and promulgation shall be made within every subsequent period of ten years. That justice shall be administered in a uniform mode of pleading, without distinction between law and equity, they shall provide for abolishing the distinct forms of action, and for that purpose shall appoint some suitable person or persons, whose duty it shall be to revise, simplify, and abridge the rules, practice, pleadings, and forms of the courts now in use in this State.

ARTICLE —.

EMINENT DOMAIN.

SECTION 1. The State shall have concurrent jurisdiction on all rivers bordering on this State, so far as such rivers shall form a common boundary to this and any other State bounded by the same; and they, together with all other navigable waters within the limits of the State, shall be common highways, and forever free, as well to the inhabitants of this State as to the citizens of the United States, without any tax or impost therefor.

SEC. 2. The title to all lands and other property, which have heretofore accrued to this State by grant, gift, purchase, forfeiture, escheats, or otherwise, shall vest in the State of South Carolina the same as though no change had taken place.

SEC. 3. The people of the State, in their right of sovereignty are declared to possess the ultimate property in and to all lands within the jurisdiction of the State; and all lands, the title to which shall fall from defect of heirs, shall revert, or escheat to the people.

ARTICLE —.

IMPEACHMENTS.

SECTION 1. The House of Representatives shall have the sole power of impeachment. A vote of two-thirds of all the members elected shall be required for an impeachment, and any officer impeached, shall thereby be suspended from office until judgment in the case shall have been pronounced.

Sec. 2. All impeachments shall be tried by the Senate. and when sitting for that purpose they shall be under oath or affirmation. No person shall be convicted except by vote of two-thirds of all the members elected. When the Governor is impeached, the Chief Justice of the Supreme Court, or the senior Judge, shall preside, with a casting vote in all preliminary questions.

Sec. 3. The Governor and all other executive and judicial officers shall be liable to impeachment; but judgment in such cases shall not extend further than removal from office. The persons convicted shall, nevertheless, be liable to indictment, trial and punishment according to law.

Sec. 4. For any wilful neglect of duty, or other reasonable cause, which shall not be sufficient ground of impeachment, the Governor shall remove any executive or judicial officer on the address of two-thirds of each House of the General Assembly. *Provided*, That the cause or causes for which said removal may be required shall be stated at length in such address, and entered on the journals of each House; *And provided further*, That the officer intended to be removed shall be notified of such cause or causes, and shall be admitted to a hearing in his own defence, before any vote for such address; and in all cases the vote shall be taken by yeas and nays, and be entered on the journals of each House respectively.

REPORT OF THE COMMITTEE ON EDUCATION.

THE ENCOURAGEMENT OF LITERATURE, ETC.

Whereas, we hold these statements as axioms : that education is knowledge; that knowledge is power; that knowledge rightly applied is the best and highest kind of power; that the general and universal diffusion of education and intelligence among the people is the surest guarantee of the enhancement. increase, purity and preservation of the great principles of republican liberty; therefore it shall be the duty of the General Assemblies, in all future periods of this Commonwealth, to establish, provide for, and perpetuate a liberal system of free public schools, to cherish the interests of literature and the sciences, and all seminaries and public schools, to encourage private and public institutions, rewards and immunities for the promotion of agriculture, arts, commerce, trades, manufactures, and natural history of the country, to countenance and inculcate the principles of humanity and general benevolence, public and private charity, industry and economy, honesty and punctuality, sincerity, sobriety, and all social affections and generous sentiments among the people.

Sec. 1. The supervision of public instruction shall be vested in a State Superintendent of Education, who shall be elected by the qualified electors of the State in such manner as the Legislature shall provide ; his powers, duties, terms of office and compensation shall be defined by the General Assembly.

Sec. 2. There shall be elected biennially, in each District or County, by the qualified electors of each District or County, one School Commissioner; said Commissioners to constitute a State Board of Education, of which the State Superintendent shall, by virtue of his office, be Chairman; the powers, duties and compensation of the members of said Board shall be determined by law.

Sec. 3. The General Assembly shall, as soon as practicable after the adoption of this Constitution, provide for a liberal and uniform system of free public schools throughout the State, and shall also make provision for the division of the State into suitable School Districts. There shall be kept open, at least six months in each year, one or more schools in each School District.

Sec. 4. It shall be the duty of the General Assembly to provide for the compulsory attendance, at either public or private schools, of all children between the ages of six and sixteen years, not physically or mentally disabled, for a term equivalent to twenty-four months.

Sec. 5. The General Assembly shall levy at each regular session after the adoption of this Constitution an annual tax on all taxable property throughout the State for the support of public schools, which tax shall be collected at the same time and by the same agents as the general State levy, and shall be paid into the Treasury of the State. There shall be assessed on all taxable polls in the State an annual tax of one dollar on each poll, the proceeds of which tax shall be applied solely to educational purposes. No other poll or capitation tax shall be levied in the State, nor shall the amount assessed on each poll exceed the limit given in this section. The School tax shall be distributed among the several School Districts of the State in proportion to their respective population between the ages of five and twenty-one years. No religious sect or sects shall have exclusive right to or control of any part of the school funds of the State, nor shall sectarian principles be taught in the public schools.

Sec. 6. Within five years after the regular session of the General Assembly, following the adoption of this Constitution, it shall be the duty of the General Assembly to provide for the establishment and support of a State Normal School, which shall be open to all persons who may wish to become teachers.

Sec. 7. Institutions for the benefit of all the insane, blind, and deaf and dumb, and such other benevolent institutions as the public good may require, shall be established and supported by the State, subject to such regulations as may be prescribed by law.

Sec. 8. Provisions shall be made by law, as soon as practicable, for the establishment and maintenance of a State Reform School for juvenile offenders.

Sec. 9. The respective Districts or Counties of the State shall make provisions, as may be determined by law, for all those inhabitants who, by reason of age and infirmities, or misfortunes, may have claim upon the sympathy and aid of society.

Sec. 10. The General Assembly shall provide for the maintenance of the State University, and as soon as practicable, provide for the establishment of an Agricultural College, and shall appropriate the land donated to this State for the support of such a College, by the Act of Congress, passed July 2, 1862, or the money or scrip, as the case may be, arising from the sale of said lands, or any lands which may hereafter be granted or appropriated for such purpose, for the support and maintenance of such college, and may make the same a branch of the State University, for instruction in agriculture, the mechanic arts, and the natural sciences connected therewith.

SEC. 11. All the public schools, colleges and universities of this State supported by the public funds shall be free and open to all the children and youths of the State, without regard to race or color.

SEC. 12. The proceeds of all lands that have been, or hereafter may be, granted by the United States to this State, and not otherwise appropriated by this State or the United States, and of all lands or other property given by individuals, or appropriated by the State for like purposes, and of all estates of deceased persons who have died without leaving a will or heir, shall be securely invested and sacredly preserved as a State School Fund, and the annual interest and income of said fund, together with such other means as the General Assembly may provide, shall be faithfully appropriated for the purpose of establishing and maintaining free public schools, and for no other purposes or use whatever.

Mr. R. C. DeLARGE. On the 29th of January, a resolution was introduced by the gentleman from Newberry (Mr. B. O. DUNCAN), that a Committee of eight be appointed, or a Committee of one be appointed from each District, whose duty it should be to report to this Convention the names of such persons as are disfranchised under the Acts of Congress, so that we might petition Congress for their re-enfranchisement; which was referred to the Committee on Petitions, who have so far failed to report. As Chairman of the Committee on Franchise and Elections, I would like to know what action has been taken on that subject.

Mr. W. J. WHIPPER. I move that the Committee be required to report to-morrow at twelve o'clock. Agreed to.

Mr. A. J. RANSIER. I desire to call the attention of the house to the fact that three Standing Committees have reported, and furnished business for this Convention. I move, therefore, to change the hour of the sessions by striking out twelve, A. M., and inserting ten, so that the Convention hereafter will meet at ten o'clock every morning, and continue in session until three o'clock every afternoon. Referred to the Committee on Rules and Regulations.

Mr. A. J. RANSIER moved that the Committee on Rules and Regulations be instructed to report at twelve o'clock to-morrow, which was agreed to.

The PRESIDENT announced the following gentlemen as the Committee on the division of the State into Congressional Districts: Messrs. B. O. Duncan, Newberry; Jas. H. Goss, Union; E. W. M. Mackey, Orangeburg; B. F. Whittemore, Darlington; W. J. Whipper, Beaufort; R. H. Cain, Charleston; Wilson Cooke, Greenville; D. H. Chamberlain, Berkley.

On motion of Mr. F. J. MOSES, Jr., the Convention adjourned.

NINETEENTH DAY.

Thursday, February 6, 1868.

The Convention assembled at 12 M., and was called to order by the PRESIDENT.

Prayer was offered by the Rev. E. P. SMITH, of New York.

The roll was called, and a quorum answering to their names, the PRESIDENT announced the Convention ready to proceed to business.

The Journal of the preceding day was read and approved.

Mr. R. C. DeLARGE. I rise to a question of privilege. I desire, with permission of the Convention, to amend the resolution adopted yesterday, requesting the President to draw from the State Treasury $30,000. I have been informed that it would be impossible for the State Treasurer to pay the money, unless through General Canby's order, and it would be necessary to amend the resolution by directing the President to request General Canby to draw the amount from the Treasury. I move that the house suspend the rules for the purpose of reconsideration.

The motion was agreed to, and the question being put on the proposed amendment, it was adopted.

The PRESIDENT announced the hour for the Special Order had arrived.

The Special Order being the "Bill of Rights," on motion, it was taken up and read by sections.

On motion of Mr. HOLMES, the first section was amended by striking out the words, "may be reckoned," in the sentence enumerating the inalienable rights, so as to read, "among which are the rights," &c.

Mr. B. O. DUNCAN. I desire to offer an amendment, which may be deemed harsh in some respects, but which I think is important. It is that the words "born free and equal" shall be stricken out. This sentiment is incorrect. Doubtless as understood by the framers of the Declaration of Independence, it was correct, but it is entirely false that any person is born free. No persons are free until a certain age. They are subject to their parents or guardians. If it is understood likewise to refer to equal capacity, that cannot be proved, for you cannot tell the capacity of all children. Hence, unless some definition showing what the expression means is attached, taken literally, it would be false.

I regard this doctrine as showing great weakness on the part of the early moral philosophers. Our Southern professors did not object, however, to receive it into their colleges. If this meaning had been taken and understood as it reads, falsehood would not have been promulgated. While I entirely concur with the rest of the section, I think we should have in our Constitution only what is strictly true and proper.

Mr. J. J. WRIGHT. I agree that we should incorporate in the Constitution only that which is right and proper, but I cannot concur with the gentleman in saying that it was not right and proper to insert that "all men are born free and equal." If he would put the interpretation upon these words which is given to them in moral philosophy, which is to govern them, I have no doubt that it would change the gentleman's opinion. The section says: "All men are born free and equal; endowed by their Creator with certain inalienable rights, the right of enjoying and defending their lives, liberties," &c.

That is exactly what is meant here, and just exactly what was meant by the framers of the Declaration of Independence in declaring "all men born free and equal," as far as their rights were concerned. So far as those rights which men have by birth. they are all born free and equal, free to breathe the same vital air, to exercise their bodies and to enjoy life.

I hope the section will stand as it is, and believe that the framers of the Declaration of Independence as well knew the import of those words as the gentleman who opposed them. I believe they will be concurred in by the majority of the Convention. Some of the leading politicians of South Carolina, of Massachusetts, Pennsylvania and New York have declared that the fathers of our country did not know what they said when they asserted that "all men are born free and equal." But the times have changed and these very men begin not only to see, but to confess, the great truth involved. For this Convention to set up a different standard would be ridiculous.

Mr. B. O. DUNCAN. I do not disagree with the gentleman at all, and he need not try to make it apparent that I do not agree that all men ought to have equal rights. It is only the phraseology to which I object. With the modification which comes after the words "born free and equal," I entirely concur.

Mr. B. F. RANDOLPH. It always seemed strange to me that any intelligent person should question the meaning of the phrase "born free and equal." If it was an anxiom, found in physiology or metaphysics, it might seem questionable, but in politics it ought to be clear and right.

We know that some men, physically speaking, are born tall, some short, some with good sense, some with little sense, some with big and some with little feet. But this phrase was not intended to refer to men in a physiological sense. It refers to the rights of men politically speaking, and in that sense the founders of the Government understood it. In that sense I understand and defend it. All men are born with certain inalienable rights which it is their privilege to enjoy.

Mr. C. C. BOWEN. As a question of phraseology seems to have arisen, I will offer an amendment which I think will obviate all objections. It is this: "That all men are born equally free and independent, and have certain natural, inherent and inalienable rights."

Mr. B. F. WHITTEMORE. I would like to ask the mover how people are born independent. As I understand the matter we are born dependent. The member from Orangeburg (Mr. B. F. RANDOLPH), has rightly interpreted the meaning of the phrase in the Bill of Rights that "all men are born free and equal." We do not pretend to say that all men are born free and equal in the enjoyment of the luxuries of life, but that all men are born free and equal politically; that they shall have equal political rights and equal chances, whatever their aspirations may be for position, if they possess ability for the attainment of that position.

On motion of Mr. GEORGE LEE, the amendments were laid upon the table.

The first section was then passed to its third reading.

Mr. B. O. DUNCAN moved to amend the second section by inserting the words "except as a punishment for crime," in lieu of the phrase "otherwise than," which was adopted, and the section passed to its third reading.

Mr. B. O. DUNCAN moved to substitute for the third section the following: "All political power is originally vested in and derived from the people, and all forms of government are founded on their authority and instituted for their peace, safety and happiness."

Mr. B. F. WHITTEMORE. That changes the character of the section altogether, which declares that all political power is vested in and derived from the people only, and therefore they have the right to modify the form of government, &c. I trust, therefore, the amendment will not prevail, and move to lay it upon the table.

The PRESIDENT. I call the attention of members to the fact that the only way to get rid of the amendment is to vote it down. If the amendment is laid on the table, it carries with it, according to parliamentary usage, the original proposition.

Mr. B. O. DUNCAN. I desire to say in reply to the gentleman from Darlington, that what is said in the first line is all we have a right to say. We may make provision in the Constitution for changing the constitutional law when deemed necessary. But in the Bill of Rights it is not proper to insert such a provision. There is no use in having everything

35

in the Bill of Rights that we have in other articles of the Constitution. I desire to see no repetition.

Mr. C. C. BOWEN. I hope the amendment will be passed. I certainly see a necessity for the substitution of this section. All the discussion and difficulty which led to the late long and bloody war arose upon a similar declaration to the one in that section that the people "have the right, at all times, to modify their form of government." It was upon this clause the South claimed the right to go out of the Union whenever they pleased. They rested their entire cause upon it. I, therefore, see no necessity for inserting that in the Constitution when they put in the section immediately following, a provision which repeals it. A great deal of discussion has arisen all over the United States in reference to this subject, and nearly every State in its Constitution, has a similar section. It is said that a Judge of the United States Supreme Court spent a great deal of time in drawing up that section of the Constitution. It is known in all Constitutions as the States Rights clause. But in all the late Constitutions it has been left out.

Mr. J. H. JENKS. I agree with the mover of the amendment, and the member who last spoke, that the section as it stands is revolutionary. All the questions of State Rights have arisen on this clause, or a similar one in the Constitution of the States. A war of seven years or less, and the blood and treasure spilled and wasted, ought to have settled it forever, and I object to introducing in the Bill of Rights any clause on which there ever can be again raised the question of the paramount allegiance of men to different States or to the general Government. I hope the amendment will prevail.

Mr. A. J. RANSIER. I agree with the last speaker, that the Bill of Rights should set forth that the people owe paramount allegiance to the Government of the United States. The Bill of Rights has embodied that idea, and provided for it in express terms. In doing this, it also denies the right of secession. While this section acknowledges the right of the people to change their form of Government, it does not carry with it the right of secession, and in other portions of the Constitution such a right is explicitly denied.

Mr. R. C. DeLARGE. I hope the amendment will prevail. That all power is derived from the people, no one would question, but that the people of the State have a right to change the government of the State, in such manner as deemed expedient, I do deny.

Mr. L. S. LANGLEY. If the people of the State have the right to change their government at all, who ought they change it to suit, if not to suit themselves.

Mr. R. C. DeLARGE. They have the right to change it agreeably to the compact which binds all the States in one republic. The people of South Carolina in 1860, considered it their right to modify the form of government in such a manner as they deemed expedient. We know how they construed it then ; and we are not prepared to say what others coming after us may construe this clause to mean. I therefore fully agree to the amendment of the gentleman from Newberry (Mr. DUNCAN), and hope it will prevail. The people should have the right to modify their form of government ; provided such modification does not conflict with the laws or allegiance due by the citizens of the State to the General Government.

Mr. A. C. RICHMOND. The people of this State will sometime be called upon to modify their form of government ; but in order that there shall never again be danger of revolution or secession, I desire to see it provided that while free to change their Constitution, the modification shall be in accordance with some known and clearly stated law.

Mr. W. J. McKINLAY. Section 3 says that "all political power is vested in and derived from the people." If we admit this fact, the people certainly have a right at all times to modify their form of government. I hope, therefore, the original section will be adopted.

Mr. B. F. RANDOLPH. The only argument urged against this section seems to be that it vests the people with the power to secede. I do not so understand it. The people of South Carolina, when they attempted to secede, did not attempt to change their State government, but to sever the relationship with the General Government. They were fighting to perpetuate the form of government established here. When gentlemen say this proposes to vest the people of South Carolina with the right to change their form of government, they say what is in accordance with Republicanism. Therefore I hope the section will be passed as it stands.

Mr. F. L. CARDOZO. I trust the amendment will not prevail. The gentleman from Newberry wishes to amend the section simply to avoid repetition in the Constitution. I do not think such would be the case. The section simply lays down a general law for the future, and states the manner in which a change is to be made. Several gentlemen have endeavored to give to it a States Rights signification, but I cannot see upon what they base that theory. They all admit that the people have the power to modify their own form of government, and this section only acknowledges that the people have the same right which is now being exercised through their representatives here in Convention assembled. As the section says the motive or inducement which may cause them to change, shall be the public good. I fail to discover any repetition in the section or the theory of State Rights, either asserted or implied.

Mr. J. H. CRAIG offered the following amendment:

That all political power be vested in and derived from the people only, and they, therefore, have a right to modify their form of government, as herein provided by this Constitution, whenever the public good demands it.

Mr. N. G. PARKER. I believe that the amendment of the gentleman from Newberry is an extract from the Constitution of South Carolina of 1808. I do not object to it on that account, but it does seem to me that we are making too much of a Constitution—doing more than is absolutely necessary. The same idea is contained in section 3, and is asserted something like fifteen times in the Bill of Rights. I see no reason why we should pass either the section or the substitute. As to the amendment of the gentleman from Colleton (Mr. CRAIG), I do not think that helps the matter at all. If his amendment is to be adopted, I shall move to strike out the five last words, "whenever the public good demands."

Mr. B. O. DUNCAN. I agree with the gentleman who has last spoken, that the section may be left out altogether. The latter part comes within the province of the Legislative Committee, which I know has had the subject under consideration. As regards the original section, which states that "all political power is derived from the people," I would like to know whether civil power does not likewise belong to the people? In my amendment, I say that which is more broadly true, namely, that all power is vested in the will of the people, and I think it may properly be inserted in the Bill of Rights.

Mr. R. J. DONALDSON. It seems to me that so far as regards State Rights, that idea is completely exploded in the two following sections. It is, therefore, needless to discuss the subject, and to bring the question to a vote, I move that all the amendments be indefinitely postponed.

The motion was agreed to.

Mr. C. C. BOWEN offered the following as a substitute: "That all power is inherent in the people, and that all free governments are founded on the consent of the governed. Therefore, no attempt shall ever be made to abridge the right of suffrage in this State except as provided in the Constitution."

Mr. B. F. WHITTEMORE. The gentleman will find, as he proceeds, that there is a clause which provides for that which he has proposed, in Sections 33 and 35.

Mr. R. C. DeLARGE. I would like to know in how many clauses are the people defended and protected.

Mr. B. F. WHITTEMORE. We propose to protect the people in all the clauses in the Bill of Rights. We are here for the purpose of modifying the laws of this Commonwealth, and in this department of the Constitution, we propose to lay down the general principle that the people have a right to modify their form of government in such manner as they deem expedient when the public good demands it. The Legislative part of the Constitution will define how this change is to be made.

Mr. F. J. MOSES, Jr. I do not desire to speak of the debate on this subject, or to prevent any gentleman from using all proper arguments in reference to the discussion of the subject, which can properly be brought to bear. But it does seem to me extraordinary, that in debating this Bill of Rights, the amendments to each section offered should be attempted to be defeated by a reference to other provisions or sections which are not before the Convention at all, except in the form of a report from the Committee. I understand this Bill of Rights to be nothing more nor less than simply a report from the Committee. After adopting the first section, it may be the good sense of the house to arrest and lay the report upon the table. I think it is a dangerous precedent to be setting, to defeat an amendment by reference to other provisions we have not yet attempted to discuss.

Mr. A. J. RANSIER. I will remind the gentleman that I, for one, referred to the Bill of Rights, because the declaration was made by some gentlemen who favored the amendment, that it provided for and advocated the right of secession, and I referred to other clauses in the hope of throwing light on the subject.

Mr. F. L. CARDOZO. I hope the voice of the gentleman from Sumter will not prevail with us. I think it very natural and proper for the Chairman of the Committee on the Bill of Rights to remind us of any amendments or substitutes offered that are already provided for in the Bill of Rights, and especially to a case in point. For instance, in the case of the amendment of the gentleman from Charleston (Mr. BOWEN), who has his own Bill of Rights printed in a newspaper. He reads from the newspaper the section he wishes to be substituted for the report of the Committee, and if that is done on any large scale, we may as well throw this report aside and adopt his. I think we had better go by this report of the Committee, especially as it touches upon all the points the gentleman from Charleston refers to. I hope this section will be adopted just as it is, and if other points are to be provided for, we will discuss them as they come up. I think it wise that the Chairman of the Committee should not let us jumble the sections together.

Mr. C. C. BOWEN. I did not intend to say anything more upon this section. I must say I am surprised. The whole gist of the matter has come out. The objection to the amendment is this: the gentleman who spoke last did not write it; he did not have a hand in it. I simply wish to inform the gentleman from Charleston (Mr. CARDOZO), that I was elected by the people to come here and do my duty. I was sent here to represent them in framing a Constitution for the State of South Carolina. I will remind him that on every occasion when necessary, I shall get up and lift my voice against anything wrong. I care not how much he objects to it. If I see fit to devote my time in writing up a Constitution, I claim the right to do it, and let it not be made a matter of imputation now because a man has the sense to do it. I certainly did have leisure time and I devoted that time to putting on paper my views in regard to the Constitution of South Carolina. I have that document here now, and I intend to insist, as far as I can, on getting these provisions adopted, simply because I think they are right. If any man will show anything better I will yield to it. I will not be so ungrateful as the delegate from Charleston, as to say, because he wrote it, it shall be thrown out. If no man has a right to offer an amendment, let us put this report to a vote, adopt it as a whole, and get rid of it at once. I am here as a representative of the people to protect their rights. I certainly do think, with due deference to the delegate from Charleston, that the substitute I offered is a proper substitute.

It has been urged on the other side that three or four separate clauses are already in the Bill of Rights, which covers the same point. My answer to that is, if we can get it into one section, make it brief and concise, you will shorten a document which is already too long. Therefore, if the point is covered in the substitue I offered, and we can get rid of two or three other sections, I say, in God's name, let us adopt it. I will say this much, that I spent some little time upon that individual section. I read and re-read it; I wrote and re-wrote it; "that all power is inherent in the people, and all free governments are founded upon their authority, and established for the peace, safety and happiness of the whole people, therefore no attempt shall ever be made to abridge or destroy the right of suffrage that is now enjoyed by any person or persons, except as provided for in this Constitution."

I would say this much more. It has been but once that a large majority of the people of South Carolina has ever taken any part in its elective franchise. I supposed, as a matter of course, something would be said under the head of elections, as to the qualifications of an elector; secondly, I closed by saying, "except such persons are made in the Constitution." I do think something should be put in the section besides that which is totally superfluous. I contend that the section just read is entirely superfluous. I start out by saying that, "men are born free and equal; that they are endowed by their Creator with certain inalienable rights." I certainly fail to see the necessity of reminding the people in in the very next section that they have a right to alter their form of government. I will state here that no proposition has been laid down by me, or the party who advocated the adoption of my amendment, that the people did not have that right. No one would be insane enough to get up here and say the people did not have the right upon the proper occasion to change their form of government. But I say that it is usual in all Constitutions to insert an article under that head, whenever experience dictates a change should take place, showing how or in what manner it should take place. I therefore see no necessity of putting it in half a dozen places.

Mr. F. L. CARDOZO. I desire not to be misunderstood. The gentleman from Charleston says that I object to his amendment because I did not write it. I am not a member of the Committee on the Bill of Rights. I certainly did not write either this one or any other. I therefore do not claim authorship either one way or the other. He clung to that as his text roving all over creation. What I said was this, that it was better for us to adhere to the printed document of the Committee before us, which embraced all the points referred to in the document which he read. We were informed that the gentleman just arose with the newspaper in his hand and offered the proposed amendment. That was unexpected. I still think we had better adhere to the report of the Committee. As to his imputation of jealousy he is mistaken. I have not written any Constitution. I stand just as he does.

Mr. C. C. BOWEN. I would simply state that I thought I complied with the rules of the house, as I reduced my substitute to writing and sent it to the Chair.

Mr. L. S. LANGLEY. I move that the amendment be indefinitely postponed.

The motion was agreed to.

Mr. L. S. LANGLEY called for the previous question, which was not sustained.

Mr. S. CORLEY offered the following amendment :

" All political power is vested in and derived from the people only ; therefore they have a right at all times to modify their form of government as provided for in the Constitution."

Mr. C. C. BOWEN. I move that we adopt the declaration or Bill of Rights as a whole.

The PRESIDENT. That motion is not in order. The house has already adopted a resolution to take up the Bill of Rights, clause by clause.

The question was then taken on the passing of Section 3 to a third reading, which resulted affirmatively.

Mr. F. J. MOSES, Jr. I move a re-consideration of the vote by which the second section was adopted. I presume it was the intention of the Committee who framed the section, that it should mean that slavery should never exist in this State, and at the same time that involuntary servitude might exist as a punishment for crime. But this intention has not been carried out. As the matter now stands, the Legislature have the right, as a punishment for crime, either to place a citizen in positive slavery or involuntary servitude. There is a great deal of difference in the two. The amendment I have to offer is this: "Slavery shall never exist in this State, neither shall involuntary servitude, except as a punishment for crime, whereof the party shall have been duly convicted."

The motion to reconsider was then agreed to.

Mr. A. J. RANSIER. I am glad that the gentleman from Sumter has been able to solve this problem. The Committee had the matter under consideration, but were unable to separate the idea and express it in the clear and unmistakeable manner in which it is now presented.

The question on agreeing to the amendment was then taken and decided in the affirmative, and the section was passed to its third reading.

Section 4 was read a second time, and without amendment passed to its third reading.

Section 5 was read as follows: "This State shall ever remain a member of the American Union, and all attempts from whatever source, or upon whatever pretext to dissolve the said Union, ought to be resisted with the whole power of the State.

Mr. G. PILLSBURY moved that the words "ought to" be stricken out, and the word "shall" be inserted.

Mr. B. F. WHITTEMORE. The Committee on the Bill of Rights originally had it "shall," but finally concluded to leave the matter to the decision of the Convention.

The amendment was agreed to.

Mr. F. J. MOSES, Jr., moved to amend the section by striking out the words "dissolve said," and insert "disconnect it from the."

Mr. N. G. PARKER moved to insert "sever from," instead of "disconnect."

Mr. W. J. McKINLAY. I hope the amendment will not prevail. The

States compose the Union; if one State leaves that Union, she dissolves it. The term is both correct and expressive.

Mr. F. J. MOSES, Jr. It seems to me that the gentleman is entirely oblivious of the fact that the United States Government during the prosecution of the war, insisted that the Union was not dissolved. Such a thought as that ought not to emanate from this Convention.

Mr. D. H. CHAMBERLAIN. I am anxious that the phraseology of this section should remain as it was reported from the Committee, for the term "dissolve" pledges us to more than the proposed amendment of the gentleman from Sumter. It not only pledges us to resist an effort to dissolve in this State, but in any other State.

Mr. F. J. MOSES, Jr. I do not see why it is necessary that we should say that an attempt made by any other State to dissolve her connection with the Union shall be resisted with the whole power of South Carolina. If I understand the spirit of this Declaration of Rights, the principle is emphatically announced that South Carolina is and shall forever remain a member of the Union. Hence, we are already pledged as a State to resist, at whatever cost, the dissolution of that Union.

Mr. R. J. DONALDSON. I hope the section will stand as reported by the Committee. We are here first, to unequivocally declare that our State shall ever remain a part of the Union, and we are to guard, at the same time, a certain amount of State Rights. I am, therefore, for one, willing to pledge this State to the protection of the Union, so that in the future, we shall not stand in such an anamolous condition as did Kentucky during the late rebellion.

Mr. F. J. MOSES, Jr. Does the State from which you come contain such a clause in the Declaration of Rights?

Mr. R. J. DONALDSON. Yes. sir.

Mr. R. C. DeLARGE. What State do you come from?

Mr. R. J. DONALDSON. From South Carolina.

Mr. F. L. CARDOZO. I desire to see this section adopted as it stands, because it not only pledges South Carolina not to go out of the Union, but that no other State shall go out without being resisted with all our force. Massachusetts, in the late war, acted practically in the spirit of this section. She used her power to prevent South Carolina from going out of the Union; and, if Massachusetts should, at any time, undertake to secede, I want South Carolina to return the compliment to her and prevent the act.

The question was now taken on agreeing to the amendment, and it was decided in the negative.

36

Mr. B. F. RANDOLPH moved to amend by striking out the words "American Union," and inserting "United States of America."

The motion was not agreed to.

Section 5 was then passed to its third reading.

Section 6 was read a second time and passed to its third reading without debate.

Section 7 was read as follows :

"All persons resident in this State, born in the United States, or who have been naturalized, and shall have legally become citizens of the United States, are hereby declared citizens of South Carolina, possessing equal civil and political rights and public privileges as hereinafter declared by this Constitution."

Mr. C. C. BOWEN. I move to strike out this entire section as superfluous. It was decided long ago by the Supreme Court of the United States, that a citizen of the United States residing in any State was a citizen of that State. The Supreme Court of the United States is the highest tribunal of the land, and I, therefore, see no necessity of our declaring what has already been decided by that Court. The decision I allude to was delivered by Chief Justice Marshall, in the case of Gasses vs. Ballou, 6 Peters, and was that any citizen residing in any State of the Union was a citizen of the United States and of the State in which he so resided.

Mr. F. L. CARDOZO. I would like to ask what political rights the citizen in the State by that section would be entitled to.

Mr. B. F. WHITTEMORE. The section says, "to all political rights and privileges as hereinafter declared."

Mr. C. C. BOWEN. That comes under the consideration of the Committee on Franchise and Elections.

Mr. R. C. DeLARGE. The Committee on Review and Consolidation agreed that that section should not be reported.

Mr. B. F. WHITTEMORE. I know of no such agreement, and think the gentleman is mistaken. There was a conflicting clause, and it was settled in the committee room, but not that this section should be stricken out.

Mr. F. J. MOSES, Jr. If I understand the Chairman of the Committee on the Bill of Rights (Mr. WHITTEMORE) correctly, that this section prescribes that all persons resident in this State are citizens of the State, in accordance with what is hereinafter declared by the Constitution, then the section does not carry out the object. After declaring that they are citizens of South Carolina, it goes on to say that the citizens of

South Carolina possess equal civil and political rights and public privileges as hereinafter declared by this Constitution. If the words used can be construed in any other light than that, I would like to be informed. All residents are declared citizens, with all the privileges as such, subject to no limitations made in the Constitution. If this section is adopted as it stands, there will be no need of the Committee on Franchise and Elections saying how long a man shall be a resident of the State.

Mr. F. L. CARDOZO. I agree with the gentleman from Sumter. It will be observed there are four conditions necessary to make a man a citizen of South Carolina : First, residence in the State; second, he must be born in the United States; third, naturalization, and fourth, he shall have legally become a citizen of the United States. He may then, after obtaining all these four, become a citizen of South Carolina. After obtaining these four, a residence here of one hour will make him a citizen.

Mr. D. H. CHAMBERLAIN. I desire to call attention to the fact that the term resident used here is a legal term. Residence is a well known legal term, and it will be defined hereafter what constitutes residence in the State, and, with that being settled, it is proper and right that this term should be used here. The Constitution will provide how long a man shall remain to acquire a residence, but to imagine that because a man is here for a short time it makes him a resident is absurd. It is a legal provision, and this Constitution will define what a man's residence is, how long they shall remain, and, that being determined, I think it is right it shall say all persons having a residence in this State shall be citizens of South Carolina. It seems to me the phraseology is precisely right.

Mr. B. O. DUNCAN. I shall not speak on the motion to strike out this section, but I am opposed to its standing here, on the ground that I think it belongs elsewhere, in another part of the Constitution. It seems to me this Bill of Rights contains a good deal that belongs to other parts of the Constitution. This question, in particular, I think belongs to the report of the Committee on Franchise and Elections.

Mr. R. J. DONALDSON. Taking into consideration the position and condition of our State at the present day, I think the Committee on the Bill of Rights have done well in introducing this section, which unequivocally declares that all men residents here or born in the State are citizens. Had South Carolina always been a free State we would have concluded there was no necessity for such a clause as this. I think the Committee have done well in engrafting in their Bill of Rights this clause, which forever sets at rest all questions as to the inalienable rights of citizenship. In our State formerly one class of men were declared not possessed of these inalienable rights. As the gentleman who has just taken his seat (Mr. CHAMBERLAIN) very ably remarks, residence is a legal term. A man may be in South Carolina twelve months or ten years and not be a citizen of the State. I think there is nothing in this section that trenches upon the report of the Committee on Franchise and Elections. I hope it will pass as it is.

Mr. F. J. MOSES, Jr. I do not agree with the gentleman from Chesterfield (Mr. R. J. DONALDSON) in reference to his law point. The word resident is not used in a technical sense, nor will it be unless used where a technical sense applies to it. In order to make the word " resident" a legal term, you must put the word legal before it. I suppose you will agree with me on that point. If gentlemen would confine themselves to the subject under discussion, and not rove off and talk about inalienable rights, we could get along much faster. The objection I have to this section is that every man in the State of South Carolina is declared a citizen. You can read it any way you please and it must amount to that, and if you adopt the section you may as well dispense with the report of the Committee on Franchise and Elections.

I agree with the gentleman from Chesterfield, that the Committee on the Bill of Rights has done well. I do not believe any other Committee could have done so well, and produced such an instrument in so short a space of time.

Mr. J. J. WRIGHT. I am surprised that there has been so much discussion over this section I consider it entirely useless, and hope it will be stricken out. As far as citizenship is concerned, that has already been decided, and the Constitution of the United States declares what is meant by the word citizen, when it says that the citizens of one State shall be entitled to the rights and privileges of the citizens of the several States. If a man is a citizen of Massachusetts, North Carolina, Georgia, or any other State in the Union, when he comes to the State of South Carolina and rebels, or tramples upon any laws of this State, he is subject to the jurisdiction and laws of the State. We cannot admit, however, the latter part of the clause, which declares all citizens of the United States entitled to all the privileges and rights of citizens of this State. The Committee on Franchise and Elections will report a clause defining those who are citizens entitled to be electors and their privileges ; I am, therefore, in favor of striking out the section.

On motion of Mr. B. F. WHITTEMORE, section 7 was stricken out.

The PRESIDENT announced Messrs. C. P. Leslie, W. E. Rose, and S. A. Swails, Auditing Committee.

On motion of Mr. F. L. CARDOZO, the rules were suspended to enable the Committee on Rules and Regulations to make a report, which was made as follows :

SOUTH CAROLINA CONSTITUTIONAL CONVENTION, {
Charleston, February 6, 1868. {

Your Committee, to whom was referred the resolution to amend the first section of Rule first, by striking out the word " twelve" and inserting " ten," beg leave to state that they had the matter under consideration, and respectfully report through their Chairman the following amendment : To strike out the word " ten," and insert " half-past ten," and strike out the word " three" and insert " half-past two," so that it will read : " The sessions of this Convention shall commence at half-past ten o'clock, A. M., and continue until half-past two o'clock, P. M. each day, unless otherwise ordered." With these alterations, your Committee would respectfully recommend the adoption of the resolution.

Respectfully submitted.

S. A. SWAILS, Chairman.

Mr. A. J. RANSIER moved the adoption of the report.

Mr. F. J. MOSES, Jr. As I expect the argument on the Constitution is coming up, and we will all have to make a free use of our lungs, I move to amend by striking out half past two, and inserting two o'clock.

Mr. J. J. WRIGHT moved as an amendment, to strike out " ten" and insert " half past ten o'clock," and strike out " three o'clock" and insert " one o'clock," and add " shall meet at three o'clock and adjourn at five."

Mr. M. MAULDIN moved that the old establishment be sustained.

Mr. B. O. DUNCAN. I do not agree with the amendment of the gentleman from Beaufort (Mr. WRIGHT). I think we would prefer an evening session, and that we should meet at seven, or half past seven, and continue until nine or ten o'clock.

Mr. F. J. MOSES, Jr. I trust that amendment will be voted down, and for this reason. I am here, any how, absent from home, and I would just as leave be in this Convention, listening to sparkling, eloquent speeches from the members ; but I would simply remind members we are not sitting here on unimportant business, that our work is a serious one, and that we should apply ourselves to it in a serious and proper mode. Framing a Constitution is most important, and I, for one, will acknowledge I am not competent to the task of sitting here all that time the gentleman proposes, then to come back the next day and vote understandingly on all those important questions, without having had time to consider them outside of the Convention. When a member is up speaking it is no time for him to be considering these questions. We must have sometime outside the Convention hall. When we come here we come to vote on the matters brought before us. If it is the desire simply to get through here as quickly as possible, and rush these things through with speed, let us commence by adopting the whole Bill of Rights as it stands, and take up and dispose of all the other departments in the same way. If not, then let us, for Heaven's sake, take our time, and not for the sake of economy destroy the permanency and grandeur of our work.

The time for the suspension of the Special Order having expired, the consideration of the Bill of Rights was resumed.

Section 8 was taken up and passed without amendment, as follows:

All persons may freely speak, write and publish their sentiments on any subject, being responsible for the abuse of that right; and no laws shall be enacted to restrain or abridge the liberty of speech or of the press.

Section 9 was taken up as follows:

" In prosecutions for the publication of papers investigating the official conduct of officers or men in public capacity, or when the matter published is proper for public information, the truth thereof may be given in evidence; and in all indictments for libel, the jury shall determine the law under the direction of the Court."

Mr. B. O. DUNCAN. It seems to me this is something belonging entirely to the laws enacted by the Legislature, and not properly belonging to the Bill of Rights. It is more of a law making provision than a Constitutional one.

Mr. C. C. BOWEN. I am in favor of striking out anything superfluous, but not in favor of striking out when there is no necessity. I consider it the business of this Convention to lay down certain fundamental principles for legislative guidance, such as is contained in this section.

Mr. J. S. CRAIG. As I believe the gentleman is a lawyer, I would like to ask him what is meant in saying, " that the jury shall have the right to determine the law and the facts ;" whether the jury are to judge of the law or take it as given by the Court. It appears vague and susceptible of different constructions.

Mr. N. G. PARKER moved to amend by adding after the word "jury" in the third line, " shall be judges of the law and fact."

Mr. R. C. DeLARGE. I move to strike out the entire section.

Mr. B. O. DUNCAN. It seems to me the first part of that section belongs entirely to the Legislature, and the second to the Committee on the Judiciary. It is very clearly going into particulars which have no connection with the Bill of Rights.

Mr. J. S. CRAIG. I understand the proposition is to establish Courts for the purpose of judging of the law. That proposition is calculated to destroy the effect of a Court, and makes the jury judges of the law as well as of the fact. I understand it is the duty of the Judge to expound the law to the jury, and the duty of the jury to determine the fact under the law. Does any man here suppose that a jury picked up all over the country can determine the law. I have always understood that juries are to determine facts not law.

Mr. F. J. MOSES, Jr. I hope, if this amendment proposed by the gentleman from Barnwell (Mr PARKER) is adopted, the Legislative Committee will be instructed to insert a clause providing for the establishment of a college for the education of jurymen for the performance of their duties. The idea of putting twelve gentlemen, however intelligent, however learned they may be, the one a capital merchant, a judge of good silk, another a capital sculptor, and so on, to pick them up all over the State to put them in a box and tell them they are qualified to judge of the law, is certainly the most preposterous proposition I ever heard of. The gentleman from Barnwell (Mr. PARKER) certainly could not have comprehended the scope of his amendment. Men may be intelligent, cultivated, talented, brilliant, and all that kind of thing, but that does not make them lawyers or qualified to judge of the law. The spirit and letter of the law has been heretofore—and for heaven's sake do not let us make dangerous innovations—has been that the jury should judge of facts, and the Judge should give them the law. The Judge must give the law and the jury must judge of the facts in connection with that law. That is the spirit and letter of the law, and that is the custom. I do hope an innovation will not be put in this Constitution which constitutes twelve men a jury to judge of the law and the fact. Suppose a Judge should tell the jury such and such is the law, and the jury go into their room and after deliberation, come to the conclusion that such and such is not law. In what a nice position you put the people. I tell you you are trifling with the rights of citizens, and the most sacred rights. You are, perhaps, fixing a plan to cast away the lives of many thousand innocent men under this Constitution. You put men in a jury box who know nothing of law, perhaps to try a man for his life, and say they shall judge the law. I earnestly entreat every man on this floor to consider it and vote down the amendment, otherwise you will regret it hereafter, and the blood of many an innocent man will be upon the head of the members of this Convention.

Mr. A. C. RICHMOND. I would like to know what is meant by a declaration of rights unless it specifies the rights of the people. I believe all important rights ought to be put down plainly in order in the Constitution. If the people have rights, let them be enumerated, and then let the necessary legislation come in the proper place. The enumeration of rights is not a legislative act, but the laws to give force to the rights of the people are and should be found in their proper place. I hope this section will be supported, and not voted down as proposed by the gentleman from Sumter (Mr. MOSES). I believe the amendment proposed by him is a dangerous amendment, and that the section reads right in its present form.

Mr. T. HURLEY The language of this section is exactly the same as the language of a similar section in the Constitution of Pennsylvania, and of some fifteen or sixteen other States. It has been copied int ͻ this Bill of Rights.

Mr. C. C. BOWEN. There is a very important difference in the language, as this section says "in all prosecutions for libel as in other cases." The insertion of those words "as in other cases," makes a material difference.

Mr. J. J. WRIGHT. We are not here to settle upon what Pennsylvania, North Carolina, California, or any other State has done. We are here for the purpose of looking after what we consider to be the rights of the people of the State of South Carolina. The gentleman has alluded to what Pennsylvania has done, but when he reads the clause as in the Constitution of Pennsylvania it is found to be entirely different from this clause. It winds up by giving juries the same power that the jury has in other cases. I happen to know something about the practice of law in Pennsylvania, and I say, as a lawyer, it matters not what Pennsylvania has done, this law has no business here. We give the jury the right, in certain cases, to determine the law and the fact. Well, there may arise a hundred and a thousand other cases, and the jury have not the right to determine the law and the fact. Then, I say, I agree with my friend from Sumter, it would be one of the most dangerous things we could do, to pick up men who cannot read and put them in a jury box to judge of the law, when they cannot read the law, and they are to be called upon to determine the law in certain cases where men are being tried for their lives. Would it be right or proper? I have been taught that the jury are to judge of the facts, that the Judge is to be the judge of the law, that he is to give the jury the law, and they are to determine the case by associating the law with the facts as presented in the evidence. I hope this clause will be struck out, and the powers of the Judge and jury respectively enumerated in the report of the Committee on the Judiciary as far as mention is made of all rights men are entitled to in the Declaration of Rights. I believe that all the rights and privileges men are entitled to could be printed in this one count on a little sheet. Let us strike this clause out and we are safe.

Mr. B. F. WHITTEMORE. In order that the minds of the members of this Convention may not be prejudiced either one way or the other, I move that the further consideration of this section be postponed until to-morrow, and that we invite the Solicitor to give us his views concerning the necessity of incorporating this section in the Bill of Rights.

Mr. W. J. WHIPPER. I move that the consideration of the entire Bill of Rights be postponed, and the Solicitor be requested to give his views.

Mr. F. J. MOSES, Jr. I would like very much to get the Solicitor's opinion in writing, but not in the Convention, personally.

Mr. A. J. RANSIER. I hope this question, with all the amendments, will be voted upon without reference to the Solicitor. I question very much the propriety of referring this matter to the Solicitor and getting his opinion. It might be reached without getting it in open Convention.

Mr. B. F. WHITTEMORE. I would say that one of the Solicitors was present when each and every section of the Legislative part of the Constitution was read in his presence.

The question being taken on the motion to invite the Solicitor to communicate his opinion in writing, it was not agreed to.

The question then recurred on the original motion to postpone the consideration of the section until to-morrow at one o'clock, at which time one of the Solicitors be invited to be present and give his views to the Convention.

Before the question was put the hour of three having arrived the Convention adjourned.

37

TWENTIETH DAY.

Friday, February 7, 1868.

The Convention assembled at 12 M., and was called to order by the PRESIDENT.

Prayer was offered by Rev. D. HARRIS.

The roll was called, and a quorum answering to their names, the PRESIDENT announced the Convention ready to proceed to business.

The Journal of the preceding day was read and approved.

On motion of Mr. B. F. RANDOLPH, the report of the Committee on Rules and Regulations was taken up.

The Convention proceeded to consider the amendment of Mr. J. J. WRIGHT to the report, to strike out "ten" and insert "half past ten o'clock," and strike out "three o'clock" and insert "one o'clock," and to add "shall meet at three o'clock and adjourn at five."

Mr. E. W. M. MACKEY moved that the amendment be indefinitely postponed, which was agreed to.

Mr. E. W. M. MACKEY moved that the report be adopted.

Mr. B. O. DUNCAN. The time of the daily sessions mentioned in the report is only four hours, which is entirely too short for work on this Constitution. I think we ought to give more time to it. Congress has both a morning and a night session, and I do not concur with the gentleman from Sumter (Mr. MOSES), in reference to a night session. The plan of having a night session I think a good one. One of the Judges of the court told me yesterday that he had to sit on the bench from ten in the morning to five in the afternoon, seven hours, and if they can do that, we should not complain of at least five hours.

Mr. C. C. BOWEN. I fully agree with the gentleman from Sumter that the session is already long enough. It may be that some here do not work enough, but since the adjournment at three o'clock yesterday I have been hard at work. We are not here to administer law, as the Judges. We are here for the purpose of framing a Constitution, to fix the machinery by which the laws can be administered. I think men who come in here ought certainly to have some relaxation from business. If it is proposed to rush the Constitution right through, why then let us adopt these things as a whole, and go home.

Mr. F. L. CARDOZO. I differ with the gentleman from Newberry, and hope the time recommended by the Committee will be adopted. The mere length of the time we have to work is, after all, not a matter of so much consequence. It is the manner in which we do our work.

A great many questions we can decide upon by pondering over in our rooms, and then we can come fully prepared, and do more work than we would without such preparation. In the afternoons and evenings we can prepare at home for our work here.

Mr. B. F. RANDOLPH. I hope the report will not be adopted as it stands. I think we can well afford to have two sessions. The objections heretofore urged against two sessions, or longer sessions, was that the Committees needed time to work. The Committees have now prepared the work for us, and we may expect so much talking any how. I think it would be much better for the members to meet here in the evening and digest matters than to go off in squads in different places. If Congress, whose sessions are six months long, can afford to have two sessions a day, I would like to know why we cannot.

Mr. E. W. M. MACKEY. Where did you get your information from? You certainly could not get it from the Congressional reports.

Mr. F. J. MOSES, Jr. Congress meets at 12 M. and adjourns at 3 P. M. Whenever pressed for time they call an evening session.

Mr. B. F. RANDOLPH. That is true; and they frequently find themselves pressed and frequently have evening sessions. I see no reason why we should not have two sessions a day, unless the Treasury of the State is full of specie. If that was the case, we could well afford to sit here and talk over constitutional matters. But the State Treasury is empty, and I am in favor of doing our work well, and getting through just as soon as we can. I hope we shall have two sessions a day.

The PRESIDENT. The hour for the resumption of the Special Order has arrived.

Mr. W. J. WHIPPER. I move that the Special Order be postponed until this subject is disposed of.

The motion was agreed to.

Mr. J. J. WRIGHT. I hope the report will not be adopted. We are here to work, and the people are paying our expenses. We have most of us in this Convention been in the habit of working, and I think we can stand more than three hours a day in this assembly; we can also work in our rooms just as much as we see fit. I work in my room and expect to do so; but then we work in our rooms and come here to do the work over again. The Committees, with the exception of the Committee on Franchise and Elections, have all prepared their work, and now we ought to come here to adopt or reject it. There are but few persons in this assemblage who have not been in the habit of working, and of getting up in the morning at six o'clock, while we do not get to work here before nine or ten o'clock and work until three. We can certainly come here at nine, work until twelve, and adjourn for dinner, and then come back and work until three o'clock. I desire to get through our work and go home.

Mr. R. C. DeLARGE. I trust the report of the Committee will be adopted. I hope every delegate will rise above the mere question of dollars and cents, and, if necessary, stay here twice as long, and even pay his own expenses if the State Treasury should be exhausted. The report of the Committee provides for a four hours session instead of three. ₄We certainly can do more work by working four hours continuously, than by working three hours in the morning and two in the evening.

Mr. N. G. PARKER. As a compromise, I move that we meet at half-past ten and sit until three o'clock. I think we can get through as much business in that time as if we held two sessions.

Mr. B. O. DUNCAN seconded the motion.

Mr. A. J. RANSIER. The gentleman from Orangeburg (Mr. B. F. RANDOLPH) introduced a resolution to request the agent of the Associated Press to inform the country we did not get more than seven dollars a day. Now he says in consideration of the fact that we are getting eleven dollars per day, we ought to work longer and get through as speedily as possible. I would like to know in what broker's office he gets his greenbacks for bills receivable. When I introduced the resolution, I thought it necessary to get a little more time ; but did not for a moment suppose it would give rise to so much debate. I think two sessions objectionable. I move to amend by striking out " half-past ten" and inserting " eleven o'clock," and to strike out " half-past two" and insert " half-past three o'clock."

Mr. C. M. WILDER moved that that amendment be indefinitely postponed, which was agreed to.

Mr. WM. McKINLAY. I hope the resolution will pass in its present form. The gentleman from Sumter, I think, expressed himself very eloquently and properly on that subject. The matter we have before us is evidently very important. We are making a Constitution for the entire State of South Carolina to last for years, perhaps for this generation and for generations to come. All we do should be well done. In my opinion, every line and paragraph in every section should be perfectly understood by every member of the Convention before he votes, and that cannot be done in hasty action or in the heat of debate. But after members retire from here to their homes, they can study and examine and deliberate upon the matters embraced in the several sections of the bills now before us, and when they come here they will come prepared to act

understandingly upon the matter before they give their votes. It ought
to be recollected that this is now as an hymenial knot that is to be tied,
and when tied there is no such thing as untying again. Therefore, in
tying it, it ought to be done understandingly. I do not think from half
past ten to half-past two is any too much. I move the previous question.

The call for the previous question was sustained, and being put, the
report of the Committee was adopted.

On motion of Mr. R. C. DeLARGE the Convention went into Committee of the Whole, on the 9th section of the Bill of Rights.

Mr. J. M. RUTLAND took the Chair.

Mr. C. C. BOWEN. Mr. Chairman : The question now before the
Convention is one of immense magnitude and importance ; one in which
the liberties of the people are, in my opinion directly concerned. I feel
that it is of the utmost magnitude. It is important as it regards the
boundaries of power between the constituent parts of our constitutional
tribunals, to which we are for the law and the fact to resort. It is important, also, to our Judges and to our juries as regards settling the right
principles that may be applied to the case, in granting to either the one
or the other the authority delegated to them by the spirit and letter of
the law. It is important on account of the influence it must have on the
rights of the citizens. Viewing it, therefore, in this light, I hope I shall,
in this arduous attempt, be supported by the importance of the question,
and if any doubt exists in the minds of the members of this Convention,
I shall, I trust, be able to satisfy them that the section now under consideration ought to be adopted. Therefore, Mr. Chairman, to prevent any
misunderstanding of the subject, I would ask that the Clerk be instructed to read the section.

Whereupon the Clerk read as follows :

SECTION 9. " In prosecutions for the publications of papers investigating
the official conduct of men in a public capacity, or where the matter published is proper for public information, the truth thereof may be given
in evidence ; and that in all indictments for libel, the jury shall have the
right to determine the law and the facts, under the direction of the
Court."

Sir, the question as I understand it is, whether the section just read
by the Clerk, shall remain as it now stands or be stricken out ; in other
words, to state the proposition perhaps plainer, shall the jury in cases of
libel have the right to judge of the law as well as the facts ? It has
been remarked by one of the opponents of this section, that we are not
here to legislate. Of that I have only to say, we are here the representatives of the people to frame a Constitution for the State of South Caro-

lína, and in that Constitution it is necessary that we should lay down some guide or rule by which the Legislature will be governed. I think it is right and proper. Nay, I think it is due to our constituents, that the 9th section of this bill should pass; that it should be engrafted in this Constitution, and thereby become a portion of the supreme law of the State. In an action for libel, three questions are necessary to be decided. First, was the article or paper published by the defendant. Second, has the inuendoes set forth by the plaintiff's been made out. And third, is the writing a libel; or in other words, was it published with intent to defame the character or injure the reputation of the plaintiff. Previous to Mr. Fox's Libel Act, this subject was one of great controversy in England. It had invariably been held by the Courts that but two of these questions should be decided by the jury; first, the fact that the defendant published the article, and second, the truth of the inuendoes in the proceedings, leaving the third and last question entirely to the Judge to say whether the publication was libellous or not. But the justice of this doctrine had always been questioned. When after a long and bitter struggle between the Government and the people, participated in on one side by the Judges, who contended that they had the exclusive right to say whether the defendant, in publishing the article, had been guilty of a criminal intent or not, and on the other side by juries, who claimed the right to decide the whole matter in issue. Mr. Fox, that successful reformer, succeeded in getting Parliament to pass his famous Libel Act, which gave to the jury the right to determine the law and facts, or in other words, the jury sworn to try the case, might give a general verdict of guilty or not guilty, upon the whole matter put in issue, and should not be required or directed by the Court or Judge before whom such case should be tried, to find the defendant guilty merely of publication, which is nothing more nor less than the proposition laid down in the section now under consideration. It is in vain to say that, allowing the Judges exclusive right to declare the law, on what the jury has found, can work no ill, for, by this privilege, they can assume and modify the fact so as to make the most innocent publication libellous. It is, therefore, no security to say, that this exclusive power will but follow the law. It must be with the jury to decide on the intent; they must, in certain cases, be permitted to judge of the law, and pronounce on the combined matter of law and of fact. If a libel is a crime, which no one will pretend to deny, why take it out of the rule that allows, in all criminal cases, when the issue is general, the jury to determine on the whole matter. Lord Camden said, that he has never been able to form a satisfactory definition of libel, but Blackstone and Hawkins declare that it is any malicious defamation, with an intent to blacken the reputation of any one, dead or alive. The criminal quality is its maliciousness. The next ingredient is, that it shall have an intent to defame. I ask, then if the intent be not the very essence of the crime? It is admitted that the word falsity, when the proceedings are founded on a statute, must be proved to the jury, because it makes the offence. Why not then the malice, when, to constitute the crime, it must necessarily be implied. In reason there can be no difference.

A libel is a complicated matter of fact and law with certain things and circumstances to give them a character; if so, then the malice is to be proved. The tendency to provoke is its constituent. The question depends on time, manner and circumstances, which must ever be questions of fact for jury determination. The Court, to be sure, may, like a jury, and in common with them, have the legal power and moral discernment, to determine on such a question; yet it does not arise out of the writing, but by adverting to the state of things and circumstances. If an article is published with a good intent, it ought not to be a libel, for it then is an innocent transaction; and it ought to have this intent, against which the jury have, in their discretion, to pronounce. It shows itself as a sentence of fact. Crime is a matter of fact by the code of our jurisprudence. In my opinion, every specific case is a matter of fact, for the law gives the definition. It is some act in violation of law. When we come to investigate, every crime includes an intent. Murder consists in killing a man with malice prepense. Manslaughter, in doing it without malice and at the moment of an impulse of passion. Killing may even be justifiable, if not praiseworthy, as in defence of chastity about to be violated. In these cases the crime is defined, and the intent is always the necessary ingredient. When a man breaks into a house, it is the intent that makes him a felon. It must be proved to the jury that it was his intention to steal; they are the judges of whether the intent was such, or whether it was innocent. And so, I say, it should be in cases of libel; let the jury determine, as they have the right to do in all other cases, on the complicated circumstances of fact and intent.

The criminal intent, says Lord Mansfield, in the Dean of Asaph's case, is what makes the crime. I contend that no act is criminal abstracted and divested of its intent. Trespass is not in itself innocent. No man has a right to enter another's land or house. Yet it becomes in this latter case felony only in one point of view, and whether it shall be held in that point, is a subject of jury determination. Suppose a man should enter the apartments of the King, this, in itself, would be harmless, but if he do it with an intent to assassinate, it would be treason. To whom must this be made to appear in order to induce conviction but to a jury?

Let it rather be said, that crime depends on intent, and intent is one parcel of the fact. Unless, therefore, it can be shown that there is some specific character of libel, that will apply in all cases, intent, tendency and quality, must all be matters of fact for a jury. A trial by jury has been considered, in the system of English jurisprudence, as the palladium of public and private liberty. In all the political disputes of that country, this has been deemed the barrier to secure the subjects from oppression. If, in that country, juries are to answer this end. if they are to protect from the weight of State prosecutions, they must have this power of judging of the intent, in order to perform their functions; they could not otherwise answer the end of their institution. I do not deny the well known maxim, that to matters of fact, the jury, and to matters of law, the judges, shall answer. I do not deny this, because it is not necessary for the purpose for which I am contending, or for any other purpose, that it should be denied. The jury have the power to decide in criminal cases, on the law and the fact. They have the right, because they cannot be restricted in its exercise; and, in politics power and right are equivalent; to prove which, let us suppose the Legislature to have laid a tax, which, by the Constitution, they certainly are entitled to impose, yet still the Legislature may be guilty of oppression; but who can prevent them or say they have not the authority to raise taxes. Legal power, then, is the decisive effect of certain acts without control; therefore it will readily be conceded that the jury may decide against the direction of the Court, and that their verdict of acquittal cannot be impeached, but must have its effect. This, then, I take to be the criterion, that the Constitution has lodged the power with them, and they have the right to exercise it. It is nothing to say, in opposition to this, that they, if they act wrong, are to answer between God and their consciences. This may be said of the Legislature, and yet, nevertheless, they have the power and the right of taxation. I do not mean to say that it would be proper for jurors thus to conduct themselves; but only to show that they do possess the legal right of determining on the law and the fact, and as far as the safety of the citizen is concerned, it is necessary that the jury should be permitted to speak to both. They ought not wantonly to depart from the advice of the Court; they ought to receive it, if there be not strong and valid reasons to the contrary; if there be, they should reject it. To go beyond this is wrong. Because it is to say, when they are obliged to decide, by their oath, according to the evidence, they are bound to follow the words of the Judge. After they are satisfied from him what the law is, they have the right to apply the definition. If they are convinced that the law is as stated, let them pronounce the person guilty; but never let them leave that guilt for the Judge to decide.

I have contended, and still do contend, that the jury should decide the whole matter in issue, and no one will for a moment contend that every general issue does not include the law and the fact. There is not a case in any criminal code in which it is otherwise. The construction, the publication, the meaning of the inuendoes, the intent and design, are all involved in the question of libel, and are to be decided on the plea of not guilty, which puts the whole matter in issue. It is, therefore, a subtlety to say, that the law and the fact are not in issue. In the case of the United States *vs.* Wilson & Porter, which was an indictment for robbing a mail carrier, tried before the Circuit Court of the United States for the Eastern District of Pennsylvania, in 1832, the Court in charging the jury, after stating at length the opinions entertained by them on various points of law involved in the case, proceeded as follows : " We have thus stated to you the law of this case under the solemn duties and obligations imposed upon us, under the clear conviction that in doing so we have presented to you the true test by which you will apply the evidence to the case ; but you will distinctly understand that you are the *judges both of the law and the fact in a criminal case, and are not bound by the opinion of the Court ;* you may judge for yourselves, and if you should feel it your duty to differ from us, you must find your verdict accordingly." In the case of the United States *vs.* Battiest, which was an indictment for a capital offence, Judge Story seems to have differed but little from the above decision ; if any thing he seems to have based it upon a broader ground. In charging the jury, he says : " My opinion is that the jury are no more judges of the law in a capital or other criminal case, upon a plea of not guilty, than they are in every civil case tried upon the general issue. *In each of these cases their verdict, when general, is necessarily compounded of law and fact, and includes both.* In each they must necessarily decide the law as well as the fact." This is what we ask for by the 9th section of this bill. This is what the people of England fought for and won. It is what the people of this country, years ago, claimed were the rights of the jury. It was first introduced in parliament by Mr. Fox, and became one of the laws of England. In 1812, a similar section to this was placed in the New York Constitution, and now remains a portion of the supreme law of that State. In Pennsylvania, by the 7th section of the Bill of Rights, " in all indictments for libels the jury shall have a right to determine the law and the facts, under the direction of the Court, as in other cases." In three-fourths of the other States I find the same doctrine incorporated in their Constitutions, and if precedents are worth following, it should be incorporated in ours.

38

Mr. Chairman, I have but one other case to cite and I am done ; it is a case directly in point. I allude to the case of William Bradford, the well known first printer of Pennsylvania and New York. This case is referred to by " Mr. Brown" in his "Forum," volume 1st, page 280, and is as follows: "In 1692, a quarrel took place between the Quaker Magistracy and a part of the Quaker Colonists, on a question partly civil and partly religious ; and Bradford, though taking no part, apparently, in the quarrel itself, printed a pamphlet of one of the disputants, George Keith, who had taken part against the dogmas, which the Quaker Rabbis then thundered from the seats of authority. Bradford was arrested, and the Sheriff being sent to search his office, took possession of his press, tools, type, and also of the 'form,' as the printer's call it (which he found still standing), from which the obnoxious pamphlet had been printed. The trial was had in form before two Quaker Judges, Jennings and Cooke, assisted by others. A curious cotemporary account of it still remains to us. The prisoner conducted his case in person, and managed it with a fearlessness, force, acuteness and skill, which speaks very highly for his intelligence and accurate conception of legal principles. When the jury were called. he challenged two of them because they had formed and expressed opinions, not as to the *fact* of his having published the paper, but as to its being of a *seditious character*, opinions which he himself had heard them express. The prosecuting attorney says to Bradford, after he had made his exception :

"Hast thou at any time heard them say that thou printed the paper, for that is *only* what they are to find ?"

Bradford. "That is not only what they are to find. They are to find *also whether this be a seditious paper or not, and whether it does tend to the weakening of the hands of the magistrates.*"

Attorney. "No, that *is a matter of law, which the jury is not to meddle with,* but find whether William Bradford hath printed it or not."

Justice Jennings (to the jury.) "You are only to try whether William Bradford *printed it or not.*"

Bradford. "This is *wrong*, for the jury are judges in the law, as well as in the matter of fact."

Justice Cook. "I will not allow these exceptions to the jurors."

"We have, therefore," says Mr. Brown, "in this trial, evidence of the fact, interesting to the whole press of America, and especially interesting to the bar and the press of Pennsylvania, that on the soil of Pennsylvania the father of her press asserted in 1692, with a precision not since surpassed, a principle in the law of libel hardly then conceived anywhere, but which now protects every publication in this State, and in much of our Union; a principle which English judges, after the struggles of the great Whig Chief Justice and Chancellor, Lord Camden, through his whole career, and of the brilliant declaimer, Mr. Erskrine, were unable to reach, and which at a later day became finally established in England only by the enactment of Mr. Fox's libel act in Parliament itself."

Mr. Chairman, I am done. If I have trespassed upon your patience, and that of the Convention, my only answer is I have done so in discharging what I believed to be my duty. I would gladly have remained in my seat, and not occupied the time of this Convention, but for the strong opposition manifested yesterday on this floor against the adoption of this section. Sir, I have now but one other duty to perform, which is to record my vote in favor of the ninth section of this bill, which duty I am now ready to perform.

Mr. G. PILLSBURY. The only important question that would arise in reference to this section is the right of the jury to exercise their judgment with regard to the law. I have but one objection to the section, and that is, it is entirely superfluous. Jurors always have been judges of the law. If we make this as a law for this State, jurors will not only be judges of all the other laws, but they will be judges of this law also. In Massachusetts this method of judicial proceeding is practiced with good success. I think the courts of Massachusetts will compare favorably with that of any other State. One thing I know is, that what criminals most dread there is justice, and what debtors most fear is that they will have to fork over. But that is the practice of the law in Massachusetts. There is no apparent clashing between the juries and the Judges. The Judges are stern expounders of the law. They have but one side, and that is the iron side. With jurors it is different. They have more than one side, and if the cold side is inclined to freeze harder and harder, they can turn it to the sun, and if the warm side is likely to dissolve, they can turn it to the ice. I do not believe the ends of justice will be perverted by granting this power to jurors.

I will institute a case and apply it to the common sense of every gentleman of the Convention: Suppose there had been a case upon which Judge Taney laid this down as the law favoring that case, "that black men have no rights which white men are bound to respect." Now what would have been the action of any gentleman of this Convention, if he had been on the jury when that infamous sentence was applied and intended to be forced upon them as law. If I had been there, I might have exercised the courtesy to have said, "your honor," but certainly I would add, "I myself, as a juror, will take that question under serious consideration." Therefore, from the fact that jurors have, and always will, exercise the prerogative of judging of the law, and from the other fact that experience has shown that the ends of justice are not retarded, but rather prompted, I hope the section, especially with that feature giving juries the right of judging of the law, will pass.

Dr. A. G. MACKEY. I have waited to see if any other gentleman desired to address this Convention. Presuming that all have expressed their opinions, I take this opportunity of saying a few words. I should not have addressed myself to the Convention on the subject at all, if I did not believe this the most important section in the Bill of Rights presented for your consideration.

When I find gentlemen like the gentleman from Colleton, standing up here in the middle of the 19th century, at a time when we have just passed through one of the most gigantic and most glorious revolutions the world has ever witnessed; at a time when more than half the people of the State have but recently been liberated from a state of bondage, and invested with the rights of freemen; when I see gentlemen of intelligence rising upon this floor and actually offering a resolution for your adoption, asking you to strike out the ninth section that perpetuates the great palladium of our liberties, I must confess my astonishment. It is a proposition to bring us back to the Star Chamber decisions, to the days when Judges joined with oppressive Governments to put their heels on the necks of the people. When I find gentlemen asking that we shall fling away all that we have gained through the glorious revolutionary period of the past, and submit ourselves, not to the decisions of our peers, but to the decisions of Judges—Judges who from time immemorial, with few exceptions, have always been on the side of oppression and tyranny—I boldly proclaim the fact that if you trust your liberties in the hands of the Judges of any country, your liberties are gone.

Need I call your attention to the time, a little more than a half century ago, when under the corrupt administration of John Adams, the alien and sedition laws were enacted, and when the Judges of the Supreme Court became the willing tool of that President in enforcing unconstitutional laws upon the people? Need I call your attention to the time when the Supreme Court, under the administration of that man, Chief Justice Taney, whose name has been embalmed in eternal infamy, rendered the decision declaring that the black man had no rights white men were bound to respect? Need I call your attention to the present time, when the Supreme Court is now in doubt, whether it will not, by its decision, endeavor to overthrow and destroy all the fruits of the victories we have just gained ?

Sir, I do not intend to argue this question as a lawyer. I thank God that in the investigation of this subject I am no lawyer, because I am thus free from the technical prejudices of the profession learned by lawyers in the schools, and which imbue them with reverence for a Judge, which I confess, I do not possess, unless he be honest and upright as Judge and man. I wish to investigate this question in the light of philosophy and statesmanship.

Now, what was the origin of the system by which the court was made the judge of the law in libel cases? It is the opinion of very eminent jurists—among them, of Thomas Cooper, than whom none better knew the subject under discussion, because he was himself a victim—that the common law in England in libel cases gave to the jury the right to decide the law as well as the fact; and I was yesterday astonished to hear my friend from Sumter (Mr. F. J. MOSES, Jr.,) a man who has sat at the feet of Gamaliel, declare that it was an abominable thing even to suppose that a jury should be the judges of the law. Why, there is no court in which the jury do not decide the law in all cases where the law and facts are complicated.

If a man is indicted for murder, do the jury undertake to confine themselves simply to the fact that he committed homicide or killed a man, and then leave it to the Judge to decide whether that killing amounted to murder, manslaughter or justifiable homicide ? By no means. They take the law into their own hands, and declare whether he is guilty of murder, manslaughter, or of neither. Their verdict shows whether a homicide was defencible, justifiable, or whether it was a murder with malice, or manslaughter without. The juries, in all these cases, take the law and the facts together. They first investigate the facts, and then apply the law. It is true that the Judge—and it is proper he should do so—undertakes to give the jury directions and advice. Being learned in the law, he can state authorities and precedents to them, and recommend them to be governed by his instructions ; but in many cases juries, like other people, when advice is offered, give a verdict in the very teeth of advice, and no one will undertake to say that such a verdict, though contrary to the opinion of the Judge, is illegal. If a jury has acquitted a man, he will be discharged, notwithstanding the Judge may think him legally guilty. If they find him guilty, he will hang, notwithstanding the Judge may believe him to be legally innocent.

Now it is only in cases of libel that the question has been mooted, whether juries should be judges of law as well as of fact. Why was that? As I said before, it has been supposed by eminent jurists that the common law of England gave juries power to judge of the law and fact; but in the reign of Henry VII, that iniquitous body—the Star Chamber—was established in which the right of the jury was taken from the people, and men were tried by a Court of State officers, and they instituted the doctrine that in cases of libel the Judge was to be judge of the law, and the jury to be the judge only of the facts. This condition of things existed for a long period of time, and the people suffered much oppression, until at last, in the thirty-second year of the reign of George III, Charles James Fox introduced a bill in Parliament (which the gentleman from Charleston, Mr. BOWEN, has described as being incorporated in the section before us), the provisions of which, almost in the very words of this section, were to the effect that the jury shall be the judges of the law as well as of the fact. What has been the consequence? Why, the Judges of England, who are always aspirants for power, have, in the very face of this bill of Mr. Fox's, continually endeavored to tread upon the rights of juries and decide the law. They have been continually persistent, in numerous cases, especially in cases of libel, in declaring to the jury, " all you have to do is to find the fact of publication, and we will decide whether it was either malicious, untruthful or detrimental to the public peace; we will decide whether it was a libel or not. You, the jury, have nothing to do with the libelous character of the transaction. We, the Judges, will decide whether it is of a libelous nature or not."

That is still the doctrine of the English Courts. But thanks be to God it is not the doctrine of the American Courts.

One of the first and most important cases in this country, subsequent to the case of Wm. Bradford, of Pennsylvania, quoted by my friend from Charleston (Mr. BOWEN), occurred in the city of New York, in the year 1732, when John Peter Zenger, a poor printer, having published several articles, in which the injustice and iniquities of the Provincial Governor were denounced, the Governor's Council directed him to be prosecuted under an " information," another abominable tool of tyranny, for a libel. Party politics ran then very high. The officials who were in power were all corrupt, the Governor, the Judges, and all his officers. The people themselves were groaning under this tyranny, and the lawyers of New York undertook to defend Zenger. But, unfortunately they took the ground that the Court was not valid, and entered a plea to its jurisdiction, in consequence of which, and it is in evidence of the baseness of the Court, the lawyers were stricken from the rolls of the Court. Zenger and his friends were, therefore, compelled to send to Philadelphia, and they employed the venerable Andrew Hamilton, then eighty-two years of age, a man whose name has been handed down to posterity for the defence made by him in that case. He then made an argument which caused Governeur Morris to say that "in that trial the germ of the tree of liberty was planted, which subsequently bloomed and bore fruit in 1776." It was upon that occasion that the Judge decided the jurors were simply judges of the fact and not of the law. I hold in my hand a book containing a full report of the trial of Zenger, from which I will quote. All can see it is not a law book. I will read the following sentences:

The Chief Justice said: "No, Mr. Hamilton, the jury may find that Zenger printed and published these papers, leaving it to the Court to judge whether they are libelous. You know this is very common. It is in the nature of a special verdict, where the jury leaves this matter of law to the Court."

That was the decision of the Judge at that time. That will be the decision f the Judges that you will have in this State, if you strike out that ninth section. One man will assume the authority and prerogative of deciding on your liberties. What did Mr. Hamilton say? Here is his reply: "I know, may it please your Honor, the jury may do so, and I do likewise know that they may do otherwise. I know they have a right beyond all dispute, to determine both the law and the fact and where they do not doubt the law they ought to do so."

Mr. Hamilton persuaded the jury to be of his mind and in spite of the times—in spite of a corrupt and oppressive Judge—in spite of a corrupt Attorney-General—the jury brought in a verdict of "not guilty," which was received with the enthusiastic plaudits of the people.

Many years after that, in 1805, another case occurred. It was the case of the people against Crosswell, who was indicted for libel against Thomas Jefferson, President of the United States. In that case the jury were directed to find a verdict according to the facts, and take the law from the Judge. They did so, and, in consequence, a motion for a new trial was made. There were four Judges, two of whom declared the jury were to be judges of the law, and two who declared they were not to be judges of the law but of the facts.

One of the grounds of appeal was that the Judge had given a misdirection to the jury, in saying that they could not judge of the law as well as the fact.

In consequence of there being an equal division the motion for a new trial was not sustained, and Crosswell suffered the punishment of the law. This led the Legislature of New York, at its next session, to pass a law, which was almost a copy of Mr. Fox's law in the British Parliament, and the law which the gentleman from Colleton proposes to strike out from the Bill of Rights. It provided that the jury in all cases of libel were to determine both the law and the fact.

They adopted that as a statute. Subsequently, in amendments to the Constitution of that State, it was made a Constitutional feature, and such it now remains. In that case the great Alexander Hamilton—and it is a singular coincidence that the two men who fought most strenuously for this doctrine were both of the same name, though not related—made that decision which sustains the argument by which your ninth section is supported. He lays down this principle—and, remember, I am quoting Alexander Hamilton, one of the greatest lawyers the country ever saw, one of the foremost defenders of liberty that ever stood upon our soil: "In all cases of prosecution for libel, the Court may instruct or advise the jury, but shall have no authority to require or direct them what verdict they shall bring in. The whole matter in issue, with all the circumstances of truth or falsehood, intent, motive and design, being within the right of the jury to decide upon, after hearing all the evidence and the charge of the Court." In other words, the jury are to be judges of the law as well as of the fact.

Gentlemen of the Convention, I have but little more to say; but I do not wish to see this section passed by a small vote. I am told it is probable that the motion to strike out will not prevail. I trust it will not, for I should certainly be sorry to see the Convention of South Carolina, one half of whose members are men who have just been liberated from bondage and from the heel of the oppressor, going back to the old times of the Star Chamber, and declaring that the liberties of the people shall depend no longer upon the decision of their peers—the juries of the country, empannelled under the fairest regulations of law—and that they are willing to throw themselves, body and soul, into the power of a Judge, who history records in nine cases out of ten, is likely to be a corrupt one, and who may wield his power with sway almost unlimited. History, which is merely a revolving wheel, continually repeating its lessons, shows, in all disputes between the throne and people, the Judges have been on the side of the throne, and in cases where the Government has been oppressive, the Judiciary lean on the side of the Government and against the people.

Mr. Madison, a profound statesman, years ago observed that if the liberties of this country are ever to be endangered, it would not be from the encroachments of the Executive or Legislative Departments, but from the encroachments of the Judiciary.

A Judge may be virtuous, but by the very character of his office, and the duties he has to perform, he is disposed to claim for himself powers and prerogatives that ought not, and really do not belong to him. When such a Judge finds himself on the one side supported by an oppressive and tyrannical King or Government, and on the other opposed by a people who demand that he shall not exercise the unjust privileges which he claims, in his indignation at the assumptions of the people, and his willingness to submit to the corruptions of the "powers that be," he becomes their willing tool; and in no better way can he oppress than under the law of libel, when "informations" being lodged against individuals for writing political articles, they are tried and to be punished, and he teaches his victims that "truth is not to be said when the truth hurts the King."

Now, gentlemen, suppose I paint a picture not drawn from romance, but from sad and sober reality. Suppose you strike this section out of your Bill of Rights, and give to the Judges the power to decide the law, while the jury have the facts alone to consider. By a solemn decision, the question being before you, you declare that juries are not judges of law, but simply of fact. The first effect you produce is this—the effect it would not produce had you said nothing about it; because in that case the good sense of the people and the very general decisions of our Courts, more especially that of that leading authority, Chancellor Kent, who has declared juries judges of the law as well as of fact, would have probably saved you from oppression. But now, having it before you, you make your solemn decision and say that juries are not judges of the law, but simply of fact, you then establish a code and precedent for the conduct of the Judges, which, at a time not far distant, will be of avail to those who oppress you. Perhaps some members of this Convention may be the victims.

Suppose that one of you, who should now vote for striking out this section, and thereby declaring that in the State of South Carolina the juries are not to decide the laws, but the Judges—suppose, I say, that at some future period, not far distant, one of you, who is seated here for the purpose of endeavoring to frame a Constitution for your country that will protect the rights of the people, should find, by the corruptions of time, another party shall have come into power; a party that thinks the slave oligarchy have been wronged, in being robbed of the blood, bones and muscle they made their living out of; suppose that member finds laws established by this new party affecting his privileges, the privileges of colored men, and he should undertake to write an article and publish it in a paper, denouncing the infamy of such a proceeding. Suppose, then, the Attorney General arrests him and has him indicted for libel, the Judge is

39

a good Democrat—and when I say that, in my opinion I say all that is politically bad of him—and he is brought up for trial. Suppose he undertakes by his counsel to demand that he shall have the right to prove to the jury that the laws enacted by the Legislature were unjust, infamous, tyrannical and oppressive, and that the jury should judge the law, what will be his position? The Judges will answer, "no sir, you yourself some years ago decided that the jury shall have no judgment or discretion upon that subject; you placed in my hands the rod with which I intend to chastise you. You have said the jury shall simply find as to the fact whether you wrote or published the article, and when they have rendered their verdict as to the publication of the article, I will decide whether it is a libel or not; and if it be a libel you shall go to jail, there to deplore in the darkness of a loathsome dungeon the fact that you trusted the Judge and gave him the power to decide upon your liberties."

In conclusion, I would say that I have but a single objection to the section as it stands. I prefer to see the words "under the direction of the court" stricken out. They prevail in but few of the Constitutions of the United States. Arkansas, California, Kentucky, New York, Delaware, Florida, Indiana, Iowa, Kansas, Mississippi, Nebraska, Nevada, New Jersey, Ohio, all unqualifiedly say that the jury shall be the judges of the law as well as of the fact.

Pennsylvania, West Virginia, Illinois, Maine, Oregon and Rhode Island have the qualification that it must be under the direction of the court, but say that the jury shall decide upon the law and the fact. There are eleven of the States that say nothing. But twenty-three States of the American Union have declared that the jury shall be judges of the law and the fact. Why add these words, "under the direction of the court?" I know what they mean. The Committee did not intend anything more than an advisory direction. I presume that the jury were to avail themselves of the wisdom and law learning of the Judge. I have no objection to that, but they get that. The Judge is not going to give up his prerogative. He is not very apt to give up anything he claims, but certainly will direct the jury and will advise with them. But when you say they (the jury) are to be Judges of the law under the direction of the court, there is a possible implication there that the jury must decide the law as the court directs them. There may be a period when some Judges shall decide that to be the case. I therefore prefer that the section should be without it. I therefore offer the following:

Resolved, That the Committee do now rise and report to the house that they have had the ninth section of the Bill of Rights under consideration, and recommend that the words "have the right to determine the law and the facts under the direction of the court," be stricken out, and the following words inserted, "the jury shall be the judges of the law and the facts;" and, with this amendment, recommend its adoption to the house.

The motion was carried with but two dissenting votes, Mr. F. J. MOSES, Jr., and Mr. CRAIG.

The Committee rose, and Dr. A. G. MACKEY resumed the Chair.

Mr. RUTLAND made the report of the Committee, which was adopted, and the ninth section, as amended, passed to a third reading.

Sections 10, 11, 12, 13, 14, 15, 16 and 17 were then severally passed to a third reading, when the hour of half-past two having arrived, the Convention adjourned.

TWENTY-FIRST DAY.

Saturday, February 8, 1868.

The Convention assembled at 12 M., and was called to order by the PRESIDENT.

Prayer was offered by the Rev. J. M. RUNION.

The roll was called, and a quorum answering to their names, the PRESIDENT announced the Convention ready to proceed to business.

The Journal of the preceding day was read and approved.

The PRESIDENT announced the unfinished business before the Convention, was the continuation of the reading of the Bill of Rights.

The 18th section declaring "that the privilege of the writ of *habeas corpus* shall not be suspended, except when in cases of insurrection, rebellion or invasion, the public safety may require it," was read, and after a verbal amendment by Mr. R. G. HOLMES, passed to its third reading.

The 19th section, forbidding the second trial of any person for the same offence, was read; and after verbal amendments by Mr. WILLIAM McKINLAY and Mr. B. F. RANDOLPH, passed to its third reading.

The 20th section, declaring that "no person shall be proceeded against criminally, by information, for any indictable offence, except in cases arising in the land and naval service, or in the militia when in actual service, in time of war or public danger, or by leave of the Court, for oppression or misdemeanor in office," was read.

Mr. R. C. DeLARGE moved to amend by striking out the words, "by leave of the Court," so as to read, "or for oppression, misdemeanor, or malfeasance in office."

Mr. R. G. HOLMES deemed the section unnecessary, and moved to strike it out.

Mr. J. D. BELL moved to strike out the words, "by leave of the Court."

Mr. J. S. CRAIG. If the word "information" is intended to prevent persons from appearing before a magistrate or other officer, to file his affidavit and obtain a writ against any other that had committed an offence, I am opposed to it.

Mr. B. F. WHITTEMORE. The intention of the Committee is that no person shall be proceeded against criminally by any information without having been indicted by a grand jury.

Mr. J. M. RUTLAND. If the section is adopted at all, it ought to be with the words "by leave of the Court." It is not intended to confer powers upon the Judge, but to restrain actions, many of a frivolous or unwarrantable character that occur so frequently against the people. It is a dangerous practice to indict citizens without a grand jury. If a person undertakes to bring information against any number of citizens without grounds, and the matter is brought before the Court, it can investigate the charge, and it may not permit an indictment. The provision "by leave of the Court" is a protection for the citizen. Even the very fact of a person being brought up before the Court on the charge of having committed crime, though he may be perfectly innocent, is likely to affect his reputation, and it ought not to be the prerogative of every citizen to file an information against another by which he may be committed to jail, or suffer in his reputation on grounds of complaint that would not be sustained by a Court.

Mr. C. C. BOWEN. I move to strike out the entire section. I am opposed entirely to the grand jury system. A great deal has been said here about Star Chamber proceedings, but I know of no greater Star Chamber than the grand jury. As an illustration, I will suppose, for instance, that I went before a Magistrate and made an affidavit that any man in the Convention had stolen my pocket book. On the instant the man is arrested or taken to jail. By the present laws of South Carolina, the Magistrate cannot enquire into the charge, but if the accused is not able to give bail, must commit. If a stranger, the accused very frequently cannot give security for his appearance. I go before the grand jury. repeat my charge, but the accused is not heard before them, nor has any voice. The grand jury return a true bill for larceny without giving the man a chance to be heard. The party against whom a true bill is thus found by a grand jury, may be continued in jail for months awaiting his trial. In other cases, where the grand jury fail to find a true bill, there is an end of the matter, though the prosecuting officer may have sufficient evidence to convict the party. A party in the up country, tried and convicted of murder, was awaiting execution of the sentence, and a few days before the time another party was lodged in jail, who, together with the party convicted, made it convenient to leave. An order was issued to prosecute the jailor upon the charge of allowing the prisoners to escape. The grand jury failed to find a true bill and there was the end of it. But suppose the prosecuting attorney had been allowed to have made up his case again and brought it into Court, and, as it was believed, could have satisfied the jury that there was evidence enough to convict the jailor of receiving money to let the prisoners go. But no! the grand jury's decision was the last of it. He would, when the subject came up, advocate that if the grand jury system was to be continued. it should be upon a modified principle.

Mr. W. J. WHIPPER. I hope the section will not be stricken out I differ with the speaker who has just taken his seat, as to abolishing the grand jury system. It is one of the principal means by which the liberties of the people have been protected for years. The mere fact that there has been a few instances in which the grand juries have liberated parties unwarrantably, is no reason why that useful body should be abolished. The jury system is the bulwark of the rights of the people, and the grand jury, with the State Attorney-General's information before them, decide whether or not there is probable cause for a public trial. The grand jury is one of the great safeguards of republicanism.

Mr. R. C. DeLARGE. I desire to ask whether the party accused is ever allowed to produce witnesses, and make in person his defence before the grand jury.

Mr. W. J. WHIPPER. According to the laws of the State he is not. But we are here to make laws for the State, and if we find it advisable to alter the law in that respect, and allow the accused to be heard before the grand jury, it could be done here. The grand jury is one of the great checks the people have upon prosecutions brought by officers of the Government, and to take it away would be to take away the liberties of the people. Enough had been said upon the floor yesterday with regard to the value of juries, and he hoped that the speech of the gentlemen from Charleston (Mr. BOWEN) would not tend to influence a single vote for the suppression of either the grand or petit juries.

Mr. C. C. BOWEN   I said nothing against petit juries, or juries in general.   I objected to the present system of grand juries.

Mr. W. J. WHIPPER.   I hope the grand jury will forever remain as one of the great safeguards of the liberties of the people.

Mr. J. M. RUTLAND.   I heartily and cordially endorse the views of the gentleman from Beaufort (Mr. W. J. WHIPPER).   To abolish the grand jury system would be one of the severest blows ever struck against the liberties of this country.   If they wiped out the grand jury system, the very Star Chamber system, which the President so eloquently portrayed yesterday in Committee of the Whole, would be resumed in all its force and evil phases.

Mr. B. F. WHITTEMORE.   I consider this section as of the highest importance.   Some of us within the last two or three years have been made painfully aware of the fact that many persons have been proceeded against without any indictment whatever.   Parties have been proceeded against before tribunals, and even sentenced without having been heard in their defence.   I hope we will not ourselves abridge the protection offered through the establishment of juries.   Allusions have been already made to the eloquent remarks made by our honored President in relation to the rights and privileges of juries, that they should guard them with jealous care, and surround them with everything that would secure those rights and privileges.   All I desire is, as the section expresses it, that no person shall be brought before any tribunal, or proceeded against for crime, or any information given, unless an indictment had been made out against him.   ·I concur entirely with the delegate from Beaufort (Mr. W. J. WHIPPER), and hope the section will pass.

The question being taken on striking out the section, it was lost.

Mr. E. W. M. MACKEY offered the following as a substitute:

No person shall be held to answer a criminal offence unless on the presentment or indictment of a Grand Jury, except in cases of impeachment, or in cases cognizable by Justices of the Peace, or arising in the army or navy, or in the militia when in actual service in time of war or public danger.

Mr. J. J. WRIGHT.   I am in favor of the adoption of the original section, which has been wisely considered and framed, and was just what is needed.   It protects the people against being proceeded against, except through regular indictment, unless sufficient cause is shown for a Court to take cognizance of the case.

Mr. R. C. DeLARGE.   I agree with my colleague (Mr. C. C. BOWEN) that the grand jury is what may be termed the Star Chamber of America. The member from Beaufort has endeavored to make it appear that the charge of men being kept in jail till the grand jury meets, was all gammon. But he has not told the Convention what is to become of a man between the time a Justice of the Peace commits and the grand jury meets. I think if we visit the jail once in six months, we will come to the conclusion it is not all gammon. I am opposed to the law where the accused has not a fair and equal showing with his or their accuser, and this is the case with the grand juries. The hearing before the grand jury is *ex parte* altogether. If that is protecting the liberties of the people, the gentleman has learned a definition of protection in an entirely different sense from that understood by the speaker. But I am also opposed to the substitute, the only difference between that and the original being the distinction made by physicians in their pills, that is, "sugar coated," so that they may be more easily swallowed.

Mr. F. L. CARDOZO. I will not take up the time of the Convention by discussing the nature of a grand jury, but will leave that to my legal friends. But I take the ground that there is no necessity for the substitute, as it simply states affirmatively what the original section states negatively, and both will bring about the same result. I heartily agree with the eloquent remarks of the President, yesterday, in having juries watch vigilantly the rights of the people. Whatever faults grand or petit jurors might have, I feel sure they have not one-fifth the tendency to evil results which generally follow the action of a bad or corrupt Judge.

Mr. W. E. JOHNSTON. I have been deprived ever since the meeting of the Convention of the privileges accorded me by the Mercury of "crying aloud and spare not." Every day members are getting up here and talking for the space of one hour, and then go home and do a great deal of business besides. I only wished to "line out" a single word. I moved that the substitute be indefinitely postponed.

The motion was agreed to, and the 20th section passed to its third reading.

On motion of Mr. J. M. RUTLAND, the Convention adjourned.

TWENTY-SECOND DAY.

Monday, February 10, 1868.

The Convention assembled at 10 A. M., and was called to order by the PRESIDENT.

Prayer was offered by the Rev. F. L. CARDOZO.

The roll was called, and a quorum answering to their names, the PRESIDENT announced the Convention ready to proceed to business.

The Journal of Saturday was read and approved.

Mr. J. M. RUTLAND, from the Committee on the Legislative part of the Constitution, submitted the following reports, which, on motion, were severally adopted :

IN CONVENTION, CHARLESTON, S. C., February 7, 1868.

The Committee to whom was referred an "Ordinance allowing a homestead of one hundred acres of land to each head of a family," etc., beg leave respectfully to report that they have had the same under consideration, and have agreed to incorporate the substance of the said "Ordinance" in a section in the "Legislative part of the Constitution," and it is so incorporated.

Respectfully submitted,

J. M. RUTLAND, Chairman.

IN CONVENTION, CHARLESTON, S. C., February 7, 1868.

The Committee to whom was referred the resolution "that the several Districts of this State shall hereafter be known and denominated Counties," beg leave respectfully to report that they have had the same under consideration, have approved of the resolution, and have incorporated the substance thereof in a section in the "Legislative part of the Constitution."

Respectfully submitted,

J. M. RUTLAND, Chairman.

IN CONVENTION, CHARLESTON, S. C., February 7, 1868.

The Committee to whom was referred the resolution requiring the Legislature "as soon as possible after their first assembling under the Constitution prepared by this Convention," to enact laws securing certain property from levy and sale, and suspending the sale of such property till the Legislature shall enact such laws, etc., beg leave respectfully to report that they have had the same under consideration, and have incorporated in a section of the "Legislative part of the Constitution," so much of the substance of said resolution as looks to the providing of a homestead for the unfortunate debtor.

As to that part of the resolution pertaining to the suspension of the sales of property under execution, and stay laws, your Committee recommend that the same be laid upon the table.

Respectfully submitted,

J. M. RUTLAND, Chairman.

In Convention, Charleston, S. C., February 10, 1868.

The Committee to whom was referred the resolutions authorizing the State to issue bonds to the amount of ———— millions, "to be paid in twenty years, and, if possible, to secure the endorsement of Congress on the same, the money raised from the sales thereof to be invested in lands when forced into the market," etc., also setting forth a plan of relief and securing homesteads to the people, beg leave respectfully to report that they have had the same under consideration, and are unanimously of the opinion that the whole scheme is impracticable.

Mr. WM. E. ROSE, from the Committee on Petitions, submitted the following report, which was adopted:

The Committee on Petitions, to whom was referred the resolution for the appointment of a Committee to report to this Convention the names of such persons as should have their disabilities removed, ask leave to report that they have duly considered the same, and are of opinion that persons desiring their disabilities removed, should apply individually to this Convention by petition. When such application shall be made, the Convention will be competent to judge of their respective merits. Your Committee, therefore, respectfully recommend that the resolution referred to them, be laid on the table.

W. E. ROSE, Chairman.

Mr. B. F. RANDOLPH submitted the following report from the Committee on the Miscellaneous Provisions of the Constitution, which was adopted:

The Committee on the Miscellaneous Provisions of the Constitution, to whom was referred a resolution declaring it to be the duty of this Convention, or the Legislature created by it, to make it a penal offence to use the epithets, "negro," "nigger" and "Yankee," have considered the same, and respectfully ask leave to report that in the opinion of your Committee it is inexpedient for this Convention to take any action in the premises, and they respectfully recommend that the resolution be laid on the table. L. BOOZER, Chairman.

Mr. B. F. RANDOLPH submitted the following report from the Committee on the Miscellaneous Provisions of the Constitution, which, on motion of Mr. R. O. DUNCAN, was read a first time and ordered to be printed:

The Committee on the Miscellaneous Provisions of the Constitution,

40

to whom was referred certain resolutions in regard to the organization of the militia, ask leave to report that they have duly considered the subject referred to them, and respectfully recommend that the following Article be adopted as a part of the Constitution of this State, to wit:

"Article —. The militia of the State of South Carolina shall consist of all able-bodied male residents of the State between the ages of eighteen and forty-five years, except such persons as now are or may hereafter be exempted by the laws of the United States or of this State, and shall be organized, armed, equipped and disciplined as the General Assembly may by law provide."

Respectfully submitted,

L. BOOZER, Chairman.

Mr. S. A. SWAILS submitted the following report, which was adopted:

South Carolina Constitutional Convention,
Charleston, S. C., February 8, 1868.

Your Committee to whom the bill of Mr. H. Judge Moore (printer) was referred to for the purpose of auditing, beg leave to report that they have not had sufficient time to investigate the same, but respectfully recommend that $100 be paid to Mr. H. Judge Moore on account, until such time as your Committee shall investigate the matter fully.

S. A. SWAILS,

For Chairman.

Mr. N. G. PARKER moved that two additional members be appointed on the Auditing Committee, which was agreed to.

The report of the Committee on the Legislative part of the Constitution was taken up the first time, and read a first time as follows:

ARTICLE II.

Section 1. The legislative power of this State shall be vested in two distinct branches, the one to be styled the "Senate," and the other the "House of Representatives," and both together the "General Assembly of the State of South Carolina."

Sec. 2. The House of Representatives shall be composed of members chosen by ballot every second year, by the citizens of this State, qualified as in this Constitution is provided.

Sec. 3. The judicial Districts shall hereafter be designated as Counties, and the boundaries of the several Counties shall remain as they are now established, except the County of Charleston, which shall be divided into two Counties, one consisting of the late Parishes of St. Philip and St. Michael, to be designated as the County of Charleston; the other, consisting of all that part of the late Judicial District of Charleston, which is without the limits of the said Parishes, to be known as the County of Berkley; *Provided*, That the Legislature shall have the power at any time, by a vote of two-thirds of both Houses, to organize new Counties by changing the boundaries of any of the old ones; but no new County shall be hereafter formed of less extent than 625 square miles, nor shall any existing Counties be reduced to a less extent than 625 square miles. Each County shall constitute one election district.

SEC. 4. The House of Representatives shall consist of one hundred and twenty-four members, to be apportioned among the several Counties according to the number of inhabitants contained in each. An enumeration of the inhabitants, for this purpose, shall be made in 1869, and again in 1875, and shall be made in the course of every tenth year thereafter, in such manner as shall be by law directed ; and representatives shall be assigned to the different Counties in the above mentioned proportion, by act of the General Assembly at the session immediately succeeding every enumeration ; *Provided*, That until the apportionment, which shall be made upon the next enumeration, shall take effect, the representation of the several Counties, as herein constituted, shall be the same as the number of delegates allowed to each County in this Convention.

SEC. 5. If the enumeration herein directed shall not be made in the course of the year appointed for the purpose, it shall be the duty of the Governor to have it effected as soon thereafter as shall be practicable

SEC. 6. In assigning representatives to the several Counties, the General Assembly shall allow one representative to every one hundred and twenty-fourth part of the whole number of inhabitants in the State ; *Provided*, That if in the apportionment of representatives any County shall appear not to be entitled, from its population, to a representative, such County shall nevertheless send one representative ; and if there be still a deficiency of the number of representatives required by section four, such deficiency shall be supplied by assigning representatives to those Counties having the largest surplus fractions.

SEC. 7. No apportionment of representatives shall be construed to take effect, in any manner, until the general election which shall succeed such apportionment.

SEC. 8. The Senate shall be composed of one member from each County, to be elected, for the term of four years, by the qualified voters of the State, in the same manner by which members of the House of Representatives are chosen.

SEC. 9. Upon the meeting of the first General Assembly which shall be chosen under the provisions of this Constitution, the Senators shall be divided, by lot, into two classes, as nearly equal as may be ; the seats of the Senators of the first class to be vacated at the expiration of two years after the Monday following the general election, and of those of the second class at the expiration of four years ; so that, except as above provided, one-half of the Senators may be chosen every second year.

SEC. 10. No person shall be eligible to a seat in the Senate or House of Representatives who at the time of his election is not a citizen of the United States; nor any one who has not been for one year next preceding his election a resident of this State, and for three months next preceding his election a resident of the county whence he may be chosen, nor any one who has been convicted of an infamous crime. Senators shall be at least twenty-five, and Representatives at least twenty-one years of age.

Sec. 11. The first election for Senators and Representatives under the provisions of this Constitution shall be held on the —— Wednesday of March of the present year; and the second election shall be held on the third Wednesday in October, 1869, and forever thereafter on the same day in every second year, in such manner and at such places as the Legislature may hereafter provide.

Sec. 12. The first session of the General Assembly after the ratification of this Constitution, shall be convened on the —— Monday in April of the present year in the city of Columbia (which shall remain the seat of government until otherwise determined by the concurrence of two-thirds of both branches of the whole representation), and thereafter on the fourth Monday in November annually. Should the casualties of war or contagious diseases render it unsafe to meet at the seat of government, then the Governor may, by proclamation, appoint a more secure and convenient place of meeting.

Sec. 13. The terms of office of the Senators and Representatives chosen at a general election shall begin on the Monday following such election.

Sec. 14. Each House shall judge of the election returns and qualifications of its own members; and a majority of each House shall constitute a quorum to do business; but a smaller number may adjourn from day to day, and may be authorized to compel the attendance of absent members, in such manner and under such penalties as may be provided by law.

Sec. 15. Each House shall choose its own officers, determine its rules of proceeding, punish its members for disorderly behavior, and with the concurrence of two-thirds, expel a member, but not a second time for the same cause.

Sec. 16. Each House may punish by imprisonment during its sitting any person not a member, who shall be guilty of disrespect to the House by any disorderly or contemptuous behavior in its presence; or who, during the time of its sitting, shall threaten harm to body or estate of any member for anything said or done in either House, or who shall assault any of them therefor, or who shall assault or arrest any witness or other person ordered to attend the House, in his going thereto or returning therefrom, or who shall rescue any person arrested by order of the House.

Sec. 17. The members of both Houses shall be protected in their persons and estates during their attendance on, going to, and returning from, the General Assembly, and ten days previous to the sitting, and ten days after the adjournment thereof. But these privileges shall not be extended so as to protect any member who shall be charged with treason, felony, or breach of the peace.

Sec. 18. Bills for raising a revenue shall originate in the House of Representatives, but may be altered, amended or rejected by the Senate; and all other bills may originate in either House, and may be amended, altered or rejected by the other.

Sec. 19. The style of all laws shall be, "Be it enacted by the Senate and House of Representatives of the State of South Carolina, now met and sitting in General Assembly, and by the authority of the same."

SEC. 20. Every act or resolution having the force of law shall relate to but one subject, and that shall be expressed in the title.

SEC. 21. No bill shall have the force of law until it shall have been read three times, and on three several days, in each house, has had the seal of State affixed to it, and has been signed in the Senate house, by the President of the Senate and the Speaker of the House of Representatives.

SEC. 22. No money shall be drawn from the Treasury, but in pursuance of an appropriation made by law; and a regular statement and account of the receipts and expenditures of all public moneys shall be published annually, in such manner as may be by law directed.

SEC. 23. Each member of the first General Assembly under this Constitution shall receive six dollars per diem while in session; and the further sum of twenty cents for every mile of the ordinary route of travel in going to and returning from the place where such session is held; after which they shall receive such compensation as shall be fixed by law; but no General Assembly shall have the power to increase the compensation of its own members. And when convened in extra session they shall receive the same mileage and per diem compensation as fixed by law for the regular session, and none other.

SEC. 24. In all elections by the General Assembly, or either House thereof, the members shall vote "*viva voce,*" and their votes thus given shall be entered upon the journals of the House to which they respectively belong.

SEC. 25. Neither House, during the session of the General Assembly, shall, without the consent of the other, adjourn for more than three days, nor to any other place than that in which the Assembly shall be at the time sitting.

SEC. 26. Each House shall keep a journal of its own proceedings, and cause the same to be published immediately after its adjournment, excepting such parts as in its judgment may require secrecy; and the yeas and nays of the members of either House, on any question, shall, at the desire of any two members present, be entered on the journals. Any member of either House shall have liberty to dissent from, and protest against, any act or resolution which he may think injurious to the public or to an individual, and have the reasons of his dissent entered on the journals.

SEC. 27. The doors of each House shall be open except on such occasions as, in the opinion of the House, may require secrecy.

SEC. 28. No person shall be eligible to a seat in the General Assembly whilst he holds any office of profit or trust under this State, the United States of America, or any of them, or under any other power, except officers in the militia, Magistrates or Justices of Inferior Courts, while such Justices receive no salary. And if any member shall accept or exercise any of the said disqualifying offices he shall vacate his seat.

SEC. 29. If any election district shall neglect to choose a member or members on the day of election, or if any person chosen a member of either House shall refuse to qualify or take his seat, or shall resign, die, depart the State, accept any disqualifying office, or become otherwise disqualified to hold his seat, a writ of election shall be issued by the

President of the Senate, or Speaker of the House of Representatives, as the case may be, for the purpose of filling the vacancy thereby occasioned, for the remainder of the term for which the person so refusing to qualify, resigning, dying, departing the State, or becoming disqualified, was elected to serve, or the defaulting election district ought to have chosen a member or members.

SEC. 30. And, whereas, the ministers of the gospel are, by their profession, dedicated to the service of God and the cure of souls, and ought not to be diverted from the great duties of their functions; therefore, no minister of the gospel, or public preacher of any religious persuasion, whilst he continues in the exercise of his pastoral functions, shall be eligible to the office of Governor, Lieutenant-Governor, or to a seat in the Senate or House of Representatives.

SEC. 31. Members of the General Assembly, and all officers before they enter upon the execution of the duties of their respective offices, and all members of the bar, before they enter upon the practice of their profession, shall take and subscribe the following oath:

" I do solemnly swear (or affirm, as the case may be,) that I am duly qualified according to the Constitution of the United States and of this State, to exercise the duties of the office to which I have been elected (or appointed), and that I will faithfully discharge to the best of my abilities the duties thereof, and that I recognize the supremacy of the Constitution and laws of the United States over the Constitution and laws of any State, and that I will support, protect and defend the Constitution of the United States and the Constitution of South Carolina, as ratified by the people on ———. So HELP ME GOD.

SEC. 32. Officers shall be removed from office for incapacity, misconduct, or neglect of duty, in such manner as may be provided by law, when no mode of trial or removal is provided in this Constitution.

SEC. 33. The House of Representatives shall have the sole power of impeaching; but a majority of all the members elected must concur in the impeachment. All impeachments shall be tried by the Senate; and when sitting for that purpose, the Senators shall be upon oath, or affirmation, to do justice according to law and evidence. No person shall be convicted without the concurrence of two-thirds of the Senators present.

SEC. 34. The Governor, Lieutenant-Governor, and all other civil officers, shall be liable to impeachment for high crimes and misdemeanors, for any misbehavior in office, for corruption in procuring office, or for any act which shall degrade their official character. But judgment in such cases shall not extend further than to removal from office and disqualification to hold any office of honor, trust or profit under this State. The party convicted shall, nevertheless, be liable to indictment, trial, judgment and punishment according to law.

SEC. 35. There shall be exempt from execution or other final process of any Court issued for the collection of any debt, a homestead in the country, consisting of one hundred acres, and the dwelling and appurtenances thereon, to be selected by the owner thereof. And in a city, town or village, in lieu thereof, a lot with the dwelling and appurtenances thereon: *Provided*, that such homestead, either in a city, town, village or country, shall not exceed in value two thousand dollars. There shall also be exempt from such execution or other final process of any Court issued for the collection of any debt, the necessary articles of furniture, apparel, subsistence and implements of husbandry, trade or other employment to the value of five hundred dollars. But no property shall be exempt from sales for taxes, or for the payment of obligations contracted for the purchase of said homestead, or for the erection or improvement thereon. It shall be the duty of the Legislature, at its next session, to pass such laws as may be necessary to carry this provision into effect.

SECTION 36. All taxes upon property, real or personal, shall be laid upon the actual value of the property taxed, as the same shall be ascertained by an assessment made for the purpose of laying such a tax.

The PRESIDENT announced next in order the second reading of the remaining sections of the Bill of Rights.

Mr. R. G. HOLMES moved a reconsideration of the 20th section.

Mr. N. G. PARKER. I second the motion, and hope that motion will prevail. If good and sufficient reasons are not shown why this section should not be adopted as it now stands, it will certainly be an easy matter to adopt it again. If, however, good and sufficient reasons are shown why it should not be adopted, we shall all be glad that we obtained the opportunity to vote against it. I trust that those who voted in the affirmative are not opposed to listening briefly to the objections that will be urged against this section. They will stand very much in their own light if they do, and may have cause to regret it when it is too late. For my part, as much as I desire to accomplish quickly the purpose of this Convention, I desire more to accomplish it well.

The motion to reconsider was then put and agreed to.

Mr. N. G. PARKER. I propose the following substitute:

"That all offences less than felony, and in which the punishment does not exceed a fine of $100, or imprisonment for thirty days, shall be tried summarily before a Justice of the Peace or other officer authorized by law, on information, under oath, without indictment or the intervention of a grand jury, saving to the defendant the right of appeal; and no person shall be held to answer for any higher crime or offence unless on presentment by a grand jury, except in cases arising in the land and naval service, or in the militia when in actual service, in time of war or public danger."

I do not claim any originality in introducing that substitute. It is a copy of a clause from the Bill of Rights in the Constitution of the State of Iowa. I have examined, since our last meeting, all the Constitutions of all the States, and I find all the improvements of the last ten years embodied in that section. While I desire to accomplish the purpose for which we were elected as speedily as possible; while I realize the importance of drawing this Convention to a close at an early day, in order that a Constitution may be submitted to the people for ratification, and that we may gain admission to the Union, and become again one of the family of States, I desire also that we shall perform the work in such a manner that we shall be satisfied with it ourselves; that the people will be satisfied with it, and that it shall be in all respects a model Constitution. We are here to make a Constitution for the State of South Carolina. We are all alike interested in this important duty. If we do our duty well, we shall be entitled to the plaudits of "well done, good and faithful servants." If we do it ill, we shall not only be entitled to censure, but we shall be victims to our own wrong doings. I do not like the phraseology of the article as it now stands, neither do I like its signification. I want something more; the people need something more. I find, upon looking over the Constitutions of all the States, that this article, as it stands, is a part of the Bill of Rights of four States. First, I find it in the Constitution of Mississippi as adopted in 1832. I cannot hold up that State as a pattern for us, but even in that State they found it was insufficient, and in 1846 they adopted the following amendment: "*Provided*, That the Legislature, in cases of petty larceny, assault and battery, or riot, may dispense with the inquest of the grand jury, and may authorize summary proceedings in such cases, under such provisions as shall be regulated by law." With such an amendment I would be satisfied. I find this provision in four other States of the Union. Missouri and Alabama adopted the same, including the amendment. Kentucky in 1850 adopted the same, without the amendment. Pennsylvania the same in 1838, without the amendment. Thus you will perceive that only two States of the United States contain a section like the one under discussion, Pennsylvania adopting it in 1838, and Kentucky in 1850; one forty years ago, and the other eighteen years. But Pennsylvania, Kentucky, Missouri and Alabama all adopted it originally in their first Constitutions. Now let us see how it is in other States. It may be said that it matters not to us how it is in other States; that we can make our own Constitution, and not follow other States. That would not be so easy a matter. First, we have the Constitution of the United States, then all the Constitutions of all the other States before us, and what we cannot find worth having in some one of these we may well expect not to find at all. Originality in Constitution making is almost out of the question.

Iowa, Minnesota, Nebraska, and Nevada, contain a section very much alike, and, in my opinion, preferable to a corresponding section in any Constitution of the States. These are all modern Constitutions. Navada,

1862, Nebraska 1867, Minnesota 1858, and Iowa 1857. I do not object to either. I consider them just right, and I propose that of Iowa as a substitute for the one which the Committee have reported. Rhode Island passed one in 1842, and New Jersey one in 1844, which are both good and very nearly alike, but they do not come up to that of Iowa. The Constitution of Iowa is regarded as a model Constitution. I consider it so myself. Let us gather from the best, if we gather at all. A few of the States are silent upon the questions involved in this section, but nearly every one contain either in express language or implied, the substance of the Iowa declaration.

I am surprised that the learned gentleman, Chairman of the Committee of the Bill of Rights, whom I know to be fully imbued with the spirit of liberality, and fully alive to the wants of to-day, should have recommended the section as it stands. I trust, however, that he is as open to conviction as any one of us, and glad to substitute the one proposed. I do not know as the Committee were aware that they were presenting any declaration of the Bill of Rights of the State of Mississippi. I think if they had been aware of it, that they would have had some doubts about recommending it. I am a little surprised that the Committee did not examine well the Constitutions of the new States, or of Vermont, Ohio, Illinois, Rhode Island, or any of the great and prosperous States of the North and West, and select from them rather than from the secession States. But it is really no matter where a good thing is obtained from. It seems that the State of Mississippi could not get along without the amendment, so that in 1846 they applied it. I would put up with it now with the amendment, but why adopt it with the amendment when we can adopt a simple article covering the whole ground without an amendment? We cannot afford to enter into a new State government with any extra load upon us. We need some manner to dispose of the thousand little petty larceny cases, and other misdemeanors, without the costly and tedious process of a jury trial.

Section fifteen, which has passed to its third reading, says, that " the Legislature shall not enact any law that shall subject any person to punishment without trial by jury ;" and in the one under discussion, " no person shall be proceeded against criminally, by information, for any indictable offence." What does this mean? Does it mean that no person can be proceeded against criminally by information, unless a grand jury take action? Must a man be arrested, held to bail or go to jail, and lay months for being suspected of stealing a chicken, or for a little boisterous behavior in the street, and have no opportunity for a trial, until the grand jury take action, and the Legislature have no power to

41

aid him? The first expenditure the Legislature would authorize, would better be for new jails, for the old ones would not hold the candidates if such be the effect of the adoption of this section. I am not opposed to a grand jury system. I want every person accused to have the right of a trial by jury if he demands it. Let Justices of the Peace or other officers designated by the Legislature, take cognizances of all petty cases. giving the accused the right of appeal, and the whole matter is properly disposed of. The Courts and jails will be relieved, and innocent persons will be kept out of jail, and justice will be obtained for all.

Mr. B. BYAS. I am heartily in favor of the substitute offered by the gentleman from Barnwell, and hope it will be adopted. While it does not curtail the duties of the grand jury, it proposes and does alleviate many suffering, and perhaps innocent, persons who are confined in jail to await the action of that body.

The question was then taken on the adoption of the substitute, and it was agreed to.

Section twenty-first received its second reading, as follows :

SECTION 21. No person shall be imprisoned for debt except in cases of fraud ; and a reasonable amount of property, as a homestead, shall be exempted from seizure or sale for the payment of any debts or liabilities, except for taxes, that may be contracted after the adoption of this Constitution.

Mr. WM. J. McKINLAY moved to amend by striking out in the second line all after the word " except," and substituting the words " those provided for in this Constitution."

Mr. G. PILLSBURY moved to amend by substituting the word " and" for " or" before the word " sale," which was not agreed to.

Mr. J. S. CRAIG. The report of the Committee on the Legislative portion of the Constitution, read here this morning, provides for a homestead for every family in the State. I think, therefore, it would be best to strike out in this section the provision for the exemption of " a reasonable amount of property as a homestead." I propose this substitute for the section :

" No person shall be imprisoned for debt except in cases of fraud, whereof the party shall have been duly convicted according to law."

Mr. R. G. HOLMES moved to amend the latter by saying, " except upon conviction of fraud."

Mr. J. S. CRAIG accepted the amendment.

Mr. T. K. SASPORTAS moved to amend the fourth line by striking out all after the word " taxes."

Mr. F. L. CARDOZO. I hope both the amendment of the gentleman from Colleton (Mr. J. S. CRAIG), and the amendment of the gentleman from Orangeburg (Mr. T. K. SASPORTAS), will be voted down. The objection of the gentleman from Colleton rests upon the repetition. He fears a repetition in the Bill of Rights and in the Legislative Department. It is a misconception. There is no repetition. In the Bill of Rights, we say, a reasonable amount of property as a homestead shall be exempted, and in the Legislative report, we state what that amount shall be. One states the general principle, and the other the manner in which that principle is to be applied.

Mr. S. J. WRIGHT moved that the substitute of the member from Colleton (Mr. J. S. CRAIG), be indefinitely postponed.

Mr. C. C. BOWEN. I am in favor of striking out the words proposed by the gentleman from Orangeburg (Mr. T. K. SASPORTAS). There are two classes of debts already settled, and with which the Convention cannot interfere. I think it would be useless to attempt to establish a homestead bill, and leave it open for people to come in and get judgments on debts contracted prior to the homestead bill. If there is any mortgage on the homestead property, that mortgage is duly recorded, and there is but one way of discharging it; that is, by paying the money. In the next place, if any judgment be entered in any Court of Record, that judgment is a lien upon any property the person may have held. These two classes of debts are recognized and cared for. There may be parties in debt in which the other parties have neither a mortgage or judgment. Leaving the section as it is, will leave this class of debts open for parties to come in and sue upon. I am, therefore, in favor of striking out the words proposed by the gentleman from Orangeburg.

Mr. J. L. NEAGLE. I see no objection to the section remaining as it now stands. I think the amendment of the gentleman from Orangeburg (Mr. T. K. SASPORTAS) is out of place. I object to striking out the section, as it makes it necessary that the Constitution shall provide for a homestead law.

Mr. WM. J. McKINLAY. The object of the amendment offered by myself was to prevent a conflict of this section with the thirty-fifth section reported by the Legislative Committee This Committee, in section thirty-five of their report, provides that the homestead shall be exempt from sale except for debts due for the purchase of the homestead and for taxes. I think the provisions wise, for if a person purchases a homestead, and pays but part of the money, the homestead should still be liable for the balance.

Mr. T. K. SASPORTAS The gentleman from Charleston (Mr. C. C.

BOWEN) has explained the precise object of the amendment offered by myself. I do not think we should refer to any part of either the Legislative or Judiciary reports whilst acting on the Bill of Rights. When we consider those reports it will be time enough then to strike out anything that conflicts with what has already been adopted.

Mr. B. F. WHITTEMORE. I believe it to be the duty of this body to make proper laws for the protection of the homestead. I think it is a humane act. But while we should have a proper regard for those who are liable to be ejected from their homes, we should at the same time endeavor to be just in every direction. The language made use of here is simply to show that we do not desire to make this section retrospective, but is intended to be prospective altogether. I am perfectly well aware of the provision made by the Legislative Committee. It defines what the exemption shall be. I presume the discussion will come more directly and properly upon that provision in the Legislative part of the Constitution, than here. I wish to lay down the principles in the Bill of Rights which shall cover the entire ground. I shall oppose anything that looks to retro-active action.

I move to amend by striking out all after the words " shall be exempted from seizure or sale," and inserting " except for the payment of such obligations as are provided for in this Constitution."

Mr. WM. J. McKINLAY and Mr. SASPORTAS withdrew their amendments.

Dr. N. J. NEWELL. If we are only to have a prospective homestead, and not a retro-active law, I shall oppose the homestead provision in every shape or form. A homestead law to be of any benefit to the people in their present condition must be retro-active.

Mr. R. J. DONALDSON. I hope the substitute offered by the gentleman from Colleton will be voted down. If we wait for a conviction in cases of fraud, before the Court gives a warrant of arrest, the party or parties convicted may leave the State. We are told that a large emigration is coming here, and among them may be swindlers who would get outside the State before the persons injured could get redress. That matter should be left to the discretion of the officers of the law. We should be careful to do nothing here that the Courts will decide to be unconstitutional. We have no right, no authority, to pass an *ex post facto* law. While I have been urged to advocate a retro-active law, I cannot conscientiously do it. The parties who are in an unfortunate position with regard to past debts must take the benefit of the bankrupt law, which reserves to every man a certain portion of his goods.

Mr. R. C. DeLARGE moved that the further consideration of the entire section be postponed until the second reading of the section in the report of the Committee on the Legislative part of the Constitution relative to the same matter.

Mr. F. J. MOSES, Jr. I hope that motion will prevail. It is certainly the intention of the Convention to adopt some kind of a homestead law. I do not presume to say what the law may be, but, in the opinion of the gentlemen who have just spoken, there are many members who desire to debate the question as to whether the law should be retro-active or prospective. That question is inseparably connected with the subject. I am, therefore, in favor of postponement until the question of homesteads comes up, then we can have the debate upon it all at once.

Mr. F. L. CARDOZO. I disagree with the gentleman from Sumter, (Mr. F. J. MOSES, Jr.) I think it would be a bad precedent to postpone action on a report before us on account of a pending matter. If we proceed in that way, we will never have anything complete. If we decide now whether the law is retro-active or prospective, how can it come up again. I think we should take decisive action on the questions as they come up before us. If we postpone action on any section because of what may occur, we may find ourselves deceived, as what we expect may not occur. I cannot understand why any gentleman should wish to postpone simply upon this question as to whether the law will be retro-active or prospective only, especially as last week we invalidated all debts contracted for the purchase of slaves, and, therefore, the homestead cannot be sold for those debts, and I think should not be sold for any other. I hope we will not take any retro-active action on any debts. It would seriously impair credit. I voted against the Ordinance invalidating debts for slaves, because I thought it to be just, and we had no right to impair the obligation of contracts.

Mr. B. F. RANDOLPH. I am in favor of a homestead law, and opposed to the latter clause of this section which says, " except for taxes that may be contracted after the adoption of this Constitution." If it is our purpose, or the purpose of the Legislature, to provide homesteads for the people, I think it would be a most uncharitable act to levy upon that homestead for taxes.

Mr. E. W. M. MACKEY. Suppose the time came when nine-tenths of the people of the State owned nothing more than a homestead, I would like to know how the State Government is to be supported if those nine-tenths are exempted from paying taxes ?

Mr. B. F. RANDOLPH. Suppose nine-tenths of the people are thrown out in the public highway because unable to pay their taxes, what then becomes the condition of the people in South Carolina? They would be the most wretched, poverty-stricken people in the world. I would rather see the people of South Carolina in a good, prosperous condition, even if we have to let the Treasury of the State be kept empty.

Mr. B. F. WHITTEMORE. The remarks of the last speaker, it appears to me, are entirely irrelevant. We know very well the State must levy taxes upon the property of the citizens of the State, and unless the taxes are paid, their estates must be sold. I would like to know what kind of a community we should have, after exempting their property from sale for other debts, they could not earn sufficient to pay their taxes. It would certain'y be a lazy community. It has already been said of many communities that they are lazy. Now I am not in favor of providing a homestead for that class of people. If we have any class of people who cannot pay a tax within a year, I would be in favor of making some exemption. But I have too good an opinion of the people of the State to believe they desire an exemption from taxes, after exempting a certain amount as a homestead, except for other taxes. We must levy taxes to pay the expenses of the State.

Mr. A. C. RICHMOND. I think there is a very simple method of settling this matter. I hope the section, with the amendment of the gentleman from Darlington (Mr. WHITTEMORE) will pass. It seems to be very proper that it should be stated as a fundamental right of the people that there should be a homestead. This section, as amended, will simply state that there shall be a homestead for the people of the State. By and by, when the Legislative department comes up, it may then be tested whether it shall take effect now or in the future. I think the homestead law should take effect immediately.

Mr. J. M. RUTLAND. I will renew my motion to postpone this matter until the thirty-fifth section of the Legislative part of the Constitution comes up. Everything can be effected by considering them together. It is a mistake to say we may never come to that because it is in the future. The matter is in possession of the house, and the Legislative report has been read a first time. I, therefore, move that the debate on this be postponed until the thirty-fifth section of the Legislative report be taken up, and that they then be considered together.

Mr. B. F. WHITTEMORE. If we are to defer our action upon these sections until we have taken up all the other departments of the Constitution, why would it not be as well to defer action upon any other clause until we have decided the Constitution.

Mr. R. H. CAIN. I can see no necessity of postponement at this stage of our proceedings. It appears to me that in settling questions in the Bill of Rights, it stands foremost. When we have declared what our rights are under the Constitution, then all the other laws and regulations are to be made under the Constitution. I think, therefore, we should proceed at once with the discussion of this question. I do not think it would make any material difference to anticipate some action on the homestead question.

Mr. B. F. RANDOLPH. What we act upon to-day, we will not be called upon to do another time, and while we have a portion of the work before us let us finish it.

Mr. A. C. RICHMOND. If we are not careful we will have the city papers saying we have not passed more than three sections to-day. The only thing necessary now is to assert the fundamental right of the people to have a homestead. I hope that the motion to postpone the section will be voted down.

Mr. R. B. ELLIOTT. I hope the motion to postpone will not prevail. I think if this matter is to be discussed at all this is the proper time to do it. Let it be discussed while we have the twenty-second section before us. That says "no bill of attainder or *ex post facto* law shall be passed." Whilst we have that before us, we can determine whether it is right and proper to pass the twenty-first section and make it retro active or prospective. I do not think it will benefit the matter to leave it until the thirty-fifth section of the Legislative report comes up. Let us determine what are our rights while we have the bill before us.

Mr. J. S. CRAIG. I opposed any action on this section simply because I considered it inappropriate. I do not think the homestead law should have a place in the Bill of Rights. No man is more in favor of a liberal homestead than myself, and no man is willing to go farther than I am. But I do think the proper place for a homestead provision is in the legislative part of the Constitution. That was my object in offering the substitute. I do not propose to go into the merits of the question of postponement.

Mr. W. B. NASH. I hope the house will not postpone this question, but decide it at once. I think this provision is in its proper place. There is no place more proper to state what our rights are, than in the Bill of Rights, and that is the very reason why I am opposed to the postponement of this section. If the people have any rights, I think one of them is that they should pay their debts. I think it ought to be laid down in the Bill of Rights, that the people have no right to repudiate their debts. I believe if we postpone the consideration of this section, and adopt that proposed by the thirty-fifth section of the Legislative Committee, it would be recognizing repudiation. I must say I am in favor of the twenty-first section as it stands.

Mr. N. G. PARKER. I hope it will not be postponed. I think this is the proper time to dispose of the question.

Mr. B. F. WHITTEMORE. I have but a few words to say. I hoped with the amendment offered by myself that the debate would have ended, and that we could have taken it up in some other place. Inasmuch as so much has been said upon the subject, I trust the amendment I have offered will be lost, and I shall withdraw it. I believe there is an intention to make this law retrospective. My object was to make it prospective altogether. It appears to me the action of this Convention already has covered the debts and liabilities of this people sufficiently. The homestead law is intended to protect more particularly the poor people of the State; those who may come into possession of property hereafter, and who may own homesteads. If we make it retrospective, we cannot touch the cases of those we propose to provide for in the future; for, if we cover all the people of the State with all the means to cover their property, I question whether we will be able to provide for the homesteads of the people in the future. We have already shown as much charity to the rich people of the State as could be expected. If we are to provide for all the people, let us take into consideration one great fact, that there are liabilities and obligations which we cannot by our action impair, that we have a duty to perform, and we declare in the twenty-second section "that no law impairing the obligation of a contract, and no *ex post facto* law shall be passed." If we make this section retrospective in our action here, or if we do not declare that whatever exemptions we make shall be for debts contracted after the adoption of this Constitution, it appears to me we are taking upon ourselves what we have no right to do; what, in accordance with the Constitution of the United States, we have no right to do, namely, to impair the obligation of a contract. Since I offered the amendment, it has been admitted to me there was an intention to make the action on this retrospective, and in accordance with that fact I am now speaking. I believe when the conviction comes from the heart and mind no gentleman has a right to retract anything he has already said

I might have been willing, in the first place, to allow this question to come upon the Legislative part of the Constitution. I trust, however, it will be decided now. We cannot do any injury to the people if we make it prospective instead of retro-active. I voted steadily against the Ordinance annulling all contracts for the purchase of slaves, and I voted upon the principle simply that I believed we had no right to impair the obligation of a contract. I believe all we have a right to do is to look forward. We must leave the past and look forward to the future in our action upon these matters. I trust this question will be decided by this Convention, and such a decision made here that the people of this Commonwealth shall see we intend not only to frame a new Constitution under which the people may live, but to frame it exactly in accordance with the Constitution of the United States. I hope we shall take no action we shall regret in the future. With these explanations, I believe I have set myself right before this body. When I offered my amendment, I had no idea of presenting any proposition that would make the measure retrospective. I, therefore, will vote against my own amendment, and hope the section will pass as it now is in the Bill of Rights.

The question was then taken on the amendment offered by the delegate from Colleton (Mr. CRAIG), and the amendment was not agreed to

The next question taken, was upon the motion of the Chairman of the Committee to strike out all after the word "sale," and insert "except for the payment of such obligations as is provided for in this Constitution," which was agreed to.

The question was then taken on the section as amended, and it passed to a third reading.

SECTION 22. No bill of attainder, *ex post facto* law, nor any law impairing the obligation of contracts, shall ever be enacted; and no conviction shall work corruption of blood or forfeiture of estate.

Mr. J. J. WRIGHT moved to strike out the words "nor any law impairing the obligation of contracts."

Mr. R. H. CAIN. I hope those words will not be stricken out. I think we will find that provision one of the bulwarks of the Constitution of the United States, as well as of most other States. We should not strike out such landmarks which have guided our country so long.

Mr. B. O. DUNCAN. I hope the words will not be stricken out.

Mr. C. C. BOWEN. I am not in favor of striking those words out altogether. I would amend by saying, "except certain contracts." I certainly think the hands of the Legislature ought not to be tied at this stage of our proceedings. A contract may have been made partly on a confederate basis. It is nevertheless a contract. If you tie the hands of the Legislature, parties may go into Court and insist on the fulfillment of contracts entered into on a Confederate basis, between the 19th day of December, 1860, and the 1st day of June 1865. I would leave the Legislature free to act in regard to these contracts.

Mr. F. L. CARDOZO. I hope the words will not be stricken out.

Mr. J. J. WRIGHT. I accept the amendment offered by my friend from Charleston (Mr. BOWEN), "except contracts entered into between the 19th of December, 1860, and the 1st of June, 1865."

42

Mr. J. M. RUTLAND. It seems to me we are doing unnecessary work in attempting to alter anything in the Constitution of the United States on this subject. The language used here is in the identical language of the Constitution of the United States, and I care not what may be the decision of the Convention, that will be the law of the land. I do not see why any motion should be entertained for one moment to encourage the idea that this Convention is in favor of impairing the obligation of contracts. I hope all our action will be in conformity to the Constitution of the United States. The language in that instrument is plain and palpable. If we attempt to ignore that we may roam where we please, but it will surely be a waste of time to undertake to pass any act or ordinance in contravention of the Constitution of the United States. I hope the section will pass as it stands, and move the indefinite postponement of the amendment.

The motion was agreed to, and the twenty-second section passed to a third reading.

Section twenty-third was read as follows:

SECTION 23. Treason against the State shall consist in levying war against the same, or in adhering to its enemies, giving them aid and comfort. No person shall be convicted of treason unless on the testimony of two witnesses to the same overt act or on confession in open Court.

Mr. E. W. M. MACKEY. I move to strike out this section altogether. It seems to me absurd to speak of treason against the State. I regard it as impossible to commit treason against South Carolina. A citizen of this State can commit treason against the United States, but he never can be guilty of treason towards South Carolina or any other State. Treason can only be committed against a sovereign power, and for this Convention to incorporate in the Constitution a section defining treason against the State, would be equivalent to admitting the treasonable doctrine of State sovereignty and States rights, a political heresy which has already cost the nation thousands of lives and millions of dollars.

This section reads, "Treason against the State shall consist in levying war against the same, or in adhering to its enemies, giving them aid and comfort." According to this doctrine, all the citizens of this State, who, during the late rebellion, adhered to the Union and aided and abetted Union soldiers in levying war against the State, were guilty of treason against South Carolina, and every Carolinian in this Convention must be a traitor. I regard it just as impossible to commit treason against a State as to commit treason against a city or a county. Chancellor Kent has said "levying war against one State is a levying of war against all in their federal capacity, and is a crime belonging exclusively to the Federal Government." A citizen of this State can only commit treason against the United States, to which he owes his paramount, and, in fact, only allegiance. It is impossible to commit treason against any portion of the United States, much less against a thirty-sixth part of it. As allegiance is due to the General Government alone, and not to South Carolina, how is it possible to commit treason against a power to which no allegiance is due. If the constituted authorities of this State were again to attempt to wage war, or rebel against the General Government, it would be the duty of all loyal Carolinians to levy war against the State. But could any of us do this without violating this section of the Constitution and committing treason against South Carolina ? The Constitution of the United States defines treason as levying war against the United States and aiding and abetting its enemies. The section in our Constitution proposes to define treason as levying war against South Carolina. Where would our citizens stand in case of civil war ? To aid the United States would be to commit treason against South Carolina, and on the other hand to aid South Carolina would be treason against the United States. Standing between two fires, the citizens would be guilty of treason which ever way they acted. It was this very doctrine, the doctrine which admitted that a citizen could commit treason against a State, that dragged thousands of Unionists and ignorant men into the rebellion, because they thought that to aid or abet the Union was to commit treason against South Carolina. As I have already said, treason can only be committed against a sovereign power, and there is no gentleman in this Convention who will undertake to prove now that a State is sovereign. It is unnecessary for me to go into any lengthy argument to prove that a State is not sovereign and does not possess sovereign powers. The war has proved to the most bitter rebels that we are one and not thirty-six nations, and therefore, that treason can only be committed against the nation itself and not against any portion of it. For these reasons, Mr. President, I move to strike out the entire clause.

Mr. R. G. HOLMES. I hope that motion will not prevail. It is certainly a correct statement that treason can be committed against a State. The gentleman is correct in his theory, that treason can only exist against a sovereign, and this is the very rock on which South Carolina split before; that was, if the State was sovereign, the United States are not sovereign. That is not the case. The State has sovereign power over the inhabitants of the State, and the Federal Government is sovereign over the inhabitants of the State. The State is sovereign over her citizens in her sovereign capacities. The principle, I think, therefore, is correct, and I hope the section will pass.

The question was taken on the motion to strike out the section, and the motion was not agreed to.

Mr. N. G. PARKER. I propose the following amendment: To insert the words "United States" in lieu of "State."

Mr B. O. DUNCAN. I voted in the majority, and therefore move to reconsider the vote by which the section was adopted.

The motion was agreed to

Mr. C. C. BOWEN. I desire to ask the members who seem to think treason can be committed against a State, in what tribunal outside of the United States Court could such a case be tried. I am satisfied treason can only be committed against the United States Government; or, in other words, if it is committed against the State, it must be against the United States. I wish to know in what tribunal a man would be tried if he is charged with committing treason against South Carolina.

Mr. F. L. CARDOZO. If I understand treason correctly it is against a sovereign power, South Carolina is a subordinate power. If a sovereign power calls upon you to obey, and the subordinate power declares you shall not, which one are you to obey? I think there can be no treason against a subordinate power, but only against the supreme and sovereign power. The Constitution of the United States provides "that treason shall consist in the levying of war against the United States," therefore any obedience to a State law in opposition to that will be a violation of the supreme law. No State has a right to set itself up as supreme. There can be no treason then except against a supreme paramount power. If we adopt this section, it will be assuming sovereign power, the very cause of all the war and all the troubles of the country.

Mr. R. B. ELLIOTT. I move the following amendment: "Treason in this State shall consist in levying war against the United States or in adhering to its enemies, giving them aid and comfort."

Mr. CARDOZO. There is no necessity for that amendment. The United States has already provided for that.

Mr. R. H. CAIN. We have already said in the first article (section fourth), that "every citizen owes paramount allegiance to the Government of the United States, and no law or Ordinance in contravention or subversion thereof can have any binding force." Gentlemen say no treason can be committed against a State, yet in most of the States a similar provision is inserted in their Constitutions. The hypothesis of the gentlemen is that we can only commit treason against the United States. I am not a lawyer, and possibly do not understand the question, but it does appear to me if the State passes laws, and those laws are in harmony with the Constitution of the United States, any act which any citizen may do against the State is clearly an act against the United States.

Mr. J. M. RUTLAND. I presume no man in this Convention would be more opposed to introducing anything into this Constitution that would hereafter recognize anything like secession or nullification than myself. I hope no clause will ever be introduced that will countenance or sanction those measures. But so far as this particular clause is concerned, while I care nothing about it, I am inclined to think it may well remain and have its proper consideration. I do think there is such a thing as treason against the State of South Carolina, notwithstanding we owe paramount allegiance to the Constitution of the United States. Levying war against the State of South Carolina, as properly said, is levying war against the United States. I do not think it necessary to waste time upon a point like this, but the State certainly does retain some attributes of sovereignty. I cannot, however, like Mr. Calhoun, contend that sovereignty is one and indivisible. Sovereignty is divisible. We have an illustration of this fact. The Government of the United States has the highest attributes of sovereignty; the right to declare war, make peace, lay duties and imposts, and collect them, all of which are the highest attributes of sovereignty, higher than those which remain to the State; but South Carolina has still some of those attributes. She has the right, under certain circumstances, to dispose of the lives of its citizens, their liberties and their property.

Mr. C. C. BOWEN. Before what tribunal would you try a man for committing treason against the State?

Mr. J. M. RUTLAND. That would be a matter of indifference to me. I think John Brown was tried in a State Court.

Mr. C. C. BOWEN. Was not John Brown tried for creating insurrection?

Mr. J. M. RUTLAND. I think for treason. In my opinion the State retains some of the rights of sovereignty. If disposing of a man's life, property and liberty are not attributes of sovereignty, I do not know what are. South Carolina most assuredly has the right to do some of these things. But I would repeat that I acknowledge paramount allegiance to the Constitution of the United States, and only secondary allegiance to South Carolina. I believe treason against the State to be treason against the General Government; I would let the section stand as it is.

Mr. R. H. CAIN. I would like to ask, first, can a citizen of a State levy war against a State; and, secondly, can a citizen give aid to the State?

Mr. E. W. M. MACKEY. I will answer that in the words of Chancellor Kent, "levying war against one State is levying war against all in their federal capacity, and is a crime to be punished exclusively by the Federal Government."

Mr. W. J. WHIPPER. The section now in question in the first place defines treason as levying war against the State. This I agree with the gentleman from Charleston is wrong. There is no such thing as levying war against the State of South Carolina, and the same may be said of the sentiment "in adhering to its enemies, giving them aid and comfort." This provision would have been invaluable had it been passed as inserted in the Constitution of South Carolina, while the State was out of the Union, when the authorities of the State were very desirous of punishing Union men who adhered, and gave food and drink to Union soldiers. Then this provision would have been of invaluable service. Every man who fed a Union soldier, or comforted any man who did not agree as to the doctrine of States Rights, would have been an object of prosecution had this provision existed at that time. Had that law existed at that time, our worthy President might have been hung under it, and the very best men whom we most love and honor would have been victims. The very fact that it would have been an instrument in the hands of bad men at one time is sufficient to induce us to vote it down. It is not impossible that the State of South Carolina may attempt to secede again; not impossible that other States may attempt to secede, and we should not attempt to establish a doctrine that will work injury to the Government in such a case.

Again, it is laid down by Chancellor Kent that levying war against a State is levying war against the United States; that whatever a man may do that amounts to treason in a State, is treason against the United States. It is not simply a violation of municipal law, but a violation of the law of the United States and the supreme law of the land. There is no tribunal under heaven in which you can try a case of this kind save in the Courts of the United States. You cannot go into the county Courts or any other Courts of the State. It is a national offence, and must be tried by the United States Courts. There is more States Rights doctrine contained in that section than the most ardent secessionist could desire. I hope it will be stricken out. I am willing to be charitable, and presume that the Committee who reported it did it inadvertently.

Mr. B. F RANDOLPH. Suppose the Federal Government passes a law and the majority of the people in this State favor that law; suppose there are thousands of men opposed to that law, and they attempt to oppose the laws of the State in the event of the majority attempting to carry out the law of the United States by making it also a State law. I want to know what they would consider that. I know in the State of Ohio, when the fugitive slave law of the United States was attempted to be executed, when the slave hunters came to recapture a fugitive, two thousand men were supposed to be in readiness to execute the law of the United States, and at the same time put down the State law, for there we had a law making every man a freeman brought there by his master. That fugitive slave was carried there by his master.

Now these men were engaged in sustaining the Federal Government and putting down the laws of the State. They would have gone to Columbus, the capital of the State, thrown out the Government and taken possession. Now I want to know if a thousand men were to go to Columbia and attempt to slay the Governor and overthrow the State government, if that is not treason against the State—if it is not, then there is no such thing as treason at all.

Mr. R. C. DeLARGE. I trust the section will be stricken out. If the Constitution of the United States is the supreme law of the land, which I claim it is, then there is no necessity for the insertion of this provision here. The Constitution of the United States defines treason to be levying war or giving aid and comfort to the enemies of the general government. If the allegiance of the citizen of the State is due to the Government of the United States, and is paramount to that due by him to the State, then I cannot see how the citizen of any State can commit treason against that State without committing treason against the General Government; and if it is treason against the General Government, it is not treason against the State. From the statement of my legal friends, I feel confident no citizen can levy war against a State without levying war against the General Government. Allusion has been made by my friend from Fairfield (Mr. RUTLAND) to the hanging of John Brown. Let me say that John Brown was hung for insurrection, and if a number of citizens of the State had to do what my learned friend from Orangeburg (Mr. RANDOLPH) says they might do, it would be an insurrection, and they could be tried and hung for it just as John Brown was. I see no necessity for this provision. If anything was settled by the late contest, it was that the paramount allegiance of the citizen is due to the General Government and not to the State. It is not unlikely that South Carolina, along with some of her sister States, may attempt to secede from the Federal Union, and attempting reconstruction now on a firm basis, we should place no clause in the Constitution that may be construed by lawyers in favor of States Rights. Some gentleman may attempt to show that liberty-loving Massachusetts has the same provision in her Constitution ; but I believe even Massachusetts has more of the doctrine of States Rights in her Constitution than any State in this Union. But I trust if other States have committed the error to suppose that a citizen can commit treason against a State, that the State of South Carolina will declare to the people of the world that the allegiance due by them to the Federal Government is paramount to the allegiance due to the State.

Mr. R. G. HOLMES. We all admit that treason cannot exist against a State, but we all maintain that the State has the sovereign power to make laws for themselves. It is argued that the laws made by the Legislature may not be obeyed. If not, they must be enforced by the military, and if they are resisted, it is treason. If the State cannot enforce her laws, she may call upon the General Government. I see no reason why the section should not be passed as it is.

Mr. J. J. WRIGHT. I think sufficient has been said to convince members that the clause before us is certainly unnecessary. I do not come here to follow the Constitutions of the States of North Carolina, Pennsylvania, Massachusetts or Georgia. We are to make a Constitution to suit affairs in South Carolina. That is our bounden and imperative duty. If any other States have committed a blunder it should serve only as a warning for us. One gentleman asks the question, if one or more persons should convene together in the State of South Carolina, could they commit treason against the State. In answer to that, I say they can. Treason consists in levying war. Persons levying war, for instance, in the State of South Carolina, levies war against the United States, and it is the bounden duty of the other States, as members of the Union, to put that treason down. When South Carolina seceded, by the act she levied war against every State in the Union ; against Massachusetts, against Pennsylvania, against New York, and all the other States, and it was the duty of all the other States to rally their forces and put it down. The very fact that it is impossible for a State to punish treason is certainly *prima facie* evidence that the framers of the Constitution did not intend that treason should be levied against the State in such a manner as to give the State the right to punish it. If the State of South Carolina has the right to punish treason, it is certain that the offenders liable to be punished by the State would also be liable to be punished by the United States.

Mr. L. S. LANGLEY. When South Carolina seceded and committed treason against Massachusetts and other States, did she commit treason against herself ?

Mr. J. J. WRIGHT. As I have already said when any State levies war against a portion of her own State, or against any other State, she has committed treason against every State in the Union, and against every person in the State, inasmuch as she aims a dagger to knock out the great prop that protects her rights and priviliges.

Mr. J. M. RUTLAND. Suppose there was no law of Congress which had any bearing on this point, and within the limits of South Carolina a party should organize themselves for the purpose of overthrowing the party holding the government in South Carolina, and suppose they should attempt to dethrone the authorities and take possession of the government upon the ground that they were not administering the government honestly, and were actually to commit overt acts, could any of the Courts of South Carolina arrest them for treason ?

Mr. J. J. WRIGHT. The Courts of South Carolina are capable of attempting anything But if the persons of whom he speaks levied war against the party in power, they could be arrested by any power or authority in the State, but I deny that they could be tried by any tribunal in the State. They must be tried by the United States Court. I will cite the case of John Brown. He was tried by the State Court of Virginia, not for treason, but for insurrection. If I were to gather a dozen men here to clean out this room it would be insurrection.

Mr. B. F. WHITTEMOBE. Does not insurrection mean sedition or rebellion, and is not that treason ?

Mr. J. J. WRIGHT. Insurrection as I understand it does not mean sedition. Insurrection consists in the getting up of a mob in such a way as to excite the people around them to gain a certain object. For instance, a certain class go to work to excite the minds of people against another portion of the people, so that this people would believe the other portion had encroached on their rights, and they would be so excited as to lay hold of arms, get hundreds together and commit outrages upon that people ; that I understand to be treason, and the ring leaders would be liable to be tried and punished for treason. I desire that we should show to the world we intend to frame our Constitution in accordance with the civilization of the age which shall protect the entire people in their rights and privileges.

Mr. L. S. LANGLEY. It seems to me that the word treason is to be received and is used with a limited meaning. I believe we are all here good Republicans, and I believe it is the principle of the great party that now rules the destinies of the nation, and will rule this State, that no State can go out of the Union. If no State can possibly go out of the Union, I would ask when South Carolina seceded, did she not, in committing treason against the Federal Government and the other States,

43

commit treason against herself? I think it necessarily follows; and if she committed treason against herself as well as against the United States, what objection can there be to having treason defined in this section of our Constitution? If we go upon the principle of striking out because it is already defined in the Constitution of the United States, we may as well strike out section one of the Bill of Rights, because it is similar to another section in that instrument.

Mr. B. F. WHITTEMORE. I remember, in my boyhood, of what was considered in Rhode Island not only an insurrection, but an act of treason committed by Governor Dorr, so-called. I remember troops from Massachusetts went upon the border line, and recollect also that the United States soldiers were called upon. It was never defined in any way but as the treason of Dorr and Dorr's insurrection. I have looked into Webster, which says insurrection is equivalent to sedition, and that sedition is equivalent to rebellion. Suppose Congress should pass further reconstruction acts and declare that no legitimate government exists in South Carolina except the Constitutional Convention, and it should devolve upon the Convention to take the government into our hands. Suppose the people of South Carolina should rise in revolt, rebellion or treason; I would like to ask whether they are not in rebellion and insurrection, and committing treason against the only existing State authority here I know there is a fear upon the minds of some gentlemen here that if we give sanction to this section in the Bill of Rights, we are ourselves placed in a peculiar position, namely, that the State of South Carolina does not acknowledge we are a legal body. I believe the Governor does as long as the reconstruction acts are not declared unconstitutional by the Supreme Court. As long as the Supreme Court does not declare us illegal he is not disposed to question the legality of this Convention. Some here, under these apprehensions, believe if we pass this section we immediately acknowledge we are traitors, and that we can be arrested, from the President to the most silent members of this body. Now, we have nothing to do with the past. We are here for the purpose of making a government for the people in the future, and when this Constitution shall have been passed upon by the people, and it becomes law, it appears to me if the people who look upon us as an illegal body should attempt to overthrow it and wage war, they are committing treason against the only acknowledged authority in the State, and should be punished for treason accordingly. In this view of the effect of the section I cannot see why we should erase it from the Bill of Rights.

Mr. B. F. RANDOLPH. This seems to me to be a question of words. It is evident to every member of the Convention that there is such a thing as a State rising in rebellion or insurrection against the regularly constituted laws of the State. For instance, a thousand men may go to Columbia armed, and those thousand men, in attempting to change or overthrow the Government of the State, would be guilty of insurrection and rebellion against the people of the State. If the loyal people could catch these thousand men they would try them all, and hang them as high as Haman. We would not apply to the United States Courts to try those men.

I move to amend the section so as to read, "Treason against the State shall consist in levying war, and no person shall be convicted of rebellion," so that when any number of men attempt to overthrow the State Government, they can be punished by the laws of the State.

Mr. C. C. BOWEN. The gentleman from Darlington (Mr. WHITTEMORE) has referred to the case of Dorr s rebellion. I would like to know whether he was tried for treason or rebellion, or whether he was tried for any offence.

Mr. B. F. WHITTEMORE. I am not able to say what the trial was, but he was tried and imprisoned in Rhode Island.

Mr. C. C. BOWEN. Governor Dorr was imprisoned in jail, and they opened the doors and let him out. They did not dare go to a trial for treason, for the reason that the United States Government would not step in and prosecute, and the State Court could not do it.

Mr. B. F. WHITTEMORE. Where was John Brown tried.

Mr. C. C. BOWEN. John Brown was tried in the State Court of Virginia for insurrection. If he had been tried in the United States Court, he would have been pardoned. An appeal was made on the ground that it was within the jurisdiction of the United States. This was denied, and it was claimed that the United States Supreme Court had decided in a similar case that the Courts of Virginia had exclusive jurisdiction; that John Brown was not indicted for treason, but for creating an insurrection within the limits of Virginia. Upon that indictment he was found guilty and executed. It is upon such a section as this in the several Constitutions of the State, that the people heretofore have claimed the right to go against the Government, and it was upon this that the people were advised in going for the State they were not guilty of treason. If any future offender is acquitted, it will be upon that plea. I hope the entire section will be stricken out.

Mr. G. PILLSBURY. I am sorry to see so much feeling on this question. This section has certainly one virtue which many enactments of rights do not possess, and that is, it can do no harm. The main argument used against it is that it is provided for in the Constitution of the United States. Many other things are enumerated in our Bill of Rights which are guaranteed in the Constitution of the United States, and which we do not deem improper to reiterate and place in the Declaration of Rights for this State. I opine that the law-givers in this State for the last twenty years, have not very particularly studied the Constitution of the United States. I fancy they might have lost their spectacles for the last twenty years, as the pretended pious old lady lost hers when the Bible was offered her to read. She had not seen her spectacles for twenty years. If, as heretofore, the people will again begin and condescend to make our Constitution their Bible, I wish every time they open on that Bill of Rights, every section of it would say to them, "Death to traitors." I deem it perfectly proper that this section should be inserted.

Mr. J. S. CRAIG. It has been already settled there can be no such thing as levying war against a State. The Constitution of the United States provides that in case of insurrection, which the civil-government cannot quell, the State can call upon the General Government to put it down. But it is not treason against the State. It is impossible to separate the State as one of the branches of the General Government.

The question recurring on striking out the section, Mr. BOWEN moved a call of the house.

Mr. F. L. CARDOZO called for the yeas and nays on the main question.

Before proceeding to the call of the yeas and nays, the hour of three having arrived, the Convention adjourned.

TWENTY-THIRD DAY

Tuesday, February 11, 1868.

The Convention assembled at half-past 10 A. M., and was called to order by the PRESIDENT.

Prayer was offered by the Rev. JOS. H. RAINEY.

The roll was called, and a quorum answering to their names, the PRESIDENT announced the Convention ready to proceed to business.

The Journal of Monday was read and approved.

Mr. S. G. W. DILL offered a resolution authorizing the President of the Convention to request General Canby to draw from the State Treasury a sufficient amount of bills receivable to pay the members the amount of their mileage on Saturday next, at 3 P. M.

Mr. R. C. DeLARGE moved to lay. the motion on the table, which was agreed to.

Mr. J. J. WRIGHT moved to take up the unfinished business of yesterday, which was carried.

The PRESIDENT announced the unfinished business to be the call of the yeas and nays on the question of striking out the twenty-third section of the Bill of Rights, which reads as follows :

"Section 23d. Treason against the State shall consist in levying war against the same, or in adhering to its enemies, giving them aid and comfort; no person shall be convicted of treason, unless on the testimony of two witnesses to the same overt act, or on confession in open Court."

Mr. B. F. WHITTEMORE moved to suspend the calling of the yeas and nays.

Mr. F. L. CARDOZO hoped not, as there had already been sufficient discussion on the subject.

Mr. B. F. WHITTEMORE said that there had been a great deal of caucussing on this matter since adjournment. He had no desire to retain in the Bill of Rights anything detrimental to the people of the State, but he thought arguments could be brought forward to show that the people of the State could not be injured by the introduction and retention of this clause.

The PRESIDENT stated all debate after the call for yeas and nays was out of order.

The yeas and nays were then taken, and resulted as follows :

YEAS.—The President; Messrs. Alexander, Arnim, Becker, Bell,

Bowen Bonum, Burton, Brockenton, Bryce, Byas E. J. Cain, Camp, Cardozo, Collins, Corley, Craig, Darrington, DeLarge, Dickson, Dogan, Driffle, Foster, Gentry, Goss, Gray, Harris, J. N. Hayne, H. E. Hayne, Henderson, Humbird, Hunter, Hurley, Jackson, Jacobs, Jervey, Wm. B. Johnson, J. W. Johnson, Dr. L. B. Johnson, Joiner, Henry Jones, Geo. Lee, Samuel Lee, Lomax, Leslie, E. W. M. Mackey, Mauldin, W. J. McKinlay, Wm. McKinlay, Miller, Milford. F. J. Moses, Jr., Nance, Newell, Neckles, Owens, Parker, Perry, Rainey, Ransier, Richmond, Rivers, Robertson, Rose, Runion, Sanders, Sasportas, Shrewsbury, Stubbs, Swails, Thomas, Augustus Thompson, Benj. Thompson, Viney, Webb, White, Williamson, Chas. M. Wilder, Wingo, Wright—80.

NAYS.—Chamberlain, Chestnut, Clinton, Davis, Dill, Duncan, H. D. Edwards, Holmes, Jenks, Jillson, Samuel Johnson, Wm. E. Johnston, Charles Jones, Lamb, Langley, McDaniels, Mead, Nash, Nelson, Neagle, Pillsbury, Randolph, Rutland, S. B. Thompson, Whittemore, Francis E. Wilder—26.

ABSENT.—Allen, Boozer, R. H. Cain, Coghlan, Cooke, Crews, Donaldson, Elliott, Chas. D. Hayne, Mayer, Middleton, Olsen, Smalls, Whipper, Wooley—15.

Mr. N. G. PARKER, Chairman of the Finance Committee, stated that it was well known to the members that the money ($30,000) to pay their per diem had arrived, and they also knew in what manner it was to be received and paid out. He, therefore, moved that the house do now adjourn to attend to that business.

On the motion being put, it was not agreed to.

Mr. E. W. M. MACKEY moved that when the house adjourn, it adjourn at half-past twelve o'clock.

Mr. N. G. PARKER moved to amend by making it half-past eleven o'clock.

The question then being taken on the original motion, it was lost, and the amendment adopted.

The Convention then adjourned.

TWENTY-FOURTH DAY

Wednesday, February 12, 1868.

The Convention assembled at 10 A. M., and was called to order by the PRESIDENT.

Prayer was offered by the Rev. B. F. WHITTEMORE.

The roll was called, and a quorum answering to their names, the PRESIDENT announced a quorum present and the Convention ready to proceed to business.

The Journal was read and approved.

The PRESIDENT laid before the Convention a communication from the Georgia Constitutional Convention praying Congress for a loan of Thirty Million Dollars for the relief of destitution and suffering among the people of the States now in course of reconstruction, and recommending that the several Conventions in session join in the petition to Congress for said loan.

On motion of Mr. B. F. WHITTEMORE the communication was referred to the Committee on Petitions.

Mr. N. G. PARKER moved that in the absence of Mr. L. BOOZER, who was likely to be away for the balance of the session, a Chairman be appointed to the Committee on Miscellaneous Provisions of the Constitution.

Mr. J. J. WRIGHT thought no such necessity existed, as the next member on the Committee would properly occupy the place of the absent Chairman.

Mr. E. W. M. MACKEY moved to lay the motion on the table, which was agreed to.

The Convention resumed the consideration of the Bill of Rights.

Section twenty-four was read as follows:

All persons have a right to be secure from unreasonable searches or seizure of their persons, houses, papers or possessions. All warrants therefore are contrary to this right if the cause or foundation of them be not previously supported by affirmation or oath, and if the order in the warrant to a civil officer, to make search in suspected places, or to arrest one or more suspected person, or to seize their property, be not accompanied with a special designation of the persons or objects of search, arrest or seizure; and no warrant shall be issued but in cases and with the formalities prescribed by the laws.

Mr. J. D. BELL, of Beaufort, moved to amend after the word warrant as follows: "shall be supported by affirmation or oath, and the order in the warrant to a civil officer to make search in suspected places, or to arrest one or more suspected persons, or to seize their property, shall be accompanied with." The amendment was agreed to

The section as amended was then passed to its third reading.

Section twenty-five was then read as follows:

Private property shall not be taken or applied for public use, or for the use of corporations, other than municipal or for private use, without the consent of the owner and a just compensation being made therefor ; *Provided, however*, that laws may be made securing to persons or corporations the right of way over the lands of either persons or corporations, and for works of internal improvement the right to establish depots, stations, turnouts, etc., but a just compensation, in all cases, shall be first made to the owner.

Mr. J. J. WRIGHT moved to strike out the word "and" before a just compensation, and insert "or", which was agreed to.

Mr. A. C. RICHMOND moved to strike out the words "other than municipal," which was agreed to, and the section passed as amended to its third reading.

Section twenty-six received its second reading as follows :

The power of suspending the laws, or the execution of the laws, ought never to be exercised but by the Legislature, or by authority derived from it ; to be exercised in such particular cases only as the Legislature may expressly provide for.

Mr E. W. M. MACKEY moved to strike out this section, which was not agreed to.

The section then passed to its third reading.

Section twenty seven was read a second time as follows :

No person shall, in any case, be subject to law martial, or to any pains or penalties by virtue of that law, except those employed in the army or navy, and except the militia in actual service, but by authority of the Legislature.

Messrs. B. O. DUNCAN, N. G. PARKER and L. S. LANGLEY offered several verbal amendments which were not agreed to.

Mr. C. C. BOWEN moved a substitute for the section which was rejected, and the section was then passed to its third reading.

Section twenty-eighth received its second reading as follows :

In the government of this Commonwealth, the Legislative Department shall never exercise the executive and judicial powers, or either of them ; the executive shall never exercise the legislative and judicial powers, or either of them ; the judicial shall never exercise the legislative and executive powers, or either of them, to the end it may be a government of laws and not of men.

Mr. B. F. WHITTEMORE offered the following amendment in lieu of the entire section after the word " Legislative," in the first line, viz :

The legislative, executive and judicial powers of the Government shall be forever separate and distinct from each other, and no person or persons exercising the functions of one of said departments shall assume or discharge the duties of any other.

Mr. C. C. BOWEN moved to strike out the entire section, which was not agreed to.

Mr. F. L. CARDOZO offered a verbal amendment, which Mr. SASPORTAS moved to lay on the table.

The motion was agreed to, and the section passed to its third reading.

Section twenty-ninth was read as follows :

SECTION 29. The Legislature ought frequently to assemble for the redress of grievances—for correcting, strengthening and confirming the laws, and for making new laws as the common good may require.

Mr. F. L. CARDOZO moved to substitute the word " shall " in place of the word " ought " after the word "Legislature."

Mr. J. J. WRIGHT moved to strike out the words " for correcting, strengthening and confirming the laws," which was agreed to.

Messrs. HOLMES and PILLSBURY moved to strike out the whole section, which was not agreed to.

Messrs. JILLSON, GEO. LEE and CORLEY offered various verbal amendments, which were not agreed to.

Mr. F. J. MOSES, Jr., moved to strike out the word "ought" and insert the word " shall " after the word "Legislature," which was agreed to, and the section passed to its third reading.

Section thirtieth received its second reading, as follows :

SECTION 30. The people have a right to keep and bear arms for the common defence. As in times of peace, armies are dangerous to liberty, they shall not be maintained without the consent of the Legislature. The military power shall always be held in exact subordination to the civil authority and be governed by it.

Messrs DUNCAN, HOLMES and RANSIER offered some verbal amendments, which were all indefinitely postponed.

44

Mr. J. J. WRIGHT. Mr. President and gentlemen, a great deal has been said here to convince us that the civil authorities should be held in subordination to the military, and be governed by it. Those who advocate that doctrine have utterly failed to produce an argument in its favor, because they had no foundation to build upon. The clause is right as it is, and I hope will pass as it is. One gentleman who has spoken, stated that to preserve true liberty, the civil authorities should be governed by the military. I shall not lay down any proposition that I can not prove. True liberty only exists in a Republican form of government. and a Republican form of government is one in which the people, by their votes, choose their own rulers. The President of the United States is chosen by the people, and his office is the highest in their gift; and by virtue of that office, he is Commander-in-Chief of the army and navy of the United States. Hence, the subordination of the military to the civil authorities. If the military authority were superior to the civil, then the military should make laws for the government of the civil. What power is it that declares war, raises and supports armies, provides and maintains the navy, makes rules and regulations for the government of the land and naval forces, provides for calling forth the militia to execute the laws, and the organizing, arming and disciplining the militia? Every one within the sound of my voice can unhesitatingly respond, that that power is civil and not military. There is no real liberty to be found under a despotic government; and a military form of government cannot be otherwise than despotic. Orders are issued one day and revoked the next. They are enforced, whether right or wrong, at the point of the bayonet. The gentleman whom I have alluded to, said that military orders were law. I differ with him. There is no foundation for such an opinion. It is true, that the military orders have the force of law while the music is playing, but the orders, like dancers, stop with the music. I would ask the gentleman where are the multitude of military orders that were issued during the revolutionary war? I will answer for him by saying, that they have passed away with the occasion that called them into existence. Look, for a moment, at Abraham Lincoln's proclamation of freedom, and General Sherman's special field order No. 40; neither of them had any validity after the bayonet was withdrawn; neither would they now, had not the civil authorities given them their sanction.

Mr. President and gentlemen, when you make the civil authorities subordinate to the military, then it is that you destroy the right of trial by jury, and barter away the liberties of the people.

Mr. B. F. RANDOLPH. I heartily concur with the gentleman who has just taken his seat. I would like to ask the question where and how, even in time of war, the military force of the State should be under the control of other than the civil authority. I would like to know whether the Constitution we are now framing will have a provision in it that in time of war the Governor should control the forces of the State. I understand we are framing a Constitution to control the local affairs of the State, and no further. We cannot look beyond the limits of the State. I hope the military force of the State will always be under the command of the Governor.

Mr. A. J. RANSIER. I move to strike out the entire section, and substitute the following : " The people shall always have a right to keep and bear arms in the common defence, but the military power shall always be held subject to the civil power, except in times of war and public danger."

Mr. B. F. WHITTEMORE. I would like to ask the gentleman what he proposes to do with the military power except in times of war and public danger, whether they shall be under the command of the civil authorities, or whether they take commands from no one. It is properly placed in the Bill of Rights as it is, under the civil authority. I move that the motion of the gentleman from Charleston be indefinitely postponed.

The motion was agreed to.

A motion was then made to strike out the last sentence in the section, and insert " the military shall always be held subject and in obedience to the civil authorities."

Mr. B. O. DUNCAN. Gentlemen may talk as much as they will about the military being subject to the civil authority. It never is and never will be the case. If we have a riot or insurrection in any part of the State, the Governor then acts in his capacity as Commander-in-Chief. The military, under his orders, are in control of affairs for the time, and the civil authorities set aside. It is simply nonsense to pass a resolution of this kind that cannot be carried out in times of war.

Mr. B. F. RANDOLPH. The difficulty with the gentleman from Newberry is evident. While he admits that the militia force of the State is under the control and command of the Governor, he does not seem to understand how it is the Governor can use that militia to suppress subordinate civil authority. For instance, suppose the civil authority of Charleston, by some means, should take possession of the Government. That would bring one portion of the civil authority into conflict with a superior civil authority. In that case, the Governor being the superior civil authority, would have the right to use the militia to put down the subordinate. He has the right to arrest the Sheriff or other officers if they are not acting in accordance with the laws of the State. It is understood, of course, that in case of rebellion of the State, the strong arm of the United States can step in and proclaim martial law.

Mr. F. L. CARDOZO. I entirely disagree with my friend from Newberry, that the military cannot and has not always been held in subordination to the civil power. It has always been the case in this country. Much of the troubles of other countries have arisen from the military power assuming to be supreme over the civil authority. To guard against this, a clause was inserted in the Constitution of the United States to the effect that the military authority shall always be held in exact subordination to the civil. The gentleman says the military in times of war will rise superior to the civil. Whenever the military do it, they are obeying the authority of the civil powers.

Mr. L. S. LANGLEY. I move to strike out the word "always," if, after the ratification of the present Constitution, it should be found necessary that the Governor should exercise his powers as commander-in-chief of the militia. A man in command of the militia of the State is a better judge of what the militia are to do than the civil authorities, and in cases of emergency ought to be independent. I move to substitute the word "ought" for "always."

Mr. F. L. CARDOZO. The Governor in such cases exercises two powers—one civil, the other military.

Mr. L. S. LANGLEY. He exercises his rights as Governor, and military powers as commander-in-chief.

Mr. J. J. WRIGHT. If the civil authority is subordinate to the military, how is it that the Governor calls the military out?

Mr. L. S. LANGLEY. He calls the military out by virtue of his power as commander-in-chief.

Mr. J. M. RUTLAND moved the previous question.

Mr. F. J. MOSES, Jr., called for the yeas and nays.

The call for the yeas and nays was sustained, and the roll was called, with the following result:

YEAS.—The President, Messrs. Alexander, Bell, Burton, Brockenton, Bryce, Camp, Coghlan, Chestnut, Clinton, Corley, Darrington, Davis, Dill, Dogan, Donaldson, Edwards, H. E. Hayne, Henderson, Hurley, Jackson, Jillson, Sam'l. Johnson, W. B. Johnson, J. W. Johnson, Dr. L. B. Johnson, W. E. Johnston, Charles Jones, Lang, Langley, Lomax, Leslie, Mauldin, Milford, Nash, Nelson, Neagle, Newell, Nuckles, Rivers, Rose, Runion, Rutland, Sanders, Swails, B. A. Thompson, White, C. M. Wilder, Wooley—49.

NAYS.—Messrs. Becker, Bowen, Bonum, Byas, R. H. Cain, F. J. Cain,

Cardozo, Craig, DeLarge, Dickson, Driffle, Duncan, Elliott, Foster, Goss, Gray, Harris, J. H. Hayne, C. D. Hayne, Holmes, Humbird, Jacobs, Jervey, Henry Jones, George Lee, Saml. Lee, E. W. M. Mackey, Mayer, W. J. McKinlay, Wm. McKinlay, McDaniels, Middleton, Moses, Jr., Nance. Olsen, Owens, Parker, Pillsbury, Randolph, Rainey, Richmond, Sasportas, Shrewsbury, Smalls, Stubbs, Thomas, S. B. Thompson, A. Thompson, Viney, Whittemore, F. E. Wilder, Wingo, Wright—53.

ABSENT.—Messrs. Allen, Arnim, Boozer, Chamberlain, Cooke, Collins, Crews, Gentry, Hunter, Jenks, Joiner, Mead, Miller, Perry, Robertson, Webb, Whipper, Williamson—19.

So the main question was not put.

Mr. R. H. CAIN. I hope we will not rush through questions of so much moment under the spur of the previous question. The question now turns upon whether or not the military power shall be in subordination to the civil authorities. My conception of government leads to this conviction, that republican governments especially, and in fact despotic governments, have for their object the protection of civil liberty, and armies and navies are brought into power especially for the purpose of maintaining the civil liberties of the people. If I understand the Constitution of the United States, the army was originally under the jurisdiction of the civil authorities, and the existence of the army and navy is for the express purpose of maintaining peace, law and government in the country, and without that we would have a despotism, with Commanding Generals overturning our State and municipal governments. We would have despots throughout the whole country. Therefore it was that the great idea was incorporated into the constitutional law of this country that all armies and navies are subject to the civil authorities. Chief Justice Marshall takes this ground when he says that the civil authorities must control the military for the safety, peace and perpetuity of the liberties of the people. If we were to admit the hypothesis that there can be a time when the military are not in subordination to the civil, then we have an end to all civil government and the establishment of a military despotism. General Grant is General-in-Chief of the army, but he is subordinate to the President, who is Commander-in-Chief. The President, in his letter to General Grant, claims the right to command General Grant as a subordinate, inferior officer. Congress is supreme over the President. I think we should retain this section in our Bill of Rights, and assert that at all times the army or militia shall always be in subordination to the civil authorities. When we admit the contrary doctrine, we admit that which is dangerous to our liberties and destructive of our best interests.

Mr. L. S. LANGLEY. Does the gentleman think in case of insurrection in this State, civil officers who have had no military experience whatever, could possibly plan and suppress that insurrection better than the men who have made military tactics their profession?

Mr. CAIN. The Governor of the State is the head of the civil authority, and the militia and all the officers in the government in the army department are but servants to the superior civil authority.

Mr. J. S. CRAIG. Suppose we had an insurrection, and the Governor calls out the militia and finds it necessary to suspend the execution of the civil law for certain reasons in order to arrest parties considered dangerous to the community, cannot a co-ordinate branch of the government refuse to recognize the charges, and set at liberty those dangerous characters. If the military in that case is subordinate to the civil, the Judiciary would set them at liberty as fast as the Governor would arrest. You cannot get higher than the Governor. In him are all the powers of the civil government. He is, to use a common expression, the "top shelf," the highest executive authority known to the Constitution, the highest civil as well as the highest military officer of the State; therefore the civil, in that sense, should be subordinate to the military in case of insurrection.

Mr. R. C. DeLARGE. I trust the section will pass in its present form. I agree with what my colleague (Mr. CAIN) has said, and I also concur with him in his rebuke to those who are disposed to rush through such important matters as these under the parliamentary dodge known as the gag law.

Mr. C. P. LESLIE. I voted for what the gentleman calls the gag law. I wish to ask him if any member has moved the previous question more frequently than himself.

Mr. R. C. DeLARGE. I have failed as yet to move or sustain the previous question on any section of the Constitution, and as long as I retain any sound sense do not believe I would, but I do not think there is anything to fear by the passage of this section as it reads, or that it will take any proper authority from the military. My friend from Beaufort (Mr. L. S. LANGLEY) being a soldier, is naturally jealous of the rights of the military. I, perhaps, as a civilian, am as equally jealous of the rights of the civil power, and therefore desire to see just such a provision in the Constitution. If the civil is made subservient to the military or militia as some propose, we would see a Major-General of militia trying a citizen of this State, at some future day, before a drum head court martial.

Mr. C. C. BOWEN. I find men very zealous of the liberties of the people, now willing to put those liberties in the hands of the military.

They supported it on the eighteenth section, which was adopted. I think they all pretty well agreed here that the civil power should have supreme control in times of peace, but the moment war was declared, I found a good many would go over to the military, horse, foot and dragoons. My impression is, that you will find these very gentlemen as anxious to get under the wing of the civil authority then as they are now anxious to be military men. I contend if you say in this Constitution that the military shall have supreme control in times of war ; in other words, that the military shall have such power, that if any military sees fit to press into the ranks any citizen of the State, he will have the right to do so and you will have no power of relief. It will be left discretionary with him. Much has been said with regard to the Governor planning a campaign. I suppose the State will be provided with the necessary military officers. I contend the Governor would have a right to appoint a commander of militia with sufficient instructions to put down insurrection. I apprehend the Governor would first call on the civil authorities, and if they failed to quell a disturbance, he would then call out the militia, and send with that militia force a competent officer to accomplish the object. I do not suppose the Governor, unless it became actually necessary, would suspend any of the privileges guaranteed by the Constitution. A great deal has been said too about court martials ; we know that military authorities heretofore have taken the responsibility to declare certain ports, towns and cities under martial law, but whether they had a right to do so is still an open question, though if a military officer has a sufficient number of bayonets to carry out his edict, he may enforce it by simple force of arms, and yet have no right to do so.

It needs no order from the President to any person invested with the command of an army. If he thinks it necessary for the safety of his troops to declare martial law he will do it. But I contend he has no right do it. But it is still left an open question.

Mr. J. S. CRAIG. But suppose a citizen should get up an insurrection, though the proof would not be sufficient to convict him in Court, the Governor has him arrested because satisfied that the party was responsible for the insurrection, and the Court releases the prisoner, how could the Governor help himself if the military are to be kept in subjection to the civil authority.

Mr. C. C. BOWEN. I think that can be best answered by telling an anecdote of a character named Toodles. He had a wife who bought everything sold at auction, and amongst other things bought a doorplate that bore the name of Thompson. Toodles asked his wife what she wanted that for, his name was not Thompson. She said, " well, my dear, we may have a child, and that child may be a female child, and she may marry a man by the name of Thompson, and then it will be just the thing to put on their door." Well, now, there is just about as much probability in the one case as in the other.

Mr. L. S. LANGLEY. A great deal has been said by gentlemen against military power. I am willing to admit that the military power is not always the best to have supreme power. But when I hear gentlemen denouncing the military as generally oppressive, and taking measures that do not conduce to the public weal, I ask if they have forgotten all the lessons which the late rebellion taught. I think the military then performed one of the grandest, one of the most sublime works ever performed in the annals of a nation.

Mr. R. H. CAIN. For what purpose did they perform that work except to preserve civil liberty?

Mr. L S LANGLEY. I acknowledge they did do it for that purpose, and they should have the credit due them for the manner in which their work was executed. I contend that the military are capable of performing a great work of defending the civil power, and without the military in the late rebellion the civil authority could not have stood one hour I believe the members of this Convention will not so soon forget the debt of gratitude they owe as a class to the nation and to the military. I hope, therefore, the section will not be adopted as it is now, and thus make the military always subject to the civil power.

Mr. C. P. LESLIE. I desire just to say one word. I believe when a man makes a mistake he ought always to be honest enough to apologize, and I desire to apologize for my vote. I voted for the previous question to save time, thinking it would be a sensible thing to do. I find now how mistaken I was. The able, ingenious, masterly, lucid, overwhelming arguments, pro and con, on the section under discussion has convinced me that my mind was not altogether made up, and that I was not perfectly safe in voting as I did. The delegate from Colleton (Mr. CRAIG), who is peculiarly lucid, put the question in such a definite shape that I was surprised, he was surprised, and so surprised that I did not understand it perfectly after he got through his ifs and buts, and knows, and writs of *habeas corpus*, &c.

Mr. B. F. RANDOLPH. The gentleman is criticising other gentlemen's remarks.

Mr. C. P. LESLIE. I will be brief. I am about to answer the question of the gentleman from Colleton, who wants to know if such things happen what will be the condition of the country? I have waited patiently to hear the learned argument in reply, and find how mistaken I was to try to cut off the debate and save time. Our friend from Charleston, whose name I will not mention, (Mr. R. C. DeLARGE,) who has been brought to task over and over again for moving the previous question, he, too, delivered an argument so profound, so learned, so completely overwhelming, that I apologize to him also; and the last delegate closed with a wonderful anecdote about Thompson and Toodles. Well now we do not, or I do not know one whit more about the subject, and if there is anything in the world clear, it is that we are going farther off every speech that is made. In that sense I voted, and I think the good sense of the house will sustain it. The gentleman from Charleston (Rev. R. H. CAIN) did make a suitable argument.

Mr. B. F. WHITTEMORE moved the indefinite postponement of the amendment of the gentleman from Beaufort (Mr. J. J. WRIGHT.)

The motion was agreed to, and the thirtieth section passed to its third reading.

Section thirty-first was read a second time, and after a verbal amendment, passed to its third reading, as follows :

In time of peace no soldier shall be quartered in any house without the consent of the owner; and, in time of war, such quarters shall not be made but in a manner prescribed by law.

Section thirty-second was read as follows :

No person who conscientiously scruples to bear arms shall be compelled so to do, but he may pay an equivalent for personal service.

Mr. WM. McKINLAY moved to amend by substituting the word "shall" for "may," before the word "may," which was agreed to.

Mr. R. G. HOLMES moved to strike out the entire section. If there is any person who does not want to bear arms in times of danger and trouble, and he asks for protection from the government, I hope he will move off to some other State.

Mr. R. J. DONALDSON. I hope the section will prevail. A great number cannot conscientiously bear arms, but may provide a substitute. Some of these are the best citizens, Quakers for instance, who are an ornament to society wherever they may reside. I am opposed to the idea of the gentleman from Beaufort, that we should not have such citizens among us.

Mr. B. F. RANDOLPH. I second the motion to strike out, not that I am opposed to the principle laid down in the section, but because I do not think it in its proper place. I think it should be in the report of the Committee on the Militia.

45

Mr. B. F. WHITTEMORE. We have defined here who shall not go into the militia. It has already been said that persons who are Friends, who have conscientious scruples about bearing arms, should not be compelled to go into the army, but pay an equivalent for personal services. That is provided for here.

The motion to strike out was not agreed to.

Mr. S. CORLEY. There is one objection to this section. No provision is made for the poor man who is unable to pay an equivalent for personal service. Though he might have conscientious scruples, he would, under this clause, for want of means to pay, be compelled to go out and do the fighting. I do hope this compelling poor men to bear arms against their will, will be done away with.

The question was then taken, and the section passed to its third reading.

Section thirty-three was read a second time, as follows :

SECTION 33. All elections shall be free and open, and every inhabitant of this Commonwealth possessing the qualifications provided for in this Constitution, shall have an equal right to elect officers and be elected to fill public employments.

Mr. WM. McKINLAY. I move to amend by striking out the word "employments" and substituting the word "office." The word "employment" is rather too indefinite.

Mr. A. J. RANSIER. I move to amend by inserting after the word Constitution, "shall have equal, civil and political rights and public privileges."

The question was taken on the amendment to strike out "employment" and substitute "officers," and the amendment was agreed to.

The question was then taken on the amendment offered by Mr. RANSIER.

Mr. N. G. PARKER. I hope that amendment will not prevail. We have already passed a section which refers to the right of being elected to office. If you adopt this, it makes the section cover two ideas.

Mr. F. L. CARDOZO. I think this amendment much more definite and clear.

Mr. A. J. RANSIER. I desire to know whether the principle is provided for that every citizen, possessing equal qualifications as provided for in this Constitution, shall have equal, civil and political rights, and that such citizen could be elected to hold office or have the benefit of public carriages. My amendment embraces everything essential to these rights.

Mr. B. F. WHITTEMORE. It appears to me the language of the section, as amended by the gentleman from Charleston (Mr. McKINLAY), is sufficiently plain and distinct, and that the amendment of the gentleman is unnecessary.

The question was then taken on the proposed amendment, and it was not agreed to.

The thirty-third section was then passed to its third reading.

Section thirty-four was read, as follows:

SECTION 34. No property qualification shall be necessary for an election to or the holding of any office, and no office shall be created, the appointment to which shall be for a longer time than good behavior. After the adoption of this Constitution, any person who shall fight a duel, or send or accept a challenge for that purpose, or be an aider or abetter in fighting a duel, shall be deprived of holding any office of honor or trust in this State, and shall be otherwise punished as the law shall prescribe.

The hour of half-past two having arrived, the Convention adjourned.

TWENTY-FIFTH DAY.

Thursday, February 13, 1868.

The Convention assembled at half-past 10 A. M., and was called to order by the PRESIDENT.

Prayer was offered by the Rev. ABRAHAM MIDDLETON.

The roll was called, and a quorum answering to their names, the PRESIDENT announced the Convention ready to proceed to business.

The Journal of the preceding day was read and approved.

The consideration of the thirty-fourth section of the Bill of Rights was resumed.

Mr. WM. McKINLAY moved to amend by inserting after the word office, a provision that "the General Assembly shall provide for the taking of such bonds, with sufficient sureties, from all persons elected to office, as it may deem expedient."

Mr. R. SMALLS moved that the amendment be indefinitely postponed, which was agreed to, and the thirty-fourth section passed to its third reading.

The next section was passed to a third reading without debate, as follows :

SECTION 35. The right of suffrage shall be protected by laws regulating elections, and prohibiting, under adequate penalties, all undue influence from power, bribery, tumult or improper conduct.

Section thirty-six was read a second time, as follows :

SECTION 36. Representation shall be apportioned according to population, and no person in this State shall be disfranchised, or deprived of any of the rights or privileges now enjoyed, except by the law of the land, or the judgment of his peers.

Mr. WM. McKINLAY moved to amend by striking out the words " now enjoye l."

Mr. S. CORLEY. By the adoption of that amendment we would make it constitutional to place certain electors in power, and at the same time allow future Legislatures to displace them.

Mr. B. F. WHITTEMORE. It is impossible for us as yet to know what the Committee on Franchise and Elections will declare shall be the privileges of the people of the State. It appears to me we are going it blind on this matter until we know what will be the action of the Committee on Franchise and Elections. The idea embodied in the section as it is, that no person, white or black, possessing any privileges, shall be deprived of those existing privileges. Some of the members appear to desire that the word color should be introduced to make the application definite and emphatic. I have endeavored throughout the Bill of Rights to avoid using that word.

Mr. WM. McKINLAY. The object of the amendment is not to impair any of the rights now enjoyed by citizens of the State. It is intended to secure them all the rights enumerated in the Constitution.

Mr. F. L. CARDOZO. With reference to the remarks made by the Chairman of the Bill of Rights, it is true we have not the report of the Committee on Franchise before us, and in one sense acting without anything definite, yet in another sense we know what we are going to demand, for we intend to see that our rights are guaranteed by this Constitution. So in one sense we know what we intend to have.

The question was then taken on the amendment and it was not agreed to.

Section thirty-six then passed to a third reading.

The following sections were then read a second time, and passed to a third reading without debate :

SECTION 37. Temporary absence from the State shall not forfeit a residence once obtained.

SECTION 38. All property subject to taxation ought to be taxed in proportion to its value. Each individual of society has a right to be protected in the employment of life, property and liberty, according to standing laws. He should, therefore, contribute his share to the expense of his protection, and give his personal service when necessary.

SECTION 39. No subsidy, charge, impost tax or duties ought to be established, fixed, laid or levied, under any pretext whatsoever, without the consent of the people or their representatives lawfully assembled.

SECTION 40 Excessive fines shall not be imposed, nor cruel and unusual punishment inflicted, nor shall witnesses be unreasonably detained.

Section forty-one received its third reading as follows:

No title of nobility or distinction, or hereditary emolument shall ever be granted in this State.

Mr. B. F. RANDOLPH offered the following amendment: " Distinction on account of race or color in any case whatever shall be prohibited, and all classes of citizens, irrespective of race and color, shall enjoy all common, equal and political privileges."

It is, doubtless, the impression of the members of the Convention that the Bill of Rights as it stands, secures perfect political and legal equality to all the people of South Carolina. It is a fact, however, that no where is it laid down in the instrument, emphatically and definitely, that all the people of the State, irrespective of race and color, shall enjoy equal privileges. Our forefathers were no doubt anti-slavery men, and they intended that slavery should die out. Consequently the word color is not to be found in the Constitution or Declaration of Independence. On the contrary, it is stated distinctly " all men are created free and equal." But that was too general, too comprehensive, and our forefathers made a mistake, the result of which was that the land has been drenched in blood to perpetuate slavery. The Constitution of the United States was too vague; it was misinterpreted. On the one hand, the ablest statesmen of England and America had pronounced it anti-slavery; on the other, equally able minds regarded it as pro-slavery in its character.

In our Bill of Rights, I want to settle the question forever by making the meaning so plain that a " wayfaring man, though a fool," cannot misunderstand it. The majority of the people of South Carolina, who are rapidly becoming property holders, are colored citizens—the descendants of the African race—who have been ground down by three hundred years of degradation, and now that the opportunity is afforded, let them be protected in their political rights. The words proposed as an amendment were not calculated to create distinction, but to destroy distinction ; and since the Bill of Rights did not declare equality, irrespective of race or color, it was important that they should be inserted. Here I would say that all of my radicalism consists in believing one thing, namely, that all men are created of one blood ; that " God created all nations to dwell upon the earth."

Mr. C. P. LESLIE. I would ask the delegate if it would not have been a little better for his theory if the Scriptures had added "without distinction of race or color."

Mr. B. F. RANDOLPH. If the gentleman will tell me why Congress saw fit to say "all men are born free and equal," I may answer his question.

Mr. C. P. LESLIE. I can't tell why Congress did this or that. They do a great many curious things, but it does strike me that God in his infinite wisdom knew fully as much about this business as Congress.

Mr. B. F. RANDOLPH. I will say to the gentleman that if God did not see fit to prepare such laws as we may adapt to the present condition of society, it becomes us to add to God's laws in such a manner as to suit circumstances, and yet not conflict with them.

Mr. A. J. RANSIER. I favor the spirit of the amendment, but wish to see the clause inserted in some other portion of the Bill of Rights.

Mr. B. F. WHITTEMORE. This whole subject is covered by previous sections, and it is unnecessary to be more explicit We discussed this matter in Committee, and the determination arrived at was not to introduce the word color in the Bill of Rights. All citizens duly qualified are entitled to equal privileges, and it is unnecessary to draw lines of distinction. The colored man was a citizen, his rights had been declared, and I propose to defend those rights wherever called upon, whether it be in the halls of legislation or upon the field of contest.

Mr. A. J. RANSIER. While I want the principle laid down clearly, that in all matters my race are civilly and politically equal with, and entitled to all the privileges of other men, I am not in favor of employing the words "race and color" in the Constitution.

Mr. F. L. CARDOZO. It is a patent fact that, as colored men, we have been cheated out of our rights for two centuries, and now that we have the opportunity, I want to fix them in the Constitution in such a way that no lawyer, however cunning or astute, can possibly misinterpret the meaning. If we do not do so, we deserve to be, and will be, cheated again. Nearly all the white inhabitants of the State are ready at any moment to deprive us of these rights, and not a loop-hole should be left that would permit them to do it constitutionally. Not one of them scarcely were in favor of this Convention, and just so soon as they had the power, whether by the election of a Democratic President, or by an increase of emigration, they would endeavor to overthrow the Constitution. Hence, while they (the Convention) had a chance to do it, by all means let them insert the words "without distinction of race or color," wherever it was necessary to give force and clearness to their purpose.

Mr. G. PILLSBURY. I am in favor of the amendment offered by the gentleman from Orangeburg. I rise simply to amend his amendment. I am in favor of this expression being incorporated into our Bill of Rights, "persons of color." You will recollect in the Constitution of the United States, modesty or some other thing prevented the use of the word slave in that Constitution. Such persons were indicated through the Bill of Rights as "persons held to service," but in the history of the country, after this unfortunate polite allusion to this class of property began to bear upon a certain portion of the inhabitants of the United States, then the profoundest statesmanship, the astutest legal ability in the country was expended to do it away, but it all failed, and nothing but the cannon of the United States knocked the sentiment of slavery out of the Constitution. That sentiment had been expressed in polite language; but in the Bill of Rights of South Carolina, it should be recognized beyond peradventure that the colored man is, in fact, a citizen, although he had been recently told by a white man that all the legislation to be accomplished could not make a citizen out of a nigger.

Mr. C. P. LESLIE. What is meant by the word "inhabitant" in section thirty-three. If the delegate from Charleston, in explicit terms, admitted that colored men are inhabitants, there could be no doubt in the minds of sensible men that their rights were already guaranteed. Why then all this anxious concern about race and color.

Mr. G. PILLSBURY. I understand the word "inhabitant" to mean a person or citizen, a black or a white man. I will do the gentleman the credit to suppose that he so understands it. What does he suppose was meant in the Declaration of Independence by the phrase "all men are born free and equal."

Mr. C. P. LESLIE. As a considerable portion of the inhabitants of the United States at the time of the adoption of the Declaration of Independence were held as slaves, the phrase was evidently not intended to apply to this class. But had the declaration said "every inhabitant" was born free and equal, it would then have covered colored men.

Mr. G. PILLSBURY. Where is the word "inhabitant" mentioned here. In this Declaration of Rights, the word "men" is used. Which

has the most significance, man or inhabitant ? In the Declaration of
Independence, the word men is used in the phrase "all men are born
free and equal," and yet four millions of men and women now living,
and millions passed away, have been slaves, deprived of all the privileges to which men were entitled under that Declaration of Independence.
I was about to say to the gentleman there could be no question in his
mind what constitutes citizenship in the State of South Carolina, but
there is a wide difference of opinion. I stated this difference of opinion
no longer than a week ago, and was told by a white man that all the
legislation of this Convention would not nor could not make a negro a
citizen. It would do no harm to have this right defined in so many
words. I do not wish it hereafter to require the profoundest statesmanship, or the most skilful lawyer to explain and define the meaning of this
Bill of Rights. The adoption of the amendment offered by the gentleman from Orangeburg, will set at rest this mooted right now and forever.
I am in favor of the amendment, except the word "common." I move,
as an amendment, to strike out the words "irrespective of race and color,"
where they occur a second time, and also the word "common."

Mr. B. F. RANDOLPH. I am opposed to the last amendment. The
word "common" expressed exactly what was meant. Common, public
and political privileges are what we wanted, and nothing less.

The motion to strike out was not agreed to.

Mr. B. F. WHITTEMORE moved to amend verbally, which was
agreed to.

The entire section, as amended, was then read a second time and
passed to its third reading.

Section forty-one received its second reading and was passed without
debate, to a third reading, as follows :

SECTION 41. No title of nobility or distinction, or hereditary emolument
shall ever be granted in this State.

Section forty-two received its second reading, as follows :

SECTION 42. All navigable waters shall remain forever public highways, free to the citizens of the State and the United States, without tax,
impost or toll imposed ; and no tax, toll or impost or wharfage shall be
imposed, demanded or received from the owner of any merchandise or
commodity, for the use of the shores or any wharf erected on the shores,
or in or over the waters of any navigable stream, unless the same be
expressly authorized by the Legislature.

Mr. W. J. McKINLAY, of Charleston, offered as a substitute, the fol-

SECTION 42. All navigable waters shall remain forever public highways, free to the citizens of the State and the United States, without tax, impost, or toll imposed ; and no tax, toll or impost shall be imposed, demanded or received from the owner of any merchandise or commodity, for the use of any navigable stream, unless the same be authorized by the Legislature

The amendment was agreed to, and the section passed to a third reading.

The next and last section of the Bill was read a second time, and passed to a third reading without debate, as follows :

SECTION 43. The enumeration of rights in this Constitution shall not be construed to impair or deny others retained by the people, and all powers not herein delegated remain with the people.

Mr. B. O. DUNCAN submitted the following as additional sections:

" The Legislature shall have no power to levy a poll tax except for educational purposes."

Referred to the Committee on the Bill of Rights.

" The Legislature shall enact such laws as it may deem proper and necessary to punish the carrying of concealed deadly weapons."

Referred to the Committee on Miscellaneous Provisions of the Constitution.

" No lottery office shall hereafter be allowed for the sale of lottery tickets in this State."

Referred to same Committee.

The preamble and title were read a second time.

Mr. J. J. WRIGHT moved several verbal amendments.

Mr. D. H. CHAMBERLAIN moved to indefinitely postpone the amendments, which was lost.

Mr. B. O. DUNCAN proposed the following amendment, which was finally withdrawn :

We, the people of the State of South Carolina, by our delegates in Convention assembled, in order to establish impartial justice, insure domestic tranquillity, promote the general welfare, and secure the blessings of liberty to ourselves and our posterity, do ordain and establish the following Declaration of Rights and Form of Government as the Constitution of the Commonwealth of South Carolina.

The preamble was therefore passed to its third reading with the only
46

amendment being a substitution of the word "people" for the words "body politic."

The Bill as amended was then ordered to be printed for the third reading.

Mr. N. G. PARKER offered the following resolution :

Resolved, That this Convention request Brevet Major General E. R. S. Canby to abolish at once the District Courts of South Carolina, and to declare vacant all offices connected therewith.

Mr. R. C. DeLARGE moved to refer it to the Judiciary Committee to be reported to-morrow at two o'clock, which was not agreed to.

Mr. C. P. LESLIE moved to amend, as follows :

"That this Convention request Brevet-Major General E. R. S. Canby to dismiss all the Judges of Courts known as District Courts in South Carolina."

Mr. T. J. ROBERTSON. I hold in my hand a petition signed by nearly every member of the Convention, asking General Canby to abolish the District Courts, and to dismiss from their offices the Judges and all the officers connected with that Court. These District Courts I regard as the offspring of the infernal code adopted by the Legislature in 1865, a code only intended to punish the colored people. These Courts also discriminated against the poor. No person could bring a suit in them against another unless a deposit is made in advance to meet the costs. A person unable to make this advance is debarred the privileges of the Court and the rights he should enjoy in common with the more fortunate and wealthy. He also knew that most of the Judges of the District Courts elected by the Legislature of 1865, are unfriendly to the colored people and opposed in toto to the Reconstruction Acts of Congress. Their prejudices are so bitter that it is impossible for the colored man to obtain justice. These Courts are now in session in the different country districts every week, and colored persons are being tried, convicted and sent to the penitentiary on the most trivial offences. It was upon these grounds, and in the performance of what he felt to be his duty, that he had drawn a petition requesting General Canby to abolish the District Courts of the State.

Mr. R. J. DONALDSON. What disposition does the gentleman propose to make of the vast amount of business now in litigation in the District Courts.

Mr. T. J. ROBERTSON. I would let it lay over until the establishment of a sound loyal Government. Some men might be kept in jail a little longer awaiting the decision of a Court to try the offence, but it would be better for them to remain there a little time than to be sent to the penitentiary.

Mr. LESLIE asked Mr. ROBERTSON to amend the petition by making the request of General Canby to dismiss the Judges, not to abolish the Courts. He doubted whether General Canby had any authority to abolish the Courts.

Mr. ROBERTSON declined to accept the proposed amendment.

Mr. R. C. DeLARGE moved that the resolution and petition be referred to the Committee on the Judiciary, with instructions to report to morrow. He did not wish to see this matter rushed through in favor of abolishing the Courts.

The Convention refused to refer, and the question being put on the original motion, it was adopted.

Mr. C. P. LESLIE desired to have his name recorded as voting " no."

Mr. B. F. WHITTEMORE offered the following resolution, which was referred to the Committee on the Legislative Part of the Constitution :

ARTICLE —.

AMENDMENT AND REVISION OF THE CONSTITUTION.

Section 1. Any amendment or amendments to the Constitution may be proposed in the Senate or House of Representatives. If the same be agreed to by two thirds of the members elected to each House, such amendment or amendments shall be entered on the journals respectively, with the yeas and nays taken thereon ; and the same shall be submitted to the electors, at the next general election thereafter, and if a majority of the electors, qualified to vote for members of the Legislature, voting thereon, shall vote in favor of such amendment, or amendments, and two thirds of each House of the next Legislature shall, after such an election and before another, ratify the same amendment or amendments, by yeas and nays, the same shall become part of the Constitution : *Provided*, that such amendment or amendments shall have been read three times, or on three several days, in each House.

Section 2. Every fifteenth year after the next general election, or ratification of this Constitution, and also at such other times as the Legislature may provide, the question of a general revision of the Constitution shall be submitted to the electors qualified to vote for members of the Legislature, and in case a majority of the electors so qualified, voting at such election, shall decide in favor of a Convention for such revision, the Legislature, at the next session, shall provide by law for the election of delegates to such Convention. All the amendments shall take effect at the commencement of the political year after their adoption.

Mr. H. E. HAYNE offered the following resolution, which was referred to the Committee on Petitions:

Resolved, That this Convention petition Congress for the removal of the disabilities of such persons in the State as accept in good faith the Reconstruction Acts of Congress and the Constitution of the United States as amended

Mr. J. M. RUNION offered the following resolution, which was laid on the table:

Resolved, That the President of this Convention be requested to see that the manuscript of the journal of the proceedings of this Convention be immediately furnished to the printer to enable him to commence the work of printing, in order that the same may be complete on or about the time that this Convention adjourns; and that one thousand copies be published for the use of the members of this Convention.

Mr. F. J. CAIN offered the following resolution, which was adopted:

Resolved, That the Committee on Petitions be hereby requested to report to this house to-morrow, at one o'clock, a preamble and resolutions relative to petitioning Congress for a grant of one million dollars to be appropriated for the purchase of land in this State.

Mr. C. P. LESLIE asked leave to record his vote against the resolution of Mr. CAIN, which was granted.

Mr. D. H. CHAMBERLAIN offered the following resolution, which was adopted:

Resolved, That the President of this Convention be directed to forward, without delay, to Brevet Maj. Gen. Ed. R. S. Canby, a copy of the resolution requesting the abolition of the District Courts of this State.

Dr. N. J. NEWELL presented the petition of sundry citizens of Anderson District, in reference to the division of that District, which was referred to the Committee on the Legislative part of the Constitution.

Mr. C. C. BOWEN offered the following resolution, which was adopted:

WHEREAS, The Ordinance passed by this Convention on the 1st of February, 1868, entitled "An Ordinance declaring null and void all contracts, judgments and decrees heretofore made or entered up, where the consideration was for the purchase of slaves," is regarded by some as of doubtful validity prior to the organization of the State under the new Constitution, and this question is likely to give rise to delays and vexatious discussions in Court, therefore,

Resolved, That Brevet Major-General Ed. R. S. Canby, Commanding

Second Military District, be respectfully requested to enforce said Ordinance.

Dr. J. L. NEAGLE moved that the President of this Convention furnish Brevet Major-General Ed. R. S. Canby with a certified copy of the resolution of Mr. C. C. BOWEN.

Mr. J. J. WRIGHT called for the second reading of the report of the Committee on the Legislative part of the Constitution.

The report was taken up, and sections 1, 2, 3, 4, 5, 6, 7, 8, 9 and 10 were read a second time, all of which, with the exception of No. 3, which was recommitted to the Legislative Committee, to alter in accordance with the Ordinance adopted by the Convention dividing Pickens District, passed to a third reading.

The eleventh section received its second reading, and pending its consideration, the Convention adjourned.

TWENTY-SIXTH DAY.

Friday, February 14, 1868.

The Convention assembled at half-past 10 A. M., and was called to order by the PRESIDENT.

Prayer was offered by the Rev. WM. DARRINGTON.

The roll was called, and a quorum answering to their names, the PRESIDENT announced the Convention ready to proceed to business.

The Journal of Thursday was read and approved.

Mr. C. P. LESLIE made a report of the Auditing Committee on several bills for printing, stationery and furniture for the hall, as follows:

The undersigned, the Committee appointed by this House to audit the contingent expenses, &c., beg leave to submit the following report:

The Committee have had under consideration the account of H. Judge Moore, Printer, and have, after patient enquiry and thorough examination, concluded to recommend to this Convention that the sum of $406.75 in bills receivable, in full settlement of his account for printing from the 19th day of January to the 10th day of February A. D. 1868, be paid, on filing with the President of this Convention the vouchers, and account properly receipted, &c.

The Committee have also had under consideration an account of Mr. J. W. Denny for stationery, &c., and recommend that the sum of $228 86 in bills receivable be paid in full payment of said account, on his filing with the President said account properly receipted.

The Committee have also had under consideration the account of Messrs Mackey & Baker, for use and hire of furniture, and after careful consideration do recommend that the sum of $267.19 in bills receivable be paid them, on their filing with the President of this Convention said account properly receipted, &c.   C. P. LESLIE,
Chairman Com. on Audit.

After the reading of the report, on motion of Mr. N. G. PARKER, it was adopted.

Mr. N. G. PARKER, Chairman of the Finance Committee, submitted the following report as a part of the Constitution, which was ordered to be printed:

ARTICLE —.

FINANCE AND TAXATION.

SECTION 1. The Legislature shall provide by law for a uniform and equal rate of assessment and taxation, and shall prescribe such regulations as shall secure a just valuation for taxation of all property, real, personal and possessory, except mines and mining claims, the proceeds of which alone shall be taxed; and also excepting such property as may be exempted by law for municipal, educational, literary, scientific, religious or charitable purposes.

SEC. 2. The Legislature may provide annually for a poll tax not to exceed one dollar on each poll, which shall be applied exclusively to the public school fund. And no additional poll tax shall be levied by any municipal corporation.

SEC. 3. The Legislature shall provide for an annual tax sufficient to defray the estimated expenses of the State for each year; and whenever it shall happen that such ordinary expenses of the State for any year shall exceed the income of the State for such year, the Legislature shall provide for levying a tax for the ensuing year sufficient, with other sources of income, to pay the deficiency of the preceding year, together with the estimated expenses of the ensuing year.

SEC. 4. No tax shall be levied except in pursuance of a law, which shall distinctly state the object of the same; to which object only such tax shall be applied.

SEC. 5. It shall be the duty of the Legislature to enact laws for the exemption from taxation of all public schools, colleges, and institutions of learning, all charitable institutions in the nature of asylums for the infirm, deaf and dumb, blind, idiotic and indigent persons, all public libraries, churches and burrying grounds; but property of associations and societies, although connected with charitable objects, shall not be exempt from State, County or Municipal taxation.

SEC. 6. The Legislature shall provide by a State Board for the valuation and assessment of all lands and the improvements thereon prior to the assembling of the Legislature of 1870, and thereafter on every fifth year.

SEC. 7. For the purpose of defraying extraordinary expenditures, the State may contract public debts; but such debts shall never in the aggregate exceed five hundred thousand dollars beyond that already incurred. Every such debt shall be authorized by law for some single object, to be distinctly specified therein; and no such law shall take effect until it shall have been passed by the vote of two-thirds of the members of each branch of the Legislature, to be recorded by yeas and nays on the journals of each House respectively; and every such law shall levy a tax annually sufficient to pay the annual interest of such debt, and also a tax sufficient to pay the principal of such debt within twenty years from the final passage of such law, and shall specially appropriate the proceeds of such taxes to the payment of such principal and interest.

SEC. 8. The corporate authorities of Counties, Townships, School Districts, Cities, Towns and Villages may be vested with power to assess and collect taxes for corporate purposes; such taxes to be uniform in respect to persons and property within the jurisdiction of the body imposing the same. And the Legislature shall require that all the property within the limits of municipal corporations belonging to individuals shall be taxed for the payment of debts contracted under authority of law

SEC. 9. The credit of the State shall not be granted to, or in aid of, any person, association or corporation.

SEC. 10. The State shall not subscribe to or be interested in the stock of any company, association or corporation.

SEC. 11. The Legislature shall provide for the incorporation and organization of cities and towns, and shall restrict their powers of taxation, borrowing money, contracting debts, and loaning their credit.

SEC. 12. No scrip, certificate, or other evidence of State indebtedness shall be issued, except for the redemption of stock, bonds, or other evidences of indebtedness previously issued, or for such debts as are expressly authorized in this Constitution.

SEC. 13. An accurate statement of the receipt and expenditures of the public money shall be published with the laws of each regular session of the Legislature.

SEC. 14. No money shall be drawn from the Treasury but in pursuance of appropriation made by law.

SEC. 15. The fiscal year shall commence on the first day of November in each year.

SEC. 16. There shall be annually assessed and collected, in the same manner as other State revenue may be assessed and collected, a tax of two mills upon each dollar's worth of taxable property, in addition to all other taxes, to be applied as follows, to wit: The fund so created shall be kept separate, and shall annually, on the first day of January, be apportioned and paid over *pro rata* upon all such State indebtedness as may for that purpose be presented by the holders of the same, to be entered as credits upon, and, to that extent, in extinguishment of the principal of said indebtedness; *Provided*, That no debt contracted in behalf of the rebellion, in whole or in part thereof, shall ever be paid.

SEC. 17. No county shall subscribe for stock in any incorporated company, unless the same be paid for at the time of such subscription; nor shall any county loan its credit to any incorporated company, nor borrow money for the purpose of taking stock in any such company; nor shall the Legislature ever on behalf of the State assume the debts of any county, city, town or township, nor of any corporation whatever.

SEC. 18. Any debt contracted by the State shall be by loan on State bonds, of amounts not less than ($500) five hundred dollars each, on interest, payable within twenty years after the final passage of the law authorizing such debt. A correct registry of all such bonds shall be kept by the Treasurer in numerical order, so as always to exhibit the number and amount unpaid, and to whom severally made payable.

SEC. 19. Suitable laws shall be passed by the Legislature for the safe keeping, transfer and disbursement of the State and school funds, and all officers and other persons charged with the same shall be required to give ample security for all moneys and funds of any kind, to keep an accurate entry of such sum received, and of each payment and transfer; and it shall be the duty of the Legislature to pass laws making embezzlement of such funds a felony, and the party convicted of such felony shall be disqualified from ever holding any office of honor or emolument in the State.

The unfinished business was then resumed, being the report of the Committee on the Legislative Provisions of the Constitution.

The consideration of the eleventh section of the report of the Committee on the Legislative Department was resumed.

Mr. C. C. BOWEN moved a reconsideration of the eighth section, which is as follows:

SECTION 8. The Senate shall be composed of one member from each county, to be elected for the term of four years, by the qualified voters of the State, in the same manner by which members of the House of Representatives are chosen.

The motion was agreed to.

Mr. C. C. BOWEN. A proposition has been made to change the name of the districts into counties, and Charleston will, therefore, become a county. Heretofore Charleston has always been entitled to two Senators when she was only an election district. Now the Convention proposes to make the city a county, and the section read, that each county shall be entitled to but one Senator. No matter how great a population Charleston might have, she would be entitled to but one Senator. Any other district or county having sufficient territory could be divided and immediately obtain another Senator. It was apparent to every gentleman upon the floor that the City of Charleston never can be divided into two counties. Take the case of Pickens District which has been recently divided. It now becomes two counties and gets two Senators. He would make a motion, which, upon the principles of equity and justice, he thought, when they come to consider it, there would be no difficulty in adding an amendment to the section. He moved to add : " Except Charleston, which shall be allowed two Senators."

Mr. L. S. LANGLEY. I am opposed to the amendment, as I see no justice or propriety in its adoption. I think the Constitution of the United States should be our model, and by that the little State of Rhode Island, and the great State of New York are on an equality of representation in the United States Senate. New York possesses a population and extent of territory more than twenty times that of Rhode Island.

Mr. N. G. PARKER. Do you think Charleston, with a large and increasing population, would be equally represented by one Senator, with other districts having a small population and entitled to the same representation in the Senate.

Mr. L. S. LANGLEY. Representation in the United States Senate is not based upon population, but upon a political division. If Charleston has a larger population than any other county, she will have a greater weight and influence by her representation in the other branch I hope the amendment will be voted down.

Mr. C. M. WILDER moved that the amendment be indefinitely postponed.

Mr. F. L. CARDOZO. I hope the motion to postpone will not prevail. Charleston always had two Senators, and she is now entitled to two. She has one seventeenth of the whole population of the State, and one thirteenth of the voting population. There being thirty-two counties in the State, notwithstanding Charleston possesses one seventeenth of the whole population, by this section she would have only a thirty-second part of the influence. In addition to that, Charleston pays one-third of the whole of the taxes of the State. I think she is eminently entitled to two Senators to watch over and protect her interests.

Mr. C. P. LESLIE. I desire to ask the gentleman who last spoke, why it is that in the city and county of New York the number of Senators are in proportion to her population ? For instance, the city and county of New York is entitled to four Senators in the State Senate, and the city of Brooklyn, or Kings County, is entitled to two, while all the other counties are entitled to but one.

Mr. F. L. CARDOZO. I suppose it was for the same reasons I have already given, viz : larger population and larger influence. It is another argument against the postponement of this question.

Mr. F. J. MOSES, Jr. I beg leave to call the attention of the Convention that it is certainly not the right way to mete out justice and
47

equity to move an indefinite postponement of a motion like this, before it can be fairly and freely discussed.

Mr. D. H. CHAMBERLAIN. I hope every opportunity will be afforded for the fullest discussion. We can then feel when final action was had on the subject, that no improper advantage has been taken.

Mr. J. K. JILLSON moved that the motion to postpone be laid on the table.

Mr. B. F. RANDOLPH. I am of opinion that in justice to Charleston she should have two Senators. New York, because of her great population, has four Senators in the Legislature of that State, and the city of Boston, with not quite so large a population as New York, has six Senators in the Legislature of Massachusetts, and so on, more or less, all through the United States.

Mr. T. HURLEY asked what part of Boston had six Senators.

Mr. B. F. RANDOLPH said the city of Boston is divided into six Senatorial districts.

Mr. J. S. CRAIG. No member is more disposed to do justice to Charleston, or any other portion of the State, than myself. I believe it wrong, however, to fix the basis of representation to the Senate, in the Constitution of the State, as set forth in the section. The apportionment, I think, should be made according to the population of every district. In some of the districts this method might decrease the representation while in others it might increase it. I propose the following amendment: "The Senate shall be composed of sixty members to be apportioned to the several districts or counties according to their population."

Mr. B. O. DUNCAN moved the indefinite postponement of this amendment.

Mr. D. H. CHAMBERLAIN: I hope the motion to postpone will not prevail. I am in favor of giving an opportunity to discuss every amendment offered, and to allow the same to other members I claim for myself.

Mr. B. O. DUNCAN. I am in favor of free discussion, but I think this amendment is carrying the thing too far.

Mr. L. S. LANGLEY. If the Convention propose to give two Senators to Charleston, then I am in favor of the amendment offered by the gentleman from Colleton (Mr. CRAIG). But if the Convention is determined to keep Charleston on an equality with the other counties of the State, although they might not possess one-tenth of the population, then I am opposed to the amendment.

Mr. R. SMALLS moved that the motion to postpone be laid on the table, which was agreed to.

Mr. W. B. NASH. I am opposed to giving one county in the State a larger representation than another. I am aware that under the old Constitution of South Carolina, Charleston had some four or five Senators. Under the old government, efforts were made to divide the districts of the upper portion of the State, but the parishes in the lower country always resisted it. It arose from the latter's greed for power. There had always been a contest between the upper districts and the lower for power. In the Constitution adopted in 1865, the parish representations were reduced. I think this nothing but an effort on the part of the gentleman from Charleston, since Pickens was divided, to get the balance of power again, by allowing Charleston two representatives to the floor of the Senate. This I deem very unjust to the other counties of the State. Berkley has a larger population than Charleston, and if this representation is given to it on the ground of population, why should not Berkley, Beaufort, or any other county, make the same request. If the motion of the gentleman from Charleston prevails, I will be in favor of the motion of the gentleman from Colleton. In that event I am in favor of giving every county in the State two Senators. I am not willing that Charleston should assume itself to be South Carolina. An opinion had prevailed in the lower part of the State that Charleston was the State of South Carolina, but I am not disposed that that opinion should prevail any longer. South Carolina should be South Carolina, and Charleston a portion of South Carolina. I am not willing Charleston should have a larger representation than any other district. I believe this to be nothing but a trick of power. I concur with the gentleman from Beaufort, that when the time comes that Charleston has a sufficient population to entitle her to another Senator, I will be in favor of an amendment to the Constitution so as to give her what she would then be entitled to.

Mr. W. J. McKINLAY. The best argument I have heard in support of the amendment, was that made by the member from Richland (Mr. NASH). He says there has always been a difference between the upper and lower country. We have seen that plainly here. We have voted for the division of a district that was not entitled to but three representatives, and that division will entitle it to two Senators. Charleston, with her nine delegates, will not be entitled to but one. If she has the preponderance of wealth and taxation, I think it no more than right and just that the amendment of the gentleman (Mr. BOWEN) should prevail.

Dr. J. L. NEAGLE. I am decidedly in favor of the amendment offered by the delegate from Charleston (Mr. BOWEN). I think it is merely common justice. I thought of it yesterday, when the section was passed on its second reading, but did not think it was my place to offer the amendment. In regard to the contest between the upper and lower country, alluded to by the member from Richland (Mr. NASH), under the new apportionment and division, the upper country will have decidedly the advantage. They will have a representation in the House of Representatives sufficiently strong to carry out any measure they please, no matter how strongly Charleston might oppose it. It is not probable that the territory of Charleston will ever be divided, and as the Constitution stands, without this amendment, there is no chance of her ever getting more than one Senator. Pickens, divided, gets two, and it has been argued that Berkley should have two, because that district has a similar voting population. Berkley has sufficient territory to be divided, and if divided they can have two Senators, or four if divided into four counties. As for the argument that we should take the Constitution of the United States for our guide, I will remind the delegates that the States are permanent political bodies. There is no chance, therefore, for any State to get any additional representation in the United States Senate. The Constitution provides for the division of counties, and any of the upper counties can, at any time, be divided, and thus gain more representation in the Senate. I am also opposed to the amendment of the gentleman from Colleton (Mr. CRAIG). I think the representation as now arranged in the sections passed was right and proper.

Mr. B. F. WHITTEMORE. I regard the request of the gentleman from Charleston (Mr. BOWEN) as very fair and just. Since the debate has been going on I have looked into the matter, and found, according to the census of 1860, the districts allowed one Senator by the section read had not more than one-half, or perhaps less than one-third, of the inhabitants of Charleston district. I understand, also, that the parishes around and near Charleston were before entitled to one Senator, which gave some ten Senators. These parishes have been absorbed in Berkley district, which, with its forty-five or fifty thousand inhabitants, is entitled to one Senator. But that district, or county, may hereafter be divided. The city of Charleston cannot be divided, and on account of her population, and her influence in the State, she should be entitled to two Senators at least.

Mr. J. J. WRIGHT. I think there is foundation for the amendment of the gentleman from Charleston (Mr. BOWEN), but I would prefer it in a different shape. I think it no more than right and proper that some provision ought to be made for cities. I propose the following amendment.

" The Senate shall be composed of one member from each county or city designated as a county, but whenever the population of any city designated as a county, shall be two-thirds greater than that of any other city or county, such city shall be entitled to two Senators.

Mr. N. G. PARKER. I concur with the views of the gentleman from Beaufort. I think we should encourage, by all means, the growth and prosperity of all cities. The great pride of the State of New York is its great city, and the great pride of Massachusetts is Boston. If there was anything we can do justly to encourage the growth and prosperity of cities, we should regard it as their highest privilege and duty to do so. Charleston is the only great and leading city of South Carolina. Her large property interests and increasing population entitles her to a larger representation than one of the little counties of the up country. I think the amendment offered by the member from Beaufort (Mr. J. J. WRIGHT) covers the whole ground. I had intended to allude to it, and to speak also of Columbia, Georgetown, and other growing cities of the State.

Mr. J. S. CRAIG. I am willing to concede that every city in the State, and every district, ought to have a fair, just and equitable representation in the Senate. If Charleston is entitled to six Representatives in the Senate according to population, I am willing to give it to her. But I want every district represented according to its population. But I do not see why Charleston should have two Senators when Colleton, with a larger population, has but one. My amendment proposes to give every district representation according to population.

Mr. J. M. RUTLAND. I rise to sanction the amendment of the gentleman from Charleston (Mr. BOWEN). Charleston always had two Senators, and I think it was only an oversight of the Legislative Committee that such a provision was not inserted in their report on this matter. I think we should cherish our cities, and allow them a just representation in both branches of the Legislature. It is almost impossible that one Senator could represent the valued interests of a large city.

Mr. C. P. LESLIE. All matters of representation in Republican forms of Government is based upon population. But there are other interests tending to fix and secure reasonable representation. The diversified interests of Charleston and its large amount of wealth, convinced people in times past that it was manifestly proper, just and right, that these diversified interests and this large capital should be protected by proper representation in the Senate of the State. For this reason I propose to vote in favor of Charleston having two Senators.

I do not claim to be a statesman, nor the son of a statesman, but a statesman, I have been told, endeavored so to legislate as to reconcile conflicting interests to all concerned, and particularly politicians. I beg my friends, and particularly the member from Richland (Mr. NASH). to bear in mind the suffering condition of the politicians of Charleston, and remember them in mercy. I would commend them to their charitable consideration, remembering always they ought not to have a representative sacrificing the interests, glory, honor and renown which necessarily accrue from a larger representation in any office whatever. Remember Charleston and its politicians, for at all times, in season and out of season, they are ready to fill all the offices in the State. I fervently pray our country members to remember the representatives of Charleston in their distress, to remember them in this Convention, and to remember that they always, on all occasions, have been the salvation of the country. I cannot go further with these prayers without forcing the tears from the delegates. In the language of the gentleman from Charleston, we should encourage the growth of Charleston ; in the language of the gentleman from Fairfield, we should cherish our cities ; in the language of the gentleman from Colleton, who is another suffering individual, whose population numbers 42,000, with, he might have added, a very large and increasing population of snakes, frogs, lizards and alligators, we should make representation according to population. I do appeal to the members from the up country, for God's sake, remember Charleston.

Mr. F. J. MOSES, Jr. It was not my intention to take up the time of the Convention on this subject, but after the remarks of the member from Barnwell (Mr. LESLIE), I fear this great and important matter has lost that serious aspect in which it deserves to be treated. Many a true word is said in jest, and though he has attempted to burlesque with that remarkable wit for which he is so distinguished, I hope no one will be influenced by the jest or burlesque of any member in considering this matter. I hope they will view it in the serious aspect it deserves. As a representative from the up country, I appeal earnestly and sincerely to every one of my fellow delegates to remember that the city of Charleston is entitled to our serious consideration. I beg them to remember that this city, saving within the last few years, has had an honorable record as a portion of our State. We should remember her greater diversified interests, her commerce, her shipping, the taxes she pays, and I would ask are we prepared to strike at that portion of the State which has reflected so much credit upon them as a thriving, prosperous community ? If we are prepared to do that, as members from the up country, I am not prepared to act with them. I came here to benefit Charleston as much as any other part of the State.

I had hoped that the dead past would be allowed to bury the differences of the past. I had hoped that the series of misfortunes that had come upon the people, with all the disasters of the war, would terminate all those unpleasant, unbrotherly differences which have existed between the up and low country. No more auspicious occasion for banishing these old unfriendly feelings offered, than on the floor of this Reconstruction Convention. We are here to work together for the honor, the glory, welfare and prosperity of the whole State.

It had been said that Charleston is very anxious to fill all the offices. That, too, might be true ; but I have no doubt the gentleman from Barnwell district (Mr. LESLIE) would like very much to fill any office coming within his grasp. Looking at the poor old city, with her crumbling walls, the wealth of her citizens wrested from them, as representatives now legislating for the whole State of South Carolina, could they consent to make one stab at the grand old city by the sea. I hope every member may bring himself strictly to the important question, "is the city of Charleston entitled to two Senators?" Is it the desire of any member to strike at the future wealth and prosperity of Charleston? I cannot believe that such a feeling can exist here. Look at the poor old city, with her crumbling walls ; think of the wealth lost and wrested from her grasp. As representatives, I deem it our duty to legislate for the whole State, and do all in our power to restore this proud commercial metropolis.

Mr. J. D. BELL. I am in favor of conforming the practice in the election of State Senators to the regulations as laid down in the Constitution of the United States. It has been said that in the representation of the United States Senate, States could not be divided. Virginia has been divided and Texas is to be divided. We must remember there are two, or perhaps more districts which have a greater population than Charleston. I will cheerfully vote for some districts, having one-fifth or less number in population than other districts, having the same number of Senators as other or larger districts. The question of population, I consider, has nothing to do with it. The former state of things has been referred to. We are not acting on the former basis. Our old Constitution says representation shall be divided according to the wealth of the inhabitants. One-half of the representation was then founded on wealth. It was not enough for the old politicians that they had a representation in the Congress of the United States for three fifths of their slaves, but they adopted a similar rule at home, and one-half of their property was represented in the State Legislature. I hope the time has passed for basing representation on property, and that we will require no property qualifications for a man to be an elector. I think it unjust to my constituents that they should have but one Senator, having the same or greater population than Charleston, and a larger territory, with greater diversified interests than a small territory possibly could have.

Mr. F. L. CARDOZO. Do you think that a larger rural territory, consisting of large plantations, has more diversified interests than a commercial city containing 50,000 inhabitants.

Mr. J. D. BELL. There are districts consisting of cities and country plantations, and necessarily with the connections between them, there must be other interests than those in a city without the country. I hope the amendment will be adopted.

Mr. T. J. COGHLAN. I differ with my colleague (Mr. MOSES) on this subject. He says he comes here not as a representative of any particular interest of the State. I came here as a representative of the up country in general, and that of Sumter in particular. But while I am proud to say that, I have as strong and ardent a feeling for my native city, Charleston, as any man in the State. But now I feel it encumbent upon me to represent the interests of my district alone, and if the interests of the up country are represented properly, the city of Charleston cannot fail to prosper. We all labor for the prosperity of our State, and as regards our representation, I think she has her full quota. In former days the low country swayed and influenced the power of the State entirely. A few simple parishes, with a white population only sufficient for a small tea party, were represented by one or two Senators. I hope the amendment of the gentleman from Charleston (Mr. BOWEN) will not succeed, not from any prejudice or ill-feelings towards the city of Charleston, but on the ground of strict justice.

Mr. B. F. RANDOLPH. I hope the amendment of the gentleman from Beaufort will prevail. It seems to be fair and just. It will secure justice to all the districts and cities in the State. I understand that amendment to be this, that when any city or county shall have one-third more population than any other city or county, then such city or county shall be entitled to two Senators. We all hope that South Carolina is growing and will continue to increase in population.

Mr. E. W. M. MACKEY. She has not more than one-third the population than Berkley. The proposition of the gentleman from Beaufort is a mere blind. It says when any county or town has one-third more population than any other, then that town or county shall be entitled to two Senators. If, for instance, Beaufort County has one-third more, she will be entitled to two Senators.

Mr. A. C. RICHMOND. I would like to know if the proposition of the gentleman from Beaufort will not prevent any county from being divided.

Mr. B. F. RANDOLPH. There is nothing in the amendment preventing the division of a district if the Legislature deem it proper.

Mr. W. J. WHIPPER. I have not the slightest objection to Charleston having two Senators, but hope if it is done it will be upon the prin ciple that would give the same number to any other city or county with the same number of inhabitants. I do not see that the amendment does anything of the kind. It proposes to give an additional Senator to Charleston or any other city or county that has one-third more population than any other city or county. If there are now in the county of Charleston, county of Colleton and Beaufort a population so nearly equal that neither of them would have one-third over the other for the next ten years, neither Charleston nor those districts would have an additional Senator.

Mr. B. F. RANDOLPH. Do you not propose to ask for the division of Beaufort District.

Mr. W. J. WHIPPER. I am not prepared to answer that question. I know not whether the people of Beaufort District will favor such a petition in sufficient numbers, nor are we to legislate with any view of what may happen. If Charleston is entitled to two Senators, give her two Senators, and do it on a basis that will give other counties the same privileges upon having the same number of inhabitants. I move that the amendment be indefinitely postponed.

The PRESIDENT. The first amendment in order is that of the gentleman from Charleston (Mr. C. C. BOWEN), to add the following words : " except the County of Charleston, which shall be allowed two Senators."

Mr. J. S. CRAIG called for the yeas and nays.

Mr. L. S. LANGLEY. I desire to set myself right. It has been said some gentlemen had some ill feeling toward Charleston. I for one am divested of that prejudice. I know that a sectional feeling has existed in South Carolina, but hope that it does not exist in this body. But when gentlemen rise and ask that Charleston should have a greater number of Senators than the County of Pickens, Lexington, Richland, or other counties in the State, I do not think it is justice. So long as representation is based on the political divisions of the State, I see no reason why Charleston is entitled to representation based on wealth, or

48

population. What are the interests of Charleston ? They are mercantile ; and it has been claimed because she has that interest she is entitled to an extra Senator. I claim that the interests of the rural districts are no less than the mercantile interests of Charleston. What would become of the mercantile, if it were not for the rural planting interests of the State protecting it ? Are not the planting interests entitled to just as much protection ? Gentlemen have risen and alluded to and deplored the sectional feeling that is exhibited. I claim that it is only sectional feeling that induced the gentleman from Charleston to offer his amendment. Hitherto in the history of this State, Charleston has been in the habit of taking and handling the rest of the State just as she wished. She has imagined herself to be South Carolina. It is the old love of power that makes her come up here and ask gentlemen from the rural districts, representing the agricultural interests of the State, to increase her power and give her a greater representation than Pickens, Lexington, Darlington or Laurens, because of greater wealth or population. Other counties in the State that have a larger population do not ask for it. Berkley has a larger population. While I am willing to do justice, I am decidedly opposed to making Charleston the pet of the State. If the amendment is agreed to, making population the basis of representation, I am in favor of it.

Mr. C. C. BOWEN. So much has been said with regard to the up country and low country. I wish to add a few words. I have already stated the Legislative Committee have made certain alterations. They had proposed to change the names of the districts into counties, and provided that any district having six hundred and twenty-five square miles could become a county. It is well known that there are but few judicial districts in the State but what could be divided, and even subdivided. Well, the gentleman from Beaufort (Mr. L. S. LANGLEY) rises, and is loud-mouthed about justice and equality, and at the same time has been harping upon this floor with his proposition to get the district which he represents divided. The representatives of Beaufort said if Pickens District was divided, they would have a petition here in less than forty-eight hours to divide Beaufort.

I would not have made this motion had it not been that Charleston, as a county, will be differently situated from the others. She can never be divided, for she has not six hundred and twenty five square miles. Beaufort, under this division, can go before the next Legislature and be divided into three counties. By that division they get three Senators. They admit the fact that the whole district has not the population of Charleston District. I fail to see the equity of this proceeding.

If they had said the city and county of Charleston can be divided, I would have kept my seat, but they commence by saying your county never can be divided, and they lay down the proposition by which they can divide their county into three. In conclusion, I move that the section be recommitted to the Committee, with instructions to report when they report on the other section committed to them.

Mr. J. J. WRIGHT. I hope the motion to recommit will prevail. I agree with the gentleman from Charleston that she should have an extra Senator whenever the case demands it. If my amendment does not prevail I shall vote for two Senators for Charleston county. The object of my amendment was simply to give the city of Columbia, or any other city, the same right and immunities as those possessed by Charleston.

The motion to recommit was withdrawn and the question was then taken on the adoption of the amendment.

The yeas and nays being called for, were taken, and the amendment adopted by the following vote :

YEAS—The President, Messrs. Becker, Bowen, Bonum, Brockenton, Bryce, Byas, R. H. Cain, Camp, Cardozo, Chamberlain, Delarge, Dickson, Dogan, Duncan, Elliott, Goss, Gray, Harris, J. N. Hayne, C. D. Hayne, H. E. Hayne, Humbird, Hurley, Jacobs, Jervey, Jillson, J. W. Johnson, Dr. L. B. Johnson, C. Jones, George Lee, Leslie, E. W. M. Mackey, Mauldin, W. J. McKinlay, Wm. McKinlay, A. Middleton, Miller, Millford, Moses, Jr., Neagle, Newell, Olsen, Parker, Pillsbury, Rainey, Ransier, Richmond, Rose, Rutland, Shrewsbury, B. A. Thompson, Thomas, Viney, Whittemore—55.

NAYS—Allen, Alexander, Arnim, Bell, Burton, F. J. Cain, Coghlan, Clinton, Cook, Corley, Craig, Crews, Darrington, Davis, Driffle, Edwards, Foster, Gentry, Henderson, Holmes, Jacobs, S. Johnson, W. B. Johnson, W. E. Johnston, Joiner, Langley, S. Lee, Mead, Nance, Nash, Mickles, B. Owens, Randolph, Rivers, Robertson, Runion, Sanders, Sasportas, Smalls, Stubbs, Swails, A. Thompson, S. B. Thompson, Whipper, White, Williamson, F. E. Wilder, C. M. Wilder, Wingo, Warley, Wright—51.

ABSENT—Boozer, Chestnut, Collins, Dill, Donaldson, Hunter, Jenks, H. Jones, Lang, Lomax, Mayer, McDaniels, Nelson, Perry, Webb—15.

Mr. R. B. ELLIOTT moved to reconsider the vote by which the amendment was adopted, and to lay the motion for reconsideration on the table, which was agreed to.

The eighth section then passed to its third reading.

The PRESIDENT announced that the hour for the Special Order had arrived.

The Special Order being the report of the Committee on Petitions, on a petition to Congress for the loan of one million dollars for the purchase of lands, was taken up.

Mr. W. E. ROSE, Chairman of the Committee on Petitions, made the following report:

The Committee on Petitions, to whom was referred the preamble and resolution relative to petitioning Congress for a grant of one million dollars to be appropriated for the purchase of lands in this State, ask leave to report that they have duly considered the same, and are of the opinion that the prayer of your petitioner should be granted, and that the President of this Convention be requested to transmit a copy of the preamble and resolution to the Congress of the United States at as early a date as practicable.

W. E. ROSE, Chairman.

Mr. C. D. HAYNE. I move that the report be adopted.

Mr. C. P. LESLIE. I know that I am now going to say what possibly may be construed to be an unkind remark towards the colored people of the State. I know that the delegates here will probably not thank me for what I am going to say, but at all times, and in all places, when called upon to discharge my duty, I mean to do it irrespective of the temporary effect it may have. If I say vote no for this resolution, the colored delegates will say he is not the friend of our race or our people. A politician is a very cunning fellow. He sometimes looks one way, like a Whitehall boatman, and rows another. It is the fashion of bogus politicians to get up resolutions that read and attract the wayfaring man and the pilgrim to the wall and say, "see how I love my people. I have recommended a million of dollars to buy lands for the free people of the State. Is there any man who has sacrificed more, or done more, than I have, in season and out of season, for your welfare? I have thought of you, and prayed for you, and when I took my position in the Convention, mindful as I have always been of your interests, I worked night and day until I framed a petition to Congress, which petition was offered to the house, and then, not contented, I went still further, and went before the Committee and urged it through there, to obtain a million of dollars for the relief of the people." At the same time that same gentleman, in his own heart a politician, knew that not one dollar of that money would ever be realized. But the wayfaring man and the pilgrim, and the poor man, think the politician has done them a great favor, but practically, he has done them no good. But it answers to get such men into office. It answers to give him great repute and possibly great glory, but of all the things in this world that I do abhor, it is these policy people, and the dishonesty and humbugs of politicians. If you ask a million of dollars ask it with the reasonable expectation that you are going to get it. But gentlemen here are tickling the fancy of the poor people of the State by petitions to Congress, that every sensible person from the coast of Maine to the Gulf of Mexico, well knows will not get a single dollar. I will not, for that reason, allow my name to be recorded in favor of fooling the people, or deceiving them for a moment. I ask now, seriously, our friend to look the figures in the face. The Treasury of the United States is called upon each month to make large disbursements of money, and I appeal to any well informed delegate, who has read the report of the Secretary of the Treasury for the last month, if he has not read that report with feelings of sorrow and regret.

Whenever I hear it said by a certain class of men, not friendly to their country, " ah, look, the money will soon be gone from the Treasury ; see how the public debt increased last month", I am pained. See how Congress has authorized a loan of $150,000,000, in order to keep up the credit of the country. Every one knows that the Treasurer is cramped to meet expenses, and has use for every cent he can get. This is strictly true. I have not spoken with an unkind disposition to any one, nor made any unkind allusion to any delegate. I am only trying to tell why we should not do so foolish a thing as to send up a petition to Congress for one million of dollars when they have not a cent to to give, and from the very nature of the case it is utterly impossible to grant it. But, says the policy man, " why don't you vote for it; because, if you dare vote against it the people will say you are the enemy of the colored people. Congress will, probably, throw it in the waste basket, and that will be the end of it. Why don't you go with the people?" Now, I am not here to humbug the people. The gentleman from Charleston, who presented that petition, in my judgment, if he knew anything about the condition of the Treasury, knew when he planned and wrote that petition, that it was all humbug. There is no more intelligent gentleman upon this floor than that same delegate from Charleston, and when his mind is brought to bear to deceive the people, I have great apprehension as to the future. I like to have my name, when it goes upon paper, go there with a reasonable expectation that I shall succeed. I shall be answered by the delegate by his saying, "we do not propose to take it out of the Treasury, but out of the Bureau Fund." But where in the world does the Bureau Fund come from if not out of the Treasury of the United States. But if the Bureau has the funds on hand, I will stake my existence, from what I know of that department and its officers, that that crowd will use up all the money, the freedmen to the contrary notwithstanding ; so that when you fetch it right home, it amounts to nothing more nor less than a cover to a proposition to see what the newspapers would say about it—what the Northern people would say about it. They would say it means to take money out of the Treasury.

It is a lamentable showing for the friends of the party that the Treasury of the United States is almost empty, scarcely able to pay the debts of the departments. I know the quartermaster-General has not had one dollar of his money for the last five weeks, and they have not been paid off at the Citadel, and everybody almost swearing against the Government for their neglect. If that is the condition of the Treasury, how can we expect to get this money. And if not, then the delegate has no right to ask me to let my name go upon such a paper.

I have said all I desire without any unkind feeling to any one. God forbid I should throw any stumbling block in the way of those endeavoring to assist unfortunate humanity. But I will not add to their unfortunate condition a false and expected hope, that sounds well to the ear, but is fatal to the hope. Most of the colored people have hired out for the year, and any preparation made to day sounds well; the petition recites "immediate relief," "something to do now," "a place, home, and habitation." Why, it would not be possible, if it were the purpose of the policy man, to give that relief in six months, so that so much of the petition of the delegate smacks of the politician and humbug, that I am sorry for my friend from Charleston, because he is a shining light.

Mr. R. H. CAIN. I desire simply to state that the gentleman's presentation of a design to deceive for the purpose of misrepresentation, is entirely gratuitous. It may be that he is a shrewd, cunning, crafty politician, as his argument certainly indicates, and having practiced possibly in the Legislature of New York, so many of those tricks of high dudgeon that he is prepared to do it here. But I shall not further notice what he has said on that score. I propose simply to state the fact that I presented these resolutions and preamble with the best intentions. It may be that he is so far removed from the interests of the poor, needy, distressed and oppressed, that his circumstances have been so far above the millions of the distressed and poor that he cannot feel. He reminds me very much of the rich man in Scripture, Dives, who it is said had but little feeling for the poor man Lazarus, and, therefore, could not sympathise with him until he found himself in my friend's (Mr. RANDOLPH) place, Hades, lifting up his eyes in torment.

Mr. B. F. RANDOLPH. I beg leave to state that is not my place.

Mr. C. P. LESLIE. I would be willing to go to Hades, provided he gets the million dollars.

Mr. CAIN. I offer this resolution with good intentions. I believe there is need of immediate relief to the poor people of the State. I know from my experience among the people, there is pressing need of some measures to meet the wants of the utterly destitute. The gentleman says it will only take money out of the Treasury. Well that is the intention. I do not expect to get it anywhere else. I expect to get the money, if at all, through the Treasury of the United States, or some other department. It certainly must come out of the Government. I believe such an appropriation would remove a great many of the difficulties now in the State and do a vast amount of good to poor people. It may be that we will not get it, but that will not debar us from asking. It is our privilege and right. Other Conventions have asked from Congress appropriations. Georgia and other States have sent in their petitions. One has asked for $30,000,000 to be appropriated to the Southern States. I do not see any inconsistency in the proposition presented by myself.

Mr. C. P. LESLIE. Suppose I should button up my coat and march up to your house and ask you for money or provisions, when you had none to give, what would you think of me.

Mr. CAIN. You would do perfectly right to run the chance of getting something to eat. This is a measure of relief to those thousands of freed people who now have no lands of their own. I believe the possession of lands and homesteads is one of the best means by which a people is made industrious, honest and advantageous to the State. I believe it is a fact well known, that over three hundred thousand men, women and children are homeless, landless. The abolition of slavery has thrown these people upon their own resources. How are they to live. I know the philosopher of the New York Tribune says, " root hog or die;" but in the meantime we ought to have some place to root. My proposition is simply to give the hog some place to root. I believe if the proposition is sent to Congress, it will certainly receive the attention of our friends. I believe the whole country is desirous to see that this State shall return to the Union in peace and quiet, and that every inhabitant of the State shall be made industrious and profitable to the State. I am opposed to this Bureau system. I want a system adopted that will do away with the Bureau, but I cannot see how it can be done unless the people have homes. As long as people are working on shares and contracts, and at the end of every year are in debt, so long will they and the country suffer. But give them a chance to buy lands, and they become steady, industrious men. That is the reason I desire to bring this money here and to assist them to buy lands. It will be the means of encouraging them to industry if the petition be granted by Congress. It will be the means of meeting one of the great wants of the present among the poor. It will lay the foundation for the future prosperity of the country as no other measure will at this time, because it will bring about a reconciliation in the minds of thousands of these helpless people, which nothing else can. This measure, if carried out, will bring capital to the State and stimulate the poor to renewed efforts in life, such as they never had before. Such a measure will give to the landholders relief from their embarrassments financially, and enable them to get fair compensation for their lands. It will relieve the Government of the responsibility of taking care of the thousands who now are fed at the Commissaries and fostered in laziness. I have gone through the country and on every side I was besieged with questions: How are we to get homesteads, to get lands? I desire to devise some plan, or adopt some measure by which we can dissipate one of the arguments used against us, that the African race will not work. I do not believe the black man hates work any more than the white man does. Give these men a place to work, and I will guarantee before one year passes, there will be no necessity for the Freedman's Bureau, or any measure aside from those measures which a people may make in protecting themselves.

But a people without homes become wanderers. If they possess lands they have an interest in the soil, in the State, in its commerce, its agriculture, and in everything pertaining to the wealth and welfare of the State. If these people had homes along the lines of railroads, and the lands were divided and sold in small farms, I will guarantee our railroads will make fifty times as much money, banking systems will be advanced by virtue of the settlement of the people throughout the whole State. We want these large tracts of land cut up. The land is productive, and there is nothing to prevent the greatest and highest prosperity. What we need is a system of small farms. Every farmer owning his own land will feel he is in possession of something. It will have a tendency to settle the minds of the people in the State and settle many difficulties. In the rural districts now there is constant discontent, constant misapprehension between the parties, a constant disregard for each other. One man won't make an engagement to work, because he fears if he makes a contract this year, he will be cheated again as he thinks he was last year. We have had petitions from planters asking the Convention to disabuse the minds of the freedmen of the thought that this Convention has any lands at its disposal, but I do desire this Convention to do something at least to relieve the wants of these poor suffering people. I believe this measure, if adopted and sent to Congress, will indicate to the people that this Convention does desire they shall possess homes and have relief.

Some of my friends say that the sum is too small, and ask why I do not make it more. I made it a million, because I thought there would be more probability of getting one million than five. It might be put into the hands of the Bureau, and I am willing to trust the Bureau.

Mr. C. P. LESLIE. I did not charge upon Gen. Scott, or any officer of the Bureau dishonesty, and I do not wish it so put in the report that I did, nor have it published in the newspapers. What I intended to show was, that if they got into their hands any sum of money they knew well how to get rid of it.

Mr. R. C. DELARGE. Was not the gentleman a distributor of coin?

Mr. C. P. LESLIE. I did that without one dollar of compensation, while the Bureau agent was paid one hundred and fifty dollars per month.

Mr. R. H. CAIN. I do not desire to have a foot of land in this State confiscated. I want every man to stand upon his own character. I want these lands purchased by the government, and the people afforded an opportunity to buy from the government. I believe every man ought to carve out for himself a character and position in this life. I believe every man ought to be made to work by some means or other, and if he does not, he must go down. I believe if the same amount of money that has been employed by the Bureau in feeding lazy, worthless men and women, had been expended in purchasing lands, we would to-day have no need of the Bureau. Millions upon millions have been expended, and it is still going on *ad infinitum*. I propose to let the poor people buy these lands, the government to be paid back in five years time. It is one of the great cries of the enemies of reconstruction, that Congress has constantly fostered laziness. I want to have the satisfaction of showing that the freedmen are as capable and willing to work as any men on the face of the earth. This measure will save the State untold expenses. I believe there are hundreds of persons in the jail and penitentiary cracking rock to-day who have all the instincts of honesty, and who, had they an opportunity of making a living, would never have been found in such a place. I think if Congress will accede to our request, we shall be benefited beyond measure, and save the State from taking charge of paupers, made such by not having the means to earn a living for themselves.

I can look to a part of my constituency, men in this hall, mechanics, plasterers, carpenters, engineers, men capable of doing all kind of work, now idle because they cannot find any work in the city. Poverty stares them in the face, and their children are in want. They go to the cotton houses, but can find no labor. They are men whose honesty and integ-

49

rity has never been called in question. They are suffering in consequence of the poverty-stricken condition of the city and State. I believe the best measure is to open a field where they can labor, where they can take the hoe and the axe, cut down the forest, and make the whole land blossom as the Garden of Eden, and prosperity pervade the whole land.

Now, the report of Major General Howard gives a surplus of over seven millions in the Freedman's Bureau last year. Out of that seven millions I propose we ask Congress to make an appropriation of one million, which will be properly distributed and then leave several millions in that Department, my friend from Barnwell notwithstanding.

I think there could be no better measure for this Convention to urge upon Congress. If that body should listen to our appeal, I have no doubt we shall be benefited. This measure of relief, it seems to me, would come swiftly. It is a swift messenger that comes in a week's time after it is passed; so that in the month of February or March the people may be enabled to go to planting and raising crops for the ensuing year. One gentleman says it will take six months or a year, but I hope, with the assistance of the Government, we could accomplish it in less time.

Mr. C. P. LESLIE. Did you ever see the Government do anything quick?

Mr. R. H. CAIN. They make taxes come quick. If this measure is carried out, the results will be that we will see all along our lines of railroad and State roads little farms, log cabins filled with happy families. and thousands of families coming on the railroads with their products. There will also spring up depots for the reception of cotton, corn and all other cereals. Prosperity will return to the State, by virtue of the people being happy, bound to the Government by a tie that cannot be broken. The taxes, that are so heavy now that men are compelled to sell their horses, will be lightened. I want to see the State alive, to hear the hum of the spindle and the mills. I want to see cattle and horses, and fowls, and everything that makes up a happy home and family. I want to see the people shout with joy and gladness. There shall then be no antagonism between white men and black men, but we shall all realize the end of our being, and realize that we are all made to dwell upon the earth in peace and happiness. The white man and the black man may then work in harmony, and secure prosperity to all coming generations.

Mr. G. PILLSBURY. I rise probably with the liability of being taken from the wall by the unique, remarkable artist from Barnwell. I may be charged with being one of those tricky, scheming politicians who like to be hung in effigy. But if I am charged with being a politician, I aver to this Convention that I have been a very unsuccessful one. It has been for thirty years one of the leading motives of my life to ask those who have to give in behalf of those who have nothing. I have often petitioned those who had money, and did not get it. I have often petitioned those who had no money, and, of course, did not get it; and on the whole, as a petitioner, my life has been a success; but as a politician, an utter failure. I ought to have learned twenty years ago that lesson, and have changed my course of life. The great objection which the gentleman from Barnwell urges to this petition is that we are making fools of ourselves, making a petition with a certain knowledge that it would be in vain, and that it would not be granted. I would ask him what he would say to a proposition by this Convention to petition Congress to spend seven millions for an iceberg. He would call us fools undoubtedly and politicians, and yet the Government has funds with which to purchase that iceberg. Again, we might be called fools for purchasing a volcano, yet Government has funds to purchase a volcano.

Mr. C. P. LESLIE. Did Government buy it because it was an iceberg, or a volcano? Did they buy an iceberg because it was an iceberg? No, sir. They bought it on account of its geographical location to this country, because it is necessary as a frontier. All I claimed was, when you knew in advance that Congress would not give a dollar in money, all this palaver is deception and a fraud on those you deceive. I will not be made a tool of in such a way. I am willing to vote any amount of money raised on the credit of the State.

Mr. G. PILLSBURY. I wish to bring forth this fact: The gentleman stated there was no money in the Treasury, and that the Government had no money to appropriate for any purpose, still it is patent the Government has purchased a volcano, and for all I know will yet purchase a thunder cloud. I speak of what the Government has done, without regard to debts. It seems to me this petition is a reasonable one. Congress has entrusted a great and priceless boon to the colored race. They have set them free. But is it just on the part of the Government, having done this great act, to leave them where they are. It is like marching them in solid phalanx before a well stored commissary and keeping them in anxious expectation through the day, while the provisions are being carried out to their former masters.

Mr. C. P. LESLIE. Secretary Seward contracted for Walrussia, and agreed to pay so much money for it. Congress refused to pay the money because they did not have the money to pay for it. Don't you know the fact that Congress said in so many words that they could not take Walrussia because they had not a dollar to pay for it.

Mr. G. PILLSBURY.   I understand the reason Congress refused to purchase was because it was an iceberg. I could place a picture upon the wall if I were an artist, which might or should touch the heart of the artist from Barnwell. Four millions of people set at liberty, thrown wholly upon their own resources, through the action of the Government, and with not one foot of soil upon this earth to claim as their own.   There is a picture I wish the gentleman from Barnwell to consider.   This is a reasonable proposition. This class of people are the wards of the Government, and they are bound in good faith, having brought them thus far out of Egypt, to advance them still further into the promised land, and, if properly addressed, I have no doubt they will be ready to accede.   I understand the Government has already sent money liberally into this State. If I am not wrongly informed, there are $600,000 already sent into the State. But how was that money expended? Who is to be benefited by it? If the benefactions of the North are hereafter to be expended as they have been heretofore, that money will be expended in repairing the dilapidated buildings of planters, in purchasing horses and carriages to contribute to their comfort, and place them, in some degree, upon the old standing which they once occupied. Very little, indeed, will the thousands and tens of thousands of colored people receive from that six hundred thousand dollars appropriation.   It will all go, or the most of it will undoubtedly go to their old masters, and I leave it to the Convention to decide to what appropriation they will be likely to apply it.

But this, as I said, is a practical question. It is a question of furnishing homes. What can a people do without homes? What can a people do out of doors, who cannot advance one yard on the earth without asking permission of some lord of the soil? They are in a pitiable, helpless, wretched and desperate condition. It cannot be doubted that there are large quantities of land in this State which can be purchased at a very cheap rate. I know when the war closed, and for a long time after, a colored man could not purchase an acre of land in this State if he had covered it with greenbacks. Thank God it is not so now. A colored man, if he has any money, can obtain land But he has not the money, and you all know why he is so poor. It is not mainly his fault.

This is a simple petition to the government to contribute still further to carry out the work which cost them millions upon millions to accomplish and carry on thus far. It is a reasonable proposition, and I believe Congress will be influenced by such a petition. I need not speak of the great benefits an appropriation of this kind would have upon this people. In conclusion, at the risk of being displayed upon the wall as being a politician, I cannot at this time of life, and under the circumstances in which I am placed, recede from the old beaten path which I have been unable to tread successfully for the last thirty years.

Mr. C. P. LESLIE. I am getting in good humor. It is now at this time when I have the kindest feeling towards all those people behind that railing who stand there ; with what little perception I have, with what little knowledge, I assert that time will prove that the petition offered, and the addresses made here to-day, were most inopportune. These addresses have been listened to by a large concourse of spectators, and have held out to them that within a very short time they are to get land. We all know that the colored people want land. Night and day they think and dream of it. It is their all in all. As these men retire from the hall and go home, the first thing they do is to announce to the people "joy on earth, and good will to all mankind." We are all going to have a home. They will say bless God, and pray that the hour will be soon. Brother CAIN has actually got up a petition, and it has passed the Convention, and what that Convention does it must stand, there is no use talking. We are certain to all get some land in a very short space of time. I know how I would feel if I was placed in the condition in which they have been. And when I know as they know, that without land a race of people, four millions in number, travelling up and down the earth without a home are suffering, I cannot but denounce those who would, for political purposes, add to their misery by raising expectations that could never be realized. The gentleman from Charleston (Mr. R. H. CAIN), knew when he offered the resolution and petition he would never get a dollar. Is it right to raise the hopes of these people to have them again dashed to the earth, and made ten fold more miserable ? I tell you you will never realize that loan.

The present financial embarrassment of the State has been a subject of much concern. We have a few dollars of bills receivable. The matter has been under consideration, and we have studied some plan to raise money. We have consulted as to whether or no Congress would make a loan, and I think those on this floor who have studied and examined the subject most, after obtaining every opinion they could get upon the subject, have arrived at this one conclusion, that we cannot get a dollar of money, whether for the freedmen or for ourselves.

Let us have a little more light upon the subject. Parson French, who, it is well known, has the welfare of the colored people at heart, did go to Washington and portrayed to leading Senators and members of Congress the terrible predicament of the colored people in the State. He said that cotton had sold so low that all the people were poverty-stricken. The white people, he told them, were not able to plant, and there being no necessity to employ laborers, the colored people were turned out of house and home, and he begged them to loan the people, or the State, a million of dollars. Their answer was, " Mr. French, for God's sake, send up no petitions for money, for we cannot give one dollar." Now, I say, there are gentlemen upon this floor who understand this thing precisely. I am honest and sincere in my desire to do anything practicable, and would go as far to serve the colored people as the gentleman from Charleston, but I will do nothing, even at the risk of my political position or otherwise, that I know will be a snare. Why should we deceive this people ? Why allow them to return to their homes and scatter widely through the State that they are going to get a home? Each one tells the other and they tell forty more, and so it goes on causing untold mischief and exciting false hopes among the freedmen. The President, but the other day, directed the attention of the house to a letter received by General Scott, reciting the fact that certain freedmen, who have been working upon a plantation in Berkley district, refused to contract or to do anything until this Convention adjourned, and the owner had to appeal to General Scott to instruct the freedmen, and in accordance with his request, a resolution was passed informing the freedmen that the Convention had no lands at their disposal.

The hour of half-past two having arrived, the Convention adjourned.

TWENTY-SEVENTH DAY.

Saturday, February 15, 1868.

The Convention assembled at half-past 10 A. M., Saturday, and was called to order by the PRESIDENT.

Prayer was offered by the Rev. J. M. RUNION.

The roll was called, and a quorum answering to their names. the PRESIDENT announced the Convention ready to proceed to business.

The Journal of the preceding day was read and approved.

The PRESIDENT called for reports of Standing Committees.

Mr. E. W. M. MACKEY, of the Committee on the Legislative part of the Constitution, reported the following, which was read a first and second time and ordered to be printed:

SECTION 3. The Judicial Districts shall hereafter be designated as Counties, and the boundaries of the several Counties shall remain as they are now established, except the County of Pickens, which is hereby divided into two Counties, by a line leaving the southern boundary of the State of North Carolina where the White Water river enters this State, and thence down the centre of said river, by whatever names known, to Ravenel's Bridge, on Seneca river, and thence along the centre of the road leading to Pendleton Village, until it intersects the line of the County of Anderson; and the territory lying East of said line shall be known as the County of Pickens; and the territory lying West of said line shall be known as the County of Oconee; and except, also, the County of Charleston, which is hereby divided into three Counties, viz: The County of Charleston, to be composed of the late Parishes of St. Philip and St. Michael; the County of Berkley, to be composed of the late Parishes of St. Thomas and St. Dennis, St. James' Santee, St. Stephen's, St. John's Berkley, Christ Church and St. James' Goose Creek; and the County of Edisto, to be composed of the late Parishes of St. Andrew's, St. John's Colleton, including Fenwick's Island, and all adjacent Islands as far South as the northern boundary of the County of Beaufort; and these three Counties shall constitute one Judicial District, the Court House and Jail of which shall be in the city of Charleston; *Provided,* That the Legislature shall have the power at any time, by a vote of two-thirds of both Houses, to organize new Counties by changing the boundaries of any of the old ones; but no new County shall hereafter be formed of less extent than six hundred and twenty-five square miles, nor shall any existing Counties be reduced to a less extent than six hundred and twenty-five square miles. Each County shall constitute one election district.

Mr. B. F. RANDOLPH, from the Committee on the Miscellaneous Provisions of the Constitution, submitted the following reports, which were adopted:

The Committee on the Miscellaneous Provisions of the Constitution, to whom was referred certain resolutions concerning corporations, have had the same under consideration, and beg leave to report that they have decided to incorporate the principles of those resolutions in their report upon corporations. All of which is most respectfully submitted.

B. F. RANDOLPH.

The Committee on the Miscellaneous Provisions of the Constitution, to whom was referred certain resolutions concerning charitable institutions, have had the same under consideration, and beg leave to report that they have decided to incorporate the principles of those. resolutions in their report upon charitable institutions. Respectfully submitted.

B. F. RANDOLPH.

The Committee on the Miscellaneous Provisions of the Constitution, to whom was referred certain resolutions declaring that all ferry charters, grants, and exclusive privileges, that may have been heretofore granted. null, void, and of no effect, after the assembling of the Legislature under this Constitution ; also, that it shall be obligatory on the Legislature to grant a charter for any proposed railroad, when said charter shall be applied for by any twelve respectable citizens of this State, have had the same under consideration, and beg leave to report that in the opinion of your Committee it is inexpedient for this Convention to take action in the premises, and they respectfully recommend that the resolutions be laid on the table. Respectfully submitted.

B. F. RANDOLPH.

Mr. B. F. WHITTEMORE, from the Committee on the Bill of Rights, submitted the following report, which was agreed to :

The Committee on the Bill of Rights, to whom was referred the resolution by the delegate from Newberry, that

"The Legislature shall enact such laws as it may seem necessary and proper to prevent the carrying of concealed and deadly weapons,"

Beg leave to report that they considered the subject, and concluded that it will be more proper for action to be passed upon it in the Legislature, and therefore recommend that the resolution be laid on the table, and the Committee discharged from its further consideration.

B. F. WHITTEMORE,
Chairman Bill of Rights.

Mr. C. P. LESLIE, from the Auditing Committee, presented the account of the Southern Express Company and the following report, which was agreed to :

We recommend that the within bill be paid in bills receivable at 80 cents, making bill amount to $37.56.

Mr. THOS. J. ROBERTSON submitted the following resolution, which was referred to the Committee of the Judiciary :

Resolved, That the General commanding this Military District be requested to issue an order, applicable to the State of South Carolina, authorizing any Attorney, Solicitor or Counsellor, admitted to practice in the Courts of the United States, or in any Court of Record in any State, and resident in this State, to appear and practice in all the Courts of this State.

Mr. R. H. CAIN called for the unfinished business of yesterday.

The PRESIDENT announced the unfinished business, the consideration of the report of the Committee on Petitions in relation to the loan of one million dollars, to be asked for from the Congress of the United States.

Mr. C. P. LESLIE, who had the floor when the Convention adjourned Friday, resumed his argument against the measure. He apologized to the Convention for taking up so much of their valuable time. From the general information and opinion of most people, that there was no money in the Treasury of the United States by which Congress could possibly make the loan, he thought, had the question been put at once, the world would say there should have been no argument, but the proposition voted down at once.

But that was not the real question before the house. The real question, when practically stated, was how far the Republican party of South Carolina will tolerate demagogism. That was the question in one of its phases. The second phase was, how much political capital could he (the mover of the petition, Rev. R. H. CAIN) make out of a petition that everybody and the world knew would not bring a dollar for the relief of the people. If the mover of the resolution had, in his argument in support of the measure, shown that there was a reasonable probability that the loan could be obtained if the petition passed the Convention, I would not have said a word. But his argument was an appeal to the passions of the colored people of the State. He undertook to hold out to them the probabilities of their getting land, and told them they were entitled to it, that it was just they should have it. He saw among the crowd of spectators behind the railing, the artizans, the working men, he saw laborers and farmers, and he appealed to them and their passions, and not to the good sense of the house. It then became clear to my mind that the member from Charleston (Rev. R. H. CAIN), from the way he handled the subject, proposed to make political capital for himself, and had he not taken that course, I would not have said a word. As I have previously said, the social position of the mover of the petition, among the colored people of Charleston, is the only unfortunate feature of the case. I am sorry to see that a delegate from Charleston, who stands so

50

well, so high in the community, both for respectability and honor, whose motto is to do right, "though the heavens fall"—a man so intelligent as he is, offer a resolution or petition upon which he knew not one dollar could be obtained, and that it was offered only for political effect.

Mr. R. H. CAIN rose to a question of privilege. He did not think the gentleman had a right to impugn his motives. He thought it unkind and gratuitous.

Mr. C. P. LESLIE disclaimed any intention of impugning the motives of the delegate from Charleston. I regard every question of State, or that concerns the people of the State, a political question; and when I said the member did certain things for political capital, I did not mean to impugn his motives. A man has a right to establish a reputation for honesty, and a character for energy and zeal in behalf of his people, and there was no way in the world of establishing it except in the way that politicians do establish it. Therefore, when I said the delegate from Charleston did this for the purpose of obtaining political capital, I did not say that it was dishonest.

Political questions are of two kinds: First, practical questions; second, impracticable. Impracticable questions are those questions of finance that appear from time to time in political society, such as the raising of funds to defray the expenses of the State, to carry on the government, and for a thousand different purposes, which from time immemorial have been presumed to be necessary to carry on the ordinary business of the government. They excite no great wonder, or cause any great shouts of applause from the populace. They are simply practical questions.

There is another kind of political question called impracticable. These are what the devil uses as instruments to make demagogues. These demagogues are of two kinds; the shrewd, calculating knave, who possesses the necessary status, skill, ingenuity and interest, to prepare his political acts so as to appeal sufficiently to the prejudices of the people as to deter honest men from opposing the schemes for fear of political death. The second class of demagogues are those who have less sense, and, consequently, are not so dangerous. To the first class, I propose to say a few kind remarks before I take my seat. First, could this money have been obtained from Congress would it have been right to have taken it? I did not discuss that question yesterday, but I have shown by facts and figures that this money can not be obtained from Congress, and it is notorious to every man capable of reading the newspapers that it is an impracticable measure. It will revive the expectations of the colored people of obtaining lands by the aid of the Government. It is well known that the whole power of this Government has been invoked to remove this impression from the minds of the colored people. Gen. Howard, the General commanding this department, and even the Radical Gen. Scott, has been repeatedly compelled to inform the colored people of the State that it would never be possible for them to obtain even an acre of ground, unless they worked for it as other people do.

Charleston is noted for possessing some of the keenest wits politically that the world ever saw. Go up Meeting street or down Queen street, or pass by the corners, and borne on the wind whistling along comes the cry of some Charleston politician, " office, office, office."

Sitting with my friends in the town hall of the little town of Blackville, proceeding in order to make nominations of delegates from Barnwell District to this Convention, the stillness of the audience was disturbed by three distinct knocks. The door-keeper was directed to inquire the cause of the disturbance, and the cry comes, " Charleston is here asking to be put upon the Barnwell ticket to go to the great Constitutional Convention." Orangeburg, Edgefield, and almost every other district had been visited in the same manner by these Charleston politicians, rapping away at the door of the nominating meetings, and asking to be put into office. I tried to resist it in my district, but they came there too strong for me, and I was overwhelmed by them.

For these two long years the colored people of these Southern States have, God knows, suffered enough. They have been the prey of merciless speculators; they have been the prey of every man almost who has taken advantage of their situation. I say, in all kindness, the sufferings of this people will never be recorded on earth, they may be recorded in heaven; and I, for one, would not add to their wrongs the deeper wrong of disappointment.

There is one way, thank God, the colored people may be provided with homes, but not in the way suggested by the gentleman from Charleston. Before the next six months roll round, every man will see land selling in this State for the nominal prices of ten to twenty-five cents an acre. I do not expect all the colored people to get land, I do not expect everybody to have money to buy, but I do expect that as many colored people in the State will have the necessary money to buy land, when it brings such low prices as the petition before the house would give, provided they got the million dollars.

I am not willing to hold out inducements to deceive the colored people by virtually telling them a lie for the purpose of making political capital. But I will go as far as any man in practical measures of relief; but I prefer not to deceive them.

Mr. A. J. RANSIER. The question of relief is certainly to the distressed people of this State of the greatest interest. None of the propositions for relief before this body do, in my opinion, appear more feasible and more likely to succeed than the present plan under discussion. It is simply a petition for a loan of one million dollars to be expended through the Bureau, in the purchase of lands of small tracts, twenty acres each, to be given to poor families, the Government to be paid back in the course of five years. The Government is to be secured by liens upon the crops. The earnest and eloquent speeches of the member from Barnwell, both yesterday and to-day, in opposition to this simple measure, has dwelt so much upon the empty condition of the United States Treasury that we might be disposed to think he had some peculiar connection with that department. Why is the gentleman here, claiming to be a representative of the people of South Carolina? I know he has the official sanction for it; but it seems strange that his whole course in this body has produced the strongest impression that he has some peculiar relations with the United States Treasury Department.

I believe he has taken an erroneous view of the measure. He certainly seems to forget the condition of the people he represents? He would have us believe that the Government could not put its hand upon a single dollar, even if it desired to do so. The gentleman, however, does not seem to remember that the Government is daily expending money here through the agency of the Freedmen's Bureau, and would save a handsome sum by the granting of this loan. Under a joint resolution of Congress, adopted in March 1867, there was expended for the relief of the destitute in this State alone, in a period of five months, $110,000. This expenditure was for rations alone to feed the destitute. About sixty-five thousand people were relieved by this means. It should also be remembered that of this number nineteen thousand were white persons. The member from Barnwell has argued as if this was a measure for the exclusive benefit of the colored people. This I deny.

The whole amount expended by that act of 1867 for the ten Southern States was something like $450,000. Now, if some measure like the one now before the Convention had been adopted by Congress in lieu of that act of 1867, I believe the Government would have saved in this State at least the sum of $110,000. If Congress had invested one million dollars through the Freedmen's Bureau for the purchase of lands, it would have enabled these people to have acquired homesteads, fed and clothed themselves, and the Government being secured by liens upon the crops would have been paid back the money.

My only purpose in rising however, was to offer a few practical remarks, and not to detain the house. The member from Barnwell had endeavored to create the impression that this was a measure solely in the interests of the colored people. This I emphatically deny. The official report of the Commissioner of the Freedmen's Bureau shows that it has relieved almost as many whites as blacks, while it is ostensibly an institution, or bureau, for the benefit of freedmen and refugees. This measure proposes to benefit the poor irrespective of color—to benefit all classes of the community.

The member from Barnwell charged the mover of the resolution (Mr. R. H. CAIN) as having appealed to the prejudices and passions of the colored portion of his constituents. I deny it. He has not made one twentieth part the effort to create that impression, or to appeal to the prejudices of the colored people, as the member has to appeal to the whites. He objects, he says, because the petitioner knows not one dollar would be forthcoming. He would have us believe that the Government of the United States is poor indeed. I know not whether he is officially connected with the Treasury Department, but if he really desires to protect it, he should advocate some such measure as this, which I am satisfied would be a saving to the Government.

The gentleman from Barnwell has said that the devil used certain political questions to make demagogues. I forbear to retort, but rather think the impression has already become wide-spread that if the devil has exercised any influence at all upon any member of this house, it has been upon the gentleman from Barnwell.

He stated, again, that the proposition contained in this petition will encourage the hope on the part of the freedmen that the Government has lands to give away. He has deprecated confiscation, and that is the unanimous sentiment of the Convention. And though the gentleman's constituents may not have advanced as high in the scale of civilization as he has himself, I think he will find they are not so entirely ignorant as to believe that from this petition, or the advocacy of it, the Government is to give them land. I would be unworthy of the position I occupy here were I not to express an opinion favorable to this measure. The Bureau of Freedmen, Refugees and Abandoned Lands has cost this Government nearly, if not quite, twelve million dollars a year. That is the estimated annual expense of the Bureau. However necessary it may have been, and however much good it may have accomplished, I am not disposed to see it perpetuated, or continued beyond the time absolutely necessary for the protection of the people. But to abolish this expensive establishment, some such measere as this, by which the wards of the Bureau may be thrown upon their resources and permitted to demonstrate to the world their fitness to earn their bread in accordance with the Almighty's command, "By the sweat of thy brow thou shalt earn thy bread," is necessary to enable them to accomplish such a result and rid the Government of this great incubus. I hope, therefore, the petition will be sustained. We do not propose to wring it from the Government whether it has the money or not. It is but a petition, but I think recommends itself more as a measure of relief than many others endorsed by this Convention.

Mr. G. PILLSBURY. I rise for two reasons. One I term a good reason, the other not. I deem this one of the most important questions appertaining to the well-being of this State before this Convention. My other reason is to give the delegate from Barnwell (Mr. LESLIE) an opportunity to propose a few more questions.

The Convention will observe a remarkable consistency between the remarks of that gentleman made yesterday and those he made to day. If I count right, he has introduced just three arguments against the passage of the petition or resolution. First, he says it will be impossible to get the money; second, that we shall not be very likely to get the money, and third, we shall not get the money. He has, however, this morning introduced one new argument since the discussion yesterday. It seems that he had an opportunity of airing himself out in the community and obtaining the voice of this loyal community, and he comes in this morning with one additional argument, namely, that it is known to the world that this resolution should have been voted down.

Now I believe there are intimations in the good book that we should resist the world; and with reference to a certain personage whom the gentleman so kindly alluded to, calling him by name—if he supposes that I am peculiarly liable to be influenced by that distinguished character, I will state to him, as far as words can go, that I am in favor of the whole scriptural injunction to "Resist the world, the flesh and the Devil."

In his very kind remarks of my colleague from Charleston (Mr. CAIN), impugning his motives very seriously, as simply acting the part of the politician and not the philanthropist or lover of his race, the member from Barnwell did mention that this resolution would have a bad effect upon the community outside, especially upon the colored portion, intimating that it would ruin their expectations of obtaining land. I know it is the old motto that "Hope deferred causeth the heart to break." We have had visions and promises of corn and soup houses, and lands; but the only fulfillment of those promises is one establishment far away up town, under military authority, which disburses soup mainly to the poor whites.

With regard to the $600,000 appropriated to the State, I would ask what encouragement the colored man derived from that appropriation? I would ask any colored delegate on this floor if he personally expects to be benefited one dollar from that appropriation, or expects one of his colored constituents will be benefited thereby. I do not know by what means that money was obtained. Perhaps the gentleman from Barnwell was instrumental in obtaining that appropriation, and thinks that was enough. He also alludes to a resolution adopted here that there was no land for a colored man unless he purchased it. Although it may not have as much bearing upon the question, but I may say that the virtual construction of that resolution was the means of incarcerating a colored man in the Penitentiary, who is still there upon the most frivolous grounds.

I think in this instance we may well imitate the example of the woman and the unjust judge. Let us continue our petition to Congress until it is heard. It is a reasonable request, and at the lowest calculation, if granted, would furnish homes for five, at least, of probably ten or twenty thousand families now out of doors. If this is not enough to excite the humanity of every gentleman in the Convention, then I am greatly mistaken.

Mr. B. F. WHITTEMORE. I might, perhaps, say much upon this subject, but it appears to me that already there has been sufficient said to warrant our minds as to what conclusion we ought to arrive at. Much has been said with regard to the deception that this petition might carry with it. I am perfectly aware of the great trouble that existed through this State with regard to the great question of the colored people receiving land. They have been told by those whom they esteemed their friends that it would be impossible to get land. At the same time it has been known that there existed in the minds of the freed people of the State, that the right person has not come along yet. Now, in order that there may be no deception in the premises, and I have no reason to believe that the delegate who offered the petition was not earnest and sincere in the presentation of it, but, in order to set ourselves right, and that any man may go to his home, or may have the opportunity to ride upon the highway of success, provided he does no wrong to any individual, I submit the following:

Resolved, That the report of the Committee be adopted, and that this petition is not supported by this Convention with a view of deceiving the poor of either race or color, who are homeless or landless, but that

an expression of Congress may be obtained as early as possible as to
how far it is in the power of the Government to aid the unfortunate in
our State in the procurement of land, and thus to assure them as to
their hopes in the whole matter.

Mr. R. B. ELLIOTT.   It is not my design to make a speech.   Sir, I
do not possess the peculiar satire of the gentleman from Barnwell (Mr.
LESLIE), who so forcibly and vehemently opposed the resolution yesterday and this morning; neither, sir, do I possess one-fourth part of
his deep learning or profound eloquence.   I bow in reverence, Mr.
President, to his vast superiority.   If the gentleman had furnished me
with a copy of his resolution which he intended to have presented, and
which differed from this of the gentleman from Charleston (Mr. CAIN)
in but one particular, viz: That it proposed to take the money more
directly out of the Treasury of the United States, inasmuch as it was
the gentleman's (Mr. LESLIE) design to take it from the cotton tax
fund, I would be better able to speak to this question; but, unfortunately, sir, he did not.

Sir, a few days ago, when the gentleman from Kershaw (Mr. JILL-
SON) offered a resolution on Franchise, to which the gentleman from
Barnwell objected.   I rose and requested the gentleman from Kershaw
to strike out the words "*non compos mentis.*"   Sir, I am *very* sorry that
I made that request, and, in reparation for that impropriety, were it
possible to do so at this moment, I would offer a resolution in this form:
That no person who is "*non compos mentis,*" or who is troubled with
no-money-mania, no-land-mania, or any kind of *mania,* shall ever be
allowed to vote or hold any office in this State.   In relation to the voice
of the politicians of Charleston being heard in Edgefield crying out
office! office! the gentleman should recollect that had not that voice been
raised in his behalf, he would not be on this floor to-day to ridicule and
assail those who assisted him when he most needed help.   When it was
unsafe for the gentlemen, on account of his former course, to canvass
his own district, the "Voice of Charleston" did it for him.

Now, Mr. President, to be serious, I claim that this resolution is one
that can result in no possible harm, while it may result in great good.
Feeling assured that this subject has been sufficiently debated on both
sides, I deem it unnecessary for me at this time to enter into a discussion on this question, I will, therefore, take my seat, with the earnest
hope that the resolution will be adopted.

Mr. R. C. DeLARGE.   I trust the resolution of the gentleman from
Darlington will be adopted.   I believe it contains everything embraced
in the petition of my colleague.   I am in favor of the petition.   Look-

ing at it from a different point of view taken by the distinguished and learned gentleman from Barnwell, I feel compelled to differ with him concerning this measure. He has endeavored to make it appear as if it was simply for the benefit of the colored people. The solicitude he has shown for the welfare of the colored people is unnecessary. They, I am confident, can take care of themselves and their interests, as well as the distinguished gentleman from Barnwell. He is one of those who always says figures won't lie. He repeatedly, in attempting to carry a point, goes to figuring, and I propose to prove by his own theory, that is by figuring, that his position is false.

My colleague (Mr. R. H. CAIN) presented a petition asking the Congress of the United States to appropriate one million dollars for a specific purpose—to purchase homesteads for the people of South Carolina ; not the colored people, as the gentleman from Barnwell has attempted to prove, but to all, irrespective of color. He has also attempted to prove that the money cannot be obtained, but has failed to carry conviction to the minds of any of the members. There is plenty of land in this State that can be purchased for two dollars per acre, and one million will buy us five hundred thousand acres ; cut this into small farms of twenty acres, and we have twenty-five thousand farms. Averaging seven persons to a family that twenty acres can sustain, and we have one hundred and seventy-five thousand persons, men, women and children, who, for a million dollars, will be furnished the means of support. That is one-fourth of the entire people of the State. In the census of 1860 the number of inhabitants is put down at 703,717. If we buy land at a dollar an acre, we can furnish three hundred and fifty thousand people with the means of support. The member from Barnwell has assumed that this petition will not be granted. He says the Treasury is empty, and the last report of the Secretary of the Treasury showed that no money could be obtained. Very often there may not be ten thousand dollars in the Treasury one day and there may be ten million dollars the next, collected by the Internal Revenue Bureau.

Again, the member from Barnwell endeavors to create the impression that every member of the Charleston delegation is seeking office. He tells us of a nominating convention at Blackville, and of spirit rapping at the door ; the wind coming through the key hole and saying Charleston, Charleston is here. Unfortunately for his district, but fortunately perhaps for the gentleman, Charleston was compelled to do for Barnwell what this measure proposes to do for the poor of South Carolina, irrespective of color: that is to supply the deficiencies of that district by giving it outside assistance, and no one has more cause to thank

51

Charleston than the distinguished member himself, for if it had not been for that spirit rapping at the door, the gentleman's spirit would not have met with the spirits in this Convention.

Again, with great solemnity, he tells us this measure is intended to deceive the people—that it is an electioneering dodge.

The gentleman, no doubt, judges from his own electioneering experience. I believe, when my colleague presented that petition, he did it with the desire to benefit the poor people of the State. So far as holding out hopes of their obtaining possession of lands from Congress without compensation, I doubt whether any members ever opposed such an idea more vehemently than did the Charleston members of my delegation. Perhaps as much cannot be said with a show of truth of some who now oppose this measure and who, sometime since, held out to the people of their district the forlorn hope that by taxation of idle lands they would be thrown into the market and sold at such a low price the people would be able to buy them. The people of that District have long since learned that they were deluded by those men who now pretend to represent them. In one breath the gentleman from Barnwell states that it would be impossible to get the million dollars from the Freedmen's Bureau, because we had voted for a resolution to continue that Bureau until reconstruction was completed, and in the very next breath he told us he believed that reconstruction would be completed in about three months, and that a measure similar to this could be carried in the Legislature of the State.

Mr. C. P. LESLIE. I said no such thing.

Mr. R. C. DeLARGE. If I knew anything I knew it would not require the seven millions of dollars in the Bureau to carry on that Department for the next three months. The statement that "if that institution had the money, they knew how to get rid of it," was a good argument in favor of this measure, which has for its object the loan of a portion of that money for the purchase of lands for the houseless people of this State. Again, he stated that not a dollar of that fund could be used for any other purpose than that of furnishing rations to the destitute. Not over three weeks ago the Assistant Commissioner of this State went to Washington to get General Howard to appropriate a portion of that fund to supply certain parties with agricultural implements to enable them to carry on their planting operations, and give work to others. But I am not confident that this money can be had, neither has the gentleman proven that he is so well acquainted with the condition of the United States Treasury as to be able to say positively that the money cannot be had. But if it can be obtained, and this land purchased, we benefit twenty thousand starving beggars, white and black, and relieve the Government of the expense of supporting them.

Again, he attempts to prove that these people can never get land without paying for it. The petition of my colleague proposes to give them land upon a credit of five years with the distinct understanding that the Government is to be reimbursed in that time.

There are over one thousand freedmen in this State who have, within the last year, purchased lands from the native whites, on the same terms. We propose that the Government should aid us in the purchase of more lands, to be divided into small tracts, and given on the above mentioned credit to homeless families to cultivate for their support. It is well known that in every District the freedmen are roaming from one side to the other, not because they expected to get land, but because the large landholders are not able to employ them, and will not sell their lands unless the freedmen have the money to pay cash for them These are facts that cannot be contradicted by the gentleman from Barnwell. I know one large landholder in Colleton District who had twenty odd freedmen working for him upon his plantation the entire year He raised a good crop; but the laborers have not succeeded in getting any reimbursement for their labor. They are now roaming to Charleston and back, trying to get remuneration for their services. We propose to give them lands, and to place them in a position by which they will be enabled to sustain themselves.

In doing this, we will add to the depleted Treasury of the State, and the large plantation system of the country will be broken up. The large plantations will be divided into small farms, giving support to more people and yielding more taxes to the State. It will bring out the whole resources of the State. I desire it to be distinctly understood that I do advocate this measure simply for the benefit of my own race.

Mr. C. C. BOWEN. It was not my purpose to have said anything, and I am sorry that so much time has been spent in this debate; I shall not go into details, but confine myself strictly to the record.

The gentleman from Barnwell has stated that the district he represents has been troubled with people from Charleston. I desire to ask him who invited the people of Charleston to his district, and for what purpose they were invited? I recollect when he called on some of us and prayed for God's sake that we should go to Barnwell and secure his nomination; we did go and helped him; but judging by his career in the past, two men were put on the same ticket to hold him in check; these men are here for that purpose. This petition has been presented here asking for relief. If there is one question that ought to claim the attention of this Convention more than another, it is the subject of relief. The people from one end of the land to the other look to this Convention for relief. I contend that that is the object for which every delegate was sent here. I disagree with the petition in this, that it does not ask for enough; I wish to God that it had asked for five millions, for I believe we could obtain that amount. Let us, at least, try and see what we can do, and having done all we can, we can do no more. We know not what we can do. The proposition is only to ask Congress to step forward and assist the suffering people of South Carolina. We do not ask the Government to give it, but simply to loan it to us. Surely there can be no impropriety in that. Other States have asked for much larger sums.

Mr. C. P. LESLIE. Have you not changed your opinion since last night.

Mr. C. C. BOWEN. I have not; I certainly think the plan feasible, and I only regret that the sum is not more. It has been charged that it is a political dodge on the part of the members of the Charleston delegation; I only ask the same measure of grains for the Charleston delegation accorded to others; and I would remind the member from Barnwell of the advice in that good old book, the Bible, "Judge not, lest ye be judged."

Mr. C. P. LESLIE. There is no grain in your neighborhood; it is all chaff.

Mr. C. C. BOWEN. Deception seems to rule uppermost in the mind of the delegate from Barnwell. Judging from his language, I would say it must have been a peculiar dodge in his own State; I know nothing that would bring prosperity to this country so quick as the relief of these people now wandering over the land, houseless and homeless. I sincerely trust every delegate will meet this question fairly, and vote for the measure.

Mr. W. J. WHIPPER. In attempting to speak upon this question, it is with no view of defeating the resolution or adoption of the report of the Committee. I intend to vote against the measure, and take this opportunity of saying so. I am the more zealous to do so when I find members of this body oscillating as they are, and openly declaring that they are going to vote for it, though believing it wrong. I am the more zealous of doing so when I find members afraid to follow their honest convictions, and then meet their constituency. Whatever may be my conviction as to the policy of this measure, I, in my heart of hearts, believe it will be detrimental to the people and detrimental to the State, and for that reason shall record my vote against it. I am not afraid to meet my constituents, nor afraid to meet the people of South Carolina, and answer for all that I shall do here, believing it to be for their best interest. I am willing that time should decide as to the propriety of the course I pursue in this body. I say it is my earnest desire that that petition should be voted down, as it should have been without discussion.

With regard to the gentleman from Barnwell, upon whom it has been the province of the delegates to pounce so wickedly, I would say he has told much that is true, and much that they will find hereafter incontrovertible. As to the office seeking of the Charleston delegates, I have nothing to do.

In the first place, I regard the petition a failure. I am opposed to one million of dollars being brought to the State of South Carolina to be disposed of as that petition proposes. I am in favor of any measure of relief that will affect the people permanently ; but if we can devise no other measure than this, then I am opposed to it. Admitting it can be done, that Congress may appropriate one million of dollars, what will be the result ? The gentleman from Charleston tells you it will give homes to one-fourth of the people of the State. What kind of homes would they be ? It would place them in possession of five and one-seventh acres ; just about enough to starve to death decently that one-fourth of the people. If you want to make a man an everlasting pauper, do as the United States did in my district, make him the owner of some ten acres. He cannot raise more than enough to feed his babies upon it. Men in this State must have more land.

Mr. B. F. RANDOLPH. One would suppose from the gentleman's question that a man having ten acres of land is worse off than if he had nothing at all, and were out in the public highway. I desire to know if that is the gentleman's opinion.

Mr. W. J. WHIPPER. The gentleman asks whether or not I think that a man with ten acres of land is worse off than a man out on the public highway. I say not. But what I do say to that is, that if a man can scarcely live upon ten acres, he cannot upon five and a half. I claim that this measure will not benefit the people of South Carolina, and upon that ground I oppose it. The very moment this resolution passes and the papers publish that a petition has been sent to Congress to buy lands for the poor of this State, a clamor for land will at once arise, the freedmen will forsake their contracts and at once leave their places of employment. You raise the hopes of the entire poor people of the country, you draw around the land offices, which they will inevitably create, a multitude, three fourths of whom will be compelled to go away with shattered hopes. Let me give you an illustration. In my district quite a scarcity of provisions existed. The Bureau, in its wisdom and charity, sent to that district twelve hundred bushels of corn, and I know that I am speaking the sentiments of my constituents when I say that that distribution of corn had an injurious effect upon labor.

This miserable meagre measure of relief but looses the laborer from the land and raises his hopes, leading him to believe he is to realize all he has longed for for years, and with that object in view goes to the land office perhaps, only to return to his house disappointed, and see his prospects for another year frustrated. You will have three-fourth without an inch of land, and another fourth with but five and one-seventh acres. If you wish to see such a state of affairs, vote for that petition. If Congress does not, in its wisdom, see fit to withhold this loan, you will see that condition of affairs to your satisfaction.

It is said we must do something here, or the people will never ratify the Constitution. There is no one would be prouder to do something that would give permanent relief than I would. If we can give any thing, give the poor man property in his labor, and we will have effected that relief. There cannot be a delegate from the coast but knows of the dire effect of holding out inducements to hold land, produced upon the laborers on the adjacent islands. Only about two years ago the Commissioner was compelled, with the bayonet, to force the people to go to work for the very reason that these inducements, with regard to owning land, had been held out to them. They had been made to believe they should hold them. The sooner the public mind is disabused of that impression, the sooner every man knows that to acquire land he must earn it; the sooner he feels the Government has no lands to dispose of or to give him, the better. Do what is necessary to protect the laborer in his labor and you will effect the greatest possible good. All these temporary and meagre measures of relief that are gotten up, I fear are too much for political purposes. I believe a majority of the members of this body do not believe this measure is permanent in its character. They look upon it as a measure of relief that in its details must fail. But they ask, must we face our constituency—go home and say we voted against that which certain members said was calculated to relieve the poor? Must we say we voted against a donation? No, it will frustrate our future prospects. But to whatever political death it may consign me, I shall vote against it.

I know members upon this floor have said in the last twenty-four hours that they intend to swim with the tide. I regret to see this disposition, for in my judgment if a measure does not meet the conscientious convictions of the members, they should vote against it and take the consequences. I believe the adoption of this measure would bring interminable difficulties upon the Assistant Commissioner of your district. But I warn you, gentlemen, against the final results. Are you not going to disappoint the people beyond all expectation ? I warn you against the indignation of the people whom you may deceive by that measure, and whose hopes you raise only to be blasted a few months hence. You may establish a measure giving to the poor man property in his labor. Do that, and you further the permanent interests of the State, build up the waste places, erect school houses, give encouragement to the mechanic and the laborer, and furnish the means for the cultivation of those lands.

If you create property in labor, the landholder will be compelled to divide and sell his lands, and the laborer will be able to purchase a home for himself. I desire to see established a system of taxation which will make it unprofitable for a man to keep lands uncultivated. We are not here to enter into any begging scheme, even if expedient to do so. I do not believe that it is for the interest of the people of this State. But protect labor and secure the laborer in all his right, and with their own strong arms and willing hands the people will accumulate property for themselves, and purchase homesteads with the results of honest industry.

Mr. A. MIDDLETON. Perhaps my voice may not be heard in this assembly. I am no speaker, no politician, and cannot make a political speech. I exceedingly regret the debate on this most important question ; if the question had simply passed without debate, I believe it would have been for us as delegates, better for the community, better for the colored people and better for the whites. As to my colleague from Barnwell, I reg et the manner in which he has spoken of those gentlemen from Charleston that represent Barnwell, and who used their influence to have him elected.

Mr. C. P. LESLIE. Are you not not aware that the colored men of that district waited upon me in a body, and I at first refused to be a candidate ?

Mr. A. MIDDLETON. I am not a politician, and therefore cannot answer a political question. If the gentleman is a sinner, I, as a clergyman, will, if he desires to know how to escape the wrath to come, enlighten him. South Carolina, my native State, lies in the dust, she needs help from somewhere—she must have aid. I feel the importance of this measure, but after the great guns that have been fired, feel a want of ability to handle this subject in a becoming manner. Since I have been here, I have written ten or twelve letters in answer to my constituents desiring to know whether the Convention will assist them in obtaining lands. I have invariably told them that the Convention had no lands to give to or divide amongst them. But here is a measure of relief proposed, to be sought from Congress, by the loan of a million of dollars from the Treasury of the United States. My colleague, I think, if it had been for five millions, would not have opposed it.

It has been said that if this measure is passed, the people will abandon their contracts. I will deny the assertion so far as concerns Barnwell District. My people will only leave their employment when they receive no pay for their labor. The gentleman does not know them as well as I do, who has sat at their firesides and eaten their hoecake. I hope the measure will be adopted, and that it may bring relief for the people of South Carolina.

Mr. F. L. CARDOZO. This question has been mingled by some of the opposition with a great deal of personality. They freely imputed the most malicious motives to their opponents, and while I sat listening to those imputations I was forcibly reminded of the proverb, "It takes a rogue to catch a rogue." I will make one remark, and then will be done with personalities. The gentleman from Barnwell has referred constantly to the gentleman from Charleston; but it is believed that the gentleman from Barnwell is an old cast off Charleston politician. I remember his obtaining a hall of me and asking me to go help him at Barnwell. I positively refused to do it, because I thought, as the gentleman from Edgefield has said, that he (LESLIE) was *non compos mentis.*

I am surprised at the gentleman from Beaufort, who just about two weeks ago rose in this Convention and advocated two measures of relief for the planters of this State, to save their property from going under the hammer of the auctioneer for debts contracted for the purchase of slaves. He was very eloquent in favor of those two measures of relief that would save to the rebel planters their old estates. But now, when a measure comes up to request help for the poor colored people, the very same eloquence is employed on the opposite side.

I would only say to him who imputed improper motives to the gentleman who originated this measure, it is currently reported that he is the tool of rebels, and his course has certainly justified that report. I opposed those two measures of relief that he favored, for two reasons; first, I said they were unjust in themselves. Men had contracted debts with their eyes wide open, knew the risks they run, took those risks, and if they were honest men, would pay their debts; but if they were dishonest, I claim they ought to be made to pay their debts. They contracted those debts in the rebel cause, to keep poor colored people down, to perpetuate slavery, and, having done that, they should suffer the consequences. Let their large estates be divided, and the poor colored people would have a better opportunity of buying lands. Those measures of relief were passed. This Convention refused to give the colored people that legal opportunity, and I would say to the gentlemen who voted for those measures of relief, if they are consistent, if they are the friends of the colored man, they may, with equal consistency, vote for this measure. The argument is used that we are not likely to get the money asked for. But how can they tell? I think we are just as likely to get it, and more likely to obtain it, than the thirty millions asked by the Georgia Convention for the planters of the South, who have tried to reduce the colored man again to slavery or its equivalent condition—serfdom.

The gentleman from Beaufort argued that this was an impolitic measure, because it would not give all the colored people lands, and I would say better that than none at all. It will do a great deal of good. It is precisely what the Assistant Commissioner of this State has been doing in this District. No later than last night he told me that he had a large quantity of provisions, amounting to a large sum, to aid the people of this State, and had been told to give it out freely. He wrote to General Howard, stating that it would be better to assist the planters, taking a lien on the crops, and he sent him word to do so; took a lien upon the crops, and said when he got the money he would build school houses with it. But the crops have failed, and it is probable he will have no return. That was a help to the white planter. The Assistant Commissioner, however, made no invidious distinction, for a truer and nobler friend, both to the colored and white man does not exist in our State. He helps all alike, and assists all alike. The poor freedmen were induced, by many Congressmen even, to expect confiscation. They held out the hope of confiscation. General Sherman did confiscate, gave the lands to the freedmen; and if it were not for President Johnson, they would have them now. The hopes of the freedmen have not been realized, and I do not think that asking for a loan of one million, to be paid by a mortgage upon the land, will be half as bad as has been supposed. I have been told by the Assistant Commissioner that he has been doing on a private scale what this petition proposes to do. I say every opportunity for helping the colored man should be seized upon. I think the adoption of this measure will do honor to the Convention. We should certainly vote for some measure of relief for the colored men, as we

52

have to the white men, who mortgaged their property to perpetuate slavery, and whom they have liberated from their bonds.

Mr. N. G. PARKER. I am glad that the gentleman who has just taken his seat has distinctly laid down the proposition that any member who votes against this petition votes against the colored man. I am a friend to the colored man, and he knows it. I have a record extending back for twenty years that shows it. I have voted for measures of relief, and intend to vote for every practicable measure of the kind introduced into this body. I voted in favor of requesting General Canby to suspend the collection of debts. I voted in favor of annulling all contracts where the purchase of slaves was the consideration. The first was an effort to procure temporary relief, but did not ask it from Congress. The second measure was a proposition which, in my opinion, will afford permanent relief to the people of South Carolina, and did not ask aid from Congress. I have been fortunate, or unfortunate, as the case may be, in having voted in the majority on most measures of importance in this House; but, judging from the debate to-day, I can see quite clearly that, unless I can convince some of the members and bring them to my way of thinking upon this question, I will be in the minority; but I am willing to be of the minority when I think the minority is right. The colored people all over South Carolina have been deceived, and now a proposition comes before this House that would continue that deception. That is my view of the case. I know we cannot get the relief this petition proposes. I do not, however, agree with the distinguished member from Barnwell, that I would not petition Congress merely because I thought Congress would not act upon it. On the contrary, I would petition Congress, in season and out of season, at any time, for any favor which I deemed beneficial to the people.

The hour of half-past 2 o'clock having arrived, the Convention adjourned, Mr. PARKER having the floor.

TWENTY-EIGHTH DAY.

Monday, February 17, 1868.

The Convention assembled at half-past 10 A. M., and was called to order by the PRESIDENT.

Prayer was offered by the Rev. B. BURTON.

The roll was called, and a quorum answering to their names, the PRESIDENT announced the Convention ready to proceed to business.

The Journal of Saturday was read and approved.

The PRESIDENT called for reports of Standing Committees.

Mr. B. F. RANDOLPH, from the Committee on the Miscellaneous Provisions of the Constitution, presented the following reports, which were ordered to be printed :

ARTICLE —.

MILITIA.

SECTION 1. The Militia of this State shall consist of all able-bodied male residents of the State between the ages of eighteen and forty-five years, except such persons as are now, or may hereafter be exempted by the law of the United States or of this State, and shall be organized, armed, equipped and disciplined as the General Assembly may by law provide.

SEC. 2. The Governor shall have power to call out the militia to execute the laws, repel invasion, repress insurrection, and preserve the common peace.

SEC. 3. The Governor may appoint the Adjutant-General, Quartermaster-General, and such other officers of his staff as the General Assembly may direct.

ARTICLE —.

CHARITABLE INSTITUTIONS.

SECTION 1. Institutions for the benefit of the insane, blind, deaf and dumb, and the poor, shall always be fostered and supported by this State, and shall be subject to such regulations as the General Assembly may enact.

SEC. 2. The Directors of the Penitentiary shall be elected or appointed, as the General Assembly may direct.

SEC. 3. The Trustees of the benevolent and other State institutions, such as may be hereafter created, shall be appointed by the Governor, by and with the consent of the Senate ; and upon all nominations made by the Governor, the question shall be taken by yeas and nays, and entered upon the journals.

SEC. 4. The Governor shall have power to fill all vacancies that may occur in the offices aforesaid, until the next session of the General Assembly, and until a successor or successors shall be appointed and confirmed.

ARTICLE —

CORPORATIONS.

SECTION 1. The General Assembly shall pass no special act conferring corporate powers.

SEC. 2. Corporations may be formed under general laws, but all such laws may from time to time be altered or repealed.

SEC. 3. The property of corporations now existing or hereafter created, shall be subject to taxation.

SEC. 4. No right of way shall be appropriated to the use of any corporation until full compensation therefor shall be first made in money, or first secured by a deposit of money to the owner, irrespective of any benefit from any improvement proposed by such corporation, which compensation shall be ascertained by a jury of twelve men, in a Court of Record, as shall be prescribed by law.

SEC. 5. Dues from corporations shall be secured by such individual liability of the stockholders and other means, as may be prescribed by law.

SEC. 6. All general laws and special acts passed pursuant to this section, shall make provisions therein for fixing the personal liability of stockholders under proper limitations ; and shall prevent and punish fraudulent misrepresentations as to the capital, property and resources of such corporations ; and shall also regulate the public use of all franchises which have heretofore been, or hereafter may be created or granted, by or under the authority of the State, and shall limit all tolls, imposts, and other charges and demands under such laws.

ARTICLE —

MISCELLANEOUS.

SECTION 1. Columbia shall be the seat of Government until otherwise ordered by the General Assembly.

SEC. 2. No person shall be elected or appointed to any office in this State, unless he possess the qualifications of an elector.

SEC. 3. Every person elected or appointed to any office under this Constitution, shall, before entering on the duties thereof, take an oath or affirmation to support the Constitution of the United States and of this, State and also an oath of office.

SEC. 4. Lotteries, and the sale of lottery tickets, for any purpose whatever, are prohibited, and the General Assembly shall prevent the same by penal laws.

SEC. 5. There shall be a seal of the State, which shall be kept by the Secretary of State, and be used by him officially, and shall be called the great seal of the State of South Carolina, and shall be attached to all official acts of the Governor (his signature to acts and resolves of the General Assembly excepted,) requiring authentication. The General Assembly shall provide for an appropriate device and motto for said seal.

SEC. 6. The people have a right peaceably to assemble together to consult for the common good, to instruct their representatives, and to petition the General Assembly for a redress of grievances.

SEC. 7. The State Library shall be subject to such regulations as the General Assembly may prescribe.

SEC. 8. The General Assembly may direct, by law, in what manner, and in what Courts, suits may be brought against the State.

SEC. 9. Divorces from the bonds of matrimony shall not be allowed but by the judgment of a Court, as shall be prescribed by law.

SEC. 10. No person who denies the existence of a God shall hold any office under this Constitution, nor be allowed his oath in any Court.

SEC. 11. Whenever any public officer shall be convicted of misdemeanor in office, he shall be removed from office, and thereafter disqualified for holding any office of trust or profit under authority of this State, unless the General Assembly shall, by a two-thirds vote, remove such disability.

SEC. 12. The printing of the laws, journals, bills, legislative documents and papers for each branch of the General Assembly, with the printing required for the Executive and other departments of State, shall be let on contract, in such manner as shall be prescribed by law.

SEC. 13. There may be established in the Secretary of State's office a Bureau of Statistics, under such regulations as may be prescribed by law.

SEC. 14. The real and personal property of a woman, held at the time of her marriage, or that which she may thereafter acquire, either by gift, grant, or inheritance, or devise, shall not be subject to levy and sale for her husbands debts, but may be bequeathed, devised, or alienated by her the same as if she were unmarried : *Provided*, That no gift or grant from the husband to the wife shall be detrimental to the just claims of his creditors.

The unfinished business of Saturday was called up.

The PRESIDENT announced the unfinished business to be the consideration of the report of the Committee on Petitions, in relation to the loan of one million dollars, to be asked for from the Congress of the United States.

Mr. N. G. PARKER. I was interrupted in my remarks on Saturday by the hour of adjournment having arrived, and I shall ask the indulgence of the Convention to but a few moments longer. I would not trespass upon its time, but I regard this as a question of too much importance to pass it by without giving expression to a few thoughts that have suggested themselves to my mind.

As I said on Saturday, I am the friend of the colored man. I can remember when was first raised the standard of anti-slavery, and, child as I was, I became at once an abolitionist, and never, for a moment, swerved from a fixed purpose to do all in my power to accomplish their deliverance from bondage. I have been familiar with every effort that has been made in this country in their behalf since the first Liberator was published in the city of Boston. I have shown my devotion to the cause by aiding in the organization of the first colored regiment of soldiers ever placed in the service of the United States. I have stood shoulder to shoulder with them in the contest which resulted in their freedom. I have no regrets for the past, and there is no man in this State or out of it who will do more, or dare do more than I will to secure, maintain, perpetuate and defend the rights of the race, their full civil, political, educational, property, and all other rights that mankind can claim than I will. I have said thus much, because some of the speakers in the opposition have said that "we who have voted so liberally for every measure of relief for the white man, now that there is a measure of relief for the colored man, are opposed to it, therefore are no friend to the colored man."

I was under the impression up to nearly the close of the debate on Saturday, that this petition asked only aid for the freedmen, the little word "white" escaped my attention when it was read. My opposition to the measure was first aroused, because I did not like the distinction. I am opposed to a distinction being made; I am opposed to legislating for a class, and defining that class by the words "white," "freedmen" and "colored."

I have said that I was opposed to legislating for a class. I do not like to hear the word white or colored spoken in debate. If it had been left to me, I would have kept both words out of debate on this floor, and out of the Constitution. I hope to live to see the time when color, as applied to men, will be expunged from the vocabulary of words. It is heathenish, and behind the ideas of this progressive age.

Nearly every member of this body, the reporters and all the speakers, on the first day understood it just as I did; and the distinguished gentleman from Charleston (Mr. CARDOZO) who preceded me in debate on Saturday, so understood it; the burden of his song was, that we who opposed the measure, opposed it because we were not friends to the colored man, appealing, as it is always his custom, to the passions and prejudices of this body whenever he enters into the discussion of any question on this floor. I am indebted to the gentleman from Charleston who sits quite near me, the Chairman of the Election and Franchise Committee (Mr. DeLARGE), for the discovery of the word white in the petition; he says this is a measure asking relief for the whites as well as the colored; he denies that it is class relief. I find the word " white" then, so little, however, was it thought of that were it not for the sharp eyes of the gentleman just referred to, it probably never would have been discovered. I am glad he found it; I take it that it means what it says, that if this measure is adopted, that the mover of it, and the Committee who reported it, so understood it. I insist, however, that the practical working of it was intended wholly to apply to the colored, and the character of the entire debate shows it. The mover of the resolution so understood it; his remarks, his speeches show it, and nothing else; the word white was a mere subterfuge, but as the word white was inserted then, and the mover of it, and at least one of the speakers, has admitted that it meant white, and said that poor whites were to be considered just as much as the poor colored, then I do not object to this measure on account of the distinction of color; that objection is entirely removed. Now, as to the measure as it really is, that is asking Congress to appropriate a million of dollars, and loan it for the purchase of homes to sell poor men on a credit, I wish the Government of the United States was able to do so. I know she is not. I have no idea that she will consent to do it.

As I understand the proposition now, it is to ask the Congress of the United States for money to buy homesteads for the poor. A very modest request I admit. Congress will certainly get one idea of us, and that is that we have plenty of assurance. I wonder what our radical friends in Massachusetts, New York and Ohio, will say to this very modest request? I wonder, still further, what they would say if Congress should grant it? I tremble for their answer. The poor are everywhere present, or in the language of Scripture, "The poor ye have always with you." They are scattered all over the earth. They are the mass of every country, every nation on the globe. There are a great number of them in all the Northern and Western States, and I tell you, Mr. President, that the destitution that prevails this winter in those snow clad States is greater than it has ever been before. Thousands, yes millions, are out of employment, and what is the cause of it. I cannot stop now to elaborate the causes, but I will only briefly allude to them. War and its results are directly the cause of it. One of the results of the war, and the principal one, was the overthrow of slavery and tyranny in the Southern States; this was the good result of it; but the expense it caused the nation to do this, and the debt it incurred, and the overthrow of the labor system and consequent disturbance of trade and commerce, was the immediate evils. The burdensome taxation which followed is another principal cause of distress which now prevails in the Northern and Western States. The fact is patent that all the manufacturing States need aid ; and let me tell you if the Congress of the United States grants additional aid to any of the unreconstructed States, for anything further than to perfect the reconstruction already half consummated, and the support of the Military and the Freedmen's Bureau, that in my opinion such a howl will go up as never was heard before, and I for one, would despair of success.

Our friends are trembling at Washington to-day, and all over the country, lest New Hampshire should cast a Democratic vote at her approaching election. I am of the opinion that if Congress should pass the appropriation called for just at this particular time, that every State from Maine to California would roll up such a Democratic vote in the coming election that was never heard of, or dreamt of, by the most ardent Democrat in this country. The result of the elections for the last year should not be unheeded.

Where would be our reconstruction if Andrew Johnson and the Democratic party had the handling of us ?

I look over and beyond the petty scheme of self-advancement in the measure now before us. I regard the triumph of the principles of the dominant party in this country as paramount to every other consideration. I am looking forward to the perfect reconstruction of these States upon the basis of equal rights and privileges to all men. And when I see, or think I see, staked upon a single die all that is worth living for, all that I have fought for, all that I hope for on earth, I have no words to express my emotions. Ah! Mr. President, the truest friend to the poor and oppressed is he who will contribute the most for them. The best friend to reconstruction is he who, leaving self out of view, will consult only the general good. The best friend of the colored man is he who has stood by them and their cause through thick and thin, through fire and sword. If now calamity befalls the poor and distressed people of South Carolina, it will, in my opinion, come to them through the bad management of ill advisers. The ingenuity of the devil could not have devised a measure so fraught with evil as the one before us—it is one that is intended to kill both ways. I do not say that the mover of it had any such intentions. I accuse no man of evil intentions. I dislike to hear such accusations, and I detest the manner in which some members discuss the intentions of other members. I will abuse no one. I believe, however, that the mover of the resolution begins already to see the evil effects of it. If I was an enemy to reconstruction, I do not know of any measure that I could introduce, better calculated for mischief, than the one before us.

I do not hesitate to say that I consider this the most serious question that has yet come before this body. If it fails to pass now, our enemies might use it to defeat reconstruction ; if it passes, it will deceive the poor unfortunate people of the State, who have so often been deceived already. This is why it will kill both ways. Fail to adopt it, and every enemy to reconstruction could say to the uneducated colored people of the country, " Your Republicans, in Convention, had an opportunity to vote you a million .of dollars to give you all homes, and they refused to do it." Therefore, between the two evils I shall choose the least. I shall vote for it, but not without a protest ; not a protest against getting the money, for I am sure that we cannot get it ; but a protest against such deceptive measures. I am expecting momentarily to hear from Washington in reply to a telegram which I sent, asking if Congress can aid us, and I expect that answer to be no. If it is no, then our action in adopting this resolution acts as deception. The poor people all over the State will hear that we have voted them all a farm, and will wait in vain expectation of getting it. This is the reason I feel so deeply upon the subject. I never believed in the policy of deceiving the people, even for party purposes.

The Government has plenty of land for all who will accept of it ; better land than there is in South Carolina. She has lands in Mississippi, Arkansas, and in all the great States West of the Mississippi River. Go anywhere where she already owns it, and it is as free to you as it is to any person. When the poor people of the East want lands they travel westward. That was the way the great West was built up to wealth and prosperity. I remember when the great State of Ohio had less population than South Carolina, and when that great city, the pride of the West, Cincinnati, was nothing but a mere village.

The Treasury of the United States has already as many drafts upon it as it can well bear. They have no money to purchase lands in South Carolina to sell on a credit—it is asking too much. Look at the almost overwhelming debt of the nation, and would you colored men, or white men, seek to increase it ? For what was it contracted ? and what keeps the expenses of Government to-day so large ? It was contracted to make you free, and it is continually increased to preserve, protect and defend your freedom.

There never was a more liberal and humane government, nor never

53

one that made such herculian efforts to retrieve the past as she has made and is making. We cannot ask her to do more than she is doing. There is such a thing as disgusting our friends. Do not let us weary them. If she will continue to afford us the protection she has afforded us in the past three years, if she will continue to the end in sustaining the reconstruction she commenced, if she will sustain the Freedmen's Bureau as long as it is a necessity, and give us the military necessary to protect and defend us, in God's name let us be satisfied.

Mr. D. H. CHAMBERLAIN. I think it is to be greatly regretted that this long discussion upon the question which we have before us this morning has induced any of the members upon the floor to indulge in abusive personalities or imputation of interested and improper motives in the position which they have severally taken. I am aware for myself of no occasion, not even the temptation, to speak under excitement, to be governed by passion in my discussion or my consideration of this question.

When my friend from Charleston (Mr. R. H. CAIN) introduced the proposition, in one of the ablest speeches to which I have had the pleasure of listening during the sitting of the Convention, it commended my hearty approval and judgment, and I sympathized with it. And not even the extraordinary speech, tone or manner of the member from Barnwell (Mr. LESLIE), or the still more extraordinary position of my other friend from that District (Mr. PARKER,) could induce me to attribute any but the most disinterested and upright motives to those gentlemen. I commence to-day by saying that I conceive and insist that every delegate upon the floor is looking upon the question with proper motives, and acting for the good of the whole people of South Carolina. A brave man, we are told, never boasts of his courage; least of all does he assail that of his neighbors, and I suggest modestly if gentlemen desire to retain the reputation of acting from pure and upright motives, there is a fairer and better way of obtaining it than indulging indiscriminately in assigning improper motives to others.

There is a pleasing but delusive word which is in the mouths of almost all men, and that is the word relief. I am astonished that not only in this Convention, but in reading the reports of other Conventions at the ideas, principles, measures and policy which that word relief is made to cover. If anybody will examine the ordinance passed by the Reconstruction Convention of South Carolina, they will find, under the delusive title of relief, that we have opened the ball of repudiation. As I have said before, I am opposed to repudiation in all its forms, or anything that looks either in principle or in fact to repudiation. But I am in favor of relief; and in this proposition for a loan, we have the plan of a pure, genuine, honest measure of relief, which even the jealous legal mind of my friend from Fairfield, (Mr. RUTLAND), could not dispute, and against which no ingenuity could raise a legal doubt.

I confess I was not a little astonished that some gentlemen, whose voices a few days ago were raised in such earnest entreaties for a measure of relief to the people of South Carolina have not been heard on this question. Where is the impassioned eloquence of my friend from Sumter (Mr. F. J. MOSES, Jr.), or the sound of the scholarly lips of my friend from Newberry (Mr. DUNCAN), that they have not been pleading the cause of the poor oppressed and loyal majority of the people of South Carolina.

It would not be kind, scarcely parliamentary to say, or even suggest, that it was because those who were to be benefited by the measure were the poor despised black people of the State.

In the first place, I want to ask the question whether there is any need of relief, and I ask a question to which I conceive there can be but one answer. There is a class, as I have already denominated them, the loyal majority, in this State, who are to-day in need of some measure of relief.

Why, Mr. President, I am not going to range on fairy ground, or paint a picture of my fancy, but I am going to tell you about a class in this community whom I know personally, and stand to-day in this situation. They do not own one foot of land. The last two years' disasters to the cotton crop have left them without anything to do. Around them are the greedy, merciless, relentless few who own every foot of the soil. On the first of January they were told if they went to work upon the lands at $5 per month for men and $3 per month for women, they could stay; if not, the United States soldiers would drive them from the soil. They declined. They went from plantation to plantation, and received the same answer. With this combination against them, there was before this people a dark and impenetrable cloud, a thick, insuperable wall, which neither my vision, nor do I think any human vision, can look beyond, which nothing but the sublime spirit which puts its trust in God can overcome.

Need I ask the question whether this relief is necessary?

But I come to the second question. Will this measure relieve them? A sufficient answer to that is, it will certainly do something towards it. I know it will not relieve all, but I know, of that community with which I am acquainted, which comprises a very large majority in this State of the colored people, I know if one worthy man out of ten received aid enough to enable him to plant himself upon his own soil, to spend his industry upon his own land, to build up a competence and independence for himself, that there is no argument in the world that could be pointed to with such effect as the example of colored men standing as owners of the soil, free and independent in their own possessions. If I knew that only one out of a hundred of the deserving men of this State, white or black, now in distress, could be relieved, I would vote for the present measure for the sake of the example I could establish, that I could point to men in their own condition in life, who had carved out for themselves competence and independence. It is no argument to point the colored man to the white man who owns the land and is wealthy and independent; but if I can point my people to their own color and condition, who have by their industry, honesty and general good character established a name and property in the community, I shall have a lever to take hold of which shall move the whole class in our community.

Much has been said and very extraordinary statements made by my friend from Barnwell (Mr. LESLIE) with reference to deceiving the colored people. This body a few days ago adopted a resolution introduced by my friend from Georgetown, which declared "that this Convention had no lands to give away, no act of confiscation had been passed, and, in our opinion, the only way in which the colored man could obtain land would be by paying for it from the sweat of his brow." I voted for that, and would vote for it every day in the week. But when I have said that, told them we have no land to give them, and did not believe the United States would give them lands, I am all the more bound when I see so much as the possibility of a chance of getting the means to enable these men to purchase lands, giving them time to pay for them. I say I am the more bound when I put myself on record against confiscation to vote for such a measure as my friend from Charleston (Mr. CAIN) has proposed here.

I am well aware that the pencils at that table (the reporters), are waiting only too eagerly to gibbet to the hatred and scorn of this community any man who dares to say that as between the landholders and landless, as between the white and the black, as between the rich and the poor, his sympathies are with the poor, the landless; and I am willing to incur all the odium of saying that I am not only in favor of this measure of positive relief, but when we are told that the Sheriff's hammer is about to fall, and scatter these hated and unjust monopolists of land, I am ready to take the odium, let the hammer fall, and pray may God speed its way.

I am no politician like my friend from Barnwell (Mr. LESLIE); I am not apt and experienced in the way of the politician, and I shall not follow that gentleman and indulge in any unparliamentary language. I shall not expose myself to the rebuke of the Chair by addressing myself to the audience behind the bar. But if it were parliamentary to address a word to my friends who are not members of this Convention, but are within the sound of my voice, I should say to them struggle on, be of good cheer, and remember whatever distress, greater if possible than those which are now upon you shall overtake you, remember there are some men here sent by your votes; there are some true enough, and still brave enough when their interests are at stake, to lift their voices and record their votes for a measure of just and honest relief to their pressing necessities.

If it were parliamentary, I would also say mark that man whose flippant tongue and biting wit is only exercised to villify your characters, and pour contempt upon an honest, faithful scheme to relieve your necessities. I believe in the independence of the representative. I believe that under proper limitations, every member who stands here should be governed by his own judgment, and be guided by the dictates of his own conscience. Yet there are times, and there are men whom it is well once in a while to remind there is a power that will call even them to account. You all remember it was a sublime advice given to the Court of the French King: "Gentlemen, posterity will judge your judgment." In that spirit I say to the gentlemen upon this floor, there is a constituency which will one day judge our judgments to-day, and that he only who to-day shall show that they have a spirit, a wish, a desire, when they are called upon by those on whom the hand of misfortune has been so heavily laid; when those who shall show by their voice and votes that they stood true to that issue; that they defended the loyal majority of this State, and they will be able to abide by that judgment.

Mr. R. H. CAIN. I regret exceedingly that this discussion has taken so wide a range, and has elicited so much acrimony in its continuance. When I, in the simplicity of my heart, and with a fervent desire for good, snatched a few moments of my time between the hours of twelve at night and two in the morning, to pen the preamble and resolutions of the petition presented, I little thought there would be five persons on this floor who would object to so reasonable, so innocent an operation as simply requesting the Congress of the United States, if in its judgment expedient, to appropriate one million of dollars of the surplus funds of seven millions now in the hands of the Freedman's Bureau, gathered into the Treasury from the sale of lands and other things, to appropriate,

I say, one million of that money for the benefit of the black men and poor white men in this State, equally involved in a state of starvation. I thought it would be no harm to ask the Government that had liberated thousands, yea, millions of bondmen, and at the same time liberated thousands of poor white men at the South, and left each class upon the platform, each in want, each resting under great necessities, penniless, poor and owning no home, no lands. I thought that to introduce a resolution of this kind would certainly evoke no opposition of any account from any party. I did not for a moment, conceive that a proposition so plain, so reasonable, would bring about a discussion of twenty-five minutes on this floor, and I was brought to this conclusion from a seeming earnest desire on the part of members to render whatever relief they could find in their power for the poor and suffering of South Carolina. The measures which had been adopted by the Convention, the arguments educed pro and con, the seeming unanimity with which the genmen voted on measures of relief, guaranteed me in believing that this measure, so simple, would meet no opposition. I regret that I find myself mistaken.

I now proceed without deigning to notice the aspersions made last week. In debate, I concede to every gentleman the right to present his arguments in such language and in such manner as may to him seem good and proper. I accord that right to the gentleman from Barnwell, who at the time saw fit in his remarks to characterize the motion offered with malice aforethought, and with the purpose of deceiving the poor, the needy and the weary in this State. I will say here at once that such a purpose was far from my intentions, and when I say this, I think I have said all that I need say as a gentleman, in opposition to what any other gentleman may say on the question. I propose, at no time, to permit my zeal to overtop my better judgment, nor let my judgment carry me beyond the bound of decent respect for the gentleman in the opposition, and proceed to notice the arguments adduced against this measure. The gentleman from Barnwell made two points in his argument; first, that the mover had an intention to deceive, which I deny. Second, that the mover did not believe that he would get what he asked for; that I deny. He also said that the mover had an intention to deceive the people that he might ride into political power by virtue of a scheme, shrewdly and cunningly devised to deceive those who have no better judgment; that I also deny. Again, it has been asserted that this measure will disturb the peace and quiet of the people now preparing to contract upon the plantations. I shall take the propositions, gentlemen, up in regular order. It was proposed to place this one million dollars under the supervision of General O. O. Howard, head of the Freedman's Bureau, for the express purpose of making purchase, under his direction, of such lands as may be offered for sale—not confiscated— but simply offered for sale by the citizens who owned the lands, to make the very best bargains they could possibly make. The appropriations could be made in three directions; first, to the purchase of lands; second, to the purchase of sites; third, to the purchase of necessary agricultural implements. It was said that this appropriation, if carried out, would give homes to but few. I think it was said that it would give one hundred and twenty-five thousand persons homes. According to my friend from Beaufort (Mr. WHIPPER), it would allow but five and one-seventh acres to each head of a family, and he claims that that would not be sufficient to do any good. Well, if we can give homes to one hundred and twenty-five thousand persons, we shall thereby take out from the jurisdiction of the Freedman's Bureau that number who still linger at the door of the Commissary, waiting for something to eat. It will, therefore, be a measure of relief to three parties; first, a measure of relief to the poor; second, to the Freedman's Bureau; third, to the landholders who will receive just compensation for the lands they own, and thus spread a million of dollars in circulation, giving to every class of men something to eat and something to do. That much good will be accomplished. But to answer the gentleman, that it will give discontent to the poor colored people, is it not better to give one hundred and twenty-five thousand people homes by a measure so judicious, so complete and so swift as this will be, than to let four hundred thousand go without any homes at all. It is objected by the gentleman also, that it will create discontent in the minds of others. I prefer to cut off one hundred and twenty-five thousand grumblers than none at all. I believe it a measure of relief, such as the people do need, such as they want, and such as they shall have.

I can see no reason why any gentleman should object to the proposition; I believe the Government will be benefited by it, and I reiterate what I said last week. I am opposed to the people constantly going up to the Commissary Department and receiving rations; I believe that if the money expended by the Commissary Department of the Freedman's Bureau was given for the purchase of land it would have a more permanent and beneficial effect. Four hundred and fifty thousand dollars has been expended in that Bureau in five months for the simple item of rations, yet that Bureau has not reached one-tenth of the people in this State. Again, I would not call into question the honesty of the officers of the Bureau, I believe there are some honest men there at any rate.

Mr. C. P. LESLIE. I deny that I ever questioned the honesty of any officer of the Bureau.

Mr. R. H. CAIN.   I was about to state that I had unbounded confidence in the Freedman's Bureau and in its operations.   I believe that the gentlemen at the head of that Bureau, from their antecedents and long experience in these matters, will do justice in this case.

The gentleman from Beaufort opposed the measure on the ground that it would create discontent, but was in favor of bringing up a resolution either in the Convention or by the Legislature, fixing such a tax upon the lands as to compel the sale of those lands, whether the owners wanted to or not.

Mr. W. J. WHIPPER.   I deny it.

Mr. R. H. CAIN.   I may be mistaken, but I watched very closely the arguments made by the gentleman last Saturday, and I distinctly understood him to say he was in favor of taxing the lands so as to compel the sale of them, and throw them into the market.   The poor would then have a chance to buy.   I am unqualifiedly opposed to any measure of taxation for the simple purpose of compelling the owners to sell their lands.   I believe the best measure to be adopted is to bring capital to the State, and instead of causing revenge and unpleasantness, I am for even-handed justice.   I am for allowing the parties who own lands to bring them into the market and sell them upon such terms as will be satisfactory to both sides.   I believe a measure of this kind has a double effect: first, it brings capital, what the people want; second, it puts the people to work; its gives homesteads, what we need; it relieves the Government and takes away its responsibility of feeding the people; it inspires every man with a noble manfulness, and by the thought that he is the possessor of something in the State; it adds also to the revenue of the country.   By these means men become interested in the country as they never were before.   It was said that five and one-seventh acres were not enough to live on.   If South Carolina, in its sovereign power, can devise any plan for the purchase of the large plantations in this State now lying idle, divide and sell them out at a reasonable price, it will give so many people work.   I will guarantee to find persons to work every five acres.   I will also guarantee that after one year's time, the Freedman's Bureau will not have to give any man having one acre of land anything to eat.   This country has a genial clime, rich soil, and can be worked to advantage.   The man who can not earn a living on five acres, will not do so on twenty-five.   I regret that another position taken by gentlemen in the opposition, is that they do not believe that we will get what we ask for.   I believe that the party now in power in the Congress of the United States, will do whatever they can for the welfare of the people of this State and of the

South. I believe that the noble men who have maintained the rights of the freedmen before and since their liberation, will continue to do everything possible to forward these great interests. I am exceedingly anxious, if possible, to allay all unpleasant feeling—I would not have any unpleasant feeling among ourselves.

I would not have any unpleasant feelings between the races. If we give each family in the State an opportunity of purchasing a home, I think they will all be better satisfied.

But it is also said that it will disturb all the agricultural operations in the State. I do not believe if the Congress of the United States shall advance one million of dollars to make purchase of lands, the laborers will abandon their engagement and run off. I have more confidence in the people I represent. I believe all who have made contracts will fulfill those contracts, and when their contracts have expired, they will go on their own lands, as all freemen ought to go. I claim it would do no harm. It would be a wonderful concatenation of circumstances indeed, to find that because the Government had appropriated one million of dollars for the purchase of lands, to see all of four hundred thousand people, rushing pell mell down to Charleston to get a homestead. I know the ignorance of the people with whom I am identified is great. I know that four hundred years of bondage has degraded them, but I have more confidence in humanity than to believe the people will leave their homes and their families to come to Charleston just to get five acres of land.

If I understood the speaker in the opposition this morning, he offered it because he said it was simply a scheme for colored men. I wish to state this question right. If there was one thing on which I thought I had been specific, it was on that point. The clock had struck two and I had dashed down my pen when the thought struck me it might be misunderstood. I retraced my steps and so shaped the petition as simply to state the poor of any class. I bore in mind the poor whites of the upper districts. I saw, not long ago, a poor white woman walk eighteen miles barefooted to receive a bag of corn and four pounds of meat, resting all night on the roadside, eating one-half and then go away, living on roots afterwards and half starved. I desire that class of people to have homes as well as the black man. I have lost long since that hateful idea that the complexion of a man makes any difference as far as rights are concerned. The true principle of progress and civilization is to recognize the great brotherhood of man, and a man's wants, whatever he may be, or whatever clime he comes from, are as sacred to me as any other class of men. I believe this measure will advance the interests of all classes.

54

A few more words and I am done. Gentlemen of the Convention, I wish to appeal to you and ask have we not had suffering enough in this country? Has not the rude hands of war, with its fiery sword, trampled out the commercial interests of the States? Hath not the rude hand of war laid up the ships in our harbors, torn down fences and barns, and left our country almost a wilderness? Hath not war set the whole country in commotion? Look at the former rich white man, now walking poor and penniless; look at those formerly in opulence, now poor and brought down low. Can the gentleman from Barnwell, formerly from New York, last from Charleston, understand the fact that the people of the State want relief? I came to identify myself with the interests of the country. If she falls, I fall with her. If she rises, I rise with her. I have a kind of South Carolina pride, because my broad heart reaches out to all men's interests wherever I am. I have identified myself with the country, and I claim it is no time in the reconstruction of the State to seek revenge upon the head of any person, or to disregard the cries of millions for relief. The freed people, in connection with the poor whites of this State, are in great want. Let us see the number of destitute in this State. General Howard reports in South Carolina five thousand colored and five thousand whites, March 7th, 1867. There are other reports here which show a larger number of persons, and as I before remarked, the Bureau hath not met one-tenth of the wants of the people. This measure, if carried out, therefore, will meet a want which the Bureau never can meet. A man may have rations to-day and not to-morrow, but when he gets land and a homestead, and is once fixed on that land, he never will want to go to the Commissary again. It is said that I depicted little farms by the roadside, chickens roosting on the the fence, and all those poetical beauties. But however poetical the gentleman may be in his remarks, I prefer to see chickens roosting on the fence, and the lambs frisking round the place, and all other things which may be desired, than to see four hundred thousand people without homes, without owning even the sand they carry in their shoes. I prefer to see each one of them the owner of a log cabin, than to be compelled to work for five or ten dollars per month. I prefer to see that than to see the bayonets of the United States brought into requisition to drive poor, helpless men, women and children, because of the relentless hearts of those planters who will not pay. I prefer this to seeing strong men working for the paltry sum of five or ten dollars a month, and some for even three dollars a month. How can a man live at that rate. I hate the contract system as I hate the being of whom my friend from Orangeburg (**Mr. RANDOLPH**) spoke last week (the devil). It has ruined the people. After fifty men have gone on a plantation, worked the whole year at raising twenty thousand bushels of rice, and then go to get their one-third, by the time they get through the division, after being charged by the landlord twenty-five or thirty cents a pound for bacon, two or three dollars for a pair of brogans that costs sixty cents, for living that costs a mere song, two dollars a bushel for corn that can be bought for one dollar ; after I say, these people have worked the whole season, and at the end make up their accounts, they find themselves in debt. The planters sell their cotton, for it is said that a negro has not brain enough to sell his own cotton. He can raise anything ; he can dig ditches, pick cotton, but has not the sense to sell it. I deprecate that idea. I would rather see these people have little cottages and farms for themselves.

It is but a few days ago I went to a plantation on Cooper river. The first place I visited, I said to the men there, go to work, work honestly, stay on the plantation, do the best you can, make yourselves as comfortable as possible. After awhile your old masters may do you justice. Those people have remained on those plantations. What was the result. Week before last they came and said to me, we took your advice, have worked hard, but as God is our judge, we have not as much as when these men got back their place again. I looked and saw four mule teams rolling off bales of cotton. I saw corn cribs piled with corn, and fodder houses filled with fodder. I went into the cabin of the negroes and found but a scanty morsel of corn dodger and a scanty ration of bacon.

I say, therefore, it is time to relieve these people, and if this is not a measure of relief I know not what is. I desire to relieve all classes. I desire to relieve the planters of the large plantations they cannot attend to, and which must be so great a burden on their minds. They are pressed down ; do not know what to do with their great plantations. I propose to bring money and say to them, " here gentlemen, you want to sell, we want to buy ; we will give you a reasonable price ; you will have the greenbacks, we will have the land ; you can apply that money to banking purposes or buy bank stock, we will deposit the money with you." I want to see a change in this country. Instead of the colored people being always penniless, I want to see them coming in with their mule teams and ox teams. I want to see them come with their corn and potatoes and exchange for silks and satins. I want to see school houses and churches in every parish and township. I want to see children coming forth to enjoy life as it ought to be enjoyed. This people know nothing of what is good and best for mankind until they get homesteads and enjoy them.

With these remarks, I close. I hope the Convention will vote for the proposition. Let us send up our petition. The right to petition is a jealous right. It was a right guaranteed to the Barons of England. The American people have always been jealous of that right, and regarded it as sacred and inviolate. That right we propose to maintain. It is said here that some high officers are opposed to it. I do not care who is opposed to it. It is none of their business. I do not care whether General Scott, General Grant, or General anybody else is opposed to it, we will petition in spite of them. I appeal to the delegates to pass this resolution. It will do no harm if it does no good, and I am equally confident that some gentleman will catch what paddy gave the drum when they go back to their constituents.

At the conclusion of the speaker's remarks, Mr. R. B. ELLIOTT called for the previous question.

Mr. R. C. DeLARGE claimed that he had risen and taken the floor prior to the call for the previous question.

The Chair decided the member entitled to the floor.

Mr. R. B. ELLIOTT appealed from the decision of the Chair, but the appeal was not sustained.

Mr. R. C. DeLARGE said he was glad his colleague (Mr. R. H. CAIN) had denied that the petition offered by him was intended so as to benefit a class. He hoped now that every member of the house understood distinctly that it was not the desire of the mover of the petition, nor of any other member who advocated it (himself among the number), to make this a class measure, other reports in the newspapers to the contrary notwithstanding. With this explanation, he yielded the floor to his friend from Sumter (Mr. F. J. MOSES, Jr.)

Mr. F. J. MOSES, Jr. It was my intention on arising to address the Chair, to allude to the many extraordinary scenes that had transpired in this Convention during the discussion of this important subject, but before noticing these scenes I desire to state that I have never yet witnessed so extraordinary a measure as that which was attempted to be enacted on this floor just now. For gentlemen, who have wasted the time of this Convention, after exhausting its time and patience in addresses in support of their side of the question, to attempt to gag a member who desires to answer, is so extraordinary a scene that I, for one, trust that it will never again be witnessed on this floor.

After saying that, I desire to state that I rise in the kindest feeling and in best of good humor towards every member of the Convention. I feel that I could not do otherwise after the laughable, humorous and ridiculous incidents which we have witnessed during the last two days. We have heard allusions to the politicians of Charleston. We have heard from the gentleman from Barnwell that he could not wend his lonely way upon the streets without hearing cries from the thirsty politicians of Charleston, " office, office, office."

But it seems to me that there must be a picture quite as plain as that which he has drawn in the minds of every member of this Convention, it is this : we have witnessed one of the most unparalleled horseback riders perform one of the most remarkable political acrobatic feats ever witnessed by the members of this Convention or the people generally. I know of no rider who has attempted to ride two horses at once so admirably as the gentleman from Barnwell, and these scenes could not but have inspired us with pleasure, amusement and enjoyment. There are others who have been jealous of the reputation achieved by the gentleman from Barnwell. They desired to have a place in the ring, and after having taken one position on this subject, they came toddling in after him with all sorts of amendments ; those amendments were to this effect : We want to tell the people why we vote for it, but cannot consent to tell them we are in favor of giving them lands. Why? Because we dread the public opinion of South Carolina. That is the true answer to be made to those men. When they say they are unwilling to sustain this measure, which is for the purpose of giving the poor people of South Carolina homes and lands, their hearts tremble with fear, and their cheeks turn pale at the thought that the pencils (the reporters) at that table will tell the story in the districts whence they came, that they have attempted to strike at the prosperity of the white men. As for myself, I say if this measure was introduced solely for the benefit of the black man, solely for the benefit of those men who have stood true to the United States Government through all the late terrible years of war and bloodshed, I would be ready to support it and give my aid in any shape or manner that would ask from the United States Government a reward for this people. I came here pledged to do it. I told my constituents before I left home that I intended to give my voice and my vote in support of any measure which would help them. I stand here to-day, and when the gentleman from Berkley (Mr. CHAMBERLAIN) this morning asked where is the gentleman from Sumter, he knew very well where I stood, and that I was but wanting an opportunity to follow him.

The measure before the Convention, it seems to me, is a very plain one. On the secession of South Carolina from the Federal Union, the Government determined that the Union should be sustained. The cry went out from the North for men to sustain it, and they came from all quarters of the country, and among them came the gentleman from

Charleston. I yield him all honor for it, and all honor for what he has done in behalf of this.

The war was waged, as the Government said, for the perpetuity of the Union, but inseperably connected with that question was the question of slavery. The war was to decide whether slavery was to exist with all its accompaniments, and that question was decided in the negative. Now, I desire to ask how these people, who were living in South Carolina in a state of bondage, with not even a soul perhaps they could call their own, living under task masters, some of whom deserved to be betrayed by those whom they owned ; how did they behave during this terrible ordeal ? It can be answered from every quarter of the State, when almost every citizen of the State was absent from his home , when his wife and little ones were left alone, without any one to guard, shield or protect them, these men, black though their faces were, with white hearts rallied round those families, and protected them from danger. I say that the purity of the home of every South Carolinian during that terrible struggle is owing to the freedmen, owing to the slave, owing to the black man, who protected those homes when their masters were absent to forge for the black man the chains of slavery. It comes, therefore, with little grace from any South Carolinian whatever to attempt to keep these people in poverty and under a despotism, which in time to come will be as odious as the despotism of slavery. If you keep one class without land, or leave the lands in the hands of those monopolists who desire not to extend the hand of assistance to this people, I say their condition will be twice as bad as slavery, and in years to come they will have no liberty or will of their own, but will be dependant upon the will and wish of those who own the land ; therefore I stand in favor of giving them land by any system, or in any shape or manner, except by a system of robbery. I am not in favor of confiscation ; I do not desire to take from any man's property, real or personal ; but after the loyalty exhibited by these people to the United States Government ; after their behavior during the terrible ordeal ; after the indulgence and the magnanimity extended to their masters, I say they deserve it from the Government, and we demand it as a right. I regret but one thing in this petition : it does not ask enough, I would prefer to ask for ten or twenty millions of dollars—give them all homes, and let them keep them. It has been said that charity begins at home. If you meet a man on the street without a coat, and he wants one, it will not do to take off and give him your own. I admit all that, but I deny that this is taking money from Northern citizens. I say the colored citizens, as tax payers, have as deep a stake in the existence and perpetuity of the Government as any Northern citizens, and I say it should come from the Government in that shape. The gentleman from Barnwell (Mr. LESLIE) in that humorous spirit which he always displays, has alluded to two kinds of politicians being in this Convention : one kind he terms practical politicians, and the other as impracticable. I go further than that, and say there are three kinds; the first class are those who desire to say oh ! yes, we are all friends of yours, we are going to give the freedmen lands, and do everything we can for you ; you shall be equal before the law, but, for God's sake, don't ask me to incur the enmity of the white man in doing it ; don't you know I am a white man ; how can we give you land if every white man is opposed to it ? That is the first class of politicians, and the gentleman from Barnwell (Mr. LESLIE) can decide for himself whether he belongs to that class.

The second class are those who really believe, and I give them credit for so believing, that this measure will not be of benefit to the colored population, and the poor whites of South Carolina. One speech has been made this morning by one politician of that class (Mr. PARKER), which speech I was bound to respect for its manliness, truth and justice.

The third class of politicians, if you choose to call them so, are those who have come here to stick to their principles ; who have come here to betray no man or set of men ; to redeem their promises, and when they return home, desire to be able to say that they have not shirked any question that has been brought upon this floor. To that class I claim to have the honor of belonging.

Mr. C. P. LESLIE. Are you a candidate for Congress ?

Mr. F. J. MOSES, Jr. I think the best way I can answer that question would be by asking another, so as to show the manœuvreing going on between the gentleman who asked the question and the gentleman in this city. Does he expect to be a candidate for the distribution of corn in Barnwell District ? As far as I am concerned individually, I answer the gentleman emphatically, I stand here a candidate for no office, I came here to do my duty for my people, and I intend to do it, undeterred alike by the frowns of open enemies, or the inuendoes of pretended friends.

Mr. C. P. LESLIE. Bully for MOSES.

Mr. F. J. MOSES, Jr. I must say, as a member of the Republican party, for it has been alluded to, that this Convention, as I understand it, is of no party, but simply for the purpose of restoring South Carolina to the Union. As that has been mentioned, and as the gentleman from Barnwell (Mr. PARKER) has had so many tremblings and nightmares creeping over him, with regard to the Republican party, I confess, since

I have heard so many things said on the floor to-day, I tremble, too, for the Republican party. When I see how fast certain men, prominent Republicans, can, in the words of the gentleman from Charleston, "swing round the circle," it seems to me we should all fear for the Republican party and for ourselves hereafter.

Mr. C. P. LESLIE. Have you not swung round?

Mr. F. J. MOSES, Jr. It is true these men who are here have had what they may call a glorious example before them for the betrayal of this party. But I, for one, do not propose to follow it. They have had, in the person of one who sits at the head of the United States Government, who has been a Judas Iscariot to his race, an example of betrayal of his party. I am not only ready to resist that betrayal of the party to any man, but to resist the attempts of any man in the Convention who dares to show a disposition to follow in his footsteps. There is but one way of betraying the Republican party in South Carolina, and that is to deceive the people who have sent us here; that is the only way in which you can betray the party. Thank God, it is now so strong in the affections of the people that it could not be betrayed, except by the treachery of those who are at its head. The gentleman from Barnwell (Mr. PARKER) has said, what will our Radical friends at the North say, if we propose to dip our hand into the United States Treasury and take one million of dollars from it for the benefit of the freedmen? And I deny that any such proposition will be presented to them.

Perhaps the gentleman has not read the petition, and does not know what is embodied in it; but I have read it, and I see it is simply a proposition to divert from the course in which it is now going one million of dollars in the possession of the Freedman's Bureau, and instead of wasting that money in the distribution of rations, giving, as the gentleman from Charleston (Mr. CAIN), said about a peck of corn and a small piece of bacon to each head of a family, for which they have to walk twenty-miles. We propose to take from that fund one million of dollars, and put it into the pockets of the freedmen permanently and forever. Now I ask if our friends at the North can hoot at any such proposition as that. If that will give the Democrats any help and put them in the majority, then we had better request Congress to take back the seven millions of dollars from the Freedman's Bureau, and abolish that institution altogether. We propose to ask Congress to lend us one million of dollars. As it is given out now, it will never be returned. It is known, as a fact, that the greater portion of the money in possession of the Freedman's Bureau has been loaned out by the Government of the United States to white planters of South Carolina under liens of their

crops. Will the gentleman from Barnwell, or anywhere else, demand
that the United States shall appropriate money to help along men who
still have their hands stained with the gore of this bloody civil war.
Shall the Government go on assisting those men, and refuse to help the
freedmen? That is a plain proposition. The Government, since the
war, has been aiding almost every white man who goes to the Bureau
for assistance. We know they were engaged in the war, and raised
their fratracidal hands against the Government, and that the only class
of people who stood firm and loyal are the very people whom we propose
to ask aid for. Will our proposition be hooted at because we propose to
give help to the freedman? If that is to be the decision here, the sooner
it is known the better, for the freedmen and poor whites in my part of
the country are under the impression that this Convention was called
for the purpose of assisting them. I do not know how it was over in
Beaufort, Berkley, or other parts of the State, but as for Sumter, I can
vouch that the loyal portion of that District looked forward to this Convention, not only to form a civil government under which to live in
peace, friendship and brotherly love, but to give them any means of relief that the circumstances will prove were justifiable. If they are to
be told they were mistaken in this Convention, that all the money of the
United States Government is to be given to those people who waged the
war for the purpose of keeping them in slavery, the sooner you send the
gentleman from Barnwell on that mission of mercy to tell them so, the
better it will be for all. I contend that this is a right that these people
have. I say it is a right which they have to petition the Government to
aid them in their necessities. They have been freed, taken from the
care of masters, many of whom were kind in their treatment of them.
They have fed, clothed and housed them through all their years of
slavery; they have not had to buffet with the cares, storms and turmoil
of the world; they have not been taught to encounter all those toils and
labors, and they have been suddenly cast out into the position of freedmen, where they have to work for themselves, and they have not the
intelligence to do it. It is not their fault that these people are ignorant.
God knows they ought to be ignorant, after all they have passed through.
It is admitted on all sides that it was the policy of the Southern country
to keep them in ignorance, because you could not keep a man in slavery
who was intelligent. They were debarred all the privileges that white
men enjoyed to learn what their rights were, or knowing their rights,
dared to maintain them. Having been cast out by the United States
Government, having been granted this gracious boon of freedom, it
behooves that Government to continue its charge over them, and give

55

them something whereby they can begin to work. I say what we propose to give is simply a lein on the crops. We propose to borrow the money, and just here I would say, if this measure is carried out, it will be a benefit to every landholder in South Carolina. For this reason the large majority of them having idle lands will be able to sell them. I have, therefore, come to the conclusion that all this doubt and wavering in the minds of gentlemen, as to the white people of South Carolina, thinking they are injuring them, is all misplaced and unnecessary.

The gentleman from Barnwell (Mr. PARKER) with that candor for which he is remarkable, has confessed that he felt warmly on this subject. I follow in that confession. I also feel warmly on the subject. I say there has been no subject presented to this Convention on which I have felt so much interest as this, and I think every member of the Republican party should feel warmly on the subject. He has asked would it not be best to avert danger to the Republican party by not granting this petition. I tell him no. I say if it was the intention of the Republican party to free these people, and leave them in the position in which they would be under, a despotism worse than slavery, and let them go where a gentleman from South Carolina said South Carolina had gone, then you drive them to another party which does not keep the word of promise to the ear, and break it to the sense; not like the Democratic party which the gentleman fears may succeed, but the party which will go forward on the broad principles of equity and justice to all men, and will not fear the result, provided it does what is just and right. To that party I for one claim to belong. I say I am prepared to desert that party whenever it deserts those whom I represent, whenever they propose to draw back and take back their fostering hands from the wards of the nation, I am willing to leave that party and seek those ready and willing to help them.

I consider all the arguments which I have heard brought forward to the notice of the Convention by the gentleman from Barnwell, as to taking from the United States Treasury money for the purpose of giving lands to the freedmen, have been answered by my reading from the petition the first few lines of the first resolution: "Resolved, that this Convention do petition, and they hereby petition the Fortieth Congress of the United States to make an appropriation of one million of dollars of the funds in the possession of the Bureau of Freedmen, Refugees and Abandoned Lands." In that we do not call on the United States Government to appropriate one cent. The money has been appropriated, and we say the money, to a certain extent, is being wasted. I am informed if the Bureau Bill now before Congress is passed, a great deal more money will be appropriated. I do not for one moment mean to charge upon the officers of the Freedman's Bureau any malfeasance in office, misappropriation, or anything of that kind. I have the utmost respect for every officer of the Bureau in the State of South Carolina. I know them intimately, and never found one dishonest man among them. I know that the man stationed in my district honors the uniform of the United States Government, and is true to all his trusts. I believe he is in all respects a fit representative of the General who stands at the head of the Bureau in this State. I do say the intention of the Government is not met by the distribution of provisions, provided the intention was to assist the freedmen. For although the freedmen may have been assisted to the utmost extent, there is still want and destitution, and I believe this will be the status of affairs until the Bureau ceases to administer its functions. I believe the means of relief, as provided by the Bureau, are totally inadequate. I am, therefore, willing to ask the Government to give us at least one million of money for the purpose of attempting to prove that our plan of relief is the best for all the people. I do not believe it will add one feather to the cap of the Democratic party in the approaching struggle, if this petition were to go to Congress.

The argument of the gentleman from Barnwell (Mr. PARKER) in the first place, took it for granted that if the petition was sent in to Congress, it would not be granted. But if Congress granted this petition, he at once augurs ill, and says Congress will kill the Republican party by granting it. Now he says, suppose Congress refuses it, don't you believe it will add to the influence of the Republican party. Don't you think if this petition was sent to Congress to appropriate from the Bureau one million of dollars now in their possession, and Congress says, "oh, no, we have done enough for the freedmen;" don't you think it will help the Republican party at the North. If the gentleman's view is correct, if the mere fact of sending up a petition can insure the Republican party, then I argue many gentlemen in South Carolina must well swing on that party. There is but one way of getting rid of this question. This argument is an attempt to shirk it. It is a plain question, and admits of no subterfuge. The question is, will you or not petition. Everything else is subterfuge, and he whom the cap fits let him wear it.

Mr. C. P. LESLIE. Put it on him. He is your co-operator. Cry aloud and spare not.

Mr. F. J. MOSES, Jr. It seems to me there is a power behind the throne in politics; the lever is not in this Convention. We represent the mass of people, and I tell you here, you who profess to be friends of this people, you who profess in one breath to be laboring for their prosperity and advancement, and in the next hold aloft a long amendment, which qualifies the thing you do. I will tell you that the day of accountability may come, and that these people will ask, where are the duties you were entrusted to perform? I say every man in South Carolina has his eyes turned to this Convention, and every heart is beating with hope that this Convention will do something for them. And right here I take the position that so far from the passage of this petition creating dissatisfaction and unrest, the agitation in the minds of all this people for whose relief we ask, I say this spirit of unrest and dissatisfaction which prevails now, which has been raised up by the United States Government like Banquo's ghost, "it will not down at its bidding," and it takes some such measure as this to put it down.

I say we owe it to the landholders of South Carolina; we owe it to those people who have freedmen employed under them this year; we owe it to every freedman who walks the streets; to every artizan, every mechanic, every wheelwright, every mason, and all the rest; we owe it to them to let them know exactly where this Convention stands on the subject of relief. My constituents are sufficiently intelligent to know that the mere sending up of this petition to the United States Congress does not guarantee that they will get the money; and after having performed my duty here, after having raised my voice, feeble as it is, in behalf of this petition, I do not expect to qualify my work with any explanatory amendment, but expect to go home to my people with a clear conscience and tell them what I did do and what my expectations are. I expect to tell them the truth, the whole truth. I expect to tell them there is a possibility of Congress giving them this money. I expect to tell them why I took the stand I did. Not because I committed myself to that measure of relief, not because I raised my voice on all measures of relief, for I think I am independent enough to occupy any position on any subject I please; it makes no difference who dares to threaten. I say I entertained my present impression simply from a sincere conviction that in working for this I am working for the good of the whole State of South Carolina; and I tell you now, if from the fear of what the people would say, if from the fear of not being able to ride two horses at once; if from the fear of all these things you refuse and table this petition, refuse to send it forward, I tell you it will not be the last time we will meet. We will meet where the sovereign power resides; we will meet where we can appeal from Cæsar drunk to Cæsar sober. From the representatives of the people, frightened and trembling, with cheeks blanched, we can appeal to Cæsar sober in the guise of the sovereign people themselves. It is there we intend to appeal. If we fail here to get this help, if we have come to this reconstruction Convention for the purpose of aiding this people, if we have to go back and tell them we have failed to get relief, I give you warning here that the blast must come, the storm cannot be averted, and you will be accountable for the deeds you have done here. I ask you are you prepared to meet it?

I have a memorandum before me which shows that the cost of rations for the State of South Carolina alone, as expended through the instrumentality of the Freedman's Bureau, is $375,000. What does that amount to after all? Does it keep soul and body together? If the Government intends this as a method of assistance to the people, I say it has been proved that the method was a wrong one. I say there has been no perceptible change in the destitution and starvation which has prevailed among the colored people and poor whites since 1865 up to this time. The Freedman's Bureau has been at work all the time, and has performed the duty it was intended to perform, but we still have the same starvation and destitution staring us in the face wherever we go. We find men not willing to work. How can they work when they know they have a wife and little ones in a state of starvation, and that working from sunrise until the dead hour of midnight cannot bring sufficient to keep their loved ones from starvation. How can you work when you know your brawny right arm can bring no relief; when, on going home at night, you see the wife of your bosom and your little ones clustering around you asking for bread, and you have to answer I have none to give? How can any man work in this condition of affairs? When they start out in the morning from the house to go to the fields, with God's sun shining brightly above their heads, do their hearts leap in gladness to meet it; do they feel they are going forth to work for the support of those who are dependent upon their labor? No! They go forth with hearts borne down with sorrow; they go forth knowing they may toil as manfully as ever man toiled, still the demon of starvation will hover around their homes. Will you give them no help from the reconstruction Convention? How do you propose to reconstruct the Union? There are a thousand ways of picking up the broken fragments and reconstructing a vessel, but how do we propose to do it? Do we propose to build it up on a solid foundation, that shall resist the storms of ages; or do we expect to patch up here and there, to build it up with men not devoted to the Government whom the Government has merely freed to put in a worse condition than before? Shall we build it up with those who will rebel, or who will tremble with alarm, who will refuse a cordial support to the Government because they believe they have been betrayed by it, or will we build it up with stout and strong hearts, out of material that shall never flinch, but will defend the Government? If we will, how can we do it? There is but one way of making a man love his country. I love my country town, I love the house I live in, the land I live on, the sand I walk on; because in that sand, in that house, and that town, I have an interest. I have an interest in the wealth and prosperity of the State. When misfortune strikes at her, it strikes at me. You cannot make citizens out of these people unless you give them those things which make men citizens. I say you must bind them to the Government with ties that can never be broken. Give them lands; give them houses. They deserve it from the people of South Carolina. They deserve it for protecting the families of those who were away from their homes during the late war. If you propose to reconstruct this Union, to carry South Carolina back on the shoulders of strong, stalwart men, and do not, Sampson-like, intend to carry down the pillars with it, you must pass this petition. If you refuse it, beware of the consequences. Most especially do I tell those representatives who are afraid of public opinion, who are afraid of the pencils at the table reporters over there; and look and tremble, I say I do not desire my name to go on the record so. I tell these men if they have come here to betray the people they stand in danger, and they will be held to a strict accountability, and so help me God I will be one to hold them.

Mr. C. P. LESLIE. Records are dangerous things.

Mr. F. J. MOSES, Jr. In conclusion, having noticed all the arguments, I propose to go a little further and steal some of the thunder which some of the gentlemen are collecting for the purpose of attacking me. It has been said that records are dangerous things. I grant it. I grant the proposition, and I propose to meet that record which the gentleman from Barnwell is preparing, and meet it as it should be met. The records which he intends to present is one, perhaps, that will be gotten up in his usual and ridiculous style, drawing, no doubt, a very vivid picture of some of the scenes which transpired at the beginning of the war, having in his mind's eye the picture of a flag being raised, and one who helped to raise that flag standing here as the representative of the Republican party of South Carolina. He will draw you a picture of just such scenes as that, but for fear he would make capital of it, I propose to meet him right here.

The picture was the picture of an officer raising the State flag of South Carolina. It was the picture of an officer raising the State flag over a dismantled fortress of the United States Government after that fortress had been surrendered. I am that officer. I am the man who raised that flag, and I stand here now, and tell the gentleman who follow me with that picture if they propose by drawing it to question my fidelity to the party with which I am now connected, I brand the accusation beforehand as an infamous falsehood. That is the proposition A man's antecedents are not to be cared for now. As far as I am individually concerned I had my own opinions about the war.

I do not propose to state what those opinions were. Nobody on this floor has a right to demand it. But since the war is over, and the troubles ended, I have done my duty to Carolina, and have acted with that party which alone can save the State, and I say it is better to remain faithful to that party than to patch up pictures to frighten the souls of those not brave enough to face them. As far as I am individually concerned, I cannot be frightened by it. I stand the equal of every man in the Convention, not only equal as far as my election is concerned, but far ahead of some of them, I trust, in fidelity to the Republican party, and in my devotion to the interests of our people.

Mr. B. F. WHITTEMORE. I do not intend to tire the Convention with a long speech, nor do I intend to establish a record here, nor do I consider it necessary I should do so. We are very glad to hear the affirmations of the newly fledged, and we are very glad to know where they are going to stand. We are very glad to hear of their honesty, their purity of motives and character. I claim that imputations cast as they have been upon this floor, upon those who have argued either the affirmative or negative side of the question, have been altogether out of place. In discussing this subject we should meet the large majority kindly, fairly and squarely. Whatever position other men take in regard to this measure, in my opinion, it is our duty to accord to every gentleman honesty of motive and of intention. I do not believe there stands upon this floor a single individual who is not my peer in every respect, and when he rises to his feet and gives us his individual views, it is our duty to accord to him all credit and honor in the presentment of those opinions. I believe when the gentleman from Charleston (Mr. R. H. CAIN) presented the petition in behalf of the poor of the Commonwealth, that he did so with a desire to alleviate their distress, to better their condition and inspire them with a brighter hope for the future. I believe, too, there might have been something in that petition that, perhaps, might have brought about some remedy for the disorders in the country to which he has alluded. It has been my duty, in the character of a public teacher for the last two years, to become acquainted with the wants and condition of the people. I have been up and down through the districts, and I know what the voice of the poor has been, white and black. I have seen them upon the plantation; I have met them upon the highway; I have seen them as they came from their labors, and my office has been thronged for two years and a half with complaints of the people of this Commonwealth. I did not come here to turn my back upon the people. I did not come here to ask any individual as to whether I had a right to offer an amendment, or anything else I was disposed to present to this body, and when he tells me that which I offered is a deception, I say it comes from that portion of his heart which I have a right to question as to honor and honesty.

It has been already said that the motives in bringing forward this petition were to deceive the people. I cannot believe it, nor do I believe it. My conversations with that gentleman, who introduced the petition, assure me that my opinion was correct.

We saw and regretted the acrimonious course the debate was taking, that district was being pitted against district; we saw the gladiatorial display on this floor, and the intention of gentlemen to forget the question we were considering, in order that they might battle one with the other. The reason I offered the amendment, was to stay this tide of abuse in order that we might act at once upon the question before us, and having got it out of the way, we might proceed to the business for which we have been sent here. I regret the side issues that have taken us away from the consideration of the great question for which we have been sent here, namely, the constitutional provisions of Government, which we are looked upon as delegates and citizens to attend to. I do not question the intentions of any gentleman who desires to relieve the distress of the people. I believe every heart beats in sympathy with the words of the gentleman who has just taken his seat (Mr. MOSES), in the desire to relieve all the people. I know this, that it has been said that delegates here obtained their seats upon this floor by promises to the credulous people that they should possess land. It has been said of me that for the past two years I have held out inducements to the people that if they continued in the hope to which allusion has been made that they would become possessors of land. I know how hard it was to beat down that idea. It has been in their minds that Government would some day present them with their old homes and old farms.

There is no gentleman on this floor from the country who does not know how much he has had to contend with when he has had to oppose that desire which has been uppermost in the hearts of the people. I have no desire to question that wish, and that hope which inspires every man. I believe with the gentleman who has just taken his seat, that we may make citizens of all the people, and the best way to make them citizens is to make them possessors of little homes and farms. Why give a man a home, a cow, a horse, a few acres of land, and he is wedded to the soil. He is a better citizen than ever before. He cannot be an itinerant, and leave the State as he has done before, with all he has upon his shoulders. I believe in creating homes for all the people, and the fear that came to my mind was not the fear of meeting the white man, whether upon this floor or in Sumter District, or any other District; it was not the fear of meeting the white man face to face, and talking over these questions that not only agitate our hearts but inspire the minds of our constituency. No, sir, I turn back to him the record. I ask the gentleman from Sumter if he thinks I fear any white man in South Carolina wherever I have stood? I ask him if he has done what others have done? We are glad to understand he is going forth into the great contest to make his appeals, and show to the people that, whereas, he raised a flag that was at enmity, he now stands under the stars and stripes, and is willing to be held forward a defender of that country.

I do not believe there is a gentleman on the floor who will not extend every measure of relief required by the people, but when any gentleman attempts to divine my feelings and my opinions by his own interpretations, he undertakes too much.

Mr. F. J. MOSES, Jr. I desire to know if I am the person the gentleman has been alluding to.

Mr. B. F. WHITTEMORE. If the coat fits the gentleman he can wear it I do not say I allude to this gentleman, and yet if the coat fits he can wear it.

Mr. F. J. MOSES, Jr. I would like to say that the gentleman never entered my mind, and that he shirks that question as he does others.

Mr. B. F. WHITTEMORE. I shall not require any new comers in the flock to tell me that I shirk my duty. I have already stated where I stood on this question and the opposition I made. The gentleman who is the author of the petition (Mr. R. H. CAIN) well knows why I did it. It has already been said upon this floor that the gentleman who has been so kindly alluded to in his honorable connection with the Bureau (Gen. Scott) to which he is attached, has given us a word in relation to the necessity of caution in all these proceedings. There is no necessity to petition for one million, or five, or twenty millions of dollars, if Congress can give us the means of relief. But the mischief has been already done. The fear, in my mind at the time, was that the people throughout the State might expect and anticipate that this Convention had a right

56

and could demand land, and give it to them, no matter how far the loan asked for might go, or how many homes it might furnish.

I desire to deal honestly with the people, and I believe I need not go back to the people in order that I may sustain the declaration which I make here. There are men upon this floor representing districts through which it has been my pleasure to pass. If they give here the true declaration of their constituency they will say that in no way, or in no part have I ever deceived them, nor do I intend to deceive them, and last of all am I to be told that I feared to meet any issue, and when the gentleman said I shirked my position, I ask him not to sit in judgment over me; the time will come when judgment will begin at home.

The amendment was offered on Saturday last, but in order that speedy action may be obtained upon the subject, and in order to show that I have no desire to qualify the terms of the petition, or otherwise, I had prepared a resolution which I will read and submit to the Convention:

Resolved, That the President of the Convention be authorized to telegraph to the President of the United States Senate and Speaker of the national House of Representatives, and request them to present before their respective branches of Congress the great need of our people, and their homeless and landless condition, with the view of securing an early expression from the Government as to whether a petition of every member of this Convention would be productive of a loan from the national Treasury to enable our people to buy farms on a reasonable credit, and if so, how large an amount should be petitioned for.

At the conclusion of Mr. WHITTEMORE'S remarks, Mr. E. W. M. MACKEY called the previous question, which was sustained.

The question was then put on the adoption of Mr. WHITTEMORE'S amendment, offered on Saturday.

The yeas and nays were demanded, and on being taken, resulted as follows:

YEAS.—The President, Messrs. Allen, Alexander, Bell, Olsen, Parker, Swails, Whittemore—8.

NAYS—Bowen, Bonum, Burton, Brockenton, Bryce, R. H. Cain, F. J. Cain, Camp, Cardozo, Coghlan, Chamberlain, Clinton, Cooke, Collins, Corley, Craig, Crews, Darrington, Davis, DeLarge, Dickson, Dill, Dogan. Driffle, Duncan, Edwards, Elliott, Foster, Gentry, Goss, Gray, Harris, J. N. Hayne, C. D. Hayne, H. E. Hayne, Henderson, Holmes, Hurley, Jackson, Jacobs, Jenks, Jervey, Jillson, W. B. Johnson, J. W. Johnson, Dr. L. B. Johnson, Johnston, Joiner, Charles Jones, Langley, G. Lee, S. Lee, Lomax, Leslie, E. W. M. Mackey, Mayer, Mauldin, W. J. McKinlay, W. McKinlay, McDaniels, Mead, Middleton, Miller, Milford, Moses, Nance, Nash, Nelson, Newell, Nuckles, Owens, Pillsbury, Randolph, Rainey, Ransier, Richmond, Rivers, Robertson, Rose, Runion,

Rutland, Sanders, Sasportas, Smalls, Stubbs, Thomas, A. Thompson, B. A. Thompson, S. B. Thompson, Viney, Webb, Whipper, White, Williamson, F. E. Wilder, Wingo, Wooley, Wright—98.

ABSENT.—Messrs. Arnim, Becker, Boozer, Byas, Chestnut, Donaldson, Humbird, Hunter, S. Johnson, Henry Jones, Lang, Neagle, Perry, Shrewsbury, C. M. Wilder—15.

So the amendment was not agreed to.

The question recurring on the main question, viz: the adoption of the report of the Committee, recommending the passage of the petition, the yeas and nays were demanded, and being taken, resulted as follows :

YEAS—The President, Messrs. Allen, Alexander, Bell, Bowen, Bonum Burton, Brockenton, Bryce, Byas, R. H. Cain, F. J. Cain, Camp, Cardozo, Coghlan, Chamberlain, Clinton, Cooke, Collins, Corley, Craig, Crews, Darrington, Davis, DeLarge, Dickson, Dill, Dogan, Driffle, Duncan, Edwards, Elliott, Foster, Gentry, Goss, Gray, Harris, J. N. Hayne, C. D. Hayne, H. E. Hayne, Henderson, Hurley, Jackson, Jacobs, Jenks, Jervey, Jillson, W. B. Johnson, J. W. Johnson, Dr. L. B. Johnson, Johnston, Joiner, Jones, Langley, G. Lee, S. Lee, Lomax, E. W. M. Mackey, Mayer, Mauldin, W. J. McKinlay, Wm. McKinlay, McDaniels, Mead, Middleton, Miller, Millford, Moses, Nance, Nash, Nelson, Newell, Nuckles, Olsen, Owens, Parker, Pillsbury, Randolph, Rainey, Ransier, Richmond, Rivers, Robertson, Rose, Runion, Rutland, Sanders, Sasportas, Stubbs, Thomas, A. Thompson, B. A. Thompson, S. B. Thompson, Viney, Webb, Whittemore, White, Williamson, F. E. Wilder, Wingo, Wooley, Wright—101.

NAYS—Holmes, Leslie, Smalls, Swails, Whipper—5.

ABSENT—Arnim, Becker, Boozer, Byas, Chestnut, Donaldson, Humbird, Hunter, S. Johnson, H. Jones, Lang, Neagle, Perry, Shrewsbury, C. M. Wilder—15.

So the report of the Committee was adopted.

Mr. E. W. M. MACKEY submitted the following resolutions, which, on motion of Mr. F. J. MOSES, Jr., was laid on the table :

Resolved, That the consideration of the Constitution be made the special order for eleven o'clock to-morrow, and be so continued from day to day, immediately after the reading of the Journal, until the whole Constitution shall have been finally disposed of, and during this time no other business except reports from the Finance and Auditing Committees shall be considered.

Resolved, That this resolution shall not be rescinded or suspended except by a three-fourths vote of the Convention.

The hour of half-past two having arrived, the Convention, adjourned to half-past ten o'clock to-morrow.

PROCEEDINGS

OF THE

CONSTITUTIONAL CONVENTION

OF

SOUTH CAROLINA,

Held at Charleston, S. C., beginning January 14th and ending March 17th, 1868.

———o———

INCLUDING THE

DEBATES AND PROCEEDINGS.

———o———

REPORTED BY J. WOODRUFF, PHONOGRAPHIC REPORTER.

VOL. 2.

PUBLISHED BY ORDER OF THE CONVENTION.

CHARLESTON, S C.
PRINTED BY DENNY & PERRY.
163 Meeting Street.
1868.

PROCEEDINGS

Constitutional Convention

OF

SOUTH CAROLINA.

TWENTY-NINTH DAY.

Tuesday, February 18, 1868.

The Convention assembled at half-past 10 A. M., and was called to order by the PRESIDENT.

Prayer was offered by the Rev. B. F. RANDOLPH.

The roll was called, and a quorum answering to their names, the PRESIDENT announced the Convention ready to proceed to business.

Mr. N. G. PARKER offered the following resolution, which was agreed to :

WHEREAS, it has come to the knowledge of this Convention that the Hon. Jacob M. Howard, United States Senator from the State of Michigan, proposes in a few days to visit Richmond, and address the Constitutional Convention of Virginia, now sitting in that city ; be it

Resolved, That the Constitutional Convention of South Carolina respectfully and cordially invite the distinguished Senator to extend his trip to Charleston, and address this Convention on the important subjects which are now exciting our country.

Mr. E. W. M. MACKEY moved to call up from the table the resolution offered by him yesterday, previous to adjournment, in reference to confining the business of the Convention to the framing and adoption of the Constitution, which was not agreed to.

The PRESIDENT announced the unfinished business was the continuation of the second reading of the report of the Committee on the Legislative Part of the Constitution, which was suspended by the call of the house for the Special Order, the house having under consideration the eleventh section, as follows:

SECTION 11. The first election for Senators and Representatives, under the provisions of this Constitution, shall be held on the —— Wednesday of March of the present year; and the second election shall be held on the third Wednesday in October, 1869, and forever thereafter on the same day in every second year, in such manner and at such places as the Legislature may hereafter provide.

Mr. T. HURLEY moved to fill the blank in the eleventh section so as to fix the period of the first election for State Senators and Representatives, under the new Constitution, on the fourth Wednesday in March next.

Mr. E. W. M. MACKEY moved to amend, making it the third Wednesday in March next.

Mr. L. S. LANGLEY moved to postpone its consideration, as it was impossible for them then to fix the time of the first election.

Mr. B. O. DUNCAN moved that it be postponed until after the remaining part of the Constitution was adopted, which was agreed to.

Section twelve was read a second time, as follows:

SECTION 12. The first session of the General Assembly, after the ratification of this Constitution, shall be convened on the —— Monday in April of the present year in the city of Columbia (which shall remain the seat of government until otherwise determined by the concurrence of two-thirds of both branches of the whole representation), and thereafter on the fourth Monday in November annually. Should the casualties of war or contagious diseases render it unsafe to meet at the seat of government, then the Governor may, by proclamation, appoint a more secure and convenient place of meeting.

Mr. B. F. WHITTEMORE. The same reason exists for the postponement of this section as for that of the eleventh section. I therefore move that the further consideration of this section be postponed until the remaining parts of the Constitution is adopted. The motion was agreed to.

Section thirteen received its second reading, and passed without debate, as follows:

SECTION 13. The terms of office of the Senators and Representatives, chosen at a general election, shall begin on the Monday following such election.

Section fourteen received its second reading, as follows:

SECTION 14. Each House shall judge of the election returns and qualifications of its own members; and a majority of each House shall constitute a quorum to do business; but a smaller number may adjourn from day to day, and may be authorized to compel the attendance of absent members, in such manner and under such penalties as may be provided by law.

Mr. L. S. LANGLEY moved to strike out the words "be authorized to" so as to read "may compel," which was agreed to, and the section passed to its third reading.

Section fifteen received its second reading, as follows:

SECTION 15. Each House shall choose its own officers, determine its rules of proceeding, punish its members for disorderly behavior, and with the concurrence of two-thirds, expel a member; but not a second time for the same cause.

Mr. CRAIG moved to strike out the word "cause" in the last line, and substitute the word "offence."

The question was then taken on the amendment, which was not agreed to, and the section passed to its third reading.

Section sixteen was read, and passed without debate, as follows:

SECTION 16. Each House may punish by imprisonment, during its sitting, any person not a member, who shall be guilty of disrespect to the House, by any disorderly or contemptuous behavior in its presence; or who, during the time of its sitting, shall threaten harm to body or estate to any member for anything said or done in either House, or who shall assault any of them therefor, or who shall assault or arrest any witness or other person ordered to attend the House, in his going thereto or returning therefrom, or who shall rescue any person arrested by order of the House.

Section seventeen received its second reading, as follows:

SECTION 17. The members of both Houses shall be protected in their persons and estates during their attendance on, going to, and returning from, the General Assembly, and ten days previous to the sitting, and ten days after the adjournment thereof. But these privileges shall not be extended so as to protect any member who shall be charged with treason, felony, or breach of the peace.

Mr. J. J. WRIGHT moved to strike out the last clause, and substitute, "The members of both Houses shall be protected in their persons; but treason, felony or breach of the peace shall be dealt with according to the laws of the land."

Mr. B O. DUNCAN. I hope the amendment will not pass. It is a mere question of words.

Mr. B. F. WHITTEMORE. We have decided that treason cannot exist against the State.

Mr. B. O. DUNCAN. The original clause is framed in the usual form, but I hope the amendment will be adopted. It might be held, if the section is allowed to remain as it is, it might be held that a member charged with treason, felony, or breach of the peace, had no protection in his person. For instance, a member coming from the General Assembly after the close of the session, if he was charged with assault or breach of the peace, and was then assaulted, this portion of the Constitution might be quoted against him, for it says he is not to be protected in his person in case of his being charged with a breach of the peace or felony.

Mr. W. J. WHIPPER. The clause as it stands, I think, is much better than the proposed amendment. It is certainly understood to mean only that a member charged with breach of the peace shall not be protected from arrest. I hope the original clause will be carried.

The question was then taken on the amendment, which was disagreed to, and the section, as it stood, passed to its third reading.

Mr. F. J. MOSES, Jr. We are hurrying through this part of the Constitution with such speed that some of us cannot keep up, and we have to consider some of the sections after their adoption by the house. I therefore move, for the purpose of making a section just passed more perfect, a reconsideration of the sixteenth section. As it stands, I do not think, and others agree with me, that the term of imprisonment which the legislature is authorized to inflict is strictly defined. I therefore propose to reconsider it. I wish to have it so strictly defined that a sharp lawyer cannot misinterpret it.

Mr. F. L. CARDOZO. If that is the only argument, I do not think it worthy of reconsideration. A sharp lawyer may interpret any part of the Constitution as he pleases, only give him a loop hole.

The motion to reconsider was not agreed to.

The following sections then passed without debate to a third reading :

Section 18. Bills for raising a revenue shall originate in the House of Representatives, but may be altered, amended or rejected by the Senate ; and all other bills may originate in either House, and may be amended, altered or rejected by the other.

Sec. 19. The style of all laws shall be, " Be it enacted by the Senate and House of Representatives of the State of South Carolina, now met and sitting in General Assembly, and by the authority of the same."

Sec. 20. Every act or resolution having the force of law shall relate to but one subject, and that shall be expressed in the title.

Sec. 21. No bill shall have the force of law until it shall have been read three times, and on three several days, in each House, has had the seal of State affixed to it, and has been signed in the Senate House by the President of the Senate and the Speaker of the House of Representatives.

Sec. 22. No money shall be drawn from the Treasury, but in pursuance of an appropriation made by law; and a regular statement and account of the receipts and expenditures of all public moneys shall be published annually, in such manner as may be by law directed.

Sec. 23. Each member of the first General Assembly under this Constitution shall receive six dollars per diem while in session; and the further sum of twenty cents for every mile of the ordinary route of travel in going to and returning from the place where such session is held; after which they shall receive such compensation as shall be fixed by law; but no General Assembly shall have the power to increase the compensation of its own members. And when convened in extra session, they shall receive the same mileage and per diem compensation as fixed by law for the regular session, and none other.

Sec. 24. In all elections by the General Assembly, or either House thereof, the members shall vote "*viva voce*," and their votes thus given shall be entered upon the journals of the House to which they respectively belong.

Sec. 25. Neither House, during the session of the General Assembly, shall, without the consent of the other, adjourn for more than three days, nor to any other place than that in which the Assembly shall be at the time sitting.

Section twenty-six was read a second time, as follows:

Section 26. Each House shall keep a journal of its own proceedings, and cause the same to be published immediately after its adjournment, excepting such parts as in its judgment may require secrecy; and the yeas and nays of the members of either House, on any question, shall, at the desire of any two members present, be entered on the journals. Any member of either House shall have liberty to dissent from, and protest against any act or resolution which he may think injurious to the public or to an individual, and have the reasons of his dissent entered on the journals.

Mr. L. S. LANGLEY. I move to amend by striking out the words " any two" before members, and to insert the words " one-fifth of the." As the section stands, a small minority might clog the wheels of legislation by simply calling the yeas and nays on every question, however unimportant, and the wishes of the majority prevented from being carried into effect.

Mr. W. J. WHIPPER. I hope the amendment will not prevail. I certainly think it should be the right of any two members to call for the yeas and nays whenever they pleased. I hope if changed at all it will be reduced to one.

The amendment was not agreed to, and the section passed to its third reading.

The following were then passed without debate :

SECTION 27. The doors of each House shall be open, except on such occasion as, in the opinion of the House, may require secrecy.

SEC. 28. No person shall be eligible to a seat in the General Assembly whilst he holds any office of profit or trust under this State, the United States of America, or any of them, or under any other power, except officers in the militia, Magistrates or Justices of inferior Courts, while such Justices receive no salary. And if any member shall accept or exercise any of the said disqualifying offices he shall vacate his seat.

Mr. N. G. PARKER moved a reconsideration of section twenty-eight, which was agreed to.

Mr. N. G. PARKER then offered the following amendment: "Provided that the prohibition herein mentioned shall not extend to the members of the first General Assembly.

The amendment was agreed to, and the section passed to its third reading.

Section twenty-nine was read as follows :

SECTION 29. If any election district shall neglect to choose a member or members on the day of election, or if any person chosen a member of either House shall refuse to qualify and take his seat, or shall resign, die, depart the State, accept any disqualifying office, or become otherwise disqualified to hold his seat, a writ of election shall be issued by the President of the Senate, or Speaker of the House of Representatives, as the case may be, for the purpose of filling the vacancy thereby occasioned, for the remainder of the term for which the person so refusing to qualify, resigning, dying, departing the State, or becoming disqualified, was elected to serve, or the defaulting election district ought to have chosen a member or members.

Mr. L. S. LANGLEY. I move to amend by striking out the words "by the President of the Senate or Speaker of the House of Representatives, as the case may be," and insert " by the Governor of the State."

Mr. W. J. WHIPPER. I hope the amendment will fail. The President of the Senate and Speaker of the House of Representatives are the proper persons to issue writs of election in all cases of necessity, and is conformable to the practice heretofore adopted. I do not know as it will be necessary for the Governor to be present all the time during the session of the General Assembly, and if a vacancy should occur, the House should not be compelled to wait for the Governor before issuing a writ of election. The President of the Senate and Speaker of the House are the proper persons, as they can do it at once.

Mr. J. S. CRAIG. The amendment of the gentleman from Beaufort (Mr. LANGLEY) occurred to me as a very proper one to be made before it was presented.

It appears to me that the Governor would have just as much opportunity to know when a vacancy occurred as the President of the Senate or Speaker of the House of Representatives. I hope the amendment will be sustained.

Mr. S. G. W. DILL moved the indefinite postponement of the amendment, which was agreed to, and the section then passed to its third reading.

Section thirtieth was read as follows:

SECTION 30. And whereas the ministers of the gospel are, by their profession, dedicated to the service of God and the cure of souls, and ought not to be diverted from the great duties of their functions; therefore, no minister of the gospel, or public preacher of any religious persuasion, whilst he continues in the exercise of his pastoral functions, shall be eligible to the office of Governor, Lieutenant-Governor, or to a seat in the Senate or House of Representatives.

Mr. B. F. RANDOLPH. I move to amend by striking out "ministers of the gospel" and substitute "whereas doctors and apothecaries are by their profession dedicated to the preservation of health and the cure of *soles*," &c.

Mr. F. J. MOSES, Jr. I move to strike out the whole section.

Mr. E. W. M. MACKEY. I move to lay the amendment offered on the table.

The motion to lay on the table was agreed to.

Mr. F. L. CARDOZO. I move to reconsider the motion to lay on the table, and to lay the motion for reconsideration on the table.

The motion was agreed to, and the PRESIDENT stated that according to parliamentary usage, the laying of an amendment on the table carried with it all that cohered to that amendment. The gentleman from Charleston (Mr. CARDOZO) having moved a reconsideration, and to lay the motion for reconsideration on the table, both having been agreed to, it was out of the power of the house to ever take it up again. The section was therefore laid on the table.

Section thirty-first was read as follows:

SECTION 31. Members of the General Assembly, and all officers before they enter upon the execution of the duties of their respective offices, and all members of the bar, before they enter upon the practice of their profession, shall take and subscribe the following oath:

"I do solemnly swear (or affirm, as the case may be) that I am duly qualified according to the Constitution of the United States and of this State, to exercise the duties of the office to which I have been elected, (or appointed,) and that I will faithfully discharge to the best of my abilities the duties thereof, and that I recognize the supremacy of the Constitution and laws of the United States, over the Constitution and laws of any State, and that I will support, protect and defend the Constitution of the United States and the Constitution of South Carolina, as ratified by the people on ————. So HELP ME GOD.

Mr. B. F. WHITTEMORE moved that the blank be modified as follows: " On the ———— day of ———— 1868," and the following words were added: " And the President of this Convention is authorized to fill up the blanks with the proper date when he shall have received satisfactory information that this Constitution has been ratified by the people."

Section thirty-first was then passed to its third reading.

Section thirty-second was read, and passed without debate, to a third reading, as follows :

SECTION 32. Officers shall be removed from office for incapacity, misconduct, or neglect of duty, in such manner as may be provided by law, when no mode of trial or removal is provided in this Constitution.

Section thirty-third received its second reading, as follows :

SECTION 33. The House of Representatives shall have the sole power of impeaching ; but a majority of all the members elected, must concur in an impeachment. All impeachments shall be tried by the Senate ; and when sitting for that purpose, the Senators shall be upon oath, or affirmation, to do justice according to law and evidence. No person shall be convicted without the concurrence of two-thirds of the Senators present.

Mr. R. G. HOLMES. It strikes me that this section comes in conflict with the twenty-eighth section of the Bill of Rights, which forbids the legislative power exercising any judicial power or authority. It says here that the Senate shall judge of impeachment cases. We should add "that the Senate shall be a Court consisting of the members of the Senate and Judges of the Supreme Court, of which the Chief Justice shall be President." I move to amend by striking out the words " and when sitting for that purpose " and substitute that amendment ; also, to strike out the word " Senators " in the last line, and say " members of the Court."

The amendment was not seconded.

Mr. N. G. PARKER. I simply desire to suggest that the section be stricken out here and be incorporated in the proper place in the Judiciary part of the Constitution. I find, upon examination, that there is a special article upon impeachment in the Judiciary report. It might perhaps be as well to postpone this at the present, and let it be taken up in connection with the section on the same subject in the report of the Judiciary Committee.

Mr. R. C. DeLARGE moved that the consideration of this section be postponed.

Mr. A. J. RANSIER. I move as an amendment that it be recommitted to the Committee, with instructions to refer it to the Committee on the Judiciary.

Mr. J. M. RUTLAND. I have no doubt we shall find similar sections in all the several departments of the Constitution. That, it appears to me, is no good reason why we should strike out a section from one of these departments. As I understand it, the Committee on Review and Consolidation will arrange that matter. They will consolidate the whole, so that that objection falls to the ground. I hope we will act upon each section as if there was no section of the kind in the other departments. I hope the house will not strike out this section.

The question was taken on the motion to recommit. The motion was not agreed to, and the motion to postpone being withdrawn, the section passed to its third reading.

Section thirty-fourth was read a second time, as follows:

SECTION 34. The Governor, Lieutenant-Governor, and all other civil officers, shall be liable to impeachment for high crimes and misdemeanors, for any misbehavior in office, for corruption in procuring office, or for any act which shall degrade their official character. But judgment in such cases shall not extend further than to removal from office and disqualification to hold any office of honor, trust or profit, under this State. The party convicted shall, nevertheless, be liable to indictment, trial, judgment and punishment according to law.

M. J. M. RUTLAND. I think there is a repetition in this section. I move to strike out the two clauses after the word "misdemeanors" The Senate is the Court to decide what the high crimes and misdemeanors are. I do not see why the Senate should try, if the members are not to be the judges of what the misdemeanors are.

Mr. W. J. WHIPPER. A man might be guilty of some misbehavior which might not be a high crime and misdemeanor.

Mr. S. CORLEY. I prefer the words "for corruption" retained in the section.

Mr. B. O. DUNCAN. I hope the amendment will not prevail. One
58

of the great troubles of the country now is the misunderstanding of that word "misdemeanor."

The question was taken on the amendment, which was not agreed to and the section passed to its third reading.

Section thirty-fifth was read a second time, as follows :

SECTION 35. There shall be exempt from execution or other final process of any Court issued for the collection of any debt, a homestead in the country, consisting of one hundred acres, and the dwelling and appurtenances thereon, to be selected by the owner thereof. And in a city, town or village, in lieu thereof, a lot with the dwelling and appurtenances thereon ; provided that such homestead, either in a city, town, village or country, shall not exceed in value two thousand dollars. There shall also be exempt from such execution or other final process of any Court issued for the collection of any debt, the necessary articles of furniture, apparel, subsistence and implements of husbandry, trade or other employment, to the value of five hundred dollars. But no property shall be exempt from sales for taxes, or for the payment of obligations contracted for the purchase of said homestead, or for the erection or improvement thereon. It shall be the duty of the Legislature, at its next session, to pass such laws as may be necessary to carry this provision into effect.

Mr. T. J. ROBERTSON. I move to amend by adding after "two thousand dollars" the following : "No homestead shall be exempt from levy for any just debt existing prior to the passage of this Constitution." I have only a few words to say in relation to this amendment. I am willing and shall insist upon a homestead law for the future. But I am not willing to go back and give men twenty-five hundred dollars worth of property which they are not justly entitled to. I am not willing to make this body the instrument of class legislation, by giving to the men who brought on the war, staked their all on secession, and who have turned off and driven the colored men, to whom they owe their property, from their plantations without a dollar. Can we give twenty-five hundred dollars worth of property to such men for nothing? This section, as it is, leaves room for mischief. I am in favor of every man having a home, provided he pays for it; but I do not believe in any resolution or law that is retrospective in its operations. The men who made this war did not count the cost; they did not care whose property was sacrificed. They drove men like cattle into slaughter pens, and I want to know if this body is prepared to relieve them at the expense of the loyal men of the country. I hope the amendment will be passed.

Mr. R. C. DeLARGE. I trust that clause of the homestead will be passed just as it is reported by the Committee. I also hope that if any amendment is offered it will be such as will not prevent that act from being even retrospective in its action. I appeal for no particular class of men. I am sorry to differ with the distinguished member from Richland, but I do not consider this a class measure.

It is not, I feel assured, the desire of any individual to legislate for any special class of people. It is not, perhaps, within the power of the Convention to pass any act that will not benefit some class. Consistency is a jewel, and having voted for all measures of relief to the impoverished condition of the people of the State, I deem it but right and proper to support a homestead for the same reasons I have supported other measures of relief. That this act gives to the men who carried the State into rebellion the same rights and privileges given to others who have stood steadfastly by the Union I will admit, and as far as I am concerned, I stand here upon this floor with higher motives than those of revenge towards any class of citizens of this State. I do not think this act will come, or is intended to be, in conflict with any mortgage, or even any judgment, already existing upon a homestead. But no one would surely pretend to say that because I owed five hundred dollars last year the law knows or recognizes me as a debtor until I am proved such. It would be just as consistent for the gentlemen to tell us that the law knows a man to be a murderer before convicted by his countrymen. A homestead act to be beneficial, must be retrospective. My distinguished friend from Richland has forgotten that while a homestead act will benefit a large class of men who carried the State into rebellion, it will also benefit another very large class of men, who were, as he well describes it, dragged into that slaughter pen to which he has alluded. I desire a just and liberal homestead act, which will relieve all classes of the people. I trust the amendment of my friend from Richland will be voted down by the Convention.

Mr. J. S. CRAIG. If I understand the amendment of the gentleman from Richland, it is to add a clause, so that the section shall not act retrospectively. I consider this one of the most important measures of relief that has come before this body. It will effect more good to the people generally than any act which has come before this body. Believing this, I shall endeavor, in my humble way, to defend it. If we frame the act so that it will not be retrospective, it will accomplish the end we have in view, but very poorly. I am in favor of this section acting retrospectively as far as possible without coming in conflict with the laws of the country. I understand, however, and have my opinion from good authority, that we can act retrospectively and not come in conflict with any law, provided there is no lien upon the property. This I learn has been the decision in many Northern Courts, that where the

property has no lien upon it a homestead law can act retrospectively. I
believe that to be the fact. I am desirous of doing all the good I can
for the people of the country in providing measures for their relief. I
am willing to leave the question of its acting retrospectively to the
Courts. If the Courts say it can act retrospectively, then I claim it
should do so. I am opposed to the amendment of the gentleman from
Richland for the reason I have assigned, and do not think it necessary
to go into any lengthy discussion of the subject.

Mr. N. G. PARKER. In advocating the passage of the section now
under discussion, I desire to say in the outset, that I am governed by no
other motive than to secure the welfare of all the inhabitants of South
Carolina. I desire to accomplish all that it is possible for this Convention to do, to relieve the people of this State, our constituents, from the
terrible distress which they are now suffering, and from the danger that
threatens them. I do not say to do this that I would yield one iota of
principle, or sacrifice a long cherished opinion ; but, sir, I would open my
heart to extend towards them all the sympathy that a decent regard to
principle and justice would permit. I am aware that I may be charged
by some with possessing more sympathy than judgment; but, sir, I would
rather be subjected to that imputation than on the other hand to be
charged with a lack of sympathy. I thank God that the milk of human
kindness forms a large part of the material of which I am composed, and
that my devotion from boyhood to the present time to the interests of
the oppressed and down trodden of my country cannot be questioned.

I trust that I may be pardoned here for alluding to the colored race.
I would gladly avoid all allusion to them as a separate people. I would
gladly see the word color expunged from the vocabulary of terms applied
to men, and I confidently look forward to a period when there will be no
distinctions on account of race or color ; but sir, while it exists, it is
necessary occasionally to allude to it. I only do it now because the
argument has been presented to me, that an effort to secure the passage
of this section was a stab at the rights of the colored man.

It has been said that to secure the present landholders in the possession of a homestead will prevent the sale of lands ; consequently none
will be put on the market, and the colored man will get no land. Why,
sir, this bill provides for a homestead of only one hundred acres ; few
of the landholders of this State who own one hundred acres of land
own less than five hundred acres, and from that to ten thousand, and
even more. It is not proposed to make a homestead exemption for the
very rich man of ten thousand acres, and for the rich man of five hundred acres, and for the man of moderate means of one hundred acres,

and for the poor man of one acre, but sir, taking all things into account in this State in the present condition, it is a broad and liberal proposition of exempting one hundred acres of land to every man the head of a family who has already, or may hereafter acquire the same, as a homestead, which shall forever be inviolate and exempt from all claims, and be forever the property of the family who acquired it.

I am aware that the amount or value of the exemption named in this ordinance is larger than the average of such exemptions ; but, sir, I do not consider this an objection to it : on the contrary, for several reasons, it is one of its principal merits.

I have said, on a former occasion, that I would have this Convention offer a Constitution to the people of this State which would stand forth pre-eminent among the Constitutions of the States of our national Government for humanity, justice and liberality. To pass this section of the Constitution will be to go far to establish its merits for these great qualities. I desire to remove every obstacle that stands in the way of the prosperity of this State. Circumstances over which the great majority of our people had no control, has brought them into this suffering condition. I desire to show that the great war through which we have passed was not a curse but a blessing, not only to the colored man, but to the whites. That the emancipation of slavery was not the only emancipation that was effected by it. The emancipation of the mind of the great mass of my brother whites was quite as great an event to them as the emancipation of slavery was to the colored race. It is not yet comprehended by all our people, but that is no sign that it will not be ; it is our duty as legislators, as representatives of the people, to force this conclusion home upon our constituents. And, sir, in my opinion there is no way in which we can do so much by any one act as to pass this homestead exemption. We can afford to be generous, and we must be both generous and just.

The tables have turned ; for the first time in the history of this State, a race hitherto denied not only the right to sit in assemblies like this, but the right to have any voice whatever in the election of any one to sit here, are now not a mere minority, but a clear majority. Being clearly in the majority, it is doubtless the belief of nearly all of our white brethren throughout the State that you will imitate their example, and legislate exclusively for your own benefit and not for all.

We, the few white Republicans in the State, are satisfied that no such thing is contemplated, nor ever was. We have all along been satisfied on this point, but it is incumbent on us all to satisfy all persons of the fact and pass this homestead exemption, and all doubts will be expelled.

I have heard it said that the colored man would get no land if this bill was passed, that it would keep all lands out of the market, and this was what the landholders wanted; but, sir, this will not follow, it is not true, and I will show it. This exemption, as I have before repeated, exempts only one hundred acres. There are plenty of debts hanging over the heads of the great majority of landholders, in my opinion, and within my positive knowledge, to show the utter falsity of this presumption. It is to be deplored that there are so many debts hanging over our people that must be paid if they have the property to pay it with, for it cripples their means, destroys to a great extent their hopes and energies, and retards not only their prosperity but the prosperity of all. Those who own land cannot prosper unless those who do not own prosper. No one can dispute this, hence you desire, we all desire the prosperity of the present landholders. I do not, however, desire any man to hold ten thousand acres of land, nor five thousand, nor hardly in any instance one thousand acres. I hope to live to see the time when there will not be a large plantation in the State; but to see those that now exist cut up into one hundred thousand farms, and all of them prospering.

But, sir, this exemption does not provide for any person retaining a large plantation; it is only for one hundred acres. Now, I would ask, if this bill is passed would the colored men be injured by it? Supposing all the land of the State to pass under the auctioneers hammer to-day for debt, or to-morrow, or next month, or next spring, or next year, at any time, would the colored man get much of it? Have they the means to purchase now? I do not believe it. And precious little would they be able to purchase at any price. I verily believe, and I say it in no disparagement to them, that if it was sold to-day for one dollar per acre, there is not one in a hundred throughout the State who could purchase a single acre.

They are not ready to purchase lands yet, and I fear that unless more prosperity is established among the present landholders that they never will be ready to purchase. Pass this homestead exemption, and one step will be taken in the right direction; do not be afraid of it because it seems to please many of the whites. There may be some white men who take the view of the case that I have endeavored to overthrow; they may believe that they can keep you out of land if such an act is passed, but they are really mistaken. They will be glad enough to sell it, they cannot afford to keep it, it will ruin them if they do; they cannot work it profitably in such large tracts, and they will be ruined if they persist in the attempt. It may be the motive of some for wishing this exemption passed ; but never mind that, we must pass it if at all upon its merits alone, regardless of any ones opinions.

I want to see the colored men of this State, and of all the States, whenever they acquire property, own farms, houses, and other property. I want them to keep it after they acquire it. It is one of the reasons for pressing this exemption. A good many own lots and houses in towns and cities now, a few in the country ; they are as much interested in securing them to themselves and families as are the whites. There are sharpers all over the world ; the war did not kill them all off. North or South, they will coax, steal, swindle, and tear away the property of one man as quickly as another. They are no respectors of persons ; they will take a colored man's house away from him and turn his family into the street just as quick as they would a white man ; we are to legislate for the future and not wholly for to-day. We have an opportunity now to do what we may not have for ten, twenty or fifty years ; let us take the whole responsibility and do that which seemeth right, whatever may be thought of us or our acts. It is a mistaken idea that to pass this homestead exemption will keep land out of the market ; it will do no such thing, there will be plenty of it on the market at all times in our day for all who want it, and I believe at a reasonable price. There are debts due from the landholders that must be paid, and their land must pay them ; they have nothing else wherewithal to pay them ; they can sell their surplus lands, pay their debts, and be better off. Taxes are always (at least in hard times) a burden, will be assessed yearly upon all lands, and they must be paid. The expenses of the State (constantly increasing, will be a continual drag upon those who attempt to carry on large landed estates with a small amount of money,) will alone force sufficient lands upon the market at all times to meet the wants of all the landless. This Convention will cost the State quite a large sum of money. A Legislature will soon assemble, and that will cost money. Education, once limited, is to be general, and that will be expensive ; and, to keep up with the age, it is fair to presume that the State tax will be greater next year than this, and increase yearly ; this will be felt, and will be the stimulus to many for owning less land, and cause them to see the necessity of disposing of their surplus.

Now, as to the amount, I do not consider it too great ; it is no argument that it is because other States have made it less ; we have been in times past an exception to other States, and we can be again. We have been more unjust and illiberal in many things, let us be more just and liberal now in some things. It is said by some that it will be unconstitutional to pass this homestead exemption. Why, sir, I propose to make it constitutional; we are here to make a constitution; those who think we have no right to pass this exemption must reflect but a moment, when I think they'will be convinced that we have a right to do so, and a great many other things. A Constitutional Convention has, in my opinion, a clearer right to legislate upon all matters that interest the State than any other body possibly can have. The reconstruction acts of Congress under which we are elected, gives us all power to "frame and adopt a Constitution and a civil government for the State of South Carolina." To adopt, or organize a civil government of a State, certainly covers all the ground that we ask. Our right to pass any Ordinance of relief to the State, or of interest to the people, cannot be questioned; it is as clear as the noon day sun.

Again, the State protects itself in the adoption of this act. Every State must protect all the inhabitants of it and itself, as an organization, from that which would destroy it. The poor of the State must be maintained. Every law of justice and humanity requires this. To prevent pauperism, then, is but a measure of self protection. The State and every county, town, city, and every individual in it who owns a dollar's worth of property for which they will be taxed, are interested in preventing pauperism. The City of Charleston alone appropriates the present year $80,000 for the support of its orphans and almshouse. What the amount in the State is I have not taken the pains to ascertain; but, sir, it must be quite a large amount, and we are all interested in keeping it at the lowest possible point. Refuse to pass this exemption act, suffer the property of the people of this State to pass under the auctioneer's hammer now, and pauperism will so increase that the next purchaser of the lands will shortly be compelled to suffer the same penalty, in order to pay the taxes that will necessarily be imposed upon him. I am glad rather than otherwise, that his Excellency the Governor of the State recommends the passage of a homestead law.

When, however, this Ordinance was introduced here, I had not been informed what were the views of his Excellency upon this subject. That they are in harmony with the principle contained in this act, cannot be any reason for us to oppose it; but if we receive it without prejudice, and I believe we do, it should be additional reasons for adopting it. I trust, therefore, sir, that we shall pass this section, and establish at once the claim of this Convention to the thanks of the entire people of this State, and the respect of all men everywhere throughout the world.

Mr. L. S. LANGLEY. I move to amend the ninth line (printed bill), by adding the words "or for debts contracted for labor." Under the section as it now reads, a homestead worth $2,000 is exempt from levy or sale of property under execution for debts due by the owner, but I think some provision should be made for the security of the laborer, and that men who employ others to work for them should pay for that labor. I am in favor of a homestead law in the State for the future, and to protect those now in possession of a homestead, but I am not willing to release a man who owns ten thousand acres of land, and is divested of that property by virtue of a legal process through his creditors levying on it for just debts. We certainly should not adopt a section in the Constitution whereby the laborer might be defrauded or cheated of the reward of his labor. As the section stands, it would exclude the laborer even who has obtained a decree of Court securing him pay for his labor. That I feel assured is not the desire of the Convention ; I therefore offer this amendment.

Mr. C. C. BOWEN. I am sorry to have to disagree with some of the proposed amendments. I am a little surprised that the delegate who has just taken his seat insisted that the homestead should be exempt so far as labor was concerned ; he might have added and for a certain amount for whiskey and provisions, and thereby rendered the homestead law ridiculous. If a party has a homestead set aside for the use of himself and family, is it not better for the laborer, the merchant, and the world around. I see no necessity of encumbering the section with such amendments, unless it is the object of the delegate to defeat it.

Mr. L. S. LANGLEY. I desire to ask the gentleman whether as the section stands, the laborer who has performed work on the plantation last year, can collect his wages that remain unpaid after the ratification of the Constitution ?

Mr. C. C. BOWEN. As I understand the proposition, is that the homestead shall not be taken by any one for any debt whatever. There are two classes of debts that are secured ; the first is a mortgage in which all the premises are described. If a man holds a mortgage upon a piece of property, and that property is described in the mortgage, there is but one way to discharge it, and that is to pay the money. No homestead law can affect that. There is but one other class, and that is where a judgment has been already entered up in a Court of record of a lien upon any property. No homestead law can affect that.

Mr. T. J. ROBERTSON. A gentleman is now in this city who has made application to Brevet Major-General E. R. S. Canby, to allow him to get back a homestead sold two years ago. I desire to know whether Brevet Major-General E. R. S. Canby can relieve him, if he has not paid for it, whether he has or has not given a mortgage ?

Mr. C. C. BOWEN. I do not propose to go into any argument of
59

that kind. I do not think it has anything to do with the question of a homestead. The object of this section is to secure to heads of families a homestead, consisting of a certain amount named. There are two classes of debts, as I have already said, which I consider secure. The amendment of the gentleman from Richland (Mr. ROBERTSON), is to make this section prospective only ; in other words, that all debts contracted heretofore, whether covered by judgment or mortgage or not, shall have the same standing. I object to that; I am in favor of letting it have as broad a scope as possible under the circumstances. This does not propose to interfere with any contract. It is a proposition to secure a man or head of a family a certain amount of property. I move to strike out these words, "but no property shall be exempt from sale for taxes, or for the payment of obligations contracted for the purchase of such homestead."

It is usual where parties sell lands, especially if the sale is on credit, to take a bond and mortgage as soon as sold. I have said a mortgage covers the debt, and if the party selling a homestead has not taken a mortgage for the purchase money, he must have been a very poor business man, and ought to suffer, for it is his own fault if he has not secured himself. But I venture to-day there is not one case in five thousand where a party sells real estate property on credit and does not take a mortgage. If he has taken this precaution, the homestead bill cannot affect him. But against all other debts, or in any way possible, I say a man's homestead should be protected.

Mr. T. K. SASPORTAS. I think the sum mentioned too large, though I am in favor of a homestead law. I move to strike out $2,000 and insert $1,000.

Mr. F. L. CARDOZO. I have opposed heretofore the cancellation of any debt whatever that a man contracted, and the violation of any obligation or contract entered into. I desire to make a special exception for a homestead law. I think every head of a family should have a homestead of about the value mentioned in this section. But at the same time, I favor the sale of all the rest of a debtor's property to pay his just debts. Such a law would establish a more permanent and settled character among the American people, who heretofore have been distinguished for their migratory character, simply because they were not protected in their homesteads. It would not only give a greater permanence, but a greater security to our people. I hope the section will pass just as it is, and that all the amendments will be voted down. I like that part of the section particularly which my colleague (Mr. BOWEN) wanted to amend, and which says, "No property shall be exempt from

sale for taxes or for the payment of obligations contracted for the purchase of a homestead." I think the gentleman from Beaufort (Mr.
LANGLEY), who desires to haye his amendment attached to this, was
surely battling against a creature of his own imagination, for if any
labor is expended in the erection of a homestead, this clause gives the
laborer the right to levy. For any debts contracted for the purchase of
the homestead or its erection any person has the right to levy on that
homestead. I would like to ask my colleague (Mr. BOWEN), if he
means to say that a homestead should be exempt from levy or sale on a
mortgage. If I understand him correctly, a person can levy and sell on
a mortgage. Cannot a person be the mortgagee and another person
hold the mortgage. It appears to me that a person who holds a mortgage can sell the mortgage and pay off the debts due him. The proposition of my colleague to strike out the last clause, if agreed to, might
make it impossible for the owner of a homestead, who desired to improve it, to borrow one or two thousand dollars on that property for that
purpose.

Mr. L. S. LANGLEY. The gentleman has stated that my apprehension was not well founded, or, in other words, if the section passes as it
is, it would not preclude the laborer from collecting the debts due him
for wages. His colleague (Mr. BOWEN) admitted it would be utterly
impossible for the laborer to collect his wages, under this section. I
desire to know whether the gentleman, after supporting so eloquently
the petition for the purchase of lands, in order that laborers might obtain them on a credit of five years from the Government, is now willing
to prevent the laborer from collecting the honest wages of his toil.

Mr. F. L. CARDOZO. I have not the slightest objection to the
laborer collecting the honest wages of his toil, if that is for the erection
of the homestead. Let him collect debts due for work on the homestead by levying on the homestead, and for debts due for the cultivation
of the soil by levying on the produce. Let him collect his wages on
whatever his labor has been expended. I think we only differ as to the
method in which the laborer shall collect his wages. I say I favor this
last clause because it allows a man who has only a homestead to borrow
money on that homestead, and thus be enabled to improve it. If we
strike this clause out, it prevents him from improving his grounds, because no person will lend him the money if he cannot give a mortgage
on his homestead It seems to me he could not mortgage it for any
other business transaction. I hope, for these reasons, and from the fact
that it will have a tendency to produce a permanent settled character
among the American people, and for the just preservation of a man's

family, the wife and children of him who may become involved in debt and bankruptcy in the course of business transactions, I hope the section will pass, and all the amendments be voted down. With regard to its retrospective action, this section does not state its character in that respect, and, I think, for a good reason. We cannot pass any retrospective law whatever. We have not incorporated into our Constitution an *ex post facto* law, and if we do not do that, then our Constitution cannot conflict with the Constitution of the United States. The Courts are compelled to abide by the organic law we frame. They must consider the Constitution as their guide; and they could not, nor would the Constitution of the United States justify them in pronouncing this or any other section retrospective and unconstitutional.

Mr. W. J. WHIPPER. I hope, with the gentleman who last addressed the Convention, that every amendment offered to this section will be voted down, and the section passed as it now stands. The member from Orangeburg (Mr. SASPORTAS) proposes to amend by making the sum one instead of two thousand dollars.

The object of this homestead law is to protect the homeless, and there are very few in any State that would have or could have a home, if the amount reserved was only one thousand dollars. The ground upon which your home would necessarily be erected would cost more money. It would be only a protection to some who live in the country; but by making it two thousand dollars, protection is afforded to all classes in city or country. Two thousand dollars in the city of Charleston would cover a moderate homestead, whilst the same amount in some portions of the country would be large. The amount of two thousand dollars I believe to be small enough.

With regard to the retrospective character of the section, there is no question but that it will to a certain extent act retrospectively. It was designed to act retrospectively as to all debts not really vested; but against any other it cannot so act. It cannot destroy any vested rights, such as a judgment or mortgage. In any case where a judgment has not been obtained on a mortgage it will act retrospectively. Such was the intention of the Committee in framing this section.

The member from Richland says we will protect men who bet their all on secession. This will be a very poor reason for leaving all poor men exposed to the mercy of the heartless speculators who are now scattered throughout the State. We should not refuse protection to a man simply because he bet his all on secession. We are framing laws for the whole people, and are not to consider the fact that the law protects the man who was once a political criminal. We are not to refuse to pass an act that will benefit the great masses of the people, lest we should protect somebody in favor of secession.

Mr. T. J. ROBERTSON. Is it not entirely class legislation?

Mr. W. J. WHIPPER. I answer the gentleman most emphatically, no. As one of the Committee, I distinctly assert that no class legislation was intended. It proposes to protect every man in a given amount of property. Even if it was a fact that there was not a colored man in South Carolina who had an acre of land, it is to be remembered that their chances in the race of life are now equal, and the fact that they may now become owners of land creates the necessity for such a provision in the Constitution as is now offered.

Mr. T. J. ROBERTSON. That is the very reason I offered my amendment.

Mr. W. J. WHIPPER. There are many colored people in the State of South Carolina who have already obtained lands, who have property, and who desire this protection, not because they are black men or white men, but simply because they are men, and the homesteads of men should be protected.

Mr. L. S. LANGLEY. I desire the gentleman to state distinctly whether laborers who labored hard last year could, after the adoption of this Constitution, collect their wages for their labor, and whether the homestead could be levied on and sold for the payment of such debts.

Mr. W. J. WHIPPER. The gentleman inquires whether the laborer who labored hard last year could levy on the homestead for the payment of his wages. I answer most emphatically he could not.

It is the design of the homestead law to protect this amount of property against all past debts where the rights of property have not been vested. We cannot set aside a judgment obtained. We cannot set aside a mortgage. For the present, the laborer must depend for his protection upon the general orders of the Military Commander of the District. The Legislature will meet within the next six months, and it will be the business of that body to provide, by a lien upon the crops, for the payment of the wages of the laborer. All debts that arise after this section is adopted for labor may be secured by the laborer, who will have a right to levy on that which he produces, and the Legislature when it meets, as the guardian of the country, will enact measures to secure the laborer just compensation.

I hope therefore the section will pass as it came from the hands of the Committee. I hope it will be adopted without any regard to race or color, and the mere fact that it may at the present time protect more white men than black men is certainly no argument against it, for it is

to be hoped and presumed that the poor people of this country, irrespective of color, will become possessed of homesteads. It is the duty
of this body to afford them this protection. Other States have done it,
and we can only give this much needed protection to the poor people by
passing a homestead law. I hope every member here will vote for it,
and vote down every amendment offered to it.

Mr. T. J. ROBERTSON. Retrospective laws, according to my understanding and version of the Constitution of the United States, and of
the sections of the Bill of Rights we have already passed, are unconstitutional. The Constitution of the United States says, "No State shall
pass any laws violating the obligation of a contract." I cannot see how
we can adopt this section and not come in conflict with that provision.
It cannot be denied that this proposed homestead law is retrospective.
No one can collect his debts. I contend that no debt can be collected
on a homestead if the section should pass as it is. It does not benefit
the colored man; it only gives the very class who inaugurated the war a
bonus of $2,500. I will sustain this bill, if we make no class legisla-
tion. If we will go back, let us purchase every man a homestead to the
value of $2,500.

Mr. C. P. LESLIE. Which side are you going to vote on?

Mr. T. J. ROBERTSON. I did not ask the gentleman from Barnwell for his opinion. I say, if we want a retrospective law, let us go
back and give every man, white or black, a homestead. A great deal
has been said about the poor debtor, but I would like to know what the
Convention will do for the poor creditor. I know a man in possession
of a home, who bought it on credit, but now, though the money is long
since due, refuses to pay, and claims under General Canby's order, that
he has a right to it, after having given a mortgage upon the property.
I know, too, that since the close of the war several millions of dollars
could have been brought to this State, if capitalists had confidence in
our people. Want of that confidence has prevented them from coming
here. My version of this section is that it applies to all debts; that it
exempts the homestead to the amount of $2,500 free of all debts.

Mr. C. P. LESLIE. Are you making laws for yourself?

Mr. T. J. ROBERTSON. I am trying to make laws for the benefit
of the whole people.

Mr. J. J. WRIGHT. It matters not to me what the State of Alabama
has done, or what the State of Georgia, or North Carolina, or Virginia,
has done. We are here to exercise our judgment, and to devise measures for the relief of the people of the State. If Alabama has undertaken to appease the wrath of those whose wrath could not be appeased,

and if she has failed, it is no reason why we should fail. It is the duty of every member of this Convention, and every person in the State of South Carolina, to do what they conceive to be their duty. If we differ in our views of what that duty is, it is no reason why we should attempt to crush one another. I do not, and I trust there is not a man here who does cherish any feeling of hatred or malice towards any person. We are about to lay a new foundation. Let us see that it shall be so broad and wide that all the people of the State can stand, live and flourish upon it. It is not for the black man or the white man, but for the whole people that we should legislate. If we conceive it to be our duty to incorporate a homestead law into the Constitution, and that Constitution is ratified by the people of the State of South Carolina, it then becomes the supreme law of the land, to which all the Courts and the Legislature of this State must be subservient.

If we review the history of past nations, we shall find that no people can live and flourish as they ought to, unless protected in their homesteads. In laying, therefore, our new foundation, and building a new fabric, as representatives of the people of South Carolina, it is a duty incumbent upon us to incorporate into the Constitution a homestead law, and just such a one as is proposed in this thirty-fifth section. I take a somewhat different view of this case from some of the gentlemen who have already spoken. With regard to this being class legislation, I would say there is no class of persons mentioned in the act, and hence it extends to the white man, the black man and the red man if he owns property. A homestead of this kind protects the people in various ways. In the first place, it keeps them from running in debt; in the second place, it makes a man more independent, and keeps a poor man from the necessity of hiring to a certain class of persons who would cheat them out of their labor. If these persons who own large plantations hire them, and they do not pay the wages agreed upon, the laborer can have his action at law, and the right to levy upon those large plantations and sell them, if necessary. As far as the Courts are concerned, and with regard to judgments, I contend, when the Constitution is adopted and ratified, no Court can order a sale of property of the amount exempted here and claimed as a homestead, whether there is a judgment on that property or not. If an action is commenced in a Court against a plantation worth $10,000, the person who holds a judgment against that plantation may call on the Court to sell, and he may collect all but what is exempted in this thirty-fifth section. This protects every man, and in laying our new foundation we desire that every man will be protected, and none robbed of their rights. There are certain things for which the homestead may be attached, such as taxes and the payment of obligations contracted for the purchase of the homestead.

Mr. L. S. LANGLEY. Are not debts contracted for labor as sacred as those contracted for the purchase of the homestead ?

Mr. J. J. WRIGHT. They are, but I consider all debts for labor contracted for the erection or the improvement of the homestead are covered by this clause, so that the laborer is secure in his labor.

Mr. L. S. LANGLEY. It has been stated by two legal gentleman that the laborer who has worked last year, and whose wages are still due, that he could not collect his wages on the property of a man who possessed only a homestead. I ask the gentleman who concurs in that view ?

Mr. J. J. WRIGHT. I am not responsible for the opinions of any gentleman upon the floor. I have stated already that any person whose labor secured any other person a homestead, was secure in his labor by this clause. If it were not so, I would not advocate it. I hope all the amendments will be voted down and the section passed as it stands.

Mr. W. E. JOHNSTON. I rise with no intention of making a speech ; but a great deal has been already said about the matter, and to shorten discussion, I move that all amendments be indefinitely postponed.

Mr. J. M. RUTLAND, I hope the gentleman will withdraw that motion and let the matter be discussed. I hope no snap judgment will be taken. It is our desire to ascertain the sense of the house as to whether this section is intended to act prospective only, or retrospective also.

Mr. W. E. JOHNSTON. I was under the impression that all our legal gentlemen had not gathered steam enough to go ahead again. As it appears I am mistaken, I will withdraw my motion.

Mr. J. M. RUTLAND. I desire to state my position upon the subject of homesteads and stay laws. I desire it to be distinctly understood, that so far as these laws are to operate in the future, I am a homestead man. I am in favor of a homestead law, and think we should have had a homestead law long ago for the protection of the unfortunate debtor, but not having had such a law heretofore, it would be against all right to pass a law here like this that would operate retrospectively. I favor no stay law, but I desire a homestead law that shall operate from this time henceforward. You may fix any amount you please, from one up to five thousand dollars, and I will support it. I will support it because it is necessary to the prosperity of the country and of the State. If you contract with a man knowing that it is the law of the land that the homestead is preserved by law, you contract with a full and fair notice that you are not allowed to sell the homestead for the payment of obligations assumed by that contract; but it is different when you apply such a law to the past. A great deal has been said in relation to retrospective and *ex post facto* laws. To illustrate to the Convention the effect of an *ex post facto* law, let us suppose a case; suppose that some member of this Convention committed a small larceny; that he had stolen a watermelon out of somebody's patch, and the offence at the time according to the laws was punishable with fine and imprisonment, and that it was known that a party convicted of such an act would be imprisoned a few days, and a small fine imposed. With this knowledge he takes the chances and steals a watermelon. He is taken in the act, but before the trial comes to a conclusion, a law is passed by a body like this or the Legislature, that any man who commits larceny should receive the same penalty as he who commits murder. Would it not be an outrage upon justice, that a man who stole a watermelon should suffer such a penalty, not attached to the crime at the time he committed it? That is an *ex post facto* law. It is an outrageous injustice. An *ex post facto* law applies strictly to criminal matters, and retrospective or retro-active laws apply to matters of contract, and all other matters not criminal. An *ex post facto* law, as applied to criminal matters, is strictly analogous to retrospective laws as applied to civil matters. We come here to-day with debts existing all over the country, and pass a section of the Constitution which gives every man a homestead law, which you might as well say is to run back as far as debts go back, and no man is allowed to sell that property though he has a $10,000 bond upon it, given in accordance with the law of contract existing at the time. I say it is strictly analogous to hanging a man for stealing a watermelon; I ask you if this is not gross injustice, when the man who gave the credit did it without any notice that any such law would ever come into existence.

Mr. C. C. BOWEN. Would you, as a lawyer, give your opinion in writing that this section would impair the obligation of any contract.

Mr. J. M. RUTLAND. If it is intended to act retrospectively, of which I have no doubt, I emphatically would give my opinion in writing, and bind myself to show I was right, and the section as it is is unconstitutional and contrary to law.

Mr. F. L. CARDOZO. Can the intentions of the framer of any constitution or section have any effect on the legal interpretation of such section or Constitution? Can this legally be interpreted an *ex post facto* law?

Mr. J. M. RUTLAND. Most unquestionably it is the province of the

60

Court to determine what is the intention of the law as passed. It is for the Court to tell us exactly what is meant. If the amendment of my friend from Richland (Mr. ROBERTSON) is adopted, we will know what is meant, and if it is rejected there will be no difficulty in interpreting the section, as the rejected amendment will be known and referred to as showing the intention of this body.

A great deal has been said from time to time about an authority or two in the State of New York, which it is alleged supports the position that it is constitutional to exempt a homestead from prior existing debts. I have not myself been able to get a reference or access to any volumes on the subject, but I consulted a legal friend who had read these cases. He told me that Chief Justice Marshall, perhaps one of the brightest ornaments that ever graced the bench of this or any other country, decided *in totidem verbis* "that stay laws intended to act retrospectively were unconstitutional." I think he said the case was to be found in 6th Peters. As to the New York authority that has been quoted, my friend said this was a case of this character. Some years ago the legislature of New York passed an act which exempted the homestead, and a case came up of a man's property to be sold for debt. He claimed the homestead. The case went to the Supreme Court. It was in evidence that the creditor had slept upon his rights and could have availed himself of the facilities the law afforded him. It was therefore decided against the creditor.

Mr. C. C. BOWEN. In the case you speak of was the judgment entered up previous to the passage of the homestead law, or subsequent to it.

Mr. J. M. RUTLAND. The Legislature passed the homestead law, and this debt existed prior to the passage of the act.

Mr. C. P. LESLIE. Will the delegate say whether the act of Congress known as the Bankrupt Act, allowing five hundred dollars to the bankrupt was complete against *back* debts? According to your tactics that was unconstitutional.

Mr. J. M. RUTLAND. There is a provision of the Constitution of the United States which allows Congress to pass a uniform bankrupt law. I think the bankrupt act allows the unfortunate debter five hundred dollars. Many members of Congress contended that they had no right under the Constitution to do so. The majority voted that they had the right. We are bound by that Constitution, tied hand and foot, and any Ordinance of this Convention in contravention of that instrument is null and void.

Mr. F. J. MOSES, Jr. What more right has Congress to violate the Constitution of the United States than this Convention ?

Mr. J. M. RUTLAND. The Constitution of the United States gives Congress the power to pass a bankrupt bill.

Mr. C. P. LESLIE. Is not that an *ex post facto* law. Did not the bankrupt act exempt five hundred dollars against past debts. You answer me by stating they did make that exemption under authority of the Constitution, which gave Congress that power. They passed a general bankrupt act. I wish to know where in the Constitution of the United States they got the authority to pass what is deemed by some an *ex post facto* law. You said it was impairing the obligation of contracts. I ask where the Congress of the United States got authority to release the debtor ?

Mr. J. M. RUTLAND. There was a division upon that very question. Many members did not believe they had the right, and the decision of Congress is not infallible. The Supreme Court of the United States has heretofore declared some acts of Congress unconstitutional.

Mr. C. P. LESLIE. Do you know of any Court that at any time ever questioned the legality of the provisions of the bankrupt act, or the right of Congress to pass it ?

Mr. J. M. RUTLAND. It does not follow because a case has not been brought before the Court that the law is constitutional.

Mr. C. P. LESLIE. What members of Congress asserted that that body had no right to pass such an act ?

Mr. J. M. RUTLAND. I did not go there; do not know their names They were divided upon the question, and it is not absolutely certain that Congress did do right. There are laws in existence now passed by Congress, the constitutionality of which is gravely questioned; questions, however, which have never been raised before the Supreme Court. I do not suppose there is a man here but what knows Congress has passed laws the constitutionality of which has been gravely questioned. I would state it as a law of the State of South Carolina, that where a marriage settlement is undertaken to be made by the parties married, and the husband desires to settle a certain portion of property upon his wife, he must answer certain questions. Among others, how many debts do you owe. Are you able to pay your debts before making this settlement. If he cannot answer this affirmatively, any lawyer will tell him he cannot make such a settlement until he has paid every dollar of his debts. You can make a settlement *in futuro* but not upon property for which the party is already in debt. That is strictly analogous to this law. The law cannot act retrospectively upon debts past due, the credit of which has been supported upon the face of this property. It is unconstitutional to allow a homestead out of property upon which another has a prior claim.

Mr. F. J. MOSES, Jr. Did not both cases of the homestead law quoted by you come under the statutes of fraud, or only one?

Mr. J. M. RUTLAND. I think they both came under that provision of the Constitution which says, "no *ex post facto* law shall be passed." That is the broad platform upon which I stand, the Constitution of the United States and the laws of Congress passed in pursuance thereof. If we are bound by those laws of the United States, I would not give the paper you write your Ordinances upon for what the Ordinance is worth. If you undertake to make your homestead law operate retrospectively, I confess its moral influence might to some extent demoralize the sense of justice. I am satisfied I am right upon the law of the case, wrong perhaps upon its morality.

Look at the morality of retrospection in a case distinguishing between the creditor who has a judgment upon the homestead and one who has not. If a man owes me a debt, and I choose to give him an opportunity of paying that debt without prosecuting him in Court, the argument of the opposite side is I must lose my debt, and the land shark who has secured his judgment against that land shall have his money, because he has a lien upon the property.

I desire to see justice done, though the heavens fall. I do not think it fair to appeal to the sympathies of a grave body like this, to tell them of the families, widows and orphans that will suffer if we do not pass this law, or do not pass that law. That is not the way to argue a great constitutional question. Let us do our duty and let the consequences take care of themselves.

The gentleman from Beaufort (Mr. WRIGHT) tells us in broad terms that it does not make any difference whether Alabama, or any other State has passed such a law as this, and that it is no guide for us. He is very un-lawyer like. The gentleman is a lawyer and should acknowledge the force of precedents, for he practices almost exclusively upon precedents; and, as a lawyer, he rises here and tells us not to act in this case according to precedent, that is as far as the practice of justice is concerned in this case.

Mr. J. J. WRIGHT. If Alabama or Massachusetts pass a law to cut their own throats, would it be a precedent for us?

Mr. J. M. RUTLAND. That would be a precedent that would never happen, for no sane people would pass such a law. I contend that lawyers do like precedents, and wherever passed upon or decided by a sensible judge or people they should be respected, no matter what country they come from.

We ourselves have slavishly almost regarded the precedents of England, because of the profound learning and ability which have characterized and established those precedents. It seems to me it is an acknowledgment of weakness on the part of my friend, because when he does so, I know if he was sustained by precedents no one would be more ready to battle for them than he would. A great deal has been said about the laborer being paid for his labor; that is exactly what I want. I want every man to have justice; not for another to get his labor or his money, and then be permitted to get off upon the cry that he is poor and cannot pay. Has not one as much right to his property in labor as the other has in the land?

Again, Mr. Brown credits Mr. Smith with provisions enough to last him until he has gathered his crop. Mr. Smith is called upon to pay, and raises the cry of "look at this shark, Mr. Brown; this greedy creditor, he comes to claim everything I have got. If you want pay for your laborers, for the provisions you sold, or any other property, look to it that you do not let this section act retrospectively. Suppose you pass an ordinance so as to act retrospectively, and it should be decided by the Courts that it is constitutional; that the Courts sustain you. Ten or twelve years from now the country has again become overwhelmed with debt. Men owe large amounts. You meet again in Convention, pass another Constitution not limited in the amount of homesteads. Is it not wholesale repudiation? If you pass the homestead provision in that section, you pass a repudiation law in every case where a man has nothing but a homestead. It is true the Convention has repudiated negro debts upon a principle which I think a very wrong principle. They argued that question upon its moral phase. I deny that they had a right to do so. Whilst, however, they have passed that ordinance to repudiate slave debts, they say they are not in favor of repudiation. If they are not in favor of repudiation, then they are not in favor of passing a law to act retrospectively. I say make every man pay his debts, and let the State be restored the credit she once had, but has not now, nor never will have as long as she enacts stay laws and laws that act retrospectively. It does seem to me the Convention ought to be satisfied on the merits and justice of the case. Pass this section upon the eternal principle of right and justice, and if you do you will vote for the amendment offered by my friend from Richland (Mr. ROBERTSON.) If not, if you are willing to sweep away the rights of creditors for the debtors, it is class legislation. If you legislate against the creditor in favor of the debtor, are they not two classes of people ? What right have you under the mild word "relief" to take away another's property ? If you want relief, the proper way to get it for the poor is this : Apply to the Legislature to enact laws, and collect taxes upon the whole community according to the value of their property, and appropriate these taxes to relieve the poor black and poor white, the widows and orphans ; I will then put my hand in my pocket as deep as any other man, but will never consent to rob one man for another.

Mr. C. C. BOWEN. I have but a few words to say, believing it useless to take up more time in discussing this question. The theory advanced by the gentleman who has just taken his seat, namely, that a party cannot make over to his wife any of his property while he owes certain debts, unless he has the wherewithal to pay those debts, I will grant is law, but it is not analogous to this case. That case would come under the statute of frauds, whereas this would not. The one is the act of a legislative body, the other the act of a private individual, performed for the purpose of defrauding other parties. He has said that retrospective laws have been declared unconstitutional. I think he would fail in any attempt to show a solitary case where any judge ever decided the question of unconstitutionality against an ordinance ; if he can, I will vote against this section in the Constitution. The very cases cited show that no homestead law or stay law can be set up against any judgment entered up. We do not propose by this section to interfere with any of those classes of debts, that is debts covered by mortgage ; those will take care of themselves under those clauses of the Constitution so much quoted this morning. The gentleman has said a creditor may be merciful, but in nine cases out of ten we expect to hear him say, " give me the bond." I, therefore, hope that this Convention will pass this section just as it is.

Mr. C. P. LESLIE. In early life I undertook to study law. I went to a law office and staid there several years. It may be that I did not read as attentively as I might have done. I have read Kent's Commentaries, Coke, and most every similar work that had any law proposition stated in it. This morning, though, I have not had the pleasure of reading a work which might be properly called "Rutland on Constitutional law," yet I have observed that whenever poor men are concerned in any measure, I have always found the delegate from Fairfield and the delegate from Richland hunting together in couples against them. I want it distinctly understood that this homestead law is not to prevent the collection of a debt. He has argued, from beginning to end, that because we pass a homestead law that the creditor can never get his money. That is the case. If a steamship should start from New York, and in rounding Hatteras, by divers gales, the vessel is sunk so deep that the passengers lose all their baggage and almost their entire wearing apparel, if the debtors of our friends from Richland and Fairfield were on board, the first thing they would do on her arrival in port would be to rush down, and, though the poor debtor stood nearly as bare as our first parents, the gentleman from Richland would ask him to pay that little debt he owed him. If the poor victim happened to be so unfortunate that he could not pay it then, and should appeal to them as he stood, my Richland friend would call to his assistance our friend from Fairfield to talk about constitutional law.

The people of South Carolina, and I speak for Barnwell more especially, ask no favors of the Convention. They only ask for time. They do not wish to impair their obligations; they do not wish to deny their honest debts; but, for heaven's sake, give the debtor time, and such an amount of property as will enable him to work and pay his debts, and not leave him in possession with an execution over his head that at any moment may allow the creditor to come and take his home from him. I will venture to say that there is as much due me in Barnwell District as any man, and if this law passes, I will run the risk of being as large a loser as any man. I hold a note of one person alone for $2,250. I cannot now get a dollar of it. But I desire to give my debtor a homestead, and afford him an opportunity to pay me after he shall have raised a crop. If he gets a homestead over and above so much money, I can say to him pay me my debt.

We have just received over the wires intelligence of the defeat of the Alabama Constitution. We all desire to prevent such a result in South Carolina. The Constitution of Alabama is a good one, but they have omitted a homestead law, and the result is a defeat by 15,000 majority. Write down the word "Alabama;" spell it, dream over it, reflect upon it, and let it be a lesson. Adopt this clause, and it will enable the planter to make a crop and to secure his provisions for the coming year. It will identify both races with the soil, and create in the hearts of the people a more durable affection for it than has ever before existed. It is for these reasons that I press this measure. It will aid in the reconstruction of the State, because it will indicate to the whole people that we have endeavored to act faithfully towards them in this our representative capacity.

I want to see the white men and the black men in Barnwell District all going to the polls to ratify this Constitution. If this provision for a homestead be adopted, I assure the member from Fairfield (Mr. RUT-

LAND) and the member from Richland (Mr. ROBERTSON) that if, on the day of election, they may be traveling that road, unless they expedite their movements, they will be run over by the people going to ratify the Constitution. The people would come from every direction. They have never had a Constitution that took care of the grand masses. If we assure the people that we are looking after their rights and interests, the roads on all sides will be filled, and when the votes are counted on the last night of the election every friend who has at heart this Constitution will have the pleasure of knowing it is ratified beyond all kind of doubt, and will have the consolation of knowing we have done our duty. I am speaking for my people, for I love them with all my heart.

[Here Mr. LESLIE was so overcome by his feelings as to burst into tears, and sat down amidst intense silence, having evidently enlisted the warmest sympathies of the members of the Convention.]—*Reporter.*

Mr. L. S. LANGLEY. I do not suppose any member of the Convention doubts that this measure will be adopted, but I desire that we shall vote upon it intelligently. According to my construction of one of its clauses the laborer cannot collect the wages that may be due him for his work. To illustrate: A. owns a thousand acres of land, and is indebted to B, who is a landshark in Charleston, to the amount of $10,000. A. perhaps employed last year twenty-five laborers in the cultivation of his crop. That crop, however, fails, and the creditor, B, levies on the estate. It is sold under the Sheriff's hammer, and with the exception of the homestead reserved, is transferred to the creditor. Now what becomes of the wages due the laborer? He has no protection, and suffers a loss, while his employer has been cared for by the law to the extent of $2,500. For one, I desire to prevent the perpetration of any such injustice. Labor is the only property of the poor man, and he is as much entitled to the protection which the law can throw around him as the rich, and it is expedient and just to surround him with these safeguards. If it is expedient for us for the purpose of securing the ratification of the Constitution to protect the property of the real estate owner, is it not just as right and expedient to protect the property of the laborer. I, therefore, hope the amendment I have proposed will be adopted, and that the poor man, be he black or white, may have the protection to which he is entitled. I need not refer the Convention to the fact that the Freedman's Bureau in this State has encountered the utmost difficulty and opposition in endeavoring to collect the amounts due to the freedmen that labor on large plantations. Shall we throw any further obstacle in its way by deliberately declaring that a man may possess property to the amount of $2,500 free from all legal process for debt, even the debt due to honest, poor laboring men for work performed during the last twelve months. I trust not. If we are so lost to all sense of justice as that, the sooner we adjourn and go home the better for our constituents, and the sooner they will call us to account.

Mr. B. F. WHITTEMORE. It can be hardly possible for those who listen to the eloquent, appealing and touching remarks of the gentleman from Barnwell, to sit here without a feeling at least that is interested for his constituency. It is no doubt our duty to do all we can in order that we may relieve the necessities of the people of the State. They are very great and burdensome, and while it is our duty to allow our hearts to expand feelingly towards those who are suffering around us, I feel it is also our duty that we should be just and fear not.

It has been said by those who best know the intention of those who framed the section before us that there was a retrospective idea in that intention. The house will bear me witness, when I accepted the amendment, or rather a similar proposition offered to a section of the Bill of Rights, that I afterwards discovered it was the intention of the party to make this clause retrospective, and I opposed it. I find now that the course I took on that occasion was correct. I find that the intimations given me had some foundation. In fact, I am not at all surprised to-day to find that there are advocates in favor of making this clause retrospective as well as prospective. In the Bill of Rights, which I had the honor of assisting to frame, it is well understood by this Convention that provisions were made for a homestead. The language was that the homestead should cover all debts that should be created after the passage of the Constitution. The Convention passed it with the amendment offered. I trust that while our hearts may be touched by the appeals made on account of the debtor, we shall not forget creditors who are not always rich. Some creditors may be poor on account of their liabilities which these parties have against them. I trust, if this section is what some gentlemen say it will do, cover all mortgages, we will erase it.

The gentleman from Charleston says we must be consistent; we do not desire to benefit any particular class. I think if we are consistent in our considerations upon this subject we will find we are legislating especially for a class, and that the poor will not receive the benefits of our legislation. We have shown our liberality—we have shown our willingness to stay the collection of liabilities for a long time. We have shown our willingness to obliterate debts for slaves. We are now trying to show still more liberality by making homesteads so sure as not only to provide for the future and present, but for the past.

I but wish to ask a single question. Is it not known that the South-

61

ern people, in order to enable them, after coming out of the ruins, to get on their feet, after coming from the din of the conflict and smoke of battle, and finding their horses, mules and farm implements taken away, is it not known that they have been compelled to call upon their friends from without to assist them to save the country? During the past few years gentlemen of this city have implored me to use what little influence I had in procuring money and assistance, not only for agricultural pursuits, but for other business. I did so. Were it necessary I could call upon factors whom I have assisted, to stand here by my side to testify to that fact. When I went to my Northern home two years ago, factors who followed me there were introduced to capitalists, and obtained assistance for the impoverished planters and assistance to employ the starving people of their neighborhood. The capital came. Shall I then, occupying this position and standing here upon this floor, for the purpose of making laws for the future government of the State, and dealing justly with men, shall I say these claims upon these people shall not be paid? that the people who have been so kindly assisted shall not meet their obligations? Shall I stand here and annex my vote or name to a project which shall impair the obligation which they have entered into? I trust while we try to be generous we will be just. Were it necessary I could present letters from all parts of the State, from honorable men with honorable intentions, and men who intend to meet their liabilities whenever called upon, or else suffer their large estates to be taken for the payment thereof; I say I could give letters from prominent gentlemen saying that they have no desire for this Convention to relieve them of the claims against them, or the responsibilities they are under to their fellow men. I believe there is honor in this Commonwealth. I believe it is the intention of every honorable man here, though he may have but little left him, to meet his creditor face to face and settle upon a fair and just principle that which he owes him, and from whom he has received an equivalent. I believe it is our duty to remember we should not always be exercised by our sympathies, but apply sometimes to our reason and our judgment; and were we to act upon our sense of duty, we would do unto all men as we would that men should do unto us.

I ask no extreme measure. I ask no gentlemen here to do that which will injure any man throughout the domain of South Carolina. I ask no man to take from another man that which belongs to him. I reiterate the expression, and wish it might reverberate throughout the entire State, let us act consistently not only with ourselves, but with our neighbors, in order that we may stand in the broad sunlight of heaven, looking every man in the face, and say we have done our duty, striving to mete out full justice to all, taking no man's property from another. Would it be right to cheat the men who loaned funds to carry on the plantations for the last two years when the people were on the verge of the grave, when starvation was staring them in the face; would it be right to say to these gentlemen, who helped these people out of their ruin, that the debt shall never be paid. I hope not.

The hour of half past two having arrived, the Convention adjourned.

THIRTIETH DAY

Wednesday, February 19, 1868.

The Convention assembled at half-past 10 A. M., and was called to order by the PRESIDENT.

Prayer by the Rev. B. F. WHITTEMORE.

The roll was called, and a quorum answering to their names, the PRESIDENT announced the Convention ready to proceed to business.

Mr. F. J. MOSES, Jr., made the following report of the Committee on the Executive Provisions of the Constitution, which was ordered to be printed.

REPORT OF THE COMMITTEE ON THE EXECUTIVE DEPARTMENT OF THE CONSTITUTION OF SOUTH CAROLINA.

SECTION 1. The Supreme Executive authority of this State shall be vested in a Chief Magistrate, who shall be styled "The Governor of the State of South Carolina, and whose title shall be "His Excellency."

SEC. 2 The Governor shall be elected by the electors duly qualified to vote for members of the House of Representatives, and shall hold his office for one year, and until his successor shall be chosen and qualified, and shall be re-eligible.

SEC. 3. No person shall be eligible to the office of Governor who does not profess a belief in the existence of a Supreme Being, and unless he hath attained the age of thirty years, and hath been a citizen and resident of this State for the four years next preceding the day of election. And no person shall hold the office of Governor, and any other office or commission, civil or military (except in the militia) under this State, or any of them, or any other power, at one and the same time.

SEC. 4. The return of every election of Governor shall be sealed up by the managers of elections in their respective Districts, and transmitted by mail to the seat of Government, directed to the Secretary of

State, who shall deliver them to the Speaker of the House of Representatives at the next ensuing session of the General Assembly, and a duplicate of said return shall be filed with the Clerks of the Courts of said Districts, whose duty it shall be to forward to the Secretary of State a certified copy thereof, upon being notified that the return previously forwarded by mail has not been received at his office. It shall be the duty of the Secretary of State, after the expiration of seven days from the day upon which the votes have been counted, if a return thereof from any District has not been received, to notify the Clerk of the Court of the said District, and order a copy of the return filed in his office to be forthwith forwarded. The Secretary of State shall deliver the returns to the Speaker of the House of Representatives, at the next ensuing session of the General Assembly; and during the first week of the session, or as soon as the General Assembly may have organized by the election of the presiding officers of the two Houses, the Speaker shall open and publish them in the presence of both Houses. The person having the highest number of votes shall be Governor; but if two or more shall be equal, and highest in votes, the General Assembly shall, during the same session, in the House of Representatives, choose one of them Governor *viva voce*. Contested elections for Governor shall be determined by the General Assembly in such manner as shall be prescribed by law.

Sec. 5. A Lieutenant Governor shall be chosen at the same time, in the same manner, continue in office for the same period, and be possessed of the same qualifications as the Governor, and shall *ex-officio* be President of the Senate.

Sec. 6. The Lieutenant Governor, while presiding in the Senate, shall have no vote, unless the Senate be equally divided.

Sec. 7. The Senate shall choose a President, *pro tempore*, to act in the absence of the Lieutenant Governor, or when he shall exercise the office of Governor.

Sec. 8. A member of the Senate, or of the House of Representatives, being chosen and acting as Governor or Lieutenant Governor, shall thereupon vacate his seat, and another person shall be elected in his stead.

Sec. 9. In case of the removal of the Governor from his office, or his death, resignation, removal from the State, or inability to discharge the powers and duties of the said office, the same shall devolve on the Lieutenant Governor, and the General Assembly, at its first session after the ratification of this Constitution, shall, by law, provide for the case of removal, death, resignation, or inability, both of the Governor and Lieutenant Governor, declaring what officer shall then act as Governor, and such officer shall act accordingly, until such disability be removed, or a Governor shall be elected.

Sec. 10. The Governor shall be commander-in-chief of the army and navy of this State, and of the militia, except when they shall be called into the actual service of the United States.

Sec. 11. He shall have power to grant reprieves and pardons after conviction (except in cases of impeachment), in such manner, on such terms, and under such restrictions as he shall think proper; and he shall have power to remit fines and forfeitures, unless otherwise directed by law. It shall be his duty to report to the General Assembly at the next regular session thereafter, all pardons granted by him, with a full statement of each case, and the reasons moving him thereunto.

SEC. 12. He shall take care that the laws be faithfully executed in mercy.

SEC. 13. The Governor and Lieutenant Governor shall, at stated times, receive for their services a compensation, which shall be neither increased nor diminished during the period for which they shall have been elected.

SEC. 14. All officers in the Executive Department shall, when required by the Governor, give him information in writing upon any subject relating to the duties of their respective offices.

SEC. 15. The Governor shall, from time to time, give to the General Assembly information of the condition of the State, and recommend to their consideration such measures as he shall judge necessary or expedient.

SEC. 16. He may, on extraordinary occasions, convene the General Assembly; and should either House remain without a quorum for five days, or in case of disagreement between the two Houses with respect to the time of adjournment, may adjourn them, to such time as he shall think proper; not beyond ——— then next ensuing.

SEC. 17. He shall commission all officers of the State.

SEC. 18. There shall be a Great Seal of the State, for which the General Assembly, at its first session, shall provide, and which shall be used by the Governor officially, and shall be called "The Great Seal of the State of South Carolina."

SEC. 19. All grants and commissions shall be signed by the Governor, countersigned by the Secretary of State, and sealed with the Great Seal.

SEC. 20. The Governor and the Lieutenant Governor, before entering upon the duties of their respective offices, shall, in the presence of the General Assembly, take the following oath of allegiance and qualification, and also the following oath of office:

Oath or Affirmation of Allegiance and Qualification.—"I do swear (or affirm) that I am duly qualified, according to the Constitution of this State, to exercise the office to which I have been elected; that I will preserve, protect and defend the Constitution of this State and that of the United States, and that I will not, directly or indirectly, do any act or thing injurious to the Constitution or Government thereof, as established by Convention. (If an oath) So help me God. (If an affirmation) under the pains and penalties of perjury."

Oath or Affirmation of Office.—"I do solemnly swear (or affirm) that I will faithfully discharge the duties of the office of Governor (or Lieutenant Governor) for the State of South Carolina, and will therein do equal right and justice to all men, to the best of my judgment and abilities, and according to law. (If an oath) So help me God. (If an affirmation) under the pains and penalties of perjury."

SEC. 21. The Governor shall reside at the capital of the State; but during the sittings of the General Assembly he shall reside where its sessions are held, except in case of contagion.

Sec. 22. Every bill which shall have passed the General Assembly, shall, before it become a law, be presented to the Governor; if he approve, he shall sign it; but if not, he shall return it, with his objections, to that house in which it shall have originated, who shall enter the objections at large on their journal, and proceed to reconsider it. If, after such reconsideration, a majority of the whole representation of that House shall agree to pass the bill, it shall be sent, together with the objections, to the other House, by which it shall likewise be reconsidered; and if approved by a majority of the whole representation of that other House, it shall become a law. But in all such cases the votes of both Houses shall be determined by yeas and nays; and the names of the persons voting for and against the bill shall be entered on the Journal of each House respectively. If any bill shall not be returned by the Governor within five days (Sundays excepted) after it shall have been presented to him, the same shall be a law in like manner as if he had signed it. And, that time may always be allowed the Governor to consider bills passed by the General Assembly, neither House shall read any bill on the last day of its session, except such bills as have been returned by the Governor as herein provided.

Mr. W. E. ROSE, Chairman of the Committee on Petitions, made the following report, which, on motion of Mr. W. J. WHIPPER, was agreed to:

The Committee on Petitions, to whom was referred "a preamble and resolution asking in behalf of Southern planters a loan of thirty million dollars from the United States Government," passed by the Constitutional Convention of the State of Georgia, February 1st, 1868, beg leave to report:

Your Committee have had under consideration said preamble and resolution, and while they admit Southern planters are and have been much embarrassed by the failure, or partial failure, of the crops during the past two years, and by the prostrations consequent upon or growing out of, the late war, they cannot recommend the Congress of the United States to furnish the opportunity, or the means, of involving themselves and their plantations for the purpose of a temporary loan, as their all may become forfeited by a failure. We think that planters should struggle on with the means that private enterprise will supply, rather than imperil all by a single venture, a simple loan.

A debt created to the Government of the United States would have to be paid, at all hazards, on a certain day, and would take precedence of all other debts. Such is the law relative to public debtors. But we deprecate the whole system of borrowing, into which planters seem willing and anxious to plunge. It will only eventuate in their financial ruin, the sale of their long cherished plantations to strangers and speculators.

Let them battle manfully with the difficulties before them, bringing to their aid fortitude, courage and sound practical sense, and gather up the slumbering elements of prosperity lying about them, and we believe prosperity and even wealth are within their grasp.

We are further opposed to this measure of relief on the ground that if permanently beneficial to the planters, it would only be so to the rich, those who have lands and other property to pledge for the payment of the loan. The poor would get or gain nothing from it.

And finally we oppose it on the ground of its utter improbability of success. We have never learned to look upon the Government as a banking institution, except for its own benefit, and are not aware of its ever having gone into the market to loan money. It frequently goes as a borrower, and, we believe, is there as such now.

The financial condition of the Government at this time would prevent this application from meeting with any success. The certainty of refusal by Congress of the loan, together with the impolicy of the loan, could it be effected, we think sufficient grounds for the Convention to refuse the adoption of the resolution, and, therefore, your Committee recommend that the preamble and resolution be laid on the table.

All of which is respectfully submitted.

WM. E. ROSE, Chairman.

Mr. B. F. RANDOLPH made a report of the Committee on Miscellaneous Provisions of the Constitution, and asked leave to report the following ordinance, introduced by the member from Laurens (Mr. J. CREWS). The Committee recommend that it do pass:

Be it ordained, That it shall be the duty of the Legislature at its first session, to appoint Commissioners to investigate and ascertain what obligations of the State are entitled to be held as valid and binding upon the State in conformity with the provisions of this Constitution and the ordinances adopted by this Convention, and to report thereon to the Legislature; and until the Legislature shall have ascertained the validity of such obligations, no payment for either the principal or interest shall be made on any outstanding obligations created or incurred prior to the 29th of April, 1865.

Mr. E. W. M. MACKEY moved that the ordinance be made the Special Order for Wednesday next, at 12 M., which was agreed to.

Mr. C. P. LESLIE made the report of the Auditing Committee on sundry bills for printing, fuel, &c., which were ordered to be paid on proper vouchers being filed with the President.

Mr. R. SMALLS called for the unfinished business of Tuesday.

The PRESIDENT announced the unfinished business to be the consideration of the thirty-fifth section of the second article of the Constitution, reported by the Legislative Committee, in reference to homesteads.

Mr. L. S. LANGLEY offered the following amendment on the ninth line:

" Or for debts contracted for labor prior to the ratification of this Constitution."

Which was not agreed to.

Mr. T. J. ROBERTSON offered the following amendment on the ninth line, which was not agreed to :

" No homestead shall be exempt from levy and sale for any just debt existing at the time of the ratification of this Constitution ; and every creditor shall be entitled to all the legal remedies for the enforcement of his contract which existed at the time it was made and entered into petition."

Mr. B. F. WHITTEMORE, who had the floor at the hour of adjournment yesterday, resumed his argument.

Mr. President and gentlemen of the Convention, unfortunately for myself the hour of adjournment came, and as every gentleman can well understand, the thread of the discourse cannot be so well taken up after the time has expired when the inspiration of the theme may be upon him, and the hour has passed away.

I want the Convention and the gentlemen present to understand that in no way do I oppose a homestead law, that is in its provisions prospective only. I conceive that act consistent with myself, with all the positions I have taken upon this floor, and it would be impossible to retrace my steps unless I could be convinced that morally I have the right to step between the debtor and the creditor, and divorce them from their claims and liabilities.

I have no doubt in my mind but what there may be precedents sufficient to found an action in this Convention, so that they may pass an ordinance retrospective in its character. Yesterday an appeal was made by the gentleman from Barnwell (Mr. LESLIE), a very effective one, too, as it appears from the ready pencils at those tables (the reporters), which have already given him sufficient credit. He not only appeals to the best sympathies of our hearts, but he depicted the condition and position of the people of the State in a manner that would warrant almost every person to look kindly towards them. I trust that neither he nor those who support the side of the question he has supported, will give me credit for anything else than sympathy with all in distress ; but whilst I should be actuated towards those who are oppressed on account of their burdens and liabilities, their debts and all that makes life miserable ; whilst I should look towards the debtor, shall I divorce him from all claims existing against him. Is it not my duty to look also towards the creditor ? Does it follow naturally that creditors must all be rich and debtors all be poor, and, consequently, that we are to legislate for the poor debtors alone ?

It appears to me it could be possible that there may be as many poor creditors as debtors, and, therefore, if the sympathies of our heart are to be called out, those sympathies should be exercised towards all. If we are to apportion out the burdens among the people, let us make a proper apportionment and a proper division. If we desire to benefit all the people as well as the debtor, let us take all these claims and divide the burdens, and spread them so that they may fall equally upon the debtor as well as the creditor. Methinks there are many poor families to-day dependent upon the collection of debts that exist, and claims which they hold against others.

I do not desire by what I might say here to prevent the protection of a homestead for the people. The gentleman from Barnwell yesterday alluded to the vessel stranded upon the shore by the fury of the storm, and the people, on account of the calamity that came upon them, thrown into the water almost in the condition in which they came into the world, with nothing saved from the wreck, and the relentless creditor coming upon them with his stern and rash demand for that which belonged to him. While this was a picture that demanded our sympathies, it was not a picture which would be parallel to the condition of the people to-day. We admit they are wrecked; but while the vessel was passing the stormy Cape they had no volition in the matter, and could not control the winds and the waves. But whatever the condition of the people to-day, however ruinous, however great their claims may be upon our sympathy and our best feelings, that condition has been brought about to a great extent by their own volition, and by their own act. If they be poor to-day, it appears to me they have no one to blame except themselves. As I have said in some of the debates that have sprung up upon this floor, that when the people of this Commonwealth and other Commonwealths of the South went into the war, they went in with the understanding that if they did not succeed, whatsoever they held as property would be swept away from them, and while I might pity their unfortunate condition, brought about by the results of their own contest, at the same time it appears to me that when we come to pass upon the right as to whether the debtor shall pay the creditor, we have to look at the moral question as well as the legal points that may be produced here ; whether it is morally right for me or you to step between gentlemen, between the first and second party, or between the second and third party, and wrest from one to give to the other.

The difference between a prospective homestead and a retrospective

62

law is this : If we pass an act here which shall protect the citizens of the State in their homesteads in the future, we certainly can do no harm to any individual, for whatever may be the condition of any people hereafter, if they go into the market for the purpose of carrying all their stores, and ask whatever it may be, a loan or anything else, they go with the understanding of appealing to the world for assistance, that the world understands that there is a homestead law which protects them, in so much as they hold a homestead. No man will then be deceived when he loans his money to assist in protecting them from disaster or losses in whatever they may be engaged.

I alluded yesterday to the assistance that has already come to the State. I presume it will be said by the opposite side that those gentlemen who furnished assistance, furnished it with a compensation. It is true; but I have yet to learn and find a man who acts so disinterested in the loaning of his funds for the purpose of helping other men as not to require some compensation for them. It would be impossible for a man to do business unless he was protected in having compensation for so doing ; it would be impossible for men to have capital to invest. I do claim that when these gentleman came forward, forgetting all past differences and bitterness that might have existed on account of what the war produced, and were willing to assist their brethren in distress, and extended a helping hand, it would be wrong for us on the floor of this Convention to say these gentlemen should not collect those debts, and those who owe for whatever they had from these gentlemen should not pay their liabilities.

I can easily imagine how a man with ten thousand acres of land, wanting to defraud his creditors, can cover every acre by the proposed law. Suppose he has a sufficiently large family to settle them on ten thousand acres of land. Suppose he has children enough, he may build log cabins and put these children into them. He may divide his land, calling each cabin, with so many acres, a homestead, and thus protect his whole estate. That might be done very easily, and, therefore, we should be exceedingly careful how far we extend that privilege.

With regard to a retrospective homestead, I look upon it in this light : I say that whatever may have been the condition of a man, whatever his liabilities were in, this provision of the Constitution provides that he shall hold at least two thousand dollars' worth of property. The gentleman from Beaufort went on to say that as long as the property was not worth two thousand dollars the laborer can collect his wages. I understand from those who framed this provision that it was their intention that the limit should be two thousand dollars; but it does not say it shall not be under that amount.

Mr. B. O. DUNCAN. It was the intention of the framers that the laborer should have his hire out of the two thousand dollars. It was the understanding that no property should be exempt for the purchase of said homestead, or the erections and improvements thereon.

Mr. B. F. WHITTEMORE. The gentleman from Beaufort says no hatred should be treasured in our land.

Mr. J. J. WRIGHT. What I intended to say was that no hatred towards any one should be exhibited by this Convention.

Mr. B. F. WHITTEMORE. It appears to me that it has become unnecessary to attribute any feeling of that kind to any one. It is the duty of this Convention to act in perfect harmony and good faith. I understand that about 1850 there was a law passed in South Carolina providing homesteads for the people, and that the provisions of that law were not found to work well, and its abolishment subsequently followed. So far as these obligations of the past are concerned, we should be exceedingly careful how we legislate.

Mr. F. J. MOSES, Jr. I would inquire of the gentleman whether the character of that law was prospective or retrospective. Was it for the benefit of the rich or the poor man?

Mr. B. F. WHITTEMORE. I am unable to say; but I presume that it was not for the benefit of the poor man, because the poor man was not at that period represented in the councils of the State. We, on the contrary, are here to legislate for all; not to form a black, nor yet a white code, but a system of laws which shall do justice to all people, the creditor and the debtor, the rich and the poor, the white and the colored man. Now, much has been said with reference to the protection of the widow and orphan. I admit that we should provide for them in their necessities; but ought we to provide for the widow of the debtor more than the widow of the creditor, who may have orphan children, and perhaps only one-third of her estate to live upon? I think not. We should be careful to exercise true wisdom and justice towards all. That is our mission here.

Mr. W. J. WHIPPER. There seems to be some doubt concerning the intention of the Committee in framing the section relative to homesteads. I will declare what my views were as a member of that Committee, and if I misrepresent any one, it will be his province to correct me. I certainly hoped that we could surround a homestead with every protection. It was my desire to do so. The gentleman from Richland (Mr. ROBERTSON) says that the section as it now stands protects a homestead against mortgages. I wish to God his view was correct. I hope the Courts will so hold; but I know they will not. My desire is to protect the homestead against any claims on earth, and this provision will do so, except where rights have already vested, as in mortgages and judgments.

The opposition claim that this is wronging the creditor. The gentleman who has just taken his seat has labored a long time to demonstrate that fact; but I can assure the Convention that it was not the intention of the Committee to interfere at all with the collection of debts. The measure does not prohibit a man from collecting his debts. We only seek to protect the unfortunate debtor from utter ruin, and without repudiating his obligations, to place him in a position in which he can pay his debts. Take a man who possesses a thousand acres. A comparatively small indebtedness may sweep away every foot of his land. If he owes a large amount, he will be left still in debt. How is he to be protected to that degree even in which, as an honest man, he can recuperate and cancel these obligations. Certainly not by depriving him of his all. It is to promote this generous object that the present section was reported.

The gentleman has spoken of those who advanced money within the last two or three years to planters. I certainly desire that every dollar may be repaid; but were those funds advanced with any expectation that failure to meet the obligation would result in the utter ruin of the debtor? I think not. It was done speculatively, but the speculation was unsuccessful, and the lender has been as unfortunate as the borrower. To protect the creditor we are willing, though his debtor may have ten thousand acres, that all should be sacrificed to the claims except one hundred acres. which in mercy we reserve as a protection to the poor man's family, and to enable him once more to commence a business career. If we have any humanity, we will see to it that this protection is accorded, and that the unfortunate debtor, with his family, shall not be deprived of every remnant of what was once his own, and turned out upon the world to starve with his wife and little ones, or to become perhaps a burden upon society.

Again, if we care anything for the prosperity of the State, it is important to adopt some measure of this kind. If we do not, the citizen will be driven abroad, and his place be filled by foreigners and aliens, who possibly can have no interest in the soil. The gentleman from Darlington (Mr. WHITTEMORE) says that he can readily see how a man can defeat the payment of his creditors. First, he may have a numerous family; and secondly, by dividing his ten thousand acres among its several members, and erecting log cabins thereon, secure for each member a homestead. This idea is worthy of the gentleman's legal profundity. In my mind he has mistaken his calling, and in wearing the clerical garb, has robbed our profession of a shining and illustrious ornament. I appeal to the members of that profession on the floor, even to my critical friend from Fairfield (Mr. RUTLAND) whether such a preposterous thing can be done.

The gentleman says that the case supposed by the gentleman from Barnwell (Mr. LESLIE), of persons distressed by shipwreck is not analogous to the present condition, for the reason that they could not control the winds and waves which produced the distress, and that the distress of the people of this State is the result of their own action. This is far from correct. There are comparatively few of the people of the South who are responsible for the existing condition of affairs ; nor is it wise, just, magnanimous, or statesmanlike to allow them to suffer from a want of confidence, simply because in following their laws and their leaders they may have committed a grave error. The facts are, the masses are not responsible for these acts. Taking the voting population of South Carolina at the time of secession, and it will be found that a comparatively small minority are now to be injured by the sale of their homes, and certainly they should not be robbed of their all, simply as a punishment for the commission of these acts.

With reference to the various amendments to this section that have been offered, I hope they will all be voted down. Their effect is only to injure the clause itself. My colleague offers an amendment, that the homestead shall be exempt from all claims, save for the wages of laborers. I can see no reason for this, because it will not affect any considerable class of persons. In the majority of cases, where labor has been performed in this State, it has been based upon the contract system, and out of the net proceeds, owing to the misfortunes of the period, nothing has been left to divide, so that there is nothing due to the laborer for which he can hold the land.

Mr. L. S. LANGLEY. Does the gentleman mean to state there is nothing due the laborers in this State ?

Mr. W. J. WHIPPER. I claim to speak sufficiently plain for any one to understand me. I say that, under the contract system, even though the proceeds were not divided, they do not constitute a lien upon the land. Although many persons have, no doubt, been wronged by this contract system, there is not a debt for which they can sell the land of their employer. If they were to have one-third of the crop, that was the basis upon which they labored, and if cheated, they must seek redress by some other means than levying upon the land.

Mr. L. S. LANGLEY. What would the gentleman do in those cases

in which the planter has sold the laborer's portion, and made no return
to him? Would not that be a debt for which the homestead would be
liable in the event of the adoption of my amendment?

Mr. W. J. WHIPPER. The gentleman must see that his amendment would not cover cases of that kind. If a man takes a bale of cotton belonging to me, and disposes of it without making a return to me,
I could not prosecute him for wages. He must be proceeded against
not for wages, but for the proceeds of the crop.

The second amendment is that of the gentleman from Richland, which
is that the section shall not be retrospective. I earnestly hope it will be
made retrospective as far as possible, and that it will work against all
debts of every character, I have not the slightest doubt. We owe it to
the prosperity of the State to secure to every man a home, and in doing
this we shall invite capital to the State, identify every man, woman and
child with the soil, and create in his heart a stronger love of country
than has ever before existed. If we fail to do it, we shall be overrun by
legalized robbers who infest this and every community. Notwithstanding the energetic effort, therefore, that is being made by men of wealth
to defeat this measure, and the intrigue which is employed to that end,
I earnestly hope that it will be adopted by an overwhelming majority.

Mr. WM. J. McKINLAY. This certainly is a measure of relief, and
one which requires cautious action, for all of the errors we have committed have been in questions of relief. I am not possessed of sufficient
legal acumen to say whether this clause will act retrospectively or not;
but I do know the law of right, and upon that platform I intend to
stand. We must admit that the provisions of this homestead are very
liberal. It is proposed to exempt two thousand dollars of real estate as
a homestead and five hundred dollars worth of furniture, the whole exemption to amount to two thousand five hundred dollars. The gentleman from Barnwell (Mr. LESLIE) yesterday depicted to us in a graphic
and sympathetic manner the fate of the unfortunate debtor, but he ought
at the same time to have had some consideration for the equally unfortunate creditor. While I am in favor of a limited and moderate homestead law, let me suppose a case, which illustrates that the present
section is calculated to do injustice to one class, and the picture is not
overdrawn. Suppose there are forty men, each of whom owes fifteen
hundred dollars to a certain individual, making sixty thousand dollars
due to one man. The forty are protected by this liberal homestead law
which covers twenty-five hundred dollars of property and puts them beyond the reach of the creditor, while he is compelled to sustain a large
loss without a single measure of redress. This is wrong. For this

reason I object to the section. I am, however, in favor of the amendment of the gentleman from Beaufort (Mr. LANGLEY), because I think it is no more than an act of justice to the laborer that he should be especially protected. On the whole, however, I am opposed to this homestead section, and hope it will be voted down.

Mr. R. B. ELLIOTT. I rise to offer an amendment so that the section will read as follows :

'It shall be the duty of the first Legislature that shall assemble after the ratification of this Constitution, at its first session, to pass such laws as may be necessary to carry this provision into effect."

I think it unnecessary for me to state the reasons which have caused me to move such an amendment. Every member reading the section will see the necessity of such an amendment.

Mr. B. F. RANDOLPH. If I have failed to speak upon the several measures of relief before the Convention, it has not been because I did not favor their adoption. Concerning the proposition now before the body I give it my hearty support just as it has been reported from the Committee, and I hope it will be incorporated in the Constitution.

I regard it as a most efficient measure of relief to the people of South Carolina, and hence it is one of the most important subjects with which we have to deal.

When we look over the State, what do we behold ? Not a people happy, contented and in the enjoyment of the luxuries of life, rolling in wealth and ease, but a people without regard to complexion, poverty-stricken and financially embarrassed. Go to the office of the Registers in Bankruptcy and look at the long list of landholders who are themselves among the sufferers Every day and hour swells the number on that fated list. Look at the plantations levied upon by the Sheriffs and Marshals. There is no capital in the country. Labor is plenty, but want of ability to remunerate the labor leaves the State in a woful condition, which demands prompt, generous and merciful relief.

This is the important question which we have to determine to-day, and I beseech you one and all to reflect well, and whatever be your race and color, to remember only the great interests at stake and the misfortunes of the people you represent. It has been asserted here, much to my regret, that certain measures were intended to benefit only white men, while others were exclusively for the advantage of the colored race. For one I shall support no such class legislation.

The principle is laid down in political economy that to make a State prosperous, the prosperity of its people must be first secured, and whatever government best achieves this end succeeds best in the formation of a perfect system of goverment. How can we attain so desirable an object as that which secures independence, comfort and happiness to the masses? Certainly not by impoverishing any class, and especially those who may be the owners of the soil. I know there are those here who desire to see the once wealthy landholders of this State—its aristocrats—reduced to utter poverty; but we cannot afford to turn these persons out into the highway. The attempt is inconsistent with the principles of political economy and the purposes of a justly constituted society. On the contrary, I desire to see every man in South Carolina a landholder, so that in traversing from one end of the State to the other, instead of desolated farms we could see the land blooming with cotton bolls and the fruits of agriculture on every side, and the owners, whether they be white or colored men, owning large or small farms, enjoying results of independent and honest industry. But God forbid, Mr. President, that while seeking to attain so noble an object we should ruin or debase any class of men. I think it desirable, however, that as a matter of policy and progress, the large landholders should be induced to break their possessions into small farms and populate them with an industrious community. I am opposed to a landed aristocracy.

As regards this homestead law, I know that it will act retrospectively in its present shape. And the very moment it is passed every man may select his hundred acres, or property to the value of two thousand five hundred dollars, and plant himself upon that property as a homestead. Hence I desire to see it adopted, so that though a person may have owed another five thousand dollars for fifty years, he shall be protected under this clause of the Constitution, which secures him in the possession of a home. And I defy the creditor to deprive him of that homestead. I do not dispute that every man should pay his just debts. But he who lends money on credit must take the consequences. As a general thing, the debtor is the larger class, and the creditor is mercenary and grasping; and therefore to the end that the poor and unfortunate man may be protected in at least a home for his family and himself, I desire to see the adoption of this section.

Mr. SIMEON CORLEY. I will state at the outset that I am not individually interested in the passage of this clause in the Constitution, if viewed as retrospective, as it is perhaps opposed to my individual pecuniary interest. But when it is remembered that this body has stamped as "impracticable" a plan which proposed the issuing of bonds by the State, and securing thereon the loan of a few millions of dollars, based upon the value of the lands said loan would purchase, at forced sales,

soon to be made at a very low figure, for the express purpose of furnishing the otherwise poor wonderers of our own loved Carolina with homes,
for which they could pay in the future, on the best security that ever
can be given, *the land itself*, and which time will demonstrate to be the
only practicable plan of relief that can be offered, then it is time to
inquire whether or not a large portion of the members of this Convention really desire any plan of relief whatever. I fear that there are gentlemen here who, after repudiating the obligations of our wealthiest class
of citizens for slave property, are now willing to see that same class take
the identical funds which they heretofore held to pay their honest debts,
and buy with the same their late creditors homestead—the amount of
which they have robbed him, in order to worse than rob him of his
home. I do not impugn the motives of any gentleman here. I speak
of the matter only in a practical point of view, and not as based upon
metaphysical theories, which are of no practical value whatever. It
matters not what epithet may be applied to me; it may be demagogue,
fanatic or fool, as best suits the calibre and moral status of those who
may utter it; yet I, for one, demand a system of relief which can be
applied to all classes and conditions of our society. I do not plead for
color or class, but for down trodden humanity! Wherever there is a
heart to suffer, whether it throbs beneath a white or a black skin, there
I hold it to be our duty to apply every remedy which God and nature
hath placed in our hands. If we are so foolish as to fear the risk of a
few millions, by entering the market with the land-sharks, which some
propose to turn loose upon the suffering poor, to purchase the lands which
they intend to monopolize, and realize therefrom fortunes of colossal
magnitude; I say, if we are so nearly beside ourselves as to stand here
with our arms folded, and listen to their syren songs of "impractica-
bility," while they play the practical, individually, personally and *alone*,
in feathering their own nests, at the sacrifice of the dearest interests of
humanity, and of freedom itself, then we are not worthy of our noble
ancestry as freemen ; and we, with those from whose hands the shackles
have just been struck, are alike recreant to duty, and alike deserve to
wear the chains! If our cowardly hearts are really afraid of the grand
investments which organized bands of land monopolists will fatten upon,
while our poor are turned from their houses to meet thousands of those
who never had a home, together to become alike wanderers and serfs in
the land of their birth, at the bidding of men whose love of gold denies
the nobler aspirations of humanity, then we simply stultify ourselves,
and are not worthy representatives of the free people of this Commonwealth.

63

There are those here who were, at one time, ready to scale debts, pass stay laws, or do almost anything else for relief to the people, until the slave debts were repudiated by the Convention; and now, since that step imperatively demands another to remove the sufferers from its worst effect, *and give all something like an equal chance*, they are as quiet as they need be. The lions have become lambs, at least, and startle us no longer by their *roar*. If this homestead clause smacks of repudiation in any sense whatever, it finds a precedent in the previous action of this body, and is the only *redeeming* part of the general swindle growing out of the rebellion. Let us but consider that the entire property of the people has depreciated to one half its original value, and that the great basis of Southern wealth has been entirely swept away. The issues of the Bank of the State, pledges of the people to the people, are worthless in our hands—practically repudiated. Class repudiation has been already authorized by the action of this Convention, in the repeal of contracts for slave property, and these precedent conditions demand further action on our part, in order to avert the worst features incident to such a disturbed condition of our pecuniary relations. And, again, we may ask if the rebellion has changed our constitutional and legal relations in a political sense—of which there can be no doubt; may we not reasonably ask if it has not also, in some sense, affected those of only a pecuniary character? At any rate, justice and equal rights demand some measures of relief of more than ordinary character under the extraordinary circumstances of the hour, and I will not voluntarily close the labors of this Convention, until every owner of a homestead is, if possible, secure in its possession, and some plan is adopted whereby any and every citizen, however poor he may be, can purchase a homestead on his own account, backed by the credit of the State or of the United States The freedom of the people cannot be long preserved unless they obtain an interest in the soil. Let them have but a few acres of ground to *squat* on, and I defy the demagogues to coax or force them into his meshes; but leave them homeless and houseless, and they must necessarily be penniless and powerless. As more equal and better plans have been ignored by the Convention as "impracticable," I shall not hesitate to vote for this or any other which promises the least chance of relief for the poor, and will support it at all hazards and against all odds.

It is questionable whether we *can* make a homestead retrospective. It has been asserted by legal gentlemen on this floor that we can, while others of the same cloth have denied it. I design, then, to pass the clause as it stands, and let the Courts decide the points of conflict with higher authority. I have no desire merely to assert anything. The bare assertion does no good in itself, and this clause is couched in as strong retrospective language as we can possibly give it, without possibly defining the intention, which is evidently to make it good against all debts whatsoever, as far as the common law will allow. If we cannot save the homestead against present liens, let it then be good against those of the future, and thus save something from the general wreck for those who are best entitled to it. If a retrospective homestead be unconstitutional, let it be remembered that secession and the bloody war which followed were also unconstitutional! Let us not forget that a majority of the people of South Carolina, who are to be benefited by this action, were driven into *both* like sheep to the slaughter, by the most corrupt and damnable of all political leaders; and if those leading specimens of concentrated depravity are permitted to partake of the crumbs we hereby offer to our betrayed and suffering countrymen, it is simply because we are unable to make a distinction in favor of the deserving; and rather than deny those who are worthy of our regard, we are willing to include also the unworthy. Sir, if I thought we could do nothing whatever to save the poor man his home, I should at once plead for confiscation, and call upon the Government to take all our lands, and permit us to sweat out our lives upon them as tenants, rather than see them pass into the hands of the vilest traitors to the Union and humanity that ever cursed the soil of South Carolina. I have the honor to represent a considerable number of white constituents who are loyal to the Government. They are, generally, men of small landed estates, such as the "pie-crust," copper-clad reporter of the *News* would, doubtless, call *only* "poor whites," and the expelled wretch of a still dirtier sheet would delight to besmear with *mercurial ointment.* Yet they are, nevertheless, patriotic men, who would prefer surrendering their homes to the Government rather than to the authors of the rebellion; those who preached treason and then forced poor Union men into the fight, while they remained at home to watch over their slaves, swindle their unprotected neighbors, and at all hazards hoard their gold, that when the war was over they might *legally* rob better men of their property, and plead the Constitution for their crime. If the Constitution is now claimed to demand such a foul wrong upon the poor, who were generally as loyal as they were permitted to be, I beg leave to say that the *loyal* nation has completely outgrown it; and, however nicely it might at one time have fitted the limbs of the infant giant while reposing upon the shoulders of "*Sombo*," the full grown gentlemen cuts rather a poor figure in that garment *now!* It is true that our distinguished "*ninth*," at the "other end of the political avenue," declares this *constitutional* garment, *as it was,* to be an exact fit, and for that reason seems to be intently bent on darning its small rents ; but his eyes growing dim, and he having entirely ignored *our latest and most approved styles,* I deny that he is a competent judge in the matter. I would prefer to piece the garment to the proper dimensions of the wearer, or cut another out of *whole cloth,* according to the most approved pattern, which shall exactly fit the full grown scion of American freedom! In short, the Constitution was intended for the people, and not the people for the Constitution ; and *if it be unconstitutional to do right,* then I am forced by the stern logic of events to yield my constitutional predilections to a plain common sense view of our situation and the duty it involves. I feel satisfied that the remedy sought in that direction is infinitely worse than the disease, to the cure of which some gentlemen has proposed to apply it, and so utterly devoid of the essential elements of justice and humanity withal, that I am compelled to accept instead the principles of our common manhood, and the injunctions of the moral law, rather than the supposed teachings of any and all the musty parchments of the past.

Mr. F. J. MOSES, Jr. I regret that in the discussion of this important subject some of the gentlemen who have preceded me have not seen fit to confine themselves to that subject. It seems they desire to follow that fashion, which has become so frequent in this Convention, of starting out in the discussion of every important measure that arises by venting their malice on other subjects. We have had several exhibitions of this desire, not only this morning, but yesterday, and I desire to say here to the delegates, that I really trust that they will earnestly consider the strength of the arguments presented solely on account of the arguments themselves, and not on account of any virtue which gentlemen on the opposite side may seek to attach by venting their personal and individual regrets.

It has been said that we propose in the measure before us to legislate for poor men. That proposition I most emphatically deny. I will even go farther than that, and say that if it was necessary, in order to ensure tranquillity to the State, and good to the majority of the population of the State, to legislate only for the poor man against the rich, I, for one, would not hesitate to do it. I remember in times gone by the State of South Carolina has been ruled by the rich for the rich. I remember that the rights of the poor man, personally, and his rights of estate, always have been trampled under foot by that aristocratic element. I for one am not willing to bring up measuress for the sole sake of benefiting the down-trodden aristocrats, while the poor man is calling upon us for relief.

I cannot understand any such arguments as these, and I submit that there never could be a place in which it is more improper to bring them than in this reconstruction Convention, met for the purpose of forming a Constitution for the State hereafter. It may be that these gentlemen differ. It may be that the gentleman from Fairfield (Mr. RUTLAND), for instance, who has sat at his table, kept quiet, heard debate after debate arise, and has not arisen to open his lips until the question of money came up. He may be willing, in consequence of some debts owing him, to attempt to use this Convention against the poor man.

I trust, however, delegates will remember we are here to be guided by no personal considerations; that no gentleman should attempt to use the Convention for the benefit of himself and associates, and that no aristocrat has the right to ask us to use ourselves for his exclusive benefit. The gentleman from Fairfield has kept perfectly quiet when there were just as important constitutional questions under debate. I recollect there are only three subjects in which he has taken a special interest, and that is where he sought to stab at the evident prosperity of the poor man, where he sought to enforce the right of creditors and forgot all the past, forgot all the bloodshed, all the property wrested from every man in the State, forgot all simply for the purpose of pouring the coffers of the State into the hands of people whom he intends shall be monopolists. Thank God, it is not the intention of the Convention to support him or any other man in that. Thank God, we intend to be retrospective, to wipe out forever, if possible, this terrible heel of despotism. We propose to erect a fabric in the future in which the poor man himself shall be concerned. Thank God, the poor man's arm is no longer to be confined to the moltening of iron, but to uphold the pillars of the State. I know no prouder spectacle in the world than to see at the close of the labors of the Convention a Constitution submitted to the people of the State which will let the poor man see for the first time in our history his rights have been respected.

Again, it has been said in reference to personal regrets by the gentleman from Darlington (Mr. WHITTEMORE), that having taken the positions he has heretofore assumed in this Convention, he cannot afford to retrace his steps. It would not be consistent to retrace his steps. I am glad, if that is his view, he has not attempted to retrace his steps, for we all know that,

> "A man convinced against his will,
> Is of the same opinion still."

Perhaps it would be dangerous for him to retrace his steps to come over to our side. I am willing he should stand just where he stands, on the platform of injustice. I am willing he should stand on that platform from which he has proclaimed that the past is not to be forgotten, and that men are to be punished simply because they rebelled against the Government. I am glad he has confessed that he never read that line, "to err is human, to forgive divine." I am glad he had the candor to confess that he stands just where he does against the people, and that he is going to stand there hereafter.

It is argued that we must look to the creditor; I ask are you not looking to the creditor? The creditor can only be aided by framing such a system of laws, by adopting such a Constitution as will allow the debtor to go to work with a manly and a stout heart for the purpose of making money to pay his debts. Everybody knows that the creditors of the State are the largest number. Creditors are not only made by sales of property. Does the gentleman from Fairfield know that creditors loan out money? Where one creditor is found you will find a dozen debtors. We are working just so much more for the creditor if we make this law prospective. What would be the consequence? Gentlemen say we are willing to aid the people of the State. I say it would not be aiding the people of the State if we pass a law merely prospective in its character. It would not operate upon the people at present; it might benefit a future generation. But cannot you see the object of the gentleman in the opposition? It is to punish the people of the State merely because they were concerned in the rebellion. We desire to help the people of the State as they stand at present. Nobody owes debts but those who rebelled. How many outstanding debts are there due by citizens of the State incurred since the existence of the war? I know the majority of sales effected were paid for in cash; I know the greater number of cases of debt incurred during the war were solely for borrowed money. The largest number of debts standing at present are those which were incurred during the war. These gentlemen will not help the rebel, and at the same time refuse to help the loyal man. I say that the only object under heaven that can be had by the gentlemen who propose to make this homestead prospective; their only object in the world is to defeat the benefit which we propose it shall be to the people. I trust this Convention will not use its strength in that manner. I trust it will be proved to those gentlemen who come here, in whatsoever livery they choose, in any garment they choose, and coats in any shape they choose to wear them, that they cannot make us believe, because of their back record, as persons sent "to preach peace on earth, good will to all men," that in this Convention they can use us as an instrument of revenge to all men. I represent loyal citizens, I represent none of those men who rebelled against the Government, but, as part of my constituents, I protest against this Convention seeking to injure by its legislation those who rebelled. What has the United States Government done? Where was the blow struck? It was struck at the heart of the Government, at the prosperity of the United States Government. What has the Government, I say, done since the close of the war, and ask yourselves if you can consent to blot out one line which bears the record of magnanimity? That Government has refused to punish the leaders of the rebellion. That Government has forwarded even to those men who came fresh from the conflict, supplies by which they could manage to live. That Government, even with a Radical Congress, has refused to commit one act of revenge against the people who rebelled against the Government, but you are asked to do it. We saw the scene enacted here yesterday. The gentleman from Barnwell (Mr. LESLIE), with a heart as honest and true as that which beats in the breast of any, spoke, and you saw him get up here and paint a vivid picture of the condition of his people. Then with tears in his eyes he was compelled to sit down, simply saying, I love my people, I love them all. I ask the members of the Convention if, after witnessing that scene, they can steel their hearts against this measure.

In justice to the gentleman from Barnwell, towards whom, on another occasion which sprung up, much bitterness was displayed, I take cordial pleasure in saying that I believe he stood where his truth and honesty induced him to stand, and all the slings and shafts hurled at him has fallen harmless at his feet; and he has come out like "the purest gold, thrice tortured in the furnace."

If it be true, as has been declared, that the war was a rich man's war and the poor man's fight, let us, in God's name, stop it here, and not by a system of legislation seek to persecute the poor man any longer. We do not propose by this measure to impair the obligation of contracts; but, on the contrary, to surround them with all the sanctity of law, while at the same time we protect, to a humane degree, the debtor.

A good deal has been said about the retrospective character of this section. I ask the Convention if it is more retrospective than the Bankrupt Act of the United States, which allows a man $500 clear of debts? If it be morally right to free these men from debt, and reserve a portion of their property in one case, does not the principle apply with equal force in the present instance, and may we not by this provision confer the intended boon upon the people. The only manner in which we can aid the creditor is to give the debtor means to recuperate. Enforce the collections now, and the creditor will not have one-tenth, or perhaps one-fifteenth of his demands satisfied; but let time and industry aid the unfortunate debtor, and eventually he will be able to cancel his obligation. We do not say that this homestead law will operate retrospectively against judgments. A judgment is a lien upon property; we do not propose to interfere with vested rights, but that this section shall operate retrospectively against all outstanding debts, except judgments and mortgages. We do not intend to wipe out debts in any degree.

The gentleman from Darlington says he is willing to meet us half way, and proposes to divide the burden between the debtor and creditor. How can he do it, except by impairing the obligation of contracts?

Mr. B. F. WHITTEMORE. I am not in favor of disturbing any existing contracts whatever.

Mr. F. J. MOSES, Jr. Now, in the legal argument of the gentlemen from Fairfield (Mr. RUTLAND), he has entirely confounded the right of action with the remedy. We do not propose to interfere with this right of action. Let it stand. And I warn the Convention against the subterfuges piled upon each other with the intention of defeating this provision. Our duty is plain. It is the duty of the law making power always to prescribe the remedy for the collection of debts. That remedy has been prescribed, and we do not propose to interfere with it, except as has been provided by the gentleman from Darlington in the Bill of Rights, which abolishes imprisonment for debt. We simply propose that so much property shall be exempt from execution as is not subject to mortgage and judgment entered up. The fact that the remedy may possibly defeat the collection of the debt does not necessarily impair the obligation of the contract. The remedy may be ill advised, but no sane lawyer would on this ground declare it to be unconstitutional. This measure is not an *ex post facto* law within the meaning of the provisions of the Constitution of the United States.

If there were a particle of doubt in reference to the constitutionality of this measure, I think we should recollect that the unanimous will of the people regulates the construction of Constitutions. And right here, so far as the unconstitutionality of this measure is concerned, I would direct the attention of the gentlemen from Fairfield to one fact in reference to this law of reconstruction measure. I do not suppose we can point to a single instance that would have a stronger effect with him, if he is sincere. Does he not know that one of the leaders of the Republican party in Congress boldly asserts and maintains the doctrine that the reconstruction acts are totally unconstitutional? Does he not know that Thaddeus Stevens proclaimed from his seat in the House of Representatives that he has encamped outside of the Constitution, so far as the settling of this reconstruction is concerned? Does he not know that Mr. Stevens admits that the Constitution of the United States was not adequate to meet the emergency, and that he argues in this way, that as the Constitution did not provide for this emergency, as it did not say what should be done on the breaking out of the rebellion, at the close of the war the United States Government were the victors, and that that victory gave them all the rights which belongs to the victors over the conquered?

Now I say, is it not just as constitutional for us to admit here, for almost as grand a purpose as that which Mr. Stevens has in view, for his purpose is to reconstruct the States, and our purpose is to save the State of South Carolina, one consequence must follow the other? Have we not the same right, taking his view generally to be the true one, is it not necessary, in order to reconstruct the State, to encamp outside of the Constitution. Have we not just as much right, if it is necessary, to aid the people of the State to build up South Carolina as an integral part of the American Union? Have we not the same right to pass anything, even if it was unconstitutional? As far as I am concerned, there is no man on the floor of the house who has more reverence for the Constitution of the United States than I have, no matter how loyal he had been during the war. I say, if it is necessary now, with the knowledge that Congress will not interfere with our Constitution, provided it is a proper one; with that knowledge, without the slightest doubt that, if this homestead law is passed, the people of the State will ratify our Constitution; knowing all these things, if it is necessary to go outside of the Constitution of South Carolina, in order to help the State, I, for one, am willing to do it. I am willing to follow the lead of those who have camped outside of the Constitution. I do not agree with those or commit myself to the opinion of those who say that the reconstruction measures are unconstitutional. But, knowing that Congress will ratify our proceedings, I am willing to swallow it, even if it is unconstitutional.

It has been said that this is class legislation. I deny it, and am prepared to prove it. It has been asserted that the movement will only benefit the white man; only those who have imbued their hands in blood.

In looking over the list of tax payers of Charleston in 1860, I find three hundred colored tax payers, paying taxes on real estate of the value of three hundred thousand dollars. I ask you is this class legislation within the city of Charleston? I know colored persons living in

64

different parts of the State who did own real estate before the war, and who own it now. Many have bought property since the close of the war. ₄ I beg you to remember that on almost all the land bought by colored men, since the close of the war, very little of it has been paid for. To make the homestead prospective only, would sweep almost every colored man, who owns a homestead, from his possession. I know that in my District it would be so. The other delegate from Sumter, I know, can substantiate that statement.

Mr. T. J. COGHLAN. I know that what you state is true.

Mr. F. J. MOSES, Jr. We have just passed a resolution asking Congress to give them more land, and now, because they have by honest hard toil bought those lands, it is proposed by some to take it from them. That will be the effect if you do not pass this homestead law. The whites can stand it a great deal better than the colored people. The white owe a great many debts, but, at the same time, the colored people will have much more trouble. The whites, as a class, will stick to each other, particularly rich men. They will lend each other money to save their plantations from being sold. But to whom can the poor man appeal? Will those who propose to make this homestead law prospective, will they vote money to help him to keep his lands? What answer will they give these colored men when they go home? Will they answer that they did it simply to have some revenge on those persons who brought on the war? I leave it to the consciences of those gentlemen to say if they would like to give an answer like that. They have come here to build up a system of laws, and provide a Constitution, which shall protect them in all their rights of present property and hereafter. Still, one of the first and most important things we do is to take away that little home, around which clusters every emotion of their hearts. We know how their hearts have been set on land; we know how everything they have made has been treasured up for the purpose of buying land. They say give me a home and place to shelter my wife and children, and we ask no more. We are willing to work out our destinies by the side of the white man. I say, if you make this law prospective only, you hurt the colored man more than you hurt the white man, because there are thousands of schemes by which the colored man may be deprived of his home. The white men are always smart enough to employ lawyers to do everything for them, smart enough, as a great many of them heretofore have been, to avoid the penalty of their just debts. They can avoid the Sheriff, but when the Sheriff comes to the colored man he has no sympathy for him. He says the white people don't want you to have lands anyhow. You have got it by your industry, perseverance and honesty, but we are determined to take it from you, and you will whistle for it when you get it again. Another point I would make is in reference to the bearing this subject will have on the adoption of our Constitution, and as to whether or not it will help our Constitution to have this clause in it, which guarantees a homestead. If every member could have sat with me by my fireside one night last week, and heard an account of the scene that occurred at the gentleman's home in Barnwell, when he first heard that the calling of the Convention was defeated, if you could hear the tale that fell from his lips, as in the agony of his heart he asked, " What must I do here? I have taken a stand for the rights of the colored people, and almost every white man is raised up against me. I have been looking forward to the calling of this Convention to have their rights recognized. I can live here no longer."

If that was the effect then, what will be the effect if our Constitution is defeated?

The gentleman from Barnwell (Mr. LESLIE,) has already felt that agony of mind ; he has already endured that perturbation of spirit and suffering of heart which enured to him when he heard of the defeat of the calling of the Convention. I ask you, for God's sake, if you desire to feel, when you go from here, that you have put this Constitution upon such a broad foundation of justice, equity and equality before the law, and of the rights of all men ; if you desire to feel that you have made the hearts of every one of your citizens leap for joy when he reads your Constitution ; if you desire to feel that there is no combination of circumstances which can give the Democratic party in this State the victory over our Constitution ; if you desire to feel that your Constitution has not only been carried by a number of voters prepared to vote for it anyhow, but by a large majority of all classes, because you framed it in a spirit of equity and justice for all men ; then, for God's sake, I say, make this homestead law retrospective.

Mr. R. B. ELLIOTT moved the previous question.

Mr. S. G. W. DILL called for the yeas and nays.

The call was not sustained.

Mr. J. M. RUTLAND. ' I do not intend to detain the house more than fifteen minutes. I confess I am not exactly prepared to speak on this subject to-day. I had hoped from the course the debate has taken that I would have had an opportunity to arrange my thoughts by to-morrow morning.

There seems to have been a misunderstanding among a great many colored persons as to the effect of the amendment offered by the gentleman from Richland (Mr. ROBERTSON). I wish to explain the effect of that amendment. Some of these colored persons think it will deprive them forever of the right to have a homestead. That is not the case. This amendment does not interfere with homesteads which may be acquired hereafter by white men or colored men, or any other class of men. It is simply intended to prevent a retro-active or retrospective bearing on this homestead law. In other words, it is intended that those men who were in debt before the war shall be compelled to let the property which they held at that time, and got credit upon, be responsible for their debts. That is all the amendment is intended to effect. It is intended to make those men who owed and contracted debts before the war, and now owe those debts and do not desire to pay, give up the property they hold. It does not interfere with our having a homestead law for the future ; and if you vote for that amendment you will have a sound homestead law in the future. When a man who makes a contract, if it is the law of the land that you shall have a homestead, and the man knows you are entitled to a homestead, then he contracts with his eyes open, and has no right to complain if you unfortunately should not be able to pay that debt, and you are allowed to retain the homestead.

Mr. J. J. WRIGHT. Who were the creditors before the war ?

Mr. J. M. RUTLAND. Their name is legion. I cannot remember them. If you vote for this amendment you are not depriving yourselves of a homestead in the future, if you are able to procure one. I hope you will all be able to do so. I have not my notes arranged and shall not be able to speak from them about the Constitution. I must, however, make a few remarks in reply to the gentleman from Sumter, who is the main gentleman who attacked my argument. He commences his speech, which is a most extraordinary one, by stating we should bury the past, forget all records and know nothing that has happened heretofore. That may suit him very well, but I do not know exactly whether it is right or not. At the same time, if we want to know something of the man addressing me as to his sincerity, we do trace him back to find out what his record has been upon the various questions before the body. I have no doubt the gentleman would be glad it should be forgotten that there was such a place as Fort Sumter, or that there ever was such a flag as a secession flag.

Mr. F. J. MOSES, Jr. I would like very much to have the gentleman go on.

Mr. C. P. LESLIE. Will the gentleman refer to his own record ?

Mr. J. M. RUTLAND. I have not heretofore boasted of my record, but I claim as clean a record upon union principles as any man in the

United States of America. I have never faltered from those principles from the opening of the war to the present time, and nó man can undertake to assert to the contrary. Even the Mercury, with all its concentrated venom and malice, cannot say aught to that character in its paragraph this morning. Surely there is malice enough in this world if there was anything wrong on my part to have given the Convention all the information that can be given. I presume I am moving against wind and tide in this Convention, for the appeals are made to poor men ; for it is said to be a relief measure, and any man opposed to relief is opposed to the poor man, and, therefore, you are to vote him down. I presume I may be in the minority, and have been threatened if I held to this measure that my political head would be taken off. Some of my friends who left me gave me notice that if I opposed this measure it would take my head. But I am willing to stand here upon principle.

Mr. B. F. RANDOLPH. The gentleman has appealed to the colored men. There are colored men here who own property and who may be in debt. If that amendment is carried, will not their property go for their debts?

Mr. J. M. RUTLAND. I suppose a good many do own property. If they contracted honest debts and got the value, I do not think any honest colored man would want to shield himself from the payment of those debts when he got credit upon the faith of his property. I do not believe a colored man would desire to do it. But their homesteads will be protected to them hereafter. I do claim that every man is bound to pay his debts, whatever they may be.

Mr. R. B. ELLIOTT. I would desire to ask the gentleman whether white men would be glad to shield themselves from their debts ?

Mr. J. M. RUTLAND. I think a great many of the white population desire to shield themselves from paying their honest debts.

Mr. B. O. DUNCAN. I would like to know whether the white people are more disposed to shirk their debts than any other class.

Mr. J. M. RUTLAND. There are a great many who want to dodge their debts and hold on to their lands. It has been said that I was a rich man, and that my friend from Richland was a rich man. I concede that my friend is a rich man, but deny that I am, or that I advocate this measure as a rich man. I come from the ranks of the poorest class. I had a competency before the war, but the war has swept it away from me. What little I do now own they propose by this retrospective homestead law and stay law to take it from me. Let them do so if they think it is right.

My friend from Sumter laughs at Constitutions, and is willing to override the Constitution if necessary to pass a measure of this sort. Relief for what? It is relieving a man who has landed possessions from the payment of his honest debts with his property upon which he proposes to sacrifice everything. He tells you he is the friend of the poor. If the gentleman lived in Utah he would marry all the poor women in the territory, and no doubt would kiss all the poor men's babies. This gentleman, so passionately fond of the poor man, tells us this is a poor man's measure. I deny it. I intend to introduce some resolutions which will be really for the benefit of the poor of this State, and which will operate universally all over the State. Any man who will introduce such a measure as that will not get my support; I am not willing to override all Constitutions.

I am honest in my convictions of this principle I am advocating; I feel I am walking upon velvet, however you decide this case. You may vote against me, vote down the amendment, have retrospective laws, stay laws or any other laws you choose that will interfere with contracts, but, notwithstanding, you can effect nothing. The Courts of the country will never respect an Ordinance of this Convention which conflicts with the Constitution of the United States; and, notwithstanding my friend from Sumter has endeavored to laugh me out of my doctrine of constitutional rights, I still contend for constitutional law. I do not know whether he wants anarchy, but he is not disposed to be bound or restrained by constitutional law. He is for the poor man and for nothing else. The poor man is his God.

Mr. F. J. MOSES, Jr. Do you not think it possible that sweeping everything in the world that a man owns from him might bring on anarchy?

Mr. J. M. RUTLAND. I believe that whenever the debtor and creditor are interfered with by outside parties, it is like interfering between a man and his wife in a quarrel. The man who does it is left to come out with a bloody nose, and it does not make any difference which side he takes. I think if we pass this, we will, eventually, come out here with a bloody nose. I think the Courts of the country will decide all this work to be unconstitutional, null and void. I may be in the minority—I suppose I am; nevertheless, I stick to my principles. My eloquent friend from Barnwell (Mr. LESLIE), yesterday made an appeal not to be resisted. I would say to him, "Weep not dearest, thy victory is sure, for who can resist that most powerful of all appeals, beauty bathed in tears?" I feel, therefore, I may weep on this question. I am willing to stand on the issue. I am right sure I will never surrender. Vote me down if you choose, but give me credit for honesty of purpose.

Mr. C. P. LESLIE. Will the gentleman allow me to ask him a question before he takes his seat? I understand him to claim sincerity for any purpose for which he recorded his vote. I ask if you question the fact, if all the votes cast in this house do express the honest sentiments of your heart, whether you did not tell me, fifteen minutes before you cast the affirmative vote, you could not concur in the petition to Congress for a loan of one million of dollars.

Mr. J. M. RUTLAND. When a measure is brought up to which I am indifferent, and which I think will go for nothing, I thought I would get in the boat with all the rest of the gentlemen and ride along, although I thought it would be a failure and a miscarriage. I went with the tide, because I did not think it worth while to oppose it. I cared not about this little petition; I would vote for far more money than that if I thought there was any chance for it. I would not stop at one million. I really thought that was got up for political effect, and I was willing to go with the rest of the gentlemen; get in the boat, vote, and ride along with them.

Mr. C. P. LESLIE. That is what he calls sincerity of purpose, I expect.

Mr. J. M. RUTLAND. I frequently have heard it said we have lost all, save honor, in this great war. I am willing to acknowledge that as pretty nearly true. If we have any honor left, I trust this Convention to the extent of its ability will preserve its honor. It is all we have to expect. If a man owes a just debt, contracted previous to that time, and has a lot of land, let him sell that land and pay his debt. But so long as we continue to pass stay laws, retrospective homestead laws, and repudiation laws, we will never have credit in South Carolina. Millions of capital are ready to be distributed among us as investments. If the owners think well of it to put it out with the proper interest, they will need confidence. Credit is worth more than the little pittance of homesteads. I contend that the country will not be the poorer by making men pay their debts, and give up their lands if necessary. If one man is dispossessed of an estate, another becomes possessed of it. The gentleman from Barnwell says he goes for the benefit of the entire State at large; then I am sure he will not injure the State by protecting a man from paying his debts.

I could say a great deal more, but I think this question has been presented in the light we cannot doubt. I contend if any man is disposed to do justice between the creditor and debtor, or if he is disposed to deprive the creditor of his rights, and to make a present to the debtor, who claims it of his just debts to another, then let him vote against that amendment; but, I trust, upon second reflection, you will sustain the laws and Constitution of the country, notwithstanding the gentleman from Sumter (Mr. MOSES) is disposed to laugh them to scorn.

Mr. R. B. ELLIOTT. I move the previous question.

The motion was sustained, and the question being taken on the various amendments offered, they were all lost with the exception of the amendment offered by Mr. R B. ELLIOTT.

The main question was then taken, upon which Mr. S. G. W. DILL called for the yeas and nays, which were ordered.

Mr. B. F. WHITTEMORE asked leave to explain his vote, which was granted.

Mr. B. F. WHITTEMORE stated he voted "no," because the section is proclaimed to be retrospective, and because he cannot support any project that would commit a violation of the Constitution of his country ; but he was in favor of a just homestead act.

Mr. W. J. McKINLAY said he would have voted no, but he understood that it would be left for the Courts to decide whether the law was retrospective or not. He therefore voted yea.

Mr. C. M. WILDER said he wanted it understood he did not oppose a homestead. He believed it to be the means of identifying the people with the State. But he was opposed to any homestead or stay law that would rob one portion of the people to satisfy the other. He, therefore, would vote no.

The yeas and nays being taken, resulted as follows :

YEAS—The President, Messrs. Allen, Alexander, Becker, Bell, Bowen, Bonum, Burton, Brockenton, Bryce, Byas, R. H. Cain, E. J. Cain, Camp, Cardozo, Coghlan, Clinton, Cooke, Collins, Corley, Craig, Crews, Darrington, Davis, DeLarge, Dickson, Dill, Dogan, Driffle, Duncan, Edwards, Elliott, Foster, Gentry, Goss, Gray, Harris, Jas. N. Hayne, Charles D. Hayne, H. E. Hayne, Henderson, Holmes, Humbird, Hurley, Jacobs, Jervey, Jillson, W. B. Johnson, J. W. Johnson, Dr. L. B. Johnson, W. E. Johnston, Joiner, Chas. Jones, Lang, Langley, Samuel Lee, Lomax, Leslie, E. W. M. Mackey, Mayer, Mauldin. W. J. McKinlay, W. McKinlay, McDaniels, Mead, Middleton, Miller, Milford, Moses, Nance, Nash, Nelson, Newell, Nuckles, Olsen, Parker, Pillsbury, Randolph, Rainey, Ransier, Richmond, Rivers, Robertson, Rose, Runion, Rutland, Sanders, Sasportas, Smalls, Stubbs, Swails, Thomas, Augustus Thompson, B. A. Thompson, S. B. Thompson, Viney, Webb, Whipper, White, Williamson, Wingo, Wooley, Wright—103.

NAYS—Messrs. Owens, Whittemore, C. M. Wilder, J. H. Jenks—4.

ABSENT—Messrs. Arnim, Boozer, Chamberlain, Chestnut, Donaldson, Hunter, Jackson, L. Johnson, H. Jones, George Lee, Neagle, Perry, Shrewsbury, F. E. Wilder—14.

The thirty-fifth section then passed to its third reading, and the President announced the Convention adjourned.

THIRTY-FIRST DAY.

Thursday, February 20, 1868.

The Convention assembled at half-past ten o'clock, and was called to order by the PRESIDENT.

Prayer was offered by the Rev. H. D. EDWARDS.

The roll was called, and a quorum answering to their names, the PRESIDENT announced the Convention ready to proceed to business.

The Journal of yesterday was read and confirmed.

The PRESIDENT called for reports of Standing Committees.

Mr. R. G. HOLMES asked and obtained leave to introduce the following proposed ordinance:

The Special Committee to whom was referred the annexed draft of an article proposed to be embodied in the Constitution of the State, respectfully report that they have given mature consideration to the subject referred to them, and submit hereby the conclusion to which they have arrived.

Your Committee recognize the necessity of the relief for the financial and industrial interest intended to be conferred upon the people of the State by the measure proposed; that relief consists in part in furnishing lands for purchase by actual settlers, upon terms and conditions as to payment so moderate that it will assure to the industrious the means of success in surrounding themselves with the comforts, the conveniences and the independence of homes; while those, who might be disposed to abuse the provision thus made, will be deprived of the opportunity of turning the bounty of the State into a scheme for speculation and land monopoly.

Another portion of the intended objects of the measure proposed is to make the State a purchaser for that portion of the lands of the State that is forced by the indebtedness of its owners upon public sale, and thus, by stimulating competition at such public sale, prevent those lands from passing into the hands of speculators at merely nominal rates, impoverishing the debtor, while the creditor realizes but little in satisfaction of his legal demands.

As to the first object of the measure stated above, the general policy of offering inducements to actual settlers in the manner proposed is not only commended by the principles of justice and economy involved, but by the practice of the Federal Government and of many of the States. The principle has become too well settled and has been too often practically applied to need either argument or illustration at the present time. It is, however, proper to remark that special reasons for its adoption exist in the present condition of the State. This State embraces an undue proportion of uncultivated lands; the number of the landless is out of proportion to the total number of inhabitants of this as compared with other political communities depending for stability upon the morality,

65

intelligence and property interests of the body of the people. The low rates at which property is sold at public sales offers the greatest inducements to enter upon a plan of relief that cannot fail under good management to be a success.

The means proposed by the measure under consideration for attaining this end, appears to be practical and free from objection. It is necessary that the credit of the State should be brought to aid in arresting the downward tendency of the property, and in providing the means of supplying a certain kind of capital to give employment to the industry of the country, while it is not desirable that the public debt should be increased; but, on the contrary, that every practicable and legal means of curtailing it should be adopted, yet the issue of stock to a reasonable extent for the purpose contemplated by this act, will not only avoid what is really objectionable in increasing the public debt, but will have a direct effect in aiding the liquidation of the outstanding debt. In the first place, the issue for the purpose will be based on the specific lands purchased with such securities and on the proceeds of the sales thereof, and therefore, will never call for taxation for its liquidation. In the second place, at the rates at which land is sold at public sales, the State will be able to acquire property which, before the stock based upon it matures, will be worth much more than the amount paid for it, and which, or its proceeds, if judiciously sold, will be more than sufficient to pay the debt incurred for its purchase, and this surplus value may be applied to a sinking fund to take the place of taxation on the final liquidation of the public debt at large.

Your Committee regard the creation of a Board of Public Lands as of importance, in order to carry out the provisions of the measure proposed; but independent of this consideration, such a Board is needed to give peculiar attention to what is demanded for the preservation and care of the public lands of the State.

Your Committee, therefore, recommend the adoption of the plan proposed, and that it be introduced in the body of the Constitution in its proper connection.

SECTION 1. It shall be the duty of the Legislature to provide for the establishing of a Board, to be known and designated as Commissioners of Public Lands, of which Board the Comptroller General of the State shall be a member; and to define the powers and duties of said Board, and fix the compensation of the members, and to provide for the current expenses thereof.

SEC. 2. The Commissioners of Public Lands shall have authority, under regulations provided by law, to purchase at public sales, improved and unimproved real estate within this State, which in the judgment of such Commissioners shall be suitable for the purposes intended by the fourth section of this Article; *Provided*, that the aggregate amount of purchases made in any fiscal year shall not exceed the par value of the public stock of this State, created and appropriated by the Legislature for the purposes contemplated in the fourth section of this Article, for such fiscal year; *And provided also*, that the rate at which any such purchase shall be made shall not exceed 75 per cent. of the value of the land so purchased, including the improvements thereon.   Such valuation to be ascertained in the manner hereinafter provided for by law.

SEC. 3. The Legislature shall have authority to issue to said Commissioners public stock of this State to such amount as it may deem expedient; which stock, or the proceeds thereof, the Commissioners shall have authority to apply in payment of all purchases made in accordance with the second section of this Article; *Provided*, that such public stock shall not be negotiated at a rate less than the par value thereof.

SEC. 4. The said Commissioners shall have authority, under such regulations as shall be established by the Legislature, to cause the said lands to be surveyed and laid off in suitable tracts to be sold to actual settlers, subject to the condition that one half thereof shall be placed under cultivation within three years from the date of any such purchase. And that the purchaser thereof shall annually pay interest upon the amount of such purchase money remaining unpaid, at the rate of 7 per cent. per annum; and also all taxes imposed thereon by or under the authority of the United States or of this State, and in addition thereto, shall, in every year after the third from the date of said purchase, pay such proportion of the principal of said purchase as shall be required by the Legislature.   The titles to said lands shall remain in the State until the amount of said purchase shall be paid, principal and interest. But a certificate of such purchase shall be issued to the purchaser, which shall be assignable after three years from the date thereof.

SEC. 5. All lands purchased by said Commissioners, or the proceeds of the sales thereof, shall be and remain pledged for the redemption of the public stock issued under section third of this Article; but the Legislature shall have authority, subject to such lien and pledge, to make upon the faith and credit of such fund, further issues of public stock; but the stock issued as last aforesaid, and the proceeds thereof, shall be used exclusively for the redemption of the public debt of the State outstanding at the date of such issue and which shall not be funded.

SEC. 6. The Legislature shall provide by law for the security of the funds in the hands of the Commissioners of Public Lands, and for the accountability of such officers, and shall require bonds to be given therefor.

Mr. E. W. M. MACKEY offered the following resolution, which was agreed to :

Resolved, That this Convention request Brevet Major-General E. R. S. Canby, commanding second Military District, to remove Mr. Lee, the present Superintendent of the State Penitentiary, and appoint in his place Mr. Wm. E. Rose, of Yorkville.

Mr. J. M. ALLEN offered the following :

Resolved, That the President be requested to take such steps as are necessary to draw twenty thousand dollars from the Treasury of the State for the purpose of paying the *per diem* and mileage of the members of this Convention, and that the same be paid on Saturday, the 22d of February, 1868.

Mr. J. J. WRIGHT moved to lay the resolution on the table, which was not agreed to, and the resolution passed.

Messrs. J. N. HAYNE and J. K. JILLSON desired to be recorded as having voting nay on the above resolution.

Mr. R. SMALLS moved to take up the unfinished business of yesterday, which was not agreed to.

The PRESIDENT stated that he had received a communication from the State Treasurer requesting information as to whether the amount of $75,000, appropriated under the ordinance levying a tax to pay the expenses of the Convention, would be sufficient for that purpose. The PRESIDENT, after a careful review of the condition of the work before the Convention, had to state that if it was the intention of the Convention to carry it beyond the first of March, it would be necessary for the body to direct the Finance Committee to draw up a new ordinance for an additional tax upon the people of South Carolina.

Mr. J. H. JENKS offered the following preamble and resolution, which was referred to the Committee on Petitions :

WHEREAS, we regard it the duty and true policy of the General Government to carefully husband, encourage and protect the agricultural resources of the several States ; and whereas, the culture of rice forms one of the principal resources of the State of South Carolina, therefore,

Resolved, That we humbly petition Congress that they will take no action looking toward the reduction or repeal of the present import duty on rice, believing that any abatement of the present tariff will render the culture of the staple unprofitable, thereby depriving the State of one of its chief resources, and the inhabitants thereof of one of their principal sources of sustenance ; at the same time denying the country at large a reasonable luxury which the inferior articles from foreign markets cannot afford.

Mr. N. G. PARKER offered the following resolution, which was agreed to.

Resolved. That no member shall speak upon any question but fifteen minutes, and only once, unless by the unanimous consent of the Convention.

The consideration of the report of the Committee on the Legislative Part of the Constitution was resumed.

Section thirty-sixth, the concluding section, providing for the taxation of all real and personal property, according to its actual value, to be ascertained by assessment, was read and passed to its third reading.

Section third, in reference to the division of Charleston and Pickens Districts, which had been recommitted, came up for a second reading.

Mr. L. S. LANGLEY. A few days ago, when a motion was made here to allow the County of Charleston two Senators, I objected to it, and I voted against that measure, because I contended then, as I do now, that it is unjust to the other counties of the State. The adoption of the motion proposed by the delegate from Charleston has emboldened that delegation to make new demands, which will give them a still further preponderance in legislation over the other counties in the State. I have no prejudices in this matter, but I consider myself bound to protect the rights of my constituents, and to see that Beaufort District has an equal representation in the State Senate with the County of Charleston. As I understand this section, it will give what was formerly known as Charleston district, including Berkley and Charleston, five Senators, whereas the other counties have but one.

If we intend a division of the late districts, let us make a general division of all, and not single out Charleston, or any other particular district, for the purpose of benefiting one portion of the State at the expense of the other. That is all the objection I have to this section, and I hope it will be duly considered.

Mr. E. W. M. MACKEY. I cannot see any reason in the objections urged by the gentleman from Beaufort against this section. It only proposes to make three counties out of a large tract of territory which was formerly known as the Judicial District of Charleston, but which was divided into nine election districts and entitled to ten Senators. We now propose to make only three election districts or counties in place of the nine, and to these three counties only four Senators in place of the ten, a reduction of six Senators. There certainly can be no reasonable objection to this. The gentleman says we desired to grasp power and to give an undue influence to Charleston. Now, these three counties will be amongst the largest in the State. Charleston will contain nine thousand voters, Berkley six thousand, and Edisto four thousand, and they will also cover as much territory as any of the other counties. It would certainly be very unjust to make only two counties out of a section of the State containing nineteen thousand voters, when very few of the other counties contain more than five thousand voters, and some of them only two thousand voters. Moreover, to make the division into two counties, as the gentleman from Beaufort desires, would be extremely absurd. Charleston County would be in the middle of Berkley, and half of Berkley would be on one side of Charleston, and the other half on the other side. As the proposed division of the Judicial District of Charleston, or rather I should say the consolidation of these nine election districts into three counties, is nothing more than just and right, I hope this section will pass, as it has been reported by the Committee. Instead of showing a grasping disposition on the part of Charleston, it evinces a disposition rather to be generous; for instead of gaining any representatives we are really loosing six Senators, and the gentleman from Beaufort, before he makes any such charges, should be better informed upon the subject under discussion, or else say nothing.

Mr. J. J. WRIGHT. This division of a district is a matter of vital importance, and should receive the grave and earnest consideration of the Convention. We should not act blindly. The delegation from Charleston, no doubt, understand this matter perfectly, and perhaps the section, as it stands, is perfectly proper. But before recording my vote I desire to be more fully informed, and I shall, therefore, make a motion to postpone its consideration. I believe Charleston should have two Senators. Prior to the war she had ten, but we must remember that representation was based upon taxation, and not alone upon population. We are not now sending men to the Senate upon a property representation or taxation, but upon population.

As the rest of the delegates, with myself, are somewhat ignorant on this subject, and desire time to investigate it, so as to vote understandingly, I move that it be made the Special Order for to-morrow at 1 o'clock.

The motion was agreed to.

Mr. N. G. PARKER. I desire to correct a mistake in the resolution offered by myself this morning, and agreed to limiting the members to fifteen minutes' speech on any one question. It was my intention to have it read twice instead of once, as it now appears. I move a reconsideration of the resolution.

Mr. A. J. RANSIER. I would remind the gentleman that, if he amends the resolution as proposed, it would simply be as the rules now provide.

Mr. B. F. RANDOLPH. I hope the motion to reconsider will prevail. It would seem strange, and I think it unprecedented, in parliamentary bodies, to gag themselves, which would be the effect of this resolution, if allowed to stand as it is. We are here to deliberate, and want all the light we can have thrown on the subject. I am, therefore, opposed to any resolution cutting off debate. No such thing exists in Congress, but great latitude is allowed there in debate.

Mr. J. J. WRIGHT. I hope the resolution will not be considered. I consider it just exactly what we want in this body. I believe most every member of this Convention, who has anything important to say upon any subject, can say it in fifteen minutes. If allowed to stand as it is, it will afford a better opportunity for more members to express themselves upon questions coming before this body, and thus give us more light. I am opposed to extending the time. If we want to facilitate business, let the resolution stand as it is.

Mr. S. A. SWAILS. I move to lay the motion to reconsider on the table.

The motion was agreed to.

Mr. C. C. BOWEN offered the following resolution, which was referred to the Committee on the Legislative Part of the Constitution:

Resolved, That it shall be the duty of the first General Assembly convened under this Constitution, at their first session, to ratify the amendment to the Constitution of the United States, known as Article Fourteen, proposed by the Thirty-ninth Congress.

The report of the Committee on the Executive Department of the Constitution was taken up for a second reading.

Mr. J. J. WRIGHT. As this printed report has not been before us, prior to the second reading, I am unprepared to consider it, and would therefore enter my objection.

The PRESIDENT. In parliamentary usage the first reading is simply for information. If, when presented, any question is made, or the report laid on the table, or it is postponed, that, of course, would place it out of the hands of the house.

Mr. L. S. LANGLEY. I move that the report of the Committee on the Executive Part of the Constitution be read and considered its first reading.

Mr. E. W. M. MACKEY moved a reconsideration of the first section, which was agreed to.

The report was then taken up, and received its first reading.

Mr. E. W. M. MACKEY called for the second reading of the report of the Committee on the Judiciary.

Section first was read a second time, and, on motion of Mr. BOWEN, the provision for District Courts was stricken out. The section then passed to its third reading.

Section second was read a second time.

Mr. C. C. BOWEN moved to strike out the words "three Judges," and amend so as to make the Supreme Court consist of "a Chief Justice and two associate Judges, to be so classified that one of the Judges shall go out of office every two years."

The amendment was agreed to, and section second passed to its third reading.

Mr. L. S. LANGLEY. In view of the fact that nearly half the members have no copy of the report before them, I move a postponement of the further consideration of the report.

The PRESIDENT stated that the Secretary had delivered copies to the members, and had none left. A postponement, therefore, would not mend the matter, unless they ordered more printed.

Mr. E. W. M. MACKEY supported the motion to postpone. as he believed a large majority of the members were in the same situation, without copies.

Mr. L. S. LANGLEY moved that it be postponed until Saturday next at 1 o'clock.

Mr. E. W. M. MACKEY moved to amend by fixing the time after the consideration of the report of the Committee on Education.

Mr. J. J. WRIGHT moved that one hundred and fifty copies be printed.

Tne PRESIDENT stated that, as the Chairman of the Committee on Education was absent, according to parliamentary courtesy, the consideration of that report would be postponed.

Mr. C. C. BOWEN. I hope we will proceed with the consideration of the report on the Judiciary. If members had left their copies at home, it was their own fault. A school boy would hardly dare go to school with that plea in his mouth, and say he had left his books at home.

Mr. R. C. DeLARGE moved to lay the motion to postpone on the table, which was not agreed to.

Mr. CRAIG moved to adjourn for half an hour, to allow members to go home and get their papers.

The motion was not seconded.

Mr. WM. McKINLAY. I hope the motion to postpone will prevail. There is not a more important part of the Constitution than the Judicial Department, and it is very evident members are not prepared to act upon it. I think it important they should all have the report before them.

Mr. N. G. PARKER moved to lay the motion to print one hundred and fifty copies on the table, which was not agreed to.

Mr. B. BYAS. I hope the motion to postpone the present consideration of the Judiciary report will not prevail. I happened to know that one hundred and fifty copies of this report were printed, and duly distributed in the house. If the members have not taken care of their copies, it is their own fault. I have reason to believe that a number of copies have been sent in the country, and now it is asked to have one hundred and fifty copies more printed. I regard this as an unnecessary expense, as they will, in all probability, be again distributed among the friends of the members.

Various members here rose a second time to speak, and were decided by the Chair, under the rule adopted, to be out of order.

The demand being made for the previous question, it was sustained.

The question was then taken on the motion to postpone, and print one hundred additional copies, which was agreed to.

The report of the Committee on the Miscellaneous part of the Constitution was then taken up, and sections one, two, three and five passed to a second reading.

Mr. E. W. M. MACKEY. I move to strike out the sixth section.

The motion was agreed to.

Sections seven, eight and nine, were read a first time.

Mr. L. S. LANGLEY. I move to strike out the tenth section.

Mr. L. S. LANGLEY afterwards withdrew the motion.

Section ten was passed to a second reading.

Mr. E. W. M. MACKEY. I move to strike out the eleventh section, as there is an almost identical section in the report of the Committee on the Legislative Department.

Section twelve was passed to a second reading.

Mr. D. H. CHAMBERLAIN. I move that section thirteen be stricken out. At the capital of all or nearly all the States there is a Bureau of Statistics, and they are regarded of great importance. At that Bureau may be obtained information concerning the population, etc., of the Districts, Parishes, Counties, etc., in the State. This does not require the Legislature to establish it. It is put in the subjunctive mood. It says it *may be* established. It is left to the disposition of the Legislature.

The motion to strike out was agreed to.

The report of the Committee on Miscellaneous Provisions of the Constitution, on Corporation, on Militia, and on Charitable Institutions, were then severally taken up, and read a first time.

The report of the Committee on Finance and Taxation was taken up, and read from section one to the eighteenth, inclusive.

On motion of Mr. N. G. PARKER, section nineteen was stricken out.

Mr. D. H. CHAMBERLAIN moved to reconsider the Special Order made for consideration on Wednesday next, being the Ordinance reported by the Committee on the Miscellaneous Provisions of the Consti-

66

tution, for the appointment of Commissioners to ascertain what obligations are binding on the State.

The motion was agreed to, and the Ordinance taken up for consideration.

Mr. B. O. DUNCAN. This motion, as it now stands, it seems to me will be somewhat objectionable. It is not our intention to repudiate any State debts. This measure proposes to stop the payment of all debts, or interest on a debt contracted prior to the 29th of April, 1865. I would propose, as an amendment, to say between the 19th of December, 1860, and the 29th of April, 1865.

Mr. C. C. BOWEN. I do not think this is the business of this body or of the Legislature. Under that portion of the Constitution already adopted, if a party has claims against another in this State he can go into the United States Courts, and once there it is the province of the Judge to decide whether he is rightfully there or not. Unless it is proposed to inaugurate some system by which the obligation of contracts are impaired, we had better let this thing alone. I know of no authority by which the Legislature of any State can appoint Commissioners to say whether one claim is valid or another not. They have no authority for anything of the kind. It is a question exclusively for the Courts of the State. The Convention has no right to entertain this motion. Some say claims may be introduced for Confederate money; but suppose the parties appointed as Commissioners say that debts contracted when Confederate money was used were not valid, would not that be impairing the obligation of contracts?

Mr. B. F. RANDOLPH. If the State itself were a party to borrow money for the purpose of carrying on the war, would you have that transaction investigated by any county or district of the State? Would it not be the duty of the Legislature to do it?

Mr. C. C. BOWEN. I suppose the Legislature will make all necessary laws in regard to any money borrowed in aid of the rebellion. Whether they do or not, there is an amendment to the Constitution of the United States that has to be adopted before these States go back into the Union, and that once adopted, it settles the whole question. In other words, money borrowed in aid of the rebellion cannot be made a valid debt. It is perfectly useless to go on with legislation that amounts to nothing in the end. I was in favor of accepting certain debts, but the Convention did not see fit to touch that section of the Bill of Rights, and as it stands I know of no authority by which the Legislature can appoint Commissioners to inquire into the validity of these contracts. It is a question solely for the Courts, and no other tribunal can exercise that authority.

Mr. J. S. CRAIG. As I understand it, the Commissioners appointed under this ordinance are simply to determine and report what contracts were entered into by the State for the purpose of carrying on the war. I do not see the force of the objections made to such a measure as that.

Mr. W. J. WHIPPER. It seems to me that the Legislature would have the right to do all that this ordinance contemplates. The gentleman from Charleston states that he knows of no authority but the Courts to inquire into the validity of these debts. The Legislature would be compelled to refuse payment of any debts contracted in aid of the rebellion. The 14th amendment to the Constitution of the United States provides that this class of debts shall not be paid. This ordinance proposes to appoint a certain Board of Commissioners to ascertain what portion of the debts of the State belong to that class. I remember reading in the proceedings of the Convention of 1865, that Andrew Johnson requested the Convention to repudiate the rebel debt incurred by the State. Governor Perry replied that the rebel debt was so mixed up with other debts that it was almost impossible to separate them. This makes the ordinance more necessary.

Mr. R. G. HOLMES. I hope the ordinance will pass as it is. I am not prepared to discuss the proposition, but we certainly need it. In looking over the proceedings of the Legislature of 1865, we find a large amount of appropriations made for Confederate purposes; among the rest one thousand dollars for removing marble from the State House, one thousand dollars for removing a few marble monuments, and a great many other things, all of which need investigation.

Mr. B. F. RANDOLPH. It is known to everybody acquainted with the financial condition of the State that it is bad. These Commissioners called for by the ordinance, are to investigate and see that the State is held responsible for no debt incurred for carrying on the rebellion. I have been informed that there are certain obligations now existing, certain bonds in England, which were held against the State, and that certain parties have compounded to pay that debt. A great many things of that character need investigation. This ordinance merely does not authorize the Legislature to investigate financially the condition of the State, and see all its honest debts paid. I am also informed that the State did borrow money from other States just before the breaking out of the war, for the purpose of carrying on the rebellion. That is a matter to be investigated. I hope, therefore, this ordinance will be passed, and the Legislature authorized to appoint a Board of Commissioners to investigate all these matters.

Mr. B. BYAS. I certainly concur in all the gentleman has said as to the necessity of an investigation. No matter how small any debt created in aid of the rebellion may be, it should not be paid by the State. We cannot do it with a consistent regard to principle, or the present condition of our State Treasury. I hope the ordinance will pass.

The question was then taken and the ordinance passed as follows :

Be it ordained, That it shall be the duty of the Legislature at its first session to appoint Commissioners to investigate and ascertain what obligations of the State are entitled to be held as valid and binding upon the State, in conformity with the provisions of this Constitution and the ordinances adopted by this Convention, and to report thereon to the Legislature; and until the Legislature shall have ascertained the validity of such obligations, no payment for either principal or interest shall be made on any outstanding obligation created and incurred prior to the 29th day of April, 1865.

Mr. B. F. RANDOLPH moved to reconsider the action of the Convention on the report of the Committee on Petitions in regard to the loan of $30,000,000 by Congress to Southern Planters. Lost.

On motion of Mr. B. O. DUNCAN, the Convention adjourned.

THIRTY-SECOND DAY.

Friday, February 21, 1868.

The Convention assembled at half-past 10 A. M., and was called to order by the PRESIDENT.

Prayer was offered by the Rev. J. M. RUNION.

The roll was called, and a quorum answering to their names, the PRESIDENT announced the Convention ready to proceed to business.

The Journal of yesterday was read and approved.

Mr. C. P. LESLIE rose to a question of privilege, and asked that the Reading Clerk, with the permission of the Convention, would read an article contained in the Mercury attacking his character.

No objection being made, the article was read.

Mr. C. P. LESLIE said : Mr. President and Delegates to the Convention, under ordinary circumstances I should not have noticed the article that has just been read by the Clerk of the house. The motive that induced the editor to write the article at this time and under the circumstances of political affairs, has compelled me to notice it.

I have observed with pain and regret, that the editor of the Charleston Mercury has seen fit, from time to time, to publish furious onslaughts upon every member of this body, and more particularly the conservative members of this house. Just in proportion as the member has displayed anything like conservative action, or advocated justice for the unfortunate white people of this State, just in that proportion has the Mercury endeavored to assail their private character and bring them into ridicule or contempt. Conservative action in this body seems to be a high crime and misdemeanor with our friend, the editor of the Mercury, and woe be to the unfortunate wretch who shall dare to advocate sympathy for the whole people, the people of its own color, the people of its own race. A sympathetic word, an exhibition of kindly feeling for their distress, is sure to bring down upon its victims the wrath and vengeance of the Mercury. Why is all this ? Does the Mercury hate or loathe the masses of the people in this State, the poor, the unfortunate people of his own native State ? If not, why does the Mercury assail me, standing upon the floor of this house, appealing for the white people in their distress ? If he would convince the Northern people that he was sincerely conservative; if he would convince the people of his own State that he had their relief at heart, I submit the editor of the Mercury takes a very queer way of showing it. Does my conservative action militate against the people of the State? Would the distress of the people of this State, by unkindly action on my part be aided or as-sisted ? I think not.

I think I understand the motive of the editor of the Mercury. "This Convention," to use the language which the editor is reported to have used, explains in a word the secret of his wrath : "This Convention,' said the editor, "is too damned conservative."

Mr. D. H. CHAMBERLAIN called the gentleman to order. He said the article was merely a matter for personal explanation so far as it abuses his personal character, but the substance of the gentleman's remarks appeared to be more of the character of a defence of his politi-cal course.

The PRESIDENT stated that questions of privilege were always, in parliamentary bodies, allowed great latitude and courtesy. It appeared to the Chair that the member having risen for the purpose of defending himself from the attack of a licentious paper published in this city, it was for the house to decide whether they should limit the time to be taken by the member.

Mr. L. S. LANGLEY objected, on the score of economy of time, to the member proceeding any further. The gentleman rose to defend his personal character, and he was speaking of his political character.

The question being put, the house allowed the member to proceed.

Mr. C. P. LESLIE continued, saying he would go back to where he was interrupted. The editor of the Mercury is reported to have said, "this Convention is too conservative." Consistent Mercury ! thy con-sistency is a rotten stone that falls to pieces the moment it is touched.

I am aware that any explanations I may make upon the floor of this house, in regard to what I know to be a libellous article, is only an ex-planation made once. The editor always has the last say. He always has the opportunity to write and publish the last word. Probably this is the last time that I shall trouble the attention of the house with any comment upon the conduct of the Mercury. I only desire to say now that this article is false from beginning to end. There is not, either as a whole or in part, one particle of truth in it.

I know it is within the power of a newspaper, within the power of a cunning reporter, a fruitful man, to assail any man now living upon the earth. I have yet to see the man who cannot by a play upon words be brought into ridicule and contempt. But there is another body—there is the people, who will judge of the article and determine for themselves whether the article itself, when so cunningly written, is not a charge, not an offence; is in no respect a calumny, or in any respect tends to dis-grace he party he seeks to write about.

I will say, in the beginning, that I do not find fault with the style in which the reporter prepares his articles. Certain subjects in all newspapers are commonly treated in about the same vein. For instance, the Mercury says: "C. P. LESLIE (white) hails from Brooklyn, New York, and claims to have once represented that city as Senator in the New York Legislature." He desires to have the world understand that I am a braggadocio, that with great pomp and full of boasting, I have gone up and down the earth, riding up and down on top of wind and wave, proclaiming everywhere that I was a member of the State Senate from Brooklyn, New York. This is a style peculiar to reporters. I cannot correct his style of writing, but we see in that style of writing, if it be untrue, a disposition to do all he can within his power to bring him into contempt.

It is not true I was ever a member of the Senate of the New York State Legislature; but were I such a member, it is the last confession to any public body that I would ever deliberately make.

I was once, it is true, a member of the lower House of the New York Legislature, but I have taken a great deal of pains, never even to reveal the fact to any one here. The astute cunning reporter of the Mercury never discovered that fact by my proclaiming it on the housetops.

The speaker again quoted from the Mercury: "While in business there he came to Charleston, bought nearly a thousand dollars worth of goods from one of our principal wholesale and jobbing dry goods houses, for which he gave a draft on a prominent factor. The draft was presented and acceptance refused, on the ground of no funds being placed in his hands to meet it."

I am aware that, in the judgment of the law, it is not illegal to have bought a thousand dollars worth of goods, nor to have given a draft in payment upon a respectable factor of the city of Charleston, and that the factor of the city of Charleston refused to accept it. That is merely an every day transaction. I hold it to be a moral offence for a man to purchase one thousand dollars worth of goods upon the faith or representation that he has in the hands of a factor some money upon which his draft will be honored, and knows when he purchases the goods that he has no money with the factor, and knows also the draft will not be honored.

I desire to tell the truth about it. It is true I kept a store at Ninety-Six. It is true I came to Charleston with over $10,000 and bought large quantities of goods. It is true, as a rule, I bought my goods against rough rice and cotton, consigned by me to the city.

It is true I did not buy $1,000 worth of goods against rough rice and cotton, but it is true I bought, of Marshall, Burge & Co., about $275 worth. Our friend of the Mercury has only multiplied it four times. I gave a draft upon a respectable factor of this city. I believe him to be a gentleman, and out of respect and kindness to him I will not present his name, although the Mercury would nearly compel me to do so. Well, the goods were bought. The factor says to the merchant, I know Mr. Leslie, and if he says the rough rice will arrive, you may depend upon it, and when it arrives I will sell it and pay you, provided the bill does not exceed $300. The rough rice did arrive, the factor sold it; but did the factor keep his word? What became of the factor?

I will simply say that the poor unfortunate man became overwhelmed in business. He was a man of high honor, of high social position, a South Carolinian by birth. He became overwhelmed by financial embarrassments and he failed, owing a very large sum of money. His word was not kept, his obligation and his bond was not kept, and the result was that Marshall, Burge & Co. lost, but they had no one to complain of except the respectable factor, a citizen of South Carolina. They certainly cannot charge fraud upon me for that which I was not responsible for. The factor agreed to pay the claim, but never did it, though he received the consignment of rice made by myself and sold it. Had the Mercury, in its wrath, seen fit to charge upon the factor, who is a native to the manor born, dishonesty in that he did not keep his solemn word to Marshall, Burge & Co., it perhaps would have had some foundation for the charge. I certainly kept my word in all respects.

The Mercury says the Sheriff got after me. When I closed my accounts of the store I kept, I had, as the net result of my operations, $10,000 in property, which consisted of cash, corn, bacon and goods. I embarked in a plantation with my all. After I had been planting three months, carrying on the most extensive planting operations in Barnwell District, by the unfortunate position in which the factor had placed me, not only in the account with Marshall, Burge & Co., but with others, I was unable to make immediate settlement of all the claims against me. None questioned my desire to settle; but the merciless creditor said, Leslie, I don't care how hard you struggle to get through, I don't care if you work yourself to death to try to make a crop to repay your investments, I must have forthwith and immediately my pound of flesh. He knew I could not pay it, but knowing there was such a law in South Carolina as imprisonment for debt, he proceeded to bring a writ against me for the debt. I did not desire to publish to the world the exact position I was placed in. I did not desire to parade in print what I regarded as a fact, that there was no sort of justice for a Northern man in South

Carolina ; I would have avoided such an allegation. It had been charged by the papers of the South that any story that went to the North and published by the Northern press of ill treatment of Northern men here, was unfounded and untrue. I know in my own heart how they treated me ; what protection I received from the civil law of South Carolina.

In the month of March, when I was upon my plantation, had robbed no one, stolen from no one, had committed no offence against the country, when the Courts were open and prepared to try any offence, if I had committed any ; in the month of March, when the wind had dried every thing upon the plantation, when everything is like lightwood, a South Carolinian put fire in my broom-sedge, and on four separate occasions I had in the day time the whole of my fences on fire, defying all the power I had on the plantation to put it out.

It is unnecessary for me to describe the intensity or rapidity of its burning. All that is simply necessary for me to do is to say that the demon of fire was applied to the property of a man who had not interfered with them, but was trying to make a crop to replace the money he invested, and to pay his creditors and his laborers.

Such I claim was notoriously done because I allowed the sunlight of heaven to shine upon me the other side of Mason and Dixon's line.

While the fire was on one side, while it was consuming my property, four fiends and ruffians, armed with revolvers, each of them citizens of South Carolina, rode upon my plantation in the open day time, and wanted to know where Leslie was. The proof is recorded in the Provost Marshal's office. They said they had come there to kill him, and that they meant to do it. They said that there was a clan of them, like unto Morgan's brigade, and it was a lucky thing for Leslie that he was not there. They swore that no Yankee should make a crop in Barnwell District ; that if I did not leave there, they would hang and lay around me until they had killed me.

Let us see what these same men did. They went to the barn, took therefrom a saddle horse, that I used for my own riding, and one for which, I can tell the Mercury, I paid three hundred dollars, and they carried him away. My trunk was robbed of even the last shirt I had. I do not suppose they knew much about mathematics, but in my trunk they discovered my mathematical instruments and they took them. They even took my very socks. They took the last thing I had, every thing they could lay their hands on, and then went towards Aiken, passed it, and then went towards Edgefield.

If the same men had found me, they would have murdered me. They took even all the colored people possessed, some of whom happened to

67

be riding in a wagon from Edgefield to Aiken. They took them, tied them to a tree, cut off their ears and did other things which modesty forbids me to mention. That was their character. That was the way I was treated. I would rather these things had slept.

In this condition of things, with the fire on one side, the ruffians on the other, and the Sheriff in the rear with a writ against me, and with a certainty that that would have sent me to jail, I ask you what any sensible man would have done. I simply took to the swamp. I did not want to leave the State, and the truth is I went to the swamp. There I cleared a little place of about half an acre of ground. I turned my plantation over to the foreman. I afterward returned in the night time, made an appointment with a certain man, and sold out my plantation, taking a note of $1900, and that was the last I had left of my $10,000 dollars. That note is the one to which I had occasion to allude in appealing in behalf of the white people of the State for homesteads. That note was three times greater in amount than any debt I owed in the State of South Carolina. That note was made payable at the First National Bank in Charleston, on the 18th of October last. That note was protested for non-payment, and from that day to this I have not received one dollar, or one cent of that money.

He says I had the Sheriff after me, and he implies that I had committed some great offence, which was simply that I owed somebody a little money. He says the detectives of Brooklyn were put upon my track. If the detectives in Brooklyn do not know me, or where I am, it is because I committed no crime. I have only further to make an emphatic denial of the rest of the article. If any one was ever after me they knew where I was. The truth is, they did not mean to charge me with any offence, but the creditor has taken this cowardly mode of attacking me on account of that debt.

The Government of the United States was perfectly advised of my situation, and knowing well my misfortune, the Treasurer of the United States gave me a commission as Inspector of Internal Revenue. A more important office can scarcely be found in any department of the Government. It was my business and my duty to see that the Government was not cheated or defrauded out of money. I say, if the Treasurer of the United States, who knew me when he appointed me, knew my character, and saw fit to give me a commission, it is a complete refutation to these slanders and all the inuendoes of the editor of the Mercury. The balance of the report is not worthy of any special notice. I know who furnished the Mercury with the information. It was one of the same men who had his writ out to put me in jail, because he knew the feeling existing in Barnwell against Yankees, and knew there was not an old citizen there who would dare risk his reputation by going my bail. But, notwiths'anding the attacks upon me, I am willing to forget the past, and work for the interest of the poor men of South Carolina, be they white or colored, against merciless and unrelenting creditors, one of whom has been instrumental in raising this attack upon me.

The PRESIDENT announced the first unfinished business before the Convention to be the consideration and second reading of the report of the Committee on the Executive Part of the Constitution. The report was taken up.

Section first was read, as follows:

Section 1. The supreme executive authority of this State shall be vested in a Chief Magistrate, who shall be styled "The Governor of the State of South Carolina," and whose title shall be "His Excellency."

On motion of Mr. E. W. M. MACKEY, the first section was amended by striking out the words "His Excellency," recommended by the Committee as the title to be given to the Governor. The first section then passed to its third reading.

Section second was read, as follows:

Section 2. The Governor shall be elected by the electors duly qualified to vote for members of the House of Representatives, and shall hold his office for one year, and until his successor shall be chosen and qualified, and shall be re-eligible.

Mr. L. B. JOHNSON moved to amend by striking out the word "one" in third line, and insert the word "two."

Mr. C. M. WILDER moved to substitute the word "one" with the word "four," which was not agreed to.

The amendment of Mr. L. B. JOHNSON was then put and carried, and the Section, so amended, passed to a third reading.

Section third was read, as follows:

Section 3. No person shall be eligible to the office of Governor who does not profess a belief in the existence of the Supreme Being, and unless he hath attained the age of thirty years, and hath been a citizen and resident of this State for the four years next preceding the day of election. And no person shall hold the office of Governor and any other office or commission, civil or military (except in the militia) under this State, or any of them, or any other power, at one and the same time.

Mr. E. W. M. MACKEY moved to amend by striking out the words, "who does not profess a belief in the existence of a Supreme Being."

He did not think it necessary to question a man's religious belief, in order to make him eligible to the office of Governor.

Mr. S. A. SWAILS moved to strike out the word "four" in the fourth line, and insert "two."

Mr. J. K. JILLSON moved to substitute the word "hath" with "has" in the third line.

Mr. N. G. PARKER moved to substitute the words "unless he" with the word "not" in second line.

Mr. B. F. RANDOLPH. I regret very much that a motion has been made to strike out the word "Supreme Being." I cannot conceive what can be the motive of the gentleman in making such a motion. He intimated that by incorporating this into the Constitution it would appear as if we were disposed to be Puritanical, or calling in question some religious belief. That is not the case. I believe we are a Christian people. We all, as a people, believe in the existence of a Supreme Being. Does that gentleman know that any people who do not believe in the existence of a Supreme Being have no organized government?

Mr. B. O. DUNCAN. I would like to ask the gentleman if he knows of any people who do not acknowledge the existence of a Supreme Being?

Mr. B. F. RANDOLPH. I believe missionaries have said there is a people of that character somewhere near the jumping off place. They have said that this people, above all the people on the earth, are sunk in the deepest depths of degradation. A man who does not believe in the existence of a Supreme Being does not feel any obligations, and his oath is not worth the drippings of a straw.

Mr. R. C. DeLARGE. I desire to know who is to decide for that person what that Supreme Being is. For instance, an infidel may believe his idol a Supreme Being.

Mr. B. F. RANDOLPH. I do not know of any infidel who believes in idols. I have never heard of an idol being a Supreme Being. Heathens acknowledge their idols as being representatives of a Supreme Being. I hope the amendment will not prevail. It would seem strange to me if we, as an enlightened people, in the hey-day of the nineteenth century, were to take such a gigantic step backward as to elect a man to be Governor of the State who does not believe in a Supreme Being. We do not say the Governor must be a Methodist, a Presbyterian, an Episcopalian, or a Catholic. We only ask him to believe in a Supreme Being, to whom he is under obligations, and by whom he will be held accountable as a moral being.

Pending these amendments, the hour for the consideration of the

Special Order arrived, which was section third of the report of the Committee on the Legislative Provisions of the Constitution.

Mr. W. J. WHIPPER moved that the Special Order be discharged.

Mr. R. C. DeLARGE. I trust that the delegates will not forget what is due to a portion of their brother delegates, as to attempt to do them an injustice by killing off an important measure with such a motion. It was the boast of the opposition, composed almost entirely of the delegation of which the mover and seconder of that motion are members, on yesterday, that they did not desire, neither did they intend, that the friends of this measure should have an opportunity of advocating its claims.

Mr. W. J. WHIPPER. The gentleman has stated what he knows to be false.

Mr. R. C. DeLARGE. I trust the house will excuse the gentleman for using such a remark; he is noted for them. This question is one of very grave importance. It affects the interests and the rights of over eighteen thousand voters; and I think their representatives upon the floor, the members of the respective delegations of Berkley and Charleston, should have an opportunity of laying before this Convention the claims of their constituents. I trust no one is afraid of having this question argued. We ask no favors in behalf of our constituents, but desire simply to present our claims for what we believe we are entitled.

The great objection urged to this measure yesterday was that it would give Charleston a greater amount of influence than she deserved. It can hardly be necessary to answer that argument. The delegations from Charleston and Berkley have shown the greatest degree of liberality in voting for every measure proposed by any of the other delegations that would advance their interests. I feel that we have a right to demand that they should do the same by us. When the question on the division of Pickens District came up, we voted boldly in its favor. We did it, believing it would be just to the people of that District, and promote their welfare. I trust, then, the motion will be voted down.

Mr. D. H. CHAMBERLAIN. I am much surprised at the source from which the motion to discharge the Special Order has come. It was with reference to the feelings of the delegation from Beaufort that we forebore to press this question to a final vote yesterday, and it was on the motion of a gentleman from Beaufort that it was postponed to allow further consideration of the subject. It is important, however, that we should come to a square vote upon the matter, and that we discuss it in a spirit of comity and kindness.

Mr. W. J. McKINLAY. I hope the motion to discharge the Special

Order will not prevail. It is certainly due to the Committee who reported that the subject should be fully considered, so that its merits may be properly understood.

The question then being on the motion to discharge the Special Order, it was decided in the negative.

Mr. A. C. RICHMOND. I wish to address myself to the judgment of this Convention for a moment. Look at the counties as they stood when this body assembled. Pickens was anxious to be divided. Her claim was considered, granted, and Pickens was divided into two counties. This was for the benefit of the up country. Now, the city of Charleston is the commercial metropolis of the State—the centre of its Railroads and enterprise. If it was deemed important to the interests of the upper portion of the State that one of the districts should be, by division, entitled to two Senators, how much more important is it to this wealthy and largely populated locality, that it likewise shall be entitled to additional representation. For instance, the County of Berkley extends one hundred and fifty miles around the coast. Commencing at the lower Edisto, reaching to the mouth of the Santee River, and embracing ten or twelve parishes. Is there any reason why this district, having more registered voters than any other, should not be divided? None that I can conceive of certainly ; and, therefore, as a matter of good feeling, of reciprocation, of justice to the population, and to the interest involved, I do hope that the delegates from the up country will unite in securing an object so eminently desirable.

Mr. J. S. CRAIG. I am in favor of doing justice to every district in the State. This section has been very cunningly drawn, and I presume it is not understood by the majority of the delegates from the rural districts. While I am willing that Charleston shall have her share of representatives, I desire that other localities may not be entirely ignored. When this subject was under consideration before, I offered an amendment giving representation to Charleston in proportion to her population. But Charleston is not satisfied with this. She seems to think that she is the State of South Carolina, and if this belief is encouraged by allowing her to fix this matter to suit herself, there will not be many districts in the State to be divided hereafter, because she will have a controlling power in the Senate. If we are going into a general division of counties let us do so on an equitable basis. But if you propose to divide Berkley alone, which it may be said is a part of Charleston, we cannot afford to allow the excess of power which she will thereby necessarily possess in the Senate over and above that of any other district in the State.

Mr. B. BYAS. I feel some diffidence in speaking upon this question, because I am from the district in question, Berkley. The gentleman from Colleton is mistaken in the supposition that Charleston will be benefited by the division of Berkley. That district includes some nine parishes, which formerly were in the district of Charleston, and it is entitled by every consideration to a large and proportionate representation. When the question is made with reference to Beaufort, I shall be prepared to fight on the same line, and as a simple matter of justice, vote for its division, and representation by two Senators.

Mr. R. B. ELLIOTT moved to amend the tenth line by striking out "three" and inserting "two."

Also to amend so as to make the section read :

"The County of Berkley, to be composed of the late Parishes of St. Thomas and St. Dennis, St. James' Santee, St. Stephen's, St. John's Berkley, Christ Church and St. James' Goose Creek, St. Andrew's, St. John's Colleton."

In the fourteenth line, after the words "and these," the word "three" be stricken out, and the word "two" be inserted.

Mr. ELLIOTT said. I offer these amendments because I believe the Committee were instructed to give Charleston what she asked for ; but, somehow, like Oliver Twist, they always cry for "more." I deprecate everything that looks like sectional interest. I do not like to see the upper and lower sections of the State arrayed against each other. We are here to legislate for the general welfare of the people of South Carolina, and I believe in dispensing justice to every portion of the State, and not in taking from one portion for the purpose of strengthening another, at the expense of the people.

The interests of Edisto and Charleston are identical, and there is no reason why, if Berkley is divided, we should not be entitled to our share of representation. It is but a short time ago that those who now favor a division of Berkley opposed legislation for the division of any other district, the cry being that this was not the place to make these changes ; but I contend that it is proper and legitimate for us in all cases, where the area or the population justifies the change, to make the division and allow the excess to be represented. It is for this reason that I urged the other day the division of Edgefield into two districts, one of which it can be shown would contain a larger population than the proposed County of Edisto. I, therefore, hope the measure of the Committee will not be adopted, and that my amendment will prevail.

Mr. B. F. RANDOLPH moved as an amendment that all the Parishes be designated as townships.

Mr. W. J. WHIPPER. I hope the amendment will be voted down. I am willing that Charleston shall have two Senators, but am not willing they shall manufacture, as this section proposes, some two more, which will be the case if Berkley, which formerly was a part of Charleston, be divided in the manner suggested. To my mind it is not a real, but pretended division, for the purpose of subserving political ends.

The question was then taken on the amendment of Mr. ELLIOTT, and it was decided in the negative.

Mr. N. G. PARKER moved to amend in the sixteenth line by striking out the words " two thirds of both Houses."

He said : I am in favor of the adoption of this section, if it be amended in the manner I have proposed. I favored the division of Pickens District, and have not for one moment regretted that I did so. I favored the division of the district I have the honor to represent, and there are good reasons why that district should be divided. We are told that petitions will come here from other districts ; and for one, I wish we had time to attend them, and accede to their requests, if they be reasonable. I believe the districts in the State are all too large. Their separation would undoubtedly promote their prosperity. For these reasons, I hope the section will be so amended as that the Legislature may, by a bare majority, divide any district which so desires.

Mr. S. A. SWAILS. By passing this measure we do for Berkley what we would do for Colleton, or Charleston, and what we would like to do for all the up country. It will promote civilization and education in this State to divide it into small counties. It will tend to the establishment of Courts of Record, to the multiplication of law offices, newspapers, and all that is calculated to educate and civilize a country.

Mr. R. SMALLS called for the previous question.

The Chair decided that the call was sustained.

Mr. R. C. DeLARGE appealed from the decision of the Chair.

The appeal was sustained, and the decision of the Chair was reversed.

Mr. C. M. WILDER. I oppose any such springing of the question, as has been brought upon us by the Charleston delegation. They first proposed to divide Charleston, so as to allow this city two Senators. Upon the heel of that action they bring in a proposition to give Berkley two Senators. I do not blame the Charleston delegation, but I do blame the representatives of the up country, if they allow Charleston to have four Senators.

We must recollect that when legislating power into the hands of Charleston, we are legislating rights that do not belong to us, but to those who sent us. It is generally understood that Charleston men cut their teeth before they are done sucking, and they intend, if they can, to monopolize the power of the State. If they obtain it, they will say, now divide your districts if you can ; we control the majority. Many a man in this city has, no doubt, been promised office, and these offices are to be created by the Senate ; and in less than four years, if they have this power, they will have every office filled with Charleston men. They do not propose to give Berkley a county seat, but to locate her jail and court house in Charleston, and by means of their patronage they will be enabled to control a very considerable portion of the up country. I appeal to the up country delegates to say whether they intend to sell their rights for a " mess of potage."

Mr. C. C. BOWEN. I am glad to see Charleston men are held in such high esteem, but amazed, however, to see delegates from other districts rise up and attempt to judge of others, when, perhaps, they would not like to be judged of themselves. The imputation has been cast that this section has been devised solely for the purpose of giving Charleston so much the more power to wield against other districts. No such idea could ever have been entertained, and I ask if members from the up country really do believe their fellow members from the low country to be governed by any such mercenary motives. Is it believed that Charleston delegates would be unjust, and deal unjustly by other districts ? I was in hope that all this feeling of the up country against the low country was swept away forever. This old charge has been mooted in the legislative halls of South Carolina ever since it had any existence. It has been continued up to this day. I find men coming from different districts, whose only question is simply this : Do you suppose the people of the up country are going to be ruled by the people from the low country ? I find members coming from the sea-board asking : Do you suppose the people of the coast are going to be ruled by you of the up country ? I say such should not be, and is not the feeling of the Charleston delegation. The proposition laid down by the gentleman from Richland is not the proposition of the delegates from Charleston. The question was asked the other day and settled. Two Senators were asked for the County of Charleston, and it was granted. This settled the question forever as far as Charleston was concerned ; therefore, as regards immediate locality, Charleston has nothing to do in this measure. It is asked for Berkley simply as a matter of justice. They are entitled to it as a matter of right. In regard to the Court House, I can answer that question. The last delegate upon the floor stated that it was a trick of the Charleston delegation to create offices, and complained that we had concentrated them all right here in Charleston.

68

The proposition in regard to the Court House and Jail is simply this : It was intended to keep the public buildings just as they were, to be used by the District of Berkley so long as they pleased. Provision was made by which the citizens applying might go to work, erect the necessary public buildings, and sit down under their own vines and their own fig trees. But care was taken in the drafting of the bill not to create any unnecessary expense. If they had provided in the bill for the immediate erection of a Court House on one of the islands, the election of a Sheriff and other county officers, etc., and had provided for the same thing over in the Santee country, then there would have been a hue-and cry against the expenses intended to be put upon the State.

In this section as it stood at first, the word county had been used, and it was impossible to remove it. If the word county could have been erased, and the words " election districts" substituted, then the words " election districts" would have appeared instead of county. Edisto and Berkley constitute one election district.

It was proposed to let the people from the islands have the privilege of the public buildings in Charleston so long as they saw fit to bring their business here. The proposition was simply laid down as a matter of convenience to the people to allow them the use of the public buildings in the City of Charleston, until such time as new buildings were erected. The Committee took a small piece of territory, and proposed to call that the County of Charleston. They proposed that the balance of territory outside of that should constitute the County of Berkley. If this division is made as we propose, it will save a number of islands by taking them into Edisto District. That proposition in this section was made from the fact, and I wish it rung in the ears of the delegate from Colleton, that five hundred citizens of Colleton have not had their names placed upon the registry book from the simple fact that they knew not where to go. If the delegate from Colleton (Mr. CRAIG) had been as zealous for them as he has been in opposing this measure, they would have had a vote and had their rights. The proposition is now to put them into a district where they will enjoy their privileges.

Mr. J. S. CRAIG. I wish to know if the gentleman desires to hold me responsible.

Mr. C. C. BOWEN. I hold him or any other man responsible who proposes to leave these people in the same identical position they were at the time this thing happened. This proposition is to give that portion of the people the same rights and privilges others have and nothing more.

As regards the City of Charleston, I am satisfied. Two Senators have been granted to this city. This proposition has nothing to do with it, and I hope it will not be held up in this Convention to the detriment of the people of Berkley District. I contend that the geographical line of Berkley demands a division. I ask it for no other cause. I might have some objection to the phraseology where it alludes to the late parishes. In my opinion the State exists now just as it always existed; you can change the parishes to counties, but the same limits and the same boundaries exist that have always existed. It was observed the other day that Charleston was entitled to ten Senators. All we ask for here is, that Berkley District, having a larger amount of territory, and certainly a larger population, should be divided according to its natural geographical line. Whether this Convention does it or not, the day is not far distant when it will be done.

Mr. L. S. LANGLEY. I rise for the purpose of offering an amendment, but before doing so, desire briefly to state my position.

A few days ago, when we were considering that portion of the Constitution which fixes the basis of representation in the State Senate, it was found it would be necessary to recognize, in the Constitution, the Ordinances passed by this Convention, whereby the District of Pickens was divided; and, in order to do so, this subject was referred to the Committee which reported this section under consideration, for the purpose of engrafting into the Constitution a clause recognizing the division of Pickens District. That Committee was not instructed to say anything about the division of Charleston District; but observe the cunning. The subject referred to them was the division of Pickens; but they go to work and report, in addition, a measure whereby Charleston will be divided into three counties, and thereby be entitled to two more Senators. The last speaker said it was a matter of indifference to Charleston whether Berkley was divided or not; that Charleston already had got what she wished. He says the clause which requires the Court House of Berkley District to be in Charleston simply means until the other counties choose to have their own Court Houses, and incur the expense of building them. And he makes this statement, notwithstanding the plain reading of the section, which says, "The Court House shall be in Charleston." The gentleman from Charleston has said, "consistency is a jewel." I agree with him, and I oppose this measure, because I believe I have been consistent. I opposed the division of Pickens District. I opposed giving Charleston two Senators, because I thought it doing injustice to the other counties of the State. I was opposed to this Convention taking up this matter of the division of Districts, or going into any other legislation than was necessary to frame a Constitution for the civil government of the State. I hope this measure will be defeated. The subject was referred to that Committee simply for the purpose of recognizing the division of a district, which has already been accomplished. It referred simply to what was known as Pickens District. I move to strike out all after the word "Oconee" on the eighth line.

Mr. J. M. RUNION. I move to strike out all between the words "Oconee" and "the city of Charleston."

Mr. R. C. DeLARGE. I move the indefinite postponement of the amendments.

The question being taken, the house refused to postpone.

Mr. J. J. WRIGHT. I am somewhat surprised that this measure should have been brought before this body. It really seems to me inconsistent. I know the member on my right (Mr. BOWEN), in his remarks cited the old, but truthful, saying, "O consistency, thou art a jewel." But, from the inconsistency of his speech, I cannot conceive that he is a jewel. When this matter came up a few days ago, I was willing Charleston should have more than one Senator. That measure I advocated, but desired it shaped differently.

Mr. C. M. WILDER. Is it not now differently shaped from what you expected the other day?

Mr. R. C. DeLARGE. I desire to ask whether the members from Charleston are responsible for the shape in which it has been offered?

Mr. J. J. WRIGHT. I think, from the manner in which they argue, they are responsible for it. It is framed in a very intelligent and acute manner. We have already adopted a section which gives one Senator to each county, and two Senators to the city of Charleston. That, I admit, is but simple justice. Prior to the war, when representation was based upon taxation, as well as upon population, Charleston had ten Senators, and Beaufort had four. Beaufort now will have but one, and if this measure passes, Charleston will have four. That is injustice. I do not charge the gentleman with being unjust for bringing it up. I make no such charges against any delegation. I do not appeal to the up or to the low country, but I appeal to every delegate upon the floor to express himself, by his vote, against this measure. Berkley and the districts around Charleston may be divided, just as Beaufort or any other district may be divided, by the Legislature, whenever the people shall make application to that effect. I simply ask that this matter be left as it is. The division of Pickens District has already been accomplished. I opposed that measure, because I believed we had simply to frame a Constitution for our civil government. But because Pickens is divided is no reason why we should go on with work that can be left to the Legislature. I also desire it to be understood, when it is said that the Beaufort delegation are so much united against this measure, that when I came upon the floor I knew not where my colleagues stood, and I acted independently. I want it understood that upon all these matters we have sufficient vim to act independently. My colleagues have opposed me in more measures than one, and that is sufficient to show that we did not consult each other, but each took such positions as he believed to be consistent with the welfare and general good of the whole people. One gentleman, on the opposite side, says we have representatives in this body opposed to all measures introduced by the Charleston delegation. That charge is entirely gratuitous and out of order. I appeal to their sense of justice, and to the sense of every member of this body, to vote down this measure. Let us make no further division of districts. If the territory around Charleston was not sufficient, that it could not be divided as prescribed in the clause already adopted, then I would be willing to vote Charleston more Senators. But some gentlemen say, when Charleston is divided as heretofore, that there may be Court Houses in the new counties. I know we would presume so; but the manner in which this proposed section reads makes it very questionable. It says these three counties shall constitute one judicial district, the Court House and jail of which shall be in the city of Charleston. What benefit, then, are the people in the surrounding country to derive by the division, with the Court House and jail in Charleston? Why should not each county have their own Court House and jail. The legal business should be transacted at the county seat, so that whenever one man wants to sue another, or anything of the kind, it will not be necessary for him to run to Charleston. Again, the proposition made in this section goes on to provide that the Legislature shall have the power at any time, by a vote of two-thirds, to organize new counties, and I hope all these questions will be left to that body.

Mr. W. E. JOHNSTON. A great deal has been said upon this subject, and I was in hopes that the Charleston delegates, particularly, had expended all their steam yesterday, but it appears I was mistaken.

Now, all we of the upper districts ask is fair play. We do not intend to allow Charleston to overrule all we do, and in this matter we do intend " to cry aloud and spare not." One of the Charleston members has said this provision was only a provision of convenience, meaning, I suppose, for the Charleston and Berkley delegates; but we want to cover all the delegates in the house; we want every district fairly represented; I have an abhorrence to any one-sided transaction. I am compelled to say I believe this section was gotten up by Charleston delegates, and the scheme has been detected by myself and a great many others. I move to strike out in the sixteenth line, between the word "time" and "is," the words "by a vote of two-thirds," so that it shall read "that the Legislature shall have the power at any time to organize new counties," etc.

Mr. T. HURLEY. I believe I stand here independent on this question. It has been asserted several times by members from other portions of the State, that the delegates who reside in the City of Charleston, representing rural districts, are actuated by no higher motive than that of creating offices in order to hold them. I am always opposed to monopolies, and am frank enough to say that in a time like the present I acknowledge its force. But, although I reside in Charleston, representing Berkley, I deny that I am actuated by any other motive than that of benefiting the whole people of this State. I believe with others, that were there offices enough to fill, Charleston would have men enough to fill them. I remember reading in the Scriptures an account of the devil taking our Saviour up on the highest mountains, and showing him all the kingdoms of the world, promising, if he would fall down and worship him, they should be his. I am not one of those who believe that our Charleston friends, if taken up in the mountains by his Satanic majesty, and pointed out all the offices, would say, "get thee behind me, Satan."

It has been said by other delegates that we will have the Court House and jail in Charleston. That I desire to see stricken out. A petition is now in the hands of Brevet Major General E. R. S. Canby, asking that a jail be established in Berkley District; also, a petition from Judge Richardson asking an appropriation for a jail. Whether or not the gentlemen selected to occupy the prominent position of Sheriff of that district is proposed, I do not know. I hope the up country delegates will vote this question down. I know there are young men in the Charleston delegation who can afford to wait a few years. I am prepared to vote, and, in order to close this debate, I move the previous question.

The demand for the previous question was sustained, and a call of the house ordered.

Mr. F. J. MOSES, Jr., moved that the Sergeant-at-Arms be directed to bring in all absentees, which was agreed to.

The amendments of Messrs. ELLIOTT and LANGLEY were lost. The amendments of Messrs. PARKER and RUNION were adopted.

The main question being put, the yeas and nays were ordered, and resulted as follows:

YEAS—Messrs. Allen, Alexander, Arnim, Becker, Burton, Brockenton, Bryce, F. J. Cain, Camp, Coghlan, Chestnut, Clinton, Cooke, Collins, Corley, Craig, Crews, Darrington, Davis, Dill, Dogan, Driffle, Edwards, Elliott, Foster, Gentry, Goss, Harris, James N. Hayne, Charles D. Hayne, H. E Hayne, Henderson, Humbird, Hurley, Jacobs, Jillson, Samuel Johnson, W. B. Johnson, J. W. Johnson, L. B. Johnson, W. E. Johnston, Joiner, Charles Jones, Lang, George Lee, Samuel Lee, Lomax, Mayer, Mauldin, McDaniels, Mead, Middleton, Nance, Nelson, Neagle, Nuckles, Owens, Randolph, Robertson, Rose, Runion, Sanders, Sasportas, Shrewsbury, Smalls, Swails, Thomas, A. Thompson, B. A. Thompson, S. B. Thompson, Viney, Whittemore, Whipper, White, Williams, Charles M. Wilder, Wingo, Wright—79.

NAYS—The President, Messrs. Bell, Bowen, Bonum, Byas, Chamberlain, DeLarge, Duncan, Gray, Holmes, Jervey, Leslie, E. W. M. Mackey, W. J. McKinlay, W. McKinlay, Moses, Jr., Olsen, Parker, Pillsbury, Rainey, Ransier, Richmond, Webb—23.

ABSENT—Messrs. Boozer, R. H. Cain, Cardozo, Dickson, Donaldson, Hunter, Jackson, Jenks, H. Jones, Miller, Milford, Nash, Newell, Perry, Rivers, Rutland, Stubbs, F. E. Wilder, Wooley—19.

So the third section, as amended, was adopted.

The following gentlemen were appointed a Special Committee on Mr. R. G. HOLMES' ordinance for the establishment of a board designated as Commissioners of Public Lands:

Messrs. R. G. HOLMES, of Beaufort; C. M. WILDER, of Richland; J. L. NEAGLE, of York; J. M. RUTLAND, of Fairfield; JOSEPH H. RAINEY, of Georgetown.

On motion, the Convention adjourned.

THIRTY-THIRD DAY.

Saturday, February 22, 1868.

The Convention assembled at half-past ten A. M., and was called to order by the PRESIDENT.

Prayer was offered by the Rev. DAVID HARRIS.

The roll was called, and a quorum answering to their names, the PRESIDENT announced the Convention ready to proceed to business.

Mr. S. G. W. DILL offered the following :

Resolved, That in respect to the memory of the birth-day of the Father of his Country, this Convention adjourn to half-past ten A. M., Monday.

Mr. B. F. RANDOLPH opposed the motion, and called for a division of the house, which was taken, and resulted—yeas 38, nays 29.

Mr. B. F. RANDOLPH and Mr. A. BRYCE desired to have their names recorded in the negative.

The PRESIDENT thereupon declared the Convention adjourned to half-past ten, A. M., Monday.

THIRTY-FOURTH DAY.

Monday, February 24, 1868.

The Convention assembled at half-past 10 A. M., and was called to order by the PRESIDENT.

Prayer was offered by the Rev. W. E. JOHNSTON.

The roll was called, and a quorum answering to their names, the PRESIDENT announced the Convention ready to proceed to business.

The Journals of Friday and Saturday were read and confirmed.

The PRESIDENT called for reports of Standing Committees.

Mr. B. F. RANDOLPH, Chairman, made a report of the Committee Miscellaneous Provisions of the Constitution, and asked leave to submit the following ordinance, introduced by Mr. JOSEPH CREWS, delegate from Laurens. The Committee recommend that the ordinance do pass :

WHEREAS, during the late war between the two sections of the country, resulting disastrously to the Southern people, by which all classes have suffered beyond reparation, therefore

Be it ordained, That equity and justice demand for the minor children of this State, in all cases where the real estate was transferred, either at public sale or otherwise, for Confederate securities or currency, during the existence of the late rebellion, the said transfer, no matter by whom made, shall be absolutely null and void, wherever based upon such sureties, and the original owners or guardians may enter upon, and take possession of, such real estate in behalf of such minor children, unless the same is paid in the currency of the United States.

Mr. W. E. JOHNSTON moved that it be printed, and made the Special Order for Saturday, at one o'clock.

Mr. T. K. SASPORTAS moved that it be indefinitely postponed, which was not agreed to.

Mr. G. LEE moved that the ordinance be made the Special Order for two weeks from Saturday next, which was lost.

Mr. A. C. RICHMOND presented a petition for the arrest of the sentence of death in the case of Ben. Hagen, colored, convicted of arson at the recent sittings of the Court of General Sessions, and sentenced to be executed in April next. The petition sets forth that the prisoner is of unsound mind, and was induced by others to participate in the act, and afterwards turned State's evidence, but was convicted as principal. The petition concludes with a resolution that General Canby be requested to arrest the execution of the sentence passed upon said prisoner, and that the President of the Convention be requested to transmit this resolution to the General commanding the District. Referred to the Committee on Petitions, with instructions to report on Wednesday.

Mr. C. P. LESLIE presented the petition of sundry citizens of Barnwell District, in relation to opening to navigation a creek in their vicinity running to the Savannah river. Referred to the Committee on Petitions.

Mr. B. F. RANDOLPH presented the petition of Thomas Owens, praying the Convention to recommend the removal of his disabilities, the petitioner having been convicted of felony, and was, therefore, under the Reconstruction Act, disfranchised. The petitioner claims to have been a loyalist during the war.

Mr. J. J. WRIGHT. Do we understand that this petitioner is disfranchised on account of felony. If such is the case, I hope the consideration of the petition will be indefinitely postponed. It is not the province of this body to ask relief from punishment for a person convicted of felony or criminal offences.

Mr. B. F. RANDOLPH. I am not personally acquainted with Mr.

69

Owens, but he is represented by other delegates here as a worthy man, whom the Convention can safely recommend to have his disabilities removed. The petition is endorsed by gentlemen who can be relied on. I hope therefore, out of respect, the petition will be referred to the Committee on Petitions. I think we should not treat any matter, much less a petition, with contempt, by dashing it upon the table without any consideration. I move that the petition be referred to the Committee on Petitions.

Mr. T. J. ROBERTSON. Without knowing anything about the petitioner I hope the petition will not be laid upon the table. The Legislature of 1865, composed in great part, if not in toto, of the disloyal men of South Carolina, enacted laws which made the most trivial offence a felony, and the intent of those laws was to deprive every colored man of their right of citizenship. If a colored man struck a white man, all he had to do was to go before an officer of the law, and declare that the colored man struck him with intent to kill, and that offence, according to the law of 1865, constituted a felony. I hope this matter will receive its due consideration.

Mr. R. C. DeLARGE. My motion to lay the petition upon the table was offered because I regarded it as an unusual movement for a delegate to rise and present a petition for the removal of a person's disabilities, when the person applying had been convicted of felony, and no explanation made by the delegate presenting the petition. As reasons have been given, however, I withdraw my motion, and hope the matter will be referred to the Committee on Petitions.

Mr. Y. J. P. OWENS. I have the honor to represent Laurens District, and am acquainted with the petitioner. He accidentally killed his brother, was tried, convicted and imprisoned, and consequently disfranchised. He has worked faithfully for reconstruction, was loyal at the outset and during the war.

The objections being withdrawn, the matter was referred to the Committee on Petitions.

Mr. E. W. M. MACKEY offered the following resolution, which was adopted:

Resolved, That a Special Committee of nine be appointed to draft an ordinance prescribing the mode in which the Constitution shall be submitted to the people for ratification, and providing for the election of State officers.

Mr. N. G. PARKER, Chairman of the Committee on Finance, presented the following substitute for the nineteenth section of the report of that Committee, which was read and ordered to be printed:

SECTION 19. Suitable laws shall be passed by the Legislature for the safe keeping, transfer and disbursement of the State, county and school funds; and all officers and other persons charged with the same, shall keep an accurate entry of each sum received, and of each payment and transfer, and shall give such security for the faithful discharge of such duties as the Legislature may provide. And it shall be the duty of the Legislature to pass laws making the embezzlement of such funds a felony, punishable by a fine and imprisonment. proportioned to the amount of deficiency or embezzlement, and the party convicted of such felony shall be disqualified forever from holding any office of honor or emolument in this State : *Provided, however*, that the Legislature, by a two-thirds vote, may remove the disability upon payment in full of the principal and interest of the sum embezzled.

Mr. R. C. DeLARGE offered the following :

Resolved, That so much of the rule of this house as allows only fifteen minutes to each speaker in the discussion of any subject, be amended so as to allow thirty minutes.

The PRESIDENT decided the resolution out of order, as that question had already been debated. A resolution on the subject was passed, a motion to reconsider afterwards made, and a motion to lay the motion to reconsider on the table carried. It could not, therefore, be taken up again during this session.

Mr. R. C. DeLARGE moved to suspend the rules of the Convention. What he wished was to amend by allowing thirty minutes for any member to speak upon any subject. The Judiciary Bill was about to come before them for their consideration, and it was impossible for any member to speak as he wished upon the questions that would arise on this subject in fifteen minutes.

The question being taken, the Convention refused to suspend the rules.

Mr. H. E. HAYNE offered a resolution changing the hours of the sittings of the Convention, so as to have a day and evening session. Lost.

On motion of Mr. C. D. HAYNE, the Convention proceeded to take up the unfinished business, which was the consideration of the third section of the report of the Committee on the Executive Part of the Constitution.

Mr. A. J. RANSIER moved the following amendment : After the word " Governor," to insert " unless he has attained the age of thirty years, is a citizen of the United States, and has been a resident of this State two years next preceding the day of election. And no person shall hold the office of Governor, or any other office or commission (except in the militia) in this State, under the United States, or either of them, or under any other power, at one and the same time."

Mr. R. C. DeLARGE moved to amend by striking out "thirty" and inserting "twenty-five," as the age at which a person may be eligible to the office of Governor.

Mr. GEORGE LEE moved to strike out the word "four," and insert the word "two."

Mr. R. G. HOLMES moved to amend by making eligible to the office of Governor, any person who is a citizen "from the time of the adoption of this Constitution."

Mr. B. BYAS moved to amend by striking out "twenty-five" and inserting "twenty-one."

Mr. R. B. ELLIOTT moved to indefinitely postpone the amendment, which was agreed to.

Mr. D. H. CHAMBERLAIN moved to amend by substituting the following :

"No person shall be eligible to the office of Governor who is not a qualified elector of the State, and who, at the time of the election, has not attained the age of thirty years, and a resident of the State for two years next preceding the day of election.

Mr. J. L. NEAGLE moved the indefinite postponement of all the amendments.

Mr. R. C. DeLARGE. This is a species of dumb eloquence which I hope the Convention will not sustain. I want to have a fair discussion of all amendments offered, and also wish the section framed in such a manner as to give the people the widest range in their selection of candidates for Governor. If we adopt the section as it stands, we should find ourselves reduced to a choice between two or three men for the most important position in the State, unless we take up men opposed to reconstruction.

Mr. J. L. NEAGLE. I am surprised at the member getting up and making a political harangue. There is no one here but feels satisfied there are enough loyal men in South Carolina competent to fill all the offices in the State. I object to the reduction of the required term of four years' residence to two years to make a person eligible to the office of Governor. To reduce it below that, we might as well invite any man from any portion of the United States to come here and become Governor of South Carolina.

Mr. C. P. LESLIE. Are you talking for an expected nominee, or discussing the merits of certain men for Governor at this time. Don't you know if the four years provision is adopted you defeat the chances of a well-known gentleman, who has been proposed as a candidate, by his friends upon this floor?

Mr. E. W. M. MACKEY. I hope the motion to indefinitely postpone will be voted down. I cannot see any impropriety in arguing all these amendments. Indeed, the importance of some demands all the light that can be thrown upon the subject.

Mr. A. J. RANSIER. There seems to be a mania in this Convention to indefinitely postpone everything that may not be agreeable to some of the members. I submit to the good sense of the house that amendments so important as these should be voted upon separately, and that a motion sweeping them away is supremely ridiculous. Should it be done, I certainly will be ashamed of this portion of the Constitution. It ought, at least, to be made euphonious.

This amendment, referring to four years, does not suit us, under the circumstances of the case. The Constitutions of Iowa, Massachusetts, Texas and other States provide various terms of residence. I am not disposed to ignore distinguished residents in this State. There are men here of great ability, competent to fill any office in the gift of the people. I do not know that a man is necessarily unfortunate who has been born outside of the limits of South Carolina; but I do think it important that the amendment offered by me, requiring two years' residence in the State, should be adopted.

Mr. WM. J. McKINLAY. I do not agree with my friend who has just taken his seat, that the two years residence in the State is a just and proper limitation. Four years, under the circumstances, is a necessary term, because even an intelligent and observing man cannot acquire the knowledge of the people and institutions in so short a period. I hope, therefore, the amendment will be voted down.

Mr. B. F. RANDOLPH. Tactics are very useful things in parliamentary practice, as well as on the field. If you cannot bring an enemy squarely up in line of battle, you must take to the bushes and flank him. I think I understand the object of one of these amendments. There happen to be, in the section, two words which appear to trouble several of the members. They are the words "Supreme Being." If they can get these words out of the section, their object will be accomplished.

Mr. R. C. DeLARGE. Would it require a four years' residence in South Carolina before a man could be known as a believer in the Supreme Being?

Mr. B. F. RANDOLPH. I have no answer for the gentleman. But I am in favor of the indefinite postponement of this amendment, and shall, therefore, vote in favor of that proposition, so that the several amendments may be separately renewed and discussed.

Mr. J. J. WRIGHT. I wish to offer an amendment to the section, so that it will read, "He shall be a citizen or resident for four years from the adoption of this Constitution." I hope none of the amendments will be postponed, but that they will be acted upon in a manner consistent with the general welfare of the people.

Mr. N. G. PARKER offered the following amendment: To insert after the period in the third line the words, "who shall have been a resident of the United States five years."

Mr. C. C. BOWEN. In my judgment, this is one of the questions on which the Convention should not tie their hands, and until members commenced discussing the qualifications of the Governor, I was satisfied to allow the section to remain as reported. Since, however, it has been brought before this body, it is important that the question should be fully discussed, and I am, therefore, opposed to an indefinite postponement.

The question being on the motion to postpone indefinitely all the amendments, Mr. E. W. M. MACKEY called for the yeas and nays, and the call was sustained.

Mr. F. J. MOSES, Jr. I would like to ask if it is in order for remarks to be made on the question at issue any time before the first name was called.

The CHAIR decided that it was in order.

Mr. W. J. WHIPPER. I am somewhat surprised at the disposition manifested upon the part of members to tie their own hands. You have already passed a rule prohibiting members from speaking more than fifteen minutes, and now, when amendments of great importance are offered, to attempt to postpone them indefinitely is a very novel course of procedure, to say the least. If it is a fact that this movement is for the purpose of electing certain men to office, I am opposed to it.

Mr. C. M. WILDER. Is the gentleman speaking to the question? The house decided to call the yeas and nays.

Mr. W. J. WHIPPER. It has been urged in favor of postponement, that there are plenty of men who are able to fill the various offices in the State. I would like to inquire whether these men are afraid to be brought into competition; whether they are afraid to show it to the world. If such is the fact, it does not speak well for that ability of which they boast. If they have such men, they certainly should not be afraid of having them brought into competition with any man. If we have these men here, they certainly have nothing to fear. I hope these amendments will be acted upon deliberately, and not disposed of in a summary manner. I hope we will not tie our own hands any further. I have forborne the privilege of speaking upon questions, for the very reason that it has not been possible to make a speech in reference to subjects requiring much reflection. If it is proposed to tie our hands much further by indefinite postponements, is it not better to adopt the various reports as they come from the Committees? If we are denied the freedom of speech upon the floor, why question the report of the Committee at all?

Mr. F. J. MOSES, Jr. I desire to say, for myself, that while occupying the position of Chairman of the Committee who reported this article of the Constitution, and apart from any importance which these amendments may have, I could not be guilty of such an act of discourtesy towards any gentleman on this floor, who introduced an amendment to the report, as refuse him an opportunity of discussing it. I do not believe there is a delegate on this floor who would be so recreant to his high and solemn duty to his constituents and the State as to attempt to introduce a section in our Constitution looking forward only to the advancement of men, and not for the future prosperity of the State. I would not cast reflections upon any gentleman on this floor. I have nominated no one for Governor, nor do I believe any one has. I desire the Convention to bear in mind this fact: that in deciding whether this section shall stand as the Committee have reported it, and as to the propriety of leaving it to stand in that form, I am not deciding because of any argument I have heard from those gentlemen who reported it. It strikes me, if it should be inserted in this section, "that no person shall be eligible to the office of Governor, unless a citizen and resident of this State for four years next preceding the day of election," this might be tying up our hands in a way that would be a matter of regret hereafter. It is to be hoped that no member is working to advance the interest of any man for Governor. We are here, not working for men, but for measures.

Mr. B. BYAS. I trust the motion to postpone indefinitely will not prevail. I am the advocate of no particular man for the office of Governor. When a person has resided a sufficient time in the State to entitle him to a vote, I think he should be eligible to any office within the gift of the people of South Carolina.

Mr. C. P. LESLIE. There has been times when I have spoken that I would have been perfectly contented to have recorded my vote in silence upon some questions. But I never will give my vote on a question likely to affect the people, unless I give some explanation of why I make it. I do not believe, as an axiom in politics, that it is worth while ever to tell a lie, if a statesman or a man wants to deal justly with the people. I stand upon the truth, and the truth will triumph.

I knew when these four years were inserted in that section, and I know why it was inserted. I do not particularly care myself if you make it four hundred and forty-four thousand years. But the times in which we are living import some trouble. There is no member upon the floor of the house that does not know that the times are portentous of troubles and storms. A candidate may be available to-day for Governor, who would not answer to-morrow. I may want my quiet friend from Richland, Colonel THOMAS J. ROBERTSON to-day, and for certain other reasons may want some other gentleman of an entirely different and opposite profession to-morrow. Again, questions of constitutional law may arise, and we may have to call upon our legal friend from Fairfield (Mr. RUTLAND). I want the greatest possible latitude, and, therefore, hope the four years' proposition will be stricken out, and two years inserted. I think the times demand it.

Mr. B. F. WHITTEMORE. I trust the motion to postpone will not prevail, but that the amendments will be taken up in their order. In the sections in the Legislative Department we have declared how long a person must be in the State to be eligible to a seat in the General Assembly, and it appears to me, with the exception of correcting a few grammatical errors, the section might be allowed to remain as it is. I hope the motion to postpone will be voted down.

The question was then taken on the motion to postpone indefinitely all the amendments, and the ayes and nays being called, resulted as follows:

AYES—Messrs. Alexander, Burton, Bryce, Camp, Coghlan, Chestnut, Clinton, Davis, Dill, Driffle, Edwards, Henderson, Hurley, Jacobs, Jenks, S. Johnson, Dr. L. B. Johnson, Joiner, C. Jones, Lang, G. Lee, Lomax, W. J. McKinlay, McDaniels, Mead, Milford, Nelson, Neagle, Owens, Randolph, Robertson, Rose, Rutland, Sanders, L. B. Thompson, White, Williamson, Wilder—38.

NAYS—Messrs. President, Allen, Arnim, Bell, Bowen, Bonum, Brockenton, Byas, F. J. Cain, Chamberlain, Cooke, Collins, Corley, Craig, Crews, Darrington, DeLarge, Dogan, Duncan, Elliott, Foster, Gentry, Goss, Gray, Harris, J. H. Hayne, C. D. Hayne, H. E. Hayne, Holmes, Humbird, Jervey, Jillson, W. B. Johnson, J. W. Johnson, W. E. Johnston, Langley, S. Lee, Leslie, E. W. M. Mackey, Mayer, Mauldin, W. McKinlay, Middleton, Moses, Nance, Nuckles, Parker, Pillsbury, Rainey, Ransier, Richmond, Runion, Sasportas, Shrewsbury, Smalls,

Swails, Thomas, B. A. Thompson, Viney, Webb, Whittemore, Whipper, Wingo, Wooley, Wright—65.

ABSENT—Messrs. Becker, Boozer, R. H. Cain, Cardozo, Dickson, Donaldson, Hunter, Jackson, H. Jones, Miller, Nash, Newell, Olsen, Perry, Rivers, Stubbs, A. Thompson, F. E. Wilder—18.

So the Convention refused to postpone.

The question was then taken on the motion to strike out the words, "who does not believe in the existence of a Supreme Being."

Mr. L. S. LANGLEY. I do not think these words comprehensive enough. In the report of the Committee on Miscellaneous Matters, section tenth, we find this provision: "No person who denies the existence of a God shall be eligible to office," &c. I am in favor of not only the Governor being required to acknowledge the existence of a Supreme Being, but I am opposed to any man holding an office who does not recognize the Supreme Being. As I believe the provision of section tenth in the report of the Committee on Miscellaneous Matters to be more comprehensive, I hope these words, "Supreme Being," will be stricken out, and that provision substituted.

Mr. B. F. WHITTEMORE. I trust these words, "Supreme Being," will be allowed to remain. It appears to me we should have some regard to the judgment and reflection of the members of the Committee that drafted this section. If we by a vote erase those words, we commit ourselves to the acknowledgment that we do not consider it necessary that a person who shall be elected by our suffrages as Governor, shall be compelled to believe in the existence of a Supreme Being. I scarcely think there is a member of this body, who would be willing to allow his vote to be recorded for any such proposition, and I trust, without any extensive debate upon the subject, the amendment will be voted down.

Mr. E. W. M. MACKEY. I am sorry to disagree with the gentleman from Darlington on this subject, but I cannot see the necessity of these words in this section. It has been said that this motion to strike out these words was taking a backward step in civilization. On the contrary, I regard it as going forward. I am opposed to religious intolerance in any shape or form. But how are we to tell whether the person elected to the office of Governor entertains the belief here asked of him. He may profess to believe in order to be able to hold the office. Shall we have a court of ministers instituted to question the gentlemen elected as to their religious belief? Are they to ask him whether he believes in this or that doctrine? They would have just as good a right to question his belief in the Trinity, or whether he was an Episcopalian, Methodist, or Catholic. It would be but one step further to require him to answer

70

to all these questions. We have just as much right, I say, to question a man's belief in the Trinity, as to question his belief in the existence of a Supreme Being It has been urged that we could not believe any person on oath, unless he believes in the existence of a Supreme Being ; why not also add in the existence of Jesus Christ. It appears to me that is as important as the Supreme Being, and would be so regarded by every trinitarian. These words "Supreme Being" convey no idea of the Deity. Different nations have different ideas of a Supreme Being. The ancient Romans characterized the Deity as their idea of the Supreme Being, and the moderns have their various ideas.

I notice that it is mostly ministers who rise and ask questions with reference to the Supreme Being. It seems to me they are alone advocating it. The gentleman from Darlington says he desires to put his vote on record against the proposition to strike out the words "Supreme Being," and would be ashamed to do otherwise. I am not ashamed to put my vote on the journals against retaining those words in this section.

Mr. N. G. PARKER moved to strike out the words "does not profess " in the first line, and insert "denies," and to strike out "had" in the second line, and insert "has," which was agreed to.

Mr. H. L. SHREWSBURY moved to strike out the word "thirty" and insert the words "thirty-five," which was not agreed to.

The question was then taken on striking out the words "who denies the existence of a Supreme Being," which was decided in the negative.

Mr. D. H. CHAMBERLAIN moved to strike out the word "thirty" and insert "twenty-five."

Mr. R. C. DeLARGE. I sincerely trust that will be voted down. I have heard that to be old is a misfortune ; to be young and intelligent is no crime. A man may well be questioned as to his ability, still we may find men who have ability, and who have not obtained the age of thirty-five years.

Mr. H. L. SHREWSBURY. Do you not think experience is a very useful quality.

Mr. R. C. DeLARGE. Experience has taught us that this State has been injured by the former doctrine of the aristocracy, that a man did not know anything unless he had attained a certain number of years. That policy carried the State into rebellion. It was considered a crime to elevate a man who had not attained the requisite age, or who had not been tutored in the then exclusive social circles, and the doctrine of the country. But I rose for the purpose of offering an amendment to that of my friend from Chesterfield (Mr. SHREWSBURY). I move to insert "eighty-five years of age."

Mr. B. BYAS. I hope the section will pass as it stands. I think thirty years a happy medium between the extremes proposed in the amendments offered, and that the Committee have prepared the section with good sense and judgment.

The question was then taken on the motion to strike out thirty and insert thirty-five, which was decided in the negative.

The question being taken on striking out thirty and inserting twenty-five, it was decided in the negative.

The next question was taken upon the amendment offered by the delegate from Williamsburg (Mr. SWAILS), to strike out "four" and insert "two," so as to read "unless he hath been a citizen and resident of this State for two years next preceding the day of election."

Mr. J. M. RUTLAND. I regret that this particular portion of the section has been attempted to be argued in the Convention upon personal grounds, or in reference to any candidates for the office of Governor. Such considerations ought not for one moment to influence our action upon this section of the Constitution. The Committee, when they passed upon it in the Committee room, I feel assured had no such question before them, and it is only within the last day or two I have heard that this part of the section would be contested. The subject having been divested of all personal considerations. in the Committee room, should be considered in the same spirit in this body. The Committee determined that the number of years requisite for a man to be a resident of the State, in order to qualify him for the office of Governor, should be four. That was the result of their deliberate judgment. If I had been called upon to give an opinion, I should have said five years, because it is analogous to the Constitution of the United States, which requires, before a man is admitted as a member of the House of Representatives in Congress, that he shall have been a citizen of the United States for seven years; and shall be admitted as a Senator of the United States after he has been a citizen of the State nine years. A man who is to be Governor of our State should, at least, have resided amongst us a sufficient length of time to become familiar with all the different interests of the State over which he is to preside. That is one of the first and highest qualifications to know the wants of the people in the State. Can any man become familiar with those interests in the short period proposed by the amendment. He certainly could not, unless he makes it the special business of his whole term to travel from the mountains to the sea-board, and enquire everywhere as to the character and wants of the people of the State.

I say then we should divest ourselves of all personal considerations or feelings on this question, and take a calm and intelligent view of it. Four years will give a man sufficient time to familiarize himself with the wants of the people of the State. Two years I regard as entirely too short, and I really think four years not sufficient, unless the person elected makes it his business to travel from one end of the State to the other during his term of office. I hope the section will be left as it stands.

Mr. D. H. CHAMBERLAIN. I quite agree with my friend from Fairfield (Mr. RUTLAND), in hoping that in the consideration of this question we shall divest ourselves of all personal feeling and friendship for the candidates of the office of Governor. I would be sorry to believe that there were certain classes of persons in this Convention influenced by such motives. If any gentleman thinks I am influenced by any interested motives, or by my desire to see any person made a candidate for Governor of this State, I shall know how to treat such a charge. I hope we will consider this question upon its merits. I consider the State of South Carolina to-day very much in the condition of a territory about to transfer itself into a State of the Union. Without raising the legal question whether we are a territory or State, I say our practical condition is very analogous to that of a territory, the delegates of which have met in Convention to form a Constitution, and make itself a member of the Union. I believe no one will dispute that in all such instances it is the rule and custom to make citizens of the United States, resident in that territory at the time, citizens of the future State without imposing any restrictions, or taking from them any privileges either as electors or as officers of the State. Upon that same ground I think every restriction should be removed, and that an exception should be made. If we fix upon two years as the length of time the Governor holds his office, then I propose that the first elections shall except from the operations of the rule, requiring four years residence, anybody who is here to-day a citizen of the United States, residing on tho soil of South Carolina. I propose that nobody now here, who are citizens of the United States, shall be deprived of the opportunity of being a candidate for Governor, or any other office within the gift of the people. We do not know what the interests of this State may require of the person we shall select as our candidate for Governor. I desire as wide a range as possible in our selection and nomination of that candidate.

My friend (Mr. RUTLAND) thinks nobody understands the affairs of South Carolina unless he has resided here a long time. I beg leave to say, though I desire to raise no question between old and new citizens of South Carolina, that there are reasons why men who have not been identified with South Carolina in the past, who have formed their opinions in a different atmosphere, should not only have an equal chance, but be preferred for the most important offices in the gift of the people of this State. I say distinctly there may be cases where a man who does not know but little of the State, but who has none of the prejudices against color or race, which is almost universal with the natives of the soil, but to which there are honorable exceptions, as I am bound to say, when I speak in presence of you, sir, (the President) ; yet I say it is an advantage in a candidate that he should not have been born and bred on the soil of South Carolina. I say, my friends, that I consider that the point which touches their (the old South Carolinians) interest and pride in the most vital point, is that there is a man with a South Carolina education, who professed during the war to stand with the loyal men of the country, and who is to-day the hope and expectation of every republican in this country. I am sorry that question has been raised, but since it has been raised, let us look at the situation. I say that, at least, it is no objection to a man that he was not born in South Carolina. It is rather to his advantage that he was born where he could not have imbibed the prejudices of South Carolina, and which are in danger of again controlling the public mind of South Carolina. Is it not better for us, in the first place, to select for the position of Governor of South Carolina a man who is familiar with the ways of freedom by birth and education—who would not exclude anybody from any privileges or right ; and, second, that, as a practical question, not to narrow our choice and exclude those familiar with the ways of freedom from having a share in the offices of the State. Upon these two grounds, I hope this section will be so decided that any man to-day a citizen of the United States, living in South Carolina, shall be eligible to any office within the gift of the people of South Carolina.

Mr. A. J. RANSIER. In my proposition to amend this third section, one of the features proposed to be stricken out was the word " four." This does not prevent us from taking up any South Carolinian who has been here all his life, while it allows the selection of another person equally competent, who may have settled in the State since the war. It is not merely a question of republicanism, of mere party, but it is a question which involves in the choice of honest and true men, the welfare of the State.

Mr. J. L. NEAGLE. Did you get that idea from the copperheads of this State or from Northern copperheads?

Mr. A. J. RANSIER. I got the idea from the principles and practice of those by whom I am surrounded. This is not a question of Southern

men or Northern men.   We want an able man; and if we can find such
a one who has resided here even for two years, we wish to put him in
the position.   If a person who has resided in South Carolina two years
does not know enough about the habits of the people to fill the office of
Governor, he is a poor creature, indeed.   It is important that the people
of the State shall be untrammeled in this matter, and I say let them
have an opportunity to secure a gentleman of ability, even though he
may have been in the State but two years.   I hope the motion to strike
out the word "four" will prevail.

Mr. T. K. SASPORTAS.   Hitherto I have refrained from speaking
upon questions before the house, chiefly from considerations of economy;
but on the present occasion I am compelled to speak without reserve.
I am an advocate for no individual—neither for a man from South Carolina, nor a man from Massachusetts—not for a general, or a colonel, or
any other person.   I can, therefore, speak freely upon the merits of the
question.

One gentleman who preceded me, stated that if a person was so unfortunate, as he termed it, to be born out of South Carolina, he ought to
be debarred from the privileges of this office.   Such is not my belief—
I cannot go so far; but I do contend that a candidate for the office of
Governor shall have remained in the State a sufficient time to become
acquainted with the wants of the people.   A question has been raised
with reference to Northerners and Southerners.   The gentleman who
has preceded me, said that only those persons who were born and educated in a land of freedom should be candidates.   Now, as regards this
curious preference, allow me to say there are men raised in the land of
freedom who are just as much opposed to the principles which actuate
us as many of the white citizens of this State.   And when it comes to
the question whether we shall trust a Northerner or a Southerner, I say
if he accepts the situation in good faith, I will always trust the Southerner in preference.   I have resided in both sections.

Mr. HAYNE.   I would like to ask the gentleman how long he has
been a resident of South Carolina?

Mr. T. K. SASPORTAS.   Six years and a half, sir; but I claim the
honor of having been born in South Carolina.   It is my State, and I
think it proper and important that a candidate for the office of Governor
shall be required to reside here at least four years, in order to learn the
habits and characteristics of the people.

Mr. R. C. DeLARGE.   My friend from Fairfield says that in considering the subject we should ignore all individual questions.   I was glad
to hear such words drop from his lips, for it grieved me to see even one

member upon this floor who could so far forget the interests of his State and constituents as to allow mere personal preferences govern his action. My friend from Fairfield says the Committee reported four years as the limit required for the Governor's residence, because they believed it best. No doubt of it, and we yield the Committee credit for its wisdom ; but I do not think this house will accept the idea of nine gentlemen in preference to one hundred and thirteen, who, I believe, are in favor of two years. My genial friend has also referred to the importance of having four years named in the Constitution, on the ground that it is necessary to be a citizen of the United States for seven years before one can be a candidate for some of the offices of the United States. I admit the force of the reasoning, but the provision in the Constitution of the United States, to which my friend refers, was made to guard against the foreigners from being elected before they had resided here long enough to become naturalized. Now, gentlemen, I am opposed to this section, because it proposes to operate ungenerously and harshly towards those who have had the misfortune to be born out of the State. It is showing a degree of ingratitude I did not expect to see, to a class of men to whom we are indebted for the privileges we are enjoying as members of this Convention, and to whom we must still continue to look for support. To be a good Governor, there is no doubt that a man should thoroughly understand the people of the State, but he need not possess more than ordinary intelligence to require the desired knowledge in a residence of two years. There is a class of men able and brilliant in South Carolina, who have not learned the people of the State, yet they plunged that State in rebellion, and it would take until the judgment day for them to learn the people that we represent. They are a class whom his Satanic majesty has learned, and they cannot be learned by any other influence. But any man in this State who has been here since the war, especially if a Northern man—and Northern men are noted for learning people—is, in my judgment, sufficiently familiar with the condition of affairs to qualify him, in that respect at least, for the office of Governor. There are some who have travelled the State very extensively, especially those who belonged to Sherman's army, and they possess a degree of familiarity with the people superior to any others. I wish it to be understood that I have no preference for any man on account of his place of birth ; ability, integrity, and a proper discharge of duty, should be the only points in the character of a candidate in which we should raise any question. I trust, therefore, that the time will be limited to two years instead of four, and that every man will be allowed a free fight and a fair race. I am desirous of seeing a liberal policy carried out by this

Convention. I stand here as ready to forgive those who have imbued their hands in blood as I am willing to welcome the loyal men of the country. I desire to be generous to those who have injured us, and to reward those who have stood by the truth. My friend from Berkley said it was an advantage to be born off the soil; I differ with him, for I am proud of the land of my birth; there is no better place on earth to be born in, provided the man is tutored aright after his birth.

I repeat, again, that there are competent and able gentlemen in the State who have resided here since the war, and if it be determined that one of them shall become a candidate for Governor, the lack of a four year's residence ought not to be a bar to his selection.

Mr. C. C. BOWEN. It is not my purpose to discuss the claims of any person who may be a candidate, at this stage of the proceeding. I hope the Convention will forget all that, and leave the question open; that it will attach to the section such an amendment as will allow any person residing here at the time of the adoption of the Constitution, who has the requisite ability, to enter the race for office. Much has been said here in regard to Northern and Southern men, but when the time arrives for a nomination to be made for any office in South Carolina, I shall not stop to ask whether a man was born here, or in Maine, or Massachusetts, or Georgia. All I want to see is ability, and an affiliation to the party with which I am myself allied. I hope the amendment limiting the required term of residence to two years will be adopted.

Mr. B. BYAS. I am opposed to this section as it stands. No doubt, a Committee of nine men may act with commendable judgment in making a report, and deciding upon the merits of questions submitted to them; but in this case, I am satisfied their action will not be sustained by the majority of this Convention. The State of South Carolina is not so large that a man must live in it four years before he knows the people; and whether our choice be of a Southern or a Northern man, I shall stand by the nominee, if I am satisfied of his ability to fill the position and do justice to the State, whether he has been here two years or a life time.

Mr. B. F. RANDOLPH. In my opinion, it is impossible for any man to come to South Carolina and gain the affections and confidence of the people, unless worthy of it; and when such a one can be found, I take it for granted that he will be their choice, even in the face of another, who may have lived here twenty, forty, or fifty years. If a man can be found who is a native born South Carolinian, and possesses the full confidence of the State, I think it would be better to elect him.

Mr. W. J. WHIPPER. What advantage does a South Carolinian possess over a Northern man of equal ability and knowledge?

Mr. B. F. RANDOLPH. I do not say he possesses any advantage, but the people of every State and nation feel a peculiar respect for those born upon the soil. And it is human nature that they prefer to see such a man elected to the highest office in their gift, rather than one who is a comparative stranger. It is so with the French, the English, the Americans, and eminently so with the people of South Carolina, who have more respect for their own citizens than for others, possessing not a superior degree of ability.

Mr. S. A. SWAILS. I would like to ask if there is a man here in the interest of any Northern man?

Mr. B. F. RANDOLPH. I know of no such person on this floor.

Mr. R. C. DeLARGE. Does the gentleman believe in that portion of the Constitution of the United States, which says that the citizens of one State shall be entitled to the privileges and immunities of the citizens of the several States.

Mr. B. F. RANDOLPH. Certainly I do. I do not object to any man coming into South Carolina. I say, if any Northern man here now can be elected Governor by the people, so be it.

Mr. R. C. DeLARGE. If the gentleman believes what he says, how can he stretch his conscience and declare his preference for a Southern over a Northern man, especially when he knows that the natives of the State are opposed to the work of reconstruction in which we are engaged?

Mr. B. F. RANDOLPH. I only referred to the preference as a characteristic of the people, as a law of human nature.

Mr. W. J. WHIPPER. Did not the gentleman assert that it was better to elect a native South Carolinian?

Mr. B. F. RANDOLPH. I say if a competent native of the State can be found, who is the choice of the people, let him be elected.

Mr. L. S. LANGLEY. I would ask the gentleman if he thinks the people of Tennessee are proud of the fact that Andrew Johnson is a native of that State?

Mr. B. F. RANDOLPH. I do not think any State has reason to be proud of a criminal, especially one charged with high crimes and misdemeanors.

Mr. B. O. DUNCAN. Do you think the State of Tennessee would be proud of Admiral Farragut, or the State of Virginia of General Thomas?

Mr. B. F. RANDOLPH. Once for all, I wish it to be understood that I do not object to any man on account of the place of his birth. I am a Northern man myself, and doubt not that I shall vote for a Northern man as the Governor of South Carolina, for I am in favor of the

71

amendment which will allow a man to become eligible for the office, who has resided here two years. I stated it as my honest conviction, however, that it would be better, if we could find a competent South Carolinian, to elect him Governor of the State, because I believe it would be more agreeable to the masses. Still, I do not lay it down as the policy which we should adopt. I am perfectly willing to trust to the good sense and judgment of the people.

Mr. T. K. SASPORTAS. In speaking, I said that I would trust a man born in South Carolina quicker than others. I did not intend to make such a broad assertion as that. What I meant was, that I would trust a man from South Carolina, who would accept the situation in truth, as soon as I would trust any man from any other portion of the United States.

Mr. W. J. WHIPPER. I hope the amendment will prevail. I certainly see no necessity for four years ; and it does seem to me it would be very inconsistent in this body to establish four years as the term of residence necessary to qualify a man to fill an office. If the same rule had been applied to this body, there are comparatively few members upon this floor who would have been here to-day. Not even the member from Orangeburg (Rev. Mr. RANDOLPH), if his own doctrine is correct, would have been here. If what he alleges of outsiders is true, I do not see how he got here any how.

Mr. B. F. RANDOLPH. I got here just as you did.

Mr. W. J. WHIPPER. It has been alleged by the gentleman from Fairfield (Mr. RUTLAND), that it is necessary for a man to live here some time in order to know the wants of the people of the State. I will admit that it is necessary for persons to know the wants of the people of any State where they are made officers of it. But it seems to me they have not shown in the administration of affairs in this State, that the ruling powers ever knew the wants of the people of the State. I think Henry Wilson was correct when he said the Northern people have always known the people of South Carolina better than the South Carolinians knew themselves. But for the Northern people knowing the people and the wants of this State, the natural advantages and resources of the State would have remained in obscurity. When you want men who know the wants and resources of your State, you do not find them in persons to the manor born. You will find those persons who came here with their bayonets, who relieved you from the condition in which you were so long anxious to be relieved ; who actually knew, and still know, your wants quite as well as any native in the State.

You did not inquire, when yonder island was aligned with men and bayonets, whether they knew you or not. Every loyal heart welcomed them to this community, and presumed they knew your wants. I believe there are many persons who have not resided here four years, who know your wants thoroughly, and they know them just as well now as when they were divided from you by the hostile shores of Sullivan's and Morris Islands. It would certainly be ungenerous, unkind and impolitic, to debar those who thus came to you in your hour of greatest need, from holding the positions created by them or their friends. I, therefore, hope the amendment will be adopted. I desire to see the section read " from the adoption of this Constitution," because we may then use the very best material we have at hand.

We are starting anew, and every man is presumed to know what laws are best required for the protection of the community, and for providing for the necessities of the people. And yet if you adopt this report as it stands you will exclude a great majority of the members of this body from any office in the gift of the people.

I disclaim being the representative of any Northern or Southern man. It is principles, and not men of which I speak. This is a question that should rest upon a broad and well defined basis, and not be confined to narrow limits ; and hence, I urge that the section be so amended as to embrace all who live upon the soil and who possess ability to represent the people.

Mr. N. G. PARKER. It is my intention to occupy the time of this body but a few minutes. I simply desire to offer the following amendment :

" Provided that the four years qualification shall not extend to the first election held under this Constitution for Governor."

I think the term, four years, is none too long. When the State has become thoroughly organized, I should feel jealous myself of the eligibility for the office of Governor that might be acquired by an outsider in a shorter period. Under the present circumstances, however, I do not think the rule should be applied. It is better to leave the question open, so that we may be free to support any one who will best sustain the interests of the State.

Mr. J. F. CAMP called for the previous question.

The call was sustained, and the question being taken on the motion to strike out " four " years residence and insert " two," it was decided in the affirmative.

Mr. D. H. CHAMBERLAIN offered the following amendment :

"Provided that the two years qualification shall not apply to the first election for Governor under this Constitution."

The amendment was rejected.

Mr. C. P. LESLIE called for the reading of the section.

Mr. B. O. DUNCAN moved to add after the words "thirty years" "and is a citizen of the United States."

Mr. N. G. PARKER proposed to add "for five years."

Mr. B. O. DUNCAN hoped the amendment would not prevail. He did not see the justice of requiring a man to be a citizen of the United States for five years, and a citizen of the State for two years.

The amendment of Mr. DUNCAN was agreed to.

Mr. J. H. JENKS. I wish to ask for information, whether the section as now amended does not provide that any man who enters the State of South Carolina the day before the ratification of this Constitution is not eligible to the office of Governor.

The PRESIDENT. That will be a question for the lawyers to settle. I do not undertake to decide it myself.

On motion of Mr. R. G. HOLMES the question was reconsidered.

Mr. C. C. BOWEN then moved to amend as follows :

"And has been a citizen and resident of the State for two years next preceding the day of the election, or was one at the time of the adoption of this Constitution."

On motion of Mr. R. B. ELLIOTT, the amendment was indefinitely postponed, and the Convention adjourned.

THIRTY-FIFTH DAY.

Tuesday, February 25, 1868.

The Convention assembled at half-past 10 A. M., and was called to order by the PRESIDENT.

Prayer was offered by the Rev. E. J. SNETTER.

The roll was called, and a quorum answering to their names, the PRESIDENT announced the Convention ready to proceed to business.

The Journal of Monday was read and approved.

Mr. E. W. M. MACKEY offered the following resolution, which was referred to the Committee on Rules and Regulations, with instructions to report to-morrow :

Resolved, That the Convention will meet hereafter from half-past ten to two o'clock every day, and from half-past seven to ten every night.

Mr. T. K. SASPORTAS submitted the following, which was referred to the Committee on Rules and Regulations :

WHEREAS, provisions are made for the payment of the per diem of members only to the 5th of March, therefore be it

Resolved, That after the 5th day of March no pay be drawn by members of this Convention.

The unfinished business was resumed, and the consideration of section three of the report of the Committee on the Executive Part of the Constitution was taken up.

Mr. B. F. WHITTEMORE submitted the following substitute for section three :

SECTION 3. No person shall be eligible to the office of Governor who denies the existence of the Supreme Being, or who at the time of such election has not attained the age of thirty years, and who, except at the first election under this Constitution, shall not have been a citizen of the United States and a citizen and resident of this State for two years next preceding the day of election. No person while Governor shall hold any other office or commission (except in the militia) under this State, or any other power, at one and the same time.

Mr. L. S. LANGLEY. I regret exceedingly that the gentleman from Darlington (Mr. B. F. WHITTEMORE) has offered that substitute I am opposed to it for the same reason that I opposed yesterday the amendment as it now stands. I am in favor of making it obligatory upon all candidates for office to believe in a Supreme Being, but it should not be upon the Governor only. The amendment is not comprehensive enough. I am willing to support any amendment excluding from office any man who does not believe in a Supreme Being. I hope the amendment or substitute will be voted down.

Mr. WM. J. McKINLAY. I hope the amendment of the gentleman from Darlington will prevail. The objections of the gentleman from Beaufort are simply that the substitute does not include other officers besides the Executive. We are considering the report of the Committee on the Executive Department, and are, therefore, regulating the duties and qualifications of the Governor. This is the proper place to legislate for that office.

Mr. J. S. CRAIG. I hope we shall go into no further discussion of this matter. The question was fully discussed and settled yesterday. The substitute of the gentleman from Darlington simply embodies the amendments already offered. I hope the question will be taken at once.

Mr. J. J. WRIGHT. I consider this one of the most important questions presented to this body. It involves a question of the constitutionality or unconstitutionality of the Constitution we are to frame. No person in the world has a greater respect and reverence for the Supreme Being than I have. I believe it is the duty of all persons who desire to prosper, to recognize the Supreme Being in all their acts, and in all their legislative assemblies. But we must remember we are assembled to frame a Constitution, and that Constitution is to be framed in accordance with the Constitution of the United States. If we do not make it to accord with the Constitution of the United States, then the work we have performed here, and the monies we have drawn out of the treasury, will all be for nothing. I contend we have no constitutional right to make a religious test. But no man can become an officer of the State without taking the prescribed oath of office, and in that oath the Deity or Supreme Being is already recognized. I believe this subject was thoroughly discussed by the framers of the Constitution of the United States, and in their discussions they alluded to this very matter. They came to the conclusion that every one before entering upon the duties of his office, would be obliged to take the oath which recognized the existence of a Supreme Being, and any person unable to take the oath would be of course disqualified from holding office. They did not, therefore, incorporate that feature into the Constitution of the United States. They incorporated that clause which says: "The Senators and Representatives before mentioned, and the members of the several State Legislatures, and all the executive and judicial officers, both of the

United States and of the several States, shall be bound by oath or affirmation to support this Constitution, but no religious test whatever shall ever be required as a qualification to any office of public trust under the United States."

The Constitution of the United States is an example for us. We are to frame a Constitution in accordance with the reconstruction acts under which we are operating. The Constitution of the United States tells us that no religious test should be made for any office in the State. There is no person who takes the oath to support the Constitution of the United States, or the Constitution of a State, but recognizes the existence of a Supreme Being. I hope, therefore, that as we have recognized in our Reclaration of Dights the Supreme Being, that we shall not say that a man shall believe in the existence of a Supreme Being before he shall be eligible to the office of Governor, or any other office in the State. The oath, or affirmation, already required of any person before entering on the duties of his office is sufficient.

Mr. S. G. W. DILL. Do the officers when taking the oath to which you allude, swear to discharge the duties of the office, or swear that they believe there is a God.

Mr. J. J. WRIGHT. When a man takes an oath or affirmation to support the Constitution of the United States and of the State at its close, he says, " so help me God."

Mr. B. F. RANDOLPH. If a man who does not believe in God takes that oath, does he really and sincerely believe what he says, when he believes there is no God.

Mr. J. J. WRIGHT. He clearly believes what he says. But the people will always choose a man in whom they can confide, and one who does recognize the existence of a Supreme Being. But I simply rise to defend the motion to strike out the words " who denies the existence of a Supreme Being," believing the passage of a section with those words would be in direct conflict with the Constitution of the United States.

Mr. B. F. RANDOLPH. The Constitution says there shall be no religious test. What does the word test mean? Does it mean a belief in some particular doctrine, or does it apply to a belief in the Deity.

Mr. J. J. WRIGHT. If the gentleman will read the Constitution of the United States, he will find that it says, Congress shall make no law for the establishment of any certain religion. It declares there shall be no religious test. That certainly means that a man's religious belief shall not be questioned as a qualification for any office of trust. He cannot be excluded from holding office if the people desire to choose him for that office.

Mr. R. G. HOLMES. I am surprised at the gentleman's argument. There is no religious test in this section as proposed. There is simply the affirmation of a person who takes the oath of office that he believes what he says. The oath of a man who does not believe there is a God, is not worth having. I hope we will engraft this section into the Constitution, and prohibit any man from holding office who cannot take the oath that he believes in a Supreme Being.

Mr. R. C. DeLARGE. It is certainly a strange argument for a member to use, that the words "Supreme Being," in this section, cannot be considered a religious test. We know that there are a great many who do not believe in the existence of what we call a Supreme Being; who believe in an entirely different Supreme Being. I have always believed that the section of the Constitution of the United States, in reference to this subject, was intended to prevent any such words or phrases being inserted as a test in the Constitutions of the several States. If it can be shown that this is not a test, and not in conflict with the Constitution of the United States, I would be very willing to have it placed in our Constitution. I am not disposed, however, to have an infidel hold the position of Governor of this State. But whilst that is my individual opinion, I am not prepared to say a religious test should be incorporated into the Constitution of the State.

Mr. R. J. DONALDSON. What denomination possessing any religion in our country is there that does not acknowledge a Supreme Being?

Mr. R. C. DeLARGE. I hope there is no class or sect of people who do not acknowledge the existence of the Supreme Being; and believing so, I see no necessity for placing this provision in the Constitution. I desire to be put right on this question. There are a great many races of men, unless my information is incorrect, who do not acknowledge, or recognize, the Supreme Being.

But I question whether it would be constitutional to insert those words in our Constitution, believing that it will be in conflict with the clause of the Constitution of the United States, read this morning.

Again, it has been argued that this section allows the party to explain what they regard as the Supreme Being. I cannot see that it does. No one can take the oath or affirmation of office who does not believe in the existence of a Supreme Being. It might be that a person would be compelled to conform his religious opinions according to those of the leaders of a political party in power.

Mr. B. F. RANDOLPH. I had hoped this question was permanently settled yesterday. The Bible says the fool saith in his heart there is no God. Well, if the Bible be true, I trust no fool will ever be elected

Governor of South Carolina. The principal ground of opposition appears to be because the Constitution of the United States says no religious test shall be required of any one who may be elected to office. It is well known that when the Constitution of the United States was framed, that religious tests were required of persons holding office by the New England States. Roger Williams was banished because he did not believe in certain religious tenets of that day. And all the old thirteen States, more or less, required religious tests. It was with the view of abolishing these tests that the framers of the Constitution introduced that clause. But they had no idea that to require a man to believe in the existence of God was a religious test. How can we believe that a man who stands up with one hand pointing to heaven and the other upon the Bible, and closing with "so help me God," does not believe in God. If he does not believe in God, he swears to a lie. I hope this may be retained in the Constitution. It would be inconsistent for us to insert an oath in one part of the Constitution, which says "so help me God," and then to say in another part that no religious test shall ever be required. Congress must have meant when they added those words to the oath, "so help me God," that a man should believe in God. When you find a man who does not believe in God, you find a man whose conscience will stretch like India rubber. In his opinion there is no God to hold him accountable for his moral conduct. I believe in having men in office who have conscientious scruples, and who believe there is a God who will hold them accountable for their deeds.

Mr. R. C. DeLARGE. How will you discover whether the Governor elect believes in the existence of God or not? Do you propose to appoint a commission to examine into his religious belief?

Mr. B. F. RANDOLPH. It would be very strange for a man to profess belief in God who does not entertain that belief. This, I understand, is intended for a man who is so lost, so far gone in depravity, as to come out boldly and deny his belief in the existence of a Supreme Being. When a man is so far gone as that, in the name of heaven, would you trust him to be Governor of South Carolina. I am in favor of the amendment proposed by the gentleman from Darlington (Mr. WHITTEMORE), and hope it will be adopted. I hope we will not here in Convention brand South Carolina as being opposed to inserting in our Constitution these words, and thus brand ourselves as atheists.

I did not intend to say a word upon this question. It is a very delicate subject; yea, it is shouldered with more of solemnity than any question that has come before this body. I well know the hazard to which one exposes himself, by opposing a measure like this. Indeed, I should

72

not be surprised if, with blanched cheeks and quivering lips, and glaring eye, a hundred voices should break forth against any one who should oppose this measure, " lo ! an atheist ! "

But, to quiet any apprehensions or misapprehensions of delegates, I now declare (a thing which I never before in my life felt compelled to do,) that I ever have, and do now, entertain a firm belief in the Supreme Being, who created, and now sustains all things ; who rules over and controls the destinies of individuals and of nations.   In the dark period through which our country has passed during the past six or eight years, when the cloud hung over us, I have looked through the darkness, and with implicit reliance upon the great Ruler of events, have exercised the strongest faith that the glorious results would eventuate which now our eyes behold.

But why, at this late day, incorporate this test in the Constitution of this State ? If those who drafted and those who advocate this section could point us to custom, which is law, then I should cheerfully join with the delegates of this Convention, and incorporate it in our Constitution.   But I have looked in vain to find this test, either in the Constitution of the United States, or in those of any of the thirty-six States. It was formerly found in some of the earlier Constitutions.   It was so in that of my native State, Massachusetts.   But, it must be recollected, that was in the comparatively dark and superstitious ages, two hundred years ago, when the Church whipped, and hung, and banished from the country Baptists and Quakers.   It was when Christians had their gibbet upon which to hang witches, and kept their crushing machines, with which to mash to atoms the bodies and bones of men, women, and children even, whom they supposed to be possessed of familiar or infernal spirits.   But do we wish to go back to that superstitious period, and, taking our latitude and longitude from thence, grope our way over the foggy, boisterous waters through which our country has struggled for two hundred years to the bright and beautiful haven which we now occupy?   It seems to me too Pharisaical.   It would seem that we are willing to lift our eyes to heaven, and thank God that we are not like other States, composed of atheists, infidels and traitors.   To me it would seem more appropriate for South Carolina to smite upon her breast and to cry out, " God be merciful to me, a sinner."   But why apply this test to an individual, when we have accorded to every citizen the fullest enjoyment of any faith or religious belief which he may adopt ?

It has been said no man can be believed who refuses to take an oath. But we have excepted individuals and whole classes from taking the oath.   There are the Quakers, who regard it as a sin to swear ; and they take their authority direct from the Bible, which says, "Swear not at all; neither by heaven, for it is God's throne, nor by the earth, for it is His footstool." And yet, who hesitates to believe the testimony of Quakers? I had rather trust my life, and reputation, and property, to the simple, honest affirmation of the "broad brim" than to all the oaths and "so help me Gods" that fall flippantly from thoughtless tongues in all our Courts. The gentleman from Orangeburg has said that belief in a God was required of all officers in this State, under its original Constitution. What has been the result? Take the State for the last two hundred years. It has constantly denied God by crushing man, His noblest work, to the lowest level of the brutes, and that, too, with this sacred clause in its Constitution. Again, declaring my firm belief and abiding confidence in the true and living God, I hope we shall not feel compelled to go back two hundred years, and drag forth from that austere, relentless age this effete, obsolete test, and incorporate it in the new Constitution of South Carolina.

Mr. C. P. LESLIE. Up to this time it has cost, by figures, $800 to get God out of the third section of the report of the Committee on the Executive Part of the Constitution. I am a sinner, and expect to confess it in a reverent way. I do so seriously. But while I am a sinner, and while I am not ashamed to confess it, I do believe in a God; I do believe in a Supreme Being, and I do believe that He controls all events that govern us as a people. When the winds and the storm comes in the night and overtakes the people, when armies are summoned and meet in deadly conflict, then it is that man turns with a conscientious satisfaction to the thought that the God of battles and of justice will determine for the right. It is on occasions like these that the Christian, and even the sinner, may turn with a consolation and a satisfaction that to the great God that controls the events of nations and of the world he looks for the final triumph of right.

I would not say an unkind word to any man who has seen fit to make an argument against this provision of the section requiring belief in the existence of a Supreme Being. But I declare before God, who witnesses me now and hears every word I say, that I was not prepared to believe that a man could be found in this Convention, or outside of this Convention, in the nineteenth century, in an age when we claim to be civilized, and in an age when every day makes manifest to us the continued mercies of a kind Providence, by whom we are allowed to breathe and live, and enjoy the blessings of life, I say I was not prepared to believe that any civilized being would have dared to have said what these men have uttered on this floor. Great God, sinner as I am, I would no sooner have asserted that I did not believe in the great Jehovah than I would have denied my own existence.

I know, in the stormy years gone by, I have watched the overrulings of Providence, and in every result of a battle my conviction and judgment has been strengthened in the superintending hand of a Supreme Being. The next two years will, perhaps, be one of turbulence and discord. We are upon revolutionary times to-day, and the man who takes the Executive office, who cannot hold up his hands and ask God to help him, who cannot look to his Father in heaven to ask his counsel, and to enable him to execute the laws without enmity to any, without malice, has taken the first direct step to those dark, mercurial regions, from which there will be no return. When a man declares that he does not want in these times to rely upon God, that man, I believe, is demented, has lost his reason, and is unfit for any office whatever.

There is another class of men who have tried to appeal to the passions of the delegates as against God. I have seen those passions appealed to. I never supposed that any delegate would undertake to appeal to the political prejudices that anybody has against God.

There is another argument used here. Every time a proposition of relief is offered for the people, or anything done that looks well as a Christian people, some delegate jumps up from the back part of the hall, or in front, and cries out, "Mr. President, this is unconstitutional." My friend from Fairfield (Mr. RUTLAND) in his arguments, in his anxiety that we should do nothing of a legislative character that was unconstitutional, has always quoted in full some clause of the Constitution of the United States which might be in conflict with our action, but this morning we heard a new version of the Constitution, and it was left, seemingly, to a Charleston politician to prove that it was unconstitutional to put God into the Constitution. I believe there was no other politician in the world from whom we could have expected such a proposition. I want as many Charleston politicians to vote the way they have been talking as they can muster. I want the world to see them, to loathe them, to look upon them with contempt, and if they come into our society, I want them to be driven out. I don't want to see them ; don't want to know them. I want them to be known as unworthy of a seat in this Convention, or anywhere else in civilized society.

Mr. E. W. M. MACKEY. Did you not make a request to have them come up to Barnwell and help you in your election?

Mr. C. P. LESLIE. What I did at Barnwell has nothing to do with their taking God out of the Constitution. The Charleston politicians are excessively important people, a remarkable people, and if it were

not for Charleston politicians, the people and the whole State of South
Carolina would sink out of sight, go down and never be heard of again.

Mr. B. F. WHITTEMORE. We have acknowledged in our Bill of
Rights that we are grateful to Almighty God for preserving our nation,
and I am well aware that we have adopted a clause of a section that has
the same effect as the words that have occasioned so much debate this
morning. Perhaps, if I had been wise, I should simply have offered an
amendment, beginning where that clause ends. We have also in sections
of the Bill of Rights declared that no "person shall be deprived of the
right to worship God according to his own conscience." We have in a
section of the Executive report required an oath, or affirmation, of a
person taking an office, which closes with "So help me God;" and in
that we have recognized the existence of a Supreme Being. No person
can, therefore, become an officer without taking that oath; and if in
taking it he acknowledges an overruling Deity, and the necessity of
calling upon that Deity for assistance, why should we stagger at a section that recognizes our dependence upon a Supreme Being? It is no
matter what a person believes that Supreme Being to be. The Indian
believes in the Great Spirit, and different nations have their peculiar
deities, and worship them as a Supreme Being. When the oath is taken,
it is taken in accordance with their peculiar views of a Supreme Being.

Much has been said with regard to the disavowals by South Carolina
of the manhood of man, but it appears to me there has been too much
disavowal of the Deity by the nation at large, and it was not until after
it had passed through a terrible conflict and bloodshed all over the land,
that the people acknowledged the necessity for their trust in God. And
now if we look upon the coin as it passes from hand to hand, we see
inscribed thereon, "trust in God." Shall we, in forming a new Constitution, thrust out of that instrument our belief in a Supreme Being? I
trust every man will allow the section to pass, and require not only of
the Governor of the Commonwealth, but of every man elevated to office,
to acknowledge his belief in an overruling Providence. God forbid we
should ignore him here to-day. As has well been said, we know we
stand in the midst of troublous times, as it were upon a crater, and we
know we must look to a higher than an earthly power for a deliverance
from our troubles. I trust that we, in whose hands is confided all the
power of making the new laws, will not refer to old South Carolina, or
old Massachusetts, but lead the people to look forward to what new
South Carolina shall be, will move forward in accordance with our high
sense of duty, and pass the section recognizing our dependence on the
Supreme Being. I care not whether you accept the substitute proposed

by myself, or the section as it stood. I trust no man will suffer himself to blot from existence an acknowledgment of the responsibility which he holds towards God, and of requiring from the officers of the State, whoever they may be, an acknowledgment of the same responsibility to an overruling Providence.

Mr. W. E. JOHNSTON. This appears to be one of the greatest questions ever brought up in the house. I hope the section, or the substitute of the gentleman from Darlington (Mr. WHITTEMORE) may be adopted.

One of the gentlemen from Charleston has said that the words "Supreme Being" are unconstitutional. I have not been able to come to his conclusion, but think I have, finally, ferreted out the ideas and wishes of those gentlemen, and have drawn up a resolution that may settle the legal question involved. I offer the following:

Resolved, That the Governor, nor any other man, shall hereafter be a professor of Judaism, Mohommedanism, Christianity, or Mormonism. I move the previous question.

The call for the previous question was not sustained.

Mr. R. H. CAIN. I trust it will not be necessary to prolong a discussion on a question that certainly is so clear to the mind of every gentleman on this floor as the propriety of retaining, in the Constitution of our State, an acknowledgment of the existence of a Supreme Being, as well as the recognition that every person occupying a place of so much note to the interests of the State as that of Governor should be, at least, a person recognizing the existence of God.

I hardly believe even the gentlemen who have argued the question on the other side are prepared to drag God out of the Constitution of the State. I think it highly necessary that persons occupying prominent public positions should certainly have a belief in the existence of an overruling power. If we take away this idea, we snap the foundations of our Government. It seems to me, such a precedent would be dangerous to reason and justice, and dangerous to society at large. Take God out of the Government, and we shall have anarchy, bloodshed, and crime of every class and every kind stalking abroad at noon-day and at midnight. There will be no security for society, no security for the sacred relationship of life, no security of law, no security anywhere. We shall have midnight assassinations. An individual who disbelieves in the existence of a Supreme Being is a dangerous man in the community, and into whose hands the people should not intrust their interests. If a man fear not God, he cares little for mankind. What oath will bind him, what law rests in him, or what law will keep him in due bounds, if he regards not the Almighty? A man who calmly and reasonably, under no excitement, disbelieves in the existence of a God, cannot be trusted with any interest dear to mankind. If you will admit this hypothesis, we shall only inaugurate or set in motion a theory destructive of all our social interests. It was this idea of the existence of a God that moved the Pilgrim fathers to leave the shores of England on the "May Flower," and take their winding way over the ocean to Plymouth Rock. There they laid the foundation, sure and steadfast, which has given prosperity to our nation, and redounded to the glory and honor of American citizens, inviting, as it did, all to come and take shelter under its benign influence. I cannot see why any one should desire to have this acknowledgment of a Supreme Being stricken out. Do you not take the Bible in your schools? Are not your children instructed upon this point? It is one of the most glorious features of the English Government that, in every place where her flag floats, there the Bible is carried. It was this idea of the existence of God impressed upon the minds of the people that has made all civilized nations great, glorious and prosperous.

I know it has been said by some gentlemen on the floor that this is not necessary. One gentleman from Charleston said it was unconstitutional. I think this idea of the existence of God was before there ever was any Constitution. The existence of God seems to take priority. But I will not detain the Convention. I believe the delegates on this floor are prepared to vote on this question, that no person who denies the existence of a Supreme Being shall be eligible to the office of Governor. I submit the question for your consideration. Keep the banner still flying, keep bright the idea, and children of unborn generations will have reason to bless you for not throwing away this great strength and power.

Mr. C. M. WILDER called for the previous question, which was sustained.

The substitute of Mr. WHITTEMORE was then taken up and adopted.

The main question being put, it resulted affirmatively, and section third, as amended, was passed to its third reading.

The ayes and nays, being ordered, were taken, and resulted as follows:

YEAS—The President, Messrs. Allen, Arnim, Becker, Bell, Bowen, Bonum, Brockenton, Bryce, R. H. Cain, E. J. Cain, Camp, Coghlan, Chamberlain, Chestnut, Clinton, Cooke, Collins, Corley, Craig, Crews, Darrington, Davis, DeLarge, Dill, Donaldson, Driffle, Duncan, Edwards, Foster, Gentry, Gray, Harris, J. N. Hayne, H. E. Hayne, Chas. D.

Hayne, Henderson, Holmes, Humbird, Jacobs, Jenks, Jervey, Jillson, S. Johnson, W. B. Johnson, J. W. Johnson, L. B. Johnson, W. E. Johnston, Joiner, Henry Jones, Chas. Jones, Lang, Langley, Samuel Lee, Lomax, Leslie, Mayer, Mauldin, W. McKinlay, McDaniels, Mead, Middleton, Milford, Nance, Nelson, Neagle, Nuckles, Parker, Pillsbury, Randolph, Rainey, Ransier, Rivers, Rose, Runion, Rutland, Sanders, Shrewsbury, Smalls, Swails, Thomas, Augustus Thompson, B. A. Thompson, S. B. Thompson, Viney, Webb, Whittemore, White, Williamson, F. E. Wilder, Chas. M. Wilder, Wingo, Wooley—93.

Nays—Messrs. Alexander, Byas, Elliott, George Lee, E. W. M-Mackey, Owens, Wright—7.

Absent—Messrs. Boozer, Burton, Cardozo, Dickson, Dogan, Goss, Hunter, Hurley, Jackson, W. J. McKinlay, Miller, Moses, Nash, Newell, Olsen, Perry, Robertson, Richmond, Sasportas, Stubbs, Whipper—21.

Mr. R. B. ELLIOTT, before the question was taken on the above, asked and obtained leave to explain his vote, and said yesterday an amendment was offered to that section, which was intended to make an exception of those who were in the State at the first election, that is before the ratification of this Constitution. I move to indefinitely postpone that amendment. To-day, when this substitute was presented, the same exception was contained in that substitute. That is the reason I cannot vote in its favor. I am in favor of the acknowledgment of the Supreme Being, but against that provision of the section which makes an exception of those in the State at the ratification of the Constitution. I, therefore, vote "No."

Mr. R. C. DeLARGE moved that the vote whereby the substitute was adopted be reconsidered, and the motion to reconsider be laid upon the table, which was agreed to.

Brevet Major-General E. R. S. Canby and Captain Caziarc here entered the hall.

The PRESIDENT introduced the General to the Convention as follows:

Gentlemen of the Convention, I have the honor and pleasure of introducing to you Brevet Major-General E. R. S. Canby, Military Commander of the Second Military District, a gentleman whose efficiency, judgment and courtesy, in the discharge of the onerous, responsible duties entrusted to him, has met the approval of the citizens of both the States under his control.

Brevet Major-General E. R. S. Canby rising, was greeted with warm applause. He returned his thanks to the Convention, and resumed his seat alongside the President.

On motion of Mr. R. C. DeLARGE, the Convention took a recess of five minutes to pay their respects to the General.

Business being resumed, sections four, five, six, seven and eight were passed to their third reading without debate.

Section nine was read as follows :

In case of the removal of the Governor from his office, or his death, resignation, removal from the State, or inability to discharge the powers and duties of the said office, the same shall devolve on the Lieutenant Governor, and the General Assembly, at its first session after the ratification of this Constitution, shall, by law, provide for the case of removal, death, resignation, or inability, both of the Governor and Lieutenant Governor, declaring what officer shall then act as Governor, and such officer shall act accordingly, until such disability be removed, or a Governor shall be elected.

Mr. B. F. WHITTEMORE moved to amend on sixth line by inserting the words "shall have been" instead of the word "be," which was adopted, and the section so amended was passed to its third reading.

Section ten was taken up, and Mr. F. J. MOSES, Jr., offered the following substitute :

SECTION 10. The Governor shall be commander-in-chief of the Militia, and other military organizations of the State, except when they shall be called into the actual service of the United States.

Mr. E. W. M. MACKEY moved to strike out the words "and other military organizations."

Mr. B. O. DUNCAN. There is such a thing as volunteer companies that are not included in the militia.

Mr. L. S. LANGLEY. Will the gentleman inform us what those organizations are if they are not military ?

Mr. B. O. DUNCAN. Volunteer companies have formerly existed in the State, and will exist in the future, but I do not think they properly can be included in the volunteer organization.

Mr. R. G. HOLMES. Volunteer companies will certainly go under the head of militia.

The question then being taken on the amendment of Mr. MACKEY, and agreed to, the section, as amended, was passed to its third reading.

Section eleven was passed to its third reading without amendment.

Section twelve received its second reading as follows :

He shall take care that the laws be faithfully executed in mercy.

73

Mr. R. G. HOLMES. I move that the words " in mercy" be stricken out.

Mr. E. W..M. MACKEY. I move to strike out the whole section.

Mr. L. S. LANGLEY. I hope that motion will be voted down. It seems to me that the history of the past two or three years furnishes every reason why we should retain this section in our Constitution. It simply says the Governor shall take care that the laws shall be faithfully executed, and unless we intend that the Governor shall not execute the laws we should retain the section.

Mr. E. W. M. MACKEY. Does not the gentleman know that the oath of office prescribed in the legislative department requires every officer to swear that he will faithfully execute the duties of his office ?

The question was taken, and a division of the house being called for, it was decided in the affirmative.

Sections thirteen and fourteen were passed to their third reading without amendment.

Section fifteen was read as follows :

The Governor shall, from time to time, give to the General Assembly information of the condition of the State, and recommend to their consideration such measures as he shall judge necessary or expedient.

Mr. N. G. PARKER moved to add to the section, after the word "expedient" in the third line, as follows : " The General Assembly, at its first session after the adoption of this Constitution, shall elect an Adjutant and Inspector General, whose term of office shall be the same as that of the Governor, and whose pay shall be provided for by law," which was agreed to.

Section sixteen was read as follows :

SECTION 16. He may. on extraordinary occasions, convene the General Assembly ; and, should either house remain without a quorum for five days, or in case of disagreement between the two houses with respect to the time of adjournment, may adjourn them to such time as he shall think proper, not beyond ——— then next ensuing.

Mr. N. G. PARKER moved to postpone the filling up of the blank until the last day of the session.

Mr. F. J. MOSES, Jr. I move to recommit this section. It appears to me to need a little alteration. I do not believe the Governor ought to have the power to discharge the house if there is no quorum in five days.

Mr. L. S. LANGLEY. I move to fill the blank as follows, " to the next regular annual session then next ensuing."

The motion was not agreed to.

Mr. F. J. MOSES, Jr. I move to fill the blank with " the first day of the next session."

Mr. L. S. LANGLEY. I move to fill it with "may adjourn them to the next regular session."

Mr. E. W. M. MACKEY. If the Legislature assembles at the regular session, a quorum is not present, and the Governor has the power to adjourn them over until the next session, would it not give him the power to adjourn them for the entire year. I think it is giving the Governor too much power.

Mr. L. S. LANGLEY. If the Legislature of the State should meet in extra session, it would be on the call of the Governor, and his power, therefore, to adjourn them to the next regular annual session, would not be detrimental to the State.

Mr. R. C. DeLARGE. I would like to know whether the gentleman has been reading English history lately.

Mr. L. S. LANGLEY. That question is irrelevant to this subject.

Mr. L. S. LANGLEY'S amendment was disagreed to.

Mr. B. O. DUNCAN. I move to insert these words, " the time of the annual session." The amendment was agreed to, and section sixteen passed to its third reading.

Section seventeen was read as follows :

"He shall commission all officers of the State."

Mr. R. B. ELLIOTT moved to add " by and with the advice and consent of the Senate."

Mr. R. G. HOLMES. I move to add " all officers of the State holding by commission."

Mr. R. C. DeLARGE. If the State Senate should not be in session how would it be possible for the officers of the State to be commissioned?

Mr. C. C. BOWEN. I am opposed to the section as it stands. If the people elect a man, it is a commission. I will admit that, if the office is held by appointment, it would be necessary for the Governor to issue a commission, but in all cases of election by the people I see no necessity. The election returns, regularly made, will be, in my opinion, commission enough. If you pass this section as it is, all Justices of the Peace and Constables elected by the people cannot serve a process, unless he has a commission from the Governor. If the Governor happens to be absent, much time is lost in getting the commission.

Mr. B. F. WHITTEMORE. I move to insert after the word State, "He shall commission all officers of the State by him appointed, or those appointed by the General Assembly."

Mr. C. M. WILDER. I move that the entire section be stricken out.

Mr. H. E. HAYNE. I cannot see the propriety of striking out the whole section. Officers of the State militia, appointed by the Governor, would certainly like to have a commission to show that they had been duly appointed as commissioned officers of a regiment or company. I move to indefinitely postpone the motion of the gentleman from Richland.

The motion to postpone indefinitely was agreed to.

Mr. B. O. DUNCAN. I propose the following amendment as a substitute: "He shall commission all officers of the State appointed by the Executive, or chosen by the General Assembly."

Mr. J. S. CRAIG. If the Governor is not to commission the officers of the State, what evidence would they have of their election to any office. Suppose a question is raised, how would it be settled? I think every officer should have the Governor's commission, as a warrant of authority to act.

The PRESIDENT stated that the question of striking out had been decided in the negative.

The question was then taken on the motion to insert, "holding by commission."

The next question was on the amendment offered by Mr. WHITTEMORE.

Mr. J. S. CRAIG. I hope the Convention will vote down every amendment to this section. Some of the amendments propose that only certain officers shall be commissioned. I think every officer elected by the people, as well as those appointed, should have the Governor's commission as their warrant of authority. I consider it very important that every officer should be commissioned. In every State of the Union commissions are issued to every officer, from Constable up.

Mr. L. S. LANGLEY. Would the gentleman like to have members of the Legislature commissioned by the Governor?

Mr. J. S. CRAIG. Members of the Legislature have a certificate of election.

Mr. J. M. RUTLAND. I agree with the gentleman from Colleton. I really think Sheriffs, Clerks of Courts, Ordinaries, Commissioners in Equity, District Judges, and all such officers, should have their commissions from somebody, to show by what authority they are exercising their offices. If they do not obtain them from the Governor, I do not know from what source they are to obtain them. It is a very easy matter to do so. These commissions can be struck off in a blank. It is not considered a very heavy tax. I am in favor of the section as it is, and hope the Convention will pass it. The question being taken on the proposed amendments, they were decided in the negative, and the seventeenth section passed to its third reading.

SECTION 18. There shall be a Great Seal of the State, for which the General Assembly, at its first session, shall provide, and which shall be used by the Governor officially, and shall be called "The Great Seal of the State of South Carolina."

Mr. E. W. M. MACKEY. I move to strike out this section, for the reason that a similar section occurs in the Miscellaneous Provisions of the Constitution, which, I think, is the right place for it.

Mr. C. C. BOWEN. I hope the section will not be stricken out, as I think this is the proper place for it. We are now considering the report to which the gentleman has alluded.

Mr. D. H. CHAMBERLAIN. I think we can, with great propriety, let it stand where it is. It provides a seal for the Governor of the State, and we are now providing in this part of the Constitution for the efficient discharge of the duties of the office of Governor.

The motion to strike out was decided in the negative.

Mr. C. C. BOWEN moved to strike out on the first line the word " Great," which was agreed to, and the section then passed to its third reading.

Section nineteenth was read, as follows :

SECTION 19. All grants and commissions shall be signed by the Governor, countersigned by the Secretary of State, and sealed with the Great Seal.

Mr. E. W. M. MACKEY. I propose the following substitute : " All grants and commissions shall be issued in the name and by the authority of the State of South Carolina, sealed with the Great Seal, signed by the Governor, and countersigned by the Secretary of State."

The substitute was agreed to, and the section passed to a third reading

Section twentieth was read, as follows:

SECTION 20. The Governor and the Lieutenant Governor, before entering upon the duties of their respective offices, shall, in the presence of the General Assembly, take the following oath of allegiance and qualification, and also the following oath of office :

Oath or Affirmation of Allegiance and Qualification.—"I do swear (or affirm) that I am duly qualified, according to the Constitution of this State, to exercise the office to which I have been elected ; that I will preserve, protect and defend the Constitution of this State and that of the United States, and that I will not, directly or indirectly, do any act or thing injurious to the Constitution or Government thereof, as established

by this Convention. (If an oath), So help me God. (If an affiirma-
tion), under the pains and penalties of perjury."

Oath or Affirmation of Office.—"I do solemnly swear (or affirm) that
I will faithfully discharge the duties of the office of Governor (or Lieutenant Governor) for the State of South Carolina, and will therein do
equal right and justice to all men, to the best of my judgment and abilities, and according to law. (If an oath), So help me God. (If an
affirmation), under the pains and penalties of perjury."

Mr. B. F. WHITTEMORE moved to transpose: "I will protect and
defend the Constitution of the United States and this State," which was
agreed to.

Mr. B. O. DUNCAN moved to amend by striking out all of the section after the words "General Assembly," and inserting these words,
"take and subscribe the oath of office as prescribed in article I, section
thirty-first, of this Constitution," which was agreed to, and the section,
so amended, passed to its third reading.

Section twenty-first was read a second time, and passed to a third
reading, as follows:

SECTION 21. The Governor shall reside at the capital of the State; but
during the sittings of the General Assembly he shall reside where its
sessions are held, except in case of contagion.

Section twenty-second was read, as follows:

SECTION 22. Every bill which shall have passed the General Assembly,
shall, before it become a law, be presented to the Governor; if he approve, he shall sign it; but if not, he shall return it, with his objections,
to that House in which it shall have originated, who shall enter the objections at large on their journal, and proceed to reconsider it. If, after
such reconsideration, a majority of the whole representation of that
House shall agree to pass the bill, it shall be sent, together with the objections, to the other House, by which it shall likewise be reconsidered:
and if approved by a majority of the whole representation of that other
House, it shall become a law. But in all such cases the votes of both
Houses shall be determined by yeas and nays; and the names of the
persons voting for and against the bill shall be entered on the journal of
each House respectively. If any bill shall not be returned by the Governor within five days (Sundays excepted) after it shall have been presented to him, the same shall be a law in like manner as if he had signed
it. And that time may always be allowed the Governor to consider bills
passed by the General Assembly, neither House shall read any bill on
the last day of its session, except such bills as have been returned by
the Governor as herein provided.

Mr. C. C. BOWEN offered the following as a substitute for the twenty-
second section, which was agreed to, and the section passed to its third

reading: "Every bill or joint resolution which shall have passed the General Assembly, except on a question of adjournment, shall, before it becomes a law, be presented to the Governor, and, if he approve, he shall sign it; if not, he shall return it, with his objections, to the House in which it shall have originated; which shall enter the objections at large on its journals, and proceed to reconsider it. If, after such reconsideration, two-thirds of that House shall agree to pass it, it shall be sent, together with the objections, to the other House, by which it shall be reconsidered, and, if approved by two-thirds of that House, it shall have the same effect as if it had been signed by the Governor; but in all such cases the vote of both Houses shall be taken by yeas and nays, and the names of the persons voting for and against the bill or joint resolution shall be entered on the journals of both Houses, respectively. If a bill or joint resolution shall not be returned by the Governor, within three days after it shall have been presented to him (Sundays excepted), it shall have the same force and effect as if he had signed it, unless the General Assembly, by their adjournment, prevents its return, in which case it shall not have such force and effect, unless returned within two days after their next meeting."

Mr. E. W. M. MACKEY called up the report of the Judiciary Committee.

The PRESIDENT announced the following Special Committee, appointed under a resolution adopted by the house to draft an Ordinance, prescribing a mode in which the Constitution shall be submitted to the people for ratification, and providing for election of State officers:

Messrs. E. W. M. MACKEY, of Orangeburg; F. L. CARDOZO, of Charleston; A. C. RICHMOND, of Berkley; H. E. HAYNE, of Marion; Dr. J. C. NEAGLE, of York; J. J. WRIGHT, of Beaufort; B. O. DUNCAN, of Newberry; JOS. H. RAINEY, of Georgetown; Dr. N. J. NEWELL, of Anderson.

On motion of Mr. C. P. LESLIE, and without further action on the first section of the Judiciary report, the Convention adjourned.

THIRTY-SIXTH DAY.

Wednesday, February 26, 1868.

The Convention assembled at half-past 10 A. M., and was called to order by the PRESIDENT.

Prayer was offered by the Rev. B. F. WHITTEMORE.

The roll was called, and a quorum answering to their names, the PRESIDENT announced the Convention ready to proceed to business.

The Journal of Tuesday was read and approved.

The PRESIDENT called for reports of Standing Committees.

Mr. S. A. SWAILS made a report of the Committee on Rules and Regulations, on a resolution changing the time of sittings of the Convention, so as to meet from half-past ten to two o'clock every day, and from half-past seven to ten every night. The Committee recommend that the resolution be laid upon the table.

Mr. B. O. DUNCAN. I hope the report of the Committee will not be adopted. I think we are getting along altogether too slow, and have been here much too long for the interests of the country we represent. I wish to have an evening session.

Mr. J. M. RUNION. I hope the report will be voted down, and that we will have two sessions a day.

Mr. R. C. DeLARGE. I desire to expedite business; but while in favor of lengthening the daily sessions to five hours, I am opposed to an evening session.

Mr. J. J. WRIGHT. I hope the report will not be adopted, and that we shall have two sessions. I think it is ample time that we were getting through with this work, and we are all aware that the work is not going on as fast as it ought to go on; perhaps all of us do not exactly realize the situation we are occupying before the country. In facilitating this business it may be the salvation of the entire people. We cannot meet and counsel with each other too often. We cannot give too much of our time to this work. The more we are together, the more we talk matters over; the more we exchange opinions with each other, the better we are prepared to mature our work. I hope, for the sake of our constituents and ourselves, and the entire people of the State, we will not adopt the report of the Committee, but have two sessions. Gentlemen say they desire time to labor at home; we have ample time for that and yet have two sessions, if we would spend our leisure time at home after leaving the Convention.

Mr. J. S. CRAIG called for the yeas and nays on the motion for the adoption of the report.

The yeas and nays were taken, and resulted as follows:

YEAS—Messrs. Arnim, Becker, Bowen, Bonum, Burton, Brockenton, Byas, F. J. Cain, Chamberlain, Collins, Crews, Davis, LeLarge, Dill, Donaldson, Driffle, Elliott, Foster, Gentry, Gray, Harris, J. N. Hayne, C. D. Hayne, Jenks, Jervey, Joiner, Henry Jones, Lang, Langley, Lomax, Leslie, Mayer, Mauldin, W. J. McKinlay, W. McKinlay, McDaniels, Mead, Miller, Moses, Nance, Nelson, Nuckles, Owens, Pillsbury, Ransier, Richmond, Rivers, Sanders, Stubbs, Thomas, Thompson, Viney, Webb, White, Wingo—55.

NAYS—The President, Messrs. Allen, Alexander, Bell, Bryce, Camp, Coghlan, Chestnut, Clinton, Cooke, Corley, Craig, Darrington, Duncan, Edwards, Goss, H. E. Hayne, Henderson, Holmes, Jacobs, Jillson, Saml. Johnson, W. B. Johnson, J. W. Johnson, L. B. Johnson, W. E. Johnston, Chas. Jones, George Lee, Samuel Lee, Middleton, Milford, Neagle, Newell, Parker, Randolph, Rainey, Robertson, Runion, Rutland, Sasportas, Smalls, Swails, B. A. Thompson, S. B. Thompson, Whittemore, Williamson, F. E. Wilder, Chas. M. Wilder, Wooley, Wright—50.

ABSENT—Boozer, R. H. Cain, Cardozo, Dickson, Dogan, Humbird, Hunter, Hurley, Jackson, Mackey, Nash, Olsen, Perry, Rose, Shrewsbury, Whipper—16.

Yeas 55, nays 50; absent 16.

Mr. R. C. DeLARGE asked leave to explain his vote, which the house refused.

Mr. R. C. DeLARGE asked permission not to vote, which was refused, and he voted nay.

Mr. C. P. LESLIE also asked permission of the house to explain his vote, but it was refused, and he voted aye.

Mr. C. P. LESLIE moved a reconsideration of the vote whereby the report of the Committee on Rules and Regulations was adopted. Pending this, the President announced the presence in the Convention of Bishop Janes, of New York, and introduced him to the Convention.

Mr. C. P. LESLIE. A few moments ago when the report of the Committee was read, I sat in my place and opposed it.

I say if there was such a thing as deadly opposition to the report of a Committee, then I am deadly opposed to this. I did not suppose there was a member of the house who, when the yeas and nays were called, would announce to the people of this State that they were in favor of sitting here, leeching upon the people, and drawing one dollar more than was absolutely necessary.

Every one knows it is necessary to discharge our duties as quickly as

74

possible. It was astonishing that any man would have it go to the world
that he wanted to continue to sit here indefinitely, so as to get the last dollar or the last cent from the poor unfortunate people of the State? We
must know how sensible men will look at it, and it behooves us to act
with sense and judgment. We may not be able to get as much money as
some of us want; but I will vote right, vote for justice, vote on the side of
the people, and for the interest of the party. I desire that we shall be
above the suspicion of our enemies that we are working to get the last dollar or the last cent out of the Treasury. What will be said of us at a time
like this, when everybody is watching our action, when we are appealed
to by our friends to hurry up, if we postpone the business and vote for
only one session a day? Whoever desired to vote against two sessions,
I want their names published, so that the people of the State can mark
them down as they deserve to be marked. I hope every man who wants
to do what is right will vote against that report.

There are some members of the body always ready to give a convenient excuse for everything they do. They are Conservative when it is
policy to be Conservative, and they are the most Radical men in the
world when it is policy to be Radical. These same men were able to
twist their conscience which ever way it suited them, and they were
always trying to prove nothing could be gained by two sessions. But
when it came to be figured up it means : "I want the last eleven dollars
I can get." That was just what it meant, and nothing else. These
men, who have no earthly business to engage in at home, want to stay
here and get their per diem.

Mr. R. C. DeLARGE rose to a point of order. The member was
speaking of the motives that induced others to vote.

The PRESIDENT said if the member on the floor had spoken anything of a personal character, the party objecting could write down the
objectionable language and submit it to the house.

Mr. R. C. DeLARGE withdrew his objection.

Mr. C. P. LESLIE. I am inside the Club House to-day, and there is
no one to molest me or make me afraid. I know in my heart we are
doing wrong if we adopt the report. The laugh may be against me,
because the money is against me, but if we adopt that report it will hurt
us as a party. Every dollar we take from the Treasury, unless we can
furnish a really good excuse, it will help our foes. We have been over
a month in session, and I know what our opponents will say. They will
say, "this great ring-streaked-and-striped Convention, down at the
Club House, when there was a chance of expediting business, refused to
do it. Those fellows never had any business before, never had any

money, and they intend to keep their hands in the State Treasury. They kept their seats and voted solidly against a measure to facilitate and get through their business. Until they voted "yea," you could not get them to look up or down, toward heaven or toward the earth. I tell you it will ring in the ears of the delegates and in the ears of the peo_ ple of this country, and the people of the North ; and even the people of the old Radical State of Massachusetts will pronounce their judgment upon us. I tell you this thing ought not to be.

Mr. B. F. RANDOLPH. I am favor of reconsidering the motion whereby the report of the Committee was adopted. I propose in a few words to appeal to your judgment and calm reason. While I am in favor of reconsideration, in the first place, allow me to say that I care not what outsiders, rebels, or anybody else may say. I hold, we ought to do what we conceive to be our duty. This question should be discussed on its merits. We now have one session a day. We meet at half past 10 o'clock in the morning, and about 11 o'clock get to business. We adjourn at half past 2. That gives us only about three hours and a half to work. We work then about three hours and a half out of twenty-four. Well now, it is a fact, and I defy any man upon this floor to dispute it, the men who voted to adopt the report of the Committee are not the working men of the Convention. They are not the working men upon this floor. It seems to me it is a pretty nice thing to get eleven dollars a day, if it is in bills receivable, they are now selling at eighty-two cents ; and to come here and spend two or three hours in the forenoon, and then go and pass all the afternoon and evening among our friends. Look at Congress. Congress holds in session sometimes six months out of the year, and the greater part of the time have two sessions a day. Nearly all the State Legislatures have very frequently two sessions a day, and they continue in session from three to four months in the year. I know we are neither Congress nor the Legislature, but we are a Convention of the people of South Carolina, called in an emergency. It becomes us to do our work just as speedily as possible. Our Constitution should be before the people of South Carolina now for their ratification. The word comes from Washington, hurry up. I want to appeal to those men who voted against two sessions, and ask them why they voted for only one session a day.

Mr. R. B. ELLIOTT. I regard the language of the delegate as insulting. He has already charged that those who oppose two sessions a day do not work, either in Committee or on the floor. He said, "In fact they do not work at all." I demand that he shall either apologize to the Convention, or take his seat.

The PRESIDENT. The Chair can scarcely deem these remarks of so personal a nature as to require an explanation from the speaker. It is a mere charge that the members of the Committee do not work on the floor, or in the house at all.

The question was then taken as to whether the gentleman should be allowed to proceed in his speech, and a division of the house being taken, resulted 48 to 48.

The PRESIDENT. It becomes the duty of the Chair to exercise his privilege. It is impossible in a deliberative assembly to check the latitude of debate so as to prevent gentlemen sometimes making remarks that may be offensive to some gentlemen in the room. But the offence may be committed and not intended, having arisen in the heat or excitement of debate. When remarks are so offensive as to attack the personal character of any gentleman, they should always be checked. But if the house takes notice of every little act of discourtesy in debate, not an actual charge against the character of a member, it would be continually interrupted in its business, and no gentleman would be able to get through his speech. The Chair, believing that the gentleman did not intend any personal application, but was rather strengthening his argument, he is compelled to cast his vote aye, and permit the gentleman to proceed. The casting vote is equivalent to a decision that the gentleman has not transgressed the rules of order.

Mr. B. F. RANDOLPH. I am sure it was far from my intention to say anything which had any tendency to criminate any gentleman upon this floor. No one regrets when any such thing is said more than I. As the Chair has said, I must admit, sometimes in the heat of debate, I may say things which seem unreasonable. I was arguing in favor of two sessions a day, and I see no reason why we should not have two sessions. We can then do double the work, enable us to get through here, and get our representatives in Congress. I submit it to the cool and candid judgment of every delegate upon the floor, if it would not be better to get our Constitution before the people as soon as possible.

Mr. A. J. RANSIER. I do not rise to make a speech, for I hope I have more feeling for the condition of the poor people in this State, and take it more at heart, than to occupy the time of the house on unimportant questions like this. I favored the adoption of the Committee's report, not that I was not in favor of two sessions, for I believe I had the honor of introducing the first resolution for a prolongation of the session, changing the time. We then met from 12 to 3, and at present from half past 10 A. M. to half past 3 P. M. Therefore, my record upon that point is as favorable as the gentleman from Barnwell (Mr.

LESLIE), or any other member. I hope this motion to reconsider will not prevail. It was my intention, on moving for the adoption of the Committee's report, to make another proposition, fixing the hours of the Convention from 10 A. M. to 2 P. M., and from 4 P. M. to 6 P. M. I think that would meet the approbation of this house. I think we will all agree that too much time has been wasted. I am not opposed to two sessions, but I am opposed to meeting at 10, then adjourning at 2, and throwing away five hours, and to coming here at 7 in the evening and remaining until 10 at night. I object to a night, but not an afternoon, session. I am very much tempted to make a defence of myself, and on part of the fifty-four gentlemen who voted with me, from the ungentlemanly assaults made by some of those who have spoken. I feel as much for the poor people of this State as the gentleman from Barnwell. I regard the language he used as insulting. I move to lay the motion to reconsider on the table.

The PRESIDENT. If the report is adopted, and the motion or resolution which has reference to that is laid on the table, it cannot again be taken up to-day, nor do I know any manner in which it can be taken up at any future period. If the house refuses the present motion, then it is in the power of the house to amend the report.

Mr. C. P. LESLIE. Suppose this motion to reconsider the vote prevails, is the house in a condition to entertain any proposition which will amend the report?

The PRESIDENT. The House can either refer it back, or amend it, as they please.

Mr. F. J. MOSES, Jr. A motion has been made to lay the motion to reconsider on the table. On that question I call for the ayes and nays.

The ayes and nays were ordered, and resulted as follows:

AYES—Messrs. Becker, Bowen, Burton, Brockenton, Byas, E. J. Cain, Chamberlain, Collins, Crews, Davis, Elliott, Harris, Chas. D. Hayne, Humbird, Jenks, Jervey, Henry Jones, Lang, Langley, Mayer, W. J. McKinlay, W. McKinlay, McDaniels, Mead, Miller, Moses, Nance, Nelson, Owens, Pillsbury, Ransier, Rivers, Sanders, Stubbs, Augustus Thompson, Webb, White, Williamson—38.

NAYS—The President, Messrs. Allen, Alexander, Arnim, Bell, Bonum, Bryce, Camp, Coghlan, Chestnut, Clinton, Cooke, Corley, Craig, Darrington, DeLarge, Dill, Donaldson, Driffle, Duncan, Edwards, Foster, Gentry, Goss, Gray, Jas. N. Hayne, Henderson, Holmes, Jacobs, Jillson, Samuel Johnson, W. B. Johnson, J. W. Johnson, L. B. Johnson, W. E. Johnston, Joiner, Chas. Jones, George Lee, Samuel Lee, Lomax, Leslie, E. W. M. Mackey, Mauldin, Middleton, Millford, Neagle, Newell, Nuckles, Parker, Randolph, Rainey, Richmond, Runion, Rutland, Sasportas, Shrewsbury, Smalls, Swails, Thomas, B. A. Thompson, S. B. Thompson, Viney,

Whittemore, F. E. Wilder, Chas. M. Wilder, Wingo, Wooley, Wright—69.

ABSENT—Messrs. Boozer, R. H. Cain, Cardozo, Dickson, Dogan, Hunter, Hurley, Jackson, Nash, Olsen, Perry, Robertson, Rose, Whipper—14.

So the house refused to lay the motion to reconsider on the table, and the motion to reconsider was agreed to.

Mr. R. C. DeLARGE moved to amend the report so as to make it read thus, "respectfully recommend that the house have two sessions, as follows: From half past 10 A. M. to 2 P. M., and from 4 to 7 P. M."

I trust this motion will prevail. I desire to have two sessions. I am indeed glad to find after the attempt of my colleague from Charleston (Mr. RANSIER), to get this house to consent to have two sessions, that the very men who so earnestly opposed it at that time, have at last become convinced that they are putting their hands into the pockets of the State Treasury too deeply. Allow me to exclaim, "oh consistency, thou art a jewel!" I am, indeed, glad to find that a man, who professes to have the honor to represent a district to which he does not belong, whose conscience will allow him to charge twenty cents mileage, and give an account to the Sergeant-at-Arms for miles he never traveled, should have awakened to a sense of righteousness.

I am prepared to do anything; to remain here from daylight until dark. My only reason for voting yea on the first vote, was on account of the discourtesy shown me by the house in refusing to let me explain my vote. When I find an account of thirty-two dollars and nine cents against the State Treasury, placed in the hands of the Sergeant-at-Arms by the gentleman from Orangeburg for miles he never traveled, I think in such a state of things we should certainly have two sessions, and bring this Convention to a close.

Mr. B. F. RANDOLPH. I think it is due to myself, coming from Orangeburg, to ask to what gentleman the delegate refers?

Mr. R. C. DeLARGE. I refer to the gentleman from Orangeburg.

Mr. B. F. RANDOLPH. The charge is false.

Mr. A. J. RANSIER. I call the gentleman to order for charging a member with falsehood.

The PRESIDENT. The Chair decides that remark entirely out of order.

Mr. R. B. ELLIOTT. I move that the gentleman be reprimanded by the Chair.

The motion was agreed to.

The PRESIDENT requested Mr. RANDOLPH to step in front.

On his appearance in front of the President's stand, the latter said that it was unnecessary for the Chair to say anything more than that the member had already heard the voice of the house on the subject. The member's own good sense would make its own reprimand.

Mr. R. C. DeLARGE said he held in his hand the mileage account handed to the Sergeant at-Arms with the name of the party.

The PRESIDENT called the member to order. If any gentleman was charged with official misconduct, the charges should be reduced to writing and presented to the Chair.

Mr. R. C. DeLARGE continued. I trust this amendment will be adopted, we will then have seven hours for work, and our business will be pushed forward. I think we can work better from four to seven in the afternoon, than from seven to ten at night.

Mr. R. B. ELLIOTT. As one who voted in favor of the adoption of the report of the Committee, I think it due to myself to make a few remarks. I am as anxious to have the business of this house transacted in as speedy a manner as any other member upon the floor. I have not wasted much of the time of this Convention in useless debate; not as much, I am sure, as some of the members who said this morning that we were not anxious to get away from here. I arose this morning to ask the gentlemen from Orangeburg a question, but he refused to allow me that privilege. He afterwards stated that those who opposed the two sessions, were men who did no work either in Committee or on the floor. As one of those who opposed the resolution, I contend I am as capable of doing as much work as that gentleman, and I consider I have done as much. I think it comes with ill grace from that particular gentleman to charge other members with doing nothing. Some of the gentlemen who are so anxious for two sessions, hardly attend the one session we have now. They spend most of their time outside instead of inside the hall; yet they profess to be very anxious to facilitate the business of the Convention. They are anxious, perhaps, to have the opportunity to make two speeches a day instead of one. I am in favor of spending as much time as possible in transacting the business of the Convention as anybody else. I would be willing to spend the entire day instead of three or four hours at night. I believe it would be impracticable for us to have a night session from seven to ten o'clock. If the resolution of the gentleman from Charleston is brought up, I shall vote for it. I am in favor of two sessions, if the hours are fixed as proposed in his amendment, but I am not willing to come here at seven o'clock at night and sit until ten o'clock. I do not believe there are many members who will do that, and I think even some of the gentlemen who would vote for it, when their names are called, will be absent; but I do not think it necessary to vent our spleen by charging members who do not advocate it with being desirous of taking the last dollar out of the State Treasury. I observe those gentlemen who made the charge, are just as eager as anybody else when the time comes to receive their pay, and they are here just as promptly as anybody else at such times. I have not heard of any of them giving any thing to the orphans and widows in the State. The gentleman from Barnwell (Mr. LESLIE) declares that those who oppose it are anxious to get the last dollar and the last cent out of the Treasury of the State. I have simply to say, I believe he is just as anxious to get it as anybody else. I believe the gentleman from Orangeburg would have done better to have kept still.

Mr. B. O. DUNCAN. I offer the following amendment: "That we meet at ten o'clock in the forenoon, and adjourn at three o'clock;" that will give us five hours. The plan proposed by the gentleman from Charleston gives us six hours and a half.

The amendment was not agreed to.

Mr. C. M. WILDER. I move the following amendment:

Resolved, That on and after the 27th inst., the Convention meet at half-past ten, A. M., and adjourn at half-past one, P. M.; and meet again at four o'clock, P. M., and adjourn at seven.

The amendment was not agreed to.

Mr. F. J. MOSES, Jr., offered the following, which was not agreed to :

Resolved, That this Convention will hold but one session a day, which session shall be from 3 P. M. to half past 10 P. M.

Mr. L. S. LANGLEY offered the following, as a substitute:

Resolved, That hereafter this Convention have two sessions a day: a morning session, to begin at 10 A. M., and adjourn at 1 P. M., and an afternoon session, to commence at 3 P. M. and adjourn at 6 P. M.

Mr. L. S. LANGLEY. I desire to say a word on that resolution. I was in favor of the adoption of the report of the Committee, which recommended to lay a certain resolution on the table. I believed the afternoon session called for by that resolution, from 7 to 10, is too long. I was one of the members of the Convention who early brought forward a resolution here to have two sessions a day. I offered a resolution more than three weeks ago that was referred to the Committee on Rules and Regulations, who recommended that it be laid on the table. Some of the men who to-day advocated, with great warmth, two sessions, then voted to lay that same resolution on the table. It has been charged that some of the members who voted for the adoption of the report of the Committee are not working members. I know we have not all had the honor of being the acting Chairman of the Committee on the Miscellaneous Portions of the Constitution. It was considered equivalent to killing a measure to refer it to that Committee, of which the gentleman from Orangeburg has the honor to be Chairman.

Mr. B. F. RANDOLPH. I object to the language the gentleman.

Mr. L. S. LANGLEY. It has been said it would facilitate the business of the Convention by having two sessions a day. If true, I for one would be the last member to rise in my place and object. I believe the Louisiana Constitutional Convention, also the Virginia and Georgia Conventions, have two sessions a day. They met a month sooner than we did, and we find them in session to-day. I believe we have got along with our Constitution further than any other State, save Alabama and Florida. The gentleman from Barnwell (Mr. LESLIE) rose in his place here, and expressed his doubts of the gentlemen who saw fit to differ with him, and voted in favor of the adoption of the report of the Committee. I must say I doubt the sincerity of the gentleman. I do it for this reason; he is in the habit, when he gets up, and speaking for his people, of shedding tears, but he did not do it to-day.

Mr. C. P. LESLIE. Yes, but I don't speak one way and vote another.

Mr. L. S. LANGLEY. There is not a gentleman on this floor who wants to facilitate the business of this Convention more than I do. As a proof of that, I refer to the fact that I introduced a resolution for this very purpose, and some of those gentlemen clamoring and impugning bad motives to others are the very ones who voted that resolution down. I am in favor of two sessions a day, but am opposed to having a session after dark.

Mr. H. E. HAYNE. We have been since half past ten o'clock, and it is now twenty minutes to one, discussing whether we shall have two sessions a day or one. I think it would be economy for us to have one long session that would be as good as two sessions. The best remedy, perhaps, would be to do less talking, and more real working.

Mr. J. S. CRAIG. I voted on a former occasion, in the early part of the session, against two sessions, with the view of then allowing the Standing Committees time to prepare their work. Now, that the Committees are through, I am in favor of our devoting more time to getting through the work of the Convention.

The previous question was demanded, and the demand sustained.

75

The question was then taken on the several amendments offered, and all, with the exception of that proposed by Mr. LANGLEY, rejected.

The amendment of Mr. LANGLEY, fixing the sessions from 10 A. M to 1 P. M., and from 3 P. M. to 6 P. M., was agreed to.

Mr. F. J. MOSES, Jr., requested that his name be recorded against the amendment.

Mr. B. F. RANDOLPH moved that the vote, whereby the amendment was agreed to, be reconsidered, and that the motion for reconsideration be laid on the table, which was agreed to.

Mr. C. C. BOWEN asked leave to record his vote against the amendment providing for two sessions a day.

Mr. D. H. CHAMBERLAIN made a similar request.

Mr. S. A SWAILS made a report of the Committee on Rules and Regulations, on a resolution declaring that no pay be drawn by the members after the fifth of March. The Committee recommend that the resolution be laid on the table.

Mr. B. BYAS moved the adoption of the report.

Mr. C. C. BOWEN moved that the ayes and nays be taken, and those voting against receiving pay after the fifth of March get no pay.

The CHAIR ruled the motion out of order.

Mr. J. S. CRAIG. I do not agree with the report as it stands. I propose we strike out fifth and say the tenth of March, and then adopt the report.

Mr. J. H. JENKS. I move further to amend by making it the twenty-fifth of March.

Mr. S. G. W. DILL moved that the amendments be indefinitely postponed.

Mr. L. S. LANGLEY. I am decidedly in favor of the report of the Committee, which proposes to lay the resolution on the table. That resolution proposes that, unless we finish our work by the fifth of March. we shall receive no pay. Why, we would in that event have no quorum. Is it to be supposed that the members would remain, incurring expenses and receiving no pay to meet those expenses. The majority of the members cannot afford it, though they might otherwise be willing. If that resolution is adopted, I predict that the fifth of March will leave us without a quorum, and unless we have framed a Constitution prior to that time, it will fall to the ground.

Pending the further consideration of the report, the hour of one having arrived, the Convention adjourned.

AFTERNOON SESSION.

The Convention re-assembled at 3 P. M., and was called to order by the PRESIDENT.

The unfinished business, being the report of the Committee on Rules and Regulations, on a resolution stopping the pay of members after the fifth of March, was taken up.

Mr. T. K. SASPORTAS. I move to amend the resolution so as to make it the fifteenth of March.

Mr. C. P. LESLIE moved that after the tenth of March the members of the Convention shall receive no per diem.

Mr. J. J. WRIGHT moved to lay the matter on the table.

Mr. S. G. W. DILL moved the indefinite postponement of the subject.

Mr. F. J. MOSES, Jr., called for the yeas and nays, which was not sustained.

Mr. J. J. WRIGHT again moved to lay the whole matter on the table, and the motion was agreed to.

Mr. J. M. RUNION moved to reconsider, and that the motion of reconsideration be laid on the table, which was agreed to.

Mr. E. W. M. MACKEY moved to take up the unfinished business, which was the report of the Committee on the Judiciary.

Mr. W. E. ROSE, Chairman of the Committee on Petitions, asked and obtained leave to make the following report:

The Committee to whom the preamble and resolutions were referred relative to Benjamin O'Hagan, respectfully report that they have had the same under consideration, and no proof in the form of affidavit or otherwise, of persons who could furnish proof having been furnished of the truth of the matters and things alleged in said preamble and resolutions, your Committee recommend that the same be laid on the table, and the Committee be discharged from further consideration of the same.

Mr. L. S. LANGLEY moved that the report of the Committee be adopted.

Mr. A. C. RICHMOND. There are facts connected with that petition which are well known, though no affidavits have been produced in proof of the correctness of some of the statements in the petition. It is a very important fact though that a man is in jail, sentenced to be hung, and it is generally known to all classes of people who live in the district where the offence took place, that the petitioner is insane, and that he would not of his own accord have become implicated or connected with the transaction. It was hardly to be expected, though I presented the petition, that I should run all over the country for the purpose of bringing half a dozen white persons to the Club House in this city. This man is believed by all persons living in his section of country to be innocent. I believe if the matter goes to the Governor, the sentence will be changed very much; but it may still leave him in jail for a long time, whereas I think he should be released at once.

Mr. C. C. BOWEN. I am sorry to see such a total disregard of humanity as is exhibited here when a man's life is in the scale. I certainly think the case is one which demands the attention of the Convention, and one not to be treated lightly. I have been informed that after the return of a true bill in this case, a combination was entered into with the prosecuting attorney, by which the person who was the real perpetrator of the crime turned States' evidence, and the petitioner, who is regarded as *non compos mentis*, who happened to be present only, was put upon trial and convicted by this States' evidence of having committed the deed. If such are the facts, they should be brought to light. I hope the Convention will not lay the petition on the table, but give the case such consideration as humanity and justice demands.

Mr. L. S. LANGLEY called for the reading of the petition, which was accordingly read by the Clerk.

Mr. L. S. LANGLEY. On the first reading of the petition I was unable to hear distinctly, and was not sufficiently acquainted with its character. I supposed it to be the petition of a certain individual praying the Convention to recommend the removal of his disabilities. It was under that impression that I made the motion for the adoption of the report. I now withdraw my motion.

Mr. R. C. DeLARGE. I trust the Convention will consider the importance of the petition presented to it. I do not know as to whether other members have had the advantage of knowing as much about this case as I have. I have read everything connected with the trial. So far as my judgment goes, I have seen no substantial reason to convict the petitioner. I trust we shall have a thorough investigation, and I intend to make a motion, which I trust will be supported by every member of this house. I desire to do justice to a poor man who is *non compos mentis*, an idiot. I move that this report and the petition be referred to the Committee on the Judiciary to investigate, and that they be empowered to send for persons and papers.

Mr. R. J. DONALDSON. Is that a competent motion for this body to entertain. I do not think we have the authority to send for persons and papers.

Mr. B. F. WHITTEMORE. I move that the petition and report be referred to the Committee on the Judiciary, and that they be instructed to wait upon Brevet Major-General E. R. S. Canby, present the case to him, and request such attention to it as its importance may demand.

Mr. D. H. CHAMBERLAIN. I hope the amendment of the gentleman from Darlington (Mr. WHITTEMORE) will not prevail. The Judiciary Committee should report to this body, and whatever action the Convention may take should be made known and communicated to the Commanding General through this body officially by its presiding officer. I am in favor of an official investigation. There can be no harm in authorizing the Judiciary Committee to send for persons and papers, even if they do not find authority for it. I apprehend this, like all legislative bodies representing the sovereign people of the State, has that power. But, so as to settle that question, I hope the motion to refer this matter to the Judiciary Committee, with power to send for persons and papers, will be adopted.

Mr. S. G. W. DILL. I claim that we have no such power, nor can our Constitution be effective until after its ratification by the people. I hope the petition will be acted upon at once.

Mr. R. B. ELLIOTT. I agree with the gentleman, and hope the petition will not be referred to any other Committee. I think it can be acted upon without dwelling upon it any longer. It is sufficient for us to know that a man's life is in danger. It is sufficient for us to know even that the report which has come to us is based upon the rumor that a man did not receive justice at the hands of the Judges who tried him, and the petition simply asks Brevet Major-General E. R. S. Canby to arrest the execution of the sentence of that man, for the purpose of giving the man and his friends an opportunity to have justice done him. I see no objection to make the request of Brevet Major-General E. R. S. Canby, and think the Convention can do it without wasting any further time. It is only a few days ago that the Governor of the State was compelled, from facts brought to his knowledge, to commute the sentence of a man about to be hung. Efforts were made in behalf of that man for nearly a year, during which time he was in jail under sentence of death. A few days ago the Governor became convinced that the man was not guilty of the crime. I hope we shall act upon this matter ourselves without reference to any other Committee.

Mr. C. P. LESLIE offered the following as a substitute:

WHEREAS, it is represented that Benjamin O'Hagan, of St. John's Berkley, is now confined in prison under sentence of death, and charged, among other things, with having committed arson; and, whereas, the Convention has had brought to its attention some statements which appear to disprove the charge,

Resolved, That this Convention request Brevet Major-General E. R. S. Canby to stay the sentence, and cause all the facts connected with the case to be immediately investigated, and to take such action forthwith as will afford speedy and effectual justice.

Mr. J. M. RUTLAND. I think this is all wrong, all a mistake. I am not opposed to doing something for this unfortunate man. but I think we are taking the wrong course. All such applications as this, according to the laws of the State, and the practice heretofore, should be made to the Governor. It is the law in all the States, and even our own Constitution in its present embryo condition gives this power to the Governor. If this Convention desires to do anything in behalf of this unfortunate man, they should do it in the form of a petition to the Governor.

Mr. R. C. DeLARGE. I would like to ask who has the supreme power in what was once the State of South Carolina, the Governor or General Canby?

Mr. J. M. RUTLAND. Governor Orr is acting in this capacity, and, to my certain knowledge, did act in a similar case the other day. General Canby does not pretend to interfere in matters of this sort. If this Convention will get up a petition, sign it, and send it to the Governor, I will guarantee he will respect that petition, and, no doubt, will do what the Convention asks him to do in the premises. I admit, the military power is supreme, and if they choose, they can take the matter in their own hands. But, I insist, as affairs stand, the true and proper course is to address the Governor. I will, in such a case, be among the first to sign any paper, and I have no doubt, from his respect for this body, from his speech delivered the other evening, but that he will do anything reasonable the Convention may ask of him.

Mr. A. C. RICHMOND. It seems to me out of the line of our duty to authorize a Committee to send for persons and papers. We are here to frame a Constitution, and as these things casually come up we can give them a respectful hearing. But I think we would do better to adopt the amendment of the gentleman from Darlington, and refer the whole matter to General Canby.

Mr. A J. RANSIER. I sincerly hope the substitute offered by the gentleman from Barnwell will prevail. I regard General Canby as the proper party to whom we should send this petition, and beg his attention to the matter. I hope the petition will be sent direct to General Canby.

Mr. C. C. BOWEN. It would be a strange proceeding to send this petition and case to General Canby, without furnishing him with all the information it is in our power to procure. If the Committee find sufficient grounds to ask a hearing from General Canby, then we can go there; but if, perhaps, they should find the man properly convicted, that will be the end of it. In regard to the power of the Convention to send for persons and papers, I have not the slightest doubt. Nobody ever heard of a legislative body of a State but what had the power to send for persons and papers. I hope the petition and report will be referred to a Committee to investigate the case, before application is made to either General Canby or Governor Orr.

Mr. C. P. LESLIE. When a man's life is in jeopardy, the remedy, if any, is direct, immediate action. Such a case is now before this body, and we should not lose one second of time. An honorable member represents that a certain party is confined in prison to be executed next month. He further represents that the citizens in the neighborhood believe he is unjustly in prison, and alleges certain facts. The honorable position of the gentleman from Berkley leaves no doubt in my mind that the facts stated by him are true. I am willing to send for persons and papers, but I am not willing the man's life should be kept in jeopardy while we are searching for witnesses. If we can represent to General Canby that we have reason to believe that this poor man has been wrongfully punished and sentenced, and request him to examine into the facts, the General, in less than three days, will have the facts before him, and justice done.

Mr. J. J. WRIGHT. There is a certain degree of dignity to which this body is entitled, and I, for one, shall strive to maintain that dignity. There is but one course to pursue in this matter, and that is the right course. The gentleman from Fairfield (Mr. RUTLAND) says we have no right to petition General Canby in this matter, but that Governor Orr has the supreme power of the State at present. We are aware of that, aware that we are acting under certain laws of the State; but we must remember that wherever the Provisional Governor or the Courts fail to mete out justice, a party has the prerogative to bring his case before the military, and if he makes the request of this Convention, it is our duty to forward that request to General Canby, and ask him to make the investigation. But I hope we will first give this matter due consideration, and that it will be referred to the Judiciary Committee, that they may take such steps as to bring the evidence that will convince every person here of their duty in the premises, and as to whether or not it is our bounden duty to make the petition to General Canby to investigate the case. I consider that course no disrespect to Governor Orr. The civil authorities have already determined and settled this matter, and we are to ascertain whether they have acted justly.

Mr. W. E. ROSE. The Committee on Petitions had no facts before them. They studied the matter over very carefully and cautiously, but had no evidence of the truth of the matter stated in the petition. We were surprised that no evidence was furnished the Committee. Major Corbin, one of the solicitors, stated that it was impossible for anybody to act upon the papers before the Committee, and that the mover of the resolution should have prepared himself with the evidence to satisfy the Committee of the truthfulness of the petition.

The question was then taken on the motion of Mr. DeLARGE to commit the report and petition to the Committee on the Judiciary, and that they be empowered to send for persons and papers, and report the result of their investigation to the house, and the motion was agreed to.

Mr. C. C. BOWEN, from the Judiciary Committee, submitted the following report:

The Committee on the Judiciary, to whom was referred a resolution in regard to attorneys, and the practice of law, respectfully report that they have had the same under consideration, and respectfully recommend that the Convention pass the following resolution:

Resolved, That the General commanding this Military District be requested to issue an order applicable to the State of South Carolina, authorizing any attorney, solicitor, or counsellor, admitted to practice in the Courts of the United States, or in any Court of record in any State, and resident in this State, to appear and practice in all the Courts of this State, and that any male person twenty-one years of age, who is a citizen of the State, and who satisfies the Court of Common Pleas and General Sessions, or District Court of this State, that he possesses the requisite learning, may be licensed to practice in all of the Courts of this State, upon his taking the usual oath.

Mr. E. W. M. MACKEY moved the adoption of the report.

Mr. T. J. ROBERTSON. I had the honor of introducing that resolution, and a few words of explanation becomes necessary.

I have been informed that, according to the custom heretofore in South Carolina, no attorney nor solicitor, no matter how high his standing, not even the Hon. Caleb Cushing, can practice in our Courts without having gone through a certain process of examination. I offered that resolution so as to put all from this or from other States coming here on an equal footing with the other States. No attorney could be introduced and, by motion, admitted to practice in our Courts; and I have witnessed an attorney and solicitor of the United States Court refused permission to practice in the Court of Common Pleas and General Sessions. I want to see this changed, so that any regular practicing attorney of any other

State shall have the same privilege enjoyed in any other State. I hope the resolution will meet with the unanimous consent of the Convention.

Mr. J. M. RUTLAND. The practice heretofore has been to admit, upon a motion merely, any gentleman who was a lawyer of three years' standing in any State, without going through a regular examination. I hope the matter will be so amended, so that any gentleman who has been practicing law for three years may be admitted without examination. If he has not practiced that length of time, it might be as well for himself, as well as for his clients, that he should undergo an examination.

Mr. J. S. CRAIG moved to strike out the words " and resident in this State." He wished citizens to have the privilege of employing counsel from any part of the United States they desired.

The amendment was not adopted.

The question occurring on the adoption of the report, it was carried.

Mr. S. G. W. DILL offered the following resolution, which was referred to the Committee on Franchise and Elections :

Resolved, That every male person over the age of twenty-one years, shall be a good and legal voter in all elections given to the people of this State, unless otherwise disqualified by crime, and that this State shall recognize no other suffrage but universal.

Mr. S. G. W. DILL offered the following resolution, which was referred to the Committee on the Miscellaneous Provisions of the Constitution :

Resolved by the Convention, That on the ratification of the Constitution of this State, now forming by this Convention, that every civil office in the State be declared vacant of its present incumbent.

Mr. S. G. W. DILL submitted the following resolution, which was referred to the Committee on Finance :

Resolved by this Convention, That the members of this Convention be paid from the day they left their homes until they return to the same ; allowing them the same number of days to return that it did to come.

The unfinished business, being the consideration of the report of the Committee on the Judiciary, section one, was taken up.

Mr. J. S. CRAIG offered the following substitute :

The Judicial power of this State shall be vested in a Supreme Court, a Court of Common Pleas, having civil jurisdiction, and a Court, of

76

General Sessions with criminal jurisdiction only, and such other inferior Courts as may be provided for by the General Assembly.

Mr. J. M. RUNION moved to amend in the third line, by inserting "Courts of" before Justices of the Peace, so as to read, " and in Courts of Justices of the Peace."

Mr. N. G. PARKER. I do not propose to discuss this matter, but to produce some facts bearing upon the question of inserting the words " Courts of." I find that in the Constitutions of fifteen States of the Union the identical words used in this section, namely, "in Justices of the Peace." I know of no State that adopts the language "in Courts of Justices of the Peace." I know nothing about State Courts, but I know there are Courts of Magistrates which Justices of the Peace preside over. To insert these words, " Courts of Justices of the Peace," is something that never has existed; and in the States of Oregon, California, Delaware, Nevada, Ohio, Pennsylvania, and several others, the words are used precisely as they are here. I know this Judicial report has received great attention, not only by the legal profession in this body, but by distinguished legal gentlemen outside the Convention. On a former occasion, when this section was under discussion, the proposed amendment was opposed by the Chairman of the Judiciary Committee, and, as the Chairman, under our rules cannot speak again upon the same subject, I have risen for the purpose of calling attention to it. I hope the amendment will not be adopted, but that we will govern ourselves by precedents, and that the section will pass as it now reads.

Mr. R. B. ELLIOTT. I hope the section will be adopted as it stands without inserting the words " Courts of," for I do not know whether in this State, or in a great many other States, there are such Courts as Courts of Justices of the Peace. The section has defined in what the Judicial power of the State shall be vested. It is just the same as the devision of Executive power, which is vested in a Chief Magistrate. The other day some gentlemen asked the question whether the Judicial power should be vested in the animal, that is, in the Justices of the Peace themselves. I say it should be vested in these very animals. A Justice of the Peace in some States of the Union has the power to order arrests, issue warrants, etc., but has no power to try a case. I think that was the object of the Judiciary Committee in submitting this section for the consideration of the Convention. I do not think the substitute of the gentleman from Colleton (Mr. CRAIG) is a proper substitute for this section, and I, therefore, move its indefinite postponement.

Mr. J. M. RUNION moved the indefinite postponement of the amendment offered by the gentleman from Fairfield (Mr. RUTLAND), which requires the insertion of the word "Courts," so as to read "in Courts of Justices of the Peace."

Mr. L. S. LANGLEY. I hope that motion will not prevail. It seems to me if a party is tried by a Justice of the Peace, it is the same as a regular Court of the country. I see no objection to the word "Court" being placed between "in" and "Justices of the Peace."

Mr. WM. J. McKINLAY. I hope the motion for an indefinite postponement of the amendment will be voted down, Justices of the Peace stand in the place of Magistrates, and it is not required that they should be lawyers. In our Bill of Rights, we have given them the power to take cognizance of cases where the punishment does not exceed one hundred dollars, and thirty days' imprisonment. I think it is placing too much power in one man's hands. It is true, it provides for the right of appeal, but after you go before the Court, and you have an opportunity to appeal, what satisfaction is it when your character is blasted?

Mr. R. B. ELLIOTT. I move the indefinite postponement of the substitute.

Mr. J. S. CRAIG. It seems to me there is a disposition here on the part of some to vote down every proposition made by certain members of this Convention. I offered the substitute in good faith. I believed it was better than the original section; that it covered the whole ground in fewer words, and was couched in better language. I think that substitute will commend itself to the good judgment of every member of the Convention.

Mr. B. BYAS. I am not one of those who feel disposed to treat lightly the work of the Committee, but I hope the substitute will be calmly considered. It appears to me to embrace all the ground, and covered by the section, and, at the same time, is more comprehensive. It provides, in addition, that the Legislature shall establish such inferior Courts as may be necessary, and I think this power should be left to that body.

Mr. W. E JOHNSTON. I think we have had sufficient debate upon this subject, and, therefore, move the previous question.

The call for the previous question was sustained.

Mr. C. C. BOWEN, Chairman of the Judiciary Committee. I have but a word to say. In drawing up this article pains was taken to obviate the District Courts. A few days ago, it will be remembered, a resolution was offered requesting Brevet Major General E. R. S. Canby to abolish the District Courts, and we now find members offering substitutes which would revive them. The words "inferior Courts," would allow the Legislature to establish District Courts.

The question was then taken on the substitute, and decided in the negative, and the first section passed to its third reading.

Section second was read as follows :

SECTION 2. The Supreme Court shall consist of three Judges, two of whom shall constitute a quorum. They shall be elected by a joint vote of the General Assembly for the term of six years, and shall continue in office until their successors shall be elected and qualified.

Mr. B. F. RANDOLPH moved to amend, in the second line, by inserting "they shall be appointed by the Governor, by and with the advice and consent of the Senate, and shall serve for the term of six years," etc.

Mr. J. M. RUNION moved to change the term of service to eight years instead of six.

Mr. B. F. RANDOLPH. My reasons for offering the amendment proposed are simply these : I think that Judges, above all other officers of the State, should be dependent upon the will and pleasure of the people as little as possible, and especially the Judges of the Supreme Court. The Judges of the Supreme Court of the United States are appointed by the President.

Mr. C. C. BOWEN. In how many States are the Judges appointed ?

Mr. B. F. RANDOLPH. We do not propose to go by the example of other States. We have for our example the Federal Government. They have succeeded admirably. I do not think the Chairman of the Judiciary Committee (Mr. BOWEN) can find any fault with the manner in which the Judges of the Supreme Court of the United States are appointed. To elect our Judges by a joint vote of the General Assembly may complicate the matter. The House and Senate may differ in their choice of men, and they may consume their time voting for candidates, without an election, during the session. It certainly makes Judges very dependent on the will and pleasure of the General Assembly.

Mr. J. K. JILLSON moved to strike out "six" and insert "ten,' making ten years the term of service.

Mr. H. E. HAYNE moved to amend by striking out the word "three" on the first line, and making it read as follows : "A Chief Justice and two Associate Judges, two of whom shall constitute a quorum."

Mr. C. M. WILDER moved the following amendment : Strike out all after the words "General Assembly," on second line, and insert, "and shall continue in office during good behavior."

Mr. R. C. DeLARGE moved to strike out on the first line the word "three" and insert "four."

Mr. J. J. WRIGHT moved to amend by striking out on the first line all after the word "of" and insert, "The Supreme Court shall consist of a Chief Justice and two Associate Judges, any two of whom shall constitute a quorum."

I hope we shall not move too hastily in this matter, and do anything that will give us cause for future regret. The gentleman from Orangeburg (Mr. RANDOLPH) wishes to amend by providing that the Chief Justice and Judges of the Supreme Court shall be appointed by the Governor, with the consent of the Senate. The objection he urges against the requirement of a joint vote of the General Assembly is that that body may disagree, and that we might be without a Chief Justice and Judges for some time. In the first place, the Judges are to be elected, and hold their offices until their successors are elected and qualified. Hence, that objection falls to the ground. We desire that every portion of the State of South Carolina shall have a voice in saying who shall or shall not be the persons who shall hold this great and all-important office of the State. The people of the different counties will elect their representatives and Senators to the General Assembly, which will elect the Judges of the Supreme Court. Hence, the voice of the people of the different counties will be heard in the election of these Judges.

He next urges that the Judges of the Supreme Court of the United States are appointed by the President of the United States, and cites that for our example. These Judges are appointed for life, or during good behavior. We do not want any person in this State to hold the office of Judge for life. We do not want any such appointments made. Chief Justice Taney was appointed for life, and every person here is well acquainted with his administration. If there is anything in the world that would induce me to assassinate a person, it would be because that person was trampling upon the liberties of the people, and that he was placed in such a position that he could not be removed in any other way. Let us not have them appointed for life. With regard to the term of office, I would fix it at ten years, which I think long enough. If we get a man in the Supreme Court who is not a good man, who is not a man who desires to mete out justice to the people, he can be impeached. Some will say, perhaps, that the impeachment of Judges is in the far distance, and that it does not occur once in a century.

Another objection to a long term is this. We are just laying the foundation for a new government. We have in our ranks but a few men of legal experience, capable of discharging the high duties incumbent upon a Judge, to acquit themselves in a manner acceptable to the people. There are men in the legal profession, men of ability and experience, liberal men, who are now ready to get upon the reconstruction train, and acknowledge the principles of progress and civilization, were it not for the fear of the prejudice of that public opinion which is opposed to our plan of reconstruction. Whenever these men come in and advocate the cause of humanity and justice, they will naturally be sought for to run the machinery of our State Government, and they will run it with fidelity to all the people, and we are ready and anxious to receive them, and place them in those high positions.

Mr. N. G. PARKER moved the indefinite postponement of all the amendments, with the exception of the amendment of the gentleman from Beaufort.

Mr. R. C. DeLARGE. I sincerely trust the motion to indefinitely postpone will not prevail. It is one of the most important subjects yet brought forward during the consideration of the Constitution now being framed. I hope we will consider the various amendments as they come up, and dispose of them as in the judgment of the Convention may be deemed just and proper. There are now several important amendments before the house, including one offered by myself, that the Supreme Court shall consist of four Judges instead of three. I trust all these motions for indefinite postponement will be voted down.

The question was then put on the motion to amend by inserting after the words Supreme Court " shall consist of a Chief Justice and two Associate Judges, any two of whom shall constitute a quorum."

Mr. J. M. RUTLAND. I dislike, after the insinuations made here about lawyers, to occupy your time, but hope you will have a little patience with us now, as we are on a branch of the Constitution, which is within the peculiar province of lawyers to discuss, and certainly is as important as any other branch of the Constitution. I do think it is not dealing fairly with gentlemen who offer amendments to move that they be indefinitely postponed, without hardly a hearing. I hope the house will listen patiently to the discussion upon any amendment, unless they are manifestly absurd and ridiculous. In so important a measure as this, we should not only be willing, but glad, to listen to the discussions ; and, after mature judgment, give their votes for or against each amendment as put to the house. Let us give each proposition a thorough investigation. If you establish a poor judiciary system, it is the worst thing you can impose upon a people. If they cannot get justice in a reasonably short time, they can never be a happy people. I hope, therefore, all motions to indefinitely postpone will be avoided, and that we give the subject that consideration its importance demands.

Mr. J. K. JILLSON moved that the motion to postpone indefinitely be laid on the table, which was agreed to.

Mr. J. D. BELL. Having seconded the amendment of the gentleman from Orangeburg, I wish to state a few of my reasons for doing so. The advantages of the appointment of Judges are that the responsibility is not divided among so many persons as to make each ones share almost nothing. The cool and deliberate expression of opinion of the highest officer of the State is an expression not often obtained from a numerous body of men, who, in the excitement always incident to such bodies, are often guided more by the faithfulness of their favorite candidate to the party than by his qualifications for the office. The joint action of the Senate, in confirming the nominee of the Governor, seems to me to unite all the advantages enjoyed by the present system with those of appointments by the Governor. I, therefore, hope the amendment of the gentleman from Orangeburg will prevail.

The CHAIR stated the question to be on the amendment proposed by the gentleman from Marion (Mr. H. E. HAYNE) to insert after the words "Supreme Court shall consist of a" the words "Chief Justice and two Associate Judges, any two of whom shall constitute a quorum."

The question being taken on this amendment, it was agreed to.

The next question was on the amendment of Mr. RANDOLPH to strike out, "that they shall be elected by the General Assembly," and insert, "shall be appointed by the Governor."

Mr. D. H. CHAMBERLAIN. On that question I desire to say a few words. This section would have been reported by the Committee on the Judiciary, if my voice alone had prevailed, so as to give the election of all the Judges of the State directly to the people. I have believed, and based my opinion upon experience, that the more direct the Judges are responsible to the people, the more certain are we to have justice done. The doctrine that the people are not to be trusted with the selection of those who are to administer justice to them, I believe to be wholly unfounded. I believe in the people. I believe they are just as competent to select their Judges as they are to select their Governors. I am aware that it is thought that while you can trust the people with everything else, you cannot trust them with the selection of their Judges. I have been unable to see any ground for that belief. We may be told that the system of electing Judges has proved a failure, and perhaps we shall be pointed to the State of New York, as an example. In that State, I admit, owing to peculiar influences, the elective judiciary has proved to be corrupt, and the system, as far as that State is concerned, has been a failure. But, at the same time, I can point to more than twenty States which have adopted the elective system without any diminution of respect on the part of the people to their Judges, or any diminution of integrity in those Judges. I say the argument of a failure of the system is to be confined to the State of New York alone, where, for obvious reasons, corruption prevails, not only with the Judges, but in every other department of the Government. The Legislature of that State is corrupt, and that corruption has forced itself, at last, into the judiciary of the State. The State of New York makes a single exception. All the other States of the Union have been gradually passing from the old system of appointment to the election of Judges directly by the people.

But while I am in favor of making the Judges directly responsible to the people, I have consented to the proposition to support by my vote the provision which gives the election of Judges to the General Assembly. I am willing to take that as a compromise, but when gentlemen go further than that, and ask that the whole power shall be put in the hands of one man, I cannot give my vote in its favor.

I am willing this should be removed one step from the direct action of the people, and that their most immediate representatives should have the power to elect the Judges; but to say they shall be appointed by the Governor, and confirmed by the Senate, is taking a step backward, and making them very nearly irresponsible to the people.

Mr. C. C. BOWEN. This matter was thoroughly discussed in Committee, and after a long struggle, it was agreed that the Judges of the Supreme Court should be elected by the General Assembly. Some of the members were urgent in giving their election to the people, and the consequence was a long and stubborn fight, when a compromise was made to give the election to the General Assembly. I hope the Convention will allow the section to stand as it is; it is but one step from the people, and it is to be supposed that the General Assembly will do what is right in the selection of Judges. I am opposed to their appointment by the Governor.

Mr. B. F. WHITTEMORE. I trust the section will be left just as it stands, in the hands of the representatives of the people. The General Assembly represents the people, and the people are willing to trust their interests with their representatives.

Mr. A. J. RANSIER. I trust the section will remain as it is, though I am disposed, as far as practicable, to make every officer holding a public trust directly responsible to the people. It has, however, been deemed advisable that the Judges of the Supreme Court should be one step removed from that direct responsibility. I believe this to be taking a wise middle course.

The hour having arrived, the PRESIDENT announced the Convention adjourned.

THIRTY-SEVENTH DAY.

Thursday, February 27, 1868.

The Convention assembled at half-past 10 A. M., and was called to order by the PRESIDENT.

Prayer was offered by the Rev. J. M. RUNION.

The roll was called, and a quorum answering to their names, the PRESIDENT announced the Convention ready to proceed to business.

The Journal of yesterday was read.

Mr. J. D. BELL. I move that so much of the Journal as relates to the reprimand of Mr. RANDOLPH be expunged.

Mr. D. H. CHAMBERLAIN. I trust that the motion will not prevail. While I entertain kind feelings for the gentleman from Orangeburg, I think it unwise to obliterate from the Journal of the Convention any part of its record of these proceedings.

The PRESIDENT. We have the example of the Congress of the United States that such motions are in order, although, strictly speaking, Journals cannot be changed. Instances are on record, however, in which Congress has expunged from its record the action of the body years after it has taken place.

Mr. L. S. LANGLEY. I hope the motion of my colleague from Beaufort will prevail. I voted in favor of reprimanding the gentleman, because I thought he was entirely out of order. Several times during the sitting of this body, members have used words just as objectionable as those of the gentleman from Orangeburg, and no notice was taken of it. I regret that gentlemen should so far forget themselves as to make use of this species of language, but inasmuch as the member from Orangeburg has been reprimanded by the Chair, the dignity of the Convention has been fully sustained.

Mr. WM. J. McKINLAY. I trust the motion of the gentleman from Beaufort will not prevail, and, for the reason just stated, namely, that

77

this thing has occurred before, and no notice has been taken it. If this style of debate is permitted to continue without reproof, there would be no limit to it, and the Convention would be disgraced. It is proper, therefore, that the Journal should remain unaltered, and stand as an example and a check.

Mr. J. D. BELL. It is true that words as equally offensive have been used on other occasions, but I think it unfair that one gentleman should be punished and the others allowed to escape, especially when he has frankly declared that his utterances were made in the excitement of the moment.

Mr. C. P. LESLIE. I hope that the record will not be changed. If the gentleman from Orangeburg thought he told the truth, it is an insult to him to expunge it from the Journal. If he told a falsehood, it ought not to be expunged.

Mr. J. S. CRAIG. One of two things ought to be done; either the Journal ought to be changed, or every other member who has been guilty of a like impropriety should be brought before the bar of the house and reprimanded.

Mr. J. J. WRIGHT. The gentleman from Orangeburg has no warmer friend than myself, but I must say that it would be setting a bad example for us to erase this matter from the Journal. If I commit a murder and escape, it is no reason why my colleague should be permitted to escape. Language has been used upon the floor of an improper character, and unless notice is taken of it, other members will be encouraged to do the same thing, and trust to the generosity of the Convention for forgiveness. I hope, therefore, the Journal will be permitted to stand as it is. If I use disgraceful language I expect to be punished for it, and the reprimand is necessary to preserve the dignity of the house.

Mr. B. F. RANDOLPH. I hope no one will understand that I have any objection to the record as it stands. I am sorry so much of the time of the Convention has been consumed, and request the gentleman from Beaufort to withdraw his motion, so that we may proceed to the legitimate business before the body.

Mr. J. D. BELL. I withdraw the motion.

Mr. F. J. MOSES, Jr. I renew the motion.

Mr. H. E. HAYNE, of Marion. I move to lay the motion to renew on the table.

The motion to lay on the table was agreed to.

The PRESIDENT announced that Senator Howard, of Michigan, had addressed him a letter in reply to the invitation extended to him by this Convention, to address it on the important subjects that are now agitating the country. Senator Howard returns his acknowledgments to the Convention, and says although the present condition of affairs at Washington makes it his duty to remain at the capitol, he trusts that in a few days that necessity will be removed, and he will then send a further reply.

Mr. B. F. RANDOLPH called for the unfinished business, being the report of the Judiciary Committee, which, on motion, was suspended in order that reports from Committees might be received.

Mr. WM. E. ROSE, from the Committee on Petitions, submitted the following report, which, on motion of Mr. R. SMALLS, was adopted:

The Committee on Petitions, to whom was referred the petition of Thomas Owens, of the District of Laurens, praying that his political disabilities be removed, and he be restored to the elective franchise, have considered the same, and respectfully report that your Committee are satisfied of the loyalty of the petitioner, and recommend that the prayer of his petition be granted. Respectfully submitted.

Also, the same gentleman, from the Committee on Petitions, submitted the following report:

The Committee on Petitions, to whom was referred the resolution of the delegate from Berkley, relative to the import duty on rice, ask leave respectfully to report that they have considered the same, and recommend that said resolution be laid on the table.

Mr. J. H. JENKS. Before action is taken and finally settled by the Convention upon that question, I desire to say a few words. I hope this body will consider the grave importance of the subject therein contained. The resolution is one of most vital importance to the District (Berkley) I have the honor to represent.

The report of the Committee on that resolution petitioning Congress against the repeal of the import duty on rice certainly seems to me to be adverse to the best interests of the State.

Being the mover of the resolution, it is due to the Convention that I should state the reasons that prompted me in the drafting and presenting of the same. I am aware it may be said that I am interested in the measure now before us; some of the members on this floor have already manifested an uneasiness on that subject.

To the charge I plead guilty. To deny it would be false and unnecessary. The district which I, with my colleagues, have the honor to represent is largely a rice-growing district, so that a large proportion of the inhabitants thereof would be compelled, in honor, to plead guilty to the same imputation. Therefore, in acknowledging the accusation of self-interest in a matter of such general importance to my district, I do not regard myself as in any way disqualified to urge the adoption of this resolution by this body; but, on the contrary, believe it to be my duty not only to introduce, but to heartily support, a measure of so vital importance to a constituency, who placed me here, that their interests may be represented. If the resolution now under consideration by this body related to cotton, and the tax thereon, it would need not one word of explanation to commend itself to the good sense of this Convention.

I venture the assertion that there is not a member on this floor to-day, not a citizen of this State, nay, nor of the United States, who has not felt the unequal and unfavorable workings of the tax on that staple. The cotton tax is now repealed, and with it, also, the import duty on the same article, and it yet remains to be proved, if in obviating or remedying one error, another equally fatal has not been committed.

I deny the charge sometimes made that the cotton tax was maliciously intended, on the part of Congress, as an act of oppression to a conquered people, as false and unfounded; but that its action has been pernicious to the best interests not only of this State, but to those of every cotton growing State, I do not deny.

It is with a view of preventing errors of this kind, however well intended, that I have brought this subject before you for your action.

It is an easy matter for Congress, in legislating for South Carolina, with no representatives in that honorable body to make known our wants and necessities, to fall into other errors that shall prove dangerous to the best welfare of our State, and the prosperity of her inhabitants.

The repeal of this duty will force us into an unequal competition, resulting in the final destruction of the rice culture in our State.

The several ice companies of New York, Boston and Portland, who have grown immensely wealthy in the ice trade with India and other tropical countries, and who, in connection with that trade, have been the chief importers of Rangoon rice, as if not yet satisfied, are making the most gigantic efforts towards the repeal of the present import duty on that article. Money has been freely subscribed, and their agents, with it in hand, are now in Washington for the purpose of lobbying through the proposed repeal. So sanguine are they of the success of their efforts, that they advise their friends throughout the South against investing in the rice culture the present year.

Should their efforts in this direction prove successful, as they claim to have every reason to expect, what will be the result?

The result will be this, that Carolina rice, instead of commanding a price remunerative to the capital and labor employed in its culture, will be dragged, by an inferior article, down to a price which will not repay the expense of raising. The rice lands, the most fertile and productive in this country, yea, in the world, and suited only to the culture of rice, and which can be kept in order for cultivation only at great expense and care, will run to waste. The plantations will be abandoned, and there will be lost to us one of the chief resources of the State, and the wealth of our seaboard. The laborers, already driven from the islands and the culture of cotton, to the rice fields to avoid starvation, will again be driven to search in vain for remunerative fields for their labors. With the repeal of this duty, foreign rice can be laid down in this market at three dollars per hundred weight—the same, three cents per pound. It cannot be produced in this country for the money. You say it has been done in the past. I admit the fact, but how was it accomplished? It was accomplished, Mr. President, only by means of a system of unrequited toil—a cruel system of oppression, better known as slavery. Amid the din and shock of battle, that institution has been swept from our land, and it is not now within the power of man to resuscitate or restore it. Thank God that it is not! So far, then, as it is beyond the power of man to establish again upon our soil the authority of the slave master, so far, also, is removed from him the possibility of again growing rice in this country at old prices, or even at prices that shall in any way compete with importations from foreign markets. With the repeal of this duty we shall be forced into a competition so unequal as to result in the final destruction of the rice culture in our State. To be sure, Carolina rice stands first in the markets of the world; but when the repeal against which we now pray shall have been effected, its superior quality will command so slight a difference in price as to prove no encouragement to its cultivation. We boast to-day of a country that guarantees every man his freedom, of an emblem that, while it protects no tyrant, knows no slave. It shall be our ambition, at no distant day, to boast of a State wherein the masses are educated, intelligent and enlightened.

Would we accomplish this? Would we elevate instead of degrade labor? Would we reserve to the State one of its chief resources? Would we encourage freedom and free labor, as opposed to oppression and oppressed labor?

Let us enter our protest against the repeal of this duty. I certainly hope, Mr. President, that before this subject passes beyond our consideration, that gentlemen who have been so earnest in the support of almost every other measure before this body will declare themselves upon this. I hope to listen to the clarion voice of the delegate from Darlington (Mr. WHITTEMORE); to hear the rounded and classic periods of the gentleman from Sumter (Mr. F. J. MOSES); to be stirred by the grave eloquence of my colleague from Berkely (Mr. D. H. CHAMBERLAIN), and to see manifested in behalf of *"my people"* the pathos of the delegate from Barnwell (Mr. C. P. LESLIE.)

On motion of Mr. J. J. WRIGHT, the matter was made the Special Order for 4 P. M., Monday.

Mr. L. S. LANGLEY submitted the following resolution, which was referred to the Committee on Education:

WHEREAS, it is very desirable to form a permanent school fund for the benefit of the Common Schools of the State; and whereas, the Congress of the United States did, by an act passed in 1863, appropriate the interest of the proceeds of the sales of certain plantations and town lots, sold for taxes by virtue of the Act aforesaid, and situate in Port Royal, Ladies' and St. Helena Islands, S. C., for educational purposes; and whereas, we believe that youthful instruction in and by a well regulated system of Common Schools tends to make better citizens of all classes of our population; be it therefore

Resolved, That the Congress of the United States be, and is hereby, respectfully requested to turn over to the Commissioner of Education of this State, under the Constitution of 1868, the proceeds of the sales of the plantations and town lots aforesaid, for the purpose of aiding in the accumulation of a permanent school fund for the State.

Resolved, That the President of this Convention is hereby requested to forward, at an early day, a copy of this preamble and these resolutions to the President of the Senate and Speaker of the House of Representatives of the United States, in Congress assembled.

Mr. L. S. LANGLEY also offered the following:

Resolved, That this Convention tender to the Congress of the United States, and to the General of the Army, also to the Hon. E. M. Stanton, Secretary of War, the sincere and heartfelt thanks of the loyal people of South Carolina, for their noble devotion to constitutional law and universal liberty.

Resolved, That the President of this Convention is hereby requested to forward a copy of these resolutions to the President of the Senate, Speaker of the House of Representatives and Secretary of War, as well as a copy to the General of the Army of the United States, respectively.

Mr. B. BYAS. I cannot see any reason in tendering our sincere thanks to Congress, the President, the Secretary of War, or anybody else. These men are placed in their positions to do their duty, and they have done no more than was expected of them. Indeed, I do not think it is the time for us to pass such a resolution. It is like thanking a man for work only half done. When they have concluded their labors, we may then properly show to Congress that we recognize the same in an appropriate way.

The motion to include "and Secretary of War" was agreed to, and the resolution was then adopted.

Mr. F. J. MOSES, Jr. As I regard the subject matter of the resolutions, which have just been adopted, as entirely out of place in this Convention, I desire to have my name recorded on the Journal as having voted in the negative.

Mr. B. BYAS also requested that he should be recorded as voting in the negative.

Mr. B. O. DUNCAN, from the Committee of Congressional Districts, asked and obtained leave to submit the following "ordinance," which was read for the first time, and, on motion of Mr. E. W. M. MACKEY, was ordered to be printed, and made the Special Order for Monday next at 11 o'clock.

The Special Committee of eight, to whom was referred the duty of learning how many Representatives South Carolina is entitled to in the Congress of the United States, and of reporting a suitable division of the State into Congressional Districts, has investigated the matter, and beg leave to report as follows:

After the census of 1860 a new apportionment of Representatives was made among the States, South Carolina then being entitled to representation for only three-fifths of her slave population, was entitled under this apportionment of Congress to only four Representatives. This act of apportionment is still in force, so that we are in reality entitled by act of Congress to only four members in the lower house of Congress. But our entire population, for which we should now be represented, entitles us to six Representatives. As, however, it is doubtful if we will be granted a larger number than the act of apportionment gives us, your Committee recommends the following ordinance, to be called

AN ORDINANCE TO DIVIDE THE STATE INTO FOUR CONGRESSIONAL DISTRICTS.

We, the People of the State of South Carolina, by our Delegates in Convention assembled, do ordain, That the State of South Carolina shall be, and the same is hereby, divided into four Congressional Districts, as follows: First Congressional District, to be composed of the Counties of Lancaster, Chesterfield, Marlborough, Darlington, Marion, Horry, Georgetown, Williamsburg, Sumter, Clarendon, and Kershaw. Second Congressional District, to be composed of the Counties of Charleston, Colleton, Beaufort, and Barnwell. Third Congressional District, to be composed of the Counties of Orangeburg, Lexington, Richland, Newberry, Edgefield, Abbeville, and Anderson; and the fourth Congressional District, to be composed of the Counties of Oconee, Pickens, Greenville, Laurens, Spartanburg, Union, York, Chester, and Fairfield.

SECTION 2. That until the next apportionment be made by the Congress of the United States, each of the said Congressional Districts shall be entitled to elect one member to represent this State in the Congress of the United States.   After such new apportionment by Congress, the Legislature shall divide the State into as many Congressional Districts as we are entitled to members in the House of Representatives.

Sec. 3. At the first election under this Constitution, two Representatives shall be elected at large on the State ticket, to represent the over plus of our population.   Should they obtain seats, they shall continu to be so elected until the new apportionment after the census of 1870.

Mr. E. W. M. MACKEY called up the unfinished business, being the report of the Judiciary Committee.

Section second of the Judiciary report was then taken up.

Mr. A. J. RANSIER resumed the floor.   I repeat that I am in favor of the section as it stands, providing for the election of Judges by a joint vote of the General Assembly.   I understand the gentleman from Orangeburg (Mr. RANDOLPH) proposes to give the appointment of Judges to the Governor, with the consent of the Senate.   The gentleman from Richland proposes to make their terms of office during good behavior.   I think both of those gentlemen are at least fifty years behind the age.   In the majority of States the election of Judges has been thrown into the hands of the people, and I am in favor of throwing the election of every officer into the hands of the people.   I am aware that there are very delicate questions connected with this matter, and, perhaps, it will be sound policy to remove the Judges of the Supreme Court from a too direct responsibility to the people.   The masses of the people of this State are not, perhaps, at present in a position to use their power wisely and judiciously; were it not for that, I would give my vote and voice any time against any provision which proposed to fill any office at all, either by the General Assembly or the government.   I think the people are the best judges of who shall make their laws in any department of the government.   I hope the amendment of the gentleman from Orangeburg will not prevail.   With the influence a Governor can exercise, his recommendation would be all-powerful, and to throw the appointment into his hands would amount, after all, to the setting up of the " one man power."   As regards the term of office, I find in the original Constitutions of most of the States, it was fixed during good behavior; but, in most of the present Constitutions, the terms are variously limited to five, six, and ten years.   I am disposed to keep up with the march of events, and to profit by the advances of the civilization of the age.   I think the section might be improved by adding a provision that the Judges may be removed for causes other than impeachment on a two-thirds vote of the General Assembly.   I hope the election of the Judges of the Supreme Court will be by the General

Assembly, and that the term of office will not be extended beyond eight or ten years.

Mr. B. BYAS. I trust that the section will stand as it is. I think we have a sufficient number of men of ability in this State to fill these offices, and if the persons elected by the General Assembly discharge for a term of six years the duties of that office to the satisfaction of the people, the General Assembly will have it within their power to re-elect them. The Committee, after due reflection, have fixed the term at six years, and I think that accords with the good sense of every member of this house.

Mr. H. E. HAYNE called for the previous question, which was sustained.

The question being first put on the amendment of Mr. JILLSON, to make the term of office ten, instead of six years, it was decided in the negative.

The question was then taken on the amendment of Mr. RUNION, to substitute eight years for six, which was also decided in the negative.

Mr. C. C. BOWEN moved to amend on third line, after qualified, "they shall be so classified that one of the Judges shall go out of office every two years;" and the section so amended passed to its third reading.

Section three was read, and Mr. C. C. BOWEN moved to strike out the entire section, which was agreed to.

Section four was read, and Mr. C. C. BOWEN offered the following as a substitute, which was adopted, and the section passed to its third reading.

SECTION 4. The Chief Justice elected under this Constitution, shall continue in office for six years, and the General Assembly, immediately after said election, shall determine by lot which of the two Associate Justices elect shall serve for the term of two years, and which for the term of four years; and having so determined the same, it shall be the duty of the Governor to commission them accordingly.

Sections five and six were severally read, and passed to their third reading.

Section seven was read, and Mr. J. M. RUTLAND moved the following amendment on seventh line, strike out "law knowledge," and insert "men learned in the law," and the section so amended passed to its third reading.

Section eight passed to its third reading without debate.

Section nine, requiring the Judges of the Supreme Court, upon special occasions, to give their opinion upon questions of constitutional law, was read.

78

Mr. J. J. WRIGHT. I hope this whole section will be stricken out, it has no business in this connection; we have no right to ask the Judges of the Supreme Court to give their opinions on a case of constitutional law; when a case comes before them, it is their prerogative to give an opinion; and whenever an opinion is required by the State, it is the province of the Attorney-General to give that opinion, and not that of the Judge.

Mr. WM. McKINLAY moved to amend on second line; strike out "solemn" and insert "special," which was not agreed to.

Mr. C. C. BOWEN moved to strike out the entire section.

Mr. S. G. W. DILL moved to indefinitely postpone the motion to strike out.

Mr. R. B. ELLIOTT moved to lay the motion to postpone on the table, which was agreed to.

The motion to strike out was agreed to.

Section ten, relative to judgments and decrees, passed without debate.

Section eleven, in reference to the salaries of the Judges, was read.

Mr. J. D. BELL. I move to amend the eleventh section, by inserting after the word "be," in the second line, "shall not be increased nor diminished."

Mr. R. C. DeLARGE. I sincerely hope that the word "increased" will not prevail. We do not know what the future may bring forth, and the State may be in a condition, at some future time, to fix the salaries of the Judges in accordance with the times and the cost of living; the present salaries may not be enough to support the Judges. If we expect to have such men as we desire, we should give them a liberal compensation for their services. An able lawyer may sacrifice a large and lucrative practice to take the position of Judge in order to serve his fellow-citizens. It would be ungenerous and unfair to ask such a person to serve, and give him a salary barely sufficient to obtain the necessaries of life without any of its comforts, and not enough to sustain the dignity of his position. I hope the amendment will not be adopted.

Mr. C. C. BOWEN. I hope the section will pass as it stands. In drafting that section, reference was had to the Constitution of the United States, and the same language used as in that instrument. It was proposed not to give the power of starving the Judges, or the power to increase, but to leave it in the hands of the Legislature. I, for one, am willing to risk it with that body. In some of the States the provision is made that salaries shall not be increased nor diminished. As far as Judges are concerned, I see no necessity for such a provision. But where parties have the privilege of voting for an increase of their own salaries, there is a forcible reason for such a measure. The Judges have not that power.

The question was then taken on the amendment of Mr. BELL, and decided in the negative.

Section eleventh then passed to a third reading.

Section twelfth, providing who shall be eligible to the office of Judge of the Supreme Court or Circuit Courts, was taken up.

Mr. B. F. RANDOLPH. I move to amend in the third line by striking out the words, "five years," and inserting "one year."

Mr. S. A. SWAILS moved to amend by striking out "thirty" and inserting "thirty-five," so as to require Judges to be thirty-five years of age.

Mr. J. S. CRAIG moved to amend by striking out the word "five," and inserting "two," so as to require a residence of two years.

Mr. B. BYAS. I hope five will be stricken out, and one substituted.

Mr. C. C. BOWEN. I hope the section will remain as it is, so far as the term of qualification is concerned. We have provided in the section that a party resident in this State, when the Constitution is adopted, shall be eligible, but after that, whosoever comes must reside here five years. If a man comes here from the North a day before the Constitution is adopted, he is eligible to the office of Judge. The Constitution provides that they shall be elected for four and six years; therefore, after the first election, unless by death or resignation, there will be no vacancies. I deem this amendment totally unnecessary. The large majority of the States fix this qualification at five years, and we have taken that as a precedent. It will certainly require a man to be a resident of the State that length of time to understand the laws of the State.

Mr. J. S. CRAIG. I am in favor of the amendment. If we cannot get sufficient good timber in this State, we can take the best material, wherever found.

Mr. B F. RANDOLPH. I have no doubt that in due time we shall have abundant judicial material. In the present, as it were, territorial condition of the State, many of the ablest Southern men, who could act as Judges, are disfranchised, and would not ask to be enfranchised. They will not ask to have their disabilities removed. I would have the advantage then of able men from Massachusetts, Ohio, New York and Pennsylvania, who come here and make South Carolina their home. For these reasons, I am opposed to requiring the Judge to reside here five years before he can be elected to fill the office. It seems to me that a man who has occupied the position of a Judge in any other State, or one who is familiar with the law of any other State, or practiced law, can pick up and become acquainted with the statues of this State in a year's time.

Mr. J. J. WRIGHT. This matter has no reference to the various Judges who are to be elected for the Circuits of the State. It simply refers to the three Judges who are to be the Judges of the Supreme Court. I hope this section will stand just as it is, for, if amended, it will require, before a person can be elected to the office of Judge, that he must be a resident for five or ten years, and a citizen of the State at the time of the adoption of the Constitution. There is a difference between a resident and a citizen. A person might come here the day the Constitution was adopted, and yet be eligible to the office.

Mr. B. F. RANDOLPH. Does the gentleman know of any three Judges who can act as Supreme Judges, and five who can act as Circuit Judges, who are not disfranchised?

Mr. J. J. WRIGHT. I wish to say here that there are a sufficient number of men in the State qualified to fill these offices.

Mr. J. S. CRAIG. Are those to whom he refers loyal men?

Mr. J. J. WRIGHT. If the gentleman knows the meaning of the word loyal, he knows what I mean. There is no State in the Union in which a man is not required to reside there at least two years before he can be appointed a Judge, and then he must be well grounded in the principles of the law, and be familiar with the decisions of the Superior and Inferior Courts.

Mr. B. F. WHITTEMORE. It appears to me that the reading of this section is quite vague. No doubt, the Chairman of the Committee intended that it should be distinctly understood that a person who is a resident of the State at the time of the adoption of this Constitution should be eligible to a judgeship of the Supreme or Circuit Courts; but to make it read plainly, I desire to erase all after the word "election" in the third line, and substitute the following: "*Provided*, That the exceptions herein contained do not apply to the first election after the adoption of this Constitution."

Mr. B. O. DUNCAN moved to strike out the words "or from" in the third line, and insert, "unless he is a resident of the State at the time of the election."

Mr. J. M. RUTLAND. If I understand the amendment, it seems to me to take away the qualification of years, and we do not wish to make an exception as to age. It appears to me the clause is plain enough as it stands. I think it can hardly be misunderstood that any man who is here at the time of the adoption of the Constitution is qualified, other things being equal, to fill the office of Judge.

Mr. J. S. CRAIG moved to strike out all after the word "or" and insert "who may have been a resident of this State at the time of the adoption of this Constitution."

The question being taken, the motion was not agreed to.

The amendment offered by Mr. DUNCAN was also disagreed to.

The question recurred on adopting the amendment of Mr. WHITTE-MORE.

Mr. B. F. WHITTEMORE.   I simply desire to say that I believe we have, within the State of South Carolina, men of sufficient legal knowledge and ability to fill all the positions of Judges; but I am well aware that there is as much legal knowledge out of South Carolina as in it.   It may be there are those upon the floor of this Convention who desire to fill one of these offices, and if it so be that they possess a sufficient degree of legal ability, I do not desire them to be hampered by any clause of the Constitution which will prevent their taking the places.   If there are others in the State who are competent and qualified, I am equally willing to cast my vote for them.

The hour of 1 o'clock having arrived, the PRESIDENT announced the Convention adjourned until 3 P. M.

AFTERNOON SESSION.

The Convention re-assembled at 3 P. M.

The consideration of the twelfth section of the judiciary report was resumed.

The CHAIR stated the question was on the amendment offered before adjournment, by the member from Darlington, Mr. B. F. WHITTE-MORE, which was to add: "*Provided*, That the exceptions herein contained do not apply to the first election after the adoption of this Constitution."

Mr. G. PILLSBURY.   I have noticed that when sections are before this body for action, and amendments are offered from various parts of the house, that we are apt to be confused, and the only mode of relief is to make one full sweep of all the amendments.   I hope that will not be the case with the section under consideration.   With the little knowledge I have of the proper construction of language, I can consider the section as it stands in no other way than that no candidate is eligible for the office of Judge unless he shall have been a resident of this State for five years previous to the adoption of this Constitution. I wish to have more light upon this matter, and I take the liberty of asking the Chairman of the Judiciary Committee whether it was intended that no person, unless he had been here five years at the time of the adoption of the Constitution, should be eligible to that office ?

Mr. C. C. BOWEN. I distinctly stated that it was the intention of the Committee that any person living in this State at the time of the adoption of this Constitution should be eligible to the office of Judge.

Mr. G. PILLSBURY. Then that Committee have nicer and more discriminating views in regard to the proper construction of language than I possess. As the section reads, it seems to me the obvious conclusion to which any one would arrive would be, that in the last line commencing with "five years next preceding his election, or from the adoption of this Constitution," the meaning would be that no person who has not been a resident of the State for five years preceding the election of Judges can be eligible to that office. With the construction the Chairman has given of the section, I am the more earnest that the amendment offered by the gentleman from Darlington should be adopted I am the more in favor of it because I believe that the timber, as it has been expressed, for this important office is scarce. I doubt very much whether we shall be able to fill those offices, at the start, with competent men. I hope that, unless a better substitute is offered, the amendment offered by the gentleman from Darlington will be adopted. I hope we shall make this thing certain, so that we can avail ourselves of any proper legal talent which may be found within our borders at the start. Unless we have impartial men upon the bench, men who will administer justice with an even hand, who will recognize the equal rights of all men, the liberties of the people will be imperiled.

Mr. C. C. BOWEN. In regard to the interpretation of this section, I am willing, in order to make it more definite, if possible, to amend. I move, therefore, to strike out the word "from" in third line, and insert the words "was a resident of the State at."

The question being taken on the amendment, it was agreed to.

The question being taken upon the several other proposed amendments, they were lost, and the twelfth section passed to its third reading. The section, as passed, makes eligible to the office of Judge any person having attained the age of thirty years, who has been a resident of the State five years next preceding his election, or was a resident of the State at the adoption of this Constitution.

Section thirteenth, providing for vacancies, was read.

Mr. A. J. RANSIER offered to amend by adding to the first line the words, "as herein prescribed," which was agreed to.

Mr. S. A. SWAILS proposed to strike out all of the second, third and fourth lines, which was withdrawn, and the section passed to its third reading.

Section fourteenth, making necessary a concurrence of two of the Judges of the Supreme Court necessary to a decision, was read, and passed without amendment or debate.

Section fifteenth was read, as follows:

SECTION 15. The State shall be divided into convenient circuits, and for each circuit a Judge shall be elected by the qualified electors thereof, who shall hold his office for a term of four years, and during his continuance in office he shall reside in the circuit of which he is Judge.

Mr. C. C. BOWEN moved to strike out the word "thereof" in second line, and insert the words "of the State," which was not agreed to.

Mr. C. M. WILDER moved to strike out the words "qualified electors" in second line, and to insert the words, "by joint vote of the General Assembly."

Mr. A. J. RANSIER. For the same reasons which determined us in giving the election of the Judges of the Supreme Court to the General Assembly, I hope that motion will prevail.

Mr. J. J. WRIGHT. I hope the section will stand as it is, and that the people shall have the privilege of electing all their Judges but those of the Supreme Court, for which we have already provided. The liberties of a people are a part of their birthright, and whenever they give those liberties to a few, I consider they are sacrificing the dearest privilege which they enjoy. Now it may be claimed by some that to give the election of the Judges to the people will be an inducement to the judiciary to cater to popular prejudices. But, notwithstanding this view, which I deem an incorrect one, I desire that every Judge shall be directly responsible to the people for his office. I believe that ninety-nine out of every hundred of the people would prefer to elect their own Judges. They are a safer tribunal than the Legislature, which, however pure it may be theoretically, will necessarily yield to influences and prejudices brought to bear in favor of those who seek office at its hands. I am under no fear that men cannot be found in every judicial district in whom the people do not sufficiently confide to elect as their Judge, and in making such a popular choice, they will better satisfy themselves than if the Legislature should elect a stranger to fill the office. Let us, therefore, place this power in the hands of the people. It has been done in many of the larger States of the Union, such as Ohio and Pennsylvania, and there is no reason why all the purity of the bench shall not be thus preserved in South Carolina.

Mr. R. C. DeLARGE. Did not the Constitution of New York provide for the election of Judges by the people?

Mr. J. J. WRIGHT. It did.

Mr. R. C. DeLARGE. Was the Judiciary system of New York a model to be followed?

Mr. J. J. WRIGHT. If the gentleman thinks that a Judiciary system as corrupt as hell is a model system, then that of New York is a model.

Mr. R. C. DeLARGE. Will the gentleman inform us if the Constitutional Convention of New York did not find it necessary to change that system, and make the Judges elective by the Legislature?

Mr. J. J. WRIGHT. I will say that it did change it, but the city controlled the State of New York. The State has tried almost every method of purification, but it will never succeed until it gives the election of all the Judges to the people.

Mr. J. S. CRAIG. Was not the Judiciary formerly elected by the people, and was it not at that time the most corrupt system ever established?

Mr. J. J. WRIGHT. I do not know the time when the Judges were elected by the people.

Mr. C. P. LESLIE. I do not know when it has been otherwise. It was no unusual thing in my time to see a Judge on the stump, and he who could make the loudest noise was generally sure of his election. I am opposed to this style of doing things, because I believe a Judge should be made as independent of the will and pleasure of the people as possible, because in the proportion that he is dependent on the will of the people is his fidelity weakened. In a conversation with a distinguished lawyer of New York only last evening, he said that while it was quite consistent with republican principles to elect the Judges by the people, his experience was that the plan worked badly, and if South Carolina succeeded with the system, he should be greatly surprised. That is the opinion of a grey-headed lawyer who has had a vast experience in the practice of the law in New York. Now, if we are to respect the action of the General Assembly in other particulars, why are they not to be trusted with the election of Judges? The Legislature are the representatives of the people, and I for one can see no vast difference between the exercise of judgment by a few careful, intelligent members of such a body, and the will of the people by whom they were elected.

Mr. B. F. RANDOLPH. How would it look to see a Judge with a bottle of whiskey in one hand, and ballots in the other, begging for the votes of the people? I must admit that it would be a strange spectacle indeed for South Carolina.

Mr. E. W. M. MACKEY. I hope this amendment will pass which gives the election of the Judges of the Circuit Courts to the General Assembly, and for the very reason given by the gentleman from Beaufort. He says the Judges should be directly responsible to the will of the people. That is just what we want to avoid. We want no Judges who will cater to the prejudices of the people, or who will enter a political campaign and try to curry favor with the masses. In a majority of cases the poor people would get no justice from these men. Not that I distrust the people, but I do distrust those who become candidates for this position. The members of the Legislature are sufficiently responsible to the people for their action, and if they elect an incompetent or corrupt Judge, the people will take care that those men shall never again take their seats in the General Assembly. We wish to make the Judges sufficiently responsible to the people, but they must not be dependent upon politicians. We wish to make Judges so independent that they will not be afraid to express their opinion in accordance with justice and law. I hope, therefore, the election of Judges will remain with the Legislature.

Another very important consideration, which cannot be avoided under present circumstances, is this: It so happens that in certain portions of the State the rebels have a majority, that is in the upper districts, which will be divided into one or more circuits. This report provides that the Judges shall change circuits. Perhaps the gentleman from Beaufort may find one of these Judges elected by rebel votes coming down to his district and administering justice there, and although elected by the people, that gentleman will have no voice in his election. To prevent this contingency, we must give the election to the Legislature, which represents not one, but all the districts of the State.

Mr. W. B. NASH. I hope the amendment of my friend from Richland will prevail. If the Judges of our Courts were to get into a similar scramble for office that I have seen on this floor, it would certainly be discreditable to the judiciary. If we give the election of Judges to the people, you may be sure that the people will not be so well qualified to choose who shall be Judges as the Legislature of the State will be, because members of the Legislature will be brought in contact every day with all the members of that body, and the Judges will be chosen, more or less, from the men who have been in the General Assembly: conse-

79

quently they would possess not only a certain degree of ability, but will possess the confidence of the people.

Mr. J. J. WRIGHT. Suppose the Legislature is composed entirely of democrats?

Mr. W. B. NASH. Then we deserve the worst kind of Judges. Mr. President, I move the previous question.

Mr. R. C. DeLARGE called for the yeas and nays, and they were ordered.

Mr. C. C. BOWEN. I hope this section will stand as it is has been framed and reported by the Committee on the Judiciary. We do not know what class of representatives may be in the next Legislature, and for one I have more confidence in the people than in that body. If bad men are elected to represent us there, we cannot foresee the trouble they will create. It has been mooted that the democratic party in the up country was sufficiently strong to control the election of Judges, and the intention was to keep it out of the power of the opposite party to fill for the present, at least, any of the offices of the State. If they have the ability to elect democratic members, they may also elect democratic Judges, but I prefer to trust to the people. I will now yield the rest of my time to the gentleman from Berkley.

Mr. C. P. LESLIE. I think this an unfair way of log-rolling this question through the Convention.

Mr. D. H. CHAMBERLAIN. I have but a few words to say upon this question, and I shall bring to the mind of the Convention the arguments which I had occasion to touch upon yesterday in the discussion of another article. We all agree that the object to be attained is to secure upright, impartial, and incorruptible Judges, and the only difference between those who favor the amendment and myself, is as to the manner of securing these Judges. Upon general principles, I am clearly of the opinion that it is better to put this whole power of election, from the highest to the lowest of our judicial offices, in the hands of the people. Whenever we come to discuss this question in the light of experience, however, we are pointed to the example of the great State of New York, and told that she has an elective and corrupt judiciary. Have they not an equally corrupt Legislature; and if the argument applies to the one, does it not equally apply to the other? If corrupt influences are to be used in the election of Judges, it will be easier to corrupt a Legislature than the people. When the gentleman points us to a Judge appealing, with a whiskey bottle in hand, to the people for their votes, a much more probable picture that presents itself to my mind, is a similar appeal made to the Legislature. I care not what may be the means, but it is easier to corrupt one hundred and twenty men, at the seat of government, than the people scattered broadcast through the State.

Mr. B. F. RANDOLPH. Does the gentleman think that the people are better qualified than the General Assembly to select Judges?

Mr. D. H. CHAMBERLAIN. They are more likely, by their votes, to select an impartial Judge than the Legislature would be. In several of the Southern States in process of reconstruction, the election of Judges, from the highest to the lowest, has been given to the people, and the whole progress of the age is in favor of removing power from the hands of the few, and bestowing it on the many.

Mr. B. O. DUNCAN. Has not the State of New York recently abandoned the elective judiciary system?

Mr. D. H. CHAMBERLAIN. It is true that New York has proposed to make a change in her Constitution, but it is not probable that the people will ratify those amendments which propose to take from their hands the election of Judges. New York, however, is no criterion for the Government of South Carolina. There is an extraordinary element in that State, disturbing in its character, which has not only crept into the judiciary, but into every other department, and it does not follow, from her example, that Judges elsewhere elected by the people must necessarily be corrupt.

Mr. R. C. DeLARGE. Will the gentleman state whether he considers the people of the interior of New York as corrupt as those of the city?

Mr. D. H. CHAMBERLAIN. I understand that the country people of the State of New York are as honest as the people of any other State in the Union; but when their Representatives and Senators reach the Legislature, they become subject to every degree of corruption and infamy which can be perpetrated by legislation.

The question being taken on the adoption of the amendment of the gentleman from Richland (Mr. C. M. WILDER), and the yeas and nays being called, it was decided in the affirmative, yeas 65, nays 24:

AYES—The President, Allen, Becker, Boozer, Brockenton, Byas, Burton, F. J. Cain, Cardozo, Coghlan, Chestnut, Clinton, Cooke, Collins, Corley, Craig, Davis, DeLarge, Duncan, Edwards, Gray, J. N. Hayne, C. D. Hayne, H. E. Hayne, Humbird, Jervey, Jillson, Samuel Johnson, J. W. Johnson, Chas. Jones, Lang, George Lee, Samuel Lee, Lomax, Leslie, E. W. M. Mackey, Mayer, W. McKinlay. Mead, Milford, Nance, Nash, Neagle, Nuckles, Pillsbury, Randolph, Rainey, Ransier, Rivers, Robertson, Rose, Rutland, Sanders, Sasportas, Shrewsbury, Stubbs,

Augustus Thompson, B. A. Thompson, S. B. Thompson, Whittemore, White, F. E. Wilder, Chas. M. Wilder, Wingo, Wooley—65.

NAYS—Messrs. Bell, Bowen, Bonum, Bryce, Camp, Chamberlain, Dill, Donaldson, Elliott, Foster, Gentry, Holmes, Hurley, Jacobs, W. B. Johnson, L. B. Johnson, W. E. Johnston, Henry Jones, Langley, Mauldin, Owens, Runion, Swails, Wright—24.

ABSENT—Alexander, Arnim, R. H. Cain, Crews, Darrington, Dickson, Dogan, Driffle, Goss, Harris, Henderson, Hunter, Jackson, Jenks, Joiner, W. J. McKinlay, McDaniels, Middleton, Miller, Moses, Nelson, Newell, Olsen, Parker, Perry, Richmond, Smalls, Thomas, Viney, Webb, Whipper, Williamson—32.

Mr. L. S. LANGLEY asked permission to explain his vote, which was granted. He said, "I vote no. I do this because I believe in the people, and because I know that the body of legal voters have never been drunk with whiskey, nor sold their birthrights for gold, whereas legislators have been guilty of both. The people may have been deceived, but they never have been bought."

Section sixteenth, providing that Judges of the Circuit Courts shall interchange circuits with each other in such manner as may be determined by law, was passed to its third reading, without amendment.

Section seventeenth was read, as follows:

SECTION 17. The Courts of Common Pleas shall have exclusive jurisdiction in all cases of divorce, and exclusive original jurisdiction in all civil cases and actions *ex delicto*, which shall not be cognizable before Justices of the Peace, and appellate jurisdiction in all such cases as may be provided by law. They shall have power to issue writs of *mandamus*, prohibition, *scire facias*, and all other writs which may be necessary for carrying their powers fully into effect.

Mr. R. C. DeLARGE moved to strike out the words, "exclusive jurisdiction in all cases of divorce."

Mr. J. S. CRAIG. I hope that some gentleman will rise and defend this question as it now stands. I acknowledge my inability to do justice to the subject. Heretofore this State has denied to any person the right of divorce. I do not know any intelligent man who can deny that many individuals have suffered from the operations of this law, and it requires no imaginary picture to show that a vast amount of unhappiness has resulted between man and wife because of their inability to effect a separation. I hope the amendment, therefore, will not prevail.

Mr. B. F. RANDOLPH. The object of the gentleman is to strike out "divorces," which so dreadfully looms up in the section. I am opposed to its erasure. There are cases in which divorces are necessary and right. They are necessary for the common welfare of the parties.

It is laid down in the Scripture, that for certain causes, certain parties may be divorced.

Mr. R. C. DeLARGE. What is the construction of Scripture concerning the marital rite? Was there any provision made for a divorce in that clause of the Bible which says, "What God hath put asunder let no man join together."

Mr. B. F. RANDOLPH. I am sorry the gentleman exhibits so much ignorance in his quotations, and I would most respectfully refer him to the New Testament, that he may become more familiar with the teachings of our Saviour. I know of no law in which God has put asunder in which man has a right to join together. It seems to me, if Christianity is to be respected, if it is not a solemn farce, it is certainly the duty of every legislative body not to adopt measures which are a direct violation of the teachings of the Scripture. When parties live together without harmony in the marriage relation, it is a Christian duty to separate them and restore peace.

Mr. B. F. WHITTEMORE. I trust this section will remain unchanged.

Mr. W. J. McKINLAY. I move that the words, "in all cases of divorce" be stricken out.

Mr. B. F. WHITTEMORE. I rise to protest against any amendment of this character. In the course of my experience in this State, it has been a matter of pride that there has been no such stain upon her record as a divorce. A case has been cited to me, which occurred in this State, where a person married his own aunt, and afterwards becoming conscious that he had done a great wrong, he sought relief from that connection. By mutual consent the parties separated, and he afterwards married another woman. The case was brought before the Courts, when it was decided that there being no law in South Carolina which suffered him to be divorced from his first wife, his aunt was decided to be the only wife to whom he had been legally united. This case was especially noted by the military authorities, and the case published. All will admit that such a condition of things as that would seem to demand that we should provide the ways and means by which individuals in such a position may be relieved. A husband and wife may find uncongeniality of association. One may prove unfaithful and unworthy of the love of the other. Shall we say here to-day, with our voice and votes, that such parties shall remain bound together in affiliation without any mode of relief? Already two petitions have been brought before this body, and referred to a Committee, which certainly commend themselves to our consideration and charity. I trust that whenever such cases shall exist in new

South Carolina, means may be provided, in accordance with the law of God and man, to release these parties from their unfortunate domestic alliance.

Mr. R. C. DeLARGE.   I desire to know what portion of God's law gives a man a right to a divorce from his wife ?

Mr. B. F. WHITTEMORE.   If the gentleman will make use of his leisure and search the Scriptures for himself, he will find out.

Mr. WM. J. McKINLAY.   To my mind there is a certain degree of sacredness in the marital tie, which should make us cautious how we act upon this question.

Mr. C. P. LESLIE.   Are you a married man ?

Mr. WM. J. McKINLAY.   I am not, but soon may be, and if this section passes, and divorce is recognized as a right, to my mind it would divest the marriage relation of the sanctity which should attach to it. Not only that, but it is altogether contrary to the Scriptural injunction, which some members seem to entirely forget, that "those whom God hath joined together let no man put asunder."

Mr. J. M. RUTLAND.   I had intended to make some remarks upon this subject; but, in the course of the argument I threw out privately to another, I chose to illustrate it by saying that whoever dared to interfere in a quarrel between a man and his wife was apt to come out of that scrape with a bloody nose.   I was told by the gentleman that I, being a single man, had no experience in such matters, and, therefore, had no right to use such an illustration, on the ground that the President would rule me out of order.

Mr. C. C. BOWEN.   I do think that parties are entitled to a divorce whenever legal grounds can be shown for such a measure, and the laws of South Carolina, I certainly think, should provide for such emergencies.

The question was then taken on the amendment to strike out, which was not agreed to.   The section then passed to a third reading.

Section eighteenth was read, as follows :

Section 18. The Court of Common Pleas shall sit in each Judicial District in this State at least twice in every year, at such stated times and places as may be appointed by law.   It shall have full jurisdiction in all matters of equity, but the Courts heretofore established for that purpose shall continue as now organized until the first day of January, one thousand eight hundred and sixty-nine, for the disposition of causes now pending therein.

Mr. C. C. BOWEN offered to substitute the words "Judicial Districts" in first line for the word "County;" also to strike out the word "full" in second line, and to add after the last word in fifth line the words, "ι less otherwise provided for by law," the first of which amendments was lost, and the second carried; and the section, so amended, passed to a third reading.

Section nineteenth was read a second time, as follows:

SECTION 19. The General Assembly shall provide by law for the preservation of the records of the Courts of Equity, and also for the transfer to the Court of Common Pleas and Probate Courts for final decision of all causes that may remain undetermined.

Mr. J. M. RUTLAND. As this is an important section, I ask that its consideration may be postponed until to-morrow morning, when I believe a clause satisfactory to all parties may be agreed upon.

Mr. E. W. M. MACKEY. I wish to see the Courts of Equity killed off right here. A more diabolical institution never existed. I hope, therefore, the motion to postpone will be voted down. I move to lay that motion on the table.

The motion to lay on the table was not agreed to.

Mr. B. F. WHITTEMORE. I move that when we adjourn, it be to meet at three o'clock to-morrow afternoon.

Mr. N. G. PARKER. I move that when this house adjourns to-morrow, it adjourn at 11 o'clock.

Mr. E. W. M. MACKEY moved to amend by inserting 12.

The question was then taken on the motion of Ν. PARKER to adjourn at 11 to-morrow, and agreed to; and, on motion of Mr. J. M. RUTLAND, the Convention then adjourned.

THIRTY-EIGHTH DAY.

Friday, February 28, 1868.

The Convention assembled at 10 A. M., and was called to order by the President, Hon. A. G. MACKEY.

Prayer was offered by the Rev. ISAAC BROCKENTON.

The roll was called, and a quorum answering to their names, the PRESIDENT announced the Convention ready to proceed to business.

The Journal of Thursday was read and approved.

Mr. H. E. HAYNE. I move a reconsideration of the vote by which the house agreed to adjourn at eleven o'clock this morning. I desire that the business of the Convention should be proceeded with by calling to the Chair, temporarily, the member from Fairfield (Mr. J. M. RUTLAND), and excusing the President and Chairman of the Finance Committee, while absent at headquarters receiving the money to pay the members.

Mr. J. M. RUTLAND. I beg leave to decline, as it would require the greatest familiarity with the bills now before the Convention, and practice, to manage and keep in order the numerous amendments offered.

The question being put to the house, a division was called for, and resulted—yeas 32, nays 48. So the house refused to reconsider.

A number of applications from members for leave of absence were read.

Mr. S. G. W. DILL. I object to granting any further leaves of absence, unless the members are called home by sickness or some similar pressing necessity. I am as anxious to be at home as any one, but while there is so much work to be done, every member owes it to the State, to his constituents and himself, to finish the labor of the Convention within the shortest possible time.

Mr. B. O. DUNCAN. I fear there is danger of being left without a quorum. I think leave of absence should not be granted without a good excuse was given.

The question being put, the house refused to grant leave.

On motion, the applications were taken up separately.

The reasons of the members applying for leave of absence were given, and leave granted.

On motion, the consideration of the unfinished business was suspended for a short time.

Mr. W. J. McKINLAY submitted the following resolutions:

Resolved, That delegates to this Convention, to whom leave of absence has been granted, be required to report to this body on their return.

Resolved, That in the event the time granted in said leave be extended, they be required to render, on honor, a satisfactory excuse to this body, or be debarred the payment of their per diem for every day so absent, and that leave of absence shall not be granted to more than eight members at the same time, except in case of sickness.

Mr. C. D. HAYNE moved to lay the resolutions on the table, which was not agreed to, and the resolutions was adopted.

Mr. C. C. BOWEN presented the petition of Mr. F. C. Miller, of Charleston, asking to have his disabilities removed. He represents that he is disqualified from holding any office under the government of the State, or of the United States, by reason of having participated in the late war; but he participated to this extent only, that he enlisted as a private in the Marion Artillery, from the City of Charleston, about the 1st of November, 1862; did not hasten to go into the war, and kept out of it as long as he could. The petitioner looks upon the said attempt to sunder the Union as a crime, and regrets that he was ever led into it, or felt any sympathy for it. He now sincerely desires the restoration of the State to her place in the Union, under the reconstruction acts of Congress, and desires to be allowed to participate in the work of restoration.

Petitions in favor of C. W. Dudley, and Thos. C. Dudley, of Darlington; Alexander McBee, of Greenville; H. H. Kinard, A. McDaniels, S. P. Kinard, T. W. Morris, H. S. Hammett, and H. Beatty, were also presented, and all referred to the Committee on Petitions.

The hour of adjournment having arrived, the Convention adjourned to 3 o'clock this afternoon.

AFTERNOON SESSION.

The Convention re-assembled at 3 P. M.

The roll was called, and a quorum being present, the Convention proceeded to business.

Mr. E. W. M. MACKEY moved that the Convention take a recess of

80

three-quarters of an hour to allow the members to receive their pay and mileage, which was agreed to.

After the expiration of that time, the PRESIDENT called the house to order, and, on motion of Mr. J. M. RUTLAND, the Convention adjourned.

THIRTY-NINTH DAY.

Saturday, February 29, 1868.

The Convention assembled at 10 A. M., and was called to order by the PRESIDENT.

Prayer was offered by the Rev. ALLEN FRANKLIN.

The roll was called, and a quorum answering to their names, the PRESIDENT announced the Convention ready to proceed to business.

The Journal of Friday was read and approved.

Mr. B. F. RANDOLPH moved to suspend the rules of the house to take up the ordinance requiring the Legislature to appoint three Commissioners, to investigate what are the outstanding obligations of the State and their validity.

The motion to suspend was not agreed to.

The consideration of the Judiciary report was resumed from the nineteenth section.

Mr. J. M. RUTLAND offered the following as a substitute for the section:

Section 19. The Judges of the Court of Common Pleas shall, hereafter, be invested with all the powers of Chancellors to hear and determine Equity causes, and the rules and practice which now govern Courts of Equity in their proceedings, shall continue until changed by law. There shall be at least two annual sessions of the Court of Equity in each judicial district in the State, to be held at such times and places as may be prescribed by law. It shall be the duty of the Judges in Equity to file their decisions within ninety days from the day of the hearing of the causes respectively. There shall be one Commissioner in Equity for each judicial district in the State, to be elected by the people of such district, whose term of office shall be two years, and whose fees and duties shall continue the same as at the present time, till changed by law.

Mr. R. C. DeLARGE moved the indefinite postponement of the substitute.

Mr. E. W. M. MACKEY moved a postponement of the further consideration of the original section until Tuesday next, at 11 o'clock, and that in the meantime the substitute be printed and laid upon the tables of the members.

Mr. J. M. RUTLAND seconded the motion.

Mr. R. C. DeLARGE. I am opposed to the motion to postpone simply to print, on the ground that it will establish a bad precedent, and before we have finished our work on the Constitution, we may have to postpone nearly every other section, to give time for printing both substitutes and amendments. The substitute as read was well understood, as it proposes to introduce into the Constitution what we proposed to keep out, that is Courts of Equity.

Mr. D. H. CHAMBERLAIN. I differ entirely with the delegate from Charleston (Mr. R. C. DeLARGE.) It is at least an important and open question, whether something in the nature of the provision proposed by the delegate from Fairfeld (Mr. J. M. RUTLAND), shall be adopted, or whether, at one stroke, it will be safe to abolish the Court of Equity and all the officers connected with that Court. In my opinion, and I believe the majority of the Convention will agree with me, that it is better to have the elaborate and carefully prepared substitute of the distinguished member from Fairfield printed, and that we have time to consider it.

The question being put, the further consideration of the nineteenth section was postponed, and the substitute ordered to be printed.

Section twenty, providing exclusive jurisdiction of the Court of General Sessions over criminal cases, and for three terms every year in each judicial district, was read.

Mr. J. L. NEAGLE moved to amend by striking out "judicial district" and inserting "county," and the section, so amended, passed to its third reading.

Section twenty-one, providing for the election every two years of a Board of County Commissioners, to have jurisdiction over roads, highways, ferries, bridges, and in all matters relating to taxes, disbursements of money for district or county purposes, internal improvements and local concerns of the respective districts, was read.

Mr. J. L. NEAGLE moved to amend by substituting "county" for "district," which was agreed to.

Mr. B. F. WHITTEMORE moved to strike out the words " District

Court" in second line, and insert "Board of County Commissioners," which was agreed to.

Mr. J. L. NEAGLE moved to substitute the word "county" for the word "district," throughout the sections, which was agreed to.

Mr. WM. McKINLAY. In my opinion this section, as it reads, confers unlimited and dangerous powers upon the boards it proposes to create; powers capable of great abuse, and, if injudiciously exercised, calculated to entail ruin not only upon the district, but the entire State. It is very evident that these boards, under this section, would have the power, if they chose to exercise it, to purchase the right of way in their respective districts, and construct main roads where, perhaps, main roads are not needed, and might, even if they desired it, purchase the right of way and construct railroads where railroads are not needed. If they deemed it expedient for the benefit of the district, they could undertake to clean our rivers and make them navigable. They might make navigable streams where a ship never could reach. They have, also, the power to collect taxes. With the view of putting this section in form, I move to amend in second line by striking out the words "which shall have full jurisdiction over," and insert the words "who under the authority of the General Assembly shall supervise," and likewise to strike out all in the section after the word "and" in third line, and insert in place thereof the following: "to discharge such other duties appertaining to the counties as may be authorized by law."

The amendment was not agreed to.

Mr. F. L. CARDOZO moved to strike out the section, which was not agreed to.

Mr. F. L. CARDOZO. I object to this section for various reasons. In the first place, I do not think it essential to the completeness of the judicial report. It refers to ferries, highways, bridges, internal improvements, taxes, and other local concerns. I would like to know in what respect these things are essential to a judicial report? This is a matter for the Legislature. If we establish this body, we tie the hands of the Legislature, and prevent their making laws that might suit county purposes better. If essential, as it evidently is, to have some board to attend to this matter, and the Legislature to make a law, they can repeal it from year to year to suit all circumstances. The Constitution ought not to go into such details; we should simply state the general principles, and leave it to the General Assembly, to time, and to the development of circumstances, to make the proper applications. In what sense is it essential to a judicial report, that we should provide a a Board of Commissioners for a ferry? The Legislature can create these

Boards of Commissioners. If we make the law, when the Legislature meets they can make provision for carrying it out in all its details. I move, therefore, that the amendment be laid on the table.

At the request of Mr. N. G. PARKER, the motion to lay on the table was withdrawn to allow the Chairman of the Committee on the Judiciary an opportunity to be heard.

Mr. C. C. BOWEN. I certainly see great necessity for the section remaining just as it is. The only objection that seems to be raised is to giving these Boards jurisdiction in matters of fine and disbursements. wish to add, that under the laws of South Carolina, subject to no alteration by the Legislature, there are three different Boards of Commissioners, having power in each district to assess taxes, and they are responsible to no one. They can assess taxes under the Sheriff, and nobody has any business to open their mouth as to the propriety of the assessment, or where the money goes to. The provision proposed in the section can be found in nearly every State Constitution of the Union. In some they are styled Boards of Commissioners, in others Boards of Supervisors. In regard to the construction of railroads, I will state that I presume no body or set of men will attempt such an enterprise without having that indispensable instrument—a charter from the Legislature.

These persons only have jurisdiction in county matters. There may be many things we have already done that could have been left to the Legislature. We could have said that the judicial power of the State shall consist of such inferior courts as the Legislature shall establish. If we wanted to leave this to the Legislature, we could have said that; but we deemed it advisable to lay down general rules, by which the Legislature shall be governed.

A clause similar to this can be found in the Constitution of nearly every State in the Union. In some of the States the Boards of Commissioners consist of five persons instead of three, and are more generally known as Boards of Supervisors. I certainly think there should be something of the kind here. There is now a Board who have the right to assess. They make out their returns, and hand them to the Sheriff. The Sheriff hands them to the collectors to collect the money, and fifteen or twenty per cent. is taken off from the amount collected. The proposition is to consolidate, to put this matter in the hands of three persons, who shall be held directly responsible. If these Commissioners do anything wrong, the persons wronged have the right to appeal to any Court in South Carolina. In regard to leaving this to the Legislature, I am not in favor of doing it. We do not know what that body may do. If it passes laws covering this section now, the next Legislature may change them entirely to our detriment. I am, therefore, in favor of settling the question right here. A proposition will be made in the Legislature defining the several counties, and I am a little surprised that it has not been brought up here. I am in favor of putting it into the Constitution. If so, it will be essential that these Boards shall have been constituted by law. If the counties are divided into townships, men will be elected to conduct the affairs of each town.

It is not intended that these Boards shall interfere with any person having a chartered ferry, who complies with the condition of the charter. It will be the business of the Commissioners, however, if roads are impassable, to repair them, to remove any obstacles in a public highway, or to go into Court and move an injunction against any party who places obstructions in a public road. Any party feeling themselves aggrieved by any acts of these Commissioners, as I have said before, can go into Court and make their appeal. In other words, the jurisdiction of these Commissioners is not final. I, therefore, move to strike out the word "full" on the second line, before the word "jurisdiction." With that amendment I hope the section will be passed.

Mr. R. C. DeLARGE. I move to amend so as to read: "The Legislature shall, at its first session, make provision for the election of three Commissioners in each county, and shall prescribe their duties and powers." I trust this amendment will be adopted. It can truly be called the olive branch between the two parties.

Mr. WM. McKINLAY. Will the gentleman from Charleston explain the difference between his amendment and the substitute proposed?

Mr. S. A. SWAILS. I move that the substitute be indefinitely postponed.

Mr. R. C. DeLARGE. In answer to my colleague, I would say that my substitute proposes to give the Legislature the power to pass a law, by which three Commissioners shall be elected, in what manner they shall be elected, and to whom they shall be responsible. I trust that substitute will be adopted.

Mr. J. S. CRAIG. I offer the following amendment: "The qualified electors of each judicial county shall elect three persons for the term of two years, to constitute a Board of County Commissioners, who shall have jurisdiction over public roads, highways, ferries, bridges and public buildings, and in all matters relating to taxes and disbursements of money for county purposes, in such manner as shall be provided by law." That, I consider, covers all the ground, and obviates all objections to the original section.

Mr. F. J. MOSES, Jr. I move to strike out the word "full," before the word "jurisdiction," and to insert the word "original," and to insert after the word "districts," at the conclusion, "*Provided*, That in all cases there shall be the right to appeal to the State Courts from the decision of the said Commissioners."

Mr. S. A. SWAILS moved to strike out in the last line, "and local concerns."

Mr. R. C. DeLARGE moved that the section be recommitted to the Judiciary Committee, with instructions to report thereon on Monday.

Mr. J. J. WRIGHT. This matter has received the most careful attention of the Judiciary Committee, and they have reported it for the consideration of this house. This is the time and place to act upon it. If we desire to adopt or reject the section, it is our prerogative to do so. If we wish to offer amendments or substitutes, that, also, is within our province. But if we recommit it to the Committee, it will only result in the loss of so much time, for I do not believe that there are any members on that Committee who would make any change in the section. In regard to the amendments offered by the Chairman of the Committee to strike out the word "full," before jurisdiction, and the word "district," so as to make it "Boards of County Commissioners," there was considerable diversity of opinion. There was a hitch in the Committee in relation to this matter, from the fact that the established Courts in some of the districts, including my own (Beaufort), had failed to mete out justice to the people. There are a class of people whose cases might be brought before a District Court composed of County Commissioners. That was the reason it was proposed to constitute these Boards a Court, with power, in cases where they were not able to collect district taxes, to issue their summons to defaulters, without being compelled to apply to a Justice of the Peace. I believe it is the usual practice in every State to have a Board of County Commissioners, who are entrusted with powers similar to what we propose to invest them with here, in this twenty-first section. I believe it would be impossible for us to get along without some such Board of Commissioners. Experience is the best test, and those States that have tried a different experiment from this have failed, and have finally resorted to this measure. These Commissioners will have all the power over roads, ferries, &c., and they should have the power to collect taxes to keep them in a good condition. If I am driving a horse over a road unfit for travelling, and the horse becomes injured in consequence of it, I want a remedy, and it will be my privilege to bring a charge against the county. I have known many cases brought up against a county for loss of property or damage caused by roads being in an unfit condition for travelling.

The gentleman from Charleston (Mr. DeLARGE) proposes, in his substitute, to make it obligatory upon the next Legislature to devise such ways and means as they think proper for the establishment of these Boards. If his substitute be adopted, it would give rise to this difficulty: In the first place, a special election would have to be ordered to elect these Commissioners. In the next place, if there was not a special election at once, then nothing could be done until 1869. We want this measure to go into effect as soon as possible after this Constitution is ratified. We want to commence work on our highways, and to put them in travelling condition. I trust that this section will not be recommitted, or that we shall lose any further time. Let us make no further change, for I believe it is just what we want and what we should have.

Mr. F. L. CARDOZO. I renew my motion to lay the amendment of the gentleman from Charleston (Mr. DeLARGE) on the table.

The motion to lay on the table was not agreed to.

Mr. B. BYAS. I hope the section will not be recommitted. Most of the amendments offered have been made by the Chairman of the Judiciary Committee. I agree with the gentleman from Beaufort, that to recommit would be only a loss of so much time. I hope all the amendments will be voted down, with the exception of the amendment offered by the gentleman from Sumter (Mr. MOSES), and that the section, with that amendment, will pass to its third reading.

Mr. J. H. JENKS. I move to amend in the second line by inserting before the word roads the words "public buildings," in the third line, after the word bridges, "public buildings," and at the close, after the word district, the words, "subject to the enactments of the General Assembly."

Mr. R. B. ELLIOTT called for the previous question, which was sustained.

The question was first taken on the amendment offered by the gentleman from York (Mr. J. L. NEAGLE) to strike out the word "district," and insert "county," which was agreed to.

The next was on the amendment of Mr. F. J. MOSES, Jr., to strike out the word "full," before jurisdiction, which was decided in the negative.

The next question, was on the amendment offered by Mr. C. C. BOWEN, Chairman of the Judiciary Committee, to strike out the word "full," which was agreed to.

The next question, was on the motion of Mr. S. A. SWAILS to strike out "and local concerns," which was decided in the negative.

The question was then taken on the amendment offered by Mr. B. O.

DUNCAN, to strike out " roads, bridges and ferries," and insert " public buildings," which was decided in the negative.

The amendment offered by Mr. F. J. MOSES, Jr., to add "provided that, in all cases, there shall be the right to appeal to the State Courts from the decision of said Commissioners," was agreed to.

The amendment offered by Mr. J. H. JENKS, of Berkley, was disagreed to.

The amendment offered by Mr. WM. McKINLAY was also decided in the negative.

The amendment offered by Mr. R. C. DeLARGE was decided in the negative.

The amendment proposed by Mr. J. S. CRAIG was also disagreed to.

Section twenty-one, as amended, then passed to its third reading.

Section twenty-two was read as follows :

SECTION 22. A Court of Probate shall be established in each judicial district, with jurisdiction in all matters testamentary and of administration, in business appertaining to minors and the allotment of dower in cases of idiotcy and lunacy, and persons *non compos mentis.* The Judge of said Court shall be elected by the qualified electors of the respective districts for the term of two years.

Mr. B. F. RANDOLPH. I move to amend in the fourth line by striking out " qualified electors of the respective districts," and inserting the words " General Assembly," so that it shall read " the Judge of said Court shall be elected by the General Assembly for the term of two years." The question of the election of Judges by the people has been before this body twice. I am opposed to the elective system of Judges. We have in both previous cases decided that the General Assembly shall elect these Judges. I am also in favor of it in this case. I do not propose now to give my reasons at length, as I have heretofore given them. A very experienced gentleman from New York, as we heard the other day, said if it did not fail in South Carolina it would be a strange business. I ask, gentlemen, if they can show such elements of character in the people of South Carolina as will guarantee the success of this system, that are not found in the people of the State of New York ? If you can show more experience, more intelligence in the people of South Carolina than in those of New York, which will guarantee the complete success of this system, then I will vote for the election of Judges. There are those who seem to think it is in accordance with republicanism. I do not propose to make republicanism go down on all-fours. I believe in republicanism and in radicalism, but I do not

81

believe in carrying it to extremes. I am opposed to the election of Judges, because, in my opinion, it weakens their fidelity.

Mr. L. S. LANGLEY. I would like to know whether the gentleman considers vesting power in the hands of the people extreme?

Mr. B F. RANDOLPH. I do. It was urged by that same gentleman that the people were better qualified to elect and judge of the qualifications of men than the General Assembly. Does he suppose that the members of the Legislature will be no more intelligent than the people at large? It seems to me that that is a strange proposition. If the members of the General Assembly are to be no more intelligent than the people are, then I say God help South Carolina. It is to be supposed that the General Assembly will be composed of select men, who are capable of making laws, and who possess qualifications that the people do not generally possess. It may be said that it has been the custom in the State of South Carolina to have the Probate Judges elected by the people. It matters not what South Carolina has done in the past, we are now acting under new circumstances; we are preparing for the future. South Carolina, in the past, went to a great many extremes. South Carolina, in the past, supposed she possessed more intelligence than all the other States in the Union; she set herself up as a model, and dictated to the General Government; and, finally, defied the General Government. It defied God. She refused to grant divorces. God wills there should be divorces. South Carolina even went so far as to say God was wrong and South Carolina was right. I think it is time for us to cease going to these extremes.

Mr. R. C. DeLARGE. What page of the Bible, or chapter and verse, does the gentleman quote from?

Mr. L. S. LANGLEY. What connection has the election of Judges with divorces?

Mr. B. F. RANDOLPH. I do not see the sense or wisdom of the gentleman's question. For the reasons I have given, I hope these words "qualified electors" will be stricken out, and the words "General Assembly" substituted.

Mr. R. G. HOLMES. I move to strike out the words "judicial district" and insert "county."

Mr. J. M. RUTLAND. I move to strike out the word "*compos,*" on the third line.

Mr. J. L. NEAGLE moved the previous question.

The call for the previous question was not seconded.

Mr. R. C. DeLARGE. I trust the motion of the gentleman from Orangeburg will prevail,

Mr. S. G. W DILL. I have consumed as little time on this floor as any man in this house, but I hope I have done as much good as any member of the house in effectual work. I am tired of seeing the people of South Carolina robbed of their rights. The gentleman from Orangeburg has said more than he would have dared to say to the people at home, that he did not believe in the people electing their officers. We have come to this Convention to discharge the duty that our constituency at home require of us; what I proposed and promised to do before I left home, I propose to do now. I hold the same opinions that I held when I first became a candidate of the republican party in my district. I am a Union man out and out. I was born and reared by Union parents, God knows it is my highest pride to have been a Union man; I have taken the pledge of unionism to the mother who embraced me; I am not willing to take away the suffrage of my people. If I had told them that, I never would have left home, neither would the gentleman from Orangeburg.

Mr. B. F. RANDOLPH. I beg leave to deny that.

Mr. S. G. W. DILL. I have kept quiet on this floor and seen my people robbed of their rights. I say they should have the privilege of electing all their officers, from the Supreme Judges and Governor, down to and including their Magistrates and Constables.

The PRESIDENT announced that the hour for the Special Order had arrived.

Mr. R. B. ELLIOTT moved to postpone the consideration of the Special Order for ten minutes.

Mr. B. F. WHITTEMORE moved to postpone the Special Order until the twenty-second section was disposed of.

Mr. R. C. DeLARGE moved to postpone the Special Order until 12 o'clock Monday.

The PRESIDENT stated the Special Order to be, an ordinance proposed by the Committee on the Miscellaneous Provisions of the Constitution, for the protection of the rights of minors.

Mr. J. J. WRIGHT. As this is a matter of vital importance, and we have not had time to consider it, I hope it will be postponed until Monday. I have no copy of the ordinance before me, and cannot give it the consideration it should receive.

Mr. B. F. RANDOLPH. The Committee have had that ordinance under consideration, and proposed to refer it back to the Judiciary Committee, that it may be reported back to the house. If this motion to postpone is voted down, a proposition will be made to refer it to that Committee with instructions. A certain distinguished legal gentleman, in connection with the Committee, considered that ordinance as it is framed.

Mr. B. BYAS. I hope the motion to postpone will not prevail. It has been before the Convention already and argued at great length, and I trust we will now take it up and dispose of it at once.

Mr. B. F. WHITTEMORE. I trust it will be taken up for the purpose of allowing the Chairman of the Committee on the Miscellaneous portion of the Constitution, to make a motion to refer it back to the Jueiary Committee.

The motion to postpone the Special Order until Monday was not agreed to, and, on motion, its consideration was postponed in order to allow Mr. DILL to conclude his remarks on the twenty-second section of the Judiciary report.

Mr. S. G. W. DILL. If I have wounded any gentleman's feelings in this Convention I do not know it, and did not intend it. It was said by the gentleman from Orangeburg that the State of New York, and other States north and west of us, have adopted this rule of election by a joint ballot of their Legislatures. The New Yorkers are in New York, and the Iowa people are in Iowa, and South Carolinians are in South Carolina. I do not think we are compelled to follow the example of any other State; the city of New York, in particular, I do not regard as an example for anybody; she has always gone head and heels for the democratic party, no matter how corrupt or how debased its leader may have been. She is not an example for me, for the people of my district, nor for the people of South Carolina; but every argument brought up here seems to be in favor of pleasing and appeasing democrats; God knows I would not follow in their footsteps if it cost me my existence. I have been asked here in the streets of Charleston, where I resided nearly forty years, and have only been out of it three years : " Mr. DILL what are you doing in this ring-streaked-and-striped Convention ? I am surprised at you, I would not stay in that damn nigger Convention ?" My reply was, I have always been a poor man, and was always known to be on the side of the poor. These people, I said, have been robbed heretofore, their wives, daughters and sisters, taken from them and sold ; they have been maltreated, and I asked who made this Convention ring-streaked-and-striped, and who consorted with their families ? Their complaint is like that of the wolf, who complained of the sheep muddling the water above him.

The gentleman from Orangeburg said, if the members of the Legislature were no more competent to elect officers, from the highest to the lowest, than the people of the State, then, "God help South Carolina."

I say, God help the people of South Carolina, if they allow the power they now have to again slip out of their hands. I am through, but let me say, in conclusion, the people of Kershaw District demand that these elections shall be left in the hands of the people. I, as their humble representative, answer with all my heart, amen. For those who have acted differently I can only pray that God in his great wisdom may bring them to repentance; for I tell them the people will hold them responsible for their action.

The consideration of the Special Order was resumed.

Mr. B. O. DUNCAN submitted the following, which was agreed to:

Resolved, That this report of the Committee on Miscellaneous Provisions be referred to the Judiciary Committee, with instructions to consider the propriety of inserting a section in the Constitution to protect minors and other *cestui que* trusts against Trustees, Guardians and other fiduciary agents who invested the funds of their trusts in Confederate or State bonds during the war. Also, to consider the propriety of annulling all debts still unsettled, either public or private, made in aid of the rebellion, or by order of the Confederate authorities, or by order of the State authorities during the war. Also, to consider the propriety of inserting in the Constitution a section annulling all obligations contracted for slaves, and taking from the Courts jurisdiction over all claims of this nature.

The unfinished business, being the consideration of the twenty-second section of the Judiciary Report, was then resumed.

The question was then taken on the motion of Mr. B. F. RANDOLPH to strike out the words "qualified electors," and insert "General Assembly."

Mr. C. M. WILDER moved the indefinite postponement of the motion, which was agreed to, and section twenty-second then passed to its third reading.

Section twenty-third was read, as follows:

SECTION 23. A competent number of Justices of the Peace and Constables shall be chosen in each district by the qualified electors thereof, in such manner as the General Assembly may direct; they shall hold their offices for a term of two years and until their successors are elected and qualified. They shall reside in the district, city or beat for which they are elected, and the Justices of the Peace shall be commissioned by the Governor.

Mr. J. L. NEAGLE moved to strike out "district," and insert "county," which was agreed to.

Mr. R. G. HOLMES moved to strike out the word "beat" in the fourth line, and to insert the word "township," which was not agreed to.

Mr. C. C. BOWEN moved a call of the house. The call was ordered, and a quorum being present, the discussion was continued; and Mr. J. S. CRAIG moved a reconsideration of the vote by which the word "beat" was not stricken out, which was lost, and section twenty-third passed to its third reading.

Mr. R. C. DeLARGE gave notice that on Monday next he would move a reconsideration of the vote whereby section twenty-second passed to its third reading.

Section twenty-fourth was read as follows, and passed to a third reading, without debate:

SECTION 24. Justices of the Peace, individually, or two or more of them jointly, as the General Assembly may direct, shall have original jurisdiction in cases of bastardy, and in all matters of contract, and actions for the recovery of fines and forfeitures, where the amount claimed does not exceed one hundred dollars, and such jurisdiction as may be provided by law in actions *ex delicto*, where the damages claimed do not exceed one hundred dollars; and prosecutions for assault and battery, and other penal offences less than felony, punishable by fines only.

Section twenty-fifth was read, as follows:

SECTION 25. They may also sit as examining Courts, and commit, discharge, or recognize persons charged with offences not capital, subject to such regulations as the General Assembly may provide; they shall also have power to bind over to keep the peace, or for good behavior. For the foregoing purposes they shall have power to issue all necessary process.

Mr. C. C. BOWEN moved to insert after the word "or," on first line, the words, "except in capital cases;" and to strike out in second line the words, "not capital," which was adopted, and the section passed to its third reading.

Sections twenty-sixth and twenty-seventh, relative to the regulation of actions before Justices of the Peace, and compensation of Judges of Probate, Justices of the Peace, and Constables, were read, and passed to their third reading, without debate.

Section twenty-eighth was read a second time, as follows:

SECTION 28. No person who has arrived at the age of seventy years shall be appointed or elected to fill the office of Judge in this State.

Mr. R. C. DeLARGE. I move to strike out the entire section.

Mr. B. F. WHITTEMORE. I move to substitute "eighty" for "seventy."

Mr. B. F. RANDOLPH. I move to amend by inserting "one hundred."

Mr. B. BYAS. I move to amend by making it "seventy-five."

Mr. N. G. PARKER. I move to postpone indefinitely all the amendments.

Mr. B. BYAS. I hope they will not be indefinitely postponed.

Mr. J. L. NEAGLE. I second the hope. God in his omnipotent wisdom hath decreed that man's existence should be three score years and ten. I hope we will take up and discuss the various amendments.

Mr. R. C. DeLARGE. I trust the house will not gag the friends of the various measures proposed by postponing them in a bunch, but that we will discuss and act intelligently upon them.

The question was then taken upon the motion to postpone, and decided in the negative.

The question next recurred on the motion to strike out "seventy" and insert "one hundred."

Mr. B. F. RANDOLPH. I have known, and, perhaps, other members of this body have known men who at the age of ninety, or over, were better qualified, and had more experience for the responsible position of Judge than men at the ages of twenty-five or thirty. I hope, therefore, the word "seventy" will be stricken out and "one hundred" inserted.

Mr. R. H. CAIN. I think we could pass this just as it is without doing any harm; I think we are only losing precious time. When a person arrives at the age of seventy he has spent the greater portion of his best days, and should be permitted to retire.

Mr. J. S. CRAIG. We have already provided that our Judges shall be elected for six years. It appears to me it should be left to those who elect a person to that office to decide for themselves whether his mind or judgment is likely to be impaired by old age before his time will expire. It seems to me unnecessary to make it seventy, one hundred, or any other age. I, therefore, propose to strike out the whole section.

Mr. S. G. W. DILL. I am in favor of the motion to strike out the section. I regard it as but another attempt to rob the people of their rights. I was disposed to let the people choose the Judges themselves. If a man is eighty years or over, and chooses to become a candidate and he can be elected, it should be his privilege to serve.

Mr. R. C. DeLARGE. I trust the house will consent to strike out this section. Some of the most prominent men in the country are those who have attained the age of seventy years.

The speaker was proceeding, when the PRESIDENT announced the hour of one having arrived, and the Convention stood adjourned to three P. M.

AFTERNOON SESSION.

The Convention re-assembled at three P. M., and was called to order by the PRESIDENT.

Mr. S. G. W. DILL. I rise to a question of privilege. I desire to finish my remarks in relation to the attack of the Mercury upon my character. Prudence forbade me, this morning, from saying what I desired to say in this Convention about that sheet.

Mr. J. J. WRIGHT. I object to any further explanation.

The PRESIDENT. Every member of a deliberative body has the right to vindicate himself from any attack made upon him in any of the public journals of the city.

Mr. F. J. MOSES, Jr. I desire to ask the Chair if the privilege accorded the gentlemen is under the rules of the house. If it is, I desire to make a motion to suspend the rule in order to debar him that privilege ?

The question was taken on the motion to suspend the rules of the house, and was decided in the negative.

Mr. L. S. LANGLEY moved that the Convention adjourn, which was not agreed to.

Mr. S. G. W. DILL. I hope my friend of the Mercury will stand here forever.

The Mercury has said that I oppressed people with my laws. I pronounce it a willful fabrication. My more respectable neighbors they allude d to are men and persons I never had communication with, nor never expect to. They are men of no character, and not worthy of my notice. The assertion that I came into Camden on Court day with an escort is a fabrication. A goodly number of people did come there, but not as my escort; that I can prove. The assertion that I indicted a gentleman for assault and battery may be true, but that any were placed on the stand and swore they would not believe me on oath is not true; that is a wilful fabrication. They did say they would not believe me;

but when the Solicitor put the question, "is it not Squire DILL'S political views you allude to and not his word?" the answer was, "mostly that." It is false when they say "no bill was found." A *nol. pros.* was ordered to be entered on the Journal. It was a verification of the old saying, "sue the devil and try the case in hell." I was attacked on the highway by this ruffian, who leaped into my buggy and attempted to draw me out, and I broke his arm for him. So much for that.

The Mercury calls us a ring-streaked-and-striped Convention; I admit it is all that; but who made it ring-streaked-and-striped but just such men as conduct the Mercury? It would not have been ring-streaked-and-striped, if such men as manage the Mercury office and newspaper had been exterminated long ago. They put the stripes into it.

Mr. B. F. RANDOLPH. The gentleman is certainly out of order in going into the character of the Convention.

Mr. S. G. W. DILL. I beg to say that as I am one, though a small part of the Convention, it is a stigma towards me, and I have a right to relieve myself. These men are fond of "Ariel;" they believe in "Ariel," and they say colored beasts are best, and we in the Convention are beasts.

Mr. B. F. RANDOLPH. I object to the gentleman's discussing the Mercury's fondness for "Ariel;" I do not think it applicable.

Mr. S. G. W. DILL. I say if what "Ariel" states is true, the State will have a fine time in trying these gentleman for violations of law, for it is against the law of God, as well as against the law of the land, to lie down and have carnal connection with beasts ; therefore they must die, and should have suffered the penalty of their crimes long ago.

The PRESIDENT decided that the gentleman's time was up, and the consideration of the twenty-eighth section of the Judiciary report was resumed.

Mr. R. C. DeLARGE. I repeat the hope that this section will be stricken out. I believe it to be inconsistent with the principles of justice and equity. Some of the most prominent and leading men in the country are those whose minds are brightest, and their intellects shine with the greatest brilliancy at the age of seventy. I may refer to the honored President of the Convention, who has arrived at the age of sixty, and whose presiding over the deliberations of this body is, of itself, one of the strongest arguments against this section being retained. One of the most learned men of this State—one of the ablest South Carolina jurists and Judges who have graced the bench of the State, though differing with them in politics, is Chief Justice Dunkin, now over seventy

82

years of age, retaining and exercising his full intellectual powers—an ornament to the bar and the State. Turning to the past history of my native State, I might refer you to the late Chief Justice O'Neall, Chancellor Johnson, and others, who, during their time, rendered the ablest decisions at seventy years of age, and who, as far as ability and learning were concerned in the dispensation of law, had no superiors. That any of our learned Judges on the bench differed with us in politics is not to be taken in question in the administration of law. I know it will be argued that men at that age become imbecile and childish; but in the present Constitution which we are framing, we have a safeguard in having restricted the term for which a Judge is elected to six years. But to send forth such a doctrine, that to be old, to be experienced, to be wise, is a crime, is certainly not in accordance with republican principles, which we all desire to perpetuate. One of our most ardent advocates is Mr. Thaddeus Stevens, now over seventy-five years of age. It is true, the opponents of reconstruction may say he is unable to deliver his own speeches, but no one can for a moment doubt the brightness of his mind, or his consistency to his country and to mankind.

In the cabinet of the present Administration we find Mr. Seward, who, although said by some to be a wily politician, is a man of undoubted ability, and is over seventy years of age. I might go on and cite hundreds of other cases.

Mr. J. J. WRIGHT. How old was Chief Justice Blackstone when he died?

Mr. R. C. DeLARGE. According to the best information I have, he was, at the time of his death, in the sixty-ninth year of his age. Where you find a man who once possessed a brilliant mind becoming an imbecile at seventy, you will find hundreds who have retained the brilliancy of their intellects to the hour of their death. It was a settled principle heretofore in South Carolina, that unless a man had attained a certain age, or was gray-headed, he was unfit to take part in the government of the State, and unfit to be a legislator. That sentiment ruined the State. It kept out of the offices of the State the ideas of progress. It kept young men from reaching any position, and placed the State in the hands of the ruling aristocracy, and a set of men who were taught all the prejudices of the heretofore ruling classes, and the prejudices of the social circles of that class, before they were allowed to get into any position. You propose to go to the other extreme. I trust our test will be ability, integrity, and honesty, the true test and key-note to republicanism. I trust the section will be stricken out.

Mr. C. C. BOWEN. The gentleman has undertaken to show that

persons at the age of seventy years are just as eligible to office as a person in the meridian of life. In support of that, he has cited various other officers. I would remind the gentleman that the cases cited by him are not analogous to that of the Circuit Judges to be elected here, and who are expected to ride over the circuits, and hold at least five terms a year in each county. The State of New York retire their Judges at sixty-five. It was to avoid any necessity to impeach or try a Judge for inability or infirmity in the discharge of his duty that this section was inserted. The object is to prevent the offices of Judge being filled with imbeciles. I propose to offer an amendment, which I hope will be accepted as a compromise. I propose to strike out on the second line the words, "who shall," and insert, "after he arrives at the age of seventy years," and to add at the close, "*Provided*, That the prohibition herein contained shall not extend to the Judges of the Supreme Court." I contend that when a man arrives at the age of seventy he is unfit to be put upon any circuit. Though Judge Dunkin may be an able man, I contend it is no criterion in this case. I hope the Convention will pass the section with the amendment I propose.

Mr. R. G. HOLMES. My objection to the section is that I do not think we should limit the people in their choice of Judges. If it was left to the Governor to appoint, I might favor the passage of the section as it is. I have been looking over to find the ages at which some of our Presidents died. Washington died at seventy, Adams at eighty-four, Jefferson at eighty-three, Madison at seventy-five, Monroe at seventy-four. No one will say that these men were *non compos* at the age of seventy. Men are as sound in their judgment at the age of seventy as they are at any time of their life. We have left it in the hands of the people to say whether they shall be Judges, and we certainly should not limit them to age. Suppose a man is sixty-eight or sixty-nine years old, and we wanted to elect him Judge for six years. By this section we would be deprived of that privilege. There are many reasons why we should strike out the whole section.

Mr. B. F. RANDOLPH. Do you not think the rule by which the Judges of the Supreme Court of the United States are allowed to hold their position for life a good one?

Mr. R. G. HOLMES. I do not.

Mr. F. L. CARDOZO. I think gentlemen are fighting a shadow. The amendment would allow a Judge to continue in office until he was seventy-five years and eleven months old.

Mr. A. J. RANSIER. I hope this section will neither be stricken out nor passed in its present form. The cases of John Quincy Adams and our own Chief Justice Dunkin, cited here, are known to be exceptions. In this case, we are endeavoring to lay down a certain principle, according to what is a well known and acknowledged fact. Men at the ages of fifty and sixty may certainly be said to be going down the hill of life. Our efforts, in my opinion, should be to select those who still retain the vigor of their intellect. It is asserted that the Legislature will exercise this prerogative discreetly, and will see to it that no person is selected who is incompetent to fill the position of Judge. But if we leave it entirely open, we do not know what will be the result. We are called upon to settle this question here, and I hope we will not leave it to an uncertainty. The Constitutions of the several States limit the number of years, as this section does, to seventy. I think it will be found in the Constitutions of Massachusetts, Rhode Island, Connecticut, and several others. I do not propose to vote for the section as it is. I move to amend by inserting " eighty-five" instead of " seventy."

Mr. WM. J. McKINLAY. Could I be convinced by any force of argument that Judges were not human, and consequently that the same effect that time has upon other men did not influence them, I would be willing that this section should be stricken out. But, as I entertain a contrary opinion, I am opposed to the motion to strike it out. I think it should be retained in our Constitution. The duties to be performed by the Judges of the Circuit Courts are arduous, and for that reason we should have hale and hearty men. I do not see how a man, at the age of seventy, can travel through the circuits, and perform his duty to his own or to the satisfaction of the people.

Mr. S. A. SWAILS called for the previous question, which was sustained.

The question being taken on the various amendments, the motion of Mr. B. F. WHITTEMORE, to insert " eighty " instead of " seventy years of age," was agreed to.

The question was then taken on the motion to strike out the entire section, which was agreed to, and the section was stricken out.

Section twenty-ninth, providing that Judges shall not charge juries in respect to matters of fact, but may state the testimony and declare the law, passed to a third reading, without amendment or debate.

Section thirtieth, providing for the election of Clerks of Courts of Common Pleas, was, on motion of Mr. E. W. M. MACKEY, amended so as to insert the word " county" for " judicial district," and to fix the term of office for four years, and then passed to a third reading, without debate.

Section thirty-first, relative to the election of an Attorney-General of the State was read.

Mr. C. C. BOWEN moved to amend by striking out the words "shall reside at the seat of government and," in first and second lines, and also to strike out the words "by a joint vote of both branches of the General Assembly," in second and third lines, and to insert in the place thereof the words "by the qualified electors of the State;" and also to strike out the words "a compensation to," in the fourth line, and insert "such compensation as shall."

The amendments were agreed to.

Mr. F. J. MOSES, Jr., moved to strike out the word "two," in third line, and to insert the word "four," so as to fix the term of office at four years.

Mr. R. C. DeLARGE. The term of Governor has been fixed at two years, and I trust that of the Attorney-General will be the same. I propose two instead of four.

Mr. F. J. MOSES, Jr. It certainly seems to me that the term of the Attorney-General should be for four years. The office of Attorney-General is not connected in any manner with that of Governor. It may, with some reason, be said that the term of the Adjutant-General, as he is a salaried officer under the Governor, should be the same as that of the Governor; but the Attorney-General is an officer of the Court, the chief prosecuting officer of the State, and should, at least, hold his office as long as the Judges.

Mr. J. M. RUTLAND. I regard the term of four years as short enough for the Attorney-General to become familiar with the duties of his office. It requires much practical experience to discharge the duties of that office in a proper manner. It is somewhat analogous to the office of Judge, and the Judges are to be elected for six years. The Attorney-General is the adviser of the State of South Carolina, and the adviser of all the important officers of the State. It is necessary, first, to become acquainted with the routine of the office, which I will venture to say even the ablest lawyer can scarcely accomplish in less than two years. I would fix his term the same as that of the Judges, but I am willing to support the term of four years. I believe that it is necessary to fix that period to render his services valuable to the State. These officers were intended to serve the State of South Carolina. I am satisfied no man can be qualified at the end of the half term proposed.

The question was then taken on the motion to strike out "two" and insert "four," which was agreed to. Section thirty-one then passed to its third reading.

Section thirty-two, providing for the election of a Solicitor for each circuit, for a term of four years, was read a second time.

Mr. B. F. WHITTEMORE moved to amend by substituting for the word "to" in third line, the words "as shall;" which was agreed to, and the section passed to its third reading.

Section thirty-three, in relation to the election of a Sheriff, Coroner, and a District Surveyor was read, and Mr. S. A. SWAILS moved to amend: Strike out the word "district" wherever it occurs, and insert the word "county," which was agreed to.

Mr. R. C. DeLARGE moved to strike out the words "County Surveyor."

Mr. J. S. CRAIG. It appears to me there is a necessity for a Surveyor for each county. A great deal of land will, no doubt, have to be surveyed, and we should have a regularly commissioned and authorized Surveyor in each county, whose surveys would be recognized as legal. It is customary in nearly all the States to have a Surveyor, who, as a general thing, receives certain fees for their services from the land owners, or the parties employing them. It is, generally, no additional expense to the State.

Mr. HAYNE moved to indefinitely postpone the amendment offered.

Mr. J. J. WRIGHT. I hope that motion will not prevail. It is true we want these Surveyors; but we do not want more than those whom we expect to survey and lay off the land in school districts, and after that is accomplished we want to be able to discharge them. If this clause remains as it is, we will be compelled to have Surveyors in every county in the State; we do not wish to be compelled to have them, especially after their work has been accomplished. Let us leave it to the Legislature to provide for county or district Surveyors; but if it is inserted in the Constitution it cannot be repealed. I hope the motion to postpone will not prevail but that the amendment to strike out "County Surveyor" will be adopted.

Mr. HAYNE withdrew the motion to postpone.

Mr. R. C. DeLARGE. My only object in offering the amendment was the protection of the people. It is a well known fact that monopolies are dangerous. Give this Surveyor the exclusive privilege of surveying the land, and he will always take advantage of the necessities of the people, especially in large counties, where, perhaps, there are six hundred square miles. The people in some cases, perhaps, would have to wait for weeks, perhaps for months, before he could be induced to come and survey the land. There are in each county a number of Surveyors, and we can leave this business to them just as we leave other business to the doctors or lawyers. There is nothing to be gained by having a Surveyor elected for the district. It has been thought that a County Surveyor would be better able to settle disputes that might arise concerning lands. That impression has been proved by experience to be incorrect. The County Surveyor cannot settle disputes, and, therefore, cannot benefit the people. I would leave the business open for competition, and let the men of that profession cope with each other just as other professional men do.

Mr. J. S. CRAIG. Would not official records have more weight in Court than records of a private character?

Mr. R. C. DeLARGE. It is not so in the case of Surveyors, the evidence goes for just what it is worth. In a very large portion of some districts there is certainly no need of a Surveyor, because there is nothing but ponds.

Mr. C. C. BOWEN I see no real necessity for a District Surveyor; it might do very well for a new country, but in this State there are a great many private Surveyors, men who gain a livelihood by surveying. The Legislature may fix the price, if necessary, to prevent extortion; I, therefore, hope the words "District Surveyor" will be stricken out. I also move to strike out the words "commissioned by the Governor" and the word "two," and insert "four," so as to make the terms of Sheriff and Coroner "four years."

Mr. S. CORLEY. I hope that amendment in relation to the term of years will not prevail. We have been cursed too much with long terms of office. It has made office holders careless, indifferent, reckless, and unmindful of the interests of the people.

The question was then taken on striking out the words "County Surveyor," which was decided in the affirmative, and the words stricken out.

The next question, was on striking out "two," and inserting "four."

Mr. S. CORLEY. I believe it to be to our interest and the interest of the people, that we should confine ourselves strictly to the term of two years—I would prefer to make it one. When a man is once elected to an office, and feels that he is safely ensconced there, as I have said, he becomes ungrateful to the people who elected him. They sit down until near the time for another election, when they begin to log-roll again. Make it two years only, and they will discharge their duties faithfully. The people can then keep the reins in their own hands, and cause the officers to be more faithful to the public.

Mr. C. C. BOWEN. I think if the gentleman has proved anything, it is that he is in favor of keeping up log-rolling. He is not satisfied with log-rolling once in four years, but wants to bring it about every year. I desire to see the duties of an officer faithfully discharged, and ample provision has been made to remove persons for any delinquency. I hardly think it is necessary to presume that every man, however faithful, will be re-elected on the recurrence of an election. I am willing to be charitable, and if a man attends to the duties of his office, permit him to retain it at least for four years. I hope the amendment will prevail, and that the section will read "four years" instead of "two."

Mr. S. G. W. DILL. I move to add "Tax Collectors."

The question being taken on the motion to strike out "two" and insert "four," it was agreed to.

The motion to amend, by striking out the words "commissioned by the Governor," was also agreed to.

Mr. N. G. PARKER. No provision seems to be made for County Treasurer. I move to add after the word Coroner, "and County Treasurer." We have provided for County Commissioners, Coroners, Sheriffs, and I think there should be, at the same time, a Tax Collector and a County Treasurer.

Mr. E. W. M. MACKEY. I hope the amendment will not succeed. This can be left to the Legislature. Let that body provide how Tax Collectors shall be appointed or elected. I see no necessity for incorporating it in here.

Mr. N. G. PARKER. I know it is the custom in other States to have all these county officers. I do not know but that provisions have already been made in other reports; but if not, this is the very section in which to insert it.

Mr. N. G. PARKER afterwards withdrew his motion, and section thirty-three passed to its third reading.

Sections thirty-four and thirty-five, relative to writs, processes, prosecutions, the publications of the decisions of the Supreme Court, after being amended, on motion of Mr. BOWEN, so as to provide that all prosecutions be conducted in the name of the people of South Carolina, and that all writs shall be tested by the Clerk of the Court from which they shall be issued, unless otherwise provided by law, passed to their third reading.

This being the closing section of the judicial department, on motion, the Convention adjourne

FORTIETH DAY.

Monday, March 2, 1868.

The Convention assembled at 10 A. M., and was called to order by the PRESIDENT.

Prayer was offered by Rev. J. M. RUNION.

The roll was called, and a quorum answering to their names, the PRESIDENT announced the Convention ready to proceed to business.

The Journal of Saturday was read and approved.

Mr. J. M. RUTLAND presented the petitions of sundry citizens of Fairfield District, praying the Convention to recommend the removal of their political disabilities.

Mr. B. O. DUNCAN called for the report of the Committee on Franchise and Elections. The members, he said, were getting very anxious to have the report of that Committee before them. They regarded it as one of the most important questions with which they have to deal, and wanted time to consider it. He moved that the Committee be required to report Wednesday morning.

Mr. R. C. DeLARGE said the Committee were ready to report, but, to save time, had not sought to introduce it before the house was ready to act upon it.

Mr. J. J. WRIGHT moved to amend the motion, so as to require the Committee to report Tuesday morning, which was agreed to, and the motion carried.

Mr. R. G. HOLMES made the report of the Special Committee of Five, appointed to consider a proposition for the establishment of a Board of Land Commissioners. The Committee reported an ordinance, previously introduced, and asked that it be drafted into the new Constitution. The ordinance provides for the establishment, by the General Assembly, of a Board of Commissioners of Public Lands, with authority to purchase, at public sales or otherwise, improved and unimproved real estate within the State. The Commissioners are also authorized to cause the lands to be surveyed, and laid off in suitable tracts, to be sold to actual settlers, on condition that one-half be placed under cultivation within three years from date of purchase, the purchaser paying interest upon the amount of the purchase money, at the rate of seven per cent. per annum. The titles to the lands thus sold are to remain in the State until the principal and interest is paid.

Mr. B. F. WHITTEMORE moved that the ordinance be printed, and copies laid on the tables of the members, which was agreed to.

83

On motion of Mr. L. S. LANGLEY, the ordinance was made the special order for 4 o'clock P. M., Wednesday.

Mr. R. SMALLS called for the unfinished business.

The unfinished business, which was the consideration of article fifth, on jurisprudence, in the report of the Committee on the Judiciary, was taken up, and after an amendment, substituting the word "county" for "district," passed to a third reading, without debate. This article, which comprises three sections, provides that the General Assembly shall pass all necessary laws, and appoint some suitable person or persons to revise, simplify and abridge the rules, practice, pleadings and forms of the Court now in use in this State.

Article sixth, on eminent domain, included in the report of the Committee on the Judiciary, was taken up.

Section first was read, as follows:

SECTION 1. The State shall have concurrent jurisdiction on all rivers bordering on this State, so far as such rivers shall form a common boundary to this and any other State bounded by the same; and they, together with all other navigable waters within the limits of the State, shall be common highways, and forever free, as well to the inhabitants of this State as to the citizens of the United States, without any tax or impost therefor.

Mr. B. F. WHITTEMORE moved to amend by adding after the word "therefore," in the fifth line, the words "unless the same be expressly provided for by the General Assembly," which was agreed to.

Mr. B. O. DUNCAN moved to amend, so that the section would read: "The Legislature shall have such control over all rivers and other streams as may be necessary to keep them open and clear, and for drainage purposes."

I think it is very necessary that this power shall be given to the Legislature. In many parts of the State the streams are clogged up, and it has been found impossible, through any power or authority conferred, to keep them clear. This is particularly the case in the low country, where there are many swamps which are constantly overflowed, and, therefore, rendered incapable of proper cultivation, besides producing sickness.

Mr. W. B. NASH. I object to the first clause in the first section, giving the State joint or concurrent jurisdiction on all rivers bordering on other States. I think the United States Court decided, in the case of the City Council of Augusta, against Schultze, that the boundaries of the State of Georgia came over to this side of the river. If we pass this clause, therefore, it will probably cause a conflict between that State and South Carolina in regard to the Savannah River.

Mr. C. C. BOWEN. If a river is out of the State of South Carolina, it is evident that the State can have no jurisdiction.

Mr. B. BYAS. I hope the amendment will prevail. It will be remembered by this house that a man owning a stream of water may, by running a wharf across it, stop the navigation of the whole of the river. A man may own a ferry, and run a wharf so far as to impede its navigation. I know this from actual observation, for I live upon the head of a creek which connects the Ashley with the Stono, and if a man felt disposed to do so, he could blockade it effectually by running a bridge or dam across it. I believe, therefore, that it is right for the Legislature to have special jurisdiction over this important subject, and prevent individuals from injuring the interests, perhaps, of an entire community.

Mr. S. A. SWAILS. The section declares that all navigable waters in the State shall become highways.

The question was then taken on the amendment of Mr. B. O. DUN-CAN, and decided in the negative. The section was then passed to its third reading.

The hour for the Special Order, which was an ordinance for the division of the State into Congressional Districts, having arrived, the ordinance was called up, and, on motion of Mr. B. O. DUNCAN, it was postponed until Friday at half-past 10 o'clock.

The unfinished business was then resumed.

Section second, providing that the title to all lands and other property heretofore accrued to the State, shall vest in the same as though no change had taken place, was passed to a third reading, without amendment or debate.

Section third was read, as follows:

SECTION 3. The people of the State, in their right of sovereignty, are declared to possess the ultimate property in and to all lands within the jurisdiction of the State; and all lands, the title to which shall fail from defect of heirs, shall revert, or escheat to the people.

Mr. L. S. LANGLEY moved to strike out the words "of sovereignty," in the first line.

Mr. B. F. RANDOLPH. I would like to know the reasons for that motion?

Mr. L. S. LANGLEY. I make the motion from the fact that the State has no sovereignty. The old and false idea has long since been exploded that there is any sovereignty in a State. These are my reasons for offering the amendment; but, if wrong, I am open to conviction.

Mr. B. F. WHITTEMORE moved to strike out "in their right;"

which amendments were adopted, and the section passed to its third reading.

Article seventh, on impeachments, was taken up.

Mr. E. W. M. MACKEY suggested that this subject matter had been disposed of in the Legislative Part of the Constitution.

Mr. R. C. DeLARGE. I hope the section will pass as it stands.

Mr. C. C. BOWEN. I think that this is the proper place for the insertion of this article. In no less than eighteen Constitutions this subject is embodied in a separate article. If it is to be stricken out at all, it is to be stricken out of the Legislative Part of the Constitution.

The PRESIDENT. The error is not irretrievable, because the whole of the article must be read a third time, and when the question then comes up, the Convention can reject it from either part of the Constitution which it sees proper.

Section second was then passed to its third reading.

Section third was read, as follows:

SECTION 3. The Governor, and all other executive and judicial officers, shall be liable to impeachment; but judgment in such cases shall not extend further than removal from office. The persons convicted shall, nevertheless, be liable to indictment, trial and punishment, according to law.

Mr. R. G. HOLMES moved to amend by adding at the end the words "and disqualification from holding his office thereafter."

Mr. L. S. LANGLEY. I hope the amendment will not prevail. Where an officer of the State has been impeached and removed, I am willing to trust to the judgment of the people to replace him. I am not one of those who believe in eternal damnation, but, on the contrary, I believe in forgiveness, especially where there are signs of repentance.

The amendment was rejected, and the section passed to its third reading.

Section fourth was passed to a third reading, without amendment.

The CHAIR announced that the next business in order was the report of the Committee on Education.

Section first was read, and, on motion of Mr. J. K. JILLSON, the words "General Assembly" were substituted for "Legislature," and the section then passed to its third reading.

Section second was read.

Mr. B. O. DUNCAN moved to substitute for the word "biennially" the words "every second year." The amendment was not agreed to.

Mr. L. S. LANGLEY moved to strike out the words "district or," in the first and second lines.

The motion was agreed to.

Mr. J. K. JILLSON moved to amend the last two lines, so that it would read "the powers and duties of said board, and the compensation of the members thereof, shall be determined by law."

Mr. F. L. CARDOZO. I think the section reads better in its present shape than it would if amended as proposed by the member from Kershaw.

Mr. J. J. WRIGHT moved to amend by striking out the words "of each county" after words "qualified electors," and inserting the word "thereof."

The motion was agreed to.

Mr. J. K. JILLSON withdrew his amendment, and the section then passed to its third reading.

Section three was passed to a third reading without debate.

Section four was read as follows :

SECTION 4. It shall be the duty of the General Assembly to provide for the compulsory attendance, at either public or private schools, of all children between the ages of six and sixteen years, not physically or mentally disabled, for a term equivalent to twenty-four months.

Mr. B. O. DUNCAN moved to strike out the word "compulsory," and insert after the word "provide," the words "enforce as far as practicable."

Mr. R. C. DeLARGE. I move that the word "compulsory" be stricken out.

Mr. H. E. HAYNE. I trust that the members of the Convention will consent to postpone the consideration of this section, and allow it to be recommitted to the Committee, and I make that motion.

Mr. F. L. CARDOZO. I would state that the object in deferring the consideration at this time, is to enable a member of the Committee, who is now absent, to discuss this question, as he has specially prepared himself for the purpose.

Mr. N. G. PARKER. I hope if we postpone any section, we shall postpone the whole, so that we may bring up the report of the Committe on Finance and Taxation.

The PRESIDENT here introduced Bishop Wayman, of the African Methodist Church, to the Convention.

Mr. B. F. RANDOLPH. I hope the motion to postpone will prevail. The subject is certainly one of great importance, and we should like to give it further consideration.

Mr. J. K. JILLSON. I hope, as a matter of courtesy to the Committee, the report will be postponed. I do not propose, as a member of the Committee, to indulge in a long speech, but, unfortunately, we did not expect the subject would be called up to-day.

Mr. R. C. DeLARGE called for the previous question, but the call was not sustained.

Mr. B. BYAS. I hope the motion to postpone will not prevail. The report of the Committee has been printed and circulated freely, and we are as well prepared to discuss the subject to-day as we would be to-morrow. We can get along with it as well this morning as at any other time, and in the name of God and the people of South Carolina, let us do so.

The question then being taken on the motion to postpone, it was decided in the affirmative.

The CHAIR announced that the next business in order, was the report of the Committee on Finance and Taxation.

The report was taken up, and sections one, two, three, four, five and six, passed to a third reading without amendment.

Section seven was read as follows :

SECTION 7. For the purpose of defraying extraordinary expenditures, the State may contract public debts ; but such debts shall never, in the aggregate, exceed five hundred thousand dollars beyond that already incurred. Every such debt shall be authorized by law for some single object, to be distinctly specified therein ; and no such law shall take effect until it shall have been passed by the vote of two-thirds of the members of each branch of the Legislature, to be recorded by yeas and nays on the journals of each house respectively ; and every such law shall levy a tax annually sufficient to pay the annual interest of such debt, and also a tax sufficient to pay the principal of such debt within twenty years from the final passage of such law, and shall specially appropriate the proceeds of such taxes to the payment of such principal and interest.

Mr. J. D. BELL moved to strike out the words " shall never, in the aggregate, exceed five hundred thousand dollars beyond that already incurred."

Mr. N. G. PARKER. I hope the amendment will not prevail. The Committee have agreed, after full consultation, that the clause is just right as it stands, and while there may be good reasons why South Carolina should go in debt, she ought not to be allowed to exceed reasonable bounds.

Mr. F. L. CARDOZO. I also object to the amendment of the gentleman from Beaufort. It leaves the matter too indefinite. It would be injustice to the people of the State to require them to pay enormous taxes, for fifteen or twenty years, upon a debt largely in excess of that which now exists.

Mr. L. S. LANGLEY. I am opposed to tying the hands of the Legislature. Contingencies may arise which will require that body to contract debts that may amount to more than five hundred thousand dollars. For one, I am willing to trust to the good sense of the General Assembly, and to leave the amount indefinite, because the faith and credit of the State may be absolutely demanded in behalf of great and profitable enterprises. I hope, therefore, that the amendment will prevail.

Mr. R. C. DeLARGE. I would ask if the gentleman does not contemplate the building of a railroad at some future time.

Mr. L. S. LANGLEY. I hope that a great many railroads will be built in South Carolina.

Mr. B. O. DUNCAN. The State of South Carolina owes one of the smallest public debts that has been contracted, before or since the war, in any State of the Union, and if we have faith in the judgment of the Legislature, I see no reason why we should not confide to that body the regulation of financial affairs, in the making of such provisions as may be necessary to preserve the public credit, or to foster the great undertakings calculated to redound to our benefit. To my mind, even a million of dollars is a small limit.

Mr. R. C. DeLARGE moved to strike out "five hundred thousand dollars," and insert "one million dollars."

Mr. R. G. HOLMES. Why should the State be limited at all, when an opportunity exists of making a good bargain? There is already a proposition that the State shall buy in land about to be sacrificed. How can she do so with such a restriction put upon her finances?

Mr. B. F. RANDOLPH. I move to amend by striking out all in the sixth line after the word "respectively." We are judging now from a certain stand-point. Two years from to-day that stand-point may change. Circumstances may arise which will make it necessary for us to borrow one, or, perhaps, two million of dollars, and we may then be in a condition to do so. For this reason, I hope the amendment of the gentleman from Beaufort will prevail; and, also, the one offered by myself, because I am not in favor of tying the hands of a future Legislature, when some great opportunity may arise for placing the State upon a healthy financial footing.

Mr. A. C. RICHMOND. I hope that "five hundred thousand dollars" will be stricken out, and "one million dollars" inserted. Every gentleman upon this floor knows that within five or six years from this time the condition of the State will be greatly improved, and it is impossible for this Convention to exercise that foresight which can declare the proper action for a Legislature to take at that time. There is no general rule which we can adopt that will apply to all future contingencies likely to arise ; and I, for one, am opposed to any restrictions upon the Legislature.

Mr. A. J. RANSIER. I hope the motion of the gentleman from Beaufort will prevail. Our resources are crippled ; all branches of trade paralyzed, and the very circumstances which exist now demand that the Legislature shall have the largest room in which to operate for the benefit of the State, even though it be the privilege of contracting a debt of three or five millions of dollars.

Mr. J. L. NEAGLE. My reason for favoring the amendment, is that the Legislature is necessarily the best judge of the wants of the State, and the manner of supplying those wants. It is proposed by an ordinance to establish a Board of Land Commissioners, to use the credit of the State for the purpose of buying land ; but if we limit the credit, as is proposed, to five hundred thousand dollars, we might as well lay that ordinance on the table. I think the policy an unjust and narrow-minded one, and that we arrogate to ourselves too much in assuming to judge of the necessities of the State, and the proper course for a Legislature to pursue two, three, or five years from this time.

The question then being taken on the amendment of Mr. BELL, it was decided in the affirmative.

Mr. B. O. DUNCAN. I move that all after the word "debt," in the seventh line, be stricken out.

The motion was agreed to.

On motion of Mr. J. J. WRIGHT, the word "Legislature" was stricken out, and the words "General Assembly" inserted.

Section seven was then passed to a third reading.

Section eight was read, and, on motion of Mr. J. L. NEAGLE, the words "General Assembly" were substituted for "Legislature," and the section then passed to its third reading.

Section nine was read as follows :

SECTION 9. The credit of the State shall not be granted to, or in aid of any person, association or corporation.

Mr. J. D. BELL moved to strike out the entire section.

Mr. N. G. PARKER. I hope the motion will not prevail. The credit of the State has already been too frequently granted in aid of persons, associations and incorporations, when it ought not to have been done.

Mr. B. F. RANDOLPH. I disagree with the gentleman. There are many associations and corporations in South Carolina largely dependent upon the State, and States have frequently loaned their faith and credit to foster and encourage such corporations. Unless this section is erased, it will be a death stroke to all internal improvements, which, in South Carolina, especially at this time, require to be nourished as much as possible.

Mr. A. C. RICHMOND. I hope this section will remain just as it is. South Carolina has been ruined by loaning her faith and credit to corporations. Look at the Charleston and Savannah Railroad; every good business man knew it would not pay, and yet South Carolina made itself responsible for its bonds to a large amount. Look at the Blue Ridge Railroad—a good while ago the State became responsible for a million. If such a section as that proposed had existed in the Constitution formerly, the State of South Carolina would not owe millions of dollars.

Mr. J. L. NEAGLE. Do you not think the members of the Legislature are as competent to judge as to the propriety of loaning the credit of the State as this Convention?

Mr. A. C. RICHMOND. Patrick Henry says that we should judge of the future by the past; and, judging by the past, this section ought not to be here.

Mr. B. F. RANDOLPH. Is it not our duty to judge from the present circumstances? Does not the Federal Government lend its faith and credit to persons and corporations?

Mr. A. C. RICHMOND. I say also let us judge by present circumstances. There is no similarity between the State of South Carolina and the General Government. The General Government has resources beyond those of any nation on earth, whilst South Carolina is feeble in her power, and we know not whether her resources are to increase or diminish. The sum and substance of the whole thing is, that the State owes five millions of dollars, and we do not know how to pay it.

Mr. GEORGE LEE moved to amend by adding after the word "corporation," in second line, "except by a joint vote of both houses of the General Assembly."

Mr. J. J. WRIGHT. I hope that the motion to strike out this clause will prevail. The provision has no business here. The welfare of the people is to be cared for by the Legislature, and we are deliberately tying the hands of that body. Adopt this clause, and the Legislature will be powerless. This is a progressive age. The Legislature will be responsible to the people, and the people will see that they do their duty. Some gentlemen seem to think that all this discussion refers to the Port Royal Railroad. Let me say that we do not intend to ask any money

84

from the State Treasury for this purpose; nevertheless we intend that that railroad shall be built, because we know that it will redound to the interests of the people of the whole State. On general principles, however, I think that the Legislature ought to be left free to do those things for the public good which the public good requires. It may happen that portions of the State, in which the people are poor, will require aid in the erection of schools, or poor houses, or other public works. Shall it go forth from this Convention that their own representatives shall not have the power to render such assistance? I think not, for I read in the eye of every man assembled here to do all they can to promote the welfare of the people, be it now or in the future.

Mr. R. C. DeLARGE. I move that the amendment of the gentleman from Berkley (Mr. GEO. LEE) be laid upon the table; which was agreed to.

The question was then taken on the motion to strike out section ninth, and was decided in the affirmative.

On motion of Mr. N. G. PARKER, section eighth was reconsidered.

Mr. E. W. M. MACKEY moved to insert between the words "property" and "within," in fourth line, the words "except that heretofore exempted."

The amendment was agreed to, and the section then passed to its third reading.

Section tenth, prohibiting the State from subscribing to, or becoming interested in, the stock of any company, association or corporation, was taken up, but before taking the question on its passage to a third reading, the hour of 1 having arrived, the house adjourned to 3 o'clock.

AFTERNOON SESSION.

The Convention re-assembled at 3 P. M.

On motion of Mr. J. M. RUNION, the rules were suspended for five minutes, for the purpose of offering the following:

Resolved, That this Convention fix the 11th of March as the day to adjourn, at 12 o'clock, M., *sine die*.

Mr. R. C. DeLARGE. I move the indefinite postponement of that resolution. I hope the members of the Convention will not go grovelling in the dark. In the first place, we should not adjourn *sine die*. We do not know what urgent reasons we may have to call us together again. I am as anxious as any one that the Convention should adjourn as early as possible, but I cannot see how we can get through business by the 11th of March Again, matters are undergoing important changes at the capital of the nation, and we do not know what powers may be given to this Convention.

Mr. A. J. RANSIER. I hope the resolution will not prevail. There is no necessity to limit the adjournment to the 11th inst., and I do not believe it is possible for us to finish our work by that time. With all due respect to the gentleman who offered it, I move to lay the motion on the table.

Mr. J. S. CRAIG. There seems to be some anxiety about adjourning. I think the best way to get ready to adjourn is to let all such resolutions alone. I do not see how any one can tell whether we will be ready to adjourn or not on the 11th inst. I think it would be better to let the resolution stay in our pockets, and adjourn when we get through. I hope it will be voted down at once.

Mr. J. M. RUTLAND. I hope the resolution will be sustained. If we go to work, and not lose too much time in speeches and useless debate, we can get ready by the 11th. It is not impossible for us to change this decision hereafter. The Convention should take into consideration the necessity of hurrying up their business, not only on account of the expenses of the Convention, but for the success of our party. Our friends at Washington have written to various members, urging all possible haste to get through, to get the Constitution before Congress, and get our members in that body. I hope some such resolution will pass this house.

Mr. J. J. WRIGHT. As I have once before said, there is a certain amount of dignity which should be sustained in this body, and as long as I am in this house I shall raise my voice to maintain that dignity. I do say that whenever a resolution of this kind is presented to this body, it is trampling upon the dignity of the body. I do believe there is sufficient judgment among the members of the Convention to go to work diligently and do what we are sent here for. It would be one of the worst things we could do to pass a resolution of this kind. It would show to the people of the State and of the world that we are not capable of such a work as framing a Constitution. I believe we are all anxious to accomplish the business before us, and that it does not need a driver to whip us up to our duty.

The question was then taken on the adoption of the resolution, and was decided in the negative.

The Convention then resumed the consideration of the tenth section of the report of the Committttee on Finance.

Mr. J. D. BELL moved that the section be stricken out.

Mr. J. S. CRAIG. I second that motion. If we adopt that section, the State cannot subscribe or take any stock in any company organized for internal improvements, or any enterprise whatever. There are a great many necessary internal improvements which will, no doubt, need assistance from the State.

Mr. A. C. RICHMOND. I protest against striking out this section. The State is suffering now from evils which this measure is designed to guard against. It is a part of political philosophy, if any enterprise does not pay, it is better for the State not to touch it. Here is a canal that has been surveyed, the stock bought, and the directors elected, for the purpose of connecting the Edisto River with the Ashley River, and because it is not supposed to be profitable, the enterprise has never been carried into completion, although there are some reasons why it is desirable, and why it should be done. Now, nobody here will rise and ask the State to subscribe fifty thousand dollars to that stock? If this section is stricken out, I desire to have my vote recorded in the negative. It will require the utmost watchfulness and care to prevent the Legislature incurring unlimited debts in this State, and if they should be allowed to enter into all the projects of corporations, our condition will be worse than it is now.

Mr. B. F. RANDOLPH. I am in favor of striking out this section. I consider the State the foster mother, so to speak, of the internal improvements and enterprises; and, so far as consistent for the State to do it, it should lend its aid and assistance to its internal improvements. These corporations and associations are all taxed. From them there flows into the treasury of the State a vast amount. It is the duty of the State to foster all these corporations as far as possible. I hope that every gentleman who feels that the State should aid in her own internal improvements will vote for the striking out of this section.

The gentleman from Berkley refers to the fact, that there are quite a number of railroads to which the State has pledged its faith and credit. That I consider no argument at all; all the States in the Union have done the same thing. The Federal Government has done the same thing. Some States have assisted corporations running railroads, not only within their own State, but running into other States.

The hour for the Special Order, being the petition to Congress, praying that the present import duty on rice be not repealed having arrived, was taken up for consideration.

Mr. R. SMALLS moved to postpone the consideration of the Special Order until four o'clock to-morrow.

Mr. J. H. JENKS. I hope that motion will not prevail. I am certainly very anxious that the question should be acted upon immediately.

The question was then taken on the motion to postpone, and decided in the negative.

Mr. J. H. JENKS. Feeling deeply interested in the question which has been made the Special Order of this hour to-day, I again beg the indulgence of the Convention for a few moments.

It may be urged that a petition of this kind, at this particular time, is premature. Such, I contend, is not the case. This, sir, is a question of the most vital importance, and one which affects the immediate and future welfare and prosperity of our State.

The people of this Commonwealth can now be heard at Washington through their delegates here in Convention assembled. Should this opportunity for expressing our disapprobation of the proposed reduction or repeal of the import duty on rice pass unheeded by us; should this Convention adjourn, having sent forward no word of protest against a measure aimed at the very heart of our financial prosperity, it would be indeed strange ! This State, more than any other, is interested in the measure now before us. Previous to the war, South Carolina raised and sent to market more than three times the amount of rice produced by North Carolina, Georgia, and Florida. The crop of 1860, amounted to 190,000 tierces, of which South Carolina produced 150,000; Georgia 30,000, and North Carolina 10,000. This, reckoning 22 bushels to the tierce, the common average, amounts to 3,300,000 bushels, which, at the moderate price of one dollar per bushel, afforded the State a revenue of $3,300,000.

The estimated value of our real estate in rice lands, is set as high as $15,000,000, giving employment to the labor and capital of 16,000 of her inhabitants.

This, Mr. President, to a State like our own, whose resources are solely agricultural, is an item of no little moment.

This measure, which although at first seemed destined to be lost, without due consideration by this body, is now, I trust, to receive the time and thought which its importance merits. This measure, while receiving only a passing thought by this Convention, has been for several weeks under consideration by the appropriate Committee in Congress ; and, to-day, that body is only awaiting the report of that Committee, when final action will be taken.

I have reason greatly to fear, Mr. President, that such report may be received and acted upon before our voice of petition can be heard. The rice culture, as it now stands, is rightly protected by a duty of 2 9-10 cents per pound against foreign imports. This may seem an excessive tariff, but the results and experience of the two past years, as deduced by both factors and producers, prove quite the contrary.

Against 150,000 tierces produced in this State in the year 1860, there were produced in 1866, 23,000 ; and, in the past year, from 25 to 30,000 ; about one-sixth of the average crops before the war. Three-fifths of the rice lands remain uncultivated. This, certainly, argues very strongly against the repeal of the present duty.

The expense attendant upon the putting in condition for cultivation, the lands so sadly out of order, in consequence of neglect during the great civil struggle through which we have recently passed, is necessarily heavy. The increase of expense in cultivation by *free labor*, is proportionally much larger than that of cotton, as on the major proportion of the better lands and those most productive, manual labor alone can be employed.

Rice is a luxury, a reasonable luxury; subject, like all others from abroad, to its contribution for the increase of the revenue of our common country. To those of our body from the upper districts, this may seem a local question. I cannot so regard it. It is a subject of great interest to our whole Commonwealth ; and it would certainly appear to me out of place for any citizen thereof to oppose it on that ground, especially while the Northern States, who have no interest in the matter whatever, except to buy their rice as low as possible, can be persuaded further to afford us that protection. I contend, Mr. President, that any man who has the interest of his State at heart, will oppose the interest of no part of our State. Rangoon rice can, to-day, be laid down in this market at $7\frac{1}{2}$ cents per pound, duty paid. Remove this duty, which must be paid in gold, and which in our currency, at the present quotation, amounts to $4\frac{1}{4}$ cents, and you have the same article here in our market at $3\frac{1}{4}$ cents a pound. Can we compete with these prices ? I can assure you no one will attempt it. And why ? Because having once breathed the air of freedom, and having tested the virtue of American liberty, no one can be found so low and degraded as to be compelled to labor at the starving rates of those countries where this import is produced.

The peculiar adaptation of our sea-board to the cultivation of rice is certainly remarkable. Other countries there are that possess the same facilities of clime as our own; in others still can be found the requisite alluvial lands but no where has nature so harmoniously blended all the necessary concomitants of climate, soil and tides, as in our beautiful Carolina.

To repeal this duty is to defraud our State of fifteen million dollars' worth of taxable property; to deprive sixteen thousand of her inhabitants of a profitable occupation, and to bankrupt the balance. Charleston, "the Queen City of the South," once so proud and arrogant, now so humble and unfortunate, will crumble and decay. When the unwelcome news of this repeal shall reach us, severing the last artery of her former prosperity, let the bells in yonder tower chime tenderly her funeral knell.

Mr. B. BYAS. This measure is directly connected with the interests of our State and the interest of the nation. About two-fifths of the best land in our State, the low country, is specially adapted and devoted to the raising of rice. This is one of the great resources of our State. Its cultivation should be encouraged by the nation, limited, as it mostly is, to two States, South Carolina and Georgia, and it is only in those two States that it may with any propriety be called a staple article. There are other States that raise the article in small or limited quantities. In Wisconsin, we find, an article of wild rice is raised, which grows spontaneously, but that cannot be called a staple article. I have had some experience in this matter, having been engaged in the importation of rice into the United States when but a boy. In California there are forty thousand persons whose principal consumption is rice, and who actually depend upon the importation of that article there for the maintenance of life itself. I say this from actual experience. There are forty thousand Chinamen in California, whose principal consumption is rice. These people come to our country, make money, hoard it up, and send it to China. They are of no benefit to this country, yet if the duty upon rice is repealed, we only assist them the more, and discourage our own rice planters. We will not, under the present high price of labor and provisions, be able to raise rice here at three and a half cents a pound, while it may be brought into the California market from China, and sold at two cents per pound. Labor is so plentiful in China that it can be procured at ten cents per day. Men are so numerous there that they have no use for mules or horses, or any beasts of burden. They carry their rice on their shoulders, and load a ship in that way in a very few hours. In fact, labor is so cheap that they can bring the rice here into the States, and make a good profit upon it by selling it for two cents a pound. We cannot compete with them now, much less if the duty is repealed. I hope the measure before the house will prevail. Let us endeavor to keep hold of and promote the full development of all such resources as we have left to us.

Mr. R. C. DeLARGE called for the previous question, which was sustained.

The question being taken on the preamble and resolutions, they were passed to a second reading.

On motion of **Mr. R. C. DeLARGE**, the rules were suspended, for the purpose of passing the petition to a third reading.

The petition then received its third reading, and on motion of Mr. B. F. WHITTEMORE, the preamble and resolutions were ordered to be engrossed, and copies sent to the President of the United States Senate and the Speaker of the House of Representatives at Washington.

The Special Order being discharged, the consideration of the tenth section was resumed.

Mr. L. S. LANGLEY moved to lay the amendments offered on the table, which was agreed to, carrying the section with them.

Section eleventh, relative to the incorporation and organization, by the Legislature, of cities and towns, and restricting their powers of taxation, borrowing money, contracting debts, and loaning their credit; and section twelfth, prohibiting the Legislature from issuing scrip, certificate, or other evidence of State indebtedness, except for bonds, stock, &c., or those previously issued, or for such debts as are expressly authorized in this Constitution, after being amended by striking out the word "Legislature" and inserting "General Assembly," wherever Legislature occurred, were passed to a third reading, without debate.

Section thirteenth was read, as follows:

SECTION 13. An accurate statement of the receipts and expenditures of the public money shall be published with the laws of each regular session of the Legislature.

Mr. B. F. WHITTEMORE moved the following as a substitute: "There shall be published by the Treasurer, in at least one newspaper published in the State, during the first week in November, detailed statements of all monies drawn from the Treasury during the preceding year; for what purpose drawn, to whom paid, by what law authorized; and, also, of all monies received, and by what authority, and from whom."

On motion, the substitute was indefinitely postponed.

Mr. E. W. M. MACKEY moved to amend by inserting "that the

statement be published by the General Assembly, in such manner as may be provided by law," which was agreed to.

The section then passed to a third reading.

Sections fourteenth and fifteenth, relative to appropriations and the commencement of the fiscal year on the 1st of November, passed to a third reading, without debate.

Section sixteenth, providing for the assessment and collection of a tax of two mills upon each dollar's worth of taxable property, for a sinking fund, was read.

Mr. R. C. DeLARGE moved to amend by inserting the following substitute: "The General Assembly shall pass the necessary laws for the creation of a fund by taxation, to be known as a Sinking Fund, &c."

Mr. B. F. RANDOLPH. I move to strike out the whole section. My reason for making that motion is that this section describes how taxes are to be collected, levied, &c., and that matter it has been usual to leave to the Legislature. I think it can be safely left to that body.

Mr. J. M. RUTLAND. I have but a word to say on this subject. I presume this measure of taxation is meant to create what is commonly called a sinking fund, for the purpose of paying a debt, and any one who has studied that question of a sinking fund must have come to the conclusion that it is as thorough a humbug as ever existed in political economy. The only way, if we want to pay a debt, is to raise the taxes. To sustain me in this position, I refer any gentleman to an article on that subject in Brande's Encyclopedia. It does not raise one cent more than can be raised by taxation. It never has done it, never can do it, and never will do it. This is still continuing the humbug and bauble of a sinking fund. I hope it will be stricken out.

Mr. R. C. DeLARGE. I agree with the gentleman who has just taken his seat, that the whole section should be stricken out.

The section as it now reads assesses a tax of two mills upon each dollar's worth of real estate; a tax almost unheard of unless in times of war, and assessed for war purposes. Two mills on a dollar might sound as a small trifle in the ears of some men in this Convention; but, upon examination, we find it to be one cent on every five dollar's worth of property, twenty cents on a hundred, two dollars upon a thousand, or one hundred and forty thousand upon seventy millions of dollar's worth of property; now that tax is more upon a hundred dollars than the entire State tax before the war. The State tax before the war was fifteen cents on a hundred dollars, including every tax, and this report proposes twenty cents special tax upon the hundred dollars, five cents more for a specific purpose alone than the whole tax before the war. It pro-

85

poses also to carry out an old system of South Carolina, that the owners of real estate shall not only bear an equal proportion and burden of taxation, but bear a special proportion. Now, I do not desire to see real estate owners specially burdened; I desire to see everybody pay their share of taxes, and that every dollar may be realized which can be collected on a fair and equitable basis.

I move to lay the amendment on the table.

The motion was agreed to, and the amendment with the section was laid on the table.

Mr. R. C. DeLARGE moved a reconsideration of the vote just taken, and that the motion to reconsider be laid on the table, which was agreed to.

Section seventeen, prohibiting any county from subscribing in any incorporated company, unless paid at the time of subscription, was read.

Mr. R. G. HOLMES. I hope this section will be stricken out, and that we will not tie the State, or compel it to issue bonds only of the denomination of five hundred dollars. I move to strike out the section.

Mr. J. J. WRIGHT. I hope the section will not pass as it is. States and counties, in one respect, occupy a similar position to that of individuals. No member in this house, I feel assured, would desire to have his hands tied in this way. If I had an opportunity of making a few dollars by subscribing to any institution whatever, I should certainly desire to have the privilege of doing so, and it would be an outrage upon my rights for any man or class of men to rise up and say I should not have the privilege of doing it. If the City of Charleston desires to convene together in a common body, and take stock in any railroad or canal, they have the right to do it, and we have no right to introduce any provision into this Constitution denying them that right; therefore I hope this clause will be amended so as to strike out "no county shall subscribe." If there is a company we wish to support in this State, or any other State, and the people in any county of this State believe that they can make something for the good of the people in that county, if that institution, whatever it may be, desires and will give the people in any county credit; if they will loan their funds to erect school houses, to support a canal or railroad, or any other improvement for the State, or that which may be considered an improvement; if the State of New York, or Georgia, or North Carolina, will loan the county of Charleston, or Beaufort, or Berkley money, then they have the right and power, and that State which lends money can only hold the county accountable for the money they borrowed. If there is a county in this State that shall be successful, and shall pledge themselves to the support and the aid of any other county in this State, or any other State, they have the right to do it; and the fact that they are doing it does not, necessarily, make the Legislature responsible for their acts. Let us leave this to the people, and let them be untrammelled. I believe in the patriotism and fidelity of the people of the State. Do not tie their hands; because, if this section is incorporated into this Constitution, we must remember it cannot be repealed as a law can be repealed, from year to year.

Mr. R. B. ELLIOTT moved, the indefinite postponement of the section.

Mr. A. C. RICHMOND. I hope the section will not be indefinitely postponed. The gentleman from Beaufort reminds me of a little friend of mine who was accustomed to borrow little sums of money, and always expressing himself ready to pay; when called upon he would reply, "oh never mind, never mind, I am perfectly able to owe you;" when remonstrated with, he never had anything to pay. When counties have such a privilege, they are very apt to abuse it. Instead of borrowing twenty-five thousand dollars, they would be more likely to borrow one hundred thousand dollars. It is because of this that one-half of the counties in the Northern States are so deeply in debt. Perhaps repudiation follows; it is very difficult to pursue a middle course.

The question was then taken on the motion to postpone indefinitely, and decided in the negative.

Section eighteen was read, and Mr. J. D. BELL moved to amend by striking out a provision requiring State bonds to be not less than "five hundred dollars," and inserting "fifty dollars," which was agreed to.

Mr. B. F. WHITTEMORE moved to strike out from word "bond" in first line to end of period, which was agreed to; and the section, so amended, was passed to its third reading.

Mr. B. F. WHITTEMORE'S substitute for section nineteen was read, and Mr. WHITTEMORE moved to amend by striking out "Legislature" and inserting "General Assembly," which was agreed to.

Messrs. B. O. DUNCAN and S. A. SWAILS offered verbal amendments, which, on motion of Mr. R. C. DeLARGE, were indefinitely postponed, and the substitute being adopted, the section passed to its third reading.

Mr. L. S. LANGLEY submitted the following additional section:

SECTION 20. No debts contracted by this State in behalf of the late rebellion, in whole or in part, shall ever be paid.

Mr. R. C. DeLARGE moved a suspension of the rules that the additional section may pass to its second reading, which was agreed to, and the section was read a second time, and passed to a third reading.

Mr. B. F. WHITTEMORE moved a reconsideration of section five, which was adopted, and offered the following amendment: Strike out fourth and fifth lines after the word "grounds," and insert the following, which was adopted, and the section, so amended, was passed to its third reading:

Provided, That this exemption shall not extend beyond the buildings and premises actually occupied by such schools, colleges. institutions of learning, asylums, libraries, churches, and burial grounds, although connected with charitable objects.

Mr. R. G. HOLMES moved a reconsideration of section four, which was adopted.

Mr. R. G. HOLMES moved to strike out the word "only," which was carried, and the section passed to its third reading.

Mr. E. W. M. MACKEY called for the second reading of the report of the Committee on Miscellaneous Provisions of the Constitution on the Militia.

Before taking the question, the Convention adjourned.

FORTY-FIRST DAY.

Tuesday, March 3, 1868.

The Convention assembled at 10 A. M., and was called to order by the PRESIDENT.

Prayer was offered by the Rev. B. F. RANDOLPH.

The roll was called, and a quorum answering to their names, the PRESIDENT announced the Convention ready to proceed to business.

The Journal of Monday was read and approved.

Mr. A. C. RICHMOND desired his vote to be recorded against Mr. BELL'S amendment to section seven, article six, of the report of the Committee on the Judiciary.

Mr. B. F. RANDOLPH made the following report of the Committee on Miscellaneous Provisions of the Constitution:

WHEREAS, No constitutional and legal assembly of the General Assembly of this State has been convened since the commencement of the rebellion against the authority of the Government of the United States; and, whereas, the body assembled from time to time at the capital of the State, since the commencement of said rebellion, assuming to possess and exercise the powers of the General Assembly of the State, had no authority to pledge the faith and credit of the State for the benefit of any corporate body or private individual, and its actions can be validated only by the confirmatory authority of the legal government of this State; and, whereas, it is expedient that when the credit of the State is advanced or pledged for the benefit of public enterprises, and works in which the people of the State are interested, that power should be lodged in the General Assembly to exercise a salutary control over such public enterprises and works, to the end that the commerce and industry of the State should be adequately fostered and promoted; therefore be it

Ordained, That all Acts or pretended Acts of legislation, purporting to have been passed by the General Assembly of the State, since the 20th day of December, A. D., 1860, pledging the faith and credit of the State for the benefit of any corporate body or private individual, are hereby suspended and declared inoperative until the General Assembly shall assemble and ratify or modify the same.

Mr. R. G. HOLMES moved that the report be made the Special Order for Thursday next, at 12 o'clock, which was agreed to.

Mr. R. C. DeLARGE, Chairman of the Committee on Franchises and Elections, made a verbal report, stating the Committee would be ready to report to morrow morning.

Mr. N. G. PARKER offered the following resolution, which was agreed to:

Resolved, That the President of this Convention be instructed to request Brevet Major-General E. R. S. Canby, to draw from the Treasury of the State the sum of thirty-eight thousand dollars, for the purpose of defraying the expenses of the Convention.

Mr. J. S. CRAIG called up the report of the Committee on Miscellaneous Provisions of the Constitution, on an ordinance providing for the organization of the Militia of the State.

The article on the militia was taken up, and section first read, and passed to a third reading, as follows, without debate:

SECTION 1. The militia of this State shall consist of all able-bodied male residents of the State between the ages of eighteen and forty-five years, except such persons as are now, or may hereafter be, exempted by the laws of the United States, or of this State; and shall be organized, armed, equipped, and disciplined, as the General Assembly may by law provide."

Section second was read, and passed to a third reading, as follows, without debate:

SECTION 2. The Governor shall have power to call out the militia to execute the laws, repel invasion, repress insurrection, and preserve the common peace.

Mr. N. G. PARKER. It was my intention to have offered an amendment to the first section, the passage of which accidentally escaped my notice. I move a reconsideration of the first section.

The motion was agreed to.

Mr. N. G. PARKER. I move to strike out, in second line, the word "eighteen" and insert "twenty-one," and also to insert, in second line, after the word "years," the words "who are electors."

Mr. B. F. RANDOLPH. It is quite evident we have passed over these sections very rapidly. I hope this subject will receive due consideration, and I would like to hear the gentleman's reasons for his amendment.

Mr. N G. PARKER. My reason is this: I do not think boys ought to be put into the militia. My reason for offering the second amendment is, that I do not desire to see those who are disfranchised put into any militia organizations.

Mr. R. G. HOLMES. I hope this amendment will not prevail. Eighteen and forty-five are the usual ages fixed in every State. We certainly shall be obliged to depend upon independent companies, and I would like to inquire whether it would prevent persons over twenty-one from forming themselves into independent companies.

Mr. L. S. LANGLEY. I hope the amendment to strike out the word "eighteen" will not prevail. During the late unhappy rebellion it was my fortune, or misfortune, to have some experience in the military, and I can bear testimony that some of the best soldiers in the Union army were under eighteen years of age. I know that in the march from Jacksonville, Fla., to Olustee, Fla., when the Fifty-fourth Massachusetts marched under heavy marching orders, that is with their knapsacks and all their little personal property, in that march of fifty miles, soldiers of eighteen, and some only fifteen years of age, stood the march better, with all its fatigues, than men who were older. I saw soldiers in that march, who were in the prime of life, succumb to fatigue, while others, from fifteen to eighteen years of age, bore it without a murmur, and seemed to have greater power of endurance than their less fortunate comrades. I, therefore, hope that the amendment will be voted down.

Mr. S. CORLEY. It would be highly dangerous to allow men who are disloyal or disfranchised to remain at home, while the loyal citizens are compelled to bear arms. The safest place would be to put them into the military, where they would be under restraint. There is some danger in going into a military organization to maintain the laws. I am not willing to support laws while disloyal men are forced to remain at home. I know, when I was forced to go into the Confederate service, many of those men said that the next best thing to my being made to shoot Yankees would be to get shot myself.

Mr. B. F. WHITTEMORE. I would like to ask the gentleman who offers the amendment if a young man eighteen years of age is an elector?

The PRESIDENT stated that the adoption of the second amendment would be equivalent to the adoption of the first.

Mr. N. G. PARKER withdrew the first part of his amendment.

Mr. B. O. DUNCAN moved to insert the words " who are not disfranchised."

Mr. D. H. CHAMBERLAIN moved to amend by inserting after the word " now," in the second line, the word " disfranchised."

Mr. N. G. PARKER withdrew both his amendments.

Mr. J. J. WRIGHT. I was in hopes the gentleman would withdraw the second amendment.

I think it would be rather a dangerous thing for us to insert such a clause as this into our Constitution. I claim that any person who is subject to the laws of the United States, or protected under those laws, should help to defend the State in which they live, or the United States whenever the nation is in danger. Here are a class of persons that you wish to exempt from this duty, and they cordially reciprocate the wish. I hope we will not gratify their wishes in this respect.

Mr. L. S. LANGLEY. Does the gentleman mean to say that this section as it now stands will exempt any from being obliged to serve in times of war?

Mr. J. J. WRIGHT. I say it would be unwise for us to exempt a class of persons from serving in the militia who are disqualified from holding office or from being electors. If this State was invaded, or an insurrection arose, and these persons were exempt, as we propose to exempt them, they would support our enemies. When they have the right of having their disabilities removed, they certainly should not be exempt from serving in the militia of the State. They should bear their part. They have disfranchised themselves, but by their fidelity and loyalty to the Government of the United States, they can have their disabilities removed. If there was no danger of the State being invaded they would stand in this situation : instead of coming up and striving to be faithful to the country, they would hold themselves aloof, and when an opportunity offered would go on the other side and claim the right to do it. Let us vote this amendment down. Unless we do it disloyalty will be encouraged, and those who desire our destruction would like nothing better than to be kept out of the militia. Let us establish it so that they will be compelled to go into the militia, and should an insurrection or invasion occur, they will be compelled to aid in its suppression.

Mr. A. J. RANSIER. I hope the amendment inserting the word disfranchised will be voted down, but not for the reason advanced by the gentleman from Beaufort. I do not believe there is a citizen of South Carolina who would commit a crime in order that he might be disqualified from serving in the militia. I propose to insert in the first line the words "who are or may become electors." That will provide for that class disfranchised under the present law, but whose disabilities I hope to see removed.

The hour for the Special Order having arrived, the consideration of a substitute, reported by the Judiciary Committee for section nineteen of the Judiciary Report, was taken up.

Mr. J. M. RUTLAND. I move to amend the fifth line by striking out the word "decisions" and inserting the word "decrees," and the sixth line by striking out the words "day of hearing of the causes respectively," and inserting the words "last day of the term at which the causes were heard," which was granted.

This I suppose will be voted upon as an amendment. It has been common to attribute selfish motives to lawyers in arguing judicial questions even in this body. Whilst I do not admit that lawyers are any more obnoxious to such charges than any other person, yet, if you will insist that lawyers have certain motives, I say in the beginning that so far as that matter is concerned it would be to the interest of lawyers to let the nineteenth section remain as it originally was, because it would create inextricable confusion or uncertainty in the State, and when that is the state of the law, it is the time for lawyers to make fortunes. Make the law clear and certain, and you check the disposition to go to law. But when the law is uncertain, almost any man will take his chances of success at law rather than comply with his contracts. If you attribute motives to lawyers, be it understood my interest is on the other side to that which I am now advocating.

Mr. RUTLAND here read the original section.

Now, the transfer of these records of the Court of Equity is one of the most important matters that I can well conceive of. It is a thing which I contend will create that very confusion of which I have just spoken. You mix up the records of the Court of Equity with those of the Court of Common Pleas, and it will very soon be impossible to trace out records. There will be no end of the confusion it will create. Besides, there is no necessity for such a thing. Where is the necessity of taking them from the offices of the Court of Equity and mixing them up with the Court of Common Pleas. There can be none, and I hope this Convention will not think of it for one moment. I have had some experience in our Courts, and I say, according to the best of my judgment, that the Court of Equity in some form must exist in this country if we intend to administer justice properly. It is proposed to make the Judges of the Court of Common Pleas take charge of these cases. This would be impracticable, if not totally impossible. I assure you if a party was to take it into his head to delay his case in Court, and most persons do when they think the law will go against them, if a skillful lawyer were to undertake to manage the delay, he could pick out three cases, in my opinion, of the District Courts that would keep the Judge and jury sitting six months, and they would have nothing else to do. In matters of account, where executors, trustees, merchants' accounts, and all such things, are to be brought before a Court and investigated, we would find it exceedingly cumbersome. Suppose in one case, there are from one to fifty vouchers, a lawyer may take a single voucher, and, in taking testimony upon it, consume an entire day before procuring the verdict of the jury upon that one voucher.

This work, according to the present law, is the duty of the Commissioners in Equity, who investigate these matters in their offices and make their report. They can do it in much less time and expense than a Judge and jury.

Mr. C. C. BOWEN. What necessity is there for the jury to try any of these questions you speak of?

Mr. J. M. RUTLAND. I say there is none the world, and that is what I am arguing against. The original section leaves it to them, and according to that, a Judge of the Court of Common Pleas will take a case as he may take it, and determine it according to the rules of practice in that Court. What are our rules of practice in that Court? They are that the testimony shall be given before the Judge and the jury. The Judge takes down the testimony in writing and delivers the law to the jury in his charge, and he generally reads over his notes of evidence. The jury retire and agree upon a verdict. This verdict may dispose of one voucher which may have taken several hours, or a whole day, to examine. But allow the shortest time to each voucher, I ask gentlemen to say what time it would take for the Court of Common Pleas to get

86

through two or three hundred vouchers. I want to get rid of all this difficult machinery. The costs of trying these cases before the Court of Common Pleas would be almost incalculable. It would entail the heavy expense of a Court of Common Pleas sitting constantly to try cases. A single Commissioner in Equity could do five times more work by himself hearing parties and examining the case in his office. Where you have a Commissioner, he orders his references, the lawyers appear before him, he takes the vouchers, hears the proof, and decides for or against according to his judgment that is made when he has finished looking over the vouchers, and makes up his reports in the nature of a decree. He decides the case according to his best judgment. If the lawyers to the suit are not satisfied with his report, they file their exceptions. The report is taken before the Chancellor when he comes to hold his Court of Equity, and that case, which otherwise might take three months, can be decided in three hours, because the Commissioner has already done the business. A case is thus determined in three hours that would perhaps take a Judge and jury three months.

I have conceded that the Judges of the Court of Common Pleas may act as Chancellors as a mere act of concession, but I do believe it would be much better for Chancellors to have them entirely separate from the Court Judges of the State. Let them hold their Courts in the manner in which the Courts of Equity have been held heretofore. But I feel assured you will never get through without the Courts of Equity. I believe it to be indispensable for the proper administration of justice, that Courts of Equity should be held twice a year. Heretofore they have held only one session a year. In my amendment, I make it imperative upon the Judges of the Court of Equity to hold two sessions. I see no reason why we should not have as many sessions as the Court of Common Pleas. If this is done, then I think the great objection heretofore existing to the Court of Equity will be removed.

It has been said by some that they prefer to have the decision of a jury to that of a Chancellor. Admit that; but what is the practice of the Court of Equity in all cases of complicated facts. It is rather to yield to the Court of Common Pleas. If a party is dissatisfied with the report of the Commissioner, the lawyer can apply for a jury to try any of the facts he wants to try.

This section is but an effort to wipe out the Court of Equity. What constitutes the difference between civilized society and the society of barbarians. It is their Courts. Were we to wipe out all the Courts, we will have barbarism. If we wipe out the Court of Equity, a motion will be brought up from some quarter to wipe out other Courts. I hold that civilization requires there should be a Court of Equity. We need it to investigate the complicated accounts of merchants, comprehending perhaps the business of eight or a dozen years, the accounts of trustees, administrators, comprehending perhaps the business of a man's life, all of which requires accounting skill of the highest order. I hold there is no tribunal we can organize that can do that business except a Court of Equity.

There is another improvement which I think my substitute makes upon the original section ; that is, requiring the Chancellor to file their decrees, containing their reasons for their decision, within ninety days from the trial of the case. That will prevent Chancellors and Judges from delaying a case beyond three months, and if the party is not satisfied with the decision, he can carry his case in that time to the Court of Appeals at Columbia. So instead of six months you will have every three months to make your appeals.

It seems to me that all that is necessary is to show the absolute necessity of a Court of Equity. I feel the deepest interest in the passage of this substitute. It is no personal interest, for my personal interest as a lawyer would run all the other way. If you adopt this substitute I feel assured that the Judiciary system thus established will not only work well, but that all the citizens of South Carolina will be benefited in due time.

Mr. C. C. BOWEN. I am in favor of the nineteenth section as originally proposed by the Committee. I deny that there is any such complication as has been stated by the gentleman who has just spoken. I will also say right here that if you adopt the substitute you will have to go back and reconsider the eighteenth section, which says that the Court of Common Pleas shall sit twice a year, and that it shall have jurisdiction in matters of Equity. What originally was the object of the Court of Equity ? Enough has been said about it then ; but I contend that the real question was not touched, that the object of a Court of Equity was to get the testimony from the parties understood at the time they were established to be precluded from the law Court.

There is nothing now to prevent men from taking the stand. Chancellors formerly issued writs requiring parties to render under so and so certain rights. At first there was no Court of Chancery, or Court of Equity, but finally those powers were erected. If a party was dissatisfied with the writ issued by a Chancellor, then he went before the King to have the matter set right. It was only by the Chancellor's issuing innumerable writs that the Courts were established, and finally triumphant. It was contended that parties could not be made to give evidence in a Law Court. Hence they had to resurrect the Court of Equity. These have passed away. I am aware that it will perhaps be a struggle to give them up. But they have been given up in New York, Kentucky, Louisiana, Missouri, and all those States followed. I think they now combine the two Courts together.

The gentleman from Fairfield (Mr. RUTLAND) in his substitute would continue them, for I see no difference as to whether you call them Judges of the Court of Common Pleas or Chancellors. It proposes the same machinery to be kept up. I see no impropriety in taking the time of the Court of Common Pleas for citizens. The first two weeks of the term might be devoted to other law or criminal business, and the jury discharged. Then the Equity docket could be taken up. I see no necessity of the jury being called upon to determine every voucher. No such complications are presented. Where a case in equity comes up, if the Court sees fit it can appoint a referee to decide.

The gentleman from Fairfield contends that we are going to mix the records of the two Courts. There is no need of that. These records still remain. All we have to do is to transfer them from the Clerk of the Court of Equity to the Clerk of the Court of Common Pleas. Two separate books can be kept, one for the equity docket, another for law cases.

I know parties have made strenuous efforts, parties holding these identical positions, to have these Courts continued. The gentleman alludes to the expense of the proposed system, but I feel assured it will not be one-fourth of the expense of the old system. As the section now stands, there is no Court of Equity. It is not proposed to mix the records of the two Courts. The next Legislature will, no doubt, require the Clerks of the Courts of Common Pleas to keep these records in such a manner as to be able to put their hands on any paper at any time. It is only combining them. The gentleman stated that it was ruled now in the Court that the Court should decide upon the law. Provisions, however, have been made in this section to simplify and abridge all the rules and proceedings as they now exist in the Courts. I have not the slightest doubt but that, when the Legislature convenes, every single vestige of the old system will be swept away, and that the improvements adopted in other States will be adopted in South Carolina. The practice now existing in South Carolina is one hundred and fifty years behind any State in the Union, and still the gentleman from Fairfield asks us to continue that practice. Under the present practice in South Carolina, there are some sixty different Courts, and when you come to trace them out, nine-tenths amount to the same thing. They go on with the same count, and each writ classes with the other in debt, covenant, or detinue, trover, or what not. They start out with these, and the leaving out of any of those technicalities will be a non suit.

In drawing this section great care was taken to give the people all their rights in law and equity, and at the same time to give them a plan by which there would be no complication, or, at least, as few complications as possible. Special reference was had to the codes and proceedings of those States which have departed from the old rule which was in vogue a century ago in England, and now still in operation in South Carolina. I certainly hope the Convention will allow the nineteenth section to stand as it is. If this is wrong, then the whole practice of New York, Kentucky, Iowa, Missouri, California and Oregon are all wrong; in other words, all the modern practice introduced since 1848 is wrong, and the old practice, which has been in vogue since the days of the colonial government, is right.

In 1846 the English Government abolished the Court of Equity, and put it upon the same basis proposed in this section. It was changed on that basis, and upon that basis the system of Kentucky and New York was changed. They were followed by the other States I have already named, and we propose that South Carolina shall follow them.

Mr. R. C. DeLARGE. I would like to ask the Chairman who will perform the duties now devolving upon the Special Commissioners in Equity?

Mr. C. C. BOWEN. If a case arises, and it becomes necessary, the Court can appoint referees, whose business it would be to act in that capacity, but in ninety-nine cases out of a hundred there would be no necessity for such a reference.

Mr. R. C. DeLARGE. It is evident, from what has been said here on this subject, that something should be done to relieve the people of the present burdens borne by them in going into Courts of Equity in this State. While I disagree with much of the substitute of the gentleman from Fairfield, I also disagree with the section as it now reads in the judiciary report. I desire the law Judges to be the Judges in Equity; but I would not have it left to them to appoint the time for the hearing and taking of testimony, and who shall act as referees. But I think it would be wise to have the law Judges Judges in Equity. I believe it would facilitate business. Some responsible person, however, should act as Commissioner of the Court. It has been argued by the Chairman of the Judiciary Committee that if we adopt this substitute, or any portion of it, or change the section reported, we will be compelled to go back and change the eighteenth section. If necessary for the proper administration of justice, and for the protection of the rights of the people, I hope we will go back and change the eighteenth section.

Mr. J. J. WRIGHT. I am in favor of the substitute with the nineteenth section, as reported by the Judiciary Committee. The Courts of Equity in this State are indispensable, and I believe I can safely say, without fear of successful contradiction, that nine-tenths of the cases that for the next ten years will be brought in the Courts will be equity cases. I am also heartily in favor of Commissioners in Equity. We want to understand how it is so very expensive to carry a case through the Court of Equity. As I have said, for the next ten years I believe that nine-tenths of the cases will be brought into some Court of Equity. In order to mete out justice to the citizens of this State, I consider it indispensable to have Commissioners in Equity.

Mr. C. C. BOWEN. Under the practice of the Court of Equity can a man get any remedy at a Court of Law?

Mr. J. J. WRIGHT. What I insist upon is, that nine cases out of ten will go into the Court of Equity. Nine-tenths will be cases that will be recognizable in a Court of Equity, to be dealt with in the spirit of the law as it heretofore existed, and as it will continue, perhaps, for the next ten years. With regard to the expense, every gentleman that knows anything about Equity, knows the expense is enormous. For the safety and welfare of any people, I believe that a petit jury is indispensable. The Commissioners in Equity stand in the same relations to the Court of Equity that a petit jury does to the Court of Common Pleas. All Equity matters should at first be brought before the Commissioner in Equity. He has the right then to order all the vouchers and to hear all the evidence, to determine the case before him, and if the lawyers wish to appeal from the decision of the Commissioner, they have the right to appeal to the Chancellors when they sit, and they are to determine the case. Perhaps nine-tenths of the cases that come before a petit jury would be stopped there and go no further. So with a Court of Equity. Nine-tenths of the cases that would come before a Commissioner in Equity would be settled there without any expense whatever. He would sit as a Justice of the Peace, getting paid out of the cases that come before him. Perhaps there would not be an appeal in one case out of twenty; and if a person takes his case before a Court of Law, and it goes against him, he may still go before the Commissioner in Equity. If there is no Commissioner in Equity, the case goes before the Equity Court. It goes through the same form as in the Court of Common Pleas. The witnesses go there, take the stand, the evidence is heard, arguments made, and the Chancellor then takes his time to pronounce his decree. Our State in her present condition is not prepared for any such thing as that. We cannot sustain a Court of Equity in this State without a Commissioner in Equity. If we have not Commissioners, we must have another separate Court, because it would be just as impossible to lay hold of the meridian sun, as for the Judge of the Court of Common Pleas to act as Judge of Equity cases without the assistance of a Commissioner in Equity. As I said before, nine-tenths of the cases that will come up in the next ten years, should go before a Court of Equity or Commissioner in Equity. If they have to come directly before a Court, it will have to sit from January to December, without any vacation, in order to mete out that justice which every person is entitled in law and equity. I am in favor of the substitute, but desire to see it amended as follows :

" The General Assembly shall make provision by law for the preservation of the records of the Courts of Equity, and also for their transfer to the Judges of the Courts of Common Pleas, or those who have jurisdiction in cases of Equity, and the Judges of the Court of Common Pleas shall keep a separate record."

The very fact that the Judges of the Court of Common Pleas have jurisdiction in cases of Equity, makes it evident they should have the records. Just as soon as the Judges of the Court of Common Pleas take their seat to try such cases, they are Chancery Judges, and invested with that power.

Mr. D. H. CHAMBERLAIN. I have but a word or two to say on this question. I am in favor of the original section as reported by the Chairman on the Judiciary, and if we are to be consistent with other sections, which I have not as yet heard a proposition to change, I think it necessary to allow the section to stand as reported by the Committee. It has been attempted to convey an impression that the report of the Judiciary Committee shuts up some of the facilities for bringing actions and cases in equity. I desire to say that it is not the intention, and it is not the effect of the provisions of the original report to narrow at all the jurisdiction of our Courts in matters of equity. The object is not to abolish, but to combine. We have declared that the Judges of the Circuit Courts shall have full jurisdiction in matters of equity, but neither the intention, nor the effect of these provisions, will in any way be so desirable in the future that a majority of the cases should be brought in equity. There is one objection, one difficulty, in the way of the change proposed to be made by my distinguished friend from Fairfield. He has attempted to show that at present there is an immense amount of business in the Courts of Equity as now constituted. Whilst some special provisions will have to be made by the Legislature in cases now pending, I do claim that it is demonstrative that the Circuit Courts are lumbered with thousands of cases which it is impossible, under the present system, ever to bring to a conclusion. That is one of the strongest reasons against the continuation of the system, a system that has brought us to that dilemma. As far as I am informed, there are six hundred cases upon the Equity docket in Charleston. It is evident that something will have to be done to dispose of these cases now pending; but that there is such a multitude of cases pending now, is an argument against the present system. It is contended by some who are not anxious that law and equity should be separated, that it is necessary to have these Equity officers with a Commissioner. In other States, where law and equity are combined, and where it has been found possible to carry on that system with success, no such officer has been found necessary. If cases occasionally arise which require it, it is within the province of those Courts to appoint a referee, to continue so long as complicated cases require his services, and when those cases are ended, his duties end.

My friend from Beaufort has said that going into equity is terribly expensive. The object of the change is to make those expenses less than terrible. I believe that in retaining the old equity system of South Carolina, we are blindly going against the legal spirit of the age. I am aware, of my own knowledge, that the equity system and equity practice of South Carolina, is pointed to in other States as one of the strongest arguments against its continuation. We have equity cases in South Carolina which more than rival the famous case of Jaryndice *vs.* Jaryndice; and, in order that we may not continue such cases, in order that we may not lumber up, or make it possible that the dockets of our Courts shall be lumbered up as they are now by these undecided cases in equity, I hope the original report will be retained and adopted.

Mr. J. J. WRIGHT. Are you not aware that the substitute provides that the Legislature may, at any time, alter the practice of the Courts as they now are?

Mr. D. H. CHAMBERLAIN. I am aware of that, and have made no argument which overlooks it. The substitute provides for a Commissioner, and simply requires that the Judges of the Court of Common Pleas shall act as Chancellors, and the system is not in any respect changed. I am aware that at some future time, with the view of conforming to the substitute, a change may be made in the mode of proceeding, but, if so, it will only be effected by establishing separate equity offices.

Mr. R. B. ELLIOTT moved the indefinite postponement of the substitute.

Mr. B. O. DUNCAN. I hope that the motion will not prevail. I think the question should be brought up in proper form and voted on in a proper way.

Mr. L. S. LANGLEY. I regret to observe that whenever a measure is introduced into this body that is not popular with certain members, they forget the courtesy due to others. I think it is certainly due, when a motion in the form of a resolution or substitute is introduced by a member, that it should receive that consideration which its merits demand. I believe others desire to speak upon this substitute. There are others, like myself, who do not fully understand it, and desire to hear a full discussion so as to vote intelligently upon the matter. I shall never give my vote for summarily cutting off the consideration of so important a measure as the one offered by the gentleman from Fairfield. I hope, therefore, the motion to postpone will not prevail.

Mr. WM. J. McKINLAY. I sincerely hope the motion to postpone will not prevail. My knowledge of law, I am free to confess, is extremely limited, and I desire to hear both the original section and the substitute fully debated. I feel sure, if the gentleman who called the previous question had reflected a moment, he would not have made the motion.

Mr. R. B. ELLIOTT. I consider it the right and privilege of any member of this body, to offer any motion in a parliamentary form as he sees fit. I claim the right to make the motion I did. Other members have made similar motions in matters to which they were opposed, and measures which I advocated. I have never yet complained of any gentleman for so doing, and I do not see any reason why gentlemen should take any exception to the motion I made, especially when the very same gentlemen are noted for such motions themselves.

In regard to the advisability of the motion, I think enough light has been shed upon this subject, and I consider the further discussion of it an effort on the part of some members to let off extra steam, and I really think one half the debate upon this substitute has not been at all to the point. I ask that the motion to postpone indefinitely be put.

Mr. B. BYAS. I, as well as many others, not lawyers, desire to get as much information as possible in reference to this matter, and hope the motion to postpone will not prevail. We wish to vote intelligently upon the subject. I move to lay the motion to postpone indefinitely on the table.

The motion was not agreed to.

87

Mr. E. W. M. MACKEY moved the previous question, which was not sustained.

The question then recurred on the motion to indefinitely postpone the substitute.

Mr. R. C. DeLARGE moved that the Sergeant-at-Arms be directed to bring in absent members, which was agreed to.

Mr. J. M. RUTLAND called for the yeas and nays, which was sustained, and they were ordered and resulted as follows:

YEAS—Messrs. Alexander, Becker, Bowen, Bonum, Burton, Brockenton, R. H. Cain, E. J. Cain, Camp, Cardozo, Coghlan, Chamberlain, Chestnut, Darrington, DeLarge, Edwards, Elliott, Gentry, Goss, Harris, C. D. Hayne, Holmes, Humbird, Hurley, Jacobs, Jervey, Jillson, Sam'l Johnson, Wm. B. Johnson, W. E. Johnston, Henry Jones, Charles Jones, Samuel Lee, Leslie, E. W. M. Mackey, Mayer, Mead, Middleton, Miller, Milford, Neagle, Newell, Nuckles, Owens, Parker, Pillsbury, Randolph, Ransier, Richmond, Rivers, Runion, Sanders, Smalls, Stubbs, Swails, Thomas, A. Thompson, Viney, Whittemore, White, Wingo—62.

NAYS—The President, Messrs. Allen, Boozer, Bryce, Byas, Cooke, Collins, Corley, Craig, Davis, Dickson, Dill, Donaldson, Duncan, H. E. Hayne, L. B. Johnson, Lang, Langley, George Lee, Mauldin, W. J. McKinlay, Wm. McKinlay, Nance, Nash, Olsen, Rainey, Robertson, Rutland, Shrewsbury, S. B. Thompson, F. E. Wilder, Wooley, Wright —34.

ABSENT—Messrs. Arnim, Bell, Crews, Clinton, Dogan, Driffle, Gray, J. N. Hayne, Hunter, Henderson, Jackson, J. W. Johnson, Joiner, Lomax, McDaniels, Moses, Nelson, Perry, Rose, Sasportas, B. A. Thompson, Webb, Whipper, Williamson, C. M. Wilder—25.

So the substitute was indefinitely postponed.

Mr. R. B. ELLIOTT moved to reconsider the vote, and to lay the motion to reconsider on the table, which latter motion was adopted.

Section nineteen, as reported from the Judiciary Committee, was then taken up.

Mr. D. H. CHAMBERLAIN moved to amend as follows, which was adopted:

Add after the last word, in Section 19, "It shall be the duty of the Judges of the Supreme and Circuit Courts,, to file their decisions within sixty days from the last day of the term of Court at which the causes were heard."

The section so amended was passed to its third reading.

The PRESIDENT stated that the next Special Order was the ordinance in relation to the rights of minor children.

Mr. R. C. DeLARGE moved a suspension of the Special Order for five minutes, in order to allow Mr. CARDOZO to submit a petition to the Convention.

Mr. F. L. CARDOZO presented the following petition, which, he said, was one of the greatest importance, and required prompt action :

To the Honorable the Senate and House of Representatives
of the United States in Congress assembled :

Your petitioners, citizens of South Carolina, respectfully represent that by authority of Act of Congress, approved February 6, 1863, entitled "An Act to amend an Act entitled an Act for the collection of direct taxes in the insurrectionary districts within the United States, and for other purposes," approved January, 7, 1862, certain lands in South Carolina were bid in by the United States at public tax sales, and that by the limitation of said Act right of redemption has expired ; and,

Whereas certain tracts of said lands have not been sold by the United States, but are now in the hands of the Tax Commissioners as the property of the United States, your petitioners humbly pray that said lands may be allotted in parcels, to the extent your honorable body may designate, to those citizens of South Carolina who are destitute and deserving ; the necessities and merits of the applicants for this benefit to be determined by such measures as your honorable body may direct, and your petitioners will ever pray.

On motion of Mr. R. C. DeLARGE, the petition was referred to the Committee on Petitions, with instructions to report to-morrow (Wednesday) morning.

Mr. H. E. HAYNE called for the next Special Order, which was the report of the Committee on Education.

The report was taken up, and the consideration of the fourth section was resumed, the question being on striking out the word " compulsory."

Mr. B. F. RANDOLPH moved to strike out the words " twenty-four" and insert " thirty."

Mr. H. E. HAYNE. I hope the word "compulsory" will not be stricken out. There is every reason why we should have compulsory attendance at school. When we look around and observe the vice and ignorance with which we have to contend, it becomes apparent that force should be exercised to make parents send their children to school. It is contended by some that compulsory attendance will work badly. But the system has worked well in Germany and Massachusetts, and there is no reason why it should not work as well here. I have never yet seen a German without a good education. I hope the section will pass as reported by the Committee.

Mr. B. BYAS. I hope the word " compulsory " will be stricken out. If a father or mother have not interest enough in their children to provide for their education, let the consequences be on their own heads. When such parents are in their graves, their children will rise up and damn them. Let us have a Republican form of government. A man should not be compelled to educate his children, any more than he should be forced to direct them to heaven or hell. Man is a free, moral agent, and he should be left where God put him.

Mr. J. K. JILLSON moved to adjourn, but the motion was not agreed to.

Mr. R. C. DeLARGE. One of the speakers from Marion (Mr. HAYNE) has alluded to the education of the German people, as well as to the practice of the people of Massachusetts. In the language of my friend from Beaufort, yesterday, if Massachusetts chooses to do wrong, it is no reason why South Carolina should follow the example. I claim to be in favor of Republican institutions, and I desire to see the liberties of the people perpetuated—not restricted, or subject to such encroachments as that which is involved in this remarkable section.

The hour of one o'clock having arrived, the Convention adjourned.

AFTERNOON SESSION.

The Convention re-assembled at 3 P. M.

The unfinished business was resumed.

Mr. R. C. DeLARGE. Although laboring under great inconvenience, I shall attempt to defend the amendment proposing to strike out the word "compulsory." In the first place, we have a report which is to become a portion of the Constitution, and that Constitution emphatically declares, in terms that cannot be misunderstood, that "no distinction shall be made on account of race, color, or previous condition." It has been remarked this morning that in the Constitution of Massachusetts, and other Northern States, the same proviso exists. But any one who reflects for a moment upon the condition of the people of Massachusetts, and those of South Carolina, will fully appreciate the great difference between them. As already stated, I object to the word "compulsory," because it is contrary to the spirit and principles of republicanism. Where is the necessity for placing in the Constitution a proviso that can never be enforced. It is just as impossible to put such a section in practical operation, as it would be for a man to fly to the moon. No one will deny that an attempt to enforce it would entail the greatest trouble and expense. Who, I ask, do we propose to set up as a censor of learning? Perhaps the opponents of the measure will say the School Commissioner. I deny that he can do it. He may be the father of half a dozen children. I, too, am the father of children; but will any body tell me that, as a free citizen of South Carolina, I have not the right to choose whether I shall send those children to school or not. Will any one say I shall not teach my child myself? It may be said, such a right is not denied me. Whether it be so or not, I plant myself upon the broad principle of the equality of all men as the basis of true republicanism; and to compel any man to do what this section provides is contrary to this principle.

Again, this clause will lead to difficulties of a serious character, to which neither you nor myself can blind our eyes. In Massachusetts there is a population cradled in the arms of freedom and liberty, free of all prejudice and devoid of passion, to a great extent. In South Carolina we have an entirely different set of people. We are about to inaugurate great changes, which it is our desire shall be successful.

Mr. C. P. LESLIE. Do I understand you to say that the people of Massachusetts have no prejudices of race?

Mr. F. L. CARDOZO. I would also like to ask the gentleman where he gets his authority for saying that the people of Massachusetts are cradled in the principles of freedom and liberty. Is it so provided in the Constitution of Massachusetts?

Mr. R. C. DeLARGE. I am not well acquainted with all the clauses in the Constitution of Massachusetts, and speak only from my historic knowledge of that people. This section proposes to open these schools to all persons, irrespective of color, to open every seminary of learning to all. Heartily do I endorse the object, but the manner in which it is to be enforced meets my most earnest disapproval. I do not propose to enact in this report a section that may be used by our enemies to appeal to the worst passions of a class of people in this State. The schools may be opened to all, under proper provisions in the Constitution, but to declare that parents "shall" send their children to them whether they are willing or not is, in my judgment, going a step beyond the bounds of prudence. Is there any logic or reason in inserting in the Constitution a provision which cannot be enforced? What do we intend to give the Legislature power to do? In one breath you propose to protect minor children, and in the next to punish their parents by fine and imprisonment if they do not send their children to school. For these reasons I am opposed to the section, and urge that the word "compulsory" shall be stricken out.

Mr. A. J. RANSIER. I am sorry to differ with my colleague from Charleston on this question. I contend that in proportion to the education of the people so is their progress in civilization. Believing this, I believe that the Committee have properly provided for the compulsory education of all the children in this State between the ages named in the section.

I recognize the importance of this measure. There is a seeming objection to the word "compulsory," but I do not think it of grave importance. My friend does not like it, because he says it is contrary to the spirit of republicanism. To be free, however, is not to enjoy unlimited license, or my friend himself might desire to enslave again his fellow men.

Now I propose to support this section fully, and believe that the more it is considered in all its bearings upon the welfare of our people, the greater will be the desire that every parent shall, by some means, be compelled to educate his children and fit them for the responsibilities of life. As to the particular mode of enforcing attendance at school, we leave that an open question. At present we are only asserting the general principle, and the Legislature will provide for its application.

Upon the success of republicanism depends the progress which our people are destined to make. If parents are disposed to clog this progress by neglecting the education of their children, for one, I will not aid and abet them. Hence, this, in my opinion, is an exceedingly wise provision, and I am content to trust to the Legislature to carry out the measures to which it necessarily leads.

Vice and degradation go hand in hand with ignorance. Civilization and enlightenment follow fast upon the footsteps of the schoolmaster; and if education must be enforced to secure these grand results, I say let the compulsory process go on.

Mr. R. C. DeLARGE. Can the gentleman demonstrate how the Legislature is to enforce the education of children without punishment of their parents by fine or imprisonment.

Mr. A. J. RANSIER. When that question arises in the Legislature, I hope we shall have the benefit of my friend's counsel, and he himself may possibly answer that question. If there is any one thing to which we may attribute the sufferings endured by this people, it is the gross ignorance of the masses. While we propose to avoid all difficulties which may be fraught with evil to the community, we shall, nevertheless, insist upon our right to provide for the exercise of the great moral agencies which education always brings to bear upon public opinion. Had there been such a provision as this in the Constitution of South

Carolina heretofore, there is no doubt that many of the evils which at present exist would have been avoided, and the people would have been advanced to a higher stage of civilization and morals, and we would not have been called upon to mourn the loss of the flower of the youth of our country. In conclusion, I favor this section as it stands. I do not think it will militate against the cause of republicanism, but, on the contrary, be of benefit both to it and to the people whom we represent. Feeling that everything depends on the education of the rising generation, I shall give this measure my vote, and use all my exertions to secure its adoption into this Constitution.

Mr. B. F. RANDOLPH. In favoring, as I do, compulsory attendance at school, I cannot for the life of me see in what manner republicanism is at stake. It seems to have been the fashion on this floor to question a man's republicanism because he chooses to differ with others on general principles. Now this is a question which does not concern republicanism at all. It is simply a matter of justice which is due to a people, and it might be just as consistently urged that it is contrary to republican principles to organize the militia, to force every man to enroll his name, and to arm and equip them, as to urge that this provision is anti-republican because it compels parents to see to the education of their children.

Mr. B. O. DUNCAN. Does the gentleman propose to educate children at the point of the bayonet, through the militia?

Mr. B. F. RANDOLPH. If necessary we may call out the militia to enforce the law. Now, the gentlemen on the other side have given no reasons why the word "compulsory" should be stricken out.

Mr. R. C. DeLARGE. Can you name any State where the provision exists in its Constitution?

Mr. B. F. RANDOLPH. It exists in Massachusetts.

Mr. R. C. DeLARGE. That is not so.

Mr. F. L. CARDOZO. This system has been tested in Germany, and I defy the gentleman from Charleston to deny the fact. It has also been tested in several States of the Union, and I defy the gentleman to show that it has not been a success. It becomes the duty of the opposition if they want this section stricken from the report, to show that where it has been applied it has failed to produce the result desired.

Mr. J. J. WRIGHT. Will you inform us what State in the Union compels parents to send their children to school?

Mr. B. F. RANDOLPH. The State of New Hampshire is one. It may be asked what is the object of law? It is not only for the purpose of restraining men from doing wrong, but for the protection of all the citizens of a State, and the promotion of the general welfare. Blackstone lays it down as one of the objects, the furthering, as far as it can consistently be done, of the general welfare of the people. It is one of the objects of law, as far as practicable, not to restrain wrong by punishing man for violating the right, but also one of its grand objects to build up civilization, and this is the grand object of this provision in the report of the Committee on Education. It proposes to further civilization, and I look upon it as one of the most important results which will follow the defeat of the rebel armies, the establishment among the people who have long been deprived of the privilege of education, a law which will compel parents to send their children to school.

Mr. R. B. ELLIOTT. Is it not regulated by general statutes in the State of Massachusetts, that parents shall be compelled to send their children to school?

Mr. B. F. RANDOLPH. We propose to do that here. I consider this one of the most important measures which has yet come before this body. I think I can read it in the eyes of the members of this Convention to favor this measure. I feel that every one here believes it to be his duty to the people he represents. I believe every one here is zealous in doing all he can to further civilization, in building up educational institutions in the State, and doing all that is calculated to diffuse intelligence among the people generally. I had the honor of being principal of a free school two years; and, in the midst of one of the most intelligent system of schools, the most trying thing which teachers had to contend with was the want of regular attendance on the part of the children. The most intelligent parents would sometimes neglect to send their children to school. The teachers had to adopt rules closing their doors to those who were irregular in their attendance. This law will assist the teachers and assist our school system. It will prove beneficial to the State not only for the reasons I have given, but for various other reasons. I hope you will all vote for it. I shall vote for it with all my heart, because I believe it to be something beneficial to the welfare of the people of the State.

Mr. A. C. RICHMOND. I desire to say but a few words on this subject. I shall speak principally in reference to our common schools and public funds. We expect to have a public school fund, although it may not be very large. We expect our parishes to be divided into school districts of convenient size. We can erect only a limited number of school houses each year, and it may be five or ten years before school houses are erected in all the districts, and the fund becomes large enough to assist in the education of all the people. If the word "compulsory" remains, it will be impossible to enforce the law for sometime to come. We say the public schools shall be opened to all. Every school district will have its school houses and its teachers. There is to be a particular school fund, school districts, and school houses. It is supposed by legislators and others that it is an excellent thing to have the children to go to school. It opens up a vast field for discussion, and affords a beautiful opportunity for making buncombe speeches. It is admitted by all legislators in every State of the Union, that cheap education is the best defence of the State. There must be schools to which colored children can go; but we wish to look into the propriety of compelling parents to send their children to school. I believe the efforts of the teachers, preachers, and all those interested in the welfare of the State, and the efforts of all those interested in the welfare of the colored people, will bring out nearly all the colored children. I believe nearly all the colored children of the State will go to school. We have societies that will help to furnish the books; we have preachers who are much interested; we have missionaries, all of whom are interested in this class of our people, and who will see to it that the colored children are educated, so that settles that point. The next point is, how are the white children going to school? By means of moral suasion nearly all the colored children will be brought to school; and by means of white schools, nearly all the white children will go to school and be educated. It will regulate itself. The word "compulsory" is used to compel the attendance of children in one or the other class of schools.

Mr. R. C. DeLARGE. What does the tenth section of that report say?

Mr. A. C. RICHMOND. I believe it is the meaning, that if families of white people are not able to send their children to private schools, they shall be obliged to send their children to the public schools, in which all white and colored shall be educated.

Mr. F. L. CARDOZO. We only compel parents to send their children to some school, not that they shall send them with the colored children; we simply give those colored children who desire to go to white schools, the privilege to do so.

Mr. A. C. RICHMOND. By means of moral suasion, I believe nearly all the colored people, as well as a large number of the children of white parents will go to school; such schools as their parents may select. If parents are too proud to take advantage of the means of education afforded, why then I say let their children grow up in ignorance.

Mr. J. A. CHESTNUT. So far as I have been able to see and judge,
88

this report of the Committee is a sensible one, and ought to be adopted as it stands. How it can affect the rights of the people, or interfere with the spirit of republicanism, I am at a loss to discover. On the contrary, from all the experience I have had among the people, I unhesitatingly declare that no measure adopted by this Convention will be more in consonance with their wishes than this, or more productive of material blessings to all classes. Sir, you cannot by any persuasive and reasonable means establish civilization among an ignorant and degraded community, such as we have in our country. Force is necessary, and, for one, I say let force be used. Republicanism has given us freedom, equal rights, and equal laws. Republicanism must also give us education and wisdom.

It seems that the great difficulty in this section is in the fact that difficulty may arise between the two races in the same school, or that the whites will not send their children to the same schools with the colored children. What of that? Has not this Convention a right to establish a free school system for the benefit of the poorer classes? Undoubtedly. Then if there be a hostile disposition among the whites, an unwillingness to send their children to school, the fault is their own, not ours. Look at the idle youths around us. Is the sight not enough to invigorate every man with a desire to do something to remove this vast weight of ignorance that presses the masses down? I have no desire to curtail the privileges of freemen, but when we look at the opportunities neglected, even by the whites of South Carolina, I must confess that I am more than ever disposed to compel parents, especially of my own race, to send their children to school. If the whites object to it, let it be so. The consequences will rest with themselves.

I hope, therefore, that the motion to strike out the word "compulsory" will be laid upon the table.

Mr. R. H. CAIN. It seems to me that we are spending a great deal of unnecessary time in the discussion of this subject. It is true, the question is one of great interest, and there are few who are not anxious that provisions shall be made by this Convention for the education of all classes in the State. But I am confident that it will not be necessary to use compulsion to effect this object. Hence, I am opposed to the insertion of the obnoxious word. I see no necessity for it. You cannot compel parents to send their children to school; and if you could, it would be unwise, impolitic, and injudicious. Massachusetts is fifty years ahead of South Carolina, and, under the circumstances which exist in that State, I might, if a resident, insist upon a compulsory education; but in South Carolina the case is different. There is a class of persons here whose situation, interests and necessities are varied, and controlled by surroundings which do not exist at the North. And justice is demanded for them. To do justice in this matter of education, compulsion is not required. I am willing to trust the people. They have good sense, and experience itself will be better than all the force you can employ to instill the idea of duty to their children.

Now, as a compromise with the other side, I propose the following amendment, namely that "the General Assembly may require the attendance at either public or private schools," &c.

This is a question that should be left to the Legislature. If the circumstances demand it, compulsion may be used to secure the attendance of pupils; but I do not believe such a contingency ever will occur.

As to the idea that both classes of children will be compelled to go to school together, I do not think it is comprehended in the subject at all. I remember that in my younger days I stumped the State of Iowa for the purpose of having stricken from the Constitution a clause which created distinction of color in the public schools. This was prior to the assembling of the Constitutional Convention. All we claimed was that they should make provision for the education of all the youth. We succeeded, and such a clause was engrafted in the Constitution, and that instrument was ratified by a majority of ten thousand. We said nothing about color. We simply said "youth."

I say to you, therefore, leave this question open. Leave it to the Legislature. I have great faith in humanity. We are in a stage of progress, such as our country never has seen, and while the wheels are rolling on, depend upon it, there are few persons in this country who will not seek to enjoy it by sending their children to school. White or black, all will desire to have their children educated. Let us then make this platform broad enough for all to stand upon without prejudice or objection. The matter will regulate itself, and to the Legislature may safely be confided the task of providing for any emergency which may arise.

Mr. R. G. HOLMES. If there is anything we want in this State, it is some measure to compel the attendance of children between the ages of six and sixteen at some school. If it is left to parents, I believe the great majority will lock up their children at home. I hope, therefore, we shall have a law compelling the attendance of all children at school. It is the statute law in Massachusetts, and I hope we will have the provision inserted in our Constitution. The idea that it is not republican to educate children is supremely ridiculous. Republicanism, as has been well said, is not license. No man has the right, as a republican, to put his hand in my pocket, or steal money from it, because he wishes to do it. I can conceive of a way in which my child may be robbed by that system of republicanism which some members have undertaken to defend. My child may be left an orphan, poor and dependent on the kindness of neighbors or friends. They may think it to the best interest of that child to bind it out as an apprentice to some person. My child may be robbed of an education, because the person to whom it was bound does not think it advisable to send that child to school, as there may happen to be some objectionable children in the school. I have seen white children sitting by the side of colored children in school, and observed that there could not have been better friends. I do not want this privilege of attending schools confined to any exclusive class. We want no laws made here to prevent children from attending school. If any one chooses to educate their children in a private school, this law does not debar them that privilege.

But there are some who oppose all education. I remember the case of an individual who refused to have his children educated beause, as he said, he himself had got along well enough without it, and he guessed his children could do the same. There is too much of that spirit in our State, and we want to contrive something to counteract it. In the case to which I have alluded, that individual some fifteen years afterwards, when his children had grown up, regretted his action, and was very much mortified because his children had no education. I hope we will engraft something into the Constitution, making it obligatory upon parents to send their children to school, and with that view, I hope the section will pass as it is.

Mr. R. B. ELLIOTT. I do not rise to make a speech, but simply and briefly to express the hope that the section as reported by the Committee on Education will be adopted. Some gentleman have said it is anti-republican. I deny it. It is in conformity with the ideas of republicanism to punish crime. It is republicanism to reward virtue. It is republicanism to educate the people, without discrimination. That has made New England great, and made her citizens, poor as well as rich, low as well as high, black as well as white, educated and intelligent. The gentleman from Berkley (Mr. Richmond) has said this law is to force the white and colored children into the public schools together. The only question is whether children shall become educated and enlightened, or remain in ignorance. The question is not white or black united or divided, but whether children shall be sent to school or kept at home. If they are compelled to be educated, there will be no danger of the Union, or a second secession of South Carolina from the Union. The masses will be intelligent, and will become the great strength and bulwark of republicanism. If they remain uneducated, they will inevitably remain ignorant, and it is a well known fact, that ignorance is the parent of vice and crime, and was the sustainer of the late gigantic slaveholder's rebellion. If the children remain at home, instead of a harbor of peace and prosperity, we will have a stone blockade.

I have been astonished at many of the grounds taken by many of the gentlemen who have spoken upon this subject. Some have gone into discussion, not on the merits of the fourth section, but either of the eleventh section or some other clause. Many have left that report altogether, and have entered into a statement of what they had the privilege of undergoing already, and what they would like to have the privilege of undergoing in the future. I think if this question was fairly discussed, there would be found but few gentlemen on this floor who was opposed to the report of the Committee. It is not a question of color, but simply as to whether white or black shall keep their children at home uneducated, bringing them up in ignorance, useless to society, or be compelled to send them to school, where they can be made intelligent and useful in the community where they reside. This is the only question to be answered. I appeal to gentlemen of the Convention to know whether they desire to see a state of anarchy, or a state of confusion in South Carolina in the future. I desire to know whether they wish to see an independent people, engaged in industrious pursuits, living happy and contented. The child that remains in ignorance until grown up will never learn the first duty that ought to be learned by every man, which is to love his country and to love his State. If a man is so ignorant as to know nothing of political economy of his State or country, he can never be a good citizen. To be a good citizen every one should know what are the duties of a citizen, and the laws of the State and country in which he resides. He must be able to tell what is a violation of law. We blame a man if he violates the law, though he is ignorant. It will not be denied that it is republicanism to punish a man if he commits a crime. If you give a man the privilege of remaining in ignorance, it is anti-republicanism to punish him. You must compel them to learn. Do that and you will have peace in the future. If you neglect to do this, you must expect confusion, vice, and everything of the sort. I hope the section will pass as reported by the Committee.

Mr. J. K. JILLSON. Hitherto I have refrained from entering into the arena of debate, but this subject before us, and the principles involved, are of such vast importance, that I must claim the indulgence of the Convention while I offer a few remarks in regard to the matter.

The report received the most careful attention from the Committee, and section four more than any other. We discussed it in all its various points before bringing it before the Convention. The subject of education is one that should command the attention and interest of all nations, all people, and every individual; but in a country or nation where the republican form of government prevails, where the government is of the people, and in, through, and by the people, it is of the most vital importance that the interest of education be cherished and enlarged as second to no other interest. A celebrated modern writer makes the following statement: "It is the clearest duty, prescribed by nature herself, under silent but real and awful penalties, of governing persons in every society, to see that the people, so far as possible, are taught; that wherever a citizen is born, some chance be offered him of becoming a man. This is for ever the duty of governors and persons in authority in human societies," and if we carefully examine the history and status of nations, that the above statement is verified by incontrovertible evidence, and by facts that cannot be gainsayed; for those nations in which the most liberal, careful, and efficient provisions for the education of the people at large are made, stand foremost in the ranks of civilization, progress, humanity, national greatness and glory, and Christianity. But, to come more directly to the question now before us, in my humble opinion, the only rational objection that can be urged against the principles involved in this section, is that they militate against the great and comprehensive principles of republicanism, that they are indicative of an abridgement of, an infringement upon, and a subversion of the rights and liberties of the people, that they assume to dictate as to what a certain class *must* and *shall* do. Mr. President, I am willing to accept, the widest, highest, and most expansive definition of freedom, but I am not disposed to accept the term as synonymous with unbridled license. Sir, while I hold that it is the sacred, solemn, and imperative duty of the State to vouchsafe to all its citizens all their rights, and all their privileges, I also maintain that it is just as much its bounden duty to check and restrain the abuse of those rights and privileges, that the government has the prerogative to assume to act as the regulator, and monitor, as well as the faithful defender and preserver of liberty. No one will deny that individual rights should and ought to be subservient to the great interests of the common weal and prosperity. "No one has a right to do as he pleases, unless he pleases to do right."

In Switzerland, that stronghold of liberty, whose snow clad Alpine crags ring with the bugle notes of freedom, the birth-place of the patriot Tell, a country whose people are noted for their intelligence, morality, patriotism, and piety, the law compels parents to send their children to school six months in each year. In Massachusetts, a State second to none in the Union in regard to the general intelligence, industry, liberality, morality, patriotism, piety, and public enterprise of its people, the pioneer State in the cause of education, there is a law which says parents *must* send their children between certain ages, to either public or private schools, three months in each year; and if the parents are not able to provide the children with the necessary school books, they are furnished by the School Committees. In Massachusetts, only one person in about every three hundred and fifty, is unable to read and write, and I venture the assertion without fear of contradiction, that there is not a single adult person of native parentage, born and raised in the State, and having ordinary mental capacity, who cannot read, write, and cipher. In South Carolina, where there has never been any system of free public schools, there is one person in every eight who cannot read and write. Here is what a celebrated advocate says of compulsory education in Prussia :

In the Kingdom of Prussia, every child is compelled to attend some school, whether his parents will or not. The annual report has these words : "There is not a single human being in Prussia who does not receive education, intellectual and moral, sufficient for all the needs of common life." This law of compulsion has been in operation but fourteen years, when pauperism and crime had diminished thirty-eight per cent.

In the present relationships of our mixed population in the United States, this law of compulsion is called for as a defence of our liberties. We have in our country more than a million of children between the ages of five and sixteen who can neither read nor write ! Do you ask what we are going to do with them ? That is not the question. The question is, what are *they* going to do with *us ?* Think of their future power at the ballot-box !- We can disarm their animal ferocity and traditional prejudices only by intellectual culture and moral principle; and this preventive process can be effectually applied, in nineteen cases out of twenty, *only* during the period of youth. Society has a right to defend itself against crime, against murder, arson, etc. Has it not an equal and prior right to defend itself against the *cause* of crime, which is ignorance ? If you force a young man into prison because he is a thief, we call upon you to force him, while a boy, into a schoolhouse, to prevent his becoming a thief. Here surely "an ounce of prevention is worth a pound of cure."

At this period, when four millions of freedmen are to carry their votes to the ballot-box to help shape the destinies of the republic, what language can overstate the pressing necessity of their being educated to comprehend their new position, exercise their new rights, and obey their new laws ? It is the command of Nature's God, that all children should be educated in order to answer the purposes of their creation. If a parent be so weak or wicked as to refuse his child the daily bread of knowledge, let the Legislature stand in the place of parent to that child, and do for him what his nature demands, and the public safety requires. To enforce the law, let the selectmen of a town be empowered to impose on that delinquent parent a fine not less than one dollar, and not more than five dollars. This fine would not need to be imposed in any neighborhood more than half a dozen times, because public sentiment would so heartily approve its benevolent aim, that it would silently change all objections, as it did in Prussia.

I hope we will profit by the experience of others. I am in favor of the section as it stands, and opposed to any change being made in the phraseology of it. It is said the word compulsory is harsh. I say it is right. Another point has been made, that we cannot enforce the law. I hope there will be no occasion for its harsh enforcement. I want to have public opinion brought to bear upon those parents who keep their children from school. I hope the section will pass as it is.

Mr. J. J. WRIGHT. Although indisposed and scarcely able to speak, I feel it my bounden and indispensable duty, as one deeply interested in this matter and as one who desires to look after the general welfare of the people, to raise my feeble voice against the adoption of this clause. I have had seven years experience in teaching school, and I know something about the influence that should be brought into communities, and the influence that should be brought upon children to cause them to attend at schools, and I say here that whenever we place in our Constitution such a clause as this we are trampling upon the liberties of the people. We are depriving them of those rights, privileges and immunities which belong to every free people.

Many gentlemen have referred to Massachusetts, New Hampshire, and several other States, to prove their case; but they have, so far, failed. They have not shown us that any of the States referred to have any such law, and we stand upon the defensive and deny that they have. But suppose Massachusetts, New Hampshire, North Carolina, or any other State in the Union, had a law of that kind, it is no reason why we should have it. We occupy an entire different position from what those States do. We have just been born to a new life, and we are not prepared at this stage of our proceedings to enact or enforce any such law, or to incorporate it into the Constitution. Millions of our people now upon the plantations can hardly get bread to satisfy their hunger and to sustain life. It is simply a matter of impossibility for us in the next one, two or even three years, to compel those people to send their children to school. If the young men in Charleston and elsewhere, who are qualified, will go out and organize schools, then we might think about such a measure. But would you put such a clause into your Constitution now, when in many places there are no schools, and children would be compelled, perhaps, to walk ten or twenty miles to reach one. It is absurd. When the time shall come that we have our schools in operation all over the State, and schools enough in every district, then we may enact such a law as to compel the attendance of children at school, and enforce it.

I have had some experience among these people, and I know of no class of people upon this earth who desire to abide by the law, when they know what the law is, more than they do. But if we put such a law into the Constitution, it may be five or ten years before we can put that law into execution. Again, how are we going to enforce a law without a penalty. Here are these people that cannot send their children to school. What are you going to do with them? I propose this amendment: "The General Assembly may by law provide for the compulsory attendance at either a public or private school of all children between the ages of six and sixteen."

I simply offer this to meet the exigencies of the case. The General Assembly is elected to provide for the general welfare of the people, not only in respect to schools, but in every respect. If you confer this power upon the General Assembly, then that body, whenever in its judgment it may be deemed prudent and such a law can be enforced, can provide for the compulsory attendance of children at school.

If, at the first session of the Legislature, that body does not make a law that comes up to the provision of this Constitution, the people have a right to complain and murmur, and to say that persons we have elected to the Legislature have not performed their duty. The Legislature is bound to fulfill every requirement of the Constitution we are about to frame. If they do not, they are not faithful servants of the people. I know New England is the glory of the land. She is an example for us. Why? It is not her vast fiscal resources, not her wealth, not her military resources. It is the superior knowledge and zeal which they have given their children. But when you undertake to say there is a law compelling parents to send their children to school, I deny it and challenge the proof. I know that Massachusetts, New Hampshire, and other States have a provision making it obligatory upon every town and every county to have a school for children. If a town or county does not establish a school, then a fine or penalty is imposed upon that county to twice the amount of the cost to establish schools. But I contend that it is incompatable with the general welfare of any people, and even with

89

the Christian religion, to compel men to send their children to school.
Mr. WRIGHT then read his amendment.

Mr. B. F. WHITTEMORE. I did not expect it would be necessary
for anything to be said in defence of the clause as reported by the Committee on Education. I was perfectly well aware of the ability
of the framers of this clause to defend whatsoever they have reported. I am very glad to find that, so far as the discussion has gone, that
the general feeling and impression made by the debaters is that it should
continue just as reported. I am glad to find so strong a feeling, with
regard to the compulsory attendance of children at school. It has been
said, with regard to the condition of the people of this State, that it is
not to be compared to that of the people of other States; and, secondly,
that a provision like this is not adapted to the present condition of the
people of South Carolina. I am aware, so far as the children of the
State are concerned, it needs no special enactment for the purpose of
sending them to school. If we establish school houses at convenient
places, I am persuaded that the children themselves will be anxious to
go to school. But I am aware that even now, with the scanty provisions
made, that in some localities there are parents who endeavor to prevent
their children from going to school. I would be in favor of taking away
the power from the parent to prevent their children from receiving educational advantages. I believe, if there is a parent so far forgetful of
the interests of his child, if there is a guardian, or any one into whose
hands a child has been entrusted, so far forgetful of the welfare of that
child and of the benefits that attach to educational advantages to prevent it from partaking of those advantages, I hope that that child will
be taken out of that parent's or guardian's hands. Show me school
houses, show me children going willingly to school, or compelled to go to
school, and I will show you a community that has high considerations
not only for its own respectability, but a community that will increase
and prosper, and whose example is worthy to be followed.

If we provide for the children, we shall provide for the condition of
the people. Make children intelligent, give them an opportunity to understand and read their own laws, to understand the constitutional provisions of the law under which they live, let them understand the penalties that attach to a violation of the law, and you protect the children
and protect the communities against crime, and in place of a prison,
there will be a school house. In other words, let us provide for the diffusion of intelligence, and we keep out of the jails and penitentiaries a
large number of people.

It has been said that the punishment inflicted · upon the parent, also punishes the children. I wish the ancient Lacedemonian law might be the law which governed us in this State ; that the punishment of children found guilty of crimes was visited upon the parents, for it was held that if these children were properly educated they might have grown up good members of society, and have been prevented from committing crime.

The ancient Hebrews had a law among them that a child not taught a trade was, consequently, taught to steal. If it was in my power to make laws for the government of the people, I would not only make it compulsory that the children attend schools a certain number of weeks, or months, but I should make it compulsory that they should have a trade. I would say that no man or woman should be allowed to enter into the solemn relation of marriage until they could read and write, and it is my solemn opinion you would very soon see the people all over the State going to their books.

We simply mean by this section to say that the Legislature, by its enactment, shall provide for the compulsory attendance of all the children in the State at some school. The laws in Connecticut and Massachusetts, which have been cited, make it imperative for children to attend school so many months in the year. Corporations themselves have established schools within their own corporate limits for the purpose of giving education to the children working in their factories, or in their employ. If we had to provide a school house at every cross road in the State, we should provide for the attendance of every child in every section of the State. I am well aware that children walk great distances to go to school. Many little children tramp eight or ten miles to attend school, so earnest are they in their hearts to attain knowledge. Wisdom is above all rubies, above all price. As I look into the faces of the members, I think I can see what the vote will be upon this question. I believe, when we come to declare our verdict, that the large majority will vote for the section as it stands. I trust there will be no half way provision adopted. I trust the cheek will not blanch, nor the lip tremble, when we come to stand upon this question. Let us not say that the General Assembly can, but that it shall, provide for the compulsory attendance at school of all the children within this Commonwealth.

Mr. W. E. JOHNSTON. I do not rise to make a speech. But it has been said by the member from Beaufort (Mr. WRIGHT) that we have just been born. I wish to deny that, and inform the member that we are three years old. Having made such tremendous strides in three years, I think it highly necessary that some method should be adopted by which these three year old children should, instead of running around

molasses barrels or stealing cotton, be compelled to go to school. I noticed with regret, on my way here this morning, some eighteen colored
children standing before the door of the Guard House of this city. If
those little boys and girls were at school they would not have been
arrested for stealing. But I think enough has already been said upon
this question, and I move an indefinite postponement of all the amendments.

Mr. C. P. LESLIE. If our friends from Massachusetts can be kept
quiet a little while, it will gratify me exceedingly to have a little talk
with them. When this Convention was first called, some of the delegates in the house, and many of the friends outside, if they met with
the slightest possible misfortune, if a man lost his watch, or his pocket
book, the first thing he did was to run into the menagerie, when some
delegate would immediately offer a resolution that some sort of relief
should be extended. After a good deal of nonsense, it was at last
thought not really proper to present that style of resolution. Time run
on, and the few delegates here in this body from somewhere have seemed
so to act, that they were picked out, and told by our enemies to do some
pretty thing or things, that would, beyond any question, tend to defeat
the adoption of the Constitution we are endeavoring to frame for this
State, they could not be doing better than they are now. Sometime ago
our friends looked anxiously forward to the various questions that should
arise. One important question was that of the judiciary. That, fortunately for all, has been settled in a way that gives satisfaction to every
reflecting right-minded man in the State. There were a number of
questions that directly affected the fate of the pending Constitution. One
important question was the homestead, and our friends again looked
forward to see what action the delegates would take in that direction.
I know the homestead provision put in our Constitution was one of the
very best strokes of policy we have yet made. Right upon the heel of
that, and at a time when everything is going on sensibly, so that it is
believed no power in the State can by any possibility defeat the adoption
of our Constitution, comes a proposition that must be odious to a large
class of people in the State. Now, I can live in South Carolina whether
the Constitution is adopted or not, and I can vote in this State. I can
have every right and privilege that any white voter has; but I say to
the colored members of this body if this Constitution is not adopted
they cannot do it. I do not suppose, in the present condition of affairs,
that we can make a Constitution that is in all respects just exactly what
we would have it. There are many good provisions that we may from
absolute necessity have to leave out. There are a great many provis-

ions that I myself would be glad to insert in that Constitution, but I will never be guilty of doing an act when my own good sense condemns that act. It is as important to the colored people of the State as to the white; it is important to me, and important to every man in the State, that a fair, liberal, just and generous government should be established. It is important to the rising generation, both white and colored. If you do not happen to get all you want; if you do not want to insert a provision which will endanger the result of the vote on the Constitution when it goes before the people, then for heaven's sake have sense enough to leave it out. Some people think they can come in here and can make just such a Constitution as they in their playful judgment may think proper. They think that a poor miserable South Carolinian can be taken up here and led just where they wish to take him. Another says he shall have nothing but gingerbread; and still another comes from Massachusetts, and insists that this miserable South Carolinian shall eat anything he chooses to cram him with, and brings in a long doctor's bill. Another from Massachusetts says he shall not have anything to drink, and so on until you have enough before you, which, if adopted, will bring our Constitution beyond any hopes of resurrection.

I appeal to the good sense of the delegates, to reflect that every time you undertake to force a people to do what you know they do not want to do, it can never be carried out. I am to-day a South Carolinian; I am going to live and die a loyal man; to be loyal to the government, but by the eternal heavens I will never be forced to do what in my own judgment no one has the right to force upon me. Who is going to execute this law if made? That is a direct question, and I want the delegates from Massachusetts to come up squarely and fairly and answer it. Our friend from Massachusetts undertakes to tell us the loyal men are going to do it. Who are they? Are they the black people in the State? You cannot force them any more than you can the whites. There is no use making a law unless you can enforce it; but if you undertake to go on with this wild business, I warn you of the consequences.

Mr. F. L. CARDOZO. The gentleman from Barnwell (Mr. LESLIE) has made an appeal to the fear of the colored delegates on this floor, by holding up before them the bugbear of the defeat of our Constitution. I would simply say, that I do not think there is a colored delegate but what knows that we have carried the Convention against the white people of this State, and will carry the Constitution also. I will qualify my language, by saying that we do not fear those whom the gentleman from Barnwell tells us to fear.

Mr. R. J. DONALDSON. Will the gentleman be kind enough to

inform the Convention how many native born South Carolinians are upon the Committee on Education ?

Mr. F. L. CARDOZO. There is but one Massachusetts man on the Committee.

Mr. C. P. LESLIE. Did any South Carolinian vote for that provision ? If so, I would like to know it ?

Mr. F. L. CARDOZO. I would say that one style of argument, of appealing to our fears, or cowardice, or our unmanliness, is scarcely worth noticing.

Mr. C. P. LESLIE. The gentleman has asserted or misstated what I said. I did not appeal to the cowardice of the colored delegates; I appealed simply to their good sense.

Mr. F. L. CARDOZO. I still maintain my position, that the style of argument to which I have alluded is low, mean, and unmanly. I desire, in the first place, to divest this question of the false issues which some cunning political demagogues on the floor have connected with it. They have said this section would compel colored and white children to go together in the schools.

Mr. J. J. WRIGHT. I rise to a point of order. I object to the words " political demagogues," used by the gentleman ln his argument.

Mr. C. P. LESLIE. He had reference to himself; what do you want to interrupt him for ?

Mr. F. L. CARDOZO. I referred to the gentleman from Barnwell.

Mr. C. P. LESLIE. I refer to him.

Mr. F. L. CARDOZO. I will state again, that it is the habit of some members of the Convention, when they want to defeat a measure, to connect false issues with it, and make it appear as odious as possible. I ask members to look at the strategy kept up by members of the opposition. They have said that we compel white and colored to go together in these schools, and by that means they attempt to defeat this section. Their assertion is ungentlemanly, and it is untrue.

The hour of six having arrived, the PRESIDENT announced the Convention adjourned.

FORTY-SECOND DAY.

Wednesday, March 4, 1868.

The Convention assembled at 10 A. M., and was called to order by the PRESIDENT.

Prayer was offered by the Rev. B. F. JACKSON.

The roll was called, and a quorum answering to their names, the PRESIDENT announced the Convention ready to proceed to business.

The Journal of yesterday was read and confirmed.

The Convention resumed the consideration of the fourth section of the report of the Committee on the Executive part of the Constitution, providing that it shall be the duty of the General Assembly to provide for the compulsory attendance, at either public or private schools, of all children between the ages of six and sixteen years, not physically or mentally disabled, for a term equivalent to at least twenty-four months.

The first question was striking out the word "compulsory."

Mr. F. L. CARDOZO. Before I resume my remarks this morning, I would ask the favor of the Convention, and especially the opposition, to give me their close attention, and I think I can settle this matter perfectly satisfactory to every one in the house.

It was argued by some yesterday, with some considerable weight, that we should do everything in our power to incorporate into the Constitution all possible measures that will conciliate those opposed to us.

No one would go farther in conciliating others than I would. But those whom we desire to conciliate consist of three different classes, and we should be careful, therefore, what we do to conciliate.

In the first place there is an element which is opposed to us, no matter what we do will never be conciliated. It is not that they are opposed so much to the Constitution we may frame, but they are opposed to us sitting in Convention. Their objection is of such a fundamental and radical nature, that any attempt to frame a Constitution to please them would be utterly abortive.

In the next place, there are those who are doubtful, and gentlemen here say if we frame a Constitution to suit these parties they will come over with us. They are only waiting, and I will say these parties do not particularly care what kind of a Constitution you frame, they only want to see whether it is going to be successful, and if it is, they will come any way.

Then there is a third class who honestly question our capacity to frame a Constitution. I respect that class, and believe if we do justice to them, laying our corner-stone on the sure foundation of republican government and liberal principles, the intelligence of that class will be conciliated, and they are worthy of conciliation.

Before I proceed to discuss the question, I want to divest it of all false issues, of the imaginary consequences that some gentlemen have illogically thought will result from the adoption of this section with the word compulsory. They affirm that it compels the attendance of both white and colored children in the same schools. There is nothing of the kind in the section. It means nothing of the kind, and no such construction can be legitimately placed upon it. It simply says all the children shall be educated ; but how is left with the parents to decide. It is left to the parent to say whether the child shall be sent to a public or private school. The eleventh section has been referred to as bearing upon this section. I will ask attention to this fact. The eleventh section does not say, nor does the report in any part say there shall not be separate schools. There can be separate schools for white and colored. It is simply left so that if any colored child wishes to go to a white school, it shall have the privilege to do so. I have no doubt, in most localities, colored people would prefer separate schools, particularly until some of the present prejudice against their race is removed.

We have not provided that there shall be separate schools; but I do not consider these issues as properly belonging to the question. I shall, therefore, confine myself to the more important matter connected with this subject.

My friend yesterday referred to Prussia and Massachusetts as examples that we should imitate, and I was much surprised to hear some of the members who have spoken, ridicule that argument. It was equivalent to saying we do not want the teachings of history, or the examples of any of those countries foremost in civilization.

It was said that the condition of affairs in Prussia and Massachusetts was entirely different. But they are highly civilized countries, with liberty-loving, industrious citizens, and the highest social order exists there. I want South Carolina to imitate those countries, which require the compulsory attendance of all children of certain ages for fixed periods, at some school. If you deem a certain end worthy of being attained, it must be accompanied by precisely the same means those countries have attained it.

Prussia, in her late victories over Austria, reaped the fruits of the superiority of her school system and the intelligence of her people, and in every conflict with the powers of darkness and error we should imitate just such a country as Prussia. To ignore the example of a country because far from us, would be to ignore all philosophy and history.

It was also remarked that there was no other State that compelled the attendance of their children at schools. Arkansas does it in her Constitution, and notwithstanding assertions to the contrary, I would say that Massachusetts does it in her statutes.

Another argument was that this matter had better be left to the Legislature. I have been charged with appealing to the prejudices and feelings of the colored delegates to this Convention. It is true to a certain extent. I do direct their attention to matters concerning their peculiar interests, but if it is meant to charge me with appealing to their passions as against the white people, I respectfully deny the charge, and stamp the assertion as gratuitous. But I do desire we shall use the opportunities we now have to our best advantage, as we may not ever have a more propitious time. We know when the old aristocracy and ruling power of this State get into power, as they undoubtedly will, because intelligence and wealth will win in the long run, they will never pass such a law as this. Why? Because their power is built on and sustained by ignorance. They will take precious good care that the colored people shall never be enlightened.

Again, it has been argued that it was anti-republican, and an infringement of individual rights to pass such a law. Men living in a savage, uncivilized state are perfectly free, and should be untrammeled. But the first thing, when a man goes into society, is to concede certain individual rights necessary for the protection and preservation of society. If you deny this great principle, there can be no law, for every law you propose is an infringement of my individual right. If you tax me for the education of the poor people of the State, I simply say that it shall not be exclusively for the rich to build up their power, but that it is for all the people, the poor as well as the rich.

I hope every gentleman will see that the argument against it is anti-republican and utterly groundless. Some may think that we go too far, and take away too many individual rights. I maintain that in this instance it is only for the benefit of the State, as well as for the benefit of society.

The question is, will you pay the poll tax to educate your children in schools, or support them in penitentiaries? No intelligent person will prefer to support them as criminals.

Some ask how it is to be enforced, and say it is impossible. I will simply say what has been done elsewhere can be done here. Our Legislature will at first, of course, make the penalties very light, will consider all the circumstances by which we are surrounded, and will not make the law onerous. Every law should be considered in a two-fold aspect

90

—in its moral effect and its penalties. The moral power of a law almost always compels obedience. Ninety-nine out of one hundred men who may be indifferent to their children, when they know there is a law compelling them to send their children to school, will make sacrifices in order not to violate that law.

I have had several years experience as a teacher, and I know exactly its effects. I can best satisfy the house by simply describing one out of the one hundred cases that have come under my own observation.

In my school I have the highest class of boys who were kept under my own special care and tuition. Among these boys was one highly gifted, universally loved, and talented. He was not only superior in regard to intellectual qualities, but also in regard to moral qualities. He was a noble boy, truly loveable and talented. I had watched the development of that boy's mind, and took the highest pleasure in assisting that development. I spent much time in assisting the development of that boy's mind, and watched his career with much interest and jealousy. At the commencement of our last session, he came to me with tears in his eyes, and bid me good bye. I asked him, "are you really going to leave school?" "Yes," he answered, "I must go; my parents are going to take me away." "Tell them," I said, "that I will consult with them." The mother, with tears, said she did not want the child to leave, but the father insisted upon it. I talked with him, but with no effect. He was a low, degraded, besotted drunkard. I endeavored by every argument in my power, by praising his boy as he deserved, and by offering to adopt him and take him North to one of the best institutions in the country, to effect my object in giving that boy a thorough education. What do you think was the reply? "No," he said, "I cannot spare him. In the morning he chops the wood, gets the water, and I want him to run on errands." Those errands, I learned, were running to the corner to buy beer and brandy for his father. If by a law of the State we could have taken that boy from his drunken father, and educated him, he would have been an ornament to us and an honor to the State. As I meet him in the street now, he slinks away from me to go, perhaps, to the corner to get liquor for his father. He told me from the time his father takes a glass in the morning till night he is never sober, and he wished his father was dead.

I am anxious to reconcile all differences on this question, and I move a reconsideration of the previous question, in order to offer an amendment, to the following effect:

Provided, That no law to that effect shall be passed until a system of public schools has been thoroughly and completely organized, and facilities afforded to all the inhabitants of the State for the free education of their children.

The motion to reconsider was agreed to, and the question being taken on the adoption of this amendment, it was agreed to, and the fourth section passed to its third reading.

Section fifth, providing for the levying of a poll tax, was taken up and read, as follows:

SECTION 5. The General Assembly shall levy, at each regular session after the adoption of this Constitution, an annual tax on all taxable property throughout the State for the support of public schools, which tax shall be collected at the same time and by the same agents as the general State levy, and shall be paid into the Treasury of the State. There shall be assessed on all taxable polls in the State an annual tax of one dollar on each poll, the proceeds of which tax shall be applied solely to educational purposes. No other poll or capitation tax shall be levied in the State, nor shall the amount assessed on each poll exceed the limit given in this section. The school tax shall be distributed among the several School Districts of the State, in proportion to their respective population, between the age of five and twenty-one years. No religious sect or sects shall have exclusive right to, or control of, any part of the school funds of the State, nor shall sectarian principles be taught in the public schools.

Mr. A. J. RANSIER. I move to amend by striking out all after the word "purposes" down to and including the word "section." My reasons for that amendment are that there is a provision in the report of the Committee on Finance and Taxation, which regulates this question.

Mr. B. O. DUNCAN. I have an amendment to propose for a portion of that section, which makes a material change, and which I think is much to be preferred. It will come in from the beginning and goes down to the word section. It is as follows: "The General Assembly may appropriate for public school purposes as much as, but not exceeding, one-fourth of the entire revenue of the State, and may at its discretion levy a poll tax of not exceeding one dollar on every able-bodied voter between the ages of twenty-one and fifty years old solely for public school purposes. No other poll or capitation tax shall be levied by the State." It will be seen that this makes a material difference. Instead of levying a tax simply for public school purposes it allows a general tax by which more can be procured without taking it directly out of the pockets of the tax payers.

Mr. B. F. WHITTEMORE offered the following amendment to Mr. DUNCAN'S amendment: Strike out the word "may" and insert the word "shall," and strike out "at its discretion."

Mr. J. S. CRAIG asked and obtained leave to have his name recorded as voting against section fourth.

The CHAIR stated the first question to be on the amendment of the gentleman from Charleston (Mr. RANSIER).

Mr. J. L. NEAGLE. I would state that that portion of the section, when under consideration of the Committee, was inserted there with the intention to meet cases not met in any other portion of the Constitution. As it is in another portion, however, the Committee on Consolidation and Review can strike out whatever belongs to, or is met in, another portion.

The CHAIR stated that the Committee on Consolidation and Review have no other power than that of arrangement, and could not strike out anything adopted by the house. They could only arrange the Articles in their order.

Mr. N. G. PARKER. I wish to offer an amendment, to strike out from the period in the fourth line to and including the word "State," and to insert in lieu thereof the words "they may also assess." I would state that the Committee on Finance omitted the word "shall" after mature deliberation; and after hearing the views of gentlemen from all sections of the State with reference to taxation upon the polls, in the peculiarly unfortunate condition which now exists, the general impression is not that there shall not be a poll tax, but that it be left with the Legislature, when it assembles, to make such a provision as in its judgment it may see fit. Should it be too severe the first year, it may be imposed the second year. I insist upon it that the property of the State ought to pay the taxes of the State, and not that class of people who do not own one acre of ground.

Mr. H. E. HAYNE. Is it possible that there is a man in South Carolina so poor that he cannot pay one dollar for the education of his children?

Mr. N. G. PARKER. I answer the question, yes. Hence, while I do not object to the assessment of a poll tax by the next Legislature, I do say unhesitatingly that it would be an imposition to require the payment of a poll tax, even though it is to enure to the benefit of the colored people in the education of their children. They have no property. I say let property pay the taxes and start the machine; then, if the people are able to pay the tax, put it on. I don't believe in tying them down now.

Mr. J. L. NEAGLE. I am opposed to the gentleman's amendment, "may." If we leave this matter to the Legislature, we may destroy one of the great resources of the State for carrying out the plan of education which is proposed. The Committee on Education framed their report with the expectation and desire of establishing a system of free schools at as early a day as possible, and the only chance we saw for raising a revenue was by means of a capitation tax, which ought to give us at least $150,000 to start on. The gentleman speaks of the State being in an impoverished condition. I acknowledge it; but if she is so poor that the people cannot pay a capitation tax of one dollar, the property holders of the State will certainly be unable to pay the vast amount of taxation that will be required of them, and what is to become of us? The schools cannot possibly be established. The property holders are few in number, and their property is not remunerative. They are likely to remain poor, especially if burdened by an excessive taxation imposed for the support of the public schools. I hope, therefore, the capitation tax will be enforced, and this section be passed as it stands.

Mr. W. J. McKINLAY. It seems to me that it is important to this section that the amendment offered by the gentleman from Barnwell should prevail.

It says here, "there shall be assessed on all taxable polls an annual tax on each poll," but it does not take into consideration the grants or gifts that may be made for educational purposes, which would greatly relieve the people from taxation for these purposes. It is made obligatory to assess the tax, although an amount may be raised more than sufficient for the educational plan.

Mr. F. L. CARDOZO. The gentleman's fear that too much money will be raised, will never be realized. Again, the gentleman from Barnwell need have no fear that the colored people are not able to pay this tax. For his benefit, and that of other gentlemen here from Massachusetts, I will state that there are many children of slave parents before the war, who paid two dollars a month. They now pay in my school from three to five dollars a year. We need not, therefore, be alarmed about their ability to pay.

Mr. R. B. ELLIOTT. What is the penalty to be attached to non-payment?

Mr. F. L. CARDOZO. We did not provide for that, because we knew it would never occur.

Mr. F. J. MOSES, Jr. I would like to ask the gentleman how it is proposed to enforce the collection of the poll tax.

Mr. F. L. CARDOZO. There will be no need of compulsion. Everybody will be glad to pay.

Mr. R. B. ELLIOTT. It is not often that I rise to take part in debate, but if there is any thing in the Constitution of vital importance to the people, and in which I am deeply interested, it is that which provides for the education of the people. While favoring every measure that will contribute to this end, I cannot support this section in its present shape. Had it been stated more definitely, the case might have been different. While we may secure the education of our children by adopting the clause as it stands, we run the risk of depriving many of the parents of the right of suffrage. Wherever a poll tax has been levied in any State of the Union, the penalty attached to its non-payment is always the deprivation of the right to vote.

Mr. H. E. HAYNE. Does not the State provide means for the collection of taxes due? Is not the Sheriff empowered to issue writs against persons for the non-payment of their taxes?

Mr. R. B. ELLIOTT. If that should be done. South Carolina would be the first State in the Union in which an execution upon property has been levied for the non-payment of a poll tax. The penalty has been a deprivation of the right to vote. If an educational tax is to be levied, it should be distinctly laid down that the non-payment of that tax should not deprive the parent of this privilege.

Mr. F. L. CARDOZO. Do we say in this report that it shall prevent the right to vote?

Mr. R. B. ELLIOTT. That is what I am driving at. You have not made it here.

Mr. F. L. CARDOZO. As we expect the services of the eloquent gentleman from Edgefield in the Legislature, we hope he will make this matter all right there.

Mr. R. B. ELLIOTT. Whether on this floor or in the Legislature, I contend that this subject should be regulated so that no doubt can attach to it. If left to the General Assembly, that body may in the future pass the same law which exists in other States, and there may be men in it too glad to deprive the poor of the freeman's right, because of his inability to pay this capitation tax. If this section be amended so that no man shall ever be deprived of his right to vote, I will sustain it heart and soul. Like the gentleman from Charleston (Mr. CARDOZO), I believe the citizens of the State will be willing to pay this poll tax, although I doubt the ability of a great proportion to do so. I know many in the upper portion of the State who are unable to pay twenty-five cents. They do not own one foot of land. They have labored, it is true, but have been robbed of the fruit of their industry.

Mr. F. L. CARDOZO. There is no need of the gentleman making such a splendid speech. I will accept his amendment with pleasure.

Mr. R. B. ELLIOTT. Then I move as an amendment the following:

"*Provided*, That no person shall ever be deprived of the right of suffrage for the non-payment of said tax."

Mr. J. DONALDSON called for the previous question, but the call was not sustained.

Mr. H. E. HAYNE. I hope the amendment of the gentleman from Edgefield will not prevail. There is no man in this State so poor as to be unable to pay one dollar for the education of his children; I therefore move its indefinite postponement.

Mr. L. S. LANGLEY. I would like t ask what penalty is proposed to be inflicted?

Mr. F. L. CARDOZO. The gentleman from Edgefield merely proposes to deprive the Legislature of the power of taking away the right to vote; but there are a thousand other penalties which may be inflicted, as for instance working upon the public roads. We do not know what may be the complexion of the Legislature, and as a safeguard against the action of a certain element, we propose to incorporate this prohibiting clause.

Mr. B. F. RANDOLPH. I regret that the amendment has been offered, for I am opposed to it. In all of the States great difficulty exists in the collection of poll tax, and as a penalty the right of suffrage is suspended. Now it may be difficult to get men to work on the public roads, and to my mind a man would much rather pay his poll tax than do so. There certainly is a necessity of some law which will force men to the payment of this tax. We cannot compel men to work upon the public roads. There is no way of reaching them.

Mr. J. S. CRAIG. What class of men cannot be compelled to work upon the roads?

Mr. B. F. RANDOLPH. If the gentleman will go to the Mills House, or the Charleston Hotel, he will find scores of this description. I appeal to the gentleman from Edgefield, why is it that other States, after long experience, have been compelled to enact these laws? It is because they have been taught that the most efficacious mode of collecting the poll tax has been to deprive the voter of his right of suffrage as a penalty for non-payment. That argument the gentleman from Edgefield cannot refute. In this State there are thousands of persons who own no property who will take advantage of the Sheriff, and whom there is no possible means of reaching but to squeeze the tax out of them. A man does not like to have it said he cant vote, because he has not paid his dollar. This law has been found to induce people to pay this tax when nothing else would.

Mr. R. B. ELLIOTT. I move that the motion to indefinitely postpone be laid on the table.

Pending this motion, the hour arrived for the consideration of the Special Order, being the report from the Committee on Petitions, relating to a petition for donating lands by the United States on sales for non-payment of direct taxes, as may remain at the disposal of the government.

Mr. F. L. CARDOZO moved a postponement of the Special Order until five o'clock this afternoon.

The PRESIDENT presented the petition of A. G. Baskin, of Columbia, praying the Convention to recommend the removal of his political disabilities.

The petition was referred to the Committee on Petitions.

Mr. C. P. LESLIE asked leave to offer the following in connection with the petition offered by Mr. F. L. CARDOZO, and obtained permission of the house to read it. It reads as follows:

Your petitioners further represent, that in their opinion said law was enacted for the purpose of collecting taxes to enable the Government to sustain itself, etc., and not in any manner to confiscate land or operate as an Act of confiscation. And, whereas, by the terms of said Act the space of — years was allotted to the owner to reclaim said land, after the same had been seized and sold, on paying to the United States said taxes, costs and expenses; and, whereas, by the operations of war, it is well known that many Union people were driven from their homes, and compelled by the Confederate forces to come within the Confederate lines, and were afterwards wholly unable to return to reclaim their lands and homes, within the time allowed by the law itself; and, whereas, it is the opinion of your petitioners, that from the peculiar circumstances under which the owners of the land were placed by the operations of the war, that the provision allowing — years to reclaim said land was wholly inoperative, and did not afford the privilege to reclaim designed by the framers of said law.

And your petitioners further represent, that it is their opinion that the time to reclaim said land should be extended for the space of six months, to every person or party in interest who can show, or prove to the satisfaction of the authorities in charge, that they were unable by the operations of the war to reclaim the land within the time allotted by law, and on paying said taxes, proper costs and charges. In case any land shall remain unclaimed after the space of six months, may be sold at a reasonable price and on reasonable time, and in such quantities as will suit purchasers.

And your petioners will ever pray, etc.

THOMAS JONES.
ROBERT NOAKES.

Mr. C. P. LESLIE. I desire to say that this matter is of such extreme importance as to require, in my judgment, immediate action. I desire also to say that I have received no instructions from any proper authorities in the matter, but I have presented this petition as I have a right to do, and because I think it a sensible thing to do. This petition is signed by various parties interested in the subject matter, but I will not detain the Convention by reading their names.

Mr. F. L. CARDOZO. I move the petition be referred to the Committee on Petitions, to report Saturday morning.

Mr. L. S. LANGLEY moved that the petition be laid on the table, which was agreed to.

Mr. J. J. WRIGHT submitted the following resolution, which was adopted:

Resolved, That it be referred to a Special Committee of five to report an ordinance appropriating the Citadel, and the grounds connected therewith, in the City of Charleston, to educational purposes. Said buildings and grounds to be devoted to the establishment of a College, which, in connection with primary and grammar schools, shall be managed by a Board of Trustees, and their successors, who shall be chosen by the General Assembly, and shall be subject to visitation by the Superintendent of the Board of Public Instruction of this State.

The PRESIDENT, in accordance with the above resolution, announced the following as the Special Committee:

Messrs. J. J. WRIGHT, of Beaufort; J. M. Rutland, of Fairfield; J. L. Neagle, of York; F. L. Cardozo, of Charleston; D. H. Chamberlain, of Berkley.

Mr. F. L. CARDOZO called up the unfinished business, which was the consideration of the fifth section of the report of the Committee on Education.

Mr. D. H. CHAMBERLAIN. I move in the eighth line to strike out the words "respective population between the ages of five and twenty-one years," and insert the words "the number of scholars attending the public schools."

Mr. F. L. CARDOZO. As Chairman of the Committee, I accept that amendment.

Mr. B. BYAS. I have most always been in favor of the passage of the reports as they come from the Committee. These reports have been deliberately considered in the Committee room, and, therefore, come to us with that great argument in favor of every section in them. Occasionally, however, something important may have escaped the notice of the Committee and be detected by this body. In this section I am in favor of striking out the word "shall," and substituting the word "may." If the word shall is left there, it gives the Legislature too much power over those who do not pay their poll tax. Now it may be that in some

91

of the up country districts, according to my friend from Marion (Mr. H. E. HAYNE), that the people can afford to pay ten dollars tax, but in my district, as has been said of another district, by the gentleman from Edgefield, many have not got twenty-five cents, let alone paying a school tax of one dollar. I know if they had it, they would certainly cheerfully pay the money. Should there, however, be a failure of the crops, which is not at all impossible, then my constituents would be in a deplorable condition. It would scarcely be right then to deprive them of the right to vote because they are unable to pay their poll tax. You might thus keep three-fourths of the legitimate voters of the State away from the polls. I hope, therefore, the amendments will be adopted.

Mr. R. J. DONALDSON. I regret that we are wasting so much time over this matter. The gentleman from Edgefield has referred to the poverty of his district. I say unqualifiedly that there is not a man in my district but who is able to pay ten dollars, if necessary, for educational purposes.

Mr. R. B. ELLIOTT. Have you got a poor house in your district?

Mr. R. J. DONALDSON. No, sir; we do not need one; men not able to pay one dollar a year for educational purposes should not be entitled to vote, and they are no honor, nor of any use in any community. I do not believe we could get fifty cents by adopting the suggestion of compelling men to work out the poll tax on the public roads. I am in favor of the Legislature insisting upon a poll tax.

Mr. B. F. RANDOLPH. As a general rule, are the freedmen in the up country better off than those on the sea coast?

Mr. R. J. DONALDSON. In the upper districts they are more driving, more moral and religious, better workmen, and when they get a few dollars they do not go to a miserable rum shop and spend it all. But, in fact, the property holders will be the parties who will be the chief support of the educational interests of our State. If the Educational Committee had recommended five dollars, I would not have considered it too much; and when they put it down to one dollar, they fixed it at its lowest limit.

Mr. W. E. JOHNSTON. If you were in a position to know the miserable condition of some portions of the people of South Carolina, you would take back that word. On the 5th of January, when the State taxes became due they were not able to pay one cent.

Mr. R. J. DONALDSON. I have had the pleasure of looking over the returns of the Sheriff for Chesterfield District, and find, as a general thing, that the colored people paid more taxes in proportion than the property holders. I was shown receipts of freedmen who paid over eight and ten dollars, whereas white men owning hundreds of acres only paid eight dollars. I think it is a mistaken idea about freedmen being unable to pay their taxes. They have time, muscle, strength and intelligence. So far from being in a deplorable state, they are the only independent people in our State.

Mr. R. B. ELLIOTT. I assert, that it is not only the freedmen who are too poor to pay their taxes but many of the gentleman's own race.

Mr. R. J. DONALDSON. I admit that ; but I say men who are not able to pay one dollar for educational purposes, are of no manner of use to any community. Men who are not able to bear the burdens of society are not entitled to the privileges of that society.

Mr. B. BYAS. Do you think if you had told your constituents that, you would have been in this Convention ?

Mr. R. J. DONALDSON. I told my constituents I would vote for the education of all the people and equality before the law. I went further, and told them that any man who was uneducated could be a good republican. I am opposed to the amendment offered by the gentleman from Edgefield, but heartily in favor of the section as reported by the Committee on Education.

Mr. A. J. RANSIER. I have but one word to say. I propose to strike out after the word " purposes, " in the fifth line in this section, and ending with the word "section" in the seventh line. I offered that because the second section of the report of the Committee on Finance and Taxation already adopted, provided that the Legislature may provide for annual levy of a tax, not exceeding one dollar on each poll, to be applied to school purposes and a public school fund. That I thought embodied the idea of the Committee on Education, as proposed in this section. I am in favor of the amendment of the gentleman from Edgefield. I believe that the people of the State should bear equally as far as possible the burthen of expenses of the State. And I see no better way by which the masses can share in bearing those expenses than by levying a poll tax. I claim this is no class measure. The friends of this measure advocate it upon the broad ground of the greatest good to the greatest number. Believing that the majority of the people of the State will share in the advantages to be derived from this measure, it is but reasonable that they should share equally in the expense. But I am not disposed to allow the people of this State to deprive any individual who may find it impossible to pay his poll tax of the right to vote. I believe there are various modes by which some penalty may be inflicted and the poll tax collected. It is not to be denied that there is a disposition among a certain class to take away the franchise of a majority of the people of this State. I have no desire to gratify that class. I hope, therefore, the amendment of the gentleman from Edgefield will prevail, and that we will leave it to the Legislature to determine the manner in which the poll tax shall be collected.

Mr. R. J. DONALDSON. Suppose those men who do not pay are put to work upon the public roads, how much money think you will go into the school fund ?

Mr. C. P. LESLIE. The delinquents can be sent catching opossums, the skins of which can be sold to pay the poll tax.

Mr. R. B. ELLIOTT. I would like to ask whether any money will go into the school fund by disfranchising voters ?

Mr. R. J. DONALDSON. If that punishment is imposed, not a single individual would be disfranchised, for every man would pay his poll tax.

Mr. A. J. RANSIER. I think those members who desire to defeat this measure, if they truly represent the people of this State, will leave it to the Legislature to determine the ways and means by which the people will be compelled to pay their obligations to the State.

Mr. J. S. CRAIG. Does not the amendment propose to cut off from the Legislature the only means by which they may compel the collection of the debt.

Mr. A. J. RANSIER. The amendment simply proposes to deprive the Legislature or any power in the State, of the right to take away from any delinquent tax payer the privilege of voting.

Mr. B. F. WHITTEMORE. I only desire to say a very few words upon this subject. The Educational Committee have provided in this section the means by which schools shall be sustained, namely : by levying a poll tax for the erection of school houses and for the payment of teachers. According to the declaration of the Chairman of the Committee, it is supposed this measure would reach one hundred and fifty thousand dollars for the support of schools in the State ; that is to say, there are one hundred and fifty thousand persons from whom a poll tax of one dollar a head can be collected. This proviso, which is offered in the nature of an amendment, declaring that no person shall be deprived of the right of suffrage for the non-payment of their poll tax, affords an opportunity for those who have no property upon which the Sheriff can levy, to say that they are unable to pay their taxes. Suppose one-third takes the advantage of that proviso. It would cut down the sum to one hundred thousand dollars. We have then no definite school fund established, and yet we say in the same report that children shall be compelled to go to school. I would like to know how the educational system of the State is to be established if we accept a proviso like this. It appears to me that we would have but a poor opinion of the energies of the people of South Carolina, if we could not believe that they would put forth an extra effort to raise an extra dollar to become electors. One dollar will pay two cents per week for having the advantage of a thorough educational system established in the State. A man may be sending even twelve children to school for the sum of one dollar per year, and enjoying himself the right of franchise. Even a child can go out upon the highway and pick up sufficient substance, sell it in a very few hours and make up the school fund for a family. We should not keep back the principal resources from which we are to gain an amount sufficient to regulate and establish our schools. It appears to me, if men would use less tobacco and drink less whiskey, they would always have money enough to pay their poll tax. It is asking but very little of the people of the State to pay one dollar for the poll tax to sustain a system of public schools.

Mr. L. S. LANGLEY. The amendment of the gentleman from Edgefield proposes to take away from the Legislature a part of its power. It proposes to prevent it from imposing a penalty for the non-fulfillment of an organic law of the State. I have, on several previous occasions, expressed my opposition to tying up the hands of the Legislature, or binding them down to cases that may arise in the future. What will be the advantage of our incorporating this section into the Constitution of the State— a section providing for a poll tax—if we take from the Legislature the power of prescribing the penalty. How are the laws to be executed if the Legislature have not the power of affixing the penalty for non-compliance with the laws ? There is nothing of more importance than that the Legislature should have the power to enforce the collection of taxes. How many men do you suppose there are in this State who are now disfranchised, who would refuse to put their hands into their pockets, though poor men, and pay one dollar or one hundred dollars if they thought by so doing they would have the right of franchise restored to them. I claim for the freedman that he has some feeling of pride left, notwithstanding the iron heel of oppression has degraded him. I believe when you say a man need not pay any taxes into the treasury of the State, you make him feel degraded. Take away from the Legislature the power of imposing a penalty, whereby every freedman in the State will be compelled to pay taxes, and you will take from that body the power of saying there should be any poll tax at all collected. Who are they that would refuse to pay one dollar per year for the education of their children ? They are the men, be they black or white, who will sell their votes for less than one dollar to the republicans or to the democrats, or to any set of men who will pay the most for them. I think the freedmen, with the poor whites of the State, are willing to make almost any sacrifice whereby the education of their children will be secured. There has, however, been sufficient debate on this subject, and I therefore move the previous question.

Mr. B. F. RANDOLPH called for the ayes and nays, which were ordered.

Mr. R. SMALLS moved that the call for ayes and nays be indefinitely postponed, which was agreed to.

Mr. L. S. LANGLEY now called for ayes and nays, which was pronounced out of order by the Chair, on the ground that the House had ordered it to be dispensed with.

Mr. L. S. LANGLEY appealed from the decision of the Chair.

The House unanimously sustained the decision of the Chair.

The question was then taken on the amendment of Mr. R. B. ELLIOTT, and decided in the affirmative.

The hour of one o'clock having arrived, the Convention adjourned to three P. M.

AFTERNOON SESSION.

The Convention re-assembled at 3 P. M., and was called to order by the PRESIDENT.

The unfinished business being the continuation of the consideration of the fifth section, it was taken up.

The question was taken on the amendment of Mr. D. H. CHAMBERLAIN, to strike out in the third line, the words " their respective population between the ages of five and twenty-one years, and to insert in lieu thereof the words " the number of pupils attending the public schools," and decided in the affirmative.

The next question was on the amendment offered by Mr. A. J. RANSIER, and was decided in the negative.

The various amendments offered by Messrs. N. G. PARKER, B. F. WHITTEMORE and B. O. DUNCAN, were taken up and decided in the negative.

The main question was then put on the passage of the section as amended, to a third reading, and decided in the affirmative.

The section then passed to a third reading.

Mr. R. B. ELLIOTT moved a reconsideration of the vote whereby the section, as amended, was passed to its third reading, also moved to lay the motion to reconsider on the table.

The motion to reconsider was agreed to, but the motion to lay on the table was lost.

Mr. R. B. ELLIOTT moved to indefinitely postpone the motion to reconsider.

Mr. J. J. WRIGHT. I hope that motion will not prevail. It was not my intention to speak to-day, in consequence of the feebleness of my health and my voice. But when an important measure springs up which involves the future welfare of the State, I feel it to be an indispensable duty to exert whatever power I have for an expression of my views in relation to the subject matter before us.

This question involves the future interests of the people of South Carolina. It is for your interest, for my interest and for the interest of posterity, that this matter should receive due consideration. It should be presented fairly and discussed fully by this body, so that we may all vote in such a manner as will secure the rights and privileges of everybody. I hope we will have a reconsideration, so that all who desire it can be heard. Let us forget, for this time, the appeals made that we are wasting time and spending money. This question involves vital interests. Let us fight it out in such a way that we will know we have done our duty to the people of the State and the community in which we live.

Mr. B. F. RANDODPH. I believe, with all my heart, that there is an amendment now attached to the fifth section of the school report, which is no more or less than a death stroke to the schools of South Carolina. We are dependent more upon the poll tax than upon any other tax. I ask that this question be allowed to come before the house again, that we may give it further consideration. I hope the house will vote against postponement.

Mr. F. L. CARDOZO. I do not particularly desire the indefinite postponement of the motion to reconsider. I agree to a certain extent with the gentleman from Orangeburg (Mr. B. F. RANDOLPH) that these questions should be left to reconsideration, so that the subject may again be taken up, if at any future time we should have any further light. But I do hope that the motion to reconsider now, after several hours discussion, after all the light has been thrown upon the matter, will not prevail. It would be useless and a simple rehash of the arguments we had this morning. If between this and the next week anything new and important on this subject can be given then let us reconsider.

Mr. R. B. ELLIOTT.   I rise to withdraw the motion for an indefinite postponement, and move that the motion to reconsider be postponed for six days.

Mr. J. K. JILLSON.   I am strongly opposed to any motion for a postponement of the reconsideration of this question.   I believe the action on this question, if made final, will be to our detriment.   I hope, therefore, the members will vote against postponement, and let the issue be frankly and squarely made.

Mr. L. S. LANGLEY.   When I see what I consider a desire to take undue advantage of members of the Convention by moving the postponement of a very important motion, I cannot refrain from raising my voice against it.   Why did the gentleman from Edgefield move to postpone the motion to reconsider?   Is he afraid that justice will be the loser?   Is he afraid that something which took place in the hasty action of the Convention this morning will be brought to light, and that it will be found that some of the members of the Convention did not understand the question at the time of voting.   Truth never loses anything by continual consideration, and must in the end prevail.   I hope the motion to postpone will be voted down, and if any new light can be thrown upon the subject, we will receive it.

The question was then taken on the motion to postpone the motion to reconsider, and decided in the negative.

Section five was again taken up for reconsideration.

Mr. J. J. WRIGHT.   I have but a few words to say in relation to this matter.   The perpetuation of all good governments depends upon the intelligence of the people.

The hour for a Special Order in relation to the appointment of a Board of Land Commissioners having arrived, on motion of Mr. E. W. M. MACKEY, the Special Order was postponed until 12 o'clock, Saturday.

On motion of Mr. R. C. DeLARGE, the unfinished business was postponed to enable the Committee on Franchise and Elections to make their report.

The report was then read a first time, and ordered to be printed.

It reads as follows:

The Committee on Franchise and Elections have had the subject under consideration, and beg leave to submit the following report:

RIGHT OF SUFFRAGE.

SECTION 1.   In all elections by the people the electors shall vote by ballot.

SEC. 2.   Every male citizen of the United States of the age of twenty-one years and upwards, not laboring under the disabilities named in this

Constitution, without distinction of race, color, or former condition, who shall be a resident of this State at the time of the adoption of this Constitution, or who shall thereafter reside in this State one year, and in the county sixty days next preceding any election, and every male inhabitant of foreign birth of the age aforesaid, who shall have resided in this State one year, and in the county sixty days immediately preceding such elections, and shall have declared his intentions to become a citizen of the United States conformable to the laws of the United States on the subject of naturalization, shall be entitled to vote for all officers that are now, or hereafter may be elected by the people, and upon all questions submitted to the electors at any election: *Provided,* That every person coming of age after the year A. D. 1875, to vote, be able to read and write; but this qualification shall not apply to any person prevented by physical disability from complying therewith. *Provided, further,* That no person shall be allowed to vote or hold office who is now, or hereafter may be, disqualified therefor by the Constitution of the United States, provided that the General Assembly shall have the power to remove said disability by a two-thirds vote. *Provided, further,* That no person while kept in any almshouse or asylum, or of unsound mind, or confined in any public prison, shall be allowed to vote or hold office.

SEC. 3. It shall be the duty of the General Assembly to provide from time to time for the registration of all electors.

SEC. 4. For the purpose of voting no person shall be deemed to have lost his residence by reason of absence while employed in the service of the United States, nor while engaged upon the waters of this State or the United States, or of the high seas, nor while temporarily absent from the State.

SEC. 5. No soldier, seaman or marine in the army or navy of the United States shall be deemed a resident of this State in consequence of having been stationed therein.

SEC. 6. Electors shall, in all cases, except treason, felony or breach of the peace, be privileged from arrest and civil process during their attendance at elections, and in going to and returning from the same.

SEC. 7. Every person entitled to vote at any election shall be eligible to any office which now is, or hereafter shall be, elective by the people in the county where he shall have resided sixty days previous to such election, except as otherwise provided in this Constitution, or the Constitution and laws of the United States.

SEC. 8. No person convicted of treason, murder, robbery, or dueling, shall exercise the right to vote at any election until he be expressly restored thereto by the act of the Legislature.

SEC. 9. Presidential Electors shall be elected by the people.

SEC. 10. In all elections held by the people under this Constitution, the person or persons who shall receive the highest number of votes shall be declared elected.

R. C. DeLARGE.

On motion of Mr. R. C. DeLARGE, the report was made the Special Order for eleven o'clock Friday.

92

Mr. C. P. LESLIE gave notice that he would offer a minority report to-morrow.

Mr. J. L. NEAGLE offered the following, which was agreed to :

Resolved, That a Committee of seven be appointed to report an ordinance upon deeds and conveyances made between the 19th of December, 1860, and the 15th of May, 1865.

Mr. C. C. BOWEN moved that leave be granted the Judiciary Committee to meet during the hours the house is in session, for the purpose of investigating the case of B. Hagens, referred to them. Granted.

The Convention then resumed the consideration of the fifth section of the report of the Committee on Education.

Mr. J. J. WRIGHT. I was about to say, when interrupted, that it was important to consider this resolution in all its bearings. We are not to legislate for a day or a week, but to lay a foundation that will be for the general welfare of the people in all future time ; and, as I was about to say before, the foundation of all good government is education. Where there is no education, vice thrives, and the people sink deeper and deeper in misery. We desire to establish a school system, and to maintain a school system by a tax upon real and personal property, and a capitation tax of one dollar upon persons who have no real or personal property. We are all aware that there is a large number of persons in every State who own no real or personal property. These persons, however, have children to be educated, and we claim that they should pay a tax for the support of the schools. There are a multitude of young men who have no property, and they should be made to pay a tax to contribute to the general good. Wherever persons are protected by a government, or by the laws of that government, they should contribute their portion to the maintenance of that government which in its laws deals to them at all times, and under all circumstances, justice and mercy. Every male person who has attained the age of twenty-one years and upwards, I claim is capable of paying at least one dollar for the support of schools. Let him smoke less segars, or chew less tobacco. If a person is interested in the people ; if he desires to see millions scattered upon the plantations throughout the various States of the Union ; if he desires to see millions rise up from the dark and turbid streams of dust in which they are now grovelling, let him contribute his share to the education of the people of the State. It is urged that there are many persons who cannot pay a capitation tax of one dollar. Provision can be made for those persons. We are here to make new laws, to make the supreme law of the State. By all the energies and vitality within us we intend that this Constitution shall be ratified by the people of the State. In this Constitution we have made it a matter of impossibility for the Courts of this State to imprison a man for debt. We have considered imprisonment for debt to be a relic of barbarism. We decided to deprive the Legislature of the power to imprison a man for debt. We decided that the poor debtor should have the free use of his limbs in order to support his family, and that he should not be shut up in a dungeon. There is no way by which the Legislature can compel a man to pay his capitation tax, and no way to make him work upon the streets or public roads, unless he has been convicted as a criminal. What way shall we devise then for the payment of the poll tax? We must instill into the minds and hearts of the people the sacredness of the ballot-box. The people must be taught that the votes they hold in their hands are their only great defence of the rights and privileges which God has granted to man. I lay this down as a proposition, that a person who has not sufficiently at heart the interest of the State as to voluntarily pay one dollar for the education of the masses of the people who have been kept in ignorance, is not fit to vote. If the people are aroused to a sense of the importance of the ballot, then you will see every man coming up and paying his dollar into the treasury. They will pay it if compelled to labor day and night to procure it. But there is a class of men in the State who, unless compelled to do so, will never pay their capitation tax. I believe that if we say no person shall be deprived of the right to vote, these persons will always shirk from the poll tax. We are dependant upon persons who have accumulated a little property, for the support of schools, and shall those persons who have the same advantages and protection of the law, be exempt altogether from contributing to the support of that law, or that government which gives them those advantages? If that class of persons who are not property holders will not go to work and pay one dollar a year into the State Treasury, for the purpose of educating the children of the State, then they should not have the right to vote. But there is a class of persons whom we all know expect to have their disabilities removed, who expect to vote, and who will pay every dollar of school tax before they will lose their vote. They consider that vote their greatest weapon.

At the election for the ratification of the Constitution, this matter will not be presented. Every male person of age can vote upon that instrument. I have the utmost confidence in my people. I have been among them sufficiently to know that there is no person among them but who, if he has been taught the sacredness of the use of the ballot, if he has been taught the duty he owes to himself and his country, will have a dollar when the time comes to pay into the Treasury of the State.

The great cry throughout the State has been, send us teachers, send us men, send us women, who will teach us how to read and write, and we will pay them for it. The people are hungry and thirsty after knowledge. They seem to be inspired with spirit from on high that tells them knowledge is the only source by which they can rise from the low and degraded state in which they have been kept. Put the proviso in the Constitution that no person shall ever be deprived of the privilege to vote for non-payment of poll tax, and I believe we divest ourselves of a great power to perpetuate the Government of South Carolina.

Mr. C. C. BOWEN. It was not my intention to say a word upon this question. I was in hopes that it had passed, and was settled. I know not whether the last speaker's occupation is that of a schoolmaster or not. Judging from his remarks, I should suppose he was fearful that Othello's occupation would be gone. While I am in favor of a poll tax, I am unwilling that the non-payment of it should be made a penalty, and that that penalty should be the taking away of a vote. If experience proves anything, if speeches prove anything, an effort will be made in the next Legislature to take away this right, and the very moment you do it, you lose the next election. You could not get your Constitution, if you make that test. Other people of the opposite party are prepared to pay the poll tax of those who cannot do it, because they have not got the money. The opposition now sprung up proves there will be an attempt to force this thing now. I say put your foot upon it. Just the moment you cut off the right to vote of these poor men you allow the power to go into the hands of the opposite party.

Mr. L. S. LANGLEY. Are there any members in this Convention who propose to take away the ballot from any one?

Mr. C. C. BOWEN. If the Legislature should say, unless you pay a dollar you cannot vote, it is just the same as depriving those who have no dollar of the right to vote.

Mr. B. F. RANDOLPH. Provided the Legislature passed such a law, how many years will it be before that law could go into effect?

Mr. C. C. BOWEN. If the Legislature pass such a law, it will go into operation immediately, and it would apply to all elections held after that. I am in favor of passing the section as amended by the gentleman from Edgefield (Mr. ELLIOTT.) If that amendment is struck out, you strike out the votes of hundreds of people. I hope the section will pass as amended.

Mr. B. F. WHITTEMORE. I desire to say only a few words relative to this matter. The Committee on Education have made it imperative that the Legislature shall, as soon as practicable, draft a liberal, uniform system of public schools. They have, also, in the fourth section, provided for the compulsory attendance of all children at school. There is probably no man upon this floor who knows better than the Chairman of the Committee on Education, how much has been done by the sympathisers all over the country towards assisting the people of this State and other States of the South, in the establishment of schools for the cultivation of the mind. They have continued to listen to the appeals made to them, expecting that whenever the people come together in their sovereign capacity, they would provide for these institutions themselves. And they said, after we had provided for the instruction of the people and the erection of school houses, they would be compelled to take away their charity from us. We are here to-day, and we should in our legislation, or in our enactments upon this subject, provide so securely for the establishment of schools for the education of our children that there need be no apprehension of the future. If we cripple the General Assembly, if we make a provision like that offered by the gentleman from Edgefield (Mr. ELLIOTT), whereby any of the people shall shield themselves, saying they are not equal to the task imposed upon them, that they cannot pay one dollar a year for the education of their children, then our condition will be deplorable indeed. There is no compulsory process to make a man pay his tax. You cannot take him upon the highway. We have not only abolished the barbarous law of imprisonment for debt, but have said there shall be no involuntary servitude. You cannot compel a man to work out his poll tax upon the public road.

Mr. F. L. CARDOZO. Does not the gentleman know that there are other revenues besides poll taxes.

Mr. B. F. WHITTEMORE. I am not in favor of decreasing the amount proposed to be raised for the purpose of establishing schools. We have to build school houses. The Chairman of the Committee ought to know it is an expensive piece of work to build school houses. We cannot legislate for one particular portion of the State. Their requirements are alike. All desire that their children should receive the advantages of a school in their neighborhood. Suppose a poll tax of one dollar raises an annual revenue of one hundred and twenty-five thousand dollars, and that amount is distributed through thirty-one districts ; that will be about four thousand dollars in each district for the building of school houses, and making provision for the education of the children in the schools. I do not believe any gentleman here should have the privilege of sitting in the Legislature, who intends to deprive any man of his right to vote for non-payment of the poll tax.

It is a declaration unfounded in fact. I do say, however, if there is a person in South Carolina who has not the ambition to raise one-third of a cent per day for the purpose of paying a capitation tax for the education of his children, if he will not pay eight cents per month for that purpose, besides enjoying himself the privilege of the elective franchise, that man is no benefit to the community, and as has been well said, his vote can be purchased. Let us repeal the amendment already made to this section. I do not believe the proviso will aid us at all in the great educational work of the State in which the people will engage. I believe we should be liberal and generous, and the only way is to look to the future as well as the present. The people who are to vote upon the ratification of the Constitution are not to be affected by this poll tax. They are coming forward to vote upon that instrument without being trammelled in the least, and I appeal to every father upon the floor, every man interested in the youth of the State, if it is not our duty, beyond any peradventure whatever, to provide a law for the education of our youth in the State, and not cripple the General Assembly, but to leave it open so that body may make a provision which will enable the people all over the State to enjoy the same privileges.

The PRESIDENT announced that the hour had arrived for the consideration of the next special order, which was the report of the Committee on Petitions, on the petition offered by Mr. F. L. CARDOZO, praying Congress for the donation to this State of certain lands in South Carolina, bought in at public sales by the United States Government, and on which the right of redemption had expired.

Mr. Y. J. P. OWENS, of the Committee to whom it was referred, reported favorably.

On motion of Mr. R. C. DeLARGE, the report was recommitted to the Committee, with instructions to report by resolution to-morrow at eleven o'clock.

The Convention then resumed the consideration of the fifth section of the report of the Committee on Education.

Mr. R. C. DeLARGE. I trust section five will pass to its third reading as amended, and that the proviso will not be stricken out. The gentleman from Darlington (Mr. B. F. WHITTEMORE), has failed to prove to the satisfaction of the Convention that the proviso should be stricken from the section. I believe the majority of delegates here regard all men entitled to vote, simply because they are men, and I am opposed to any restriction, save the restriction that is required for the good order and protection of society. While I desire that every man should pay his poll tax, and that every citizen should pay his portion towards the support of the government of the State, I, nevertheless, do not desire to see a citizen disfranchised and deprived of the rights of citizenship simply because he is poor. It has also been said by the gentleman from Darlington (Mr. B. F. WHITTEMORE), that any one could pay this tax, that they certainly could earn a dollar to pay it, and if not they should not be allowed to vote. The very same gentleman, less than nine months ago, was the framer of the platform of a certain party, one of the main planks of which was universal suffrage, without any distinction, and if I mistake not, that gentleman owes his seat in the Convention to the endorsement of the plank he proposes to throw overboard. In that very platform, which he not only advocated, but was one of the main builders, and, perhaps, one of the most noisy of all advocates, there is an express provision which is entirely opposed to any poll tax in any shape or form.

Mr. B. F. WHITTEMORE rose to a question of privilege, and requested that the speaker be called to order for making the broad assertion that the gentleman from Darlington owed his seat upon the floor to a certain plank in a platform, and that the speaker should state the number of the plank in that platform. He felt personally aggrieved by the assertion made by the speaker that he (Mr. B. F. WHITTEMORE) was attempting to overthrow universal suffrage.

The CHAIR decided that the language used was not a breach of the privileges of the House, and on Mr. B. F. WHITTEMORE taking an appeal, the decision of the Chair was sustained by the House.

Mr. R. C. DeLARGE. If there ever was any system devised by man that could act as a perfect curse upon his fellows, it would be a system of poll tax without limitation. Unless we insert in this Constitution an explicit provision that no man shall be disfranchised for nonpayment of poll tax, in a year's time, we may see a political party in position who will use it as an instrument against us for partisan purposes, and to our injury. While I am desirous that every citizen should bear an equal proportion of the burdens of government, I am not willing to see a man less fortunate, perhaps, than myself, and not able to pay a dollar poll tax, deprived of the right to say who shall make the laws that are to govern him. As to the question that has been raised whether this measure should not come more properly in the report of the Committee on Franchise and Elections, that I regard as an unimportant consideration. The same men who have opposed the measure here would oppose it if inserted in any other report. They desire to defeat what they were sent here to carry out, and will work just as hard to do it in any other part of the Constitution. I hope the section will pass as amended.

Mr. R. B. ELLIOTT. I do not rise to discuss the merits of the section or of the amendment, but simply to make a few remarks in relation to the various statements made by those who have spoken in opposition to the measure. One of the gentlemen from Beaufort says, it is our duty to teach the people of the State the importance of keeping the ballot box pure. I agree with that gentlemen, that it is of the most vital importance that the ballot should be kept pure, and I would ask him whether he thinks by allowing any future Legislature the privilege of abridging the right of the citizen to cast his vote, simply because he could not pay his poll tax, is teaching that citizen the importance of the purity of the ballot box, or whether it would not be better to give him the privilege of exercising that right without any hindrance.

It is a well known fact that in Massachusetts and other States, where citizens are prevented from voting unless able to pay their poll tax, that the ballot box has been perverted, and many a time true republican men defeated by that very prohibition. Men who have been unable to pay their taxes have been drummed up by the opposite parties, their poll taxes paid for them, and their votes thus secured. If the privilege was given any Legislature to prohibit a man from casting his vote, simply because unable to pay one dollar poll tax, I doubt whether in two years hence a Republican Legislature would control the State of South Carolina.

The gentleman from Darlington quotes elaborately from the declaration of rights. He says this section is in violation of that great instrument, which says there shall be no involuntary servitude, and that a man compelled to work on the public road, because unable to pay the tax, would be involuntary servitude. I was surprised to hear a gentletleman so eloquent and so distinguished as the member from Darlington, make such an assertion.

Mr. J. S. CRAIG. Do you know of any way to compel a man to work on the roads except by imposing fines upon him?

Mr. R. B. ELLIOTT. I am not here to point out in what way such things could be done. We are here to lay down general principles upon which the Legislature of the State are to act. It will be their duty to devise the ways and means to do so.

Mr. J. S. CRAIG. I deny that there is any other way except by imposing a fine, and you cannot collect a fine from a man who has not got money enough to pay a dollar poll tax.

Mr. R. B. ELLIOTT. I would rather lose the fine and the dollar also, than cause a man to lose his vote. I cannot, for the life of me, see how the gentleman from Darlington can prove that this section has anything to do whatever with the question at issue. The question is simply, whether or not men shall be deprived of that highest gift that can be given to an American citizen. Deprive a man of his vote because he could not pay a dollar poll tax, and it would do no good. I think that a tax is required, but the amount required for the payment of expenditures for educational purposes in this State could be raised by other means besides the deprivation of the right to vote. So much for the gentleman's opinion in regard to involuntary servitude.

The gentleman from Beaufort (Mr. WRIGHT), in a very eloquent and fiery speech, appealed to the delegates not to allow this section, as amended, to pass to its third reading.

Upon what ground has he done so? He gets up, as is his usual wont, to tell the delegates about trampling upon this right and that right; about the horrors it will bring upon the community, and all that; but I cannot see the essence of his argument. I fail to see where he has touched upon the merits of the case at all. Lawyer like, he has been going all around it. He has been around the entire circumference, but has never bridged the centre. The gentleman from Darlington seemed like him, but though not a lawyer, like a preacher, has spun out a sermon and made an elaborate argument, without approaching the real issue of the case. I would like to meet the gentleman squarely. There are no side issues attached to this question. The gentleman from Beaufort says truth must prevail. I think the truth in his case will prevail. I think the delegates will reiterate the same votes they gave this morning, when this question was decided favorably. I think the vote will be again that this section, as amended, shall pass to the third reading in spite of the legal argument of the gentleman from Beaufort, or the able sermon of the gentleman from Darlington. As I said before, it is useless for me to dwell upon the merits of the case. It is plainly to be seen here that gentlemen do not now avow their intention of depriving a citizen of the privilege of voting. Gentlemen speak confidently of what the Legislature may be in the future. I have my fears upon that question. It is difficult for me or for any other gentleman to tell whether or not the Legislature will be filled with Copperheads or Republicans. We heard a good deal of the organizations being effected throughout the State. We have heard of the labors that are to be put forth during the campaign for the defeat of the Constitution we are now debating. I do not believe that the Republican party of South Carolina is imbecile. I believe we can prove ourselves equal to the emergency, but I would say, do not be so sure of success. Do not trust too much to the

93

Legislature, but let us act in such a manner that the Legislature will not be able to deprive any citizen of his rights.

Mr. B. F. RANDOLPH. When this subject was under consideration in the morning, I listened carefully to the gentlemen upon the other side. I listened to the sophistry of the gentleman from Charleston, and the warlike tones of the gentleman from Edgefield. I listened to the other gentleman who attempted to prove it would not do for us to fail to incorporate in this section the amendment of the gentleman from Edgefield. In my humble opinion the gentlemen have failed to prove the logic of that amendment. They have used a great deal of circumlocution, and I wonder some of the gentlemen did not caution us of an attempt to rob the people of their rights. I wonder the gentleman from Kershaw (Mr. DILL), did not rise up and charge an attempt to rob the people of their rights. They did not go so far as to tell us we would lose the election. The gentleman from Charleston was not coming out in plain terms, but there was a probability, they said, that we would fail in the election. I am no candidate; I do not know but that these gentlemen are. Probably they are very anxious in regard to this matter, looking forward to future offices. I wish, in the first place, to divest your minds of the idea some of you may entertain. You probably think or suppose that if a man is disfranchised, or if he once fails to vote, because he fails to pay his tax, he is forever disfranchised. That is not the case; he is disfranchised only as far as he cannot pay the poll tax.

Mr. F. J. MOSES, Jr. The gentleman makes a broad assertion, that a person would only be disfranchised for that one election. I ask him if he can tell what disfranchising act may be passed?

Mr. B. F. RANDOLPH. By striking out the amendment it leaves the matter solely with the Legislature.

Mr. F. J. MOSES, Jr. Can you say that the Legislature will not pass such a law.

Mr. B. F. RANDOLPH. I hope it will. If, in the judgment of the Legislature, it is necessary in order to collect the poll tax, then that body, in my humble judgment, will pass such a law at the first session The gentleman from Charleston (Mr. BOWEN), says it will cause us to lose the election, but it will be at least four years before this question can effect any election. The Senators will be elected under the new Constitution for four years, and the members of the House of Representatives for two years. The people of the State are improving their condition every year, and will be able to pay this poll tax. I have no fear that striking out the proviso will affect any election. We have provided here for the compulsory attendance of scholars at schools. The State of South Carolina is in great need of school property and school houses. We want to pay our school teachers, and will be dependent mostly upon the poll tax. If we fail to collect the poll tax our State will not be able to establish a school system. By securing the poll tax a sufficient amount of money will be raised for school purposes. There is but one way of securing the poll tax, and that is by saying you cannot vote at the election following the failure to pay. Gentlemen have asserted that there are various other means by which we could compel the payment of the poll tax. I challenge them to show any other way. I hope the proviso will be stricken out, and that it will be left to the Legislature to adopt such measures as it may deem necessary to collect the poll tax. I move that the proviso appended to the fifth section of the report of the Committee on Education be stricken out.

The hour of six having arrived, the Convention adjourned.

FORTY-THIRD DAY.

Thursday, March 5, 1868.

The Convention assembled at 10 A. M., and was called to order by the PRESIDENT.

Prayer was offered by the Rev. T. W. LEWIS.

The roll was called, and a quorum answering to their names, the PRESIDENT announced the Convention ready to proceed to business.

The Journal of Wednesday was read and approved.

The Convention took up the unfinished business, and resumed the consideration of the fifth section of the report of the Committee on Education.

The question recurred on the amendment offered by Mr. B. F. RANDOLPH, to strike out the provision, "that no persons shall be deprived of the right of suffrage for non-payment of poll tax."

Mr. J. C. NEAGLE called for the previous question, which was sustained.

The question was then taken on the amendment offered by Mr. B. F. RANDOLPH, and was decided in the negative.

The question then recurred on the passage of the section as amended.

The PRESIDENT announced that on that question, the Chairman of the Committee on Education (Mr. F. L. CARDOZO), would be allowed fifteen minutes.

Mr. F. L. CARDOZO. This subject has been sufficiently discussed and ought to be understood. I have observed, however, that some of the speakers opposed to the amendment of the gentleman from Edgefield have endeavored to bring in a number of issues which do not belong to the subject, and have enveloped it in a cloud of mystery. All I desire to do now is simply to state the proposition. We have provided two means to sustain a system of public education, namely : a heavy tax upon property, and an additional tax in the nature of a poll tax. This last was freely discussed in the committee rooms. Some of the members of the Committee questioned it, but it was finally adopted. Your committee did not pretend to arrogate to itself the wisdom of the Convention, and agreed that it should be fairly discussed in the House. I, for one, was willing to receive amendments and suggestions from any gentleman, and to have the subject considered and reconsidered. When we provided for the poll tax, I had not at the time reflected upon the wisdom of the proposition of the gentleman from Edgefield (Mr. ELLIOTT), that we should forever deprive the Legislature of the power to take from any person the privilege of voting. Let the poll tax be forever lost; let the whole report be sunk to the bottom of the ocean rather than lose a ballot. I believe if we want to secure the ballot, we should never allow the Legislature to deprive any one of the privilege of exercising the right of suffrage. If it is once lost, it may never be given again. I now yield the floor to my friend from Sumter.

Mr. F. J. MOSES, Jr. I simply desire to notice one or two of the arguments brought up yesterday, and then give my reasons why I think it is outside of the power of this Convention to take away the ballot from any man, because he is not able to pay the poll tax.

Yesterday the collection of this tax was urged, because it was said the charitable societies of the North were about to stop the aid they had hitherto furnished. That I consider no argument whatever.

I desire to call the attention of the Convention to the fifth section of the "Act to provide for the more efficient government of the rebel States." I desire to ask, gentlemen, if we have any power in the face of that section to take away the elective franchise from any man, or to take away the ballot from any man. It is the Constitution of the United States as far as we are concerned, for if we go outside the Reconstruction Act, the probability is our measures will go by the board.

An argument brought out by the gentleman from Darlington, was that as we have adopted in this Constitution a clause that "slavery shall never be established nor involuntary servitude," we would not be able to get any work on the roads out of men in the place of the poll tax. I refer the gentleman to Article Tenth of the Constitution of 1865, which says: "Neither slavery nor involuntary servitude, except as a punishment for crime, shall ever be re-established in this State." Since that Constitution has been adopted men have been made to work on the streets, either because they refused, or were unable to pay, not only their State but town taxes. We have re-enacted this section almost precisely in the same language, and if constitutional under that of 1865, it is certainly constitutional under ours. I take the ground that the State has the right to demand service from any man in lieu of paying his taxes. I believe there is but one question involved in this matter. I believe that question to be connected with the success and prosperity of the Republican party in this State. I believe that narrowing the issue down to the point it should be; but one question, and that is whether the delegates on this floor are prepared now, or in years to come, to sell out the Republican party of South Carolina; for I tell you just as certain as you strike out that proviso, you strike at the freedmen of South Carolina, who are among the poorest of the poor. There will be scarcely a white man in the State but will be able to raise a dollar from our enemies. You will allow all power to again go into the hands of the aristocratic element. If you are willing to sell out the Republican party, do it now; do not wait to go through the coming campaign. On the success of the Republican party depends your political and civil salvation for years to come. These people will not be able to raise this money, and the Democratic element will go forward. The freedmen cannot be bribed to vote against the Republican party. I believe they would rather die first than yield up their vote to the Democratic party; but by depriving them of the right to vote, you strengthen so much the hands of your enemies. In giving these views I may be called an extremist, but I regard it my duty to preserve to my constituents the privilege granted them by the Constitution of the United States, to preserve the integrity and success of that party to which I belong. If you strike out this proviso, you may prepare yourselves for a total uprising of the political elements; and though you may not lose the first election, in four years time the top rail, which had gone under, will be on top again. How will you feel then, having deprived these men of the inestimable rights of the ballot for one dollar? For that pitiful sum, you propose to take away the elective franchise from the man to whom it has just been given by the blood of thousands of loyal men.

Mr. L. S. LANGLEY. I object to the gentleman charging that the opposition proposed to take away the right of franchise from the men who cannot pay the poll tax.

Mr. F. J. MOSES, Jr. I accuse no man of the opposite side of doing any such thing, but I say such will be the result of their proposed action. I heard the gentleman from Orangeburg say he hoped to God they would do it.

Mr. B. F. RANDOLPH. I did not use those words.

Mr. F. J. MOSES, Jr. Whether he said it or not, the Legislature will have it in their power to do it. If you are prepared, and can afford to restrict your party; if you are prepared to sell out the rights of your constituents, and the Republican party of South Carolina, then strike out the proviso. If, on the contrary, you come here for the purpose of perpetuating a Republican form of government in this State, then pass the section as it stands amended,

Mr. F. L. CARDOZO. I just rise to say that I am very glad the subject has been so fairly stated, and will yield the balance of my time to the gentleman from Edgefield.

Mr. R. B. ELLIOTT. I do not rise to make a speech, for I am willing to leave it to the sense of the House. I believe the majority of members have heard enough, and if I may judge from the indications of their countenances, I believe that the amendment proposed by myself will be adopted. I hope the amendment offered by the gentleman from Orangeburg will be buried so deep in the sea of oblivion, that it will never be resurrected again.

Mr. J. S. CRAIG. I rise to protest against the course of proceedings taken. The majority have labored very hard to show that it is our purpose to deprive parties of the right of suffrage, and have carried the previous question, cutting off debate, and not giving us an opportunity to reply. I consider this unfair and unjust.

Mr. J. S. CRAIG asked to be excused from voting, which was not granted.

Mr. L. S. LANGLEY obtained permission to explain his vote. Said he would vote " No;" not that he was in favor of disfranchising any man unable to pay his poll tax, but because he was opposed, as he had always been since he had the honor of sitting in Convention, to tying up the hands of the Legislature.

Mr. WM. McKINLAY, of Charleston, also obtained leave to explain his vote, and said he voted " No." He did so because the colored element is largely in the majority in this State, and he thought they could well afford to leave it to the Legislature to determine the mode or means of collecting the poll tax.

Mr. JOS. H. RAINEY obtained leave to explain his vote, and said he was not in favor of disfranchising any citizen of South Carolina, believing it to be the prerogative of every one to vote, but he really and conscientiously also believed that if a man could not raise one dollar a year poll tax for the educational fund of the State, they should look upon him as a pauper that has no right to vote. He would, therefore, vote "No."

Mr. J. M. RUNION asked leave to explain his vote, which was granted. He said it had never been his disposition to arrogate to himself any unconstitutional right, nor to impose his views or opinions upon other men. He was utterly opposed to any system that would disfranchise any of the citizens of the State, and he heartily concurred in the section as proposed by the committee. But he would vote "No" upon the amendment, as he thought that every man who enjoys all the rights, immunities, and privileges of citizens of South Carolina, ought to help, in some degree, to support that Government. But he was perfectly willing to leave that matter to the Legislature.

Mr. C. M. WILDER. I want it understood I am not opposed to any man having the right of suffrage, but after seeing such a liberal provision made for the free schools of this State, and thinking that the section they were about to pass with the amendment or proviso, destroys every support of those schools, I am compelled to vote "No."

Mr. C. P. LESLIE said, when the section with the proviso came under consideration yesterday, his first impression was that the purpose of the section, as amended by the delegate from Edgefield (Mr. ELLIOTT), or the tendency of it, would be to compel the white people to educate the colored people. That it was his first impression, and just to that extent he was opposed to the amendment; but, on reflection, it was his judgment that it could not operate in that direction to any great extent or harm.

But another thought struck him, which was, that in a Republican form of government, where a man is human, and has a soul, who is accountable to the laws, and has, or may have, a dollar that he may lose or gain, that man has an unqualified right to vote, and no earthly or heavenly power can take that right from him. He asked, therefore, to record his vote "Aye."

The ayes and noes on this question, were as follows:

AYES—The President, Messrs. Alexander, Arnim, Becker, Bell, Bowen, Bonum, Boozer, Burton, Brockenton, Bryce, Byas, E. J. Cain, Camp, Cardozo, Coghlan, Chamberlain, Chesnut, Clinton, Cook, Collins, Corley, Craig, Darrington, Davis, DeLarge, Dickson, Dill, Driffle, Duncan, Edwards, Elliott, Gentry, Goss, Gray, Harris, James H. Hayne, Chas. D. Hayne, Henderson, Humbird, Jacobs, Jervey, J. W. Johnson, W. E.

Johnston, Henry Jones, Chas. Jones, Lang, George Lee, Lomax, Leslie, E. W. M. Mackey, Mayer, Mauldin, Mead, Middleton, Miller, Milford, F. J. Moses, Jr., Nance, Nelson, Neagle, Newell, Nuckles, Owens, Parker, Ransier, Rivers, Robertson, Rose, Rutland, Sanders, Shrewsbury, Stubbs, Swails, Thomas, S. A. Thompson, Samuel B. Thompson, Viney, White, Williamson, Wingo—81.

Nays—Messrs. Allen, Donaldson, H. E. Hayne, Holmes, Jillson, W. B. Johnson, Dr. L. B. Johnson, Langley, W. J. McKinlay, W. McKinlay, Nash, Olsen, Randolph, Rainey, Runion, B. A. Thompson, Webb, Whittemore, F. E. Wooley, Wright, Wilder—21.

Absent—Messrs, R. H. Cain, Crews, Dogan, Foster, Hunter, Hurley, Jackson, Jenks, S. Johnson, Joiner, McDaniels, Perry, Pillsbury, Richmond, Sasportas, Smalls, Whipper—17.

Section five then passed to its third reading.

Mr. R. C. DeLARGE. I move that the unfinished business be suspended, in order to allow the Committee on Petitions to make a report.

Mr. J. J. WRIGHT. I hope we will finish the report before us, and then take up the report of the Committee on Petitions. I trust the motion to suspend will not prevail.

Mr. F. L. CARDOZO. I hope the motion to suspend will prevail. The petition offered by myself was made the special order twice, and the committee failed to report at the hours fixed upon. It will not take more than fifteen minutes.

Mr. R. C. DeLARGE The report of the Committee on Education will not suffer by being delayed half an hour. Unless we act speedily upon this petition, the object of it will, perhaps, be placed beyond our reach and that of those who desire to act with us.

Mr. C. P LESLIE. The motion, as it now stands. is to suspend the rules for a certain specific purpose. I have a very brief minority report of the Committee on Franchise and Elections, and I desire to read it. If the friends who make this motion will allow me three minutes, I will favor the motion.

Mr. L. S. LANGLEY. I am not in favor of a suspension of the rules. We have made good progress with the report of the Committee on Education, and when we have a subject under consideration, I like to see it finished. I do not consider the petition for which the gentleman from Charleston proposes to suspend the rules, so important as to warrant the delay of the consideration of the report of the Committee on Education.

Mr. D. H. CHAMBERLAIN. I hope this motion to suspend the rules will prevail. I am not well informed of the objects of the petition, but it is understood to be a very important question. It concerns the interests of the State in the subject we are now discussing. I desire to state further, without expressing an opinion, that it is understood to be a question between the Port Royal Railroad and the other interest of the States alluded to. If certain action should be taken upon the petition, the Port Royal Railroad will not get a certain grant of land, but the educational and other interests of the State will receive a certain amount from Congress. But whatever we do must be done speedily.

The question was then taken on the motion to suspend, and decided in the affirmative.

Mr. W. E. ROSE, Chairman of the Committee on Petitions, presented the following report :

The Committee on Petitions, to whom was referred a certain paper, purporting to be a petition of citizens of South Carolina, but without signature, praying that certain lands held by the Government of the United States, may be allotted to deserving citizens of said State, respectfully report—

That while your Committee are impressed with the importance and utility of the measure proposed, they deem it entirely foreign to their duty to take any action on a document of this character. If in fact this be a *bona fide* petition, it should be signed by the petitioners, and endorsed by the delegate presenting it. Your committee, therefore, respectfully ask to be discharged from the further consideration of the said document.

Mr. J. L. NEAGLE. I move that the whole matter be referred to the Committee on Education.

The CHAIR stated that the report of the committee must first be disposed of.

Mr. R. G. HOLMES. I move the adoption of the report of the Committee.

Mr. F. L. CARDOZO. I hope the report of the committee will not be adopted. The real question before us is whether a half a million dollars shall be given for the educational purposes of our State, or shall go to a heartless railroad corporation. That corporation is making the most strenuous efforts to secure this grant, and unless we take speedy action on that petition they may succeed.

Mr. L. S. LANGLEY. The question of the Port Royal Railroad is not under consideration. The question is, whether the report of the Committee on Petitions shall be adopted.

Mr. F. L. CARDOZO. This is an effort to kill the petition. But we are to consider whether forty thousand acres of land and a half million of dollars shall be given for the benefit of the poor colored people, and for educational purposes, or whether we shall permit this heartless rail-

94

road corporation to get before Congress in advance with their petition. If this corporation succeeds, they will make the colored people work on their railroad, and will give them bonds in payment to purchase the lands. I was told by the Chairman of the Committee on Public Lands to foil this scheme, and the Assistant Commissioner of the Freedmen's Bureau heartily favored this petition. If this petition is passed we will secure a fund for educational purposes, and deprive the railroad corporation of the opportunity of speculating in the poor freedman's labor. If this railroad is worth building, there are plenty of private capitalists to enlist in its favor.

Mr. J. J. WRIGHT. I rise to a question of order. The question before the House is on the adoption or non-adoption of the report of the Committee on Petitions. The gentleman is now discussing the propriety or impropriety of this Convention taking part for or against the Port Royal Road.

The CHAIR decided the point of order not well taken.

Mr. F. L. CARDOZO. If we adopt the report of the committee we deprive the school fund of this State of one hundred thousand dollars, and prefer that the railroad should get the money and the land.

Mr. L. S. LANGLEY. I agree with the gentleman from Charleston, who has just resumed his seat, on one point; and that is, when he speaks of a heartless railroad corporation. I do not believe any railroad corporation has a heart.

The reasons advanced by the gentleman from Charleston why the report of the committee should not be adopted have no foundation whatever. Where is this land located that the gentleman from Charleston is so anxious about? Is it located in Charleston?

Mr. R. B. ELLIOTT. We are not now considering the location of any land. The question is as to the propriety of adopting the report of the committee.

Mr. L. S. LANGLEY. These lands are said to be situated in Beaufort District. I doubt very much whether the gentleman from Charleston ever saw these lands. He does not know whether they are worth half a million or not. I claim to know something about the circumstances under which the United States hold these lands. Allow me to say, if the measure of the gentleman from Charleston is carried out, it will benefit no person from Charleston District; it will benefit those persons residing in Beaufort District. He has stated that the real issue is whether the land shall be given to a heartless railroad company, or for educational purposes. I will inform him that Congress has already provided that the proceeds shall go for educational purposes, and ever since the sale of the lands those proceeds have been largely applied for educational purposes, in erecting school houses and establishing schools at St. Helena and St. Luke's.

This petition simply proposes to give these lands to certain persons. Congress in 1863 wanted to give them to the freedmen, but, that they should appreciate them, deemed it wise and best to ask the nominal sum of one dollar and a half per acre. Two-thirds of the schools of the Parishes of St. Helena and St. Luke's have been supported from the proceeds of the sale of the lands. When the people of Beaufort District, whose interests are most concerned in this scheme, see these proceeds given to a heartless railroad company, they will take care of the matter themselves, without asking assistance from Charleston. The petition proposes to give the lands to "deserving persons," while the gentleman from Charleston asks them for educational purposes. I know that the proceeds have been given for educational purposes, for I taught school there, and am personally aware of the fact that my pay was drawn from that fund. The people of Beaufort, who are receiving the benefit of those schools, appreciate the wisdom of Congress, and do not want a change.

Mr. F. L. CARDOZO. The gentleman has mis-stated this question. The facts are these. There are $660,000 in the possession of the United States Tax Commissioners of this State, arising from the past sales of lands, and there are forty thousand acres remaining unsold. I was advised by the Chairman of the Committee on Public Lands in the House of Representatives, and the Chairman of a similar committee in the Senate, and by General Scott to draw up this petition.

The PRESIDENT announced that the half hour for which the rules were suspended had expired.

Mr. R. C. DeLARGE moved a further suspension of the rules until this question was decided.

Mr. L. S. LANGLEY moved to lay the motion to suspend on the table.

A division of the house was called for, and the motion to suspend the rules decided in the affirmative.

Mr. F. L. CARDOZO. The gentleman is right when he says my petition refers only to the land unsold. It does so, because General Scott is going to take of the money for school purposes. I have one object, and General Scott has the other in view.

Mr. R. B. ELLIOTT. I hope the report of the committee will not be adopted, but that we take it up and consider it, if not now, let it be made the special order for some other time. It is a question which involves the interest of the poor of this State, and demands the serious consideration of every member upon this floor. I hope if there are a few who, from their peculiar connections with the Port Royal Railroad, are willing to sink this petition into oblivion that the majority will not sacrifice the feelings of humanity in behalf of any railroad. I move that the motion for the adoption of the report be indefinitely postponed.

The motion was agreed to.

The PRESIDENT then stated that as the paper had now come into the hands of the Chair, as there was no signature or no endorsement, it would be returned to the member from whom it eminated.

The petition was returned, and after being signed by Mr. F. L. CARDOZO and Mr. W. B. NASH, on motion, the rules were suspended, the document again introduced, and, on motion, referred to the Judiciary Committee, to report at half-past three P. M.

Mr. C. P. LESLIE then presented the following, which was read, and a motion made to print, which was not agreed to :

CLUB HOUSE, March 5th, 1868.

As a member of the Committee on Franchise and Elections, I am compelled by a sense of duty to submit a minority report.

I confess that I agree with the very liberal report of the committee on every proposition save that contained in the second priviso to the second section of said report, which reads as follows : "That no person shall be allowed to vote or hold office who is now, or hereafter may be, disqualified therefor by the Constitution of the United States ; provided that the General Assembly shall have power to remove said disability by a two-thirds vote." This proviso I am opposed to from beginning to the end thereof. I am in favor of allowing every person who has been disqualified from voting by the reconstruction laws of Congress, or who may hereafter be disqualified by what is commonly known as the Howard amendment, to vote and hold office. I assert and maintain that in a Republican form of Government every citizen has the absolute right to vote, unqualified and unrestricted, unless convicted of crime, &c. If it be contended that "necessity" justifies disqualification and furnishes any excuse for abridging the right to vote, then, I contend, that in this State there is no such necessity existing, nor has there been. I do not think it advisable at this time to enter into a lengthy discussion of the rights and privileges of citizens to vote, nor a long recitation of census reports, or the more recent and conclusive evidence furnished by the list of the names registered by authority of the Reconstruction Acts of Congress. I simply state that the evidence is clear and conclusive against disfranchisement, and there can be no excuse for a continued disqualification, unless it be the aim of a large and admitted majority to sustain and perpetuate themselves in power and office at the expense of a to be continued and oppressed minority, besides subjecting us to the suspicion that we are afraid of the people, because it may be supposed that they might vote against the Republican party unless disfranchisement is continued.

A continuance of this oppression continues discontent, and certainly accomplishes no good, but on the contrary invites disorder and revolution.   C. P. LESLIE.

On motion of Mr. JOSEPH H. JENKS the minority report was received as information, and on motion of Mr. A. J. RANSIER was ordered to be printed.

The PRESIDENT announced the hour had arrived for the consideration of the special order which was the following ordinance reported by the Committee on Miscellaneous Provisions of the Constitution.

AN ORDINANCE

To repeal all Acts of Legislation pssed since the twentieth day of December, one thousand eight hundred and sixty, which pledge the faith and credit of the State for the benefit of any Corporate body.

WHEREAS, it is inexpedient that when the credit of the State is advanced or pledged for the benefit of public enterprises and works, in which the people of the State are interested, that power should be lodged in the General Assembly to exercise a salutary control over such public enterprises and works, to the end that the commerce and industry of the State should be adequately fostered and promoted ; therefore,

We, the People of South Carolina, in Convention met, do ordain,. That all Acts or pretended Acts of legislation purporting to have been passed by the General Assembly of the State since the twentieth day of December, A. D. 1860, pledging the faith and credit of the State for the benefit of any corporate body or private individual, are hereby suspended and declared inoperative until the General Assembly shall assemble and ratify the same. And it shall be the duty of the General Assembly at its first session after the passage of this Ordinance to attend to the same.

The Ordinance was read a first and second time, and then passed to a third reading.

The Convention then resumed the consideration of the report of the Committee on Education.

Section sixth was read as follows :

SECTION 6. Within five years after the regular session of the General Assembly, following the adoption of this Constitution, it shall be the duty of the General Assembly to provide for the establishment and support of a State Normal School, which shall be open to all persons who may wish to become teachers.

Mr. J. S. CRAIG moved to amend so as to read : "It shall be the duty of the General Assembly, as soon as practicable after the ratification of this Constitution, to provide for the establishment and support of a State Normal School, which shall be open to all persons who may wish to become teachers."

Mr. J. K. JILLSON moved that the amendment be indefitely postponed, which was agreed to, and the section pased to its third reading.

Section seven was read as follows :

SECTION 7. Institutions for the benefit of all the insane, blind, and deaf and dumb and such other benevolent institutions as the public good may require, shall be established and supported by the State, subject to such regulations as may be prescribed by law.

Mr. B. F. WHITTEMORE moved to amend as follows : Prefix to the word "institutions" the word "educational," and strike out the word "insane," in first line, which was agreed to.

Mr. B. F. RANDOLPH offered an amendment, which, on motion of Mr. J. L. NEAGLE was indefinitely postponed, and Section Seven, as amended, passed to its third reading.

Section eight passed to a third reading without debate, as follows :

SECTION 8. Provisions shall be made by law, as soon as practicable, for the establishment and maintenance of a State Reform School for juvenile offenders.

On motion of Mr. J. K. JILLSON, section nine, requiring the respective counties to make provisions for the infirm and unfortunate, was stricken out.

Section ten was read as follows :

SECTION 10. The General Assembly shall provide for the maintenance of the State University, and as soon as practicable, provide for the establishment of an Agricultural College, and shall appropriate the land donated to this State, for the support of such a college, by the Act of Congress, passed July 2d, 1868, or the money or scrip, as the case may be, arising from the sale of said lands, or any lands which may hereafter be granted or appropriated for such purpose, for the support and maintenance of such college, and may make the same a branch of the State University, for instruction in Agriculture, the Mechanic Arts, and the Natural Sciences connected therewith.

Mr. J. K. JILLSON moved to amend by striking out the word "donated" and to inserting "given," pending the consideration of which the hour of one having arrived, the Convention adjourned to three, P. M.

AFTERNOON SESSION.

The Convention re-assembled at three P. M., and was called to order by the President.

Mr. J. M. RUNION presented the petition of certain citizens of Greenville praying the division of that District ; also the petition of John W. Twitty praying the Convention to recommend the removal of his political disabilities, which were referred to the Committee on Petitions.

Mr. S. A. SWAILS presented the petition of Samuel W. Maurice, Esq., in regard to his pay as Assistant Assessor, which was referred to the Committee on Petitions.

The PRESIDENT stated that the first business in order was the report of the Committee on the Judiciary, on the petition presented to them this morning.

Mr. C. C. BOWEN, from the Judiciary Committee presented the following report :

The Committee on the Judiciary, to whom was referred the petition of Mr. F. L. CARDOZO and Mr. W. B. NASH, requesting the Congress of the United States to allot certain lands in parcels to those citizens of South Carolina who are destitute and deserving, under such regulations as may be established by Congress, respectfully report that they have duly considered the subject, and recommend the adoption of the following resolutions :

I. *Resolved*, That this Convention do recommend to the Congress of the United States that the prayer of Mr. F. L. CARDOZO and Mr. W. B. NASH, as set forth in the accompanying petition, be granted.

II. *Resolved*, That this Convention do hereby further pray the Congress of the United States that the proceeds of the sales already made of lands within the State of South Carolina for taxes due the United States, or so much thereof as may now remain unappropriated, may be granted to the State of South Carolina for the support of the public schools of the State, under such regulations as the Congress of the United States may prescribe.

III. *Resolved*, That a copy of the petition aforesaid, together with a copy of the foregoing resolutions be forwarded at once by the President of this Convention to the President of the Senate and the Speaker of the House of Representatives of the United States.

Mr. A. J. RANSIER moved the adoption of the report.

Mr. L. S. LANGLEY moved that the report be printed and made the special order for to-morrow at half-past four o'clock.

Mr. R. C. DeLARGE moved to indefinitely postpone that motion.

Mr. J. L. NEAGLE hoped the resolutions would be printed, so that they might have copies placed before the members. From simply hearing it read, he could not tell whether the land was to be given and sold or not.

Mr. J. J. WRIGHT. I hope we shall meet this question at once. These lands are situated in St. Helena and St. Luke's Parishes, and belong to the United States. I would like to see this matter, for several important reasons, discussed to-day.

Mr. C. C. BOWEN. I hope no postponement will be agreed upon. In the first resolution, we have agreed to ask Congress to denote certain lands upon certain terms. The reasonable supposition is, that Congress would put it upon the basis of one dollar and twenty-five cents per acre. We think we could get that money. The next resolution asks that certain monies be appropriated for school purposes, and that the money already in the hands of the United States, for lands sold in this State, be given for school purposes in South Carolina, under such regulations as the Congress of the United States may prescribe.

Mr. L. S. LANGLEY. It was with the best of motives that I made the motion to print, and that the subject be made the special order for half-past four o'clock to-morrow. I am opposed to all hasty action on important questions, and believed that the members having the resolutions on their tables in printed form, would be able to fully understand them before acting upon these resolutions. I appeal to the delegates to vote for the printing of the resolutions. It is for your benefit, and when you have them on your table, you can offer any amendment that may suggest itself to your minds.

Mr. F. L. CARDOZO moved to indefinitely postpone the motion, which was adopted.

Mr. F. L. CARDOZO called the previous question, which was sustained.

The question was then taken on the adoption of the resolutions, and was decided in the affirmative.

Mr. C. P. LESLIE. I rise to a question of privilege. I wish to know whether when any gentleman desires to make a statement, the President is disposed so to rule as to force the thing through; notwithstanding that should be the case, I thought this an important question, and wanted to inquire into the status of the subject matter.

The PRESIDENT. I would state to the gentleman when the previous question has been moved and seconded, and the main question put, it is not in the power of the Chair to permit any gentleman to address the Chair or the Convention. By seconding the previous question, and the ordering of the main question, the majority of the house have signified a desire to have no more debate on the subject before it.

The Chair is only carrying out the orders of the house when he refuses to permit any further debate.

Mr. S. A. SWAILS moved a reconsideration of the vote, whereby the report of the Committee on the Judiciary was adopted, and the motion for reconsideration laid on the table. The motion was agreed to.

The unfinished business, which was the report of the Committee on Education, was taken up.

The consideration of section ten was resumed, and the verbal amendments offered by Messrs. JILLSON and DUNCAN agreed to; after which, the section passed to its third reading.

Section eleven was read as follows :

SEC. 11. All the public schools, colleges, and universities of this State supported by the public funds, shall be free and open to all the children and youths of the State, without regard to race or color.

Mr. F. L. CARDOZO. I move that this section be recommitted to the committee. We desire to give the subject further consideration. The motion was agreed to.

Mr. B. F. RANDOLPH. I move that the committee be instructed to report upon that subject to-morrow.

Mr. J. K. JILLSON moved that it be instructed to report on the 11th inst.

Mr. B. F. RANDOLPH. The object of this motion is evidently to get rid of those two little words race or color. I understand it all, and I ask the house not to allow it. There is no use in our backing down from these questions. We are laying the foundation of a new structure here, and the time has come when we shall have to meet things squarely, and we must meet them now or never. The day is coming when we must decide whether the two races shall live together or not, and I appeal to the gentlemen in this Convention to sustain the motion I have made, so that this question can be brought up to-morrow and discussed.

Mr. F. J. MOSES, Jr. I move to amend by requiring that the committee shall report a week hence, at half-past twelve o'clock ; and I wish to say here that, as far as I or the Chairman of the Committee are concerned, there exists no intention of striking out the words to which the gentleman from Orangeburg has alluded. I do not care to state my reasons publicly for desiring that the consideration of the section shall be postponed until to-morrow week, but I pledge my honor that when they hear my reasons privately given, every one will be thoroughly satisfied of the propriety of such a step.

Mr. L. S. LANGLEY. I hope the amendment offered by the gentle-

95

man from Sumter will not prevail. There are no good reasons *why* this section should be postponed by recommittal to the committee who reported it, and especially that it should be postponed for one week. I believe it has been thoroughly considered, and I for one will not change my mind, even if we are kept in session two months longer. I hope the Convention will refuse to postpone until to-morrow week, but I have no objection to postpone it until to-morrow.

Mr. B. F. RANDOLPH. I propose three o'clock to-morrow.

Mr. L. S. LANGLEY. I hope the Convention will vote in favor of that motion. I am a little astonished at this motion to postpone until the 11th of March, for it seems to me that the gentleman has backed down from the sentiments he uttered in the committee. If we are Republicans, let us have a Republican Government, and stand by our principles.

Mr. J. K. JILLSON. I have my reasons for making this motion; others know them, and, therefore, I deny the charge that I have backed down.

Mr. D. H. CHAMBERLAIN. I think it due to the Convention that the reasons should be stated. Unless it is done, it will be unwise to postpone the consideration of this section. I think I know the reasons which are kept hidden from the majority of this Convention, and if they are not stated by other gentlemen, I think it will be my duty to give them, so that the Convention may understand why it is proposed to postpone this section until next Wednesday.

Mr. B. F. RANDOLPH. Do you understand the reason?

Mr. D. H. CHAMBERLAIN. I think I do.

Mr. J. S. CRAIG. As there seems to be some very important reasons for the postponement of this section, and we do not want the public to know them, I move that we go into secret session.

The PRESIDENT. The rules of the Convention do not permit such a thing to be done.

Mr. A. J. RANSIER. I think that as a matter of courtesy, the request of the Chairman of the Committee should be favorably considered. I am not prepared to say for how long a time the subject should be recommitted, but I am decidedly in favor of sending the section back.

Mr. B. BYAS. If this committee was not prepared to have their reports discussed in the house, they had no business to bring them in here I hope the motion to recommit will not prevail. I believe the two words " race and color " should remain, and I will have them there, if I am compelled to talk for three weeks.

Mr. R. C. DeLARGE. I trust the motion to recommit will prevail.

I think that much courtesy is due to the Chairman of the Committee. My colleague made the motion for the purpose of having an opportunity to assemble his committee together once more, to submit to them important information received upon the subject, within the last week. The business of the Convention will not be retarded by the delay of this section. I know the committee will report speedily, and those who may oppose any change made by the committee can discuss the whole subject upon its merits when it comes before the Convention. The aspersion attempted to be cast upon the Chairman of the Committee, that his desire for recommitment arises from a want of backbone, is something beneath the notice and dignity of any gentleman.

Mr. B. F. RANDOLPH. I call the gentleman to order. He has used words reflecting upon me personally, and accused me of things I did not say.

Mr. B. F. RANDOLPH then sent up the following as the objectionable language of Mr. R. C. DeLARGE.

"The gentleman (Mr. RANDOLPH), said it would test the backbone of the Chairman of the Committee, which is beneath the dignity of a gentleman."

The CHAIR decided that the language was enigmatical.

Mr. HAYNE moved that the Convention go into secret session.

The CHAIR decided the motion out of order, the rules of the house not providing for secret sessions.

Mr. F. J. MOSES, Jr., called for the previous question, and it being sustained, the motion to recommit to the committee was agreed to, all amendments being voted down.

Section twelve was read, as follows:

SEC. 12. The proceeds of all lands that have been, or hereafter may be, granted this State or the United States, and of all lands or other property given by the United States to this State, and not otherwise appropriated by by individuals, or appropriated by the State for like purposes, and of all estates of deceased persons who have died without leaving a will or heir, shall be securely invested and sacredly preserved as a State School Fund, and the annual interest and income of said fund, together with such other means as the General Assembly may provide, shall be faithfully appropriated for the purpose of establishing and maintaining free public schools, and for no other purposes or uses whatever.

Mr. B. O. DUNCAN. I move to amend on the second line, after the word "State," by striking out the words "and not otherwise appropriated by this State or the United States," and to insert "for educational purposes," after the word State.

Mr. B. F. WHITTEMORE. This section, as it reads, appropriates all the proceeds of lands and other causes mentioned, to the establishment and maintenence of free public schools. There is, therefore, no necessity for inserting the words, " for educational purposes."

Mr. F. L. CARDOZO. I hope the amendment of the gentlemen from Newberry will not prevail. We have already said that the proceeds shall be appropriated to a State School Fund unless otherwise appropriated by the United States. If already appropriated, how can we get it for a school fund? We propose, however, to appropriate all we can get for a definitive purpose, and that purpose is education.

Mr. B. F. RANDOLPH. I hope this section will pass. If members will examine the section they will see that the words, "race or color," are stricken out.

I understand it all. The Convention will understand it all. Some of you have accused me of being too conservative; but you will see who are the conservatives in this house. Well, I hope this section will pass; that lands will be appropriated to schools, and that the colored children in the State will get as much as they can; but I tell you that for one I am not afraid of the New Hampshire elections, or any other elections.

The PRESIDENT. The gentleman must come to order.

The question was then taken on the first amendment, offered by Mr. B. O. DUNCAN, and decided in the negative.

Mr. B. O. DUNCAN moved to amend, by striking out "granted," and inserting "given," which was agreed to, and the section, so amended, was passed to its third reading.

Mr. B. O. DUNCAN proposed the following additional section, which was referred to the Committee on Education :

SECTION —. All donations for the support of public schools, or for other purposes of education, which may be received by the General Assembly, shall be applied according to the terms prescribed by the donor.

On motion of Mr. R. G. HOLMES, the preamble to the report of the Committee on Education, was stricken out.

Mr. F. L. CARDOZO moved to reconsider the vote whereby section one of the report on education was passed, which was agreed to, and the following substitute offered, which was adopted, and the section, so amended, passed to its third reading :

SEC. 1. The supervision of public instruction shall be vested in a State Superintendent of Education, who shall be elected by the qualified electors of the State, at the same time, and in the same manner as the other State officers; his powers, duties, term of office, and compensation, shall be defined by the General Assembly.

The Convention then proceeded to the consideration of the article on the militia.

Section one was read as follows:

Sec. 1. The militia of this State shall consist of all able bodied male residents of the State, between the ages of eighteen and forty-five years, except such persons as are now, or may hereafter be, exempted by the laws of the United States, or of this State, and shall be organized, armed, equipped and disciplined as the General Assembly may by law provide.

Mr. N. G. PARKER. I move to amend by inserting after the word "now" the word "disfranchised." I am not inclined to organize those who are disfranchised into companies, and put arms into their hands.

Mr. J. J. WRIGHT. I would organize the militia of the State from the able bodied men in the State. We have men enough of the right material to put down any insurrection on the part of those who may attempt it. When the laws are to be enforced by the use of arms, we should make no exceptions; and if a certain class attempt resistance, we must teach them their duty to the United States, and to the State. The severe lessons they have already been taught are so impressed upon their minds, that I do not believe there is any danger of their taking them up again. If they co-operate with us, and repent of their former action, we may recommend the removal of their disabilities. I hope we will make no such provision as that proposed by the gentleman from Barnwell (Mr. PARKER.)

Mr. R. C. DeLARGE. I move to indefinitely postpone all the amendments

The motion was agreed to.

Mr. B. F. WHITTEMORE. I move to amend by striking out the words "of this State," in the third line, and to insert in place thereof the words, "who may be adverse to bearing arms as provided for in this Constitution.

The amendment was agreed to, and the section, as amended, passed to its third reading.

Section two was read, as follows:

Sec. 2. The Governor shall have power to call out the militia to execute the laws, repel invasion, suppress insurrection, and preserve the common peace.

Mr. B. F. WHITTEMORE. I move to strike out the word, "common," and insert "public." The amendment was agreed to.

Mr. R. G. HOLMES. I move to insert after the word "power," " under regulations provided by law."

The question was taken on this amendment, and decided in the negative. The section then passed to its third reading.

Section third was read, as follows:

SEC. 3. The Governor may appoint the Adjutant-General, Quarter-master-General, and such other officers of his Staff as the General Assembly may direct.

Mr. N. G. PARKER offered the following substitute:

There shall be an Adjutant and Inspector-General elected by the qualified electors of the State, at the same time and in the same manner as other State officers, who shall rank as Brigadier-General, and whose duties and compensation shall be prescribed by law.

The Governor shall appoint, by and with the advice and consent of the Senate, such other staff officers as the General Assembly may direct.

This will throw the election of that very important officer into the hands of the people. It is of the highest importance that the people should elect that officer. I am in favor of retaining all the power in the hands of the people that we can.

Mr B. F. RANDOLPH. The committee gave that matter due consideration. They thought the Governor should be allowed to appoint certain military officers, constituting, as it were, his military family. We thought he should be allowed to select who they should be, on the same principle that the President of the United States selects his cabinet.

Mr. B. F. WHITTEMORE. I trust that the motion, as presented by the gentleman from Barnwell (Mr. PARKER), will prevail, and that the election of the Adjutant-General will be given to the people. It is a very important office, and as we propose to organize the militia of the State soon, we propose to let the people elect that officer, who will have to superintend the work of organization.

Mr. E. W. M. MACKEY called the previous question, which was sustained.

The question was then taken on the adoption of the substitute, and decided in the affirmative. The section then passed to its third reading.

Mr. R. C. DeLARGE moved that the vote by which the third section was passed to a third reading be reconsidered and the motion for reconsideration laid upon the table, which was agreed to.

The Convention then proceeded to the consideration of the article on charitable institution.

Section one was read as follows:

SECTION 1. Institu ions for the benefit of the insane, blind, deaf and dumb, and the poor, shall always be fostered and supported by this State, and shall be subject to such regulations as the General Assembly may enact.

Mr. B. O. DUNCAN. I move to strike out this section. We have but a short time ago passed a similar section in the report of the Committee on Education, and it is unneccessary to have the same provision in two places.

Mr. R. C. DELARGE. Will it not be the duty of the Committee on Review and Consolidation to transpose the sections.

Mr. B. F. WHITTEMORE. It is understood that the Committee on Review and Consolidation can only arrange the articles in their order.

The question was taken on a motion to strike out the words "blind, deaf and dumb," and decided in the negative.

The next question was on striking out the section, which was decided in the negative, and the section passed to its third reading.

Section two was read as follows :

SEC. 2. The Directors of the Penitentiary shall be elected or appointed, as the General Assembly may direct.

Mr. B. F. WHITTEMORE. I move to substitute the word "trustees" in place of "directors."

Mr. B. F. RANDOLPH. I move to strike out "directors" and insert "commissioners."

Mr. R. J. DONALDSON. I move to amend by inserting "Governors of Penitentiaries."

Mr. E. W. M. MACKEY. I move to postpone indefinitely all the amendments. I think the word "directors" most appropriate.

Mr. B. F. RANDOLPH. Directors duties are specific. If we say commissioners it will include not only those who may be directors, but other persons who have the management of the penitentiary.

The question was taken on the motion to postpone the amendments, and decided in the affirmative.

Mr. G. W. S. DILL. I move that the second section be stricken out.

Mr. R. C. DELARGE. I move to indefinitely postpone that motion. The motion was agreed to, and section two passed to its third reading.

Section three was read as follows :

Sec. 3. The Trustees of the benevolent and other State institutions, such as may be hereafter created, shall be appointed by the Governor, by and with the consent of the Senate ; and upon all nominations made by the Governor, the question shall be taken by yeas and nays, and entered upon the journal.

Mr. B. F. WHITTEMORE moved to change the word "trustees" to "directors," so as to agree with the preceding section. The motion was agreed to, and the section, as amended, passed to its third reading.

Section four was read a second time and passed to a third reading without debate, as follows :

Sec. 4. The Governor shall have power to fill all vacancies that may occur in the offices aforesaid, until the next session of the General Assembly, and until a successor or successors shall be appointed and confirmed.

Mr. N. G. PARKER moved a suspension of the rules in order to allow Mr. J. L. NEAGLE to introduce, as a fifth section of article on charitable institutions, section nine of the Educational Report, which was agreed to.

The section was read twice, and passed to its third reading as follows :

Sec. 5. The respective counties of this State shall make such provision, as may be determined by law, for all those inhabitants who by reason of age and infirmities or misfortunes, may have a claim upon the sympathy and aid of society.

Mr. J. L. NEAGLE also introduced the following, which was adopted :

Sec. 6. The Physician of the Lunatic Asylum, who shall be super-intendent of the same, shall be appointed by the Governor, with the advice and consent of the Senate. All other necessary officers and employees shall be appointed by the Governor.

The Convention proceeded to the consideration of the article on corporations.

Section one was read as follows :

Section 1. The General Assembly shall pass no special act conferring corporate powers.

Mr. R. G. HOLMES. I move to add "except for municipal purposes."

Mr. N. G. PARKER. Provisions have already been made in the constitution for the incorporation of towns and cities.

Mr. J. J. WRIGHT. What is the real meaning of this provision, which says, "the General Assembly shall pass no special act ?"

Mr. B. F. RANDOLPH. It has been customary for the General Assembly to pass special acts incorporating cities, towns, &c. For instance, a church would make application and the General Assembly would pass a special act incorporating that particular body. The committee deemed it best to have the law general, so that corporations may come under a general act, as they are in all other States.

Mr. R. G. HOLMES. I trust my amendment will prevail. The article referred to does not cover the ground. If this section should pass as it is the only way a town or city could be incorporated, would be to pass a general act. The first provision in the charter would be to decide and fix the boundaries. An act might be passed whereby any six or ten miles square could be incorporated. That would not be at all consistent. I consider my amendment absolutely necessary.

Mr. F. J. MOSES, Jr. A clause in the second section of the report of the Committee on Taxation says, "the General Assembly shall provide for the incorporation of cities, towns &c."

Mr. R. G. HOLMES. This section, however, says no special act shall be passed. Then it must be a general charter. But there can be no general charter for the incorporation of cities and towns.

Mr. R. C. DeLARGE. I move to indefinitely postpone the amendment.

Mr. E. W. M. MACKEY. I move to lay the amendment on the table.

The motion was agreed to, and the amendment laid on the table, which also carried the section with it.

Section two was read as follows, and passed without debate :

SEC. 2. Corporations may be formed under general laws; but all such laws may, from time to time, be altered or repealed.

Section three was read as follows :

SEC. 3. The property of corporations now existing or hereafter created, shall be subject to taxation.

Mr. BOWEN moved to amend by adding to it " except in cases otherwise provided for in this Constitution." The amendment was agreed to, and the section passed to a third reading.

Section four was read as follows :

SEC. 4. No right of way shall be appropriated to the use of any corporation until full compensation therefor shall be first made in money, or first
96

secured by a deposit of money to the owner, irrespective of any benefit from any improvement proposed by such corporation, which compensation shall be ascertained by a jury of twelve men, in a Court of Record, as shall be prescribed by law.

Mr. CRAIG offered to amend by striking out the second word " first " in second line, which was agreed to.

Mr. W. J. McKINLAY offered to amend by striking out the words "in money," second line, which was agreed to, and the section passed to a third reading.

Section five was passed as follows without debate :

SEC. 5. Dues from corporations shall be secured by such individual liability of the stockholders and other means, as may be prescribed by law.

Mr. E. W. M. MACKEY proposed the following additional section :

SEC. 6. All general laws and special acts passed pursuant to this section, shall make provions therein for fixing the personal liability of stockholders under proper limitations; and shall prevent and punish fraudulent misrepresentations as to the capital, property and resources of such corporations; and shall also regulate the public use of all franchises which have heretofore been, or hereafter may be, created or granted by or under the authority of this State, and shall limit all tolls, imposts, and other charges and demands under such laws.

The section was read a first time, and the hour of six having arrived, the Convention adjourned.

FORTY-FOURTH DAY.

Friday, March 6, 1868.

The Convention assembled at 10 A. M., and was called to order by the PRESIDENT.

Prayer was offered by the Rev. WM. DARRINGTON.

The roll was called, and a quorum answering to their names, the PRESIDENT announced the Convention ready to proceed to business.

The Journal of Thursday was read and approved.

Mr. N. G. PARKER moved a suspension of the rules of the house for fifteen minutes, for the introduction of resolutions, which was agreed to.

Mr. C. M. WILDER offered the following, which was referred to the Committee on the Legislative part of the Constitution :

Resolved, That it be referred to the Legislative Committee to inquire into and report by Ordinance or otherwise, as to the propriety of requiring all railroads in this State to charge the same rates for passage and freight over the entire length of their road in the State.

Mr. N. G. PARKER offered the following:

Resolved, That all chartered cities and incorporated towns shall hold their municipal elections within thirty days from the ratification of the Constitution. All municipal offices, cities, and towns, shall be declared vacant within thirty days from the adoption of this Constitution.

Referred to the Special Committee of Nine, appointed to consider the matter of the approaching elections.

Resolved, That a clause in the Constitution is necessary for defining the qualifications of jurors.

Referred to the Committee on the Judiciary.

Resolved, That the General Assembly, at its first session, shall provide suitable laws for the registration of all qualified electors and for preventing frauds at elections.

Referred to the Committee on Franchise and Elections.

Resolved, That the General Assembly may declare the cases in which any office shall be deemed vacant, and also the manner of filling the vacancy, when no provision is made for that purpose in this Constitution.

Referred to the Special Committee of Nine, on the approaching elections.

Mr. B. F. WHITTEMORE asked and obtained leave to introduce the following as a portion of the legislative part of the Constitution.

There shall be elected by the qualified electors of the State, a Comptroller-General, State Treasurer, and Secretary of the State, who shall hold their respective offices for four years, and whose duties and compensation shall be prescribed by law.

The section was read a first time, and ordered to be printed.

Mr. J. M. ALLEN presented the petition of Colonel John D. Ashmore and Jacob Kepler, praying the Convention to recommend the removal of their political disabilities.

Referred to the Committee on Petitions.

Mr. T. J. ROBERTSON submitted the following, which was read, and, on motion, referred to a Special Committee of Nine.

Whereas, the financial condition renders it necessary that the General Assembly, at its first session, should adopt the measures requisite to apply its available resources to the discharge of its valid obligations; and, whereas, it is essential to that end that an investigation of the financial resources of the State should be made without delay, in order that the results thereof may be submitted to the General Assembly at such first session, we, the people of South Carolina, in Convention assembled, do ordain :

SECTION 1. That three Commissioners be appointed in the manner hereinafter provided, whose duty it shall be to investigate the financial condition of the State, and the situation and value of all property, assets, securities, and other resources applicable to the discharge of its valid obligations, and to report thereon, with their recommendations, to the General Assembly upon its being convened, or as soon thereafter as practicable.

SEC. 2. Such Commissioners shall have authority to inspect all public records, accounts and vouchers; to call for reports under oath, in such form as they shall prescribe, from all public officers having knowledge of facts or possession of matters pertinent to such investigations; to summon witnesses, to administer oaths, and to examine all persons, who, in their judgment, may have knowledge of any such matters.

SEC. 3. It shall be the duty of any person or officer, under a penalty of five hundred dollars, to be recovered in any Court of Record, in the name of said Commissioners, upon notification or summons, to make such report, and to attend at any time and place at which they may be requested to appear for such examination, and to produce any document or writing, the production of which shall be required by such notification or summons. Witnesses attending for such examination may be allowed the customary rates, to be paid as a part of the contingent expenses of the commission   Any person guilty of knowingly and willingly making any false statement under oath or affirmation in respect thereto, shall be guilty of wilful and corrupt perjury, and liable to the pains and penalties therefor prescribed by law.

SEC. 4. Said Commissioners shall be appointed by the President of this Convention, and shall receive the same per diem allowance as members of this Convention, and actual expenses incurred in travelling in the performance of said duties.

SEC. 5. The sum of ——— dollars is hereby appropriated for the pay of said Commissioners, and the contingent expenses of said Commissioners, which sum shall be placed by the Treasurer of the State in the currency of the United States, or the bills receivable of this State, guaranteed under the authority of this Convention, to the credit of the Commission, and shall be drawn upon the warrant of the Chairman of this Commission, countersigned by the President of this Convention, and shall be drawn for no other account whatsoever.

SEC. 6. The General Assembly shall have authority to extend the powers of said Commission, or to modify the same, when, in their judgment, the objects of this Ordinance are fully attained, to terminate said Commission, making provision by law for the payment of any deficiency of the appropriation hereby made to meet the lawful expenses of said Commission.

The PRESIDENT announced the following members to constitute the committee on the above: Messrs. T. J. Robertson, of Richland; W. J. McKinlay, of Orangeburg; W. E. Rose, of York; D. H. Chamberlain, of Berkley; Wilson Cook, of Greenville; R. G. Holmes, of Beaufort; Joseph H. Rainey, of Georgetown.

Mr. L. S. LANGLEY offered the following, which was referred to the Committee on Petitions:

Resolved, That this honorable body unite and join in with the citizens of Beaufort in praying Gen. Canby to relieve them from the oppressive abuse under which they are now suffering at the hands of their town officers, by removing the present incumbents, and substituting to act in their place gentlemen of acknowledged morality, integrity, and loyalty.

Mr. L. S. LANGLEY offered the following:

Resolved, That this Convention will not receive nor act upon any petition or resolution except petitions for removal of political disabilities, after to-morrow's session, and until the Constitution is completed.

Mr. R. B. ELLIOTT moved that the resolution be laid upon the table, which was not agreed to.

Mr. W. H. W. GRAY moved that the resolution be indefinitely postponed, which was agreed to.

The unfinished business, which was the consideration of the seventh section of the Committee on Incorporations, was taken up, and the section passed to its third reading.

Mr. F. E. WILDER offered the following as an additional section :

The credit of the State shall not be granted to, or in aid of, any person, association or corporation, nor shall the State subscribe to, or be interested in, the stock of any company, association or corporation.

Mr. E W. M. MACKEY said a similar section had already been voted upon and stricken out of the report of the Committee on Finance. The subject was then fully discussed, and he, therefore, moved that the section be laid on the table.

The PRESIDENT decided the proposed section to be out of order, as the matter had already passed out of the hands of the house by the adoption of a motion to reconsider the vote taken upon the section, and to lay the motion to reconsider upon the table.

The report of the Committee on Miscellaneous Provisions of the Constitution, was taken up for a second reading.

The first section, providing that Columbia shall be the seat of Government, on motion of Mr. E. W. M. MACKEY was stricken out, there being a similar provision already adopted in the Legislative part of the Constitution.

Mr. J. M RUTLAND moved that the Committee on Review and Consolidation have power to transfer any section of the Constitution, either from one article to another, or to change its position in the same article ; provided, however, that they do not change the sense of the sections so transferred. The motion was agreed to.

Mr. J. K. JILLSON moved a suspension of the rules, in order to take up the additional section to the executive part of the Constitution, proposed by the delegate from Darlington (Mr. WHITTEMORE).

The section was then read as follows :

Section 10. The election for all State officers shall take place at the same time as is provided for that of members of the General Assembly, and the election for those officers whose terms of service are for four years, shall be held at the time of each alternate general election.

Mr. B. O. DUNCAN. I move to amend by making the term of service of the Secretary of State two years, the same as Governor.

Mr. C. P. LESLIE. I desire to say a few words on this subject, though I am satisfied I shall be voted down, or in other words, the good sense of what I propose to say, in my judgement, will not be appreciated. If I understand what a Republican form of government is, and I think I do, on the broad principles of right as distinguished from political ambition and party tactics; if I can rise high enough above the political expectations of certain parties and look honestly forward to the establishment of true Republican principles, I think I can say clearly that if this section should pass, injustice to Republicanism will be the result. I assert this broad proposition, and am willing to leave it to time to determine its correctness. As long as there is a human being in a Republican form of government, whether he be white or black or any other color, and he is accountable before the law ; as long as he has a dollar to gain or loose, that man has the inalienable right in a Republican form of government to cast his vote. I assert that as a grand truth, and am willing to leave it to time to determine. It makes no difference how humble or unfortunate a man may be, if he can be brought before the law and be held in any manner accountable, that man, in a Republican form of government, has an undisputed and unqualified right to vote. The rule of oppression may shut out that right for awhile; it may hide, it may cover it up, but it cannot stand the test of time.

We are well aware that a certain portion of the people of this State did, for a long time, preclude the colored people of the right to vote. That was kept up for two hundred years. The Constitution of the United States in some manner or other was brought into requisition, the whole political world was arrayed against the colored man, the whole political power and influence of wealth was against the colored man, but through the Providence of God all these powers and wealth have passed away. The great principle at last triumphed, and whenever a man will keep his eye upon the holy principle of right, he may be defied by arms, by political power; nations may override and trample him under foot, but justice will ultimately triumph as sure as God is in Heaven.

The illustration I wish to apply is this. There is a class of white men in this State who according to every principle of Republicanism, although they do not believe at all with me in politics, nor accord in sentiment with one single thought or act of mine, should have the right to vote. I assert the proposition I have already made, just as strongly in their behalf, that in a Republican form of government they have the inalienable, absolute, fixed and unqualified right to cast their vote. To-day we know that although these men are paying taxes to the government, they are unable to vote. They may be arraigned before the courts, they may be brought here in person, they have property to lose and property to gain, and all this in a Republican form of government. I assert it as a great American principle, which will apply to our political enemies as well as to our political friends. I say that whilst these people have the right to vote, and that right is not conceded, we should not foist or fasten upon them a class of officers for four years, because we think we have the power and can do it. I think I can truthfully state why it is that this

four years rule is insisted upon.   Are those who seek office fearful that they cannot hold them after all the people in the State shall be
allowed to vote ?   To state such a proposition would be simply to merit
the contempt of every Republican throughout the length and breadth of
the land.   I do not say this unkindly, for God knows my heart; but I
submit, when you seek to fasten upon the people of this State who cannot vote a class of officers for four years, I have a right to utter my voice
against it.

Mr. B. O. DUNCAN. The motion made by myself to fix the term of
office of the Secretary of State for two years was, because I regard it as
an unheard of precedent for a Governor to hold his office only two years,
and his Cabinet, as it were, for four years.   If the Governor's term be
extended to four years, I will vote in favor of the terms of service of
the other officers be fixed for the same time.

Mr. F. J. MOSES, Jr. I feel it my duty to say a few words upon this
subject, for two reasons : first, I happen to be Chairman of the Executive Committee ; second, I feel a deep interest in the section as it stands.
I believe it is absolutely essential to the welfare of South Carolina for
the next few years that those officers named in that resolution, more
especially the Comptroller-General and the Treasurer of the State, should
be elected to their offices for as long a term as possible, and as far as
consistent with the principles of a Republican form of government.

It has become the fashion on this floor that whenever a gentleman desires to kill a resolution or measure, which does not agree with their own
opinion, to surround it with false issues, to cover it up in a mass of reasoning or rhetoric which has no reference to the subject under discussion;
they strive by that means to produce a false impression upon the minds
of the delegates on this floor.

This subject, I consider, has but one bearing, and that bearing I regard
as of vast importance to the interests of our State.   We propose to adopt
a new constitution, to build up a new government which is to be founded
on the consent of the governed, and I believe that section as introduced will reflect the sentiments of a majority of the loyal people of
South Corolina.   I believe it is the wish and intention of these loyal
people that we should do anything or pass any measure necessary to the
preservation of good government in South Carolina.   The Comptroller-
General and the State Treasurer are two of the most important officers
the people of the State have to elect.   It is true, they will not be as high
officers as the Governor, or Senators, or Members of Congress, but they
are to assist the Governor of the State in wielding its destinies, and upon the proper performance of their duties by these officers depends the

question whether we are to have a proper State government for the next two years. Suppose we say these gentlemen shall hold their offices for only two years. We know how complicated the duties of those officers are. If we take them out of office at the end of two years, we remove them just when they thoroughly understand and appreciate the duties appertaining to those offices.

Mr. B. O. DUNCAN. Does not this reasoning apply to the office of Governor as well as any other officer.

Mr. F. J. MOSES, Jr. I do not believe my reasoning applies in any one particular to the office of Governor. The duties of the office of Governor are not half as responsible, or half as difficult to understand as the duties of the Comptroller-General and State Treasurer. While we can put a man in the office of Governor for two years and not endanger the stability of the government, I believe it to be one of the most dangerous steps we can take to put a man in those other offices for only two years, and then, just as they are accustomed to their duties, take them out and put in other men. This talk about taking the ballot from the people is all stuff and nonsense. The Governor of the State is controlled simply by the recollection of the fact that unless he performs his duties to the satisfaction of the people of the State, they can remove him from office. It is different with the Comptroller-General and the Treasurer of the State. They are required to give heavy bonds to the State, and will be held strictly responsible for the faithful performance of their duties; consequently, I fail to see the analogy between these two officers and the Governor. I hope gentlemen in voting on this subject will recollect that we are about entering on a new stage of government in South Carolina. We have been at the hands of our enemies with remarks and abuse, all striving to show that the delegates on this floor were not capable of making a Constitution under which the rights and liberties of the people could be preserved or the affairs of the State faithfully and safely administered. Those gentlemen who propose to put irresponsible parties for a term of two years in office, are playing into the hands of those people. We are making a new start, making an experiment in government, and God alone knows whether it is to succeed. But I have faith in the good sense and judgment of the delegates upon this floor. I ask, in the name of the loyal people of the State, that you shall give them officers who shall have full time to prove to the people of the State that they are fit and worthy to occupy their positions.

It is not so extraordinary that the Comptroller-General and State Treasurer should be elected for a longer time than the Governor. They have been called the Cabinet officers of the Governor; I deny that they

97

are. I regard them as entirely independent of the Governor. The Governor has no right to control any of their actions, save under the laws which the General Assembly may provide. There is nothing, therefore, in that argument which would limit the term of these officers to that of the Governor. We intend to make this experiment so safe that it cannot fail of success. I do hope a provision for a term of four years will be adopted.

Mr. D. H. CHAMBERLAIN. I shall not be able to do much more than express my concurrence with the views of my friend from Sumter. I think it very important that the false issues attempted to be drawn around this question; should be exploded, when the gentleman from Barnwell (Mr. LESLIE), talks about foisting upon the people of the State a class of officers, he uses one of those shrewd tricks which he has so frequently attempted upon this floor. We have a right, without subjecting ourselves to the charges made by the gentleman, of attempting to foist upon or furnish any set of men, to determine the length of time officers of the State shall hold their position. I go further, and say that if the argument of the gentleman from Newberry be good; if it is desirable that the term of office of the Governor, and that of the other State officers should be the same, I will join with him in the reconsideration of that section already adopted, which limits the term of office to two years. If at the first election we should be so unfortunate, as I feel sure we shall not be, as to elect an unworthy officer to position, it is by the provisions we have already passed within the power of the Legislature to remove that officer. I am entirely in favor, regardless of the term of the office of the Governor, to have those officers elected for a term of four years; but, rather than that this provision should be defeated, I would accept the proposition of my friend from Newberry.

The call was made for the previous question, but was not sustained.

Mr. J. J. WRIGHT. I thank the members that the previous question was not sustained. The gentleman from Sumter says we are about to lay the foundation of a new government, and that we should lay that foundation on a sure basis. That is true, and we want to lay that foundation in such a manner that the people shall have the right at any time to oust a man from office, and to elect another in his place. If we get bad men in office for a term of four years, what is the result? Impeachment is not a very easy thing. What the other side call their strongest argument appears to me to be the most forcible reason that can be urged in favor of short terms. If we put a man in office for two years, and he proves to be a faithful public servant, we can re-elect him. The section which provides for a term of two years, does not deprive us of the right of re-electing an officer. Let us look for a moment at the office of Governor. First, it is the most important office in the State. He executes the laws for at least a period of two years; but would it not be hard to bear with him even two years, if he is not the right sort of a man? Now, those we are about to put into office are new men. They are like children; they have had no experience, and are necessarily on trial. Is it right, under these circumstances, to imperil, perhaps, the existence of the State, by consigning it to the care of irresponsible and unqualified persons? It has been alleged here that some are trying to rob you of your rights and liberties; but I say if you put a bad man in office for four years, you will be sure to rob the people of their rights, and they have no redress. The work is your own, and it has been accomplished. You may talk about impeachment, but what does it amount to? Mr. Johnson has done everything to overthrow the Government for two years, but he has had such shrewd counsellors around him that it has taken two years even to impeach him, and there is doubt expressed whether the attempt will now prove successful. I say, therefore, under these circumstances, let the term of office of the Governor be two years, and the terms of the other offices remain as they are.

Mr. F. J. MOSES, Jr. It is only because I wish to reply to some of the arguments of the gentleman that I rise a second time. And here I desire to say, that it seems to me whenever a gentleman desires to carry a special point on this floor, with reference to a term of office, they bring in the name of Andrew Johnson, and discourse about his betrayal of the rights and liberties of the country. I beg the members of this Convention to remember that the action of the President of the United States has nothing to do with questions pending here.

By refering to section four of the Article on Impeachment, it will be seen that the Governor may, for any willful neglect of duty, remove any executive or judicial officer, on the address of two-thirds of each House of the General Assembly, provided the causes are stated at full length, etc.

There, Mr. President, is an unanswerable refutation of the argument advanced by the gentleman from Beaufort. If we place a man in the office of Treasurer or Comptroller-General, incapable or unworthy of the confidence of the people, what is easier than to adopt the course suggested by the Constitution? It has been said we desire to foist these officers on the people for four years; I deny the proposition. The officers nominated by the Republican Convention cannot be "foisted" upon the people; and, as regards the hue and cry about robbing the people of their liberties, why, sir, in my judgment, the way to preserve them is to put men in office for a term sufficient to enable them properly to carry out the duties devolved upon them. It is absolutely essential for the success of the Republican party in South Carolina that we should elect our officers from the Legislature, upwards and downwards, for as long terms as possible. If we can ensure the success of the Republican party here for four years, there is no power under Heaven that can keep us from advancing hereafter. The next four years is to decide the question who shall rule in this State and country, and I propose to place the matter beyond doubt. Put gentlemen in office for a short term, and you defeat the measures we have met here to enforce. Tell the Democrats of the State, or the aristocratic element, that in two years from this time they will have a chance to vote for or fill these offices, and you will fill their hearts with gladness. It is to their interest that we should have frequent elections, and they would be more than delighted if we should decide upon but one year as the term of office. Make the term short if you please then, but do not allege that we who favor the long term are robbing the people, when every fact and argument conclusively proves the reverse I am not interested in the section personally, or in behalf of any man, but because I believe the political salvation of South Carolina is concerned in the measure now pending Having said thus much, I yield the remainder of my time to the gentleman from Darlington.

Mr B. F. WHITTEMORE. I did not suppose, Mr. President, that this subject would create so much discussion as has arisen, for the question is a practical one, and appeals to common sense. I cannot see how the rights of the people are to be trampled upon by making the tenure of office four years instead of two. Delegates are to appear in a few days in the nominating Convention, which will assemble here, who will come fresh from the people, and instructed by the people as to their duties. When they vote, the people themselves will have voted and uttered their voice. It has been well said, we are passing through a crisis, and we have before us such examples as make it necessary for us to be cautious in our movements. But when it is alleged that we cannot oust from his position an incompetent or dishonest official before the expiration of his term, it does not speak well for the intelligence of those who express such a novel and erroneous opinion We propose, in the first place, that no man who is not qualified in every respect shall enter upon the discharge of the duties of any office.

Mr. R. SMALL. I would like to ask if the gentleman is not himself a candidate for office ?

Mr. B. F. WHITTEMORE. Not one.

Mr. J. D. BELL. If you were to hire a man to do your work, would you hire him for four years?

Mr. B. F. WHITTEMORE. Give me an opportunity of selecting the man, and I will hire him for four years. What we want are good men, and believing we shall nominate only such men, I favor the long term. The State needs improvement in everything. Its financial condition is at an ebb; its railroad system; its land, its people, all require nourishment and strength, and this can only be secured by choosing gentlemen who will carry out a liberal policy, and have an abundance of time. in which to perfect their measures of relief. The truth is, our dangers are not from within, but from without, and if we succeed in guarding against these, the future of the State and of the party are safe in our hands. Eternal vigilance is the price of liberty, and we propose to be vigilant in all things that pertain to the honor of the State, its integrity, salvation and prosperity in the future.

Finally, I trust that this provision will pass just as it has been framed, and that we shall see to it that in electing men to office for four years, their ability, honor and loyalty shall be beyond all question. Then, South Carolina will enter upon a career of progress, to which posterity will point as an evidence of good faith the fervent desire for advancement, which I believe actuates every member of the Republican party within her borders.

Mr. C. D. HAYNE, called for the previous question, which was sustained.

The question was then taken on the amendment of Mr. B. O. DUNCAN to strike out "four" and insert "two," so as to make the terms of office two instead of four years.

The yeas and nays were ordered.

Mr. B. O. DUNCAN, was granted leave to explain his vote, and stated that he was in favor of the long term, but desired that it should be extended also to the office of Governor.

The yeas and nays were then taken and resulted as follows:

YEAS.—Messrs. Allen, Alexander. Arnim, Bell, Byas, Cardozo, Corley, DeLarge, Dickson, Dill, Dogan, Donaldson, Elliott, Foster, Gentry, Goss, Harris, J. N. Hayne, C. D. Hayne, Henderson, Holmes, Hurley, Jervey, S. Johnson, W. B. Johnson, Langley, George Lee, Leslie, W. McKinlay, McDaniels, Mead, Middleton, Miller, Nance, Newell, Nuckles, Olsen, Owens, Randolph, Rivers, Robertson, Shrewsburry, Smalls, Swails, Webb, Wingo, Wright.---47.

NAYS—The President; Messrs. Bowen, Boozer, Burton, Brockenton, Bryce, F. J. Cain, J. P. F. Cain, Coghlan, Chamberlain, Chestnut, Clinton, Collins, Darrington, Davis, Driffle, Duncan, Edwards, Gray, H.

E. Hayne, Jacobs, Jillson, J. W. Johnson, Dr. L. B Johnson, John-
ston, Joiner, H. Jones, C. Jones, Lang, S. Lee, Lomax, E. W. M.
Mackey, Mayer, Milford, Moses, Nash, Neagle, Parker, Rainey, Ransier,
Rose, Runion, Rutland, Sanders, Stubbs, A. Thompson, B. A. Thompson,
S. B. Thompson, Whittemore, White, Williamson, F. E. Wilder, Wool-
ey.---50.

ABSENT.—Messrs. Becker, Bonum, R. H. Cain, Cook, Craig, Crews,
Humbird, Hunter, Jackson, Jenks, Mauldin, W. J. McKinlay, Nelson,
Perry, Pillsbury, Richmond, Sasportas, Thomas, Viney, Whipper, C. M.
Wilder.—21.

Mr. L. S. LANGLEY. I am satisfied that the passage of that section
on the first vote was rejected by the house. A division of the house
was then called for, and, by the count, the section was rejected. I hope
the yeas and nays will be called again, with the question stated fairly,
in order to satisfy all parties.

The PRESIDENT. The Chair is very reluctant to oppose the views
of any gentleman, but it is apparent that a deliberative body would soon
descend to the character of a mob, unless it had rules and regulations to
control it. There would be no possibility of transacting business unless,
having resolved to abide by those well settled rules which have been
established by the learned in parliamentary law, that determination is
adhered to. If the house is bent upon upsetting its former proceedings
every moment---to pass a resolution at one moment, and another resolution the next moment---to decide a question, and immediately afterwards
declare that it was not decided, it must be evident that no business can be
transacted. It would be in the power of two or three disorderly persons
to keep a deliberative body in a constant state of confusion.

Now, no point is more definitely settled in parliamentary law than this:
that where a decision has been made, and declared by the Chair, that
decision must stand, and can only be overcome by a resolution of the
house rescinding the same. The proper time for calling the yeas and
nays is when a question is about to be put. If the gentlemen who are
in the minority did not think proper to call for the yeas and nays at first,
it is to be taken for granted they did not desire the yeas and nays to be
called at all. The Chair, therefore, hopes it is apparent to every member of the house, that a call for the yeas and nays after a question has
been decided, if permitted by the Chair, would result only in protracting
useless discussion, and instead of being a purely deliberative body we
should degenerate to a mere collection of gentlemen guided by no rules,
holding colloquial conversation upon the floor, every person talking as
long as he may please, and upon any subject. Hence deliberative bodies
appoint a moderator or chairman, to the end that this state of anarchy

may be avoided. That officer should act with the utmost impartiality, and sacrifice everything else to the preservation of order. In the present instance, the Chair, therefore decides, that when the question was taken and decided by a proper count, and the count was reported to the house, it was a decision which cannot be overturned, except by a resolution rescinding the action of the body. It is always in the power of the Convention to pass upon the decision of its presiding officer, and it may be done, if it is thought necessary, on the present occasion.

Mr. B. O. DUNCAN. I call for the special order of the day, which is the Ordinance to divide the State into four Congressional districts.

Mr. R. C. DeLARGE moved that the special order be discharged, or indefinitely postponed.

On motion of Mr. W. E. JOHNSTON, of Sumter, the motion to discharge or indefinitely postpone was laid upon the table.

The ordinance was then read a second time.

Mr. R. B. ELLIOTT. I move the ordinance now be made the special order for to-morrow. There are certain changes proposed which do not meet the approbation of the people of some portions of the State, and I do not propose to allow so important a matter to be hurried through this body. I know that if time is given us, this ordinance never can be passed in its present shape.

Mr. F. L. CARDOZO. Why can you not discuss it now, as well as at any other time ?

Mr. R. B. ELLIOTT. Because there are certain facts to be presented which are not at present in our possession, but which we may have to-morrow. I hope under these circumstances that the motion will prevail.

The hour of recess having arrived, the Convention adjourned until three o'clock, P. M.

AFTERNOON SESSION.

The Convention re-assembled at three P. M.

Mr. T. J. COGHLAN moved to suspend the rules in order to move a reconsideration of the section prolonging the term of the Comptroller-General, Secretary of State and Treasurer.

Mr. R. B. ELLIOTT. I hope the rules will be suspended for the purpose of considering this subject again. If the rules are suspended, I hope the motion to lay the motion to reconsider on the table will be voted down. I am confident if this matter is brought before the house a second time for its consideration, that it will be decided in a different manner from what it was this morning. Many of the members voted under a mistake. I think everything we do should be done only after the most careful consideration. I hope the motion to suspend the rules will be carried.

The question was then taken on the motion to suspend, and decided in the negative.

The special order, which was the consideration of the Ordinance to divide the State into four Congressional Districts, was taken up.

Mr. E. W. M. MACKEY moved to postpone the special order to ten A. M. to-morrow.

Mr. F. J MOSES, Jr. I hope the motion to postpone this matter will be voted down. I see no reason why this Ordinance should be postponed from day to day. We are ready to discuss it now.

The question being taken on postponement, it was decided in the negative.

On motion of Mr. B. F. WHITTEMORE, the Ordinance was taken up by sections, and section one was read as follows :

SECTION 1. *We, the People of the State of South Carolina, in Convention assembled, do ordain,* That the State of South Carolina shall be, and the same is hereby, divided into four Congressional Districts, as follows: First Congressional District to be composed of the Counties of Lancaster, Chesterfield, Marlborough, Darlington, Marion, Horry, Georgetown, Williamsburg, Sumter, Clarendon, and Kershaw ; Second Congressional District, to be composed of the Counties of Charleston, Colleton, Beaufort, and Barnwell; Third Congressional District, to be composed of the Counties of Orangeburg, Lexington, Richland, Newberry, Edgefield, Abbeville, and Anderson; and the fourth Congressional District, to be composed of the Counties of Oconee, Pickens, Greenville, Laurens, Spartanburg, Union, York, Chester, and Fairfield.

Mr. C. M. WILDER. I move to amend by striking out " Anderson" from the Third District, and substitute " Fairfield," and to insert " Anderson" in the Fourth in place of "Fairfield."

Mr. B. O. DUNCAN. I would merely state with regard to this matter, that we considered it very carefully in committee, and after comparing statistics with registered voters, we divided them as nearly equal as we could, and as we thought best for all four Congressional Districts. The committee are entirely united in the plan proposed.

Mr. E. W. M. MACKEY. I really hope, as this subject is of such a peculiar nature, and many members are not prepared to discuss it, that it will be postponed. It is a matter altogether of party issues, and the arguments are hardly proper to be brought up in the Convention. If postponed, we may consider it in caucus. I move that it be postponed until half-past ten Monday morning.

The motion was agreed to.

Mr. J. L. NEAGLE reported the following Ordinance of the Special Committee of Nine, appointed to draft an Ordinance providing for the ratification of the Constitution and Ordinances of the Convention, and for the election of State officers:

AN ORDINANCE

To provide for the Ratification of the Constitution and Ordinances, and for the Election of Certain Officers.

SECTION 1. *We, the People of South Carolina, by our delegates in Convention met, do ordain,* That on the 14th, 15th and 16th days of April, 1868, the Constitution and Ordinances adopted by this Convention shall be submitted for ratification or rejection to the registered voters of this State, and also that, at the same time, an election shall be held for Governor, Lieutenant-Governor, Secretary of State, Comptroller-General, Treasurer, Attorney-General, Superintendent of Education, Adjutant and Inspector-General, and members of the General Assembly; and, furthermore, that at the same time an election shall be held in each Congressional District for a member of the House of Representatives of of the United States Congress.

SEC. 2. That the election for the ratification or rejection of the Constitution and Ordinances, and for the aforementioned officers, shall be held at such places, and under such regulations as may be prescribed by the Commanding General of this Military District, and the returns made to him, as directed by law.

SEC. 3. That in voting for or against the adoption of the Constitution and Ordinances, the words "For Constitution and Ordinances," or "Against Constitution and Ordinances," shall be printed on the ballot of each voter; but no voter shall vote for or against the Constitution and Ordinances on a separate ballot from that cast by him for officers.

SEC. 4. That a Board of Commissioners is hereby appointed, to consist of Messrs. E. W. M. Mackey, F. L. Cardozo, A. J. Ransier, and C. C. Bowen, who shall keep an office for the transaction of business in the City of Charleston, and who may employ such clerical forces as may be necessary, and who are empowered to cause to be appointed suitable persons for managers of election in each county in the State, to hold the election provided for by this Ordinance. Said Commissioners shall have power to use all the necessary means to secure a full and fair vote upon the Constitution and Ordinances, and the election of officers.

SEC. 5. In case of the death, resignation or inability to serve of any member, or members of said Board of Commissioners, the President of this Convention shall have power to fill such vacancy.

SEC. 6. That should the said Board of Commissioners deem it neces-

98

sary or expedient, they are hereby authorized to extend in any county or counties, election precinct or precincts, the number of days during which the election aforesaid is to be held, from three to five.

SEC. 7. That within thirty days after the ratification of this Constitution, an election shall be held in and for each county, at such time and under such regulations as may be prescribed by said Board of Commissioners, for the election of all county officers required by this Constitution to be elected by the people. And the Board shall have authority to call elections for all municipal officers, at present elected by the people, at the same time and place, and subject to such regulations as said Board may prescribe, not inconsistent with this Constitution or the charters of such municipal bodies.

SEC. 8. That the Commissioners herein appointed shall receive for their services five dollars per day in United States currency, or its equivalent in bills receivable of this State.

SEC. 9. That the President of this Convention, upon the requisition of said Board of Commissioners, shall have power to draw from the Treasury of the State all money necessary to pay the expenses incurred under this Ordinance, and which the General Commanding this Military District is not authorized to assume.

SEC. 10. That the said Board of Commissioners, as soon as they have carried out the provisions of this Ordinance, shall make to the General Assembly a report of their proceedings, and a statement of the moneys expended by them.

Mr. J. L. NEAGLE. I move that this Ordinance be printed, and made the special order for half-past ten to-morrow. I make this motion because the military are anxious to have this Ordinance passed, so as to make arrangements concerning the election.

Mr. R. B. ELLIOTT moved to amend by making it the special order for half-past three o'clock Monday.

Mr. E. W. M. MACKEY. I have been in consultation with some of the military officers who have this matter in charge, and they have urged the passage of this Ordinance as soon as possible. The only reason it has been postponed to this time, was the illness of General Canby. The committee waited to have a full consultation with General Canby in reference to the county elections. The military desired the appointment of a Board of Commissioners to arrange the different districts, appoint managers of elections, select the different voting places, and so on.

Mr. R. B. ELLIOTT. It seems to me the views presented are not weighty enough to justify us in hurrying a measure of this kind through. It is, apparently, a very important Ordinance, and demands serious consideration.

The question being taken on the motion to postpone until half-past three o'clock Monday, it was decided in the negative.

Mr. F. L. CARDOZO. I move that the Ordinance be printed, and made the special order for four o'clock to-morrow afternoon. The Ordinance is a very simple one ; simply providing the time and manner in which the election shall take place. The military authorities always require a long routine, and they must have a week at least before issuing the necessary orders. We desire to have the elections about the middle of April.

The question was then taken on the motion to make the Ordinance the special order for half-past four o'clock to-morrow, and decided in the affirmative.

The unfinished business, which was the consideration of section three of Article — of the Constitution, on Miscellaneous Provisions of the Constitution, was taken up.

On motion of Mr. B. O. DUNCAN, section three was stricken out, the provisions therein contained having been already inserted in a previous part of the Constitution.

Section four, prohibiting lotteries and the sale of lottery tickets, passed without debate.

On motion of Mr. F. J. MOSES, Jr., section five, providing for a Great Seal of the State, was stricken out, the provision having been already incorporated in the executive part of the Constitution.

Section six, relative to the right of the people to assemble peacably, already provided for in the Bill of Rights, was stricken out.

Section seven, relative to the State Library, passed to a third reading without debate.

Section eight was read as follows :

SECTION 8. The General Assembly may direct by law in what manner, and in what courts suits may be brought against the State.

Mr. R. G. HOLMES moved to strike out the section and substitute the following :

The Supreme Court shall have authority to inquire upon petition as to the validity of all obligations or damages alleged to be due from this State to any resident or citizen of the United States, and certify its opinions to the General Assembly for its consideration. The General Assembly shall provide by law, for carrying into operation the provisions of this section.

Mr. B. F. RANDOLPH. After the committee reported this section, they again had the matter under consideration, and concluded it was not possible for a citizen to sue the government of which he was a subject.

They, therefore, proposed to arrange it, so that a citizen could apply by petition to the Supreme Court, which could decide upon a case, and the decision be presented to the General Assembly for its action. For instance, suppose the militia were called out. Private property may be destroyed, or a house burned, in an attempt to suppress a riot. The person owning the property should have some means by which he can recover the value of his property. In a case of that kind, we propose the person who has suffered loss may make application to the Supreme Court, which shall consider the case, and present its decision to the General Assembly. The General Assembly may then pass upon the claim, and if substantiated, order it to be paid.

Mr. R. C. DeLARGE. I move an indefinite postponement of the substitute.

Mr. J. J. WRIGHT. I hope that motion will be voted down, and I hope the the substitute will not be adopted. Such a clause should not be inserted in our Constitution. We expect to establish a Superior or a Supreme Court of the State, and the General Assembly will provide what the appellate jurisdiction of that Court shall be. It is rather a novel course of procedure for a citizen of the United States to present a petition to the Supreme Court of a State, and after a decision has been rendered by that Court, to present such decision to the General Assembly for final decision.

Mr. R. G. HOLMES. How do you propose to collect dues from a State ?

Mr. J. J. WRIGHT. I propose to collect them by filing a declaration or petition in the Supreme Court of the United States. I might file it with the Court of Common Pleas, but if tried there, and I am not satisfied with the decision of the jury, I have a right to appeal to the highest Court of the State, or the Supreme Court of the United States. But it would be a novel procedure for a citizen of another State—Georgia or North Carolina, for instance—to file a petition in the Supreme Court of the State, and if not satisfied with its decision, to appeal to the Legislature of the State. If there is any appeal from the decision of the Supreme Court of the State, it should go to the Supreme Court of the United States. To provide otherwise, would be a direct blow at the Supreme Court of the United States, which exercises jurisdiction over all the States for the benefit of any citizen of the United States.

Mr. R. G. HOLMES. It is only proposed that the Supreme Court should pass an opinion, and that the opinion should go before the Legislature.

Mr. J. J. WRIGHT. All we get from the Supreme Court is their opinion, and that opinion is final. We do not propose, after the highest judicial power in the State has rendered an opinion, that there shall be any appeal unless to the Supreme Court of the United States. If a case comes to the Supreme Court of the State, and the decision is made, unless a question of constitutionality is moved, there is no appeal from that decision. To refer a decision of the Supreme Court of the State to the General Assembly, would not only be an outrage upon the people of our own State, but also upon the people of other States having cases before the Supreme Court of this State. We do not want the General Assembly to consume their time over such matters. If citizens of our own State, or of any other State, are dissatisfied with the decision of the Supreme Court of the State, then let them go into the United States Courts, where such cases properly belong. For the purpose of giving every citizen of each State an opportunity to present his case and obtain justice in any State, United States Courts have been established in every State of the Union. Whenever any citizen considers he has been wronged or deprived of his rights, he has the remedy of final petition in any United States Court.

Mr. J. M. RUTLAND. It seems to me that the gentleman from Beaufort has taken up this matter with too much zeal and feeling. It occurs to me, that the proposition embraces a very simple process by which the citizen of a State may obtain his rights, without being harrassed or annoyed by going through the long process of applying to the United States Courts and suing a State. It is a simple mode of giving a citizen redress who may have suffered at the hands of the State. I hope it will receive every consideration. The mode is by petition upon oath to the Supreme Court of the State, to ask its opinion upon a question of justice. It simply asks the opinion of the Supreme Court as to whether there is justice in the demand of the citizen who has a suit against the State. Suppose the Supreme Court certifies to the Legislature that, in their opinion, this citizen has a just claim against the State ; there is scarcely a doubt but that in nine cases out of ten the Legislature would be governed by that opinion. I regard this as a simple mode of redress for a citizen who has suffered wrong from the State, and is a much less expensive and troublesome mode than has heretofore existed.

Mr. J. J. WRIGHT. Would you desire a citizen of Georgia or North Carolina to come here and file a petition in the Supreme Court of the State for any claims against this State ?

Mr. J. M. RUTLAND. I do not think this contemplates any such proceeding, unless that citizen had property in the State, which property has been destroyed by the authority of this State. If that is the case, let him come here and obtain redress in the same manner as if he had sold property in the State. It is to facilitate the settlement of claims of citizens of South Carolina against the State of South Carolina.

Mr. J. J. WRIGHT. Is it the duty of the Judges of the Supreme Court, or the Attorney-General, to give an opinion upon matters of this kind?

Mr. J. M. RUTLAND. That depends upon the action of this Convention. If the Ordinance passes, then it is made the duty of the Supreme Court. If not passed, the Attorney-General might or might not be called upon to give an opinion.

Mr. B. F. RANDOLPH. Do you think if this Ordinance passes, the Supreme Court would entertain a case not really just and proper in itself?

Mr. J. M. RUTLAND. I might have to entertain a case possibly improper, in order to hear it on its merits. The Supreme Court cannot say whether a case is just or unjust until it has heard the testimony.

Mr. C. P. LESLIE. Are you not of the opinion that, sooner or later, if a man desires to petition the Almighty for forgiveness of sins, he will have to go into some political operation to get at Him?

Mr J. M RUTLAND. I do not give spiritual advice.

Mr. F. J. MOSES, Jr. Is it proposed that a man should petition the Legislature for the settlement of his claims, and then that the Legislature shall refer the case to the Supreme Court for its opinion?

Mr. B. F. RANDOLPH. The design of the substitute is that a citizen may present his petition with the evidence before the Supreme Court for its opinion. If the Judges decide in favor of the petition, then the case may go before the General Assembly.

Mr. F. J. MOSES, Jr. That does not take away the absurdity of the proposition. It is certainly setting a new precedent in South Carolina. Although the gentleman from Fairfield says we are not dealing with the past, still while this Convention proposes to reconstruct everything, we do not go upon the principle that nothing good can come out of Nazareth, but wherever we find any thing good, we desire to adopt it as ours. The State has always had in office an Attorney-General and five Solicitors. It has always been the duty of those gentlemen to be present during the sessions of the General Assembly, and any member or members desiring legal advice of any kind, on any question in which the General Assembly or either House was interested, had the privilege of applying to the Attorney-General or Solicitors. Suppose such a measure as this substituted, and the decision of the Supreme Court, after it is rendered, goes to the Legislature, what a scene will be witnessed! Members of the Legislature would undertake to argue the validity of the law points made in that decision. It would be additional expense and trouble. You will put too much work upon the shoulders of your Judges. The Attorney-General and Solicitors are paid to attend to this business. Their salaries are paid out of the State for that purpose. It would be a new scene to have lawyers applying to the Legislature for every little claim or account. I am unwilling to degrade the Judiciary, or depart from the excellent practice set us in the past. In addition to this, it will be remembered we have in every State, as has been said, United States Courts organized and established for just such cases as this. This measure would take these cases out of those Courts and send them to the Supreme Court of the State. What an absurdity; I hope the substitute will be voted down.

The previous question was called and sustained. The President stated the Chairman on Miscellaneous Provisions of the Constitution was entitled to the floor for fifteen minutes.

Mr. B. F. RANDOLPH. I yield my time to the gentleman from Beaufort (Mr. HOLMES).

Mr. R. G. HOLMES. This is a very simple measure proposed to obtain speedy justice. The design is to permit a man who has a claim against the State to petition the Supreme Court, and have a hearing. When the claim is heard, then he can go before the Legislature. There is no way by which a State can be sued in the United States Courts. This is a simple, easy, and most expeditious mode for a party having claims against the State to obtain justice. The decision of the Supreme Court in such cases would have great weight before the Legislature.

Mr. F. J. MOSES, Jr. Does the gentleman not know, that in every Legislature there is among the committees a Committee on Claims, to whom all such matters are referred? After it has been so referred, that committee can easily apply to the Attorney-General or Solicitors for their opinion.

Mr. R. G. HOLMES. I know all that; but this is prevented by bringing the case before a competent tribunal.

Mr C. C. BOWEN. If a man has a suit against the State for five hundred dollars, is he not entitled to a trial before a jury?

Mr. R. G. HOLMES. The State cannot be sued. I endeavored to sue the State, but could find no way to do it. I could not get the case in the United States Court, or any other Court. There is no way to arrive at cases of this kind, except through the Legislature.

Mr. R. SMALLS. Did you obtain the services of a lawyer?

Mr. D. H. CHAMBERLAIN. Is not the Supreme Court the highest judicial power of the State, and does not this substitute make it subordinate to the Legislature? Does it not, in fact, make the Legislature the supreme judicial power of the State?

Mr. R. G. HOLMES. Of course, it makes the Legislature above the Supreme Court. We desire the decision of the Supreme Court in these to be submitted to the Legislature.

Mr. B. F. RANDOLPH. I desire to submit two propositions. First, that citizens in this State, and many other States, in order to recover against a State claims or damages, have been in the habit of petitioning the Legislature. That being the case, some means must be provided by which those citizens can recover their claims. The next point is, what is the best and most simple and effective method to recover? The citizen cannot sue a State. Therefore, is it not better for the citizen to be permitted to file his petition in the Supreme Court, appear before that Court with his evidence, and if the Court decide in his favor, then the petition goes to the Legislature. And I submit, when the Supreme Court shall have passed upon any such matter, the Legislature will acquiesce in the decision.

Mr. F. J. MOSES, Jr. How long do you propose to give the Supreme Court to make up its decision? Suppose the Judge puts the petition in his pocket and keeps it there.

Mr. B. F. RANDOLPH. If we have such a Justice or such a Supreme Court that cares nothing about the welfare of the citizens of the State, then it would be better perhaps to abolish the Supreme Court altogether. The gentleman proposes to submit these claims to the Attorney-General, the Solicitors, Committee on Claims, &c., but I submit that such a proceeding will only complicate matters. I submit to the Convention whether the opinion of those officers would be regarded as much in the eye of the Legislature as the opinion of the Supreme Court.

The question has been asked if the Supreme Court is not the highest judicial power in the State. We do not propose to make it superior to the Legislature, but when the Supreme Court sends its decision, accompanied by a recommendation, to the Legislature, then the Legislature, we expect, will act in accordance with that recommendation.

Mr. F. J. MOSES, Jr. Suppose the Legislature does not agree, then which is the superior or inferior power?

Mr. B. F. RANDOLPH. Suppose your Solicitor or Attorney-General, or Committee on Claims decide, and the Legislature decide to the contrary.

Mr. D. H. CHAMBERLAIN. Is it not true, that under this provision you propose that citizens of other States may appear before the Supreme

Court and file their claims? Would not that be an unconstitutional proceeding?

Mr. B. F. RANDOLPH. I think the Supreme Court could decide whether it would be proper to entertain such cases. I suppose we will have judges who know their business, and who will not undertake to investigate a case that does not come properly before them.

The question being put on the adoption of the substitute, it was rejected.

Mr. D. H. CHAMBERLAIN moved to reconsider the vote by which section eight passed to its third reading, which was agreed to.

Mr. D. H. CHAMBERLAIN moved to strike out all after the word "manner" and insert "claims against the State may be established and adjusted." I consider the word "suits" improper. It should be claims. Claims may be for actions, damages and everything else brought against the State.

Mr. R. G. HOLMES. I hope the amendment will not prevail, but that the section will be stricken out. We cannot afford to have claims established against the State but in one way, and that is through petitions.

Mr. J. J. WRIGHT. I hope the section will not be stricken out. There are many persons in this State who have claims against the State, and whose property was destroyed by the State. It is the prerogative of the Legislature to devise means by which claims can be adjusted. A committee is usually appointed by the Legislature for the purpose of investigating these claims, and the report of that committee is either sustained or rejected by the Legislature. If the citizen of this State or any other State is dissatisfied with the decision of the Legislature, then his final remedy is to file his declaration in the United States Court.

The question being taken on the adoption of the amendment, it was agreed to, and section eight passed to its third reading.

Section nine was read as follows:

SEC. 9. Divorces from the bonds of matrimony shall not be allowed, but by the judgment of a Court, as shall be prescribed by law.

Mr. E. W. M. MACKEY moved to strike out this section and to insert it in the judiciary department of the Constitution.

Mr. B. F. RANDOLPH. There is considerable difference between the two sections. This section declares that the Court only shall grant a divorce. According to the section in the legislative department, the Legislature may grant them also.

Mr. F. J. MOSES, Jr. The section referred to in the judiciary

99

report provides that the Supreme Court alone shall have jurisdiction of divorce cases. This section is simply declaratory of the fact that divorces shall be granted. There is no necessity for striking out the section.

Mr. E. W. M. MACKEY withdrew his motion.

Section ten was read as follows :

SEC. 10. No person who denies the existence of a God shall hold any office under this Constitution, nor be allowed his oath in any Court.

Mr. E. W. M. MACKEY moved to strike out the entire section.

Mr. B. F. RANDOLPH moved to strike out the letter "a" before the word "God."

Mr. B. F. WHITTEMORE moved to strike out the words "a God" and substitute the words "Supreme Being."

Mr. E. W. M. MACKEY moved to lay that motion on the table, which was not agreed to.

The question was taken upon striking out the entire section and decided in the negative:

Mr. D. H. CHAMBERLAIN. I desire to ask the Chairman of the Committee what is meant by the last clause of this section. Is it meant that no person who believes in the existence of a Supreme Being shall be allowed to give evidence in Court, or does he mean what the language says, he shall not take oath or affirm.

Mr. B. F. RANDOLPH. He could affirm, but not take his oath.

The PRESIDENT. The Chair understands, that a man who does not believe in a Supreme Being must not take an oath, but one that does must take an oath.

Mr. C. C. BOWEN. I move to strike out all after the word "constitution."

Mr. B. F. RANDOLPH. I hope the clause will not be stricken out. A person who has not the confidence of the people, so that he may hold office, should not be allowed to take an oath. I would not believe him at all.

Mr. C. C. BOWEN. It is always left to the rules of evidence of a Court to say whether a man's oath or affirmation shall be taken. It is to be hoped the clause will be stricken out.

Mr. R. C. DeLARGE. I trust the motion will prevail. It has been customary to either take a witness' oath or affirmation, and if a man did not believe in the existence of a Supreme Being, he was permitted to affirm. His evidence can be taken for what it is worth.

The question was taken on striking out the words "nor be allowed his oath in any Court," and decided in the affirmative, so the words were stricken out, and the section, as amended, passed to its third reading.

Section eleven was stricken out on the first reading.

Section twelve was read and passed to a third reading, as follows:

SEC. 12. The printing of the laws, journals, bills, legislative documents and papers for each branch of the General Assembly, with the printing required for the Executive and other departments of State, shall be let, on contract, in such manner as shall be prescribed by law.

Section thirteen was stricken out on its first reading.

Section fourteen was read as follows:

SEC. 14. The real and personal property of a woman, held at the time of her marriage, or that which she may thereafter acquire, either by gift, grant or inheritance, or devise, shall not be subject to levy and sale for her husband's debts; but may be bequeathed, devised, or alienated by her, the same as if she were unmarried; *Provided,* That no gift or grant from the husband to the wife shall be detrimental to the just claims of his creditors.

Mr. F. E. WILDER offered the following substitute.

SEC. 14. The Legislature shall provide for the protection of the rights of women in acquiring and possessing property, real, personal, and mixed, seperate and apart from the husband; and shall also provide for their equal rights and possession of their children.

Mr. R. C. DeLARGE moved to postpone the consideration of the substitute until to-morrow, and make it the special order for 11 o'clock, which was adopted.

Mr. E. W. M. MACKEY introduced the following as additional sections to the article on the Miscellaneous Provisions of the Constitution were read a first time.

SEC. 15. The General Assembly shall provide for the removal of all causes which may be pending when this Constitution goes into effect to courts created by the same.

SEC. 16. The provisions of this Constitution concerning the terms of residence necessary to enable persons to hold certain offices, therein mentioned, shall not be held to apply to officers chosen by the people at the first election, or by the General Assembly at its first session.

SEC. 17. All laws of this State now in force, not inconsistent with this Constitution, shall continue in force until they shall expire by their own limitation, or be amended or repealed by the General Assembly.

On motion of Mr. D. H. CHAMBERLAIN, section sixteen was referred to the Committee on Franchise and Elections.

Mr. B. O. DUNCAN moved that section seventeen be referred to the Committee on the Judiciary.

Mr. E. W. M. MACKEY. I hope that motion will not prevail. This provision is in nearly all miscellaneous portions of the Constitutions of other States.

Mr. R. B. ELLIOTT. I hope the section will be referred to the Committee on the Judiciary. I think it the duty of the Committee on the Judiciary to find out whether it would be expedient or safe to make any such provision in this Constitution at the present time, and if so, whether it is proper to insert it in the miscellaneous portions of the Constitution.

Mr. C. C. BOWEN. I think it is usual to make a separate article of schedules. It appears in that way in almost all other constitutions of the State.

The question being put on the motion to refer to the Judiciary Committee, a division was called for, and resulted : ayes 37, nays 29.

On motion of Mr. R. J. DONALDSON the rules were suspended, and sections fifteen and sixteen of the Miscellaneous Provisions of the Constitution were read a second time and passed to a third reading.

The PRESIDENT announced that all portions of the Constitution which had been submitted by the different committees had passed to a third reading, with the exception of the report of the Committee on Franchise and Elections.

Mr. T. J. ROBERTSON asked and obtained leave to present a petition from Mr. R. M. Wallace, a citizen of Columbia, for the removal of political disabilities. The petition was referred to the Committee on Petitions.

The hour for the consideration of the special order having arrived, being the consideration of an Ordinance to create a Board of Land Commissioners : it was read a second time.

Mr. L. S. LANGLEY moved to strike out the word "thereof" in the 4th line, in section one, which was adopted, and sections one, two and three passed to a third reading.

Section four was read, and Mr. R. G. HOLMES offered to amend by inserting after the word "the" in sixth line, the words "authority of the," which was adopted, and the section, so amended, passed to a third reading.

Sections five and six were read, and severally passed to a third reading

On motion of Mr. E. W. M. MACKEY the Convention adjourned to 10 o'clock to-morrow morning.

The Convention then adjourned.

FORTY-FIFTH DAY.

Saturday, March 7, 1868.

The Convention assembled at 10 A. M., and was called to order by the PRESIDENT.

Prayer was offered by the Rev. J. M. RUNION.

The roll was called, and a quorum answering to their names, the PRESIDENT announced the Convention ready to proceed to business.

The Journal of Friday was read and approved.

The special order, which was the consideration of the fourteenth section of the report of the Committee on Miscellaneous Provisions of the Constitution, was taken up.

Mr. WM. McKINLAY. I desire to offer an amendment to the substitute offered by the member from Beaufort (Mr. F. E. WILDER). I regard the matter as of the highest importance, and do not think it should be inserted in the Constitution. This matter should be left to to the Legislature. Let that body pass some special act upon the subject, or let them alter and amend whatever law they make upon the subject, as experience may deem expedient.

I move to strike out all after the word "further," in the first line, and insert "the General Assembly shall pass laws to secure to married women the right to their separate estates."

Mr. R. C. DeLARGE moved to amend the section by adding the following:

And, provided further, that a schedule of such real and personal property, under the hands and seals of husband and wife, if held at the time of marriage, shall, within sixty days of the time of marriage, be recorded in the office of the Register of Mesne Conveyance of the Judicial District, in which the said wife was at the time of her marriage resident. And, provided further, that a schedule of such real and personal property as may be acquired by the said wife subsequent to marriage, shall, within thirty days from such acquisition, be recorded in the office of the Register of Mesne Conveyance of the Judicial District, of which the said wife, at the time of such acquisition, is resident.

The subject of this section, as I understand it, is the protection of a woman in the rights of property that she may have had, or secured previous to marriage, and to protect her in such property as she may acquire by gift, grant, or bequest after marriage. I agree with the section, but I think it is necessary that some such clause as I have presented here, should be added to prevent fraud. Unless this is done, a wide field will be opened to fraud. It would be an easy matter for married persons to defraud a creditor, unless the property of the wife is registered in due form before marriage, so that the creditors of the husband may be able to ascertain what property actually belonged to the woman. A schedule of the property owned before marriage by the woman, would give all the necessary information ; what we desire is to protect the woman who is so unfortunate as to marry a profligate or a drunkard; to protect the property she has at the time of marriage, so that it shall not be forfeited by a drunken husband. We also propose to secure the hard earnings that may be bequeathed by a mother on her death bed to a child, so that it cannot be taken and squandered by the husband or father of the child.

Mr. C. C. BOWEN. I desire to offer an amendment, and to insert after the word " before," on the third line, the words " shall be held as her separate property and." I shall be decidedly in favor of the section reported by the committee, if this amendment be adopted, for I conceive that it affords full protection to the property of the wife. It has been urged that the husband, becoming in debt, may transfer his property to his wife, but such a transfer is almost impossible under the last clause of the section. To the plan suggested by the delegate from Charleston, of filing a schedule of property, I object.

Mr. R. C. DeLARGE. It is provided that a schedule of all property acquired by the wife shall be filed, whether acquired after or before marriage.

Mr. C. C. BOWEN. I think that is unnecessary. Should the question be raised, it will be easy enough for the wife to go into Court, and show whether she came in possession of her property by will, gift, or otherwise. There is no chance for anybody to be defrauded. Our proposition is to secure to the wife all of her property against the debts contracted by her husband. If left to the Legislature, as has been suggested, that body may pass no such law of protection, and the wife's property will still be held responsible for her husband's misfortunes. This, therefore, is the proper time and place to put the matter beyond all doubt.

Mr. B. F. RANDOLPH. I move to amend by inserting after the

words " a devise," the words "or otherwise." I deem this addition necessary to complete the protection which we propose to secure; and hope, likewise, the amendment last offered (by Mr. BOWEN), will be adopted. The Solicitor has given his opinion upon this subject, and I am astonished that men of no legal experience whatever should rise upon this floor and attempt to counteract that opinion. The gentleman from Charleston (Mr. DeLARGE), looking far into the foggy future, has thus attempted to oppose the experience of gentlemen more learned than himself; but I am inclined to follow the counsels that have been given.

Mr. C. P. LESLIE. Do I understand that the Solicitor has fully approved of that section?

Mr. B. F. RANDOLPH. The Solicitor has given his opinion as to the bearing of this section upon the rights of woman, and her ability to possess and control her own property.

Mr. R. C. DeLARGE. Did not the Solicitor disapprove of the section?

Mr. B. F. RANDOLPH. He did not.

Mr. J. M. ALLEN. I did not think it was necessary to rise on this floor in defence of woman, nor did I believe there was a man in this Convention unwilling to secure to woman the property to which, in the eyes of the law and of mankind, she should be justly entitled.

Mr. R. C DeLARGE. Is the gentleman from Greenville in favor of woman's suffrage?

Mr. J. M. ALLEN. I am not, nor do I believe in that class of persons who carry poodle dogs, and follow in the trail of mere fashion; but I do love and honor those noble women of South Carolina, who, while their husbands were in the field fighting for a cause which I detested, exhibited a spirit of heroism and devotion to what they conceived to be principle, and suffered to make that principle successful. It is consistent with the character of the sex; and, whether right or wrong, I am not one who will take revenge upon women for showing such a virtue. Nearly all of the States of the Union have passed laws for the protection of women's property; and shall we, when we have passed page after page of enactments, explaining the rights of man, stop here and make a wry face at a single clause? These women may be sneering at us to-day; but, for one, I wish to see the law laid down which will protect them in the enjoyment of every dollar of property which they own, or may hereafter acquire, and I hope that this measure will pass without a dissenting voice. I appeal to you who have lived here all your lives, and seen women suffer from the hands of the fortune hunters; the plausible villains, who, after securing the property of their wives, have squandered it in gambling and drinking; a class of men who are still going about the country boasting that they intend to marry a plantation, and take the woman as an incumbrance. A great deal has been said about injustice and fraud. What greater fraud can be perpetrated than to spend the inheritance of a wife in debauchery and crime? Shall we allow this to be done in order to prevent some smaller fraud? There are plenty of men incapable of taking care of property, and for such there should be a law which shall itself protect the portion which belongs to the wife. We are ourselves poor men now, but should we succeed in saving a little property, and leaving it to our wives, it is not a comfortable thought that when we are dead, some villain may marry our widows, and squander what we have saved for the care and comfort of those we love. It is for these reasons that I hope this section, which promises protection to woman, will be adopted.

Mr. B. F. RANDOLPH. Without making a speech, I desire to say a word or two, by way of explanation. After this report had been considered by the committee, I presented it to the Solicitor for his consideration, and it met with his unqualified approval. It is due to the gentleman from Greenville (Mr. ALLEN,) to say that he presented this section to the committee just as it stands.

Mr. R. B. ELLIOTT. I rise to express the hope that the section will pass with the amendment offered by the gentleman from Charleston (Mr. BOWEN), to insert the words " shall be held as her separate property." I believe that it will secure all the legal rights of a woman in this State. Enough has been said upon the subject to put us in possession of the facts, and to enable us to form our judgment, and I, therefore, call the previous question.

The call was sustained.

Mr. B. F. RANDOLPH—(Under the rule being entitled to the floor). I presume that if this section meets with much opposition, it will come from the unmarried members of the Convention who may be looking for rich wives. But there are those here who are already married, who have mothers, sisters and daughters, all of whom may come into possession of property; and I ask if it is just that those who are so near and dear to us, shall be left in a position where a man without principle may, by marriage, take possession of their property, and leave them dependent upon the cold charities of the world? It is a common thing for men to talk about marrying rich wives, and to marry them for no other purpose than to squander their property. To protect this class of women, and to prevent them from falling into the hands of scoundrels, is the object of this section, and I confidently look to this Convention to pass it. I yield the balance of my time to the gentleman from Charleston.

Mr. C. C. BOWEN. The object of this section has been so often explained that it is scarcely necessary for me to dwell upon it. It has been said that a husband may give all of his property to his wife. I admit it, and on what principles are you going to stop him from so doing? It cannot be done. Nor does this measure contemplate it. All this section proposes to do is to protect the woman against the bad debts of her husband, to secure that to her of which she has come into possession, and enable her to hold separately the property which is by right her own. Suppose, for instance, a person was going to buy a piece of property from a man's wife, what would be the first thing he would do? First, he would ascertain whether she had any property to dispose of; and secondly, how she came in possession of it? If obtained within the purview of this section, her right to sell would be unquestionable. If fraud is perpetrated, it may be proved in the same manner as any other fraud under the insolvent debtors act. I can, therefore, see no objection to the passage of this section as amended. I hope this Convention will not leave the matter to be acted upon by the Legislature; for if we acknowledge the principle at all, it is competent for us to declare it, and incorporate it in the Constitution which we are about to give to the people of South Carolina.

The question then being taken on the amendment of Mr. B. F. RANDOLPH, it was decided in the affirmative.

The amendment offered by Mr. C. C. BOWEN was also agreed to.

The amendment offered by Mr. R. C. DeLARGE was rejected; also the amendment offered by Mr. McKINLAY.

The main question now being upon the passage of section fourteen as amended to a third reading, the yeas and nays were called, and resulted as follows: Yeas, 88; Nays, 8. Absent, 25.

YEAS.—Messrs. Allen, Arnim, Becker, Bell, Bowen, Bonum, Boozer, Burton, Brockenton, Byas, E. I. Cain, Camp, Coghlan, Chamberlain, Clinton, Cook, Collins, Corley, Darrington, Davis, DeLarge, Dickson, Dill, Dogan, Driffle, Duncan, Edwards, Elliott, Foster, Gentry, Goss, Gray, Harris, C. D. Hayne, J. N. Hayne, Henderson, Holmes, Humbird, Hurley, Jacobs, Jillson, S. Johnson, W. B. Johnson, J. W. Johnson, L B. Johnson, W. E. Johnston, Joiner, H. Jones, C. Jones, Langley, George Lee, S. Lee, Lomax, Leslie, E. W. M. Mackey, Mayer, Mead, Miller, Milford, Nance, Nash, Nelson, Neagle, Newell, Nuckles, Parker, Randolph, Rainey, Ransier, Rivers, Robertson, Rose, Runion, Rutland, Sanders, Stubbs, A. Thompson, S. B. Thompson, B. A. Thomp-

100

son, Viney, Webb, Whittemore, White, F. E. Wilder, C. M. Wilder, Wingo, Wooley, Wright—88.

NAYS—The President; Messrs. Alexander, Bryce, W J. McKinlay, Wm. McKinlay, McDaniels, Owens, Shrewsbury—8

ABSENT.—Messrs R. H. Cain, Cardozo, Chestnut, Craig, Crews, Donaldson, H. E. Hayne, Hunter, Jackson, Jenks, Jervey, Lang, Mauldin, Middleton, Moses, Olsen, Perry, Pillsbury, Richmond, Sasportas, Smalls, Swails, Thomas, Whipper, Williamson—25.

Section fourteen was then passed to its third reading, as follows :

SECTION 14. The real and personal property of a woman, held at the time of her marriage, or that which she may thereafter acquire, either by gift, grant, inheritance, devise or otherwise, shall not be subject to levy and sale for her husband's debts, but her seperate property may be bequeathed, devised or alienated by her, the same as if she were unmarried ; *Provided*, That no gift or grant from the husband to the wife shall be detrimental to the just claims of his creditors.

The PRESIDENT announced the next unfinished business was the consideration of the report of the Committee on Franchise and Elections.

Mr. B. O. DUNCAN moved that the consideration of that report be postponed, and made the special order for Monday, at eleven o'clock, which was agreed to.

The next special order was the consideration of an Ordinance to create Land Commissioners, which was taken up, passed its third reading, and declared an Ordinance of the Convention.

Mr. F. J. MOSES, Jr., moved that the vote whereby the above Ordinance passed to its third reading, be reconsidered, and that the motion for reconsideration be laid on the table, which was carried.

The Convention then proceeded to the third reading of the first article of the Constitution, known as the " Bill of Rights."

The article was read by sections, and after several ineffectual motions to recommit certain sections, was finally passed.

The PRESIDENT then put the question, "shall the first article pass," which was unanimously carried.

The PRESIDENT then announced it as follows :

" This is the first article, and, I hereby declare, has become a part of the Constitution of South Carolina."

The announcement was followed with great applause by the delegates, who gave vent to the expression of their feelings by clapping of hands and continued applause for several minutes, during which the President was unable to proceed.

The following is the article as passed, which, under the Ordinance of the Convention, is to be submitted to the people of the State for ratification on the 14th, 15th, and 16th days of April next.

We, the People of the State of South Carolina, in Convention assembled, Grateful to Almighty God for this opportunity, deliberately and peaceably of entering into an explicit and solemn compact with each other, and forming a new Constitution of civil government for ourselves and posterity, recognizing the necessity of the protection of the people in all that pertains to their freedom, safety, and tranquillity, and imploring the direction of the Great Legislator of the Universe, do agree upon, ordain, and establish the following

DECLARATION OF RIGHTS AND FORM OF GOVERNMENT AS THE CONSTITUTION OF THE COMMONWEALTH OF SOUTH CAROLINA.

ARTICLE I.

DECLARATION OF RIGHTS.

SECTION 1. All men are born free and equal—endowed by their Creator with certain inalienable rights. among which are the rights of enjoying and defending their lives and liberties, of acquiring, possessing and protecting property, and of seeking and obtaining their safety and happiness.

SEC. 2. Slavery shall never exist in this State; neither shall involuntary servitude, except as a punishment for crime, whereof the party shall have been duly convicted.

SEC. 3. All political power is vested in and derived from the people only; therefore they have the right, at all times, to modify their form of government in such manner as they may deem expedient, when the public good demands.

SEC. 4. Every citizen of this State owes paramount allegiance to the Constitution and Government of the United States, and no law or ordinance of this State in contravention or subversion thereof, can have any binding force.

SEC. 5. This State shall ever remain a member of the American Union, and all attempts, from whatever source, or upon whatever pretext, to dissolve the said Union, shall be resisted with the whole power of the State

SEC. 6. The right of the people peaceably to assemble to consult for the common good, and to petition the Government, or any department thereof, shall never be abridged.

SEC. 7. All persons may freely speak, write and publish their sentiments on any subject, being responsible for the abuse of that right; and no laws shall be enacted to restrain or abridge the liberty of speech or of the press.

Sec. 8. In prosecutions for the publication of papers, investigating the official conduct of officers or men in public capacity, or when the matter published is proper for public information, the truth thereof may be given in evidence; and in all indictments for libel, the jury shall be the judges of the law and the facts.

Sec. 9. No person shall be deprived of the right to worship God according to the dictates of his own conscience; *Provided*, That the liberty of conscience hereby declared shall not justify practices inconsistent with the peace and moral safety of society.

• Sec. 10. No form of religion shall be established by law; but it shall be the duty of the General Assembly to pass suitable laws to protect every religious denomination in the peaceable enjoyment of its own mode of worship.

Sec. 11. The right of trial by jury shall remain inviolate.

Sec. 12. No person shall be disqualified as a witness, or be prevented from acquiring, holding and transmitting property, or be hindered in acquiring education, or be liable to any other punishment for any offence, or be subjected in law to any other restraints or disqualifications in regard to any personal rights than such as are laid upon others under like circumstances.

Sec. 13. No person shall be held to answer for any crime or offence, until the same is fully, fairly, plainly, substantially and formally described to him; or be compelled to accuse or furnish evidence against himself; and every person shall have a right to produce all proofs that may be favorable to him, to meet the witnesses against him face to face, to have a speedy and public trial by an impartial jury, and to be fully heard in his defence by himself or by his counsel, or by both, as he may elect.

Sec. 14. No person shall be arrested, imprisoned, despoiled or dispossessed of his property, immunities or privileges, put out of the protection of the law, exiled or deprived of his life, liberty, or estate, but by the judgment of his peers, or the law of the land. And the General Assembly shall not enact any law that shall subject any person to punishment without trial by jury; nor shall he be punished but by virtue of a law already established, or promulgated prior to the offence, and legally applied.

Sec. 15. All Courts shall be public, and every person, for any injury that he may receive in his lands, goods, person or reputation, shall have remedy by due course of law, and justice administered without unnecessary delay.

Sec. 16. All persons shall, before conviction, be bailable by sufficient sureties, except for capital offences, when the proof is evident or the presumption great; and excessive bail shall not, in any case, be required, nor corporeal punishment inflicted.

Sec. 17. The privilege of the writ of *Habeas Corpus* shall not be suspended, except when in case of insurrection, rebellion or invasion, the public safety may require it.

Sec. 18. No person, after having been once acquitted by a jury, shall again, for the same offence, be put in jeopardy of his life or liberty.

Sec. 19. All offences less than felony, and in which the punishment does not exceed a fine of one hundred dollars, or imprisonment for thirty days, shall be tried summarily before a Justice of the Peace, or other officer authorized by law, on information under oath, without indictment or intervention of a Grand Jury, saving to the defendant the right of appeal; and no person shall be held to answer for any higher crime or offence, unless on presentment of a Grand Jury, except in cases arising in the land and naval service, or in the militia when in actual service in time of war or public danger.

SEC. 20. No person shall be imprisoned for debt, except in cases of fraud; and a reasonable amount of property, as a homestead, shall ba exempted from seizure or sale for the payment of any debts or liabilities, except for the payment of such obligations as are provided for in this Constitution.

SEC. 21. No bill of attainder, *ex post facto* law, nor any law impairing the obligation of contracts, shall ever be enacted; and no conviction shall work corruption of blood or forfeiture of estate.

SEC. 22. All persons have a right to be secure from unreasonable searches or seizures of their persons, houses, papers or possessions. All warrants shall be supported by oath or affirmation, and the order of the warrant to a civil officer to make search or seizure in suspected places, or to arrest one or more suspected persons, or to seize their property, shall be accompanied with a special designation of the persons or objects of search, arrest or seizure; and no warrant shall be issued but in the cases, and with the formalities prescribed by the laws.

SEC. 23. Private property shall not be taken or applied for public use, or for the use of corporations, or for private use, without the consent of the owner or a just compensation being made therefor; *provided, however*, that laws may be made securing to persons or corporations the right of way over the lands of either persons or corporations, and, for works of internal improvement, the right to establish depots, stations, turnouts, etc; but a just compensation, shall in all cases, be first made to the owner.

SEC. 24. The power of suspending the laws, or the execution of the laws, shall never be exercised but by the General Assembly, or by authority derived therefrom; to be exercised in such particular cases only as the General Assembly shall expressly provide for.

SEC. 25. No person shall, in any case, be subject to martial law, or to any pains or penalties by virtue of that law, except those employed in the army or navy of the United States, and except the militia in actual service, but by authority of the General Assembly.

SEC. 26. In the government of this Commonwealth, the Legislative, Executive and Judicial powers of the Government shall be forever separate and distinct from each other, and no person or persons exercising the functions of one of said departments shall assume or discharge the duties of any other.

SEC. 27. The General Assembly ought frequently to assemble for the redress of grievances, and for making new laws as the common good may require.

SEC. 28. The people have a right to keep and bear arms for the common defence. As in times of peace, armies are dangerous to liberty, they ought not to be maintained without the consent of the General Assembly. The military power ought always to be held in an exact subordination to the civil authority and be governed by it.

SEC. 29. In time of peace no soldier shall be quartered in any house without the consent of the owner; and, in time or war, such quarters shall not be made but in a manner prescribed by law.

SEC. 30. No person who conscientiously scruples to bear arms shall be compelled so to do, but he shall pay an equivalent for personal service.

SEC. 31. All elections shall be free and open, and every inhabitant of this Commonwealth possessing the qualifications provided for in this Constitution, shall have an equal right to elect officers and be elected to fill public office.

SEC. 32. No property qualification shall be necessary for an election to or the holding of any office, and no office shall be created, the appointment to which shall be for a longer time than good behavior. After the adoption of this Constitution, any person who shall fight a duel, or send or accept a challenge for that purpose, or be an aider or abetter in fighting a duel, shall be deprived of holding any office of honor or trust in this State, and shall be otherwise punished as the law shall prescribe.

SEC. 33. The right of sufrage shall be protected by laws regulating elections, and prohibiting, under adequate penalties, all undue influences from power, bribery, tumult or improper conduct.

SEC. 34. Representation shall be apportioned according to population, and no person in this State shall be disfranchised or deprived of any of the rights or privileges now enjoyed except by the law of the land or the judgment of his peers.

SEC. 35. Temporary absence from the State shall not forfeit a residence once obtained.

SEC. 36. All property subject to taxation shall be taxed in proportion to its value. Each individual of society has a right to be protected in the enjoyment of life, liberty and property according to standing laws. He should, therefore, contribute his share to the expense of his pretection and give his personal service when necessary.

SEC. 37. No subsidy, charge, impost tax or duties shall be established, fixed, laid or levied, under any pretext whatsoever, without the consent of the people or their representatives lawfully assembled.

SEC. 38. Excessive fines shall not be imposed, nor cruel and unusual punishment inflicted, nor shall witnesses be unreasonably detained.

SEC. 39. No title of nobility or hereditary emolument shall ever be granted in this State. Distinction on account of race or color, in any case whatever, shall be prohibited, and all classes of citizens shall enjoy equally all common, public, legal and political privileges.

SEC. 40. All navigable waters shall remain forever public highways, free to the citizens of the State and the United States, without tax, impost, or toll imposed; and, no tax, toll, impost or wharfage shall be imposed, demanded or received, from the owner of any merchandize or commodity, for the use of the shores or any wharf erected on the shores, or in or over the waters of any navigable stream, unless the same be authorized by the General Assembly.

SEC. 41. The enumeration of Rights in this Constitution shall not be construed to impair or deny others retained by the people, and all powers not herein delegated remain with the people.

On motion of R. C. DeLARGE, the vote whereby the above was passed was reconsidered, and the motion for reconsideration laid on the table.

LEGISLATIVE DEPARTMENT.

Mr. E. W. M. MACKEY called up for a third reading the report of the Committee on the Legislative Department, and sections one and two were passed.

Mr. N. G. PARKER moved that section three be recommitted to the committee, with instructions to provide for the formation of a new county from the contiguous portions of Barnwell, Edgefield, Lexington and Orangeburg.

Mr. R. B. ELLIOTT. I hope the members will vote in favor of recommitment. It is important that this question should be settled here. I would like to ask the gentlemen of the Convention to bear with me while I give my reasons.

The hour of adjournment having arrived, the Convention adjourned to three P. M.

AFTERNOON SESSION.

The Convention met pursuant to adjournment, and the unfinished business, being the report on the Legislative Department, was resumed.

Mr. R. B. ELLIOTT, who was speaking at the hour of adjournment, on the motion to recommit section three, resumed his argument, and said:

As the judicial system of the State is now to undergo a revision, we deem this a fitting opportunity for presenting the claim of the citizens of those portions of Barnwell, Orangeburg, Lexington and Edgefield Districts, lying contiguous to each other, for the establishment of a new district, with a court house to be located at Aiken.

For forty years past it has been the desire of the people of this section to have these large and cumbrous districts divided, so as to afford them additional judicial facilities. Memorial after memorial has been

presented to the various Legislatures unavailingly ; still they have per-
sisted in their efforts, hoping ultimately to succeed.

The aggregate size of the four districts, from whose territory it is proposed to form the new District of Sumner is nearly 6,000 square miles,
having a population in 1850 of over 100,000 inhabitants, or more than
one-seventh, the total population of the State : $1,200,000 was then
employed in manufactures. and wares to the amount of $160,000
annually produced, profitably employing two thousand operatives ,
50,000 bales of cotton was produced, and animals to the value of
$750,000 slaughtered.

As embodying some of the arguments in favor of the proposed measure, I append a circular addressed to the members of the Legislature
in 1856, the citizens of Aiken being then desirous of establishing said
district under the name of Calhoun :

AIKEN, November, 1856.

Dear Sir : We take the liberty of addressing you on a subject of deep
interest to us, as citizens of South Carolina, and inhabitants of Barnwell
District, and would solicit your attention, whilst we present, as briefly
and concisely as possible, *some* of the facts and arguments upon which
our claim is founded.

A Bill will be brought before the Legislature, at the present session,
for the formation of a new Judicial District, to be composed of portions
of the Districts of Barnwell, Edgefield, Lexington and Orangeburg,
with the town of Aiken as the centre. We beg you to observe that
the object of the Bill will be the organization merely of a *Judicial* District. We are well aware that many grave considerations might be
urged against the project of establishing an additional *Electoral* District.
We would, however, expressly disclaim any such purpose as this. We
do not propose to disturb the balances and compromises of the Constitution, or to innovate upon the principles on which, under our organic
law, are based the right and ratio of representation in our State Legislature. In this matter, we claim to be conservatives— we are quite con
tent that the political relations between the several sections of our State
should remain as they are, and are no agitators in behalf of any scheme
of *Parliamentary Reform* in South Carolina. Our sole object, we
repeat, is the establishment of another *Judicial District*, in order to
relieve ourselves of what we consider to be a grievance and a burden.

Such a measure we now beg leave to recommend very briefly to your
serious and earnest consideration, for the following reasons :

One of the main objects of all political associations, we hold to be the
proper administration of justice between man and man. It is this which
distinguishes the regulated liberty of civilized society from the unbridled
license of savage life; and we must ever regard it as among the most
sacred duties, as well as the best marks of a good government, to endeavor to secure by every means in its power, this inestimable blessing to

its citizens. To effect this, we require not only good laws, correctly administered, but what is obviously not less essential, that the aggrieved citizens possess the privilege of a cheap and easy access to the Courts of Justice. When the appeal to the authorized tribunals is burdened with heavy costs, and can only be pursued at much expense of time and money, a judicial system, however excellent otherwise, is to the poor man—to the man of moderate means—but a solemn mockery, for it amounts virtually to a denial of justice. In the administration of the law, we all admit there should be no distinction between rich and poor; and it should, therefore, be the paramount aim of every government, not only in the enactment of its laws, and in the appointment of its officers, but in the *arrangement of its Judicial Districts*, to extend the ægis of its protection equally over all. Under a Government professedly popular and free, it becomes a solecism of the grossest nature, if, either in what it does, or what it omits to do, it excludes any class of its citizens from the benefits of its Courts of Justice, and leaves them in the condition of outlaws. And least of all, should this disability be allowed to fall upon the poor—the class which most needs the supporting arm of the Government—for while wealth is said to be in itself a tower of strength to its possessor, according to Solomon, "the destruction of the poor man is his poverty." Now, this is substantially the character of the grievance of which many of the inhabitants of these districts complain. Living as they do, thirty, forty, and some even fifty miles from the respective seats of Justice, it is utterly impossible for most of them, thus situated, to afford the expense of frequent journeys to the Court House, to consult lawyers and attend to the trial of their causes, with perhaps a long train of reluctant witnesses, for whose expense they must also make provision. Independently of law suits, there is also a vast amount of business that can be transacted only at the Court House—such as returns of trustees, executors, guardians, commissioners, &c. Now, the man of wealth may afford occasionally to be absent from his home and business for the requisite time, but the poor man, who earns his bread by the sweat of his brow, has little time to spare, and every extra day, and every extra dollar, is a serious loss to him.

To avoid this burden of expense, the only alternative for the aggrieved is, to submit to the wrong, or take the law into his own hand, and seek satisfaction in the blood of his adversary, a result ·pernicious in the extreme, but we think not more dangerous to the peace of the community than the impunity of the offender, since the tendency of either case is to subvert the foundation of society. These views apply in force to the state of things at the present time. The effect of all this cannot but be to alienate the feelings of many of our citizens from the Government under which they live. The sentiment is not less common than just, that protection and obedience are reciprocal obligations—when the one ceases, the other is cancelled; and this may serve to account for the fact that Barnwell and Edgefield, the two largest Districts in the State, are notorious for their affrays and homicides, and as long as they retain their present extent of territory, there will be but little hope of any amendment.

But the question may be asked, and we allow it to be strictly relevant

101

to the issue, where is this system of division and sub-division of our Judicial Districts to end ? Assuredly some limit must be assigned to this process of partition ? To this we answer, that the expediency of forming a new D strict will depend on various circumstances, such as the extent, population, wealth, intelligence, and commercial business and wishes of the citizens embraced within the area of the District which it is proposed to organize. We are quite willing to submit our claim on this occasion to any or all of these tests of propriety.

The proposed new District of Calhoun would include an area of more than 700 square miles, nearly $6,000,000 of taxable property, with a population of 5 or 6,000 whites, and as many colored persons. It would contain the towns of Aiken, Hamburg, Graniteville, Bath and Vaucluse, and more than a hundred saw and flour mills.

Barnwell would then be much larger than most of the present Districts. It would still have about 1200 square miles, with a population of 20,000.

According to the Comptroller's report in 1854, taxes were paid in this District on 1,032,750 acres of land, which, after taking into the estimate, town lots, water courses, ponds, &c., omitted in this enumeration, and making allowances for defective surveys, would give us an area of nearly 1800 square miles of territory, being twice as much as each of seventeen Districts in the State.

Barnwell District has nearly three times the extent of an average county in the older settled States of the Union ; and is larger than the State of Rhode Island, which has five counties.

The average size of counties in Kentucky is 376 square miles; in Indiana, 371 ; Virginia, 444 ; Georgia, 550 ; and Barnwell has over 1600 square miles.

When the present population and wealth of Barnwell is compared to what it was in 1808, the necessity for increased Judicial facilities will be apparent. In a sparsely settled country it was advisable to have an extended area. Now, that wealth and population have increased, some change is demanded. Then there was but little business for the Courts ; now a two weeks' term is hardly sufficient to clear the docket. Edgefield and Barnwell are the only rural Districts which have a two weeks' term. This fact speaks for itself. Much might be brought to your notice regarding the ill effects of a two weeks' term, but the fear of trespassing on your patience prevents us from dwelling at length on this subject.

The arguments that were brought to bear during the past session of the Legislature, in the case of Sumter District, apply with equal force to this case.

Upon a question like this, necessarily connected with local interests and sympathies, it is, we think, quite appropriate to consider what is the voice of the people in those Districts which are to be principally affected by the passage of the Bill. It, therefore, may not be amiss to state, that in the late election of the four members chosen for Barnwell, three declared themselves, during the canvass, favorable to the establishment of a new District. In the adjoining District of Edgefield, there is also a strong feeling in favor of this measure, so that of those who are most concerned, and we may reasonably suppose, best qualified to judge of the policy of the measure, and whose views and wishes are, therefore, most entitled to the consideration of the Legislature, a decided maj rity are desirous of forming the new District of Calhoun.

There are other forcible arguments which we might present, but we forbear, believing that you will give this matter due consideration. As Legislators for the State, the interests of each integral portion demand your attention, and we respectfully submit our case, with the views we have taken the liberty to suggest, to the dispassionate and unprejudiced judgment of the Legislature of South Carolina.

These views, it will readily be conceded, have an important bearing on and show the importance of the measure.

1. By it law and justice would be more perfectly administered, and lawlessness and crime diminished. Living as the people of this section do, from twenty to fifty miles from their respective Court Houses, they are virtually without law, for the expenses incident to transacting business at such a distance from their homes, induces men to neglect duties incumbent on all good citizens, and to frequently redress their injuries with their own strong arms. Witnesses evade, by every possible means, attendance at a distant Court House; thus insufficent evidence is obtained to procure conviction. Malefactors escape before the proper officer can be reached, or when arrested the constables refuse to convey them to a distant jail, as the fees are not enough to pay the expenses incurred. The duties of the various commissioners are neglected; managers of elections refuse to open the polls, and in various ways the community suffers.

2. That these causes act as an indirect tax, which amount far exceeds the direct tax levied by law, and which might be saved by establishing the additional District.

3 Barnwell and Edgefield are the only rural Districts, whose size and population require a two weeks' term of the Court, and not unfrequently even that extended time is insufficient to clear the docket. Moreover, the notoriety of these Districts for frays and fights, indicate the effect of over-large Judicial Circuits.

4. That this policy is in accordance with the experience of all other States, and the custom formerly of this State, as well as with the teachings of the most advanced thinkers of the present day, such as Mill, Ricardo, McCulloch, etc.

5. That it would give a centre to and an impetus in the development of the peculiar interests of this section. Within the proposed limits are the factories of Graniteville, Vaucluse, Hampton, etc.; Bath Paper Mills, Kaolin Works, several large potteries, and over one hundred saw mills. That, as the want of machinery and skilled mechanics has been sorely felt in this State, encouragement should be extended to such enterprises, and the establishment of this District is a practical step in that direction. Here also are the largest vineyards and orchards. Any measure which tends to diversify pursuits, and give employment to the poor and needy, should be carefully considered. By this means emigra-

tion from this section would, be checked, and immigration encouraged; new channels of industry be opened, wealth and business increased, and the general prosperity advanced.

Several of the factories have recently been enlarged and improved, and others are now being built, and it is probable that in a few years ten thousand persons will be supported by the manufacturing interests of this section alone. The Kalmia Mills are intended to employ one thousand operatives when completed.

The establishment of Sumner District, as proposed, would still leave Barnwell, Edgefield and Orangeburg, near one thousand three hundred square miles each, and Lexington near one thousand. A cursory glance at a map of the State will show the adaptation of the site selected (Aiken) for the new Court House, being nearly equi-distant between the present Court Houses of Barnwell and Edgefield, and on the line of the South Carolina Railroad, so that it is easily accessible from all quarters.

If conservation consists in avoiding extremes, then, in respect to the size of her Judicial Districts, South Carolina is not conservative, for they are the largest of any of the older settled States of the Union, averaging as they do, nearly one thousand square miles each, whilst, for example, in Kentucky they have only three hundred and seventy-six square miles; Indiana, three hundred and seventy-one; Georgia, five hundred and fifty; and Virginia, four hundred and forty-four. Barnwell has nearly one thousand seven hundred square miles, being larger than the State of Rhode Island, which has five counties, and fully three times the size of counties in other States.

CALHOUN.

The boundaries we would propose for the new district are as follows: Commencing at the mouth of Fox's Creek, where it empties into the Savannah River, thence in a direct line to where the "Old Ninety-Six," or Edgefield and Charleston road crosses the dividing line of Edgefield and Lexington; thence down said road to where it is intersected by the road leading to Guignard's Bridge, on the Edisto River; from said intersection in a straight line to the mouth of Pond Branch, where it empties into the Edisto; thence up that stream (Pond Branch) to its head, and then across to the head of Tinker's Creek, and down the centre of that creek to where it empties into the Runs; and then down the middle of the Runs to where it empties into the Savannah River, and thence up the Savannah River to the initial point.

If these are not weighty reasons which should induce members of the Convention to recommit the third section of the report, with instructions to the committee to create this county, then no weighty reasons can ever be brought forward. I say it is the duty of the Convention to regard the voice of the majority of the people in every section of the State. If there was any objection, I had the best grounds for opposing it. We should, however, consider the good of the people of every section of the

State before our own mere personal interest. From the portions of the districts out of which this new district is to be created, Edgefield gives almost everything that will enable this county to support itself. All the factories, mills, and other manufacturing interests that this new county will have comes from Edgefield District, and I do not see why gentlemen who represent other portions of the State, who really know nothing of the wants of this section, should object to the measure recommended by the representative of the district most concerned.

Mr. L. BOOZER. It has not been my habit to intrude myself upon this Convention. I had laid down a rule when I came here not to do so, and I would not violate that rule if I had not believed that it was absolutely required that I should do it now. I am surprised by this proposition. It was understood by the Convention that this matter was to be left to the Legislature. When this clause in the Constitution was adopted, that was the understanding of all parties. Now, when we are about approaching the close of the session, on the third reading of an article, a motion is made to recommit a section, with instructions to the committee to do that which this Convention had refused to do. I am surprised at the course of gentlemen on this subject. Is there such an urgency for the passage of this measure now that they cannot wait until the Legislature assembles, who will have ample power under this very section to do what these gentlemen propose? Is there any necessity for it at this late day of the session, after the question had been already settled and fairly understood? I am not prepared to say whether I should oppose it or not, for my constituents of Lexington have not been consulted. It is proposed to disintegrate, to cut off a portion of my district without asking the consent of the people. I enter my solemn protest against it. I have not seen a man from that district who has been consulted on the subject, and my colleague informs me he has not. We are a weak district with but two representatives here, while Barnwell has five or six, and Edgefield seven. They propose to take off a portion of Lexington District, which now has only two representatives. Are we to lose a member by this process? Who is to tell? The census has not been taken, and we have no data. Let it alone as it is; let the Legislature act upon it; and when this measure is brought up before that body, when it is brought before the Legislature with all the proper information and evidence, then we will be prepared to act upon it.

The question was taken on the motion to lay the motion to recommit on the table, and decided in the affirmative.

The question then recurred on the passage of the section to a third reading.

Mr. J. J. WRIGHT moved that the consideration of the third section be postponed.

On motion of Mr. E. W. M. MACKEY, the motion to postpone was laid on the table, and the section then passed to its third reading.

Section four was read, and Mr. C. C. BOWEN moved the following, which was adopted, and the committee instructed to report on Monday at ten o'clock :

Recommit, with instructions to report this section, so as to allow the County of Charleston the same number of representatives as the present District of Charleston and Berkley are allowed in this Convention, and the names of each county appear with its number of representatives in the Lower House of the General Assembly.

The hour for the consideration of the special order having arrived, which was an Ordinance to provide for the ratification of the Constitution and Ordinances, and for the election of certain officers.

Mr. L. BOOZER. I wish to inquire whether it is proper now to fix the time for this election. The Constitution has not yet been adopted, and, according to my understanding of the reconstruction acts by which we are governed, thirty days' notice of the election is required.

Mr. E. W. M. MACKEY. The reconstruction acts only require thirty days' notice of the election should be given after the ratification of the Constitution. The Commanding General of the military district is required to give thirty days' notice of the election. We can go on and complete our Constitution up to within so many days. Unless this Ordinance is passed to-day, the military will not have the necessary time. The reason why the committee fixed the election for the 14th, 15th and 16th of April, is that the 14th is the anniversary of the assassination of President Lincoln, the anniversary of the hauling down of the flag of Fort Sumter, and the anniversary of replacing the flag over Fort Sumter. It was deemed by your committee a most glorious time for holding the election. It will be of great assistance to our speakers too.

The question was put on the passage of the first section, and decided in the affirmative.

Mr. J. M. ALLEN. I move to strike out the words "and Ordinances" in the section. I think there is no necessity for incorporating those words with it. If the Constitution is ratified, the Ordinances are certainly ratified by it, and everything is legalized.

Mr. E. W. M. MACKEY. I hope that motion will not prevail, as there is much doubt expressed as to the legality of the Ordinances passed by this Convention, and in order to put it beyond a doubt, it is much better for us to submit the Constitution and Ordinances together. A great many important Ordinances have been passed by this body. We have passed an Ordinance nullifying slave debts; declaring all such debts null and void. It will, at least, do no harm to submit the Ordinances of the Convention with the Constitution, and forever place our acts of legislation beyond any doubt or

Mr. A. J. RANSIER. I hope the motion to strike out the words "and Ordinances" will not prevail. I do not believe any of the Ordinances we have passed here, will have the force of law, unless made part of the Constitution, to be submitted and ratified by the people. I have heard it said here that we have no precedent for any such step. It will be found, however, that in many of the States the Ordinances are made part of the Constitution.

Mr. J. M. ALLEN. I withdraw the motion to strike out "and Ordinances."

Mr. F. J. MOSES, Jr. I do not desire to do aught to endanger the Constitution. I desire, as far as possible, to avoid any conflict that might ensue between voting upon the Constitution and the Ordinances. I desire to have the Constitution voted upon entirely separate. I, therefore, offer the following as an amendment:

"*Provided*, That the Commanding General be requested to order separate boxes, to be opened for voting upon the Constitution and the Ordinances respectively."

Mr. C. P. LESLIE. I would like to ask the delegates if they do not know beforehand what will be the result if these Ordinances are submitted r t y to the people for ratification. Suppose we submit the Ordinance raising seventy-five thousand dollars. Do the delegates believe the people will ratify that?—will the people ratify the Ordinance abolishing debts contracted for slave property? I have seen men busy about this Convention, who want this Ordinance submitted separately. They think it will not have the force or effect it would have if put in the Constitution. They say we are authorized to make a Constitution, but not authorized to legislate. I submit, your only hope or chance is to submit them in the Constitution. The white people of the State want a homestead, and they are willing to take and swallow all you have done, provided, that you put it all together and not undertake to make them swallow the pills separately. If you do, you will get the Constitution, but they will cheat you out of the balance.

Mr. J. M. RUNION. I move the indefinite postponement of the amendment.

Mr. J. M. RUTLAND. I hope the amendment will not be postponed. I desire to have this Constitution submitted seperately to the people of South Carolina for ratification or rejection.

Mr. E. W. M. MACKEY. Is not the gentleman entirely opposed to the adoption, by the people, of the Ordinance invalidating contracts for slaves ?

Mr. J. M. RUTLAND. I am, but I am also in favor of other Ordinances. As far as my recollection goes, it has always been the rule for a Constitution to be submitted alone. I never heard of a string of Ordinances tacked on and made so much dead weight. Many are opposed to the Ordinances who favor the Constitution. It is of the utmost importance that the Constitution should not be encumbered with any dead weight whatever : so far as the Republican party is concerned, it does not matter whether a single Ordinance is ratified. The Constitution is what we want, and I, for one, am not willing that anything of any sort of dead weight should, by any possibility, be so attached as to induce a single vote against it. I would cast my vote in favor of the Ordinances in a mass, though I do object to some of them, as you all know. But I hope you will not permit the Ordinances to be tacked on and to give others an excuse to say, we would have voted for your Constitution if you had not attached to it those Ordinances.

Mr. R. H. CAIN. It appears to me that the Ordinances passed by the Convention, were passed for the purpose of laying the foundation upon which the Constitution might rest, and if the parties would not sanction by their votes the Ordinance nullifying contracts for slaves and all the other Ordinances, they would not accept the work in good faith. The Ordinances are the ground work upon which we raised our Constitution. These Ordinances have been discussed and acted upon in good faith, by the Convention, and passed, as believed, for the well-being of the State It strikes me, to say to the people that you can vote on the Constitution, but you may reject the Ordinances, would be fatal. We suggest the propriety of voting on one part and rejecting the other part of our work.

Mr. N. G. PARKER. I do not regard it absolutely necessary to submit the Ordinances at all to the people. We submit the Constitution to the people to say whether they will ratify or reject it. The Ordinances will be enforced by the General Commanding until such time as the new government goes into operation. I have consulted several legal gentlemen upon this point, and they have decided the same way. I am, therefore, in favor of striking out the words "and Ordinances", and submitting the Constitution just as it is to the people. I move, therefore, to strike out the words "and Ordinances."

Mr. A. J. RANSIER. If the military enforce the Ordinances until the new government goes into operation, we may certainly leave them with the judges to determine their legality.

If we submit to the Ordinances, it may lead to confusion, some favoring one Ordinance and some another. I would not take the least risk of anything that would endanger the Constitution. I am not willing to trust the submission of any Ordinance separately to the people. I know an Ordinance passed by this Convention, to have any effect or force of law, must be approved by the military, and they will hold good just so long as the military choose; but if they rescind Ordinances, it falls. I am in favor of every Ordinance passed by the Convention becoming a part of the Constitution. I have never believed that this Convention had legislative powers, but that our duty was specific to frame a Constitution, and nothing else. Believing, therefore, that the Ordinances, to have the force of law, must be attached to the Constitution, I hope we shall make that necessary provision. My legal friend from Beaufort, has said that such a thing as an Ordinance in a Constitution was unknown to him. I think if he looks, he will find it in Louisiana, Missouri, Nevada, Mississippi and several other States.

Mr. E. W. M. MACKEY called for the previous question, which was sustained.

Mr. E. W. M. MACKEY. I hope the motion to strike out the words " and Ordinances," will be voted down. The gentleman from Barnwell (Mr. PARKER) says it is not absolutely necessary to submit the Ordinances with the Constitution. That may be; but it will not be denied that much doubt has been expressed as to the validity of all the Rrdinances passed by this Convention. I regard it as much better for us to submit the Ordinances along with the Constitution, and ensure their ratification.

Mr. N. G. PARKER. My object is simply to avoid all risks to the Constitution that might be incurred by attaching the Ordinances.

Mr. E. W. M. MACKEY. The fear is that many persons opposed to the Ordinances may vote against the Constitution. All those in favor of abolishing debts contracted for slaves, and those in favor of a homestead, will vote for the Constitution if those Ordinances are attached; so that if we lost one vote, we would gain two, or perhaps more. We might, perhaps, gain four or five thousand votes. Would it not be better to place the question of the validity of these Ordinances beyond litigation in our State Courts by having them ratified by the people. I, therefore, hope the motion to strike out the words " and Ordinances" will be voted down.

102

The question was taken on the motion to strike out the words "and Ordinances," and decided in the negative.

Section two then passed to its third reading.

Section three passed to its third reading without debate.

Second four received its second reading.

Mr. T. HURLEY moved to amend by striking out after the word appointed, the words "to consist of Messrs. E. W. M. Mackey, F. L. Cardozo, A. J. Ransier, and C. C. Bowen," and to insert "of two persons in the district, who shall not be candidates for any office at the time of the ratification of this Constitution."

Mr. B. F. WHITTEMORE moved that the amendment be indefinitely postponed.

Mr. B. F. RANDOLPH. With all due respect for the gentlemen whose names are mentioned here, I would like to ask as to the propriety of candidates for office being commissioners of elections, or being interested in them personally.

Mr. F. L. CARDOZO. I simply would say that it is necessary for the Board to reside in Charleston, in order to be in constant communication with the military commander. The Convention, if it deems proper, can erase those names and substitute others, but some board is necessary, and is requested by the General Commanding the military department. My name has been used without my knowledge. It has not been the result of any consultation with me. I am no candidate for office.

Mr. B. F. WHITTEMORE. This is simply to be an advisory board for the military authorities. As I understand it, these commissioners are to consult the different delegations, and obtain information from all sections of the State, then to act and advise with the military authorities. I hope the amendment will be indefinitely postponed.

Mr. F. J. MOSES, Jr. I hope this section will pass as reported from the committee. The object of the committee has been to report an Ordinance for the purpose of carrying through the next election in the best manner possible. After a long consultation, they came to the conclusion they could devise no better plan for the success of the next election than to send in the Ordinance now under consideration. I am gratified to find that the committee have recommended the names of the gentle-men designated in the fourth section. This idea about their being candidates for office is one which I hope the Convention will not entertain for one moment. Their office will be in connection with the office of the Commanding General in the City of Charleston. The Commanding General has requested that an Ordinance embodying these features should be passed by this Convention. These gentlemen, as has been said, will sit simply as an advisory board with the Commanding General. They are to nominate, on consultation with the different district delegations, managers of elections for the various counties in the State, and the Commanding General in accordance with their recommendation will appoint.

Mr. E. W. M. MACKEY. As my name is mentioned in this section, I rise to say that I have no particular desire to be a member of the Board of Commissioners, and if the Convention think best, will cheerfully give way to my friend from Berkley (Mr. HURLEY). With reference to the Ordinance and the Board itself, I would say that the matter has been delayed on account of the sickness of General Canby. The Ordinance, as submitted to him, meets with his approval. He desires that a board shall be created and located at the Citadel, so as to be able to consult with the military at all times, in regard to the appointment of managers and everything else necessary for the successful ratification of this Constitution.

The question being put on the indefinite postponement of the amendment of the gentleman from Berkley (Mr. HURLEY), it was decided in the affirmative.

Section four then passed to its third reading.

Section five was read, and Mr. T. HURLEY moved to strike out the section, which was rejected, and the section passed to its third reading.

Sections six and seven were passed to a third reading.

Section eight was read, and Mr. C. D. HAYNE moved to strike out the section.

Mr. J. M. RUNION moved to strike out "five" and insert "three," which was not agreed to.

A motion was made to strike out "five" and insert "four," which was not agreed to

Mr. B. F. WHITTEMORE moved to indefinitely postpone the motion to strike out the section.

Mr. W. E. JOHNSTON moved to lay the motion on the table, which was agreed to.

The question recurred on the motion to strike out the section.

Mr. W. B. NASH. As the Convention has decided to create the board, I certainly think we should be generous enough to pay the members composing it for their services. I was opposed to the section creating a · Board of Commissioners, but after it has been adopted and gentlemen are to be employed, I think they should be paid whatever their services are worth. They will certainly earn five dollars a day.

Besides they will have clerks, and if they perform their duty just about one-half as they ought to, they will probably have more than they can attend to.

Mr. C. P. LESLIE. I desire to say a few words on this matter. Alabama, before submitting her Constitution, passed a similar Ordinance to this, with the exception that it provided no compensation to any commissioner. It did provide, that the clerical force of the board should be paid. Why should we adopt a different rule? There is no objection to carrying out this Ordinance, or doing whatever is necessary, in order to enable the Commission appointed to carry out the election It appears strange, however, that the gentlemen who reported this Ordinance have added, somehow or other, perhaps unintentionally, for I do not think a man from Charleston could do a thing of this kind, two more as disinterested men as there are in the whole country, and they all had to be from Charleston. Why, in the world, could not one or more just as well resided at Columbia? But, what I desire particularly to ask is, why could not two good men have performed this work as well as four? What in the world have they got to do? A clerical force is provided for, and it does really appear, as if two would be sufficient. It may be necessary to give somebody an office, but I tell you it is one of those private things that we do very reluctantly.

Mr. F. E. WILDER. Don't you think these plans could be carried out better with four than with two, provided one was accorded to each Congressional District?

Mr. C. P. LESLIE Certainly, that is an excellent suggestion.

Mr. CAIN. It appears to me this Ordinance authorises a great amount of work to be done. As one of the committee that reported that Ordinance, I can say we considered it in all its phases. We considered that the members of the Convention were now receiving eleven dollars a day, in bills receivable, equal to eight or nine dollars in United States currency, and arrived at the conclusion that five dollars a day for each member of this board would not be too much. The commissioners will have to devote their whole time to the work, and have but thirty days in which to arrange all matters connected with the elections. We desire to have the work well done. There is much at stake in this coming election, and I think we ought to place all the power we can in the hands of this board. I am willing to pay them generously, in order to have the work properly and fully performed. The Commanding General has requested the establishment of this board, and deems it imperative that the parties composing it should reside in Charleston. I hope the section will be adopted.

On the question being taken, the Convention refused to strike out, and the section passed to its third reading.

Sections nine and ten were passed to a third reading.

Mr. E. W. M. MACKEY moved a suspension of the rules to enable the house to put the Ordinance on its third reading, and the motion, being decided in the affirmative, the Ordinance was read a third time by the title and passed.

It was moved to reconsider the vote just had, and to lay the motion on the table. Adopted.

The Convention then adjourned.

FORTY-SIXTH DAY.

Monday, March 9, 1868.

The Convention assembled at 10 A. M., and was called to order by the PRESIDENT.

Prayer was offered by the Rev. B. F. WHITTEMORE.

The roll was called, and a quorum answering to their names, the PRESIDENT announced the Convention ready to proceed to business.

The PRESIDENT announced, as the first business, the special order for the consideration of the Ordinance for a division of the State into Congressional Districts.

Mr. N. G. PARKER. I move a suspension of the rules for the purpose of reconsidering section three of article two on the legislative part of the Constitution, which passed a third reading last Saturday. The motion to suspend was agreed to.

Mr. N. G. PARKER. I move that section three of the legislative report be reconsidered for the purpose of placing it once more in the hands of the committee, with power to examine the voluminous papers in reference to the formation of a new county out of Barnwell, Lexington, Edgefield and Orangeburg, received since the section was passed. It is not often we have such an opportunity as is here offered by the formation of a new county to benefit seventy thousand people.

Mr. E. W. M. MACKEY moved to lay the motion for reconsideration on the table, which was not agreed to.

Mr. L. BOOZER. I am opposed to the amendment to reconsider, on the ground that we have much more important business before us than the formation of a new district. The question has been disposed of twice before by the Convention. I desire, and it is no doubt the wish of a great majority of the Convention, to refer the subject to the Legislature, where it will receive a fair and full hearing. Lexington is a portion of the county out of which this new district will be formed, and my constituents have not been consulted. I protest against the mutilation and disintegration of Lexington District before the voice of the people has been heard on the subject. I move that the motion to reconsider be laid on the table.

The motion was agreed to.

The next business was the consideration of "an Ordinance to divide the State into Congressional Districts."

Mr. C. M. WILDER moved to amend by striking out from the third Congressional District the County of "Richland" and insert "Fairfield" and to strike out "Fairfield" from the fourth Congressional District and insert "Anderson" and to strike out "Anderson" in the Third district and insert "Fairfield."

Mr. B. BYAS. I hope the amendment will not prevail. The Committee have given this subject the most careful attention, and I think we should abide by their report. They have considered all the points involved, and their judgment in the matter should certainly have great weight. Probably the amendment might be the means of casting a few more votes in Richland District, but I do not think it would be wise to reject the report. Until a division of the State is made, under Congressional provisions, I think we can get along very well with the report of the committee.

Mr. W. B. NASH. I hope the amendment will prevail. The gentleman from Berkley (Mr. BYAS) thinks the committee have done well; I entertain a contrary opinion. They have not given any reasons why our district should be divided. I also believe that the delegates from our part of the State know best what is for our welfare, as surely as well as the gentleman from Berkley (Mr. BYAS), or from any other section of the State. We are not willing for our district to be divided. We want it to stand just as it is, with Fairfield in the third. I hope the Convention will not divide our district without our consent.

Mr. R. B. ELLIOTT. I hope the amendment will prevail. It may suit one district to have the section as it stands, but on the other hand, it does not suit five others. The district I have the honor to represent is as large as any other district in the State. I am unable to perceive in what way the division, as reported by the committee, will benefit us. I find that those who are most clamorous in the desire that this section should go as reported, are not those who are interested in the district, or reside anywhere near it, and I think the duty of the Convention to regard the voice of those most immediately interested. It is the desire of the delegations from those respective districts, which comprise the Third Congressional District, that the amendment of the gentleman from Richland (Mr. WILDER) should prevail.

Mr. B. F. RANDOLPH. This matter of re-arranging Congressional Districts was referred to a committee, which we supposed thoroughly understood the matter. That committee has had the subject under consideration, and made their report. I hope the Convention will adopt the report of the committee without amendments. It would not be wise for me, nor do I think it necessary to give the reasons why the committee arranged the districts as they are, and made their report accordingly. The matter is known to you all, and that is sufficient for me to say this much to you. I shall vote for the arrangement as reported by the committee, for reasons best known to all.

Mr. R. SMALLS moved that the amendment be indefinitely postponed, which was not agreed to.

Mr. W. J. WHIPPER. I am glad that the motion to postpone indefinitely has not prevailed, and I hope the amendment will not be adopted. I was one upon that committee. There is in the new arrangement a majority of loyal voters in every Congressional District. If the change is made, proposed by this amendment, you give the Fourth Congressional District a disloyal majority of sixteen hundred. If that is the desire of this body, or those who favor the amendment, then make it, but if you would preserve a loyal majority in each Congressional District, adopt the Ordinance as it came from the committee.

Mr. C. C. BOWEN. I certainly have no individual or selfish interest in this matter. A committee has been appointed to draft an Ordinance, and they have presented the result of their consultation to this body. I hope the Convention will adopt the report. I claim to have a common interest with the balance of South Carolina, and when it is evident, by the proposed amendment, to deliver into the hands of the opposite party one member of Congress, I must say I protest against it.

Mr. A. BRYCE Who is the opposite party?

Mr. C. C. BOWEN. I know of but two parties in South Carolina— the Republican and the Democratic party. There is legally no objection to the Ordinance presented by the committee. No county is separated from another. These are all adjoining, and everything has been done required by any custom or rule whatever. I think it due to the people of the State at large to adopt that report. We have no business to jeopardize the interests of any class of loyal voters in the territosy over which they have control. I hope the amendment will be voted down.

The question being taken on the amendment of the member from Richland, it was decided in the negative.

Section one then passed to its third reading.

Section two passed to its third reading without debate.

Mr. J. J. WRIGHT. I move to strike out the third section. In all our deliberations it becomes us to review the past and look well to the future; to understand perfectly as near as possible what we are doing. I have no doubt gentlemen will differ with me, but I believe the view I take to be correct. The third section reads as follows:

SECTION 3. At the first election under this Constitution, two representatives shall be elected at large on the State ticket, to represent the overplus of our population. Should they obtain seats, they shall continue to be so elected until the new apportionment after the census of 1870.

The Congress of the United States is composed of a certain number of Representatives and Senators, and that number is fixed by law, which remains as such until it is changed upon the statute books. The apportionment of representatives to Congress is made by the Congress of the United States itself. It may be that South Carolina will have six representatives in the Lower House of Congress, or she may not. It is to be determined by Congress, after the State is re-admitted to representation in Congress, and a new apportionment is made in 1870. It will, perhaps, be remembered that this matter came up for consideration in Congress upon a bill which was introduced, providing that South Carolina should elect two representatives for the State at large. The bill failed.

A MEMBER. That bill was withdrawn.

Mr. J. J. WRIGHT. I consider it equivalent to a failure. There is, united and sitting together, a body of wise men in Congress, who are working for the general welfare of the people of the United States. They are looking to South Carolina, and are willing we shall have all we are entitled to, and if they had thought it proper to give us two representatives at large, the bill introduced would have passed. I simply desire that we shall not attempt to arrogate to ourselves any privilege that may be denied by Congress. I believe if we elect two representatives of the State at large in the coming election, they will not be permitted to take seats upon the floor of Congress as representatives. I am not anxious to have this done. If we have two men in South Carolina who possess the requisite ability to take seats at large in the House of Representatives, let us have their services where we know they are most needed. I am told there are members of the Convention who have addressed members of Congress upon the subject, and that the reply has been that they did not believe members at large would be admitted as representatives. We had better not undertake to elect any such representatives. We can get along without it; we must not be too eager for power. We are entitled to four, and the reconstruction act allows us as many Congressmen as were entitled in 1860. Until a new apportionment is made, or Congress sees proper to give the State of South Carolina one or more members, we should be content, and not claim seats upon the floor of Congress for two more members than allowed by the reconstruction act.

Mr. B. O. DUNCAN. It was not the object of this Ordinance to arrogate to themselves any privilege which we did not have, or claim rights which we are not entitled to. Our population entitles us to six representatives in the Lower House. When the apportionment was made, we were entitled to but four members of Congress, because two-fiths were not entitled to representation at all. That is not the case now ; we are entitled to the representation of our entire people. By special act of Congress, of 1860, we have four members of Congress. As the gentleman from Beaufort (Mr. J. J. WRIGHT) has very properly said, Congress has this matter in its own hands and can change that apportionment. Congress is composed of two hundred and forty-one members. Under the apportionment, South Carolina at present is allowed but four ; but if Congress sees fit to give us more, that body can very easily make the change.

Mr. Stevens' plan, as proposed by him, was exactly in accordance with this part of the report. For reasons unknown to myself, he withdrew that plan, by which we would have been enabled to have obtained the two other members to which we are entitled. The committee felt very doubtful as to whether they would have the two additional members, so they placed the matter in a seperate section.

Mr. B. BYAS. I hope the section will not be stricken out, but that it will be adopted as it came from the committee. I think the committee have shown wisdom in introducing this matter. It is the prerogative of all the States to have such representation on the floor of Congress as is necessary to defend its rights, and according to the number of its population. Some said heretofore, if we disfranchise the black people of South Carolina they would lose a large representation in the House of Representatives. If we enfranchise them, that will give the negro the power. Then they said, we will have nothing to do with them, we will keep neutral. If South Carolina, along with the rest of the Southern

103

States, had adopted the Constitutional Amendment, they would have been represented upon the floor of Congress to-day, and we would not have had a voice in the matter. The gentleman from Beaufort (Mr. J. J. WRIGHT) says that representation is established by law of Congress. Very true. Congress is the law making power of the land. Is it not, then, in the power of Congress to pass an act at any moment giving this State two more representatives upon the floor of Congress. It certainly can, and I believe it will yet be done. The same gentleman also states that we want material amongst ourselves. So we do; but if we elect these representatives, it is not necessary to send them to Washington immediately. We can elect them, and they can stay until Congress decides what representatives to allow us.

Mr. W. J. WHIPPER. It is true we have been informed from a public source, that we are not entitled to more than four representatives in the Lower House of Representatives. It must be remembered, however, that representation was then based upon a census since changed. At that time the colored people were only counted as three-fifths; now we are entitled to representation for all of them, and that representation on one hundred and twenty-five thousand voters, entitles us at least to five if not six representatives. This is the rule both of law and population. It was fair to presume, without knowing just exactly what would be done by Congress, that we would be warranted in electing two representatives at large. We did not feel warranted however, in changing the districts. We knew four would certainly be admitted, and we thought through their influence, the two others might secure admission. As to the measure spoken of which was before Congress, I need only say that Mr. Stevens withdrew it to avoid the opposition springing up in his own ranks, and in order to try to get the measure through some other time, he was willing to withdraw it. But it shows clearly that Mr. Stevens thought it was due to us that those unrepresented should be represented. But we may proceed to elect two members at large, and if they obtain admission, we will then have the representation to which we are entitled according to our population. Congress may change the act at any time, and at any rate no inconvenience is likely to grow out of the election of two members at large of the State. If they do not secure admission, no harm is done. If they do, so much the better.

Mr. C. C. BOWEN. I hope the third section will not be stricken out. I, at one time, entertained a somewhat similar opinion to that of my friend from Beaufort (Mr. WRIGHT), but, upon examination, I have changed that opinion. By an act of Congress provision is made for the admission of members from Territories. For instance, a Territory is entitled to one member. The moment she is admitted as a State, she is entitled to representation under the act. Suppose these men are elected at large and go on to Washington. They ask for admission but are not admitted. No harm is done. They can go home and the State will have need of their services. If they should be admitted as members of Congress, then they immediately do us a great deal of good. I, therefore, hope the section will remain as it is.

Mr. R. B. ELLIOTT moved the previous question, which was sustained.

The question was taken on the motion to strike out the section, and decided in the negative.

The Ordinance then passed to its third reading.

Mr. E. W. M. MACKEY, from the Committee on the Legislative part of the Constitution, to which had been recommitted section four of the report of that Committee, reported back the same amended.

The section was read, passed and declared an integral portion of the Constitution.

Sec. 4. The House of Representatives shall consist of one hundred and twenty-four members, to be apportioned among the several counties according to the number of inhabitants contained in each. An enumeration of the inhabitants, for this purpose, shall be made in 1869, and again in 1875, and shall be made in the course of every tenth year thereafter, in such manner as shall be by law directed ; and Representatives shall be assigned to the different counties in the above mentioned proportion, by act of the General Assembly at the session immediately succeeding every enumeration ; *Provided*, That until the apportionment, which shall be made upon the next enumeration shall take effect, the representation of the several counties, as herein constituted, shall be as follows :

Abbeville 5, Anderson 3, Barnwell 6, Beaufort 7, Charleston 18, Chester 3, Clarendon 2, Colleton 5, Chesterfield 2, Darlington 4, Edgefield 7, Fairfield 3, Georgetown 3, Greenville 4, Horry 2, Kershaw 3, Lancaster 2, Laurens 4, Lexington 2, Marion 4, Marlboro 2, Newberry 3, Oconee 2, Orangeburg 5, Pickens 1, Richland 4, Spartanburg 4, Sumter 4, Union 3, Williamsburg 3, York 4.

The PRESIDENT announced the next special order to be the report of the Committee on Franchise and Elections.

On motion of Mr. R. C. DeLARGE, the consideration of the special order was suspended for fifteen minutes.

Mr. R. C. DeLARGE. On Saturday last we passed an Ordinance entitled, "an Ordinance to provide for the ratification of the Constitution and Ordinances, and for the election of certain officers." We desire a reconsideration of that Ordinance, in order to amend in a manner that I believe will give more general satisfaction, and place the ratification of the Constitution beyond all doubt.

On motion of Mr. B. F. WHITTEMORE the rules were suspended for thirty minutes.

Mr. R. C. DeLARGE. I ask leave to introduce the following:

We, the People of South Carolina, in Convention assembled, do ordain: That the second and third sections of an Ordinance to provide for the ratification of the Constitution and Ordinances, and for the election of certain officers be and the same are hereby rescinded.

I trust that the Convention will agree to rescind those two sections. The object is not to destroy them entirely. We desire to amend by striking out the words "and Ordinances." After consultation among our friends it was deemed advisable to submit the Constitution free and untrammelled to the people. We do not wish, by any measure, to place weapons in the hands of the enemies of reconstruction, with which they might thwart the desires of the loyal people.

Mr. E. W. M. MACKEY. In order to prevent further discussion, and to meet the views of all parties more generally, I ask leave to introduce an Ordinance amendatory of the Ordinance passed last Saturday, striking out the words "and Ordinances" wherever they occur in the latter.

Since I reported the Ordinance, my views as to the propriety of submitting all of the Ordinances passed by the Convention to the people with the Constitution, have undergone a change. I was of the opinion, that some of these Ordinances would secure us a large number of votes, but on account of the strenuous opposition that has been made here, I am, myself, disinclined to adopt such a course. It has been said here, that if these Ordinances were submitted with the Constitution, members would be compelled to vote against the ratification of that instrument. These are sufficient reasons to induce me to offer the following Ordinance:

AN ORDINANCE

To amend an Ordinance entitled "An Ordinance to provide for the Ratification of the Constitution and Ordinances, and for the election of certain Officers.

We, the people of South Carolina, by our Delegates in Convention met, do ordain: That the aforesaid Ordinance is so amended as to strike out the words "and Ordinances" in the following places:

In the title—

On the second line of section one.

On the first line of section two.
On the first line of section three.
On the second line of section three.
On the third line of section three.
On the sixth line of section four.

Mr. R. C. DeLARGE. I withdraw the Ordinance offered by myself and accept this as a substitute.

Mr. N. G. PARKER. I hope this amendatory Ordinance will be adopted. On Saturday I made a motion to strike out the words "and Ordinances," and after considerable debate, it was almost unanimously decided that my amendment should be indefinitely postponed. I am glad to see some persons coming to their senses. Now, I hope to see this Ordinance pass as unanimously as the amendment. was voted down. I wish to congratulate members on the disposition they have always shown, whenever they have found any measure that had been adopted to be wrong, to turn right square about and set things right again.

Mr. B. F. WHITTEMORE. I was well aware that the members of the Convention, when this Ordinance passed on Saturday, had not given it that consideration which its importance demanded. There is, probably, not one on this floor but is anxious when the Constitution is submitted to the people to have it ratified. I believe it will be ratified. There are some members who have been compelled, from conscientious scruples, to vote against some of the Ordinances, as they have arisen from time to time. They have been consistent in their action. If we append the Ordinance to the Constitution when it is submitted to the people, they would again be compelled to vote against that Constitution. I believe no gentleman here desires to place that instrument in such a position that even members of the body will be compelled to vote against it. I look upon this matter as very important, and am glad that the committee have reported this morning against the adoption of the Ordinance with the words "and Ordinances." I trust the good sense of the Convention will be exercised, and that each and every man will vote for striking out from the Ordinance the words the committee desire.

Mr. B. F. RANDOLPH. The substitute for this Ordinance proposes to strike out the words "and Ordinances." I am opposed to that for various reasons. These Ordinances have been passed by this Convention, and it is not right for the members now to go back upon them, and to do what would appear to be an act of nullification. The argument of the gentleman from Darlington, is that there are certain delegates to the Convention who are opposed to these Ordinances; that they voted against them, and cannot now conscientiously vote for them, when the Constitution is submitted to the people for ratification.

Mr. N. G. PARKER. I desire to state, I voted for every Ordinance.

Mr. B. F. RANDOLPH. The gentleman from Darlington favors the substitute for the reasons I have stated. Then there are delegates upon the floor of the Convention who voted against different sections of the Constitution; sections in the Bill of Rights and other articles. These sections are part and parcel of the Constitution. According to the gentleman's argument, those who voted and argued against certain sections, cannot now vote conscientiously for the Constitution, and they must go back to their constituents, and induce them also not to vote for the Constitution, because they are opposed to certain sections.

Mr. B. F. WHITTEMORE. I rise to a point of order. The gentleman from Orangeburg is accusing the gentleman from Darlington of an intention to go back to his constituents, and induce them not to vote for the Constitution.

The PRESIDENT. The point of order is not sustained. It would be a problematical matter as to what the gentleman from Darlington will do, and the gentleman from Orangebnrg is entitled to his theory.

Mr. B. F. RANDOLPH. I said that according to the gentleman's argument, the members who voted against certain sections and certain amendments would not vote for the Constitution, and, as a matter of course, would not advise their constituents to vote for it. I did not charge that the gentleman from Darlington would do so. If we are going to vote for the Constitution, we may as well vote for the Ordinances. If the Ordinances do not accompany the Constitution, it would only complicate matters in such a way that the great mass of people will not understand it.

Mr. R. C. DeLARGE. I desire to ask the gentleman whether, if this Convention should pass an Ordinance of a legislative character, it would have any more validity after submitting it to the people than before?

Mr. B. F. RANDOLPH. Of course it would, and I suppose the gentleman knew it. I have before me now Ordinances which were ratified with the Constitutions of other States, and are as legal and binding as the Constitutions themselves. To all intents and purposes South Corolina is still a Territory; and, like eleven other States, will be so regarded until they are readmitted to representation on the floor of Congress. In this attitude they may, with perfect propriety, vote for these Ordinances. I claim, therefore, if the Ordinances are submitted at all, they should be submitted with the Constitution, or the voters of South Carolina will not understand for what they are voting. They are as much a law of the State as the Constitution itself. They are but clauses of the Constitution under another name, and I see no reason why, in their present shape, they can endanger that instrument. There are certain gentlemen opposed to invalidating slave debts; but this Convention has passed just such an Ordinance, and, for one, I am in favor of submitting it to the people. I hope, therefore, the words "and Ordinances" will not be stricken out.

Mr. WILDER. I have not risen to make a speech, but simply to suggest one or two plans. In my judgment this Ordinance should go with the Constitution. The question has arisen which policy is best? I am decidedly of the opinion that this Ordinance, if attached to the Constitution, will prove a great wedge with which we shall break asunder the opposite party. There are many men who intend to vote against this Constitution under any circumstences; but chiefly because it was drawn up by the ring-streaked-and-striped Convention. There are a great many persons who will be benefitted by the passage of this Ordinance; as for instance, those who have been relieved from debt; and from this class we shall receive a strength which we cannot obtain from the Constitution alone.

The hour for the special order having arrived, Mr. B. F. RANDOLPH moved that the rules be suspended until the Ordinance was disposed of, which was agreed to.

Mr. J. S. CRAIG. I rise simply to say that I will not vote for anything in direct conflict with what I conceive to be the law of the land. If you want to kill this Constitution, add to it these Ordinances, and you will not only compel a number of the members of this Convention to vote against that instrument, but thousands of people throughout the State will either vote against the Constitution or remain away from the polls.

Mr. W. J. WHIPPER. I am opposed to submitting these Ordinances to the people. They were adopted by the Convention in a purely legislative capacity; they are themselves strictly legislative, and not a portion of the organic law which we have been called here to create; hence they are subject to the action of a future Legislature. It is not proper that they should be submitted to the people for ratification; because, being matters purely within the control of the people, they must be modified or changed at their pleasure. There are some of these Ordinances which are not likely to be affected by legislative action, but there are others which undoubtedly will be changed by the next body which assembles in this city in a representative capacity. It is, therefore, unwise as well as unnecessary to declare them a portion of the organic law of the State, and then place them beyond the control of the Legislature. I take it that this Convention has certain legislative powers, such for instance as are created by the necessities of the times, and the people in their Conventional capacity may enact such laws as may meet this necessity ; but we must take care that while acting in such capacity, not to legislate on any subject which is not clearly within our province, and on which the will of the people may, at some future time, desire to assert itself ; for this reason, I claim we have no right to submit these Ordinances as a whole for ratification in connection with the Constitution. Again, why burden the Constituion with Ordinances, many of which have been vehemently opposed by gentlemen on the floor of the Convention. I believe to attach these Ordinances to the Constitution, in all probability if it does not defeat it, will at least largely diminish the majority. There are Ordinances I would oppose. There are no doubt a number, perhaps a very large number, outside the Convention who would vote for the ratification of the Constitution, but would not vote for the Ordinances. I, therefore, hope the Ordinances will not be submitted to the people at all.

Mr. B. F. RANDOLPH. Are there not sections in the Constitution that you are opposed to ?

Mr. W. J. WHIPPER. I have just stated I was not one that would oppose the Constitution on account of the Ordinances. But I hope that the Constitution as framed by this body will be submitted to the people unburdened by any act of legislation whatever. If it then is rejected, no man will be able to say hereafter, it was because the Ordinances were attached to it. I do not wish our own friends to say we cannot conscientiously vote for your Constitution, because of the Ordinances submitted with it. If there is a necessity for submitting the Ordinances, then let them be submitted by themselves.

Mr. A. J. RANSIER. I opposed on Saturday the amendment proposed by the gentleman from Sumter (Mr. MOSES), and favored the indefinite postponement of that amendment. It was proposed then to strike out in the Ordinance referred to the words " and Ordinances."

Mr. F. J. MOSES, Jr. The gentleman has referred to the amendment introduced by myself. I desire to state that was not the ground covered by my amendment. I do not wish the Convention to suppose that I am in favor of adopting the Ordinances without submitting them to the people.

Mr. A. J. RANSIER. If I mistake not, the amendment proposed by the gentleman from Sumter was to submit the Ordinances and Constitution separately to the people. An amendment to strike out the words "and Ordinances" was proposed by the gentleman from Barnwell (Mr.

PARKER), and a motion to indefinitely postpone that amendment was made. Upon both of these I expressed an opinion. I was not in fav-ᵣ of striking out the words "and Ordinances," simply because I had supposed that this Convention was satisfied with every Ordinance that had received a majority of votes and passed the Convention. I believed the Convention looked upon them as framed and introduced by gentlemen impressed with a sense of their obligations to act only in the interests and for the good of the whole people. I supposed that to be the case, and was, therefore, perfectly willing for one to put these Ordinances beyond the risk of possible defeat. But it seems that some entertain the opinion that there is something unconstitutional and illegal connected with some of these Ordinances. Especially does this apply to the Ordinance invalidating contracts based upon the purchase of slaves. I attach no force to the argument. There seems to be a dread in the mind of some in the Convention, that the people would not ratify that Ordinance in particular. I had the pleasure of expressing an opinion upon that Ordinance, and I repeat, that I do not believe that any contracts based upon the purchase of slaves ever did have any binding force. Suppose the constitutionality of that Ordinance is questioned at all, how will it tend to defeat the ratification of our Constitution, if passed as a part of that Constitution. The constitutionality of it may be questioned, as if simply passed by the Convention and not incorporated into the Constitution. The courts will have the same opportunity to take hold of it, and make it matter perhaps of litigation. If I felt assured, in common with the apprehension of some gentlemen here, that submitting these Ordinances for ratification as a part of the Constitution was calculated to defeat the ratification of that Constitution, I stand prepared to say let them not, for God's sake, go with the Constitution. But I do not share in this apprehension; I am impressed with the idea that every Ordinance passed by this Convention has been made in the best interests of the people. I believe the class of people who would vote against these Ordinances would vote against the Constitution, whether these Ordinances are or are not submitted with it. But if the majority deem this apprehension well founded, that the Ordinances would endanger the ratification of the Constitution, then I am prepared to detach them, and take no risk of their connection with the Constitution. But, as I have said, the argument is intended to apply principally to the Ordinance invalidating contracts based upon the purchase of slaves. There are a large number of men in this State who would vote for that Ordinance, and the Constitution with it, if it were necessary to ratify the latter, in order to carry the former. Perhaps a larger number would vote for the

Constitution with it, than there would if it be detached. That is my mpression. But, if this apprehension is well founded, I am prepared to vote for the Ordinance, as amended by the gentleman from Orangeburg, (Mr. E. W. M. MACKEY), though I am not at all convinced, by any argument offered, as to the injurious effect of attaching the Ordinances to the Constitution. I propose to give those gentlemen, however, who are alarmed, the benefit of any doubt on the subject.

Mr. J. J. WRIGHT. I entertain no doubt but that the Constitution we are about to frame will be ratified. I feel assured of that, whether the Ordinances are or are not attached to it. I am in favor of every Ordinance passed by this Convention. I have made every effort in this Convention to pass them, and especially the Ordinance invalidating contracts where slaves were the consideration. But what I desire to say in relation to the Ordinances is this : it would be a new wrinkle to me, a new wrinkle in the history of American jurisprudence, for the Ordinances of a Convention to be submitted to the people with the Constitution.

Mr. B. F. RANDOLPH. Do you pretend to say it never has been done by any State ?

Mr. J. J. WRIGHT. I say it would be a new wrinkle for an Ordinance to be submitted to the people with the Constitution, as a part of that Constitution. I wish to state in what light I regard these Ordinances ; their force, and how they stand before the courts, and then to consider whether it would be necessary for us to submit them to the people for ratification.

In the first place then, I contend that the Ordinances passed by the Convention are a part of the laws of South Carolina, made such by the legislation of a portion of the people sent here to represent the people of South Carolina in Convention assembled. We claim that it is the prerogative of the Convention at any time to pass an Ordinance, or resolve themselves into a legislative body and pass an Ordinance or Ordinances. The Constitution we expect to frame will be a seperate law of South Carolina. The Ordinances will be law, just as if enacted by the Legislature of the State. These Ordinances are law, and have the force of law, and will so stand until they are either pronounced as unconstitutional by the Supreme Court of this State, or until the Legislsture of the State repeals them. The Legislature of the State at its first session may repeal every Ordinance passed by the Convention, and they will have the right and power to do it. But they have no right to repeal any clause inserthe in tde Constitution of the State. We pass these Ordinances because we believe them to be right and proper. We believe it was for the general welfare of the State of South Carolina. If there are any persons in the State who do not believe the Ordinances are law, it is their privilege, when any suit is brought in, to plead the validity of these Ordinances, and the courts cannot do otherwise than decide that these Ordinances are law, and they are compelled to abide by them. It is not necessary to submit these Ordinances to the people for ratification any more than it is to submit a law passed by the Legislature of the State.

Mr. B. F. RANDOLPH. Did you ever hear of any Constitution of South Carolina being submitted to the people for ratification?

Mr. J. J. WRIGHT. I did not. But we all know that wherever a Republican form of government exists, wherever the people are not divested of their rights, there a Constitution, whenever framed, is submitted to the people. I am in favor of submitting these Ordinances to the people with the Constitution, and I believe the majority of the people of the State are in favor of the Ordinances themselves, notwithstanding that some gentlemen upon the floor seem to think that the tendency of such a course will be to defeat the Constitution. For one, I do not imagine it will make any difference whether they are attached to the Constitution or not. The class of persons who favor the Ordinance will vote for the Constitution, and those who will vote for the Constitution will, as a general thing, vote for these Ordinances. In either case the Constitution will be ratified. I know it; you know it, and God knows it, as well as the people of South Carolina.

These Ordinances are clearly in the nature of laws, and yet the Constitution has not gone through the necessary steps to become the law of the land. It yet requires to be submitted to the people. The Ordinances are already familiar to the majority of the people; and they secure certain rights and privileges which we have not expressed in the organic law. The Constitution, on the other hand, affords security to the people.

They have got a good school system, ways and means have been devised for future legislation, and various reforms have been introduced, which look to their advancement and the general prosperity of the State. Who can doubt that when this instrument is submitted to the people, they will not sustain it? I consider it unnecessary to append to the Constitution, therefore, any law which we have adopted outside of it, and favor the proposition that has been made.

Mr. C. C. BOWEN. I am also opposed to attaching all the Ordinances passed by this Convention to this Constitution. Among the several that have been passed by this body, I contend there is but one which it is necessary shall be ratified by the people, and in order to make that valid, I am convinced that it is best to incorporate it as an article of the instrument itself. If I am rightly informed, the fourteenth article of the Constitution of Louisiana was originally an Ordinance. I do not now remember the number of Ordinances that we have adopted, but will refer to some of them. 1st. There was an Ordinance for the division of Pickens Distrtct. Now there is no use in submitting that to the people, from the fact that it has been incorporated as a section of the Constitution, and there shows for itself. Next was an Ordinance to raise money to pay the expenses of the Convention. There is no necessity of attaching it to the Constitution, because that expense will have been met and the amount will be re-imbursed to the State Treasury. Therefore, there is no necessity of submitting that to the people. Next was an Ordinance invalidating all contracts where the consideration was for the purchase of slaves. This, I contend, it is absolutely necessary we should incorporate in the Constitution, so that it may be ratified by the people, and made of binding force and effect.

It has been declared here that the Legislature will have the right to change this Ordinance, unless it is made a part of the Consttiution. That cannot be denied; but I do contend it was not intended that this Ordinance should ever be altered; and, to prevent such an act, it should be made a distinct article of the Constitution. If I understand the proposition under consideration, it is that all the Ordinances passed by the Convention may be submitted to the people in connection with the Constitution. Such a policy will be of no use whatever, since the ratification of these Ordinances will have no binding force or effect. There is but one way in which you can submit any of them, and that is by incorporating them in an article of the Constitution itself; and the only one which I care to see there, or which it is absolutely necessary should be there, is that which invalidates all contracts binding upon the purchase and sale of slaves. For these reasons I hope the amendment will be adopted, and that the word Ordinances will be stricken out.

The question now being taken, was decided in the affirmative, and the Ordinance passed to a second reading.

On motion of Mr. R. C. DeDARGE, the Ordinance was then read a third time and passed.

Mr. R. C. DeLARGE moved to reconsider, and to lay the motion to reconsider on the table, which was not agreed to.

Mr. E. W. M. MACKEY offered the following resolution:

Resolved, That upon the ratification of this Constitution, all Ordinances passed by this Convention shall be valid and binding as a part of the Constitution

On motion, the resolution was referred to the Committee on the Miscellaneous Provisions of the Constitution.

Mr. L. S. LANGLEY moved to suspend the rules, to allow the Chairman on Petitions to submit his report on the petition of the citizens of Beaufort. The motion was agreed to.

Mr. J. N. NEAGLE then made a report of the Committee on Petitions, to whom was referred the petition of the citizens of Beaufort, asking the Convention to unite with them in praying General Canby to relieve them from the oppressive abuse under which they are now suffering from their town officers. The committee recommend that the prayer of the petitioners be granted. The report was adopted.

The report of the Committee on Franchise and Elections, which had been made the special order for the day, was taken up.

Mr. S. G. W. DILL. I move to strike out all between the word provided on the ninth line, to the same on the twelfth line.

Mr. President: I think I discover here an attempt to rob the poor man of his rights, and I am sick and weary of witnessing the efforts that have been silently made to ignore him. I have seen many things in the course of my experience, but never a plainer attempt to deprive an unfortunate creature of that highest and most appreciative right—the right of suffrage. It is the only thing the poor man has left, and yet it is proposed to take even this poor boon from him. It is proposed in this section that if he is not worth a certain amount of taxable property, or happens to be illiterate, that he shall not have the right to go up like a man and cast his ballot, and declare who shall be his ruler or mine! Nay, more, I have heard it stated on the floor of this house, that men of this class were not fit to cast a vote. I denounce this section, and I denounce the man who put it here. I do not believe that any person who has a Christian heart in his body, or expects to see the light of Heaven, would introduce such a bill. It is a fraud, a swindle, or anything you please. I know there are hundreds of members in my district who are not paupers, and yet because one cannot write his name, he is, according to this phraseology, to be denied the privilege of the ballot box.

Mr C. P. LESLIE. I rise not to a point of order, but to have the gentleman called to order for language used here to-day. He has said that no Christian man would endorse the report, and made use of other expressions that were disrespectful to this body.

The PRESIDENT. The gentleman will reduce the objectionable language to writing.

Mr. C. P LESLIE. I will do so. The words used by the gentleman, as nearly as I can recollect, are these: "The section is a fraud, a cheat, a swindle, or anything else you please. No man can be an honest or a Christian man, who would dare to give his assent to any such proposition."

The PRESIDENT. The Chair decides that this language is disrespectful to the members of the house, and in violation of parliamentary rules, which regulates this and every other body of a like character.

The question before the house is, shall the gentleman be permitted to proceed?

The point of order being sustained, the house refused Mr. S. G. W. DILL to proceed with his remarks, and the delegate accordingly resumed his seat.

The hour of one o'clock having arrived, the Convention adjourned to three P. M.

AFTERNOON SESSION.

The Convention re-assembled at three P. M., and resumed the consideration of the report of the Committee on Franchise and Elections.

Section two was taken up as follows:

SECTION 2. Every male citizen of the United States, of the age of twenty-one years and upwards, not laboring under the disabilities named in this Constitution, without distinction of race, color, or former condition, who shall be a resident of this State at the time of the adoption of this Constitution, or who shall thereafter reside in this State one year, and in the county sixty days next preceding any election, and every male inhabitant of foreign birth of the age aforesaid, who shall have resided in this State one year, and in the county sixty days immediately preceding such election, and shall have declared his intention to become a citizen of the United States, conformably to the laws of the United States on the subject of naturalization, shall be entitled to vote for all officers that are now, or hereafter may be, elected by the people, and upon all questions submitted to the electors at any elections; *Provided*, That every person coming of age after the year 1875, to be entitled to the privilege of an elector, shall be able to read and write; but this qualification shall not apply to any person prevented by physical disability from complying therewith; *Provided, further*, That no person shall be allowed to vote or hold office who is now, or hereafter may be, disqualified therefor by the Constitution of the United States; but the General Assembly shall have power to remove such disability by a two-thirds vote; *Provided, further*, That no person, while kept in any alms house or asylum, or of unsound mind, or confined in any public prison, shall be allowed to vote or hold office.

Mr. W. J. McKINLAY moved to strike out in the tenth line "1875," and to insert "1878," which was not agreed to.

Mr. W. J. McKINLAY also moved to strike out the words, "the General Assembly shall have power to remove such disabilities by a two-thirds vote," which was agreed to.

Mr. S. G. W. DILL. I rise to a question of privilege. I wish to say that the accusation made against me, that I attributed, in my remarks this morning, dishonesty to some of the members, was false and without foundation. I am willing to leave it to the reporters.

Mr. R. B. ELLIOTT. I move to amend section two, in the ninth line, by striking out the word "provided," and all the words following, to the word "provided" in the twelfth line.

Mr. B. F. WHITTEMORE. I move to strike out on the sixth line the word "sixty," and insert the word "ninety," so that it shall correspond with the requisition of section ten, in the legislative department of the Constitution; also, to strike out on the tenth line the figures "1875," and insert "1890;" also, in the fourth line, to strike out "sixty," and insert "ninety."

Mr. S. A. SWAILS moved to amend by striking out all after the words "United States," on the thirteenth line.

Mr. F. L. CARDOZO. I hope the Convention will give this matter their earnest attention. It is one of the most important propositions brought before us since we have assembled in Convention. I am surprised at the indifference shown by gentlemen in passing over this section. This indifference is placing the interests of our party in jeopardy. According to this section, in the course of seven years all the people, not educated, are to be deprived of the right of voting. This is one of the most momentous subjects yet brought before us. It will take until 1875 to establish a system of schools.

Mr. B. O. DUNCAN. Does the gentleman understand this section to deprive any one of the right to vote who is twenty-one years of age before that period?

Mr. F. L. CARDOZO. Every person now fourteen years of age, who cannot read at the time fixed in this section, cannot vote on coming of age. I say it will take ten years to establish a school system in the State. There is but one place in the State where there is a system of common schools, that is in Charleston; and yet there are seven hundred thousand people in the State. I would not be surprised if it takes twenty years to establish a thorough system of common schools. It will take several millions to erect school houses. Where are we to get the money? I hope the amendment of the gentleman from Edgefield, (Mr. R. B. ELLIOTT), to strike out altogether the reading and writing qualification of a voter, will be adopted. I think it would come with bad grace from any individual in this State, who has helped to deprive men for two centuries, of the means of education, to demand that in seven years all unable to read should not be allowed to vote. It not only comes with bad grace from those opposed to us, but it is extremely ridiculous, coming from ourselves. We scarcely know what we are doing. The adoption of this section would be fatal to our success. I am convinced, if gentlemen allow this section to pass, with the reading and writing qualification proviso, before two months have passed over their heads, they will repent of their action. They will desire that that section should be reconsidered and struck out altogether. I hope gentlemen will exercise now that "ounce of prevention" which is so much "better than a pound of cure," by striking out the section altogether, or putting the time to such a distance that every one will have a fair chance to vote. It will take to 1875 to establish our system of schools. If you fix it at 1890, that will be fifteen years; then every child six or seven years of age will have fifteen years. At fourteen, parents generally demand the services of their children. I hope we will not, by our action here to-day, deprive a poor man of the only means to protect himself. I feel sure no further argument is needed. I call the attention of members to this important matter. I hope the period will be stricken out, or fixed at 1890.

Mr. R. B. ELLIOTT. Hitherto, I have taken little or no part in the debates arising in regard to other sections of the Constitution, but when it comes to the educational department, I can no longer keep silence. It is a question of too great moment to allow it to pass by quietly, especially when such a clause, as is proposed in this section, restricts the right of suffrage in the largest degree of that oppressed class with which I am doubly identified. It is proposed here to restrict the right of suffrage to every person coming of age after the year 1875.

For nearly two hundred and fifty years, we,—I say we, because I believe this to be aimed more directly at the people with whom I am identified than at any other—have been deprived of the rights of education. Even if it had been limited to thirty or forty years, I should still object to this section as it stands. I claim that this Convention has met for the purpose of laying down a basis of universal suffrage. The reconstruction act declares that all male citizens of the State shall possess the right to vote; the right to select their own officers. Here we, who have met together under that very act, under that very authority, propose to say to Congress, you are wrong; you had no right to give any such privileges to the people, and, therefore, we will restrict the privilege. How could you face your constituents? Would you say to them, you sent us to lay the foundations of liberty deep and br. ad for your children and your childrens' children, but after getting to Charleston we found out you were not fit for it; neither do we believe your children would be fit for it; consequently we have taken it away from you? Will you face your constituents and tell them this is the case? I, for one, will not do it. I ask that the amendment to strike out this clause may be accepted. If we are true to the great charge entrusted to us, we cannot hesitate a moment. Some gentlemen believe 1875 would be ample time for the education of all this large class of people. I believe the time fixed by the gentleman from Darlington, 1890, insufficient. Some one will, perhaps, reply and say, that the Constitution of Massachusetts has such a proviso. That proviso, however, did not become a part of the Constitution of Massachusetts until 1857, and I would ask, gentlemen, how long the Constitution of the State of Massachusetts had been in existence before that proviso was adopted? Since its adoption it has worked as much, if not more, injury than good. The ballot box has been perverted. Men, not able to read, have got others to go with them, read the Constitution of the United States, write their names, say they were the men, and after having taken a false oath, have voted, though not able to read and write. Do we propose to encourage any such pernicious practice? If we do, then we will vote for the section as it stands; if we do not, it is our duty to strike it out at once. If such a proposition were submitted to the people to decide, and the majority saw fit to change from universal to qualified suffrage, it is their privilege to do so; but it would certainly be wrong for us to attempt to insert any such provision in the Constitution. I trust we will vote down such a provision, by voting for the amendment I have proposed.

Mr. C. P. LESLIE. I am aware that when the committee made this report to the Convention, they embodied in it such sentiments and opinions as the committee thought right and proper. They were considered with a good deal of care, so that when they took the shape and form of a report, they should eminently reflect the popular sense, or the best sense that the committee had upon the subject in hand. Our friends upon the floor of the Convention thought that we took a long time in making the report. But they made it as their deliberate and calm judgment. I desire to state why the committee did not strike out that section. The member from Orangeburg (Mr. B. F. RANDOLPH)

105

offered a resolution to the Convention, which is, in substance, the same as the provision in this report, that none should be allowed to vote who were unable to read after a certain period. The committee took that under consideration. As a member of that committee, I thought, upon first reflection, the resolution a good one. But on second reflection, I came to the conclusion that a man in a Republican form of government, if he was responsible to the government for a dollar, is liable to be taxed ; has a dollar to gain or to lose, has a right to go to the ballot box to deposit his vote, and you cannot deprive him of it. Although I helped to insert that provision, I afterwards concluded to move to strike it out.

Mr. W. J. McKINLAY. There are some subjects which are extremely unpopular to advocate upon the floor of this Convention. Nevertheless, I think it is but right that a man should divest himself of all prejudices, and look only for the good of the whole country. I have done so, and I have conscientiously come to the conclusion that the amendment I offered should prevail, namely : that all persons coming of age after the year 1878, unless they had certain qualifications and were able to read and write, they should not be allowed to vote. I shall endeavor to give my reasons why I have come to that conclusion. As far as 1890 is proposed by the gentleman from Darlington, we are living in a Republican government, where the rulers of the government are chosen by the people. Now, in order to have wise men at the head of our government, it is necessary that the people should be educated and have a full sense of the importance of the ballot. The public schools are to be supported by the public. The revenue for the support of the public schools was principally to be derived through a capitation tax. If that provision for such a tax had not been stricken out, I would have favored the section as it stands. But that having been withdrawn, I am willing to give my vote to extend the time to 1890. It is but right if this State establishes a system of free schools, supported by the taxes and money of the people, that it should be demanded by the State that the people should avail themselves of the privileges of those public schools, so as to, at least, be able to read and write. The delegates, I hope, will take all these matters into consideration and come to a calm, deliberate judgment upon the subject that will be of benefit to the whole people.

Mr. R. C. DeLARGE. There are now two amendments before the Convention. I shall address myself to the question of striking out the figures "1875." I contend that the General Assembly have no right to insert any provision in the Constitution that will disfranchise any citizen of the State. If citizens are disfranchised by the general government, it rests altogether with the general government to restore their franchise. I, therefore, hope the amendment of the gentleman from Darlington, to insert 1890, will prevail.

Mr. A. J. RANSIER. When the report of the Committee on Franchise and Elections was made, I came to the conclusion that the proposition made by the gentleman from Kershaw would prevail. My learned friend and colleague (Mr. CARDOZO) was surprised that this section should be acted upon with such apparent indifference. I can assure him that there were others besides myself who were only waiting our opportunity to get a hearing in order to express an opinion upon the subject. The question involved is, whether the right of suffrage is a natural or acquired right, or an established privilege, which may be given or withheld at pleasure under a Republican form of government.

All men have a natural and unalienable right to life, liberty and the pursuit of happiness, and I am, therefore, in favor of every means by which these can be protected and defended. The right to vote is among them, and it is by this means that the citizen is best enabled to protect the great interest which must concern his manhood. It is the right which belongs alike to the wise and the ignorant, to the virtuous and vicious, and I cannot give my consent in this Convention, met under the genius of American liberty, as interpreted by a Republican Congress, to any qualification upon this privilege. It has been declared upon this floor that certain of the speeches made here have been intended to produce simply an effect outside. I care not what impression may be made upon the public mind, so that I am secure in the consciousness that I am discharging, to the best of my ability, the duty which I owe to the people of South Carolina, whom I have the honor in part to represent. In venturing an expression of opionion upon this subject, I am guided by a conscientious regard for my duty. This is not a question that we should deal with lightly. I hope that the music of the nineteenth century will inspire every man upon the floor to view it in the light of progress and of reason, and to strike from it every word that puts a limitation upon the manhood of the citizen, so far as regards his right to vote. Let the section go forth untrammelled by any qualification whatever. I do not like to use the words colored or white in discussing this matter, but the necessity of the case compels me to do so. So long as the question of suffrage to the white man was concerned, I have never heard of an educational or other qualification. So soon, however, as the colored man applies for this privilege, you at once, on every side, hear the demand that he must be surrounded with both property and educational restrictions, which would deprive a large portion of our race of this ines-

timable privilege. As I said before, it is our chief means for self-defence
This section will be a weapon in our hands, if we shall use it properly
and I do hope that we shall clog it by no qualifications whatever. Th
Congress of the United States deemed it proper, after the l pse of ninet:
years, to dispense tardy justice to the colored man, and to declare uni
versal suffrage over every portion of this country which they control
And the moment we attach a qualification to this right, even in the
manner proposed, we give the lie to the justice of their legislation and
to the wisdom of their measures.

Mr. R. H. CAIN. I would have been perfectly content to let other
gentlemen discuss this matter, for I did not suppose there would be a
prolonged debate on the striking out of this provision. It appears to me,
however, there are certain persons who are making an endeavor to
enforce this proviso, and I cannot see the necessity for its existence in this Constitution at all. It has been claimed by some that the
effect of this provision will be to establish schools, and induce a greater
proportion, perhaps a large majority, of the colored people to educate
themselves. On the other hand, it has been contended that it will disfranchise a large portion of the present citizens of the State after a certain period. In my judgment, no advantage whatever can occur from
the qualification, even though the proviso should run until 1890. I see
no use for it. The right of suffrage ought not to be abridged under any
circumstances, and under no provision of our Constitution ought any
citizen of the State to be deprived of the enjoyment of that right, which is
his by virtue of his creation, by virtue of the act of Congress, and by virtue of that justice which is due to all men. Why should we place any
restriction whatever upon a vote ? It is said that man must learn to
read. Why, if you go into New York city, or among those States
where the Democratic party have the strongest power, and muster their
cohorts in double file, you will find that probably not one-tenth of them
can read and write.

Mr. S A. SWAILS. Are they white or colored voters ?

Mr. R. H. CAIN. They are white voters; but, as Burns says, "a
man's a man for a' that." A man may not be able to educate himself.
The circumstances of his childhood may possibly have prevented the acquisition of knowledge, but for all that he is a man, the noblest work of
God ; and I would not deprive any being, rich or poor, of the enjoyment
of that franchise, by which alone he can protect himself as a citizen.
Whether learned or ignorant, he is subject to government, and he has an
inalienable right to say who shall govern him ; to say what shall be the
character of that government. He may not understand a great deal of the

knowledge that is derived from books; he may not be generally familiar with the ways of the world; but he can, nevertheless, judge between right and wrong, and to this extent he has as much ability to cast his vote and declare his opinion as any other man, no matter what may be his situation in life. It has too long been the right of tyrants to rule over man and prescribe for him a line of action, and never again will this right be conceded to any class, especially in South Carolina, where, as I believe, we have entered upon a new era, and obliterated those peculiar distinctions which made the ruling class the tyrants of those held in subjection. For two hundred years it has been the curse of the slave States, that a certain class of men have dictated the laws that guided the multitude, and have deprived the majority of their God-given right to express their will in the creation of those laws, in which they themselves were most interested. In remodelling the institutions of this country, we propose to establish them upon a broad basis, so that the halo of liberty may overshadow every class of men, and no right, however small, shall be withheld from those entitled to enjoy it. I am surprised to find gentlemen who, through life and amid all its fortuitous circumstances, have been permitted to enjoy the blessings of education, are not willing to confer the same blessings upon the poorer classes by whom they have been surrounded. One of the greatest reasons why I feel thankful to my Maker for the present condition of things, is that it has opened to us an age of progress, in which mankind will take a forward bound towards humanity, developing its purest principles and bringing out its greatest results. Hence it is that in this Constitution we do not wish to leave a jot or tittle upon which anything can be built to remind our children of their former state of slavery. On the contrary, I would have this instrument so comprehensive as to embrace all classes, and hold up to every man an inducement to become, in mind and estate, an honest, educated and efficient citizen of the country.

But it is said that a certain class of citizens are not qualified to vote : be that as it may, I desire to state here especially, that, for my part, I will never, never, give my influence to establish one barrier against any class of men. I care not whether they be white or black, rich or poor, I shall never interfere with their possession of this sacred right. Now, I propose to strike out this article entirely, and, in doing so, believe I shall be doing justice to ourselves, to posterity, to the coming generation, and, at the same time, we shall lay the foundation of a career in which equity, and every principle of right will be possessed, and the prosperity of man advanced.

Mr. R. C. DeLARGE. Mr President, I have not allowed any opportunity to pass, either in committee, upon the floor of the house, or before the public, when I could raise my voice in behalf of the principles of justice and equality. The resolution from which this portion of the report was taken, was introduced by the gentleman from Orangeburg, who was the first speaker this afternoon. In committee, the opponents of the measure were voted down, and we were compelled to support it. As I have always stood upon the platform of universal suffrage, I feel that I would be recreant to the trust reposed in me by my constituents if I did not advocate the striking out of that proviso. I look upon suffrage as the inherent right of man. When God creates man in his own image, I believe that he also put upon him the stamp of equality ; and with equality insured him all the rights which we claim as citizens. I do not think the Almighty ever intended to prescribe any rights or liberties which all men were not entitled to enjoy. Now, sir, my clerical friend, I desire that this proviso shall be stricken out for certain reasons which he has eloquently assigned, but I cannot see the force of his argument. No one will deny that the most critical period in the history of this State ; the most critical period of the government which we are about to inaugurate, will be during the next five years. If, upon the sound basis of universal suffrage, this State can be wheeled into line with the other States of the Union, I hold it will be proof positive that it will exist hereafter upon an equally sound basis. If the argument holds good, that suffrage can be advantageously restricted in 1875, for the life of me, I cannot see why that argument should not hold good to-day. I am not one of those who believe it is right to require a man to eat bread, and afterwards lock him in a cellar where he can get no more. We know the impoverished condition of the State. We know the amount of money that we will be required to raise for schools. We know the present condition of the people. We will not be permitted, for the next ten years, successfully to carry out that system of education which is necessary for these people. We know, furthermore, that the class of men, both white and black, who will come within the scope of this proviso, cannot afford to educate their children, even gratuitously ; they belong to the agricultural portion of the people, and are compelled to employ themselves, and their children, at the handle of the plough and in the field to obtain their daily subsistence. Now, how is it possible to take this class from their labor, in the present prostrate condition of the country, and place them at school? Were I in Massachusetts, I would advocate this proviso heartily. In South Carolina, I oppose it. I admit that some incentive should be given to education, but let it not be such an incentive as shall restrict the people in that employment which gives them their daily bread. It has been suggested that certain qualifications should be imposed in 1878 and 1890. Sir, we have enjoyed the pleasure of seeing the blessed principles established, which declare that all men are born free and equal; and yet I find many upon this floor to-day, to whom this very privilege has been heretofore denied, advocating that that doctrine may be ignored. I feel confident and grateful that there are but few of this class here; would to God there were none; for, sir, nothing pains a friend of freedom more; nothing could pain a man inspired with the truthfulness of the language of that declaration more than to find the members of the Constitutional Convention of South Carolina, at such a time as this, attempting to restrict the right of suffrage, and advocating the establishment upon a new basis different from that which now prevails. I wish it to be distinctly understood that I am here for the purpose of doing what I believe will advance the interests of the people of the entire State; for the purpose of showing the greatest amount of liberality to those who plunged this State into a rebellion and antagonism to the Union, I ask of you to show the same liberality to the men who stood by the Government; who are loyal, and prepared at this time, if necessary, to sacrifice their lives in behalf of their country. While extending the hand of friendship and good will to every one, I would not brand the other class who have ever been, and always will be, faithful to the Union, and intent on maintaining its glorious principles.

Mr. HAYNE. Did you not sign that report with the proviso?

Mr. R. C. DeLARGE. I cannot see the force of the question, especially as I have been arguing against the proviso, and signed it only that I might have the privilege of doing so, and occupying the floor, under the rule of the house, which gives me an opportunity to say the last word upon the subject. I now yield the balance of my time to my friend from Charleston.

Mr. C. C. BOWEN. If I have read the Constitution of the United States aright, you are expressly forbidden to disfranchise any person twenty-one years of age, unless it be for participation in rebellion or crime; and in the fifth section of the reconstruction acts, it is laid down that when you form a Constitution in conformity with the laws of the United States, which declares that all persons of proper age, and of whatever race or color, may be entitled to vote, you will be admitted again into the Union. I contend that the moment you attempt to abridge the right of any man to vote, you will not only jeopardize the ratification of this Constitution, but you will be acting contrary to the laws of Congress, and may not be admitted into the Union. Unless you are prepared to carry out your portion of the contract, you have no right to demand recognition at the hands of Congress. I will go further, and say that if you place such a clause in the Constitution, I tremble for the result that will follow when you go before the people of South Carolina, and ask them to ratify your work. For one, I would not dare to do so ; and, if there were any clause in the Constitution which would induce me to vote against its adoption, it would be that which we have now under discussion, and which involves all that is unjust, unwise, impolitic, and at variance with the spirit of Republicanism, and of the age.

The question then being taken on the amendment of the member from Darlington (Mr. WHITTEMORE), to strike out the figures " 1875," and insert " 1890," it was decided in the negative.

The amendment of the member from Williamsburg (Mr. SWAILS) was also rejected.

The amendment offered by Mr. McKINLAY, to strike out the words " the General Assembly shall have power to remove such disabilities by a two-thirds vote," was adopted.

The amendment of the member from Darlington (Mr WHITTEMORE), to strike out the words " seventy-five," and insert " ninety," was not agreed to.

The motion of Mr. W. J. McKINLAY, to strike out the words " 1875," and insert " 1878," was lost.

The question then recurring on the amendment of Mr. R. B. ELLIOTT, to amend by striking out the word " provided," on the ninth line of the bill, and all the words following to the word " provided," on the twelfth line, the vote was taken by yeas and nays, and resulted as follows :

YEAS--The President, Messrs. Allen, Alexander, Arnim. Becker, Bell, Bowen, Boozer, Burton, Brockenton, Bryce, Byas, R. H. Cain, E. I. Cain, Camp, Cardozo, Coghlan, Chamberlain, Chestnut, Clinton, Cook, Collins, Corley, Craig, Darrington, Davis, DeLarge, Dickson, Dill, Dogan, Donaldson, Driffle, Duncan, Edwards, Elliott, Foster, Gentry, Goss, Gray, Harris, J. N. Hayne, C. D. Hayne, H. E. Hayne, Henderson, Holmes, Humbird, Hurley. Jacobs, Jenks, Jervey, S Johnson, W. A. Johnson, J. W. Johnson, Dr. L. B. Johnson, W. E. Johnston, Joiner, Jones, Lang, Langley, G. Lee, S. Lee, Lomax, Leslie, E. W M. Mackey, Mayer, Mauldin, McDaniels, Mead, Miller, Milford. Moses, Nance, Nash, Nelson, Neagle, Newell, Nuckels, Olsen. Owens, Parker, Pillsbury, Randolph, Rainey, Ransier, Richmond, Rivers, Rose, Runion, Rutland, Sanders, Sasportas, Shrewsbury, Smalls, Stubbs, Swails, Thomas, A Thompson, B. A. Thompson, S. H. Thompson, Whittemore, Whipper, White, F. E. Wilder, C. M. Wilder, Wingo, Wooley, Wright—107.

NAYS--Messrs. Williamson and Webb--2.

ABSENT—Messrs. Crews, Donaldson, Hunter, Jackson, Jillson, Wm. J. McKinlay, W. McKinlay, Middleton, Perry, Viney—10

The amendment of Mr. R. B. ELLIOTT was adopted.

Mr. B. F. RANDOLPH. I wish to have it entered upon the Journal that I vote " Yea," for these reasons: My object in introducing the resolution, which was incorporated in the report, was to give an incentive to the people to educate themselves, in order that they might become intelligent and worthy of their new relation as citizens ; but there having been incorporated in the report on the educational department a clause requiring compulsory attendance at schools, my views are met in that section, and my object having been accomplished, I shall vote as I have indicated on the present occasion.

Mr. T. K. SASPORTAS. I vote " Yea," for the reason that it has been reported in my district that I was the introducer of this resolution. Not wishing such an opinion to prevail, I desire especially to make this explanation, to the end that those misrepresentations may not be repeated.

The section, as amended, then passed to its third reading.

Mr. J. J. WRIGHT moved the reconsideration of the vote by which the section was passed, which was adopted.

Mr. J. J. WRIGHT moved to amend by striking out all between the word " birth," in fifth line, and the word " shall," in eighth line, and to insert in place thereof the words " being a citizen of the United States, and possessing the above qualifications."

Mr. R. C. DELARGE moved to amend the amendment, by striking out all between the word " and," in fifth line, and the word " shall," in eighth line.

Mr. R. C. DELARGE. I cannot see the force of the amendment. Although I understand perfectly well what the gentleman is trying to get at. According to the section reported any person who has declared his intention of becoming a citizen of the United States, and who shall have resided in the city or county sixty days previous to the election is entitled to vote. The United States law is that no person is entitled to vote until after a residence of three or five years, I forget which. It is a matter of perfect indifference whether the foreigner be required to remain three or five years. I cannot see the force or necessity of the amendment. My friend from Beaufort says it is necessary that the Constitution should conform in this respect to the Constitution of the United States I desire to state that over twenty-one States have the clause in their Constitutions just as it reads here Some of them, Kansas, for instance, require a residence of only six months. I shall move

106

to strike out all after the word "and," in the fifth line, to the word "shall" in the eighth line, so that it will read, "every male citizen of the United States of the age of twenty-one years or upwards."

Mr. B. BYAS. I hope the amendment of the gentleman from Beaufort will prevail, and the amendment of the gentleman from Charleston will be voted down. I move to further amend the section by striking out in the fourth line the words "one year" and inserting "six months." If the section is allowed to remain as it is, a man who has lived here twenty-one years has no more right to vote than a man who has just crossed the Atlantic.

Mr. W. E. JOHNSTON. I rise to a point of order. The gentleman is making no point that we can understand.

Mr. B. BYAS. Then I will go on and explain. If a man comes from England, Ireland, Russia or Prussia, he ought to have the same right to vote after living here six months, as the citizen of South Carolina possesses. But as there has been no second to my amendment, I take it for granted that it is contrary to the sense of the Convention. I hope, however, that the motion of the gentleman from Beaufort will prevail, and I move the previous question.

The previous question was not sustained.

Mr. W. J. WHIPPER. I move to strike out the word "male," in the second line, so that it shall read "every citizen of the United States."

Mr. D. H. CHAMBERLAIN. I wish to offer another amendment, namely: to add in the twelfth line after the words "United States," the words "until such disqualification may be removed by the Congress of the United States." I hardly think it necessary to say a single word on the propriety or necessity of the amendment.

Mr. A. J. RANSIER I desire to further amend by inserting after the word "county," in the fourth, fifth and sixth lines of the bill, the words "in which he offers to vote."

Mr. B. O. DUNCAN. I trust that amendment will not prevail. We need all the population possible in this State, no matter from what locality they may come. If they come from Europe, so much the better. We are anxious to see emigrants, and we cannot get a better population than the Germans. The Irish are not likely to come, but the Germans are intelligent, frugal and industrious, free from prejudice, and well adapted to live permanently upon a soil so inviting as South Carolina. By giving to them political privileges we shall ally them with us, and that is doing no more than is done in the States of the Northwest, many of which allow the emigrants to vote after a six months' residence, or after a declaration of their intention to become citizens.

Mr. J. J. WRIGHT. I wish to say a few words in answer to the gentleman who has just taken his seat. I think the safest and surest plan for us to follow in the formation of a Constitution, is to make it as much as possible in accordance with the laws of the Unsted States. Every gentleman of intelligence will agree with me.

Mr. B. O. DUNCAN. Is that violating any law of the United States, to allow foreigners to vote after a six months' residence in the State?

Mr. J. J. WRIGHT. I do not say so; I remarked that the surest and safest way for us to form our Constitution, was to make it in accordance with the laws of the United States. Congress has framed the naturalization laws of the country in such a way that foreigners are compelled to remain here five years before becoming voters. I simply make this point in answer to what a gentleman says about emigrants. The great mass of the people who ship from the old country are not members of the wealthier or better classes of that country. The aristocracy generally send off the poorest of the poor. They desire to make the United States a poor house for Ireland. I have no objection to their coming here; I will hold out both hands and welcome them; but, at the same time, I wish to comply with the laws of Congress in relation to naturalization.

Mr. B. O. DUNCAN. Does the gentleman know what he asserts to be a fact?

Mr. J. J. WRIGHT. I believe, from my observations, that the statement I have made is true. I known this, that the people who come here, generally, are the poorer classes of the old country. I say that, without fear of successful contradiction. Now, I have been here twenty-seven years, a citizen of the United States, but I have only had the right to vote about one year. Yet we propose to bring these people, contrary to the laws of the United States, to this country, and after they have been here but one year and declared their intention to become citizens of South Carolina, to allow them to go to the polls and vote. I am perfectly willing, as I said before, to welcome these emigrants, but I am not willing that they shall become citizens of South Carolina, unless they can do so under the laws of the United States. We desire to form a Constitution as liberal as possible, but we shall be striking a blow at ourselves if we insert a clause of the kind proposed in our Constitution. We have a demonstration of some of the evils likely to occur in the experience with which some of us who have lived in New York are familiar. It is well known that emigrants are there carried from the ships to the polls and allowed to vote, and thus to influence elections which they do not understand and in which they have no personal concern. To avoid such a condition of things in South Carolina, we should, if possible, throw around this class all proper legal restrictions. If we abide by the laws of the United States, we shall show our wisdom, and at the same time be liberal without endangering the liberties of the people. I repeat, however, that one of the worst things we could do, would be to bring a mass of inexperienced emigrants to South Carolina, and, in a comparatively short time, allow them to exercise the same privileges that are enjoyed by a life-long citizen. I want those emigrants to remain here at least three years, and to cultivate social relations with the people, before they are permitted to vote.

Mr. W. J. WHIPPER. I offered my amendment, not thinking that it would be adopted. I would be pleased if it were adopted, but I am aware that this body will not show themselves so liberal and progressive as to act favorably upon this subject at the present time. For my part, I believe in universal suffrage; yet here is a word inserted in the first line of the report which prevents, perhaps, one-half of the people of this State from voting, and who, I claim, have the same rights at the ballot box that I possess I wish to have the word "male" stricken out. Whether it be done or not; however lightly the subject may be treated; however frivolous you may think it, I tell you here that I know the time will come when every man and woman in this country will have the right to vote. I acknowledge the superiority of woman. There are large numbers of the sex who have an intelligence more than equal to our own, and I ask, is it right or just to deprive these intelligent beings of the privileges which we enjoy? Sir, I look upon that disposition which denies them suffrage as essentially contemptible and wrong. Governments will continue to totter and fall until the rights of all parties are respected—womankind as well as mankind. We have seen the uprising and downfall of Republics everywhere, and the great secret of revolution has been, that governments have not extended the rights of the people to this sex. The systems of legislation have been laid upon insecure foundations, and they never will be permanent until women are recognized as the equal of men, and with him permitted to enjoy the privileges which appertain to the citizen. However frivolous you may deem it, the time will come when you will have to meet this question. It will continue to be agitated, until it must ultimately triumph. Sooner or later, everything in the shape of tyranny must yield; and, however derisively we may treat these noble women who are struggling for their sex, we shall yet see them successful in the assertion of their rights.

The question was taken on the motion of Mr. W. J. WHIPPER, to strike out the word "male," and decided in the negative.

Section eight was read, and **Mr. B. O. DUNCAN** moved to amend: "But the General Assembly shall have no right to disfranchise any person except for offences herein mentioned;" which amendment was put to the house and rejected.

Mr. B F. WHITTEMORE proposed the following as a substitute for section eight, which was adopted, and the section passed to a third reading:

SECTION 8. The General Assembly shall never pass any law that will deprive any of the citizens of this State of the right of suffrage, except for treason, murder, robbery or dueling, whereof the persons shall have been duly tried and convicted.

Sections nine and ten were read and passed to a third reading.

The hour of adjournment having arrived, the Convention adjourned to ten 10 o'clock to-morrow morning.

FORTY-SEVENTH DAY.

Tuesday, March 10, 1868.

The Convention assembled at 10 A. M., and was called to order by the PRESIDENT.

Prayer was offered by the Rev. F. L. CORDOZO.

The roll was called, and a quorum answering to their names, the PRESIDENT announced the Convention ready to proceed to business.

The Journal of Monday was read and approved.

Mr. S. G. W. DILL moved a suspension of the rules for five minutes, and offered the following resolution:

Resolved, That this Convention adjourn on Saturday, the 14th instant, at twelve o'clock, Meridian, *sine die*.

Mr. J. S. CRAIG moved that the motion to adjourn be laid on the table, which was agreed to.

The Convention then proceeded with the third reading of Article 2d of the Constitution, in relation to the legislative department.

Sections one, two, three, four, five, six, seven, were read a third time and passed.

Section eight was read, and Mr. J. S. CRAIG moved to recommit it to the committee, with instructions to report an amendment, providing that the Senate shall consist of forty-five members, apportioned among the several counties according to population, provided that each county shall be entitled to one Senator.

The motion was not agreed to.

Mr. E. W. M. MACKEY moved to recommit the section to the committee, with instructions to report, instanter, an amendment, striking out the word "city" before Charleston, and substituting the word "county," so as to read "County of Charleston," which was agreed to.

The committee, through their Chairman, made the following report, which was adopted, and the section, so amended, received its third reading:

The legislative committee beg leave to recommend that the word "city," in the eighth section of the legislative part of the Constitution be stricken out, and the word "county" inserted in its stead.

Sections nine and ten were read a third time, and passed without amendment.

Section eleven was read a second time, and Mr. E. W. M. MACKEY moved to fill up the blank by inserting "14th, 15th and 16th of April," and to strike out "1869" and insert "1870," which was adopted, and the section, thus amended, received its third reading.

Section twelve was read, and Mr. E. W. M. MACKEY moved to fill up the blank by inserting "first Monday in May."

Mr. B. F. WHITTEMORE moved to insert "first Wednesday in May."

Mr. B. O. DUNCAN moved to insert "second Tuesday in May," which was adopted.

Mr. C. P. LESLIE. I move to strike out of the twelfth section the words "casualties of war," which is made one of the exceptions to Columbia being always the Capital of the State. I want to assert one thing right now; there is to be no such thing hereafter as war in this State; there is going to be no blood shed; no such thing as strife; all is to be peace and sunshine; everything is to be serene; glistening bayonets are to be done away with, and the hordes of armed men are forthwith to quietly disperse and go to their homes.

Mr. B O. DUNCAN. How does that statement correspond with those of a previous speech which you made on this same subject?

Mr. C. P. LESLIE. I have got another idea or two in my head within two or three days that has changed my opinions, and it has been done since the nominating Convention was called. We are to have a chieftain soon who is a civilian, and we have just to manage that he shall be nominated, and every border ruffian; every outlaw in the State; every man who wants to disturb the peace and good order of this community, are to forthwith retire to their homes. There is one phase of the question we may take into consideration. Suppose a President of the United States should happen to be elected who is a Democrat, and Congress, of course, follows with the House of Representatives, I want to know what man on the floor believes, for a moment, that such a President, backed by the House of Representatives, would, by proclamation, declare all of our proceedings out of order, and order us to disperse? Is it in the order of things? If not in the order of things that such an event might possibly happen, what do we want to be talking about the casualties of war? Some of our friends say there is going to be peace, and nothing but peace, and that a certain man ought to be and should be elected Governor; I ask those men to vote on striking out these words, so that the nominee can stand squarely on the peace platform. I call upon the friends of the civilian nominee to give him such a vote as will demonstrate their strength. I predict that, under his administration, the next two years will be one of the quietest times ever witnessed in this State, and it will be a sensible thing to strike out all about "casualties of war."

The question being put, the house unanimously refused to strike out the words "casualties of war," Mr. C. P. LESLIE himself voting in the negative.

Sections twelve, thirteen, fourteen and fifteen, then received their third reading.

Section sixteen was read.

Mr. F. J. MOSES, Jr. When this section was before the Convention, on its second reading I introduced an amendment, which was as follows: to insert after the last word in the section, the word "provided, that such imprisonment shall in no case extend beyond the session of the General Assembly."

I think that amendment vitally necessary. As the section now stands, it leaves the Senate and House of Representatives the discretion to imprison members a year or more. The term is indefinite. I, therefore, ask the Convention to recommit the section to the committee, with instructions to report, instanter, the following proviso:

Provided, That such imprisonment shall, in no case, extend beyond the session of the General Assembly.

The Chairman of the Committee handed in the following report, which was adopted, and the section, as amended, passed:

Provided, Such term of imprisonment shall not, in any case, extend beyond the session of the General Assembly.

Section seventeen, and all the sections down to section thirty-three, inclusive, were severally read a third time, and passed without amendment.

The article as amended, and declared an integral portion of the Constitution, is as follows :

ARTICLE II.

LEGISLATIVE DEPARTMENT.

SECTION 1. The legislative power of this State shall be vested in two distinct branches, the one to be styled the "Senate," and the other the "House of Representatives," and both together the "General Assembly of the State of South Carolina."

SEC. 2. The House of Representatives shall be composed of members, chosen by ballot, every second year, by the citizens of this State, qualified as in this Constitution is provided.

SEC. 3. The Judicial Districts shall hereafter be designated as Counties, and the boundaries of the several counties shall remain as they are now established, except the County of Pickens, which is hereby divided into two counties, by a line leaving the southern boundary of the State of North Carolina where the White Water River enters this State, and thence down the centre of said river, by whatever names known to Ravenel's Bridge, on Seneca River, and thence along the centre of the road leading to Pendleton Village, until it intersects the line of the County of Anderson ; and the territory lying east of said line shall be known as the County of Pickens ; and the territory lying west of said line shall be known as the County of Oconee ; *Provided*, that the General Assembly shall have the power at any time to organized new counties by changing the boundaries of any of the old ones ; but no new county shall be hereafter formed of less extent than six hundred and twenty-five square miles, nor shall any existing counties be reduced to a less extent than six hundred and twenty-five square miles. Each county shall constitute one election district.

SEC. 4. The House of Representatives shall consist of one hundred and twenty-four members, to be apportioned among the several counties according to the number of inhabitants contained in each. An enumeration of the inhabitants, for this purpose, shall be made in 1869, and again in 1875, and shall be made in the course of every tenth year thereafter, in such manner as shall be by law directed ; and Representatives shall be assigned to the different counties in the above mentioned proproportion, by act of the General Assembly at the session immediately succeeding every enumeration ; *Provided*, That until the apportionment, which shall be made upon the next enumeration shall take effect, the representation of the several counties, as herein constituted, shall be as follows: Abbeville' 5, Anderson 3, Barnwell 6, Beaufort 7, Charleston 18, Chester 3, Clarendon 2, Colleton 5, Chesterfield 2, Darlington 4 Edgefield 7, Fairfield 3, Georgetown 3, Greenville 4, Horry 2, Kershaw 4, Lancaster 2, Laurens 4, Lexington 2, Marion 4, Marlboro' 2, Newberry 3, Oconee 2, Orangeburg 5, Pickens 1, Richland 4, Spartanburg 4, Sumter 4, Union 3, Williamsburg 3, York 4.

SEC. 5. If the enumeration herein directed shall not be made in the course of the year appointed for the purpose, it shall be the duty of the Governor to have it effected as soon thereafter as shall be practicable.

SEC. 6. In assigning representatives to the several counties, the General Assembly shall allow one representative to every one hundred and twenty-fourth part of the whole number of inhabitants in the State; *Provided*. That if, in the apportionment of representatives, any county shall appear not to be entitled, from its population, to a representative, such county shall, nevertheless, send one representative; and if there be still a deficiency of the number of representatives required by section four of this Article, such deficiency shall be supplied by assigning representatives to those counties having the largest surplus fractions

SEC 7. No apportionment of representatives shall be construed to take effect, in any manner, until the general election which shall succeed such apportionment.

SEC. 8. The Senate shall be composed of one member from each county, to be elected, for the term of four years, by the qualified voters of the State, in the same manner in which members of the House of Representatives are chosen; except the County of Charleston, which shall be allowed two Senators.

SEC. 9 Upon the meeting of the first General Assembly which shall be chosen under the provisions of this Constitution, the Senators shall be divided, by lot, into two classes, as nearly equal as may be; the seats of the Senators of the first class to be vacated at the expiration of two years after the Monday following the general election, and of those of the second class at the expiration of four years; so that, except as above provided, one half of the Senators may be chosen every second year.

SEC. 10. No person shall be eligible to a seat in the Senate or House of Representatives who at the time of his election is not a citizen of the United States; nor any one who has not been for one year next preceding his election a resident of this State and for three months next preceding his election a resident of the county whence he may be chosen, nor any one who has been convicted of an infamous crime. Senators shall be at least twenty-five, and Representatives at least twenty-one years of age.

SEC 11. The first election for Senators and Representatives under the provisions of this Constitution shall be held on the 14th, 15th and 16th days of April, of the present year; and the second election shall be held on the third Wednesday in October, 1870, and forever thereafter on the same day in every second year in such manner and at such places as the Legislature may hereafter provide.

SEC. 12. The first session of the General Assembly after the ratification of this Constitution, shall be convened on the second Tuesday in May

107

of the present year, in the city of Columbia, (which shall remain the seat of Government until otherwise determined by the concurrence of two-third of both branches of the whole representation), and thereafter on the fourth Tuesday in November annually. Should the casualties of war or contagious diseases render it unsafe to meet at the seat of government, then the Governor may, by proclamation, appoint a more secure and convenient place of meeting.

SEC. 13. The terms of office of the Senators and Representatives chosen at a general election, shall begin on the Monday following such election.

SEC. 14 Each House shall judge of the election returns and qualifications of its own members ; and a majority of each House shall constitute a quorum to do business ; but a smaller number may adjourn from day to day, and may compel the attendance of absent members, in such manner and under such penalties as may be provided by law.

SEC. 15. Each House shall choose its own officers, determine its rules of proceeding, punish its members for disorderly behavior, and, with the concurrence of two-thirds, expel a member, but not a second time for the same cause.

SEC. 16. Each House may punish by imprisonment, during its sitting, any person not a member, who shall be guilty of disrespect to the House by any disorderly or contemptuous behavior in its presence ; or who, during the time of its sitting, shall threaten harm to body or estate of any member for anything said or done in either House, or who shall assault any of them therefor, or who shall assault or arrest any witness or other person ordered to attend the House, in his going thereto or returning therefrom, or who shall rescue any person arrested by order of the House ; *Provided*, That such time of imprisonment shall not in any case extend beyond the session of the General Assembly.

SEC. 17. The members of both Houses shall be protected in their persons and estates during their attendance on, going to, and returning from, the General Assembly, and ten days previous to the sitting, and ten days after the adjournment thereof. But these privileges shall not be extended so as to protect any member who shall be charged with treason, felony, or breach of the peace.

SEC. 18. Bills for raising a revenue shall originate in the House of Representatives, but may be altered, amended or rejected by the Senate ; and all other bills may originate in either House, and may be amended, altered or rejected by the other.

SEC. 19. The style of all laws shall be, "Be it enacted by the Senate and House of Representatives of the State of South Carolina, now met and sitting in General Assembly, and by the authority of the same."

SEC. 20. Every act or resolution having the force of law shall relate to but one subject, and that shall be expressed in the title.

SEC. 21. No bill shall have the force of law until it shall have been read three times, and on three several days, in each House, has had the Great Seal of State affixed to it, and has been signed in the Senate House, by the President of the Senate and the Speaker of the House of Representatives.

SEC. 22. No money shall be drawn from the treasury, but in pursuance of an appropriation made by law; and a regular statement and account of the receipts and expenditures of all public moneys shall be published annually, in such manner as may be by law directed.

SEC. 23. Each member of the first General Assembly, under this Constitution shall receive six dollars per diem while in session; and the further sum of twenty cents for every mile of the ordinary route of travel in going to and returning from the place where such session is held; after which they shall receive such compensation as shall be fixed by law; but no General Assembly shall have the power to increase the compensation of its own members. And when convened in extra session they shall receive the same mileage and per diem compensation as are fixed by law for the regular session, and none other.

SEC. 24. In all elections by the General Assembly, or either House thereof, the members shall vote "*viva voce*," and their votes, thus given, shall be entered upon the journal of the House to which they respectively belong.

SEC. 25. Neither House, during the session of the General Assembly, shall, without the consent of the other, adjourn for more than three days, nor to any other place than that in which the Assembly shall be at the time sitting.

SEC. 26. Each House shall keep a journal of its own proceedings, and cause the same to be published immediately after its adjournment, excepting such parts as in its judgment may require secrecy; and the yeas and nays of the members of either House, on any question, shall, at the desire of any two members present, be entered on the journals. Any member of either House shall have liberty to dissent from and protest against, any act or resolution which he may think injurious to the public or to an individual, and have the reasons of his dissent entered on the journals.

SEC. 27. The doors of each House shall be open, except on such occasions as in the opinion of the House may require secrecy.

SEC. 28. No person shall be eligible to a seat in the General Assembly whilst he holds any office of profit or trust under this State, the United States of America, or any of them, or under any other power, except officers in the militia, magistrates, or justices of inferior courts, while such justices receive no salary. And if any member shall accept or exercise any of the said disqualifying offices, he shall vacate his seat; *Provided*, That this prohibition shall not extend to the members of the first General Assembly.

SEC. 29. If any election district shall neglect to choose a member or members on the day of election, or if any person chosen a member of either House shall refuse to qualify and take his seat, or shall resign, die, depart the State, accept any disqualifying office, or become otherwise disqualified to hold his seat, a writ of election shall be issued by the President of the Senate, or Speaker of the House of Representatives, as the case may be, for the purpose of filling the vacancy thereby occasioned, for the remainder of the term for which the person so refusing to qualify, resigning, dying, departing the State, or becoming disqualified, was elected to serve, or the defaulting election district ought to have chosen a member or members.

Sec. 30. Members of the General Assembly, and all officers before they enter upon the execution of the duties of their respective offices, and all members of the bar, before they enter upon the practice of their profession, shall take and subscribe the following oath :

"I do solemnly swear (or affirm as the case may be) that I am duly qualified according to the Constitution of the United States and of this State to exercise the duties of the office to which I have been elected, (or appointed,) and that I will faithfully discharge to the best of my abilities the duties thereof; that I recognize the supremacy of the Constitution and laws of the United States over the Constitution and laws of any State ; and that I will support, protect and defend the Constitution of the United States and the Constitution of South Carolina, as ratified by the people on the ———— day of ————, 1868. So HELP ME GOD." And the President of this Convention is authorized to fill the blanks in this section whenever he shall receive satisfactory information of the day on which this Constitution shall be ratified.

Sec. 31 Officers shall be removed for incapacity, misconduct or neglect of duty, in such manner as may be provided by law, when no mode of trial or removal is provided in this Constitution.

Sec. 32. The family homestead of the head of each family, residing in this State, such homestead consisting of dwelling house, out-buildings and lands appurtenant. not to exceed the value of one thousand dollars, and yearly product thereof, shall be exempt from attachment, levy or sale on any mesne or final process issued from any court. To secure the full enjoyment of said homestead exemption to the person entitled thereto, or to the head of any family, the personal property of such person, of the following character, to wit : household furniture, beds and bedding, family library, arms, carts, wagons, farming implements, tools neat cattle, work animals, swine, goats and sheep, not to exceed in value in the aggregate the sum of five hundred dollars, shall be subject to like exemption as said homestead, and there shall be exempt in addition thereto all necessary wearing apparel ; *Provided,* That no property shall be exempt from attachment, levy or sale, for taxes, or for payment of obligations contracted for the purchase of said homestead, or the erection of improvements thereon ; *Provided further,* That the yearly products of said homestead shall not be exempt from attachment, levy or sale, for the payment of obligations contracted in the production of the same. It shall be the duty of the General Assembly at their first session to enforce the provisions of this section by suitable legislation.

Sec. 33. All taxes upon property, real or personal, shall be laid upon the actual value of the property taxed, as the same shall be ascertained by an assessment made for the purpose of laying such tax.

Mr. B. F. WITTEMORE moved that when the House adjourn, it adjourn to meet to-morrow morning at ten o'clock, which was agreed to.

Mr. E. W. M. MACKEY moved a reconsideration of the vote, by which sections thirty-two and thirty-three were passed, which was agreed to.

Mr. C. P. LESLIE stated that he had a substitute, embracing a very liberal homestead measure, to offer for the thirty fourth section. This substitute had been shown to all the friends of the homestead law, and they had all agreed to it as just the thing, and much better than the homestead provision of the section as it stood. It had, however, been left with the Chairman of the Committee on the Judiciary who had not brought it with him. He moved, therefore, to postpone the further consideration of the report, which was agreed to.

The PRESIDENT stated to the Convention that he had been informed, to his great grief and mortification, that a bar-room had been opened in the basement room of the building, and that some fifteen or twenty intoxicated persons were at that time in the basement. As the house had not been put in his hands he could issue no order, but hoped that the bar-keeper would be expelled from the house, and the bar-room closed, in order to preserve the dignity and character of the Convention.

Mr. R. C. DeLARGE denied that there was a bar-room kept in the building, but that there was a refreshment saloon, where the members obtained lunch. He had just come from that room, and could say there was not a single intoxicated person there.

Mr. B. F. WHITTEMORE moved that the house be put in charge of the President of the Convention, and that the bar-room be from this time and henceforth closed, which was agreed to.

The PRESIDENT then directed the Sergeant-at-Arms to see the order of the house forthwith carried into execution.

On motion, the Convention then adjourned.

FORTY-EIGHTH DAY.

Wednesday, March 11, 1868.

The Convention assembled at ten A. M., and was called to order by the PRESIDENT.

Prayer was offered by the Rev. H. D. EDWARDS.

The roll was called, and a quorum answering to their names, the PRESIDENT announced the Convention ready to proceed to business.

The unfinished business was resumed, being the consideration of section thirty-two and thirty-three, Article 2. legislative department.

Mr. C. C. BOWEN moved that section thirty-two be stricken out, which was agreed to.

Section thirty-three was read, and, on motion of Mr. C. C. BOWEN, this section was also stricken out.

The Convention proceeded to the consideration of the thirty-fourth section of Article 2, on the legislative part of the Constitution.

Mr. C. P. LESLIE moved a recommitment of the section, and offered the following substitute:

The family homestead of the head of each family residing in this State, such homestead consisting of a dwelling and lands appurtenant, occupied by such person as a homestead, not to exceed the value of one thousand dollars, and the yearly product thereof shall be exempt from attachment, levy or sale, or any mesne or final process issued from any Court, To secure the full enjoyment of such homestead to the person entitled thereto, the personal property of such person of the following character. to wit: household furniture, bed and bedding, wearing apparel, school books, arms, carts, wagons, farming implements, tools, neat cattle, work animals, swine and sheep, not to exceed in value in the aggregate the sum of five hundred dollars, shall be subject to like exemption as said homestead; provided, further, that the wearing apparel, bed and bedding herein exempted, shall not be appraised or included in the exemption of personal property, and shall be absolutely exempt from levy and sale, provided, no property shall be exempt from attachment, levy or sale for taxes, or for payment of obligations contracted for the purchase of said homestead, or the erection of improvements thereon; provided, further, that the yearly products of said homestead shall not be exempt from attachment, levy or sale, for the payment of obligations contracted in the production of the same. It shall be the duty of the General Assembly to enforce the provisions of this section by suitable legislation.

Mr. C. P. LESLIE. The attention of the friends of the homestead law, adopted in Convention, has been directed by a distinguished Judge of the State Courts to the fact that the very provisions of that law defeated the law itself. The homestead law passed, says: "One hundred acres of land, with the buildings and appurtenances thereon, and a town lot or building in the city," provided that it does not exceed two thousand five hundred dollars. Here they were caught. If the property is worth ten dollars more than the two thousand five hundred dollars, the sheriff can seize the whole, sell it, and take the money or debt out of it.

This substitute has been carefully prepared by the Solicitor to the Convention, Major D. T. Corbin, and I desire it, with the section, to go to the committee on the legislative part of the Constitution.

The motion was agreed to, and, on motion of Mr. F. J. MOSES, Jr., the committee were instructed to report on Friday next.

Section thirty-five was then taken up, and passed its third reading.

Mr. F. L. CARDOZO rose to a question of privilege, in reference to a matter which occurred in the house to-day This had gone out to the world in the public prints, and he desired to call the attention of the house to it, as it effected the dignity of the Convention.

The President publicly stated that a bar-room was kept in the basement, and that some fifteen or twenty intoxicated men were then in that room.

The PRESIDENT. I desire to give the language as nearly as possible that was used by the Chair.

The CHAIR did not state directly that there were fifteen or twenty intoxicated men in the bar-room, but that it had been informed that fifteen or twenty intoxicated men were in the basement of the building at the time.

Mr. F. L. CARDOZO. The statement was given as you have just said, Mr. President. You simply stated what had been told you. I simply wish to say that while the gentleman from Charleston (Mr. DeLARGE, who, naturally feeling jealous of the dignity of the Convention, and very properly I think, immediately rose and challenged the truthfulness of the statement), was on the floor, one or two gentlemen made a few jesting remarks in reference to his statement of having just come from that room. Nothing in those remarks was intended to convey the unfortunate false impression that seems to have gone out from the house, for every gentleman on the floor could see that the gentleman was perfectly sober. I wish to state that the President was misinformed in the representations made in reference to a bar-room. I visited the basement immediately afterwards to see if the statements were true, and found them utterly incorrect. All the gentlemen in the basement affirmed that the President had been wholly misinformed. I think it due to the dignity of the Convention, and my colleague from Charleston, than whom there is no more industrious member on the floor, and due to myself, to say, in relation to that report of intoxicated men made yesterday, that there was nothing of the kind in this house.

The PRESIDENT. This matter having been made a question of privilege, it is left for the house to say what course it will take—whether to received it as a question of privilege, or as information.

Mr. J. M. RUNION moved that it be received as information.

Mr. R. C. DeLARGE. As one of the parties directly implicated, and who have made the denial, I desire to ask the gentleman from Darlington (Mr. WHITTEMORE), who gave the information to the Chair, whether, in his judgment, the remarks of my colleague Mr. CARDOZO) were correct or incorrect, or whether he was jesting?

Mr. B. F. WHITTEMORE. I am not in the habit of jesting with this Convention. I informed the President of the condition of things in the basement from what was told while in conversation with the President by a delegate, namely: that fifteen or twenty persons were there at the time intoxicated. The delegate said the bar room ought to be closed, and I repeated to the President the information that had been given to me. It is not the first time the subject of closing the bar room has been brought up. The gentleman himself said the bar room should be closed during the sitting of the Nominating Convention. My intention was nothing more nor less than to preserve the dignity of the Convention, and not for the purpose of reflecting upon the character of any individual of the Convention. It was not my intention to make the inference that the gentleman from Charleston was in such a condition as did not reflect credit upon him, but simply that his remarks gave a sufficient warrant for the closing of the bar room.

The PRESIDENT decided the question of privilege to be exhausted by the explanations made.

On motion of Mr. T. J. ROBERTSON. the rules were suspended to enable the Special Committee of Nine to report.

The following report was then submitted by Mr. T. J. ROBERTSON, Chairman of the Committee, which, on motion of Mr. D. H CHAMBERLAIN, was ordered to be printed and made the special order for Friday morning:

The Special Committee of Nine, to whom was referred an Ordinance, appointing three commissioners ' to investigate the financial condition of the State, and the situation and value of all property, assets, securities, and other resources applicable to the discharge of its valid obligations," &c., beg leave respectfully to report that they have had the same under consideration, and unanimously recommend that the Ordinance do pass.

Mr. T. J. ROBERTSON presented the petition of D. B. Miller, praying the Convention to recommend the removal of his political disabilities. Referred to the Committee on Petitions.

Mr. B. O DUNCAN presented similar petitions from Henry Summer and other citizens of Newberry, which were referred to the same committee.

The regular business was resumed, being section thirty-five of the Legislative report, which was read a third time and passed.

On motion of Mr. D. H. CHAMBERLAIN, the Convention adjourned to ten o'clock to-morrow.

FORTY-NINTH DAY.

Thursday, March 12, 1868.

The Convention assembled at ten A. M., and was called to order by the President, Hon. A. G. MACKEY.

Prayer was offered by Rev. J. M. RUNION.

The roll was called, and a quorum answering to their names, the PRESIDENT announced the Convention ready to proceed to business.

The journal of Wednesday was read and approved.

Petitions from the following persons, praying the Convention to recommend the removal of their political disabilities, were presented, and referred to the Committee on Petitions: Jesse K. Stone, Greenville; H. W. Lawson, Mathew McDonald, Abbeville; E. P. Lake, Newberry; John W. Twitty, Lancaster; John T. Green, Sumter.

His Excellency Governor J. L. Orr visited the Convention, and was received with becoming demonstrations.

The report of the Committee on the Executive part of the Constitution, Article III., was taken up for a third reading.

Section one was read a third time, and passed.

Section two was read, and Mr. F. J. MOSES, Jr., moved to recommit, with instructions to fix a day for the installation of the Governor elect, Agreed to.

108

Sections five, six, seven, eight, nine, ten, eleven, twelve, thirteen and fourteen were read a third time, and passed.

Mr. B. F. WHITTEMORE moved to recommit section fifteen to the committee, with instructions to strike out all after the word "expedient," which was agreed to.

The committee reported in accordance with the motion, and the section, as amended, passed.

Section sixteen and all the sections down to twenty-three inclusive, then were severally read a third time and passed.

The Article, as thus adopted, is as follows:

ARTICLE III.

EXECUTIVE DEPARTMENT.

SECTION 1. The Supreme Executive authority of this State shall be vested in a Chief Magistrate, who shall be styled "The Governor of the State of South Carolina."

SEC. 2. The Governor shall be elected by the electors duly qualified to vote for members of the General Assembly, and shall hold his office for two years, and until his successor shall be chosen and qualified, and shall be re-eligible. (Recommitted).

SEC. 3. No person shall be eligible to the office of Governor who denies the existence of the Supreme Being or who at the time of such election has not attained the age of thirty years, and who, except at the first election under this Constitution, shall not have been a citizen of the United States and a citizen and resident of this State for two years next preceding the day of election. No person while Governor shall hold any other office or commission (except in the militia) under this State, or any other power, at one and the same time.

SEC. 4. The returns of every election of Governor shall be sealed up by the managers of elections in their respective counties, and transmitted, by mail, to the seat of Government, directed to the Secretary of State, who shall deliver them to the Speaker of the House of Representatives at the next ensuing session of the General Assembly, and a duplicate of said returns shall be filed with the Clerks of the Courts of said Counties, whose duty it shall be to forward to the Secretary of State a certified copy thereof, upon being notified that the returns previously forwarded by mail have not been received at his office It shall be the duty of the Secretary of State, after the expiration of seven days from the day upon which the votes have been counted, if the returns thereof from any county have not been received, to notify the Clerk of the Court of said County, and order a copy of the returns filed in his office to be forwarded forthwith. The Secretary of State shall deliver the returns to the Speaker of the House of Representatives, at the next ensuing session of the General Assembly; and during the first week of the session, or as soon as the General Assembly shall have organized by the election of the presiding officers of the two Houses, the Speaker shall open and publish them in the presence of both Houses. The person having the highest number of votes shall be Governor; but if two or more shall be equal, and highest in votes, the General Assembly shall, during the same session, in the House of Representatives, choose one of them Governor *viva voce.* Contested elections for Governor shall be determined by the General Assembly in such manner as shall be prescribed by law.

SEC. 5. A Lieutenant-Governor shall be chosen at the same time, in the same manner, continue in office for the same period, and be possessed of the same qualifications as the Governor, and shall *ex officio* be President of the Senate.

SEC. 6. The Lieutenant-Governor, while presiding in the Senate, shall have no vote, unless the Senate be equally divided.

SEC. 7. The Senate shall choose a President *pro tempore,* to act in the absence of the Lieutenant-Governor, or when he shall exercise the office of Governor.

SEC. 8 A member of the Senate, or of the House of Representatives, being chosen and acting as Governor or Lieutenant-Governor, shall thereupon vacate his seat, and another person shall be elected in his stead.

SEC. 9. In case of the removal of the Governor from his office, or his death, resignation, removal from the State, or inability to discharge the powers and duties of the said office, the same shall devolve on the Lieutenant-Governor, and the General Assembly, at its first session after the ratification of this Constitution, shall, by law, provide for the case of removal, death, resignation, or inability, both of the Governor, Lieutenant-Governor, declaring what officer shall then act as Governor, and such officer shall act accordingly, until such disability shall have been removed, or a Governor shall have been elected.

SEC. 10. The Governor shall be Commander-in-chief of the militia of the State, except when they shall be called into the actual service of the United States.

SEC. 11. He shall have power to grant reprieves and pardons after conviction, (except in cases of impeachment) in such manner, on such terms, and under such restrictions as he shall think proper; and he shall have power to remit fines and forfeitures, unless otherwise directed by law. It shall be his duty to report to the General Assembly at the next regular session thereafter, all pardons granted by him, with a full statement of each case, and the reasons moving him thereunto.

SEC. 12. He shall take care that the laws be faithfully executed, in mercy.

SEC. 13. The Governor and Lieutenant-Governor shall, at stated times, receive for their services a compensation which shall be neither increased nor diminished during the period for which they shall have been elected.

SEC. 14. All officers in the Executive Department shall, when required by the Governor, give him information in writing upon any subject relating to the duties of their respective offices.

SEC. 15. The Governor shall, from time to time, give to the General Assembly information of the condition of the State, and recommend to their consideration such measures as he shall judge necessary or expedient.

SEC. 16. He may, on extraordinary occasions, convene the General Assembly; and should either House remain without a quorum for five days, or in case of disagreement between the two Houses, with respect to the time of adjournment, may adjourn them to such time as he shall think proper; not beyond the time of the annual session then next ensuing.

SEC. 17 He shall commission all officers of the State.

SEC. 18. There shall be a Seal of the State, for which the General Assembly, at its first session, shall provide, and which shall be used by the Governor officially, and shall be called "The Great Seal of the State of South Carolina."

SEC. 19. All grants and commissions shall be issued in the name and by the authority of the State of South Carolina, sealed with the Great Seal, signed by the Governor and countersigned by the Secretary of State.

SEC. 20. The Governor and the Lieutenant-Governor, before entering upon the duties of their respective offices, shall take and subscribe the oath of office as prescribed in Article two, section thirty of this Constitution.

SEC. 21. The Governor shall reside at the capital of the State; but during the sittings of the General Assembly he shall reside where its sessions are held, except in case of contagion.

SEC. 22 Every bill or joint resolution which shall have passed the General Assembly, except on a question of adjournment, shall, before it becomes a law, be presented to the Governor, and, if he approve, he shall sign it; if not, he shall return it, with his objections to the House in which it shall have originated; which shall enter the objections at large on its journals, and proceed to reconsider it. If, after such reconsideration, two-thirds of that House shall agree to pass it, it shall be sent, together with the objections, to the other House, by which it shall be reconsidered, and, if approved by two-thirds of that House, it shall have the same effect as if it had been signed by the Governor; but, in all such cases the vote of both Houses shall be taken by yeas and nays, and the names of the persons voting for and against the bill or joint resolution, shall be entered on the journals of both Houses respectively. If a bill or joint resolution shall not be returned by the Governor within three days after it shall have been presented to him, Sundays excepted, it shall have the same force and effect as if he had signed it, unless the General Assembly, by their adjournment, prevent its return, in which case it shall not have such force and effect unless returned within two days after their next meeting.

SEC. 23. There shall be elected by the qualified voters of the State a Comptroller-General, a Treasurer, and a Secretary of State, who shall hold their respective offices for the term of four years, and whose duties and compensation shall be prescribed by law.

The Convention next proceeded to the consideration of Article IV., which was read by sections, and passed for ratification, as follows:

ARTICLE IV.

JUDICIAL DEPARTMENT.

SECTION 1. The judicial power of this State shall be vested in a Supreme Court, in two Circuit Courts, to wit: A Court of Common Pleas, having civil jurisdiction, and a Court of General Sessions, with criminal jurisdiction only; in Probate Courts, and in Justices of the Peace. The General Assembly may also establish such municipal and other inferior Courts as may be deemed necessary.

SEC. 2. The Supreme Court shall consist of a Chief Justice and two Associate Justices, two of whom shall constitute a quorum. They shall be elected by a joint vote of the General Assembly for the term of six years, and shall continue in office until their successors shall be elected and qualified. They shall be so classified that one of the Justices shall go out of office every two years.

SEC 3. The Chief Justice elected under this Constitution shall continue in office for six years, and the General Assembly immediately after the said election shall determine which of the two Associate Justices elect shall serve for the term of two years, and which for the term of four years; and having so determined the same, it shall be the duty of the Governor to commission them accordingly.

SEC 4. The Supreme Court shall have appellate jurisdiction only in cases of Chancery, and shall constitute a Court for the correction of errors at law, under such regulations as the General Assembly may by law prescribe; *Provided*, The said Court shall always have power to issue writs of injunction, *mandamus, quo warranto, habeas corpus,* and such other original and remedial writs as may be necessary to give it a general supervisory control over all other Courts in the State

SEC. 5. The Supreme Court shall be held at least once in each year, at the seat of Government. and at such other place or places in the State as the General Assembly may direct.

SEC. 6. No Judge shall preside on the trial of any cause in the event of which he may be interested, or where either of the parties shall be connected with him by affinity or consanguinity, within such degrees as may be prescribed by law, or in which he may have been counsel, or have presided in any inferior Court except by consent of all the parties. In case all or any of the Judges of the Supreme Court shall be thus disqualified from presiding in any cause or causes, the Court or the Judges thereof shall certify the same to the Governor of the State, and he shall immediately commission, specially, the requisite number of men learned in the law for the trial and determination thereof. The same course shall be pursued in the Circuit and inferior Courts as is prescribed in this section for cases of the Supreme Court.

SEC. 7. There shall be appointed by the Judges of the Supreme Court a reporter and clerk of said Court, who shall hold their offices for two years, and whose duties and compensation shall be prescribed by law.

SEC 8. When a judgment or decree is reversed or affirmed by the Supreme Court, every point made and distinctly stated in writing in the cause, and fairly arising upon the record of the case, shall be considered and decided; and the reasons therefor shall be concisely and briefly stated in writing, and preserved with the records of the case.

Sec. 9. The Judges of the Supreme Court and Circuit Courts shall, at stated times, receive a compensation for their services, to be fixed by law, which shall not be diminished during their continuance in office. They shall not be allowed any fees or perquisites of office, nor shall they hold any other office of trust or profit under this State, the United States, or any other power.

Sec. 10. No person shall be eligible to the office of Judge of the Supreme Court or Circuit Courts, who is not at the time of his election a citizen of the United States, and has not attained the age of thirty years, and been a resident of this State for five years next preceding his election, or from the adoption of this Constitution.

Sec. 11. All vacancies in the Supreme Court or other inferior tribunals shall be filled by election, as herein prescribed; *Provided*, That if the unexpired term does not exceed one year, such vacancy may be filled by Executive appointment. All Judges, by virtue of their office, shall be conservators of the peace throughout the State.

Sec. 12. In all cases decided by the Supreme Court, a concurrence of two of the Judges shall be necessary to a decision.

Sec. 13. The State shall be divided into convenient circuits, and for each circuit a Judge shall be elected by joint ballot of the General Assembly, who shall hold his office for a term of four years, and during his continuance in office he shall reside in the circuit of which he is Judge.

Sec. 14. Judges of the Circuit Court shall interchange circuits with each other in such manner as may be determined by law.

Sec. 15. The Courts of Common Pleas shall have exclusive jurisdiction in all cases of divorce, and exclusive original jurisdiction in all civil cases and actions *ex delicto*, which shall not be cognizable before Justices of the Peace, and appellate jurisdiction in all such cases as may be provided by law. They shall have power to issue writs of *mandamus*, prohibition, *scire facias*, and all other writs which may be necessary for carrying their powers fully into effect.

Sec. 16. The Court of Common Pleas shall sit in each Judicial District in this State at least twice in every year, at such stated times and places as may be appointed by law. It shall have jurisdiction in all matters of Equity, but the Courts heretofore established for that purpose shall continue as now organized until the first day of January, one thousand eight hundred and sixty-nine, for the disposition of causes now pending therein, unless otherwise provided by law

Sec. 17. The General Assembly shall provide by law for the preservation of the records of the Courts of Equity, and also for the transfer to the Court of Common Pleas and Probate Courts for final decision of all causes that may remain undetermined. It shall be the duty of the Judges of the Supreme and Circuit Courts to file their decisions within sixty days from the last day of the term of court at which the causes were heard.

Sec. 18. The Court of General Sessions shall have exclusive jurisdiction over all criminal cases which shall not be otherwise provided for by law. It shall sit in each county in the State at least three times in each each year, at such stated times and places as the General Assembly may direct.

SEC. 19. The qualified electors of each county shall elect three persons for the term of two years, who shall constitute a Board of County Commissioners, which shall have jurisdiction over roads, highways, ferries, bridges, and in all matters relating to taxes, disbursements of money for county purposes, and in every other case that may be necessary to the internal improvement and local concerns of the respective counties; *Provided*, That in all cases there shall be the right of appeal to the State Courts.

SEC. 20. A Court of Probate shall be established in each county, with jurisdiction in all matters testamentary and of administration, in business appertaining to minors and the allotment of dower in cases of idiotcy and lunacy, and persons *non compotes mentis*. The Judge of said Court shall be elected by the qualified electors of the respective counties for the term of two years.

SEC. 21. A competent number of Justices of the Peace and Constables shall be chosen in each county by the qualified electors thereof, in such manner as the General Assembly may direct; they shall hold their offices for a term of two years and until their successors are elected and qualified. They shall reside in the county, city or beat, for which they are elected, and the Justices of the Peace shall be commissioned by the Governor.

SEC 22. Justices of the Peace, individually, or two or more of them jointly, as the General Assembly may direct, shall have original jurisdiction in cases of bastardy, and in all matters of contract, and actions for the recovery of fines and forfeitures where the amount claimed does not exceed one hundred dollars, and such jurisdiction as may be provided by law in actions *ex delicto*, where the damages claimed do not exceed one hundred dollars; and prosecutions for assault and battery and other penal offences less than felony, punishable by fines only.

SEC. 23. They may also sit as examining courts and commit, discharge, or recognize (except in capital cases) persons charged with offences subject to such regulations as the General Assembly may provide; they shall also have power to bind over to keep the peace, or for good behavior. For the foregoing purposes they shall have power to issue all necessary processes.

SEC. 24. Every action cognizable before Justices of the Peace instituted by summons or warrant, shall be brought before some Justice of the Peace in the county or city where the defendant resides, and in all such causes tried by them, the right of appeal shall be secured under such rules and regulations as may be provided by law.

SEC. 25. The Judges of Probate, County Commissioners, Justices of the Peace, and Constables, shall receive for their services such compensation and fees as the General Assembly may from time to time by law direct.

SEC. 26. Judges shall not charge juries in respect to matters of fact, but may state the testimony and declare the law.

SEC. 27. There shall be elected in each county, by the electors thereof, one Clerk for the Court of Common Pleas, who shall hold his office for the term of four years, and until his successor shall be elected and qualified. He shall, by virtue of his office, be Clerk of all other Courts of Record held therein ; but the General Assembly may provide by law for the election of a Clerk, with a like term of office, for each or any other of the Courts of Record, and may authorize the Judge of the Probate Court to perform the duties of Clerk for his Cour , under such regulations as the General Assembly may direct. Clerks of Courts shall be removeable for such cause, and in such manner as shall be prescribed by law.

SEC. 28. There shall be an Attorney-General for the State, who shall perform such duties as may be prescribed by law   He shall be elected by the qualified electors of the State for the term of four years, and shall receive for his services such compensation as shall be fixed by law.

SEC. 29. There shall be one Solicitor for each circuit, who shall reside therein, to be elected by the qualified electors of the circuit, who shall hold his office for the term of four years, and shall receive for his services such compensation as shall be fixed by law.   In all cases where an Attorney for the State, of any circuit, fails to attend and prosecute, according to law, the court shall have power to appoint an Attorney *pro tempore.*

SEC. 30. The qualified electors of each county shall elect a Sheriff and a Coroner, for the term of four years, and until their successors are elected and qualified ; they shall reside in their respective counties during their continuance in office, and be disqualified for the office a second time, if it should appear that they or either of them are in default for moneys collected by virtue of their respective offices.

SEC. 31. All writs and processes shall run, and all prosecutions shall be conducted in the name of the State of South Carolina ; all writs shall be· attested by the Clerk of the Court from which they shall be issued ; and all indictments shall conclude against the peace and dignity of the State.

SEC. 32. The General Assembly shall provide by law for the speedy publication of the decisions of the Supreme Court made under this Constitution.

Mr. B. O. DUNCAN stated that the Chairman of the Committee on the Judiciary was not present, and he would state that the Chairman had prepared an additional section to the above department, making it section thirty-three, which covers an Ordinance passed by this Convention annulling all slave debts.

Mr. J. S. CRAIG opposed the introduction of such a section in the Constitution as coming in conflict with that part of the Constitution of the United States which prohibits any State from impairing the validity of obligations and contracts.   If adopted, he would be compelled to vote against the Constitution.

Articles V., VI., and VII., were then read a third time and passed as follows :

ARTICLE V.

JURISPRUDENCE.

SECTION 1. The General Assembly shall pass such laws as may be necessary and proper, to decide differences by arbitrators, to be appointed by the parties who may choose that summary mode of adjustment.

SEC. 2. It shall be the duty of the General Assembly to pass the necessary laws for the change of venue in all cases, civil and criminal, over which the Circuit Courts have original jurisdiction, upon a proper showing, supported by affidavit, that a fair and impartial trial cannot be had in the County where such trial or prosecution was commenced.

SEC. 3. The General Assembly, at its first session after the adoption of this Constitution, shall make provision to revise, digest and arrange, under proper heads, the body of our laws, civil and criminal, and form a penal code, founded upon principles of reformation, and have the same promulgated in such manner as they may direct; and a like revision, digest and promulgation shall be made within every subsequent period of ten years. That justice may be administered in a uniform mode of pleading, without distinction between law and equity, they shall provide for abolishing the distinct forms of action, and for that purpose shall appoint some suitable person or persons, whose duty it shall be to revise, simplify, and abridge the rules, practice, pleadings, and forms of the courts now in use in this State.

ARTICLE VI.

EMINENT DOMAIN.

SECTION 1. The State shall have concurrent jurisdiction on all rivers bordering on this State, so far as such rivers shall form a common boundary to this and any other State bounded by the same; and they, together with all other navigable waters within the limits of the State, shall be common highways, and forever free, as well to the inhabitants of this State as to the citizens of the United States, without any tax or impost therefor, unless the same be expressly provided for by the General Assembly.

SEC. 2. The title to all lands and other property, which have heretofore accrued to this State by grant, gift, purchase, forfeiture, escheats, or otherwise, shall vest in the State of South Carolina, the same as though no change had taken place.

SEC. 3. The people of the State are declared to possess the ultimate property in and to all lands within the jurisdiction of the State; and all lands, the title to which shall fail from defect of heirs, shall revert, or escheat to the people.

ARTICLE VII.

IMPEACHMENTS.

SECTION 1. The House of Representatives shall have the sole power of impeachment. A vote of two-thirds of all the members elected shall be required for an impeachment, and any officer impeached, shall thereby be suspended from office until judgment in the case shall have been pronounced.

SEC. 2. All impeachments shall be tried by the Senate, and when sitting for that purpose, they shall be under oath or affirmation. No person shall be convicted except by vote of two-thirds of all the members elected. When the Governor is impeached, the Chief Justice of the Supreme Court, or the senior Judge, shall preside, with a casting vote in all preliminary questions.

SEC. 3. The Governor and all other executive and judicial officers shall be liable to impeachment; but judgment in such cases shall not extend further than removal from office. The persons convicted shall, nevertheless, be liable to indictment, trial and punishment according to law.

SEC. 4. For any willful neglect of duty, or other reasonable cause, which shall not be sufficient ground of impeachment, the Governor shall emove any executive or judicial officer on the address of two-thirds of each House of the General Assembly; *Provided*, That the cause or causes for which said removal may be required, shall be stated at length in such address, and entered on the journals of each House; *And, provided further*, that the officer intended to be removed shall be notified of such cause or causes, and shall be admitted to a hearing in his own defence, before any vote for such address; and in all cases the vote shall be taken by yeas and nays, and be entered on the journals of each House respectively.

The PRSIDENT announced that this concluded all the matter entitled to a third reading, in the hands of the printer. The remaining sections would be given to the printer at once.

The PRESIDENT also suggested that the Convention take some action in reference to printing a certain number of copies of the Constitution, which, as it was already in type, would be less expensive. No order, however, could be issued until the House prescribed what number of copies they desired.

Mr. WHITTEMORE said he would, in the afternoon, offer a resolution in relation to that matter.

Mr. N. G. PARKER moved a suspension of the rules, for the purpose of introducing two resolutions.

The rules were suspended and the resolutions adopted as follows:

Resolved, That J. J. Wright, D. H. Chamberlain, J. M. Rutland, B. F. Whittemore and W. B. Nash, be declared Vice-Presidents of this Convention, and shall perform the duties of President of this Convention in the event of the inability, by death or otherwise, of the President.

Resolved, That when this Convention adjourn, it shall be on Tuesday next, March 17th, at 12 M., subject to the call of the President or the Vice-President, in the order in which they stand, at any time the public exigences shall demand; *Provided*, that as soon as the presiding officer shall have received official notice of the ratification of this Constitution by the people, he shall, by public proclamation, adjourn the Convention *sine die*.

Mr. B. F. RANDOLPH called up the following Ordinance, which was read a third time, passed, and declared an Ordinance of the Convention :

We, the People of South Carolina, by our Delegates in Convention assembled, do ordain, That it shall be the duty of the General Assembly, at its first session, to appoint commissioners to investigate and ascertain what obligations of the State are entitled to be held as valid and binding upon the State, in conformity with the provisions of this Constitution and the Ordinances adopted by this Convention, and to report thereon to the General Assembly ; and until the General Assembly shall have ascertained the validity of such obligations, no payment for either principal or interest shall be made on any outstanding obligation created and incurred prior to the 29th day of April, 1865.

Mr. S. CORLEY offered the following resolutions, which were adopted:

Whereas, the Registrars in some of the counties of the State during the period of our late registration, forgetting that virtue itself is meanness in a slave, refused to enter the names of colored men on their lists, simply because while slaves they had been punished as felons by an incompetent autocratic court, held for the trial of petty offences; therefore,

Resolved, That no offences heretofore committed by a slave, nor punishment inflicted on the same, can now be held as coming within the intent and meaning of the reconstruction laws in reference to felony; and, hereafter, every loyal citizen should hold it to be his imperative duty to report all Registrars so offending to the Commander of the Second Military District, in order that they may be visited with the just penalties of violated law.

Whereas, the provisions of the present Bankrupt Law are beyond the reach of the really poor man, and, therefore, a practical nullity in their application to the very cases they should, above all others, reach,

Resolved, That we, the members of this Constitutional Convention, do hereby petition Congress to amend the said laws in such manner as to secure its benefits to all, without reference to the precise amount of the indebtedness of the applicant or the payment of advance fees, which are now required.

Mr. D. H. CHAMBERLAIN obtained leave and introduced the following Ordinance, and moved its reference to a special committee of five ·

Whereas, during the recent rebellion against the authority and Government of the United States, many dishonest practices were resorted to in order to enhance, in the public estimation, the nominal value of the currency and securities issued by the States confederated in rebellion, and divers agents were employed and acting for that purpose in this State, who while misrepresenting the condition and prospects of said Confederacy, with the view of deceiving the people as to the value of its obligations, took advantage of the credulity of the people, inducing them to part with real estate, and other property, for such obligations, for the private and personal benefit of such agents, and those associated with them for such speculative purposes ; and, whereas, without special aid from the General Assembly, the persons thus defrauded, being stripped of their property and means, will, in many instances, be unable to prosecute, with effect, their said legal demands,

Be it ordained, That it shall be the duty of the General Assembly, at its first session, to provide the means of facilitating the recovery of all such property and damages; and, to that end, shall have power to authorize the Attorney-General to prosecute one or more actions or proceedings in behalf of the persons so injured, and against all officers, agents and employees of the said Confederacy, and their associates implicated as hereinbefore mentioned, and in such actions or proceedings, the interests or liabilities of two or more individuals, growing out of separate transactions, may be united either as plaintiff or defendant, as may be deemed most expedient.

The President appointed as Special Committee on the above: D. H. Chamberlain, T. J. Robertson, J. M. Rutland, W. H. Webb and F. E. Wilder, with instructions to report to the Convention to-morrow afternoon.

Mr. G. W. DILL offered the following :

Resolved, That the President of the Convention be instructed to have five thousand copies of the Constitution now framing, printed for distribution among the members of the Convention, and the people of the State generally.

Mr. B. F. WHITTEMORE stated that he had given notice of his intention to offer a resolution in regard to that matter, and Mr. G. W. DILL withdrew his resolution.

Mr. B. F. RANDOLPH moved that the Committee on Education be instructed to report the eleventh section of Article 2 back to the house, at three o'clock to-morrow, which was agreed to.

Mr. W. E. JOHNSTON offered the following :

Resolved, That we, the members of the first Constitutional Convention of South Carolina, do affectionately greet our President, A. G. Mackey, on this the sixty-first anniversary of his birthday.

This was followed by great applause, during which the Secretary of the Convention put the question, and it was unanimously decided in the affirmative.

The PRESIDENT rising was again greeted with applause, and said :

Gentlemen of the Convention : I receive your kind greeting with grateful affection. I am unable to give utterance to an expression of my feelings for the kindness you have always shown me. But you will allow me to make one sentiment alone in response to your greeting, which is, that I thank God that he has preserved my life long enough to let me see the renovation of South Carolina, and her elevation to a condition of liberty and universal equality.

The speech was followed by renewed and prolonged applause.

On motion of Mr. R. C. DeLARGE the Convention then adjourned to three P. M.

AFTERNOON SESSION.

The Convention re-assembled at three P. M.

Mr. B. F. WHITTEMORE offered the following resolution, which was agreed to :

Resolved, That ten thousand copies of the Constitution of South Carolina, as adopted by this Convention, and the several Ordinances passed by the same, be printed in pamphlet form, for distribution among the members, and that an amount sufficient be drawn from the Treasury of the State by the President of this Convention to pay for the same.

On motion of Mr. T. J. ROBERTSON, the special order for four o'clock this afternoon, being an Ordinance introduced by himself, was postponed until twelve o'clock to-morrow.

On motion of Mr. N. J. NEWELL, the Convention then adjourned.

FIFTIETH DAY.

Friday, March 13, 1868.

The Convention assembled at ten A. M., and was called to order by the PRESIDENT.

Prayer was offered by the Rev. I. BROCKENTON.

The roll was called, and a quorum answering to their names, the PRESIDENT announced the Convention ready to proceed to business.

The Journal of Thursday was read and approved.

General Canby visited the Convention this morning, and was introduced by the PRESIDENT to the members, who rose and greeted the General with enthusiastic applause.

The PRESIDENT read the following communication, which was received as information:

HEADQUARTERS ARMY OF THE UNITED STATES, }
WASHINGTON, D. C., March 9, 1868. }

Hon. A. G. Mackey, President of the Convention:

SIR:—General Grant directs me to acknowledge the receipt of a copy of resolutions adopted by the Constitutional Convention of South Carolina, and forwarded to me by you.

I am, sir, with great respect, your obedient servant,

ADAM BADEAU,
Brevet Brigadier-General, A. D. C.

The President also read a communication from the Ladies' Juvenil Benevolent Society, (colored,) tendering their compliments to the gentlemen of the Convention, and inviting them to attend their fair and musical entertainment at Bonum's Hall, John-street, at eight o'clock this evening.

On motion of Mr. WM. McKINLAY, the invitation was accepted by the Convention.

The PRESIDENT announced the unfinished business to be the report of the Committee on Finance, Article IX. of the Constitution.

Mr. F. J. MOSES, Jr., from the Committee on the Executive Department, presented the following section (section two) as amended. The section was read twice and passed to a third reading.

The rules were then suspended and the section was read a third time and passed:

SECTION 2. The Governor shall be elected by the electors duly qualified to vote for members of the House of Representatives, and shall hold his office for two years, and until his successor shall be chosen and qualified, and shall be re eligible He shall be elected at the first general election held under this Constitution for members of the General Assembly, and at each general election thereafter, and shall be installed during the first session of the said General Assembly after his election, on such day as shall be provided for by law. The other State officers elect shall, at the same time, enter upon the performance of their duties.

Mr. J. M. RUTLAND, from the Committee on the Legislative Provisions of the Constitution, reported the following substitute for section thirty-four, Legislative Department, which was read, and, on motion of Mr. F. J. MOSES, Jr., was ordered to be printed and made the special order for to-morrow at 11 o'clock:

SECTION 34. The family homestead of the head of each family, residing in this State, such homestead consisting of dwelling house, out-buildings and lands appurtenant, occupied by such person as a homestead, not to exceed the value of one thousand dollars, and yearly product thereof, shall be exempt from taxation, levy or sale on any mesne or final process issued from any court. To secure the full enjoyment of said homestead exemption to the person entitled thereto, the personal property of such person, of the following character, to wit: household furniture, bed and bedding, wearing apparel, school books, arms, carts, wagons, farming implements, tools. neat cattle, work animals, swine and sheep, not to exceed in value in the aggregate the sum of five hundred dollars, shall be subject to like exemption as said homestead; *Provided,* That no property shall be exempt from attachment, levy or sale, for taxes, or for payment of obligations contracted for the purchase of said homestead, or the erection of improvements thereon; *Provided further,* That the yearly products of said homestead shall not be exempt from attachment, levy or sale, for the payment of obligations contracted in the production of the same.

It shall be the duty of the General Assembly to enforce the provisions of this section by suitable legislation.

Article IX. was then taken up, read a third time, by sections, and finally passed as follows:

ARTICLE IX.

FINANCE AND TAXATION.

SECTION 1. The General Assembly shall provide by law for a uniform and equal rate of assessment and taxation, and shall prescribe such regulations as shall secure a just valuation for taxation of all property, real, personal and possessory, except mines and mining claims, the proceeds of which alone shall be taxed; and also excepting such property as may be exempted by law for municipal, educational, literary, scientific, religious or charitable purposes

SEC. 2. The General Assembly may provide annually for a poll tax not to exceed one dollar on each poll, which shall be applied exclusively to the public school fund. And no additional poll tax shall be levied by any municipal corporation.

SEC. 3. The General Assembly shall provide for an annual tax sufficient to defray the estimated expenses of the State for each year; and whenever it shall happen that such ordinary expenses of the State for any year shall exceed the income of the State for such year, the General Assembly shall provide for levying a tax for the ensuing year sufficient, with other sources of income, to pay the deficiency of the preceding year, together with the estimated expenses of the ensuing year.

SEC. 4. No tax shall be levied except in pursuance of a law, which shall distinctly state the object of the same; to which object such tax shall be applied.

SEC. 5. It shall be the duty of the General Assembly to enact laws for the exemption from taxation of all public schools, colleges, and institutions of learning, all charitable institutions in the nature of asylums for the infirm, deaf and dumb, blind, idiotic and indigent persons, all public libraries, churches and burying grounds; but property of associations and societies, although connected with charitable objects, shall not be exempt from State, County or Municipal taxation; *Provided*, That this exemption shall not extend beyond the buildings and premises actually occupied by such schools, colleges, institutions of learning, asylums, libraries, churches and burial grounds, although connected with charitable objects.

SEC. 6. The General Assembly shall provide for the valuation and assessment of all lands and the improvements thereon prior to the assembling of the General Assembly of one thousand eight hundred and seventy, and thereafter on every fifth year.

SEC. 7. For the purpose of defraying extraordinary expenditures, the State may contract public debts; but such debts shall be authorized by law for some single object, to be distinctly specified therein; and no such law shall take effect until it shall have been passed by the vote of two-thirds of the members of each branch of the General Assembly, to be recorded by yeas and nays on the journals of each House respectively; and every such law shall levy a tax annually sufficient to pay the annual interest of such debt.

SEC. 8. The corporate authorities of Counties, Townships, School Districts, Cities, Towns and Villages may be vested with power to assess and collect taxes for corporate purposes; such taxes to be uniform in respect to persons and property within the jurisdiction of the body imposing the same. And the General Assembly shall require that all the property, except that heretofore exempted within the limits of municipal corporations, shall be taxed for the payment of debts contracted under authority of law.

SEC. 9. The General Assembly shall provide for the incorporation and organization of cities and towns, and shall restrict their powers of taxation, borrowing money, contracting debts, and loaning their credit.

SEC. 10. No scrip, certificate, or other evidence of State indebtedness shall be issued, except for the redemption of stock, bonds, or other evidences of indebtedness previously issued, or for such debts as are expressly authorized in this Constitution

SEC. 11. An accurate statement of the receipt and expenditures of the public money shall be published with the laws of each regular session of the General Assembly in such manner as may, by law, be directed.

SEC. 12. No money shall be drawn from the Treasury but in pursuance of appropriations made by law.

SEC. 13. The fiscal year shall commence on the first day of November in each year.

SEC. 14. Any debt contracted by the State shall be by loan on State Bonds, of amounts not less than fifty dollars each, on interest, payable within twenty years after the final passage of the law authorizing such debt. A correct registry of all such bonds shall be kept by the Treasurer in numerical order, so as always to exhibit the number and amount unpaid, and to whom severally made payable.

SEC. 15. Suitable laws shall be passed by the General Assembly for the safe keeping, transfer and disbursement of the State, County and School funds, and all officers and other persons charged with the same, shall keep an accurate entry of each sum received, and of each payment and transfer; and shall give such security for the faithful discharge of such duties as the General Assembly may provide. And it shall be the duty of the General Assembly to pass laws making embezzlement of such funds a felony, punishable by fine and imprisonment proportioned to the amount of deficiency or embezzlement, and the party convicted of such felony shall be disqualified from ever holding any office of honor or emolument in this State; *Provided, however*, That the General Assembly, by a two-third vote, may remove the disability upon payment in full of the principal and interest of the sum embezzled.

SEC. 16. No debt contracted by this State in behalf of the late rebellion, in whole or in part, shall ever be paid.

Mr. S. G. W. DILL offered the following:

Resolved, That no land owner or other persons having charge of lands in the county or State, shall be allowed to receive more than one-half of the crop made or raised upon lands rented by him or her to any tenant, for the use of the lands so cultivated by said tenant, and no landlord in any city, town or village, shall charge more than ten per cent. on any house or lot, according to its assessed value by the assessor.

Mr. J. H. RAINEY moved to lay the resolution on the table.

Mr. S. G. W. DILL called for the yeas and nays, which was not seconded, and the motion to lay on the table was agreed to.

Mr. S. G. W. DILL offered the following:

Resolved, That the committee to whom were referred three resolutions, namely: one on Universal Suffrage; one declaring all the civil offices in the State vacant on the ratification of the Constitution, and one claiming pay for the members of the Convention from the time they left their homes until they return, be instructed to report at half-past three o'clock to-morrow.

110

Mr. S. A. SWAILS moved to lay the resolution on the table.

Mr. S. G. W. DILL moved to lay the man that made the motion on the table.

The motion to lay on the table was agreed to.

Mr. S. G. W. DILL rose to a question of privilege, and said he thought he had the right to make a few remarks.

The PRESIDENT decided that not to be a question of privilege.

Mr. S. G. W. DILL said he was in earnest.

Mr. B. F. WHITTEMORE moved that the floor be given to the gentlemen from Kershaw (Mr. DILL), for fifteen minutes, which was agreed to.

The PRESIDENT informed the house that the gentleman from Kershaw had the floor for fifteen minutes, to speak on any subject he pleased.

Mr. S. G. W. DILL. I am in earnest in what I have to say. As I am not confined to any specific subject, I will take the opportunity to make a few general remarks. We have had a long and pleasant time together, and I hope this pleasantness will continue to the close of the Convention. I have voted in every instance, while here, to the best of my knowledge and ability, for everything that I thought would benefit the poor. At the same time that I claimed to be the friend of the poor man, I was no enemy to the rich. While I insist on giving the poor man justice and all that truly belongs to him, I would not rob the rich of any of their rights or privileges. Thank God! I have enough to live on at home, but that is not the case with the majority of my constituents. Numbers of them are oppressed; numbers are without homes, without shelter, and cannot obtain it unless they give more than one-half of their physical labor to their landlords for shelter. I have received numerous letters and communications from my constituents in reference to the rent of lands, and I am begged to do something for them towards keeping the landlords in cheek.

Mr. R. C. DELARGE requested the privilege of asking the gentleman a question.

Mr. S. G. W. DILL said he desired not to be interrupted, and if the member did not keep still, he would have to get him in his friend's (Mr. RUTLAND'S) cage of hyenas. (Laughter.)

Mr. H. E. HAYNE rose to call the speaker to order, for having called the gentleman from Charleston a hyena.

Mr. S. G. W. DILL said he only alluded to hyena cages building for the hyenas here.

Mr. R. C. DELARGE asked the speaker if he was not one of the hyenas.

Mr. S. G. W. DILL said he might come to it, when a poor man could not live without turning hyena.

Mr. R. C. DELARGE asked how much time was to be allowed the speaker, and on what subject he was speaking.

The PRESIDENT said the gentleman was allowed fifteen minutes to speak on all subjects, and such other things besides as he might desire.

Mr. S. G. W. DILL. First, I am sorry to see so many contending opinions relative to this homestead matter. I intend to fight that to the day of my death. I don't think its right or just The amendment calls for too little. I want to get out of the old channel. The old laws of the State dragged us all to perdition, and they still threaten to do so. I want to get rid of them. Now, I say the homestead should be, at least, one hundred acres of land, and such a house as I choose to erect on it. I should have the privilege of spending on that house one or five thousand dollars, and that ought to be secured to me against all debts. By the proposed amendment, if I built a house worth more than one thousand dollars, I can be sold out of house and home if I get in debt. I say, let it be as first reported—one hundred acres of land and twenty-five hundred dollars. I don't wonder that the demagogues outside laugh at us in their sleeves. Our actions here are making laws that will make the rich man richer and the poor man poorer. Now, I want a change. We have come here to represent the great Union Republican party ; that party is to-day composed of the poor men and those who were but recently in slavery. I want to see this class treated fairly. Secure suffrage to them all firmly, fixedly, so that they can protect themselves. Let these rich nabobs know that at last they have equals at the ballot box, and my word for it, we can take care of ourselves. I have lived in this city, off and on, for near on to forty years. I know as much about the men who call us ringed-streaked-and-striped as any body, and if I choose to tell, I could astonish you with a revelation of secrets that would account for some of these streaks. But I wont say much more; only this, that when I go from here I mean to take my horse and buggy, canvass my district and explain the Constitution, and if the people of Kershaw don't ratify it by a handsome vote, it will not be the fault of their delegate in this Convention.

The fifteen minutes having expired the PRESIDENT called the gentleman to take his seat, when Mr. R. C. DELARGE moved that his time be extended, provided he stated the subject matter to be discussed.

The motion was not agreed to, and the PRESIDENT decided that the member could speak no longer.

Mr. T. J. ROBERTSON called up the Ordinance introduced by him for the appointment of three commissioners to investigate claims against the State, &c., which had been referred to a special committee of nine, who had recommended the passage of the Ordinance.

Mr. B. F. RANDOLPH. I would state that an Ordinance somewhat similar in its provisions, but leaving the matter to be acted upon by the Legislature, has been passed, and I, therefore, consider this Ordinance unnecessary.

Mr. T. J. ROBERTSON. I advocate the passage of the Ordinance, simply on the ground that by the appointment of these Commissioners, all the information necessary for the Legislature to have upon the subject of claims against the State, and its financial condition and resources could be collected by the Board previous to the meeting of that body, and would also aid the credit of the State.

Mr. B. F. WHITTEMORE moved to strike out the enacting clause, which was agreed to, and the Ordinance was thereby rejected.

Mr. E. W. M. MACKEY, from the Committee on the Legislative Provisions of the Constitution, submitted an additional article to the Constitution, which was read twice and ordered to be printed, and made the special order for to-morrow morning :

ARTICLE —

AMENDMENT AND REVISION OF THE CONSTITUTION.

SECTION 35. Any amendment or amendments to this Constitution may be proposed in the Senate or House of Representatives. If the same be agreed to by two thirds of the members elected to each House, such amendment or amendments shall be entered on the journals, respectively, with the yeas and nays taken thereon ; and the same shall be submitted to the qualified electors of the State, at the next general election thereafter for Representatives, and if a majority of the electors, qualified to vote for members of the General Assembly, voting thereon, shall vote in favor of such amendment or amendments, and two-thirds of each of the next Legislature shall, after such an election, and before another, ratify the same amendment or amendments, by yeas and nays, the same shall become part of the Constitution : *Provided*, That such amendment or amendments shall have been read three times, on three several days, in each House.

SEC. 36. If two or more amendments shall be submitted at the same time, they shall be submitted in such manner that the electors shall vote for or against each of such amendments separately ; and while an amendment or amendments which shall have been agreed upon by one General Assembly shall be awaiting the action of a succeeding General Assembly, or of the electors, no additional amendment or amendments shall be proposed.

Sec. 37. Whenever two-thirds of the members elected to each branch of the General Assembly shall think it necessary to call a Convention to revise, amend, or change this Constitution, they shall recommend to the electors to vote at the next election for Representatives, for or against a Convention; and if a majority of all the electors voting at said election shall have voted for a Convention, the General Assembly shall, at their next session, provide by law for calling the same; and such Convention shall consist of a number of members not less than that of the most numerous branch of the General Assembly.

Mr. WRIGHT, from the Special Committee of Five, submitted the following report and Ordinance, which were ordered to be printed, and made the special order for to-morrow:

The Special Committee to whom as referred the resolution of the Convention providing for the appropriation of the Citadel, in the city of Charleston, for educational purposes, respectfully report that they have complied with the instructions conveyed by said resolution, and herewith transmit an Ordinance in conformity therewith, and recommend the adoption of the same:

Be it ordained, That the General Assembly is hereby instructed to provide, by suitable laws, for the appropriation of the Citadel and grounds, in the city of Charleston, for educational purposes, said buildings and grounds to be devoted to the establishment of an institution of learning, which shall be a body politic and corporate, and shall be managed by a Board of Trustees, and their successors, who shall be chosen by the General Assembly, and shall be subject to visitation by and under its authority. Said institution of learning shall have power to establish schools of law and medicine, and to issue diplomas that shall entitle the holders to practice said professions, as shall be prescribed by law.

Mr. E. W. M. MACKEY moved that the Committee on Franchise and Elections be instructed to report to-morrow on the Article that has been referred to them. Adopted.

Mr. B. F. RANDOLPH moved to take up an Ordinance in relation to corporate bodies, which was read, and

Mr. J. M. RUTLAND moved to strike out the preamble.

Mr. B. F. WHITTEMORE moved to strike out the words from "whereas" on the first line to "whereas" on the seventh line, which was adopted.

Mr. J. J. WRIGHT moved to strike out the words "or modify" in fourth line. Adopted.

Mr. B. F. WHITTEMORE moved to add, "And it shall be the duty of the General Assembly, at its first session after the passage of this Ordinance, to attend to the same." Adopted, and the Ordinance was read a third time, as follows, and passed.

AN ORDINANCE

To repeal all acts of Legislation passed since the twentieth day of December, one thousand eight hundred and sixty, which pledge the faith and credit of the State for the benefit of any Corporate Body.

Whereas, it is inexpedient that when the credit of the State is advanced or pledged for the benefit of public enterprises and works, in which the people of the State are interested, that power should be lodged in the General Assembly to exercise a salutary control over such public enterprises and works, to the end that the commerce and industry of the State should be adequately fostered and promoted ; therefore,

We, the People of South Carolina, in Convention met, do Ordain, That all acts or pretended acts of legislation purporting to have been passed by the General Assembly of the State since the twentieth day of December, A. D. 1860, pledging the faith and credit of the State for the benefit of any corporate body or private individual, are hereby suspended and declared inoperative until the General Assembly shall assemble and ratify the same. And it shall be the duty of the General Assembly at its first session after the passage of this Ordinance to attend to the same.

The Convention then adjourned.

FIFTY-FIRST DAY.

Saturday, March 14, 1868.

The Convention assembled at ten A. M., and was called to order by the PRESIDENT.

Prayer was offered by the Rev. J. M. RUNION.

The roll was called, and a quorum answering to their names, the PRESIDENT announced the Convention ready to proceed to business.

The Journal of Friday was read and approved.

The PRESIDENT read the following communication, which was received with applause.

WAR DEPARTMENT, WASHINGTON, D. C., March 9, 1868.

Sir :—I have the honor to acknowledge the receipt of your communication of the 2d instant, transmitting a copy of resolutions adopted by the Constitutional Convention of South Carolina on the 27th ult. I beg you to communicate to the Convention my thanks for the expressions contained in the resolutions in reference to my official action.

I am, with great respect, your obedient servant,

EDWIN M. STANTON.

Hon. A. G. MACKEY,
President of the Constitutional Convention of South Carolina.

Article X. of the Constitution was taken up, read a third time, and with the exception of section ten, in relation to opening the schools to all, without regard to race or color or previous condition, passed and declared an integral part of the Constitution.

The following is the article as passed :

ARTICLE X.

EDUCATION.

SECTION 1. The supervision of public instruction shall be vested in a State Superintendent of Education, who shall be elected by the qualified electors of the State in such manner and at such time as the other State officers are elected ; his powers, duties, term of office and compensation shall be defined by the General Assembly.

SEC. 2. There shall be elected biennially, in each County, by the qualified electors thereof, one School Commissioner, said Commissioners to constitute a State Board of Education, of which the State Superintendent shall, by virtue of his office, be Chairman; the powers, duties, and compensation of the members of said Board shall be determined by law.

SEC. 3. The General Assembly shall, as soon as practicable after the adoption of this Constitution, provide for a liberal and uniform system of free public schools throughout the State, and shall also make provision for the division of the State into suitable School Districts. There shall be kept open at least six months in each year one or more schools in each School District.

SEC. 4. It shall be the duty of the General Assembly to provide for the compulsory attendance, at either public or private schools, of all children between the ages of six and sixteen years, not physically or mentally disabled, for a term equivalent to twenty-four months at least: *Provided*, That no law to that effect shall be passed until a system of public schools has been thoroughly and completely organized, and facilities afforded to all the inhabitants of the State for the free education of their children.

SEC. 5. The General Assembly shall levy at each regular session after the adoption of this Constitution an annual tax on all taxable property throughout the State for the support of public schools, which tax shall be collected at the same time and by the same agents as the general State levy, and shall be paid into the Treasury of the State. There shall be assessed on all taxable polls in the State an annual tax of one dollar on each poll, the proceeds of which tax shall be applied solely to educational purposes ; *Provided*, That no person shall ever be deprived of the right of suffrage for the non-payment of said tax. No other poll or capitation tax shall be levied in the State, nor shall the amount assessed on each poll exceed the limit given in this section The School Tax shall be distributed among the several School Districts of the State, in proportion to the respective number of pupils attending the public schools. religious No sect or sects shall have exclusive right to, or control, of any part of the school funds of the State, nor shall sectarian principles be taught in the public schools.

SEC. 6. Within five years after the first regular session of the General Assembly, following the adoption of this Constitution, it shall be the duty of the General Assembly to provide for the establishment and support of a State Normal School, which shall be open to all persons who may wish to become teachers.

SEC. 7. Educational institutions for the benefit of all the blind, deaf and dumb, and such other benevolent institutions as the public good may require, shall be established and supported by the State, subject to such regulations as may be prescribed by law.

SEC. 8. Provisions shall be made by law, as soon as practicable, for the establishment and maintenance of a State Reform School for juvenile offenders.

SEC. 9. The General Assembly shall provide for the maintenance of the State University, and as soon as practicable, provide for the establishment of an Agricultural College, and shall appropriate the land given to this State, for the support of such a college, by the act of Congress, passed July second, one thousand eight hundred and sixty-two, or the money or scrip, as the case may be, arising from the sale of said lands, or any lands which may hereafter be given or appropriated for such purpose, for the support and maintenance of such college, and may make the same a branch of the State University, for instruction in Agriculture, the Mechanic Arts, and the Natural Sciences connected therewith.

SEC. 11. The proceeds of all lands that have been or hereafter may be given by the Unite States to this State for educational purposes, and not otherwise appropriated by this State or the United States, and of all lands or other property given by individuals, or appropriated by the State for like purpose, and of all estates of deceased persons who have died without leaving a will or heir, shall be securely invested and sacredly preserved as a State School Fund, and the annual interest and income of said fund, together with such other means as the General Assembly may provide, shall be faithfully appropriated for the purpose of establishing and maintaining free public schools, and for no other purposes or uses whatever.

Article VIII. on the right of suffrage was read a third time, passed, and declared an integral portion of the Constitution, as follows:

ARTICLE VIII.

RIGHT OF SUFFRAGE.

SECTION 1. In all elections by the people the electors shall vote by ballot.

SEC. 2. Every male citizen of the United States, of the age of twenty-one years and upwards, not laboring under the disabilities named in this Constitution, without distinction of race, color, or former condition, who shall be a resident of this State at the time of the adoption of this Constitution, or who shall thereafter reside in this State one year, and in the County in which he offers to vote, sixty days next preceeding any election, shall be entitled to vote for all officers that are now, or hereafter may be, elected by the people, and upon all questions submitted to the electors at any elections; *Provided,* That no person shall be allowed to vote or hold office who is now or hereafter may be disqualified therefor by the Constitution of the United States, until such disqualification shall be removed by the Congress of the United States; *Provided further,* That no person, while kept in any alms house or asylum, or of unsound mind or confined in any public prison, shall be allowed to vote or hold office.

SEC. 3 It shall be the duty of the General Assembly to provide from time to time for the registration of all electors.

SEC. 4. For the purpose of voting no person shall be deemed to have lost his residence by reason of absence while employed in the service of the United States, nor while engaged upon the waters of this State or the United States, or of the high seas, nor while temporarily absent from the State.

SEC. 5. No soldier, seaman or marine in the army or navy of the United States shall be deemed a resident of this State in consequence of having been stationed therein.

SEC. 6. Electors shall, in all cases, except treason, felony or breach of the peace, be privileged from arrest and civil process during their attendance at elections, and in going to and returning from the same.

SEC. 7. Every person entitled to vote at any election shall be eligible to any office which now is or hereafter shall be elective by the people in the County where he shall have resided sixty days previous to such election, except as otherwise provided in this Constitution or the Constitution and laws of the United States.

SEC. 8. The General Assembly shall never pass any law that will deprive any of the citizens of this State of the right of suffrage except for treason, murder, robbery, or duelling, whereof the persons shall have been duly tried and convicted.

SEC. 9. Presidential electors shall be elected by the people.

SEC. 10. In all elections held by the people under this Constitution, the person or persons who shall receive the highest number of votes shall be declared elected.

Mr. R. C. DeLARGE, the Chairman of the Committee on Franchise and Elections, submitted the following additional sections, on which the rules were suspended; the sections were read three times and passed:

SEC. 11. The provisions of this Constitution concerning the terms of residence necessary to enable persons to hold certain offices therein mentioned, shall not be held to apply to officers chosen by the people at the first election, or by the General Assembly at its first session.

SEC. 12. No person shall be disfranchised for felony or other crime committed while such person was a slave.

Mr. JAMES D. BELL presented the petition from Mr. D. L. Thompson, of Yorkville, praying the Convention to recommend the removal of

111

his political disabilities, which was referred to the Committee on Petitions.

Mr. T. J. ROBERTSON presented the petition of Mr. James Augustus Black, of Abbeville District, praying the Convention to recommend the removal of his political disabilities.

Referred to Committee on Petitions.

Mr. N. J. NEWELL presented the following resolution, which, on motion of Mr. W. J. WHIPPER, was made the special order for Monday, twelve o'clock.

Whereas, the Union Republican party has pledged itself to the support of all internal improvements ; and, whereas, a connection by railroad between the Atlantic coast of this State and the States of the West is of great importance to develop the agricultural, mineral, mechanical, and mercantile resources of the State; and, whereas, the sum of three millions of dollars have already been expended upon the Blue Ridge Railroad, connecting this State from Anderson to Knoxville, Tennessee ; and, whereas, efforts are now being made by the officers of said road to secure a large subscription of lands thereto along the line of said road by the citizens of North and South Carolina, between Walhalla and Knoxville, with reasonable prospects that such efforts will be crowned with successs ; therefore, be it

Resolved, By this Convention, that the General Assembly, so soon as satisfactory evidence shall be furnished, that 300,000 acres of land along the line of said road shall have been donated for the purpose of completing the same, be and they are hereby requested to endorse the bonds of the said Blue Ridge Railroad, heretofore authorized to be issued by the General Assembly of this State, under such restrictions as they may deem proper, to an amount not exceeding three millions of dollars, and that the General Assembly may provide, by all proper means, to secure the completion of the said road at the earliest day practicable.

The following supplementary article to the Constitution, reported by Mr E. W. M. MACKEY, was read a third time, passed, and declared an integral portion of the Constitution, as follows :

ARTICLE —.

AMENDMENT AND REVISION OF THE CONSTITUTION.

SECTION 1. Any amendment or amendments to this Constitution may be proposed in the Senate or House of Representatives. If the same be agreed to by two-thirds of the members elected to each House, such amendment or amendments shall be entered on the journals respectively, with the yeas and nays taken thereon ; and the same shall be submitted to the qualified electors of the State, at the next general election thereafter for Representatives, and if a majority of the electors, qualified to vote for members of the General Assembly, voting thereon, shall vote in favor of such amendment or amendments, and two-thirds of each branch of the next General Assembly, shall, after such an election, and before another, ratify the same amendment or amendments, by yeas and nays, the same shall become part of the Constitution: *Provided*, That such amendment or amendments shall have been read three times, on three several days, in each House.

Sec. 2. If two or more amendments shall be submitted at the same time, they shall be submitted in such manner that the electors shall vote for or against each of such amendments separately.

Sec. 3. Whenever two-thirds of the members elected to each branch of the General Assembly shall think it necessary to call a Convention to revise, amend, or change this Constitution, they shall recommend to the electors to vote at the next election for Representatives, for or against a Convention; and if a majority of all the electors voting at said election shall have voted for a Convention, the General Assembly shall, at their next session, provide by law for calling the same; and such Convention shall consist of a number of members not less than that of the most numerous branch of the General Assembly.

Mr. R. C. DeLARGE offered the following resolution:

Resolved, That this Convention petition Congress to remove all political disabilities from the citizens of this State.

Mr. W. J. WHIPPER moved that the resolution be made the special order for Monday, at four o'clock.

Mr. J. D. BELL moved that the resolution be indefinitely postponed.

Mr. R. C. DeLARGE. I desire to see this body act with the dignity and gravity which becomes a subject of such great importance. Nothing is so surprising as to see what appears to be an anxious desire on the part of some members not to meet fairly a question like the one now before us. I confess I am anxious to have this resolution discussed. I am anxious that its friends should have an opportunity of advocating its passage. At the same time, I desire to hear the reasons that may be urged against it. I hope, therefore, the Convention will not vote in favor of an indefinite postponement. I move that the motion to indefinitely postpone be laid on the table.

The motion to lay on the table was not agreed to.

Mr. W. J. WHIPPER. I hope the opponents of that resolution are not afraid to meet us in the discussion of that question. I am in favor of the resolution, and ready to give my reasons. I only ask to have it fairly argued. With regard to the merits of the proposition, it is wrong; we expect those who oppose it to show the injurious effects that would be caused by its adoption. If the friends of the resolution are right, as they believe they are, and can prove it upon a frank and calm discussion of the matter here, let us have that discussion. I ask that the motion to indefinitely postpone be voted down, and that the resolution be made the special order for this afternoon or to-morrow.

Mr. F. L. CARDOZO. I hope the motion to postpone will not prevail. I hope there will be no fear to take this subject up, and it is also to be hoped that the Convention will exercise that magnanimity and generosity which becomes every citizen of this State. A motion to postpone is only a sort of polite way of dodging a question; and this is but saying, in a polite way, we are not in favor of a removal of political disabilities. We hope those opposed to it, however, will have the courage to say so, and will not shirk the responsibility. There are some of us who favor the proposition as an act of generosity, and we wish to discuss it. We think it is a matter of expediency as well as of policy to do it; and I hope when the question comes up, it will be shown that our party can exercise a generosity and magnanimity unparalleled in the history of the world; that although our people have been oppressed and have every inducement to seek revenge; although deprived of all means of education and learning, we can rise above all selfishness and exhibit a christian universality of spirit.

Mr. S. G. W. DILL. I hope the motion to indefinitely postpone will prevail. I have not so much confidence as others in what outsiders say they will do for us. I do not think it good policy to put a weapon into the hands of our enemies; and hence, am opposed to this proposition. I am willing, however, to debate on the propriety of removing the disabilities of those who may be recommended by their delegations on this floor; but cannot favor such a sweeping resolution as this.

At this stage of the business, Mr. W. H. Sweet, a member of the North Carolina Constitutional Convention, visited the Convention, and was introduced to the members by the PRESIDENT, and made some remarks congratulatory of the body.

Mr. J. J. WRIGHT. This is a question which no doubt will strike the mass of members of this body as rather peculiar. I hope, therefore, we shall have a full and frank discussion; and that we shall determine whether it is or is not for the welfare of South Carolina to pass the resolution. It has been intimated that there are those who are timid and afraid to meet the question. I am not one of that kind. The gentleman who last spoke says he is willing to show a christian spirit whenever there is a proper evidence of repentance. So am I. The resolution has been introduced, and if we fail to meet it, it will be said by outsiders that we were afraid of the question. I am perfectly willing and ready to meet it now.

Mr A. BRYCE. That's all, Wright. (Laughter.)

Mr. L. S. LANGLEY. I hope, inasmuch as the Convention is drawing to a close, and we are about to return to our homes and constituents, no subject requiring such grave deliberation as this will be forced upon this body. I am decidedly in favor of indefinitely postponing the consideration of this resolution. While favoring an extension of the right of franchise to all men, I think this question should have been brought up at its proper time and place. Had it been introduced some weeks ago, we might have given it the consideration it deserves; but now that we are about to adjourn, to consider so grave a subject would, in my opinion, be exceedingly unwise. I, therefore, do hope the motion to postpone indefinitely will prevail, and that we shall content ourselves by acting simply on the petitions that have been introduced.

Mr. W. B. NASH. I hope that motion will not prevail. I believe this is one of the most important matters that can be brought to the attention of the Convention. I hope we shall pass this very measure. Now that we have nearly formed a Constitution to present to the people of the State, what more glorious act could we wind up our labor with than to offer to the people of the State, to those disfranchised, a universal pardon? It would show to the men who have raised their hands against us, that we can exercise a magnanimity of which we can be proud, and it would be a great stroke of policy on the part of this Convention. We should disarm our enemies. I believe I was almost the first man in this State, in the Republican party, who dared to advocate this measure, and it fills my heart with joy to find men, who, a month ago, were denouncing me in reference to this very proposition, now coming forward to my support. My heart is interested in the subject, because I believe it will redound to the welfare of the people of South Carolina, and the welfare of the whole country. Congress made a great mistake in disfranchising so many of the people of the Southern States. I wish to see every man in South Carolina have a right to cast his vote, and also the right to hold an office if he can get one. It will do us good, and when we enfranchise the people of this State it will be said, that it was the loyal masses who did it. I hope, therefore, the motion to postpone will not prevail.

Mr. R. B. ELLIOTT. I have not risen to make a speech, for I believe it to be unnecessary It is a useless consumption of time to discuss whether this matter should be postponed, and I hope the members will vote unanimously against it.

Mr. J. H. RAINEY. I regret extremely at this stage of our proceedings, that we are compelled to discuss a measure of such importance as the one before us. I cannot see why it is that members on this floor oppose a resolution which is simply an expression of peace and good will to the whole State. I am in favor of the resolution, and believe we can well afford to adopt it, and exhibit a magnanimity which has not been shown to us.

Mr. J. S. CRAIG. I hope this motion will be voted down. We have introduced and supported various generous measures here, and there is no reason why the majority should not confer upon the minority a privilege which we can afford to accord to them. If we are in favor of universal suffrage, we certainly ought not to ignore those who are politically disabled for past offences. If we adjourn without acting upon this subject, to whom are those who have petitioned for a removal of their disqualifications to appeal for redress? Let us show our sense of justice, and a desire to accord to every man the privileges which we enjoy.

Mr. R. B. ELLIOTT. I now move the previous question.

The previous question was sustained; and on the main question Mr. F. L. CARDOZO called for the yeas and nays.

The yeas and nays were ordered, and being taken resulted as follows:

Yeas—Messrs. Alexander, Bell, Burton, Camp, Coghlan, Clinton, Dill, Dogan, Foster, Goss, Henderson, Jacobs, Langley, McDaniels, Middleton, Nance, Neagle, Nuckels, Owens, Rose, White, Wingo—22.

Nays—The President, Messrs. Allen, Arnim, Becker, Bowen, Bonum, Boozer, Brockenton, Brice, Cain, Cardozo, Chamberlain, Cook, Collins, Corley, Craig, Crews, Darrington, DeLarge, Dickson, Duncan, Elliott, Gentry, Gray, Harris, J. N. Hayne, C. D. Hayne, H. E. Hayne, Holmes, Humbird, Hurley, Jervey, Jillson, S. Johnson, W. B. Johnson, J. W. Johnson, W. E. Johnston, Jones, Long, Lee, Lomax, Leslie, Mackey, Mayer, W. J. McKinlay, Wm. McKinlay, F. F. Millar, Milford, Nance, Nash, Nelson, Newell, Olsen, Rainey, Ransier, Rivers, Robertson, Runion, Rutland, Sanders, Smalls, Stubbs, Thomas, A. Thompson, B. A. Thompson, S. B. Thompson, Viney, Whittemore, Williamson, F. E. Wilder, C. M. Wilder, Wooley, Wright—72.

Absent—23.

So the motion was not agreed to.

The resolution was made the special order for Monday afternoon, at four o'clock.

The Convention proceeded to consider the thirty-fourth section of the Report of the Constitution on the Legislative part of the Constitution.

Mr. J. S. CRAIG moved to amend by inserting after the word "occupied," in line two of the bill, the words "or cultivated."

It is a well known fact that in many places of this State, the best cultivated lands are so situated that a man cannot live on them in the summer time, because of sickness.

My amendment provides that, if cultivated, the owner can claim the place as a homestead.

Mr. J. L. NEAGLE moved to strike out the words in second line from "occupied" to "homestead;" in sixth line to strike out the words "wearing apparel," and to insert after word "homestead," in ninth line, the words "and there shall be exempt in addition thereto all necessary wearing apparel."

Mr. J. M. RUNION moved to strike out "school books," in sixth line, and insert "family library;" and also to strike out in sixth line the word "bed," and insert "beds."

Mr. F. L. CARDOZO moved to strike out the words "one thousand," and insert the words "two thousand," in third line.

Mr. B. F. WHITTEMORE moved to strike out "one thousand," and insert "ten thousand."

Mr. C. P. LESLIE moved to insert in fifth line, after the word "thereto," the words "or to the head of any family," and in seventh line "or goats."

Mr. S. A. SWAILS moved to insert after the word "Assembly," thirteenth line, the words "at their first session."

Mr. C. P. LESLIE. I do not think much discussion on this subject is necessary. I wish, however, to define what a homestead is; why homestead laws are sustained, and for whom they are enacted. Lord Coke once said a man never understood the law unless he understood the reason of it. Show me a man who understands the reason of the law, and I will show you a man who understands the law. If we commence at the foundation and go back to the bottom, or the inquiry of what a homestead law is; what it means, and what it is intended to effect, we would not have a great deal of trouble in disposing of every other question connected with it. A homestead law is sustained by considerations of public policy.

It is sustained because it is a humane measure. The courts uphold and sustain it, because it is charitable in its object and purposes. By the old common law, it used to be a crime for a man to owe a debt. A man could be seized and imprisoned. All that has passed away. We have amended the laws of South Carolina so that there can be no further imprisonment for debt. Now, we propose to create a homestead. We cannot make a homestead law, unless we keep in view the fact that we are endeavoring to shelter our people from the storm, the rain and the misfortunes of the world. If we propose to make a homestead for any other than charitable purposes, the courts will not sustain it. If we pass a sweeping homestead law to secure the debtor against his just debts, we will fail in our efforts. But if we pass a fair, reasonable law, that appears to be necessary, the courts will sustain it and uphold it. If we undertake, however, to cover up an unusual sum of money from the creditor, the courts cannot sustain it, and they will declare the homestead bill, a bill to repudiate debts, and it will be defeated. Our friends must also remember that a debtor, as matter of right, is not entitled to a dollar as long as he owes his creditor. Everything granted him is granted on the score of humanity and public policy. I say, then, to our friends, we must be moderate in our demands, or we will certainly lose all. Our friends from Charleston desire that the sum of two thousand dollars should be exempt. If we strike out two thousand dollars' worth of real estate, I ask if that is applicable to the country? What will be its effect? I do not stand here to shield the rich man, nor do I speak exclusively for the poor. But I want to do what is fair and what is just. If we give to the country people two thousand dollars' worth of real estate, the effect will be that the rich planter will just shield himself under that two thousand dollars, and will deprive the poor people of an opportunity of getting any land by sale or otherwise. Every dollar allowed a debtor is so much kindness, and ought to command his gratitude. For this reason, too, I would make it moderate. Two thousand dollars would allow a certain class of persons to shield a large quantity of land that might be sold with advantage to the State. If a man cannot live upon one thousand dollars' worth of land; if he could not live upon that, I think he would be a very unreasonable man. A man that cannot be satisfied with that provision, had better go to some other place, if he can find it. There are two propositions before the body, one to exempt twenty-five hundred dollars' worth of property, and another proposing that all lands and houses shall be exempt. Now, that's extreme. Neither are right; because neither are in the nature of a fair homestead law. My first idea was that two thousand dollars' worth of real estate should be exempt, but upon consultation, I came to the conclusion that such a provision would not be sustained. It would seem too much like a repudiation of all debts.

The PRESIDENT informed the members that an artist was present who desired to take a picture of the Convention, and requested all who wished to hand down their *fac simile* to posterity, to remain seated for a short time, presenting as decorous an appearance as possible.

Mr. B. F. WHITTEMORE said it was suggested by the gentleman

from Fairfield (Mr. RUTLAND), that all the good looking men go to the front.

The PRESIDENT asked if the gentleman from Darlington (Mr. WHITTEMORE) would lead the way? (Great laughter.)

Mr. L. S. LANGLEY. I second the motion.

At the request of the artist, the members ranged themselves in seats towards the President's stand, facing the front entrance of the hall.

Two pictures were then taken, the body maintaining the most perfect silence.

The PRESIDENT begged leave to resign the Chair in favor of the photographer, who, he said, had been able to preserve better order than had been witnessed during the sitting of the Convention. He had not been compelled to call even the gentleman from Barnwell (Mr. LESLIE) to order.

The hour of adjournment now having arrived, the Convention took a recess until three o'clock, P. M.

AFTERNOON SESSION.

The Convention re-assembled at three, P. M.

The PRESIDENT said that, before proceeding to the regular business of the Convention, he desired to read the following copy of the official order of General Canby, in relation to the election ordained by the Convention, for voting on the ratification of the Constitution, and the election of members of Congress and State officers:

HEADQUARTERS SECOND MILITARY DISTRICT, ⟩
CHARLESTON, S. C., March 13, 1868. ⟨

[*General Orders, No.* 40.]

The Constitutional Convention of the State of South Carolina, in conformity with the act of Congress of March 23, 1867, supplementary to the act of March 2, 1867, "to provide for the more efficient government of the rebel States," having framed a Constitution and civil government according to the provisions of the aforecited laws; and having, by an Ordinance adopted on the 9th day of March, 1868, provided that the said Constitution shall be submitted "for ratification to the persons registered under the provisions of this act (March 23, 1867, section 4), at an election to be conducted by the officers appointed, or to be appointed by the Commanding General, as hereinbefore provided, and to be held after the expiration of thirty days after the notice thereof to be given by the said Convention;" and having further provided, by the aforesaid

Ordinance, that at the same time an election shall be held for Governor, Lieutenant-Governor, Adjutant and Inspector General, Secretary of State, Comptroller-General, Treasurer, Attorney General, Superintendent of Education, and members of the General Assembly; and, further, that in each Congressional District of the State an election shall be held for a member of the House of Representatives of the United States Congress, and for two members at large: It is ordered,

First. That an election be held in the State of South Carolina, commencing on Tuesday, the 14th day of April, and ending on Thursday, the 16th day of April, 1868, at which all registered voters of said State may vote "For Constitution" or "Against Constitution," and also on the same ballot for the State officers and members of the House of Representatives, specified in the aforesaid Ordinance.

Second. It shall be the duty of the Boards of Registration in South Carolina, commencing fourteen days prior to the election herein ordered, and giving reasonable public notice of the time and place thereof, to revise, for a period of five days, the registration lists, and upon being satisfied that any person not entitled thereto has been registered, to strike the name of such person from the lists, and such person shall not be entitled to vote. The Boards of Registration shall also, during the same period, add to such registers the names of all persons who at that time possess the qualifications required by said Acts, who have not already been registered.

Third. In deciding who are to be stricken from or added to the registration lists, the Boards will be guided by the law of March 2, 1867, and the laws supplementary thereto, and their attention is specially directed to the supplementary act of July 19, 1867.

Fourth. Any duly registered voter of this State who may have removed from the district in which he was registered, shall be entitled to vote in the district (county) to which he has removed, and has resided for the ten days next preceding this election, upon presentation of a certificate of registration from the district in which he was originally registered, or upon his affidavit or other satisfactory evidence that he was so registered, and that he has not voted at this election. It shall be the duty of the Registrars, upon the application of any duly registered voter who has removed, or is about to remove from the precinct in which he was originally registered, to furnish him with a certificate that he was so registered, and to note the fact in the registration books of the precinct. In default of the certificate, the affidavit of the voter must set forth the district and precinct in which he was originally registered, and the length of time he has resided in the county in which he desires to vote. In doubtful cases, the Registrars or Managers of Elections shall require such additional evidence as may be necessary to satisfy them that the applicant is legally entitled to vote. Blank forms for the certificates and for the affidavits herein required, will be furnished the Registrars and the Managers of Elections, and when used will be attached to the ballots cast by such voters, and will be transmitted to District Headquarters with the returns required by law.

Fifth. The said election will be held in each district at such places as may hereafter be designated, under the superintendence of the Boards of Registration as provided by law, and in accordance with instructions hereafter to be given to said Boards, in conformity with the acts of Congress, and as far as may be with the laws of South Carolina.

Sixth. The polls shall be opened at such voting places at six o'clock in the forenoon, and closed at six o'clock in the afternoon of each day, and shall be kept open during these hours without intermission or adjournment.

Seventh. All judges and clerks employed in conducting said election, shall, before commencing to hold the same, be sworn to the faithful performance of their duties, and shall also take and subscribe the oath of office prescribed by law for officers of the United States.

Eighth. No member of the Board of Registration, who is a candidate for election to any office to be filled at this election, shall serve as a Judge or Manager of the Election in any precinct which he seeks to represent.

Ninth. The sheriff and other peace officers of each county are required to be present during the whole time that the polls are kept open, and until the election is completed; and will be made responsible that there shall be no interference with Judges of Elections, or other interruption of good order. If there should be more than one polling place in any county, the sheriff of the county is empowered and directed to make such assignment of his deputies, and other peace officers, to the other polling places, as may in his judgment best subserve the purposes of quiet and order; and he is further required to report these arrangements in advance to the Commander of the Military Post in which his county is situated.

Tenth. Violence, or threats of violence, or of discharge from employment, or other oppressive means to prevent any person from registering or exercising his right of voting, is positively prohibited; and any such attempts will be reported by the Registrars or Judges of elections to the Post Commander, and will cause the arrest and trial of the offenders by military authority. The exhibition or carrying of deadly weapons in violation of General Orders No. 10, of 1867, at or in the vicinity of any polling places during the election herein ordered, will be regarded and treated as an additional offence.

Eleventh. All bar rooms, saloons and other places for the sale of liquors by retail, will be closed from six o'clock of the evening of the 13th of April, until six o'clock of the morning of the 17th of April, 1868, and during this time the sale of all intoxicating liquors at or near any polling place is prohibited. The police officers of cities and towns, and the sheriffs and other peace officers of counties, will be held responsible for the strict enforcement of this prohibition, and will promptly arrest and hold for trial all persons who may transgress it.

Twelfth. Military interference with elections, "unless it shall be necessary to repel the armed enemies of the United States, or to keep the peace at the polls," is prohibited by the act of Congress, approved February 25th, 1865, and no soldiers will be allowed to appear at any polling place, unless as citizens of the State they are qualified and are registered as voters, and then only for the purpose of voting; but the Commanders of Posts will keep their troops well in hand on the days of election, and will be prepared to act promptly if the civil authorities are unable to preserve the peace.

Thirteenth. The returns required by law to be made to the Commander of the District of the results of, this election, will be rendered by the Boards of Registration of the several registration precincts, through the Commanders of the Military Posts in which their precincts are situated, and in accordance with the detailed instructions hereafter to be given.

Fourteenth. The State officers to be voted for at this election are :

1. Governor.
2. Lieutenant-Governor.
3. Adjutant and Inspector-General.
4. Secretary of State.
5. Comptroller-General.
6. Treasurer.
7. Attorney-General.
8. Superintendent of Education.
9. Members of the General Assembly, as follows :

County of Charleston,* two Senators and eighteen Representatives.
County of Colleton, one Senator and five Representatives.
County of Beaufort, one Senator and seven Representatives.
County of Georgetewn, one Senator and three Representatives.
County of Horry, one Senator and two Representatives.
County of Williamsburg, one Senator and three Representatives.
County of Marion, one Senator and four Representatives.
County of Darlington, one Senator and four Representatives.
County of Marlboro', one Senator and two Representatives.
County of Chesterfield, one Senator and two Representatives.
County of Sumter, one Senator and four Representatives.
County of Clarendon, one Senator and two Representatives.
County of Barnwell, one Senator and six Representatives.
County of Edgefield, one Senator and seven Representatives.
County of Orangeburg, one Senator and five Representatives.
County of Kershaw, one Senator and three Representatives.
County of Richland, one Senator and four Representatives.
County of Lexington, one Senator and two Representatives.
County of Newberry, one Senator and three Representatives.
County of Laurens, one Senator and four Representatives.
County of Abbeville, one Senator and five Representatives.
County of Anderson, one Senator and three Representatives.
County of Greenville, one Senator and four Representatives.
County of Pickens,* one Senator and one Representative.
County of Spartanburg, one Senator and four Representatives.
County of Union, one Senator and three Representatives.
County of York, one Senator and four Representatives.
County of Chester, one Senator and three Representatives.
County of Fairfield, one Senator and three Representatives.
County of Lancaster, one Senator and two Representatives.
County of Oconee,* one Senator and two Representatives

---

* NOTES.—(1) The territorial sub-divisions heretofore known as "Districts," are designated as "Counties," by the new Constitution. (2) The Districts of Charleston and Berkeley are united, and constitute the County of Charleston. (3) The County of Oconee is formed by the division of Pickens District.

Fifteenth. The First Congressional District is composed of the Counties of Lancaster, Chesterfield, Marlboro', Darlington, Marion, Horry, Georgetown, Williamsburg, Sumter, Clarendon and Kershaw; the second is composed of the Counties of Charleston, Colleton, Beaufort and Barnwell; the third is composed of the Counties of Orangeburg, Lexington, Richland, Newberry, Edgefield, Abbeville and Anderson; the fourth is composed of the Counties of Oconee, Pickens, Greenville Laurens, Spartanburg, Union, York, Chester and Fairfield; in each of which one person shall be elected as Representative to the Congress of the United States. In addition, two other members of that body will be elected by the ballots of the registered voters voting at large throughout the State.

By command of Brevet Major-General Ed R. S. Canby.

LOUIS V. CAZIARC,

Aide-de-Camp, Act'g Ass't Adg't General.

The PRESIDENT also stated that he had seen an official dispatch from the General of the army, General Grant, to General Canby, approving of the order, and also stating officially that the act of Congress, requiring simply a majority of voters to ratify the Constitution, also authorizing an election for members of Congress and State officers, to be held at the same time, had been adopted, become a law, and was now in force. (Applause.)

On motion of Mr. L. S. LANGLEY, the rules were suspended for the purpose of enabling him to offer the following resolution:

Whereas, Hon. H. H. Sweet, a delegate to the North Carolina Constitutional Convention, has honored this body with a visit:

Resolved, That this Convention send its greeting and good wishes to to the Constitutional Convention of their sister State, and that the President be requested to forward a copy of this resolution to the President of the Constitutional Convention of North Carolina.

The resolution was agreed to.

The Convention then resumed the consideration of the thirty-fourth section of the legislative provisions of the Constitution.

Mr. C. P. LESLIE resumed his remarks as follows:

Several very curious propositions have been made while this subject has been under consideration, which indicate clearly that the true purpose of a homestead law is not understood. My best answer to all these propositions is a reference to this clause which I have introduced, and which, I believe, covers in theory and practice the entire design of a homestead law. Much of the credit of the preparation of this law is due to your own Solicitor, Major D. T. Corbin, and to doubt its intent or its justice, is to doubt one of the ablest and most conscientious lawyers in the Republican party. Every one should be satisfied with the law as it stands, and if a man cannot live on a hundred acres of land and the products thereof, he should emigrate to some place where more liberality is to be found. My friend from Berkley has said that the words "yearly products" is an India rubber provision. If they cannot get along with one thousand dollars and this India provision, people never will be satisfied.

Mr. J. M. RUTLAND. I desire to state, for the information of the Convention, the reasons which induced the committee to change the original section. The committee had concluded to change the provision from two thousand to fifteen hundred dollars of real estate; but the Solicitor of the Convention arriving shortly afterwards, another meeting was held. The matter was then fully discussed in his presence, and the sum was reduced to one thousand dollars. It was understood that the yearly products allowed in the substitute would more than counterbalance the difference in the amount of the value. The committee thought this would be far more preferable, inasmuch as the yearly products were in most instances more valuable. I have always been an advocate for the homestead, the only objection I had to it being its retrospective character.

Mr. J. J. WRIGHT. The more we attempt to patch this thing up, the worse we shall make it. The substitute now proposed is, I believe, as near right as we can get a homestead law. It must be conceded that the decisions of the courts on this subject have generally been favorable to the homestead acts, and we should, therefore, be liberal, without being extravagant. Too much property reserved may induce some court hereafter to decide that this was an effort to screen persons from the payment of their honest debts. One thousand dollars, in my opinion, is enough, and should satisfy any reasonable man.

Mr. J. L. NEAGLE called for the previous question, which was sustained.

The question then recurred on the amendments of Messrs. J. S. CRAIG and F. L. CARDOZO, and they were rejected.

The amendments of Messrs. J. L. NEAGLE, J. M. RUNION, C. P. LESLIE, and S. A. SWAILS, were adopted, and the section, so amended, was passed to its third reading.

The section as adopted is as follows:

"The family homestead of the head of each family, residing in this State, such homestead consisting of dwelling house, out-buildings and lands appurtenant, not to exceed the value of one thousand dollars, and yearly product thereof, shall be exempt from attachment, levy, or sale on any mesne or final process issued from any court. To secure the full enjoyment of said homestead exemption to the person entitled thereto, or to the head of a family, the personal property of such person, of the following character, to wit : household furniture, beds and bedding, library, arms, carts, wagons, farming implements, tools, neat cattle, work animals, swine and sheep, not to exceed in value in the aggregate the sum of five hundred dollars, shall be subject to like exemption as said homestead; and there shall be exempt in addition thereto, the necessary wearing apparel ; *Provided,* That no property shall be exempt from attachment, levy or sale, for taxes, or for payment of obligations contracted for the purchase of said homestead, or the erection of improvements thereon ; *Provided further,* That the yearly products of said homestead shall not be exempt from attachment, levy or sale, for the payment of obligations contracted in the production of the same."

"It shall be the duty of the General Assembly at the first session to enforce the provisions of this section by suitable legislation."

The section, as passed, was then declared to be an integral part of the Constitution.

The next regular order being the following section, Article X., from Committee on Education, to whom it was recommitted :

SECTION 11. All the public schools, colleges, and universities of this State, supported wholly or in part by the public funds, shall be free and open to all the children and youths of this State, without regard to race, color or previous condition.

Mr. B. O. DUNCAN. I regret exceedingly at this late stage of our proceedings, to be compelled to detain the Convention by a prolonged discussion of any question. But since the Committee on Education persists in urging this section, I must beg your indulgence while I enter into a discussion of the question somewhat on its merits.

The subject of education is, under the peculiar condition of our State, probably the most important one we have had to consider in this body. Its importance to our people individually, and as a whole, cannot be overlooked by any intelligent man. Our success as a party, and our success as a people, depends entirely upon our being able to educate the masses of the people. Of this, no one is more convinced than I am, and no one is more earnest in the desire than I am, to see every man, woman and child in our State educated, without regard to the complexion of their skins. In this view of the subject, I know that I am sustained by the intelligence, and virtue, and Christian feeling of the State. Where there is opposition, it comes from prejudice and ignorance. The feeling of opposition to the education of the colored people was strong at the close of the war, it is true ; but it is now rapidly dying out among sensible men ; indeed among educated Christians it is already entirely dead. I need only refer, as proof of this assertion, to the actions of the Conventions, Conferences, &c., of the different denominations of the State. The Baptist State Convention, which met at Anderson last August, unanimously adopted resolutions introduced by Dr. Furman, President of Furman University, warmly urging the education of the colored people in Sunday Schools, and in every way practicable; and expressing regret that the poverty of the denomination would not allow it to take more active steps. The resolutions provide that colored theological students, or ministers applying for instruction to the Southern Theological Seminary, at Greenville, shall receive such instructions of the professors. That Baptist Convention was presided over by Dr. Winkler, of this city, and was composed of the intelligence and learning of the denomination throughout the State. Measures of a like character have been adopted by similar bodies in the State; and all over the State you find the intelligent, educated ministers, founding Sunday Schools for colored children, and urging the necessity of their education. You find in many localities strong objections, it is true; but it must be remembered that the majority of our white people are woefully ignorant, and that many of the religious teachers are not able to read the Bible correctly. My assertion applies only to the intelligent, and there I contend that I am right. The earnest desire to educate all the people, is general among them. Their prejudices have been overcome by intelligence, and this is the only way prejudices can be overcome. And I now take the position, that the only way the prejudices of race existing among our people can be overcome, is by educating them. Let us then not begin wrong in this all important matter. Let us not begin at the top of the house to build downwards. But let us lay the foundation aright, and we may build on it with confidence that all will come out right. Let us not begin where we ought to end. If we begin by educating the masses, we end by overcoming their prejudices. But if we begin by attempting to overcome their prejudices by force, and educating them afterwards, I am convinced that the whole plan will result in a failure.

Now, what is likely to be the result of retaining this section, and thereby opening the public schools to all? Simply, that they would be attended only by the colored children. If the attempt is made to enforce a mixture in this way, I have no idea that fifty white children in the State would attend the public schools. The freedmen's schools are now, if I mistake not, open to all; and yet I believe not one white pupil in the State attends them. The result would be exactly the same with our public schools. This is a state of affairs that we should certainly desire to avoid. In the first place, the poor white children would be deprived of any chance of education. They would continue ignorant and degraded and prejudiced. The whites who have means would send their children to private schools, but the poor whites would be as heretofore, unable to do so. You would also have the strange condition of affairs, of the whites paying probably nine-tenths of the expenses of institutions, which, by their organization, they would regard themselves as shut out from using. This would be a continual barrier in the way of peaceable and friendly relations existing between the two races all over the country. It would, I fear, have a most injurious effect on the ratification of this Constitution, and go far towards counteracting the good impressions made by our moderation thus far.

Again, in attempting to enforce mixed schools, you bring trouble, quarrelling and wrangling, into every neighborhood; and that too among those who are not directly responsible to the law, and who are more likely to be governed by prejudice and passion than by reason. You come in contact with the women and children, who are more prejudiced and more difficult to control. Suppose the case that it were possible to force the whites to send to mixed schools; and let a white boy and a colored boy have a little "pass at arms," as would continually occur, and at once you have a row between the mothers, which will frequently involve the fathers. In this way every neighborhood all over the State would be kept in a continual state of turmoil and strife. In this way passion and prejudice of race will be continually nurtured, and peace and quiet will not be allowed to prevail in any portion of the country. Both races, the colored as well as the white, would have good reason to complain of our inconsiderate action in bringing about such a state of affairs.

But the very shrewd members of the committee contended a few days ago, while debating the fourth section of this article, that the question was not on compelling the white and colored children to attend the same schools. That was not the idea at all, of this remarkably competent committee, as the gentleman from Darlington expresses it. I suppose they will to-day insist that the question is not on compulsion, but on mixed schools. They thought yesterday, we could not see forward, over five sections, to the tenth, and to-day they will think we cannot see backward the same distance. Wonderfully shrewd men these are, I will admit.

Gentlemen, this is too serious a question, to the peace and welfare of the country, for me not to speak out plainly the dangers before us. The gentleman from Darlington (Mr. WHITTEMORE) has paid the Committee on Education a very high compliment for ability; and yet I venture the assertion, that it has introduced the report most fraught with

113

danger to the peace and harmony of the State, and to the friendly relations between the two races. They attempt to force upon South Carolina measures even in advance of Massachusetts, though they know that
we are, in every respect, at least one hundred years behind that much
favored State. They do not reflect that civilization is a plant of slow
growth; that we can only arrive at it gradually, and after long years of
toil. They strive to talk learnedly of Prussia, and only show their want
of knowledge of facts, by attempting to bring in a case so dissimilar.
They forgot that, even in the time of the Cæsars, before the time of
Christ, Germany was a comparatively enlightened country, and has been
in the van of civilization ever since. And yet the Prussians and Saxons,
the most advanced among the Germans, have only arrived at compulsory education within the last twenty years. The gentleman from Darlington even goes back (I suppose he would call it going forward)
to the old Lacædemonian rule, and would take the children from
their parents, and educate them at the hands of the State. I tell you,
gentlemen, these extreme measures are fraught with danger to the peace
and welfare of our country, and should be defeated at all hazards.

Now, how are we to avoid these dangers? This does not seem to me
so difficult. Let us simply strike out this section, and leave the whole
matter to the Legislature. If that body determines that the schools
shall be mixed, and it is found after a year or two that the plan does not
work well, it can easily be changed; but if we retain this section, no
matter how injurious it may be found; no matter how dangerous to the
welfare of the country, and to the cause of education, it cannot be
removed. It does seem to me that we should leave a question so untried,
so delicate, and yet of such paramount importance, where it may be
changed, if it is found that the first experiments do not work well. I
believe we have everything to gain and nothing to lose by such a course.
We would certainly gain among the whites, and I believe we would lose
nothing among the colored people. Our colored people want schools to
send their children to. That is a universal desire, and certainly a most
praiseworthy one. But I do not believe they would prefer or even desire
to have white children attending the same schools with their own. If
they can have well organized schools under competent and kind teachers, sustained by the public, I believe they will be perfectly satisfied.

Now, would it not be far better to have schools entirely impartial in
their organization, but seperate, and all classes attending them, and
acquiring an education, and everything working harmoniously together,
than for us to introduce a measure here that would very likely prove
injurious to the cause of education, but which we could not change,

because it is in the Constitution? It seems to me there should be on doubt on this point among intelligent, reasonable men. Certainly, if we look at the condition of the country, we will see the necessity of adopting such measures as will secure the education of the white people as well as of the colored. It is estimated that from twenty to thirty per cent. of the grown up white men of South Carolina are unable to read or write. I suppose, at least ninety per cent. of the grown up colored men are in that condition; and indeed, if ten per cent. of them have already learned to read and write, it speaks wonderfully well for them. We have then sixty per cent. of the grown up men, the voters of the State, unable to read or write. What a contrast does this present, in comparison with a Northern State, where almost every man is educated! In Massachusetts only one grown man in two hundred and fifty is not able to read and write and here we have at least sixty in the hundred who cannot. Now, if the general theory be true, and all history proves that it is, that only an educated people can preserve a free government, our prospects are not very bright, if we do not adopt the best and surest means of educating the masses as soon as possible. I mention these facts to show the paramount importance of doing nothing that will injure the cause of education. The future welfare of our State, and of our people, individually and collectively, depends upon our success in this cause I do most sincerely trust and entreat that this all-important question may receive the calm and careful consideration it merits; and that we will not adopt a section so sure to injure the cause of education in our State, as this most certainly would.

Mr. J. J. WRIGHT. I did not suppose that this section would elicit any discussion whatever. The gentleman who last resumed his seat has referred to the impropriety of allowing the children of the two races to attend school together. If I read the section aright, it contemplates no such thing. It simply says, "all schools, colleges, etc., supported by public funds, shall be open to all classes, without regard to race, color or previous condition." The gentleman said such a state of things would not be allowed even in Massachusetts. I must say I have read the laws of that State, and know of no such provision. The school law of Massachusetts is that all persons, without discrimination, are allowed to attend all schools, colleges or public institutions, supported by public funds. I have had the pleasure of visiting the schools in Massachusetts, New York, New Hampshire, and a large number of States, and all children can attend school in these States without regard to color. If they do not want to go, they can remain at home. I know, however, there are but few schools where white and colored children mingle together, and the same arrangements could be carried out in South Carolina. This provision leaves it so that white and colored children can attend school together, if they desire to do so; but I do not believe the colored children will want to go to the white schools, or *vice versa*. I think there will be separate schools established, and there is no clause in our Constitution that prevents it; therefore I hope this clause will be adopted exactly as it is. One thing I would have understood, the colored people do not want to force what is called social equality; that is a matter which will regulate itself. No law we can pass can compel associations that are distateful to anybody. It is useless to attempt it, and when the idea is held up before you, it is only a bugbear, with which some persons would frighten you from the performance of your duty. All you have to do is to stand up, face the music for a while, and I tell you that every man, white and black, in South Carolina will come to time. This prejudice will be broken down. We are not framing a Constitution for to-day, but for years, and we should be careful how we execute that task. Let us so enact laws that all children will have the benefit of all schools for which the public pay. We cannot leave this matter wholly to the General Assembly. We must not falter or shrink one inch, or pause in the work of doing all classes justice. Time will prove our work.

Mr. R. C. DeLARGE. I wish to know if the gentleman is in favor of compelling the children of the two races to go to school together?

Mr. J. J. WRIGHT. I am not. The gentleman knows that no person in this Convention has raised his voice louder against the compulsory attence of children than I have done.

The hour of six having arrived, the Convention adjourned.

FIFTY-SECOND DAY.

Monday, March 16, 1868.

The Convention assembled at ten A. M., and was called to order by the President, Hon. A. G. MACKEY.

Prayer was offered by the Rev. D. HARRIS.

The roll was called, and a quorum answering to their names, the PRESIDENT announced the Convention ready to proceed to business.

The journal of Saturday was read and approved.

Mr. B. F. WHITTEMORE rose to a question of privilege, and offered the following resolution. which was agreed to:

Resolved, That for the remainder of the session, the rule requiring that Ordinances and sections of the Constitution shall not receive three readings on the same day, be suspended.

The Convention resumed the consideration of Article XI, Charitable and Penal Institutions of the Constitution, which came up in regular order as the unfinished business from Saturday.

The following sections were read a third time and passed:

ARTICLE XI.

CHARITABLE AND PENAL INSTITUTIONS.

SECTION 1. Institutions for the benefit of the insane, blind, deaf and dumb, and the poor, shall always be fostered and supported by this State, and shall be subject to such regulations as the General Assembly may enact.

SEC. 2. The Directors of the Penitentiary shall be elected or appointed, as the General Assembly may direct.

SEC. 3. The Directors of the benevolent and other State institutions, such as may be hereafter created, shall be appointed by the Governor, by and with the consent of the Senate; and upon all nominations made by the Governor, the question shall be taken by yeas and nays, and entered upon the journals.

SEC 4. The Governor shall have power to fill all vacancies that may occur in the offices aforesaid, until the next session of the General Assembly, and until a successor or successors shall be appointed and confirmed.

SEC. 5. The respective Counties of this State shall make such provision, as may be determined by law, for all those inhabitants who, by reason of age, and infirmities or misfortunes, may have a claim upon the sympathy and aid of society.

Mr. J. L. NEAGLE presented the following additional section to Article XI, which was read three times and passed :

Sec. 6. The Physician of the Lunatic Asylum, who shall be Su perintendent of the same, shall be appointed by the Governor, with the advice and consent of the Senate All other necessary officers and employees shall be appointed by the Governor.

Mr. R. G. HOLMES introduced the following additional section to Article XI, which, on motion of Mr B. F. WHITTEMORE, was referred to the Judiciary Committee with instructions to report during the afternoon session, which was adopted :

Sec. 7. All records of Deeds, Wills, and other instruments made within this State, since October 1st, 1-63, under or in conformity with Military Orders of the United States, are hereby declared to be valid, and shall have the same effect as if duly registered in conformity with the laws of this State, by the officers authorized to register such instruments. The General Assembly shall provide by law for the proper authentication and safe keeping of all such records.

Article XII. of the Constitution received its third reading and finally passed for ratification, as follows :

ARTICLE XII.

CORPORATIONS.

Section 1. Corporations may be formed under general laws ; but all such laws may, from time to time, be altered or repealed.

Sec. 2. The property of corporations now existing or hereafter created, shall be subject to taxation, except in cases otherwise provided for in this Constitution.

Sec. 3. No right of way shall be appropriated to the use of any corporation until full compen-sation therefor shall be first made, or secured by a deposit of money to the owner, irrespective of any benefit from any improvement proposed by such corporation, which compensation shall be ascertained by a jury of twelve men, in a Court of Record, as shall be prescribed by law.

Sec. 4. Dues from corporations shall be secured by such individual liability of the stockholders and other means, as may be prescribed by law.

Sec. 5. All general laws and special acts passed pursuant to this section, shall make provision therein for fixing the personal liability of stockholders under proper limitations ; and shall prevent and punish fraudulent misrepresentations as to the capital, property and resources of such corporations ; and shall also regulate the public use of all franchises which have heretofore been, or hereafter may be created or granted, by or under the authority of this State, and shall limit all tolls, imports and other charges and demands under such laws.

Sec. 6. The General Assembly shall grant no charter for banking purposes, nor renew any banking corporations now in existence, except upon the condition that the stockholders shall be liable to the amount of their respective share or shares of stock in such banking institution; for all its debts and liabilities upon note, bill, or otherwise; and upon the further condition that no director or other officer of said corporation shall borrow any money from said corporation; and if any director or other officer shall be convicted upon indictment of directly or indirectly violating this section, he shall be punished by fine or imprisonment, at the discretion of the Court. The books, papers, and accounts of all banks shall be open to inspection, under such regulations as may be prescribed by law.

Article XIII—Militia—Section one was read, and Mr. C. M. OLSEN moved to recommit to the committee, with instructions to strike out the word "residents," and insert the word "citizen," and report during the morning session, which was adopted.

Sections two and three were passed.

The Committee on the Miscellaneous Provisions of the Constitution reported, in accordance with the above, and Section one, as amended, was passed.

The Article as passed is as follows:

ARTICLE XIII.

MILITIA.

SECTION 1. The militia of this State shall consist of all able-bodied male citizens of the State, between the ages of eighteen and forty-five years, except such persons as are now, or may hereafter be exempted by the laws of the United States, or who may be adverse to bearing arms, as provided for in this Constitution; and shall be organized, armed, equipped and disciplined as the General Assembly may by law provide.

Sec. 2. The Governor shall have power to call out the militia to execute the laws, repel invasion, repress insurrection and preserve the public peace.

Sec. 3. There shall be an Adjutant and Inspector General elected by the qualified electors of the State, at the same time and in the same manner as other State officers, who shall rank as a Brigadier-General, and whose duties and compensation shall be prescribed by law. The Governor shall appoint, by and with the advice and consent of the Senate, such other staff officers as the General Assembly may direct.

Article XIV., of the Constitution received its third reading and finally passed as follows:

ARTICLE XIV.

SECTION 1. No person shall be elected or appointed to any office in this State, unless he possess the qualifications of an elector.

SEC. 2. Lotteries, and the sale of lottery tickets, for any purpose whatever, are prohibited, and the General Assembly shall prevent the same by penal laws.

SEC. 3 The State Library shall be subject to such regulations as the General Assembly may prescribe.

SEC. 4. The General Assembly may direct, by law, in what manner claims against the State may be established and adjusted.

SEC. 5. Divorces from the bonds of matrimony shall not be allowed but by the judgment of a court, as shall be prescribed by law.

SEC. 6. No person who denies the existence of the Supreme Being shall hold any office under this Constitution.

SEC. 7. The printing of the laws, journals, bills, legislative documents and papers for each branch of the General Assembly, with the printing required for the Executive and other departments of State, shall be let on contract, in such manner as shall be prescribed by law.

SEC. 8. The real and personal property of a woman, held at the time of her marriage, or that which she may thereafter acquire, either by gift, grant, inheritance, devise or otherwise, shall not be subject to levy and sale for her husband's debts; but shall be held as her separate property and may be bequeathed, devised, or alienated by her the same as if she were unmarried; *Provided*, That no gift or grant from the husband to the wife shall be detrimental to the just claims of his creditors.

SEC. 9. The General Assembly shall provide for the removal of all causes which may be pending when this Constitution goes into effect to courts created by the same.

Mr. E. W M. MACKEY asked and obtained leave to introduce the following additional section to Article XIV, which was read and passed :

SECTION 10. The election for all State officers shall take place at the same time as is provided for that of members of the General Assembly, and the election for those officers whose terms of service are for four years, shall be held at the time of each alternate general election.

Mr. E. W. M. MACKEY also obtained leave to introduce the following additional section to Article XIV :

SECTION 11. All contracts, whether under seal or not, the considerations of which were the purchase of slaves, are hereby declared null, void, and of no effect, and no suit, either at law or in equity, shall be commenced or prosecuted for the enforcement of such contracts ; and all proceedings to enforce satisfaction or payment of judgments or decrees rendered, recorded, enrolled or entered upon such contracts in any Court of this State, are hereby prohibited. All orders heretofore made in any Court in this State in relation to such contracts whereby property is held subject to decision, as to the validity of such contracts, are also hereby declared null, void, and of no effect.

Mr. J. S. CRAIG presented the following as a substitute for the foregoing :

All suits or actions to recover debts or demands, the consideration of which were slaves, shall be heard, tried, and determined by the Court sitting in equity, and shall be decided according to equity on a full consideration of all the facts affected by emancipation.

Mr, R. C. DeLARGE. I move the indefinite postponement of the substitute.

Mr. J. S. CRAIG. I desire to say that I consulted the Solicitor relative to that substitute. That article was prepared by Major Corbin devoid of the objectionable features of the original proposition.

Mr. D. H. CHAMBERLAIN. In order that the Convention may understand how to act, I would say this matter was referred to the committee on the Judiciary, with instructions to report a section covering that Ordinance. The committee have had the subject under consideration, and the report is in the hands of the Chairman. I move that the consideration of the section offered and the substitute be postponed until the Committee on the Judiciary make their report.

The motion was agreed to.

The unfinished business was called up, being the consideration of section ten of the educational report which had been recommitted to the committee.

Mr. R. C. DeLARGE. I do not desire to detain the Convention ; I have not the least doubt but that the section reported by the committee will be adopted. The principle enunciated in that report I heartily endorse. I was surprised, however, to hear such an elaborate argument in opposition to the section by my friend from Newberry (Mr. DUNCAN). Perhaps, I can undertake to reply to that argument with better grace than almost any other member of the Convention. I believe it will be admitted, that as far as liberality towards those who were plunged into the late rebellion is concerned, no member has shown more leniency and charity to those people than myself. I believe we should treat them as a magnanimous, christian people would treat their former enemies. But when I find a delegate declaring that the principles for which we contend are erroneous, I feel compelled to raise my voice

114

against it. While I desire to treat that class of people with all leniency and generosity compatible with our safety, I am not desirous of sacrificing a principle to gratify them or anybody else. If there is a place in the State where no distinction should be made, or in this country, it should be in the school house, or in the church. I most heartily desire to see this section of the educational report adopted.

While I admit that people have their prejudices, I feel confident that my friend from Newberry has greatly exaggerated what he thinks will be the effect of those prejudices. I am sure the class of men nurtured and cared for together, who have been suckled at the same breast, and worshipped in the same Sunday School, will be ready to endorse the measure. I see no attempt to force them into the schools together. I opposed the word "compulsory" in the fourth section, because it sounded harsh. I feel confident that if our ticket is successful and our Superintendent of Education is elected, his administration will be of such a character that no one will have a right to complain, or have reason to regret it. I know it has been said by some gentleman on the floor that the disposition manifested by my colleague and others, was to go horse, foot and dragoons over to the opposition. Upon points of generosity, where we can afford to be magnanimous and treat our opponents in a christian spirit, both my colleagues and myself will support any measure ; but wherever a principle is at stake, I shall always be found battling earnestly in its defence, as I do now. While we intend to be liberal, we must be true to ourselves and our constituents.

Mr. H. E. HAYNE called for the previous question and it was sustained.

Mr. F. L. CARDOZO. I think the opinion of the members is so fully established on this subject, that elaborate argument is unnecessary. I shall briefly notice some of the points made by the gentleman from Newberry, (Mr. B. O. DUNCAN.)

His first point is, that this provision runs counter to the prejudices of the people. To my mind, it is inconsistent that such an argument should come from a member of the Convention, or from one who favored the reconstruction scheme of Congress. The whole measure of reconstruction is antagonistic to the wishes of the people of the State, and this section is a legitimate portion of that scheme. It secures to every man in this State full political and civil equality, and I hope members will not commit so suicidal an act as to oppose the adoption of this section.

The gentleman from Newberry said he was afraid we were taking a wrong course to remove these prejudices. The most natural method to effect this object would be to allow children ; when five or six years of age, to mingle in schools together, and associate generally. Under such training, prejudice must eventually die out ; but if we postpone it until they become men and women, prejudice will be so established that no mortal can obliterate it. This, I think, is a sufficient reply to the argument of the gentleman under this head.

We have carefully provided in our report that every one shall be allowed to attend a free school. We have not said there shall be no separate schools. On the contrary, there may be separate schools, and I have no doubt there will be such in most of the districts. In Charleston, I am sure such will be the case. The colored pupils in my school would not like to go to a white school. Without flattery, I think I may say I have not seen as good a public school in Charleston as my own. We have as able a corps of teachers as any in the country. They have come from the North, adopted teaching as their profession, and they will not, in point of efficiency, yield to any teachers in the State.

In sparsely settled country districts, where perhaps there are not more than twenty-five or thirty children, separate schools may be established ; but for ten or fifteen white children to demand such a separation, would be absurd ; and I hope the Convention will give its assent to no such proposition.

Mr. J. M. RUNION. I ask leave to explain my vote. I have always acted conscientiously, and am just as true a Republican as any other member of the Convention. I am in favor of a general system of free schools, and that these schools shall be open to all classes ; but I do not think it best to the interests of the Republican party to so arrange or construct this Constitution as to force a consolidation of the schools. Inasmuch as the Article on education contains a clause compelling children to attend schools, I am compelled to vote against the section. I shall, therefore, vote no.

Mr. W. H. W. GRAY called for the ayes and nays, and they were ordered, resulting as follows :

Ayes—The President, Messrs. Alexander, Arnim, Becker, Bell, Bowen, Bonum, Burton, Brockenton, Cain, Cardozo, Coghlan, Chamberlain, Chestnut, Clinton, Cook, Collins, Corley, Craig, Crews, Darrington, Davis, DeLarge, Dickson, Dill, Dogan, Driffle, Elliott, Foster, Goss, Gray, Harris, J. N. Hayne, C. D. Hayne, H. E. Hayne, Henderson, Holmes, Humbird, Hurley, Jacobs, Jenks, Jervey, Jillson, S. Johnson, W. B. Johnson, J. W. Johnson, W. E. Johnston, Joiner, Jones, Lang, Langley, G. Lee, S. Lee, Lomax, Mackey, Mayer, W. J. McKinlay, W. McKinlay, McDaniels, Middleton, Mead, Milford, Nance, Nash, Nelson, Neagle, Newell, Nuckels, Owens, Parker, Pillsbury, Rainey, Ransier, Rivers, Robertson, Rose, Rutland, Sanders, Sasportas, Shrewsbury, Smalls, Stubbs, Swails, Thomas, A. Thompson, B. A. Thompson,

S. B. Thompson, Viney, Webb, Whittemore, Whipper, White, Williams, F. E. Wilder, C. M. Wilder, Wingo, Wooley, Wright—98.

NAYS—Messrs. Bryce, Duncan, L. B. Johnson, Runion—4.

ABSENT — Messrs. Allen, Boozer, Byas, Cain, Camp, Donaldson, Edwards, Gentry, Hunter, Jackson, Jones, Leslie, Mauldin, Miller, Moses, Olsen, Perry, Randolph, Richmond—19.

And section ten of the educational reports was passed.

Mr. J. M. RUNION asked and obtained leave to explain his vote; not believing in the consolidation of the schools, he voted nay.

Mr. W. E. ROSE, from the Committee on petitions, presented the following report, which was adopted.

The Committee on Petitions, to whom was referred the Petitions of various persons, praying that this Convention recommend to Congress that their political disabilities be removed, and they be restored to the elective franchise, have considered the same, and respectfully report that your committee are satisfied of the loyalty of the petitioners, and recommend that the prayer of their petitions be granted, viz :

Jacob Kibler, Newberry County; R. M. Wallace, Richland County; Henry Summer, Newberry County; John P. Kinard, Newberry County; E. P. Lake, Newberry County; John W. Twitty, Lancaster County; Mathew McDonald, Abbeville County; A. G. Baskin, Richland County; W. W. Houseal, Newberry County; D. B. Miller, Richland County; H. P. Hammet, Greenville County; Calvin S. Rutland, York County; J. Bolton Smith, York County; Daniel A. Burton, York County; Elihu Moore, Lancaster County; Samuel B. Clowney, Fairfield County; Lewis Dial, Laurens; Walter W. Herbert, Fairfield; Thos. Jordan, Fairfield County; H. H. Kinard, Newberry; J. C. Miller, Charleston; A. P. Kinard, Newberry; Thomas E. Dudley, Bennettsville; Alex. McBeel Greenville; H. Beatie, Greenville; J. B. Tollesoh, Spartanburg; Samuel W Mourice, Williamsburg County; B. F. Bates, Spartanburg; D. L. Thompson, Beaufort; Wm M. Thomas, Greenville; F. C. Gower, Greenville County; H. C. Markley, Greenville County; Thomas Cox, Greenville County; James A. Black, Abbeville; Willis Allen, Spartanburg, John D. Ashmore, Greenville; John S. Green, Sumter; Elijah W. Horne, Edgefield; William B. Johnson, Richland County.

Also the following, which was adopted :

The Committee on Petitions, to whom was referred the petition of the citizens of Beaufort County, praying that the Hall of Records be removed to this point, and that the courts in future should hold their sittings in this town, ask leave to report that they have duly considered the same, and are of opinion that the petition of the persons desiring the removal of said Court House should be granted; at the same time, your committee recommend that the expense of removing said Court House should be paid by the citizens of Beaufort, and not by the State of South Carolina.

Mr. R. C. DeLARGE moved a reconsideration of the resolution submitted by the Committee on Franchise and Elections, relating to petitioning Congress to remove all political disabilities from citizens of this State, which was adopted.

Mr. R. C. DeLARGE then moved to recommit the resolution to the committee with instructions to report at four P. M., which was agreed to.

On motion of Mr. C. P. LESLIE, the rules were suspended, and Mr. N. G. PARKER, submitted the following resolution, which was adopted :

Resolved, That the President of this Convention be instructed to request Brevet Major-General E. R. S. Canby, Commanding Second Military District, to draw from the State Treasury the sum of ($16,000) sixteen thousand dollars, to complete the payment of the expenses of the Convention.

Mr. J. L. NEAGLE presented the following resolution, which was adopted :

Resolved, That the President of this Convention is hereby authorized to have two copies of the Constitution engrossed, one of which he shall deposit in the office of Secretary of State of this Commonwealth, and the other he shall present to the President of the United States, in accordance with the Reconstruction Acts of Congress, and that for the payment of the expenses of engrossment, and the actual expenses of going to, remaining in, and returning from Washington, the sum of $500 is hereby appropriated, if so much be necessary.

Mr. B. F. WHITTEMORE submitted the following, which was adopted :

Whereas, the State of South Carolina is largely interested in the stock of the Greenville and Columbia Railroad ; and, whereas, a meeting of the Stockholders of said Road, for the election of President and Directors and other officers, will take place at Columbia about the first week in May, and before the General Assembly under this Constitution can convene ; and, whereas, it is essential that the State should be represented at the meeting to be held at Columbia ; therefore,

Resolved, That the President of this Convention request Brevet Major-General E. R. S. Canby, Commanding Second Military District, to appoint *two* persons to represent the State at the before mentioned meeting, in order that the interests of South Carolina may not suffer or be imperilled.

Mr. E. W. M. MACKEY, by leave, presented the following Ordinance :

AN ORDINANCE

To provide for the organization of the General Assembly at its first session, and for the inauguration of the Governor and Lieutenant-Governor.

We the people of South Carolina, in Convention met, do ordain :

1. That the members of the General Assembly elected under the provisions of the Constitution shall assemble in the Capitol at the city of Columbia, on Tuesday, the twelfth day of May, 1868, at twelve o'clock, M.

2. That each House shall be temporarily organized by the election of a presiding officer, to whom the oath of office shall be administered by the President of this Convention, and which presiding officer shall then administer the said oath to the other members.

3. That as soon as the House of Representatives is permanently organized by the election of a Speaker, and shall have appointed a day for that purpose, the Governor shall be installed into office in the presence of both Houses, and the oath of office shall be administered to him by the President of this Convention, who shall immediately thereafter administer the said oath to the Lieutenant-Governor in the Senate Chamber.

4. That for the purpose of administering these oaths of office, the President of this Convention shall be continued in the prerogatives of his office until that duty shall have been performed. And at all subsequent inaugurations of the Governor and Lieutenant-Governor, the oath of office shall be administered by the Chief Justice of the Supreme Court, or, in his absence, by one of the Associate Justices; and the General Assembly shall, at its first session, provide by law for its organization in future.

Mr. R. G. HOLMES submitted a substitute for Mr. E. W. M. MACKEY'S Ordinance, which, on motion of Mr. J. L. NEWEL, was indefinitely postponed.

The Ordinance then received three readings and was passed.

Mr. E. W. M. MACKEY submitted the following Ordinance, which was read three times and passed :

AN ORDINANCE

To provide for the Ratification of the Constitutional Amendment, and for the election of United States Senators.

We, the People of South Carolina in Convention met, do ordain :

1. That the General Assembly shall, within five days after its permanent organization, proceed to ratify the Constitutional Amendment, known as the 14th Article.

2. That the General Assembly shall also, within the same period, proceed to the election of two United States Senators.

Mr. C C. BOWEN presented the following, as an additional section to Article XIV.

SECTION 11. The first General Assembly convened under this Constitution shall, immediately after its permanent organization, ratify the amendment to the Constitution of the United States, known as the 14th Article, proposed by the 39th Congress.

Mr. W. J. WHIPPER. I do not think the General Assembly should be trammelled by any article. All we have to do is to provide for the convening of that body, and it is their duty to do what they deem best for the interests of the people. For us to tie the hands of that body is to destroy its validity.

Mr. R. G. HOLMES. That 14th Article must necessarily be passed before anything else can be done by the Legislature.

Mr. C C. BOWEN. I see the necessity for the adoption of this Article by this Convention. It is essential to the welfare of the people, and the future condition of the State. Our opponents have already made their calculation to defeat this measure. In other words, they expect to get men enough into the Legislature to vote it down. It has been said, we cannot do a single thing until it has been adopted ; and it is, therefore, prudent on our part to enforce early action upon the subject by the Legislature. Until that amendment has become a portion of the supreme law of the land. we cannot get back into the Union. Let us then make it a part of the Constitution of the State, so that each man, when he comes up to swear to support the Constitution of South Carolina, will have to support that, however much he may desire to oppose the Constitutional Amendment. He will have to face the music, or stay out. The final success of all the work done here depends on the adoption of that section.

Mr. J. J. WRIGHT. I trust every gentleman on the floor will vote for the passage of this Ordinance ; first, because the Convention is the only law-making power in the State of South Carolina. When we get to work for the purpose of framing an Ordinance, we become a legislative body, and when we pass an Ordinance, it is a law of the State, until repealed. Hence, if we adopt an Ordinance, that, within five days after assembling, the Legislature shall ratify this amendment to the United States Constitution, that body will be bound to obey our law. It is the very first act they are to perform, even before they effect a permanent organization. Our enemies are at work. The voters against us are already being rallied, and we should adopt all proper means to ensure our own success and the return of this State to the Union. I hope, therefore, we shall pass this Article.

Mr. J. S. CRAIG. In order to set myself right, I desire to say I do not consider that we have a right to bind the Legislature in this respect. Every member of that body has a right to vote for or against that amendment as he chooses.

The previous question being called was sustained, and the main question being put, the section was read three times and passed.

Mr. R. C. DeLARGE asked and obtained leave to introduce an Ordinance relating to the financial condition of the State.

Mr. F. J. MOSES, Jr., moved that it be printed and made the special order for to-morrow eleven o'clock.

Mr. S. A. SWAILS moved to indefinitely postpone.

Mr. H. E. HAYNE moved to postpone until the 4th day of July, 1890.

Pending which, the hour of adjournment arrived, and the Convention adjourned to three o'clock, P. M.

———

AFTERNOON SESSION.

The Convention re-assembled at three o'clock, P. M.

The consideration of the Ordinance relating to the financial condition of the State was resumed.

The several motions to postpone were withdrawn.

Mr. R. C DeLARGE. I hope this Ordinance will pass. I have seen a petition asking for an appropriation of money for the Blue Ridge Railroad, and believing its completion is essential to the material prosperity of the State, I desire to assist every public enterprise that is likely to accomplish this purpose. It will, probably, be alleged that this commission will be an unnecessary expense to the State. I do not believe it; but if so, it is important to our interests, and I do not see how a sane man can doubt it.

Mr. T. J. ROBERTSON. I feel sure if the delegates understood this matter there would not be a dissenting voice on the passage of this Ordinance. It provides for the appointment of five commissioners to enquire into the financial condition of the State. The object of the commission is to trace out the origin of the indebtedness of the State, and the manner in which the public funds have been disbursed. The Legislature, during the war, endorsed the bonds of various railroad companies in the State, taking as security a second mortgages which I can assert is worthless. Are we to pay that debt, made by a rebel Legislature during the war ? If so, it is unneccessary to pass this Ordnance. If we leave it to the next Legislature, they will be as much in the dark as we are This anticipates the meeting of that body, and when it assembles this commission will be prepared to report the result of its investigations. I insist that if we want to restore the faith and credit of South Carolina, it is necessary this examination into the condition of the State shall take place. The cost of these five commissioners will not equal the cost of the Legislature one day.

Mr. W. J WHIPPER. While I favor the Ordinance, it seems to me that the commission should be appointed by this Convention, with instructions to report to the coming General Assembly. I, therefore, move that the Ordinance be so amended.

Mr. J. L NEAGLE. I move to strike out "five" and insert "two."

Mr. J. J. WRIGHT. We should certainly consider this thing well before acting. If it is necessary to appoint any commissioners, we should appoint enough. We must remember that this is a large State, and many of these obligations are scattered over the State. They must all be investigated, and it will be a laborious task. It is, therefore, proper to appoint a sufficient member to do the work in a manner that shall meet the approbation of the people. There ought to be one commissioner for at least every Congressional District, of which there are four in the State. I am in favor of making it five, and hope the amendment of the gentleman from York will not prevail.

The question was taken on the several sections and the Ordinance finally passed as follows :

Whereas, the financial condition of the State renders it necessary that the General Assembly, at its first session, should adopt the measures requisite to apply its available resources to the discharge of its valid obligations ; and whereas, it is essential to that end that an investigation of the condition of the financial resources of the State should be made without delay, in order that the results thereof may be submitted to the General Assembly at such session,

We, the People of South Carolina, in Convention assembled, do ordain :

SECTION 1. That Five Commissioners be appointed, in the manner hereinafter provided, whose duty it shall be to investigate the financial

115

condition of the State, and the situation and value of all property, assets, securities, and other resources applicable to the discharge of its valid obligations, and to report thereon, with their recommendations, to the General Assembly, upon its being convened, or as soon thereafter as practicable.

SEC. 2. Such Commission shall have authority to inspect all public records, accounts and vouchers ; to call for reports under oath, in such form as they shall prescribe, from all public officers having knowledge of facts, or possession of matters pertinent to investigations ; to summon witnesses, to administer oaths, and to examine all persons who, in their judgment, may have knowledge of any such matters.

SEC. 3. It shall be the duty of any person or officer, under a penalty of $500, to be recovered in any Court of Record in the name of said Commissioners, upon notification or summons, to make such report, and to attend at any time and place at which he may be required to appear for such examination, and to produce any document or writing, the production of which shall be required by such notification or summons. Witnesses attending for such examination may be allowed the customary rates, to be paid as a part of the contingent expenses of the Commission. Any person guilty of knowingly and wilfully making any false statement under oath or affirmation in respect thereto, shall be guilty of wilful and corrupt perjury, and liable to the pains and penalties therefor, prescribed by law.

SEC. 4 Said Commissioners shall be elected by the delegates of this Convention by a plurality of votes, and shall receive the same per diem allowance as members of the General Assembly, and actual expenses incurred in traveling in the performance of said duties, and the Commissioners shall commence their work on or before the 20th March, 1868 ; *Provided*, That there shall be one from each Congressional District, and one from the State at large.

SEC. 5. The General Assembly shall make provision for the compensation and expenses of said Commissioners, and shall have authority to extend the powers of said Commission, or to modify the same, and when in their judgment the objects of this Ordinance are fully attained, to terminate said Commission.

On motion of Mr. E. W. M. MACKEY, the Convention proceeded to the election of five Commissioners, required by the above Ordinance.

Mr. T. J. ROBERTSON nominated for the State at large Mr. D. H. Chamberlain, who was elected by acclamation.

On motion of Mr. H. E. HAYNE, the Convention took a recess of ten minutes, to allow the delegates from each Congressional District to nominate their respective candidates.

On being called to order, Mr. F. J. Moses, Jr., was nominated as a candidate from the First District ; R. C. DeLarge, Second District ; Colonel T. J. Robertson, Third District, and J. M. Allen, Fourth District—all of whom were elected by acclamation.

Mr. R. C. DeLARGE. I move that, when this Convention adjourns, it adjourn to meet this evening at eight o'clock, and continue in session until ten o'clock.

Mr. L. S. LANGLEY. If I could see any utility in that motion, I should certainly favor it. I do not think it necessary. Whenever the Convention has finished its work, it is simply necessary for the Committee on Review and Consolidation to present their work for the adoption of it by this Convention. If we vote to have an evening session, from seven to ten, what have we to do? After we have done all that remains for us to do, the Committee can present their report, we can adopt it, and adjourn.

The PRESIDENT. It seems proper for the Chair to state what actually remains to be done. The Chair does not know of any important business, except to receive the report of the Committee on the Judiciary, which, it is presumed will be made in a few minutes. The resolution proposed by the gentlemen from Anderson (Mr. NEWELL), which was made the special order for eleven o'clock to-day, has been staved off by other proceedings. In relation to the report of the Committee on Consolidation and Review, it seems to me that that work has been already done by the Convention. It was understood that the duty of that committee would be to take up all parts of the Constitution after it was adopted by the Convention, and see that everything had its place in the proper article. But the Convention itself has from time to time, in its own wisdom, so transposed from one article to another, that upon a careful examination of the whole, every section has been found to be in its proper place. The Chairman of the Committee on Review and Consolidation is not here. I have read every article prepared, and really do not see a single section that could be taken out of its present place without changing the symmetry of the Constitution. It seems to me that the Constitution, so far, is as perfect as it is possible to make it.

Mr. F. J. MOSES, Jr. I really hope this attempt to hasten the adjournment of the Convention will not be continued. I see no reason for it—not the slightest. I have no idea we will be able to adjourn so soon. There are several things which require our attention yet. The Committee on Review and Consolidation are to submit their report. At the same time, the members should all sign the Constitution after it has been engrossed. I really cannot see any good to be done by sitting it out here to-night. I hope the Convention will take time to finish up the work in a proper manner.

The PRESIDENT. The Chair would simply state that, in consequence of the day of adjournment having been fixed, the Chairman of the Committee on Finance and the Sergeant at-Arms, have arranged all the books and accounts up to twelve o'clock M to-morrow.

Mr. J. L. NEAGLE. If the Convention is so disposed, and will remain in session, they can finish their business. There is but one section to be acted upon.

Mr. L. S. LANGLEY. I hope the motion to convene at eight o'clock this evening will not prevail. The members of this Convention have sat here for three hours this morning and three this afternoon, and I scarcely think they desire to sit three more hours this evening. I want to get through our work. I want to see it well done. We have been here sixty days, and we can certainly spend two days longer in order to complete our work.

The question being taken on the motion that when the Convention adjourn, it adjourn to meet at eight o'clock this evening, and continue in session until ten, it was decided in the negative.

Mr. D. H. CHAMBERLAIN. I rise to make a personal remark. I was nominated by my friend from Richland, (Mr. T. J. ROBERTSON,) in view of my official relations as Chairman of the Commission. I have thought over the matter and have concluded that it is not at all important that the Attorney-General should be associated with the Commission. On personal grounds, I hope the Convention will allow me to decline, and I nominate for the position Mr R. H. CAIN.

Mr. B. BYAS. I move that the resignation of the gentleman from Berkeley be accepted, and the gentleman from Charleston elected.

Mr. J. M. ALLEN nominated Mr J. CREWS, delegate from Laurens.

Mr. B. BYAS. I second that nomination.

Mr. F. J. MOSES, Jr. I hope the Convention will not allow the gentleman from Berkeley (Mr. CHAMBERLAIN,) to resign, or allow him to nominate a successor. I object to his resignation being accepted. He is a gentleman who would be in the right place at the head of that Commission, and I think it is his duty to serve whenever or wherever we desire his services. I hope the Convention will refuse to allow him to resign.

Mr. B. BYAS. I hope the resignation of the gentleman from Berkeley will not be received. No gentleman on the floor is more competent to the task.

Mr. T. J. ROBERTSON. I had the honor to propose the name of the gentleman from Berkeley, as Chairman of that Commission. I did it for this reason : grave questions will come up before the Legislature, on which it will be necessary to obtain the opinion of the Attorney-General. Unless he is a member of that Commission, he will be in ignorance of the condition of matters upon which he will be asked to give an opinion. This Commission will take testimony, obtain all the facts in relation to the most important subjects bearing upon the interests of the State.

The question was taken, "Shall the resignation be accepted?" and decided in the negative.

Mr. C. C BOWEN, Chairman of the Committee on the Judiciary, to whom was referred a resolution concerning *cest qui trusts*, reported that they had the same under consideration, and are of opinion that this Convention ought not to exercise any jurisdiction over the subject matter, and that it should be left entirely to the courts for adjudication. They, therefore, recommend that its further consideration by the Convention be indefinitely postponed. The report was adopted.

Mr. C. C. BOWEN, of the same Committie, to whom was referred an Ordinance in regard to debts contracted where the consideration was the purchase of slaves, reported that they had consolidated the Ordinances heretofore passed, and recommended the adoption of the following:

"That all contracts, whether under seal or not, the consideration of which were for the purchase of slaves, are hereby declared null and void and of no effect; and no suit, either at law or equity, shall be commenced or prosecuted for the enforcement of such contracts, and all proceedings to enforce satisfaction or payment on judgments or decrees, rendered, recorded, enrolled or entered up on such contracts in any court of this State, are hereby prohibited, and all orders heretofore made in this State, in relation to such contracts, whereby property is held subject to the decision, as to the validity of such contracts, are also hereby declared null and void and of no effect.

The Committee report this as the thirty-fourth section of Article IV. of the Constitution. The report was adopted.

Mr. W. J. WHIPPER. I move that the report be rejected.

The motion to reject was not agreel to.

Mr. W. J. WHIPPER. Though I was one who voted for the passage of the Ordinance, rendering invalid all debts contracted for the purchase of slaves, I am not ready to have that section incorporated into the Constitution as the organic law of the State. I was as zealous to pass that Ordinance, abolishing contracts for slave debts, and on that Ordinance I am ready to meet any claims of that character that may arise. The very attempt to incorporate such a clause into the Constitution, is an admission of itself that the Ordinance was worth nothing. I am surprised at the Committee on the Judiciary, who have reported it here to-day. I am opposed to burdening the Constitution with Ordinances of this kind. We have an Ordinance which renders all such contracts worthless. Why insert it into the Constitution, when it can work nothing but detriment to that instrument? I cannot conceive what could have been the idea of the mover of that section, or the gentleman who made the motion to incorporate it, save that it was to array against the Constitution, those conscientiously opposed to the repudiation of slave debts. It can do no possible good. If the action of this Convention is worth anything at all, by the Ordinance already passed every slave debt was wiped out, and I, for one, am willing to meet even our genial constitutional lawyer, (Mr. RUTLAND,) before the Courts on that question. I would not ask the intervention of a constitution at all in the matter. I would like to be informed what we are to accomplish by this step; what is to be gained by incorporating into the Constitution what we have already established by an Ordinance of the Convention? We must necessarily array against us members of our own body, whose loyalty is unquestionable, but who conscientiously oppose this measure on its passage. I fail to see any good end to be accomplished by incorporating into the Constitution that which looks to a defeat. It is suicidal. I sincerely hope the Convention will not take special pains to go into further legislation for the protection of the men and women who went into this business; who took the desperate chances involved in it; who had years of experience with perfect liberty either to engage in it or let it alone. I hope we will not go into any further legislation to protect those classes. We ignored the claims of other women and children whose trustees or guardians invested in this business, to their everlasting ruin. I certainly hope that section will never become a portion of the Constitution. It should be remembered that there is a large class of citizens outside of this body who conscientiously believe these debts should be paid. There are large numbers who zealously support the Constitution we have framed so far, but who cannot do it with that article attached. I hope, therefore, as there is no necessity for it, we will not burden our Constitution with a clause that may, in a manner, have a tendency to defeat it. I hope the section will be voted down.

Mr. J. J. WRIGHT. I am glad to say that I can concur with my colleague in this matter. In relation to this matter of guardian and and wards, I was and am in favor of leaving that to be decided by the courts of the State. These matters can be decided in the equity courts. The Ordinance passed by the Convention in relation to slave debts, it will be remembered, had no stronger advocate than myself. That Ordinance has been passed by the supreme power of South Carolina, and has become law. It is a law of South Carolina until repealed by the courts of the State. As a law of the land, I am willing to go into court and meet any question that may arise under it. If there are any who do not regard it as law, all we have to do is, when a case is made in court to meet it. The Judge cannot but instruct the jury that this is the law of the State, and the jury must decide accordingly.

Mr. F J MOSES, Jr. Were you not in favor of the Ordinance?

Mr. J. WRIGHT. I was.

Mr. F. J. MOSES, Jr. Were you not in favor of the passage of the Ordinance, on the ground that there could be no property in man?

Mr. J. J. WRIGHT. I was.

Mr, F. J. MOSES, Jr. Is it not your opinion that any future Legislature can repeal an Ordinance passed by this Convention?

Mr. J. J. WRIGHT. It is.

Mr. F. J. MOSES, Jr. Suppose, in the course of a few years, the Democratic party should gain the ascendancy in the Legislature, are you willing this Ordinance should be repealed by them?

Mr. J. J. WRIGHT. Any act of any Legislature may be repealed by its successor. Any Ordinance passed here, can be repealed by the Legislative Assembly of the State. But the point I desire to bring to the attention of the Convention is this : After we have passed this Ordinance and it has become a law, is it requisite or necessary to again take it up and incorporate it into our Constitution? It will be a question to be decided by the Supreme Court of this State, and by the Supreme Court of the United States, whether or not the Constitution we are framing is in accordance with the Constitution of the United States. We should, therefore, be careful, and endeavor to frame the Constitution of the State, so that none of its provisions may at all conflict with the Constitution of the United States. If I was required to give an opinion as to whether that Ordinance was contrary to the Constitution of the United States, I would be compelled to say that I did believe it to be contrary to that Constitution. But I was willing to pass this Ordinance and let it be a law of the State. In going before the courts with such cases, we could plead no consideration in contracts for slaves, and the burden of proof would then be upon the other party. If they can show, beyond all doubt, that there was a consideration received, then their case is good, but I feel sure that it will be utterly impossible for any party to show there was any consideration in the contract. But they are contracts, whether there is or whether there is not a consideration, and we should not adopt any clause in our Constitution impairing the obligation of contracts. If we look back to the Constitution of the United States we will find that all the debts contracted prior to the formation of the Govern-.

ment of the United States were made valid and binding upon the United States and the several States. Now, we desire that all debts where there was any legitimate consideration shall remain, but we do not desire to impair the obligation of any contract. We should leave this matter, then, as we have already acted upon it, and let it go before the courts. But I do not desire it should be made a part of the Constitution of the State.

Mr. R. C. DeLARGE. The speech of my eminent friend from Beaufort who has just taken his seat reminds me of the story told us the other day by our friend from Sumter (Mr. MOSES.) He told a story of a man passing along the road meeting with a little boy sitting on the roadside by a large load of hay that had upset from the wagon. The boy was crying bitterly. The good Samaritan went to him and said: "My little fellow, what are you crying so hard for. It's no use for you to cry. I will assist you to load the hay again." "Oh, Sir," said the boy, "it is not so much the upsetting of the load, but daddy is under the hay." Now, when I see a gentleman, who was one of the strongest advocates of a certain measure, rising here and exhibiting such an extraordinary speedy change of opinion in such a matter, it strikes me that "daddy is under the load of hay."

I supported the Ordinance abolishing debts where the consideration was the purchase of slaves. I did it because I believed such debts were not valid. I believed no man had a right to own his fellow. I believed that property in man was not and could never be recognised by christendom, and I believed in that law which says, where there is no consideration, there is no debt. If it was right, therefore, to pass an Ordinance to that effect, it is right to place it in the Constitution. I am not responsible for the loss of those who committed the grave error and mistake of trading in that which was no property. I am not willing to sacrifice a great principle. I am not willing to admit that either myself or my fellow being ever was property. I am not willing to admit it, and when men who are identified with the race to which I belong, who have felt the heel of oppression, rise, and by their voice or action, acknowledge that they or their fellow-men were property, it stings me to the heart. They should blush to acknowledge it. I consider the vote by which this Ordinance was passed one of the most glorious acts of the Convention. Now, let that principle become a feature of the Constitution The masses, I feel confident, can be relied upon with that section in the Constitution. The Ordinance, it will be remembered, passed by a vote of yeas 104, nays 8, and I believe this section to-day will pass by the same vote. Let us place it beyond the reach of all succeeding Legislatures.

We know the uncertainty which attends the success of political parties. I desire to see this class of debts placed beyond the hope of resurrection. Let us, by our votes, deny that any human being was ever a chattel or a slave. They tell you it is in conflict with the Constitution of the United States. That assertion is not worth the time taken to make it. We all know the Constitution of the States must be subordinate to the Constitution of the United States, and if it conflicts with that instrument then the United States Courts can take the matter in hand, But we will record our votes in behalf of freedom, liberty and justice.

Mr. A. J. RANSIER. As one who supported and advocated this measure when introduced in the Convention, I desire to appeal to the members to place this question beyond any hope of repeal. I advocated and supported the measure not from any motives of policy, but because I believed that any contract, the consideration of which was based upon the property in man, was of itself invalid. I shall, therefore, cheerfully give my vote to make this section an integral portion of our State Constitution. Some of the legal members of the Convention argue that the Ordinance is of itself sufficient; that it has already all the force of law, and that, therefore, it is unnecessary to incorporate it into the Constitution. But there are those who do question the power of this Convention to legislate. Let us take the benefit of the doubt, and place the law where it cannot be misconstrued, and beyond the possibility of defeat. Do this, and we emphatically deny that there ever was or could be property in man. I believe this endorsement will rather tend to increase than diminish the vote in favor of the ratification of our Constitution. I hope the report of the committee will prevail, and that this measure will become a part of the Constitution of the State of South Carolina.

Mr. F. J. MOSES, Jr. I desire to move a reconsideration of the vote, whereby the Convention agreed to adjourn at twelve M. to-morrow. I am in favor of adjourning as soon as we can get through, but do not believe it to be possible in the time fixed.

Mr. J. M. RUTLAND. I hope no such motion will be made. I believe we can complete our work.

Mr. D. H. CHAMBERLAIN. If I had opposed the Ordinance which this Convention has passed, invalidating all existing claims for slaves, I should expect to find myself opposed to the introduction of that principle and that rule into the Constitution. But I confess I am surprised to find gentlemen on this floor who, by vote or speech, were in favor of the passage of that Ordnance, to-day unwilling that it should go into the organic law of the State. I was in favor of invalidating such contracts,

116

and of forbidding any person or any court prosecuting such claims. I was an earnest advocate of that Ordinance; and it is because that I was an honest, earnest advocate of the measure that I am equally honest and earnest to see it put into the Constitution of the State. If worth anything, let us put it, as far as lies in our power, beyond the reach of our enemies. There is great doubt among lawyers and some gentlemen of the Convention whether we have the right to pass any Ordinance beyond providing for the payment of our expenses and for the election by the people for the ratification or the rejection of our Constitution. There is great doubt, then, as to whether that Ordinance secures the great object we have at heart. There could be no stronger reason for incorporating it into the Constitution of the State.

The Convention agreed upon the measure by an overwhelming majority, that we have a right, either by the Constitution or by Ordinance, to annul all contracts where the consideration was for the purchase of slaves. If it was good to pass that Ordinance, then it is better to-day to pass this section of the Constitution. Gentlemen have argued that this would cause many to vote against the Constitution. There are many provisions in that Constitution to which I have been conscientiously opposed, but I do not, on account of my objections, oppose, in the slightest, the ratification of that instrument. I do not believe there is a member on the floor of the Convention who would desire the defeat of the Constitution. I go further and say, I do not believe there is a delegate that dare, as a member of the Republican party, go before the people of South Carolina and oppose the ratification of the Constitution.

Mr. J. S. CRAIG. I say emphatically I never will vote for anything in conflict with the Constitution of the United States.

Mr. C. P. LESLIE. My friend Mr. CHAMBERLAIN forgot you Mr. CRAIG.

Mr. D. H. CHAMBERLAIN. We have gone through a great revolution in this country. That revolution has established two principles. The first is the inviolability and perpetuity of the American Union. The second is the principle that no man can hold property in another, and the sacredness before the law of human rights. And when that great consummation has been reached and, we meet here under the protection of that rule to-day, to re-assume and re-establish the sovereignty of the Constitution of South Carolina, write it I beseech you; blazon it on that Constitution, until the blind shall see and proclaim it; until the deaf shall hear that, hereafter, in no court of South Carolina shall the question ever be raised whether one man has a valid claim to property in another man!

Mr. J. S. CRAIG. The gentleman has said that no honest man, no Republican, would oppose this proposition. I desire to say, I have been a Republican ever since I arrived at the age of twenty-one years, and before that time. I have never been anything else. While I do not oppose the proposition upon principle, I do oppose it on constitutional grounds. If I believed it to be constitutional, I should vote for it; but I believe it to be in direct violation of that provision of the Constitution of the United States, which says no law shall be passed by any State impairing the obligation of contracts. As a citizen of the United States, I feel bound by that provision. It has been said that there is no such thing as property in man. I acknowledge that principle, but I do not believe there is a man in this Convention who will deny that the Constitution of the United States did recognize and protect the institution of slavery. I am willing to go to the people on that issue.

Mr. C. C. BOWEN. I have a word to say in reply to those gentlemen who have raised the question of constitutionality. Some of them have said that if this section is incorporated into the Constitution, that they will not vote for it. I may one day meet these gentlemen before the people. I tell them right here, that in less than ten minutes this section will have become a part of the Constitution of South Carolina. I do not believe that any Republican will dare vote against that Constitution. The fourteenth amendment to the Constitution of the United States lays down this same rule, that neither the United States nor any of the States shall ever pay any claims for slaves. Does that impair the obligation of contracts? That is expected to become a part of the Constitution of the United States, and as far as South Carolina is concerned, she can only resume her place in the Union by the adoption of that amendment. We intend to make this the supreme law of the land, and if there are those who will leave us, we say, let them go and joy go with them. It will be the supreme law of South Carolina. If any man has claims of this character, and he thinks the law is unconstitutional, by impairing the obligation of contracts, let him go to the Supreme Court of the United States and test the question.

I am surprised to find some gentlemen, who advocated it, have swung so far round the circle to-day as to get on the opposite side. I fear they have fallen into the hands of the Philistines. I know not the motive. They admit that the Ordinance can be repealed by the very first Legislature that meets in South Carolina. They know, too, in that case, all our work here in discussing this question will have come to nought. I do not propose such shall be the case. Great pains were taken by the committee in framing that Ordinance. It is true, there has been outside pressure by parties to have it set aside. But that makes me all the more desirous to have it incorporated into the Constitution of the State. I have every confidence in the members of this Convention that they will, by their votes, make it a part of the Constitution of South Carolina.

The question being taken on the adoption of the section, it was decided in the affirmative, and pronounced an integral part of the Constitution of South Carolina.

Mr. R. C. DeLARGE, of the Committee on Franchise and Elections, reported the following as a substitute for the resolution offered on Saturday :

Resolved, That this Convention hereby request Congress to remove the political disabilities of such citizens of this State as may petition for the same after the adoption of the Constitution framed by this Convention ; *Provided*, Such persons make oath to support the Constitution of this State and of the United States ; said oath to be first deposited in the office of the Secretary of State, and a copy of the same forwarded with the petition to the Congress of the United States.

Resolved, That the President of the Convention is hereby directed to forward a copy of this resolution to the President of the Senate of the United States, and a copy to the Speaker of the House of Representatives.

On motion of Mr. L. S. LANGLEY, the report was ordered to be printed, and made the special order for ten o'clock Tuesday morning.

On motion, the Convention adjourned.

FIFTY-THIRD DAY.

Saturday, March 14, 1868.

The Convention assembled at ten A. M., and was called to order by the PRESIDENT.

Prayer was offered by the Rev. B. F. WHITTEMORE.

The roll was called, and a quorum answering to their names, the PRESIDENT announced the Convention ready to proceed to business.

The Journal of Monday was read and approved.

The PRESIDENT read the following extract from a letter received from a distinguished gentleman in Washington, to whom was sent copies of the Constitution as it progressed in the readings of the several articles :

" I have shown your Constitution and Bill of Rights to many of the leading Republicans here, who pronounce them as eminently fit for the corner stone of the new temple of liberty that you are engaged in erecting. The Convention has indeed done a square work." (Applause)

Mr. B. BYAS offered the following:

In order that this body may sustain its dignity against all charges made against it and its members ; be it
Resolved, That the President of this Convention appoint a committee of three to investigate the charge or charges made against one Dogan, a member of this body, which charges appeared in the public journals of this city this morning.
Resolved, That the committee be instructed to report within one hour from the present time

The resolution was unanimously agreed to, and the PRESIDENT appointed Messrs. B. BYAS, W. H. W. GRAY and M. F. BECKER the committee.

Mr. D. H. CHAMBERLAIN called up the preamble and resolutions relative to the endorsement by the State of the bonds of the Blue Ridge Railroad, which were made the special order for yesterday at twelve o'clock.

Mr. B. F. WHITTEMORE rose to a question of privilege, and Mr. CHAMBERLAIN yielded the floor for the purpose of allowing the member from Darlington to offer a resolution.

Mr. B. F. WHITTEMORE offered the following preamble and resolutions, which were unanimously agreed to with enthusiastic applause :

Resolved, That the thanks of this Convention are due Brevet Major-General Ed R. S. Canby, Commanding Second Military District, and all officers in this department who have co-operated with this body in the framing of the Constitution under the provision of the Reconstruction Acts of Congress for the future government of South Carolina.
Resolved, That this Convention will ever remember, with gratitude, the harmonious relations which have existed between the military authorities, under the command of General Canby, and its members, and that in this expression of the appreciation of such pleasant facts, we recognize how feeble words are to convey the true sentiment of the heart.
Resolved, That a certified copy of these resolutions be furnished by the President of this Convention to Brevet Major-General Ed. R. S. Canby, Commanding Second Military District.

Mr. E. W. M. MACKEY offered the following resolution, which was agreed to :

Resolved, That the Secretary and Sergeant-at-Arms of this Convention be continued in office for five days after the adjournment, for the purpose of completing the records and settling accounts, and that the President is hereby authorized to pay all just claims that may be approved and certified by the Chairman of the Finance Committee.

Mr. R. C. DeLARGE offered the following resolution :

Resolved, That the thanks of this Convention are hereby tendered to the liberal-hearted and noble minded people of the North who have taken such a lively interest in the cause of education in this State, and other States of the South, and who have aided our people in the establishment of our schools and school advantages.

Mr. B. F. WHITTEMORE offered the following resolution, which was agreed to :

Resolved, That the thanks of this Convention are due the City Government of Charleston, for the able and efficient police force placed under the charge of the President of this Convention.

Resolved, That a certified copy of the foregoing resolution be sent to the Mayor of this city by the President of this Convention.

Mr. L. S. LANGLEY offered the following resolution :

Resolved, That this Convention will not adjourn *sine die* until the Committee on Review and Consolidation have completed their work.

The PRESIDENT decided the resolution out of order. The Convention having once passed a resolution appointing a special time to adjourn, any other resolution except to rescind its action, which should be agreed to by a two-thirds vote, was not in order.

The PRESIDENT stated that he held in his hand an instrument consisting of fifteen articles and two hundred and thirteen sections, each of which had been read three times and passed by the Convention. They had from time to time been reviewed by the Convention, and properly arranged, and now purports to be the Constitution of the State of South Carolina. The question before the Convention is, whether, having passed these sections after three separate readings, they will pass this Constitution as a whole. The question is shall this Constitution be adopted ?

Mr. R. C. DeLARGE objected to voting on the Constitution as a whole, until the Committee on Consolidation and Review and the two Solicitors had examined it and arranged it, so that no sect on came in conflict with another.

Mr. S G. W. DILL hoped the Constitution would be passed without further argument or debate. He claimed that the various parts had been already arranged by the Convention, and he for one, did not wish to retard its presentation to the people a moment longer.

Mr. F. L. CARDOZO moved to rec. d the resolution whereby the Convention resolved to adjourn at twelve M., and to adjourn at six this evening.

The PRESIDENT decided the motion out of order.

The PRESIDENT stated he would be most reluctant to interfere with the expressed will of the Convention. He would content himself by saying, that if a motion of that kind was carried it would be the first time in the history of a parliamentary body that such a proceeding was recorded. It would be strange indeed, if, within three-quarters of an hour before the adjournment, the members of the body should show themselves so unfamiliar with parliamentary law and practice, and so much unacquainted with the condition of their business as to demand an extension of the time agreed upon The work of the Convention had been already accomplished, and if there were any remaining labors to be performed by the Committee on Review and Consolidation, the members of that Committee in the city could meet after adjournment for the purpose of making the final arrangement of the work. To prolong the session now, however, after a time had been fixed for adjournment, and some of the members gone home under the impression that the Convention would adjourn at that time, in his opinion would be scarcely justifiable, and might raise a question as to the legality of such action.

Mr. B. F. RANDOLPH thought if this Convention had not completed its work, it would be inconsistent for them to adjourn. He claimed that the Convention had not completed its work, as the Committee on Review and Consolidation had not made their report.

Mr. J. J. WRIGHT asked the President if it was not in his power to call this Convention together, after it had adjourned at twelve M. into another session.

The PRESIDENT answered in the affirmative

Mr. J. J. WRIGHT said, he hoped the members would keep quiet ; and, if they did not get through, they could, under the call of the President, have another session.

Mr. R. C. DeLARGE offered the following :

Resolved, That the President of this Convention is hereby directed to re-assemble this Convention at three o'clock this afternoon.

The PRESIDENT said : The chair is in a very disagreeable position, and an important and responsible duty is imposed upon the President. He has but one way in which to proceed, and that is, when the hour of 12 M. (looking at his watch) arrives, to declare the Convention adjourned *sine die.* If the President, under the rule of the House, is empowered to reconvene the body, it must be apparent to every gentleman that it must be by sending a summons to every member of the Convention, many of whom have already left. It would not be just, fair, legal or constitutional to summon only a portion of this Convention to enact any measure. The Chair, however, will obey the orders of the house, although they might be illegal and unconstitutional.

Mr. E. W. M. MACKEY. If I understand aright the question now is, whether the Constitution shall be adopted as a whole. I hope the motion will prevail. I cannot see for the life of me any necessity of waiting or putting the Constitution into the hands of the Committee on Review and Consolidation. This body has itself acted, so far, as it were, a Committee of the Whole on Review and Consolidation of the Constitution. They have reviewed the entire Constitution, section by section, and have consolidated it by altering or arranging them as they came up. Whenever a clause or a section in one article came in conflict with a clause or section in another or different article, the Convention has invariably stricken out one of the conflicting clauses. For instance, in regard to the Great Seal of the State, the same section was reported in the report of the Committee on Miscellaneous Matters, and the report of the Committee on the Executive Provisions of the Constitution. It was struck out of the first named report, and remained in that of the Executive.

Mr. L. S LANGLEY rose to a point of order, saying the question was on rescinding the resolution to adjourn.

The call for the previous question was not sustained, by a vote of 43 ayes to 45 nays

Mr. B. F RANDOLPH moved that the resolution by which this Convention was to adjourn at twelve M., be rescinded.

The PRESIDENT said : The present action of the Convention, if continued, will leave our work in danger of remaining incomplete. I am compelled, under the instructions of the house, to adjourn at twelve o'clock. The Constitution is not yet adopted. It is the first time I have to appeal to the house, and I advise it not to throw its time away. If, by a system of parliamentary tactics to protract proceedings, the Constitution is not adopted as a whole by twelve o'clock, unpleasant as the duty may be, when the hour arrives, I will be compelled to adjourn the Convention *sine die.* The Cons'itution not being adopted, the Convention would necessarily be obliged to re-assemble after a lapse of sufficient time, perhaps of twenty days, in order to give notice to the members. Time is rapidly passing, and I adjure the house not to throw away the important opportunity now offered of adopting the Constitution.

Mr. B. F. RANDOLPH said he would not have made his motion, if the President had not stated that such a motion would be in order.

The PRESIDENT said many things are in order which are unconstitutional. I believe the result of the motion. if decided affirmatively, would be illegal. Many things might be in order for the Convention to do, but the result of the action would be illegal. I do believe and think I would be sustained by any parliamentary lawyer in saying, that when the house has agreed to adjourn at any particular time, it is not in the power of the house to change its decree. Some of the members have retired; they cannot form a portion of the prolonged session without much delay, and they might reasonably protest against its subsequent action as a legal and constitutional body. Looking at it, therefore, in the very best light, such action would place the Convention in a doubtful position. At present, you are a body whose legality and constitutionality cannot be questioned, and it is my fervent wish that you shall so remain to the end

Several motions were made for indefinite postponement of the motion' to recind, which was agreed to.

Mr. L. S. LANGLEY. I desire to record my vote "no" on the question of postponement.

The question was then put upon the adoption of the Constitution, when it was unanimously carried.

The PRESIDENT. I now declare that this instrument, containing fifteen articles and two hundred and thirteen sections, having received the requisite number of readings, and passed by the Convention, has been adopted as the organic law of the land and Constitution of the State of South Carolina, subject to the ratification of its people. And may God in His infinite mercy and wisdom grant that it may work good to our whole country.

At this announcement, the Convention spontaneously rose to its feet and broke forth in loud and prolonged cheering.

After the applause had subsided, Mr. J. M. RUTLAND offered the following, which was agreed to :

117

Resolved, That the President of this Convention be requested to forward, at an early day, to the President of the Senate and Speaker of the House of Representatives at Washington, respectively, a copy of the Report of the Chairman of the Committee on Petitions, recommending that this Convention do petition Congress to remove the political disabilities of certain persons named in said report, together with a copy of this resolution.

Mr. T. J. ROBERTSON moved that the President temporarily vacate the Chair.

Mr. N. G. PARKER moved that Mr. T. J. COGHLAN, of Sumter, take the Chair, which was agreed to.

Mr. T. J. COGHLAN, on taking the Chair, returned his thanks for the honor conferred. It would, he said, be a great pleasure to render a tribute of esteem from the Convention to their noble President—such a tribute as would do him everlasting honor.

Mr. J. T. ROBERTSON then offered the following, which was unanimously agreed to, with great cheering and applause :

Resolved, That for the very able and important discharge of the responsible and arduous duties, gratuitously performed, of presiding over the deliberations of this Convention, and for the uniform kindness and forbearance shown at all times to all its members, the thanks of this Convention be tendered to Hon. A. G. MACKEY, our President

The PRESIDENT, on resuming the Chair, spoke as follows :

GENTLEMEN OF THE CONVENTION :—After an arduous labor of two months, we are at last about to part, and the time has arrived which admonishes us that having accomplished, to the best of our abilities, the duty which had been imposed upon us by our constituents, nothing is left for us to do but affectionately to bid each other farewell.

I look back, as I trust you all do, with much self-gratulation, upon the hours that we have spent together. There are with us no unpleasant reminiscences of those acrimonious bickerings which, in all deliberative assemblies, are too often incidental to the excitement of debate and the attrition of antagonistic minds. Engaged in the consideration of topics of the highest importance, differences of opinion have necessarily existed, but those differences, although always boldly expressed and sturdily maintained, have never been characterized by the petulance of personal retort. Indeed, I am sure that the history of parliamentary bodies has never presented a more uninterrupted example of the capacity of men to differ widely on certain subjects, and yet with friendly forbearance to agree to differ The members of this Convention, on all occasions, where there has not been unanimity, may have been opponents in opinion, but have always been friends in counsel.

For myself, I do not know that I have ever said one word to wound e feelings of a delegate. If I have done so, the fault has been unin tentional, and has escaped my recollection.   I am sure that no word has been uttered by any one of the members to me, which the most exacting man would have wished unsaid.   To me, as their presiding officer, the delegates of this Convention hove ever been most kind, considerate and respectful, and for these demonstrations of your good will I am most profoundly grateful.   In my own course I have endeavored to be thoroughly impartial.   Whatever have been my private opinions on any of the subjects under deliberation, I have sought, and I hope successfully, to forget them while I controlled debate, and have tried to rule on every question, not as my predilections might have led me, but as the law of parliament and the rules of the house required.   And I feel proud as well as grateful, that the house has evinced its confidence in my honesty as a presiding officer in this, that no decision I have made has ever been overruled.

The work which we were sent here to do was most momentous to the Commonwealth which we represent, and the members of this Convention are, I think, worthy of much commendation for the improvements they have made in the organic law, when their labors are compared with those of their predecessors.   We here present to our constituents a Constitution in which, for the first time in the political history of the State, the great doctrine of manhood suffrage is distinctly recognized, and all the rights are secured to every citizen to which nature and nature's God have entitled him.   Here, have we stricken every vestige of serfdom from our institutions, and that too in so emphatic and unambiguous a way, that no doubt can be entertained of our determination that this relic of barbarism shall never again, in any form, pollute our soil.   Here we have made every needful arrangement for the free education of our people, so that if future legislators shall carry out in good faith the provisions which we have ordained on this vital subject, in a few years the stain of ignorance which now pollutes our history will be forever obliterated, and the happy period will have arrived when no son or daughter of South Carolina will be unable to read and write.   Thus have we broadly sown the seeds of public education, and thus shall we, in no distant time, reap the rich harvest of public virtue.   Crime and ignorance are inseparable companions   We have stricken a heavy blow at both, and may look for the natural and inevitable result in the elevation of all our people to a social, political and religious eminence, to which, under the former Constitution and laws of the State, they had never attained.

Here, too, we have obliterated from our political system that most pernicious heresy of State sovereignty—a heresy which, for nearly half a century, taught by our leaders, had, like an *ignis fatuis*, led the people of South Carolina, on more than one occasion, to the brink of rebellion, until there arose at length, as a necessary result of this doctrine, one of the most fratracidal wars that the world ever saw.   The theory of a divided allegiance, and of a sovereignty within a sovereignty, alike incongruous with all the principles of political science and with the system of national power established by our fathers, has received from you a death blow.   No longer, if the Constitution you have adopted should be ratified by the people, will there be any danger of a future rebellion, in which the glorious flag of our common country—a flag which has often " braved the battle an the breeze "—shall be treated by a portion of the nation with insult, and for it an ensign to be substituted, consecrated by no national traditions, and simply the novel insignia of a disrupted Confederacy.   In establishing this principle of a paramount allegiance to the national Government you have thrown a protection around the national life for the future, and you have justified the acts of those Union men who, in the midst of a wide-spread and threatening rebellion, nobly stood by this doctrine you have announced, and would not acknowledge that the State, however much they loved it as their home, could supplant, in their affections, the nation from which they received protection

I speak not of these, as parts of the results of our labors, in any spirit of acrimony toward those who have heretofore neglected these great duties of legislators—for I would desire to bury the past in that oblivion which best befits it, or to hold it only as a beacon light to warn us from its follies and its perils in the future—but because as stewads of a great trust we have a right to show to our constituents how we have discharged the duties of the stewardship which they had confided to us.

To the people of South Carolina, we submit the Constitution which we were instructed to frame, in the confident expectation that its manifest superiority over all other Constitutions by which this Commonwealth has hitherto been governed, will secure for it a triumphant ratification.   We do not claim for ourselves a pre-eminence of wisdom or virture, but we do claim that we have followed, in the progressive advancement of the age ; that we have been bold and honest enou h and wise enough to trample obsolete and unworthy prejudices under foot, and thus have been enabled, with impartial legislation, to provide for the civil and political interests of all men of every rank, station or race, within the borders of our beloved State

But the painful moment of separation has arrived, and that word which friends always dread to hear has to be pronounced   Associates, I bid you an affectionate farewell, and wishing you all a safe and happy return to your respective homes, I now, in accordance with the resolution of the house, declare the Constitutional Convention of South Carolina to be adjourned *sine die*.

The Convention then adjourned *sine die*.